Social Psychology

Tenth Edition

Elliot Aronson

Timothy D. Wilson

Samuel R. Sommers

 Pearson

Portfolio Manager: Kelli Strieby
Content Producer: Cecilia Turner/Lisa Mafrici
Content Developer: Thomas Finn
Portfolio Manager Assistant: Louis Fierro
Executive Product Marketing Manager: Christopher Brown
Senior Field Marketing Manager: Debi Doyle
Content Producer Manager: Amber Mackey
Content Development Manager: Sharon Geary

Art/Designer: Blair Brown
Digital Studio Course Producer: Lindsay Verge
Full-Service Project Manager: Angel Chavez
Compositor: Integra Publishing Services, Inc.
Printer/Binder: LSC Communications
Cover Printer: Lehigh Phoenix Color/Hagerstown
Cover Design: Lumina Datamatics
Cover Credit: Noma Bar, Pentagram

Credits and acknowledgments borrowed from other sources and reproduced, with permission, in this textbook appear on the appropriate page within the text or on pages 545–548.

Library of Congress Cataloging-in-Publication Data

Names: Aronson, Elliot, author. | Wilson, Timothy D., author. | Sommers, Sam, author.
Title: Social psychology / Elliot Aronson, Timothy D. Wilson, Samuel R. Sommers.
Description: Tenth edition. | New York, NY : Pearson, [2019] | Includes bibliographical references and index.
Identifiers: LCCN 2017037187 | ISBN 9780134641287 (softcover : alk. paper)
Subjects: LCSH: Social psychology.
Classification: LCC HM1033 .A78 2019 | DDC 302—dc23
LC record available at https://lccn.loc.gov/2017037187

1   18

Rental Edition
ISBN-10:   0-13-464128-0
ISBN-13: 978-0-13-464128-7

Access Card
ISBN-10:   0-13-470064-3
ISBN-13: 978-0-13-470064-9

Books à la Carte
ISBN-10:   0-13-470066-X
ISBN-13: 978-0-13-470066-3

Instructor's Review Copy
ISBN-10:   0-13-467840-0
ISBN-13: 978-0-13-467840-5

To my grandchildren: Jacob, Jason, Ruth, Eliana, Natalie, Rachel, and Leo. My hope is that your capacity for empathy and compassion will help make the world a better place.
—E.A.

To my family, Deirdre Smith, Christopher Wilson, and Leigh Wilson
—T.D.W.

To my students—past, present, and future—for making coming to work each morning fun, educational, and unpredictable.
—S.R.S.

Brief Contents

Contents

Preface

When we began writing this book, our overriding goal was to capture the excitement of social psychology. We have been pleased to hear, in many kind notes and messages from professors and students, that we succeeded. One of our favorite responses was from a student who said that the book was so interesting that she always saved it for last, to reward herself for finishing her other work. With that one student, at least, we succeeded in making our book an enjoyable, fascinating story, not a dry report of facts and figures.

There is always room for improvement, however, and our goal in this, the tenth edition, is to make the field of social psychology an even better read. When we teach the course, there is nothing more gratifying than seeing the sleepy students in the back row sit up with interest and say, "Wow, I didn't know that! Now *that's* interesting." We hope that students who read our book will have that same reaction.

What's New in This Edition?

First a word about what has *not* changed. As mentioned, we have done our best to tell the story of social psychology in an engaging way that will resonate with students. We also have retained features that help students learn and retain the material. As before, each chapter begins with learning objectives, which are repeated in the sections of the chapter that are most relevant to them and in the chapter-ending summary. All major sections of every chapter end with review quizzes. Research shows that students learn material better when they are tested frequently; thus, these section quizzes, as well as the test questions at the end of every chapter, should be helpful learning aids. In the Revel version of the text, instructors have the option of assigning these quizzes and giving course credit for correct answers. Each chapter also has our Try It! feature that invites students to apply what they have learned to their own lives. Several of these Try It! features have been updated.

We are pleased to add several new features to the tenth edition that we believe will appeal to students and make it even easier for them to learn the material. The first is called #SurvivalTips which are brief videos recorded by students who have taken a social psychology class. Each one tells a personal story relaying how the student applied social psychology to better navigate or "survive" a real situation in their lives. For example,

one video in Chapter 9 tells the story of how a student learned to avoid process loss in her study groups. These videos are in the Revel version of the text, placed alongside the relevant concepts.

A second new feature, called #trending, is a brief analysis of a current event that illustrates a key principle in each chapter. In Chapter 11 on Prosocial Behavior, for example, we describe an incident in which a White dentist from Texas, in town for Donald Trump's inauguration, left a $450 tip for an African American waitress. Students are asked to think about how concepts in the chapter might help explain why the man acted so generously, such as Batson's empathy-altruism hypothesis. Importantly, these examples will be updated frequently in the Revel version of the text, such that students will always be able to connect what they are reading to current, real-world events.

Third, every chapter now begins with a feature called, "What do YOU think?" where students answer a survey question designed to illustrate a concept in that chapter. In Chapter 6, for example, students are asked, "Have you ever joined a group that required you to do something humiliating or dangerous in order to gain membership?" In the Revel version of the text, students get immediate feedback on how other students have answered (23% said yes to this question). Then, at the end of the chapter, there is a writing exercise tied to the survey question that instructors can assign if they wish. In Chapter 6, for example, the question is, "How does justification of effort help explain why hazing and initiation rites are common across so many different group types?"

Lastly, we have expanded a feature that proved to be very popular with users of the Revel version of the previous edition, namely videos that recreate classic experiments in social psychology. These videos, recorded exclusively for this book, give students a vivid and contemporary look at how an experiment was done and what it found.

And, of course, we have updated the tenth edition substantially, with numerous references to new research. Here is a sampling of the new research that is covered:

- Chapter 1: This chapter contains updated examples, a new Try It!, and a new section on the role of biological approaches and evolutionary theory in social psychology.
- Chapter 2: A signature of our book continues to be a readable, student-friendly chapter on research methods in social psychology. This chapter has been updated

for the tenth edition with new references and examples and a discussion of the replication debate in social psychology.

- Chapter 3, "Social Cognition: How We Think About the Social World," has been updated with more than 40 new references. There is a new section on the planning fallacy and discussions of recent research findings, such as a study on counterfactual thinking and people's belief in God.

- Chapter 4, "Social Perception: How We Come to Understand Other People," now includes several new features, including a new opening drawing on the *Black Mirror* television series, an interactive photo gallery on using first impressions to your advantage, a discussion of cross-cultural attitudes regarding karma and beliefs in a just world, and a reorganized discussion of Kelley's covariation model.

- Chapter 5, "The Self: Understanding Ourselves in a Social Context," has been updated with more than 35 new references. The chapter headings have also been reorganized into three major sections, which should make the material clearer to students. There is a new opening example about children raised by animals and how they might have influenced their sense of self. Lastly, the section on self-esteem has been updated and moved to Chapter 6.

- Chapter 6, "Cognitive Dissonance and the Need to Protect Our Self-Esteem," is one of the most extensively revised chapters in this edition. This chapter has always been a signature of the book; we are the only text to devote an entire chapter to cognitive dissonance theory and self-esteem maintenance. We proudly retain this chapter in our tenth edition, continuing to present classic work in cognitive dissonance in a highly readable manner with compelling examples designed to draw students in. At the same time we have updated the chapter, adding a major new section on advances and extensions of dissonance theory that includes discussions of self-affirmation theory and self-evaluation maintenance theory. There is also a section on narcissism and self-esteem, which previously appeared in Chapter 5. Lastly the chapter has two new Try It! exercises that students will enjoy: In one they complete a values affirmation writing exercise, and in another they can take a short version of the Narcissistic Personality Inventory and get feedback on their score.

- Chapter 7, "Attitudes and Attitude Change: Influencing Thoughts and Feelings," includes a new opening story, new examples from Election 2016 in the discussion of affectively based attitudes, and new discussion of how implicit versus explicit attitudes can vary in predicting outcomes when it comes to evaluation of job résumés based on applicant name. A new interactive feature is also included to explain the formula for persuasion according to the Yale Attitude Change approach.

- Chapter 8, "Conformity and Obedience: Influencing Behavior," now opens with a more positive focus on social influence, in the form of Pete Frates and the ALS ice bucket challenge. We have added a discussion of the proliferation of "fake news" in the section on informational social influence. The chapter also features a new interactive video demonstrating students employing various social influence techniques and added discussion of contemporary criticism of Milgram's research.

- Chapter 9, "Group Processes: Influence in Social Groups," now opens with an analysis of problematic group decision making and strategizing in Hilary Clinton's 2016 campaign team. We have also added coverage of recent research on combating the problematic effects on deindividuation online and group polarization via social media feeds. The chapter also includes expanded and updated discussion of the prisoner's dilemma and a new photo gallery regarding resource dilemmas.

- Chapter 10, "Attraction and Relationships: From Initial Impressions to Long-Term Intimacy," has a new title to better reflect the balanced focus between initial attraction and relationship trajectory/satisfaction. A new interactive photo gallery explores the relationship between mere exposure and liking, and a new interactive video illustrates the matching hypothesis in attraction. We have added coverage (including an interactive figure) of Sternberg's triangular theory of love and have reorganized and updated the concluding section on relationship satisfaction and breaking up.

- In Chapter 11, "Prosocial Behavior: Why Do People Help?" includes more than 30 new references, expanded discussions of empathy and altruism and volunteerism, and a revised discussion of religion and prosocial behavior.

- Chapter 12, "Aggression: Why Do We Hurt Other People? Can We Prevent It?," has significant content updates in addition to covering new research. Our discussion of testosterone and aggression is more nuanced, disentangling some aspects of gender and hormones and introducing the other sex hormone related to aggression, estradiol. We also introduce and evaluate two formal evolutionary theories of aggression: the challenge hypothesis and dual-hormone theory. We also streamlined the section on sexual assault to make this important section clearer. Overall, the chapter narrative now emphasizes the convergent evidence for the role of impulsivity in aggression across biological and psychological evidence.

- In Chapter 13, "Prejudice: Causes, Consequences, and Cures," has undergone a major organizational and content update. We generalized the discussion of prejudice from the strong focus on Black-White and male-female relations to relate more generally to other ethnic, gender, and stigmatized identities. Nonetheless, we maintain an important dialog on anti-Blackness, including a discussion of police shootings and activist groups. We expanded the discussion of emotions as a core component of prejudice, through which we included more physiological research on prejudice into the chapter. Under the ways to reduce prejudice, we have extended the discussion of intergroup contact to teach students about *indirect* contact, and we have streamlined the discussion of the jigsaw classroom. The entire chapter was updated with new examples from recent popular culture and interactive components in Revel.

- Social Psychology in Action chapters—"Using Social Psychology to Achieve a Sustainable and Happy Future," "Social Psychology and Health," and "Social Psychology and the Law"—have been updated with many references to new research, but remain shorter chapters. When we teach the course, we find that students are excited to learn about these applied areas. At the same time, we recognize that some instructors have difficulty fitting the chapters into their courses. As with the previous edition, our approach remains to maintain a shortened length for the applied chapters to make it easy to integrate these chapters into different parts of the course in whatever fashion an instructor deems best. SPA1, "Using Social Psychology to Achieve a Sustainable and Happy Future," includes an updated opening example about the effects of climate change and new examples of ways in which students can both act in sustainable ways and maximize their well-being. In SPA2, "Social Psychology and Health," we updated coverage on perceived control interventions among nursing home residents and included a new interactive on coping with stress. SPA3, "Social Psychology and Law," has a new video about attentional blindness and an interactive feature on best practices in eyewitness identification procedures.

Revel for Social Psychology

Revel™

When students are engaged deeply, they learn more effectively and perform better in their courses. This simple fact inspired the creation of Revel: an interactive learning environment designed for the way today's students read, think, and learn. Built in collaboration with educators and students nationwide, Revel is the newest, fully digital way to deliver respected Pearson content. Revel enlivens course content with media interactives and assessments—icluding an interactive figure) of ntegrated directly within the authors' narrative—that provide opportunities for students to read about and practice course material in tandem. This immersive educational technology boosts student engagement, which leads to better understanding of concepts and improved performance throughout the course.

Learn More about Revel

http://www.pearsonhighered.com/revel/

Rather than simply offering opportunities to read about and study social psychology, Revel facilitates deep, engaging interactions with the concepts that matter most. By providing opportunities to improve skills in analyzing and interpreting sources of psychological evidence, for example, Revel engages students directly and immediately, which leads to a better understanding of course material. A wealth of student and instructor resources and interactive materials can be found within Revel. Some of our favorites are mentioned in the information that follows.

For more information about all the tools and resources in Revel and access to your own Revel account for Social Psychology, go to www.pearsonhighered.com/revel.

Instructor Resources

We know that instructors are "tour guides" for their students, leading them through the exciting world of social psychology in the classroom. As such, we have invested tremendous effort in the creation of a world-class collection of instructor resources that will support professors in their mission to teach the best course possible.

Coauthor Sam Sommers guided the creation of this supplements package, which has been reviewed and updated for the tenth edition. Here are the highlights of the supplements we are pleased to provide:

PRESENTATION TOOLS AND CLASSROOM ACTIVITIES

- **Social Psychology PowerPoint Collection** (0134700732) The PowerPoints provide an active format for presenting concepts from each chapter and incorporating relevant figures and tables. Instructors can choose from three PowerPoint presentations: a lecture presentation set that highlights major topics from the chapters, a highly visual lecture presentation set with **embedded videos**, or a PowerPoint collection of the complete art files from the text. The

PowerPoint files can be downloaded from www .pearsonhighered.com.

- **Instructor's Resource Manual** (0134700694) The Instructor's Manual includes key terms, lecture ideas, teaching tips, suggested readings, chapter outlines, student projects and research assignments, Try It! exercises, critical-thinking topics and discussion questions, and a media resource guide. It has been updated for the tenth edition with hyperlinks to ease facilitation of navigation within the Instructor's Resource Manual.

ASSESSMENT RESOURCES

- **Test Bank** (0134700740) Each of the more than 2,000 questions in this test bank is page-referenced to the text and categorized by topic and skill level. Each question in the test bank was reviewed by several instructors to ensure that we are providing you with the best and most accurate content in the industry.

- **MyTest Test Bank** (0134677897) This Web-based test-generating software provides instructors "best in class" features in an easy-to-use program. Create tests and easily select questions with drag-and-drop or point-and-click functionality. Add or modify test questions using the built-in Question Editor, and print tests in a variety of formats. The program comes with full technical support.

Acknowledgments

Elliot Aronson is delighted to acknowledge the collaboration of Carol Tavris. He would also like to acknowledge the contributions of his best friend (who also happens to be his wife of 60 years), Vera Aronson. Vera, as usual, provided inspiration for his ideas and acted as the sounding board for and supportive critic of many of his semiformed notions, helping to mold them into more sensible analyses.

Tim Wilson would like to thank his graduate mentor, Richard E. Nisbett, who nurtured his interest in the field and showed him the continuity between social psychological research and everyday life. He also thanks the many students who have taken his course in social psychology over the years, for asking fascinating questions and providing wonderful examples of social psychological phenomena in their everyday lives. Lastly, he thanks the many graduate students with whom he has had the privilege of working for joining him in the ever-fascinating discovery of new social psychological phenomena.

Sam Sommers would like to acknowledge, first and foremost, the Sommers ladies, Marilyn, Abigail, and Sophia, for being patient with round-the-clock revision sessions, for tolerating the constantly expanding mass of papers and books on the floor of the study (he promises to clean them up before

work starts on the eleventh edition), and for frequently providing excellent real-life examples that illustrate social psychological concepts. He also gives special thanks to all of his teachers of social psychology, for introducing him to the field, for continued support, and for serving as role models as instructors, mentors, researchers, and writers.

No book can be written and published without the help of many people working with the authors behind the scenes, and our book is no exception. We need to give a special thanks to Elizabeth Page-Gould for her tremendous help in revising two of the chapters. Her deep knowledge of social psychology and wonderful writing style contributed greatly to this edition. We would also like to thank the many colleagues who read one or more chapters of this edition and of previous editions of the book.

Reviewers of the Tenth Edition

Jim Allen, *State University of New York, College at Geneseo*; Kathryn Anderson, *Our Lady of the Lake University*; Anila Bhagavatula, *California State University–Long Beach*; Amy Bradshaw-Hoppock, *Embry-Riddle Aeronautical University*; Ngoc Bui, *University of La Verne*; Bernardo Carducci, *Indiana University Southeast*; Alex Czopp, *Western Washington University*; Keith Davis, *University of South Carolina*; Michael Dudley, *Southern Illinois University Edwardsville*; Heidi English, *College of the Siskiyous*; Joe Ferrari, *DePaul University*; Christine Floether, *Centenary College*; Krista Forrest, *University of Nebraska at Kearney*; Allen Gorman, *Radford University*; Jerry Green, *Tarrant County College*; Dana Greene, *University of North Carolina*; Donnell Griffin, *Davidson County Community College*; Lisa Harrison, *California State University, Sacramento*; Gina Hoover, *Ohio State University*; Jeffrey Huntsinger, *Loyola University Chicago*; Alisha Janowsky, *University of Central Florida*; Bethany Johnson, *University of Nebraska–Omaha*; Deborah Jones, *Columbia University*; Suzanne Kieffer, *University of Houston*; Marvin Lee, *Tennessee State University*; Alexandra Luong, *University of Minnesota Duluth*; Robyn Mallett, *Loyola University Chicago*; Brian Meier, *Gettysburg College*; Andrea Mercurio, *Boston University*; Lori Nelson, *University of Iowa*; Darren Petronella, *Nassau Community College*; Jennifer Rivers, *Elms College*; Kari Terzino, *Des Moines Area Community College*; T. Joel Wade, *Bucknell University*; Angela Walker, *Quinnipiac University*; Chrysalis Wright, *University of Central Florida*; Garry Zaslow, *Nassau Community College*; Jie Zhang, *University at Buffalo*

Reviewers of Past Editions

Jeffrey B. Adams, *Saint Michael's College*; Bill Adler, *Collin County Community College*; John R. Aiello, *Rutgers University*; Charles A. Alexander, *Rock Valley College*; Sowmya Anand, *Ohio State University*; Nathan Arbuckle,

Ohio State University; Art Aron, *State University of New York, Stony Brook;* Danny Axsom, *Virginia Polytechnic Institute and State University;* Joan W. Baily, *Jersey City State College;* Norma Baker, *Belmont University;* Austin Baldwin, *University of Iowa;* John Bargh, *New York University;* William A. Barnard, *University of Northern Colorado;* Doris G. Bazzini, *Appalachian State University;* Arthur Beaman, *University of Kentucky;* Gordon Bear, *Ramapo College;* Susan E. Beers, *Sweet Briar College;* Kathy L. Bell, *University of North Carolina at Greensboro;* Leonard Berkowitz, *University of Wisconsin–Madison;* Ellen S. Berscheid, *University of Minnesota;* John Bickford, *University of Massachusetts, Amherst;* Thomas Blass, *University of Maryland;* C. George Boeree, *Shippensburg University;* Lisa M. Bohon, *California State University, Sacramento;* Jennifer Bosson, *The University of Oklahoma;* Chante C. Boyd, *Carnegie Mellon University;* Peter J. Brady, *Clark State Community College;* Kosha Bramesfeld, *Pennsylvania State University;* Kelly A. Brennan, *University of Texas, Austin;* Richard W. Brislin, *East-West Center of the University of Hawaii;* Jeff Bryson, *San Diego State University;* Melissa Burkley, *Oklahoma State University;* Amy Bush, *University of Houston;* Amber Bush Amspoker, *University of Houston;* Brad Bushman, *Iowa State University;* Thomas P. Cafferty, *University of South Carolina, Columbia;* Melissa A. Cahoon, *Wright State University;* Frank Calabrese, *Community College of Philadelphia;* Michael Caruso, *University of Toledo;* Nicholas Christenfeld, *University of California, San Diego;* Margaret S. Clark, *Carnegie Mellon University;* Russell D. Clark, III, *University of North Texas;* Susan D. Clayton, *Allegheny College;* Megan Clegg-Kraynok, *West Virginia University;* Brian M. Cohen, *University of Texas, San Antonio;* Florette Cohen, *Rutgers University;* Jack Cohen, *Camden County College;* Steven G. Cole, *Texas Christian University;* Eric J. Cooley, *Western Oregon State University;* Diana Cordova, *Yale University;* Traci Craig, *University of Idaho;* Jack Croxton, *State University of New York, Fredonia;* Keith E. Davis, *University of South Carolina, Columbia;* Mary Ellen Dello Stritto, *Ball State University;* Dorothee Dietrich, *Hamline University;* Kate Dockery, *University of Florida;* Susann Doyle, *Gainesville College;* Steve Duck, *University of Iowa;* Michael G. Dudley, *Southern Illinois University Edwardsville;* Karen G. Duffy, *State University of New York, Geneseo;* Valerie Eastman, *Drury College;* Tami Eggleston, *McKendree College;* Timothy Elliot, *University of Alabama–Birmingham;* Steve L. Ellyson, *Youngstown State University;* Cindy Elrod, *Georgia State University;* Kadimah Elson, *University of California, San Diego/Grossmont College;* Rebecca S. Fahrlander, *University of Nebraska at Omaha;* Alan Feingold, *Yale University;* Edward Fernandes, *East Carolina University;* Phil Finney, *Southeast Missouri State University;* Susan Fiske, *University of Massachusetts;* Robin Franck, *Southwestern College;* Denise Frank, *Ramapo College of New Jersey;* Timothy M. Franz,

St. John Fisher College; William Rick Fry, *Youngstown State University;* Russell Geen, *University of Missouri;* Glenn Geher, *State University of New York at New Paltz;* David Gersh, *Houston Community College;* Frederick X. Gibbons, *Iowa State University;* Cynthia Gilliland, *Louisiana State University;* Genaro Gonzalez, *University of Texas;* Jessica Gonzalez, *Ohio State University;* Sara Gorchoff, *University of California, Berkeley;* Beverly Gray, *Youngstown State University;* Gordon Hammerle, *Adrian College;* H. Anna Han, *Ohio State University;* Judith Harackiewicz, *University of Wisconsin–Madison;* Elaine Hatfield, *University of Hawaii, Manoa;* Vicki S. Helgeson, *Carnegie Mellon University;* Joyce Hemphill, *Cazenovia College;* Tracy B. Henley, *Mississippi State University;* Ed Hirt, *Indiana University;* Harold Hunziker Jr., *Corning Community College;* David E. Hyatt, *University of Wisconsin–Oshkosh;* Marita Inglehart, *University of Michigan;* Carl Kallgren, *Behrend College, Pennsylvania State University, Erie;* Stephen Kilianski, *Rutgers University;* Bill Klein, *Colby College;* James D. Johnson, *University of North Carolina, Wilmington;* Lee Jussim, *Rutgers University;* Stephen Kilianski, *Rutgers University;* Fredrick Koenig, *Tulane University;* Alan Lambert, *Washington University, St. Louis;* Emmett Lampkin, *Kirkwook Community College;* Elizabeth C. Lanthier, *Northern Virginia Community College;* Patricia Laser, *Bucks County Community College;* G. Daniel Lassiter, *Ohio University;* Dianne Leader, *Georgia Institute of Technology;* John Lu, *Concordia University;* Stephanie Madon, *Iowa State University;* John Malarkey, *Wilmington College;* Andrew Manion, *St. Mary's University of Minnesota;* Allen R. McConnell, *Michigan State University;* Adam Meade, *North Carolina State University;* Joann M. Montepare, *Tufts University;* Richard Moreland, *University of Pittsburgh;* Dave Nalbone, *Purdue University–Calumet;* Carrie Nance, *Stetson University;* Todd D. Nelson, *Michigan State University;* Elaine Nocks, *Furman University;* Matylda Osika, *University of Houston;* Cheri Parks, *Colorado Christian University;* W. Gerrod Parrott, *Georgetown University;* David Peterson, *Mount Senario College;* Mary Pritchard, *Boise State University;* Cynthia K. S. Reed, *Tarrant County College;* Dan Richard, *University of North Florida;* Neal Roese, *University of Illinois;* Darrin L. Rogers, *Ohio State University;* Joan Rollins, *Rhode Island College;* Paul Rose, *Southern Illinois University Edwardsville;* Lee D. Ross, *Stanford University;* Alex Rothman, *University of Minnesota;* M. Susan Rowley, *Champlain College;* Delia Saenz, *Arizona State University;* Brad Sagarin, *Northern Illinois University;* Fred Sanborn, *North Carolina Wesleyan College;* Connie Schick, *Bloomsburg University;* Norbert Schwartz, *University of Michigan;* Gretchen Sechrist, *University at Buffalo;* Richard C. Sherman, *Miami University of Ohio;* Paul Silvia, *University of North Carolina at Greensboro;* Randolph A. Smith, *Ouachita Baptist University;* Linda Solomon, *Marymount Manhattan College;* Janice Steil, *Adelphi University;* Jakob Steinberg,

Fairleigh Dickinson University; Mark Stewart, *American River College*; Lori Stone, *University of Texas at Austin*; JoNell Strough, *West Virginia University*; T. Gale Thompson, *Bethany College*; Scott Tindale, *Loyola University of Chicago*; David M. Tom, *Columbus State Community College*; David Trafimow, *New Mexico State University*; Ruth Warner, *St. Louis University*; Anne Weiher, *Metropolitan State College of Denver*; Gary L. Wells, *Iowa State University*; Jackie White, *University of North Carolina at Greensboro*; Paul L. Wienir, *Western Michigan University*; Kipling D. Williams, *University of Toledo*; Tamara Williams, *Hampton University*; Paul Windschitl, *University of Iowa*; Mike Witmer, *Skagit Valley College*; Gwen Wittenbaum, *Michigan State University*; William Douglas Woody, *University of Northern Colorado*; Clare Zaborowski, *San Jacinto College*; William H. Zachry, *University of Tennessee–Martin*; Leah Zinner, *University of Wisconsin–Madison*

We also thank the wonderful editorial staff of Pearson for their expertise and professionalism, including Dickson Musslewhite (Editorial Director), Cecilia Turner (Content Producer), Christopher Brown (Executive Product Marketing Manager), Louis Fierro (Editorial Assistant), and Angel Chavez (Project Manager). We would especially like to thank Thomas Finn (Developmental Editor), who provided expert guidance with constant good cheer and insight even through barrages of e-mail exchanges and attachments, and Amber Chow (Portfolio Manager), whose smart vision for the book, and commitment to making it as good as it can be, have truly made a difference. Finally, we thank Mary Falcon, but for whom we never would have begun this project.

Thank you for inviting us into your classroom. We welcome your suggestions, and we would be delighted to hear your comments about this book.

Elliot Aronson
elliot@cats.ucsc.edu

Tim Wilson
tdw@virginia.edu

Sam Sommers
sam.sommers@tufts.edu

About the Authors

Elliot Aronson

When I was a kid, we were the only Jewish family in a virulently anti-Semitic neighborhood. I had to go to Hebrew school every day, late in the afternoon. Being the only youngster in my neighborhood going to Hebrew school made me an easy target for some of the older neighborhood toughs. On my way home from Hebrew school, after dark, I was frequently waylaid and roughed up by roving gangs shouting anti-Semitic epithets.

I have a vivid memory of sitting on a curb after one of these beatings, nursing a bloody nose or a split lip, feeling very sorry for myself and wondering how these kids could hate me so much when they didn't even know me. I thought about whether those kids were taught to hate Jews or whether, somehow, they were born that way. I wondered if their hatred could be changed—if they got to know me better, would they hate me less? I speculated about my own character. What would I have done if the shoe were on the other foot—that is, if I were bigger and stronger than they, would I be capable of beating them up for no good reason?

I didn't realize it at the time, of course, but eventually I discovered that these were profound questions. And some 30 years later, as an experimental social psychologist, I had the great good fortune to be in a position to answer some of those questions and to invent techniques to reduce the kind of prejudice that had claimed me as a victim.

Elliot Aronson is Professor Emeritus at the University of California at Santa Cruz and one of the most renowned social psychologists in the world. In 2002, he was chosen as one of the 100 most eminent psychologists of the twentieth century. Dr. Aronson is the only person in the 120-year history of the American Psychological Association to have received all three of its major awards: for distinguished writing, distinguished teaching, and distinguished research. Many other professional societies have honored his research and teaching as well. These include the American Association for the Advancement of Science, which gave him its highest honor, the Distinguished Scientific Research award; the American Council for the Advancement and Support of Education, which named him Professor of the Year of 1989; the Society for the Psychological Study of Social Issues, which awarded him the Gordon Allport prize for his contributions to the reduction of prejudice among racial and ethnic groups; and the William James Award from the Association for Psychological Science. In 1992, he was named a Fellow of the American Academy of Arts and Sciences. A collection of papers and tributes by his former students and colleagues, The Scientist and the Humanist, *celebrates his contributions to social psychological theory and its application to real-world problems. Dr. Aronson's own recent books for general audiences include* Mistakes Were Made (but not by ME), *with Carol Tavris, and a memoir,* Not by Chance Alone: My Life as a Social Psychologist.

Tim Wilson

One day when I was 8, a couple of older kids rode up on their bikes to share some big news: They had discovered an abandoned house down a country road. "It's really neat," they said. "We broke a window and nobody cared!" My friend and I hopped onto our bikes to investigate. We had no trouble finding the house—there it was, sitting off by itself, with a big, jagged hole in a first-floor window. We got off of our bikes and looked around. My friend found a baseball-sized rock lying on the ground and threw a perfect strike through another first-floor window. There was something exhilarating about the smash-and-tingle of shattering glass, especially when we knew there was nothing wrong with what we were doing. After all, the house was abandoned, wasn't it? We broke nearly every window in the house and then climbed through one of the first-floor windows to look around.

It was then that we realized something was terribly wrong. The house certainly did not look abandoned. There were pictures on the wall, nice furniture, books in shelves. We went home feeling frightened and confused. We soon learned that the house was the home of an elderly couple who were away on vacation. Eventually, my parents discovered what we had done and paid a substantial sum to repair the windows. For years, I pondered this incident: Why did I do such a terrible thing? Was I a bad kid? I didn't think so, and neither did my parents. How, then, could a good kid do such a bad thing? Even though the neighborhood kids said the house was abandoned, why couldn't my friend and I see the clear signs that someone lived there? How crucial was it that my friend was there and threw the first rock? Although I didn't know it at the time, these reflections touched on several classic social psychological issues, such as whether only bad people do bad things, whether the social situation can be powerful enough to make good people do bad things, and the way in which our expectations about an event can make it difficult to see it as it really is. Fortunately, my career as a vandal ended with this one incident. It did, however, mark the beginning of my fascination with basic questions about how people understand themselves and the social world—questions I continue to investigate to this day.

Tim Wilson did his undergraduate work at Williams College and Hampshire College and received his PhD from the University of Michigan. Currently Sherrell J. Aston Professor of Psychology at the University of Virginia, he has published numerous articles in the areas of introspection, attitude change, self-knowledge, and affective forecasting, as well as a recent book, Redirect: The Surprising New Science of Psychological Change. *His research has received the support of the National Science Foundation and the National Institute for Mental Health. He has been elected twice to the Executive Board of the Society for Experimental Social Psychology and is a Fellow in the American Psychological Society and the Society for Personality and Social Psychology. In 2009, he was named a Fellow of the American Academy of Arts and Sciences. In 2015 he received the William James Fellows Award from the Association for Psychological Science. Wilson has taught the Introduction to Social Psychology course at the University of Virginia for more than 30 years. In 2001 he was awarded the University of Virginia All-University Outstanding Teaching Award, and in 2010 was awarded the University of Virginia Distinguished Scientist Award.*

Sam Sommers

I went to college to major in English. I only found myself in an Intro to Psychology course as a second-semester freshman because, well, it just seemed like the kind of thing you did as a second-semester freshman. It was when we got to the social psychology section of the course that a little voice in my head starting whispering something along the lines of, *Hey, you've gotta admit this is pretty good stuff. It's a lot like the conversations you have with your friends about daily life, but with scientific data.*

As part of the class, we had the opportunity to participate in research studies for course credit. So one day I found myself in an interaction study in which I was going to work on solving problems with a partner. I walked in and it was clear that the other guy had arrived earlier—his coat and bag were already hanging on the back of a chair. I was led to another, smaller room and shown a video of my soon-to-be partner. Then I was given a series of written questions about my perceptions of him, my expectations for our upcoming session together, and so forth. Finally, I walked back into the main area. The experimenter handed me a chair and told me to put it down anywhere next to my partner's chair, and that she would go get him (he, too, was presumably completing written questionnaires in a private room).

So I did. I put my chair down, took a seat, and waited. Then the experimenter returned, but she was alone. She told me the study was over. There was no other participant; there would be no problem solving in pairs. The video I

had watched was of an actor, and in some versions of the study he mentioned having a girlfriend. In other versions, he mentioned a boyfriend. What the researchers were actually studying was how this social category information of sexual orientation would influence participants' attitudes about the interaction.

And then she took out a tape measure.

The tape measure was to gauge how close to my partner's chair I had placed my own chair, the hypothesis being that discomfort with a gay partner might manifest in terms of participants placing their chairs farther away. Greater comfort with or affinity for the partner was predicted to lead to more desire for proximity.

And at that, I was hooked. The little voice in my head had grown from a whisper to a full-throated yell that this was a field I could get excited about. First of all, the researchers had tricked me. That, alone, I thought was, for lack of a better word, *cool.* But more important, they had done so in the effort to get me and my fellow participants to reveal something about our attitudes, preferences, and tendencies that we never would have admitted to (or perhaps even would have been aware of) had they just asked us directly. Here was a fascinatingly creative research design, being used in the effort to study what struck me as an incredibly important social issue.

Like I said, I was hooked. And I look forward to helping to introduce you to this field that caught me by surprise back when I was a student and continues to intrigue and inspire me to this day.

Sam Sommers earned his BA from Williams College and his PhD from the University of Michigan. Since 2003 he has been a faculty member in the Department of Psychology at Tufts University in Medford, Massachusetts. His research examines issues related to stereotyping, prejudice, and group diversity, with a particular interest in how these processes play out in the legal domain. He has won multiple teaching awards at Tufts, including the Lerman-Neubauer Prize for Outstanding Teaching and Advising and the Gerald R. Gill Professor of the Year Award. He was also inducted into the Tufts Hall of Diversity for his efforts to promote an inclusive climate on campus for all students. He has testified as an expert witness on issues related to racial bias, jury decision making, and eyewitness memory in criminal trial proceedings in eight states. He has written two general audience books related to social psychology: Situations Matter: Understanding How Context Transforms Your World *(2011) and* This Is Your Brain on Sports: The Science of Underdogs, the Value of Rivalry, and What We Can Learn from the T-shirt Cannon *(2016). He is also co-author of* Invitation to Psychology *(7th edition), along with Carole Wade, Carol Tavris, and Lisa Shin.*

Special Tips for Students

"There is then creative reading as well as creative writing," said Ralph Waldo Emerson in 1837, and that aptly sums up what you need to know to be a proficient student: Be an active, creative consumer of information. How do you accomplish that feat? Actually, it's not difficult. Like everything else in life, it just takes some work—some clever, well-planned, purposeful work. Here are some suggestions about how to do it.

Get to Know the Textbook

Believe it or not, in writing this book, we thought carefully about the organization and structure of each chapter. Things are presented as they are for a reason, and that reason is to help you learn the material in the best way possible. Here are some tips on what to look for in each chapter.

Key terms are in boldface type in the text so that you'll notice them. We define the terms in the text, and that definition appears again in the margin. These marginal definitions are there to help you out if later in the chapter you forget what something means. The marginal definitions are quick and easy to find. You can also look up key terms in the alphabetical Glossary at the end of this textbook.

Make sure you notice the headings and subheadings. The headings are the skeleton that holds a chapter together. They link together like vertebrae. If you ever feel lost, look back to the previous heading and the headings before it—this will give you the "big picture" of where the chapter is going. It should also help you see the connections between sections.

The summary at the end of each chapter is a succinct shorthand presentation of the chapter information. You should read it and make sure there are no surprises when you do so. If anything in the summary doesn't ring a bell, go back to the chapter and reread that section. Most important, remember that the summary is intentionally brief, whereas your understanding of the material should be full and complete. Use the summary as a study aid before your exams. When you read it over, everything should be familiar. When you have that wonderful feeling of knowing more than is in the summary, you'll know that you are ready to take the exam.

Be sure to do the Try It! exercises. They will make concepts from social psychology concrete and help you see how they can be applied to your own life. Some of the Try It! exercises replicate social psychology experiments. Others reproduce self-report scales so you can see where you stand in relation to other people. Still others are short quizzes that illustrate social psychological concepts.

Watch the videos. Our carefully curated collection of interviews, news clips, and research study reenactments is designed to enhance, and help you better understand, the concepts you're reading. If you can see the concept in action, it's likely to sink in a little deeper.

Just Say No to the Couch Potato Within

Because social psychology is about everyday life, you might lull yourself into believing that the material is all common sense. Don't be fooled. The material presented in this book is more complicated than it might seem. Therefore, we want to emphasize that the best way to learn it is to work with it in an active, not passive, fashion. You can't just read a chapter once and expect it to stick with you. You have to go over the material, wrestle with it, make your own connections to it, question it, think about it, interact with it. Actively working with material makes it memorable and makes it your own. Because it's a safe bet that someone is going to ask you about this material later and you're going to have to pull it out of memory, do what you can to get it into memory now. Here are some techniques to use:

- Go ahead and highlight lines in the text—you can do so in Revel by clicking and dragging the cursor over a sentence; you can even choose your own color, and add a note! If you highlight important points, you will remember those important points better and can scroll back through them later.

- Read the chapter before the applicable class lecture, not afterward. This way, you'll get more out of the lecture, which will likely introduce new material in addition to what is in the chapter. The chapter will give you the big picture, as well as a lot of detail. The lecture will enhance that information and help you put it all together. If you haven't read the chapter first, you may not understand some of the points made in the lecture or realize which points are most important.

- Here's a good way to study material: Write out a key concept or a study in your own words, without looking at the book or your notes. Or say it out loud to yourself—again in your own words, with your eyes closed. Can you do it? How good was your version? Did you omit anything important? Did you get stuck at some point, unable to remember what comes next? If so, you now know that you need to go over that information in more detail. You can also study with someone else, describing theories and studies to each other and seeing if you're making sense.

- If you have trouble remembering the results of an important study, try drawing your own version of a graph of the findings (you can use our data graphs for an idea of how to proceed). You will probably find that you remember the research results much better in pictorial form than in words. Draw the information a few times and it will stay with you.

- Remember, the more you work with the material, the better you will learn and remember it. Write it in your own words, talk about it, explain it to others, or draw visual representations of it.

- Last but not least, remember that this material is a lot of fun. You haven't even started reading the book yet, but we think you're going to like it. In particular, you'll see how much social psychology has to tell you about your real, everyday life. As this course progresses, you might want to remind yourself to observe the events of your daily life with new eyes—the eyes of a social psychologist—and try to apply what you are learning to the behavior of friends, acquaintances, strangers, and, yes, even yourself. In each chapter you will see how other students have done this in brief videos called #SurvivalTips. Make sure you use the Try It! exercises. You will find out how much social psychology can help us understand our lives. When you read the news, think about what social psychology has to say about current events and behaviors; we believe you will find that your understanding of daily life is richer. If you notice a news article that you think is an especially good example of "social psychology in action," please send it to us, with a full reference to where you found it and on what page. If we decide to use it in the next edition of this book, we'll list your name in the Acknowledgments.

We realize that 10 years from now you may not remember all the facts, theories, and names you learn now. Although we hope you will remember some of them, our main goal is for you to take with you into your future a great many of the broad social psychological concepts presented herein—and, perhaps more important, a critical and scientific way of thinking. If you open yourself to social psychology's magic, we believe it will enrich the way you look at the world and the way you live in it.

Chapter 1
Introducing Social Psychology

Chapter Outline and Learning Objectives

Defining Social Psychology

LO 1.1 Define social psychology and distinguish it from other disciplines.

Social Psychology, Philosophy, Science, and Common Sense

How Social Psychology Differs From Its Closest Cousins

The Power of the Situation

LO 1.2 Summarize why it matters how people explain and interpret events, as well as their own and others' behavior.

Underestimating the Power of the Situation

The Importance of Construal

Where Construals Come From: Basic Human Motives

LO 1.3 Explain what happens when people's need to feel good about themselves conflicts with their need to be accurate.

The Self-Esteem Motive: The Need to Feel Good About Ourselves

The Social Cognition Motive: The Need to Be Accurate

Why Study Social Psychology?

LO 1.4 Explain why the study of social psychology is important.

WHAT DO YOU THINK?

Survey	**What Do You Think?**	
	SURVEY	RESULTS

Do you consider yourself good at predicting how people around you will behave and react under different circumstances?

○ Yes

○ No

It is a pleasure to be your tour guides as we take you on a journey through the world of social psychology. As we embark on this journey, our hope is to convey our excitement about social psychology—what it is and why it matters. Not only do we, the authors, enjoy teaching this stuff (which we've been doing, combined, for more than 100 years), we also love contributing to the growth and development of this field. In addition to being teachers, each of us is a scientist who has contributed to the knowledge base that makes up our discipline. Thus, not only are we leading this tour, we also helped create some of its attractions. We will travel to fascinating and exotic places like prejudice, love, propaganda, education, conformity, aggression, compassion… all the rich variety and surprise of human social life. Ready? OK, let's go!

Let's begin with a few examples of the heroic, touching, tragic, and puzzling things that people do:

- Jorge Munoz is a school bus driver during the day but works a different "job" at night: Feeding the hungry. When he gets home from his last school bus run, he and his family cook meals for dozens of people using donated food and their own money. They then serve the food to people down on their luck who line up at a street corner in Queens, New York. Over a 4-year period Munoz has fed more than 70,000 people. Why does he do it? "When they smile," Munoz says, "That's the way I get paid." (http://www.karmatube.org/videos.php?id=1606)

- Kristen has known Martin for 2 months and feels that she is madly in love with him. "We're soul mates!" she tells her best friend. "He's the one!" "What are you thinking?" says the best friend. "He's completely wrong for you! He's as different from you as can be—different background, religion, politics; you even like different movies." "I'm not worried," says Kristen. "Opposites attract. I know that's true; I read it on Wikipedia!"

- Janine and her brother Oscar are arguing about fraternities. Janine's college didn't have any, but Oscar is at a large state university in the Midwest, where he has joined Alpha Beta. He went through a severe and scary hazing ritual to join, and Janine cannot understand why he loves these guys so much. "They make the pledges do such stupid stuff," she says. "They humiliate you and force you to get sick drunk and practically freeze to death in the middle of the night. How can you possibly be happy living there?" "You don't get it," Oscar replies. "Alpha Beta is the best of all fraternities. My frat brothers just seem more fun than most other guys."

- Abraham Biggs Jr., age 19, had been posting to an online discussion board for 2 years. Unhappy about his future and that a relationship had ended, Biggs announced on camera that he was going to commit suicide. He took an overdose of drugs and linked to a live video feed from his bedroom. None of his hundreds of observers called the police for more than 10 hours; some egged him on. Paramedics reached him too late, and Biggs died.

- In the mid-1970s, several hundred members of the Peoples Temple, a California-based religious cult, immigrated to Guyana under the guidance of their leader, the Reverend Jim Jones, where they founded an interracial community called Jonestown. But within a few years some members wanted out, an outside investigation was about to get Jones in trouble, and the group's solidarity was waning. Jones grew despondent and, summoning everyone in the community, spoke to them about the beauty of dying and the certainty that everyone would meet again in another place. The residents willingly lined up in front of a vat containing a mixture of Kool-Aid and cyanide, and drank the lethal concoction. (The legacy of this massacre is the term "drinking the Kool-Aid," referring to a person's blind belief in ideology.) A total of 914 people died, including 80 babies and the Reverend Jones.

Why do many people help complete strangers? Is Kristen right that opposites attract or is she just kidding herself? Why did Oscar come to love his fraternity brothers despite the hazing they had put him through? Why would people watch a troubled young man commit suicide in front of their eyes, when, by simply flagging the video to alert the website, they might have averted a tragedy? How could hundreds of people be induced to kill their own children and then commit suicide?

All of these stories—the good, the bad, the ugly—pose fascinating questions about human behavior. In this book, we will show you how social psychologists go about answering them.

Defining Social Psychology

LO 1.1   Define social psychology and distinguish it from other disciplines.

The task of the psychologist is to understand and predict human behavior. To do so, social psychologists focus on the influence other people have on us. More formally, **social psychology** is the scientific study of the way in which people's thoughts, feelings, and behaviors are influenced by the real or imagined presence of other people (Allport, 1985). When we think of social influence, the kinds of examples that readily come to mind are direct attempts at persuasion, whereby one person deliberately tries to change another person's behavior or attitude. This is what happens when advertisers use sophisticated techniques to persuade us to buy a particular brand of deodorant, or when our friends try to get us to do something we don't really want to do ("Come on, have another beer!"), or when the bullies use force or threats to get what they want.

The study of direct attempts at **social influence** is a major part of social psychology and will be discussed in our chapters on conformity, attitudes, and group processes. To the social psychologist, however, social influence is much broader than attempts by one person to change another person's behavior. Social influence shapes

Social Psychology
The scientific study of the way in which people's thoughts, feelings, and behaviors are influenced by the real or imagined presence of other people

Social Influence
The effect that the words, actions, or mere presence of other people have on our thoughts, feelings, attitudes, or behavior

Our thoughts, feelings, and actions are influenced by our immediate surroundings, including the presence of other people—even mere strangers.

Try It!

Conflicting Social Influences

Think of situations in which you feel conflicting pressures: your parents (or other influential adults in your life) would like you to do one thing, but your friends would like you to do something altogether different. Are there situations like this in which you feel conflicting pressures from your parents versus your friends? How do you decide how to act in these situations?

our thoughts and feelings as well as our overt acts, and takes many forms other than deliberate attempts at persuasion. For example, we are often influenced merely by the *presence* of other people, including perfect strangers who are not interacting with us. Other people don't even have to be present: We are governed by the imaginary approval or disapproval of our parents, friends, and teachers and by how we expect others to react to us. Sometimes these influences conflict with one another, and social psychologists are especially interested in what happens in the mind of an individual when they do. For example, conflicts frequently occur when young people go off to college and find themselves torn between the beliefs and values they learned at home and the beliefs and values of their professors or peers. (See the Try It! above) We will spend the rest of this introductory chapter expanding on these issues, so that you will get an idea of what social psychology is, what it isn't, and how it differs from other, related disciplines.

Social Psychology, Philosophy, Science, and Common Sense

Throughout history, philosophy has provided many insights about human nature. Indeed, the work of philosophers is part of the foundation of contemporary psychology. Psychologists have looked to philosophers for insights into the nature of consciousness (e.g., Dennett, 1991) and how people form beliefs about the social world (e.g., Gilbert, 1991). Sometimes, however, even great thinkers find themselves in disagreement with one another. When this occurs, how are we supposed to know who is right?

We social psychologists address many of the same questions that philosophers do, but we attempt to look at these questions scientifically—even questions concerning that great human mystery, love. In 1663, the Dutch philosopher Benedict Spinoza offered a highly original insight. In sharp disagreement with the hedonistic philosopher Aristippus, he proposed that if we fall in love with someone whom we formerly hated, that love will be stronger than if hatred had not preceded it. Spinoza's proposition was beautifully stated, but that doesn't mean it is true. These are *empirical* questions, meaning that their answers should be derived from experimentation or measurement rather than by personal opinion (Aronson, 1999; Wilson, 2015).

Now let's take another look at the examples that opened this chapter. Why did these people behave the way they did? One way to answer would simply be to ask them. We could ask Jorge Munoz why he spends so much time and money feeding the poor; we could ask the people who observed Abraham Biggs's suicide why they didn't call the police; we could ask Oscar why he enjoys fraternity life. The problem with this approach is that people are often unaware of the reasons behind their own responses and feelings (Nisbett & Wilson, 1977; Wilson, 2002). People might come up with plenty of justifications for not calling the police to rescue Biggs, but those justifications might not be the *reason* they did nothing.

Another approach is to rely on common sense or folk wisdom. Social psychologists are not opposed to folk wisdom—far from it. The primary problem with relying entirely on such sources is that they often disagree with one another. Consider what folk wisdom has to say about the factors that influence how much we like other people. We know that "birds of a feather flock together." Of course, we say, thinking of the many examples of our pleasure in hanging out with people who share our backgrounds and interests. But folk wisdom also tells us—as it persuaded lovestruck Kristen—that "opposites attract." Of course, we say, thinking of all the times we were attracted to people with different backgrounds and interests. Well, which is it? Similarly, are we to believe that "out of sight is out of mind" or that "absence makes the heart grow fonder"?

Social psychologists would suggest that there are some conditions under which birds of a feather do flock together, and other conditions under which opposites do attract. Similarly, in some conditions absence does make the heart grow fonder, and in others "out of sight" does mean out of mind. But it's not enough to say both proverbs can be true. Part of the job of the social psychologist is to do the research that specifies the *conditions* under which one or another is most likely to take place.

NATO-led soldiers inspect the site of a suicide attack in Afghanistan. What causes a person to become a suicide bomber? Popular theories say such people must be mentally ill, alienated loners, or psychopaths. But social psychologists would try to understand the circumstances and situations that drive otherwise healthy, well-educated, bright people to commit murder and suicide for the sake of a religious or political goal.

Thus, in explaining why two people like each other—or any other topic of interest—social psychologists would want to know which of many possible explanations is the most likely. To do this, we have devised an array of scientific methods to test our assumptions, guesses, and ideas about human social behavior, empirically and systematically rather than by relying on folk wisdom, common sense, or the opinions and insights of philosophers, novelists, political pundits, and our grandmothers. Doing experiments in social psychology presents many challenges, primarily because we are attempting to predict the behavior of highly sophisticated organisms in complex situations. As scientists, our goal is to find objective answers to such questions as: What are the factors that cause aggression? What causes prejudice, and how might we reduce it? What variables cause two people to like or love each other? Why do certain kinds of political advertisements work better than others? In Chapter 2 we discuss the scientific methods social psychologists use to answer questions such as these.

How Social Psychology Differs From Its Closest Cousins

Social psychology is related to other disciplines in the physical and social sciences, including biology, neuroscience, sociology, economics, and political science. Each examines the determinants of human behavior, but important differences set social psychology apart—most notably in its level of analysis. For biologists and neuroscientists, the level of analysis might be genes, hormones, or physiological processes in the brain. Although social psychologists sometimes draw on this approach to study the relationship between the brain and social behavior, their emphasis is, as we will see, more on how people interpret the social world.

Other social psychologists draw on the major theory of biology—evolutionary theory—to generate hypotheses about social behavior. In biology, evolutionary theory is used to explain how different species acquired physical traits, such as long necks.

In an environment where food is scarce, giraffes that happened to have long necks could feed on foliage that other animals couldn't reach. These giraffes were more likely to survive and reproduce offspring than were giraffes with shorter necks, the story goes, such that the "long neck" gene became dominant in subsequent generations.

But what about social behaviors, such as the tendency to be aggressive toward a member of one's own species or the tendency to be helpful to others? Is it possible that social behaviors also have genetic determinants that evolve through the process of natural selection, and if so, is this true in human beings as well as other animals? These are the questions posed by **evolutionary psychology**, which attempts to explain social behavior in terms of genetic factors that have evolved over time according to the principles of natural selection. The core idea is that evolution occurs very slowly, such that social behaviors that are prevalent today, such as aggression and helping behavior, are a result, at least in part, of adaptations to environments in our distant past (Brown & Cross, 2017; Buss, 2005; Neuberg, Kenrick, & Schaller, 2010). We will discuss in upcoming chapters how evolutionary theory explains social behavior (e.g., Chapter 10 on interpersonal attraction, Chapter 11 on prosocial behavior, and Chapter 12 on aggression).

We note here that a lively debate has arisen over the testability of evolutionary hypotheses. Because current behaviors are thought to be adaptations to environmental conditions that existed thousands of years ago, psychologists make their best guesses about what those conditions were and how specific kinds of behaviors gave people a reproductive advantage. But these hypotheses are obviously impossible to test with the experimental method. And just because hypotheses sound plausible does not mean they are true. For example, some scientists now believe that giraffes did not acquire a long neck to eat leaves in tall trees. Instead, they suggest, long necks first evolved in male giraffes to gain an advantage in fights with other males over access to females (Simmons & Scheepers, 1996). Which of these explanations is true? It's hard to tell. Evolutionary explanations can't be tested directly, because after all, they involve hypotheses about what happened thousands of years ago. They can, however, suggest novel hypotheses about why people do what they do in today's world, which can then be put to the test, as we will see in later chapters.

Well, if we aren't going to rely solely on an evolutionary or biological approach, how else might we explain why people do what they do, such as in the examples that opened this chapter? If you are like most people, when you read these examples you assumed that the individuals involved had some weaknesses, strengths, and personality traits that led them to respond as they did. Some people are leaders and others are followers; some people are public-spirited and others are selfish; some are brave and others are cowardly. Perhaps the people who failed to get help for Abraham Biggs were lazy, timid, selfish, or heartless. Given what you know about their behavior, would you loan them your car or trust them to take care of your new puppy?

Explaining people's behavior in terms of their traits is the work of personality psychologists, who generally focus on *individual differences*, that is, the aspects of people's personalities that make them different from others. Research on personality increases our understanding of human behavior, but social psychologists believe that explaining behavior primarily through personality traits ignores a critical part of the story: the powerful role played by social influence.

Consider again the tragedy at Jonestown. Remember that it was not just a handful of people who committed suicide there, but almost 100% of them. It is highly improbable that they were all mentally ill or had the same constellation of personality traits. If we want a richer, more thorough explanation of this tragic event, we need to understand what kind of power and influence a charismatic figure like Jim Jones possessed, the nature of the impact of living in a closed society cut off from other points of view, and other factors that could have caused mentally healthy people to obey him. In fact, as social psychologists have shown, the social conditions at Jonestown were such

Evolutionary Psychology

The attempt to explain social behavior in terms of genetic factors that have evolved over time according to the principles of natural selection

that virtually anyone—even strong, nondepressed individuals like you or us—would have succumbed to Jones's influence.

Here is a more mundane example. Suppose you go to a party and see a great-looking fellow student you have been hoping to get to know better. The student is looking uncomfortable, however—standing alone, not making eye contact, not talking to anyone who comes over. You decide you're not so interested; this person seems pretty aloof, even arrogant. But a few weeks later you see the student again, now being super social and witty, the center of attention. So what is this person "really" like? Aloof and arrogant or charming and welcoming? It's the wrong question; the answer is both and neither. All of us are capable of being shy in some situations and outgoing in others. A much more interesting question is: What factors were different in these two situations that had such a profound effect on the student's behavior? That is a social psychological question. (See the Try It!)

For personality and clinical psychologists, the level of the analysis is the individual. For the social psychologist, the level of analysis is the individual in the context of a social situation—particularly the individual's **construal** of that situation. The word *construal*, which means how people perceive, comprehend, and interpret the social world, is a favorite among social psychologists, because it conveys how important it is to get inside people's heads and understand how they see the world, and how those construals are shaped by the social context. For example, to understand why people intentionally hurt one another, the social psychologist focuses on how people construe a specific social situation: Do they do so in a way that makes them feel frustrated? Does frustration always precede aggression? If people are feeling frustrated, under what conditions will they vent their frustration with an aggressive act and under what conditions will they restrain themselves? (See Chapter 12.)

Other social sciences are more concerned with social, economic, political, and historical factors that influence events. Sociology, rather than focusing on the individual,

Personality psychologists study qualities of the individual that might make a person shy, conventional, rebellious, and willing to wear a turquoise wig in public or a yellow shirt in a sea of blue. Social psychologists study the powerful role of social influence on how all of us behave.

Construal

The way in which people perceive, comprehend, and interpret the social world

Try It!

Social Situations and Shyness

1. Think about one of your friends or acquaintances whom you regard as shy. (You may use yourself!) Try not to think about him or her as "a shy person," but rather as someone who has difficulty relating to people in some situations but not others.
2. List the situations you think are most likely to bring out your friend's shy behavior.
3. List the situations that might bring forth more outgoing behaviors on your friend's part. Being with a small group of friends he or she is at ease with? Being with a new person, but one who shares your friend's interests?
4. Set up a social environment that you think would make your friend comfortable. Pay close attention to the effect that it has on your friend's behavior—or yours.

The people in this photo can be studied from a variety of perspectives: as individuals or as members of a family, a social class, an occupation, a culture, or a region. Sociologists study the group or institution; social psychologists study the influence of those groups and institutions on individual behavior.

focuses on such topics as social class, social structure, and social institutions. Of course, because society is made up of collections of people, some overlap is bound to exist between the domains of sociology and those of social psychology. The major difference is that in sociology, *the level of analysis is the group, institution, or society at large,* whereas the level of analysis in social psychology is the individual within a group, institution, or society. So although sociologists, like social psychologists, are interested in causes of aggression, sociologists are more likely to be concerned with why a particular society (or group within a society) produces different levels of violence in its members. Why is the murder rate in the United States so much higher than in Canada or Europe? Within the United States, why is the murder rate higher in some geographic regions than in others? How do changes in society relate to changes in aggressive behavior?

Social psychology differs from other social sciences not only in the level of analysis, but also in what is being explained. *The goal of social psychology is to identify psychological properties that make almost everyone susceptible to social influence, regardless of social class or culture.* The laws governing the relationship between frustration and aggression, for example, are hypothesized to be true of most people in most places, not just members of one gender, social class, culture, age group, or ethnicity.

However, because social psychology is a young science that developed mostly in the United States, some of its findings have not yet been tested in other cultures to see if they are universal. Nonetheless, our goal is to discover such laws. And increasingly, as methods and theories developed by American social psychologists are adopted by European, Asian, African, Middle Eastern, and South American social psychologists, we are learning more about the extent to which these laws are universal, as well as cultural differences in the way these laws are expressed, as well as cultural influences on how people interpret the social world (see Chapter 2). *Cross-cultural research* is therefore extremely valuable, because it sharpens theories, either by demonstrating their universality or by leading us to discover additional variables that help us improve our understanding and prediction of human behavior. We will offer many examples of cross-cultural research in this book.

In sum, social psychology is located between its closest cousins, sociology and personality psychology (see Table 1.1). Social psychology and sociology share an interest in the way the situation and the larger society influence behavior. Social psychology and personality psychology share an interest in the psychology of the individual. But social psychologists work in the overlap between those two disciplines: They emphasize the psychological processes shared by most people around the world that make them susceptible to social influence.

Table 1.1 Social Psychology Compared to Related Disciplines

Biology and Neuroscience	Personality Psychology	Social Psychology	Sociology
The study of genes, hormones, or physiological processes in the brain	The study of the characteristics that make individuals unique and different from one another	The study of the psychological processes people have in common that make them susceptible to social influence	The study of groups, organizations, and societies, rather than individuals

Review Questions

1. A social psychologist would tend to look for explanations of a young man's violent behavior *primarily* in terms of:
   a. his aggressive personality traits.
   b. possible genetic contributions.
   c. how his peer group behaves.
   d. what his father taught him.

2. The topic that would most interest a social psychologist is:
   a. how the level of extraversion of different presidents affected their political decisions.
   b. whether people's decision about whether to cheat on a test is influenced by how they imagine their friends would react if they found out.
   c. the extent to which people's social class predicts their income.
   d. what passers-by on the street think of global warming.

3. Which of the following is true about evolutionary psychology?
   a. Natural selection works differently in humans than other animals.
   b. It is easy to test evolutionary hypotheses by doing experiments.
   c. Most social behaviors are genetically determined with little influence by the social environment.
   d. Evolutionary approaches can generate novel hypotheses about social behavior that can then be tested with experiments.

4. How does social psychology differ from personality psychology?
   a. Social psychology focuses on individual differences, whereas personality psychology focuses on how people behave in different situations.
   b. Social psychology focuses on the shared processes that make people susceptible to social influence, whereas personality psychology focuses on individual differences.
   c. Social psychology provides general laws and theories about societies, whereas personality psychology studies the characteristics that make people unique.
   d. Social psychology focuses on individual differences, whereas personality psychology provides general laws and theories about societies.

5. What is the "level of analysis" for a social psychologist?
   a. The individual in the context of a social situation.
   b. The social situation itself.
   c. A person's level of achievement.
   d. A person's level of reasoning.

6. Which of the following research topics about violence is one that a social psychologist might investigate?
   a. How rates of violence change over time within a culture
   b. Why murder rates vary across cultures
   c. Brain abnormalities that produce aggression when a person is provoked
   d. Why some situations are more likely to provoke aggression than others

The Power of the Situation

LO 1.2   Summarize why it matters how people explain and interpret events, as well as their own and others' behavior.

Suppose you go to a restaurant with a group of friends. The server comes over to take your order, but you are having a hard time deciding which pie you want. While you are hesitating, she impatiently taps her pen against her notepad, rolls her eyes toward the ceiling, scowls at you, and finally snaps, "Hey, I haven't got all day!" Like most people, you would probably think that she is a nasty or unpleasant person.

But suppose, while you are deciding whether to complain about her to the manager, a regular customer tells you that your "crabby" server is a single parent who was kept awake all night by the moaning of her youngest child, who was terribly sick; that her car broke down on her way to work and she has no idea where she will find the money to have it repaired; that when she finally arrived at the restaurant, she learned that her coworker was too drunk to work, requiring her to cover twice the usual number of tables; and that the short-order cook keeps screaming at her because she is not picking up the orders fast enough. Given all that information, you might now conclude that she is not a nasty person but an ordinary human under enormous stress.

This small story has huge implications. Most Americans will explain someone's behavior in terms of personality; they focus on the fish, and not the water the fish swims in. The fact that they fail to take the situation into account has a profound impact on how human beings relate to one another—such as, in the case of the server, whether they feel sympathy and tolerance or impatience and anger.

Underestimating the Power of the Situation

Fundamental Attribution Error

The tendency to overestimate the extent to which people's behavior is due to internal, dispositional factors and to underestimate the role of situational factors

The social psychologist is up against a formidable barrier known as the **fundamental attribution error**, which is the tendency to explain our own and other people's behavior entirely in terms of personality traits and to underestimate the power of social influence and the immediate situation. We are going to give you the basics of this phenomenon here, because you will be encountering it throughout this book.

Explaining behavior in terms of personality can give us a feeling of false security. When people try to explain repugnant or bizarre behavior, such as the people of Jonestown taking their own lives and killing their own children, they find it tempting and, in a strange way, comforting to write off the victims as flawed human beings. Doing so gives them the feeling that it could never happen to them. Ironically, this way of thinking actually increases our vulnerability to destructive social influences by making us less aware of our own susceptibility to them. Moreover, by failing to fully appreciate the power of the situation, we tend to oversimplify the problem, which can lead us to blame the victim in situations where the individual was overpowered by social forces too difficult for most of us to resist, as in the Jonestown tragedy.

To take a more everyday example, imagine a situation in which two people are playing a game and they must choose one of two strategies: They can play competitively and try to win as much money as possible and make sure their partner loses as much as possible, or they can play cooperatively and try to make sure they both win some money. How do you think each of your friends would play this game?

Few people find this question hard to answer; we all have a feeling for the relative competitiveness of our friends. Accordingly, you might say, "I am certain that my friend Jennifer, who is a hard-nosed business major, would play this game more competitively than my friend Anna, who is a soft-hearted, generous person." But how accurate are you likely to be? Should you be thinking about the game itself rather than who is playing it?

To find out, researchers at Stanford University conducted the following experiment (Liberman, Samuels, & Ross, 2004). They described the game to resident assistants (RAs) in a student dorm and asked them to come up with a list of undergrads whom they thought were either especially cooperative or especially competitive. As expected, the RAs easily identified students who fit each category. Next, the researchers invited these students to play the game in a psychology experiment. There was one added twist: The researchers varied a seemingly minor aspect of the social situation—what the game was called. They told half the participants that they would be playing the Wall Street Game and the other half that they would be playing the Community Game. Everything else about the game was identical. People who were judged as either competitive or cooperative played a game that was called either the Wall Street Game or the Community Game, resulting in four conditions: cooperative people playing the Wall Street Game, cooperative people playing the Community Game, competitive people playing the Wall Street Game, or competitive people playing the Community Game.

Again, most of us go through life assuming that what really counts is an individual's true character, not something about the individual's immediate situation and certainly not something as trivial as what a game is called, right? Not so fast! As you can see in Figure 1.1, the name of the game made a tremendous difference in how people behaved. When it was called the Wall Street Game, approximately two-thirds of the students responded competitively; when it was called the Community Game, only a third responded competitively. The name of the game sent a powerful message about how the players should behave. But a student's alleged personality trait made no measurable difference in the student's behavior. The students labeled *competitive* were no more likely to adopt the competitive strategy than those who were labeled *cooperative*. We will see this pattern of results throughout this book: Aspects of the social

Figure 1.1 Why the Name of the Game Matters

In this experiment, when the name of the game was the "Community Game," players were far more likely to behave cooperatively than when it was called the "Wall Street Game"—regardless of their own cooperative or competitive personality traits. The game's title conveyed social norms that trumped personality and shaped the players' behavior.

(Data from Liberman, Samuels, & Ross, 2004)

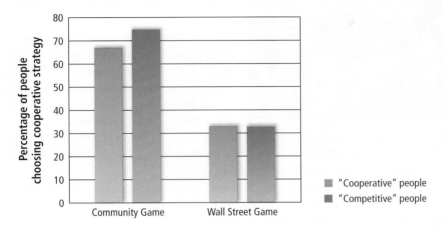

situation that may seem minor can overwhelm the differences in people's personalities (Ross & Ward, 1996).

If merely assigning a name to a game in a psychology experiment has such a large impact on the behavior of the players, what do you think the impact would be conveying to students in a classroom that the activity they were doing was competitive or cooperative? Suppose you are a seventh-grade history teacher. In one of your classes, you structure the learning experience so that it resembles the situation implied by the term "Wall Street Game." You encourage competition, you tell your students to raise their hands as quickly as possible and to jeer at any incorrect answers given by other students. In your other class, you structure the learning situation such that the students are rewarded for cooperating with one another, for listening well, for encouraging one another and pulling together to learn the material. What do you suppose the effect these different situations might have on the performance of your students, on their enjoyment of school, and on their feelings about one another? Such an experiment will be discussed in Chapter 13 (Aronson & Patnoe, 2011).

Of course personality differences do exist and frequently are of great importance, but social and environmental situations are so powerful that they have dramatic effects on almost everyone. This is the domain of the social psychologist.

The Importance of Construal

It is one thing to say that the social situation has profound effects on human behavior, but what exactly do we mean by the social situation? One strategy for defining it would be to specify the objective properties of the situation, such as how rewarding it is to people, and then document the behaviors that follow from these objective properties.

This is the approach taken by **behaviorism**, a school of psychology maintaining that to

Behaviorism

A school of psychology maintaining that to understand human behavior, one need only consider the reinforcing properties of the environment

Watch WHAT WOULD YOU DO?

Watch SURVIVAL TIPS! USING SOCIAL PSYCHOLOGY TO NAVIGATE YOUR WORLD

understand human behavior, one need only consider the reinforcing properties of the environment: When behavior is followed by a reward (such as money, attention, praise, or other benefits), it is likely to continue; when behavior is followed by a punishment (such as pain, loss, or angry shouts), it is likely to stop, or become extinguished. Dogs come when they are called because they have learned that compliance is followed by positive reinforcement (e.g., food or petting); children memorize their multiplication tables more quickly if you praise them, smile at them, and paste a gold star on their foreheads following correct answers. Behavioral psychologists, notably the pioneering behaviorist B. F. Skinner (1938), believed that all behavior could be understood by examining the rewards and punishments in the organism's environment.

Behaviorism has many strengths, and its principles explain some behavior very well. (See Chapter 10.) However, because the early behaviorists did not concern themselves with cognition, thinking, and feeling—concepts they considered too vague and mentalistic and not sufficiently anchored to observable behavior—they overlooked phenomena that are vital to the human social experience. Most especially, they overlooked the importance of *how people interpret their environments.*

For social psychologists, people's behavior is not influenced directly by the situation but rather, as we mentioned earlier, by their construal of it (Griffin & Ross, 1991; Ross & Nisbett, 1991). For example, if a person approaches you, slaps you on the back, and asks you how you are feeling, your response will depend not on what that person has done, but on how you *construe* (i.e., interpret) that behavior. You

Gestalt Psychology

A school of psychology stressing the importance of studying the subjective way in which an object appears in people's minds rather than the objective, physical attributes of the object

might construe these actions differently depending on whether they come from a close friend who is concerned about your health, a casual acquaintance who is just passing the time of day, or a car salesperson attempting to be nice for the purpose of selling you a used car. And your answer will vary also, even if the question about your health were worded the same and asked in the same tone of voice. You would be unlikely to say, "Actually, I'm feeling pretty worried about this kidney pain" to a salesperson, but you might tell your close friend.

The emphasis on construal has its roots in an approach called **Gestalt psychology**. First proposed as a theory of how people perceive the physical world, Gestalt psychology holds that we should study the subjective way in which an object appears in people's minds (the *gestalt*, or whole) rather than the way in which the objective, physical attributes of the object combine. An illustration of this point is

Figure 1.2

An illustration of the Gestalt approach to perception is optical illusions, such as the one shown in the picture below. Is this a picture of a duck looking to the left or a rabbit looking the right? Objectively it is neither; rather, it is how you are *construing* it at any particular point in time.

how people perceive optical illusions like the one shown in Figure 1.2. What do you see in that figure? Do you see a duck looking to the left or a rabbit looking the right? Objectively it is neither; rather, it is how you are *construing* it at any particular point in time. That is, according to Gestalt psychology, one must focus on the phenomenology of the perceivers—on how an object appears to them—instead of on its objective components.

The Gestalt approach was formulated by German psychologists in the first part of the twentieth century. In the late 1930s, several of these psychologists fled to the United States to escape the Nazi regime. Among the émigrés was Kurt Lewin, generally considered the founding father of modern experimental social psychology. As a young German Jewish professor in the 1930s, Lewin experienced the anti-Semitism rampant in Nazi Germany. The experience profoundly affected his thinking, and once he moved to the United States, Lewin helped shape American social psychology, directing it toward a deep interest in exploring the causes and cures of prejudice and ethnic stereotyping.

Kurt Lewin (1890–1947).

As a theorist, Lewin took the bold step of applying Gestalt principles beyond the perception of objects—such as the duck/rabbit picture above—to how we perceive the social world. It is often more important to understand how people perceive, comprehend, and interpret each other's behavior, he said, than it is to understand its objective properties (Lewin, 1943). "If an individual sits in a room trusting that the ceiling will not come down," he said, "should only his 'subjective probability' be taken into account for predicting behavior or should we also consider the 'objective probability' of the ceiling's coming down as determined by engineers? To my mind, only the first has to be taken into account" (p. 308).

Social psychologists soon began to focus on the importance of how people construe their environments. Fritz Heider (1958), another early founder of social psychology, observed, "Generally, a person reacts to what he thinks the other person is perceiving, feeling, and thinking, in addition to what the other person may be doing" (p. 1). We are busy guessing all the time about the other person's state of mind, motives, and thoughts. We may be right—but often we are wrong.

That is why construal has major implications. In a murder trial, when the prosecution presents compelling evidence it believes will prove the defendant guilty, the verdict always hinges on precisely how each jury member construes that evidence. These construals rest on a variety of events and perceptions that often bear no objective relevance to the case. During cross-examination, did a key witness come across as being too remote or too arrogant? Did the prosecutor appear to be smug, obnoxious, or uncertain?

A special kind of construal is what Lee Ross calls **naïve realism**, that is, the conviction that we perceive things "as they really are," underestimating how much we are interpreting or "spinning" what we see. People with opposite political views, for example, often can't even agree on the facts; both sides think that they are "seeing as it really is," when in fact both are probably letting their beliefs color their interpretation of the facts. We tend to believe, therefore, that if other people see the same things differently, it must be because *they* are biased (Ehrlinger, Gilovich, & Ross, 2005; Pronin, Gilovich, & Ross, 2004; Ross, 2010). Ross has been working closely with Israeli and Palestinian negotiators who are trying to resolve the decade's long conflict between Israel and Palestine. These negotiations frequently run aground because of naïve realism; each side assumes that other reasonable people see things the same way they do. "[E]ven when each side recognizes that the other side perceives the issues differently," says Ross, "each thinks that the other side is biased while they themselves are objective and that their own perceptions of reality should provide the basis for settlement" (Ross, 2010). So both sides resist compromise, fearing that their "biased" opponent will benefit more than they.

Naïve Realism

The conviction that we perceive things "as they really are," underestimating how much we are interpreting or "spinning" what we see

Research by social psychologists on construal shows why negotiation between nations can be so difficult: Each side thinks that it sees the issues clearly but that the other side is "biased."

In a simple experiment, Ross took peace proposals created by Israeli negotiators, labeled them as Palestinian proposals, and asked Israeli citizens to judge them. The Israelis liked the Palestinian proposal attributed to Israel more than they liked the Israeli proposal attributed to the Palestinians. Ross (2010) concludes, "If your own proposal isn't going to be attractive to you when it comes from the other side, what chance is there that the *other* side's proposal is going to be attractive when it comes from the other side?" The hope is that once negotiators on both sides become fully aware of this phenomenon and how it impedes conflict resolution, a reasonable compromise will be more likely.

You can see that construals range from the simple (as in the question "How do you see it?") to the remarkably complex (international negotiations). And they affect all of us in our everyday lives. Imagine that Jason is a college student who admires Maria from afar. As a budding social psychologist, you have the job of predicting whether or not Jason will ask Maria to have dinner with him. To do this, you need to begin by viewing Maria's behavior through Jason's eyes—that is, by seeing how Jason interprets her behavior. If she smiles at him, does Jason construe her behavior as mere politeness, the kind of politeness she would extend to any of the dozens of nerds and losers in their class? Or does he view her smile as an encouraging sign that inspires him to ask her out? If she ignores him, does Jason figure that she's playing hard to get, or does he take it as a sign that she's not interested in him? To predict what Jason will do, it is not enough to know Maria's behavior; we must know how Jason construes her behavior. But how are these construals formed? Stay tuned.

#trending

What's in a Name?

Politicians recognize the power of construal, namely getting the public to interpret their policies in a favorable light. One way they do so is by putting positive labels on policies they favor and negative labels on ones they do not. Republicans, for example, labeled the Affordable Care Act as "Obamacare" to convey that it was the work of a president unpopular with many of their constituents. This rhetorical move was so successful that a sizeable number of people did not realize that Obamacare and the Affordable Care Act were the same thing. Take Kentucky, a state that created a state health insurance program called "Kynect" under of the Affordable Care Act. Kentucky's Governor

Steve Beshear called Kynect "an indispubtable success," and indeed, a 2014 poll found that only 22% of Kentucky residents had an unfavorable view of Kynect. This same poll did something clever, though—half of the residents were asked how they felt about Kynect, and half how they felt about Obamacare. When the latter term was used, 57% of residents said they had an unfavorable view (Dann, 2014). And it's not just Kentuckians who are confused: A poll conducted in February of 2017 found that 35% of Americans either did not know that Obamacare and the Affordable Care Act were the same thing or weren't sure (Dropp & Nyhan, 2017).

Review Questions

1. The *fundamental attribution error* is best defined as the tendency to
   a. explain our own and other people's behavior entirely in terms of personality traits, thereby underestimating the power of social influence.
   b. explain our own and other people's behavior in terms of the social situation, thereby underestimating the power of personality factors.
   c. believe that people's group memberships influence their behavior more than their personalities.
   d. believe that people's personalities influence their behavior more than their group memberships.

2. What does the Wall Street Game reveal about personality and situation?
   a. Competitive people will compete fiercely no matter what a game is called.
   b. Cooperative people will try hard to get competitive opponents to work with them.
   c. The name of the game makes no difference in how people play the game.
   d. The name of the game strongly influences how people play the game.

3. A stranger approaches Emily on campus and says he is a professional photographer. He asks if she will spend 15 minutes posing for pictures next to the student union. According to social psychologists, Emily's decision will depend on which of the following?
   a. How well dressed the man is
   b. Whether the man offers to pay her
   c. How Emily construes the situation
   d. Whether the man has a criminal record

4. Social psychology had its origins in
   a. Gestalt psychology.
   b. Freudian psychology.
   c. behavioral psychology.
   d. biological psychology.

5. "Naïve realism" refers to the fact that
   a. most people are naïve (uneducated) about psychology.
   b. few people are realistic.
   c. most people would rather be naïve than accurate.
   d. most people believe they perceive things accurately.

Where Construals Come From: Basic Human Motives

LO 1.3   Explain what happens when people's need to feel good about themselves conflicts with their need to be accurate.

How will Jason determine why Maria smiled at him? If it is true that subjective and not objective situations influence people, we need to understand how people arrive at their subjective impressions of the world. What are people trying to accomplish when they interpret the social world? Are they concerned with making an interpretation that places them in the most positive light (e.g., Jason's deciding that "Maria is ignoring me just to make me jealous") or with making the most accurate interpretation, even if it is unflattering (e.g., "Painful as it may be, I must admit that she would rather go out with a sea slug than with me")? Social psychologists seek to understand the fundamental motives that determine why we construe the social world the way we do.

We human beings are complex organisms. At any given moment, various intersecting motives underlie our thoughts and behaviors, including hunger, thirst, fear, a desire for control, and the promise of love and other rewards. (See Chapters 10 and 11.) Social psychologists emphasize the importance of two central motives in steering people's construals: *the need to feel good about ourselves* and *the need to be accurate*. Sometimes, each of these motives pulls us in the same direction. Often, though, these motives tug us in opposite directions, where to perceive the world accurately requires us to admit that we have behaved foolishly or immorally.

Leon Festinger, one of social psychology's most innovative theorists, realized that it is precisely when these two motives pull in opposite directions that we can gain our most valuable insights into the workings of the mind. To illustrate, imagine that you are the president of the United States and your country is engaged in a difficult and costly war. You have poured hundreds of billions of dollars into that war, and it has

Leon Festinger (1919–1989) wrote: "If the empirical world looks complicated, if people seem to react in bewilderingly different ways to similar forces, and if I cannot see the operation of universal underlying dynamics, then that is my fault. I have asked the wrong questions; I have, at a theoretical level, sliced up the world incorrectly. The underlying dynamics are there, and I have to find the theoretical apparatus that will enable me to reveal these uniformities" (Festinger, 1980, p. 246). Finding and illuminating those underlying dynamics is the goal of social psychology.

This is Edward Snowden, a former computing contractor for the National Security Agency. Snowden's release in 2013 of thousands of classified documents related to the U.S. government's surveillance programs led the Department of Justice to charge him with espionage. Some have argued that Snowden is a spy, a traitor, and a criminal who should be brought back to the United States from his asylum in Russia to face trial. Others view him as a whistle-blower, a patriot, and a hero fighting to protect privacy rights and inform the American public of what its government is up to (in fact, here you see him pictured receiving a German peace prize, a prize he was only able to accept via Skype). Each side is sure that they are right. Where do differing construals come from, and what are their consequences?

consumed tens of thousands of American lives as well as thousands more lives of innocent civilians. The war seems to be at a stalemate; no end is in sight. You frequently wake up in the middle of the night, bathed in the cold sweat of conflict: On the one hand, you deplore all the carnage that is going on; on the other hand, you don't want to go down in history as the first American president to lose a war.

Some of your advisers tell you that they can see the light at the end of the tunnel, and that if you intensify the bombing or add thousands more troops, the enemy will soon capitulate and the war will be over. This would be a great outcome for you: Not only will you have succeeded in achieving your military and political aims, but history will consider you to have been a great leader as well. Other advisers, however, believe that intensifying the bombing will only strengthen the enemy's resolve; they advise you to sue for peace.

Which advisers are you likely to believe? President Lyndon Johnson faced this exact dilemma in the 1960s, with the war in Vietnam; so did George W. Bush in 2003, when the war in Iraq did not end in 6 weeks as he had predicted; so did Barack Obama and Donald Trump, in 2009 and 2017, respectively, in deciding whether to invest more troops in the war in Afghanistan. Most presidents have chosen to believe their advisers who suggest escalating the war, because if they succeed in winning, the victory justifies the human and financial cost; but withdrawing not only means going down in history as a president who lost a war, but also having to justify the fact that all those lives and all that money have been spent in vain. As you can see, the need to feel good about our decisions can fly in the face of the need to be accurate, and can have catastrophic consequences (Draper, 2008; McClellan, 2008; Woodward, 2010). In Johnson's case, the decision to increase the bombing *did* strengthen the enemy's resolve, thereby prolonging the war in Vietnam.

The Self-Esteem Motive: The Need to Feel Good About Ourselves

Self-Esteem

People's evaluations of their own self-worth—that is, the extent to which they view themselves as good, competent, and decent

Most people have a strong need to maintain reasonably high **self-esteem**—that is, to see themselves as good, competent, and decent (Aronson, 1998, 2007; Baumeister, 1993; Tavris & Aronson, 2007). Given the choice between distorting the world to feel good about themselves and representing the world accurately, people often take the first option. They put a slightly different spin on the matter, one that puts them in the best possible light. You might consider your friend Roger to be a nice guy but an awful slob—somehow he's always got stains on his shirt and empty food cartons all over his kitchen. Roger, though, probably describes himself as being casual and "laid back."

Self-esteem is obviously a beneficial thing, but when it causes people to justify their actions rather than learn from them, it can impede change and self-improvement. Suppose a couple gets divorced after 10 years of a marriage made difficult by the husband's irrational jealousy. Rather than admitting the truth—that his jealousy and possessiveness drove his wife away—the husband blames the breakup of his marriage on her; she was not responsive enough to his needs. His interpretation serves a purpose: It makes him feel better about himself (Simpson, 2010). The consequence of this distortion, of course, is that learning from experience becomes unlikely. In his next marriage, the husband will probably recreate the same problems. Acknowledging our deficiencies is difficult, even when the cost is failing to learn from our mistakes.

SUFFERING AND SELF-JUSTIFICATION Moreover, the need to maintain our self-esteem can have paradoxical effects. Let's go back to one of our early scenarios: Oscar and the hazing he went through to join his fraternity. Personality psychologists might suggest that only extraverts who have a high tolerance for embarrassment would want to be in a fraternity. Behavioral psychologists would predict that Oscar would dislike anyone or anything that caused him pain and humiliation. Social psychologists, however, have found that the major reason that Oscar and his fellow pledges like their fraternity brothers so much was *because* of the degrading hazing rituals.

These first-year students are being "welcomed" to their university by seniors who subject them to hazing. Hazing is sometimes silly, but it is often dangerous as well (and even fatal), leading college campuses to crack down on the practice. One difficulty faced by such efforts is that for all of its downsides, hazing can also build group cohesiveness. Does this explanation sound far-fetched? In Chapter 6 we will see a series of laboratory experiments that indeed show that people often come to love what they suffer for.

Here's how it works. Suppose Oscar freely chose to go through a severe hazing to become a member of the fraternity but later discovers unpleasant things about his fraternity brothers. If he were completely honest with himself he would conclude, "I'm an idiot; I went through all of that pain and embarrassment only to live in a house with a bunch of jerks." But saying "I'm an idiot" is not exactly the best way to maintain one's self-esteem, so instead Oscar puts a positive spin on his situation. "My fraternity brothers aren't perfect, but they are there when I need them and this house sure has great parties." He justifies the pain and embarrassment of the hazing by viewing his fraternity as positively as he can.

An outside observer like his sister Janine, however, can see the downside of fraternity life more clearly. The fraternity dues make a significant dent in Ocar's budget, the frequent parties take a toll on the amount of studying he can do, and consequently his grades suffer. But Oscar is motivated to see these negatives as trivial; indeed, he considers them a small price to pay for the sense of brotherhood he feels. He focuses on the good parts of living in the fraternity, and he dismisses the bad parts as inconsequential.

The take-home message is that human beings are motivated to maintain a positive picture of themselves, in part by justifying their behavior, and that under certain specifiable conditions, this leads them to do things that at first glance might seem surprising or paradoxical. They might prefer people and things for whom they have suffered to people and things they associate with ease and pleasure.

The Social Cognition Motive: The Need to Be Accurate

Even when people are bending the facts to see themselves as favorably as they can, most do not live in a fantasy world. After all, it would not be advisable to sit in our rooms thinking that it's simply a matter of time before we become a movie star, lead singer in a rock band, the best player on a World Cup soccer team, or President of the United States, all the while eating, drinking, and smoking as much as we want because surely we will live to be 100. We might say that people bend reality but don't completely break it. Yes, we try to see ourselves in a favorable light, but we are also quite good at scoping out the nature of the social world. That is, we are skilled at **social cognition**, which is the study of how people select, interpret, remember, and use information to make judgments and decisions (Fiske & Taylor, 2017; Markus &

Social Cognition

How people think about themselves and the social world; more specifically, how people select, interpret, remember, and use social information to make judgments and decisions

We rely on a series of expectations and other mental short-cuts in making judgments about the world around us, from important life decisions to which cereal to buy at the store, a conclusion with which advertisers and marketers are very well aware.

Zajonc, 1985; Nisbett & Ross, 1980). Researchers who investigate processes of social cognition begin with the assumption that all people try to view the world as accurately as possible. They regard human beings as amateur sleuths who are doing their best to understand and predict their social world.

Just as the need to preserve self-esteem can occasionally run aground, however, so too can the need to be accurate. People are not perfect in their effort to understand and predict, because they almost never know all the facts they need to judge a given situation completely accurately. Whether it is a relatively simple decision, such as which breakfast cereal offers the best combination of healthfulness and tastiness, or a slightly more complex decision, such as our desire to buy the best car we can for under $20,000, or a much more complex decision, such as choosing a partner who will make us deliriously happy for the rest of our lives, it is usually impossible to gather all the relevant information in advance. Moreover, we make countless decisions every day. No one has the time and stamina to gather all the facts for each of them.

Does this sound overblown? Aren't most decisions fairly easy? Let's take a closer look. Which breakfast cereal is better for you, Lucky Charms or Quaker Simply Granola with oats, fruit, and almonds? If you are like most of our students, you answered, "Quaker Simply Granola." After all, Lucky Charms is a kids' cereal, full of sugar and cute little marshmallows, with a picture of a leprechaun on the box. Quaker Simply Granola cereal boxes have pictures of healthy granola and fruit, and doesn't *natural* mean "good for you"? If that's the way you reasoned, you have fallen into a common cognitive trap: You have generalized from the cover to the product. A careful reading of the ingredients in small print will reveal that, per one cup serving, Quaker Simply Granola has 400 calories, 20 grams of sugar, and 12 grams of fat. In contrast, a cup of Lucky Charms has 147 calories, 13 grams of sugar, and 1 gram of fat. Even in the simple world of cereals, things are not always what they seem.

Thus, even when we are trying to perceive the social world as accurately as we can, there are many ways in which we can go wrong, ending up with the wrong impressions.

Review Questions

1. Researchers who study *social cognition* assume that people
   a. try to view the world as accurately as possible.
   b. can't think clearly with other people around them.
   c. distort reality to view themselves favorably.
   d. are driven by the need to control others.

2. Which of the following does *not* reflect the motive to maintain high self-esteem?
   a. After Sarah leaves Bob for someone else, Bob decides that he never liked her much anyway.

b. Students who want to take Professor Lopez's seminar have to apply by writing a 10-page essay. Everyone who is selected ends up loving the class.

c. Janetta did poorly on the first test in her psychology class. She admits that she didn't study enough and vows to study harder for the next test.

d. Zach has been involved in several minor traffic accidents since getting his driver's license. "There sure are a lot of terrible drivers out there," he says. "People should learn to be good drivers like me."

3. According to the social cognition approach,

a. People almost always form accurate impressions about the social world.

b. People rarely form accurate impressions of the social world.

c. When viewing the social world, people's main goal is to feel good about themselves.

d. Even when people are trying to perceive the social world as accurately as they can, there are many ways in which they can go wrong, ending up with the wrong impressions.

Why Study Social Psychology?

LO 1.4   Explain why the study of social psychology is important.

We defined social psychology as the scientific study of social influence. But why do we want to understand social influence in the first place? What difference does it make whether our behavior has its roots in the desire to be accurate or to bolster our self-esteem?

The basic answer is simple: We are curious. Social psychologists are fascinated by human social behavior and want to understand it on the deepest possible level. In a sense, all of us are social psychologists. We all live in a social environment, and we are all more than mildly curious about such issues as how we become influenced, how we influence others, and why we fall in love with some people, dislike others, and are indifferent to still others. You don't have to be with people literally to be in a social environment. Social media is a social psychologist's dream laboratory because it's all there: love, anger, bullying, bragging, affection, flirting, wounds, quarrels, friending and unfriending, pride and prejudice.

Many social psychologists have another reason for studying the causes of social behavior: to contribute to the solution of social problems. This goal was present at the founding of the discipline. Kurt Lewin, having barely escaped the horrors of Nazi Germany, brought to the United States his passionate interest in understanding how the transformation of his country had happened. Ever since, social psychologists have been keenly interested in their own contemporary social challenges, as you will discover reading this book. Their efforts have ranged from reducing violence and prejudice to increasing altruism and tolerance (Chapters 11 and 13). They study such pressing issues as how to induce people to conserve natural resources like water and energy, practice safe sex, or eat healthier food (Chapter 7). They study the effects of violence in the media (Chapter 12). They work to find effective strategies to resolve conflicts within groups—whether at work or in juries—and between nations (Chapter 9). They explore ways to raise children's intelligence through environmental interventions and better

Social psychology can help us study social problems and find ways to solve them. Social psychologists might study whether children who watch violence on television become more aggressive themselves—and, if so, what kind of intervention might be beneficial.

Watch WHY IS SOCIAL PSYCHOLOGY IMPORTANT?

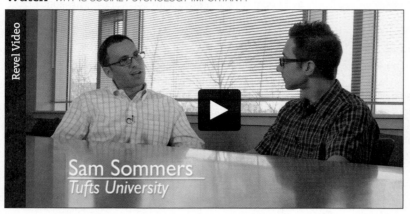

Revel Video

Sam Sommers
Tufts University

school programs, and reduce the high school dropout rate of minority students. They study happier topics, too, such as passion, liking, and love—and what sustains them (Chapter 10).

Throughout this book, we will examine many other examples of the application of social psychology to real-world problems. For interested readers, we have included three final chapters on health, the environment, and law. We hope that by understanding the fundamental causes of behavior as social psychologists study them, you will also be better able to change your own self-defeating or misguided behavior, improve your relationships, and make better decisions.

We are now ready to begin our tour of social psychology in earnest. So far, we have been emphasizing the central theme of social psychology: the enormous power of most social situations. As researchers, our job is to ask the right questions and to find a way to capture the power of the social situation and bring it into the laboratory for detailed study. If we are adept at doing that, we will arrive at truths about human behavior that are close to being universal. And then we may be able to bring our laboratory findings into the real world—for the ultimate betterment of our society.

Summary

LO 1.1 Define social psychology and distinguish it from other disciplines.

- **Defining Social Psychology** Social psychology is defined as the scientific study of the way in which people's thoughts, feelings, and behaviors are influenced by the real or imagined presence of other people. Social psychologists are interested in understanding how and why the social environment shapes the thoughts, feelings, and behaviors of the individual.

  - **Social Psychology, Philosophy, Science, and Common Sense** Social psychologists approach the understanding of social influence differently from philosophers, journalists, or the layperson. Social psychologists develop explanations of social influence through empirical methods, such as experiments in which the variables being studied are carefully controlled. The goal of the science of social psychology is to discover universal laws of human behavior, which is why cross-cultural research is often essential.

  - **How Social Psychology Differs From Its Closest Cousins** Some social psychologists attempt to explain social behavior in terms of genetic factors that have evolved over time according to the principles of natural selection, adopting the approach of *evolutionary psychology*. Such ideas are hard to

test experimentally but can generate novel hypotheses about social behavior that can be tested scientifically. When trying to explain social behavior, personality psychologists explain the behavior in terms of the person's individual character traits. Although social psychologists would agree that personalities vary, they explain social behavior in terms of the *power of the social situation* to shape how one acts. *The level of analysis for social psychology is the individual in the context of a social situation.* In contrast, the level of analysis for sociologists is the group, institution, or society at large. Social psychologists seek to identify universal properties of human nature that make everyone susceptible to social influence regardless of their social class, gender, or culture.

LO 1.2 Summarize why it matters how people explain and interpret events, as well as their own and others' behavior.

- **The Power of the Situation** Individual behavior is powerfully influenced by the social environment, but many people don't want to believe this.

  - **Underestimating the Power of the Situation** Social psychologists must contend with the *fundamental attribution error*, the tendency to explain our own and other people's behavior entirely in terms of personality traits and to underestimate the power of social influence. But social psychologists have shown time and again that social and environmental situations are usually more powerful than personality differences in determining an individual's behavior.

- **The Importance of Construal** Social psychologists have shown that the relationship between individuals and situations is a two-way street, so it is important to understand not only how situations influence individuals, but also how people *perceive and interpret* the social world and the behavior of others. These perceptions are more influential than objective aspects of the situation itself. The term *construal* refers to the world as it is interpreted by the individual.

LO 1.3 **Explain what happens when people's need to feel good about themselves conflicts with their need to be accurate.**

- **Where Construals Come From: Basic Human Motives** The way in which an individual construes (perceives, comprehends, and interprets) a situation is largely shaped by two basic human motives: *the need to feel good about ourselves* and *the need to be accurate*. At times these two motives tug in opposite directions; for

example, when an accurate view of how we acted in a situation would reveal that we behaved selfishly.

- **The Self-Esteem Motive: The Need to Feel Good About Ourselves** Most people have a strong need to see themselves as good, competent, and decent. People often distort their perception of the world to preserve their self-esteem.

- **The Social Cognition Motive: The Need to Be Accurate** Social cognition is the study of how human beings think about the world: how they select, interpret, remember, and use information to make judgments and decisions. Individuals are viewed as trying to gain accurate understandings so that they can make effective judgments and decisions that range from which cereal to eat to whom they marry. In actuality, individuals typically act on the basis of incomplete and inaccurately interpreted information.

LO 1.4 **Explain why the study of social psychology is important.**

- Why do social psychologists want to understand social influence? Because they are fascinated by human social behavior and want to understand it on the deepest possible level. Many social psychologists also want to contribute to the solution of social problems.

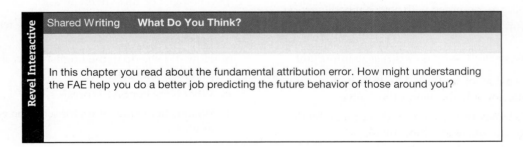

Revel Interactive

Shared Writing   **What Do You Think?**

In this chapter you read about the fundamental attribution error. How might understanding the FAE help you do a better job predicting the future behavior of those around you?

Test Yourself

1. Social psychology is the study of
   a. the real or imagined influence of other people.
   b. social institutions, such as the church or school.
   c. social events, such as football games and dances.
   d. psychological processes, such as dreaming.

2. For social psychologists, the likely explanation of the mass suicide at Jonestown was
   a. members of the cult were mentally unstable or clinically depressed.
   b. the cult leader used hypnotism or drugs to coerce his followers into obedience.

   c. processes that could ensnare almost any healthy person.
   d. the open, welcoming nature of the cult that made members feel it was safe to obey their leader.

3. In social psychology, the *level of analysis* is
   a. society at large.
   b. the individual in a social context.
   c. groups and organizations.
   d. cognitive and perceptual brain processes.

4. Which of the following does *not* illustrate the fundamental attribution error?

   a. A man says, "My wife has sure become a grouchy person," but explains his own grouchiness as a result of having a hard day at the office.

   b. A woman reads about high unemployment in poor communities and says, "Well, if those people weren't so lazy, they would find work."

   c. "The people who committed suicide at Jonestown were socially isolated and thus cut off from other points of view about their leader."

   d. "The people who committed suicide at Jonestown were mentally ill."

5. What do social psychology and personality psychology have in common?

   a. They both focus on the individual.

   b. They both focus on personality traits.

   c. They both focus on formative childhood experiences.

   d. They both focus on genetic contributions to personality.

6. What do social psychology and sociology have in common?

   a. They both examine demographic trends in society.

   b. They both study national institutions.

   c. They both are concerned with personality differences.

   d. They both are concerned with group processes.

7. In social psychology, why is *construal* so important?

   a. People's behavior is affected by their interpretation of events, not only the events themselves.

   b. People's behavior is primarily determined by the objective circumstances they are in.

   c. People are aware of their biases in perceiving events.

   d. People realize that other reasonable people see things they way they do.

8. What was the main contribution of Gestalt psychology to social psychology?

   a. It added an understanding of how the brain works.

   b. It emphasized how people perceive the physical world.

   c. It showed that the whole is larger than the sum of its parts.

   d. It added historical perspective to the study of behavior.

9. What central motives influence the way we construe the world?

   a. The need to maintain self-esteem.

   b. The need to be accurate in our perceptions and decisions.

   c. The need for self-expression.

   d. a and b.

   e. a and c.

10. Eleanor gets a bad grade on the first paper in her English class. To predict whether she will drop the course or stick with it, which question would a social psychologist be most likely to ask?

    a. How did she score on a personality test of persistence?

    b. How did she do in the English class she took the previous semester?

    c. What were her SAT scores?

    d. What is her explanation for why she got the bad grade?

Chapter 2
Methodology
How Social Psychologists Do Research

 ## Chapter Outline and Learning Objectives

Social Psychology: An Empirical Science

LO 2.1 Describe how researchers develop hypotheses and theories.

Formulating Hypotheses and Theories

Research Designs

LO 2.2 Compare the strengths and weaknesses of various research designs that social psychologists use.

The Observational Method: Describing Social Behavior
The Correlational Method: Predicting Social Behavior
The Experimental Method: Answering Causal Questions

New Frontiers in Social Psychological Research

LO 2.3 Explain the impact cross-cultural studies and social neuroscience research have on the way in which scientists investigate social behavior.

Culture and Social Psychology
Social Neuroscience

Ethical Issues in Social Psychology

LO 2.4 Summarize how social psychologists ensure the safety and welfare of their research participants, while at the same time testing hypotheses about the causes of social behavior.

WHAT DO YOU THINK?

Survey	**What Do You Think?**	
	SURVEY	RESULTS

You hear a news story describing the following research finding: the more fast food children eat, the lower their scores on reading, math, and science tests. Even though this study was with kids, does it make you want to cut down on the amount of fast food you eat?

○ Yes

○ No

In this information age, when pretty much anything can be found on the internet, pornography is more available than ever before. One survey found that 46% of men and 16% of women between the ages of 18 and 39 looked at pornography in the past week (Regnerus, Gordon, & Price, 2016). Another found that a quarter of all employees who have access to the internet visit porn sites during their workdays ("The Tangled Web of Porn," 2008). It is thus important to ask whether exposure to pornography has harmful effects. Is it possible, for example, that looking at graphic sex increases the likelihood that men will become sexually violent?

Over the past several decades there has been plenty of debate about the right answer to these questions. Legal scholar Catharine MacKinnon (1993) argued that "Pornography is the perfect preparation—motivator and instruction manual in one—for … sexual atrocities" (p. 28). In 1985, a group of experts, appointed by the attorney general of the United States, voiced a similar opinion, concluding that pornography is a cause of rape and other violent crimes. But in 1970, another commission reviewed much of the same evidence and concluded that pornography does *not* contribute significantly to sexual violence. Who are we to believe? Is there a scientific way to determine the answer? We believe there is, and in this chapter we will discuss the kinds of research methods social psychologists employ, using research on pornography as an example.

Social Psychology: An Empirical Science

LO 2.1 Describe how researchers develop hypotheses and theories.

A fundamental principle of social psychology is that many social problems, such as the causes of violence, can be studied scientifically (Reis & Gosling, 2010; Reis & Judd, 2000; Wilson, Aronson, & Carlsmith, 2010). Before we discuss how social psychological research is done, we begin with a warning: The results of some of the experiments you encounter will seem obvious because social psychology concerns topics with which we are all intimately familiar—social behavior and social influence (Richard, Bond, & Stokes-Zoota, 2001). This familiarity sets social psychology apart from other sciences. When you read about an experiment in particle physics, it is unlikely that the results will connect with your personal experiences. We don't know about you, but we have never thought, "Wow! That experiment on quarks was just like what happened to me while I was waiting for the bus yesterday," or "My grandmother always told me to watch out for positrons and antimatter." When reading about the results of a study on helping behavior or aggression, however, it is quite common to think, "Come on, I could have predicted that! That's the same thing that happened to me last Friday."

Watch SURVIVAL TIPS! ADMIT YOU DIDN'T KNOW IT ALL ALONG

Try It!

Social Psychology Quiz: What's Your Prediction?

Answer the following questions, each of which is based on social psychological research.

1. Suppose an authority figure asks college students to administer near-lethal electric shocks to another student who has not harmed them in any way. What percentage of these students will agree to do it?

2. If you give children a reward for doing something they already enjoy doing, they will subsequently like that activity (a) more, (b) the same, or (c) less.

3. When a business or governmental agency is faced with an important choice it is always better to have a group of people make the decision, because "two heads are better than one": (a) true (b) false.

4. Repeated exposure to a stimulus—such as a person, a song, or a painting—will make you like it (a) more, (b) the same, or (c) less.

5. You ask an acquaintance to do you a favor—for example, to lend you $10—and he or she agrees. As a result of doing you this favor, the person will probably like you (a) more, (b) the same, or (c) less.

6. Who do think would be *least* likely to help a stranger who drops a bunch of papers all over the ground? Someone who is in a (a) good mood (b) neutral mood, or (c) bad mood?

7. In the United States, female college students tend not to do as well on math tests as males do. Under which of the following circumstances will women do as well as men: (a) when they are told that there are no gender differences on the test, (b) when they are told that women tend to do better on a difficult math test (because under these circumstances they rise to the challenge), or (c) when they are told that men outperform women under almost all circumstances?

8. Which statement about the effects of advertising is most true? (a) Subliminal messages implanted in advertisements are more effective than normal, everyday advertising; (b) normal TV ads for painkillers or laundry detergents are more effective than subliminal messages implanted in ads;

(c) both types of advertising are equally effective; or

(d) neither type of advertising is effective.

9. What effect, if any, does playing violent video games have on how likely people are to act aggressively in everyday life? (a) playing the games increases the likelihood that they will act aggressively; (b) they become less aggressive because the games "get it out of their system"; (c) playing the games has no effect on how aggressive people are.

10. Students walking across campus are asked to fill out a questionnaire on which they rate the degree to which student opinion should be considered on a local campus issue. Which group do you think believed that students should be listened to the most? (a) Those given a light clipboard with the questionnaire attached; (b) those given a heavy clipboard with the questionnaire attached; (c) the weight of the clipboard made no difference in people's ratings.

1. In studies conducted by Stanley Milgram (1974), up to 65% of participants administered what they thought were near-lethal shocks to another subject. (in fact, no real shocks were administered; see Chapter 8.)

2. (c) Rewarding people for doing something they enjoy will typically make them like that activity less in the future (see Chapter 5).

3. (b) False: groups often make worse decisions than individuals (see Chapter 9).

4. (a) Under most circumstances, repeated exposure increases liking for a stimulus (see Chapter 10).

5. (a) More (see Chapter 6).

6. (b) People who are in good moods or bad moods are more likely to help others than people in neutral moods, though for different reasons (see Chapter 11).

7. (a) Research has found that when women think there are sex differences on a test, they do worse, because of the added threat of confirming a stereotype about their gender. When women were told that there were no gender differences in performance on the test, they did as well as men (see Chapter 13).

8. (b) There is no evidence that subliminal messages in advertising have any effect; considerable evidence shows that normal advertising is quite effective (see Chapter 7).

9. (a) Playing violent video games increases the likelihood that people will act aggressively (see Chapter 12).

10. (b) People given the heavy clipboard thought that student opinion should be weighed the most (see Chapter 3).

The thing to remember is that, when we study human behavior, the results may appear to have been predictable—in retrospect. Indeed, there is a well-known human tendency called the **hindsight bias**, whereby after people know that something occurred, they exaggerate how much they could have predicted it before it occurred (Bernstein, Aßfalg, Kumar, & Ackerman, 2016; Davis & Fischhoff, 2014; Ghrear, Birch, & Bernstein, 2016; Knoll & Arkes, 2016). After we know the winner of a political election, for example, we begin to look for reasons why that candidate won. After the fact, the outcome seems more easily predictable, even if we were quite unsure who would win before the election. The same is true of findings in psychology experiments; it seems like we could have easily predicted the outcomes—after we know them. The trick is to predict what will happen in an experiment before you know how it turned out. To illustrate that not all obvious findings are easy to predict, take the Try It! quiz above.

Hindsight Bias

The tendency for people to exaggerate, after knowing that something occurred, how much they could have predicted it before it occurred

Formulating Hypotheses and Theories

How, then, do social psychologists come up with the ideas for their studies? Research begins with a hunch, or hypothesis, that the researcher wants to test. There is lore in science that holds that brilliant insights come all of a sudden, as when the Greek scholar Archimedes shouted, "Eureka! I have found it!" when the solution to a problem flashed into his mind. Although such insights do sometimes occur suddenly, science is a cumulative process, and people often generate hypotheses from previous theories and research.

INSPIRATION FROM PREVIOUS THEORIES AND RESEARCH Many studies stem from a researcher's dissatisfaction with existing theories and explanations. After reading other people's work, a researcher might believe that he or she has a better way of explaining people's behavior. In the 1950s, for example, Leon Festinger was dissatisfied with the ability of a major theory of the day, behaviorism, to explain why people change their attitudes. He formulated a new approach—cognitive dissonance theory—that made specific predictions about when and how people would change their attitudes. As we will see in Chapter 6, other researchers were dissatisfied with Festinger's explanation of the results he obtained, so they conducted further research to test other possible explanations. Social psychologists, like scientists in other disciplines, engage in a continual process of theory refinement: A theory is developed; specific hypotheses derived from that theory are tested; based on the results obtained, the theory is revised and new hypotheses are formulated.

HYPOTHESES BASED ON PERSONAL OBSERVATIONS Social psychology also deals with phenomena we encounter in everyday life. Researchers often observe something in their lives or the lives of others that they find curious and interesting, stimulating them to construct a theory about why this phenomenon occurred—and to design a study to see if they are right. In the early 1960s, for example, a tragic murder was committed in the Queens section of New York City that led to a major research area in social psychology. Kitty Genovese, a young woman returning to her apartment late one night in 1964, was brutally killed in an attack that lasted 45 minutes. The *New York Times* reported that 38 apartment residents either saw the attack from their windows or heard Genovese's screams, and that no one attempted to help her, not even by calling the police. Although we know now that the *Times* exaggerated the number of eyewitnesses who did noth-

In October of 2011, a 2-year-old girl was struck by two vans in a row. A dozen people walked or rode past her. Why didn't they stop to help?

ing (Cook, 2014; Pelonero, 2014), the story vividly captured public fears and, for its time, "went viral." There is no doubt that bystanders often fail to help in emergencies (as we will see in Chapter 11), and the Genovese murder triggered a great deal of soul searching as to why. Some concluded that living in a metropolis dehumanizes us and leads inevitably to apathy, indifference to human suffering, and lack of caring.

Bibb Latané and John Darley, two social psychologists who taught at universities in New York, had another idea. Instead of focusing on "what was wrong with New Yorkers," Latané and Darley thought it would be more interesting and important to examine the social situation in which Genovese's neighbors found themselves. Maybe, they thought, the more people who witness an emergency, the less likely it is that any given individual will intervene. Genovese's neighbors might have assumed that someone else had called the police, a phenomenon Latané and Darley (1968) called the *diffusion of responsibility.* Perhaps the bystanders would have been more likely to help had each thought he or she alone was witnessing the murder. How can we tell whether this hypothesis is true?

Review Questions

1. Which of the following is a basic assumption that social psychologists make?
   a. Social problems have complex causes and we will never know why they occur.
   b. It is hard to study what effect looking at pornography has on people, because everyone is different.
   c. Many social problems can be studied scientifically.
   d. Many people fail to help others in emergencies because they don't care about other people.

2. Which of the following is true about social psychological findings?
   a. They sometimes seem obvious after we learn about them, because of a hindsight bias.
   b. Most people could easily predict them in advance of knowing how the studies turned out.
   c. Wise people such as our grandparents could easily predict them in advance of knowing how the studies turned out.
   d. Most people who live in the culture in which the studies were conducted could predict the findings in advance of knowing how the studies turned out.

3. How do social psychologists formulate hypotheses and theories?
   a. They are inspired by previous theories and research.
   b. They disagree with a previous researchers' interpretations of their study.
   c. They construct hypothesis and theories based on personal observations in everyday life.
   d. All of the above answers are correct.

In science, idle speculation will not do; researchers must collect data to test their hypotheses. Let's look at how different research designs are used to do just that.

Research Designs

LO 2.2   Compare the strengths and weaknesses of various research designs that social psychologists use.

Social psychology is a scientific discipline with a well-developed set of methods for answering questions about social behavior, such as the one about the effects of pornography with which we began this chapter, and the one about reactions to violence that we just discussed. There are three types of methods: the *observational method*, the *correlational method*, and the *experimental method* (see Table 2.1). Any of these methods could be used to explore a specific research question; each is a powerful tool in some ways and a weak tool in others. Part of the creativity in conducting social psychological research involves choosing the right method, maximizing its strengths, and minimizing its weaknesses.

Here we discuss these methods in detail and try to provide you with a firsthand look at both the joy and the difficulty of conducting social psychological studies. The joy comes in unraveling the clues about the causes of interesting and important social behaviors, just as a sleuth gradually unmasks the culprit in a murder mystery. Each of us finds it exhilarating that we have the tools to provide definitive answers to questions philosophers have debated for centuries. At the same time, as seasoned researchers, we have learned to temper this exhilaration with a heavy dose of humility, because there are formidable practical and ethical constraints involved in conducting social psychological research.

Table 2.1 A Summary of Research Methods

Method	Focus	Question Answered
Observational	Description	What is the nature of the phenomenon?
Correlational	Prediction	From knowing X, can we predict Y?
Experimental	Causality	Is variable X a cause of variable Y?

The Observational Method: Describing Social Behavior

There is a lot to be learned by being an astute observer of human behavior. If the goal is to describe what a particular group of people or type of behavior is like, the **observational method** is very helpful. This is the technique whereby a researcher observes people and records measurements or impressions of their behavior. The observational method may take many forms, depending on what the researchers are looking for, how involved or detached they are from the people they are observing, and how much they want to quantify what they observe.

ETHNOGRAPHY One example of observational learning is **ethnography**, the method by which researchers attempt to understand a group or culture by observing it from the inside, without imposing any preconceived notions they might have. The goal is to understand the richness and complexity of the group by observing it in action. Ethnography is the chief method of cultural anthropology, the study of human cultures and societies. As social psychology broadens its focus by studying social behavior in different cultures, ethnography is increasingly being used to describe different cultures and generate hypotheses about psychological principles (Fine & Elsbach, 2000; Flick, 2014; Uzzel, 2000).

Consider this example from the early years of social psychological research. In the early 1950s, a small cult of people called the Seekers predicted that the world would come to an end with a giant flood on the morning of December 21, 1954. They were convinced that a spaceship from the planet Clarion would land in the backyard of their leader, Mrs. Keech, and whisk them away before the apocalypse. Assuming that the end of the world was not imminent, Leon Festinger and his colleagues thought it would be interesting to observe this group closely and chronicle how they reacted when their prophecy was disconfirmed (Festinger, Riecken, & Schachter, 1956). To monitor the hour-to-hour conversations of this group, the social psychologists found it necessary to become members and pretend that they too believed the world was about to end. On the fateful morning of December 21, 1954, with no flood waters lapping at the door and no sign of a spaceship, they observed a curious thing: Rather than admitting that she was wrong, Mrs. Keech "doubled down" on her beliefs, announcing that God had spared Planet Earth because of the Seekers' faith, and that it was now time for the group to go public and recruit more members. Based on his observations of Mrs. Keech's tenacious adherence to her beliefs, Festinger formulated one of the most famous theories in social psychology, cognitive dissonance, which we discuss in Chapter 6.

The key to ethnography is to avoid imposing one's preconceived notions on the group and to try to understand the point of view of the people being studied. Sometimes, however, researchers have a specific hypothesis that they want to test using the observational method. An investigator might be interested, for example, in how much aggression children exhibit during school recesses. In this case, the observer would be systematically looking for particular behaviors that are concretely defined before the observation begins. For example, aggression might be defined as hitting or shoving another child, taking a toy from another child without asking, and so on. The observer might stand at the edge of the playground and systematically record how often these behaviors occur. If the researcher were interested in exploring possible sex and age differences in social behavior, he or she would also note the child's gender and age. How do we know how accurate the observer is? In such studies, it is important to establish agreement between two or more people who independently observe and code a set of data. By showing that two or more judges independently come up with the same observations, researchers ensure that the observations are not the subjective, distorted impressions of one individual.

ARCHIVAL ANALYSIS The observational method is not limited to observations of real-life behavior. The researcher can also examine the accumulated documents, or archives, of a culture, a technique known as an **archival analysis** (Mannes, Soll, &

Observational Method

The technique whereby a researcher observes people and systematically records measurements or impressions of their behavior

Ethnography

The method by which researchers attempt to understand a group or culture by observing it from the inside, without imposing any preconceived notions they might have

Archival Analysis

A form of the observational method in which the researcher examines the accumulated documents, or archives, of a culture (e.g., diaries, novels, magazines, and newspapers)

Larrick, 2014; Oishi, 2014). For example, diaries, novels, suicide notes, music lyrics, television shows, movies, magazine and news articles, advertising, social media, and the ways in which people use the internet all tell us a great deal about human behavior. One study, for example, analyzed millions of Twitter messages sent in 84 countries to examine daily rhythms in people's mood. Judging by the content of the messages they send, most people's positive moods appear to peak at two different times of the day: In the morning, soon after they get up, and late in the evening, before they go to bed (Golder & Macy, 2011). Researchers have also used archival data to answer questions about pornography usage. For example, do you think that people who live in some areas of the United States are especially likely to look at online pornography? Perhaps you guessed that it is those who live in more liberal "blue" states that are the biggest consumers, given that liberals tend to have more permissive attitudes toward social issues. To address this question, a researcher examined credit card subscriptions to pornography sites (Edelman, 2009). Although he was not given access to the names of people who subscribed, he did know their zip codes, which enabled him to estimate regional variations. As it turned out, residents of "blue" states and "red" were equally likely to subscribe to pornography sites (residents of Utah came in first).

LIMITS OF THE OBSERVATIONAL METHOD   The study that analyzed Twitter messages revealed interesting daily patterns, but it did not say much about *why* moods peak in the morning and at night. Furthermore, certain kinds of behavior are difficult to observe because they occur only rarely or only in private. You can begin to see the limitations of the observational method. Had Latané and Darley chosen this method to study the effects of the number of bystanders on people's willingness to help a victim, we might still be waiting for an answer, given the infrequency of emergencies and the difficulty of predicting when they will occur. And, archival data about pornography, although informative about who is accessing it, tells us little about the effects on their attitudes and behavior of doing so. Social psychologists want to do more than just describe behavior; they want to predict and explain it. To do so, other methods are more appropriate.

The Correlational Method: Predicting Social Behavior

A goal of social science is to understand relationships between variables and to be able to predict when different kinds of social behavior will occur. What is the relationship between the amount of pornography people see and their likelihood of engaging in sexually violent acts? Is there a relationship between the amount of violence children see on television and their aggressiveness? To answer such questions, researchers frequently use another approach: the correlational method.

With the **correlational method**, two variables are systematically measured, and the relationship between them—how much you can predict one from the other—is assessed. People's behavior and attitudes can be measured in a variety of ways. Just as with the observational method, researchers sometimes make direct observations of people's behavior. For example, researchers might be interested in testing the relationship between children's aggressive behavior and how much violent television they watch. They too might observe children on the playground, but here the goal is to assess the relationship, or correlation, between the children's aggressiveness and other factors, such as TV viewing habits, which the researchers also measure.

Researchers look at such relationships by calculating the **correlation coefficient**, a statistic that assesses how well you can predict one variable from another—for example, how well you can predict people's weight from their height. A correlation coefficient can range from −1 to +1. A

Correlational Method

The technique whereby two or more variables are systematically measured and the relationship between them (i.e., how much one can be predicted from the other) is assessed

Correlation Coefficient

A statistical technique that assesses how well you can predict one variable from another—for example, how well you can predict people's weight from their height

Researchers use archival analyses to test psychological hypotheses. One study, for example, analyzed millions of Twitter messages to see how people's moods varied over the course of a day.

positive correlation means that increases in the value of one variable are associated with increases in the value of the other variable. The correlation between people's height and weight is about 0.7, for example, reflecting the fact that the taller people are, the more they tend to weigh. The relationship is strong but not perfect, which is why the correlation is less than 1. A negative correlation means that increases in the value of one variable are associated with decreases in the value of the other. If height and weight were negatively correlated in human beings, we would look very peculiar; short people, such as children, would look like penguins, whereas tall people, such as NBA basketball players, would be all skin and bones! It is also possible, of course, for two variables to be completely unrelated, so that a researcher cannot predict one variable from the other. In that case the correlation coefficient would be 0 (see Figure 2.1).

Surveys

Research in which a representative sample of people are asked (often anonymously) questions about their attitudes or behavior

Random Selection

A way of ensuring that a sample of people is representative of a population by giving everyone in the population an equal chance of being selected for the sample

SURVEYS   The correlational method is often used to analyze the results of **surveys**, research in which a representative sample of people are asked questions about their attitudes or behavior. Surveys are a convenient way to measure people's attitudes; for example, people can be telephoned and asked which candidate they will support in an upcoming election or how they feel about a variety of social issues. Psychologists often use surveys to help understand social behavior and attitudes—for example, by seeing whether the amount of pornography men say they read is correlated with their attitudes toward women.

Surveys have a number of advantages, one of which is allowing researchers to judge the relationship between variables that are difficult to observe, such as how often people engage in safer sex. Another advantage is the ability to sample representative segments of the population. The best way to do this is to use a **random selection** of people from the population at large, which is a way of ensuring that a sample of people is representative of a population by giving everyone in the population an equal chance of being selected for the sample. As long as the sample is selected randomly, and is reasonably large, we can assume that the responses are a reasonable match to those of the population as a whole.

There are famous cases of surveys that yielded misleading results by failing to sample randomly. In the fall of 1936, for example, a weekly magazine called the *Literary Digest* conducted a large survey asking people which candidate they planned to vote for in the upcoming presidential election. The magazine obtained the names and addresses of its sample from telephone directories and automobile registration lists. The results of its survey of 2 million people indicated that the Republican candidate, Alf Landon,

Figure 2.1 Types of Correlations

The diagrams show three possible correlations in a hypothetical study of watching violence on television and aggressive behavior in children. The diagram at the left shows a strong positive correlation: The more television children watched, the more aggressive they were. The diagram in the middle shows no correlation: The amount of television children watched is not related to how aggressive they were. The diagram at the right shows a strong negative correlation: The more television children watched, the less aggressive they were.

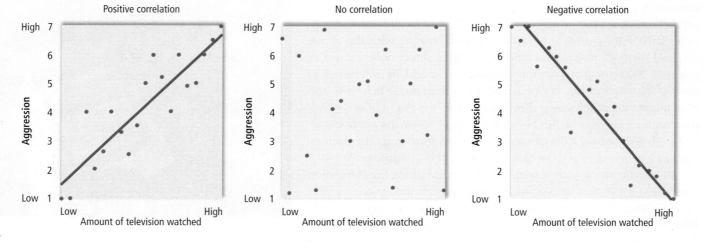

would win by a landslide. Of course, you know that there never was a President Landon; instead, Franklin Delano Roosevelt won every state in the Union but two. What went wrong with the *Literary Digest* poll? In the depths of the Great Depression, many people could not afford telephones or cars. Those who had them were doing well financially; most well-to-do voters were Republican and overwhelmingly favored Alf Landon. However, the majority of the voters were not well off—and overwhelmingly supported the Democratic candidate, Roosevelt. By using a list of names that excluded the less affluent members of the population, the *Literary Digest* surveyed a nonrepresentative sample. (the *Literary Digest* never recovered from this methodological disaster and went out of business shortly after publishing its poll.)

Modern political polls are not immune from such sampling errors. Many polling companies only contact people on their home phones (landlines), because of the difficulty of obtaining directories of cell phone numbers. They do so at their peril, because research shows that Americans who rely solely on cell phones are more likely to vote for Democratic candidates (Silver, 2012). Further, pollsters adjust their results by estimating how likely respondents are to vote and applying other statistical corrections. These adjustments can introduce further bias, which may be why several polls underestimated the percentage of votes Donald Trump would receive in key swing states in the 2016 presidential election (Newkirk, 2016).

Another potential problem with survey data is the accuracy of the responses. Straightforward questions, regarding who people intend to vote for or what they typically do, are relatively easy to answer. But asking survey participants to predict how they might behave in some hypothetical situation or to explain why they behaved as they did in the past is an invitation to inaccuracy (Schuman & Kalton, 1985; Schwarz, Groves, & Schuman, 1998). Often people simply don't know the answer—but they think they do. Richard Nisbett and Tim Wilson (1977) demonstrated this "telling more than you can know" phenomenon in a number of studies in which people often made inaccurate reports about why they responded the way they did. Their reports about the causes of their responses pertained more to their theories and beliefs about what should have influenced them than to what actually influenced them. (We discuss these studies at greater length in Chapter 5.)

In the fall of 1936, a magazine called the *Literary Digest* predicted that the Republican candidate for president would win by a landslide, based on a poll they conducted. Instead, Franklin Roosevelt won every state but two, as seen in the map below. What went wrong with the *Literary Digest* poll?

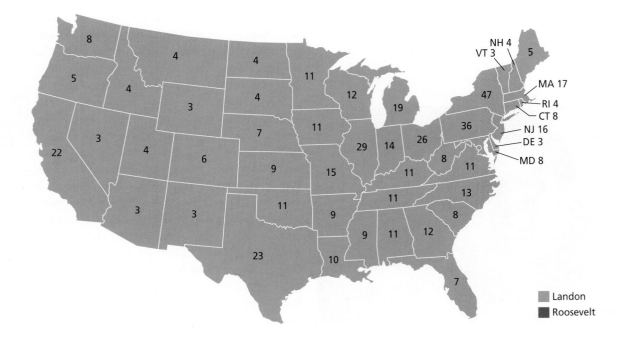

Landon
Roosevelt

A study conducted in the early 1990s found a correlation between the type of birth control women used and their likelihood of getting a sexually transmitted infection (STI). Those whose partners used condoms were more likely to have an STI than were women who used other forms of birth control. Does this mean that the use of condoms caused the increase in STIs? Not necessarily—see the text for alternative explanations of this research finding.

LIMITS OF THE CORRELATIONAL METHOD: CORRELATION DOES NOT EQUAL CAUSATION The major shortcoming of the correlational method is that it tells us only that two variables are related, whereas the goal of the social psychologist is to identify the *causes* of social behavior. We want to be able to say that A causes B, not just that A is correlated with B.

If a researcher finds that there is a correlation between two variables, it means that there are three possible causal relationships between these variables. For example, researchers have found a correlation between the amount of violent television children watch and how aggressive they are (similar to the pattern shown in the graph on the left side in Figure 2.1, though not quite as strong; see Eron, 2001). One explanation of this correlation is that watching TV violence causes kids to become more violent themselves. It is equally probable, however, that the reverse is true: that kids who are violent to begin with are more likely to watch violent TV. Or there might be no causal relationship between these two variables; instead, both TV watching and violent behavior could be caused by a third variable, such as having neglectful parents who do not pay much attention to their kids. (Experimental evidence supports one of these causal relationships; we will discuss which one in Chapter 12.) When using the correlational method, it is wrong to jump to the conclusion that one variable is causing the other to occur. *Correlation does not prove causation.*

Unfortunately, forgetting this adage is one of the most common methodological errors in the social sciences. Consider a study of birth control methods and sexually transmitted infections (STIs) in women (Rosenberg, Davidson, Chen, Judson, & Douglas, 1992). The researchers examined the records of women who had visited a clinic, noting which method of birth control they used and whether they had an STI. Surprisingly, the researchers found that women who relied on condoms had significantly more STIs than women who used diaphragms or contraceptive sponges. This result was widely reported in the popular press, with the conclusion that the use of diaphragms and sponges caused a lower incidence of disease. Some news articles urged women whose partners used condoms to switch to other methods.

Can you see the problem with this conclusion? The fact that the incidence of disease was correlated with the type of contraception women used is open to a number of causal interpretations. Perhaps the women who used sponges and diaphragms had sex with fewer partners. (In fact, condom users were more likely to have had sex with multiple partners in the previous month.) Perhaps the partners of women who relied on condoms were more likely to have STIs than were the partners of women who used sponges and diaphragms. There is simply no way of knowing. Thus, the conclusion that the birth control methods protected against STIs cannot be drawn from this correlational study.

As another example of the difficulty of inferring causality from correlational designs, let's return to the question of whether pornography causes aggressive sexual acts against women, such as rape. A recent summary of 22 studies, with more than 20,000 participants in seven countries, found a correlation of 0.28 between looking at pornography and the likelihood of committing acts of sexual aggression (Wright, Tokunaga, & Kraus, 2016). Remember what a correlation of 0.28 means? Because it's positive it means that the more pornography people consumed, the more likely they were to be sexually aggressive; though the relationship was not particularly strong.

Watch SURVIVAL TIPS! CORRELATION DOES NOT EQUAL CAUSATION

Revel Video

Try It!

Correlation and Causation: Knowing the Difference

It can be difficult to remember that, when two variables are correlated, it doesn't necessarily mean that one caused the other; correlation does *not* allow us to make causal inferences. For each of the following examples, think about why the correlation was found. Even if it seems obvious which variable was causing the other, are there alternative explanations?

1. A politician extols the virtues of the Boy Scouts and Girl Scouts. In his salute to the scouts, the politician mentions that few teenagers convicted of street crimes have been members of the scouts. In other words, he is positing a negative correlation between activity in scouting and frequency of criminal behavior. Can you think of any alternative explanations?

2. A recent study found that college students who have "helicopter parents"—moms and dads who keep close track of their kids' academic life and intervene often— actually get lower grades than college students whose parents do not hover over them so closely. Does it follow that college students would do better in school if their parents backed off a little bit?

3. A study of soldiers stationed on army bases found that the number of tattoos a soldier had was correlated positively with becoming involved in a motorcycle accident. Why?

4. A study found that adolescents who are religious are less likely to commit crimes and more likely to wear seat belts than are adolescents who are not religious. Does religion make people more likely to obey the law?

5. A correlation exists between people's tendency to eat breakfast and how long they live, such that people who skip breakfast die younger. Does eating Wheaties lead to a long life?

6. A study reported that the more milk children drank, the more weight they gained. One researcher concluded that children who need to control their weight should cut down on their milk consumption. Is this a valid conclusion?

7. A recent survey found that people who watch public television have more sex than people who do not. "Who would have thought," the researchers reported, "that National Geographic Specials or Ken Burns' history of baseball could get people in the mood?" How would you explain this correlation?

8. A recent study in Britain found that kids who ate sweets daily at age 10 were much more likely to be arrested for a violent crime later in life than were kids who did not eat

sweets daily at 10. Should we limit the number of candy bars that kids eat, so that they don't turn into violent criminals?

9. A recent study found that college students who use Facebook have lower GPAs than college students who do not. Does that mean that deleting your Facebook account will increase your GPA?

10. According to one study, the more sex that teenagers watch on television, the more likely they are to have sex themselves. Should parents limit the amount of sexual TV their teens watch?

Note: For more examples on correlation and causation, see http://jfmueller. faculty.noctrl.edu/100/correlation_or_causation.htm.

1. The politician ignored possible third variables that could cause both Scout membership and crime, such as socioeconomic class. Traditionally, Scouting has been most popular in small towns and suburbs among middle-class youngsters; it has never been very attractive or even available to youths growing up in densely populated, urban, high-crime areas.

2. Not necessarily. It might be the other way around—namely, that moms and dads are more likely to become helicopter parents if their kids are having academic problems. Or there could be a third variable that causes parents to hover and their kids to have academic problems.

3. Did tattoos cause motorcycle accidents? Or, for that matter, did motorcycle accidents cause tattoos? The researchers suggested that a third variable (unmeasured) was in fact the cause of both: A tendency to take risks and to be involved in flamboyant personal displays led to tattooing one's body and to driving a motorcycle recklessly.

4. It is possible that religion makes people more likely to obey the law. It is equally possible, however, that some other variable increases the likelihood that people will be religious and follow the rules—such as having parents who are religious.

5. Not necessarily. People who do not eat breakfast might differ from people who do in any number of ways that influence longevity—for example, in how obese they are, how hard-driving and high-strung they are, or even how late they sleep in the morning.

6. Not necessarily, because milk drinking may have little to do with weight gain. Children who drink a lot of milk might be more likely to eat cookies or other high-calorie foods.

7. It is possible that watching public television makes people want to have more sex. It is equally possible, however, that some third variable, such as health or education, influences both television preferences and sexual behavior. It is even possible that having sex makes people want to watch more public television. Based on the correlation the researchers reported, there is no way of telling which of these explanations is true.

8. Not necessarily. There could be a third variable that is causing kids to eat a lot of candy and to become violent later in life.

9. Not necessarily. Perhaps students who study less are more drawn to Facebook. Or, there is some third variable that causes people to want to use Facebook and do worse academically.

10. Not necessarily. There may be a third variable that makes kids more interested in watching sex and having sex.

But does this prove that using pornography *caused* people to commit sexual violence? That's one of the possible explanations, but can you think of others? Perhaps the causal direction is the other way around—people who are prone to commit sexual violence are more interested in pornography; that is, it is their aggressiveness causing their attraction to pornography, and not the pornography causing their aggressiveness (Malamuth, Addison, & Koss, 2000). Alternatively, there could be some third variable, such as something in people's upbringing or subculture, that makes them more likely both to commit sexual violence and look at pornography. Other examples of the difficulty of inferring causality from correlational studies are shown in the following Try It!

The Experimental Method: Answering Causal Questions

The only way to determine causal relationships is with the **experimental method**. Here, the researcher systematically orchestrates the event so that people experience it in one way (e.g., they witness an emergency along with other bystanders) or another way (e.g., they witness the same emergency but are the sole bystander). The experimental method is the method of choice in most social psychological research, because it allows the experimenter to make causal inferences.

INDEPENDENT AND DEPENDENT VARIABLES   To illustrate how this is done, let's return to our previous example of Bibb Latané and John Darley, the two social psychologists who came up with the diffusion of responsibility hypothesis, that the more people who witness an emergency, the less likely it is that any one of them will intervene. As with any experiment, they needed to vary the critical aspect of the situation that they thought would have a causal effect, in their case the number of people who witnessed an emergency. This is called the **independent variable**, which is the variable a researcher changes or varies to see if it has an effect on some other variable. The researcher then observes whether the independent variable (e.g., the number of bystanders) has the predicted effect on the outcome of interest, namely the **dependent variable**, which is the variable a researcher measures to see if it is influenced by the independent variable—in this case whether people help in an emergency (see Figure 2.2).

Sound simple? Actually, it isn't. Staging an experiment to test Latané and Darley's hypothesis about the effects of group size involves severe practical and ethical difficulties. What kind of emergency should be used? Ideally (from a scientific perspective), it should be as true to the Genovese case as possible. Accordingly, you would want to stage a murder that passersby could witness. In one condition, you could stage the murder so that only a few onlookers were present; in another condition, you could stage it so that a great many onlookers were present.

Obviously, no scientist in his or her right mind would stage a murder for unsuspecting bystanders. But how could the researchers arrange a realistic situation that is upsetting enough to be similar to the Genovese case without it being too upsetting? In addition, how could they ensure that each bystander experienced the same emergency except for the independent variable whose effect they wanted to test—namely, the number of bystanders?

Let's see how Latané and Darley (1968) dealt with these problems. Imagine that you are a participant in their experiment. You arrive at the scheduled time and find yourself in a long corridor with doors to several small rooms. An experimenter greets you and takes you into one of the rooms, mentioning that five other students, seated out of view in the other rooms, will be participating with you. The experimenter leaves after giving you a pair of headphones with an attached microphone. You put on the headphones, and soon you hear the experimenter explaining to everyone that he is interested in learning about the kinds of personal problems college students experience.

Experimental Method

The method in which the researcher randomly assigns participants to different conditions and ensures that these conditions are identical except for the independent variable (the one thought to have a causal effect on people's responses)

Independent Variable

The variable a researcher changes or varies to see if it has an effect on some other variable

Dependent Variable

The variable a researcher measures to see if it is influenced by the independent variable the researcher hypothesizes that the dependent variable will depend on the level of the independent variable

Figure 2.2 Researchers vary the independent variable (e.g., the number of bystanders people think are present) and observe what effect that has on the dependent variable (e.g., whether people help).

Independent Variable	Dependent Variable
The variable that is hypothesized to influence the dependent variable. Participants are treated identically except for this variable.	The response that is hypothesized to depend on the independent variable. All participants are measured on this variable.

Example: Latané and Darley (1968)	
The number of bystanders	**How many participants helped?**
Participant Victim	85%
Participant Victim Two others	62%
Participant Victim Four others	31%

To ensure that people will discuss their problems candidly, he explains that each participant will remain anonymous and each will stay in his or her separate room and communicate with the others only via the intercom system. The experimenter further says that the discussion will be recorded, but to encourage openness, he will not listen to it "live." Finally, the experimenter asks participants to take turns presenting their problems, each speaking for 2 minutes, after which each person will comment on what the others have said. To make sure this procedure is followed, he says, only one person's microphone will be turned on at a time.

The group discussion begins. You listen as the first participant admits that he has found it difficult to adjust to college. With some embarrassment, he mentions that he sometimes has seizures, especially when under stress. When his 2 minutes are up, you hear the other four participants discuss their problems; then it is your turn. When you have finished, the first person speaks again. To your astonishment, he soon begins to experience one of the seizures he mentioned earlier:

> I—er—um—I think I—I need—er—if—if could—er—er—somebody er—er—
> er—er—er—er—give me a little—er—give me a little help here because—
> er—I—er—I'm—er—er—h—h—having a—a—a real problem—er—right now
> and I—er—if somebody could help me out it would—it would—er—er s—s—
> sure be—sure be good … because—er—there—er—er—a cause I—er—I—uh—
> I've got a—a one of the—er—sei—er—er—things coming on and—and—and
> I could really—er—use some help so if somebody would—er—give me a little
> h—help—uh—er—er—er—er c—could somebody—er—er—help—er—uh—
> uh—uh (choking sounds) … I'm gonna die—er—er—I'm … gonna die—er—
> help—er—er—-seizure—er (chokes, then quiet). (Darley & Latané, 1968, p. 379)

What would you have done in this situation? If you were like most of the participants in the actual study, you would have remained in your room, listening to your fellow student having a seizure, without doing anything about it. Does this surprise you? Latané and Darley kept track of the number of people who left their cubicle to find the victim or the experimenter before the end of the victim's seizure. Only 31% of the participants sought help in this way. Fully 69% of the students remained in their cubicles and did nothing—just as Kitty Genovese's neighbors failed to offer assistance in any way.

Does this finding prove that the failure to help was due to the number of people who witnessed the seizure? How do we know that it wasn't due to some other factor? We know because Latané and Darley included two other conditions in their experiment. In these conditions, the procedure was identical to the one we described, with one crucial difference: The size of the discussion group was smaller, meaning that fewer people witnessed the seizure. In one condition, the participants were told that there were three other people in the discussion group besides themselves (the victim plus two others), and in this case, helping behavior increased to 62%. In a third condition, participants were told that there was only one other person in their discussion group (the victim), and in that case, nearly everyone helped (85%; see Figure 2.2).

These results indicate that the number of bystanders strongly influences the rate of helping, but it does not mean that the size of the group is the only cause of people's decision to help. After all, when there were four bystanders, a third of the participants still helped; conversely, when participants thought they were the only witness, some of them failed to do so. Obviously, other factors influence helping behavior—the bystanders' personalities, their prior experience with emergencies, and so on. Nonetheless, Latané and Darley succeeded in identifying one important determinant of whether people help: the number of bystanders that people think are present.

INTERNAL VALIDITY IN EXPERIMENTS How can we be sure that the differences in help across conditions in the Latané and Darley seizure study were due to the different numbers of bystanders who witnessed the emergency? Could something else have produced this effect? This is the beauty of the experimental method: We can be sure of the causal connection between the number of bystanders and helping, because Latané and Darley made sure that everything about the situation was the same in the different conditions *except* for the independent variable—the number of bystanders. Keeping everything but the independent variable the same in an experiment is referred to as *internal validity.* Latané and Darley were careful to maintain high internal validity by making sure that everyone witnessed the same emergency. They prerecorded the supposed other participants and the victim and played their voices over the intercom system so that everyone heard exactly the same thing.

You may have noticed, however, that there was a key difference between the conditions of the Latané and Darley experiment other than the number of bystanders: Different people participated in the different conditions. Maybe the observed differences in helping were due to characteristics of the participants instead of the independent variable. The people in the sole-witness condition might have differed in any number of ways from their counterparts in the other conditions, making them more likely to help. Maybe they were more likely to know something about epilepsy or to have experience helping in emergencies. If either of these possibilities is true, it would be difficult to conclude that it was the number of bystanders, rather than something about the participants' backgrounds, that led to differences in helping.

Fortunately, there is a technique that allows experimenters to minimize differences among participants as the cause of the results: **random assignment to condition**. This is the process whereby all participants have an equal chance of taking part in any condition of an experiment; through random assignment, researchers can be relatively certain that differences in the participants'

Random Assignment to Condition

A process ensuring that all participants have an equal chance of taking part in any condition of an experiment; through random assignment, researchers can be relatively certain that differences in the participants' personalities or backgrounds are distributed evenly across conditions

Watch THE EXPERIMENTAL METHOD

Revel Video

personalities or backgrounds are distributed evenly across conditions. Because Latané and Darley's participants were randomly assigned to the conditions of their experiment, it is very unlikely that the ones who knew the most about epilepsy all ended up in one condition. Knowledge about epilepsy should be randomly (i.e., roughly evenly) dispersed across the three experimental conditions. This powerful technique is the most important part of the experimental method.

Even with random assignment, however, there is the (very small) possibility that different characteristics of people did not distribute themselves evenly across conditions. For example, if we randomly divide a group of 40 people into two groups, it is possible that those who know the most about epilepsy will by chance end up more in one group than in the other—just as it is possible to get more heads than tails when you flip a coin 40 times. This is a possibility we take seriously in experimental science. The analyses of our data come with a **probability level (*p*-value)**, which is a number, calculated with statistical techniques, that tells researchers how likely it is that the results of their experiment occurred by chance and not because of the independent variable. The convention in science, including social psychology, is to consider results *significant* (trustworthy) if the probability level is less than 5 in 100 that the results might be due to chance factors rather than the independent variables studied. For example, if we flipped a coin 40 times and got 40 heads, we would probably assume that this was very unlikely to have occurred by chance and that there was something wrong with the coin (we might check the other side to make sure it wasn't one of those trick coins with heads on both sides!). Similarly, if the results in two conditions of an experiment differ significantly from what we would expect by chance, we assume that the difference was caused by the independent variable (e.g., the number of bystanders present during the emergency). The *p*-value tells us how confident we can be that the difference was due to chance rather than the independent variable.

To summarize, the key to a good experiment is to maintain high **internal validity**, which we can now define as making sure that the independent variable, and *only* the independent variable, influences the dependent variable. This is accomplished by controlling all extraneous variables and by randomly assigning people to different experimental conditions (Campbell & Stanley, 1967). When internal validity is high, the experimenter is in a position to judge whether the independent variable causes the dependent variable. This is the hallmark of the experimental method that sets it apart from the observational and correlational methods: Only the experimental method can answer causal questions, such as whether exposure to pornography causes men to commit violent acts.

For example, researchers have tested whether pornography causes aggression by randomly assigning consenting participants to watch pornographic or nonpornographic films (the independent variable) and measuring the extent to which people acted aggressively toward women (the dependent variable). In a study by Donnerstein and Berkowitz (1981), males were angered by a female accomplice and then were randomly assigned to see one of three films: violent pornography (a rape scene), nonviolent pornography (sex without any violence), or a neutral film with no violence or sex (a talk show interview). The men were then given an opportunity to act aggressively toward the woman who had angered them, by choosing the level of electric shock she would receive in an ostensibly unrelated learning experiment (the accomplice did not really receive shocks, but participants believed that she would). The men who had seen the violent pornography administered significantly more intense shocks to the woman than did the men who had seen the nonviolent pornography or the neutral film, suggesting that it is not pornography per se that leads to aggressive behavior, but the violence depicted in some pornography (Mussweiler & Förster, 2000). We review this area of research in more detail in Chapter 12.

EXTERNAL VALIDITY IN EXPERIMENTS For all the advantages of the experimental method, there are some drawbacks. By virtue of gaining enough control over the situation so as to randomly assign people to conditions and rule out the effects of extraneous variables, the situation can become somewhat artificial and distant from

Probability Level (*p*-value)

A number calculated with statistical techniques that tells researchers how likely it is that the results of their experiment occurred by chance and not because of the independent variable or variables; the convention in science, including social psychology, is to consider results *significant* (trustworthy) if the probability level is less than 5 in 100 that the results might be due to chance factors and not the independent variables studied

Internal Validity

Making sure that nothing besides the independent variable can affect the dependent variable; this is accomplished by controlling all extraneous variables and by randomly assigning people to different experimental conditions

real life. For example, it might be argued that Latané and Darley strayed far from the original inspiration for their study, the Kitty Genovese murder. What does witnessing a seizure while participating in a laboratory experiment in a college building have to do with a brutal murder in a densely populated urban neighborhood? How often in everyday life do we have discussions with other people through an intercom system? Did the fact that the participants knew they were in a psychology experiment influence their behavior?

External Validity

The extent to which the results of a study can be generalized to other situations and to other people

These are important questions that concern **external validity**, which is the extent to which the results of a study can be generalized to other situations and other people. Note that two kinds of generalizability are at issue: the extent to which we can generalize from the situation constructed by an experimenter to real-life situations, referred to as generalizability across *situations*, and the extent to which we can generalize from the people who participated in the experiment to people in general, referred to as generalizability across *people*.

When it comes to generalizability across situations, research in social psychology is sometimes criticized for being conducted in artificial settings that cannot be generalized to real life—for example, psychological experiments at a university. To address this problem, social psychologists attempt to increase the generalizability of their results by making their studies as realistic as possible. But this is hard to do in a laboratory setting in which people are placed in situations they would rarely, if ever, encounter in everyday life, such as occurred in Latané and Darley's group discussion of personal problems over an intercom system. Instead, psychologists attempt to maximize the study's **psychological realism**, which is the extent to which the psychological processes triggered in an experiment are similar to psychological processes that occur in everyday life (Aronson, Wilson, & Brewer, 1998). Even though Latané and Darley staged an emergency that in significant ways was unlike those encountered in everyday life, was it psychologically similar to real-life emergencies? Were the same psychological processes triggered? Did the participants have the same types of perceptions and thoughts, make the same types of decisions, and choose the same types of behaviors that they would in a real-life situation? If so, the study is high in psychological realism and we can generalize the results to everyday life.

Psychological Realism

The extent to which the psychological processes triggered in an experiment are similar to psychological processes that occur in everyday life

Cover Story

A description of the purpose of a study, given to participants, that is different from its true purpose and is used to maintain psychological realism

A good deal of social psychological research takes place in laboratory settings. How do social psychologists generalize from the findings of these studies to life outside the laboratory?

Psychological realism is heightened if people feel involved in a real event. To accomplish this, experimenters often tell participants a **cover story**—a disguised version of the study's true purpose. Recall, for example, that Latané and Darley told people that they were studying the personal problems of college students and then staged an emergency. It would have been a lot easier to say to people, "Look, we are interested in how people react to emergencies, so at some point during this study we are going to stage an accident, and then we'll see how you respond." We think you'll agree that such a procedure would be very low in psychological realism. In real life, we never know when emergencies are going to occur, and we do not have time to plan our responses to them. If participants knew that an emergency was about to happen, the kinds of psychological processes triggered would have been quite different from those of a real emergency, reducing the psychological realism of the study.

Social psychologists are also concerned with generalizability across people. Latané and Darley's experiment, for example, documented an interesting, unexpected example of social influence whereby the mere knowledge that others were present reduced the likelihood that people helped. But what have we learned about people in general? The participants in their study were 52 male and female students at New York University who received course credit for participating in the experiment. Would the study have turned out the same way if a different population had been used? Would the number of bystanders have influenced helping behavior had the participants been middle-aged blue-collar workers instead of college students? Midwesterners instead of New Yorkers? Japanese instead of American?

The only way to be certain that the results of an experiment represent the behavior of a particular population is to ensure that the participants are randomly selected from that population. Ideally, samples in experiments should be randomly selected, just as they are in surveys. Increasingly, social psychologists are conducting research with diverse populations and cultures, some of it over the internet (e.g., Lane, Banaji, & Nosek, 2007). But, unfortunately, it is impractical and expensive to select random samples for most social psychology experiments. It is difficult enough to convince a random sample of Americans to agree to answer a few questions over the telephone as part of a political poll, and such polls can cost thousands of dollars to conduct. Imagine the difficulty Latané and Darley would have had convincing a random sample of Americans to board a plane to New York to take part in their study, not to mention the cost of such an endeavor. Even trying to gather a random sample of students at New York University would not have been easy; each person contacted would have had to agree to spend an hour in Latané and Darley's laboratory.

However, concerns about practicality and expense are not good excuses for doing poor science. Many researchers address this problem by studying basic psychological processes that make people susceptible to social influence, assuming that these processes are so fundamental that they are universally shared. In that case, participants for social psychology experiments don't really have to come from all over the country or world. Of course, some social psychological processes are likely to be quite dependent on cultural factors, and in those cases, we'd need diverse samples of people. The question then is, how can researchers tell whether the processes they are studying are universal?

FIELD EXPERIMENTS   One of the best ways to increase external validity is by conducting **field experiments**. In a field experiment, researchers study behavior outside the laboratory, in its natural setting. As in a laboratory experiment, the researcher controls the occurrence of an independent variable (e.g., group size) to see what effect it has on a dependent variable (e.g., helping behavior) and randomly assigns people to the different conditions. Thus, a field experiment has the same design as a laboratory experiment, except that it is conducted in a real-life setting rather than in the relatively artificial setting of the laboratory. The participants in a field experiment are unaware that the events they experience are in fact an experiment. The external validity of such an experiment is high, because, after all, it is taking place in the real world, with real people who are more diverse than a typical college student sample.

Many such field studies have been conducted in social psychology. For example, Latané and Darley (1970) tested their hypothesis about group size and bystander intervention in a convenience store outside New York City. Two "robbers" (with full knowledge and permission of the cashier and manager of the store) waited at the checkout counter until there were either one or two other customers approaching to get in line. They then asked the cashier to retrieve the most expensive beer the store carried. The cashier said he would have to check in the back to see how much of that brand was in stock. While the cashier was gone, the robbers picked up a case of beer in the front of the store, declared, "They'll never miss this," put the beer in their car, and drove off.

Field Experiments

Experiments conducted in natural settings rather than in the laboratory

Some experiments are done in a psychology laboratory, whereas others are done in real-life settings. What are the advantages and disadvantages of each approach?

Because the robbers were rather burly fellows, no one attempted to intervene directly to stop the theft. The question was, when the cashier returned, how many people would help by telling him that a theft had just occurred? As it turned out, the number of bystanders had the same inhibiting effect on helping behavior as in the laboratory seizure study: Significantly fewer people reported the theft when there was another customer-witness in the store than when they were alone.

It might have occurred to you to ask why researchers conduct laboratory studies at all, given that external validity is so much better with field experiments. Indeed, it seems to us that the perfect experiment in social psychology would be one that was conducted in a field setting with a sample randomly selected from a population of interest and with extremely high internal validity (all extraneous variables controlled, people randomly assigned to the conditions). Sounds good, doesn't it? The only problem is that it is very difficult to satisfy all these conditions in one study, making such studies virtually impossible to conduct.

There is almost always a trade-off between internal and external validity—that is, between being able to randomly assign people to conditions and having enough control over the situation to ensure that no extraneous variables are influencing the results, and making sure that the results can be generalized to everyday life. We have the most control in a laboratory setting, but the laboratory may be unlike real life. Real life can best be captured by doing a field experiment, but it is very difficult to control all extraneous variables in such studies. For example, the astute reader will have noticed that Latané and Darley's (1970) beer theft study differed from laboratory experiments in an important way: People could not be randomly assigned to the alone or in-pairs conditions. Were this the only study Latané and Darley had performed, we could not be sure whether the kinds of people who prefer to shop alone, as compared to the kinds of people who prefer to shop with a friend, differ in ways that might influence helping behavior. By randomly assigning people to conditions in their laboratory studies, Latané and Darley were able to rule out such alternative explanations.

The trade-off between internal and external validity has been referred to as the **basic dilemma of the social psychologist** (Aronson & Carlsmith, 1968). The way to resolve this dilemma is not to try to do it all in a single experiment. Most social psychologists opt first for internal validity, conducting laboratory experiments in which people are randomly assigned to different conditions and all extraneous variables are controlled; here there is little ambiguity about what is causing what. Other social psychologists prefer to maximize external validity by conducting field studies. And many social psychologists do both. Taken together, both types of studies meet the requirements of our perfect experiment.

REPLICATIONS AND META-ANALYSIS **Replications** are the ultimate test of an experiment's external validity. Only by conducting studies in different settings, with different populations, can we determine how generalizable the results are. Often, though, when many studies on one problem are conducted, the results are somewhat variable. Several studies might find an effect of the number of bystanders on helping behavior, for example, while a few do not. How can we make sense of this? Does the number of bystanders make a difference or not? Fortunately, there is a statistical technique called **meta-analysis** that averages the results two or more studies to see if the effect of an independent variable is reliable. Earlier we discussed *p*-values, which tell

Basic Dilemma of the Social Psychologist

The trade-off between internal and external validity in conducting research; it is very difficult to do one experiment that is both high in internal validity and generalizable to other situations and people

Replications

Repeating a study, often with different subject populations or in different settings

Meta-Analysis

A statistical technique that averages the results of two or more studies to see if the effect of an independent variable is reliable

#trending

Correlation Does Not Equal Causation

Do you use a laptop or tablet to take notes in any of your classes? If so, has your attention ever wandered away from the class and onto a website, such as Facebook or Instagram? "Well sure," you might say, "sometimes the lecture is pretty boring so I check in with my friends on social media, but hey, I was still listening to what my professor had to say." But can you really message your friends and listen to a lecture at the same time? Consider this recent study done in an introductory psychology class at Michigan State University: With the permission of the university and the students, researchers tracked the students' browsing activity during the 1-hour 50-minute class. On average, students spent 37 minutes on websites that were unrelated to the class (e.g., social media, e-mail, shopping websites). And, it turned out that this was related to how well they did in the class: The more time students spent on non-class related websites, the lower their score on the final exam, with a statistically significant correlation of –.25 (Ravizza, Uitvlugt, & Fenn, 2016).

"Whoa," you may be thinking, "Maybe I should put my laptop away and listen to my professor more carefully." And that is one possible implication of the results. But we hope that after reading this chapter a sign is flashing on and off in your head

that says, "Not so fast! Correlation does not equal causation!" Indeed, there are a variety of interpretations of the results of the Ravizza et al. (2016) study. Yes, one possibility is that looking at the websites caused students to do worse in the class. But it is equally possible that doing poorly on tests caused students to give up and tune out during class, or that some third variable, such as a lack of interest in the subject, caused students to tune out during class and study less for the exams.

As we have seen, there is nothing like a good experiment to settle questions about causality. Fortunately there have been some on this very topic. In one, students were randomly assigned to multitask (e.g., surf the Web) during class or not, and those in the multitask condition did worse on a test of the material—showing definitively that multitasking during class lowered performance (Sana, Weston, & Cepeda, 2013). In another, students were randomly assigned to take notes on a laptop or by hand. Those who used a laptop tended to write more superficial notes and they did worse on a test (Mueller & Oppenheimer, 2014). So, thanks to these well-designed experimenters, the answer is clear: Consider putting your laptop away and taking notes the old fashioned way, with pen and paper.

---

us the probability that the findings of one study are due to chance or to the independent variable. A meta-analysis essentially does the same thing, except that it averages the results of many different studies. If, say, an independent variable is found to have an effect in only 1 of 20 studies, the meta-analysis will tell us that that one study was probably an exception and that, on average, the independent variable is not influencing the dependent variable. If an independent variable is having an effect in most of the studies, the meta-analysis is likely to tell us that, on average, it does influence the dependent variable.

Most of the findings you will read about in this book have been replicated in several different settings, with different populations; we know, then, that they are reliable phenomena, not limited to the laboratory or to college sophomores. For example, Anderson and Bushman (1997) compared laboratory studies on the causes of aggression with studies conducted in the real world. In both types of studies, violence in the media caused aggressive behavior. Similarly, Latané and Darley's original findings have been replicated in numerous studies. Increasing the number of bystanders inhibited helping behavior with many kinds of people, including children, college students, and future ministers (Darley & Batson, 1973; Latané & Nida, 1981; Plötner et al., 2015); in both small towns and large cities (Latané & Dabbs, 1975); in a variety of settings, such as psychology laboratories, city streets, and subway trains (Harrison & Wells, 1991; Latané & Darley, 1970; Piliavin & Piliavin, 1972); and with different kinds of emergencies, such as seizures, potential fires, fights, and accidents (Latané & Darley, 1968; Shotland & Straw, 1976; Staub, 1974), as well as with less-serious events, such as having a flat tire (Hurley & Allen, 1974). Many of these replications took place in real-life settings (e.g., on a subway train) where people could not possibly have known that an experiment was being conducted.

That said, sometimes replications fail to confirm the findings of a particular study. The question of how replicable findings are in social psychology and other sciences has become a topic of debate, with some arguing that too many studies in psychology have failed to replicate and that our methods need to be improved to make sure that research findings of studies are reliable and replicable (Open Science Collaboration, 2015). Others argue that while scientific methods can always be improved, and that there have been healthy steps in that direction, there is no evidence of a "replication crisis" (Gilbert, King, Pettigrew, & Wilson, 2016). Readers can be assured that most of the areas of research discussed in this book have been replicated. There are cases in which specific findings have been called into question, however, and when that is the case we will point that out.

BASIC VERSUS APPLIED RESEARCH   You may have wondered how people decide which specific topic to study. Why would a social psychologist decide to study helping behavior, cognitive dissonance theory, or the effects of pornography on aggression? Is he or she simply curious? Or does the social psychologist have a specific purpose in mind, such as trying to reduce sexual violence?

Basic Research

Studies that are designed to find the best answer to the question of why people behave as they do and that are conducted purely for reasons of intellectual curiosity

Applied Research

Studies designed to solve a particular social problem

The goal in **basic research** is to find the best answer to the question of why people behave as they do, purely for reasons of intellectual curiosity. The researchers aren't trying to solve a specific social or psychological problem. In contrast, **applied research** is geared toward solving a particular social problem. Here, building a theory of behavior is usually secondary to solving the specific problem, such as alleviating racism, reducing sexual violence, or stemming the spread of AIDS.

In social psychology, the distinction between basic and applied research is fuzzy. Even though many researchers label themselves as either basic or applied scientists, the endeavors of one group are not independent of those of the other group. There are countless examples of advances in basic science that at the time had no known applied value but later proved to be the key to solving a significant applied problem. As we will see later in this book, for example, basic research with dogs, rats, and fish on the effects of feeling in control of one's environment has led to the development of techniques to improve the health of elderly nursing home residents (Langer & Rodin, 1976; Richter, 1957; Schulz, 1976).

Review Questions

1. A researcher is interested in whether moods vary by the day of the week. She codes the postings on thousands of Facebook pages to see whether people express more positive comments on some days than others. Which research method has she used?
   a. Ethnography
   b. Survey
   c. Experimental method
   d. Archival analysis

2. The observational method is best at answering which of these questions?
   a. How polite are people in public places?
   b. Are people from the southern United States more polite in public places than people from the northern United States?
   c. What makes people act politely or rudely in public places?
   d. Does music played in department stores influence how polite people are in those stores?

3. The correlational method is best at answering which of these questions?
   a. How polite are people in public places?
   b. Are people from the southern United States more polite in public places than people from the northern United States?
   c. What makes people act politely or rudely in public places?
   d. Does music played in department stores influence how polite people are in those stores?

4. The experimental method is best at answering which of these questions?
   a. How aggressively do people drive during rush hours in major U.S. cities?
   b. Are people who play violent video games more likely to drive aggressively?
   c. Are people who play violent video games more likely to be rude to someone who cuts in line in front of them?
   d. Does playing violent video games cause people to be more rude to someone who cuts in line in front of them?

5. Suppose a researcher found a strong positive correlation between the number of tweets people send each day and their reported happiness. Which of the following is the best conclusion he or she can draw from this finding?
   a. Sending tweets makes people happy.
   b. Feeling happy makes people want to tweet more.
   c. Happy people are more likely to send a lot of tweets than sad people.
   d. There is a third variable that makes people happy and send a lot of tweets.

6. A researcher wants to see whether people are more likely to donate money to a charity when they receive a small gift from that charity. She sends an appeal for money from the charity to 1,000 people. For half of the people (randomly chosen) the letter includes free address labels and for half it does not. The researcher then sees whether those who got the address labels donate more money. Which of the following is true about this study?
   a. It uses the correlational method.
   b. The independent variable is whether people got address labels and the dependent variable is how much money they donate.

   c. The independent variable is how much money people donate and the dependent variable is whether they got address labels.
   d. The study is low in internal validity because the people who got the address labels may differ in other ways from the people who did not.

7. Which of the following is the best way to increase the external validity of a study?
   a. Make sure it is low in psychological realism.
   b. Conduct the study in the laboratory instead of the field.
   c. Replicate the study with a different population of people in a different setting.
   d. Make sure you have at least two dependent variables.

8. Social psychologists often do experiments in the laboratory, instead of the field, to:
   a. increase internal validity.
   b. increase external validity.
   c. conduct a meta-analysis.
   d. decrease psychological realism.

Most social psychologists would agree that, to solve a specific social problem, we must understand the psychological processes responsible for it. Indeed, Kurt Lewin (1951), one of the founders of social psychology, coined a phrase that has become a motto for the field: "There is nothing so practical as a good theory" (p. 169). He meant that to solve such difficult social problems as urban violence or racial prejudice, one must first understand the underlying psychological dynamics of human nature and social interaction. Even when the goal is to discover the psychological processes underlying social behavior, the findings often have clear applied implications, as you'll see throughout this book. For example, basic research on how people understand and construe the world has been translated into successful attempts to address many problems, including closing the achievement gap in education, reducing prejudice, reducing teenage pregnancies, and lowering the rate of child abuse (Wilson, 2011; Walton, 2014).

New Frontiers in Social Psychological Research

LO 2.3 Explain the impact cross-cultural studies and social neuroscience research have on the way in which scientists investigate social behavior.

Social psychologists are always looking for new ways of investigating social behavior, and in recent years some exciting new methods and approaches have been developed. These methodological advances have been spurred on by new questions about the origins of social behavior, because new questions and new methods often develop hand in hand.

Culture and Social Psychology

Social psychology largely began as a Western science, conducted by Western social psychologists with Western participants. This raises the question of how universal the findings are. To study the effects of culture on social psychological process, social psychologists conduct **cross-cultural research** (Gelfand, Chiu, & Hong,

Cross-Cultural Research
Research conducted with members of different cultures, to see whether the psychological processes of interest are present in both cultures or whether they are specific to the culture in which people were raised

Some basic psychological processes are universal, whereas others are shaped by the culture in which we live. For example, are people's self-concepts shaped by cultural rules of how people must present themselves, such as the requirement by the Taliban regime in Afghanistan that women cover themselves from head to toe? Cross-cultural research is challenging but necessary for exploring how culture influences the basic ways in which people think about and interact with others. We will see many other examples of cross-cultural research later in this book.

2014; Heine, 2010; Kitayama & Cohen, 2007; Morling, 2016; Wang, 2016; Nisbett, 2003). Some findings in social psychology are culture-dependent, as we will see throughout this book. In Chapter 3, for example, we will see that Westerners and East Asians rely on fundamentally different kinds of thought to perceive and understand the social world. In Chapter 5, we'll discuss cultural differences in the very way people define themselves. Whether we emphasize personal independence or social interdependence reflects our cultural values (Henrich, Heine, & Norenzayan, 2010).

Conducting cross-cultural research is not simply a matter of traveling to another culture, translating materials into the local language, and replicating a study there (Heine et al., 2002; Davidov et al., 2014). Researchers have to guard against imposing their own viewpoints and definitions, learned from their culture, onto another culture with which they are unfamiliar. They must also be sure that their independent and dependent variables are understood in the same way in different cultures (Bond, 1988; Lonner & Berry, 1986).

Suppose, for example, that you wanted to replicate the Latané and Darley (1968) seizure experiment in another culture. Clearly, you could not conduct the identical experiment somewhere else. The tape-recorded discussion of college life used by Latané and Darley was specific to the lives of New York University students in the 1960s and could not be used meaningfully elsewhere. What about more subtle aspects of the study, such as the way people viewed the person who had the seizure? Cultures vary considerably in how they define whether or not another person belongs to their social group; this factor figures significantly in how they behave toward that person (Gudykunst, 1988; Triandis, 1989). If people in one culture view the victim as a member of their social group but people in another culture perceive the victim as a member of a rival social group, you might find very different results in the two cultures—not because the psychological processes of helping behavior are different, but because people interpreted the situation differently. It can be quite daunting to conduct a study that is interpreted and perceived similarly in dissimilar cultures. Cross-cultural researchers are sensitive to these issues, and as more and more cross-cultural research is conducted carefully, we will be able to determine which social psychological processes are universal and which are culture-bound (Heine, 2010). For example, there is substantial evidence that playing violent video games makes people act in more aggressive ways and makes them less likely to help others. But is this true just in Western countries? A review of the literature compared studies of video games in the United States and Japan. As it happened, the deleterious effects of violent video games were the same in both countries (Anderson et al., 2010).

Social psychologists are studying the brain and its relation to behavior. They use technologies such as electroencephalography (EEG) and functional magnetic resonance imaging (fMRI).

Social Neuroscience

As we have seen, social psychology is concerned with how people's thoughts, feelings, and behaviors are influenced by the real or imagined presence of other people. Most research studies in social psychology, then, study just that—thoughts, feelings, and behaviors. Human beings are biological organisms, however, and social psychologists have become increasingly interested in the connection between biological processes and social behavior. These interests include the study of hormones and behavior, the human immune system, and neurological processes in the human brain. To study the brain and its relation to behavior,

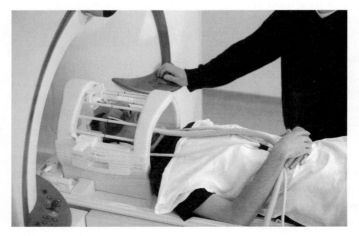

psychologists use sophisticated technologies, including electroencephalography (EEG), in which electrodes are placed on the scalp to measure electrical activity in the brain, and functional magnetic resonance imaging (fMRI), in which people are placed in scanners that measure changes in blood flow in their brains. Social psychologists take these measurements while participants think about and process social information, allowing them to correlate different kinds of brain activity with social information processing. This kind of research promises to open up a whole new area of inquiry into the relationship of the brain to behavior (Cacioppo & Cacioppo, 2013; Coan & Maresh, 2014; Connelly & Morris, 2016; Lieberman, 2013; Ochsner, 2007; Varnum, 2016).

Review Questions

1. Which of the following is true about cross-cultural research?
   a. Most social psychological findings have been found to be universal; that is, true in virtually all cultures that have been studied.
   b. The purpose of cross-cultural research is to see which social psychological findings are universal and which are culture-bound.
   c. To conduct a cross-cultural study a researcher travels to another country, translates the materials into the local language, and replicates the study there.
   d. It is relatively easy to conduct a study that is interpreted and perceived similarly in different cultures.

2. Which of the following is true about social neuroscience?
   a. This field is concerned exclusively with how different kinds of brain activity correlate with social information processing.
   b. This field is concerned primarily with how hormones influence social behavior.
   c. Social psychologists are increasingly interested in the connection between biological processes and social behavior.
   d. When it comes right down to it, the brain is not related to behavior, and there is not much to be learned by measuring its electrical activity or blood flow.

Ethical Issues in Social Psychology

LO 2.4 **Summarize how social psychologists ensure the safety and welfare of their research participants, while at the same time testing hypotheses about the causes of social behavior.**

As you read this chapter, did it bother you to learn that researchers sometimes mislead people about the true purpose of their study or that, in Latané and Darley's seizure study, people were put in a situation that might have been upsetting? In their quest to create realistic, engaging situations, social psychologists frequently face ethical dilemmas. For scientific reasons, we want our experiments to resemble the real world as much as possible and to be as sound and well controlled as we can make them. But we also want to avoid causing our participants stress, discomfort, or unpleasantness. These two goals sometimes conflict as the researcher goes about the business of creating and conducting experiments.

Above all, researchers are concerned about the health and welfare of the individuals participating in their experiments. Researchers are also in the process of discovering important information about human social behavior, such as bystander intervention, prejudice, conformity, aggression, and obedience to authority. Many of these discoveries are bound to benefit society. Indeed, given the fact that social psychologists have developed powerful tools to investigate such issues scientifically, many scholars feel it would be immoral not to conduct experiments to explore them. To gain insight into such

"DON'T TELL ME THIS NONSENSE DOESN'T VIOLATE THE CODE OF BIOETHICS."

critical issues, however, researchers often must create events that are vivid and engaging for the participants. Some of these events might make the participants uncomfortable, such as witnessing someone having a seizure. We can't resolve the dilemma by making pious claims that participants never experience discomfort in an experiment or by insisting that all is fair in science and then forging blindly ahead. Clearly, some middle ground is called for.

Informed Consent

Agreement to participate in an experiment, granted in full awareness of the nature of the experiment, which has been explained in advance

The dilemma is less problematic if researchers can obtain **informed consent** from their participants prior to their participation. To obtain informed consent, the researcher explains the nature of the experiment to participants before it begins and asks for their permission to participate. If participants are made fully aware of the kinds of experiences they are about to undergo and state that they are willing to participate, the ethical dilemma is resolved. In many social psychology experiments, this sort of description is feasible—and where it is feasible, it is done. For example, one of the authors of this text was interested in how college students would react if they were left alone with their thoughts for 15 minutes, without access to their phones or any other external distractions. Might they get so bored that they would administer to themselves a mild electric shock to relieve their boredom? To find out we asked people whether they would be willing to receive mild electric shocks in the study, and all participants gave their informed consent to do so. (As it happened, two-thirds of men and a quarter of women chose to shock themselves at least once; Wilson et al., 2014).

But sometimes it is not possible to inform people exactly what will happen in advance. Suppose Latané and Darley had told their participants that a seizure was about to be staged, that it wouldn't be a real emergency, and that the point was to see if they offered help. Such a procedure would be bad science. In this kind of experiment, it's essential that the participant experience contrived events as if they were real; this is called a *deception experiment*. **Deception** in social psychological research involves misleading participants about the true purpose of a study or the events that transpire. Psychologists use deception only if it is the only way in which they can test a hypothesis about social behavior.

Deception

Misleading participants about the true purpose of a study or the events that will actually transpire

Debriefing

Explaining to participants, at the end of an experiment, the true purpose of the study and exactly what transpired

When deception is used in a study, the postexperimental interview, called the *debriefing session*, is crucial. **Debriefing** is the process of explaining to the participants, at the end of an experiment, the true purpose of the study and exactly what transpired. If any participants have experienced discomfort, the researchers attempt to undo and alleviate it. During debriefing too the participants learn about the goals and purpose of the research. The best researchers question their participants carefully and listen to what they say, regardless of whether or not deception was used in the experiment. (For a detailed description of how debriefing interviews should be conducted, see Aronson et al., 1990.)

In our experience, virtually all participants understand and appreciate the need for deception, as long as the time is taken in the postexperimental debriefing session to review the purpose of the research and to explain why alternative procedures could not be used. Several investigators have gone a step further and assessed the impact on people of participating in deception studies (e.g., Christensen, 1988; Epley & Huff, 1998; Finney, 1987; Gerdes, 1979; Sharpe, Adair, & Roese, 1992). These studies have consistently found that people do not object to the kinds of mild discomfort and deceptions typically used in social psychological research. In fact, some studies have found that most people who participated in deception experiments reported learning more and enjoying the experiments more than did those who participated in nondeception experiments (Smith & Richardson, 1983). For example, Latané and Darley (1970) reported that, during their debriefing, the participants said that the deception was necessary and that they were willing to participate in similar studies in the future—even though they had experienced some stress and conflict during the study.

To ensure that the dignity and safety of research participants are protected, the American Psychological Association (2010) has published a list of ethical principles

Figure 2.3 The American Psychological Association, a professional organization that represents psychology in the United States, has established ethical guidelines that psychological researchers are expected to follow. Some of them are listed here.

(Adapted from American Psychological Association Ethical Principles of Psychologists and Code of Conduct, 2017)

Selected Ethical Principles of Psychologists in the Conduct of Research

1. Psychologists seek to promote accuracy, honesty, and truthfulness in the science, teaching, and practice of psychology.
2. Psychologists respect the dignity and worth of all people, and the rights of individuals to privacy, confidentiality, and self-determination.
3. When psychologists conduct research in person or via electronic transmission or other forms of communication, they obtain the informed consent of the individual.
4. When obtaining informed consent psychologists inform participants about (1) the purpose of the research, expected duration, and procedures; (2) their right to decline to participate and to withdraw from the research once participation has begun; (3) the foreseeable consequences of declining or withdrawing; (4) reasonably foreseeable factors that may be expected to influence their willingness to participate such as potential risks, discomfort, or adverse effects; (5) any prospective research benefits; (6) limits of confidentiality; (7) incentives for participation; and (8) whom to contact for questions about the research and research participants rights.
5. Psychologists have a primary obligation and take reasonable precautions to protect confidential information obtained through or stored in any medium.
6. Psychologists do not conduct a study involving deception unless they have determined that the use of deceptive techniques is justified by the study's significant prospective scientific, educational, or applied value and that effective nondeceptive alternative procedures are not feasible.
7. Psychologists explain any deception that is an integral feature of the design and conduct of an experiment to participants as early as is feasible.
8. Psychologists provide a prompt opportunity for participants to obtain appropriate information about the nature, results, and conclusions of the research, and they take reasonable steps to correct any misconceptions that participants may have of which the psychologists are aware.

---

that govern all research in psychology (see Figure 2.3). In addition, any institution (such as a university) that seeks federal funding for psychological research is required to have an **institutional review board (IRB)** that reviews research before it is conducted. The board, which must include at least one scientist, one nonscientist, and one person who is not affiliated with the institution, reviews all research proposals and decides whether the procedures meet ethical guidelines. Any aspect of the experimental procedure that this committee judges to be overly stressful or upsetting must be changed or deleted before the study can be conducted. Note that some of the research described in later chapters was conducted before IRBs were required in the early 1970s. You will need to decide whether you would have approved these studies if you were on an IRB that judged them.

Now that you have a good grounding in how social psychologists conduct research we can begin our tour of the major findings in the field. We hope you find them as fascinating as we do.

Institutional Review Board (IRB)

A group made up of at least one scientist, one nonscientist, and one member not affiliated with the institution that reviews all psychological research at that institution and decides whether it meets ethical guidelines; all research must be approved by the IRB before it is conducted

---

Review Questions

1. Which of the following is true about the ethical conduct of psychological research?
   a. It is good scientific procedure to tell participants about the research hypotheses before they participate.
   b. If research participants are misled about a study they must be fully debriefed at the end of the study.
   c. Darley and Latané could have easily tested their hypotheses about helping behavior by telling participants in advance that they would hear someone pretending to have a seizure.
   d. It is never permissible to use deception.

2. Which of the following is true about Institutional Review Boards (IRBs)?
   a. Universities can decide whether to have an IRB to approve psychological research.
   b. The purpose of IRBs is to review research after it is conducted and review any complaints.
   c. IRBs review psychological studies before they are conducted to make sure they meet ethical guidelines.
   d. IRBs must be made up entirely of nonscientists.

3. Which of the following is one of the ethical principles of the American Psychological Association?

a. Psychologists respect the dignity and worth of all people, and the rights of individuals to privacy, confidentiality, and self-determination.
b. Psychologists may not use minors (those younger than age 18) as participants in research.
c. If a study is conducted over the internet, psychologists need not obtain informed consent from participants.
d. Psychologists are not responsible for protecting the confidentiality of information they obtain from participants.

Summary

LO 2.1 Describe how researchers develop hypotheses and theories.

- **Social Psychology: An Empirical Science** A fundamental principle of social psychology is that social influence can be studied scientifically.

  - **Formulating Hypotheses and Theories** Social psychological research begins with a hypothesis about the effects of social influence. Hypotheses often come from previous research findings; researchers conduct studies to test an alternative explanation of previous experiments. Many other hypotheses come from observations of everyday life, such as Latané and Darley's hunches about why people failed to help Kitty Genovese.

LO 2.2 Compare the strengths and weaknesses of various research designs that social psychologists use.

- **Research Designs** Social psychologists use three research designs: the observational method, the correlational method, and the experimental method.

  - **The Observational Method: Describing Social Behavior** The *observational method*, whereby researchers observe people and systematically record their behavior, is useful for describing the nature of a phenomenon and generating hypotheses. It includes *ethnography*, the method by which researchers attempt to understand a group or culture by observing it from the inside, without imposing any preconceived notions they might have. Another method is *archival analysis*, whereby researchers examine documents or archives, such as looking at photographs in magazines to see how men and women are portrayed.

  - **The Correlational Method: Predicting Social Behavior** The *correlational method*, whereby two or more variables are systematically measured and the relationship between them assessed, is very useful when the goal is to predict one variable from another. For example, researchers might be interested in whether there is a correlation between the amount of violent television children watch and how aggressive they are. The correlational method is often applied to the results of surveys in which a representative group of people are asked questions about their attitudes and behaviors. To make sure that the results are generalizable, researchers randomly select survey respondents from the population at large. A limit of the correlational method is that *correlation does not equal causation*.

- **The Experimental Method: Answering Causal Questions** The only way to determine causality is to use the *experimental method*, in which the researcher randomly assigns participants to different conditions and ensures that these conditions are identical except for the independent variable. The *independent variable* is the one researchers vary to see if it has a causal effect (e.g., how much TV children watch); the *dependent variable* is what researchers measure to see if it is affected (e.g., how aggressive children are). Experiments should be high in *internal validity*, which means that people in all conditions are treated identically, except for the independent variable (e.g., how much TV children watch). *External validity*—the extent to which researchers can generalize their results to other situations and people—is accomplished by increasing the realism of the experiment, particularly its psychological realism (the extent to which the psychological processes triggered in the experiment are similar to those triggered in everyday life). It is also accomplished by *replicating* the study with different populations of participants. As in any other science, some social psychology studies are basic research experiments (designed to answer basic questions about why people do what they do), whereas others are applied studies (designed to find ways to solve specific social problems).

LO 2.3 Explain the impact cross-cultural studies and social neuroscience research have on the way in which scientists investigate social behavior.

- **New Frontiers in Social Psychological Research** In recent years, social psychologists have developed new ways of investigating social behavior.

  - **Culture and Social Psychology** To study the ways in which culture shapes people's thoughts, feelings, and behavior, social psychologists conduct cross-cultural research. This is not simply a matter of replicating the same study in different cultures; researchers have to guard against imposing their own viewpoints and definitions, learned from their culture, onto another culture with which they are unfamiliar.

  - **Social Neuroscience** Social psychologists have become increasingly interested in the connection between biological processes and social behavior. These interests include the study of hormones and behavior, the human immune system, and neurological processes in the human brain.

LO 2.4 Summarize how social psychologists ensure the safety and welfare of their research participants, while at the same time testing hypotheses about the causes of social behavior.

- **Ethical Issues in Social Psychology** Social psychologists follow federal, state, and professional guidelines to ensure the welfare of their research participants. These include having an *institutional review board* approve their studies in advance, asking participants to sign *informed consent* forms, and *debriefing* participants afterward about the purpose of the study and what transpired, especially if there was any deception involved.

Revel Interactive

Shared Writing   What Do You Think?

Now that you know correlation doesn't equal causation, you know that eating fast food doesn't necessarily cause poor test performance. What are some alternative explanations for the negative correlation between children's fast food consumption and low test scores?

Test Yourself

1. Megan reads a research study which shows that children who see a lot of violence on television are more likely to be aggressive on the playground. Megan thinks, "This is obvious; I could have predicted that!" Megan's reaction to the study is probably an example of:

   a. internal validity.

   b. the hindsight bias.

   c. external validity.

   d. psychological realism.

2. Suppose a researcher found a strong negative correlation between college students' grade point average (GPA) and the amount of alcohol they drink. Which of the following is the best conclusion from this study?

   a. Students with a high GPA study more and thus have less time to drink.

   b. Drinking a lot interferes with studying.

   c. If you know how much alcohol a student drinks, you can predict his or her GPA fairly well.

   d. People who are intelligent get higher grades and drink less.

3. A team of researchers wants to test the hypothesis that drinking wine makes people like jazz more. They randomly assign college students who are 21 or older to one room in which they will drink wine and listen to jazz or to another room in which they will drink water and listen to jazz. It happens that the "wine room" has a big window with nice scenery outside, whereas the "water room" is windowless, dark, and dingy. The most serious flaw in this experiment is that it

   a. is low in external validity.
   b. is low in internal validity.
   c. did not randomly select the participants from all college students in the country.
   d. is low in psychological realism.

4. Mary wants to find out whether eating sugary snacks before an exam leads to better performance on the exam. Which of the following strategies would answer her question most conclusively?

   a. Identify a large number of students who perform exceptionally low and exceptionally high in exams, ask them whether they eat sugary snacks before exams, and see whether high performers eat more sugary snacks before exams than do low performers.
   b. Wait for exam time in a big class, ask everyone whether they ate sugary snacks before the exam, and see whether those who ate sugary snacks before the exam do better compared to those who didn't.
   c. Wait for exam time in a big class, give a random half of the students M&Ms before the exam, and see whether the students who ate M&Ms perform better.
   d. Pick a big class, give all students sugary snacks before one exam and salty snacks before the next exam; then see whether students score lower on average in the second exam.

5. A researcher conducts a study with participants who are college students. The researcher then repeats the study using the same procedures but with members of the general population (i.e., adults) as participants. The results are similar for both samples. The research has established _____ through _____.

   a. external validity, replication
   b. internal validity, replication
   c. external validity, psychological realism
   d. internal validity, psychological realism

6. Professor X wants to make sure his study of gifted youngsters will get published, but he's worried that his findings could have been caused by something other than the independent variable, which was a

new teaching method he introduced. He is concerned with the _____ his experiment.

   a. probability level
   b. external validity
   c. replication
   d. internal validity

7. Suppose a psychologist decides to join a local commune to understand and observe its members' social relationships. This is

   a. cross-cultural research.
   b. applied research.
   c. an experiment.
   d. ethnography.

8. The basic dilemma of the social psychologist is that

   a. it is hard to teach social psychology to students because most people believe strongly in personality.
   b. there is a trade-off between internal and external validity in most experiments.
   c. it is nearly impossible to use a random selection of the population in laboratory experiments.
   d. almost all social behavior is influenced by the culture in which people grew up.

9. Which of the following is true about new frontiers in social psychological research?

   a. Social psychologists are interested in the role of culture but not in evolutionary processes.
   b. Social psychologists are interested in evolutionary processes but not the role of culture.
   c. Social psychologists use functional magnetic resonance imaging (fMRI) to correlate different kinds of brain activity with social information processing.
   d. The purpose of cross-cultural research is to show that all social psychological findings are universal with no cultural variations.

10. All of the following except one are part of the guidelines for ethical research. Which is not?

   a. All research is reviewed by an IRB (institutional review board) that consists of at least one scientist, one nonscientist, and one person unaffiliated with the institution.
   b. A researcher receives informed consent from a participant unless deception is deemed necessary and the experiment meets ethical guidelines.
   c. When deception is used in a study, participants must be fully debriefed.
   d. There must be a cover story for every study, because all studies involve some type of deception.

Chapter 3
Social Cognition
How We Think About the Social World

Chapter Outline and Learning Objectives

On Automatic Pilot: Low-Effort Thinking

LO 3.1 Explain the advantages and disadvantages of schemas.

People as Everyday Theorists: Automatic Thinking With Schemas

Which Schemas Do We Use? Accessibility and Priming

Making Our Schemas Come True: The Self-Fulfilling Prophecy

Types of Automatic Thinking

LO 3.2 Describe the types of automatic thinking.

Automatic Goal Pursuit

Automatic Thinking and Metaphors About the Body and the Mind

Mental Strategies and Shortcuts: Judgmental Heuristics

Cultural Differences in Social Cognition

LO 3.3 Analyze how culture influences social thinking.

Cultural Determinants of Schemas

Holistic Versus Analytic Thinking

Controlled Social Cognition: High-Effort Thinking

LO 3.4 Describe drawbacks to controlled thinking and ways to improve its effectiveness.

Controlled Thinking and Free Will

Mentally Undoing the Past: Counterfactual Reasoning

Improving Human Thinking

Watson Revisited

WHAT DO YOU THINK?

Revel Interactive

Survey	**What Do You Think?**	
SURVEY		RESULTS

Have you ever read your horoscope and had an eerie feeling about how accurate it was?

○ Yes
○ No

Social Cognition

How people think about themselves and the social world; more specifically, how people select, interpret, remember, and use social information to make judgments and decisions

Rodin's famous sculpture, *The Thinker*, mimics controlled thinking, where people sit down and consider something slowly and deliberately. Even when we do not know it, however, we are engaging in automatic thinking, which is nonconscious, unintentional, involuntary, and effortless.

It was an epic match on *Jeopardy!*, the television quiz show on which contestants are given an answer and have to provide the correct question. Two of the three contestants were among the best players of all time, namely, Ken Jennings, who held the record for the longest winning streak on the show (74 consecutive games), and Brad Rutter, who was the all-time money winner. What about the third contestant? Who would dare match his or her wits against these formidable opponents? Actually, it wasn't a "he" or "she," but an "it": a supercomputer named Watson, developed by IBM and named after that company's founder, Thomas J. Watson.

The match was close at first, but by the third and last day Watson had built an insurmountable lead. Time after time, the supercomputer gave correct responses to difficult clues. Ken Jennings, who described himself as "the Great Carbon-Based Hope against a new generation of thinking machines," conceded defeat by writing on his video screen, "I, for one, welcome our new computer overlords," paraphrasing a line from an episode of *The Simpsons* (Jennings, 2011; Markoff, 2011).

This was not the first time an IBM computer had outwitted human beings. In 1997, Gary Kasparov, the reigning chess champion of the world, resigned in the sixth and decisive game against an IBM computer named Big Blue. Should we all feel a little less smart, like the commentator who remarked, after Big Blue defeated Gary Kasparov, that he felt "a twinge of IQ loss and an increase in hairiness" (Dunn, 1997)?

Well, computers are getting smarter and smarter; it's probably only a matter of time before they are driving our cars, cooking our meals, and serving us at restaurants (Rao, 2016). But they have a long way to go before they can match the human brain in recognizing and understanding the complexity of human behavior. Perhaps computers will get there, as in the futuristic movie *Ex Machina* and the television drama *Westworld*, in which computers become so sophisticated that they have minds of their own and understand human beings astutely—so much so that people fall in love with them. But as for now, the human brain far outperforms the fastest computer in at least one critical task: understanding other people.

The human brain has evolved to be a powerful, finely tuned instrument for thinking about other people (Liebeman, 2013). More generally, people are extremely good at **social cognition**, which, as we saw in Chapter 1, refers to the ways in which people think about themselves and the social world, including how they select, interpret, remember, and use social information. Although no computer can match us in this kind of thinking, that's not to say we are perfect social thinkers. Social psychologists have uncovered some fascinating mistakes to which we are prone, despite our uncanny cognitive abilities. In this chapter, we will see both the power and limits of social cognition.

To understand how people think about their social worlds and how accurate their impressions are likely to be, we need to distinguish between two different kinds of social cognition: automatic versus controlled thinking. Let's take a look at automatic thinking first.

On Automatic Pilot: Low-Effort Thinking

LO 3.1   Explain the advantages and disadvantages of schemas.

People are good at sizing up a new situation quickly and accurately. They figure out who is there, what is happening, and what might happen next. When you attended your first college class, for example, you probably made quick assumptions about who people were (the person standing at the lectern was the professor) and how to behave. We doubt that you confused the class with a fraternity party. And you probably reached these conclusions without even being aware that you were doing so.

Imagine a different approach: Every time you encounter a new situation, you stop and think about it slowly and deliberately, like Rodin's statue *The Thinker*. When you are introduced to someone new, you have to excuse yourself for 15 minutes while you analyze what you have learned and how much you like the person. Sounds exhausting, doesn't it? Fortunately, we form impressions of people quickly and effortlessly, without much conscious analysis of what we are doing. We do these things by engaging in an automatic analysis of our environments, based on our past experiences and knowledge of the world. **Automatic thinking** is thought that is nonconscious, unintentional, involuntary, and effortless. Although different kinds of automatic thinking meet these criteria to varying degrees (Bargh et al., 2012; Hassin, 2013; Jonas, 2013; Moors & De Houwer, 2006; Payne & Gawronski, 2010), for our purposes we can define automaticity as thinking that satisfies all or most of them.

Automatic Thinking

Thinking that is nonconscious, unintentional, involuntary, and effortless

People as Everyday Theorists: Automatic Thinking With Schemas

Automatic thinking helps us understand new situations by relating them to our prior experiences. When we meet someone new, we don't start from scratch to figure out what he or she is like; we categorize the person as "an engineering student" or "like my cousin Emma." The same goes for places, objects, and situations. When we walk into a fast-food restaurant we've never visited, we know, without thinking, not to wait at a table for a waiter and a menu. We know that we have to go to the counter and order, because our past experience automatically tells us that this is what we do in fast-food restaurants.

More formally, people use **schemas**, which are mental structures that organize our knowledge about the social world. These mental structures influence the information we notice, think about, and remember (Bartlett, 1932; Heine, Proulx, & Vohs, 2006; Markus, 1977). The term *schema* is general; it encompasses our knowledge about many things—other people, ourselves, social roles (e.g., what a librarian or an engineer is like), and specific events (e.g., what usually happens when people eat a meal in a restaurant). In each case, our schemas contain our basic knowledge and impressions that we use to organize what we know about the social world and interpret new situations. For example, if you watch the television show *The Bachelor* or *The Bachelorette*, you have probably developed schemas for different types of contestants, such as "the snide backstabbing villain" and the "naïve one whose heart will be broken."

Schemas

Mental structures people use to organize their knowledge about the social world around themes or subjects and that influence the information people notice, think about, and remember

Schemas are useful for helping us organize and make sense of the world and to fill in the gaps of our knowledge. Think for a moment what it would be like to have no schemas at all. What if everything you encountered was inexplicable, confusing, and unlike anything else you've ever known? Tragically, this is what happens to people who suffer from a neurological disorder called *Korsakov's syndrome*. People with this disorder lose the ability to form new memories and must approach every situation as if they were encountering it for the first time, even if they have actually experienced it many times before. This can be so unsettling—even terrifying—that some people with Korsakov's syndrome go to great lengths to try to impose meaning on their experiences. Neurologist Oliver Sacks (1987) gives the following description of a Korsakov patient named Thompson:

> He remembered nothing for more than a few seconds. He was continually disoriented. Abysses of amnesia continually opened beneath him, but he would bridge them, nimbly, by fluent confabulations and fictions of all kinds. For him they were not fictions, but how he suddenly saw, or interpreted, the world. Its radical flux and incoherence could not be tolerated, acknowledged, for an instant—there was, instead, this strange, delirious, quasi-coherence, as Mr. Thompson, with his ceaseless, unconscious, quick-fire inventions, continually improvised a world around him ... *for such a patient must literally make himself (and his world) up every moment.* (pp. 109–110; emphasis in original)

In short, having continuity, being able to relate new experiences to our past schemas, is so important that people who lose this ability invent schemas where none exist.

Schemas are particularly useful in helping us figure out what is going on in confusing or ambiguous situations. Consider a classic study by Harold Kelley (1950) in which students in different sections of a college economics class were told that a guest lecturer would be filling in that day. To create a schema about what the guest lecturer would be like, Kelley told the students that the economics department was interested in how different classes reacted to different instructors and that the students would thus receive a brief biographical note about the instructor before he arrived. The note contained information about the instructor's age, background, teaching experience, and personality. One version said, "People who know him consider him to be a very warm person, industrious, critical, practical, and determined." The other version was identical except that the phrase "a very warm person" was replaced with "a rather cold person." The students received one of these personality descriptions at random.

The guest lecturer then conducted a class discussion for 20 minutes, after which the students rated their impressions of him. Given that there was some ambiguity in this situation—after all, the students had seen the instructor for only a brief time—Kelley hypothesized that they would use the schema provided by the biographical note to fill in the blanks. This is exactly what happened. The students who expected the instructor to be warm gave him significantly higher ratings than the students who expected him to be cold, even though all the students had observed the exact same teacher behaving in the same way. The students who expected the instructor to be warm were also more likely to ask him questions and to participate in the class discussion.

Has this happened to you? Have your expectations about a professor influenced your impressions of him or her? Did you find, oddly enough, that the professor acted just as you'd expected? Ask a classmate who had a different expectation about the professor what he or she thought. Do the two of you have different perceptions of the instructor based on the different schemas you were using?

Of course, people are not totally blind to what is actually out there in the world. Sometimes what we see is relatively unambiguous, and we do not need to use our schemas to help us interpret it. But the more ambiguous our information is, the more we use schemas to fill in the blanks.

It is important to note that there is nothing wrong with what the students in Kelley's study did. As long as people have reason to believe their schemas are accurate, it is perfectly reasonable to use them to resolve ambiguity. If a stranger comes up to you in a dark alley and says, "Take out your wallet," your schema about such encounters tells you that the person wants to steal your money, not admire pictures of your family. This schema helps you avert a serious and perhaps deadly misunderstanding.

People who know him consider him a rather cold person, industrious, critical, practical, and determined.

People who know him consider him a very warm person, industrious, critical, practical, and determined.

Which Schemas Do We Use? Accessibility and Priming

The social world is full of ambiguous information that is open to interpretation. Imagine, for example, that you are riding on a city bus and a man gets on and sits beside you. He mutters incoherently to himself and rocks back and forth in his seat. At one point, he starts singing an old Nirvana tune. How would you make sense of his behavior? You have several schemas you could use. Should you interpret his behavior with your "alcoholic" or "mentally ill person" schema? How will you decide?

The schema that comes to mind and guides your impressions of the man can be affected by **accessibility**, the extent to which schemas and concepts are at the forefront of the mind and are therefore likely to be used when making judgments about the social world (Higgins, 1996; Kilduff & Galinsky, 2017; Wheeler & DeMarree, 2009; Wyer & Srull, 1989). Something can become accessible for three reasons. First, some schemas are chronically accessible because of past experience (Chen & Andersen, 1999; Coane & Balota, 2009; Koppel & Bensten, 2014). This means that these schemas are constantly active and ready to use to interpret ambiguous situations. For example, if there is a history of alcoholism in your family, traits describing a person with alcoholism are likely to be chronically accessible to you, increasing the likelihood that you will assume that the man on the bus has had too much to drink. If someone you know has a mental illness, however, thoughts about how people with mental illnesses behave are likely to be more accessible than thoughts about someone with alcoholism, leading you to interpret the man's behavior very differently.

Second, something can become accessible because it is related to a current goal. The concept of mental illness might not be chronically accessible to you, but if you are studying for a test in your abnormal psychology class and need to learn about different kinds of mental disorders, this concept might be temporarily accessible. As a consequence, you might be more likely to notice the man on the bus and interpret his behavior as a sign of a mental disorder—at least until your test is over and you no longer have the goal of learning about mental illnesses (Eitam & Higgins, 2010; Masicampo & Ambady, 2014; Mun et al., 2016).

Accessibility
The extent to which schemas and concepts are at the forefront of people's minds and are therefore likely to be used when making judgments about the social world

Is this man suffering from alcoholism or just down on his luck? Our judgments about other people can be influenced by schemas that are accessible in our memories. If you had just been talking to a friend about a relative who had an alcohol problem, you might be more likely to think that this man has an alcohol problem as well, because alcoholism is accessible in your memory.

Figure 3.1 How We Interpret an Ambiguous Situation

The role of accessibility and priming.

Situation 1:

Situation 2:

Priming

The process by which recent experiences increase the accessibility of a schema, trait, or concept

Lastly, schemas can become temporarily accessible because of our recent experiences (Bargh, 1996; Higgins & Bargh, 1987; Orbell & Henderson, 2016). This means that a particular schema or trait happens to be primed by something people have been thinking or doing before encountering an event. Suppose that right before the man on the bus sat down, you were reading a newspaper account of Prince Harry's struggles with the death of his mother, Princess Diana, and how he finally sought help to deal with "the years of total chaos" (Smith, 2017). Given that thoughts about mental struggles were accessible in your mind, you would probably assume that the man had mental health issues as well. If, however, you had just looked out the window and seen a man leaning against a building drinking from a paper bag, you would probably assume that the man on the bus was drunk (see Figure 3.1). These are examples of **priming**, the process by which recent experiences increase the accessibility of a schema, trait, or concept. Reading about Prince Harry primes thoughts about mental illness, making it more likely that these thoughts will be used to interpret a new event, such as the behavior of the man on the bus, even though this new event is completely unrelated to the thoughts that were primed.

The following classic experiment illustrates the priming effect (Higgins, Rholes, & Jones, 1977). Research participants were told that they would take part in two unrelated studies. In the first, a perception study, they would be asked to identify different colors while at the same time memorizing a list of words. The second was a reading comprehension study in which they would read a paragraph about a man named Donald and then give their impressions of him. This paragraph is shown in Figure 3.2. Take a moment to read it. What do you think of Donald?

You might have noticed that many of Donald's actions are ambiguous—interpretable in either a positive or a negative manner—such as the fact that he piloted a boat without knowing much about it and that he wants to sail across the Atlantic. You might put a positive spin on these acts, deciding that Donald has an admirable sense of adventure. Or you could give the same behavior a negative spin, assuming that Donald is reckless and impulsive.

How did the participants interpret Donald's behavior? As expected, it depended on whether positive or negative traits were primed and accessible. In the first study, the researchers randomly divided people into two groups and gave them different words to memorize. People who had first memorized the words *adventurous, self-confident, independent*, and *persistent* later formed positive impressions of Donald, viewing him as a likable man who enjoyed new challenges. People who had first memorized *reckless, conceited, aloof,* and *stubborn* later formed negative impressions of Donald, viewing him as a stuck-up person who took needlessly dangerous chances.

But it was not just memorizing any positive or negative words that influenced people's impressions of Donald. In other conditions, research participants memorized words that were also positive or negative, such as *neat* or *disrespectful*. However, these traits didn't influence their impressions of Donald because the words did not

Figure 3.2 Priming and Accessibility

In the second of a pair of studies, people were asked to read this paragraph about Donald and form an impression of him. In the first study, some of the participants had memorized words that could be used to interpret Donald in a negative way (e.g., reckless, conceited), while others had memorized words that could be used to interpret Donald in a positive way (e.g., adventurous, self-confident). As the graph shows, those who had memorized the negative words formed a much more negative impression of Donald than did those who had memorized the positive words.

(Based on data in Higgins, Rholes, & Jones, 1977)

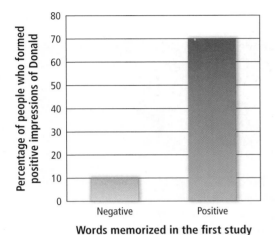

Description of Donald

Donald spent a great deal of time in his search of what he liked to call excitement. He had already climbed Mt. McKinley, shot the Colorado rapids in a kayak, driven in a demolition derby, and piloted a jet-powered boat—without knowing very much about boats. He had risked injury, and even death, a number of times. Now he was in search of new excitement. He was thinking perhaps he would do some skydiving or maybe cross the Atlantic in a sailboat. By the way he acted one could readily guess that Donald was well aware of his ability to do many things well. Other than business engagements, Donald's contacts with people were rather limited. He felt he didn't really need to rely on anyone. Once Donald made up his mind to do something it was as good as done no matter how long it might take or how difficult the going might be. Only rarely did he change his mind even when it might well have been better if he had.

apply to Donald's behavior. Thoughts, then, have to be both *accessible* and *applicable* before they will act as primes, exerting an influence on our impressions of the social world. Priming is a good example of automatic thinking, because it occurs quickly, unintentionally, and unconsciously. When judging others, people are usually not aware that they are applying concepts or schemas that they happened to be thinking about earlier.

Making Our Schemas Come True: The Self-Fulfilling Prophecy

People are not just passive recipients of information—they often act on their schemas in ways that change the extent to which these schemas are supported or contradicted. In fact, people can inadvertently make their schemas come true by the way they treat other people (Rosenthal & Jacobson, 1968/2003; Stinson et al., 2011; Snyder, 2016; Willard & Madon, 2016; Willard et al., 2012). This **self-fulfilling prophecy** operates as follows: People have an expectation about what another person is like, which influences how they act toward that person, which causes that person to behave consistently with people's original expectations, making the expectations come true. Figure 3.3 illustrates the sad self-perpetuating cycle of a self-fulfilling prophecy.

In what has become one of the most famous studies in social psychology, Robert Rosenthal and Lenore Jacobson (1968/2003) demonstrated the self-fulfilling prophecy in an elementary school. They administered a test to all the students in the school and told the teachers that some of the students had scored so well that they were sure to "bloom" academically in the upcoming year. In fact, this was not necessarily true: The students

Self-Fulfilling Prophecy

The case wherein people have an expectation about what another person is like, which influences how they act toward that person, which causes that person to behave consistently with people's original expectations, making the expectations come true

Watch THE SELF-FULFILLING PROPHECY

Figure 3.3 The Self-Fulfilling Prophecy

A sad cycle in four acts.

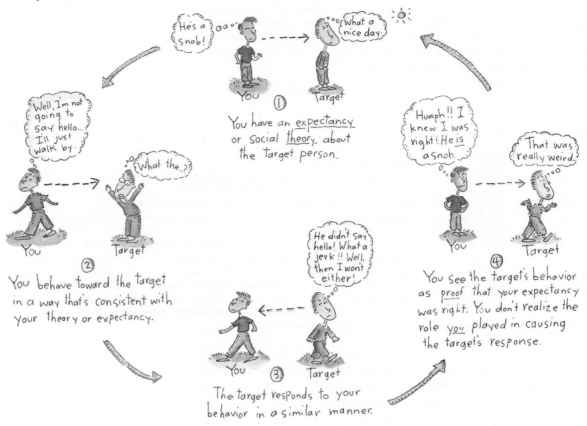

identified as "bloomers" were chosen at random by the researchers. As we discussed in Chapter 2, the use of random assignment means that, on average, the students designated as bloomers were no smarter or more likely to bloom than any of the other kids. The only way in which these students differed from their peers was in the minds of the teachers (neither the students nor their parents were told anything about the results of the test).

After creating the expectation in the teachers that certain students would do especially well, Rosenthal and Jacobson waited to see what would happen. They observed the classroom dynamics periodically, and, at the end of the school year, they gave all of the children an IQ test. Did the prophecy come true? Indeed it did. The students in each class who had been labeled as bloomers showed significantly greater gains in their IQ scores than the other students did (see Figure 3.4). The teachers' expectations had become reality. Rosenthal and Jacobson's findings have since been replicated in a number of both experimental and correlational studies (Jussim, 2012; Lamb & Crano, 2014; Madon et al., 2003; 2008; 2011; Sorhagen, 2013; Weaver, Filson Moses, & Snyder, 2016).

What happened in the classrooms studied by Rosenthal and Jacobson (1968/2003)? Did the teachers callously decide to give more attention and encouragement to the bloomers? Not at all. Most teachers are very dedicated and would be upset to learn that they favored some students over others. Far from being a conscious, deliberate act, the self-fulfilling prophecy is instead an example of automatic thinking (Chen & Bargh, 1997). Interestingly, the teachers in the Rosenthal and Jacobson study reported that they spent slightly less time with the students who were labeled as bloomers. In subsequent studies, however, teachers have been found to treat bloomers (the students

Figure 3.4 The Self-Fulfilling Prophecy: Percentage of First and Second Graders Who Improved on an IQ Test Over the Course of the School Year

Those whom the teachers expected to do well actually improved more than the other students.

(Figure adapted from Rosenthal & Jacobson, 1968/2003. Reprinted with permission of R. Rosenthal.)

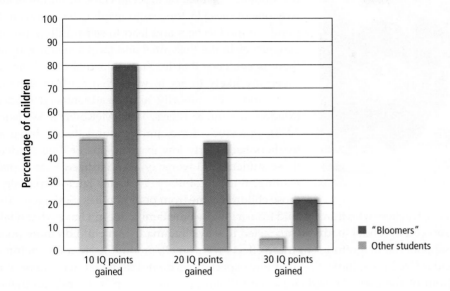

they expect to do better) differently in four critical ways: They create a warmer emotional climate for bloomers, giving them more personal attention, encouragement, and support; they give bloomers more material to learn and material that is more difficult; they give bloomers more and better feedback on their work; and they give bloomers more opportunities to respond in class and give them longer to respond (Brophy, 1983; Rosenthal, 1994; Snyder, 1984).

#trending

Do You Believe in Astrology?

At the beginning of this chapter we posed the question, "Have you ever read your horoscope and had an eerie feeling about how accurate it was?" As you saw, 50% of students answered yes. A 2014 study by the National Science Foundation found that 45% of Americans believe astrology has some scientific basis. Given that there actually is no good scientific evidence in support of astrology, where do these beliefs come from? Is it possible that a self-fulfilling prophecy is at play?

To find out, researchers randomly assigned college students to read their horoscope that was either optimistic (e.g., "There will be something amazing for me; All the health, work and money will be positive; Nothing could go wrong") or pessimistic (e.g., "It's going to be an awful day, filled with negative outcomes and unfortunate circumstances"). They then looked to see whether the horoscope students read influenced their performance on subsequent tasks.

Here's what happened: Those who read the positive horoscope did significantly better on tests of creativity and cognitive skills than did those who read the negative horoscope. We know that this wasn't due to the *actual* power of astrology because people did not get real horoscopes—remember, they were randomly assigned to get optimistic or pessimistic ones. Instead, it was the content of the horoscopes themselves that caused people to act more positively (if they got the optimistic one) or more negatively (if they got the pessimistic one). In other words, this is a classic case of a self-fulfilling prophecy, because it was people's *belief* in the horoscope that made it come true, not the actual alignment of the planets (Clobert et al., 2016). This finding may help explain why so many people believe in astrology: They may unknowingly act in ways that makes their horoscope come true.

Teachers can unintentionally make their expectations about their students come true by treating some students differently from others.

In real life, of course, psychologists do not give teachers false expectations about how well their students will do. But teachers are only human, and they may acquire faulty expectations about their students based on the students' gender, race, social class, or family history. Any one of these factors could instill expectations in the minds of the teachers and lead to self-fulfilling prophecies, just as in the Rosenthal and Jacobson study. In fact, there is evidence that teachers in actual classrooms are especially likely to act in ways that confirm their low expectations of minority and disadvantaged students (Madon, Jussim, & Eccles, 1997; McKown & Weinstein, 2008). One study, for example, found that if first-grade teachers had overly low expectations of their students, those students did worse on standardized tests of math, reading, and vocabulary 10 years later—especially if those children came from poor families (Sorhagen, 2013).

That is, teachers who think a child from a low-income family doesn't have what it takes to succeed in school inadvertently acted in ways that made that child do more poorly in school. The magnitudes of these effects were small, amounting to a few points on standardized tests, indicating that low expectations do not doom students to be at the bottom of the class. Nonetheless, self-fulfilling prophecies are real and can make it harder for capable students to perform up to their true abilities. And, we should note, the same thing can happen outside the classroom, such as in the workplace, where bosses might influence their employees' behavior via self-fulfilling prophecies.

To summarize, we have seen that the amount of information we face every day is so vast that we have to reduce it to a manageable size. In addition, much of this information is ambiguous or difficult to decipher. One way we deal with this "blooming, buzzing confusion"—in William James's words—is to rely on schemas, which help us reduce the amount of information we need to take in and help us interpret ambiguous information. These schemas are applied quickly, effortlessly, and unintentionally; in short, they are one form of automatic thinking. But schemas are only one of several examples of how we automatically process information about the social world, as we will see next.

Watch SURVIVAL TIPS! AVOIDING THE SELF-FULFILLING PROPHECY

Revel Video

Review Questions

1. Which of the following is the best summary of the function of schemas?

   a. Schemas usually result in erroneous judgments because of the self-fulfilling prophecy.

   b. Schemas are always beneficial because they help people organize the world and fill in the gaps in their knowledge.

   c. Schemas are useful in helping people organize information about the world, but they are problematic when they result in self-fulfilling prophecies.

   d. Schemas are useful for helping us organize information about other people but not about events such as what we should do when eating in a restaurant.

2. Which of the following is *not* a way in which schemas can become accessible in people's minds?

   a. The more negative in content a schema is, the more likely it is to be accessible.

   b. Schemas can be accessible because of people's past experiences.

  c. Schemas can become temporarily accessible because of priming.

  d. Schemas can be accessible if they are related to our current goals.

3. Which of the following is the best example of a self-fulfilling prophecy?

  a. A teacher believes that boys are better at math than girls, but boys in his class do worse than girls in math.

  b. Bob thinks that members of the Alpha Beta Psi sorority are unfriendly and snobby. Whenever he meets members of this sorority, they are friendly toward him.

  c. Sarah is worried that her son is not gifted in music, but he does better at his piano lessons than she expected.

  d. Jill thinks her daughter is not a good reader and doesn't spend much time reading to her. As a result her daughter falls behind in reading at school.

4. Suppose you're driving home from watching a scary movie about a hitchhiker who was a murderer when you see someone talking loudly with a friend. Because you saw the movie, you assume that you are witnessing an argument that will probably end in a fight. This is an example of

  a. priming.

  b. base rate information.

  c. belief perseverance.

  d. controlled thinking.

5. Rob is definitely not the most attractive guy in the dorms, but he is extremely confident about who he is and how he looks. He is convinced that most women find him to be very attractive, and he in fact usually gets dates with women who are much more attractive than he is. What is the best explanation of Rob's success?

  a. Self-affirmation theory

  b. Self-fulfilling prophecy

  c. The representativeness heuristic

  d. Holistic thinking

Types of Automatic Thinking

LO 3.2   Describe the types of automatic thinking.

There are several other forms of automatic thinking that help us interpret the social world and make decisions, without necessarily intending to do so.

Automatic Goal Pursuit

When it comes to setting goals for ourselves, such as what career path to follow, we often do so carefully and consciously, deliberating for some time about what we want to do. That's not the only way, however, that we choose what goals to follow. In our everyday lives there are often competing goals, and the choice of which one to follow can happen automatically. Suppose, for example, that you are taking a difficult math course in which the professor grades on a curve, guaranteeing that only a few people will get As. A classmate you don't know very well tells you he is having difficulty with some of the material and asks whether you can have coffee and go over your class notes with him. On the one hand, you want to be helpful, satisfying your goal to be a caring, compassionate person. On the other hand, you want to satisfy your goal of doing well in the class and are hesitant to hurt your chances by raising someone else's grade. Which goal do you act on? You could mull this over for a while, consciously weighing your options. Often, however, it is our nonconscious minds that choose the goal for us, basing the decision in part on which goal has been recently activated or primed (Aarts & Elliot, 2012; DeMarree et al., 2012; Hassin, 2013; Loersch & Payne, 2011; Marien, Aarts, & Custers, 2016).

Social psychologists have tested this hypothesis by priming people's goals in a subtle way and then seeing if it influences their behavior. In a study by Azim Shariff and Ara Norenzayan (2007), for example, participants were asked to make sentences out of sets of provided words—such as *felt, she, eradicate, spirit*, and *the*—from which they could make the sentence, "She felt the spirit." Next, as part of what was supposedly a different study, participants played an economic game in which they were given ten $1 coins and asked to divide them up between themselves and the next participant. Only the next participant would know what they decided, and that participant

Research has found that people's goals can be activated unconsciously by their recent experiences. For example, someone who walks by a church might have the "Golden Rule" activated without knowing it, making him or her more likely to give money to a homeless person.

wouldn't know who they were. Think for a moment what you would do in this situation. Here's an opportunity to make a quick 10 bucks, and there is a definite temptation to pocket all the coins. But you might feel a little guilty hoarding all the money and leaving nothing for the next person. This is one of those situations in which there is a devil on one of our shoulders ("Don't be a fool—take it all!") and an angel on the other ("Do unto others as you would have them do unto you"). In short, people want the money, but this conflicts with their goal to be nice to others. Which goal wins out?

It depends in part on which goal has been recently primed. Remember the sentence-unscrambling task people did first? For some participants, the words people were given had to do with religion (spirit, divine, God, sacred, and prophet), which were designed to prime the goal of acting kindly to one's neighbor. In the control condition, people received neutral words. An important detail is that participants did not make a connection between the sentence-making task and the economics game—they thought the two tasks were completely unrelated. Even so, the people who made sentences out of the words having to do with religion left significantly more money for the next participant ($4.56 on average) than did people who got the neutral words ($2.56 on average).

A recent meta-analysis has confirmed that priming religious thoughts increases the likelihood that people would act kindly toward their fellow human beings (Shariff et al., 2015), with an important qualification: only if people are religious to start with. For people who were not religious, priming religious goals, understandably, had little effect. How, then, might we increase prosocial behavior in nonreligious people? A third condition in the Shariff and Norenzayan (2007) study shows how: prime goals about being a good citizen. In this condition, the sentence task contained nonreligious words that had to do with fairness to others, such as *civic* and *contract*. People in this condition left nearly as much money for the next person as did people primed with God words ($4.44 on average).

Studies such as this one show that goals can be activated and influence people's behavior without their knowing it, because people didn't realize that the words they got in the first task had anything to do with their decision about how to divide the money in the second task (Strack & Schwarz, 2016; Weingarten et al., 2016). The moral? Your decision about whether to help your classmate in your math class might depend on which goals have recently been primed. If you are a religious person, and had just walked by your place of worship, you might be especially likely to help your classmate.

Automatic Thinking and Metaphors About the Body and the Mind

Suppose that, as you are leaving a store one day, a stranger approaches you and says that her purse was just stolen and asks if you could spare a couple of dollars so that she could take the bus home. On the one hand, the woman could be telling the truth and really need someone to help her out, but on the other, she could be making the whole thing up to get money to buy drugs or alcohol. Will you decide to help her? As we have just seen, when faced with ambiguous situations such as this one, people rely on schemas that are accessible in their minds. If the schema of helpfulness was just primed—maybe you just saw a clerk in the store go out of her way to help someone—you will be more likely to help the stranger.

But what if we told you that your decision will also depend on whether you just smelled something fresh and clean? Suppose, for example, that some window washers were cleaning the glass outside the store and that you could smell the citrusy aroma of the cleaning solution they were using. As preposterous as it may sound, research shows that the scent of cleanliness increases the degree to which people trust strangers and their willingness to help others (Kalanthroff, Aslan, & Dar, 2017; Meier et al., 2012).

It turns out that it is not just schemas that can be primed and influence people's judgments and decisions. The mind is connected to the body, and when we think about something or someone, we do so with reference to how our bodies are reacting. Sometimes this is pretty straightforward; if we are tired, for example, we might interpret the world more negatively than if we are feeling peppy and full of energy. What is less obvious is that metaphors about the body and social judgments also influence our judgments and decisions (Barsalou, 2008; Lakoff & Johnson, 1999; Zhong & Liljenquist, 2006). For example, cleanliness is usually associated with morality, and dirtiness with immorality, as seen by such phrases as "washing away our sins" and "dirty thoughts." These are just metaphors, of course—thoughts aren't literally dirty. But priming metaphors about the relationship between the mind and the body influence what we do and think (Landau, Meier, & Keefer, 2010).

In one study, for example, participants sat down in a room that had just been sprayed with citrus-scented Windex or in a room with no odor. As the researchers predicted, those who were in the room that smelled clean were more trusting of a stranger and more likely to donate time and money to a charity (Liljenquist, Zhong, & Galinsky, 2010). In another study, participants who held a cup of hot coffee thought that a stranger was friendlier than did participants who held a cup of iced coffee. Holding the hot or cold beverage seems to have activated the metaphor that friendly people are "warm" and unfriendly people are "cold," thereby influencing people's impression of the stranger (Williams & Bargh, 2008). In yet another study, college students who filled out a survey attached to a heavy clipboard thought that student opinion should be given more consideration on a local campus issue than did students who filled out the survey attached to a light clipboard. Why? There is a metaphor that associates weight with importance, as indicated by the phrases, "carries weight" and "adding weight to the argument." Apparently, feeling the weight of the heavy clipboard primed this metaphor, causing participants to believe that student opinion should be given more weight (Jostmann, Lakens, & Schubert, 2009).

Will this person's answers to the questionnaire be influenced by how heavy the clipboard is? Why or why not?

In each of these studies, a physical sensation (smelling something clean, feeling a hot beverage, holding something heavy) activated a metaphor that influenced judgments about a completely unrelated topic or person. This research shows that it is not just schemas that can be primed in ways that influence our judgments and behavior; priming metaphors about the relationship between the mind and the body can too (Krishna & Schwarz, 2014; Winkielman et al., 2015).

Mental Strategies and Shortcuts: Judgmental Heuristics

So far we have seen how people automatically use their prior knowledge about the world (e.g., their schemas and knowledge of metaphors) to make sense of the social world. Are there other ways that people deal with the vast amount of information they are confronted with at any given moment? For example, think back to your decision of where to apply to college. One strategy you might have taken was to investigate thoroughly every one of the more than 5,000 colleges and universities in the United States. You could have read every catalog from cover to cover, visited every campus, and interviewed as many faculty members, deans, and students as you could find. Getting tired yet? Such a strategy would, of course, be prohibitively time-consuming and costly. Instead of considering every college and university, most high school students narrow down their choices to a small number of options and find out what they can about these schools.

This example is like many other decisions and judgments we make in everyday life. When deciding which job to accept, what car to buy, or whom to marry, we usually do not conduct a thorough search of every option ("OK, it's time for me to get married; I think I'll consult the Census Bureau's list of unmarried adults in my town and begin my interviews tomorrow"). Instead, we use mental strategies and shortcuts that make the decisions easier, allowing us to get on with our lives without turning every decision into a major research project. These shortcuts do not always lead to the best decision. For example, if you had exhaustively studied every college and university in the United States, maybe you would have found one that you liked better than the one where you are now. Mental shortcuts are efficient, however, and usually lead to good decisions in a reasonable amount of time (Gigerenzer, 2016; Gilovich & Griffin, 2002; Griffin & Kahneman, 2003; Kahneman, 2011; Nisbett & Ross, 1980).

What shortcuts do people use? One, as we have already seen, is to use schemas to understand new situations. Rather than starting from scratch when examining our options, we often apply our previous knowledge and schemas. We have many such schemas, about everything from colleges and universities (e.g., what Ivy League colleges and big Midwestern universities are like) to other people (e.g., teachers' beliefs about the abilities of students from low-income families). When making specific kinds of judgments and decisions, however, we do not always have a ready-made schema to apply. At other times, there are too many schemas that could apply, and it is not clear which one to use. What do we do?

Judgmental Heuristics

Mental shortcuts people use to make judgments quickly and efficiently

At times like these, people often use mental shortcuts called **judgmental heuristics** (Gigerenzer, 2016; Shah & Oppenheimer, 2008; Tversky & Kahneman, 1974). The word *heuristic* comes from the Greek word meaning "discover"; in the field of social cognition, heuristics are the mental shortcuts people use to make judgments quickly and efficiently. Before discussing these heuristics, we should note that they do not guarantee that people will make accurate inferences about the world. Sometimes heuristics are inadequate for the job at hand or are misapplied, leading to faulty judgments. In fact, a good deal of research in social cognition has focused on just such mistakes in reasoning; we will document many such mental errors in this chapter. As we discuss the mental strategies that sometimes lead to errors, however, keep in mind that people use heuristics for a reason: Most of the time, they are highly functional and serve us well.

HOW EASILY DOES IT COME TO MIND? THE AVAILABILITY HEURISTIC
Suppose you are sitting in a restaurant with several friends one night when it becomes clear that the server has made a mistake with one of the orders. Your friend Alphonse ordered the veggie burger with onion rings but instead got the veggie burger with fries. "Oh, well," he says, "I'll just eat the fries." This starts a discussion of whether he should have sent back his order, and some of your friends accuse Alphonse of not being assertive enough. Suppose he turns to you and asks, "Do you think I'm an unassertive person?" How would you answer?

One way, as we have seen, would be to call on a ready-made schema that provides the answer. If you know Alphonse well and have already formed a picture of how assertive he is, you can recite your answer easily and quickly: "Don't worry, Alphonse, if I had to deal with a used-car salesman, you'd be the first person I'd call." Suppose, though, that you've never really thought about how assertive Alphonse is and have to think about your answer. In these situations, we often rely on how easily different examples come to mind. If it is easy to think of times Alphonse acted assertively (e.g., the time he stopped someone from cutting in line in front of him at the movies), you will conclude that Alphonse is a pretty assertive guy. If it is easier to think of times Alphonse acted unassertively (e.g., the time he let a salesperson talk him into an expensive cell phone plan), you will conclude that he is pretty unassertive.

Availability Heuristic

A mental rule of thumb whereby people base a judgment on the ease with which they can bring something to mind

This mental rule of thumb is called the **availability heuristic**, which is basing a judgment on the ease with which you can bring something to mind (Caruso, 2008; Pachur, Hertwig, & Steinmann, 2012; Schwarz & Vaughn, 2002; Tversky &

Kahneman, 1973). There are many situations in which the availability heuristic is a good strategy to use. If you can easily recall several instances when Alphonse stood up for himself, he probably is an assertive person; if you can easily recall several times when he was timid or meek, he probably is not. The trouble with the availability heuristic is that sometimes what is easiest to remember is not typical of the overall picture, leading to faulty conclusions.

When physicians are diagnosing diseases, for example, it might seem relatively straightforward for them to observe people's symptoms and figure out what disease, if any, they have. Sometimes, though, symptoms might be a sign of several different disorders. Do doctors use the availability heuristic, whereby they are more likely to consider diagnoses that come to mind easily? Several studies of medical diagnoses suggest that the answer is yes (Weber et al., 1993).

Consider Dr. Robert Marion's diagnosis of Nicole, a 9-year-old girl who came to his office one day. Nicole was normal in every way except that once or twice a year she had strange neurological attacks characterized by disorientation, insomnia, slurred words, and strange mewing sounds. Nicole had been hospitalized three times, had seen over a dozen specialists, and had undergone many diagnostic tests, including CT scans, brain-wave tests, and virtually every blood test there is. Still, the doctors were stumped. Within minutes of seeing her, however, Dr. Marion correctly diagnosed her problem as a rare inherited blood disorder called acute intermittent porphyria (AIP). The blood chemistry of people with this disorder often gets out of sync, causing a variety of neurological symptoms. It can be controlled with a careful diet and by avoiding certain medications.

Physicians have been found to use the availability heuristic when making diagnoses. Their diagnoses are influenced by how easily they can bring different diseases to mind.

How did Dr. Marion diagnose Nicole's disorder so quickly when so many other doctors failed to do so? He had just finished writing a book on the genetic diseases of historical figures, including a chapter on King George III of England, who—you guessed it—suffered from AIP. "I didn't make the diagnosis because I'm a brilliant diagnostician or because I'm a sensitive listener," Dr. Marion admitted. "I succeeded where others failed because [Nicole] and I happened to run into each other in exactly the right place, at exactly the right time" (Marion, 1995, p. 40).

In other words, Dr. Marion used the availability heuristic. AIP happened to come to mind quickly because Dr. Marion had just read about it, making the diagnosis easy. Although this was a happy outcome of the use of the availability heuristic, it is easy to see how it can go wrong. As Dr. Marion says, "Doctors are just like everyone else. We go to the movies, watch TV, read newspapers and novels. If we happen to see a patient who has symptoms of a rare disease that was featured on the previous night's 'Movie of the Week,' we're more likely to consider that condition when making a diagnosis" (Marion, 1995, p. 40). That's fine if your disease happens to be the topic of last night's movie. It's not so good if your illness isn't available in your doctor's memory, as was the case with the doctors Nicole had seen previously—all 12 of them (Schmidt et al., 2014).

Do people use the availability heuristic to make judgments about themselves? It might seem as if we have well-developed ideas about our own personalities, such as how assertive we are, but we often lack firm schemas about our own traits (Markus, 1977). We thus might make judgments about ourselves based on how easily we can recall examples of our own behavior. To see if this is true, researchers performed a clever experiment in which they altered how easy it was for people to remember examples of their own past behaviors (Schwarz et al., 1991). In one condition, they asked people to think of 6 times they had acted assertively. Most people readily thought of times they turned down persistent salespeople and stood up for themselves. In another condition, the researchers asked people to think of 12 times they had acted assertively. These participants had to try very hard to think of this many examples. All participants were then asked to rate how assertive they thought they really were.

Figure 3.5 Availability and Assertiveness

People asked to think of 6 times they had behaved assertively found it easy to do so and concluded that they were pretty assertive people. People asked to think of 12 times they had behaved assertively found it difficult to think of so many examples and concluded that they were not very assertive people (see the left-hand side of the graph). Similar results were found among people asked to think of 6 or 12 times they had behaved unassertively (see the right-hand side of the graph). These results show that people often base their judgments on availability, or how easily they can bring information to mind.

(Based on Schwarz et al., 1991)

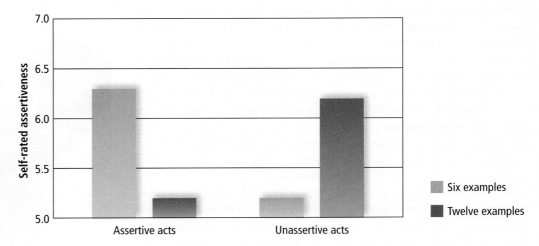

The question was, did people use the availability heuristic (the ease with which they could bring examples to mind) to infer how assertive they were? As seen on the left side of Figure 3.5, they did. People asked to think of six examples rated themselves as relatively assertive because it was easy to think of this many examples. People asked to think of 12 examples rated themselves as relatively unassertive because it was difficult to think of that many. Other people were asked to think of 6 or 12 times they had acted unassertively, and similar results were found; those asked to think of six examples rated themselves as relatively unassertive, whereas those asked to think of 12 examples had trouble doing so and thus rated themselves as relatively assertive (see the right side of Figure 3.5). In short, people use the availability heuristic when making judgments about themselves and other people (Caruso, 2008; Yahalom & Schul, 2016). Recently, a devious college professor used this technique to improve his course evaluations. He asked his students to list either 2 or 10 ways that the course could be improved and then to rate their overall impression of the course. Who gave the course the highest ratings? Those asked to list 10 ways it could be improved, because they found it hard to think of that many examples and thus thought, "If I can't come up with that many criticisms, it must be a great course!" (Fox, 2006).

HOW SIMILAR IS A TO B? THE REPRESENTATIVENESS HEURISTIC   Suppose you attend a state university in New York. At the student union one day, you meet a student named Brian. Brian has blond hair and a deep tan, seems to be very mellow, and likes to go to the beach. What state do you think Brian is from? Because Brian matches a common stereotype for Californians, you might guess that that is his home state. If so, you would be using the **representativeness heuristic**, which is a mental shortcut we use to classify something according to how similar it is to a typical case—such as how similar Brian is to your conception of Californians (Arend et al., 2016; Kahneman & Frederick, 2002; Kahneman & Tversky, 1973; Lien, & Yuan, 2015).

Categorizing things according to representativeness is often a perfectly reasonable thing to do. If we did not use the representativeness heuristic, how else would we decide where Brian comes from? Should we just randomly choose a state, without making any attempt to judge his similarity to our conception of students from New York State versus out-of-state students? Actually, there is another source of information we might use. If

Representativeness Heuristic

A mental shortcut whereby people classify something according to how similar it is to a typical case we knew nothing about Brian, it would be wise to guess that he was from New York State, because at state universities there are more in-state than out-of-state students. If we guessed New York State, we would be using what is called **base rate information**, information about the relative frequency of members of different categories in the population (e.g., the percentage of students at New York state universities who are from New York).

What do people do when they have both base rate information (e.g., knowing that there are more New Yorkers than Californians at a university) and contradictory information about the person in question (e.g., knowing that Brian is blond and mellow and likes to hang out at the beach)? Kahneman and Tversky (1973) found that people do not use base rate information sufficiently, paying most attention to how representative the information about the specific person is of the general category (e.g., Californians). Although this is not a bad strategy if the information about the person is very reliable, it can get us into trouble when the information is flimsy. Given that the base rate of Californians attending state universities in New York is low, you would need to have very good evidence that this person is a Californian before ignoring the base rate and guessing that he is one of the few exceptions. And given that it is not that unusual to find people from eastern states who have blond hair, are laid-back, and like to go to the beach, you would be wise to use the base rate in this instance.

We don't mean to imply that people totally ignore base rate information (Koehler, 1993, 1996; Obrecht & Chesney, 2016). Baseball managers consider the overall likelihood of left-handed batters getting a hit off of left-handed pitchers when deciding whom to send up as a pinch hitter, and birdwatchers consider the prevalence of different species of birds in their area when identifying individual birds ("That probably wasn't a bay-breasted warbler, because they've never been seen in this area"). The point is that people often focus too much on individual characteristics of what they observe ("But that bird did seem to have a chestnut-colored throat; hmm, maybe it was a bay-breasted warbler") and too little on the base rates.

Throughout history, for example, people have assumed that the cure for a disease must resemble—be representative of—the symptoms of the disease, even when this wasn't the case. At one time, eating the lungs of a fox was thought to be a cure for asthma, because foxes have a strong respiratory system (Mill, 1843). Such a reliance on representativeness may even impede the discovery of the actual cause of a disease. Around the turn of the twentieth century, an editorial in a Washington newspaper denounced the foolhardy use of federal funds to research far-fetched ideas about the causes of yellow fever, such as the absurd contention of one Walter Reed that yellow fever was caused by, of all things, a mosquito (which, of course, turned out to be the cause; Nisbett & Ross, 1980). How do heuristics influence your thinking? Take the quiz in the following Try It! to find out.

PERSONALITY TESTS AND THE REPRESENTATIVENESS HEURISTIC

Suppose you took a personality test, such as one of the many that are available online, and received the following feedback:

> You have a need for other people to like and admire you, and yet you tend to be critical of yourself. While you have some personality weaknesses, you are generally able to compensate for them. You have considerable unused capacity that you have not turned to your advantage. Disciplined and self-controlled on the outside, you tend to be worrisome and insecure on the inside. At times you have serious doubts as to whether you have made the right decision or done the right thing. You prefer a certain amount of change and variety and become dissatisfied when hemmed in by restrictions and limitations. You also pride yourself as an independent thinker and do not accept others' statements without satisfactory proof. But you have found it unwise to be too frank in revealing yourself to others. At times you are extroverted, affable, and sociable, while at other times you are introverted, wary, and reserved. Some of your aspirations tend to be rather unrealistic. Security is one of your major goals in life.

Base Rate Information

Information about the frequency of members of different categories in the population

Try It!

Reasoning Quiz

Answer each of the following questions.

1. Consider the letter *r* in the English language. Do you think this letter occurs more often as the first letter of words (e.g., *rope*) or more often as the third letter of words (e.g., *park*)?
   a. More often as the first letter
   b. More often as the third letter
   c. About equally often as the first and as the third letter

2. Which of these do you think cause more fatalities in the United States?
   a. Accidents
   b. Strokes
   c. Accidents and strokes in approximately equal numbers

3. Suppose you flipped a fair coin six times. Which sequence is more likely to occur: HTTHTH or HHHTTT? (H = heads, T = tails)?
   a. HTTHTH is more likely.
   b. HHHTTT is more likely.
   c. Both sequences are equally likely.

4. After flipping a coin and observing the sequence TTTTT, what is the probability that the next flip will be heads?
   a. Less than 0.5
   b. 0.5
   c. Greater than 0.5

1. The correct answer is (b), the third letter. Tversky and Kahneman (1974) found that most people thought that the answer was (a), the first letter. Why do people make this mistake? Because, say Tversky and Kahneman, they find it easier to think of examples of words that begin with *r*. By using the availability heuristic, they assume that the ease with which they can bring examples to mind means that such words are more common.

2. The correct answer is (b). Slovic, Fischhoff, and Lichtenstein (1976) found that most people think that (a) is correct (accidents). Why do people make this error? Again, it's the availability heuristic: Accidental deaths are more likely to be reported by the media, so people find it easier to bring to mind examples of such deaths than deaths from strokes.

3. The correct answer is (c). Both outcomes are equally likely, given that the outcomes of coin flips are random events. Tversky and Kahneman (1974) argue that, due to the representativeness heuristic, people expect a sequence of random events to "look" random. That is, they expect events to be representative of their conception of randomness. Many people, therefore, choose HTTHTH because this sequence is more representative of people's idea of randomness than HHHTTT. In fact, the chance that either sequence will occur is 1 out of 2^6 times, or 1 in 64. As another illustration of this point, if you were to buy a lottery ticket with four numbers, would you rather have the number 6957 or 1111? Many people prefer the former number because it seems more "random" and thus more likely to be picked. In fact, both numbers have a 1 in 1,000 chance of being picked.

4. The correct answer is (b). Many people choose (c) because they think that after five tails in a row, heads is more likely "to even things out." This is called the gambler's fallacy, which is the belief that prior random events (e.g., five tails in a row) have an influence on subsequent random events. Assuming that the coin is fair, prior tosses have no influence on future ones. Tversky and Kahneman (1974) suggest that the gambler's fallacy is due in part to the representativeness heuristic: Five tails and one head seems more representative of a chance outcome than six tails in a row.

"Wow," you might think. "This test is amazing; it is uncanny how well it captured who I am." If so, you are not alone. Bertram Forer (1949) gave this feedback to a group of students and asked them to rate how well it described them, on a scale from 0 = very poor to 5 = excellent. The average rating was 4.26—a phenomenon that has come to be known as the "Barnum effect" after the circus owner and showman P. T. Barnum.

Why do most people believe that this personality description describes them so well? One culprit is the representativeness heuristic: The statements are vague enough that virtually everyone can find a past behavior that is similar to (representative of) the feedback. Consider the statement, "At times you have serious doubts as to whether you have made the right decision or done the right thing." All of us can think of times this was true of us—that is, of examples that are representative of this statement. Who hasn't second-guessed themselves about an important decision, such as where to go to college or what major to choose? Similarly, all of us can think of times when we were independent thinkers and times when we revealed too much about ourselves. The reason the feedback seems to describe us so well is that we do not go beyond the representative examples that come to mind and think, "Actually, there are just as many times when I didn't feel or act this way." So, be wary of magazine quizzes and horoscopes that give generic feedback, which could apply to just about anyone.

Review Questions

1. Which of the following is the best summary of research on automatic goal pursuit?
   a. People can only select which goals to work toward using controlled thinking.
   b. People often pursue goals that have been recently primed, without realizing that that is why they are pursuing the goal.
   c. People often pursue goals that have been recently primed, but only if they are consciously aware that the goal has been primed.
   d. People never choose their goals consciously; they only pursue automatically primed goals.

2. Suppose you have invited a new acquaintance over to your apartment and want to make a good impression; in other words, you want this person to like you. Which of the following should you do?
   a. Serve the person a warm drink and hope that he or she holds it in their hands while you are talking to him or her.
   b. Serve the person a cold drink and hope that he or she holds it in their hands while you are talking to him or her.
   c. Bake some bread before the person comes over so that the apartment smells nice.
   d. Serve the person a snack on a very heavy plate.

3. Over Thanksgiving break, your parents ask you if you can think of 12 reasons why your college is better than its arch rival. You find it hard to come up with many reasons and end up thinking, "Hmm, maybe the schools aren't all that different." Which of the following mental strategies did you probably use to reach this conclusion?
   a. The representativeness heuristic
   b. Base rate information
   c. The anchoring and adjustment heuristic
   d. The availability heuristic

4. According to research in social psychology, why do many people believe that their horoscopes are accurate descriptions of who they are and what is likely to happen to them?
   a. Horoscopes are written in a vague way so that most people view them as representative of their personalities and past behaviors.
   b. Horoscopes trigger automatic decision making.
   c. People find it difficult to bring to mind examples that are similar to the horoscope.
   d. Horoscopes automatically prime people's life goals.

Cultural Differences in Social Cognition

LO 3.3   **Analyze how culture influences social thinking.**

It may have occurred to you to wonder whether the kinds of automatic thinking we have been discussing are present in all people throughout the world, or whether they are more common in some cultures than in others. If so, you are in good company: Social psychologists have become increasingly interested in the influence of culture on social cognition.

Watch CULTURE AND PSYCHOLOGY

Cultural Determinants of Schemas

Although everyone uses schemas to understand the world, the *content* of our schemas is influenced by the culture in which we live. One researcher, for example, interviewed a Scottish settler and a local Bantu herdsman in Swaziland, a small country in south-eastern Africa (Bartlett, 1932). Both men had been present at a complicated cattle transaction that had occurred a year earlier. The Scottish man needed to consult his records to recall how many cattle were bought and sold and for how much. The Bantu man promptly recited from memory every detail of the transaction, including from whom each ox and cow had been bought, the color of each animal, and the price of each transaction. The Bantu people's memory for cattle is so good that they do not bother to brand them; if a cow happens to wander away and gets mixed up with a neighbor's herd, the owner simply goes over and takes it back, having no trouble distinguishing his animal from the dozens of others.

Clearly, an important source of our schemas is the culture in which we grow up. Cattle are a central part of the Bantu economy and culture, and therefore the Bantu have well-developed schemas about cattle. To an American, one cow might look like any other, though this person might have well-developed schemas, and hence an excellent memory, for transactions on the New York Stock Exchange or the latest contestants on *The Voice*. Schemas are a very important way by which cultures exert their influence—namely, by instilling mental structures that influence the very way we understand and interpret the world. In Chapter 5, we will see that people in different cultures have fundamentally different schemas about themselves and the social world, with some interesting consequences (Wang & Ross, 2007). Here we point out that the schemas our culture teaches us strongly influence what we notice and remember about the world.

Analytic Thinking Style
A type of thinking in which people focus on the properties of objects without considering their surrounding context; this type of thinking is common in Western cultures

Take a quick look at these two photos and see if you notice any differences between them. As discussed in the text, the differences you notice may have to do with the culture in which you grew up.

Holistic Versus Analytic Thinking

Culture influences social cognition in fundamental ways. An analogy that is often used is that the human mind is like a toolbox filled with specific tools to help people think about and act in the social world. All humans have access to the same tools, but the culture in which they grow up can influence the ones they use the most (Norenzayan & Heine, 2005). If you live in a house that has screws instead of nails, you will use your screwdriver more than a hammer, but if your house contains nails and not screws, the screwdriver won't get much use.

By the same token, culture can influence the kinds of thinking people automatically use to understand their worlds. Not *all* kinds of thinking, mind you. The kinds of automatic thinking we have discussed so far, such as unconscious thinking and the use of schemas, appear to be used by all humans. But some basic ways in which people typically perceive and think about the world *are* shaped by culture. To illustrate these differences, take a quick look at the top picture on this page. Okay, now take a quick look at the picture right beneath it: Did you notice any differences between the two pictures? Your answer might depend on the culture in which you grew up. Richard Nisbett and his colleagues have found that people who grow up in Western cultures tend to have an **analytic thinking style**, a type of thinking in which people focus on the properties of objects without considering their surrounding context. For example, Westerners are most likely to focus on the planes because they are the main objects in the pictures. They are thus more likely to notice differences in these objects, such as the fact that the passenger plane has more windows in the second picture than in the top one (Masuda & Nisbett, 2006). People who grow up in East Asian cultures (e.g., China, Japan, or Korea) tend to have a **holistic thinking style**, a type of thinking in which people focus on the overall context, particularly the ways in which objects relate to each other (Chen et al., 2016; Miyamoto, 2013; Monga & Williams, 2016; Nisbett, 2003; Norenzayan & Nisbett, 2000).

For example, East Asians are more likely to notice differences in the backgrounds of the pictures, such as the fact that the shape of the control tower changes from one to the other. (Note that in the actual study, people saw 20-second videos of these scenes and tried to find all the differences between them. The pictures on the previous page are the last scenes from these two videos.) In Chapter 4, we will see that these differences in thinking styles also influence how we perceive emotions in other people. Suppose, for example, that you ran into a classmate who was surrounded by a group of friends. If you grew up in the West, you would likely focus only on your classmate's face (the object of your attention) to judge how he or she is feeling. If you grew up in East Asia, you would likely scan everyone's face in the group (the overall context) and use this information to judge how your classmate is feeling (Ito, Masuda, & Li, 2013; Masuda, Ellsworth, & Mesquita, 2008).

Where do these differences in holistic versus analytic thinking come from? Richard Nisbett (2003) suggests that they are rooted in the different philosophical traditions of the East versus West. Eastern thought has been shaped by the ideas of Confucianism, Taoism, and Buddhism, which emphasize the connectedness and relativity of all things. Western thought is rooted in the Greek philosophical tradition of Aristotle and Plato, which focuses on the laws governing objects, independent of their context. Recent research suggests, however, that the different thinking styles might also stem from actual differences in the environments in the different cultures. Yuri Miyamoto, Richard Nisbett, and Takahiko Masuda took photographs in randomly chosen locations in cities in Japan and the United States. They matched the scenes as best they could; for example, the sizes of the cities were equivalent, as were the buildings that were photographed in each city (e.g., hotels and public elementary schools). The researchers hypothesized that the scenes in the Japanese cities would be "busier"—that is, they would contain more objects that competed for people's attention—than the scenes in the American cities. They were right. The Japanese scenes contained significantly more information and objects than the American scenes.

Could this be one reason why Americans focus more on a foreground object, whereas East Asians focus more on the overall context? To find out, Miyamoto and his colleagues did a second study in which they showed the pictures of American or Japanese cities to a sample of American and Japanese college students. The students were asked to imagine that they were in the scene depicted in each picture, with the idea that the Japanese pictures would prime holistic thinking, whereas the American pictures would prime analytic thinking. Then the students completed the same airplane picture task described previously, in which they tried to detect the differences between two similar pictures. As predicted, the people who saw the photos of Japanese cities were more likely to detect changes in the *background* of the test pictures, whereas people who saw the pictures of the American cities were more likely to detect changes in the *main object* of the pictures. This finding suggests that people in all cultures are capable of thinking holistically or analytically (they have the same tools in their mental toolbox), but that the environment in which people live, or even which environment has been recently primed, triggers a reliance on one of the styles (Boduroglu, Shah, & Nisbett, 2009; Cheung, Chudek, & Heine, 2011; Masuda, Ishii, & Kimura, 2016; Norenzayan, Choi, & Peng, 2007; Varnum et al., 2010).

Holistic Thinking Style
A type of thinking in which people focus on the overall context, particularly the ways in which objects relate to each other; this type of thinking is common in East Asian cultures (e.g., China, Japan, and Korea)

Review Questions

1. Which of the following is true of the holistic thinking style?
   a. It involves a focus on the properties of objects without considering their surrounding context.
   b. People living in the West can think holistically if they are primed with pictures taken in Japan.
   c. The holistic style of thinking has a genetic basis.
   d. It may have its roots in the Greek philosophic traditions of Aristotle and Plato.

2. Which of the following is true about cultural differences in social thinking?
   a. Although everyone uses schemas to understand the world, the content of those schemas is influenced by the culture in which they live.
   b. Schemas influence what people notice in the world but have no influence on what they remember.
   c. Schemas influence what people remember but have no influence on what they notice in the world.
   d. Culture has no influence on automatic thinking.

3. Which is the definition of analytic thinking?
   a. A type of thinking in which people focus on the overall context, particularly the ways in which objects relate to each other.
   b. A type of thinking in which people focus on the properties of objects without considering their surrounding context.
   c. Thinking that is conscious, intentional, voluntary, and effortful.
   d. Thinking that is nonconscious, unintentional, involuntary, and effortless.

4. Where do differences in holistic versus analytic thinking come from?
   a. Genetic differences between Asians and non-Asian Westerners
   b. Different educational systems in the East versus the West
   c. Different weather patterns in the East versus the West
   d. Different philosophical traditions of the East versus the West

5. Researchers took photographs in randomly chosen locations in cities in Japan and the United States. They found that on average, city scenes in Japan contained more:
   a. businesses and advertisements.
   b. people and residences.
   c. objects that competed for people's attention.
   d. buildings and concrete.

Controlled Social Cognition: High-Effort Thinking

LO 3.4 Describe drawbacks to controlled thinking and ways to improve its effectiveness.

Controlled Thinking

Thinking that is conscious, intentional, voluntary, and effortful

It may have struck you as odd that we have spent so much of this chapter on automatic thinking, when controlled thinking is one of the hallmarks of what it is to be human. We are the only species (as far as we know) that has the ability to engage in conscious reflection about ourselves and the outside world, and we often use that ability to great purpose, solving difficult problems and planning for the future. After all, we are the ones who discovered the cures for fatal diseases, built architectural wonders, and put people on the moon. And we did so at least in part with **controlled thinking**, which is defined as thinking that is conscious, intentional, voluntary, and effortful. People can usually turn this on or turn off at will and are fully aware of what they are thinking. Further, this kind of thought is effortful in the sense that it requires mental energy. People have the capacity to think in a conscious, controlled way about only one thing at a time; they cannot be thinking about what they will eat for lunch today at the same time they are thinking through a complex math problem (Weber & Johnson, 2009).

So why so much emphasis on automatic thinking? The reason is that in the past few decades, social psychologists have discovered that this kind of thinking is much more powerful and prevalent than previously believed. As we saw earlier in this chapter, people's ability to think quickly and nonconsciously is quite impressive and is critical to our survival. Nonetheless, some social psychologists believe that the pendulum has swung too far in favor of automatic thinking and that we have underestimated the value and power of controlled thinking (Baumeister & Masicampo, 2010; Baumeister, Masicampo, & Vohs, 2015; Dijksterhuis & Strick, 2016). A lively debate has ensued over the relative importance of each type of thought.

Controlled Thinking and Free Will

One focus of this debate is on the age-old question of free will (Knobe et al., 2012). Do we really have control over our actions, such that we can freely choose what to do at any given point in time? Maybe not as much as we think, if our behavior is under the control of automatic thought processes of which we are unaware.

"Well," you might reply, "I know that I have free will because I can decide right now whether to scratch my head, stop reading this text, or stand up and dance like a chicken." Are you done with your chicken dance now? If so, consider this: Although it certainly seems like our ability to choose what we do demonstrates the existence of free will, it turns out that it is not that simple. Daniel Wegner (2002, 2004; Ebert & Wegner, 2011) demonstrated that there can be an *illusion* of free will that is very much like the "correlation does not equal causation" problem we discussed in Chapter 2. Your thought "I think I'll do the chicken dance now" and your subsequent behavior (flapping your arms and hopping around the room) are correlated, making it seem like the thought caused the action. But they might actually have been produced by a third variable—namely, an unconscious intention that caused both the conscious thought and the behavior.

Perhaps an example other than chicken dancing will make this clearer. Suppose you are sitting on the couch watching television and have the thought, "A bowl of ice cream sure would taste good right now." So you get up and go to the freezer and scoop out a serving of your favorite flavor. But maybe, as you were watching television, the desire for ice cream arose unconsciously first (perhaps primed by something you saw in a commercial). This unconscious desire led both to the conscious thought that you wanted ice cream and to your decision to get up and go to the freezer. In other words, the conscious thought "I want ice cream" was a consequence of an unconscious process and was not the cause of your decision to go to the freezer. After all, sometimes people find themselves on the way to the refrigerator *without* having had the conscious thought that it was time for a snack. Their unconscious desire triggered the action without any intervening conscious thought. As this example shows, people sometimes believe that they are exerting more conscious control over events than they really are.

But it can also work the other way: People can actually be controlling things more than they realize. A number of years ago, a new technique called *facilitated communication* was developed to allow communication-impaired people, such as those with autism and cerebral palsy, to express themselves. A trained facilitator held the fingers and arm of a communication-impaired client at a computer keyboard to make it easier for the client to type answers to questions. This technique caused great excitement, because it seemed that people who had been unable to communicate with the outside world suddenly were able to do so, voicing all sorts of thoughts and feelings with the aid of the facilitator. Parents were thrilled by the sudden opportunity to communicate with their previously silent children.

Sadly, facilitated communication was soon discredited when it became clear that it was not the communication-impaired person who was doing the typing but, unwittingly, the facilitator. In one well-designed study, researchers asked separate questions over headphones of the facilitator and the communication-impaired person. The facilitator might have heard, "How do you feel about today's weather?" while the communication-impaired person heard, "How did you like your lunch today?" The answers that were typed

Are you sure you're in control of when you choose to eat ice cream?

matched the questions the facilitator heard (e.g., "I wish it were sunnier"), not the ones posed to the communication-impaired client (Heinzen, Lilienfeld, & Nolan, 2015; Mostert, 2010; Wegner, Sparrow, & Winerman, 2004). The facilitators were not deliberately faking it; they genuinely believed that it was the communication-impaired person who was choosing what to type and that they were simply helping them move their fingers on the keyboard—but in fact, it was the facilitators doing the typing.

These examples illustrate that there can be a disconnect between our conscious sense of how much we are causing our own actions and how much we really are causing them. Sometimes we overestimate the amount of control we have, as when we believe that wearing our lucky hat will help our favorite sports team score a goal. Sometimes we underestimate the amount of control we have, as was the case with the facilitators who thought it was the client choosing what to type when they were unconsciously doing it themselves (Wegner, 2002).

Why does it matter what people believe? It turns out that the extent to which people believe they have free will has important consequences (Dar-Nimrod & Heine, 2011; Feldman, 2017; Moynihan, Igou, & van Tilburg, 2017). The more people believe in free will, for example, the more willing they are to help others in need and the less likely they are to engage in immoral actions such as cheating (Baumeister, Masicampo, & Dewall, 2009). In one study, college students either read a series of statements that implied the existence of free will, such as "I am able to overcome the genetic and environmental factors that sometimes influence my behavior," or a series of statements that implied the absence of free will, such as "Ultimately, we are biological computers—designed by evolution, built through genetics, and programmed by the environment" (Vohs & Schooler, 2008, p. 51). Next, all participants took a test composed of items from the Graduate Record Exam (GRE), scored their own tests, and paid themselves $1 for every correct answer. At least that is what participants were supposed to do. The question was, did some participants cheat and take extra money, beyond what they had actually earned? It turned out that people cheated significantly more when they read the statements implying that there is no free will than when they read the statements implying that there is free will. Why? When experiencing temptation, people who believe that they can control their actions probably exert more effort to do so, thinking, "I could easily steal some money, but I can control what I do, so it's up to me to be strong and do the right thing." In contrast, people who believe that there is no free will think, "I want the money, and I'm not really in control of my actions, so I might as well just go with that impulse." Thus, regardless of how much free will human beings *really* have, it is in society's best interest for us all to *believe* that we have it. (See the Try It! for a demonstration of how much free will people think they have compared to other people.)

Try It!

Can You Predict Your (or Your Friend's) Future?

A. Please answer the following questions about *yourself*. In each row, circle *one* of the three possible options, according to which one best captures the genuine possibilities for what might happen during the year after you graduate from college.

1. have an exciting job or be in an exciting graduate program	have a boring job or be in a boring graduate program	both are possible
2. live in a really nice apartment or house	live in a really crappy apartment or house	both are possible
3. be in a long-term relationship	be single	both are possible
4. travel to Europe	not travel to Europe	both are possible
5. do something useful	waste time	both are possible
6. keep in close contact with my college friends	not keep in close contact with my college friends	both are possible

B. Please answer the following questions about *a college friend of your choosing*. In each row, circle *one* of the three possible options, according to which one best captures the genuine possibilities for what might happen during the year after he or she graduates from college.

1. have an exciting job or be in an exciting graduate program	have a boring job or be in a boring graduate program	both are possible
2. live in a really nice apartment or house	live in a really crappy apartment or house	both are possible
3. be in a long-term relationship	be single	both are possible
4. travel to Europe	not travel to Europe	both are possible
5. do something useful	waste time	both are possible
6. keep in close contact with his or her college friends	not keep in close contact with his or her college friends	both are possible

These questions are based on ones used by Pronin and Kugler (2010), who found that people tend to believe that they have more free than do other people. In their study, they asked Princeton undergraduates to predict what would happen in the year after graduation, either to them or to a friend of their choosing. When the students answered the questions about themselves, they circled "both are possible" 52% of the time, whereas when they answered the questions about a friend, they circled "both are possible" only 36% of the time. In other words, the students seemed to think their friends' actions were more predetermined than were their own.

Mentally Undoing the Past: Counterfactual Reasoning

Another important question about controlled thinking is when people do it. When do we go off automatic pilot and think about things more slowly and consciously? One circumstance is when we experience a negative event that was a "close call," such as failing a test by just one point. Under these conditions, we engage in **counterfactual thinking**, which is mentally changing some aspect of the past as a way of imagining what might have been (Markman et al., 2009; Myers et al., 2014; Petrocelli et al., 2015; Roese, 1997; Wong, Galinsky, & Kray, 2009). "If only I hadn't erased my first answer to Question 17 and circled the wrong one instead," you might think, "I would have passed the test."

Counterfactual Thinking

Mentally changing some aspect of the past as a way of imagining what might have been

Counterfactual thoughts can have a big influence on our emotional reactions to events. The easier it is to mentally undo an outcome, the stronger the emotional reaction to it (Miller & Taylor, 2002; Myers et al., 2014; Zhang & Covey, 2014). You would probably be angrier at failing a test by one point than by 10 points, for example, because you can more easily imagine it turning out differently (i.e., going with your first answer to Question 17).

The same is true about our reactions to positive outcomes. For example, who do you think would be happier: an Olympic athlete who won a silver medal (came in second) or an Olympic athlete who won a bronze medal (came in third)? You might think the one who got the silver, because he or she did better. Actually it is the reverse, because the silver medal winner can more easily imagine having won the event and therefore engages in more counterfactual reasoning. To test these hypotheses, Medvec, Madey, and Gilovich (1995) analyzed videotapes of the 1992 Olympics. Both immediately after their event and while they received their medals, silver medal winners appeared less happy than bronze medal winners. And during interviews with reporters, silver medal winners engaged in more counterfactual reasoning by saying things like, "I

Who do you think would be happier: someone who won a silver medal at the Olympics or someone who won a bronze? Surprisingly, research shows that silver medalists are often less happy, because they can more easily imagine how they might have come in first and won a gold.

almost pulled it off; it's too bad." The moral seems to be that if you are going to lose, it is best *not* to lose by a slim margin.

There is another interesting consequence in engaging in counterfactual reasoning about positive events—it might increase your belief in God. Suppose, for example, that we asked you to write about how your life would be worse if a positive event in your past had not happened. Maybe you would choose to write about what would have happened if you had not gotten into the college you are now attending or if you had never met your current romantic partner. "I'd be miserable" you might think! But, if you are like participants in a study by Buffone, Gabriel, and Poulin (2016), you would also increase your faith in God. In that study, participants randomly assigned to write about how their lives would be worse, if something good in their lives had not happened, subsequently expressed more religious faith, compared to participants who wrote about how their lives could be better or who simply described a past event. Those who imagined a good thing happened seemed to believe that God had a hand in making sure that that good thing had, in fact, occurred.

Earlier we described controlled thinking as conscious, intentional, voluntary, and effortful. But like automatic thinking, different kinds of controlled thought meet these requirements to different degrees. Counterfactual reasoning is clearly conscious and effortful; we know we are obsessing about the past, and this kind of thinking often takes up so much mental energy that we cannot think about anything else. It is not, however, always intentional or voluntary. Even when we want to stop dwelling on the past and move on to something else, it can be difficult to turn off the kind of "if only" thinking that characterizes counterfactual reasoning (Andrade & Van Boven, 2010; Goldinger et al., 2003).

This is not so good if counterfactual thinking results in rumination, whereby people repetitively focus on negative things in their lives. Rumination has been found to be a contributor to depression (Lyubomirsky, Layous, Chancellor, & Nelson, 2015; Trick et al., 2016; Watkins & Nolen-Hoeksema, 2014). Thus, it is not advisable to ruminate constantly about a bad test grade to the point where you can't think about anything else. Counterfactual thinking can be useful, however, if it focuses people's attention on ways they can cope better in the future. Thinking such thoughts as "If only I had studied a little harder, I would have passed the test" can be beneficial, to the extent that it gives people a heightened sense of control over their fate and motivates them to study harder for the next test (Nasco & Marsh, 1999; Roese & Olson, 1997).

Improving Human Thinking

One purpose of controlled thinking is to provide checks and balances for automatic thinking. Just as an airline captain can turn off the automatic pilot and take control of the plane when trouble occurs, controlled thinking takes over when unusual events occur. How successful are people at correcting their mistakes? How can they be taught to do better?

Planning Fallacy
The tendency for people to be overly optimistic about how soon they will complete a project, even when they have failed to get similar projects done on time in the past

One barrier to improvement is that people are often too optimistic about the accuracy of their judgments. A good example of this is the **planning fallacy**, which is the tendency for people to be overly optimistic about how soon they will complete a project, even when they have failed to get similar projects done on time in the past (Buehler, Griffin, & Peetz, 2010; Kahneman & Tversky, 1979). When, for example, do you think you will finish the next paper you have to write for a class? "Oh, I'll definitely finish it by next Monday," you might think. But if you are like participants in the many studies that have documented the planning fallacy, your estimate is too optimistic—Monday will roll around and you still won't be done. In one study, for example, college honors students estimated that it would take them 34 days to finish their theses. What about the worst case, they were asked, where "everything went as poorly as it possibly could"? Well, in that case, they said, it would take them 49 days. But when push came to shove, it took the students 56 days to finish their theses (Buehler, Griffin, & Ross, 1994, p. 369).

Why are people overly optimistic about making deadlines, when they surely have lots of prior experiences with how long it actually takes to complete similar projects?

The problem is that people tend to think that this time will be different—surely nothing will get in the way of finishing *this* assignment on time, even though they know that in the past it was easy to get sidetracked by assignments in other classes, weekend trips home, social activities, and so on. If this is the case, then one way to correct people's estimates would be to remind them that working toward their next deadline is likely to be similar to working toward past deadlines, including all the things that got in the way. In one study, for example, students estimated how long it would take them to complete a computer tutorial program. As usual, they were overly optimistic: They predicted that it would take 5.5 days when in fact it took 6.8 days. In another condition, participants were first asked to think about their past experiences with completing assignments and how those experiences might be similar to completing the computer tutorial. These students made highly accurate predictions: They said it would take 7 days, and in fact that's exactly how long it took (Buehler, Griffin, & Ross, 1994). So, when thinking about how long it will take you to finish your upcoming assignments, remind yourself of all the things that got in the way of finishing previous assignments.

Another approach to improving human thinking is to directly teach people some basic statistical and methodological principles about how to reason correctly, with the hope that they will apply these principles in their everyday lives. Many of these principles are already taught in courses in statistics and research design, such as the idea that if you want to generalize from a sample of information (e.g., a group of mothers currently on welfare) to a population (e.g., all mothers currently on welfare), you must have a large, unbiased sample. Do people who take such courses apply these principles in their everyday lives? Are they less likely to make the kinds of mistakes we have discussed in this chapter? A number of studies have provided encouraging answers to these questions, showing that people's reasoning processes can be improved by college statistics courses, graduate training in research design, and even brief onetime lessons (Crandall & Greenfield, 1986; Malloy, 2001; Nisbett, 2015; Schaller et al. 1996; Sirota, Kostovičová, & Vallée-Tourangeau, 2015).

Richard Nisbett and his colleagues (1987), for example, examined how different kinds of graduate training influenced people's reasoning on everyday problems involving statistical and methodological reasoning—precisely the kind of reasoning we have considered in this chapter, such as people's understanding of how to generalize from small samples of information (see the Try It! for sample questions). The researchers predicted that students in psychology and medicine would do better on the statistical reasoning problems than students in law and chemistry would, because graduate programs in psychology and medicine include more training in statistics than programs in the other two disciplines do.

Try It!

How Well Do You Reason?

The following two questions assess methodological and statistical reasoning. For each question, choose the answer that is correct based on principles of methodology or statistics.

1. The city of Middleopolis has had an unpopular police chief for a year and a half. He is a political appointee who is a crony of the mayor, and he had little previous experience in police administration when he was appointed. The mayor has recently defended the chief in public, announcing that in the time since he took office, crime rates have decreased by 12%. Which of the following pieces of evidence would most deflate the mayor's claim that his chief is competent?

a. The crime rates of the two cities closest to Middleopolis in location and size have decreased by 18% in the same period.

b. An independent survey of the citizens of Middleopolis shows that 40% more crime is reported by respondents in the survey than is reported in police records.

c. Common sense indicates that there is little a police chief can do to lower crime rates. These are for the most part a result of social and economic conditions beyond the control of officials.

d. The police chief has been discovered to have business contacts with people who are known to be involved in organized crime.

2. After the first 2 weeks of the Major League baseball season, newspapers begin to print the top 10 batting averages. Typically, after 2 weeks, the leading batter has an average of about .450. Yet no batter in major league history has ever averaged .450 at the end of a season. Why do you think this is?

   a. A player's high average at the beginning of the season may be just a lucky fluke.

   b. A batter who has such a hot streak at the beginning of the season is under a lot of stress to maintain his performance record. Such stress adversely affects his playing.

   c. Pitchers tend to get better over the course of the season as they get more in shape. As pitchers improve, they are more likely to strike out batters, so batters' averages go down.

   d. When a batter is known to be hitting for a high average, pitchers bear down more when they pitch to him.

   e. When a batter is known to be hitting for a high average, he stops getting good pitches to hit. Instead, pitchers "play the corners" of the plate because they don't mind walking him.

1. (a) This question assesses methodological reasoning, the recognition that there are several reasons why crime has gone down other than actions taken by the police chief and that a better test of the mayor's claim is to compare the crime rate in Middleopolis with other, similar cities. The other answers might be true, but they don't involve sound methodological reasoning.

2. (a) This question assesses statistical reasoning, the recognition that large samples of information are more likely to reflect true scores and abilities than small samples of information. For example, if you flip a fair coin four times, it is not unusual to get all heads or all tails, but if you flip the coin a thousand times, it is extremely unlikely that you will get all heads or all tails. Applied to this example, this statistical principle says that when baseball players have a small number of at-bats, it is not unusual to see some very high (or very low) averages just by chance. By the end of the season, however, when baseball players have hundreds of at-bats, it is highly unlikely that they will have a very high average just by luck. The other answers might also be true, but they don't reflect sound statistical reasoning.

As Figure 3.6 shows, after 2 years of graduate work, students in psychology and medicine improved on the statistical reasoning problems more than students in law and chemistry did. The improvement among the psychology graduate students was particularly impressive. Interestingly, the students in the different disciplines performed equally well on sample items from the Graduate Record Exam, suggesting that they did not differ in overall intelligence. Instead, the different kinds of training they had received appeared to influence how accurately and logically they reasoned on everyday problems (Nisbett et al., 1987). Thus, there are grounds for being optimistic about people's ability to overcome the kinds of mistakes we have documented in this chapter. And you don't have to go to graduate school to do it. Formal training in statistics helps, at both the graduate and undergraduate levels. So if you were dreading taking a college statistics course, take heart: It might not only satisfy a requirement for your major, but improve your reasoning as well!

Watson Revisited

By now we have seen two different modes of social cognition: one that is effortless, involuntary, unintentional, and unconscious (automatic thinking) and another that is more effortful, voluntary, intentional, and conscious (controlled thinking). As we mentioned at the beginning of the chapter, these two kinds of thought, in combination, are extremely powerful, particularly when it comes to understanding the social world. The IBM computer Watson may have succeeded on the TV show *Jeopardy!*, but we

Figure 3.6 Performance on a Test of Statistical Reasoning Abilities by Graduate Students in Different Disciplines

After 2 years of graduate study, students in psychology and medicine showed more improvement on statistical reasoning problems than students in law and chemistry did.

(Figure from Nisbett, Fong, Lehman, Cheng, 1987. Reprinted with permission of AAAS.)

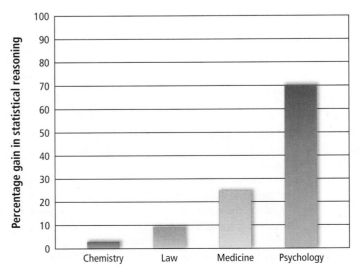

wouldn't recommend that you ask Watson to find you a romantic partner, raise your children, or help you negotiate a difficult business deal.

But as we've seen in this chapter, social cognition is by no means perfect. People make mistakes in reasoning, even to the point of unintentionally acting in ways to make their faulty theories come true (the self-fulfilling prophecy). How can we reconcile the fact that human beings have amazing cognitive abilities that have resulted in dazzling cultural and intellectual achievements but at the same time are prone to making consequential mental errors like the ones documented in this chapter?

The best portrait of the social thinker is this: Whereas people are very sophisticated social thinkers who have amazing cognitive abilities, there is also plenty of room for improvement. The shortcomings of social thinking can be quite significant, as demonstrated by examples in this chapter and in later ones (e.g., racial prejudice—see Chapter 13). An apt metaphor for human thinking is that people are like "flawed scientists," brilliant thinkers who are attempting to discover the nature of the social world in a logical manner but who do so imperfectly. People are often blind to truths that don't fit their schemas and sometimes treat others in ways that make their schemas come true—something good scientists would never do.

Review Questions

1. Sam is playing a carnival game challenging him to guess which of the 20 cups is hiding the red ball. Unfortunately, he picked the cup directly to the *left* of the winning cup and thus did not win the stuffed donkey he wanted. According to social psychological research, he is most likely to
   a. experience cognitive dissonance.
   b. engage in counterfactual thinking.
   c. blame his mistake on the noise of the crowd.
   d. subsequently avoid similar games.

2. Which of the following is true about research on free will?
   a. People rarely overestimate the amount of control they have over their behavior.
   b. Sometimes people underestimate the amount of control they have over their behavior.
   c. Studies have shown that people have free will over almost everything they do.
   d. The more people believe in free will, the more likely they are to engage in immoral actions such as cheating.

3. Which of the following is the best description of facilitated communication?
   a. It is a promising new way of letting communication-impaired people, such as those with autism, express their thoughts.

   b. The facilitators, who hold the fingers and arm of communication-impaired people on a keyboard, are deliberately faking the answers.
   c. The facilitators believe that communication-impaired people are choosing what to type, but they are probably wrong and unknowingly determining the answers themselves.
   d. Facilitated communication helps people with mild versions of autism to communicate but does not help those with severe cases.

4. Enrolling in which of the following graduate programs would be most likely to improve your statistical reasoning ability about problems in everyday life?
   a. Psychology
   b. Medicine
   c. Law
   d. Chemistry

5. According to this chapter, which is the best analogy to describe people's thinking abilities?
   a. People are cognitive misers.
   b. People are motivated tacticians.
   c. People are skilled detectives.
   d. People are flawed scientists.

Summary

LO 3.1 Explain the advantages and disadvantages of schemas.

- **On Automatic Pilot: Low-Effort Thinking** People are extremely good at *social cognition*, which refers to the ways in which people think about themselves and the social world. Although no computer can match us in this kind of thinking, we are not perfect social thinkers. Social psychologists have uncovered some fascinating mistakes to which we are prone, despite our uncanny cognitive abilities. A great deal of social cognition—how people think about themselves and the social world—involves *automatic thinking*, which is nonconscious, unintentional, involuntary, and effortless.

  - **People as Everyday Theorists: Automatic Thinking With Schemas** An important part of automatic thinking is using our past knowledge to organize and interpret new information. More specifically, people use *schemas*, mental structures for organizing their knowledge about the social world around themes or subjects and for influencing what they notice, think about, and remember. Schemas are extremely useful tools for reducing ambiguity about the social world.

  - **Which Schemas Do We Use? Accessibility and Priming** Sometimes a situation is ambiguous and it is not clear what schema applies. Schemas are most likely to be used if they are high in *accessibility*, which means they are at the forefront of our minds. Schemas can be accessible because we have used them a lot in the past, because they are related to our current goals, or because of *priming*, which is the process by which recent experiences increase the accessibility of a schema.

  - **Making Our Schemas Come True: Self-Fulfilling Prophecies** Schemas are problematic when they cause *self-fulfilling prophecies*, whereby a schema or expectation about another person influences how we act toward that person, which causes that person to behave consistently with our expectation.

LO 3.2 Describe the types of automatic thinking.

- **Types of Automatic Thinking** There are several other forms of automatic thinking that help us interpret the social world and make decisions, without necessarily intending to do so.

  - **Automatic Goal Pursuit** In our everyday lives there are often competing goals, and the one we choose to follow can happen automatically. People often act on goals that have been recently primed.

  - **Automatic Thinking and Metaphors About the Body and the Mind** In addition to using schemas to reduce ambiguity about the world, people use metaphors about the mind and the body. Physical sensations (e.g., holding a heavy clipboard) can *prime* a metaphor (e.g., that important thoughts "have weight"), which then influences people's judgments (e.g., that student opinion should be given more weight on a campus issue).

  - **Mental Strategies and Shortcuts: Judgmental Heuristics** Another form of automatic thinking is the use of *judgmental heuristics*, which are mental shortcuts people use to make judgments quickly and efficiently. Examples are the *availability heuristic*, whereby people base a judgment on the ease with which they can bring something to mind, and the *representativeness heuristic*, whereby people classify something according to how similar it is to a typical case. Heuristics are extremely useful and often produce accurate judgments, but can be misused, producing faulty judgments.

LO 3.3 Analyze how culture influences social thinking.

- **Cultural Differences in Social Cognition** The human mind is like a toolbox filled with specific tools to help people think about and act in the social world. All humans have access to the same tools, but the culture in which they grow up can influence the ones they use the most.

  - **Cultural Determinants of Schemas** Although everyone uses schemas to understand the world, the *content* of our schemas is influenced by the culture in which we live.

  - **Holistic versus Analytic Thinking** Western cultures tend to have an *analytic thinking style*, a type of thinking in which people focus on the properties of objects without considering their surrounding context. People who grow up in East Asian cultures tend to have a *holistic thinking style*, a type of thinking in which people focus on the overall context, particularly the ways in which objects relate to each other.

LO 3.4 Describe drawbacks to controlled thinking and ways to improve its effectiveness.

- **Controlled Social Thinking: High-Effort Thinking** Not all social cognition is automatic; we also engage in *controlled thinking*, which is conscious, intentional, voluntary, and effortful.

- **Controlled Thinking and Free Will** There can be a disconnect between our conscious sense of how much we are causing our own actions and how much we really are causing them. Sometimes we overestimate the amount of control we have, and sometimes we underestimate the amount of control we have. But the more people believe in free will, the more willing they are to help others in need and the less likely they are to engage in immoral actions such as cheating.

- **Mentally Undoing the Past: Counterfactual Reasoning** One form of controlled thinking is *counterfactual reasoning*, whereby people mentally change some aspect of the past as a way of imagining what might have been.

- **Improving Human Thinking** In this chapter, we documented several ways in which social cognition can go wrong, producing faulty judgments and errors in prediction such as the *planning fallacy*. Research shows that some kinds of thinking, such as statistical reasoning, can be improved dramatically with training—such as by taking a course in statistics.

- **Watson Revisited** Human beings are sophisticated social thinkers who have amazing cognitive abilities. But we are also capable of consequential mistakes, such as self-fulfilling prophecies. People are like "flawed scientists"—brilliant thinkers who are attempting to discover the nature of the social world in a logical manner but do so imperfectly.

Revel Interactive

Shared Writing   **What Do You Think?**

How does the Barnum Effect explain why horoscopes can sometimes feel eerily accurate?

Test Yourself

1. Which of the following is the best summary of research on automatic thinking?

   a. Automatic thinking is vital to human survival, but it is not perfect and can produce mistaken judgments that have important consequences.

   b. Automatic thinking is amazingly accurate and rarely produces errors of any consequence.

   c. Automatic thinking is a problem because it usually produces mistaken judgments.

   d. Automatic thinking works best when it occurs consciously.

2. Jennifer and Nate are walking along the street when they see a man walk out of a convenience store clutching a bag. The owner of the store runs out and shouts for the man to stop and come back. Jennifer immediately assumes that there has been a robbery, whereas Nate immediately assumes that the man forgot to get his change and that the store owner wants to give it to him. What is the best explanation for why Jennifer and Nate interpreted this event differently?

   a. Jennifer and Nate were engaged in controlled thinking that resulted in different assumptions about what was going on.

   b. Jennifer and Nate have different personalities.

   c. Jennifer and Nate fell prey to the self-fulfilling prophecy.

   d. Different schemas were accessible in Jennifer and Nate's minds, perhaps because they had different recent experiences that primed different schemas.

3. Which of the following is true about the use of schemas?

   a. Schemas are an example of controlled thinking.

   b. When people have an incorrect schema, rarely do they act in a way to make it come true.

   c. Although schemas can lead to errors, they are a useful way of organizing information about the world and filling in gaps in our knowledge.

   d. The schema we use is influenced only by what information is chronically accessible and not by our goals or by what has been primed recently.

4. Tiffany has a hard time trusting her friends because she believes they are irresponsible. Accordingly, when she makes dinner plans with one friend, she also makes backup plans with someone else, and she goes to one or the other. Her friends soon in turn begin to "blow off" their arrangements with Tiffany, because they are never sure whether she will show up. Tiffany thinks to herself, "See, I was right, my friends are irresponsible." Which of the following best explains why Tiffany made this conclusion?

   a. Accurate social perception due to controlled processes
   b. A self-fulfilling prophecy
   c. Holistic thinking
   d. Accurate social perception due to automatic processes

5. Suppose you wanted your friend Stephan to feel like a more assertive person. According to research on _____, you should ask him to think of _____ times in the past when he acted in an unassertive manner.

   a. Representativeness heuristic; 12
   b. Availability heuristic; 3
   c. Representativeness heuristic; 3
   d. Availability heuristic; 12

6. Which one of the following involves the *least* amount of automatic thinking?

   a. Acting according to goals that have been primed
   b. Using metaphors about the body to make judgments
   c. Counterfactual reasoning
   d. Self-fulfilling prophecies

7. Which of the following is true?

   a. All human beings have the same cognitive "tools" that they can use.
   b. When people move from one culture to another they generally do not learn to think like people in the new culture.
   c. East Asians tend to think more holistically and Westerners tend to think more analytically because of genetic differences between East Asians and Westerners.

   d. American college students were more likely to notice changes in the background of a picture whereas Japanese college students were more likely to notice changes in the main objects in the foreground of the picture.

8. Research on controlled thinking and free will shows that:

   a. There is a disconnect between our conscious sense of how much we are causing our actions and how much we are really causing our actions.
   b. It doesn't really matter whether or not people believe that they have free will.
   c. Some primates have just as much free will as human beings.
   d. People definitely do not have free will.

9. Suppose you are trying to raise money for your favorite charity and you set up a table in the lobby of a campus building. Which of the following is likely to increase the likelihood that passersby will donate money?

   a. Give them a light clipboard with information about your charity.
   b. Ask people to hold a cold bottle of water while they listen to what you have to say.
   c. Show them pictures of Japanese cities so that they think holistically.
   d. Spray some citrus-scented cleaning solution on the table.

10. Based on everything you've read in this chapter, what is the best conclusion about social cognition?

    a. People would be better off if we could turn off automatic thinking and rely solely on controlled thinking.
    b. Whereas people are sophisticated social thinkers who have amazing cognitive abilities, there is also plenty of room for improvement.
    c. Social cognition is pretty much the same throughout the world in all cultures that have been studied.
    d. One purpose of controlled thinking is to set goals for ourselves; that cannot be done with automatic thinking.

Chapter 4
Social Perception
How We Come to Understand Other People

 ## Chapter Outline and Learning Objectives

WHAT DO YOU THINK?

Revel Interactive	Survey **What Do You Think?**	
	SURVEY	RESULTS
	When you text or e-mail, do you regularly use emojis, smiley faces, or other strategies for conveying emotional tone?	
	○ Yes	
	○ No	

Social Perception

The study of how we form impressions of and make inferences about other people

Other people are not easy to figure out. Is this someone I can trust? Should I get to know him better? Why is she the way she is? Why are they doing what they're doing? The frequency and urgency with which we pose questions like these are clear across many daily situations in which we seek to evaluate others and figure out the reasons for their behavior.

In this chapter we focus on these efforts to make sense of the social world around us. Specifically, we will discuss **social perception**—the study of how we form impressions of other people and how we draw inferences about them. How important is impression formation? Consider a recent episode of the science fiction series *Black Mirror*—a show that some have called a latter day *Twilight Zone*—in which every social interaction ends with the individuals involved rating each other using the 5-point scale of a hugely popular mobile app. Seemingly every outcome in life—what job you qualify for, which neighborhood you can live in, whether or not you can get another flight when yours is canceled—depends on how high your average rating is. Meeting someone for the first time or crossing paths with an old friend? Either way, in the universe of the show, special digital contact lenses mean that you'll see their score at the same time as you see their face.

The episode follows the exploits of Lacie Pound (pictured on the previous page, in the center, in pink dress with eyes glued to pink phone), as she navigates this world and seeks, at all costs, to reach the prized rating level of 4.5. We won't spoil the plot for you, though the episode title ("Nosedive") and common sense might suggest that a life led in single-minded pursuit of popularity does not always lead to happiness. The show's satire exaggerates our contemporary emphasis on social media "likes" and other forms of superficiality. Still, aspects of the episode ring familiar. We may not walk around with popularity ratings hanging over us, but even without visible numbers, do we not use external characteristics to quickly evaluate people we meet? The clothes they wear, the car they drive, the food they buy—is it processed? Gluten-free? Organic? By making snap judgments like these, aren't we all essentially dialing rating numbers up or down, every day, all the time, much like Lacie Pound?

Social perception is also about *explaining* why others behave as they do. This desire to understand people is so fundamental that it, too, carries over into our recreational lives. We go to movies, read novels, eavesdrop on conversations, and watch people flirt at bars because thinking about the behavior even of strangers and fictional characters fascinates us (Weiner, 1985). This basic aspect of human cognition has been exploited brilliantly by reality television producers, who cast television shows with real people, not actors, and film them as they go about their lives. You can watch *Teen Mom* or *Real Housewives, Keeping Up with the Kardashians* or *The Bachelor.* Why are these shows so popular? Because we enjoy trying to figure people out.

You don't have to be a fan of any of these shows to appreciate the intrigue posed by the complex and contradictory characters around us: we have a fundamental fascination with explaining other people's behavior. From "people watching" out in public to first impressions about a new professor on the first day of class to late-night conversations with friends about why so-and-so just acted the way he did, much of our daily mental energy is devoted to analyzing other people. Why? Because thinking about other individuals and their behavior helps us understand and predict our social universe (Heider, 1958; Kelley, 1967).

The challenge, of course, is that the reasons why people behave as they do are usually hidden from us. Unfortunately, we can't read minds. All we have to go on is observable behavior: how people act, what they say, their facial expressions, gestures, and tone of voice. We rely on subtle cues and quick impressions, putting together these puzzle pieces as best we can, hoping they will lead to reasonably accurate and useful conclusions. We'll start our review of social perception with one particularly important source of information used in thinking about others: nonverbal communication, such as people's facial expressions, body movements, and tone of voice.

Nonverbal Communication

LO 4.1 Explain how people use nonverbal cues to understand others.

In the course of daily interaction, so much of what we have to say to other people doesn't require us to actually *say* anything at all. Our nonverbal expressions provide others with a wealth of information about us; we use these same nonverbal cues to learn about them (Burgoon, Guerrero, & Floyd, 2016; Hall, Gunnery, & Andrzejewski, 2011; Hall, Murphy, & Schmid Mast, 2007). **Nonverbal communication** refers to how people communicate, intentionally or unintentionally, without words. Facial expressions, tone of voice, gestures, body positions and movement, the use of touch, and eye gaze are the most frequently used and most revealing channels of nonverbal communication (Knapp, Hall, & Horgan, 2014).

Nonverbal cues serve a variety of functions in communication. They help us to express our emotions, our attitudes, and our personality (and to perceive those same characteristics in others). For example, you express "I'm angry" by narrowing your eyes, lowering your eyebrows, and setting your mouth in a thin, straight line. You communicate your personality traits, such as being an extravert, with broad gestures and frequent changes in voice pitch and inflection (Knapp et al., 2014). Just think about how difficult it can sometimes be to convey the true meaning and tone of your message when communicating on e-mail or via text. There's a reason why emojis are so popular; they help fill in gaps created by the lack of nonverbal cues in such communications. You can explore how you use one aspect of nonverbal communication—your voice—in the Try It! on the following page.

Social psychologists are not the only ones to recognize the importance of nonverbal communication. Today it seems like every political debate or press conference is inevitably followed by a panel of pundits who analyze what was said but also *how* it was said. Indeed, on today's cable news channels, the title "body language expert" appears to be just as common as "political correspondent." Some of these analyses are more informed than others. The best ones draw on an extensive scientific literature concerning nonverbal communication. Interestingly, though, nonverbal forms of communication have typically been studied individually, in their separate "channels." In other words, some studies examine eye gaze, others investigate gestures, and still others explore the role of body posture in social perception. But in everyday life, nonverbal cues of many kinds occur all at the same time in a quite dazzling orchestration of simultaneous information (Archer & Akert, 1984; Knapp et al., 2014). Let's focus on the research concerning a few of these channels now before turning to how we interpret the full symphony of nonverbal information as it occurs naturally.

Nonverbal Communication

The way in which people communicate, intentionally or unintentionally, without words, including via facial expressions, tone of voice, gestures, body position, movement, touch, and gaze

Try It!

Using Your Voice as a Nonverbal Cue

Even though the words you say are full of information, the way you say them gives your listener even more of an idea of what you mean. You can take a perfectly straightforward sentence like "I don't know her" and give it many different meanings, depending on how you say it. Try saying that sentence out loud so that it communicates each of the emotions listed below. Experiment with the pitch of your voice (high or low), the speed with which you speak, the loudness or softness of your voice, and which words you stress.

"I don't know her."

- You're angry.
- You're being sarcastic.
- You're scared.

- You're surprised.
- You're disgusted.
- You're very happy.

Now try this exercise with a friend. Turn your back to your friend as you repeat the sentence; you want your friend to have to rely on your voice as the only cue, without help from any facial expressions. How well does he or she guess the emotions you are expressing? Have your friend try the exercise too. Can you understand his or her nonverbal vocal cues? If you don't always correctly identify the emotions in each other's voices, discuss what was missing or confusing in the voice. In this way, you'll be able to figure out, for example, what a "disgusted" voice sounds like as compared to an "angry" or "scared" voice.

Facial Expressions of Emotion

The crown jewel of nonverbal communication is the facial-expressions channel. This aspect of communication has a long history of research, beginning with Charles Darwin's book *The Expression of the Emotions in Man and Animals* (1872). Its primacy is due to the exquisite communicativeness of the human face (Becker et al., 2007; Fernández-Dols & Crivelli, 2013; Kappas, 1997; Wehrle et al., 2000). Look at the set of facial expressions here. We bet you can figure out which emotions these expressions convey with very little effort.

These photographs depict facial expressions of the six major emotions. Can you guess the emotion expressed on each face?

Top row answers (L to R): anger, fear, disgust. Bottom row (L to R): happiness, surprise, sadness.

EVOLUTION AND FACIAL EXPRESSIONS   Darwin's research on facial expressions has had a major impact on the field in many areas. We will focus on his belief that the primary emotions conveyed by the face are universal: the argument that all humans **encode**, or express, these emotions in the same way and that all humans can **decode**, or interpret them, with comparable accuracy. Darwin's interest in evolution led him to believe that nonverbal forms of communication were species specific and not culture specific. He proposed that facial expressions were vestiges of once-useful physiological reactions. For example, if early hominids ate something that tasted terrible, they would have wrinkled their noses in displeasure and expelled the food from their mouths. Research by Joshua Susskind and his colleagues (2008) offers support for Darwin's view. They studied the facial expressions of disgust and fear and found, first, that the muscle movements of each emotion were completely the opposite of the other. Second, they found that the "fear face" enhances perception, while the "disgust face" decreases it. For fear, the facial and eye muscle movements increase sensory input, such as widening the visual field, increasing the volume of air in the nose, and speeding up eye movements—all useful responses to something that is frightening. In contrast, for disgust, the muscle movements decrease input from these senses: Eyes narrow and less air is breathed in, which are useful reactions to something that smells or tastes disgusting (Susskind et al., 2008).

In the Pixar movie *Inside Out*, we meet the five major emotions living inside the brain of an 11-year-old girl named Riley: Anger, Disgust, Joy, Fear, and Sadness. As you'll read, researchers have long argued that these are, indeed, five of the major emotions expressed across cultures. But psychologists usually propose a sixth major emotion as well, one not included in the movie or the image above … can you guess what it is?

Was Darwin right that facial expressions of emotion are universal? The answer seems to be yes, for the most part, for six major emotional expressions: anger, happiness, surprise, fear, disgust, and sadness. For example, in a particularly well-designed study, Paul Ekman and Walter Friesen (1971) traveled to New Guinea, where they studied the decoding ability of the South Fore, a preliterate tribe that, until that time, had had no contact with Western civilization. They told the Fore people brief stories with emotional content and then showed them photographs of American men and women expressing the six emotions; the Fores' job was to match the facial expressions of emotion to the stories. The Fores were as accurate as Western subjects. The researchers then asked the Fore people to demonstrate, while being photographed, facial expressions that would match the stories they were told. These photographs, when later shown to American research participants, were also decoded accurately. This research yielded considerable evidence that the ability to interpret the six major emotions is cross-cultural—part of being human and not a product of people's particular cultural experiences (Ekman, 1993; Matsumoto & Wilingham, 2006; Sznycer et al., 2017).

Why do we say that evidence has supported universal emotional expression, but only "for the most part"? Well, for decades, textbooks such as this one have offered an unqualified "yes" to the question of universality. But recent research paints a more complicated picture. Studies have found that individuals from Western cultures maintain more rigid boundaries between the six major emotions when applying them to faces, whereas Asian respondents show overlap in their use of these categories (Jack et al., 2012). Other research has supported universality when asking participants from across cultures to match emotional labels to faces but found evidence of cross-cultural differences when allowing people to freely sort faces into their own grouping system (Gendron et al., 2014). And still other research has demonstrated that individuals are better at decoding facial expressions from other members of their own ethnic group than they are for people of other groups (Yan, Andrews, & Young, 2016). Clearly,

Encode

To express or emit nonverbal behavior, such as smiling or patting someone on the back

Decode

To interpret the meaning of the nonverbal behavior other people express, such as deciding that a pat on the back was an expression of condescension and not kindness

The nonverbal expression of pride, involving facial expression, posture, and gesture, is encoded and decoded cross-culturally.

cultural variation in encoding and decoding remains an open research question among contemporary social psychologists.

Beyond these six emotions, are there other emotional states that are communicated with distinctive and readily identifiable facial expressions? Researchers are exploring just this question for emotions such as contempt, anxiety, shame, determination, envy, and embarrassment (Ekman, O'Sullivan, & Matsumoto, 1991; Harmon-Jones et al., 2011; Keltner & Shiota, 2003; van de Ven, Zeelenberg, & Pieters, 2011). For example, research has indicated that the emotion of *pride* exists cross-culturally (Sznycer et al., 2017). Pride is a particularly interesting emotional display because it involves a facial expression as well as body posture and gesture cues. Specifically, the prototypical pride expression includes a small smile, the head tilted back slightly, an expanded chest, and arms raised above the head or hands on hips (Tracy & Robins, 2004). Photographs of pride expressions were accurately decoded by research participants in the United States and Italy, as well as individuals from a preliterate, isolated tribe in Burkina Faso, West Africa (Tracy & Robins, 2008). Jessica Tracy and David Matsumoto (2008) explored pride and its opposite, *shame*, by coding the spontaneous expressions of judo athletes at the 2004 Olympic and Paralympic Games. Sighted and blind athletes from 37 countries were coded on their nonverbal behavior just after they had won or lost a match. The pride expression was associated with winning for both sighted and blind athletes around the world. Shame, expressed by slumped shoulders and a sunken chest, was significantly associated with losing for all the athletes except one group—sighted athletes from highly individualistic cultures, such as those of the United States and Western Europe. In individualistic cultures, shame is a negative, stigmatized emotion that one tends to hide rather than display (Robins & Schriber, 2009).

WHY IS DECODING SOMETIMES DIFFICULT? Decoding facial expressions accurately is more complicated than we have indicated, however, for multiple reasons. First, people frequently display **affect blends** (Du, Tao, & Martinez, 2014; Ekman & Friesen, 1975): One part of their face registers one emotion while another part registers a different emotion. Take a look at the photographs on the following page and see if you can tell which two emotions are being expressed in each face. An affect blend is the sort of expression you might display if a person told you something that was both horrible and inappropriate—you'd be disgusted with the content and angry that the person told you. A second complication is that aspects of the same facial expression can have different implications based on context and other cues (Hassin, Aviezer, & Bentin, 2013; Parkinson, 2013; Wenzler et al., 2016). For example, studies indicate that decoding of facial displays varies depending on eye gaze (Adams et al., 2010; Ulloa et al., 2014). For an approach-oriented emotion like anger, decoding is quickest when a face stares right at you, presumably alerting you that you are the target of the anger and might need to prepare for confrontation. But for avoidance-oriented emotions like fear, decoding is easiest when a face displays an averted gaze—the eyes looking over to the side reveal to you the exact location of the scary object, signaling to you that you should also be fearful of whatever is off in that direction (Adams & Kleck, 2003). And yet a third reason why decoding facial expressions can be challenging has to do with culture, as alluded to previously.

Affect Blends

Facial expressions in which one part of the face registers one emotion while another part of the face registers a different emotion

President Barack Obama and 2012 U.S. Olympic gymnast McKayla Maroney show off their matching "McKayla is not impressed" faces during a White House visit. Recent research suggests that beyond the six major emotion expressions, other expressions may also be universally recognized.

Culture and the Channels of Nonverbal Communication

For decades, Paul Ekman and his colleagues have studied the influence of culture on the facial display of emotions (Ekman & Davidson, 1994; Ekman & Friesen, 1971; Matsumoto & Hwang, 2010). They have concluded that **display rules** are particular to each culture and dictate what kinds of emotional expressions people are supposed to show. For instance, Japanese norms often lead people to cover up negative facial expressions with smiles and laughter and, in general, to display fewer facial expressions than are displayed in the West (Aune & Aune, 1996; Gudykunst, Ting-Toomey, & Nishida, 1996; Huwaë & Schaafsma, 2016). Here is another example: American cultural norms typically discourage emotional displays in men, such as grief or crying, but allow the facial display of such emotions in women.

There are, of course, other channels of nonverbal communication besides facial expressions. These nonverbal cues are strongly shaped by culture. Eye contact and gaze are particularly powerful nonverbal cues, as alluded to before. In American culture, people often become suspicious when a person doesn't "look them in the eye" while speaking (or, for that matter, someone who always wears dark sunglasses that obscure the eyes). However, as you can see in Figure 4.1, in other parts of the world, direct eye gaze is considered invasive or disrespectful.

Another form of nonverbal communication is how people use personal space. Imagine that you are talking to a person who stands too close to you or too far away; these deviations from "normal" spacing will affect your impressions of that person. Cultures vary greatly in what is considered normative use of personal space (Hall, 1969; Hogh-Olesen, 2008). For example, most Americans like to have a bubble of open space, a few feet in radius, surrounding them. In comparison, in some other cultures it is normal for strangers to stand right next to each other, to the point of touching; someone who stands apart may be considered odd or suspicious.

Gestures of the hands and arms are also a fascinating means of communication. Americans are adept at understanding certain gestures, such as the OK sign, in which one forms a circle with the thumb and forefinger and curves the rest of the fingers above the circle, or "flipping the bird," in which one bends all the fingers down at the first knuckle except the longest, middle finger. Gestures such as these, which have clear, well-understood definitions, are called **emblems** (Archer, 1997; Ekman & Friesen, 1975). The important thing to keep in mind about emblems is that they are not universal; each culture has devised its own emblems, and these are not necessarily understandable to people from other cultures (see Figure 4.1). Thus, "flipping the bird" will be a clear communicative sign in American society, whereas in some parts of Europe you'd need to make a quick gesture with a cupped hand under your chin to convey the same message. On one occasion when President George H. W. Bush used the "V for victory" sign (forming a V shape with his fingers), he did it backward—with the palm of his hand facing him instead of the audience. Unfortunately, he flashed this gesture to a large crowd in Australia, and in Australia this emblem is the equivalent of "flipping the bird" (Archer, 1997)!

To summarize, people's nonverbal communication can tell us a lot about their attitudes, emotions, and intentions. In some instances, as with the expression of major emotions, the conclusions people draw from these bits of social data are fairly consistent across cultures. In other instances, as with eye contact, personal distance, and gestures, the same nonverbal information is interpreted differently by people in different parts of the world. But regardless of where you're from, it's clear that much of what you pick up on in the course of social interaction is conveyed nonverbally. In short, much of what is said in daily conversations takes place before anyone actually *says* anything at all.

Display Rules

Culturally determined rules about which nonverbal behaviors are appropriate to display

Emblems

Nonverbal gestures that have well-understood definitions within a given culture, usually having direct verbal translations, such as the OK sign

Figure 4.1 Nonverbal communication

Cultural Differences in Nonverbal Communication

Many forms of nonverbal behavior are specific to a given culture. Not only do some of the nonverbal behaviors of one culture mean nothing in another, but the same nonverbal behavior can exist in two cultures but have very different meanings in each. Such nonverbal differences can lead to misunderstanding when people from different societies interact. Some of these cultural differences are noted here.

Eye contact and gaze

In American culture, direct eye contact is valued; a person who won't "look you in the eye" is perceived as being evasive or even lying. However, in many parts of the world, direct eye contact is considered disrespectful, especially with superiors. For example, in Nigeria, Puerto Rico, and Thailand, children are taught not to make direct eye contact with their teachers and other adults. Cherokee, Navajo, and Hopi Native Americans use minimal eye contact as well. Japanese use far less direct eye contact than Americans do. In contrast, Arabs use a great deal of eye contact, with a gaze that would be considered piercing by people from some other cultures.

Personal space and touching

Societies vary in whether they are high-contact cultures, where people stand close to each other and touch frequently, or low-contact cultures, where people maintain more interpersonal space and touch less often. High-contact cultures include Middle Eastern, South American, and southern European countries. Low-contact cultures include North American, northern European, Asian, Pakistani, and Native American peoples. Cultures also differ in how appropriate they consider same-sex touching among friends.

For example, in Korea and Egypt, men and women hold hands, link arms, or walk hip to hip with their same-sex friends, and these nonverbal behaviors carry no sexual connotation. In the United States, such behavior is much less common, particularly between male friends.

Hand and head gestures

The "OK" sign: The OK sign is formed by making a circle with your thumb and index finger, with your three other fingers extended upward. In the United States, this means "okay." However, in Japan, this hand gesture means "money." In France, it means "zero"; in Mexico, it means "sex." In Ethiopia, it means "homosexuality." Finally, in some South American countries, such as Brazil, it is an obscene gesture, carrying the same meaning as the American "flipping the bird" sign, where the middle finger is the only one extended.

The thumbs-up gesture: In the United States, raising one thumb upward with the rest of the fingers in the fist means "OK." Several European countries have a similar meaning for this gesture; for example, in France it means "excellent!" However, in Japan, the same gesture means "boyfriend," while in Iran and Sardinia, it is obscene.

The "hand-purse" gesture: This gesture is formed by straightening the fingers and thumb of one hand and bringing them together so the tips touch, pointing upward. This gesture has no clear meaning in American culture. However, in Italy, it means "What are you trying to say?"; in Spain, it means "good"; in Tunisia, it means "slow down"; and in Malta, it means "you may seem good, but you are really bad."

Other body movements

In the United States, nodding one's head up and down means "yes" and shaking it from side to side means "no." However, in some parts of Africa and India, the opposite is true. To complicate matters more, in Korea, shaking one's head from side to side means "I don't know," which in the United States is communicated by a shrug of the shoulders and a lifting of the hands, as pictured above.

Review Questions

1. Paul Ekman and Walter Friesen traveled to New Guinea to study the meaning of various facial expressions in the primitive South Fore tribe. What major conclusion did they reach?
   a. Facial expressions are not universal because they have different meanings in different cultures.
   b. The six major emotional expressions appear to be universal.
   c. There are nine major emotional expressions.
   d. The members of the South Fore used different facial expressions than westerners to express the same emotion.

2. Which of the following is *not* one of the six major emotional expressions examined by Ekman and his colleagues in their influential cross-cultural research on perception of emotions?
   a. Disgust
   b. Anger
   c. Embarrassment
   d. Sadness

3. Darwin's evolutionary perspective on nonverbal communication of emotion led him to predict that facial expressions were
   a. specific to particular cultures.
   b. related to physiological reactions that proved to be a useful way to respond to a particular type of stimulus.

   c. a way to increase but not decrease input through senses such as vision and smell.
   d. universal across all animal species.

4. Tracy and Matsumoso's (2008) research on Olympic athletes indicated that the nonverbal expression of shame was
   a. associated with losing for many athletes but not those from highly individualistic cultures such as the United States.
   b. different for blind athletes than it was for sighted athletes.
   c. difficult to distinguish from the nonverbals associated with pride among athletes from more collectivistic cultures such as Japan.
   d. more often displayed rather than hidden by athletes from highly individualistic cultures such as the United States.

5. Research on eye gaze and perception of facial expression indicates that which of the following tends to be most quickly decoded?
   a. An angry face looking right at us
   b. An angry face looking away from us
   c. A fearful face looking right at us
   d. A fearful face with eyes closed

First Impressions: Quick But Long-Lasting

LO 4.2   Analyze how first impressions form quickly and persist.

What do we know about people when we first meet them? We know what we can see and hear. And even though we also know we should not "judge a book by its cover," we do form impressions of others based on the slightest of cues. For example, Sam Gosling has conducted research on "what your stuff says about you," as presented in his book *Snoop* (2008). Is your room messy or orderly? What posters are on your wall? What objects are on your desk and shelves? All of these possessions can be used by observers (potential snoopers) as clues to what you are really like. For example, consider what we might learn from an individual whose office or car doesn't have much decoration in the form of personal objects or photos. One possibility, Gosling suggests, is that this is the mark of a person who wants to establish a clear separation between his or her private self and his or her work/public self. Another is that this is someone low on the personality trait of extraversion: extraverts tend to decorate public spaces more, making them inviting to other people and sparking conversations with passersby.

Of course, as you now know, another factor that plays a major role in first impressions is nonverbal communication. What we have not reviewed yet is just how quickly such communication takes place. Research indicates that we form

#trending

First Impressions Formed Online

Physical spaces are not the only contexts where we leave behind tell-tale signs of identity and personality. Snooping, of the type described above, can also be done online. Instagram posts, Twitter and Facebook feeds, and Snapchat stories can also tell us something about other people.

Now, you might be thinking, can we really trust people's online self-portraits? After all, it's no secret that people often try to put themselves in the very best (and coolest) of lights, whether by photoshopping pictures of themselves or making sure that everyone knows they're having the most epic time ever on a random Tuesday night. Surely, this propensity to exaggerate the good and downplay the bad (and boring) on social media can skew social perception.

However, research suggests that online honesty depends on a person's motivation for being on social media to begin with. Those who seek to maintain existing relationships tend to be more accurate in their social media self-depictions than those who are looking to meet new people (Hollenbaugh & Ferris, 2015). And, for that matter, just discovering that someone's profile is a bit exaggerated or dishonest might, in and of itself, teach you something notable about them.

The specific type of social media also makes a difference. For a website like Facebook, the majority of users become online friends *after* becoming friends in person. This makes it difficult to present misleading or enhanced information—your friends will know you're lying about your job title; they'll recognize that your profile picture comes from 10 years and 30 pounds ago. On an app like Tinder, however, or other media that facilitate new relationships, inaccurate profile information is more likely (Wilson, Gosling, & Graham, 2012).

Psychologists would propose that there is, indeed, valuable social perception evidence to be gathered online. For example, Facebook use can help us predict an individual's personality, such as how extraverted, or outgoing, that person is (yes, we know that Facebook is hardly the trendiest of social media sites, but it's been around the longest and most research on these issues has thus far focused on it). As you might have guessed, the more friends a Facebook user has, the more extraverted he or she tends to be. But extraverts also view and comment on other people's pages more often, add more photos of groups of people (both including and not including themselves), and spend more time on the website across the board (Gosling et al., 2011).

What other characteristics can we learn about from Facebook use? People who change their profile picture often also tend to be more open to new experiences more generally. And those individuals who score on high measures of conscientiousness—who meet deadlines regularly and avoid procrastination—also tend to spend fewer hours per week on the site (Gosling et al., 2011).

All of which is to say that trying to form impressions of people online is a lot like trying to do so in person. You often have only a small amount of data on which to base a conclusion. You have to distinguish between what someone is really like and what they *want* you to think they're like. And you have to keep in mind the broader context in which you're seeing people: are they presenting themselves to existing friends or trying to initiate new social connections?

---

initial impressions of others based solely on their facial appearance in less than 100 milliseconds (Bar, Neta, & Linz, 2006; Willis & Todorov, 2006). That's less than 1/10 of one second! And recent research indicates that we show signs of this tendency to consistently infer character from faces when we're as young as 3 years old (Cogsdill et al., 2014).

One example of these quick snap judgments is that people who have "baby faces"—features that are reminiscent of those of small children, with big eyes, a small chin and nose, and a high forehead—tend to be perceived as having childlike traits as well, such as being naive, warm, and submissive (Livingston & Pearce, 2009; Zebrowitz & Montepare, 2008). Obviously, these impressions are not always correct, but there is some evidence that we can make accurate judgments about others simply based on facial appearance. As another example, after brief glances at photographs of men's and women's faces, research participants are able to judge sexual orientation at above-chance levels of accuracy, suggesting that there may indeed be a scientific basis to the notion of "gaydar" (Rule et al., 2008; Rule, Ambady, & Hallett, 2009). Or in another set of studies, American participants rated the faces of Canadian political candidates (with whom they were totally unfamiliar) on the dimensions of powerfulness and warmth. Their first-impression ratings correlated with actual election results: The more powerful the candidates looked, the more likely they were to have won their election; the warmer they looked, the less likely they were to have won (Rule & Ambady, 2010; Todorov et al., 2008). Just think about this for a moment—all the time, money, and effort candidates expend to try to win elections, and in the end, the simple question of how powerful their face looks emerges as a significant predictor of success. Perhaps we were too dismissive previously of the importance of "body language experts"!

Indeed, it is amazing just how limited an exposure to other people is enough for us to form meaningful first impressions about their abilities or personalities. Nalini Ambady and her colleagues have referred to such social perception based on extremely brief snippets of behavior as **thin-slicing** (Ambady & Rosenthal, 1992; Rule et al., 2013; Slepian, Bogart, & Ambady, 2014). In one study, they examined an instance of social perception familiar to most readers of this book (not to mention its authors): how college students form impressions of their professors (Ambady & Rosenthal, 1993). For the study, the researchers videotaped more than a dozen instructors while teaching and then selected three random 10-second clips from each one. After removing the audio track, they showed the silent video clips to students who had never before taken a class with these instructors. Students were asked to rate the teachers on a series of variables including how competent, confident, and active they appeared to be.

Not surprisingly, participants had little trouble coming up with ratings—as we've discussed, first impressions come to us quickly. But recall that Ambady's prediction was that thin-sliced impressions would be *meaningful*, not just fast. To test this, she compared the ratings made by her participants—whose only exposure to the instructors came in the form of brief, silent video clips—with the end-of-semester teaching evaluations these instructors received from their actual students. The result was a significant correlation: the thin-sliced impressions were quite similar to the perceptions of students who spent an entire semester with the instructors. In fact, even when shorter, 6-second silent clips were used, participants were still able to accurately predict who the highest-rated teachers were (Ambady & Rosenthal, 1992). Similar findings have been observed outside the classroom: patients draw informative first impressions based on thin-slice exposures to doctors; clinicians do the same with their patients (Ambady et al., 2002; Slepian et al., 2014). Our ability to extract meaningful information from very limited encounters has also captured the attention of best-selling authors, with the research of Ambady and colleagues playing a central role in Malcolm Gladwell's *Blink* (2005).

It is clear, then, just how quickly first impressions happen. But do they last? If first impressions faded from view as quickly as they came into focus, then they might not matter much when it comes to social perception. But it turns out they do matter. Let's look at just how important and long-lasting first impressions really are.

The Lingering Influence of Initial Impressions

As we saw in Chapter 3, when people are unsure about the nature of the social world, they use their schemas to fill in the gaps. A schema is a mental shortcut: When

This is Sarah Hyland, whom you might know from her TV role as older daughter Haley Dunphy on *Modern Family*. Research suggests that her baby-faced appearance—big eyes, small chin, high forehead—might also lead you to jump to the conclusion that she is friendly, honest, and gullible.

Thin-Slicing

Drawing meaningful conclusions about another person's personality or skills based on an extremely brief sample of behavior

How much do you think you would enjoy having the professor pictured here as your instructor? Quick, just answer—don't think! Although it might seem ridiculous to suggest that you can learn anything of substance about the job performance of a college professor or anyone else from a simple photograph, research indicates that thin-slice judgments can yield meaningful information. (They can also perpetuate stereotypes, as we will discuss in more detail in Chapter 13.) This particular professor is Dr. Preethika Kumar, a faculty member in electrical engineering at Wichita State University. In 2015, the Institute of Electrical and Electronic Engineers named her their nationwide outstanding teacher of the year. Were your thin-slice judgments of this photo consistent with Professor Kumar's award-winning reputation?

all we have is a small amount of information, our schemas provide additional information to fill in the gaps (Fiske & Taylor, 2013; Markus & Zajonc, 1985). Thus, when we are trying to understand other people, we can use just a few observations of a person as a starting point and then, using our schemas, create a much fuller understanding. This idea suggests that our initial impressions have staying power—that they color the way we interpret the information we learn next.

As an example, consider a hypothetical individual you've never met before. Let's call him Keith. We want you to mull over your impressions of Keith as we tell you the following about him: Keith is an interesting guy. People who know him say he's intelligent. Another word often used to describe him is industrious. Keith can also be impulsive as well as critical. Still others have described him as stubborn and envious. Based on this information, what's your impression of Keith at this point?

Now consider another hypothetical stranger. We'll call him Kevin. Kevin is an interesting guy as well. People who know him have called him envious. Also stubborn. And you know what, it just so happens that other descriptors that people use when talking about Kevin are critical, impulsive, industrious, and intelligent.

By now, you've likely sensed the pattern. Keith and Kevin are being described the same way. Or, at least, the content of what you've been told about them is the same; the order of the descriptors has been switched around. What conclusions do you think people would draw about Keith versus Kevin? When Solomon Asch (1946) ran this very study, describing hypothetical individuals with the same descriptors you read above, he found that order made a big difference. Participants formed a more positive impression of someone described as intelligent-industrious-impulsive-critical-stubborn-envious (Keith, in our example), compared to someone described as envious-stubborn-critical-impulsive-industrious-intelligent (Kevin, in our case). Why? Because first impressions are powerful. In this instance, Keith's positive traits of being intelligent and industrious create a filter—a schema—through which subsequent traits are viewed. After learning that he is smart and hardworking, perhaps you also perceived "impulsive" and "critical" in a positive light—as in, sure, Keith may make quick decisions and critique the work of others, but that can be productive for someone who's intelligent. Kevin, on the other hand? You already know he's envious and stubborn. This makes it easy to see those same traits of critical and impulsive as negatives, bringing them in line with the initial expectations you have for him.

Asch's study demonstrates that there's a **primacy effect** in social perception: What we learn first about another person colors how we see the information we learn next. In addition to primacy effects, we also have schemas regarding which traits tend to appear together in clusters. That is, we use a few known characteristics to determine what other characteristics a person likely has (Sedikides & Anderson, 1994; Werth & Foerster, 2002; Willis & Todorov, 2006). For example, a capable, can-do person is also seen as powerful and dominant, whereas an incompetent person is seen as the opposite (Fiske, Cuddy, & Glick, 2006;

Primacy Effect

When it comes to forming impressions, the first traits we perceive in others influence how we view information that we learn about them later

In the months leading up to the 2016 U.S. presidential election, large numbers of voters continued to believe in political misinformation that had long since been discredited. For example, polls indicated that a majority of voters with a positive impression of Donald Trump continued to believe that then-President Barack Obama was Muslim and had not been born in the United States (Gangitano, 2016), a disturbing example of belief perseverance in action.

Todorov et al., 2008; Wojciszke, 2005). Or consider physical attractiveness. We often presume that "what is beautiful is good"—that people with physical beauty will also have a whole host of other wonderful qualities (Dion, Berscheid, & Walster, 1972; Eagly et al., 1991; Hughes & Miller, 2016).

But primacy effects and schemas about which characteristics go together aren't the only reasons why first impressions have lasting effects. When it comes to social perception, we also have a tendency for **belief perseverance**, or standing by initial conclusions even when subsequently learned information suggests we shouldn't. In dozens of studies over several decades, research participants have opted to stick by their original impressions even once the basis for their that judgment is contradicted or revealed as erroneous (Anderson, 1995; Ross, Lepper, & Hubbard, 1975). Indeed, belief perseverance has been cited to explain why jurors have a hard time disregarding evidence ruled inadmissible, why scientists are slow to discount published research conclusions that turn out to be based on fabricated data, and why voters remain influenced by political misinformation even after it has been discredited (Greitemeyer, 2014; Lilienfeld & Byron, 2013; Thorson, 2016). As Chapter 6 will detail, we find inconsistent thoughts unpleasant and uncomfortable. Once we make up our minds, we're inclined to keep them made up. And so first impressions, once formed, can prove pretty hard to shake.

There are clear implications of the research on first impressions: When trying to win people over, there's no overemphasizing how important it is to start off on the right foot. Getting ready for public speaking? Make sure the opening moments of your presentation are your most polished, as that thin-slice will set an influential tone. Going on a job interview? How you dress, whether you maintain eye contact, your body posture—these are immediately apparent factors that may shape how others evaluate the rest of your visit. Even the simplest of introductory actions, like the way you shake hands, can have a dramatic effect, as detailed in the following photo gallery.

Belief Perseverance
The tendency to stick with an initial judgment even in the face of new information that should prompt us to reconsider

USING FIRST IMPRESSIONS TO YOUR ADVANTAGE

Revel Interactive

Given all that you now know about the importance of first impressions, you might be even more motivated than ever to make a good one. Social psychologists refer to this tendency as *impression management*, both conscious and unconscious efforts control how people see you (Leary & Kowalski, 1990).

For example, research indicates that perceptions of handshake quality are significantly related to assessments of personality and even final hiring recommendations in an interview setting (Chaplin et al., 2000; Stewart et al., 2008). So when meeting new people, by all means, give thought to how you will dress, pay attention to eye contact, but don't overlook the importance of a firm (but not too firm) handshake.

Recent research offers the provocative conclusion that in addition to influencing how others see you, your body language can also change how you think, feel, and act. In one study, participants required to adopt a high-power pose, such as the one depicted above, reported feeling more powerful and were rated as giving a better speech in a subsequent job interview task (Cuddy et al., 2015; but also see Garrison, Tang, & Schmeichel, 2016).

Efforts to capitalize on the power of first impressions take place online as well. On social networks as well as dating websites and apps, people often strive to put their best (digital) foot forward, sometimes at the expense of accuracy (Rosenberg & Egbert, 2011). As in real life, though, too much impression management can seem disingenuous and rub people the wrong way.

Review Questions

1. Research indicates that which of the following candidates would be most likely to win a political election?
   a. Denise, whose face other people often perceive as indicating a warm personality
   b. Theo, who many people believe is gay based only on his facial appearance
   c. Vanessa, who has large eyes, a high forehead, and a small, child-like nose
   d. Rudy, whose face is usually seen by others as indicating a cold, calculating, and powerful personality

2. Ambady and colleagues were able to conclude that the thin-sliced impressions formed by their participants were based on meaningful information because
   a. their ratings based on 30-second clips were little different than their ratings based on 6-second clips.
   b. their ratings of the silent video clips corresponded strongly with the ratings that the instructors received from their actual students at the end of the semester.
   c. ratings were similar for silent video clips and for the same video clips when shown with audio.
   d. while the thin-sliced video clips were brief, it took participants a relatively long amount of time to come up with ratings of the instructors they viewed.

3. Asch's (1946) research on person perception provided evidence for which of the following conclusions?
   a. There is a primacy effect in social perception.
   b. First impressions serve as a filter through which subsequently learned information is interpreted.
   c. Even when the content of information conveyed about two individuals remains the same, the order in which we learn it can have a powerful effect on our impression.
   d. All of the above.

4. Belief perseverance can help explain which of the following?
   a. Why people who watch news programs that refer to climate change as a hoax remain convinced of that conclusion even in the face of scientific evidence to the contrary.
   b. Why during jury deliberations it is easier to convince fellow jurors to change their votes from guilty to not guilty than it is to change their minds in the opposite direction.
   c. Why weather forecasters are better at predicting rainfall totals than snowfall totals.
   d. All of the above.

5. Which of the following statements about impression management is true?
   a. It can be a conscious or unconscious process.
   b. It occurs in person but not during online interactions.
   c. It involves an effort to depict the self as accurately as possible.
   d. It tends to be counterproductive and "rub people the wrong way."

Causal Attribution: Answering the "Why" Question

LO 4.3   Explain how we determine why other people do what they do.

We have seen that when we observe other people, we have a rich source of information—their nonverbal behavior—on which to base our impressions. However, nonverbal behavior and other components of first impression formation are not foolproof indicators of what a person is really thinking or feeling. If you meet an acquaintance and she says, "It's great to see you!" does she really mean it? Perhaps she is acting more excited than she really feels, out of politeness. Perhaps she is outright lying and really can't stand you. The point is that even though nonverbal communication is sometimes easy to decode and first impressions are quick to form, there is still substantial ambiguity as to what a person's behavior really means (Ames & Johar, 2009; DePaulo, 1992; Hall, Mast, & West, 2016).

Attribution Theory

A description of the way in which people explain the causes of their own and other people's behavior

Why did that acquaintance behave as she did? To answer this "why" question, we will use our immediate observations to form more elegant and complex inferences about what people are really like and what motivates them to act as they do. How we go about answering these questions is the focus of **attribution theory**, the study of how we infer the causes of other people's behavior.

The Nature of the Attribution Process

Fritz Heider (1958) is frequently referred to as the father of attribution theory. His influential book defined the field of social perception, and his legacy is still very much evident in current research (Crandall et al., 2007; Kwan & Chiu, 2014). Heider discussed what he called "naive," or "commonsense," psychology. In his view, people were like amateur scientists, trying to understand other people's behavior by piecing together information until they arrived at a reasonable explanation or cause (Surian, Caldi, & Sperber, 2007; Weiner, 2008).

One of Heider's most valuable contributions is a simple dichotomy: When trying to decide why people behave as they do—for example, why a father has just yelled at his young daughter—we can make one of two attributions. One option is to make an **internal attribution**, deciding that the cause of the father's behavior was something about him—his disposition, personality, attitudes, or character—an explanation that assigns the causes of his behavior internally. For example, we might decide that the father has poor parenting skills or is an impatient person. Alternatively, we might make an **external attribution**, deciding that something in the situation, not in the father's personality or attitudes, caused his behavior. If we conclude that he yelled because his daughter had just stepped into the street without looking, we would be making an external attribution for his behavior.

Notice that our impression of the father will be very different depending on the type of attribution we make. For this particular example, if we make an internal attribution, we'll form a negative impression. If we make an external attribution, we won't learn much about the father—after all, most parents would have done the same thing if their child had just disobeyed them by stepping into the street. Quite a difference!

This internal/external attribution dichotomy plays an extraordinarily important role in even the most intimate parts of our lives. Indeed, spouses in happy, satisfied marriages make very different attributions about their partners than spouses in troubled, distressed marriages. Satisfied spouses tend to make internal attributions for their partners' positive behaviors (e.g., "She helped me because she's such a generous person") and external attributions for their partners' negative behaviors (e.g., "He said something mean because he's so stressed at work right now"). In contrast, spouses in distressed marriages tend to display the opposite pattern: Their partners' positive behaviors are chalked up to external causes (e.g., "She helped me because she wanted to impress our friends"), while negative behaviors are attributed to internal causes (e.g., "He said something mean because he's a self-centered jerk"). When an intimate relationship becomes troubled, this second pattern of attributions about one's partner only makes the situation worse and can have dire consequences for the future of the relationship (Fincham et al., 1997; Furman, Luo, & Pond, 2017; McNulty, O'Mara, & Karney, 2008).

Internal Attribution

The inference that a person is behaving in a certain way because of something about the person, such as attitude, character, or personality

External Attribution

The inference that a person is behaving a certain way because of something about the situation he or she is in, with the assumption that most people would respond the same way in that situation

Attributional tendencies have important consequences for relationships, including marriage. Consider Dre, the father on the TV show *Blackish*. On a weekly basis, his wife, Bow, has to decide whether to attribute his comically eccentric behavior to internal or external causes. For example, should she interpret his desire to terrify his children with Halloween pranks an indication of hopeless immaturity? Or a natural response of a loving father to the realization that his kids are getting older and spending less time with him? Whether we make charitable (or less so) attributions for the behavior of a partner is a strong predictor of relationship satisfaction in the long run

According to Fritz Heider, we tend to see the causes of a person's behavior as internal. For example, when we see a driver exhibiting signs of "road rage," we are likely to assume that he is at fault for losing his temper. If we knew the person's situation—perhaps he is rushing to the hospital to check on a family member and another driver has just cut him off—we might come up with a different, external attribution.

Covariation Model

A theory that states that to form an attribution about what caused a person's behavior, we note the pattern between when the behavior occurs and the presence or absence of possible causal factors

Consensus Information

The extent to which other people behave the same way toward the same stimulus as the actor does

Distinctiveness Information

The extent to which a particular actor behaves in the same way toward different stimuli

Consistency Information

The extent to which the behavior between one actor and one stimulus is the same across time and circumstances

The Covariation Model: Internal Versus External Attributions

The first, essential step in the process of social perception is determining whether to make an internal or an external attribution. Harold Kelley's major contribution to attribution theory was the idea that we notice and think about more than one piece of information when making this decision (Kelley, 1967, 1973). For example, let's say you ask your friend to lend you her car, and she says no. Naturally, you wonder why. What explains her behavior? Kelley's theory, called the **covariation model**, says that you will examine multiple behaviors from different times and situations to answer this question. Has your friend refused to lend you her car in the past? Does she lend it to other people? Does she normally lend you things when you ask her?

Kelley, like Heider before him, assumed that when we are in the process of forming an attribution, we gather information, or data. The data we use, according to Kelley, are about how a person's behavior "covaries," or changes, across time and place and depending on the target of the behavior. By discovering covariation in people's behavior (e.g., your friend refuses to lend you her car, but she agrees to lend it to others), you can reach a conclusion about what causes their behavior.

When we are forming an attribution, what kinds of covariation information do we examine? Kelley (1967) identified three key types: *consensus, distinctiveness*, and *consistency*. Suppose that you are working at your part-time job at the mall and you observe your boss yelling at another employee, Hannah. Automatically, you ask that attributional question about your boss: "Why is he yelling at Hannah and being so critical? Is it something about him as a person, something about what is going on around him (perhaps something about Hannah), or something else entirely?"

How would Kelley's (1967, 1973) model of covariation assessment answer this question? It would focus on three different types of information regarding the actor (your boss, the target of your attributional efforts) and the stimulus (Hannah, the person on the receiving end of the action in question) in this scenario. **Consensus information** refers to how other people behave toward the same stimulus—in this case, Hannah. Do other people at work also yell at or criticize Hannah? In other words, is there consensus to how various people respond to Hannah? If so, perhaps something about Hannah's job performance is responsible for the interaction you witnessed. But if not, you would become more confident that your boss's behavior is more unique and he is, therefore, to blame.

Distinctiveness information refers to how a person responds to other stimuli—in this case, everything other than Hannah. Is Hannah the only employee whom your boss criticizes publicly? That is, does your boss only react this way to Hannah and no one else? If so, we wonder what it is about her that seems to set him off, and we begin to think she's to blame. If, however, your boss reacts this way with multiple people, we might think that he's probably the one responsible for the confrontation.

Consistency information refers to the frequency with which the observed behavior between the same person and the same stimulus occurs across time and circumstances. Does your boss criticize Hannah regularly and frequently, whether the store is filled with customers or empty, whether it's Monday morning or Saturday evening? In other words, is yelling consistently the outcome when the boss and Hannah are together?

According to Kelley's theory, it is difficult to make either a straightforward internal or external attribution when consistency is low—when the actor and stimulus in question do not always produce the same outcome. In such instances, we usually have little choice but to chalk up the event to being a fluke. In essence, we resort to a special kind of external or situational attribution, one that assumes that something peculiar must have happened in this particular circumstance—for example, the boss just received very upsetting news that day and uncharacteristically lost his temper with the first person he saw.

But when consistency is high, specific patterns of consensus and distinctiveness information can permit a clear internal attribution, according to Kelley. People are most likely to make an internal attribution (deciding that the behavior was due to something about the boss) when the consensus and distinctiveness of the act are low (in addition to high consistency; see Figure 4.2). We would be pretty confident that the boss yelled at Hannah because he is an impatient or vindictive person if we knew that no one else yells at Hannah, that the boss yells at other employees, and that the boss yells at Hannah every chance he gets. On the other hand, people are likely to make an external attribution (in this case, perhaps about Hannah) if consensus, distinctiveness, and consistency are all high. If everyone always yells at Hannah too, and the boss never yells at anyone otherwise, we can be pretty confident that something about Hannah is triggering this response in the boss (and everyone else).

Figure 4.2 The Covariation Model

Why did the boss yell at his employee Hannah? To decide whether a behavior was caused by internal (dispositional) factors or by external (situational) factors, people use consensus, distinctiveness, and consistency information.

Your boss keeps yelling at Hannah. Is it something about who your boss is as a person (internal attribution), or something external to your boss (e.g., Hannah's work ethic or attitude, pressure your boss faces at work, a tragic event in his personal life). The covariation model can help you make this determination using three variables of consensus, distinctiveness, and consistency.

Low Consensus (No one except your boss yells at Hannah)	+ *Low* Distinctiveness (Your boss yells at everyone)	+ *High* Consistency (Your boss always yells at Hannah)	= *Internal* Attribution	This is something about your boss's personality or values.
High Consensus (Everyone yells at Hannah)	+ *High* Distinctiveness (Your boss only yells at Hannah)	+ *High* Consistency (Your boss always yells at Hannah)	= *External* Attribution	This is not about your boss, but more likely about Hannah's work ethic or attitude.
Low/High Consensus	+ *Low/High* Distinctiveness	+ *Low* Consistency	= *No* Attribution	When consensus and distinctiveness are varied, and there's no consistency to a behavior, attributions are difficult to make.

The covariation model assumes that people make causal attributions in a rational, logical way, observing the clues about consensus, distinctiveness, and consistency and then drawing a logical inference about why the person did what he or she did. Research has confirmed that people often do make attributions in this way (Hilton, Smith, & Kim, 1995; Rottman & Hastie, 2014; White, 2002)—with two exceptions. Studies have shown that people don't use consensus information as much as Kelley's theory predicted; they rely more on consistency and distinctiveness when forming attributions (McArthur, 1972; Wright, Lüüs, & Christie, 1990). Also, people don't always have the relevant information they need on all three of Kelley's dimensions. For example, what if this is Hannah's first day at work? Or your first day, and you've never seen your boss or Hannah before? In these situations, research has shown that people proceed with the attribution process using the information they do have and, if necessary, making guesses about the missing data (Fiedler, Walther, & Nickel, 1999; Kelley, 1973).

To summarize, the covariation model portrays people as master detectives, deducing the causes of behavior as systematically and logically as Sherlock Holmes would. However, people aren't always logical or rational when forming judgments about others. Sometimes they distort information to satisfy their need for high self-esteem. At other times they use mental shortcuts that, although often helpful, can lead to inaccurate judgments. Unfortunately, the attributions we make are sometimes just plain wrong. In the next section, we will discuss some specific errors or biases that plague the attribution process—we don't always follow the straightforward logic of the covariation model in a balanced and levelheaded way. One such shortcut is common: the idea that people do what they do because of the kind of people they are, not because of the situation they are in.

The Fundamental Attribution Error: People as Personality Psychologists

One day in December 1955, a Black seamstress in Montgomery, Alabama, refused to give up her seat on the city bus to a White man. At the time, segregationist "Jim Crow" laws in the South relegated African Americans to second-class status in all aspects of everyday life. They could sit in the middle section if it was empty, but they had to give up their seats to White people when the bus got full; the front 10 rows were always reserved for White people (Feeney, 2005). That day in 1955, Rosa Parks broke the law and refused to give up her seat. Later, she said, "People always say I didn't give up my seat because I was tired, but that wasn't true. I was not tired physically.... No, the only tired I was, was tired of giving in" (Feeney, 2005, pp. A1, B8). Ms. Parks was convicted of violating the segregation laws and fined. In response, African Americans boycotted the Montgomery buses for over a year and mounted a legal challenge that led to a successful Supreme Court decision in 1956 outlawing segregation on buses. Rosa Parks's brave act was the precipitating event of the American civil rights movement (Shipp, 2005).

On October 24, 2005, Rosa Parks died at the age of 92. To commemorate her, the American Public Transportation Association called for December 1 to be "Tribute to Rosa Parks Day." Buses in major cities across the country designated that one seat, behind the driver, be kept empty for the day in her honor. To alert riders, signs were posted on the windows adjacent to the seat, with Rosa Parks's photograph and the small caption "It all started on a bus" (Ramirez, 2005).

A New York City journalist rode the buses that day to see if people would honor the request—after all, an empty seat on a crowded city bus is a coveted item. He found that the vast majority of riders did so, even during rush hour, when just finding a place to stand is difficult. However, some people did sit in the special seat (Ramirez, 2005). Now this was an interesting development, both to the journalist and to his fellow travelers. Why did they do it? It seemed to be a flagrant act of disrespect. How could one not honor Rosa Parks? Were these "sitters" prejudiced? Were they selfish or arrogant, believing that their personal needs were more important than anything else? In short, negative dispositional attributions were possible about these sitters.

Being a good reporter, the journalist began asking the sitters why they chose to sit in this special seat. Wouldn't you know it, a situational explanation emerged. They hadn't seen the sign. In fact, the small signs were badly placed and easy to miss in the midst of scheduling announcements (Ramirez, 2005). After the sign was pointed out to sitters, they reacted swiftly. One man "read it quickly, shuddered, then uttered a loud profanity in dismay. He scooted out of the seat. 'I didn't realize it was there.... It's history.... It means freedom'" (Ramirez, 2005, p. B1). Another rider, a Black man, began to sit down but stopped halfway when he saw the sign. He said to another rider, a Black woman, "'But people were sitting here.' The woman said gently, 'They couldn't see the sign.' 'Well,' the man said, peeling away the sign and moving it to the edge of the seat, 'they will now'" (Ramirez, 2005, p. B1). Thus, many on the bus were making the wrong attribution about the sitters. The other riders believed that their behavior was due to the kind of people they were (bad ones) instead of due to the situation—in this case, a too small, poorly located sign.

The fundamental theory or schema most of us have about human behavior is that people do what they do because of the kind of people they are, not because of the situation they are in. When thinking this way, we are more like personality psychologists, who see behavior as stemming from internal dispositions and traits, than like social psychologists, who focus on the impact of social situations on behavior. As we saw in Chapter 1, this tendency to overestimate the extent to which other people's behavior results from internal, dispositional factors, and to underestimate the role of situational factors is called the **fundamental attribution error** (Heider, 1958; Ross, 1977; Ross & Nisbett, 1991). The fundamental attribution error has also been called the *correspondence bias* (Gilbert & Jones, 1986; Gilbert & Malone, 1995; Jones, 1979).

There have been many empirical demonstrations of the tendency to see people's behavior as a reflection of their dispositions and beliefs rather than as influenced by the situation (Arsena, Silvera, & Pandelaere, 2014; Gawronski, 2003; Miller, Ashton, & Mishal, 1990). For example, in a classic study, Edward Jones and Victor Harris (1967) asked college students to read an essay written by a fellow student on a controversial political topic. Specifically, students were asked to read an essay about what was, in that era, a hot-button issue: whether to support or oppose the regime of Fidel Castro in Cuba. (If the same study were run today, students might be asked to read an essay adopting a position that is either pro-choice or anti-abortion, or in favor versus opposed to affirmative action in college admissions.) After reading an essay that either supported or opposed Castro, the participants had to guess how the author of the essay *really* felt about Castro (see Figure 4.3).

In one condition, the researchers told the students that the author had chosen freely which position to take in the essay, thereby making it easy to guess how he really felt. If he chose to write in favor of Castro, clearly he must be sympathetic to Castro. Much like if a

Buses across the United States posted a sign like this one, asking riders to keep one seat empty to honor Rosa Parks.

Fundamental Attribution Error

The tendency to overestimate the extent to which other people's behavior results from internal, dispositional factors and to underestimate the role of situational factors

Figure 4.3 The Fundamental Attribution Error

Even when people knew that the author's choice of an essay topic was externally caused (i.e., in the no-choice condition), they assumed that what he wrote reflected, at least to some degree, how he really felt about Castro. That is, they made an internal attribution for his behavior.

(Based on Jones & Harris, 1967)

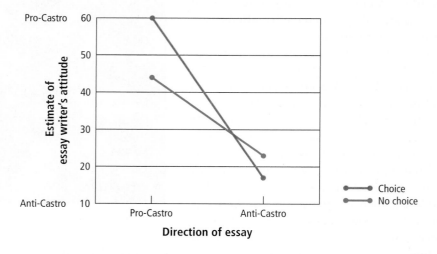

student today chose to write an essay in favor of affirmative action, we would likely assume that the student was, indeed, a supporter of the policy. In another condition of the Jones and Harris (1967) study, however, the participants learned that the author had been *assigned* the position in the essay as part of a debate. In that instance, one should not assume that the student held the same opinion as the essay's position; the student was, after all, told which position to take. Yet the participants in this study (and in dozens of others like it) assumed that the students really believed what they wrote, even knowing that they had no choice as to which position to take. As you can see in Figure 4.3, people ratcheted down their guesses a little bit, but they still assumed that the content of the essay reflected the author's true feelings to some extent. This would be like assuming that someone assigned to argue an anti-abortion position in a class debate truly was, deep down, against abortion. This is the fundamental attribution error in action, overlooking the role of the situation (the assignment of a position), and jumping to conclusions about internal explanations (the person's true attitudes).

Why is the fundamental attribution error so fundamental? It is not always wrong to make an internal attribution; clearly, people sometimes do what they do because of the kind of people they are. Some yelling bosses really are jerks. However, considerable evidence indicates that social situations can strongly affect behavior. Indeed, the major lesson of social psychology is that these influences can be extremely powerful. The point of the fundamental attribution error is that people often tend to underestimate external influences when explaining other people's behavior. Even when the influence of the situation on behavior is obvious, as in the Jones and Harris (1967) experiment, people persist in making internal attributions (Li et al., 2012; Newman, 1996; Ross, Amabile, & Steinmetz, 1977).

THE ROLE OF PERCEPTUAL SALIENCE IN THE FUNDAMENTAL ATTRIBUTION ERROR Why do people fall prey to the fundamental attribution error? One reason is that when we try to explain someone's behavior, our focus of

Watch QUIZ SHOW ATTRIBUTIONS

attention is usually on the person, not on the surrounding situation (Baron & Misovich, 1993; Heider, 1944, 1958; Jones & Nisbett, 1972). In fact, the situational causes of another person's behavior are practically invisible to us (Gilbert, 1999 Gilbert & Malone, 1995). If we don't know what happened to someone earlier in the day (e.g., she received an F on her midterm), we can't use that situational information to help us understand her current behavior. And even when we know her situation, we still don't know how she interprets it (e.g., the F may not upset her because she's planning to drop the course anyway). If we don't know the meaning of the situation for her, we can't accurately judge its effects on her behavior.

If information about the situational causes of behavior is unavailable or difficult to interpret, what does that leave us with? Although the whole of any given situation may be largely unknown or even out of sight for us, the individual is "perceptually prominent"—our eyes and ears notice people. And what we notice seems like the reasonable and logical cause of the observed behavior (Heider, 1958). We can't see the situation, so we overlook its importance. People, not the situation, have **perceptual salience** for us; we pay attention to them, think about them, and tend to assume that they alone cause their behavior (Lassiter et al., 2002; Moran, Jolly, & Mitchell, 2014).

Several studies have confirmed the importance of perceptual salience—especially an elegant one by Shelley Taylor and Susan Fiske (1975). In this study, two male students engaged in a "get acquainted" conversation. (They were actually both accomplices of the experimenters and followed a script during their conversation.) At each session, six actual research participants also took part. They sat in assigned seats, surrounding the two conversationalists (see Figure 4.4). Two sat on each side of the actors; they had a clear, profile view of both individuals. Two observers sat behind each actor; they could see the back of one actor's head but the face of the other. Thus, the conversationalist who was visually salient—that is, the individual the participants could see better—was cleverly manipulated.

After the conversation, participants were asked questions about the two men—for example, Who had taken the lead in the conversation? Who had chosen the topics

Perceptual Salience

The seeming importance of information that is the focus of people's attention

---

Figure 4.4 Manipulating Perceptual Salience

This is the seating arrangement for two actors and the six research participants in the Taylor and Fiske study. Participants rated each actor's impact on the conversation. Researchers found that people rated the actor they could see more clearly as having the larger role in the conversation.

(Based on Taylor & Fiske, 1975)

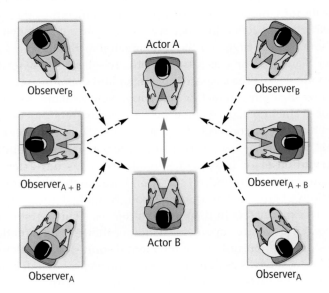

Figure 4.5 The Effects of Perceptual Salience

These are the ratings of each actor's causal role in the conversation. People thought that the actor they could see better had more impact on the conversation.

(Based on Taylor & Fiske, 1975)

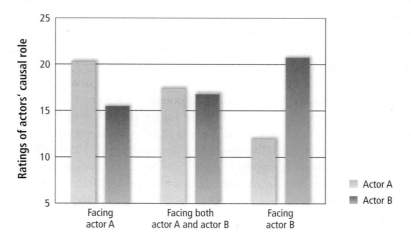

to be discussed? What happened? The person they could see better was the person they thought had more impact on the conversation (see Figure 4.5). Even though all the observers heard the same conversation, those who faced student A thought he had taken the lead and chosen the topics, whereas those who faced student B thought he had taken the lead and chosen the topics. In comparison, those who could see both students equally well thought both were equally influential.

Perceptual salience plays a role in how we view higher-stakes conversations as well. Consider a police interrogation in which investigators question a potential suspect for an unsolved crime. G. Daniel Lassiter and his colleagues (2007; Lassiter, 2010) presented 21 courtroom judges and 24 police officers with a videotape of an individual confessing to a crime. These judge and police participants were shown one of three different versions of the videotape: (a) the camera's focus was on the suspect only, (b) the camera's focus was on the detective only, or (c) there was equal camera focus on the suspect and the detective. Participants were asked to rate how voluntary the confession seemed, as opposed to it seeming coerced. For both the judge and the police respondents, the videotape that focused only on the suspect produced significantly higher ratings of voluntariness than the other two videotape versions (Lassiter et al., 2007). In other words, the perceptual salience of the suspect, when shown alone, triggered the fundamental attribution error, making him appear guiltier than when he was less perceptually salient. These results are worrisome because videotaping the suspect only is standard operating procedure in many real criminal investigations. In fact, one country, New Zealand, has adopted a rule of "equal focus" camera perspective (suspect + detective) for videotaped interrogations, in direct response to concerns about attributional bias (Lassiter et al., 2006).

Our visual point of view, or perceptual salience, helps explain why the fundamental attribution error is so widespread. We focus our attention more on the person than on the surrounding situation because the situation is so hard to see or know. So we hear a debater argue strongly against abortion, and our first inclination is to explain this in dispositional terms: "This person must be anti-abortion rights." But we are capable of realizing that this explanation might not be the whole story. We certainly have the mental sophistication to think, "On the other hand, I know she was assigned this position as part of a debate," adjusting our attributions more toward a situational explanation. However, the problem is that people often don't adjust their judgments enough. In the Jones and Harris

(1967) experiment, participants who knew that the essay writer did not have a choice of topics nevertheless thought that what he had written told them *something* about his true attitudes. They adjusted insufficiently from the most salient information—the position taken in the essay (Quattrone, 1982).

THE TWO-STEP ATTRIBUTION PROCESS In sum, we go through a **two-step attribution process** when we make attributions (Gilbert, 1989, 1991, 1993; Krull, 1993). We make an internal attribution, assuming that a person's behavior was due to something about that person. We then sometimes attempt to adjust this attribution by considering the situation the person was in. It's just that we often don't make enough of an adjustment in this second step. Indeed, when we are distracted or preoccupied, we often skip the second step altogether, making an internal attribution in the extreme (Gilbert & Hixon, 1991; Gilbert & Osborne, 1989; Gilbert, Pelham, & Krull, 1988). Why? Because the first step (making the internal attribution) occurs quickly and spontaneously, whereas the second step (adjusting for the situation) requires more effort and conscious attention (see Figure 4.6). Indeed, recent brain-imaging studies provide evidence at a neural level that our tendency to spontaneously consider the internal, mental states of actors often leaves us less likely to think later about potential situational explanations for their actions (Brosch et al., 2013; Moran et al., 2014).

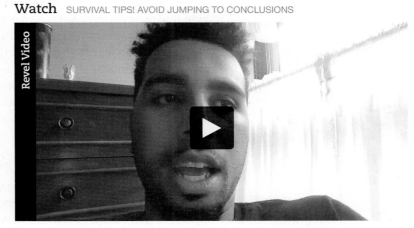

Watch SURVIVAL TIPS! AVOID JUMPING TO CONCLUSIONS

Revel Video

Two-Step Attribution Process

Analyzing another person's behavior first by making an automatic internal attribution and only then thinking about possible situational reasons for the behavior

---

Figure 4.6 Two-Step Process of Attribution

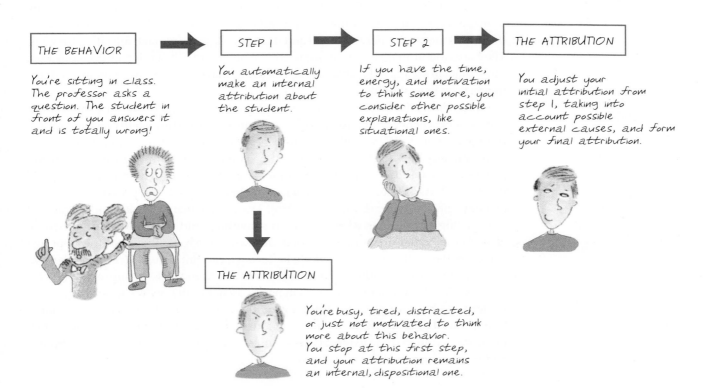

THE TWO-STEP PROCESS OF ATTRIBUTION

THE BEHAVIOR

You're sitting in class. The professor asks a question. The student in front of you answers it and is totally wrong!

STEP 1

You automatically make an internal attribution about the student.

STEP 2

If you have the time, energy, and motivation to think some more, you consider other possible explanations, like situational ones.

THE ATTRIBUTION

You adjust your initial attribution from step 1, taking into account possible external causes, and form your final attribution.

THE ATTRIBUTION

You're busy, tired, distracted, or just not motivated to think more about this behavior. You stop at this first step, and your attribution remains an internal, dispositional one.

When do we engage in this second step of attributional processing? If and when we consciously slow down and think carefully before reaching a judgment; if we are cognitively alert and motivated to make as accurate a judgment as possible; or if we are suspicious about the behavior of the target person—for example, believing that he or she has ulterior motives (Hilton, Fein, & Miller, 1993; Risen & Gilovich, 2007; Webster, 1993). Of course, this two-step model of attribution may be less applicable to individuals in cultures in which internal attributions are not a default response (Mason & Morris, 2010), as discussed in the final section of this chapter.

Self-Serving Attributions

Imagine that Imani goes to her chemistry class one day feeling anxious because she's getting her midterm grade back. The professor returns her exam. Imani turns it over and sees that she has received an A. What will Imani think explains her grade? As you might guess, people tend to take personal credit for their successes: Imani is likely to think that her success was due to the fact that she's good at chemistry and just plain smart. But what if she got a bad grade? Here, she is more likely to blame external events beyond her control, such as the professor for giving an unfair test. When our self-esteem is threatened, we often make **self-serving attributions**. Simply put, these attributions refer to people's tendency to take credit for their successes by making internal attributions but to blame the situation (or others) for their failures by making external attributions (Kestemont et al., 2014; Miller & Ross, 1975; Pronin, Lin, & Ross, 2002).

A particularly interesting arena for studying self-serving attributions is sports (Wertheim & Sommers, 2016). When explaining their victories, athletes and coaches both point overwhelmingly to aspects of their own teams. In fact, an analysis of professional athletes' and coaches' explanations for their team's wins and losses found that 80% of the attributions for wins were to such internal factors. Losses were more likely to be attributed to external causes, outside of the team's control, such as bad luck or the superior play of the other team (Lau & Russell, 1980). Roesch and Amirkhan (1997) further wondered if an athlete's skill, experience, and type of sport predicted attributional tendencies. They found that less experienced athletes were more likely to make self-serving attributions than experienced ones; experienced athletes realize that losses are sometimes their fault and that they can't always take full credit for wins. They also found that athletes in solo sports made more self-serving attributions than those in team sports. Solo athletes, such as tennis players, know that winning and losing rests on their shoulders.

Why do we make self-serving attributions? Most people try to maintain their self-esteem whenever possible, even if that means distorting reality by changing a thought or belief. (We will discuss this concept at length in Chapter 6.) Here we see a specific attributional strategy that can be used to maintain or raise self-esteem: just locate "causality"—the reason something happened—where it does you the most good (Greenberg, Pyszczynski, & Solomon, 1982; Shepperd, Malone, & Sweeny, 2008; Snyder & Higgins, 1988). We are particularly likely to engage in self-serving attributions when we fail at something and we feel we can't improve at it. The external attribution protects our self-esteem, as there is little hope we can do better in the future. But if we believe we can improve, we're more likely to attribute our current failure to internal causes and then work on improving (Duval & Silvia, 2002). Another related reason has to do not with how we see ourselves but rather with how we present ourselves to others (Goffman, 1959). We want people to think well of us, as we discussed previously. Telling others that our poor performance was due to some external cause can be a way to put a "good face" on failure and manage impressions.

Self-Serving Attributions

Explanations for one's successes that credit internal, dispositional factors and explanations for one's failures that blame external, situational factors

Yet one more reason individuals make self-serving attributions has to do with our prior discussion about the kind of information that is available to people. Let's imagine the attributional process of another student in Imani's chemistry class, Ron, who did poorly on the midterm. Ron knows that he studied very hard for the midterm, that he typically does well on chemistry tests, and that in general he is a good student. The D on the chemistry midterm comes as a surprise. The most logical attribution Ron can make is that the test was unfair—the D grade wasn't due to a lack of ability or effort. The professor, however, knows that some students did well on the test and some did poorly; given the information available to her, it is logical for the professor to conclude that Ron, not the difficulty of the test, was responsible for his poor grade (Miller & Ross, 1975; Nisbett & Ross, 1980).

People also alter their attributions to deal with other kinds of threats to their self-esteem. One of the hardest things to understand in life is the occurrence of tragic events such as random attacks, terminal diseases, and fatal accidents. Even when they happen to strangers we have never met, they can be upsetting. They remind us that if such tragedies can happen to someone else, they could happen to us. So we take steps to deny this fact. One example is the belief that bad things happen only to bad people—or, at least, only to people who make mistakes or poor choices. This allows us to rest assured that bad things won't happen to us because we won't be that careless. Melvin Lerner (1980, 1998) has called this the **belief in a just world**—the assumption that people get what they deserve and deserve what they get (Adolfsson & Strömwall, 2017; Aguiar et al, 2008; Hafer & Begue, 2005).

Belief in a Just World

A defensive attribution wherein people assume that bad things happen to bad people and that good things happen to good people

The just-world belief has some sad and even tragic consequences. For example, consider the terrible hypothetical of a female student on your campus being raped. How do you think you and your friends would react? Would you wonder if she'd done something to trigger the attack? Ask if she had been acting suggestively earlier in the evening or whether she had invited the perpetrator into her room? Problematic questions like these are examples of a defensive attribution process by which people might try to make themselves feel better about a disturbing attack by placing some of the blame onto the victim (Burger, 1981; Lerner & Miller, 1978; Stormo, Lang, & Stritzke, 1997). Indeed, research has found that the victims of crimes or accidents are often seen by others as contributing to their own fate. For example, people tend to believe that victims of rape and domestic abuse are somehow to blame for the crimes committed against them (Abrams et al., 2003; Bell, Kuriloff, & Lottes, 1994). By using this attributional bias, the perceiver does not have to acknowledge that there is a certain randomness to becoming a victim, that accidents or crimes can happen to good and careful people as well (see the photo gallery on the next page). The belief in a just world keeps anxiety-provoking thoughts about one's own safety at bay.

The "Bias Blind Spot"

By now, we've discussed a number of attributional biases. Chances are you've thought of an occasion or two when you've fallen prey to one of these biases. But chances are you also think that these are isolated incidents and this is really a bigger problem for other people. If you are thinking this way, you're not alone! Emily Pronin and colleagues have studied this tendency and found evidence for what they call a **bias blind spot**: the tendency to think that others are more susceptible to attributional biases than we are (Hansen et al., 2014; Pronin et al., 2002, 2004).

Bias Blind Spot

The tendency to think that other people are more susceptible to attributional biases in their thinking than we are

To study the bias blind spot, researchers presented participants with descriptions of a number of biases. We will focus on two here: self-serving attributions and victim blaming. The descriptions the participants read never used the word *bias* (which makes it sound like a bad thing); instead, they were described as *tendencies*

EXAMPLES OF SELF-SERVING BIAS

The attribution process is all about making sense of the world around us, but it can also play a self-serving function. Consider, for example, the attributions that a student might make upon receiving a poor grade on an exam. Blaming external factors (e.g., the test was unfair, the room was too crowded and distracting, it was just a busy time of the semester) can help protect the ego from the negative feedback.

Another form of self-serving attribution is the tendency to blame victims for their own misfortune. The conclusion that "bad things only happen to bad people" is one way to reassure ourselves that we will remain immune from such tragedy. One egregious example of this occurs when anyone suggests that a natural disaster was God's way of punishing segments of our society for supposedly immoral behavior.

Have you ever heard about a mugging or other crime in your area and convinced yourself that this would never happen to you because you'd take better precautions? Perhaps the victim was distracted on a cell phone at the time of the crime or walking alone in a poorly-lit area? While there certainly are steps we can take to reduce the likelihood of being robbed, such thoughts also serve to make us feel safer in an often unpredictable world.

One particularly problematic example of victim blaming occurs in cases of rape. By attributing such crimes, at least in part, to choices or actions made by the victim, perceivers are able to avoid acknowledging that anyone could become the victim of sexual violence. Here you see protesters speaking out against this tendency to blame sexual assault on the way a victim was dressed.

In short, the tendency to hold on to the belief that we live in a just world in which people only experience the outcomes they deserve is often a self-serving one. This underlying sentiment can be seen in sayings such as "what goes around comes around" and "he or she had it coming." Such a mindset may be reassuring in some ways, but it also prevents us from a fuller, more reasoned consideration of events in our social world.

to think a certain way. Participants were asked to rate how susceptible they thought they were to each of these thought tendencies, using a scale ranging from "not at all" to "strongly." Next, participants made the same ratings for how susceptible they thought the average American was to these tendencies. The results indicated a striking difference: Participants felt they were only "somewhat" susceptible to self-serving attributions, while the average American was rated as much more susceptible, an ironically self-serving belief in its own right. Similarly, participants felt they rarely committed the "blaming the victim" attribution, but again, they judged the average American as much more likely to do so (see Figure 4.7).

Figure 4.7 Perceived Susceptibility to Attributional Biases for Self and the Average American

Research participants rated their own susceptibility to two attributional biases and that of the "average American." They believed that others were significantly more likely to engage in biased thinking than they themselves were.

(Based on Pronin, Lin, & Ross, 2002)

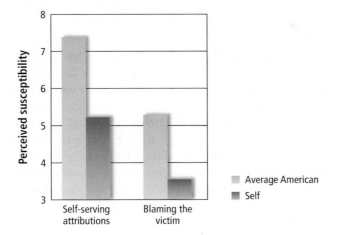

Thus, it appears that we realize that attributionally biased thinking can occur in other people, but we're not so good at spotting it in ourselves. Our own thoughts seem rational and sensible, but other people, hey, they're susceptible to biases! These findings suggest that we often need to reflect more carefully on our judgment processes, check our conclusions, and remind ourselves that a bias blind spot may be lurking.

Review Questions

1. All of the following are examples of an internal attribution *except* for which one?
   a. After winning close to $100 playing poker, Fred explains that he's always been a skilled gambler.
   b. Velma blames her poor grade on her biology exam on the idea that she's never been good at taking multiple-choice exams.
   c. Daphne thinks that the reason her brother is never able to hold a steady job is that he's lazy and quick to get angry with others.
   d. Shaggy says that the only reason for his recent van accident is that the road he was traveling on that day was wet from a recent rainfall.

2. Although he claims to hate reality television, Simon never misses an episode of *Hoarders*. Simon's behavior (i.e., watching *Hoarders*) is
   a. high in distinctiveness.
   b. low in distinctiveness.
   c. low in consensus.
   d. low in consistency.

3. The two-step process of attribution suggests that
   a. people first make an internal attribution and then correct for situational influences.
   b. people first make an external attribution and then correct for dispositional influences.

   c. Americans are less likely than Chinese to commit the fundamental attribution error.
   d. if the attribution process is disrupted at either step, no attribution will be made.

4. Which of the following is the most accurate conclusion based on the Jones and Harris (1967) Castro essay study?
   a. When a target's behavior is forced, perceivers do not attribute it to any sort of internal cause.
   b. We are less generous with ourselves when making attributions for negative events than we are when others are the actors.
   c. We are more likely to make an internal attribution for a chosen action versus a forced action.
   d. We are more likely to make an internal attribution when the actor in question is perceptually salient.

5. Who of the following individuals is most likely to make a self-serving attribution?
   a. Rory, a golfer in the early stages of his career
   b. Mariano, a baseball player who has won multiple championships in the past
   c. LeBron, a basketball player who has been playing since he was young
   d. Roger, a professional tennis player with over a decade of experience

Culture and Social Perception

LO 4.4 **Describe how culture influences our processes of social perception and attribution.**

Social psychologists are focusing more and more on the role of culture in social perception. Beyond our discussion of nonverbal communication and emblems from before, does the culture in which we grow up influence how we perceive other people and try to make sense of their behavior? Let's look at the evidence.

North American and some other Western cultures stress individual autonomy. A person is perceived as independent and self-contained; his or her behavior reflects internal traits, motives, and values (Lu, Fung, & Doosje, 2017; Markus & Kitayama, 1991). The intellectual history of this cultural value can be traced from the Judeo-Christian belief in the individual soul and the English legal tradition of individual rights (Kitayama et al., 2006; Menon et al., 1999). In contrast, East Asian cultures such as those in China, Japan, and Korea tend to stress group autonomy. The individual is more likely to derive his or her sense of self from the social group. The intellectual history of this belief derives from the Confucian tradition—for example, the "community man" (*qunti de fenzi*) or "social being" (*shehui de renge*)—as well as from Taoism and Buddhism (Menon et al., 1999, p.703; Zhu & Han, 2008).

Holistic Versus Analytic Thinking

Research has indicated that these differing cultural values predict the kind of information that people notice and pay attention to. As we discussed in Chapter 3, the values inherent in individualistic Western cultures cause people, as they grow up, to develop more of an *analytic thinking style*. This style involves focusing on the properties of objects (or people) while paying much less attention, if any, to the context or situation that surrounds that object. In contrast, the values of collectivistic cultures, such as those of East Asia (e.g., China, Korea, and Japan), cause people to develop more of a *holistic thinking style*. Here, people focus on the "whole picture"—that is, the object (or person) and the context that surrounds that object as well as the relationships that exist between them (Nisbett, 2003; Nisbett & Masuda, 2003). We don't mean to suggest that these are either–or differences, that all people in one culture think one way and all people in another culture think another way; obviously, a great deal of variability exists within cultures as well. But these generalized differences in thinking styles do predict how we perceive other people.

For example, imagine that you are talking to a group of friends. The expression on one friend's face catches your attention. She's frowning, and her mouth is set in a tight line. What is she feeling? The analytic thinking style suggests that you would focus on her face alone and reach a decision. The holistic thinking style suggests that you would scan the faces of the others in the group, compare them to hers, and then reach a decision.

Takahiko Masuda and colleagues (2008) conducted a study much like this. They presented research participants in the United States and Japan with cartoon people in groups. One person in each cartoon was the central figure, and had a facial expression that was happy, sad, angry, or neutral. The other people in the group had facial expressions that either matched the central figure or were different. The participants' task was to judge the central person's emotion on a 10-point scale. The researchers found that the facial expressions of the other group members' faces had little effect on Americans' ratings of the central figure. If the central figure was smiling broadly, he received a high rating for "happy." It didn't matter what the rest of the group was expressing. In comparison, the facial expressions of the other group members had a significant effect on Japanese participants' ratings of the central figure. A broad smile was interpreted as very happy if the group members were also smiling; the same broad smile was interpreted as less happy if the other group members looked sad or angry. In short, the

What emotion do you think the central person (the one in the middle) is experiencing in each of these cartoons? Your answer might depend on whether you live in a Western or East Asian culture (see the text as to why).

meaning of the cartoon character's facial expression depended on his "context"—what the other cartoon characters standing next to him seemed to be feeling (Masuda et al., 2008). The researchers also measured the eye-tracking movements of the participants as they looked at the cartoons. The Japanese spent more time looking at the cartoon characters in the background than did the Americans. Both groups began by looking at the central character, but after 1 second, the Japanese started to scan the other characters significantly more than did the Americans (Masuda et al., 2008).

SOCIAL NEUROSCIENCE EVIDENCE   The eye-tracking results in the study by Masuda and colleagues (2008) suggest that something very interesting is going on at a physiological level in people as they engage in analytic versus holistic thinking. Beyond eye movements, other researchers have explored how differences in cultural thinking styles predict how the brain responds to social stimuli (Knowles et al., 2001; Mason & Morris, 2010). Trey Hedden and colleagues (2008) used functional magnetic resonance imaging (fMRI) to examine where in the brain cultural experience predicts perceptual processing. Their participants, East Asians and Americans, underwent fMRI brain scans while making judgments about the length of lines inside boxes. Some participants were told to ignore the box around each line ("ignore context"), and some were told to pay attention to the box around each line ("attend to context"). Although participants from the two cultures were equally accurate at judging the lengths of the lines, they showed significantly more brain activity when they had to follow the instructions that were the opposite of their usual cultural thinking style. That is, American participants showed greater activation in higher-order cortical regions (frontal and parietal areas) when told to pay attention to the context, while East Asian participants showed greater activity in the same brain regions when told to ignore context. Greater cortical activation means that the participant had to exert more attention (in a sense, had to work harder cognitively) when asked to perceive objects in a way that was not typical (Hedden et al., 2008).

Other researchers have used event-related potentials (ERPs) to measure brain activity among individuals from different cultures (Goto et al., 2010, 2013). Although fMRI indicates which brain regions are active, ERPs provide a more fine-grained analysis of the onset and offset of neural firing by measuring electrical activity through sensors placed on the scalp. In one study, researchers presented participants with a series of simple perceptual tasks that involved visual information about "targets" and context (Lewis, Goto, & Kong, 2008). In an interesting twist, their participants were all Americans who had grown up in American culture but were of two different ethnic backgrounds: European American or East Asian American. The pattern of ERPs indicated that the European American participants paid more attention to the targets, while the East Asian American participants paid more attention to the context surrounding the targets.

Bicultural research participants were first "primed" with images from one of their cultural heritages: either images evoking American culture or images evoking Chinese culture, like these.

Next, these research participants were asked to make an attribution about the behavior of the fish in the front of the pack. Would they make dispositional or situational attributions about the fish's behavior, given the cultural priming they had experienced earlier?

Cultural Differences in the Fundamental Attribution Error

Previously we saw that people often commit the fundamental attribution error, overestimating the extent to which people's behavior is due to internal, dispositional factors and underestimating the role of situational factors. Is the fundamental attribution error stronger in Western than Eastern cultures?

As it turns out, people in individualist cultures do prefer dispositional attributions about others, relative to people in collectivist cultures, who prefer situational attributions (Newman & Bakina, 2009; Tang, Newman, & Huang, 2014). For example, Joan Miller (1984) asked people of two cultures—Indians living in India and Americans living in the United States— to think of various examples of their friends' behaviors and to explain why those behaviors occurred. The American participants used more dispositional explanations for the behaviors. In contrast, Indian participants gravitated toward situational explanations for their friends' behaviors. But, you might be thinking, perhaps the Americans and Indians generated different kinds of examples. Perhaps the Indians thought of behaviors that were really situationally caused, whereas the Americans thought of behaviors that were really dispositionally caused. To test this alternative hypothesis, Miller (1984) took some of the behaviors generated by the Indian participants and gave them to Americans to explain. The attributional difference remained: Americans still found internal, dispositional causes for the behaviors that the Indians had thought were caused by the situation.

Remember our discussion of the role of evolution in the display of facial expression? Well, Miller's (1984) cross-cultural findings serve as an important reminder that environmental forces—in this case cultural experiences— play a major role in social perception processes as well. In fact, some of the most interesting findings from Miller's (1984) research come from the American and Indian children she examined. In addition to comparing the attributional tendencies of adults from the two cultures, Miller also analyzed the attributions of 8-, 11-, and 15-year-olds. Unlike the significant differences she observed among the adults, children from the United States and India were more or less indistinguishable in terms of how they explained their friends' behaviors. In short, cross-cultural differences in social perception do not appear to be inborn; rather, we arrive in this world with a flexibility of thinking style that is molded over time by cultural (and other) influences.

A fascinating look at this flexibility is provided by Ying-Yi Hong and colleagues (2003), who investigated the fundamental attribution error among Hong Kong Chinese college students. These students were bicultural—deriving their identity not only from their Hong Kong Chinese culture but also from Western culture, to which they had had a great deal of exposure. The participants were first shown a series of images and asked brief questions about them. The purpose of the photographs was to activate, or prime, one aspect of their bicultural identity. Half the participants saw images representing American culture, such as the American flag and the U.S. Capitol building. The other half saw Chinese images, such as a Chinese dragon and the Great Wall. Participants in the control condition saw geometric figures, which did not prime either culture. Next, in a supposedly unrelated task, participants were shown a photograph of a fish swimming in front of a school of other fish. They were asked to make an attribution: Why was this fish swimming in front of the others? Their responses were coded for dispositional reasons (e.g., "The fish is leading the other fish") and situational reasons (e.g., "The fish is being chased by the other fish"). The researchers found that about 30% of the control group made situational attributions about the central fish. However, participants primed with thoughts of one culture or the other showed markedly different patterns. Those primed with Chinese cultural images were more likely to make situational attributions about the fish (nearly 50% of the participants), while those primed with American cultural images were less likely to make situational attributions (about 15% of the participants), instead making dispositional attributions (Hong, Chiu, & Kung, 1997; Hong et al., 2000).

Thus, it appears that Western cultures prompt people to think more like personality psychologists, viewing behavior in dispositional terms. In contrast, Eastern cultures seem to prompt people to think more like social psychologists, considering the situational causes of behavior. However, it would be a mistake to think that members of collectivist cultures don't *ever* make dispositional attributions. Of course they do—it's just a matter of degree. A tendency to think dispositionally about others is prevalent in many cultures. However, members of collectivistic cultures are more aware of how the situation affects behavior and more likely to take situational effects into account (Choi et al., 2003; Krull et al., 1999; Miyamoto & Kitayama, 2002). Thus, the difference is that people in collectivist cultures are more likely to go beyond dispositional explanations and consider information about the situation as well.

Culture and Other Attributional Biases

Continuing to explore the link between culture and attributional biases, social psychologists have examined the self-serving bias and found a strong cultural component to it as well. In a meta-analysis of 266 studies conducted all over the world, Amy Mezulis and her colleagues (2004) found that the self-serving bias is strongest in the United States and some other Western countries—Canada, Australia, and New Zealand. It is also prevalent in Africa, Eastern Europe, and Russia. Within the United States, samples of participants who were of White, Asian, African, Hispanic, and Native American descent did not differ significantly from each other in the degree of self-serving bias. On the other hand, some Asian cultures displayed a lower level of self-serving bias: Japan, the Pacific Islands, and India (Mezulis et al., 2004). That said, more recent studies— such as one including more than 1,300 Chinese secondary school students—have found evidence that the self-serving bias can be just as strong in Asian samples (Hu, Zhang, & Ran, 2016).

Why, though, might there be reason to suspect that self-serving biases could vary across cultures? In many traditional Asian cultures, the values of modesty and harmony with others are highly valued. For example, Chinese students are expected to attribute their success to other people, such as their teachers or parents, or to other aspects of the situation, such as the high quality of their school (Bond, 1996; Leung, 1996). Their cultural tradition does not encourage them to attribute their success to themselves (such as to their talent or intelligence), as it does in the United States and other Western countries. Indeed, in some studies Chinese research participants take less credit for their successes than U.S. participants do (Anderson, 1999; Lee & Seligman, 1997). Instead, Chinese students attribute their success to aspects of their situation, reflecting the values of their culture.

Do individualistic and collectivistic cultures differ in how they explain Olympic gold-medal success? Prior research has indicated that "cultural products" such as advertising, song lyrics, television shows, and art reflect their culture's values: more individualistic content is found in Western cultures and more collectivistic content in countries such as Japan, Korea, China, and Mexico (Morling & Lamoreaux, 2008). Hazel Markus and her colleagues (2006) found that this applies to sports commentary

Sports competitors often make very different attributions for their outcomes based on whether they win or lose as well as cross-cultural variability in attributional tendencies.

as well. They coded Japanese and American media accounts of their countries' gold medal–winning athletes. They found that U.S. media described the performance of American gold medalists in terms of their unique abilities and talents. In comparison, Japanese media described the performance of Japanese gold medalists in much broader terms, including the individual's ability but also encompassing his or her past experiences and the role of other people such as coaches, teammates, and family in his or her success. Finally, American coverage focused more on positive aspects than negative ones (e.g., "[his] strength keeps him in the running"), consistent with a self-serving attributional style, while Japanese coverage focused more equally on positive and negative aspects (e.g., "Her second Olympics is a regrettable one. She was almost at the top, but she didn't have a perfect performance"; Markus et al., 2006). The following two quotes from gold medalists summarize the different ways in which culture influences how one explains one's own behavior:

> I think I just stayed focused. It was time to show the world what I could do…. I knew I could beat [her], deep down in my heart I believed it … the doubts kept creeping in … but I just said, "No, this is my night." (Misty Hyman, American gold medalist, 200m butterfly).

> Here is the best coach in the world, the best manager in the world, and all of the people who support me—all these things were getting together and became a gold medal. So I think I didn't get it alone, not only by myself (Naoko Takahashi, Japanese gold medalist, marathon).

What about failure? Remember that in individualistic cultures such as the United States, people tend toward the self-serving bias, looking outside of themselves—to the situation—to explain failure. In collectivist cultures such as Chinese, the reverse is true: People often attribute failure to internal causes, not to external ones (Anderson, 1999; Oishi, Wyer, & Colcombe, 2000). In fact, in some Asian cultures such as Japan and Korea, self-critical attributions are a common and important "glue" that holds groups together. In response to self-criticism, others offer sympathy and compassion, which strengthens the interdependence of the group members (Kitayama & Uchida, 2003).

Finally, recall that the belief in a just world is a defensive attribution that helps people maintain their vision of life as safe, orderly, and predictable. Is there a cultural component to it as well? Adrian Furnham (1993, 2003) argues that in a society where most people tend to believe the world is a just place, economic and social inequities are considered "fair." In such societies, people believe that the poor and disadvantaged have less because they deserve less. Thus, the just-world attribution can be used to explain and justify injustice. Research suggests that, indeed, in cultures with extremes of wealth and poverty, just-world attributions are more common than in cultures where wealth is more evenly distributed (Dalbert & Yamauchi, 1994; Furnham & Procter, 1989). And more recently, Cindel White and colleagues (2017) have argued that one more way to explore cross-cultural variability in just-world beliefs is to consider endorsement of the religious concept of *karma*, the notion that good moral behavior is rewarded and bad actions will be punished, whether in this lifetime or others. More than 1.5 billion people practice religions centered on karmic principles, including Buddhism, Hinduism, and Jainism. The relationship between traditions like these and social perception tendencies remains understudied, but it has the potential to help further our understanding of how people—all people, in all cultures—seek to assess and explain the behavior of those around them.

Review Questions

1. In Masuda and colleagues' (2008) study of cross-cultural perceptions of emotion,
   a. eye-tracking technology is used to demonstrate that American participants spend less time looking at the peripheral individuals surrounding the central figure than do Japanese participants.
   b. American participants' perceptions of the central figure's emotional state are significantly influenced by the emotions of the peripheral individuals.
   c. context has little influence on the social perception processes of the participants.
   d. American participants begin by looking at the peripheral individuals before shifting their attention to the central individuals.

2. Research using fMRI brain scanning technology indicates which of the following?
   a. East Asian participants use a greater percentage of their frontal and parietal regions when making judgments than do American participants.
   b. Neither East Asian nor American participants are able to overcome their typical, learned ways of attending to (or overlooking) context.
   c. Participants from both cultures demonstrate greater activation in higher-order cortical regions when asked to perceive objects in a way that is unusual for them.
   d. Social neuroscience data provide no support for the hypothesis that holistic versus analytic thinking styles tend to vary by cultural background.

3. In Miller's (1984) cross-cultural investigation of attribution style in the United States and India,
   a. among young children, Americans were more likely to make external attributions, and Indians were more likely to make internal attributions, but few cultural differences emerged with adult participants.
   b. among young children, Americans were more likely to make internal attributions, and Indians were more likely to make external attributions, but few cultural differences emerged with adult participants.
   c. few cultural differences emerged with children, but among adults, Americans were more likely to make external attributions, and Indians were more likely to make internal attributions.
   d. few cultural differences emerged with young children, but among adults, Americans were more likely to make internal attributions, and Indians were more likely to make external attributions.

4. Who among the following individuals would you predict would be most likely to make an external attribution for any given behavior observed?
   a. A U.S.-born American adult
   b. An 8-year-old born and raised in India
   c. A Hong Kong Chinese college student who had just been shown images related to Chinese culture
   d. A Hong Kong Chinese college student who had just been shown images related to American culture

5. Whereas individuals in Western cultures tend to think more like _____, individuals in Eastern cultures tend to think more like _____.
   a. children; adults
   b. psychologists; sociologists
   c. personality psychologists; social psychologists
   d. introverts; extraverts

Summary

LO 4.1   Explain how people use nonverbal cues to understand others.

- **Nonverbal Communication** Nonverbal communication is used to express emotion, convey attitudes, and communicate personality traits. People can accurately decode subtle nonverbal cues.

  - **Facial Expressions of Emotion** The six major emotions are universal, encoded and decoded similarly by people around the world; they have evolutionary significance. *Affect blends* occur when one part of the face registers one emotion and another part registers a different emotion. Mirror neurons are involved in emotional encoding and decoding and help us experience empathy.

  - **Culture and the Channels of Nonverbal Communication** Other channels of nonverbal communication include eye gaze, touch, personal space, gesture, and tone of voice. *Display rules* are particular to each culture and dictate what kinds of emotional expressions people are supposed to show. *Emblems* are gestures with well-defined meanings and are culturally determined.

LO 4.2   Analyze how first impressions form quickly and persist.

- **First Impressions: Quick But Long-Lasting** We form impressions of other people based on their facial structure, possessions, attire, and a variety of other cues, and this process begins within milliseconds. Research on *thin-slicing* indicates that these snap judgments are not just quick; they also pick up on meaningful information and converge with the impressions formed by perceivers with even longer exposure to the target in question.

- **The Lingering Influence of Initial Impressions** Once formed, impressions remain influential because the *primacy effect* demonstrates that the first traits we perceive in another person influence our interpretation of subsequently learned information. We also tend toward *belief perseverance*, or clinging to conclusions even in the face of evidence that seems to indicate we should change our minds. Knowing what influences social perception can allow us to manage the impressions others form of us.

LO 4.3 **Explain how we determine why other people do what they do.**

- **Causal Attribution: Answering the "Why" Question** According to *attribution theory*, we try to determine why people do what they do in order to uncover the feelings and traits that are behind their actions. This helps us understand and predict our social world.

  - **The Nature of the Attribution Process** When trying to decide what causes people's behavior, we can make one of two attributions: an *internal*, or dispositional, attribution or an *external*, or situational, attribution.

  - **The Covariation Model: Internal Versus External Attributions** The *covariation model* focuses on observations of behavior across time, place, actors, and targets of the behavior. It examines how the perceiver chooses either an internal or an external attribution. We make such choices by using *consensus*, *distinctiveness*, and *consistency* information.

  - **The Fundamental Attribution Error: People as Personality Psychologists** In making attributions, people also use various mental shortcuts, including schemas and theories. One common shortcut is the *fundamental attribution error*, the tendency to believe that people's behavior corresponds to (matches)

their dispositions. A reason for this bias is that a person's behavior has greater *perceptual salience* than does the surrounding situation. The *two-step attribution process* states that the initial and automatic attribution tends to be dispositional, but it can be altered by situational information at the second step.

- **Self-Serving Attributions** People's attributions are also influenced by their personal needs. *Self-serving attributions* occur when people make internal attributions for their successes and external attributions for their failures. The *belief in a just world*, where we believe that bad things happen to bad people and good things happen to good people, allows us to avoid thoughts about our own mortality.

- **The "Bias Blind Spot"** The *bias blind spot* indicates that we think other people are more susceptible to attributional biases in their thinking than we are.

LO 4.4 **Describe how culture influences our processes of social perception and attribution.**

- **Culture and Social Perception** Social psychologists have increasingly begun to consider cross-cultural differences in how people interpret the world around them.

  - **Holistic Versus Analytic Thinking** In individualistic cultures like the United States, people tend to pay more attention to the properties of objects. In collectivistic cultures like those of East Asia, people focus more on the whole picture, including context and the relationships between objects, as demonstrated by *social neuroscience evidence* from fMRI and ERP studies.

  - **Cultural Differences in the Fundamental Attribution Error** Although people from both individualistic and collectivistic cultures demonstrate the fundamental attribution error, members of collectivist cultures are more sensitive to situational causes of behavior as long as situational variables are salient.

  - **Culture and Other Attributional Biases** There is also evidence for cross-cultural differences in self-serving attributions and belief in a just world. Typically, these differences, too, occur between Western, individualistic cultures and Eastern, collectivistic cultures.

Revel Interactive

Shared Writing **What Do You Think?**

How might you use what you have learned about the power of nonverbal cues in social perception to be more effective in daily interactions?

Test Yourself

1. What is a major assumption of Kelley's covariation model of attribution?

   a. We make quick attributions after observing one instance of someone's behavior.

   b. People make causal attributions using cultural schemas.

   c. People infer the cause of others' behaviors through introspection.

   d. People gather information to make causal attributions rationally and logically.

2. Which of the following psychological phenomena shows the least cultural variation?

   a. Self-serving attributions

   b. Preferences regarding eye contact and personal space

   c. Anger facial expressions

   d. Fundamental attribution error

3. Suppose that Mischa has found that when she sits in the first row of discussion classes, she gets a better participation grade, regardless of how much she actually participates. Her positioning in front of the teacher could have an effect on how large of a role the teacher thinks Mischa has in discussion due to

   a. the teacher's use of schemas.

   b. perceptual salience.

   c. the "what is beautiful is good" schema.

   d. the two-step process of attribution.

4. Which of the following best illustrates the idea of belief perseverance?

   a. The first time Lindsay meets Tobias, she is impressed with his intellect and ambition, but quite quickly she comes to sour on him and see him as lazy and ineffectual.

   b. Gob is quite smitten with Marta when he first gets together with her, but once they begin an exclusive dating relationship, he feels that he has made a big mistake.

   c. Michael's first impression of Anne is a negative one, and even though he comes to observe her in a variety of scenarios displaying a variety of skills, he remains convinced that she will never amount to very much.

   d. Buster was shy and awkward as a young boy and remains much the same now as an adult.

5. Mr. Rowe and Ms. Dabney meet on a blind date. They get along well until they get into his black convertible to go to a movie. Ms. Dabney is quiet and reserved for the rest of the evening. It turns out that her brother had recently been in a serious accident in that same type of car and seeing it brought up those unwanted emotions. Mr. Rowe assumes that Ms. Dabney has a cold and reserved personality, thereby demonstrating

   a. a belief in a just world.

   b. the fundamental attribution error.

   c. perceptual salience.

   d. insufficient justification.

6. Suppose a certain student, Jake, falls asleep during every chemistry class. Further suppose that Jake is the only one who falls asleep in this class and he falls asleep in all of his other classes. According to Kelley's covariation theory of attribution, how will people explain his behavior?

   a. It results from something unusual about this particular class because his behavior is low in consensus, high in distinctiveness, and high in consistency.

   b. Chemistry is really a boring class because Jake's behavior is high in consensus, high in distinctiveness, and high in consistency.

   c. It results from something unusual about Jake because his behavior is low in consensus, low in distinctiveness, and high in consistency.

   d. It results from something peculiar about the circumstances on a particular day because his behavior is high in consensus.

7. Imagine that you are in Hong Kong reading the morning news and you notice a headline about a double murder that took place overnight. A suspect is in custody. Which of the following headlines is most likely to accompany the story?

   a. Dispute Over Gambling Debt Ends in Murder

   b. Crazed Murderer Slays Two

   c. Homicidal Maniac Stalks Innocents

   d. Bloodthirsty Mobster Takes Revenge

8. Ming is from China; Jason is from the United States. Both participate in an experiment in which they take a test, are given feedback, and are told that they did very well. They are then asked to make attributions for their performance. Based on cross-cultural research on the self-serving bias, you would expect that

   a. Jason but not Ming will say that he succeeded due to his high ability.

   b. neither Ming nor Jason will say that they succeeded due to their high ability.

   c. both Ming and Jason will say that they succeeded due to their high ability.

   d. Ming but not Jason will say that he succeeded due to his high ability.

9. Which of the following statements best describes cultural differences in the fundamental attribution error?

   a. Members of collectivist cultures rarely make dispositional attributions.

   b. Members of Western cultures rarely make dispositional attributions.

   c. Members of collectivist cultures are more likely to go beyond dispositional explanations, considering information about the situation as well.

   d. Members of Western cultures are more likely to go beyond dispositional explanations, considering information about the situation as well.

10. It is 10:00 A.M. and Jamie, an American college student, is dragging himself to his next class to turn in a paper for which he pulled an all-nighter. Through a haze of exhaustion, on the way to class he sees a student slip and fall down. How would Jamie be most likely to interpret the cause of the student's behavior?

    a. Jamie's attribution will most heavily be influenced by his own personality.

    b. Given what we know about Jamie's current cognitive capacity and cultural background, he will likely assume that the student fell because he or she was clumsy.

    c. Jamie would probably attribute the cause to the situation, such as the fact that it was raining and the sidewalks were slippery.

    d. Jamie would be so tired that he would not make any causal attributions.

Chapter 5
The Self
Understanding Ourselves in a Social Context

 ## Chapter Outline and Learning Objectives

The Origins and Nature of the Self-Concept

LO 5.1   Describe the self-concept and how it develops.

Cultural Influences on the Self-Concept

Functions of the Self

Self-Knowledge

LO 5.2   Explain how people use introspection, observations of their own behavior, and other people to know themselves.

Knowing Ourselves Through Introspection

Knowing Ourselves by Observing Our Own Behavior

Using Other People to Know Ourselves

Self-Control: The Executive Function of the Self

LO 5.3   Compare when people are likely to succeed at self-control and when they are likely to fail.

Impression Management: All the World's a Stage

LO 5.4   Describe how people portray themselves so that others will see them as they want to be seen.

Ingratiation and Self-Handicapping

Culture, Impression Management, and Self-Enhancement

WHAT DO YOU THINK?

Survey **What Do You Think?**	
SURVEY	RESULTS

Do you consider yourself to be an above-average driver?

○ Yes
○ No

Over the years there have been fantastical reports of children raised by wild animals. Some are clearly fictional, such as Rudyard Kipling's Mowgli, a child raised by wolves in India (whose story is retold in Disney's *The Jungle Book*). But some accounts appear to be true—kids who, for one reason or another, were abandoned at an early age and adopted by animals. Oxana Malaya was neglected by her alcoholic parents in the Ukraine in the 1980s and was purportedly raised by dogs until she was 7 (Grice, 2006). Marie-Angélique Memmie Le Blanc, known as the "Wild Girl of Champagne," purportedly lived alone in the forests of France for 10 years in the 18th century (Douthwaite, 2002). When John Ssebunya was 2 or 3 years old, he fled into the jungle of Uganda after witnessing his father murder his mother. He was apparently adopted by green vervet monkeys, who fed him nuts and roots and taught him how to survive in the jungle as they did. A year later a villager came across a pack of monkeys and was shocked to see a little boy among them. She alerted other villagers and they were able to rescue John (though not before his green vervet family put up a fight and tried to protect him).

How does being raised by animals shape a human being? Obviously the kids don't learn human language or social niceties. But what about their very sense of self—who they think they are and how they define themselves? Do they view themselves as the animals that protected and cared for them? Or as a human living with animals? As we will see in this chapter, even something as basic as our self-concept is profoundly influenced by interactions with other people. It is impossible to say what kind of self-concept feral children would have had if they were never rescued and continued to live with animals, but as we will see in this chapter, such an experience would likely have had a profound effect on who they believed themselves to be.

The Origins and Nature of the Self-Concept

LO 5.1   Describe the self-concept and how it develops.

Who are you? How did you come to be this person you call "myself"? A good place to begin is with the question of whether we are the only species that has a "self." Although it is doubtful that other species can think of themselves as unique beings in the same way that we do, some fascinating studies suggest that other species have at least a rudimentary sense of self (Gallup, 1997). To study whether animals have a self-concept, researchers placed a mirror in an animal's cage until the mirror became a familiar object. The animal was then briefly anesthetized, and an odorless red dye was painted on its brow or ear. What happened when the animal woke up and looked in the mirror? Members of the great ape family, such as chimpanzees and orangutans, immediately touched the area of their heads marked with the red spot, whereas lesser apes, such as gibbons, did not (Anderson & Gallup, 2015; Suddendorf & Butler, 2013).

These studies suggest that chimps and orangutans have a rudimentary sense of self. They realize that the image in the mirror is themselves and not another animal, and they recognize that they look different from how they looked before (Gallup,

Anderson, & Shillito, 2002; Heschl & Burkart, 2006; Posada & Colell, 2007). What about other animals? There have been reports of individual members of other species passing the mirror test, but these studies have often failed to replicate (Suddendorf & Butler, 2013). At least as measured by the mirror test, a sense of self seems to be limited to human beings and the great apes.

Wondering when a sense of self develops in humans, researchers used a variation of the red-dye test with toddlers and found that human self-recognition develops at around 18 to 24 months of age (Hart & Matsuba, 2012; Lewis & Ramsay, 2004; Stapel et al., 2016). Then, as we grow older, this rudimentary sense of self develops into a full-blown **self-concept**, defined as the overall set of beliefs that people have about their personal attributes. One way psychologists have studied how people's self-concept changes from childhood to adulthood is by asking people of different ages to answer the simple question "Who am I?" Typically, a child's self-concept is concrete, with references to clear-cut, easily observable

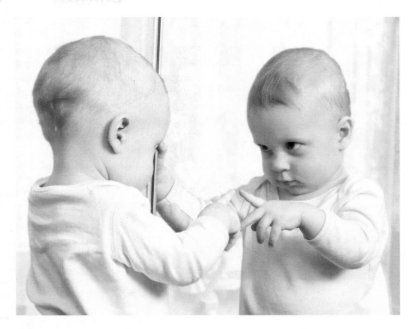

Researchers have examined whether other species have a self-concept, by seeing whether individuals recognize that an image in a mirror is them and not another member of their species. The same procedure has been used with human infants.

characteristics like age, sex, neighborhood, and hobbies. A 9-year-old answered the question this way: "I have brown eyes. I have brown hair. I have brown eyebrows.... I'm a boy. I have an uncle that is almost 7 feet tall" (Montemayor & Eisen, 1977, p. 317).

As we mature, we place less emphasis on physical characteristics and more on psychological states (our thoughts and feelings) and on considerations of how other people judge us (Hart & Damon, 1986; Livesley & Bromley, 1973; Montemayor & Eisen, 1977). Consider this 12th-grade high school student's answer to the "Who am I?" question:

> I am a human being.... I am a moody person. I am an indecisive person. I am an ambitious person. I am a very curious person. I am not an individual. I am a loner. I am an American (God help me). I am a Democrat. I am a liberal person. I am a radical. I am a conservative. I am a pseudoliberal. I am an atheist. I am not a classifiable person (i.e., I don't want to be). (Montemayor & Eisen, 1977, p. 318)

Self-Concept

The overall set of beliefs that people have about their personal attributes

Clearly, this teenager has moved well beyond descriptions of her hobbies and appearance (Harter, 2003). What do we see as key attributes of "the self" when we are adults? To answer that question, imagine that you had a good friend when you were

20 but lost track of this person and didn't see him or her again until 40 years later. You notice that your friend has changed in certain ways, and the question is, how do these changes alter your view of the person's "true self"? A recent study asked participants this question and found that some changes, such as physical declines, minor cognitive deficits, and new preferences, don't change people's basic view of who someone is. If our friend Sahil now needs prescription eyeglasses, doesn't recall things as well as he used to, and has become a vegetarian, we still see him as the same old Sahil (with some minor changes). But if an old friend has undergone

Watch   THE RED-DYE TEST WITH HUMAN TODDLERS

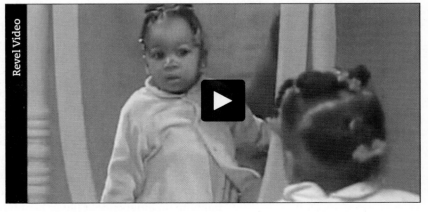

Revel Video

Figure 5.1 What Do We See as Key Attributes of Other People's Selves?

Participants were asked to imagine that they saw an old friend that they knew when they were 25 years old but had not seen in 40 years. They were given a list of ways in which their friend had changed and rated each one according to how much it would alter their view of their friend' true self, on a scale that went from 0% ("this change has no impact on his/her true self") to 100% (this change completely alters his/her true self). People thought that changes in their friend's morality (e.g., how cruel he/she was) would alter his/her true self more than other changes. People thought that changes in perceptual abilities (e.g., changes in vision) would have the smallest impact on their friend's true self.

(Data from Strohminger & Nichols, 2014)

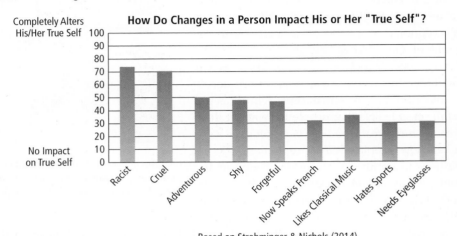

Based on Strohminger & Nichols (2014)

Independent View of the Self

A way of defining oneself in terms of one's own internal thoughts, feelings, and actions and not in terms of the thoughts, feelings, and actions of other people

When Harvard-educated Masako Owada abandoned her promising career to marry Crown Prince Naruhito of Japan and assumed the traditional roles required of her, many Western women questioned her decision. At issue for many was cultural interdependence versus independence of the self.

a moral transformation—for example, if Sahil shows signs of cruelty when he used to be kind or racist when he used to be egalitarian—we hardly recognize him as the same person (see Figure 5.1). In short, morality is viewed as central to the self-concept, more so than cognitive processes or desires (Goodwin, Piazza, & Rozin, 2014; Strohminger & Nichols, 2014).

Cultural Influences on the Self-Concept

An important influence on our self-concept is the culture in which we grew up. Consider Masako Owada, the crown princess of Japan. When she married Crown Prince Naruhito in June 1993, at age 29, she was a brilliant career diplomat in the Foreign Ministry, educated at Harvard and Oxford. She spoke five languages and was on the fast track to a prestigious job as a diplomat. Her decision to marry the prince surprised many observers because it meant she would have to give up her career. Indeed, she gave up any semblance of an independent life, becoming subservient to the prince and the rest of the royal family and spending much of her time participating in rigid royal ceremonies. Although some people hoped that she would modernize the monarchy, "the princess has not changed the imperial family as much as it has changed her" ("Girl Born to Japan's Princess," 2001).

What do you think about Masako's decision to marry the prince? Your answer may say something about the nature of your self-concept and the culture in which you grew up. In many Western cultures, people have an **independent view of the self**, which is a way of defining oneself in terms of one's own internal thoughts, feelings, and actions and not in terms of the thoughts, feelings, and actions of others (Kitayama & Uchida, 2005; Markus & Kitayama, 1991, 2010; Nisbett, 2003; Oyserman & Lee, 2008; Triandis, 1995). Consequently, many Western observers were mystified by Masako's decision to marry the crown prince. They assumed that she was coerced into the marriage by a backward, sexist society that did not properly value her worth as an individual with an independent life of her own.

In contrast, many Asian and other non-Western cultures have an **interdependent view of the self**, which is a way of defining oneself in terms of one's relationships to other people and recognizing that one's behavior is often determined by the thoughts, feelings, and actions of others. Here, connectedness and interdependence between people are valued, whereas independence and uniqueness are frowned on. For example, when asked to complete sentences beginning with "I am," people from Asian cultures are more likely to refer to social groups, such as their family or religious group, than people from Western cultures are (Bochner, 1994; Triandis, 1989). To many Japanese and other Asians, Masako's decision to give up her career was not at all surprising and was a natural consequence of her view of herself as connected and obligated to others, such as her parents and the royal family. What is viewed as positive and normal behavior by one culture may be viewed very differently by another.

Ted Singelis (1994) developed a questionnaire that measures the extent to which people view themselves as interdependent or independent. Sample items from this scale are given in the Try It! given below. Studies generally show that people who live in East Asian countries agree more with the interdependence items, whereas those who live in Western countries agree more with the independence items (Taras et al., 2014).

We do not mean to imply, however, that every member of a Western culture has an independent view of the self and that every member of an Asian culture has an interdependent view of the self. In the United States, for example, people who live in states that were settled more recently by European Americans, such as Oklahoma and Utah, tend to have more of an independent view of the self than do people who live in more "settled" East Coast states, such as Massachusetts and Connecticut. One sign of this, according to a recent study, is that babies born in recently settled states have more unusual names than babies born in other states. That is, one sign of an independent self-construal is giving your baby an unusual name, and parents are more likely

Interdependent View of the Self

A way of defining oneself in terms of one's relationships to other people, recognizing that one's behavior is often determined by the thoughts, feelings, and actions of others

---

Try It!

A Measure of Independence and Interdependence

Instructions: Indicate the extent to which you agree or disagree with each of these statements.

	Strongly Disagree						Strongly Agree
1. My happiness depends on the happiness of those around me.	1	2	3	4	5	6	7
2. I will sacrifice my self-interest for the benefit of the group I am in.	1	2	3	4	5	6	7
3. It is important to me to respect decisions made by the group.	1	2	3	4	5	6	7
4. If my brother or sister fails, I feel responsible.	1	2	3	4	5	6	7
5. Even when I strongly disagree with group members, I avoid an argument.	1	2	3	4	5	6	7
6. I am comfortable with being singled out for praise or rewards.	1	2	3	4	5	6	7
7. Being able to take care of myself is a primary concern for me.	1	2	3	4	5	6	7
8. I prefer to be direct and forthright when dealing with people I've just met.	1	2	3	4	5	6	7
9. I enjoy being unique and different from others in many respects.	1	2	3	4	5	6	7
10. My personal identity, independent of others, is very important to me.	1	2	3	4	5	6	7

Note: These questions are taken from a scale developed by Singelis (1994) to measure the strength of people's interdependent and independent views of themselves. The actual scale consists of 12 items that measure interdependence and 12 items that measure independence. We have reproduced five of each type of item here: The first five are designed to measure interdependence, and the last five are designed to measure independence. See below for scoring instructions. (Adapted from Singelis, 1994.)

To estimate your degree of interdependence, take the average of your answers to questions 1–5. To estimate your degree of independence, take the average of your answers to questions 6–10. On which measure did you come out higher? Singelis (1994) found that Asian Americans agreed more with the interdependence than the independence items, whereas Caucasian Americans agreed more with the independence than the interdependence items.

Figure 5.2 Date of Statehood and Frequency of Popular Baby Names

This graph shows selected U.S. states and the year they attained statehood. It can be seen that the more recently a state became part of the union, the less likely parents were to give their children popular names. Researchers view this as evidence that residents of these states have a more independent self-view

(Based on Varnum & Kitayama, 2011)

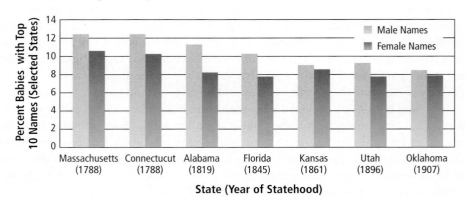

to do that in states such as Oklahoma than they are in states such as Connecticut (see Figure 5.2). The same difference was found in recently settled versus older areas of Canada (Varnum & Kitayama, 2011).

Nonetheless, the difference between the Western and Eastern sense of self is real and has interesting consequences for communication between the cultures. Indeed, the differences in the sense of self are so fundamental that it is difficult for people with independent selves to appreciate what it is like to have an interdependent self and vice versa. After giving a lecture on the Western view of the self to a group of Japanese students, one psychologist reported that the students "sighed deeply and said at the end, 'Could this really be true?'" (Kitayama & Markus, 1994, p. 18). To paraphrase William Shakespeare, in Western society the self is the measure of all things. But however natural we consider this conception of the self to be, it is important to remember that it is socially constructed and therefore may differ from culture to culture.

Functions of the Self

What exactly does the self do? There are four main functions: *self-knowledge* is the way we understand who we are and formulate and organize this information; *self-control* is the way we make plans and execute decisions, such as your decision to read this book right now instead of going out for ice cream; *impression management* is the way we present ourselves to other people and get them to see us the way we want to be seen; and *self-esteem* is the way in which we try to maintain positive views of ourselves. In the remainder of the chapter, we will discuss self-knowledge, self-control, and impression management, reserving our discussion of self-esteem for Chapter 6.

Review Questions

1. Which of the following is *least* likely to pass the "mirror" test suggesting they have at least a rudimentary self-concept?
   a. An orangutan
   b. A chimpanzee
   c. A 12-month-old human infant
   d. A 3-year-old human child

2. When thinking about other people, which of the following will we see as most central to their self-concept?
   a. Their morals
   b. Their preferences and attitudes
   c. Their physical attributes
   d. Their memories

3. Which is the best definition of an *independent* view of the self?

 a. Defining oneself in terms of one's relationships to other people

 b. Defining oneself in terms of one's own internal thoughts, feelings, and actions

 c. Someone who enjoys activities such as dancing and team sports

 d. Someone who enjoys activities such as reading and writing poetry

4. Which is the best definition of an *interdependent* view of the self?

 a. Defining oneself in terms of one's relationships to other people

 b. Defining oneself in terms of one's own internal thoughts, feelings, and actions

 c. Someone who enjoys activities such as dancing and team sports

 d. Someone who enjoys activities such as reading and writing poetry

Self-Knowledge

LO 5.2   Explain how people use introspection, observations of their own behavior, or other people to know themselves.

We've seen that the culture in which people grow up helps shape their self-concept. But how exactly do we come to know who we are and why we do what we do? Social psychologists have uncovered some interesting sources of self-knowledge that may not be all that obvious. Other people, for example, are an important source of information about who we are. But we'll begin with what might seem like a more straightforward source of self-knowledge: introspection.

Knowing Ourselves Through Introspection

Have you ever stopped for a moment to think about how you really felt about something, such as what you want to major in? Or wondered why you do what you do, such as why you binge watched the latest *Netflix* drama instead of studying for your psychology test? If so, you were using **introspection**, which is looking inward to examine the "inside information" that we—and we alone—have about our thoughts, feelings, and motives. One of the most amazing things about the human mind is that we can use it to examine ourselves.

As useful as introspection can be, however, it is by no means perfect. For one thing, it is not always pleasant to be thinking about ourselves, and for another, the reasons for our feelings and behavior can be hidden from conscious awareness. Let's take a look at some of the consequences and limits of introspection.

FOCUSING ON THE SELF: SELF-AWARENESS THEORY   Sometimes our thoughts naturally turn inward, and we think about ourselves. At other times this happens because of external circumstances, such as seeing ourselves in a mirror or in a video that a friend just took of us on her phone. When this happens, we are in a state of self-awareness. According to **self-awareness theory**, when we are focused on ourselves, we evaluate and compare our current behavior to our internal standards and values (Carver, 2003; Duval & Silvia, 2002; Duval & Wicklund, 1972; Morin, 2011; Phillips & Silva, 2005). In short, we become self-conscious in the sense that we become objective, judgmental observers of ourselves, seeing ourselves as an outside observer would.

Let's say that you feel you should quit smoking, and one day you catch an image of yourself in a store window smoking a cigarette. How do you think you will feel? Seeing your reflection will likely highlight the disparity between your behavior and your internal standards. If you can change your behavior to match your internal guidelines (e.g., quit smoking), you will do so. If you feel you can't change your behavior, being in a state of self-awareness will be uncomfortable because you will be confronted with disagreeable feedback about yourself (Duval & Silvia, 2002). This seems to happen pretty frequently. In one study, researchers asked 365 high school juniors (in two American cities) what they were thinking about at random points in their day and found that the

Introspection

The process whereby people look inward and examine their own thoughts, feelings, and motives

Self-Awareness Theory

The idea that when people focus their attention on themselves, they evaluate and compare their behavior to their internal standards and values

Figure 5.3 Self-Awareness Theory: The Consequences of Self-Focused Attention

When people focus on themselves, they compare their behavior to their internal standards.

(Based on Carver & Scheier, 1981)

① You come across a self-focusing cue in the environment (e.g., a mirror, a camera, or an audience).

② This cue creates a state of self-awareness... you become aware of and think about yourself...

③ You compare your current thoughts or behavior to your internal standards or expectations for yourself. Do they match?

④a If NO... uh-oh! What to do? (either)

④b If YES... everything's fine!

⑤a Change your behavior so it matches your standard for yourself. Feel great!

⑤b If you can't or won't change your behavior... Feel terrible! Flee from a state of self-awareness as quickly as possible!

more often people said they were thinking about themselves, the more likely they were to be in a bad mood (Mor et al., 2010). Figure 5.3 illustrates how self-awareness makes us conscious of our internal standards and directs our subsequent behavior.

When people are in a negative state of self-awareness, they often try to escape this state by, for example, avoiding looking at pictures of themselves on their friends' Facebook pages. Sometimes people go even further in their attempt to escape the self. Abusing alcohol, for example, temporarily diverts negative thoughts about oneself and even binge eating and sexual masochism can be effective, albeit dangerous, ways of turning off one's internal spotlight (Baumeister, 1991). The fact that people regularly engage in such dangerous behaviors, despite their risks, is an indication of how aversive self-focus can be (Donnelly et al., 2016; Leary & Tate, 2010; Wisman, Heflick, & Goldenberg, 2015).

Not all means of escaping the self, however, are so damaging. Many forms of religious expression and spirituality are also effective means of avoiding self-focus (Baumeister, 1991; Leary, 2004a). Further, self-focus is not always aversive. If you have just experienced a major success, focusing on yourself can be pleasant indeed because it highlights your positive accomplishments (Greenberg & Musham, 1981; Silvia & Abele, 2002). Self-focus can also be a way of keeping you out of trouble by reminding you of your sense of right and wrong. For example, several studies have found that when people are self-aware (e.g., in front of a mirror), they are more likely to follow their moral standards, such as avoiding the temptation to cheat on a test (Beaman, Klentz, Diener, & Svanum, 1979; Diener & Wallbom, 1976; Gibbons, 1978). Self-awareness, then, is particularly aversive when it reminds people of their shortcomings, and under these circumstances (e.g., right after doing poorly on a test), people try

Try It!

Measure Your Private Self-Consciousness

How much do you focus on yourself when you are alone? The following questions are taken from a scale developed by Fenigstein, Scheier, and Buss (1975) to measure private self-consciousness—the consistent tendency to be self-aware.

Instructions: Answer the following questions as honestly as possible on a scale from 1 to 5, where

1 = extremely uncharacteristic (not at all like me)
2 = somewhat uncharacteristic
3 = neither characteristic nor uncharacteristic
4 = somewhat characteristic
5 = extremely characteristic (very much like me)

	1	2	3	4	5
1. I'm always trying to figure myself out.	1	2	3	4	5
2. Generally, I'm not very aware of myself.	1	2	3	4	5
3. I reflect about myself a lot.	1	2	3	4	5
4. I'm often the subject of my own fantasies.	1	2	3	4	5
5. I never scrutinize myself.	1	2	3	4	5
6. I'm generally attentive to my inner feelings.	1	2	3	4	5
7. I'm constantly examining my motives.	1	2	3	4	5
8. I sometimes have the feeling that I'm off somewhere watching myself.	1	2	3	4	5
9. I'm alert to changes in my mood.	1	2	3	4	5
10. I'm aware of the way my mind works when I work through a problem.	1	2	3	4	5

See below for scoring instructions. (Adapted from Fenigstein, Scheier, & Buss, 1975)

Reverse your answers to questions 2 and 5. If you answered 1 to these questions, change it to a 5; if you answered 2, change it to a 4; and so on. Then add your ratings for all 10 questions. The higher your score, the more likely you are to focus your attention on yourself. Fenigstein, Scheier, and Buss (1975) found that the average score was 26 in a sample of college students.

to avoid it. At other times, however—such as when that little devil is on your shoulder pushing you into temptation—a dose of self-awareness is not such a bad thing because it makes you more aware of your morals and ideals. How self-aware do you tend to be? Complete the Try It! given above to find out.

JUDGING WHY WE FEEL THE WAY WE DO: TELLING MORE THAN WE CAN KNOW   Another function of introspection is trying to figure out *why* we feel the way we do. The problem is that knowing why is not so easy. Imagine trying to decide why you love someone. Being in love typically makes you feel giddy, euphoric, and preoccupied; in fact, the ancient Greeks thought love was a sickness. But what causes you to feel this way? We know it is something about our loved one's looks, personality, values, and background. But precisely what? A friend of ours once told us he was in love with a woman because she played the saxophone. Was this really the reason? The heart works in such mysterious ways that it is difficult to tell.

Unfortunately, it's not just love that is difficult to explain. As we saw in Chapter 3, many of our basic mental processes occur outside of awareness (Bargh, 2017; T. D. Wilson, 2002; Wilson & Dunn, 2004). This is not to say that we are thinkers without a clue—we are usually aware of the final result of our thought processes (e.g., that we are in love) but often unaware of the cognitive processing that led to the result. It's as if the magician pulled a rabbit out of a hat: You see the rabbit, but you don't know how it got there. How do we deal with this rabbit problem? Even though we often don't know why we feel a certain way, it seems we are always able to come up with an explanation. We are the proud owners of the most powerful brain to evolve on this planet, and we certainly put it to use. Unfortunately, it didn't come with an owner's manual. Richard Nisbett and Tim Wilson referred to this phenomenon as "telling more than we can know" because people's explanations of their feelings and behavior often go beyond what they can reasonably know (Nisbett & Ross, 1980; Nisbett & Wilson, 1977; T. D. Wilson, 2002).

In one study, for example, college students recorded their daily moods every day for 5 weeks (Wilson, Laser, & Stone, 1982). The students also kept track of things that might predict their daily moods, such as the weather, their workload, and how much sleep they had gotten the night before. At the end of the 5 weeks, the students estimated how much their moods were related to these other variables. An analysis of the data showed that in many cases people's estimates were wrong. For example, most people believed that the amount of sleep they got predicted how good a mood they were in the next day when in fact this wasn't true: The amount of sleep was unrelated to people's moods. People weren't clueless; most knew, for example, that how well they were getting along with their friends was a good predictor of their mood. But overall, people weren't all that accurate in knowing what predicted their moods (Johansson et al., 2005; Wegner, 2002; T. D. Wilson, 2002).

Causal Theories

Theories about the causes of one's own feelings and behaviors; often we learn such theories from our culture (e.g., "absence makes the heart grow fonder")

Why not? It turned out that participants were relying on their **causal theories** about mood. People have many theories about what influences their feelings and behavior (e.g., "My mood should be affected by how much sleep I got last night") and often use these theories to help them explain why they feel the way they do (e.g., "I'm in a bad mood; I'll bet the fact that I got only 6 hours of sleep last night has a lot to do with it"). We learn many of these theories from the culture in which we grow up—ideas such as "absence makes the heart grow fonder" and that people are "blue" on Mondays. The only problem is that, as discussed in Chapter 3, our schemas and theories are not always correct and thus can lead to incorrect judgments about the causes of our actions.

We do not mean to imply that people rely solely on their causal theories when introspecting about the reasons for their feelings and behaviors. In addition to culturally learned causal theories, people have a great deal of information about themselves, such as how they have responded in the past and what they happen to have been thinking about before making a choice (Andersen, 1984; T. D. Wilson, 2002). The fact remains, however, that introspecting about our past actions and current thoughts does not always yield the right answer about why we feel the way we do (Hassin, 2013; Wilson & Bar-Anan, 2008).

Knowing Ourselves by Observing Our Own Behavior

If introspection doesn't always reveal who we are or why we do what we do, how else do we figure it out? It turns out that an important source of self-knowledge is by observing our own behavior.

SELF-PERCEPTION THEORY Suppose that a friend asks you how much you like classical music. You hesitate because you never listened to classical music much when you were growing up, but lately you have found yourself listening to symphonies every now and then. "Well, I don't know," you reply. "I guess I like some kinds of classical music. Just yesterday I listened to a Beethoven symphony on the radio while I was driving to work." If so, you used observations of your own behavior to determine how you feel—in this case, what you chose to listen to.

Self-Perception Theory

The theory that when our attitudes and feelings are uncertain or ambiguous, we infer these states by observing our behavior and the situation in which it occurs

Self-perception theory argues that when our attitudes and feelings are uncertain or ambiguous, we infer these states by observing our behavior and the situation in which it occurs (Bem, 1972). Let's consider each part of this theory. First, we infer our inner feelings from our behavior only when we are not sure how we feel. If you've always known that you love classical music, you do not need to observe your behavior to figure this out (Andersen, 1984; Andersen & Ross, 1984). Maybe, though, your feelings are murky; you've never really thought about how much you like it. If so, you are especially likely to use your behavior as a guide to how you feel (Chaiken & Baldwin, 1981; Wood, 1982).

Second, people judge whether their behavior really reflects how they feel or whether it was the situation that made them act that way. If you freely choose to listen to the classical music station—no one makes you do it—you are especially likely to conclude that you listen to that station because you like classical music. If it was your partner and not you who turned to the station playing Beethoven, you are unlikely to conclude that you listen to classical music in your car because you like it.

Sound familiar? In Chapter 4, we discussed attribution theory—the way in which people infer someone else's attitudes and feelings by observing that person's behavior. According to self-perception theory, people use the same attributional principles to infer their own attitudes and feelings. For example, if you were trying to decide whether a friend likes classical music, you would observe her behavior and explain why she behaved that way. You might notice, for example, that she is always listening to classical music in the absence of any situational pressures or constraints—no one makes her play Mozart on her smartphone. You would make an internal attribution for her behavior and conclude that she likes Mozart. Self-perception theory says that we infer our own feelings in the same way: We observe our behavior and explain it to ourselves; that is, we make an attribution about why we behaved that way (Aucouturier et al., 2016; Schrift & Parker, 2014; Olson & Stone, 2005; T. D. Wilson, 2002). In fact, it is not only attitudes and preferences that we infer from our behavior—we also infer our emotions, as we will now see.

UNDERSTANDING OUR EMOTIONS: THE TWO-FACTOR THEORY OF EMOTION

How do you know which emotion you are experiencing at any given time? Is it fear or elation? This question probably sounds kind of silly: Don't we know how we feel without having to think about it? Not necessarily. The way in which we experience emotions has a lot in common with the kinds of self-perception processes we just discussed.

Stanley Schachter (1964) proposed a theory of emotion that says we infer what our emotions are in the same way we infer what kind of person we are or what we like. In each case, we observe our behavior and then explain to ourselves why we are behaving that way. The only difference in these types of inferences is the kind of behavior we observe. Schachter says we observe our internal behaviors—how physiologically aroused we feel. If we feel aroused, we then try to figure out what is causing this arousal. For example, suppose you go for a 3-mile run one day and are walking back to your apartment. You go around a corner and nearly walk right into an extremely attractive person from your psychology class whom you are just getting to know. Your heart is pounding, and you feel a little sweaty. Is it because love is blossoming between you and your new friend or simply because you just went for a run?

Schachter's theory is called the **two-factor theory of emotion** because understanding our emotional states requires two steps: We must first experience physiological arousal, and then we must seek an appropriate explanation or label for it. Because our physical states are difficult to label on their own, we use information in the situation to help us make an attribution about why we feel aroused (see Figure 5.4).

Imagine that you were a participant in a classic study by Stanley Schachter and Jerome Singer (1962) that tested this theory. When you arrive, the experimenter tells you he is studying the effects that a vitamin compound called Suproxin has on vision. After a physician injects you with a small amount of Suproxin, the experimenter asks you to wait while the drug takes effect. He introduces you to another participant who, he says, has

Two-Factor Theory of Emotion

The idea that emotional experience is the result of a two-step self-perception process in which people first experience physiological arousal and then seek an appropriate explanation for it

Figure 5.4 The Two-Factor Theory of Emotion

People first experience physiological arousal and then attach an explanation to it.

been given some of the same vitamin compound. The experimenter gives each of you a questionnaire to fill out, saying he will return in a little while to give you the vision tests.

You look at the questionnaire and notice that it contains some highly personal and insulting questions. For example, one question asks, "With how many men (other than your father) has your mother had extramarital relationships?" (Schachter & Singer, 1962, p. 385). The other participant reacts angrily to these offensive questions, becoming more and more furious, until he finally tears up his questionnaire, throws it on the floor, and stomps out of the room. How do you think you would feel? Would you feel angry as well?

As you've probably guessed, the real purpose of this experiment was not to test people's vision. The researchers set up a situation in which the two crucial variables—arousal and an emotional explanation for that arousal—would be present or absent, and then they observed which, if any, emotions people experienced. The participants did not really receive an injection of a vitamin compound. Instead, some participants received epinephrine, a hormone produced naturally by the human body that causes arousal (body temperature and heart and breathing rates increase), and the other half received a placebo that had no physiological effects.

Imagine how you would have felt had you received the epinephrine: As you read the insulting questionnaire, you begin to feel aroused. Remember, the experimenter didn't tell you the shot contained epinephrine, so you don't realize that the injection is making you feel this way. The other participant—who was actually an accomplice of the experimenter—reacts with rage. You are likely to infer that you are feeling flushed and aroused because you too are angry. You have met the conditions Schachter (1964) argues are necessary to experience an emotion: You are aroused, you have sought out and found a reasonable explanation for your arousal in the situation that surrounds you, and so you become furious. This is indeed what happened: The participants who had been given epinephrine reacted much more angrily than did participants who had been given the placebo.

A fascinating implication of Schachter's theory is that people's emotions are somewhat arbitrary, depending on what the most plausible explanation for their arousal happens to be. Schachter and Singer (1962) demonstrated this idea in two ways. First, they showed that they could prevent people from becoming angry by providing a nonemotional explanation for why they felt aroused. They did this by informing some of the people who received epinephrine that the injection would increase their heart rate, make their face feel warm and flushed, and cause their hands to shake slightly. When people actually began to feel this way, they inferred that it was not because they were angry but because the drug was taking effect. As a result, these participants did not react angrily to the questionnaire.

Second, Schachter and Singer showed that they could make participants experience a very different emotion by changing the most plausible explanation for their arousal. In another condition, participants received the epinephrine but did not get the insulting questionnaire, and the accomplice did not respond angrily. Instead, the accomplice acted in a euphoric, devil-may-care fashion, playing basketball with rolled-up pieces of paper, making paper airplanes, and playing with a hula hoop he found in the corner. How did the participants respond? Now they inferred that they must be feeling happy and euphoric and often joined in on the fun.

The Schachter and Singer experiment has become one of the most famous studies in social psychology because it shows that emotions can be the result of a self-perception process: People look for the most plausible explanation for their arousal. Sometimes the most plausible explanation is not the right one, and so people end up experiencing a mistaken emotion. The people who became angry or euphoric in the Schachter and Singer (1962) study did so because they felt aroused and thought this arousal was due to the obnoxious questionnaire or to the infectious, happy-go-lucky behavior of the accomplice. The real cause of their arousal, the epinephrine, was hidden from them, so they relied on situational cues to explain their behavior.

FINDING THE WRONG CAUSE: MISATTRIBUTION OF AROUSAL   Do people form mistaken emotions in their everyday lives in the same way as participants did in the Schachter and Singer (1962) study? In everyday life, one might argue, people usually know why they are aroused. If a mugger points a gun at us and says, "Give me your wallet!" we feel aroused and correctly identify this arousal as fear. If our heart is thumping while we walk on a deserted moonlit beach with the man or woman of our dreams, we correctly label this arousal as love or sexual attraction.

In many everyday situations, however, there is more than one plausible cause for our arousal, and it is difficult to identify how much of the arousal is due to one source or another. Imagine that you go to see a scary movie with an extremely attractive date. As you are sitting there, you notice that your heart is thumping and you are a little short of breath. Is this because you are wildly attracted to your date or because the movie is terrifying you? It is unlikely that you could say, "Fifty-seven percent of my arousal is due to the fact that my date is gorgeous, 32% is due to the scary movie, and 11% is due to indigestion from all the popcorn I ate." Because of this difficulty in pinpointing the precise causes of our arousal, we sometimes misidentify our emotions. You might think that most of your arousal is a sign of attraction to your date when in fact a lot of it is due to the movie (or maybe even indigestion).

If so, you have experienced **misattribution of arousal**, whereby people make mistaken inferences about what is causing them to feel the way they do (Anderson et al., 2012; Bar-Anan, Wilson, & Hassin, 2010; Rydell & Durso, 2012; Zillmann, 1978). Consider how this worked in a field experiment by Donald Dutton and Arthur Aron

Misattribution of Arousal

The process whereby people make mistaken inferences about what is causing them to feel the way they do

When people are aroused for one reason, such as occurs when they cross a scary bridge, they often attribute this arousal to the wrong source—such as attraction to the person they are with.

(1974). An attractive young woman asked men visiting a park in British Columbia if they would fill out a questionnaire for her as part of a psychology project looking at the effects of scenic attractions on people's creativity. When they had finished, she said that she would be happy to explain her study in more detail when she had more time. She tore off a corner of the questionnaire, wrote down her name and phone number, and told the participant to give her a call if he wanted to talk with her some more. How attracted do you think the men were to this woman? Would they telephone her and ask for a date?

This is a hard question to answer. Undoubtedly, it depends on whether the men were involved with someone else, how busy they were, and so on. It might also depend, however, on how they interpreted any bodily symptoms they were experiencing. If they were aroused for some extraneous reason, they might mistakenly think that some of the arousal was the result of attraction to the young woman. To test this idea, Dutton and Aron (1974) had the woman approach males in the park under two different circumstances.

In one condition, the men were walking across a 450-foot-long suspension bridge that spanned a deep canyon. The bridge was made of wooden planks attached to wire cables, and as they walked across, they had to stoop to hold on to the low handrail. A little way out over the canyon, the wind tended to catch the bridge and make it wobble from side to side. This is a scary experience, and most people who cross the bridge become more than a little aroused—their heart pounds against their chest, they breathe rapidly, and they begin to perspire. It was at this point that the attractive woman approached a man on the bridge and asked him to fill out her questionnaire. How attracted do you think the men in this condition felt toward her?

In another condition, the woman waited until men had crossed the bridge and rested for a while on a bench in the park before approaching them. They had a chance to calm down—their hearts were no longer pounding, and their breathing rate had returned to normal. They were peacefully admiring the scenery when the woman asked them to fill out her questionnaire. How attracted were these men to the woman?

Schachter's two-factor theory would predict that in comparison to those sitting on the bench, the men on the bridge would be considerably more aroused, mistakenly thinking that some of their arousal from crossing the bridge was the result of attraction to the beautiful woman. That is exactly what happened. A large proportion of the men approached on the bridge called the woman later to ask her for a date, whereas relatively few of the men approached on the bench called the woman (see Figure 5.5). This type of misattribution of arousal has been found in numerous subsequent studies in both men and women (e.g., Meston & Frohlich, 2003; Zillmann, 1978). The moral is this: If you encounter an attractive person and your heart is going thump-thump, think carefully about why you are aroused—or you might fall in love for the wrong reasons!

To sum up this section, one way that people learn about themselves—including their attitudes, motives, and emotions—is to observe their behavior and the conditions

Figure 5.5 Misattribution of Arousal

When a woman approached men on a scary bridge and asked them to fill out a questionnaire, a high percentage of them were attracted to her and called her for a date. When the same woman approached men after they had crossed the bridge and had rested, relatively few called her for a date.

(Based on Dutton & Aron, 1974)

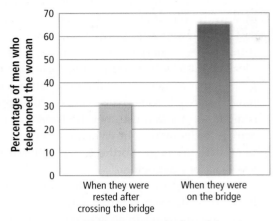

under which that behavior occurs. This includes observations of their outward behavior (e.g., whether they freely chose to listen to classical music on the radio) as well as their bodily responses (e.g., whether their heart is thumping when talking with a stranger). We turn now to another example of self-perception, namely inferring our motives.

INTRINSIC VERSUS EXTRINSIC MOTIVATION   So far we've seen that people use their own behavior as an important source of information about their attitudes and emotions. We turn now to people's attributions about their motivation. Do people think they are performing an activity because they are intrinsically interested in it, for example, or because they stand to gain something (e.g. money) by doing it? And why does this matter?

Questions about what motivates people to do what they do are important in many domains, including education. Imagine, for example, that you are an elementary school teacher who wants your students to develop a love of reading. Not only do you want your students to read more, but you also want them to develop a love of books. How might you go about accomplishing this? It is not going to be easy because so many other things compete for your students' attention, such as television, video games, and social media.

If you are like many educators, you might decide that a good approach would be to reward the children for reading. Maybe that will get them to put down those game controllers and pick up a book—and develop a love of reading in the process. Teachers have always rewarded kids with a smile or a gold star on an assignment, but recently they have turned to more powerful incentives, such as candy, brownies, and toys (Perlstein, 1999). A chain of pizza restaurants is also encouraging kids to read more, offering elementary school students a certificate for a free pizza if they read a certain number of books (see "Book It!" at www.bookitprogram.com). One school district has taken this a step further by rewarding high school students with cash prizes if they do well on advanced placement exams (Hibbard, 2011).

There is no doubt that rewards are powerful and that pizzas and money will help to motivate kids. One of the oldest and most fundamental psychological principles,

Many programs try to get children to read more by rewarding them. But do these programs increase or decrease a child's love of reading?

Intrinsic Motivation

The desire to engage in an activity because we enjoy it or find it interesting, not because of external rewards or pressures

Extrinsic Motivation

The desire to engage in an activity because of external rewards or pressures, not because we enjoy the task or find it interesting

Overjustification Effect

The tendency for people to view their behavior as caused by compelling extrinsic reasons, making them underestimate the extent to which it was caused by intrinsic reasons

called *positive reinforcement*, says that giving a reward each time a behavior occurs will increase the frequency of that behavior. Whether it be a food pellet delivered to a rat pressing a bar or a free pizza given to a child for reading, rewards can change behavior.

But people are not rats, and we have to consider the effects of rewards on what's inside—people's thoughts about themselves, their self-concept, and their motivation to read in the future. Does being paid to read, for example, change people's ideas about *why* they are reading? The danger of reward programs such as Book It! is the very self-perception process we have discussed. Kids may infer that they are reading to earn something, not because they find reading to be an enjoyable activity in its own right. When the reward programs end and pizzas are no longer forthcoming, children may actually read less than they did before.

This is especially likely to happen to children who already liked to read. Such children have high **intrinsic motivation**: the desire to engage in an activity because they enjoy it or find it interesting, not because of external rewards or pressures (Deci, 2016; Harackiewicz & Elliot, 1993, 1998; Harackiewicz & Hulleman, 2010; Hirt et al., 1996; Hulleman et al., 2010; Ryan & Deci, 2000). Their reasons for engaging in the activity have to do with themselves—the enjoyment and pleasure they feel when reading a book. In other words, reading is play, not work.

What happens when the children start getting rewards for reading? Their reading, originally stemming from intrinsic motivation, is now also spurred by **extrinsic motivation**, which is people's desire to engage in an activity because of external rewards or pressures, not because they enjoy the task or find it interesting. According to self-perception theory, in such situations people often assume that they are motivated by the rewards and not their intrinsic interest. That is, children who liked to read at the outset now assume that they are cracking open books only to get the reward. The unfortunate consequence is that rewards can make people lose interest in activities they initially enjoyed. This is called the **overjustification effect**, which results when people view their behavior as caused by compelling extrinsic reasons, such as a reward, making them underestimate the extent to which their behavior was caused by intrinsic reasons (Deci, Koestner, & Ryan, 1999a, 1999b; Harackiewicz, 1979; Lepper, 1995; Warneken & Tomasello, 2014).

In one study, for example, fourth- and fifth-grade teachers introduced four new math games to their students, and during a 13-day baseline period they noted how long each child played each math game. As seen in the leftmost line in Figure 5.6, the children initially had some intrinsic interest in the math games in that they played them for several minutes during this baseline period. For the next several days, a reward program was introduced. Now the children could earn credits toward certificates and trophies by playing the math games, and as we might expect, the amount of time they spent on the math games increased (see the middle line in Figure 5.6).

The key question is, what happened after the reward program ended and the kids could no longer earn rewards for playing the games? As predicted, an overjustification effect occurred in that the children spent significantly less time on the math games than they had initially, before the rewards were introduced (see the rightmost line in Figure 5.6). The researchers determined, by comparing these results to those of a control condition, that it was the rewards that made people like the games less and not the fact that everyone became bored with the games as time went by. In short, the rewards

Figure 5.6 The Overjustification Effect

During the initial baseline phase, researchers measured how much time elementary school students played math games. During the reward program, they rewarded the children with prizes for playing with the games. When the rewards were no longer offered (during the follow-up phase), the children played with the games even less than they had during the baseline phase, indicating that the rewards had lowered their intrinsic interest in the games.

(Adapted from Greene, Sternberg, & Lepper, 1976)

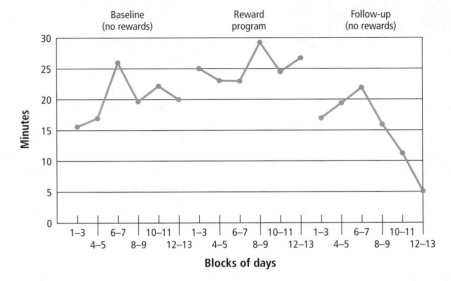

destroyed the children's intrinsic interest in the games so that by the end of the study, they were hardly playing the games at all (Greene, Sternberg, & Lepper, 1976).

It's not just in schools where this undermining of intrinsic interest can play out. What about professional athletes who are rewarded for high performance with lucrative contracts? Mark White and Ken Sheldon (2014) compared the performance of NBA basketball players and major league baseball players the year before their contracts expired, the year their contracts was being renegotiated, and the year after they were awarded new contracts. During the year contracts were being renegotiated players did better than they had previously, perhaps because extrinsic rewards were quite salient to them—the better they did, the more money they could get. But the following year—after their new contract had been awarded—performance tended to fall below what it had been each of the previous two years. NBA players, for example, had a higher scoring average during the contract year than the previous year, but their lowest scoring average came the next year after they had gotten the big contract. We can't be sure from a correlational study such as this one, but the findings are consistent with the idea that rewards can undermine people's intrinsic motivation after those rewards are removed or are no longer salient.

What can we do to protect intrinsic motivation from the dangers of society's reward system? Fortunately, there are conditions under which overjustification effects can be avoided. Rewards will undermine interest only if interest was initially high (Calder & Staw, 1975; Tang & Hall, 1995). If a child has no interest in reading, then getting him or her to read by offering rewards is not a bad idea because there is no initial interest to undermine.

Also, the type of reward makes a difference. So far, we have discussed **task-contingent rewards**, meaning that people are rewarded simply for doing a task, regardless of the quality of their performance. In the pizza program, for example, kids are rewarded for the number of books they read, not how well they read them. Sometimes **performance-contingent rewards** are used, whereby the reward depends

Task-Contingent Rewards

Rewards that are given for performing a task, regardless of how well the task is done

Performance-Contingent Rewards

Rewards that are based on how well we perform a task

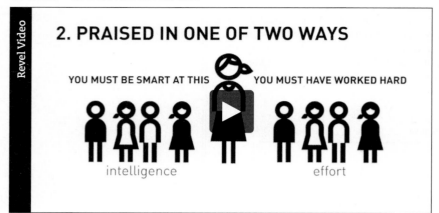

Revel Video

2. PRAISED IN ONE OF TWO WAYS

YOU MUST BE SMART AT THIS   YOU MUST HAVE WORKED HARD

intelligence   effort

Fixed Mindset

The idea that we have a set amount of an ability that cannot change

Growth Mindset

The idea that achievement is the result of hard work, trying new strategies, and seeking input from others

on how well people perform the task. An example is giving students cash prizes for doing well on advanced placement exams, not simply for taking the exams. This type of reward is less likely to decrease interest in a task—and may even increase interest—because the earned reward conveys the message that you are good at the task (Deci & Ryan, 1985; Pulfrey, Darnon, & Butera, 2013). Thus, rather than giving kids a reward simply for playing math games—a task-contingent reward—it is better to give them a reward for doing *well* in math—a performance-contingent reward. Performance-contingent rewards must be used with care, however, because they too can backfire. Even though they convey positive feedback, these types of rewards can put pressure on people by making them feel evaluated, which makes it harder for them to do well and lowers their intrinsic interest in the activity (Harackiewicz, 1989; Harackiewicz, Manderlink, & Sansone, 1984). The trick is to convey positive feedback without putting extra pressure on people by making them feel nervous and apprehensive about being evaluated.

Do you think this person was born with the ability to climb this mountain? It's likely this person has gone through years of training and practice to achieve such heights (literally). People with a fixed mindset, however, might simply believe it's impossible and never try. People with a growth mindset are likely to believe anything is possible if they find the right strategies and work hard—and consequently accomplish far more in life.

MINDSETS AND MOTIVATION   There is another way in which people's self-perceptions influence their motivations, and that is the way in which they perceive their own abilities. Some people believe that their abilities are set in stone; they either have them or they do not. Psychologist Carol Dweck (2006) calls this a **fixed mindset**—the idea that we have a set amount of an ability that cannot change. According to this view, we have a fixed amount of intelligence, athletic ability, musical talent, and so on. Other people have a **growth mindset**, which is the belief that achievement is the result of hard work, trying new strategies, and seeking input from others. Research shows that the mindset people have is crucial to their success: People with the fixed mindset are more likely to give up after setbacks and are less likely to work on and hone their skills; after all, if they fail, it must be a sign that they simply don't have what it takes. People with the growth mindset view setbacks as opportunities to improve through hard work (Claro, Paunesku, & Dweck, 2016).

Mindsets are important not only to athletic performance but also to how we view any ability, including how good we are at academics. Most students hit a bump in the road when they start college; for you, maybe it was a lower grade than you expected on a psychology or math test. How did you react to your disappointing grade? Dweck's research shows that students who have a fixed mindset about intelligence are more likely to give up and do poorly on subsequent tests, whereas those with growth mindsets are more likely to redouble their efforts and change their strategies and thus do better on subsequent tests. Thus, the next time you experience a setback—be it on the athletic field, in your classes, or in your personal relationships—you might want to view it as an opportunity to find a new strategy rather than as a sign that you "don't have what it takes."

#trending

Growth Mindset in the Classroom

Imagine a group of ninth graders who are struggling in one or more of their classes, such as math or English. According to the research on mindsets discussed in this chapter, they would be better off believing that they could improve if they worked harder and found the right strategies (a growth mindset) than if they believed they simply didn't have what it takes to do well (a fixed mindset). But can a growth mindset be taught in a standardized way to large groups of students?

To find out, David Yeager and colleagues (2016) conducted an ambitious study in nine different middle schools with more than 3,000 ninth graders. Half of the students were randomly assigned to complete a growth mindset learning module in their computer classrooms on two different occasions a week apart. The module explained what a growth mindset was and emphasized the importance of effort, developing new strategies, and asking for help with academic material. This message was reinforced with stories about other students' experiences,

testimonials from celebrity role models, and writing exercises in which the students applied the material to their own lives. The other half of the students were assigned to a control condition in which they completed a learning module about academics minus any mention of growth mindsets.

As the researchers predicted, the mindset intervention had no effect on high performing students, because they were already doing well in their classes. But as the researchers also predicted, the intervention helped low-achieving students. Compared to those in the control condition, low-achieving students who got the growth mindset modules showed a greater improvement in their grades. The difference was small; for example, the growth mindset module reduced the percentage of low-performing students who received Ds or Fs from 46% to 39%. But the fact that such an inexpensive and brief intervention—completing a computer learning module on two occasions—had any effect is encouraging.

Using Other People to Know Ourselves

The self-concept does not develop in a solitary context but is shaped by the people around us. If we never interacted with other people—like a feral child raised by animals—our own image would be a blur because we would not see ourselves as having selves distinct from those of others. Remember the mirror and red-dye test we discussed earlier, used to determine if animals have a self-concept? Variations of this test have been used to show that social contact is indeed crucial to the development of a self-concept. Gordon Gallup (1997) compared the behavior of chimpanzees raised in normal family groupings with that of chimps who were raised alone in complete social isolation. The socially experienced chimps "passed" the mirror test. However, the socially isolated chimps did not react to their reflections at all; they did not recognize themselves in the mirror, suggesting that they had not developed a sense of self.

KNOWING OURSELVES BY COMPARING OURSELVES TO OTHERS   How do we use others to define ourselves? One way is to measure our own abilities and attitudes by seeing how we stack up against other people. Suppose you work in an office that subscribes to a charity fund. You can deduct from your monthly paycheck whatever you want and have it go to worthy organizations. You decide to donate $50 a month. How generous is this? Should you be feeling particularly proud of your philanthropic nature? One way to answer this question is to compare yourself to others. If you know that your friend Hannah donated only $10 per month, you are likely to feel that you are a very generous person who cares a lot about helping others. If you find out, however, that Hannah donated $100 per month, you probably will not view yourself as quite so generous.

This example illustrates **social comparison theory**, originally formulated by Leon Festinger (1954) and refined by many others (Buunk & Gibbons, 2013; Hoorens & Van Damme, 2012; Suls & Wheeler, 2000; Swencionis & Fiske, 2014). The theory holds that people learn about their own abilities and attitudes by comparing themselves to others and revolves around two important questions: When do people engage in social

Social Comparison Theory
The idea that we learn about our own abilities and attitudes by comparing ourselves to other people

comparison? And with whom do they choose to compare themselves? The answer to the first question is that people socially compare when there is no objective standard to measure themselves against and when they are uncertain about themselves in a particular area (Suls & Fletcher, 1983; Suls & Miller, 1977). If the office donation program is new and you are not sure what amount would be generous, you are especially likely to compare yourself to others.

As to the second question—with whom do people compare themselves?—the answer depends on whether your goal is to get an accurate assessment of your abilities, to determine what the top level is so that you know what to strive for, or to feel better about yourself. To illustrate why these goals matter, suppose that it is the first day of your college Spanish class and you are wondering about your abilities and how well you will do in the class. With whom should you compare yourself: a student who mentions that she lived in Spain for 2 years, a student who has never studied Spanish before, or a student who has a similar background to yours? If your goal is to get the most accurate assessment of your abilities, then it makes sense to compare yourself to the one with the most similar background (Goethals & Darley, 1977; C. T. Miller, 1982; Suls, Martin, & Wheeler, 2000). If the student with a similar background in Spanish is doing well in the class, you probably will too (Thornton & Arrowood, 1966; Wheeler, Koestner, & Driver, 1982).

If your goal is to know what excellence is—the top level to which you can aspire—you are likely to engage in **upward social comparison**, which is comparing yourself to people who are better than you are with regard to a particular trait or ability—namely, the student who lived in Spain for 2 years (C. Johnson, 2012). A problem with upward social comparison, however, is that it can be dispiriting, making us feel inferior. We'll never learn the language like that student who studied in Spain! (Beer, Chester, & Hughes, 2013; Normand & Croizet, 2013; Ratliff & Oishi, 2013). If our goal is to feel good about ourselves and boost our egos, then we are better off engaging in **downward social comparison**—comparing ourselves to people who are worse than we are with regard to a particular trait or ability (Arigo, Suls, & Smyth, 2014; Aspinwall & Taylor, 1993; Wehrens et al., 2010). That is, if you compare your performance in the class to that of the student who is taking Spanish for the first time, you will likely feel good about your own abilities. As another example, when interviewed by researchers, the vast majority of patients with cancer spontaneously compared themselves to other patients who were more ill than they were, presumably as a way of making themselves feel more optimistic about the course of their own disease (Wood, Taylor, & Lichtman, 1985).

Another way we can feel better about ourselves is to compare our current performance with our own past performance. In a sense, people use downward social comparison here as well, though the point of comparison is a "past self," not someone else. In one study, people made themselves feel better by comparing their current self with a past self who was worse off. One student, for example, said that her "college self" was more outgoing and sociable than her "high school self," who had been shy and reserved (Ross & Wilson, 2003; Wilson & Ross, 2000).

In short, the nature of our goals determines who we compare ourselves to. When we want an accurate assessment of our abilities and opinions, we compare ourselves to people who are similar to us. When we want information about what we can strive toward, we make upward social comparisons, though doing so can make us feel inferior. When our goal is to make ourselves feel better, we compare ourselves to those who are less fortunate (including our past selves); such downward comparisons make us look better.

KNOWING OURSELVES BY ADOPTING OTHER PEOPLE'S VIEWS As we just saw, sometimes we use other people as a measuring stick to assess our own abilities. When it comes to our views of the social world, however, often we adopt the views

Upward Social Comparison

Comparing ourselves to people who are better than we are with regard to a particular trait or ability

Downward Social Comparison

Comparing ourselves to people who are worse than we are with regard to a particular trait or ability

our friends hold. Have you ever noticed that people who hang out together tend to see the world in the same way? Maybe the roommates in the apartment across the hall all tend to support liberal policies and enjoy watching *House of Cards*, whereas the roommates in the apartment next door are Libertarians and big fans of *Game of Thrones*. One explanation for people holding common views, of course, is that "birds of a feather flock together"—that is, people who have similar views are attracted to each other and are more likely to become friends than are people who have dissimilar views. In Chapter 10, we will see evidence for this "birds of a feather" hypothesis (Newcomb, 1961).

But it is also true that people adopt the views of the people they hang out with, at least under certain conditions. Charles Cooley (1902) called this the "looking glass self," by which he meant that we see ourselves and the social world through the eyes of other people and often adopt those views. According to recent research, this is especially true when two people want to get along with each other (Hardin & Higgins, 1996; Huntsinger & Sinclair, 2010; Shteynberg, 2010; Skorinko & Sinclair, 2013). If a close friend thinks that *Game of Thrones* is the best television show ever made, you will probably like it as well.

Perhaps it seems obvious that friends influence what each other thinks. What is surprising, however, is that such **social tuning**—the process whereby people adopt another person's attitudes—can happen even when we meet someone for the first time, *if* we want to get along with that person. And, social tuning can happen unconsciously. Consider, for example, a study by Stacey Sinclair and her colleagues (Sinclair et al., 2005). College students took part individually, and half of the time the experimenter wore a T-shirt that expressed antiracism views ("eracism") and half of the time she did not. The question was, did the participants unconsciously "tune" their views to the experimenter, such that they adopted her anti-racist views when she was wearing the "eracism" T-shirt?

Social Tuning

The process whereby people adopt another person's attitudes

The researchers hypothesized that this would only occur when participants liked the experimenter and wanted to get along with her. To find out, they varied how likeable the experimenter was. In the likable condition she thanked students for participating and offered them some candy from a bowl, whereas in the unlikable condition she pushed the bowl of candy to the side and exclaimed, "Just ignore this; some of the experimenters in my lab like to give subjects candy for their participation, but I think you are lucky just to get credit" (Sinclair et al., 2005, p. 588). Thus, to reiterate, half of the time the experimenter wore the "eracism" T-shirt and half the time she did not. And, in each of those conditions, she was likeable half of the time and unlikeable the other half.

The next step was to measure whether participants unconsciously adopted the experimenters' anti-racist views when she wore the eracism T-shirt. To do so, the researchers administered a test of automatic prejudice on a computer. The details of this test need not concern us here; we will discuss such tests in Chapters 7 and 13. The important point for now is that although participants didn't know what the test was measuring, it assessed their level of unconscious bias toward Blacks. As hypothesized, when the experimenter was likeable, participants showed less automatic prejudice when she was wearing the antiracism T-shirt than when she was not (see the left-hand side of Figure 5.7; low scores on the measure indicate an absence of prejudice). Without even knowing it, participants "tuned" their views toward the experimenter's.

What about when the experimenter was unlikable? As seen on the right side of Figure 5.7, participants seemed to react *against* her views: They showed *more* automatic prejudice when she was wearing the antiracist T-shirt than when she was not. These results show that we tend to automatically adopt the views of people we like but automatically reject the views of people we do not.

Figure 5.7 Social Tuning to a Likable Experimenter

Participants took a test of automatic prejudice toward Black people, after interacting with an experimenter who wore an antiracism T-shirt or a blank T-shirt and who was either likable or unlikable. When the experimenter was likable (see the left side of the graph), participants showed less automatic prejudice when she was wearing the antiracism T-shirt than when she was not (the lower the number on the scale, the lower the anti-Black prejudice). When the experimenter was unlikable (see the right side of the graph), participants reacted against her views: They showed more automatic prejudice when she was wearing the antiracist T-shirt than when she was not. These results show that people tend to automatically adopt the views of people they like, but automatically reject the views of people they do not.

(Adapted from Sinclair, Lowery, Hardin, & Colangelo, 2005)

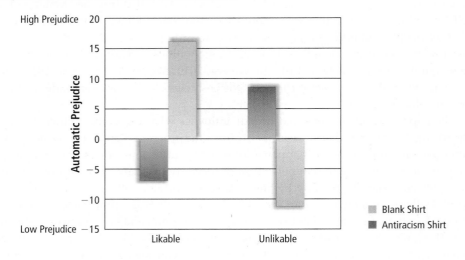

Review Questions

1. When people focus attention on themselves, they
   a. evaluate and compare their behavior to their internal standards and values.
   b. are less likely to drink alcohol or engage in binge eating.
   c. are less likely to follow their moral standards.
   d. almost always like what they see about themselves.

2. Suppose that your friend Meghan says, "If I get less than 8 hours of sleep, I'm in a terrible mood the next day." Based on research in social psychology, what is the best conclusion about her statement?
   a. She is probably right because people generally know why they feel the way they do.
   b. She is probably wrong because people rarely know why they feel the way they do.
   c. She is likely to be right only if she first made a list of all the reasons why she is in a good mood or bad mood on a typical day.
   d. Her statement is probably based on a causal theory that may or may not be true.

3. Which of the following statements best illustrates self-perception theory?
   a. "I might not know why, but I know what I like."
   b. "I often don't know what I like until I see what I do."
   c. "I like classical music because my wife is always playing it."
   d. "I get a warm feeling inside when I listen to my favorite songs."

4. Suppose you are a parent and want your children to do well in school. Which of the following is likely to work the best?
   a. Tell them that they were born with a lot of academic talent.
   b. Tell them that academic ability is something that they can cultivate and grow if they work hard.
   c. When they are young, give them money for every book they read.
   d. Tell them that intelligence is inherited and that there is a lot of it in your family.

5. Under which of the following conditions is Khalid most likely to feel the romantic attraction toward Heather?
   a. Khalid isn't sure whether he wants to go out with Heather, so he spends time introspecting about why he feels the way he does about her.
   b. Khalid isn't sure whether he wants to go out with Heather, but he agrees to do so after Heather's roommate says she will help him with his calculus homework if he does.
   c. Khalid and Heather go for a long run together. After a couple of hours, when they are well-rested, Heather gives Khalid a hug and tells him that she really likes him.
   d. Khalid and Heather nearly get into a serious car accident, and both are terrified. Then Heather gives Khalid a hug and tells him that she really likes him.

6. Mariana is a sophomore in high school who is trying out for the varsity softball team. To get an accurate assessment of her softball abilities, she should compare her abilities to:

   a. a senior who was the best player on the team last year.

   b. a sophomore who has less experience playing softball than Mariana has.

   c. the coach of the team.

   d. a sophomore who has about the same amount of experience playing softball as Marianna has.

7. Which of the following is true about social tuning?

   a. People decide consciously about whether to agree with someone else's attitudes.

   b. People will adopt someone else's attitudes only if they largely agree with that position to start with.

   c. People are especially likely to adopt someone else's attitudes when they want to get along with that person.

   d. Members of Western cultures are more likely to engage in social tuning than members of East Asian cultures.

Self-Control: The Executive Function of the Self

LO 5.3 Compare when people are likely to succeed at self-control and when they are likely to fail.

Is there something you would rather be doing right now than reading this book? Go ahead, admit it: you would just as soon be hanging out with your friends, watching something on *Netflix*, or taking a nap. Still there? If so, then you are exerting **self-control**, which is the ability to subdue immediate desires (e.g., to take a nap) to achieve long-term goals (e.g., finish this chapter and do well in your class).

An important function of the self is to be the chief executive who sets goals and makes choices about what to do in the present and in the future (Carver & Scheier, 1998; Kotabe & Hoffmann, 2015; Mischel, Zeiss, & Ebbesen, 1972; Vohs & Baumeister, 2011). We appear to be the only species, for example, that can imagine events that have not yet occurred and engage in long-term planning, and it is the self that does this planning and exerts control over our actions (Gilbert, 2006; Gilbert & Wilson, 2007). Sometimes this is easy because the path to our goal is clear and easy to achieve. But more often it's hard, because to get what we want (e.g., a good grade in a class) we need to avoid short-term pleasures that would get in the way (e.g., those *Netflix* videos). Regulating our behavior and choices in optimal ways is often easier said than done, as anyone who has been on a diet or quit a bad habit knows. But take heart, social psychologists have identified some strategies that can improve self-control.

Let's first take a look at what *doesn't* work. It is not helpful to avoid temptations simply by trying not to think about them. In fact, the more we try not to think about something, such as an ex-boyfriend or the ice cream beckoning from the freezer, the more those very thoughts keep coming to mind (Baird et al., 2013; Wegner, 1992, 1994). Second, it doesn't work well simply to focus on the long-term goal and how important it is to us (Webb & Sherran, 2006). Well, then, what does work?

First, it helps to form specific **implementation intentions** in advance of a situation in which we will need to exert self-control, making specific plans about where, when, and how we will fulfill a goal and avoid temptations (Gollwitzer, 2014; Oettingen & Reininger, 2016). That is, instead of saying to yourself, "I really want to get a good grade in my psychology class," make specific "if–then" plans that specify how and when you will study and how you will avoid temptations. For example, you might make these plans: "I'm going to the library on Thursday after dinner, and if my roommate texts me and says I should join her at a party that night, I'll tell her that I'll meet up with her after I'm done studying." Get specific and plan how you will overcome obstacles in your way.

Second, it works well to arrange our environments so that we avoid temptations in the first place (Duckworth, Gendler, & Gross, 2016). If you think it will be too hard to ignore your roommate's text, then turn off your phone and store it in your backpack until you are done studying. If it will be too hard to avoid the ice cream in the freezer,

Self-Control

The ability to subdue immediate desires to achieve long-term goals

Implementation Intentions

People's specific plans about where, when, and how they will fulfill a goal and avoid temptations

then don't put ice cream in the freezer. If you take notes on a laptop in a lecture class, but often find yourself checking social media instead, then put your laptop away and try taking notes by hand instead.

Lastly—and we warn you that this one is controversial—it might help to make sure that you are well-rested when trying to exert self-control (Baumeister, Vohs, & Tice, 2007). According to this view self-control requires energy, and spending this energy on one task, such as avoiding the ice cream in the freezer, limits the amount of energy you have to exert self-control on something else, such as deciding to study instead of going to a party. In one experiment, for example, people who were instructed to suppress a thought (don't think about a White bear) were worse at trying to regulate their emotions on a second task (try not to laugh while watching a comedy film) as compared to people who did not first have to suppress their thoughts (Muraven, Tice, & Baumeister, 1998). Although the tasks were quite different, the researchers suggest that the first one depleted the resource that people use to control their behaviors and feelings, making it difficult to engage in a subsequent act of self-control.

Although several studies have demonstrated this "depletion effect," researchers recently failed to replicate one of them and a lively controversy has ensued over whether spending energy on one self-control task really does make it harder to engage in a subsequent self-control task (Baumeister & Vohs, 2016; Carter et al., 2015; Cunningham & Baumeister, 2016; Dang, 2016; Hagger et al., 2016). Undoubtedly more replication projects will be done to resolve this controversy.

Meanwhile, we can say with more certainty that it matters how much people *believe* that willpower is a limited resource that is easily depleted (Egan, Hirt, & Karpen, 2012). People who believe that willpower is an unlimited resource are better able to keep going and avoid being depleted by a difficult task, as long as the task is not too demanding (Clarkson et al., 2016; Job et al., 2015; Job, Dweck, & Walton, 2010; Vohs, Baumeister, & Schmeichel, 2012). So, if your goal is to finish this chapter and do well on your next psychology test, despite other temptations, try to adopt the belief that you have all the energy you need to do so.

Review Questions

1. One afternoon at work Rachel has a meeting with her boss, who is wearing the silliest-looking outfit Rachel has ever seen. Rachel is tempted to laugh and make fun of her boss, but she knows this would be a bad idea. Under which of the following conditions would Rachel be most likely to resist the temptation to make fun of her boss?
   a. Rachel spent all morning writing a difficult report and believes that willpower is a limited resource.
   b. Rachel spent all morning writing a difficult report, but she believes that willpower is an unlimited resource and that she thus has a lot of it.
   c. Rachel says to herself over and over, "Don't think about the boss's outfit!"
   d. Rachel says to herself, "Remember that the most important thing is not to insult my boss."

2. Eduardo is tempted to eat some of his roommate's cookies, even though his roommate told him not to. Under which of the following conditions would Eduardo be mostly likely to resist the temptation to eat the cookies?

   a. It's the afternoon, and Eduardo has had a busy morning.
   b. Eduardo believes that willpower is fixed resource and that people have a limited amount of it.
   c. Eduardo went to the gym that morning and had a good workout.
   d. Eduardo puts the cookies in a cupboard so he doesn't have to look at them.

3. Tarek needs do his laundry but has been very busy. Under which of the following conditions is he most likely to do his laundry in the next few days?
   a. He says to himself, "I'll do my laundry at 7:00 P.M. tomorrow, and if my roommate says we should play video games then, I'll ask him if we can do that later."
   b. He vows to do it at some point the next day.
   c. He vows to do it sometime in the next 2 days.
   d. He vows not to think about video games the next day so that he doesn't spend time doing that instead of doing his laundry.

Impression Management: All the World's a Stage

LO 5.4   Describe how people portray themselves so that others will see them as they want to be seen.

The last function of the self we will consider in this chapter is **impression management**, which is the attempt by people to get others to see them the way they want to be seen (Bolino, Long, & Turnley, 2016; Goffman, 1959; Schlenker, 2003). Everyone wants to put their best foot forward and be liked by others, and many of us do so by posting flattering pictures of ourselves on Instagram or Facebook, or drawing attention to ourselves with clever Tweets. But few go to the extremes that some politicians have. In 1991, for example, David Duke decided to run for governor of Louisiana as a mainstream conservative Republican. He had some obstacles to overcome in convincing people to vote for him because for most of his adult life he had been a White supremacist and an anti-Semite who in 1989 had sold Nazi literature from his office (Applebome, 1991). To improve his appeal, he claimed that he no longer supported Nazi ideology or the Ku Klux Klan, of which he had been a leader (or "grand wizard") in the 1970s. He also tried to improve his appearance by undergoing facial cosmetic surgery. Duke's campaign rhetoric didn't fool too many Louisiana voters. They perceived the same racist message disguised in new clothes, and he was defeated by the Democratic candidate Edwin Edwards. In 2003, he was sentenced to 15 months in federal prison for allegedly using funds raised from supporters for personal investments and gambling (Murr & Smalley, 2003).

Though few politicians attempt as extreme a makeover as David Duke did, managing public opinion is hardly a new concept in politics, or, for that matter, among celebrities of all stripes. Selena Gomez and Miley Cyrus, for example, transformed themselves from child actor on kids' television shows to mature pop stars. And, as noted previously, all of us attempt to put the best possible spin on our actions and manage the impressions others have of us, both on social media and in our everyday lives. As Erving Goffman (1959) pointed out, we are all like stage actors who are trying our best to convince the "audience" (the people around us) that we are a certain way, even if we really are not.

Impression Management

The attempt by people to get others to see them as they want to be seen

Impression management in action: In the 1970s, David Duke was a leader in the Ku Klux Klan; in 1991, he ran for governor of Louisiana as a mainstream conservative Republican. A remarkable change occurred in Duke's presentation of self during this time.

Watch SURVIVAL TIPS! AVOIDING SELF-HANDICAPPING

Ingratiation and Self-Handicapping

People have many different impression management strategies (Jones & Pittman, 1982). One is **ingratiation**—using flattery or praise to make yourself likable to another, often a person of higher status (Jones & Wortman, 1973; Proost et al., 2010; Romero-Canyas et al., 2010). We can ingratiate through compliments, by agreeing with another's ideas, by commiserating and offering sympathy, and so on. If your boss drones on at a staff meeting, nearly putting the entire office to sleep, and you say, "Great job today, Sue. Loved your presentation," you are probably ingratiating. Ingratiation

Ingratiation

The process whereby people flatter, praise, and generally try to make themselves likable to another person, often of higher status

Self-Handicapping

The strategy whereby people create obstacles and excuses for themselves so that if they do poorly on a task, they can avoid blaming themselves

is a powerful technique because we all enjoy having someone be nice to us—which is what the ingratiator is good at. However, such a ploy can backfire if the recipient of your ingratiation senses that you're being insincere (Jones, 1964; Kauffman & Steiner, 1968).

The strategy that has attracted the most research attention is **self-handicapping**. In this case, people create obstacles and excuses for themselves so that if they do poorly on a task, they can avoid blaming themselves. Doing poorly or failing at a task is damaging to your self-esteem. In fact, just doing less well than you expected or than you have in the past can be upsetting, even if it is a good performance. How can you prevent this disappointment? Self-handicapping is a rather surprising solution: You can set up excuses before the fact, just in case you do poorly (Schwinger et al., 2014; Snyder et al., 2014; Wusik & Axsom, 2016).

Let's say it's the night before the final exam in one of your courses. It's a difficult course, required for your major, and one in which you'd really like to do well. A sensible strategy would be to eat a good dinner, study intensively, and then go to bed early and get a good night's sleep. The self-handicapping strategy would be to blow off

Celebrities often make a deliberate attempt to transform their public image. Selena Gomez started out as a child actor on kids' television shows, such as Barney and Friends (pictured in pink-striped shirt) and various Disney sitcoms, but then transformed herself into a pop star with quite a different image.

studying and instead do some heavy partying, and then wander into the exam the next morning bleary-eyed and muddle-headed. If you don't do well on the exam, you have an excuse to offer to others to explain your performance, one that deflects the potential negative internal attribution they might otherwise make (that you're not smart). If you ace the exam, well, so much the better—you did it under adverse conditions (hungover and no sleep), which suggests that you are especially bright and talented.

There are two major ways in which people self-handicap. In its more extreme form, called *behavioral self-handicapping*, people act in ways that reduce the likelihood that they will succeed on a task so that if they fail, they can blame it on the obstacles they created rather than on their lack of ability. The obstacles people have been found to use include drugs, alcohol, reduced effort on a task, and failure to prepare for an important event (Deppe & Harackiewicz, 1996; Lupien, Seery, & Almonte, 2010). Interestingly, research shows that men are more likely to engage in behavioral self-handicapping than are women (Hirt & McCrea, 2009; McCrea, Hirt, & Milner, 2008).

The second type, called *reported self-handicapping*, is less extreme. Rather than creating obstacles to success, people devise ready-made excuses in case they fail (Eyink, Hirt, Hendrix, & Galante, 2017; Hendrix & Hirt, 2009). We might not go out partying before an important exam, but we might complain that we are not feeling well. People can arm themselves with all kinds of excuses: They blame their shyness, test anxiety, bad moods, physical symptoms, and adverse events from their past.

A problem with preparing ourselves with excuses in advance, however, is that we may come to believe these excuses and hence exert less effort on the task. Why work hard at something if you are going to do poorly anyway? Self-handicapping may prevent unflattering attributions for our failures, but it often has the perverse effect of causing the poor performance we feared to begin with. Further, even if self-handicappers avoid unflattering attributions about their performance (e.g., people thinking they aren't smart), they risk being disliked by their peers. People do not like others whom they perceive as engaging in self-handicapping strategies (Hirt, McCrea, & Boris, 2003; Rhodewalt et al., 1995). Women are particularly critical of other people who self-handicap. Thus, as we saw earlier, women are less likely to engage in the kind of self-handicapping in which they put obstacles in their own way, and they are more critical of others who do so (Hirt & McCrea, 2009; McCrea, Hirt, & Milner 2008). Why? Research shows that women place more value on trying hard to achieve something than men do and thus are more critical of people who seem not to try hard and then make up excuses for doing poorly.

Culture, Impression Management, and Self-Enhancement

People in all cultures are concerned with the impression they make on others, but the nature of this concern and the impression management strategies people use differ considerably from culture to culture (Lalwani & Shavitt, 2009). We have seen, for example, that people in Asian cultures tend to have a more interdependent view of themselves than people in Western cultures do. One consequence of this identity is that "saving face," or avoiding public embarrassment, is extremely important in Asian cultures. In Japan, people are very concerned that they have the "right" guests at their weddings and the appropriate number of mourners at the funerals of their loved ones—so concerned, in fact, that if guests or mourners are unavailable, they may go to a local "convenience agency" and rent some. These agencies (*benriya*) have employees who are willing to pretend—for a fee—that they are your closest friends. A woman named Hiroko, for example, worried that too few guests would attend her second wedding. No problem—she rented six, including a man to pose as her boss, at a cost of $1,500. Her "boss" even delivered a flattering speech about her at the wedding (Jordan & Sullivan, 1995). Although such impression management strategies might seem extreme to Western readers, the desire to manage public impressions is just as strong in the West (as exemplified by David Duke's attempts to change the way the public viewed him).

Review Questions

1. Amanda is at a team picnic with her coach and fellow soccer players. Which of the following is the best example of ingratiation?
   a. Amanda tells her coach that the quinoa salad he made was delicious, even though she thinks it tasted like dirt.
   b. Amanda tells her coach that he might want to consider taking cooking lessons.
   c. Amanda tells the 10-year-old brother of one her teammates that she likes his sneakers, which she thinks look great.
   d. The coach tells Amanda that she is a good player but should keep practicing to improve her skills.

2. Ben is worried that he will do poorly on his psychology test. Which of the following is the best example of *behavioral* self-handicapping?
   a. He spends a couple of extra hours studying, and right before the test, he tells his friends that he studied really hard.
   b. Instead of studying the night before, he stays up late watching movies on his computer. Right before the test, he tells his friends that he saw some great movies instead of studying.
   c. He spends a couple of extra hours studying. Then, right before the test, he tells his friends that he isn't feeling very well.
   d. Right before the test, Ben tells the professor that her class is the best one he's ever taken.

3. Ben is worried that he will do poorly on his psychology test. Which of the following is the best example of *reported* self-handicapping?
   a. He spends a couple of extra hours studying, and right before the test, he tells his friends that he studied really hard.
   b. Instead of studying the night before, he stays up late watching movies on his computer. Right before the test, he tells his friends that he saw some great movies instead of studying.
   c. He spends a couple of extra hours studying. Then, right before the test, he tells his friends that he isn't feeling very well.
   d. Right before the test, Ben tells the professor that her class is the best one he's ever taken.

Summary

LO 5.1   Describe the self-concept and how it develops.

- **The Origins and Nature of the Self-Concept** Studies show that great apes such as chimpanzees and orangutans have a rudimentary sense of self because they pass the mirror self-recognition test, whereas lesser apes do not. In humans, self-recognition develops at around 18 to 24 months of age, and by adolescence the self-concept becomes much more complex. As people grow older, their sense of self develops into a full-blown *self-concept*, defined as the overall set of beliefs that people have about their personal attributes. In adulthood, people view morality as central to the self-concept, more so than cognitive processes or desires.

  - **Cultural Influences on the Self-Concept** People who grow up in Western cultures tend to have an independent view of the self, whereas people who grow up in Asian cultures tend to have an interdependent view of the self.

  - **Functions of the Self** The self serves four functions: *self-knowledge*, our beliefs about who we are and the way in which we formulate and organize this information; *self-control*, the way in which we make plans and execute decisions; *impression management*, how we present ourselves to other people; and *self-esteem*, the way we feel about ourselves.

LO 5.2   Explain how people use introspection, observations of their own behavior, or other people to know themselves.

- **Self-Knowledge** How do people come to know who they are and why they do what they do?

  - **Knowing Ourselves Through Introspection** One way we attempt to learn about our own feelings, motives, and emotions is with introspection, which is looking inward to examine the "inside information" that we—and we alone—have about our thoughts, feelings, and motives. According to *self-awareness theory*, when people focus on themselves, they evaluate and compare their current behavior to their internal standards and values. When people introspect about why they feel the way they do, they often use causal theories, many of which are learned from one's culture.

  - **Knowing Ourselves by Observing Our Own Behavior** People also gain self-knowledge by observing their own behavior. Self-perception theory argues that when our attitudes and feelings are uncertain or ambiguous, we infer these states by observing our own behavior and the situation in which it occurs. The *Two-Factor Theory of Emotion* argues that emotional experience is often the result of a two-step self-perception process in which people first experience arousal and then seek an appropriate explanation for it. Sometimes people make mistaken inferences about what is causing them to be aroused, resulting in the *misattribution of arousal*. An *overjustification effect* occurs when people focus on the extrinsic reasons for their behavior and underestimate their intrinsic reasons. Further, some people have a *fixed mindset* about their abilities, which is the idea that they have a set amount of the ability that cannot change. Others have a *growth mindset*, the idea that their abilities are malleable qualities that they can cultivate and grow. People with a fixed mindset are more likely to give up after setbacks and are less likely to work on and hone their skills, whereas people with a growth mindset view setbacks as opportunities to improve through hard work.

- **Using Other People to Know Ourselves** Our self-concepts are shaped by the people around us. According to *social comparison theory*, we learn about our own abilities and attitudes by comparing ourselves to other people. In addition, according to research on *social tuning*, people automatically adopt the attitudes of those they like and want to interact with.

LO 5.3 Compare when people are likely to succeed at self-control and when they are likely to fail.

- **Self-Control: The Executive Function of the Self** In general, exerting energy on one task limits people's ability to exert self-control on a subsequent task. However, simply believing that willpower is an unlimited resource can help people exert more self-control, as can praying in advance of a task and forming implementation intentions.

LO 5.4 Describe how people portray themselves so that others will see them as they want to be seen.

- **Impression Management: All the World's a Stage** People try to get others to see them as they want to be seen.
  - **Ingratiation and Self-Handicapping** People have many different *impression management* strategies. One is *ingratiation*—using flattery or praise to make yourself likable to another, often a person of higher status. Another is *self-handicapping*, whereby people create obstacles and excuses for themselves so that if they do poorly on a task, they can avoid blaming themselves.
  - **Culture, Impression Management, and Self-Enhancement** The desire to manage the image we present to others is strong in all cultures, although the kinds of images we want to present depend on the culture in which we live.

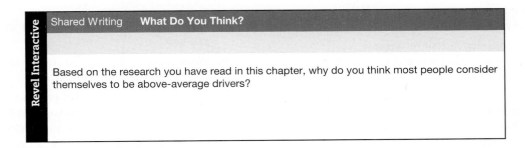

Revel Interactive

Shared Writing   **What Do You Think?**

Based on the research you have read in this chapter, why do you think most people consider themselves to be above-average drivers?

Test Yourself

1. Which of the following statements is *least* true, according to research on self-knowledge?

   a. The best way to "know thyself" is to look inward, introspecting about ourselves.

   b. Sometimes the best way to know ourselves is to see what we do.

   c. We often try to figure out ourselves by comparing ourselves to others.

   d. One way we know ourselves is by using theories we learn from our culture.

2. Which of the following is *not* a function of the self?

   a. Self-knowledge

   b. Self-control

   c. Impression management

   d. Self-criticism

3. In which state are people most likely to have an interdependent sense of self?

    a. Massachusetts

    b. Connecticut

    c. Oklahoma

    d. Alabama

4. On Halloween, you decide to do an experiment. When the trick-or-treaters arrive at your house, you have them stand in a line on your front porch. You stay outside with the group and let each child enter your house individually. You tell them they can take *one* piece of candy from the bowl that is sitting on a table. Half of the time you put the candy bowl in front of a big mirror. The other half of the time there is no mirror present. All of the children may be tempted to take more than one piece of candy. Which children will be *least* likely to give in to temptation?

    a. Those in the mirror condition

    b. Those who are between 7 and 9 years old

    c. Those in the no-mirror condition

    d. Those who experience downward social comparison

5. Which of the following is *most* true?

    a. Every member of a Western culture has an independent view of the self, and every member of an Asian culture has an interdependent view of the self.

    b. Members of Western cultures are more likely to have an interdependent sense of self than are members of Asian cultures.

    c. People with independent selves can easily appreciate what it is like to have an interdependent self.

    d. People who live in parts of the United States and Canada that were settled by Europeans more recently have more of an independent sense of self than people who live in parts of those countries that were settled earlier.

6. Your little sister enjoys taking time out of her day to make bead necklaces. A birthday party is coming up, and you decide you want to give a necklace to each person at the party. She offers to make a necklace for each of your friends, but for added motivation you give her a dollar for each one she makes. Which of the following is most likely to happen?

    a. After the party, your sister will enjoy making beads *more* than she did before because you gave her a reward.

    b. After the party, your sister will enjoy making beads *less* than she did before because you rewarded her for something she already liked to do.

    c. Because your sister already enjoys making beads, paying her for making them will have no effect on how much she enjoys the activity.

    d. Paying your sister for making the beads will increase her self-awareness.

7. Catherine did very well on her math test. Which of the following statements should her mother tell her to increase the chances that Catherine will not give up on math if it later becomes more difficult for her?

    a. "You really worked hard for this test, and your hard work paid off!"

    b. "You are such a smart kid, you excel in everything you do!"

    c. "You are so good in math, you obviously have a gift for this!"

    d. "I'm so glad to see you are doing better than all your classmates!"

8. Your friend Jane is interning at a law firm. When you ask her how it's going, she says, "I'm feeling good about it because I'm doing much better than the intern who started a month after me." What kind of social comparison is Jane making?

    a. Upward social comparison

    b. Downward social comparison

    c. Impression comparison

    d. Self-knowledge comparison

9. Which of the following is *most* true about self-handicapping?

    a. People who self-handicap tend to try harder at a task.

    b. Women are more likely to engage in reported self-handicapping than are men.

    c. Women are more critical of people who self-handicap than are men and are less likely to engage in behavioral self-handicapping than are men.

    d. East Asians are more likely to engage in behavioral self-handicapping than are westerners.

10. Elise wants to increase her ability at self-control, such as by spending more time studying. Which of the following is *most* likely to work?

    a. When she is studying, she should try hard to suppress thoughts about the party she could have gone to.

    b. Just before it is time for her to study, she should do something that requires a lot of concentration, such as a difficult puzzle.

    c. She should eat a small, sugary snack before studying.

    d. She should adopt the belief that willpower is an unlimited resource.

Chapter 6
Cognitive Dissonance and the Need to Protect Our Self-Esteem

 ## Chapter Outline and Learning Objectives

WHAT DO YOU THINK?

Revel Interactive	Survey **What Do You Think?**	
	SURVEY	RESULTS
	Have you ever joined a group that required you to do something humiliating or dangerous in order to gain membership? ○ Yes ○ No	

It was shocking news: 39 people were found dead at a luxury estate in Rancho Santa Fe, California, participants in a mass suicide. All were members of an obscure cult called Heaven's Gate. Each body was laid out neatly, feet clad in brand-new Black Nikes, face covered with a purple shroud. The cult members died willingly and peacefully, leaving behind videotapes describing their reasons for suicide: They believed that the Hale-Bopp Comet, a recently discovered comet streaking across the night skies, was their ticket to a new life in paradise. They were convinced that in Hale-Bopp's wake was a gigantic spaceship whose mission was to carry them off to a new incarnation. To be picked up by the spaceship, they first needed to rid themselves of their current "containers." That is, they needed to leave their own bodies by ending their lives. Alas, no spaceship ever came.

Several weeks before the mass suicide, some members of the cult purchased an expensive, high-powered telescope. They wanted to get a clearer view of the comet and the spaceship that they believed was traveling behind it. A few days later, they returned the telescope and politely asked for their money back. When the store manager asked them if they had problems with the scope, they replied, "Well, gosh, we found the comet, but we can't find anything following it" (Ferris, 1997). Although the store manager tried to convince them that there was nothing wrong with the telescope and that nothing was following the comet, they remained unconvinced. Given their premise, their logic was impeccable: We know an alien spaceship is following behind the Hale-Bopp Comet. If an expensive telescope has failed to reveal that spaceship, then there is something wrong with the telescope.

Their thinking might strike you as strange, irrational, or stupid, but, generally speaking, the members of the Heaven's Gate cult were none of those things. Neighbors who knew them considered them pleasant, smart, and reasonable.

What is the process by which intelligent, sane people can succumb to such fantastic thinking and self-destructive behavior? In this chapter, we will show you why their behavior is not mysterious after all. It is simply an extreme example of a normal human tendency: the need to justify our actions and commitments.

The Theory of Cognitive Dissonance: Protecting Our Self-Esteem

LO 6.1 Explain what cognitive dissonance is and how people avoid dissonance to maintain a positive self-image.

As we saw in Chapter 1, *self-esteem* refers to people's evaluations of their own self-worth—that is, the extent to which they view themselves as good, competent, and decent. And as noted in the previous chapter, an important function of the self is to maintain our self-esteem. Indeed, during the past several decades, social psychologists have discovered that one of the most powerful determinants of human behavior stems from our need to preserve a stable, positive self-image (Aronson, 1969, 1998; Boden, Berenbaum, & Gross, 2016; Kappes & Crockett, 2017; Randles et al., 2015; Steele, 1988; Tesser & Cornell, 1991). In this chapter we will see some surprising ways in which we manage to do this.

Many years ago, Leon Festinger (1957) developed and investigated the precise workings of what is arguably social psychology's most important and most provocative theory: the theory of **cognitive dissonance**. He defined dissonance as the discomfort that is caused when two cognitions conflict, or when our behavior conflicts with our attitudes. This definition was revised by Festinger's student Elliot Aronson, who showed that dissonance is most painful, and we are most motivated to reduce it, when one of the dissonant cognitions challenge our self-esteem (Aronson, 1969). In other words, it is not just any kind of inconsistency that causes dissonance, but actions or beliefs that challenge our very sense of self-worth.

When that happens, watch out—dissonance results. But unlike the ways we satisfy other uncomfortable feelings—for example, reducing hunger or thirst by eating or drinking—the path to reducing dissonance is not always simple or obvious. In fact, it can lead to fascinating changes in the way we think about the world and the way we behave.

For example, consider something that millions of people do several times a day: smoke cigarettes. If you are a smoker, you are likely to experience dissonance because you know that smoking significantly increases the risks of lung cancer, emphysema, and earlier death, which is pretty much the ultimate threat to our self-esteem. Dissonance is an uncomfortable psychological state that people want to get rid of; who wants to be reminded of all the bad effects of smoking each time they light up?

How can we reduce dissonance? There are three basic ways (see Figure 6.1):

- By changing our behavior to bring it in line with the dissonant cognition.
- By attempting to justify our behavior through changing one of the dissonant cognitions.
- By attempting to justify our behavior by adding new cognitions.

With smoking, for example, the most direct way to reduce the dissonance this causes is to change your behavior and give up cigarettes. Your behavior would then be consistent with your knowledge of the link between smoking and cancer. Although many people have succeeded in quitting, it's not easy; many others have tried and failed. What do these people do? It would be wrong to assume that they simply swallow hard, light up, and prepare to die. They don't. Instead, many smokers reduce the dissonance in by changing one of the dissonant cognitions, namely the belief that it is harmful. Researchers found, for example, that heavy smokers who tried to quit and failed managed to lower their perception of the dangers of smoking. In this way, they could continue to smoke without feeling terrible about it (Gibbons, Eggleston, & Benthin, 1997). Some smokers, even pregnant women who hear warnings all the time, convince themselves that the data linking nicotine to cancer are inconclusive, or that if they just cut down, the chance of harm is reduced (Naughton, Eborall, & Sutton, 2012). Smokers' self-justifications like these turn up in studies all over the world (Fotuhi et al., 2013).

If smokers can't manage to deny all the evidence that smoking is harmful they can reduce their dissonance in a third way, namely by adding new cognitions (or beliefs) that make them

Cognitive Dissonance

The discomfort that people feel when they behave in ways that threaten their self-esteem

Watch WHAT IS COGNITIVE DISSONANCE?

Revel Video

Figure 6.1 How We Reduce Cognitive Dissonance

There are three basic ways of reducing dissonance: change your behavior, change your cognition, or add a new cognition.

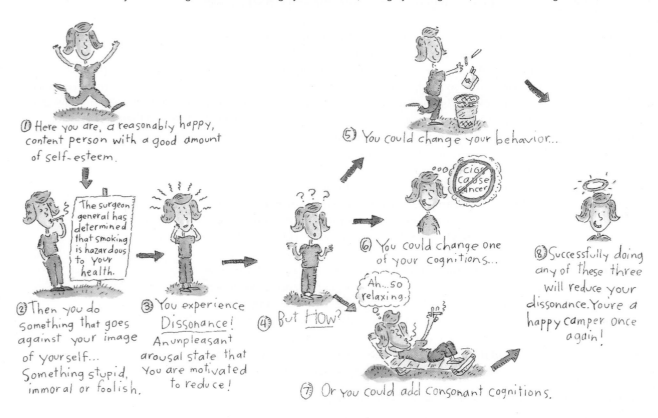

① Here you are, a reasonably happy, content person with a good amount of self-esteem.

② Then you do something that goes against your image of yourself... Something stupid, immoral or foolish.

③ You experience Dissonance! An unpleasant arousal state that you are motivated to reduce!

④ But HOW?

⑤ You could change your behavior...

⑥ You could change one of your cognitions...

⑦ Or you could add consonant cognitions.

Ah...so relaxing

⑧ Successfully doing any of these three will reduce your dissonance. You're a happy camper once again!

feel better. A study of more than 360 adolescent smokers, for example, found that the greater their dependence on smoking and the greater the trouble they had quitting, the more justifications they came up with to keep smoking (Kleinjan, van den Eijnden, & Engels, 2009). And smokers can come up with some pretty creative justifications. They say that smoking is worth the risk of cancer and emphysema because it is so enjoyable, and besides it relaxes them and reduces nervous tension and in this way actually improves their health. Teenagers who smoke usually justify their actions by adding such cognitions as "Smoking is cool"; "I want to be like my friends"; "I'm healthy; nothing is going to happen to me"; "Adults are always on my back about stuff I do," or "Who wants to live to be 90 anyway?"

When you understand dissonance, you will see it in action all around you. Here are a couple of examples.

- What happens to the people who predict the end of the world, sell their possessions and await doomsday at the top of a mountain, and who then, fortunately, turn out to be wrong? Rarely would they admit they were foolish or gullible. Instead, they would be more likely to reduce dissonance by saying something like, "Our prediction was accurate; we just used numbers from the wrong chapter of the Bible."

- How do people resolve the dissonance when two central aspects of their identity conflict? In one study, researchers wondered how gay men who were strongly identified with their Christian church

Teenagers who smoke usually justify their actions with such cognitions as "Smoking is cool"; "I want to be like my friends"; "in movies, everyone smokes"; "I'm healthy; nothing is going to happen to me"; or "adults are always on my back about stuff I do."

dealt with anti-gay pronouncements from their ministers. One way to resolve dissonance would be to change their behavior—that is, to change their church or even leave their religion. But those who decide to stay in the church resolve dissonance by focusing on the shortcomings of the minister; for example, they say, "It's not my religion that promotes this prejudice—it's the bigotry of this particular preacher" (Pitt, 2010).

In short, understanding dissonance explains why so much of human thinking is not rational, but *rationalizing*. No matter how smart they are, people who are in the midst of reducing dissonance are so involved with convincing themselves that they are right that they frequently end up behaving irrationally and maladaptively (Stanovich, West, & Toplak, 2013). Sometimes, of course, we pursue new information because we want to be accurate in our views or make the wisest decisions. But once we are committed to our views and beliefs, most of us distort new information in a way that confirms them (Hart et al., 2009; Ross, 2010). People who don't want to give up scientifically discredited ideas (such as the mistaken belief that vaccines cause autism), or who receive bad news about their health can be equally "creative" in denying evidence and reducing their discomfort (Aronson, 1997; Croyle & Jemmott, 1990; Pratarelli, 2012).

It may not come as any surprise to you that people rationalize their actions and interpret facts to fit what they already believe. The way in which people reduce cognitive dissonance is often surprising, however, and has far-reaching implications—as we will now see.

Decisions, Decisions, Decisions

Every time we make a decision we experience dissonance. How come? Suppose you are about to buy a car, but you are torn between a large SUV and a smaller, compact car. You know that each has advantages and disadvantages: You can pack the SUV full of luggage during long trips and it has plenty of power, but it gets poor mileage and it's hard to park. The compact is a lot less roomy, but it is less expensive, is a lot zippier to drive, and has a pretty good repair record. Before you decide, you will probably get as much information as you can. You go online and read what the experts say about each model's safety, gas consumption, and reliability. You'll talk with friends who own an SUV or a compact. You'll probably visit automobile dealers to test-drive the vehicles to see how each one feels. All this predecision behavior is perfectly rational.

Let's assume you decide to buy the compact. We predict that your behavior will change in a specific way: You will begin to think more and more about the number of miles to the gallon as though it were the most important thing in the world. Simultaneously, you will almost certainly downplay the fact that you don't have a lot of room. How does this shift in thinking happen?

DISTORTING OUR LIKES AND DISLIKES In any decision, whether it is between two cars, two colleges, or two potential lovers, the chosen alternative is seldom entirely positive and the rejected alternative is seldom entirely negative. After the decision, your cognition that you are a smart person is dissonant with all the negative things about the car, college, or lover you chose; that cognition is also dissonant with all the *positive* aspects of the car, college, or lover you *rejected*. We call this **postdecision dissonance**. Cognitive dissonance theory predicts that to help yourself feel better about the decision, you will do some unconscious mental work to try to reduce the dissonance.

What kind of work? In a classic experiment, Jack Brehm (1956) posed as a representative of a consumer testing service and asked women to rate the attractiveness and desirability of several kinds of small appliances. Each woman was told that as a reward for having participated in the survey, she could have one of the appliances as a

Postdecision Dissonance

Dissonance aroused after making a decision, typically reduced by enhancing the attractiveness of the chosen alternative and devaluating the rejected alternatives

Watch SURVIVAL TIPS! BEING MORE RATIONAL ABOUT POST-DECISION DISSONANCE REDUCTION

gift. She was given a choice between two of the products she had rated as being equally attractive. After she made her decision, each woman was asked to rerate all the products. After receiving the appliance of their choice, the women rated its attractiveness somewhat higher than they had the first time. Not only that, but they drastically lowered their rating of the appliance they might have chosen but decided to reject.

In this way, following a decision, we reduce dissonance to make ourselves feel better about the choice we made.

THE PERMANENCE OF THE DECISION The more important the decision, the greater the dissonance. Deciding which car to buy is clearly more important than deciding between a toaster and a coffeemaker; deciding which person to marry is clearly more important than deciding which car to buy. Decisions also vary in terms of how permanent they are—that is, how difficult they are to revoke. It is a lot easier to trade in your new car for another one than it is to get out of an unhappy marriage. The more permanent and irrevocable the decision, the stronger is the need to reduce dissonance (Bullens et al., 2013).

In a simple but clever experiment, social psychologists intercepted people at a racetrack who were on their way to place $2 bets and asked them how certain they were that their horses would win (Knox & Inkster, 1968). The investigators also approached other bettors just as they were leaving the $2 window, after having placed their bets, and asked them the same question. Almost invariably, people who had already placed their bets gave their horses a much better chance of winning than did those who had not yet placed their bets. Because only a few minutes separated one group from another, nothing real had occurred to increase the probability of winning; the only thing that had changed was the finality of the decision—and hence the dissonance it produced.

Other investigators tested the irrevocability hypothesis in a photography class (Gilbert & Ebert, 2002). In their study, participants were recruited through an advertisement for students interested in learning photography while taking part in a psychology experiment. Students were informed that they would shoot some photographs and print two of them. They would rate the two photographs and then get to choose one to keep. The other would be kept for administrative reasons. The students were randomly assigned to one of two conditions. In Condition One, students were informed that they had the option of exchanging photographs within a 5-day period; in Condition Two, students were told that their choice was final. The researchers found that *prior* to making the choice between the two photographs, the students liked them equally. The experimenters then contacted the students several days after they had made their choice to find out if those who had a choice to exchange photographs liked the one they chose more or less than did those in the no-choice (irrevocable) condition. And, indeed, the students who had the option of exchanging photographs liked the one they finally ended up with less than did those who made the final choice on the first day.

Life is full of tough choices, like where to attend college. Once we make a decision, we often inflate the importance of positive aspects of our choice (i.e., the college we selected) and minimize the positive aspects of the other alternatives (i.e., the colleges we didn't select).

Interestingly, when students were asked to predict whether keeping their options open would make them more or less happy with their decision, they predicted that keeping their options open would make them happier. They were wrong. Because they underestimated the discomfort of dissonance, they failed to realize that the finality of the decision would make them happier.

CREATING THE ILLUSION OF IRREVO-CABILITY The irrevocability of a decision always increases dissonance and the motivation to reduce it. Because of this, unscrupulous salespeople have developed techniques for creating the illusion that irrevocability exists. One such technique is called **lowballing** (Cialdini, 2009; Cialdini et al., 1978; Weyant, 1996). Robert Cialdini, a distinguished social psychologist, temporarily joined the sales force of an automobile dealership to observe this technique closely. Here's how it works: You enter an automobile showroom intent on buying a particular car. Having already priced it at several dealerships and online, you know you can purchase it for about $18,000. You are approached by a personable middle-aged man who tells you he can sell you one for $17,679. Excited by the bargain, you agree to write out a check for the down payment so that he can take it to the manager as proof that you are a serious customer. Meanwhile, you imagine yourself driving home in your shiny new bargain. Ten minutes later the salesperson returns, looking forlorn. He tells you that in his zeal to give you a good deal, he miscalculated and the sales manager caught it. The price of the car comes to $18,178. You are disappointed. Moreover, you are pretty sure you can get it a bit cheaper elsewhere. The decision to buy is not irrevocable. And yet in this situation far more people will go ahead with the deal than if the original asking price had been $18,178, even though the reason for buying the car from this particular dealer—the bargain price—no longer exists.

There are at least three reasons that lowballing works. First, although the customer's decision to buy is reversible, a commitment of sorts does exist. Signing a check for a down payment creates the illusion of irrevocability, even though, if the car buyer thought about it, he or she would quickly realize that it is a non-binding contract. In the world of high-pressure sales, however, even a temporary illusion can have real consequences. Second, the feeling of commitment triggered the anticipation of an exciting event: driving out with a new car. To have had the anticipated event thwarted (by not going ahead with the deal) would have been a big letdown. Third, although the final price is substantially higher than the customer thought it would be, it is probably only slightly higher than the price at another dealership. Under these circumstances, the customer in effect says, "Oh, what the heck. I'm here, I've already filled out the forms, I've written out the check—why wait?" Thus, by using dissonance reduction and the illusion of irrevocability, high-pressure salespeople increase the probability that you will decide to buy their product at their price.

All sales are final. When will these customers be happier with their new car: 10 minutes before the purchase or 10 minutes after?

Lowballing

An unscrupulous strategy whereby a salesperson induces a customer to agree to purchase a product at a low cost, subsequently claims it was an error, and then raises the price; frequently, the customer will agree to make the purchase at the inflated price

The Justification of Effort

Suppose you put in a lot of effort to get into a particular club and it turns out to be a totally worthless organization, consisting of boring, pompous people doing trivial activities. You would feel pretty foolish, wouldn't you? A sensible person doesn't work hard

The harsh training required to become a marine is likely to increase the recruits' feelings of cohesiveness and their pride in the corps.

Justification of Effort

The tendency for individuals to increase their liking for something they have worked hard to attain

---

Figure 6.2 The Justification of Effort

The more effort we put into becoming members of a group, and the tougher the initiation, the more we will like the group we have just joined—even if it turns out to be a dud.

(Based on Aronson & Mills, 1959)

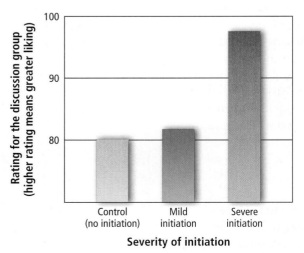

to gain something worthless. Such a circumstance would produce significant dissonance; your cognition that you are a sensible, adept human being is dissonant with your cognition that you worked hard to get into a dismal group. How would you reduce this dissonance?

You might start by finding a way to convince yourself that the club and the people in it are nicer, more interesting, and more worthwhile than they appeared to be at first glance. How can one turn boring people into interesting people and a trivial club into a worthwhile one? Easy. Even the most boring people and trivial clubs have some redeeming qualities. Activities and behaviors are open to a variety of interpretations; if we are motivated to see the best in people and things, we will tend to interpret these ambiguities in a positive way. We call this the **justification of effort**, the tendency for individuals to increase their liking for something they have worked hard to attain.

In a classic experiment, Elliot Aronson and Judson Mills (1959) explored the link between effort and dissonance reduction. In their experiment, college students volunteered to join a group that would be meeting regularly to discuss various aspects of the psychology of sex. To be admitted to the group, they volunteered to go through a screening procedure. For one-third of the participants, the procedure was demanding and unpleasant; for another third, it was only mildly unpleasant; and the final third was admitted to the group without any screening at all.

Each participant was then allowed to listen in on a discussion being conducted by the members of the group he or she would be joining. Although the participants were led to believe that the discussion was live, they were listening to a prerecorded tape. The taped discussion was designed to be as dull as possible. After the discussion was over, each participant was asked to rate it in terms of how much he or she liked it, how interesting it was, how intelligent the participants were, and so forth.

As you can see in Figure 6.2, participants who expended little or no effort to get into the group did not enjoy the discussion much. They were able to see it for what it was—a dull and boring waste of time. Participants who went through a severe initiation, however, convinced themselves that the same discussion, though not as scintillating as they had hoped, was dotted with interesting and provocative tidbits and was therefore, in the main, a worthwhile experience. These findings have been replicated under a variety of circumstances: people justify the effort they have expended on everything from a worthless self-help program to a course of physical therapy (Coleman, 2010; Cooper, 1980; Gerard & Mathewson, 1966).

A stunning example of the justification of effort comes from an observational study done in the multicultural nation of Mauritius (Xygalatas et al., 2013). Every year, the Hindu festival of Thaipusam includes two rituals: a low-ordeal ritual involving singing and collective prayer, and a severe-ordeal ritual called Kavadi. "Severe" is something of an understatement. Participants are pierced with needles, hooks, and skewers, carry heavy bundles, and drag carts that are attached by hooks to their skin for more than 4 hours. Then they climb a mountain barefooted to reach the temple of Murugan. Afterward, the researchers gave both the low-ordeal and severe-ordeal participants the opportunity to anonymously donate money

to the temple. The severe-ordeal ritual produced much higher donations than the low-ordeal ritual. The greater the men's pain, the
greater their commitment to the temple.

We are not suggesting that most people enjoy difficult, unpleasant, painful experiences, nor that people enjoy things that are merely
associated with unpleasant experiences. Rather, if a person *chooses* to
go through a demanding or an unpleasant experience to attain some
goal or object, that goal or object becomes more attractive. Consider
the sex discussion group described above: If you were walking
to the meeting and a passing car splashed mud all over you, you
would not like that group any better. However, if you volunteered to
jump into a mud puddle to be admitted to a group that turned out to
be boring, you *would* like the group better.

Counterattitudinal Behavior

Suppose your friend Jen shows you her expensive new dress and
asks your opinion. You think it is atrocious and are about to say so,
advising her to exchange it before another human being sees her
in it, when she tells you that she has already had it altered, which
means that she cannot return it. What do you say? Chances are you
go through something like the following thought process: "Jen seems
so happy and excited about her new dress. She spent a lot of money
for it, and she can't take it back. If I say what I think, I'll upset her."

So you tell Jen that you like her dress. Do you experience much
dissonance? We doubt it. Many thoughts are consistent with having
told this lie, as outlined in your reasoning. In effect, your cognition that it is important
not to embarrass or cause pain to people you like provides ample **external justification** for having told a harmless lie.

What happens, though, if you say something you don't believe when there *isn't* a
good external justification for being insincere? What if your friend Jen is wealthy and
can easily afford to absorb the cost of her ugly new dress? What if she sincerely wanted
to know what you thought? Now the external justifications—the reasons for lying to
Jen about the dress—are minimal. If you still withhold your true opinion, you will
experience dissonance. When you can't find external justification for your behavior,
you will attempt to find **internal justification**; you will try to reduce dissonance by
changing something about yourself, such as your attitude or behavior.

How can you do this? You might begin by looking harder for positive things
about the dress that you hadn't noticed before. Within a short time, your attitude
toward the dress will have moved in the direction of the statement you made. And
that is how *saying becomes believing*. Its official term is **counterattitudinal behavior**.
It occurs when we act in a way that conflicts with our private beliefs or attitudes,
such as claiming to have an opinion or attitude that differs from our true beliefs.
When we do this with little external justification—that is, without being motivated
by something outside of ourselves—what we believe begins to conform more and
more to the lie we told.

This proposition was first tested in a groundbreaking experiment by Leon
Festinger and J. Merrill Carlsmith (1959). College students were induced to spend
an hour performing a series of excruciatingly boring and repetitive tasks. The experimenter then told them that the purpose of the study was to determine whether
or not people would perform better if they had been informed in advance that
the tasks were interesting. They were each informed that they had been randomly
assigned to the control condition—that is, they had not been told anything in advance. However, he explained, the next participant, a young woman who was just

A devotee participates in a ritual
as part of the Hindu festival of
Thaipusam.

External Justification

A reason or an explanation for
dissonant personal behavior that
resides outside the individual
(e.g., to receive a large reward or
avoid a severe punishment)

Internal Justification

The reduction of dissonance by
changing something about oneself
(e.g., one's attitude or behavior)

Counterattitudinal Behavior

Acting in a way that runs counter
to one's private belief or attitude

Celebrities are paid huge amounts of money to endorse products. Do you think that Brad Pitt believes the message he is delivering about this expensive watch? Is the justification for his endorsement internal or external?

arriving in the anteroom, was going to be in the experimental condition. The researcher said that he needed to convince her that the task was going to be interesting and enjoyable. Because it was much more convincing if a fellow student rather than the experimenter delivered this message, would the participant do so? Thus, with his request, the experimenter induced the participants to lie about the task to another student—this was the counterattitudinal behavior.

Half of the students were offered $20 for telling the lie (a large external justification), while the others were offered only $1 for telling the lie (a small external justification). After the experiment was over, an interviewer asked the lie-tellers how much they had enjoyed the tasks they had performed earlier in the experiment. The results validated the hypothesis: The students who had been paid $20 for lying—that is, for saying that the tasks had been enjoyable—rated the activities as the dull and boring experiences they were. But those who were paid only $1 for saying the task was enjoyable rated the task as significantly more enjoyable. In other words, people who had received an abundance of external justification for lying told the lie but didn't believe it, whereas those who told the lie without much external justification convinced themselves that what they said was closer to the truth.

COUNTERATTITUDINAL BEHAVIOR TOWARD CONSEQUENTIAL ISSUES Can you induce a person to change an attitude about things that matter, such as racial prejudice and eating disorders? The answer is yes, and you do it not by offering people large incentives to write a forceful essay supporting issues such as equal rights, but with small incentives. For example, white college students were asked to write a counterattitudinal essay publicly endorsing a controversial proposal at their university to double the amount of funds available for academic scholarships for African American students. Because the total amount of funds was limited, this meant cutting by half the amount of scholarship funds available to White students. As you might imagine, this was a highly dissonant situation. How might the students reduce dissonance? As they came up with more and more reasons in writing their essays, they ended up convincing themselves that they believed in that policy. And not only did they believe in it, but their general attitude toward African Americans became more favorable (Leippe & Eisenstadt, 1994, 1998). Later experiments with diverse groups have gotten the same results, including a decrease in White prejudice toward Asian students (Son Hing, Li, & Zanna, 2002) and, in Germany, German prejudice toward Turks (Heitland & Bohner, 2010).

Counterattitudinal behavior has also been effective in dealing with a far different problem: eating disorders (such as bulimia) and dissatisfaction with one's body. In American society, where super-thin is considered beautiful, many women are dissatisfied with the size and shape of their own bodies, and the internalization of the media's "thin ideal" leads not only to unhappiness but also to constant dieting and

Watch COGNITIVE DISSONANCE: FESTINGER AND CARLSMITH

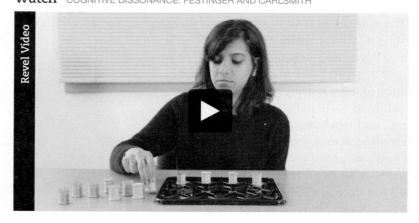

Revel Video

eating disorders. In an effort to disrupt this pattern, a team of researchers assigned high school and college women with body-image concerns to either dissonance or control conditions. Women in the dissonance condition had to compose their own arguments against the "thin is beautiful" image they had bought into, by writing an essay describing the emotional and physical costs of pursuing an unrealistic ideal body and by acting out that argument to discourage other women from pursuing the thin ideal. Participants in the dissonance condition showed significant increases in their satisfaction with their bodies, as well as a decrease in chronic dieting, and were happier and less anxious than women in the control conditions. Moreover, their risk of developing bulimia was greatly reduced (Green et al., 2017; McMillan, Stice, & Rohde, 2011; Stice et al., 2006). This intervention has been replicated with 12- and 13-year-old English girls (Halliwell & Diedrichs, 2014) as well as with Latina, African American, and Asian/Hawaiian/Pacific Island women (Rodriguez et al., 2008; Stice et al., 2008).

THE BEN FRANKLIN EFFECT: JUSTIFYING ACTS OF KINDNESS What happens when you do a favor for someone? In particular, what happens when you are subtly induced to do a favor for a person you don't much like? This is an example of counterattitudinal behavior, because you are acting in a way (helping someone) that is contrary to your beliefs (you don't like the person you are helping). As a result, will you like the person more—or less? Dissonance theory predicts that you will like the person more after doing the favor. Can you say why?

This phenomenon has been a part of folk wisdom for a long time. Benjamin Franklin confessed to having used it as a political strategy. While serving in the Pennsylvania state legislature, Franklin was disturbed by the political opposition and animosity of a fellow legislator. So he set out to win him over. He didn't do it by "paying any servile respect to him," Franklin wrote, but rather by inducing his opponent to do him a favor—namely, lending him a rare book he was eager to read. Franklin returned the book promptly with a warm thank-you letter. "When we next met in the House," Franklin said, "he spoke to me (which he had never done before), and with great civility; and he ever after manifested a readiness to serve me on all occasions, so that we became great friends and our friendship continued to his death. This is another instance of the truth of an old maxim I had learned, which says, 'He that has once done you a kindness will be more ready to do you another than he whom you yourself have obliged'" (Franklin, 1868/1900).

Benjamin Franklin was clearly pleased with the success of his blatantly manipulative strategy. But as scientists, we should not be convinced by his anecdote. We have no way to know whether Franklin's success was due to this particular gambit or to his all-around charm. That is why it is important to design and conduct an experiment that controls for such things as charm. Such an experiment was finally done—240 years later (Jecker & Landy, 1969). Students participated in an intellectual contest that enabled them to win a substantial sum of money. Afterward, the experimenter approached one-third of them, explaining that he was using his own funds for the experiment and was running short, which meant he might be forced to close down the experiment prematurely. He asked, "As a special favor to me, would you mind returning the money you won?" The same request was made to a different group of subjects, not by the experimenter but by the departmental secretary, who asked them if they would return the money as a special favor to the (impersonal) psychology department's research fund, which was running low. The remaining participants were not asked to return their winnings at all. Finally, all of the participants were asked to fill out a questionnaire that included an opportunity to rate the experimenter. Participants who had been cajoled into doing a special favor for him found him the most attractive; they convinced themselves that he was a wonderful, deserving fellow. The others thought he was a pretty nice guy but not anywhere near as wonderful as did the people who had been asked to do him a favor. (See Figure 6.3.)

Figure 6.3 The Justification of Kindness

If we have done someone a personal favor (blue bar), we are likely to feel more positively toward that person than if we don't do the favor (orange bar) or do the favor because of an impersonal request (yellow bar).

(Based on data in Jecker & Landy, 1969)

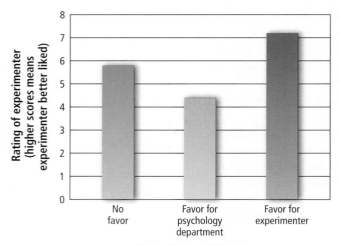

The recipient of the favor

Without realizing it, Ben Franklin may have been the first dissonance theorist.

The Ben Franklin effect starts early. In a study of 4-year-olds, some children were told to give away some of their playful stickers to a doggie puppet "who is sad today"; others had a choice of how much to share with Doggie. The children who were allowed to choose to be generous to the sad doggie later shared more with a new puppet named Ellie, compared with children who had been instructed to share (Chernyak & Kushnir, 2013). Once children saw themselves as generous kids, they continued to behave generously.

We can see how helping others might change our self-concept and our attitudes. But what if you harmed another person; what then might happen to your feelings?

DEHUMANIZING THE ENEMY: JUSTIFYING CRUELTY A sad, though universal, phenomenon is that all cultures are inclined to dehumanize their enemies by calling them cruel names and regarding them as "vermin," "animals," "brutes," and other nonhuman creatures. During World War II, Americans referred to the German people as "krauts" and portrayed them as brutes; they called the Japanese people "Japs" and portrayed them as sneaky and diabolical; during the Vietnam War, American soldiers referred to the Vietnamese as "gooks"; after the wars in Iraq and Afghanistan began, some Americans began referring to the enemy as "ragheads" because of the turbans or other headdresses that many Arabs and Muslims wear. The use of such language is a way of reducing dissonance: "I am a good person, but we are fighting and killing these other people; therefore, they must deserve whatever they get, because they aren't fully human like us."

The other side, of course, is doing the same thing: for example, the Nazis portrayed the Jews as rats; during the Cold War, the Soviets called the Americans greedy capitalist pigs; after 9/11, anti-American demonstrators called Americans "rabid dogs." Of course, many people have always held negative and prejudiced attitudes toward certain groups, and calling them names might make it easier for them to treat them ruthlessly.

How can we be certain that self-justification can *follow* acts of cruelty rather than only cause them? To test this possibility, the social psychologist must temporarily step back from the helter-skelter of the real world and enter the more controlled setting of the experimental laboratory.

In one of the first demonstrations of the way that the need to reduce dissonance can change attitudes toward an innocent victim, experimenters asked students, one at a time, to watch a young man (a confederate) being interviewed, and then describe their general opinions of him. Next, the students were instructed to provide the confederate with an analysis of his shortcomings as a human being (Davis & Jones, 1960). After telling him things they knew were certain to hurt him—that they thought he was shallow, untrustworthy, and boring—they convinced themselves that he deserved to be insulted this way, as a way of reducing their dissonance over insulting him.

It may seem a big jump from the laboratory to the battlefield, but dissonance links them. Imagine these two scenes: (1) A soldier kills an enemy combatant in the heat of battle; (2) a soldier kills an innocent civilian who happened to be in the wrong

Try It!

The Internal Consequences of Doing Good

When you walk down a city street and see people sitting on the sidewalk, panhandling, or pushing their possessions around in a shopping cart, how do you feel about them? Think about it for a few moments, and write down your feelings. If you are like most college students, your list will reflect some mixed feelings. That is, you probably feel some compassion but also think these people are a nuisance; if they tried harder, they could get their

lives together. The next time you see a person panhandling or digging through the trash looking for food, take the initiative and give him or her a dollar. Say something friendly; wish them well. Note your feelings. Is there a change in how you perceive the person? Analyze any changes you notice in terms of cognitive dissonance theory.

place at the wrong time. Which soldier will experience more dissonance? We predict that it would be the latter. Why? When engaged in combat with an enemy soldier, it is a "you or me" situation; if the soldier had not killed the enemy, the enemy might have killed him. So even though wounding or killing another person is rarely taken lightly, it is not nearly so heavy a burden, and the dissonance not nearly as great, as it would be if the victim were an unarmed civilian, a child, or an old person. Indeed, one of the major causes of posttraumatic stress disorder (PTSD) among veterans of the wars in Afghanistan and Iraq is their inability to reduce dissonance over killing children, bystanders, and other innocent civilians—a result of the difficulty of fighting a war against counterinsurgents rather than a formal army (Klug et al., 2011).

This prediction, about which soldier will feel the greater dissonance, was supported by the results of an experiment in which volunteers had to administer a supposedly painful electric shock to a fellow student (Berscheid, Boye, & Walster, 1968). As one might expect, these students disparaged their victim as a result of having administered the shock—they felt compelled to justify their actions. But half of the students were told that there would be a reversal: the other student would be given the opportunity to retaliate against them at a later time. Those who were led to believe that their victim would be able to retaliate later did not insult the victim. Because the victim was going to be able to even the score, there was little dissonance, and therefore the harm-doers had no need to belittle their victim to convince themselves that he or she deserved it. The results of these laboratory experiments suggest that, during a war, military personnel are more likely to demean civilian victims (because these individuals can't retaliate) than military victims.

Think of the chilling implications of this research: namely, that people who perform acts of cruelty do not come out unscathed. Success at dehumanizing the victim virtually guarantees a continuation or even an escalation of the cruelty: It sets up an endless chain of violence, followed by self-justification (in the form of dehumanizing and blaming the victim), followed by still more violence and dehumanization (Sturman, 2012). In this manner, unbelievable acts of human cruelty can escalate, such as the Nazi "Final Solution" that led to the murder of six million European Jews. But all tyrants and oppressors reduce dissonance by justifying their cruelty. This is how they sleep at night.

Riccardo Orizio (2003) interviewed seven dictators, and every one of them claimed that everything they did— torturing or murdering their opponents, blocking free elections, starving their citizens, looting their nation's wealth,

Unfortunately, dehumanizing outgroups, religious groups, and minorities continues to this day.

After he cheats, this student will try to convince himself that everybody would cheat if they had the chance.

launching genocidal wars—was done for the good of their country. The alternative, they said, was chaos, anarchy, and bloodshed. Far from seeing themselves as despots, they saw themselves as self-sacrificing patriots. Sound familiar? Consider President Bashar al-Assad's account of the civil war in Syria, which, since 2011, has cost the lives of more than 400,000 people, including thousands of children. President Assad is widely believed to have perpetrated deadly chemical attacks on his own citizens. His rationale? In a 2013 speech Assad stated that, "Defending the homeland is a duty that isn't up for discussion and is a legal, constitutional and religious duty and is the only choice" (Bashar al-Assad's Opera House Speech, 2013).

JUSTIFYING OUR OWN IMMORAL ACTS   Another kind of counterattitudinal behavior occurs when we decide to act contrary to our moral beliefs. Take the issue of cheating on an exam. Suppose you are a college sophomore taking the final exam in organic chemistry. Ever since you can remember, you have wanted to be a surgeon, and you think that your admission to medical school will depend heavily on how well you do in this course. A key question involves some material you know fairly well, but because so much is riding on this exam, you feel acute anxiety and draw a blank. You happen to be sitting next to one of the best students in the class, and when you glance at her paper you see that she is just completing her answer to the crucial question. You avert your eyes. Your conscience tells you it's wrong to cheat, and yet, if you don't cheat, you are certain to get a poor grade. And if you get a poor grade, you are convinced you won't get into medical school.

Regardless of whether or not you decide to cheat, the threat to your self-esteem arouses dissonance. If you cheat, your belief or cognition "I am a decent, moral person" is dissonant with your cognition "I have just committed an immoral act." If you decide to resist temptation, your cognition "I want to become a surgeon" is dissonant with your cognition "I could have nailed a good grade and admission to medical school, but I chose not to. Wow, was I stupid!"

Suppose that after a difficult struggle, you decide to cheat. According to dissonance theory, it is likely that you would try to justify the action by finding a way to minimize its negative aspects. In this case, an efficient path to reducing dissonance would involve changing your attitude about cheating. You would adopt a more lenient attitude toward cheating, convincing yourself that it is a victimless crime that doesn't hurt anybody, that everybody does it, and that, therefore it's not really so bad.

Suppose, by contrast, after a difficult struggle, you decide not to cheat. How would you reduce your dissonance? Again, you could change your attitude about the morality of the act, but this time in the opposite direction. That is, to justify giving up a good grade, you convince yourself that cheating is a heinous sin, that it's one of the lowest things a person can do, and that cheaters should be rooted out and severely punished. What has happened is not merely a rationalization of your own behavior, but a change in your system of values. Thus, two people acting in two different ways could have started out with almost identical attitudes toward cheating. One came within an inch of cheating but decided to resist, while the other came within an inch of resisting but decided to cheat. After they

Watch   "DISSONANCE AND SELF-CONCEPT" – CHEATING AND DISSONANCE

Revel Video

"Don't cheat."   "Don't be a cheater."

had made their decisions, however, their attitudes toward cheating would diverge sharply as a consequence of their actions.

Avoiding Temptations

How do we get people to avoid doing tempting things they're really not supposed to do? All societies run, in part, on punishment or the threat of punishment. You know, while cruising down the highway at 80 miles an hour, that if a cop spots you, you will pay a substantial fine, and if you get caught often, you will lose your license. So we learn to obey the speed limit when patrol cars are in the vicinity. By the same token, schoolchildren know that if they cheat on an exam and get caught, they could be humiliated by the teacher and punished. So they learn not to cheat while the teacher is in the room, watching them. But does harsh punishment teach adults to want to obey the speed limit? Does it teach children to value honest behavior? We don't think so. All it teaches is to try to avoid getting caught.

Parents can intervene to stop one sibling from tormenting another right at the moment of the incident, but what might they do to make it less likely to happen in the future?

Let's look at bullying. Imagine that you are the parent of a 6-year-old boy who often beats up his 4-year-old brother. You've tried to reason with your older son, to no avail. In an attempt to make him a nicer person (and to preserve the health and welfare of his little brother), you begin to punish him for his aggressiveness. As a parent, you can use a range of punishments, from the mild (a stern look) to the severe (forcing the child to stand in the corner for 2 hours, depriving him of privileges for a month). The more severe the threat, the higher the likelihood the youngster will cease and desist—while you are watching him. But he may hit his brother again as soon as you are out of sight. Just as most drivers learn to watch for the highway patrol while speeding, your 6-year-old still enjoys bullying his little brother; he has merely learned not to do it while you are around to punish him. What can you do?

If you used a severe threat, would your child experience much dissonance over the fact that he wasn't bullying his brother? Probably not, because he has *external justification* for not doing it. He implicitly asks himself, "How come I'm not beating up my little brother?" Under severe threat, he has a convincing answer in the form of sufficient external justification: "I'm not beating him up because, if I do, my parents are going to punish me." But what if you dialed back the threat so that it was pretty mild? As long as he still obeys you, your 6-year-old is more likely to experience dissonance. When he asks himself, "How come I'm not beating up my little brother?" he doesn't have a convincing answer, because the threat is so mild that it does not provide a superabundance of justification. This is called **insufficient punishment**. The child is refraining from doing something he wants to do, and although he does have some justification for not doing it, that doesn't seem strong enough to explain his compliance. In this situation, he experiences dissonance; therefore, the child must find another way to justify the fact that he is not hitting his kid brother. The less severe you make the threat, the less external justification there is; the less external justification, the higher the need for internal justification. The child can reduce his dissonance by convincing himself that he doesn't want to beat up his brother. In time, he can go further in his quest for internal justification and decide that beating up little kids is not fun.

To find out if this is what happens, Elliot Aronson and J. Merrill Carlsmith (1963) devised an experiment with preschoolers. They couldn't very well have young children hitting each other for the sake of science, so they decided to perform their experiment with a more benign goal: attempting to change the children's desire to play with some appealing toys. The experimenter first asked each child to rate the attractiveness of several toys. He then pointed to a toy that the child considered

Insufficient Punishment

The dissonance aroused when individuals lack sufficient external justification for having resisted a desired activity or object, usually resulting in individuals devaluing the forbidden activity or object

Figure 6.4 The Forbidden Toy Experiment

Children who had received a threat of mild punishment were far less likely to play with a forbidden toy (orange bar) than children who had received a threat of severe punishment (blue bar). Those given a mild threat had to provide their own justification by devaluing the attractiveness of the toy ("I didn't want to play with it anyhow"). The resulting dissonance reduction lasted for weeks.

(Based on data in Freedman, 1965)

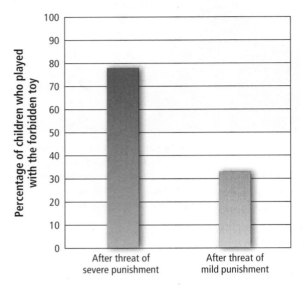

among the most attractive and told the child that he or she was not allowed to play with it. Half of the children were threatened with mild punishment if they disobeyed; the other half were threatened with severe punishment. The experimenter left the room for a few minutes, giving the children the time and opportunity to play with the other toys and to resist the temptation to play with the forbidden toy. None of the children played with the forbidden toy.

Next, the experimenter returned and asked each child to rate how much he or she liked each of the toys. Initially, everyone had wanted to play with the forbidden toy, but during the temptation period, when they had the chance, not one child played with it. Obviously, the children were experiencing dissonance. How did they respond to this uncomfortable feeling? The children who had received a severe threat had ample justification for their restraint. They knew why they hadn't played with the toy, and therefore they had no reason to change their attitude about it. These children continued to rate the forbidden toy as highly desirable; indeed, some even found it more desirable than they had before the threat.

But what about the others? Without much external justification for avoiding the toy—they had little to fear if they played with it—the children in the mild threat condition needed an *internal* justification to reduce their dissonance. Before long, they persuaded themselves that the reason they hadn't played with the toy was that they didn't like it. They rated the forbidden toy as less attractive than they had when the experiment began. That is, they reduced their dissonance over not playing with a fun toy by convincing themselves that the toy wasn't all that great to begin with.

Moreover, the effects of dissonance reduction in young children can be lasting. In a replication of the forbidden-toy experiment, the overwhelming majority of the children who had been mildly threatened for playing with a terrific toy decided, on their own, not to play with it, even when given the chance several *weeks* later; the majority of the children who had been severely threatened played with the forbidden toy as soon as they could (Freedman, 1965). (See Figure 6.4.)

To summarize, a sizable reward or a severe punishment provides strong external justification for an action. They encourage compliance but prevent real attitude change. So if you want a person (your child, for example) to do something or not to do something only once, the best strategy would be to promise a large reward or threaten a severe punishment. But if you want a person to become committed to an attitude or to a behavior, the *smaller* the reward or punishment that will lead to momentary compliance, the *greater* will be the eventual change in attitude and therefore the more permanent the effect (See Table 6.1).

Table 6.1 Internal Versus External Justification for Counterattitudinal Behavior and Avoiding Temptations

Magnitude of Reward or Threats	Counterattitudinal Behavior (People Rewarded for Doing Something They Don't Want to Do)	Avoiding Temptations (People Threatened Punishment for Doing Something They *Want* to Do)
Small (Internal Justification)	Dissonance Resulting in Long-Term Internal Change "Now I really like it"	Dissonance Resulting in Long-Term Internal Change "I really don't like it after all!"
Large (External Justification)	No Dissonance ("I did it for the money, I still really don't like it")	No Dissonance ("I avoided it because of the severe threat; I still really want to do it")

The Hypocrisy Paradigm

Understanding self-justification helps us explain the fascinating, sometimes amusing, sometimes alarming phenomenon of hypocrisy: A famous minister rants against homosexuality but has a gay lover. A politician wages a high-profile campaign against prostitution and then is caught with a high-priced call girl. A woman ends a relationship because her partner had an affair but somehow doesn't consider her own outside affairs as equally serious.

In a series of studies of what they call the "pot calling the kettle black" problem, researchers wondered how people reduce the dissonance of being guilty of ethical violations they condemn in others. Can you guess by now? Hypocrites judge *others* more harshly than do people who have not committed the same unethical acts, and they present *themselves* as being more virtuous and ethical than everyone else. That is, they typically polarize their judgments, seeing more evil in others and more righteousness in themselves (Barkan et al., 2012).

Let's delve a little deeper. It is important to understand how hypocrisy operates because people often behave in ways that run counter to their own beliefs and their best interests. For example, although college students know that sexually transmitted infections (STIs) are serious problems, only a small percentage of sexually active students use condoms. Not a surprise; condoms are inconvenient and unromantic, and they remind people of disease—the last thing they want to be thinking about in the heat of passion. No wonder that sexual behavior is often accompanied by denial: "Sure, STDs are a problem, but not for *me*."

How do you break through this wall of denial? In the 1990s, Elliot Aronson and his students developed a research design they called **hypocrisy induction** (Aronson, Fried, & Stone, 1991; Cooper, 2010; Stone et al., 1994). They asked two groups of college students to compose a speech describing the dangers of AIDS and other STDs, advocating the use of condoms every time a person has sex. In one group, the students merely composed the arguments. In the second group, after composing their arguments, they were to recite them in front of a video camera and were told that an audience of high school students would watch the resulting tape. In addition, half of the students in each group were made mindful of their own failure to use condoms by making a list of the circumstances in which they had found it particularly difficult, awkward, or impossible to use them.

The participants in one group experienced the highest dissonance: those who made a video for high school students after the experimenter got them to think about their own failure to use condoms. Why? They were made aware of their own hypocrisy; they had to deal with the fact that they were preaching behavior that they themselves were not practicing. To remove the hypocrisy and maintain their self-esteem, they would need to start practicing what they were preaching. And that is exactly what the researchers found. When they gave each student the chance to buy condoms cheaply, the students in the hypocrisy condition were far more likely to buy condoms than students in any of the other conditions. Moreover, when the researchers phoned the students several months after the experiment, they found that the effects held. People in the hypocrisy condition—the students who would have felt the most cognitive dissonance—reported far higher use of condoms than did those in the control conditions.

Hypocrisy induction—making people aware of the dissonance between what they are doing and what they are preaching to others—has since been applied to a wide array of problems: getting people to quit smoking, apply sunscreen to prevent skin cancer, stop disordered eating, and manage other health concerns (Cooper, 2012; Freijy & Kothe, 2013; Peterson, Haynes, & Olson, 2008). Hypocrisy induction has even been applied to help drivers who fall victim to road rage, which is responsible for thousands of traffic accidents and fatalities each year. An angry driver typically thinks, "Look at

Hypocrisy Induction

The arousal of dissonance by having individuals make statements that run counter to their behaviors and then reminding them of the inconsistency between what they advocated and their behavior. The purpose is to lead individuals to more responsible behavior.

Understanding dissonance can help us increase people's likelihood of making healthy, safe choices.

that selfish jerk who just cut me off! He's about to get what's coming to him!" Seiji Takaku (2006) decided to apply the hypocrisy–induction paradigm to this problem. He used video to simulate a highway situation in which a driver is cut off by another driver, which frequently causes anger. In the experimental condition, the participants themselves first accidentally cut off another driver, thus being reminded of the fact that we are all capable of making this mistake. Takaku found that when people are reminded of their own fallibility, they are quicker to go from anger to forgiveness than if this reminder is not induced. The reminder reduces their perceived need to retaliate.

You might keep Takaku's method in mind the next time you find yourself fuming in traffic or that anger you feel at *other* people texting and driving.

Dissonance Across Cultures

We can find dissonance operating in almost every part of the world, but it does not always take the same form, and the content of the cognitions that produce it may differ across cultures (e.g., Beauvois & Joule, 1996; Kitayama, Tompson, & Chua, 2014; Sakai, 1999). In "collectivist" societies, where the needs of the group matter more than the needs of a particular person (as in "individualist" societies), dissonance-reducing behavior might be less prevalent, at least on the surface (Kokkoris & Kühnen, 2013; Triandis, 1995). In such cultures, we'd be more likely to find behavior aimed at maintaining group harmony and less likely to see people justifying their own personal misbehavior but more likely to see people experiencing dissonance when their behavior shames or disappoints others.

Japanese social psychologist Haruki Sakai (1999), combining his interest in dissonance with his knowledge of Japanese community orientation, found that, in Japan, many people will vicariously experience dissonance on the part of someone they know and like. The observers' attitudes change to conform to those of their dissonance-reducing friends. Moreover, in subsequent experiments, Japanese participants justified their choices when they felt others were observing them while they were making their decision, but not later; this pattern was reversed for Americans (Imada & Kitayama, 2010). The perceived privacy or public visibility of the choice being made interacts with culture to determine whether dissonance is aroused and the choice needs to be justified.

Nonetheless, most causes of dissonance are international and intergenerational. For example, in multicultural America, immigrant parents and their young-adult children often clash over cultural values: the children want to be like their peers, but their elders want them to be like them. This conflict often creates enormous dissonance in the children because they love their parents but do not embrace all of their values. In a longitudinal study of Vietnamese and Cambodian adolescents in the United States, those who were experiencing the most cognitive dissonance were most likely to get into trouble, do less well in school, and fight more with their parents (Choi, He, & Harachi, 2008).

Review Questions

1. Which of the following techniques relating to *postdecision dissonance* could a clothing store use to increase customer satisfaction?
   a. Cut all prices in half
   b. Ask customers to make a radio ad saying how great the store is
   c. Charge a membership fee to shop at the store
   d. Make all sales final

2. You are selling $30 souvenir books for a club fund-raiser. How could you use the technique of lowballing to improve your sales?
   a. Start by offering the books at $70 each and pretend to bargain with customers, making $30 your "final offer."
   b. Start by selling the books at $25, but once the customer has retrieved his or her checkbook, tell him or her you made a mistake and the books are actually $5 more than you thought.

    c. Offer the customers additional incentives to buy the book, such as free cookies with every purchase.

    d. Start by selling the books at $40, but tell the customer he or she will get $10 back in three weeks.

3. Jake's professor tells Jake that if he is caught cheating on an exam, he will be expelled. Amanda's professor tells her that if she is caught cheating, she will have only to write a short paper about why cheating is wrong. If both students don't cheat, dissonance theory would predict that:

    a. Amanda will feel more honest than Jake will.

    b. Jake will feel more honest than Amanda will.

    c. Amanda and Jake will feel equally honest.

    d. Amanda and Jake will feel equally dishonest because were both threatened in advance.

4. After spending 2 years of tedious work fixing up an old house themselves, Abby and Brian are even more convinced that they made the right choice to buy the place. Their feelings are an example of

    a. counterattitudinal behavior.

    b. insufficient punishment.

    c. the Ben Franklin effect.

    d. justifying their effort.

5. Briana undergoes treatment for drug addiction. After she leaves the clinic, Briana is most likely to stay off drugs if the treatment at the clinic was

    a. involuntary (she was ordered to undergo treatment) and a difficult ordeal.

    b. involuntary (she was ordered to undergo treatment) and an easy experience.

    c. voluntary (she chose to undergo treatment) and an easy experience.

    d. voluntary (she chose to undergo treatment) and a difficult ordeal.

6. Your friend Amy asks you what you think of the shoes she just bought. Privately, you think they are the ugliest shoes you have ever seen, but you tell her you love them. In the past, Amy has always valued your honest opinion and doesn't care that much about the shoes, which were inexpensive. Because the external justification for your fib was ____, you will probably ____.

    a. high, decide you like the shoes

    b. high, maintain your view that the shoes are ugly

    c. low, decide you like the shoes

    d. low, maintain your view that the shoes are ugly

7. Based on the "Ben Franklin effect," you are most likely to increase your liking for Tony when

    a. you lend Tony $10.

    b. Tony lends you $10.

    c. Tony returns the $10 you loaned him.

    d. Tony finds $10.

8. Amanda's parents tell her that if she texts while driving, they will take away her car for a year. Erin's parents tell her that if she texts while driving, they will take her car away for one weekend. Both Amanda and Erin decide not to text while driving. What would dissonance theory predict?

    a. After they go to college and are away from their parents, Erin is more likely to text while driving than Amanda is.

    b. After they go to college and are away from their parents, Amanda is more likely to text while driving than Erin is.

    c. Amanda and Erin will both think that texting while driving is OK; they avoided it so that they wouldn't be punished.

    d. Amanda and Erin will both come to believe that texting while driving is bad.

9. Which of the following statements about culture and cognitive dissonance is true?

    a. Japanese people rarely experience dissonance.

    b. Dissonance occurs everywhere, but culture influences how people experience it.

    c. Cognitive dissonance is a uniquely American phenomenon.

    d. Cognitive dissonance is more likely to occur in collectivist rather than individualist cultures.

Advances and Extensions of Cognitive Dissonance Theory

LO 6.2   **Describe recent advances and extensions of cognitive dissonance theory.**

Throughout this chapter, we've seen that people generally need to see themselves as intelligent, sensible, and decent people who behave with integrity. Social psychologists have continued to explore this basic need to protect our self-esteem in greater depth and in new contexts. What are they finding?

Self-Affirmation Theory

Earlier we said that there are three ways of reducing dissonance: changing our behavior to bring it in line with the dissonant cognition, changing one of the dissonant cognitions to be in line with our behavior, or justifying our behavior by adding new cognitions. Think back to the example of people who are in a state of dissonance because they smoke cigarettes: They can stop smoking (change their behavior), convince themselves that smoking isn't bad for them (change their cognitions to be in line with their behavior), or decide that it's worth it to smoke because it's so enjoyable and who wants to live until their 90 anyway? (adding new cognitions). Sometimes, however, it is not easy to reduce dissonance in any of these ways. As anyone who smoked tobacco knows, it's darn hard to quit. And, it's not easy to convince ourselves that smoking isn't harmful to our health or that we don't really want to live a long life. What is a poor dissonance sufferer to do in this case? Are smokers doomed to wallow in a constant state of dissonance?

Self-Affirmation Theory
The idea that people can reduce threats to their self-esteem by affirming themselves in areas unrelated to the source of the threat

Fortunately not. According to **self-affirmation theory**, people can also reduce dissonance by focusing on and affirming their competence on some dimension *unrelated* to the threat (Aronson, Cohen, & Nail, 1999; Steele, 1988). "Yes, it's true that I smoke," the tobacco user might say, "but I am a great cook" (terrific tennis player, wonderful friend, promising scientist—whatever is important to the person). These justifications may sound silly to the nonsmoker, but not to people trying to reduce their cognitive dissonance. Remember, dissonance results from a threat to our self-esteem, and if we can't reduce that threat directly (e.g., by quitting smoking), we can do so by focusing on how great we are in some completely different area of our lives.

In a series of clever experiments, Claude Steele and his colleagues demonstrated that if you give people an opportunity for self-affirmation before the onset of dissonance, they will often grab it. For example, the researchers replicated Jack Brehm's (1956) classic experiment on postdecision dissonance reduction (Steele, Hoppe, & Gonzales, 1986). They asked students to rank 10 record albums, ostensibly as part of a marketing survey. As a reward, the students were then told that they could keep either their fifth- or sixth-ranked album. Ten minutes after making their choice, they were asked to rate the albums again. You will recall that in Brehm's experiment, after selecting a kitchen appliance, the participants rated the one they had chosen much higher than the one they had rejected. In this manner, they convinced themselves that they had made a smart decision. And that is what the students did in this experiment as well.

But Steele and his colleagues built an additional set of conditions into their experiment. Half of the students were science majors, and half were business majors. Half of the science majors and half of the business majors were asked to put on a white lab coat while participating in the experiment. Why the lab coat? A lab coat is associated with science. Steele and his colleagues suspected that the lab coat would serve a "self-affirmation function" for the science majors but not for the business majors. The results supported their predictions. Whether or not they were wearing a lab coat, business majors reduced dissonance just as the people in Brehm's experiment did: After their choice, they increased their evaluation of the chosen album and decreased their evaluation of the one they had rejected. Similarly, in the absence of a lab coat, science majors reduced their dissonance in the same way. However, science majors who were wearing the lab coat resisted the temptation to distort their perceptions. The lab coat reminded these students that they were promising scientists and thereby short-circuited the need to reduce dissonance by changing their attitudes toward the albums. In effect, they said, "I may have made a dumb choice in record albums, but I can live with that because I have other things going for me; at least I'm a promising scientist!"

How might we apply this in our everyday lives to mitigate threats to our self-esteem? Subsequent research has demonstrated the power of what is called a *values affirmation writing exercise*, which works like this: People are given a list of values, asked to pick the one that is most important to them, and then to write about why that value is important. As simple as this sounds, values affirmation exercises have been shown to have a wide range of lasting positive effects on people's lives, particularly when they allow people to mitigate a threat to one area of their self-esteem (e.g., doing poorly in school) by reminding themselves that there are other parts of their lives that are important to them (e.g., their families; Cohen & Sherman, 2014).

For example, some African American children believe that they "don't have what it takes" to succeed academically, plus they worry that if they do poorly they will confirm negative stereotypes about their intelligence (Steele, 2010). As a result it can be difficult for them to concentrate on their studies. To address this, a team of social psychologists had African American middle-school students complete a values affirmation writing exercise a few times in their classrooms, in which they were given a list of nonacademic values and asked to write about the one that was most important to them (Cohen et al., 2009). Compared to a control group of children who did not do the writing exercise, these students reduced their academic anxiety and did better in school. This increased performance "fed" on itself such that the students who did the values affirmation exercise continued to do better for years to come. Remarkably, they were more likely to go to college than the children in the control group, all as a result of reducing threats to their self-esteem with a simple writing exercise (Goyer et al., 2017; Harackiewicz et al., 2014; Miyake et al., 2010; Sherman et al., 2013). Give the following Try It! a whirl to see how values affirmation writing exercises work.

Try It!

Values Affirmation Writing Exercise

Below is a list of characteristics and values. Please rank them according to how important they are to you, from least important to most important.

____ Being good at art
____ Creativity
____ Relationships with family and friends
____ Government or politics
____ Independence
____ Learning and gaining knowledge
____ Athletic ability

____ Belonging to a social group (such as your community, racial group, or school club)
____ Music
____ Spiritual or religious values
____ Sense of humor

Now choose one of the values from the list and write about why this value is important to you. It is completely up to you which value you pick. Please spend the next several minutes writing about the value you pick, including times it was important to you (please write a full page or more). Don't worry about spelling or punctuation. (Adapted from Silverman, Logel, & Cohen, 2013).

Dissonance in Close Relationships: Self-Evaluation Maintenance Theory

Most dissonance research concerns how our self-image is threatened by our own behavior, such as acting contrary to our attitudes or making a difficult decision. Abraham Tesser and his colleagues have explored how dissonance arises in interpersonal relationships, where we often compare our own accomplishments with someone close to us (e.g., a friend or sibling; Beach et al., 1996; Tesser, 1988).

Suppose you consider yourself a good guitar player—in fact, you typically outshine all of your friends and band mates. Then you move to another town and discover that your favorite new friend plays like Jimi Hendrix. How does that make you feel? You are probably more than a little uneasy about the fact that your new friend outdoes you in your area of expertise.

Now instead suppose that your new best friend is not a guitar hero but a very talented artist. Will you still feel uncomfortable? Undoubtedly not; in fact, you will probably take pleasure in your friend's success. You might even brag to your other friends, "Sophie just sold some of her paintings in a really hot New York gallery!" The difference between these two scenarios is that in the first one, your friend excels at something that is important to you and may even be a central part of how you define yourself. Whatever our most treasured ability, if we meet someone who is better at it than we are, there is likely to be trouble—of the dissonance variety.

According to Tesser's (1988) **self-evaluation maintenance theory**, people will experience dissonance in relationships when three conditions are met: We feel *close* to another person, he or she is *outperforming* us in a particular area, and that area is *central* to our self-esteem. So there is no problem if a close friend outperforms us in an area that is not particularly important to us. In fact, we feel even better about ourselves for having such a talented friend. Dissonance only occurs when a close friend outperforms us on a task that is important to the way we define ourselves.

To reduce this dissonance we can change any one of the three components that produced it. First, we can distance ourselves from the person who outperforms us, deciding that he or she is not such a close friend after all. This was shown in a study in which college students competed against another student (who was actually an accomplice of the experimenter) on general knowledge questions (Pleban & Tesser, 1981). The researchers rigged it so that in some conditions the questions were on topics that were highly relevant to people's self-esteem and the accomplice got many more of the questions correct. Just as predicted, this was the condition in which people distanced themselves the most from the accomplice, saying they would not want to work with him again (Kamide & Daibo, 2009; Wegner, 1986).

A second way to reduce such threats to our self-esteem is to change how relevant the task is to our self-esteem. If our new friend is a far better guitar player than we are, we might lose interest in the guitar and decide that running is really our thing. In a test of this prediction, people received feedback about how well they and another student had done on a test of a newly discovered ability. Those who learned that the other student was similar to them and had done better on the test were especially likely to say that this ability was not very important to them—just as the theory predicts (Crawford, 2007; Tesser & Paulus, 1983).

Lastly, people can change the third component in the equation—their performance relative to the other person's. Suppose that being a good cook is important to you and your new best friend is a superb cook. You can reduce the dissonance by trying to become an even better cook. But no matter how hard you try, your friend still outdoes you. You might then resort to a more diabolical route: try to undermine your friend's performance so that it is not as good as yours. If your friend asks for a recipe, you might leave out a crucial ingredient so that the resulting dish is not nearly as good as yours.

Are people really so mean-spirited that they try to sabotage their friends' performances? Surely not always, but if our self-esteem is on the line, we may not be as helpful as we would like to think. Students in a study were asked to play a word game in which one person gives clues to help another guess a word. Students were paired with both friends and strangers, and they could choose to give clues that would make it easy or hard for the other player to guess the word. The researchers set it up so that people first performed poorly themselves, then had the opportunity to help the other players by giving them easy or difficult clues. Whom would they help more, the strangers or their friends?

You can probably see what self-evaluation maintenance theory predicts. If the task is not self-relevant to people, they should want their friends to do especially well—after all, we want good things for our friends. And this is just what happened: When the researchers made the task low in importance, by saying that it

Self-Evaluation Maintenance Theory
The idea that people experience dissonance when someone close to us outperforms us in an area that is central to our self-esteem. This dissonance can be reduced by becoming less close to the person, changing our behavior so that we now outperform them, or deciding that the area is not that important to us after all.

was just a game, participants gave easier clues to their friends than to strangers (see left side of Figure 6.5). When the researchers made the task high in self-relevance, however, by saying that performance on the game was highly correlated with intelligence and leadership skills, participants gave *harder* clues to their friends than to the strangers (see the right side of Figure 6.5). Apparently it was threatening to people's self-esteem to have their friends outperform them, so they made sure they did not (Tesser & Smith, 1980).

In sum, research on self-evaluation maintenance theory has shown that threats to our self-concept have fascinating implications for our interpersonal relationships. Though much of the research has been with college students in laboratory settings, the theory has been confirmed in field and archival studies as well. For example, Tesser (1980) found that the greatest amount of friction between siblings occurred when the siblings were close in age and one sibling was significantly better on key dimensions, such as popularity or intelligence. When performance and relevance are high, it can be difficult to avoid conflicts with family members (Tesser, 1980). Consider how the novelist Norman Maclean (1983) describes his relationship with his brother in his book, *A River Runs through It*: "One of the earliest things brothers try to find out is how they differ from each other. Undoubtedly, our differences would not have seemed so great if we had not been such a close family" (p. 83).

Figure 6.5 Self-Evaluation Maintenance Theory in Action

Students played a word game in which they could give easy or difficult clues to their partner, who was either a friend or a stranger. When the task was described as "just a game," and thus, of low relevance to self-esteem, people gave easier clues to a friend than a stranger (see left side of the graph). However, when the game was described as related to intelligence and leadership skills, and thus, was highly relevant to people's self-esteem, they gave more difficult clues to a friend than a stranger, in order to avoid the dissonance of seeing their friend do better than they had done (see right side of graph) (Based on Tesser & Smith, 1980).

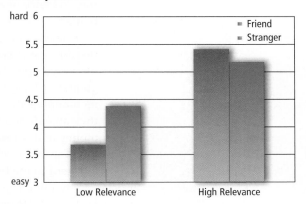

Difficulty of Clues

Review Questions

1. Suppose Juan, a premed student, is in a long-term, romantic relationship but chooses to flirt with someone else. He experiences dissonance because he sees himself as loving and trustworthy, and his flirtatious behavior is incongruent with that self-perception. According to dissonance theory he could reduce his dissonance by ____, whereas according to self-affirmation theory he could reduce his dissonance by ____.

   a. convincing himself that the flirting was harmless/ thinking about how proud he is to be a premed student

   b. thinking about how proud he is to be a premed student/ convincing himself that the flirting was harmless

   c. convincing himself that the flirting was harmless/ breaking up with his girlfriend

   d. breaking up with his girlfriend/convincing himself that the flirting was harmless

2. Kristin is one of the few women in her computer science class and gets a poor grade on the first test. According to self-affirmation theory, which of the following would help her do better in the class?

   a. Doing a values-affirmation writing exercise

   b. Getting tutoring in the class

   c. Getting study tips from the professor

   d. Joining a study group of other students in the class

3. Suppose that you and your best friend are both psychology majors and both want to go to grad school in psychology. Your friend is also a talented athlete, whereas athletics is not that important to you. One day you find out that your friend won an intramural free-throw shooting contest. Which of the following is *most* likely to happen, according to self-evaluation maintenance theory?

   a. You will become less close to your friend.

   b. You will bask in your friend's reflected glory and congratulate him or her on winning the free-throw contest.

   c. You will study really hard for the next psychology test to do better than your friend.

   d. You will decide that you are not that interested in psychology.

4. Imagine that you and your sister are both psychology majors and that you are very close to your sister. Suppose you learn that your sister's GPA in psychology classes is a lot higher than yours. According to self-evaluation maintenance theory, which of the following is *least* likely to occur?

   a. You will decide that you are not that interested in psychology.

   b. You will become less close to your sister.

   c. You will bask in your sister's reflected glory and congratulate her on her high GPA.

   d. You will study really hard for the next psychology test to do better than your sister.

Some Concluding Thoughts on Dissonance and Self-Esteem

LO 6.3   Summarize ways to overcome dissonance and the pros and cons of having high self-esteem.

At the beginning of this chapter, we raised a vital question regarding the followers of Heaven's Gate: How could intelligent people allow themselves to be led into the apparently senseless behavior of mass suicide? Of course, many factors were operating, including the charismatic power of the leaders, mutual social support among group members, and the relative isolation of the group from dissenting views, producing a closed system—like living in a roomful of mirrors.

Yet, in addition to these factors, one of the single most powerful forces was the existence of a high degree of cognitive dissonance within the minds of the participants. As we have seen, when individuals make an important decision and invest heavily in that decision (in terms of time, effort, sacrifice, and commitment), the result is a strong need to justify those actions and that investment. The more they give up to be a part of the group and the harder they work for the group, the greater will be the need to convince themselves that their views are correct. The members of the Heaven's Gate cult made monumental sacrifices for their beliefs: they abandoned their friends and families, left their professions, relinquished their money and possessions, moved to another part of the world, and worked hard and long for the particular cause they believed in—all actions that increased their commitment to the belief.

By understanding cognitive dissonance, therefore, you can understand why the Heaven's Gate people, having bought a telescope that failed to reveal a spaceship, concluded that the telescope was faulty. To have believed otherwise—"There is no spaceship after all!"—would have created too much dissonance to bear. That they went on

#trending

Politics and Cognitive Dissonance

It's bad enough when ordinary people get caught up in the self-justifying cycle, but when a political leader does so, the consequences can be devastating for the nation and the world. Virtually all leaders encounter evidence that is contrary to their positions, or make decisions that end badly. Rather than admitting they were wrong, leaders often reduce the dissonance they experience by becoming even more convinced that they were right—after all, they are human too (Tavris & Aronson, 2007).

Consider President George W. Bush's decision to invade Iraq in 2003. His original rationale was that Iraqi leader Saddam Hussein possessed weapons of mass destruction (WMD), nuclear and biochemical weapons that posed a threat to America and Europe. After the invasion of Iraq, as the months dragged on and still no WMD were discovered, administration officials had to admit that there were none. Now what? How did President Bush and his staff reduce dissonance between "We believed there were WMD that justified this war" and "We were wrong"? By adding new cognitions to justify the war: Now they said that the U.S. mission was to liberate the nation from a cruel dictator and give the Iraqi people the blessings of democratic institutions.

Of course we cannot be certain what was going on in George Bush's mind, but some six decades of research on cognitive dissonance suggests that he and his advisers may not have been intentionally deceiving the American people; it is more likely that, like the members of Heaven's Gate, they were deceiving themselves, to avoid the painful, dissonance producing conclusion that they were wrong. Needless to say, Mr. Bush was not the only leader to engage in this kind of self-justifying behavior. The memoirs of some of our most beleaguered former presidents, Democrat and Republican alike, are full of the kinds of self-serving, self-justifying statements that can best be summarized as "If I had it all to do over again, I would not change much. Actually, I wouldn't change anything except how my opponents treated me unfairly" (Johnson, 1971; Nixon, 1990). It is too early to tell how Barack Obama and Donald Trump will justify their most important decisions; stay tuned.

to commit suicide in the belief that their higher incarnation would get on that spaceship may be bizarre, but it is not unfathomable. It is simply an extreme manifestation of a process that we have seen in operation over and over again.

Much of the time, dissonance-reducing behavior can be useful because it allows us to maintain self-esteem. Yet if we were to spend all our time and energy defending our egos, we would never learn from our mistakes, bad decisions, and incorrect beliefs. Instead, we would ignore them, justify them, or, worse still, attempt to turn them into virtues. We would get stuck within the confines of our narrow minds and fail to grow or change. And, in extreme cases, we might end up justifying our own smaller Heaven's Gates—mistakes that can harm ourselves and others.

The members of the Heaven's Gate cult were just plain folks of all races, backgrounds, and walks of life. Yet almost all of them eventually committed suicide because of their commitment to the cult and its beliefs, an extreme result of the mechanism of cognitive dissonance that all of us experience.

After DNA testing proved that he could not have committed the rape he was convicted of, David Lee Wiggins was released from a Texas prison in 2012 after serving 23 years. How might dissonance explain why prosecutors in wrongful conviction cases often have a hard time accepting that the defendant is actually not guilty?

Overcoming Dissonance

It is important to consider how we can avoid compounding our failures and mistakes by blinding ourselves to the possibility of learning from them. Is there hope? We think so. Although the process of self-justification is unconscious, once we know that we are prone to justify our actions, we can begin to monitor our thinking and, in effect, "catch ourselves in the act." If we can learn to examine our behavior critically and dispassionately, we stand a chance of breaking out of the cycle of action followed by self-justification followed by more committed action.

Admittedly, acknowledging our mistakes and taking responsibility for them is easier said than done. Imagine that you are a prosecutor who has worked hard for many years to put "bad guys" in prison. You're the good guy. How will you respond to the dissonant information that DNA testing suggests that a few of those bad guys you put away might be innocent? Will you welcome this evidence with an open mind, because you would like justice to be done, or will you reject it, because it might show that you were wrong? Unfortunately—but not surprisingly for those who understand dissonance theory—many prosecutors in America make the latter choice: They resist and block the efforts by convicted prisoners to reopen their cases and get DNA tests. Their dissonance-reducing reasoning is something like this: "Well, even if he wasn't guilty of *this* crime, he was surely guilty of something else; after all, he's a bad guy."

But at least one prosecutor chose to resolve that dissonance in a more courageous way. Thomas Vanes had routinely sought the death penalty or extreme prison sentences for defendants convicted of horrible crimes. One man, Larry Mayes, served more than 20 years for rape before DNA testing cleared him of the crime. Vanes was sure that the DNA test would confirm Mayes's guilt. "But he was right, and I was wrong," Vanes wrote. "Hard facts trumped opinion and belief, as they should. It was a sobering lesson, and none of the easy-to-reach rationalizations (just doing my job, it was the jurors who convicted him, the appellate courts had upheld the conviction) completely lessen the sense of responsibility—moral, if not legal—that comes with the conviction of an innocent man" (quoted in Tavris & Aronson, 2007).

Throughout our lives, all of us, in our roles as family members, workers, professionals, and citizens, will be confronted with evidence that we were wrong about something important to us—something we did or something we believed. Will you step off the pyramid in the direction of justifying that mistake … or will you strive to correct it?

Narcissism and the Dangers of Too Much Self-Esteem

There is one group of people who seem to have a particularly hard time in recognizing their own dissonance and admitting they were wrong: narcissists. **Narcissism** is defined as the combination of excessive self-love and a lack of empathy toward others (Furnham, Richards, & Paulhus, 2013; Grubbs & Exline, 2016; Schriber & Robins, 2012; Twenge & Campbell, 2009). Narcissists are extremely self-centered, concerned much more with themselves than with other people. Take the brief measure of narcissism in the Try It! that follows to see how you score.

Narcissism

The combination of excessive self-love and a lack of empathy toward others

Try It!

Measuring Your Narcissism

Read each pair of statements below and place an "X" by the one that comes closest to describing your feelings and beliefs about yourself. You may feel that neither statement describes you well, but pick the one that comes closest. **Please complete all pairs.**

1. _____ I really like to be the center of attention
   _____ It makes me uncomfortable to be the center of attention
2. _____ I am no better or no worse than most people
   _____ I think I am a special person
3. _____ Everybody likes to hear my stories
   _____ Sometimes I tell good stories
4. _____ I usually get the respect that I deserve
   _____ I insist upon getting the respect that is due me
5. _____ I don't mind following orders
   _____ I like having authority over people
6. _____ I am going to be a great person
   _____ I hope I am going to be successful
7. _____ People sometimes believe what I tell them
   _____ I can make anybody believe anything I want them to
8. _____ I expect a great deal from other people
   _____ I like to do things for other people
9. _____ I like to be the center of attention
   _____ I prefer to blend in with the crowd
10. _____ I am much like everybody else
    _____ I am an extraordinary person
11. _____ I always know what I am doing
    _____ Sometimes I am not sure of what I am doing
12. _____ I don't like it when I find myself manipulating people
    _____ I find it easy to manipulate people
13. _____ Being an authority doesn't mean that much to me
    _____ People always seem to recognize my authority
14. _____ I know that I am good because everybody keeps telling me so
    _____ When people compliment me I sometimes get embarrassed
15. _____ I try not to be a show off
    _____ I am apt to show off if I get the chance
16. _____ I am more capable than other people
    _____ There is a lot that I can learn from other people

From Ames, Rose, & Anderson (2006) and Raskin and Terry (1988)
Scoring: Give yourself a 1 if you checked the TOP answer to Questions 1, 3, 6, 8, 9, 11, 14, or 16. Give yourself a 1 if you checked the BOTTOM answer to Questions 2, 4, 5, 7, 10, 12, 13, or 15. Then add up your score. Ames et al. (2006) found that men had an average score of 6.4, whereas women had an average score of 5.3

Is it bad to be a narcissist? After all, shouldn't we strive to have as positive a view of ourselves as we can? Well, we should definitely try to avoid low self-esteem, which is a very unpleasant state that is associated with depression and the feelings that we are ineffective and not in control of our lives (Baumeister et al., 2003). What's more, high self-esteem protects us against thoughts about our own mortality. This is the basic tenet of **terror management theory**, which holds that self-esteem serves as a buffer, protecting people from terrifying thoughts about death (Greenberg, Solomon, & Pyszczynski, 1997; Juhl & Routledge, 2016; Pyszczynski & Taylor, 2016). That is, to protect themselves from the anxiety caused by thoughts of their own deaths, people embrace cultural worldviews that make them feel like they are effective actors in a meaningful, purposeful world. People with high self-esteem are thus less troubled by thoughts about their own mortality than people with low self-esteem are (Schmeichel et al., 2009).

But if we love ourselves too much—to the point where we become narcissists—problems result. Narcissists do less well academically than others, are less successful in business, are more violent and aggressive, and are disliked by others, especially once people get to know them (Bushman & Baumeister, 2002; Twenge & Campbell, 2009). Further, narcissists are poor at looking in the mirror and seeing themselves as they really are. Remember how we said that to learn from our mistakes, it is important to be able to examine our behavior critically and admit we were wrong? Well, narcissists are especially bad at doing that, and instead do an especially good job of reducing dissonance in ways that allow them to preserve the view that they are wonderful people (Jordan et al., 2003).

If you were born after 1980, you might not want to hear this, but narcissism has been increasing among college students in recent years. Jean Twenge and her colleagues (Twenge et al., 2008; Twenge, Miller, & Campbell, 2014) tracked down studies that administered the Narcissistic Personality Inventory to college students in the United States between the years 1982 and 2008. As seen in Figure 6.6 there has been a steady increase in scores on this test since the mid-1980s. And there is some evidence that narcissism is more prevalent in America than in other cultures (Campbell, Miller, & Buffardi, 2010; Foster, Campbell, & Twenge, 2003).

Terror Management Theory
The theory that holds that self-esteem serves as a buffer, protecting people from terrifying thoughts about their own mortality

In Greek mythology, Narcissus fell in love with his own reflection in a pool of water and was so fond of his own image that he couldn't leave and eventually died. Today, narcissism refers to the combination of excessive self-love and a lack of empathy toward others.

Why the increase in narcissism? Nobody knows, though Twenge and colleagues (2008) speculate that American culture at large has become increasingly self-focused. To illustrate this, researchers coded the lyrics of the 10 most popular songs of the year between 1980 and 2007. They counted the number of first-person singular pronouns in the lyrics (e.g., "I," "me") and found a steady increase over time (see Figure 6.6; DeWall et al., 2011). True, the Beatles released a song called "I, Me, Mine" in 1970, but such self-references have become even more common, such as Justin Bieber's "Love Yourself" or Silentó's "Watch Me." This trend has spawned many spoofs, such as the song "Selfie" by the Chainsmokers, in which the singer keeps interrupting her monologue to take another picture of herself, and MadTV's parody of a Coldplay music video called *The Narcissist*. This pattern toward self-reference is also true in books. Using the Google Books ngram database, researchers searched books published between the years 1960 and 2008 and found that first-person singular pronouns ("I," "me") increased by 42% over that time period (Twenge, Campbell, & Gentile, 2013). Although the reasons are not entirely clear, Americans seem to become more focused on themselves. (Perhaps we should pause for a moment here so that we can all take selfies.)

Many young people are not so self-focused, of course, and devote countless hours to helping others through volunteer work. Ironically, in so doing they may have hit upon a way to become happier than by taking the narcissistic route. Imagine that you were in a study conducted by Dunn, Aknin, and Norton (2008). You are walking across campus one morning when a researcher approaches you and gives you an envelope with $20 in it. She asks you to spend it on yourself by 5:00 P.M. that day, such as by buying yourself a gift or paying off a bill. Sounds pretty nice, doesn't it? Now imagine that you were randomly assigned to another condition. Here you also get $20, but the researcher asks you to spend it on someone else by 5:00 P.M., such as by taking a friend out for lunch or donating it to a charity. How would that make you feel? It turns out that when the researchers contacted people that evening and asked how happy they were, those assigned to the "spend it on others" condition were happier than those asked to spend the money on themselves. A little less self-focus and a little more concern with others can actually make us happier.

To recap, having high self-esteem is generally a good thing to the extent that it makes people optimistic about their futures and work harder for what they want in life. There is a form of high self-esteem, however, that is quite problematic—namely, narcissism—which, as we have seen, is extreme high self-regard combined with a lack of empathy toward others. The best combination is to feel good about ourselves but also to be able to learn from our mistakes and to look out for and care about others.

Figure 6.6 Are People Becoming More Narcissistic?

The top (red) line shows average scores for college students on the Narcissistic Personality Inventory (NPI), a common measure of narcissism, from the years 1980 to 2008. The bottom (blue) line shows the percentage of first-person pronouns (e.g., I, me, mine) in the lyrics of the 10 most popular songs of the year from 1980 to 2007.

(Based on Twenge & Foster, 2010)

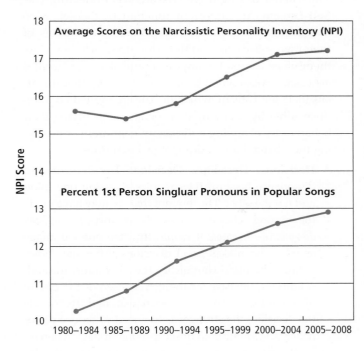

Review Questions

1. Which of the following people is most likely to be able to admit a major mistake?
   a. A prosecutor, because he or she is trained to pursue justice at all costs.
   b. A political leader, because otherwise he or she would be voted out of office.
   c. A member of a religious sect, because he or she can leave at any time.
   d. All of the above will find it hard to admit having been wrong.

2. Which of the following is most true about self-esteem?
   a. It's good to have low self-esteem because that motivates people to improve.
   b. In general, women have lower self-esteem than men.
   c. People who are optimistic try harder, persevere more in the face of failure, and set higher goals than do people who are not.
   d. The higher a person's self-esteem, the better off he or she is.

3. The basic tenet of terror management theory is that
   a. people are becoming increasingly narcissistic.
   b. it is important for governments to protect its citizens from terrorist attacks.
   c. people are less terrified of dying if they are religious.
   d. self-esteem protects people against thoughts about their own mortality.

4. Which of the following is most true about narcissism?
   a. In general, college students are becoming less narcissistic.
   b. It is characterized by excessive self-love and a lack of empathy toward others.
   c. People who are narcissistic do better academically than those who are not.
   d. People who are narcissistic have more friends and a better social life than those who are not.

Summary

LO 6.1   Explain what cognitive dissonance is and how people avoid dissonance to maintain a positive self-image.

• **The Theory of Cognitive Dissonance: Protecting Our Self-Esteem** An important function of the self is to maintain self-esteem, namely people's evaluations of their own self-worth and the extent to which they view themselves as good, competent, and decent. *Cognitive dissonance* arises when people act in a way that threatens their self-esteem, which people are motivated to reduce either by changing their behavior, justifying their behavior by changing a dissonant cognition, or justifying their behavior by adding new cognitions.

  • **Decisions, Decisions, Decisions** Decisions arouse dissonance because they require choosing one thing and not the other. The thought that we may have made the wrong choice causes discomfort—*postdecision dissonance*—because it would threaten our self-image as one who makes good decisions. After the choice is final, the mind diminishes the discomfort through solidifying the case for the item chosen or the course of action taken. The more permanent and irrevocable the decision, the stronger is the need to reduce dissonance. *Lowballing* is an unscrupulous strategy whereby a salesperson makes a decision seem irrevocable by inducing a customer to agree to purchase a product at a low cost, subsequently claiming it was an error, and then raising the price; frequently, the customer will agree to make the purchase at the inflated price.

  • **The Justification of Effort** People tend to increase their liking for something they have chosen to work hard to attain, even if the thing they have attained is not something they would otherwise like. This explains the intense loyalty that initiated recruits feel for their fraternities and military institutions after undergoing hazing.

  • **Counterattitudinal Behavior** refers to times when people act in a way that runs counter to their private belief or attitude. If there is ample *external justification* for the behavior (e.g., a large reward), then there is no dissonance and no change in people's attitudes or beliefs. However, if the reward is not big enough to justify the action people resort to *internal justification*, which is the reduction of dissonance by changing something about oneself (e.g., one's attitude or behavior). Internal justification has a much more powerful effect on an individual's long-term values and behaviors than does a situation where the external justifications are evident. Counterattitudinal behavior has been used to change people's attitudes in many ways, from their prejudices to self-defeating beliefs and harmful practices such as bulimia. Another example involves getting someone to like you by having them do you a favor. This works because the person needs to internally justify the fact that they did something nice for you. The converse is true as well. If you harm another person, to reduce the threat to your self-image that could come from doing a bad deed, you will tend to justify what you did by denigrating your victim: the person deserved it, or he or she is not "one of us" anyway. In extreme cases such as conflict and war, many people will embrace the cognition that the victim or enemy deserved everything they got because they are less than human.

  • **Avoiding Temptations** Another way of getting people to change is by giving them mild threats not to perform an attractive activity. That is, rather than using threatening severe punishment, it is better to use *insufficient punishment*, which is the dissonance aroused when individuals lack sufficient external justification for having resisted a desired activity or object, as the forbidden-toy experiment demonstrated. The less severe the threat or the smaller the reward, the less external justification the person has for compliance. The resulting internal justification lasts longer than temporary obedience to avoid a punishment.

  • **The Hypocrisy Paradigm** *Hypocrisy induction* is a method of making people face the difference between what they say and what they do. It takes advantage of the need to reduce dissonance to foster socially beneficial behaviors. In the case of an AIDS-prevention experiment, participants videotaped speeches about the importance of using condoms and they were made aware of their own failure to use them. To reduce dissonance, they changed their behavior—they purchased condoms.

  • **Dissonance Across Cultures** Although cognitive dissonance occurs in non-Western cultures as well as Western ones, the content of what creates dissonant cognitions and the process and intensity of dissonance reduction do vary across cultures, reflecting the difference in cultural norms.

LO 6.2   Describe recent advances and extensions of cognitive dissonance theory.

• **Advances and Extensions of Cognitive Dissonance Theory** Social psychologists have continued to explore this basic need to protect our self-esteem in greater depth and in new contexts.

- **Self-Affirmation Theory** holds that people can also reduce dissonance by focusing on and affirming their competence on some dimension *unrelated* to the threat. One way to do so is by completing a values affirmation writing exercise, whereby people write about why a value is important to them. This exercise has been shown to have a wide range of lasting positive effects on people's lives.

- **Self-Evaluation Maintenance Theory** holds that we will experience dissonance in relationships when three conditions are met: We feel close to another person, he or she is outperforming us in a particular area, and that area is central to our self-esteem. This dissonance can be reduced by changing any one of these factors: Becoming less close, doing better in that area, or lowering how central the area is to our self-esteem.

LO 6.3   **Summarize ways to overcome dissonance and the pros and cons of having high self-esteem.**

- **Some Concluding Thoughts on Dissonance and Self-Esteem** Much of the time, dissonance-reducing behavior can be useful because it allows us to maintain self-esteem. Yet if we were to spend all our time and energy defending our egos, we would never learn from our mistakes, bad decisions, and incorrect beliefs.

- **Overcoming dissonance** Dissonance reduction is counterproductive when it solidifies negative values and behaviors, and this applies to everyone from members of small cults to national leaders. Knowing that humans are dissonance-reducing animals can make us more aware of the process. The next time we feel the discomfort of having acted counter to our values, we can consciously pause the self-justification process to reflect on our action.

- **Narcissism and the Dangers of Too Much Self-Esteem** Most of us have high self-esteem, which has the benefits of avoiding depression, allowing us to persevere in the face of failure, and, as shown by research on *terror management theory*, protecting us from thoughts about our own mortality. There is a form of high self-esteem, however, that is quite problematic—namely, narcissism—which is extreme high self-regard combined with a lack of empathy toward others. The best combination is to feel good about ourselves but also to look out for and care about others.

Revel Interactive

Shared Writing   **What Do You Think?**

How does justification of effort help explain why hazing and initiation rites are common among so many different group types?

Test Yourself

1. You know you're eating too much junk food and that it's bad for your energy and health. Which of the following will not reduce your dissonance?

   a. Cutting out your favorite afternoon sweets

   b. Deciding that all those health warnings are stupid exaggerations

   c. Admitting you are eating too many sweets but claim that they boost your energy for studying

   d. Accepting the fact that your attitudes and behavior simply conflict

2. You are reading a blog by someone whose point of view is really making you angry. Which of her arguments are you most likely to focus on and remember?

   a. Her silliest claims, because she is a silly person

   b. Her silliest claims, because they are consonant with your opinion that she is a silly person

   c. Her smartest claims, so that you can contradict them in a post

   d. Her smartest claims, because they are so unlikely to have come from a silly person

3. Rachel was accepted at both University A and University B. She has a hard time making up her mind because she sees pros and cons to attending either university. Which of the following is true, according to dissonance theory?

   a. She will experience the most dissonance right before making up her mind because it is such a difficult choice.

   b. She will experience the most dissonance right after making up her mind.

   c. Whichever university she chooses, she is likely to regret her choice.

   d. Because the choice is so difficult, she is unlikely to fully commit herself to the university she chooses to attend.

4. When does "saying become believing"?

   a. When you claim to have an opinion that differs from your true beliefs for no strong reason.

   b. When what you say is what you believe.

   c. When someone forces you to say something you don't believe.

   d. When you're paid a lot of money to lie.

5. What is the "hypocrisy paradigm" in experimental research?

   a. Choosing participants who are hypocrites in order to study their rationalizations.

   b. Requiring participants to write essays that are critical of hypocrisy.

   c. Making participants understand that everyone is a hypocrite.

   d. Making participants aware of their own hypocrisy in not practicing what they preach.

6. In terms of dissonance theory, what is the primary reason that "we" (our side) often dehumanize "them," the enemy, seeing them as animals, brutes, or monsters?

   a. The enemy is violent and cruel and deserves whatever we do to them.

   b. The enemy started the war.

   c. Our side has treated the enemy brutally and needs to justify these actions.

   d. Our side is more moral and humane than their side.

7. Your best friend has joined a cult called "The Fellowship of Feeling." He had to spend a month in a set of increasingly severe hazing rituals; pay an $8,000 membership fee; and go along to watch older members find homeless people to harass and beat up, before having to treat these "useless animals" the same

way. Your friend loves this group and keeps urging you to join. What principle of dissonance is likely operating on your friend?

   a. The justification of effort

   b. Low self-esteem

   c. Postdecision dissonance

   d. Hypocrisy induction

   e. Insufficient punishment

8. Suppose Harold is in a long-term, romantic relationship but chooses to flirt with someone else. He experiences dissonance because he sees himself as loving and trustworthy, and his flirtatious behavior is incongruent with that self-perception. According to research on self-affirmation theory, how could Harold reduce his dissonance?

   a. He could say, "Hey, at least I'm doing good work volunteering at the homeless shelter" (assuming that being a good volunteer is important to him).

   b. He could confess to his romantic partner about what he did.

   c. He could say to himself, "I'm really an idiot, I shouldn't do that again".

   d. He could say to himself, "I guess I'm not all that trustworthy a person".

9. Rachel and Eleanor are best friends and also in the high school choir. Both of them consider themselves to be talented singers and singing is very important to them. They both try out for an important solo in the choir, which Eleanor wins. Which of the following is Rachel *least* likely to do, according to self-evaluation maintenance theory?

   a. Rachel will be very happy for Eleanor and tell all their friends about her success in winning the solo.

   b. Rachel will decide that singing isn't as important to her as she thought.

   c. Rachel will practice even harder for the next solo in order to do better than Eleanor.

   d. Rachel will feel less close to Eleanor as a friend.

10. Which of the following is *true* about self-esteem and narcissism?

   a. The best way to be happy is to focus on ourselves and our own needs.

   b. Narcissists are disliked by others but do better academically and in business than other people.

   c. People who are optimistic (but not narcissistic) persevere more in the face of failure and set higher goals than do other people.

   d. Narcissism has been decreasing among college students in the United States over the past 30 years.

Chapter 7
Attitudes and Attitude Change
Influencing Thoughts and Feelings

 ## Chapter Outline and Learning Objectives

WHAT DO YOU THINK?

Revel Interactive

Survey   **What Do You Think?**

SURVEY   RESULTS

Can you think of a time when you made a choice or acted a certain way precisely because someone said you should do the opposite?

○ Yes

○ No

It sometimes seems like advertising is everywhere we look. Ads that pop up on your computer or phone, on professional sports team jerseys, in public restrooms, on video screens at gasoline pumps, and even on motion sickness bags on airplanes (Story, 2007). But Jason Sadler, a 34-year-old based in Jacksonville, Florida, may just win the prize for advertising innovation. In 2009, he founded IWearYourShirt.com, through which he was paid by various companies to post attention-grabbing photos and videos of himself engaged in various shenanigans while wearing a t-shirt with their logo and name on it. A few years later, he auctioned off the rights to his last name, and for the price tag of $45,500 he legally became, for 12 months, Jason Headsets.com. Ridiculous? Perhaps. But the president of the Headsets.com has claimed that the investment yielded his company more than $6 million in media attention and name recognition (Horgan, 2013). And one year after that, a surf conditions travel app also made the decision to hire Jason—or, as he became known for a period of time, Mr. SurfrApp.

It is easy to laugh at the lengths to which advertisers will go, brushing them off as absurd but harmless attempts to influence our attitudes and behaviors. We should keep in mind, though, that advertising can have powerful effects. Consider the history of cigarette ads. In the 19th century, most consumer goods, including tobacco products, were made and sold locally. But as the Industrial Revolution led to the mass production of many consumer products, manufacturers sought broader markets. Advertising was the natural result. In the 1880s, cigarettes were being mass-produced for the first time, and moguls such as James Buchanan Duke began to market their brands aggressively. Duke placed ads in newspapers, rented space on thousands of billboards, hired famous actresses to endorse his brands, and gave gifts to retailers who stocked his products. Other cigarette manufacturers soon followed suit (Kluger, 1996).

These efforts were phenomenally successful, as sales of cigarettes skyrocketed in the United States. But there remained a vast untapped market—namely, women. Until the early 20th century, men bought 99% of all cigarettes sold. It was socially unacceptable for women to smoke; those who did were considered to have questionable morals. This began to change with the burgeoning women's rights movement and the fight to achieve the right to vote. Ironically, smoking cigarettes became a symbol of women's emancipation (Kluger, 1996). Cigarette manufacturers were happy to encourage this view by targeting women in their advertisements. Because it was unacceptable for women to smoke in public, early cigarette ads never showed a woman actually smoking. Instead, they tried to associate smoking with glamour or convey that cigarettes helped control weight ("Reach for a Lucky instead of a sweet"). By the 1960s, cigarette advertisements were making a direct link between women's liberation and smoking, and a new brand was created (Virginia Slims) specifically for this purpose ("You've come a long way, baby"). Women began to purchase cigarettes in droves. In 1955, 52% of men and 34% of women in the United States smoked (Centers for Disease Control and Prevention, n.d.). Fortunately, the overall smoking rate has decreased since then, but the gap between men and women has narrowed. As of 2015, 21% of adult men smoked, compared to 14% of adult women (Centers for Disease Control and Prevention, 2017).

To make up for this shrinking market in the United States, tobacco companies now have begun aggressively marketing cigarettes in other countries. The World Health Organization estimates that 50,000 teenagers a day begin smoking in Asia alone, and that smoking may eventually kill *one-quarter* of the young people currently living in Asia (Teves, 2002).

Is advertising responsible for this looming public health crisis? To what extent can advertising really shape people's attitudes and behavior? Exactly what are attitudes, anyway, and through what processes can they be changed? These questions, which are some of the oldest in social psychology, are the subject of this chapter.

It seems that no corner is left untouched in the modern advertising world. Companies go to great lengths to grab attention and influence, even if incrementally, people's familiarity with and attitudes toward their products. This Utah woman, for example, accepted a fee of $10,000 to advertise Golden Palace casino on her forehead.

The Nature and Origin of Attitudes

LO 7.1   Describe the types of attitudes and what they are based on.

Each of us *evaluates* the world around us. We form likes and dislikes of virtually everything we encounter; indeed, it would be odd to hear someone say, "I feel completely neutral toward anchovies, chocolate, Kanye West, and Donald Trump." For most people, at least *one* of those targets should elicit strong attitudes, don't you think? Simply put, **attitudes** are evaluations of people, objects, or ideas (Banaji & Heiphetz, 2010; Bohner & Dickel, 2011; Eagly & Chaiken, 2007; Petty & Krosnick, 2014). Attitudes are important because they often determine what we do—whether we eat or avoid anchovies and chocolate, download Kanye songs or change the station when they come on, and who we vote for on Election Day.

Attitudes

Evaluations of people, objects, and ideas

Where Do Attitudes Come From?

One provocative answer to the question of where attitudes come from is that they are linked, in part, to our genes (Cai et al., 2016; Lewis, Kandler, & Riemann, 2014; Schwab, 2014). Evidence for this conclusion comes from the fact that identical twins share more attitudes than do fraternal twins, even when the identical twins were raised in different homes and never knew each other. One study, for example, found that identical twins had more similar attitudes than fraternal twins did toward, say, exercise, being the center of attention, riding roller coasters, and organized religion (Olson et al., 2001). Now, we should be careful how we interpret this evidence. No one is arguing that there are specific genes that determine our attitudes; it is highly unlikely, for example, that there is a "roller coaster" gene that determines your amusement park preferences. It appears, though, that some attitudes are an indirect function of our genetic makeup. They are related to things such as our temperament and personality, which are directly related to our genes. People may have inherited a temperament and personality from their parents that make them predisposed to like thrill rides more than the Ferris wheel (or vice versa).

Even if there is a genetic component, our social experiences clearly play a major role in shaping our attitudes. Social psychologists have focused on these experiences and how they result in different kinds of attitudes. They have identified three components of attitudes: the *cognitive component*, or the thoughts and beliefs that people form about the attitude object; the *affective component*, or people's emotional reactions toward the attitude object; and the *behavioral component*, or how people act toward the attitude object. Importantly, any given attitude can be based on any one of these components or some combination of them (Aquino et al., 2016; Zanna & Rempel, 1988).

COGNITIVELY BASED ATTITUDES   Sometimes our attitudes are based primarily on the relevant facts, such as the objective merits of a car. How many miles per gallon does it get? What are its safety features? To the extent that an evaluation is based primarily on beliefs about the properties of an attitude object, we say it is a **cognitively based attitude**. An attitude of this kind allows us to classify the pluses and minuses of an object so that we can quickly determine whether we want to have anything to do with it (De Houwer, Gawronski, & Barnes-Holmes, 2013; DeMarree et al., 2017). Consider your attitude toward a basic object like a vacuum cleaner. Your attitude is likely to be based on your beliefs about the objective merits of various brands, such as how well they clean up dirt and how much they cost—not on more emotional considerations such as how sexy they make you feel.

AFFECTIVELY BASED ATTITUDES   An attitude rooted more in emotions and values than on an objective appraisal of pluses and minuses is called an **affectively based attitude** (Breckler & Wiggins, 1989; Bülbül & Menon, 2010). Sometimes we simply like a car, regardless of how many miles per gallon it gets. Occasionally we even feel strongly attracted to something—such as another person—in spite of having negative beliefs about him or her (e.g., knowing the person is a "bad influence").

As a guide to which attitudes are likely to be affectively based, consider the topics that etiquette manuals will tell you should not be discussed at a dinner party: politics, sex, and religion. People seem to vote more with their hearts than their minds, for example, caring more about how they feel about a candidate than their beliefs about his or her specific policies (Abelson et al., 1982; Westen, 2007). In fact, even those segments of the electorate who know virtually nothing about specific politicians nonetheless often have strong feelings about them (Ahler et al., 2017; Redlawsk, 2002). Consider, for example, polls taken in the wake of the 2016 U.S. election in which more than one-third of voters did not realize that "Obamacare" was the same thing as the Affordable Care Act (Dropp & Nyhan, 2017). This result helps explain the spate of examples of people who voted for Donald Trump at least in part because of his promise to repeal Obamacare, but were then shocked to find out that his proposed policies would cost them their own insurance coverage.

If affectively based attitudes do not come from examining the facts, where do they come from? A variety of sources. They can stem from people's values, such as basic religious and moral beliefs. People's feelings about such issues as abortion, the death penalty, and premarital sex are often based more on their sense of value than on a cold examination of the facts. The function of such attitudes is not so much to paint an accurate picture of the world as to express and validate one's basic value system (Maio et al., 2001; Smith, Bruner, & White, 1956; Snyder & DeBono, 1989). Other affectively based attitudes can result from a sensory reaction, such as liking the taste of a certain

Cognitively Based Attitude

An attitude based primarily on people's beliefs about the properties of an attitude object

Affectively Based Attitude

An attitude based more on people's feelings and values than on their beliefs about the nature of an attitude object

food, or an aesthetic reaction, such as admiring a painting or the shape and color of a car. Still others can be the result of conditioning (Hofmann et al., 2010).

Classical conditioning works this way: A stimulus that elicits an emotional response is accompanied by a neutral, nonemotional stimulus, and eventually, the neutral stimulus elicits the emotional response by itself. For example, suppose that when you were a child you experienced feelings of warmth and love when you visited your grandmother. Suppose also that her house always smelled faintly of laundry detergent and chicken soup. Eventually, either of those smells alone will trigger the emotions you experienced during your visits, through the process of classical conditioning (De Houwer, 2011; Walther & Langer, 2010).

In **operant conditioning**, behaviors we freely choose to perform become more or less frequent, depending on whether they are followed by a reward (positive reinforcement) or punishment. How does this apply to attitudes? Imagine that a 4-year-old White girl goes to the playground with her father and begins to play with an African-American girl. Her father expresses disapproval, telling her, "We don't play with that kind of child." It won't take long before the child associates interacting with African Americans with disapproval, and therefore adopts her father's racist attitudes. Attitudes can take on a positive or negative affect through either classical or operant conditioning, as shown in Figure 7.1 (Cacioppo et al., 1992; Sweldens, Corneille, & Yzerbyt, 2014).

Although affectively based attitudes come from many sources, we can group them into one family because they (1) do not result from a rational examination of the issues, (2) are not governed by logic, and (3) are often linked to people's values, so that efforts to change them challenge those values (Katz, 1960; Kertzer et al., 2014). How can we tell if an attitude is more affectively or cognitively based? See the following Try It! for one way to measure the bases of people's attitudes.

Some attitudes are based more on emotions and values than on facts and figures. Attitudes toward gay marriage may be such a case.

Classical Conditioning

The phenomenon whereby a stimulus that elicits an emotional response is repeatedly paired with a neutral stimulus that does not, until the neutral stimulus takes on the emotional properties of the first stimulus

Operant Conditioning

The phenomenon whereby behaviors we freely choose to perform become more or less frequent, depending on whether they are followed by a reward or punishment

---

Figure 7.1 Classical and Operant Conditioning of Attitudes
Affectively based attitudes can result from either classical or operant conditioning.

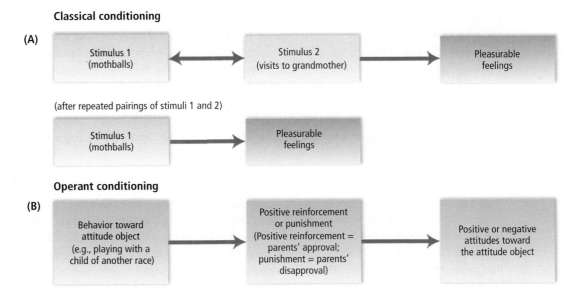

Try It!

Affective and Cognitive Bases of Attitudes

Instructions: Fill out this questionnaire to see how psychologists measure the affective and cognitive components of attitudes.

1. Circle the number on each scale that best describes your feelings toward snakes.

hateful	−3	−2	−1	0	1	2	3	love
sad	−3	−2	−1	0	1	2	3	delighted
annoyed	−3	−2	−1	0	1	2	3	happy
tense	−3	−2	−1	0	1	2	3	calm
bored	−3	−2	−1	0	1	2	3	excited
angry	−3	−2	−1	0	1	2	3	relaxed
disgusted	−3	−2	−1	0	1	2	3	acceptance
sorrowful	−3	−2	−1	0	1	2	3	joy

2. Circle the number on each scale that best describes the traits or characteristics of snakes.

useless	−3	−2	−1	0	1	2	3	useful
foolish	−3	−2	−1	0	1	2	3	wise
unsafe	−3	−2	−1	0	1	2	3	safe
harmful	−3	−2	−1	0	1	2	3	beneficial
worthless	−3	−2	−1	0	1	2	3	valuable
imperfect	−3	−2	−1	0	1	2	3	perfect
unhealthy	−3	−2	−1	0	1	2	3	wholesome

Add up the sum of your responses to Question 1 and, separately, your responses to Question 2.

Question 1 measures the affective component of your attitude toward snakes, whereas Question 2 measures the cognitive component of attitudes. Most people's attitudes toward snakes are more affectively than cognitively based. If this is true of you, your total score for Question 1 should depart more from zero (in a negative direction for most people) than your total score for Question 2.

Now go back and fill out the scales again, substituting *vacuum cleaners* for *snakes*. Most people's attitudes toward a utilitarian object such as a vacuum cleaner are more cognitively than affectively based. If this is true of you, your total score for Question 2 should depart more from zero than your total score for Question 1.

Behaviorally Based Attitude

An attitude based on observations of how one behaves toward an object

BEHAVIORALLY BASED ATTITUDES   A **behaviorally based attitude** stems from people's observations of their own behavior toward an object. This may seem a little odd: How do we know how to behave if we don't already know how we feel? According to Daryl Bem's (1972) *self-perception theory*, under certain circumstances people don't know how they feel until they see how they behave. For example, suppose you asked a friend how much she likes to exercise. If she replies, "Well, I guess I like it, because I always seem to be going for a run or heading over to the gym to work out," we would say she has a behaviorally based attitude. Her attitude is based more on an observation of her behavior than on her cognitions or affect.

As noted in Chapter 5, people infer their attitudes from their behavior only under certain conditions. First, their initial attitude has to be weak or ambiguous. If your friend already has a strong attitude toward exercising, she does not have to observe her behavior to infer how she feels about it. Second, people infer their attitudes from their own behavior only when there are no other plausible explanations available. If your friend believes she exercises to lose weight or because her doctor has ordered her to, she is unlikely to assume that she runs and works out because she enjoys it.

Explicit Versus Implicit Attitudes

Once an attitude develops, it can exist at two levels. **Explicit attitudes** are ones we consciously endorse and can easily report; they are what we think of as our attitude when someone asks us a question like "What is your opinion on affirmative action?" **Implicit attitudes**, on the other hand, are involuntary, uncontrollable, and at times unconscious evaluations (Gawronski & Bodenhausen, 2012; Greenwald & Banaji, 1995; Hahn et al., 2014; Wilson, Lindsey, & Schooler, 2000).

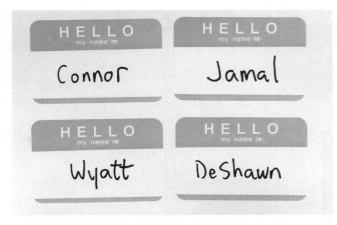

Consider Robert, a white college student who genuinely believes that all races are equal and abhors the very idea of any kind of racial bias. This is Robert's explicit attitude, in the sense that it is his conscious evaluation of members of other races that governs how he chooses to act. For example, consistent with his explicit attitude, Robert recently signed a petition in favor of hiring a more diverse faculty at his university. Robert has grown up in a culture in which there are many negative stereotypes about minority groups, however, and it is possible that some of these negative ideas have seeped into him outside of his awareness (Devine, 1989; Xu, Nosek, & Greenwald, 2014). When he is around African Americans, for example, perhaps some negative feelings are triggered automatically. If so, he has a negative implicit attitude toward African Americans, which is likely to influence those behaviors he is not monitoring or attending to, such as whether he makes good eye contact or how nervous he appears to be (Dovidio, Kawakami, & Gaertner, 2002; Greenwald et al., 2009).

People can have explicit and implicit attitudes toward virtually anything, not just other racial groups. For example, students can believe explicitly that they hate math yet still have a positive attitude at an implicit level, finding that—in spite of what they claim—they actually enjoy working through a certain type of problem (Galdi, Arcuri, & Gawronski, 2008; Ranganath & Nosek, 2008; Steele & Ambady, 2006). How do we know this? A variety of techniques have been developed to measure implicit attitudes, one of the most popular of which is the Implicit Association Test, or IAT, which we discuss in Chapter 13. But for now, let's focus on the question of where our implicit attitudes come from.

Laurie Rudman, Julie Phelan, and Jessica Heppen (2007) have found evidence that implicit attitudes are rooted more in people's childhood experiences, whereas explicit attitudes are rooted more in their recent experiences. In one study, the researchers measured college students' implicit and explicit attitudes toward overweight people. They also asked the students to report their current weight and their weight when they were growing up. Participants' implicit attitudes toward overweight people were predicted by their childhood weight but not their current weight, whereas their explicit attitudes were predicted by their current weight but not their childhood weight. An additional finding from this study was that people whose mother was overweight (and who also had a good relationship with her) had positive implicit attitudes toward overweight people, even if their explicit attitudes were negative. In short, people can often have different implicit and explicit attitudes toward the same thing, one rooted more in childhood experiences and the other based more on their adult experiences.

In sum, research on implicit attitudes is a relatively young field, and social psychologists are actively investigating the nature of these attitudes, how to measure them, when they

People can have both explicit and implicit attitudes toward the same topic. Social psychologists have been especially interested in people's explicit and implicit attitudes toward members of other races. For example, many people who evaluate job applicants would likely state that they have no biases whatsoever against people of different racial groups. But research suggests that résumés with "White-sounding" names like Emily and Greg tend to get more callbacks for interviews than résumés with "Black-sounding" names like Lakisha and Jamal (Bertrand & Mullainathan, 2004). Do you think this could be the result of implicit bias?

Explicit Attitudes

Attitudes that we consciously endorse and can easily report

Implicit Attitudes

Attitudes that exist outside of conscious awareness

Watch IMPLICIT ATTITUDES

Revel Video

converge versus diverge with explicit attitudes, their stability over time, and the degree to which they predict behavior (Briñol & Petty, 2012; Fazio & Olson, 2003; Kurdi & Banaji, 2017; Payne, Burkley, & Stokes, 2008). We will return in Chapter 13 to a discussion of implicit attitudes as they apply to stereotyping and prejudice. The focus in the remainder of this chapter will be on the more general relationship between attitudes and behavior and on the processes through which attitudes change.

Review Questions

1. Which of the following conclusions is the most consistent with research on the heritability of attitudes?
   a. Our attitudes are shaped by our surroundings and do not seem to have any genetic component to them.
   b. Our attitudes are inherited and dictated by our genetic makeup, with little influence from environmental factors.
   c. We often inherit a temperament or personality that renders us likely to develop similar attitudes to those held by our genetic relatives.
   d. Fraternal twins are just as likely to share attitudes as are identical twins.

2. People's emotional reaction to a target is referred to as the _____component of attitudes.
   a. affective
   b. behavioral
   c. cognitive
   d. operant

3. Which component of an attitude is most related to the process of examining facts and weighing the objective merits of a target?
   a. Affective
   b. Behavioral
   c. Cognitive
   d. Operant

4. Adults' tendency to experience happy, nostalgia-filled feelings when they hear the music of an ice cream truck can be best explained by the relationship of attitudes to
   a. classical conditioning.
   b. operant conditioning.
   c. self-perception.
   d. values.

5. Newman is currently overweight, but as a child he was quite thin. His current explicit attitude toward the overweight is likely to be more _____, and his current implicit attitude toward the overweight is likely to be more _____.
   a. behaviorally based; cognitively based
   b. cognitively based; behaviorally based
   c. negative; positive
   d. positive; negative

When Do Attitudes Predict Behavior?

LO 7.2   Analyze the conditions under which attitudes can predict behavior.

Remember our discussion of cigarette advertising? The reason corporations and other groups are willing to spend so much money on ad campaigns is because of a simple assumption: When people change their attitudes (e.g., cigarettes are for women too), they change their behavior as well (e.g., women start smoking). In reality, though, the relationship between attitudes and behavior is not so simple, as shown in a classic (and disturbing) study. In the early 1930s, Richard LaPiere embarked on a cross-country sightseeing trip with a young Chinese couple. Prejudice against Asians was common in the United States at this time, so at each hotel, campground, and restaurant they entered, LaPiere worried that his friends would be refused service. To his surprise, of the 251 establishments he and his friends visited, only one refused to serve them (LaPiere, 1934).

Struck by this apparent lack of prejudice, LaPiere decided to explore people's attitudes toward Asians in a different way. After his trip, he wrote a letter to each establishment he and his friends had visited, asking if it would serve a Chinese visitor. Of the many replies, only *one* said it would. More than 90% said they definitely would not; the rest were undecided. Why were the attitudes people expressed in writing the reverse of their actual behavior?

LaPiere's study was not, of course, a controlled experiment. As he acknowledged, there are several reasons why his results may have shown inconsistency between people's attitudes and behavior. He had no way of knowing whether the proprietors who answered his letter were the same people who had served him and his friends, and even if they were, people's attitudes could have changed in the months between the time they served the Chinese couple and the time they received the letter. Nonetheless, the lack of correspondence between people's attitudes and how they actually acted was so striking that we might question the assumption that behavior routinely follows from attitudes. Indeed, more recent research has also found that people's attitudes can be poor predictors of their behavior (Ajzen & Sheikh, 2013; Fishbein & Ajzen, 2010; Wicker, 1969), including one study in which researchers found results similar to LaPiere's when it came to the willingness of bed-and-breakfast owners to rent a room to two gay men on their honeymoon (Howerton, Meltzer, & Olson, 2012).

How can this be? Does a person's attitude toward an ethnic group or political candidate or cigarettes really tell us nothing about how he or she will behave? How can we reconcile LaPiere's findings—and other studies like it—with the fact that many times behavior and attitudes *are* consistent? Indeed, attitudes do predict behavior, but only under certain specifiable conditions (DeBono & Snyder, 1995; Friese et al., 2016; Glasman & Albarracín, 2006). One key factor is knowing whether the behavior we are trying to predict is spontaneous or planned (Fazio, 1990).

Predicting Spontaneous Behaviors

Sometimes we act spontaneously, thinking little about what we are about to do. When LaPiere and his Chinese friends entered a restaurant, the manager did not have a lot of time to reflect on whether to serve them; he or she had to make a snap decision. Similarly, when someone stops us on the street and asks us to sign a petition, we usually don't stop and think about it for 5 minutes; we decide on the spot whether to sign on.

Attitudes will predict spontaneous behaviors only when they are highly accessible to people (Fazio, 2007; Petty & Krosnick, 2014). **Attitude accessibility** refers to the strength of the association between an object and an evaluation of it, which is typically measured by the speed with which people can report how they feel about the object or issue (Fazio, Ledbetter, & Towles-Schwen, 2000; Young & Fazio, 2013). When accessibility is high, your attitude comes to mind whenever you see or think about the attitude object. When accessibility is low, your attitude comes to mind more slowly. It follows that highly accessible attitudes will be more likely to predict spontaneous behaviors because people are more likely to be thinking about their attitude when they are called on to act. But what makes attitudes accessible in the first place? One important determinant is the degree of experience people have behaving with the attitude object. Some attitudes are based on hands-on experience, such as a person's attitude toward the homeless after volunteering at a homeless shelter. Other attitudes are formed without much experience, such as a person's attitude toward the homeless that is based on reading newspaper articles. The more direct experience people have with an attitude object, the more accessible their attitude will be, and the more accessible it is, the more likely their spontaneous behavior will be consistent with that attitude (Descheemaeker et al., 2016; Glasman & Albarracín, 2006).

Attitude Accessibility

The strength of the association between an attitude object and a person's evaluation of that object, measured by the speed with which people can report how they feel about the object

Predicting Deliberative Behaviors

Some decisions and behaviors are less spontaneous, however. We might take our time and deliberate, for example, when it comes to matters such as where to go to college, what courses to register for, or whether to accept a job offer. Under these conditions, the accessibility of our attitude is less important. Given enough time and motivation to think about an issue, even inaccessible attitudes can be conjured up and influence the choice we make. It is only when we have to decide how to act on the spot, without time to think it over, that accessibility becomes critical (Eagly & Chaiken, 1993; Fazio, 1990).

Although some behaviors result from spur-of-the-moment, spontaneous decisions, others emerge from more thoughtful processes in which we carefully weigh pros and cons. The theory of planned behavior helps us understand the link between attitudes and these sorts of deliberative behaviors.

Theory of Planned Behavior

The idea that people's intentions are the best predictors of their deliberate behaviors, which are determined by their attitudes toward specific behaviors, subjective norms, and perceived behavioral control

The best-known theory of when and how attitudes predict deliberative behaviors is the **theory of planned behavior** (Ajzen & Fishbein, 1980; Ajzen & Sheikh, 2013; Fishbein & Ajzen, 2010). According to this theory, when people have time to contemplate how they are going to behave, the best predictor of their behavior is their intention, which is determined by three things: their attitude toward the specific behavior, subjective norms, and perceived behavioral control (see Figure 7.2). Let's consider each of these in turn.

SPECIFIC ATTITUDES The theory of planned behavior holds that the more specific the attitude toward the behavior in question, the better that attitude can be expected to predict the behavior. In one study, researchers asked a sample of married women for their attitudes toward birth control pills, ranging from their general attitude toward birth control to their specific attitude toward using birth control pills during the next 2 years (see Table 7.1). Two years later, they asked the women whether they had used birth control pills at any time since the last interview. As Table 7.1 shows, the general attitudes expressed 2 years earlier did not predict the women's subsequent use of birth control at all. This general attitude had not taken into account other factors that could influence such a decision, from concern about the long-term effects of the pill to their attitudes regarding other available forms of birth control. The more specific the original question was about the act of using birth control pills, the better the attitude predicted actual behavior (Davidson & Jaccard, 1979).

This study and others like it help explain why LaPiere (1934) found such inconsistency between people's attitudes and behaviors. His question to the proprietors—whether they would serve "members of the Chinese race"—was very general. Had he asked a much more specific question—such as whether they would serve an educated, well-dressed, well-to-do Chinese couple accompanied by a White American college professor—the proprietors might have given an answer that was more predictive of their actual behavior.

Figure 7.2 The Theory of Planned Behavior

According to this theory, the best predictors of people's planned, deliberative behaviors are their behavioral intentions. The best predictors of their intentions are their attitudes toward the specific behavior, their subjective norms, and their perceived behavioral control of the behavior.

(Adapted from Ajzen, 1985)

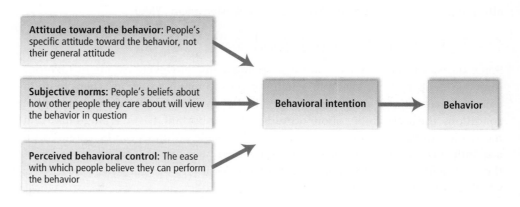

Table 7.1 Specific Attitudes Are Better Predictors of Behavior

Different groups of women were asked about their attitudes toward birth control. The more specific the question, the better it predicted their actual use of birth control over the next 2 years.

Attitude Measure	Attitude—Behavior Correlation
Attitude toward birth control	0.08
Attitude toward birth control pills	0.32
Attitude toward using birth control pills	0.53
Attitude toward using birth control pills during the next 2 years	0.57

Note: If a correlation is close to 0, it means that there is little to no relationship between the two variables. The closer the correlation is to 1, the stronger the positive relationship between attitudes and behavior.

(Adapted from Davidson & Jaccard, 1979)

SUBJECTIVE NORMS   In addition to measuring attitudes toward the behavior, we also need to measure subjective norms—people's beliefs about how others they care about will view the behavior in question (see Figure 7.2). Knowing these beliefs can be just as important as knowing the person's attitudes when it comes to trying to predict someone's intentions (Hood & Shook, 2014; Park & Smith, 2007). For example, suppose we want to predict whether Deepa intends to go to a violin concert and we know that she doesn't like classical music. We would probably say that she won't go. But suppose we also know that Deepa's best friend, Kristen, is playing in the concert, and that Deepa assumes that Kristen will be disappointed if she is not in the audience and will view her failure to show up as a slap in the face. Knowing this subjective norm—Deepa's belief about how a close friend will view her behavior—we might predict that she will go.

PERCEIVED BEHAVIORAL CONTROL   Finally, as seen in Figure 7.2, people's intentions are influenced by the ease with which they believe they can perform the behavior—perceived behavioral control. If people think it is difficult to perform a behavior, such as remembering to use a condom when having sex, they will not form a strong intention to do so. If people think it is easy to perform the behavior, such as remembering to buy milk on the way home from work, they are more likely to form a strong intention to do so.

Considerable research supports the idea that asking people about these determinants of their intentions—attitude specificity, subjective norms, and perceived behavioral control—increases our ability to anticipate how they will act. Specifically, these factors help us predict those behaviors that are planned and deliberative, such as deciding what job to accept, whether to wear a seat belt, whom to vote for, and, yes, whether to use a condom when having sex (Albarracín et al., 2001; Hood & Shook, 2014; Rise, Sheeran, & Hukkelberg, 2010; Manning, 2009).

#trending
Predicting Environmentally Friendly Action

One domain in which it is particularly important to consider the link between atitudes and behaviors involves the environment. Although many of us hold environmentally friendly beliefs, most recyclable waste is not recycled, a small number of people use energy efficient lightbulbs, and the vast majority of Americans drive to work alone. So what gives? How can we better use individuals' attitudes about the environment to predict actual behavior?

In a recent series of studies, Kate Ratliff, Jennifer Howell, and Liz Redford (2017) demonstrated that one useful predictor of environmentally friendly behavior is how people feel about the protoypical environmentalist. That is, the mental image someone conjures up when asked to think about the average environmentalist appears to be a fairly good indicator of how this person is likely to behave.

In one study, participants evaluated a variety of hypothetical individuals, including professors, bicyclists, Republicans, lobbyists, and, of course, environmentalists. They were asked to take as much time as necessary to rate each person in terms of how attractive, cool, fun, intelligent, and judgmental they were likely to be. These ratings were used to assess the participants' *explicit* attitudes about environmentalists.

The participants were then asked another series of questions, this time under extreme time pressure. Now they were shown a category—such as environmentalist—and given less than one second to indicate their rating on one of the five dimensions listed above. Immediately after this, another category and rating dimension appeared on the screen, demanding a quick response. And then another and another and another. This speeded task gave participants very little time to think and control their responses. In this manner, these ratings measured their *implicit* attitudes about environmentalists.

Finally, participants were asked to report how frequently they themselves engaged in a variety of environmentally friendly behaviors, including turning down the thermostat when leaving home, bringing reusable bags to the grocery store, and taking short showers to save energy. The researchers' primary question: Would participants' attitudes about the average environmentalist predict their own behavioral tendencies? And if so, which type of attitudes: the explicit or implicit ones?

Ratliff et al. (2017) found that people who held more positive impressions of environmentalists were indeed significantly more likely to engage in pro-environmental behaviors. This held true for explicit attitudes, the types of beliefs about which participants were consciously aware, and also for implicit, or unconscious atitudes. These findings have interesting implications, namely that when trying to predict who will avoid bottled water and go for reusable containers, asking someone whether they consider themselves an environmentalist may be less useful than asking how they feel about the *average* environmentalist.

Review Questions

1. The major finding of LaPiere's (1934) classic study on attitudes and behavior involving prejudice and hotel/restaurant owners is that
   a. people are more prejudiced than their self-reported attitudes would lead us to believe.
   b. people's attitudes are not always reliable predictors of their behaviors.
   c. the less accessible an attitude is, the more likely it is to shape behavior.
   d. when it comes to racial prejudice, people's attitudes are particularly strong predictors of their behaviors.

2. Attitude accessibility is a particularly good predictor of behavior when
   a. the behavior in question is spontaneous.
   b. the behavior in question is deliberative.
   c. the attitude in question is general.
   d. the attitude in question is an unpopular one.

3. Which of the following is the best example of a deliberative behavior?
   a. Buying a candy bar from the rack next to the check-out line at the grocery store
   b. Telling a salesman who calls you on the phone that you aren't interested in the item he's selling
   c. Deciding at the last minute to skip a class because your friends just told you that they're going to a movie you want to see

   d. Making a decision regarding where you want to travel over your next vacation break

4. Wendy is a member of a political group on your campus and is interested in finding out how many students plan to vote in the next presidential election. According to the theory of planned behavior, which of the following attitude questions Wendy could ask would be the best predictor of whether or not a particular student will vote in the next presidential election?
   a. "What are your attitudes about U.S. politics?"
   b. "What are your attitudes about voting?"
   c. "What are your attitudes about voting in the next U.S. presidential election?"
   d. "What are your attitudes about former U.S. President Barack Obama?"

5. In trying to predict deliberative behaviors, what three considerations must we evaluate?
   a. Cognitively based attitudes, behaviorally based attitudes, affectively based attitudes
   b. Attitude specificity, subjective norms, perceived behavioral control
   c. Classical conditioning, operant conditioning, self-perception theory
   d. Attitude accessibility, explicit attitudes, implicit attitudes

How Do Attitudes Change?

LO 7.3   **Explain how internal and external factors lead to attitude change.**

Thus far we have defined different types of attitudes and discussed the circumstances under which attitudes predict behavior. But another important point about attitudes also warrants our attention: Attitudes often change. In America, for example, the popularity of the president often rises and falls with surprising speed. Right after Barack Obama was first elected president, in January of 2009, 67% of Americans said they approved of the job he was doing. By November of 2010, as the economic recovery in the United

States sputtered, his approval rating had dropped to 47%. Then, right after Osama Bin Laden was killed in May of 2011, his approval rating shot back up to 60%. It stood at 57% in November 2012 at the time of his re-election, fell back into the 40s by 2014, but hit the 50% mark again as his second term neared its end in 2016 (AP-GfK Poll, 2016).

When attitudes change, they often do so in response to social influence. Our attitudes toward everything from a presidential candidate to a brand of laundry detergent can be influenced by what other people do or say. This is why attitudes are of such interest to social psychologists; even something as personal and internal as an attitude is a highly social phenomenon, influenced by the imagined or actual behavior of other people. The entire premise of advertising, for example, is that your attitudes toward consumer products can be influenced by publicity. Remember Jason Sadler—er, Jason Headsets.com? His namesake client company claimed to have made millions of dollars on the publicity. But such external influences—like an opportunistic attention-seeker's name change—are not the only forces that shape our attitudes. Let's take a look at the conditions under which attitudes are most likely to change.

Changing Attitudes by Changing Behavior: Cognitive Dissonance Theory Revisited

We have already discussed one way that attitudes change: when people behave inconsistently with their attitudes and cannot find external justification for their behavior. We refer, of course, to cognitive dissonance theory. As we noted in Chapter 6, people experience dissonance when they do something that threatens their image of themselves as decent, kind, and honest—particularly if there is no way they can explain away this behavior as due to external circumstances.

If you wanted to change your friends' attitudes toward a problematic behavior like smoking, using tanning beds, or texting while driving, one way to succeed might be to get *them* to give speeches against each practice. You would want to make it hard for your friends to find external reasons for giving the speech; for example, you would not want them to justify their actions by saying, "I'm doing it as a special favor for my friend" or "I'm getting paid to do it." That is, as we saw in Chapter 6, the goal is to get your friends to find *internal justification* for giving the speech, whereby they must seek to reduce the dissonance of giving the speech by deciding that they actually believe what they are saying. But what if your goal is to change attitudes on a mass scale? Suppose you were hired by the American Cancer Society to come up with an antismoking campaign that could be used nationwide to counteract the kind of tobacco advertisements we discussed at the beginning of this chapter. Although dissonance techniques are powerful, they are difficult to carry out on a mass scale (e.g., it would be hard to have all American smokers make antismoking speeches under just the right conditions of internal justification). To change as many people's attitudes as possible, you would have to resort to other techniques of attitude change. You would probably construct some sort of **persuasive communication**, such as a speech or television advertisement that advocates a particular side of an issue. How should you construct your message so that it would change people's attitudes?

Persuasive Communication

A message advocating a particular side of an issue

Sometimes attitudes change dramatically over short periods of time. If previous presidential administrations are any indication, Americans' approval rating of Donald Trump will go up and down during the course of his presidency.

Persuasive Communications and Attitude Change

Suppose the American Cancer Society has given you a budget to develop your advertising campaign. Should you pack your public service announcement with facts and figures? Or should you take a more emotional approach, including in your message frightening visual images of diseased lungs? Should you hire a movie star to deliver your message or a Nobel Prize–winning medical researcher? Should you take a friendly tone and acknowledge that it is hard to quit smoking,

or should you take a hard line and tell smokers to quit cold turkey? You get the point: Constructing an effective persuasive communication is complicated.

Luckily, social psychologists, beginning with Carl Hovland and his colleagues, have conducted many studies over the years on what makes a persuasive communication effective (Hovland, Janis, & Kelley, 1953). Drawing on their experiences during World War II, when they worked for the United States Army to increase the morale of soldiers (Stouffer et al., 1949), Hovland and his colleagues conducted many experiments on the conditions under which people are most likely to be influenced by persuasive communications. In essence, they studied "who says what to whom," looking at the *source* of the communication (e.g., how expert or attractive the speaker is), the *communication* itself (e.g., the quality of the arguments, whether the speaker presents both sides of the issue), and the nature of the *audience* (e.g., whether the audience is hostile or friendly to the point of view in question). Because these researchers were at Yale University, their approach to the study of persuasive communications remains known as the **Yale Attitude Change approach**.

This approach yielded a great deal of useful information on how people change their attitudes in response to persuasive communications, as summarized in Figure 7.3.

Yale Attitude Change Approach

The study of the conditions under which people are most likely to change their attitudes in response to persuasive messages, focusing on the source of the communication, the nature of the communication, and the nature of the audience

Figure 7.3 The Yale Attitude Change Approach

Researchers at Yale University initiated research on what makes a persuasive communication effective, focusing on "who said what to whom."

The Yale Attitude Change Approach

The effectiveness of persuasive communications depends on who says what to whom.

Who: The Source of the Communication

- Credible speakers (e.g., those with obvious expertise) persuade people more than speakers lacking in credibility (Hovland & Weiss, 1951; Schwarz, Newman, & Leach, 2016).
- Attractive speakers (whether due to physical or personality attributes) persuade people more than unattractive speakers do (Eagly & Chaiken, 1975; Khan & Sutcliffe, 2014).
- People sometimes remember a message longer than they do information about the message source. In this manner, information from a low-credibility source sometimes becomes more persuasive with the passage of time, a phenomenon referred to as the *sleeper effect* (Kumkale & Albarracín, 2004; Albarracín, Kumkale, & Poyner-Del Vento, 2017).

What: The Nature of the Communication

- People are more persuaded by messages that do not seem to be designed to influence them (Petty & Cacioppo, 1986; Walster & Festinger, 1962).
- It is generally better to present a two-sided communication (one that presents arguments for and against your position) than a one-sided communication (one that presents only arguments favoring your position), especially when you are sure to refute the arguments on the other side of the issue (Cornelis, Cauberghe, & De Pelesmacker, 2014; Igou & Bless, 2003).
- In terms of order effects, if speeches are to be given back to back and there will be a delay before people have to make up their minds, there tends to be a *primacy effect*: the first speech is usually more persuasive. However, if there is a delay between the speeches and people will make up their minds right after the second one, there is likely to be a *recency effect*: it is then better to give the last speech (Haugtvedt & Wegener, 1994; Miller & Campbell, 1959).

To Whom: The Nature of the Audience

- An audience that is distracted during the persuasive communication will often be persuaded more than one that is not distracted (Albarracín & Wyer, 2001; Festinger & Maccoby, 1964).
- Some individual differences predict a greater likelihood of persuadability, including having lower intelligence, being of moderate (versus high or low) self-esteem, and being between the impressionable ages of 18-25 (Krosnick & Alwin, 1989; Rhodes & Wood, 1992; Sears, 1981).
- Cultural differences have also been found for which argument types are most persuasive. For American or other "Western" audiences, personal preferences are often central to effective messages, such as an advertisement that emphasizes, "I like it because it makes me feel good." In other cultures that prioritize contextually appropriate behavior, an advertisement might be more effective by emphasizing the message, "I like it because others I am connected to like it" (Riemer et al., 2014).

As the research mounted, however, a problem became apparent: Many aspects of persuasive communications turned out to be important, but it was not clear which were more important than others—that is, it was unclear when one factor should be emphasized over another.

For example, let's return to that job you have with the American Cancer Society. The marketing manager wants to see your ad next month. If you were to read the many Yale Attitude Change studies, you might find lots of useful information about who should say what to whom in order to construct a persuasive communication. However, you might also find yourself saying, "There's a lot of information here, and I'm not sure what to emphasize. Should I focus on who delivers the ads? Or should I worry more about the content of the message?"

THE CENTRAL AND PERIPHERAL ROUTES TO PERSUASION   More recent attitude researchers have asked the same questions: When is it best to stress factors central to the communication, such as the strength of the arguments? When is it best to stress factors peripheral to the logic of the arguments, such as the credibility or attractiveness of the person delivering the speech (Chaiken, 1980; Petty & Wegener, 2014)? The **elaboration likelihood model** of persuasion (Petty, Barden, & Wheeler, 2009; Petty & Cacioppo, 1986), for example, specifies when people will be influenced by what the speech says (i.e., the logic of the arguments) and when they will be influenced by more superficial characteristics (e.g., who gives the speech or how long it is).

The theory states that under certain conditions people are motivated to pay attention to the facts in a communication, which means that the more logically compelling those facts are, the more persuasion occurs. That is, sometimes people elaborate on the messages they hear, carefully thinking about and processing the content of the communication. Petty and Cacioppo (1986) call this the **central route to persuasion**. Under other conditions, people are not motivated to pay attention to the facts; instead, they notice only the surface characteristics of the message, such as how long it is and who is delivering it. Here, people will not be swayed by the logic of the arguments, because they are not paying close attention to what the communicator says. Instead, they are persuaded if the surface characteristics of the message— such as the fact that it is long or is delivered by an expert or attractive communicator—make it seem like a reasonable one. Petty and Cacioppo call this the **peripheral route to persuasion** because people are swayed by things peripheral to the message itself. For example, if you happen to follow Khloe Kardashian on Twitter, you may have seen any of a variety of tweets related to particular products, such as one stating that a particular brand of jeans "makes your butt look scary good." Such a communication is, shall we say, light on factual evidence; if it persuaded anyone to go out and buy this brand of jeans, it is likely to have done so through the peripheral route. Indeed, companies reportedly have paid celebrities fees exceeding $10,000 per instance to tweet or post about the virtues of various products (Rexrode, 2011).

What determines whether people take the central versus the peripheral route to persuasion? The key is whether they have both the motivation and the ability to pay attention to the facts. When people are truly interested in the topic and thus motivated to pay close attention to the arguments, *and* if people have the ability to pay attention—for example, if nothing is distracting them—they are more likely to take the central route (see Figure 7.4).

Elaboration Likelihood Model

A model explaining two ways in which persuasive communications can cause attitude change: *centrally*, when people are motivated and have the ability to pay attention to the arguments in the communication, and *peripherally*, when people do not pay attention to the arguments but are instead swayed by surface characteristics

Central Route to Persuasion

The case in which people have both the ability and the motivation to elaborate on a persuasive communication, listening carefully to and thinking about the arguments presented

Peripheral Route to Persuasion

The case in which people do not elaborate on the arguments in a persuasive communication but are instead swayed by more superficial cues

Sometimes attitude change occurs via a peripheral route. For example, we can be swayed more by who delivers a persuasive message than by the strength of the message itself, such as when consumers buy certain products because a celebrity tweets about them.

Figure 7.4 The Elaboration Likelihood Model

The elaboration likelihood model describes how people change their attitudes when they hear persuasive communications.

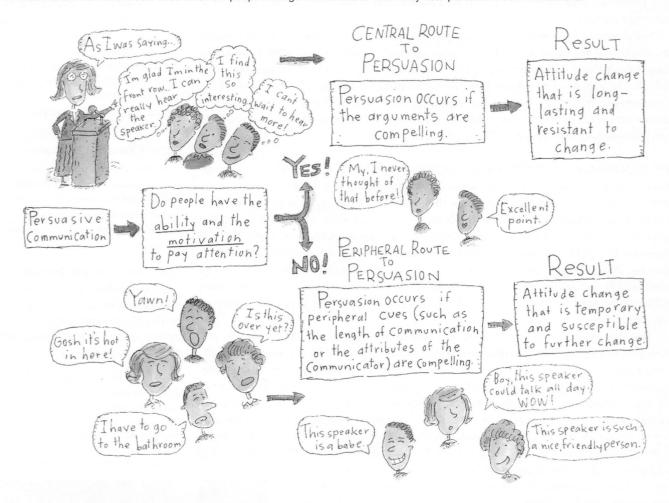

THE MOTIVATION TO PAY ATTENTION TO THE ARGUMENTS One thing that determines whether people are motivated to pay attention to a communication is the personal relevance of the topic: How important is the topic to a person's well-being? For example, consider the issue of whether Social Security benefits should be reduced. How personally relevant is this to you? If you are a 72-year-old whose sole income is from Social Security, the issue is extremely relevant; if you are a 20-year-old from a well-to-do family, it is likely less so.

The more personally relevant an issue is, the more willing people are to pay attention to the arguments in a speech and therefore the more likely they are to take the central route to persuasion. In one study, for example, college students were asked to listen to a speech arguing that all college seniors should be required to pass a comprehensive exam in their major before they graduate (Petty, Cacioppo, & Goldman, 1981). Half of the participants were told that their university was seriously considering requiring comprehensive exams. For these students, the issue was personally relevant. For the other half, it was more "ho-hum"—they were told that their university might require such exams, but not for 10 more years.

The researchers then introduced two variables that might influence whether people would agree with the speech. The first was the strength of the arguments presented. Half of the participants heard arguments that were strong and persuasive (e.g., "The quality of undergraduate teaching has improved at schools with the exams"), whereas the others heard arguments that were weak and unpersuasive (e.g., "The risk of failing

Figure 7.5 Effects of Personal Relevance on Type of Attitude Change

The higher the number, the more people agreed with the persuasive communication. Left panel: When the issue was highly relevant, people were swayed by the quality of the arguments more than the expertise of the speaker. This is the central route to persuasion. Right panel: When the issue was low in relevance, people were swayed by the expertise of the speaker more than the quality of the arguments. This is the peripheral route to persuasion.

(Based on data in Petty, Cacioppo, & Goldman, 1981)

the exam is a challenge most students would welcome"). The second variable was a peripheral cue—the prestige of the speaker. Half of the participants were told that the author of the speech was an eminent professor at Princeton University, whereas the others were told that the author was a high school student. When deciding how much to agree with the speaker's position, the participants could use one or both of these different kinds of information; they could listen carefully to the arguments and think about how convincing they were, or they could simply go by who said them and how prestigious that source was. As predicted by the elaboration likelihood model, the route to persuasion depended on the personal relevance of the issue. The left panel of Figure 7.5 shows what happened when the issue was highly relevant to the listeners. Those students who heard strong arguments agreed much more with the speech than did those who heard weak arguments, regardless of who presented them, the Princeton professor or the high school student. A good argument was a good argument, even if it was written by someone who lacked prestige. In other words, persuasion took place via the central route.

What happens when a topic is of low relevance? As seen in the right panel of Figure 7.5, what mattered then in the comprehensive exam study was not the strength of the arguments but who the speaker was. Those who heard strong arguments agreed with the speech only slightly more than those who heard weak arguments, whereas those who heard the Princeton professor were much more swayed than those who heard the high school student. Here, the persuasion took a peripheral route.

THE ABILITY TO PAY ATTENTION TO THE ARGUMENTS Sometimes even when we want to pay attention to a persuasive communication, it is difficult to do so. Maybe we're tired and sitting in a hot and crowded room; maybe the issue is too complex and hard to evaluate. When people are unable to pay close attention to the arguments, they are swayed more by peripheral cues (Petty & Brock, 1981; Petty et al., 2009). For example, consider the daunting task faced by a jury that has to evaluate a case involving complicated scientific evidence. Perhaps a trial in which the plaintiff is suing because he believes that exposure to a toxic substance at work made him ill. Now, most jurors are not scientists—they don't have the expertise needed to carefully weigh the arguments in such a case, even if they want to.

Indeed, in a study examining this very scenario, Cooper and colleagues (1996) showed mock jurors a video reenactment of a product liability trial. One of the critical witnesses was an expert biologist hired by the plaintiff to persuade the jury that the product in question had caused the plaintiff's illness. The researchers varied how qualified the expert seemed to be: some mock jurors were told that the expert had published 45 research articles in peer-reviewed journals and his multiple advanced degrees came from prestigious universities; other jurors learned that the expert had published far fewer articles and his degrees came from relatively obscure schools. When his scientific testimony was relatively simple and easy to understand, participants paid little attention to the expert's apparent credentials, instead focusing on the strength of the arguments he offered. Able to understand the persuasive arguments, they engaged in a central route. But when his scientific testimony was complicated and conveyed in jargon that only a molecular biologist could fully grasp, mock jurors relied on the expert's credentials to determine how much stock to place in his testimony. Unable to attend carefully to the persuasive communication, they were influenced by peripheral cues (Cooper, Bennett, & Sukel, 1996).

In short, your own expertise and personal tendencies shape your ability to pay attention to persuasive arguments. As one more example, those of us who are "morning people" are more likely to take the central route to persuasion the earlier in the day it is. But those of us who are "evening people" are more likely to take the central route as the hours grow later (Martin & Martin, 2013).

HOW TO ACHIEVE LONG-LASTING ATTITUDE CHANGE   Now that you know a persuasive communication can change people's attitudes in either of two ways—via the central or the peripheral route—you may be wondering what difference it makes. Does it really matter whether it was the logic of the arguments or the expertise of the source that changed students' minds about comprehensive exams in the Petty and colleagues (1981) study? Given the bottom line—they changed their attitudes—should any of us care how they got to that point?

If we are interested in creating long-lasting attitude change, we should care a lot. People who base their attitudes on a careful analysis of the arguments will be more likely to maintain this attitude over time, more likely to behave consistently with this attitude, and more resistant to counterpersuasion than people who base their attitudes on peripheral cues (Mackie, 1987; Petty & Briñol, 2012; Petty & Wegener, 1999). In one study, for example, people changed their attitudes either by analyzing the logic of the arguments or by using peripheral cues. When the participants were telephoned 10 days later, those who had analyzed the logic of the arguments were more likely to have maintained their new attitude (Chaiken, 1980).

And throughout this chapter we have considered the potential for public health messages to change attitudes and behaviors—but just how long lasting are such changes made in response to advertisements, movies, books, and other efforts? In one study, Julia Hormes and her colleagues (2013) examined the duration of attitude change effects among incoming college freshman who read *The Omnivore's Dilemma* as part of a university-wide requirement. The popular book, by Michael Pollan, addresses the politics of modern food production, and researchers asked the students a series of questions right after they had read it as well as 1 year later. Right after reading the book, students had very different attitudes regarding food production issues than did a control group that hadn't read it. One year later, many of these attitude changes had disappeared, but a few did remain intact: readers of the book continued to express greater concern about the quality of the contemporary food supply and opposition to governmental subsidies for corn production (Hormes et al., 2013). In short, the effects of attitude change campaigns do decline over time, but some attitude change can, indeed, be long lasting.

Emotion and Attitude Change

Now you know exactly how to construct your ad for the American Cancer Society, right? Well, not quite. Before people will consider your carefully constructed arguments, you have to get their attention. How can you be sure people will watch the ad when it comes on or pops up? One way is to grab people's attention by playing to their emotions.

FEAR-AROUSING COMMUNICATIONS One way to get people's attention is to scare them—for example, by showing pictures of diseased lungs and presenting alarming data about the link between smoking and lung cancer. This is an example of a **fear-arousing communication**. Public service ads often take this approach by trying to scare people into practicing safer sex, wearing seat belts, cutting down on carbon emissions, and staying away from drugs. For example, since January 2001, cigarettes sold in Canada have been required to display graphic pictures of diseased gums and other body parts that cover at least 50% of the outside label. A few years ago the U.S. Food and Drug Administration ruled that all cigarette packs sold in the United States were to contain similar images, but after legal challenges from the tobacco industry, the USFDA abandoned the plan (Felberbaum, 2013).

Do fear-arousing communications work? It depends on whether the fear influences people's ability attend to and process the arguments in a message. If a moderate amount of fear is created and people believe that listening to the message will teach them how to reduce this fear, then they are more likely to be motivated to analyze the message carefully and their attitudes via the central route (Emery et al., 2014; Petty, 1995).

Consider a study in which a group of smokers watched a graphic film depicting lung cancer and then read pamphlets with specific instructions about how to quit smoking (Leventhal, Watts, & Pagano, 1967). As shown by the bottom line in Figure 7.6, people in this condition reduced their smoking significantly more than people who were shown only the film or only the pamphlet. Why? Watching the film scared people, and giving them the pamphlet reassured them that there was a way to reduce

Fear-Arousing Communication

Persuasive message that attempts to change people's attitudes by arousing their fears

Figure 7.6 Effects of Fear Appeals on Attitude Change

People were shown a scary film about the effects of smoking, instructions about how to stop smoking, or both. Those who were shown both had the biggest reduction in the number of cigarettes they smoked.

(Adapted from Leventhal, Watts, & Pagano, 1967)

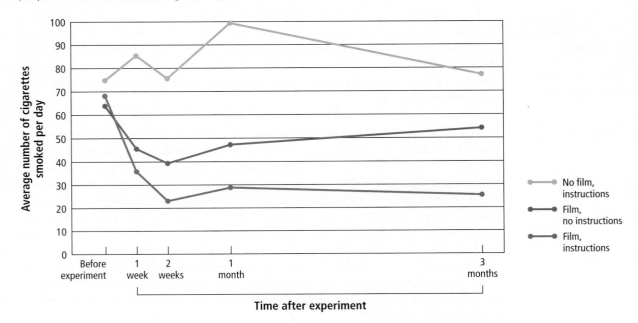

PERINGATAN

MEROKOK SEBABKAN KANKER MULUT

FILTER CIGARETTES

Marlboro

The FDA has tried to implement guidelines to require all cigarette packs sold in the United States to display pictures that warn about the dangers of smoking, such as the one shown here. Do you think that this ad would scare people into quitting?

Heuristic–Systematic Model of Persuasion

An explanation of the two ways in which persuasive communications can cause attitude change: either systematically processing the merits of the arguments or using mental shortcuts or heuristics

this fear—by following the instructions on how to quit. Only seeing the pamphlet didn't work very well, because there was little fear motivating people to read it carefully. Only seeing the film didn't work very well either, because people are likely to tune out a message that raises fear but does not give information about how to reduce it. This may explain why some attempts to frighten people into changing their attitudes and behaviors fail: They succeed in scaring people but do not provide specific ways to help them reduce that fear (Aronson, 2008; Hoog, Stroebe, & de Wit, 2005; Ruiter, Abraham, & Kok, 2001).

Fear-arousing appeals will also fail if they are so strong that they overwhelm people. If people are terribly frightened, they will become defensive, deny the importance of the threat, and be unable to think rationally about the issue (Feinberg & Willer, 2011; Janis & Feshbach, 1953; Kessels et al., 2014). So if you have decided to arouse people's fear in your ad for the American Cancer Society, keep these points in mind: Try to create enough fear to motivate people to pay attention to your arguments, but not so much fear that people will tune out what you say. And make sure to include some specific recommendations about how to stop smoking so people will be reassured that paying close attention to your arguments will help them reduce their fear.

EMOTIONS AS A HEURISTIC   Another way in which emotions can cause attitude change is by acting as a signal for how we feel about something. According to the **heuristic–systematic model of persuasion** (Chaiken & Stangor 1987), when people take the peripheral route to persuasion, they often use heuristics. Recall from Chapter 3 that heuristics are mental shortcuts people use to make judgments quickly and efficiently. In the present context, a heuristic is a simple rule people use to decide what their attitude is without having to spend a lot of time analyzing every detail about the topic. Examples of such heuristics are "Experts are always right" and "People who speak quickly must know what they're talking about."

Interestingly, our emotions can themselves act as heuristics to determine our attitudes. When trying to decide what our attitude is about something, we often rely on the "How do I feel about it?" heuristic (Forgas, 2013; Kim, Park, & Schwarz, 2010; Storbeck & Clore, 2008). If we feel good, we must have a positive attitude; if we feel bad, it's thumbs down. Now this probably sounds like a pretty good rule to follow, and, like most heuristics, it is—most of the time. Suppose you need a new couch and go to a furniture store to look around. You see one in your price range and are trying to decide whether to buy it. Using the "How do I feel about it?" heuristic, you do a quick check of your emotions. If you feel great while you're sitting on the couch in the store, you will probably buy it.

The only problem is that sometimes it is difficult to tell where our feelings come from. Is it really the couch that made you feel great, or is it something completely unrelated? Maybe you were in a good mood to begin with, or maybe on the way to the store you heard your favorite song on the radio. The problem with the "How do I feel about it?" heuristic is that we can make mistakes about what is causing our mood, misattributing feelings created by one source (our favorite song) to another (the couch; Claypool et al., 2008). When this happens, you might make a bad decision. After you get the new couch home, you might discover that it no longer makes you feel all that great. It makes sense, then, that retailers strive to create good feelings while presenting their products: salespeople play music and put art on the walls of the showroom; real estate agents bake cookies in the kitchen before staging an open house. Their underlying hope is that people will attribute at least some of the pleasant feelings that follow to the product being sold.

More generally, emotions can also influence the way that people think about persuasive messages (Petty & Briñol, 2015). For instance, when we're in a good mood, we tend to relax a bit, comfortable in the assumption that the world is a safe place, which can lead us to be content with heuristic cues like the apparent expertise of a source. A bad mood, however, often puts us on alert, sharpening our skepticism and leading us to pay more attention to message quality. Although we may be persuaded by a weak message from an attractive source when we're happy, it usually takes a strong message to sway us when we're sad (Schwarz, Bless, & Bohner, 1991).

EMOTION AND DIFFERENT TYPES OF ATTITUDES   The success of various attitude-change techniques also depends on the type of attitude we are trying to change. As we saw previously, not all attitudes are created equally; some are based more on beliefs about the attitude object (cognitively based attitudes), whereas others are based more on emotions and values (affectively based attitudes). Several studies have shown that it is best to fight fire with fire: If an attitude is cognitively based, your best bet is to try to change it with rational arguments; if it is affectively based, you're better off trying to change it with emotional appeals (Conner et al., 2011; Fabrigar & Petty, 1999; Haddock et al., 2008).

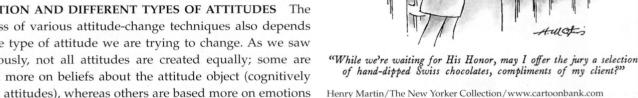

"While we're waiting for His Honor, may I offer the jury a selection of hand-dipped Swiss chocolates, compliments of my client?"

Henry Martin/The New Yorker Collection/www.cartoonbank.com

Consider a study of the effectiveness of different kinds of advertisements (Shavitt, 1990). Some ads stress the objective merits of a product, such as an ad for an appliance that discusses its price, efficiency, and reliability. Other ads stress emotions and values, such as ones for designer jeans that associate the brand with sex, beauty, and youthfulness rather than saying anything about the objective qualities of the product. Which kind of ad is most effective? To find out, participants were shown different kinds of advertisements. Some were for "utilitarian products" such as air conditioners and coffee. People's attitudes toward such products tend to be formed after an appraisal of the functional aspects of the products and thus are cognitively based. The other items were "social identity products" such as perfume and greeting cards. People's attitudes toward these types of products tend to reflect a concern with how they appear to others and are therefore more affectively based. Participants in the study reacted most favorably to the ads that matched the type of attitude they had. If their attitudes were cognitively based, the ads that focused on the utilitarian aspects of these products, such as the energy efficiency of the air conditioner, were most successful. If their attitudes were more affectively based, the ads that focused on values and emotions were most successful.

Attitude Change and the Body

Although you know a lot by now about how to craft your persuasive message for the American Cancer Society, there is yet one more thing you might want to take into account: what will your audience be doing when they hear it? Reclining comfortably on a living room couch? Sitting in a crowded school auditorium during a required assembly? Our physical environment and even our body posture play surprising roles in the process of attitude change (Briñol & Petty, 2009, 2012). Consider, for example, a study by Briñol and Petty (2003) in which participants were asked to test out the durability of some new headphones. Some were asked to shake their heads from side to side while wearing them, whereas others were asked to nod their heads up and down. While doing this, the participants listened to an editorial arguing that all students should be required to carry personal identification cards on campus. One final twist was that half of the participants heard strong, persuasive arguments (e.g., that ID cards would make

Figure 7.7 Effects of Confidence in One's Thoughts on Persuasion

People who nodded their heads up and down, compared to those who shook their heads from side to side, had greater confidence in their thoughts about the message (e.g., "Wow, this is really convincing" when the arguments were strong, and "Wow, this is really dumb" when the arguments were weak).

(Figure adapted from Briñol & Petty, 2003)

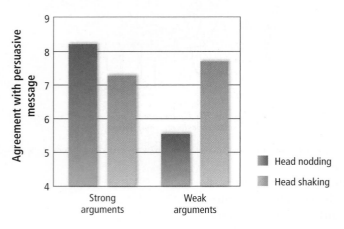

Head nodding

Head shaking

Strong arguments | Weak arguments

Agreement with persuasive message

Watch BODY MOVEMENT AND PERSUASION

Revel Video

the campus safer for students) whereas the other half heard weak, unconvincing arguments (e.g., that if students carried the cards, security guards would have more time for lunch).

As you have no doubt gathered, the point of the study was not to test the headphones but to see whether shaking or nodding one's head while listening to a persuasive communication influenced the likelihood of persuasion. The idea was that even though the head movements had nothing to do with the editorial, these actions might influence how confident people felt in the arguments they heard. Nodding one's head up and down, as people do when they say yes, might increase feelings of confidence compared to shaking one's head side to side, as people do when they say no. This is exactly what happened, with interesting consequences. When the arguments in the editorial were strong, people who nodded their heads agreed with them more than did people who shook their heads, because the head-nodders had more confidence in the strong arguments that they heard (see the left side of Figure 7.7). But when the arguments were weak, head nodding had the opposite effect. It gave people more confidence that the arguments they heard were in fact weak and unconvincing, making them *less* convinced than people who shook their heads from side to side (see the right side of Figure 7.7).

The moral? What people are doing when you try to persuade them makes a difference. Sitting in a soft, cushy chair at the computer store just might make you more comfortable with the idea of spending more on your new laptop than you had originally budgeted. Getting customers to smile even before they hear about your product may get them to transfer positive feelings to the item you're trying to sell them. And anything you can do to increase audience members' confidence in their thoughts about your message will make that message more effective—just as long as your arguments are strong and convincing in the first place.

Review Questions

1. One way to change someone's attitude is to get that person to give a speech arguing against his or her actual viewpoint. This strategy can lead to attitude change through cognitive dissonance as long as _____ is (are) present.
   a. peripheral cues to persuasion
   b. a motivated audience that feels a sense of personal relevance
   c. two-sided arguments
   d. insufficient justification for making the speech

2. Which of the following is *not* one of the three factors considered by the Yale Attitude Change approach?
   a. Nature of the audience
   b. Message source
   c. Fear
   d. Nature of the communication itself

3. A debate breaks out at the town hall meeting over whether local real estate taxes should be raised to pay for a new public school building. Which of the following individuals is most likely to process the persuasive information raised during this debate through the *peripheral* route?
   a. Gob, who has no school-aged children of his own and owns no real estate
   b. Lindsay, whose daughter still has 3 years left of public school
   c. Michael, who is a real estate executive whose business is affected by local tax rates
   d. Buster, a local teacher, who is working in a temporary classroom because the current school building is too small for the number of students enrolled

4. The physical attractiveness of the source of a persuasive communication would be best described as which of the following?
   a. Systematic cue
   b. Central cue
   c. Peripheral cue
   d. Rational cue

5. Fear-arousing persuasive communication is most likely to be effective when
   a. very high levels of fear are induced.
   b. very low levels of fear are induced.
   c. a plan for reducing the fear is provided.
   d. the target of the communication is a utilitarian or functional object.

6. Briñol and Petty (2003) conducted a study in which participants tried on headphones while listening to a persuasive editorial. Half of the participants shook their heads side-to-side while listening; the other half nodded up-and-down while listening. Which group of participants expressed the greatest agreement with the arguments expressed in the editorial at the end of the study?
   a. The head-shakers who heard weak arguments in the editorial
   b. The head-shakers who heard strong arguments in the editorial
   c. The head-nodders who heard weak arguments in the editorial
   d. The head-nodders who heard strong arguments in the editorial

The Power of Advertising

LO 7.4   Describe how advertising changes people's attitudes.

As alluded to elsewhere in this chapter, many examples of when, why, and how we change our attitudes are provided by considering the influence of advertising. In many respects, advertising is a direct application of social psychology—it's a concerted effort to change the way that consumers think about and act toward a certain product. Consider, for example, this insight into human nature provided by perhaps the most famous (albeit fictional) advertising executive of recent memory, Don Draper, lead character of the TV show *Mad Men*: "People want to be told what to do so badly that they'll listen to anyone." Is this an exaggeration? Of course it is—you already know from the preceding sections that whether or not people listen depends on factors such as a message's source and the nature of a communication itself. But there remains a kernel of truth underlying the comment. Advertising *is* powerful, and people are surprisingly susceptible to its influence.

One curious thing about advertising is that most people think it works on everyone but themselves (Wilson & Brekke, 1994). But it turns out that people are influenced by advertisements more than they think, even when it comes to those annoying online pop-up ads (Capella, Webster, & Kinard, 2011; Courbet et al., 2014; Wilson, Houston, & Meyers, 1998). Evidence that advertising can change attitudes (and behaviors) is provided by successful public health campaigns. As we've discussed, advertising, product placement, and the behavior of admired figures can have powerful effects on people's behavior, including tobacco and alcohol use (Pechmann & Knight, 2002; Saffer, 2002). A meta-analysis of studies that tested the effects of a media message (conveyed via television, radio, electronic, and print media) on substance use among youths yielded encouraging results (Derzon & Lipsey, 2002). After a campaign that targeted a specific substance, such as tobacco, kids were less likely to use it. Television and radio messages had even bigger effects than messages in the print media (Ibrahim & Glantz, 2007).

Advertising is just one aspect of the broader category of marketing, the effort to communicate with potential customers about the value of a product or service. Hopeful entrepreneurs appearing on the TV show *Shark Tank*, for example, must make a compelling pitch to potential investors (i.e., the "sharks") to raise money for their idea. They have to market their product to the sharks by convincing them that they will also be able to market it to paying customers. The successful entrepreneur can use social psychological principles of attitude change to make any product seem attractive, personally relevant, useful, and even necessary.

How Advertising Works

How does advertising work, and what types of ads work best? The answers follow from our earlier discussion of attitude change. If advertisers are trying to change an affectively based attitude, then, as we have seen, it is best to fight emotions with emotions. Many advertisements take the emotional approach—for example, ads for different brands of soft drinks. Given that different brands of colas are not all that different, and that they have little nutritional value to be touted, many people do not base their purchasing decisions on the objective qualities of the different brands. Consequently, soda advertisements do not stress facts and figures. As one advertising executive noted, "The thing about soda commercials is that they actually have nothing to say" ("Battle for Your Brain," 1991). Instead of presenting facts, soft drink ads play to people's emotions, trying to associate feelings of excitement, youth, energy, and attractiveness with the brand.

Of course, advertising is even harder if you have a product that does not trigger people's emotions and is not directly relevant to their everyday lives. The trick is to *make* your product personally relevant. Consider the case of Gerald Lambert, who early in the 20th century inherited a company that made a surgical antiseptic used to treat throat infections—Listerine. Seeking a wider market for his product, Lambert decided to promote it as a mouthwash. The only problem was that no one at the time used a mouthwash or even knew what one was. So having invented the cure, Lambert invented the disease. Advertisements for Listerine began to appear in countless magazines over the years, including one ad that today we would find incredibly sexist, depicting a solitary woman with the text "Often a bridesmaid, never a bride." This tagline became one of the most famous in the history of advertising, successfully playing on people's fears about social rejection. In a few carefully chosen words, it succeeded in making a problem—bad breath—personally relevant to millions of people. The sharks on *Shark Tank* (and Donald Draper) would be proud.

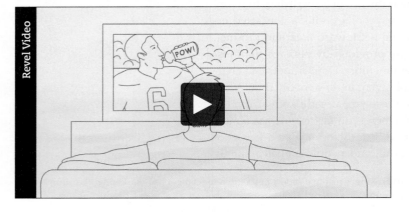

Watch THE SOCIAL PSYCHOLOGY OF ADVERTISING

Revel Video

Subliminal Advertising: A Form of Mind Control?

Effective advertising tells consumers what they want, sometimes even before they know they want it. But what happens when we don't even recognize that an attempt at persuasion is underway? This question brings us to the idea of subliminal advertising. For example, in September 2000, during the heat of the U.S. presidential campaign between George W. Bush and Al Gore, a man in Seattle was watching a political advertisement on television. At first the ad looked like a run-of-the-mill political spot in which an announcer praised the benefits of Bush's prescription drug plan and criticized Gore's plan. But the viewer thought that he noticed something odd. He videotaped the ad the next time it ran and played it back at a slow speed, and sure enough, he *had* noticed something unusual. As the announcer said, "The Gore prescription plan: Bureaucrats decide ..." the word RATS (as in the last four letters of "bureaucrats") flashed on the screen very quickly—for just one-thirtieth of a second. The alert viewer notified officials in the Gore campaign, who quickly contacted the press. Soon the country was abuzz about a possible attempt by the Bush campaign to use subliminal messages to create a negative impression of Al Gore. The Bush campaign denied that anyone had deliberately inserted the word RATS, claiming that it was "purely accidental" (Berke, 2000).

During the 2000 U.S. presidential race, George W. Bush aired a television ad about his prescription drug plan, during which the word RATS was visible on the screen for a split second. Do subliminal messages like this one have any effect on people's attitudes?

The RATS incident was neither the first nor the last controversy over the use of **subliminal messages**, defined as words or pictures that are not consciously perceived but may influence people's judgments, attitudes, and behaviors. In the late 1950s, James Vicary supposedly flashed the messages "Drink Coca-Cola" and "Eat popcorn" during movies at his theater and claimed that sales at the concession counter skyrocketed (according to some reports, Vicary made up these claims; Weir, 1984). Wilson Bryan Key (1973, 1989) has written several best-selling books on hidden persuasion techniques, which claim that advertisers routinely implant sexual messages in print advertisements, such as the word *sex* in the ice cubes of an ad for gin, and male and female genitalia in everything from butter to the icing in an ad for cake mix. Key (1973) argues that these images are not consciously perceived but put people in a good mood and make them pay more attention to the advertisement. More recently, gambling casinos in Canada removed a brand of slot machines after it was revealed that the machines flashed the winning symbols on every spin, at a speed too fast for the players to see consciously (Benedetti, 2007).

Subliminal messages are not just visual; they can be auditory as well. There is a large market for audiotapes that contain subliminal messages to help people lose weight, stop smoking, raise self-esteem, and even shave a few strokes off their golf game. But are subliminal messages effective? Do they really make us more likely to buy consumer products or help us lose weight and stop smoking? Most members of the public believe that subliminal messages can shape their attitudes and behaviors (Zanot, Pincus, & Lamp, 1983). Are they right?

DEBUNKING THE CLAIMS ABOUT SUBLIMINAL ADVERTISING Few of the proponents of subliminal advertising have conducted controlled studies to back up their claims. Fortunately, many studies of subliminal perception have been conducted, allowing us to evaluate their sometimes outlandish claims. Simply stated, there is no evidence that the types of subliminal messages encountered in everyday life have regular influence on people's behavior. Hidden commands do not cause us to line up and buy popcorn any more than we normally do, and the subliminal commands on self-help tapes do not (unfortunately!) help us quit smoking or lose weight (Brannon & Brock, 1994; Nelson, 2008; Trappey, 1996). For example, one study randomly assigned people to listen to subliminal self-help recordings designed to improve memory or to one designed to raise their self-esteem (Greenwald et al., 1991). Neither of the recordings had any effect on people's memory or self-esteem. Even so, participants were convinced that they had worked, which explains why you can still today find subliminal self-help audio sold online and in bookstores.

Subliminal Messages
Words or pictures that are not consciously perceived but may nevertheless influence judgments, attitudes, and behaviors

PEOPLE HAVE BEEN TRYING TO FIND THE BREASTS IN THESE ICE CUBES SINCE 1957.

The advertising industry is sometimes charged with sneaking seductive little pictures into ads.

Supposedly, these pictures can get you to buy a product without your even seeing them.

Consider the photograph above. According to some people, there's a pair of female breasts

hidden in the patterns of light refracted by the ice cubes.

Well, if you really searched you probably *could* see the breasts. For that matter, you could also see Millard Fillmore, a stuffed pork chop and a 1946 Dodge.

The point is that so-called "subliminal advertising" simply

doesn't exist. Overactive imaginations, however, most certainly do.

So if anyone claims to see breasts in that drink up there, they aren't in the ice cubes.

They're in the eye of the beholder.

ADVERTISING

ANOTHER WORD FOR FREEDOM OF CHOICE.

American Association of Advertising Agencies

There is no scientific evidence that implanting sexual images in advertising boosts sales of a product. In fact, subliminal advertising is rarely used and is outlawed in many countries. The public is very aware of the subliminal technique, however—so much so that advertisers sometimes poke fun at subliminal messages in their ads.

LABORATORY EVIDENCE FOR SUBLIMINAL INFLUENCE You may have noticed that we said that subliminal messages don't work when "encountered in everyday life." There *is* evidence, however, that people can be influenced by subliminal messages under carefully controlled laboratory conditions (Dijksterhuis, Aarts, & Smith, 2005; Verwijmeren et al., 2011). In one study, for example, Dutch college students saw subliminal flashes of the words "Lipton Ice" (a brand of ice tea) or a nonsense word made of the same letters (Karremans, Stroebe, & Claus, 2006). All the students were then asked whether they would prefer Lipton Ice or a brand of Dutch mineral water to drink. If students were not thirsty at the time, the subliminal flashes had no effect on what they chose. But if students were thirsty, those who had seen the subliminal flashes of "Lipton Ice" were significantly more likely to choose that beverage than were students who had seen subliminal flashes of the nonsense word. Several other laboratory studies have found similar effects of pictures or words flashed at subliminal levels (e.g., Bargh & Pietromonaco, 1982; Bermeitinger et al., 2009; Snodgrass, Shevrin, & Abelson, 2014).

Does this mean that advertisers will figure out how to use subliminal messages in everyday advertising? Maybe, but it hasn't happened yet. To get subliminal effects, researchers have to make sure that the illumination of the room is just right, that people are seated just the right distance from a viewing screen, and that nothing else is occurring to distract people as the subliminal stimuli are flashed. Recent research indicates that warning participants that someone is about to try to persuade them subliminally decreases the potential influence of such manipulations on their subsequent ratings of consumer products (Verwijmeren et al., 2013). And even in the laboratory, there is no evidence that subliminal messages can get people to act counter to their wishes, values, or personalities (Neuberg, 1988). Thus, it is highly unlikely that the appearance of RATS in the Bush campaign ad convinced any Gore supporters to vote for Bush. For more on the relationship between automatic thinking and consumer attitudes, check out the following Try It!

Try It!

Consumer Brand Attitudes

Here are two exercises to test the role of automatic thought processes in consumer-related attitudes. You can do the exercises on your own, but the first one in particular might be easier to test on a friend.

A. Let's start with a baseline memory assessment. Below are four word pairs. Read each pair aloud to your friend (or to yourself), who should pay close attention and try to remember them—yes, there will be a test!

    i. Blue-duck

    ii. Ocean-moon

    iii. Window-hammer

    iv. Ski-climb

OK, while your friend is rehearsing these four word pairs and trying to remember them, you should read the following questions and ask for immediate, first-instinct responses:

    1. Name the first automobile brand that comes to mind.

    2. Name the first laundry detergent brand that comes to mind.

    3. Name the first soft drink brand that comes to mind.

Was your friend's laundry detergent Tide? Was the soft drink Mountain Dew? There actually is no memory test here—what we're interested in is whether the word pairs from the first half of the exercise primed particular brand names in the second half. Perhaps *ocean-moon* made your friend more likely to think of Tide, a semantically related brand name. Perhaps learning *ski-climb* made your friend think of a mountain, and therefore Mountain Dew. Information does not have to be subliminal in order to affect how (and how often) we think of particular consumer goods. Priming, as discussed in Chapter 3, can make certain thoughts, concepts, and attitudes more accessible, including those related to the purchases we make.

B. Consider the following eight companies. From this list, see if you can guess the Top 3 in terms of total sales revenue (not profit, but revenue) for 2016, according to *Fortune* magazine:

- Berkshire Hathaway
- McKesson
- Cardinal Health
- Boeing
- Microsoft
- Target
- Coca-Cola
- American Express
- Starbucks

Ready? Do you have your Top 3 selected? Keep reading for the correct answers …

The list above is already in the right order. So starting at the top, the companies with highest total sales revenue on the list were Berkshire Hathaway, McKesson, and Cardinal Health. Our guess is that these weren't your answers. We know that they wouldn't have been our guesses! For that matter, you may never have heard of some of the companies at the top of this list, and therein lies the explanation for what just happened. Remember the availability heuristic from Chapter 3? Microsoft, Target, American Express, Starbucks … these are familiar brand names. And the more easily a brand name comes to mind, the more popular, more successful, and even just flat-out better we often assume that brand to be. Of course, there is a wide and complex range of economic factors that contribute to a company's success; such questions are beyond the scope of our present focus. But for our purposes, this example provides yet another reason why advertising may pay off in the long run: we tend to think pleasant thoughts about that which is familiar.

Advertising and Culture

Ironically, the hoopla surrounding subliminal messages has obscured the fact that media messages are most powerful when people consciously perceive them. And it is important to note that in addition to trying to change attitudes towards consumer products via advertising, the media also shapes and reflects cultural attitudes in less direct ways. The attitudes we form toward women and men, members of different races, people of different ages, and so on, are all related to the manner in which members of these groups are portrayed in advertising, television shows, movies, and the internet. For a fuller discussion of how the media influences stereotypes, see Chapter 13.

And on questions of culture, there also appear to be notable differences across societies in the kinds of attitudes people have toward consumer products, perhaps reflecting the differences in self-concept we discussed in Chapter 5. As we saw, Western cultures tend to stress independence and individualism, whereas many Asian cultures stress interdependence and collectivism. These differences seem to predict the kinds of attitudes people have as well as how advertisements affect those attitudes (Aaker, 2000; de Mooij, 2014).

In one such series of studies, researchers created different print ads for the same product that stressed independence (e.g., an ad for shoes said, "It's easy when you have the right shoes") or interdependence (e.g., "the shoes for your family") and showed them to both Americans and Koreans (Han & Shavitt, 1994). The Americans were persuaded most by the ads stressing independence, and the Koreans were persuaded by the ads stressing interdependence. The researchers also analyzed actual magazine advertisements in the United States and Korea and found that these ads were in fact different as well: American ads tended to emphasize individuality, self-improvement, and benefits of the product for the individual consumer, whereas Korean ads tended to emphasize the family, concerns about others, and benefits for one's social group. In general, then, advertisements, like other forms of persuasive communication, work best if they are tailored to the kind of attitude they are trying to change and the expectations and thinking styles of the target audience (Markus & Kitayama, 2010).

Cross-cultural studies of advertising have revealed various differences, such as the finding that American ads place a greater emphasis on individuality and Korean ads place a greater emphasis on interdependence and social groups. Interestingly, the frequency and nature of celebrity endorsements also varies by culture, with more than half of Korean ads including a celebrity, a rate far exceeding that of American ads. Celebrities are also more likely to play a role of some sort in Korean ads (see example above on right), whereas they appear as themselves, as spokespeople, in American ads (see example above on the left). According to Sejung Choi, Wei-Na Lee, and Hee-Jung Kim (2005), these tendencies reflect the importance of social hierarchy in Korean society, as well as a greater emphasis placed on consuming the very same products that famous individuals are consuming.

Review Questions

1. Research on public service ads designed to promote healthy behavior indicates that such efforts
   a. almost always fail.
   b. are more effective at changing the attitudes of men versus women.
   c. are more effective via television than print ads when their target is young people.
   d. are most effective when they are subliminal.

2. The best way for an advertisement to change an affectively based attitude is to use a(n) _____ appeal.
   a. cognitive
   b. behavioral
   c. affective
   d. fact-filled

3. Serafina, an advertising executive, is trying to figure out the best way to market a product that does not evoke a strong emotional, personal response from people. Her most effective strategy would be to adopt a campaign that focuses on
   a. logical, fact-based arguments.
   b. creating such an emotional connection.

   c. avoiding behavioral references.
   d. subliminal strategies.

4. Research on subliminal influence in advertising demonstrates that subliminal efforts at persuasion are
   a. less effective than people assume them to be.
   b. more effective than people assume them to be.
   c. more effective in individualistic versus collectivistic cultures.
   d. more effective in collectivistic versus individualistic cultures.

5. Which of the following is true regarding cross-cultural comparisons of advertising?
   a. Korean ads are more likely than American ads to focus on utilitarian products like shoes.
   b. Korean ads are more likely than American ads to portray women and men in a state of complete or partial undress.
   c. Korean ads are more likely than American ads to focus on family and concern for others.
   d. Korean magazines have fewer ads than American magazines.

Resisting Persuasive Messages

LO 7.5   Identify strategies for resisting efforts at persuasion.

By now you very well may be getting nervous (and not just because the chapter hasn't ended yet). With all these clever methods out there designed to change your attitudes, are you ever safe from persuasive communications? Indeed you are, or at least you can be if you use some counterstrategies of your own. Here's how to make sure all those persuasive messages that bombard you don't turn you into a quivering mass of constantly changing opinion.

Attitude Inoculation

One step you can take is to consider the arguments against your attitude before someone attacks it. The more people have thought about pro and con arguments beforehand using the technique known as **attitude inoculation** (Banas & Miller, 2013; Compton, Jackson, & Dimmock, 2016; McGuire, 1964), the better they can ward off attempts to change their minds using logical arguments. The process functions much like a medical inoculation, in which patients are exposed to a small amount of a weakened version of a virus to protect them from developing the full-blown viral disease upon subsequent exposure. Here's how it works for protecting against attitude change: By considering "small doses" of arguments against their position, people become more resistant to later, full-blown attempts to change their attitudes. In other words, having thought about the counterarguments beforehand, people are relatively immune to the effects of the later persuasive communication. In contrast, if people have not thought much about the issue ahead of time—for example, if they formed their attitude via the peripheral route—they are particularly susceptible to an attack on that attitude that uses logical appeals.

Thinking ahead of time about the various directions in which counterarguments might go can make you less susceptible to efforts to change your existing attitude.

In one study, for example, William McGuire (1964) "inoculated" people by giving them brief arguments against *cultural truisms*, beliefs that most members of a society accept uncritically, such as the idea that we should brush our teeth after every meal. Two days later, people came back and read a much stronger attack on the truism, one that contained a series of logical arguments about why brushing your teeth too frequently is a bad idea. The people who had been inoculated against these arguments earlier were much less likely to change their attitudes than were those in a control group who had not been inoculated. Why? The individuals who were inoculated with weak arguments had time to think about the limitations of these arguments, making them more able to contradict the stronger attack they heard 2 days later. The control group, though, never having thought about how often people should brush their teeth, was particularly susceptible to the strong communication arguing against frequent brushing.

Attitude Inoculation

Making people immune to attempts to change their attitudes by initially exposing them to small doses of the arguments against their position

Being Alert to Product Placement

When an advertisement comes on during a TV show, people often decide to press the mute button on the remote control or the fast-forward button on the DVR; we've also all learned to try to ignore pop-up ads and other efforts at persuasion when we're online. To counteract these efforts to avoid ads, advertisers look for ways of displaying their wares during the show or movie itself. Many companies pay the producers to incorporate their products into the script (Kang, 2008). If you have ever watched *American Idol*, you've probably noticed that ever-present Coca-Cola cup in front of each judge. Maybe the revolving groups of judges over the years have all genuinely and personally loved Coke. But more likely the Coca-Cola company paid to have their product prominently displayed. They are not alone: By many estimates, more than $3 billion is now spent annually on similar product placements; Heineken reportedly paid $45 million just for one movie, enough to convince James Bond to abandon his usual penchant for martinis and drink the Dutch beer instead in 2012's *Skyfall* (Olmsted, 2012; Van Reijmersdal, Neijens, & Smit, 2009).

Most television and movie audiences are quite familiar by now with the idea of product placement. More recent releases have blurred—if not annihilated entirely—the boundary between advertisement and entertainment. In *The Lego Movie*, for example, where does the product placement end and the film begin?

One reason product placement can work is that people do not always realize that someone is trying to influence their attitudes and behavior. Our defenses are down; when we see a character like James Bond drinking a certain brand of beer, we're often more focused on the movie itself than on the fact that someone is trying to influence our attitudes. As a result, we don't generate counterarguments (Burkley, 2008; Levitan & Visser, 2008; Wheeler, Briñol, & Hermann, 2007). Children are especially vulnerable. One study, for example, found that the more children in grades 5 to 8 had seen movies in which adults smoked cigarettes, the more positive were their attitudes toward smoking (Heatherton & Sargent, 2009; Wakefield, Flay, & Nichter, 2003).

This leads to the question of whether forewarning people that someone is about to try to change their attitudes is an effective tool against product placement, or persuasion more generally. It turns out that it is. Several studies have found that alerting people about an upcoming attempt to change their attitudes makes them less susceptible to that attempt. When people are forewarned, they analyze what they see and hear more carefully and as a result are likely to avoid attitude change. Without such warnings, people pay little attention to the persuasive attempts and tend to accept the messages at face value (Sagarin & Wood, 2007; Wood & Quinn, 2003). So before letting kids watch TV or sending them off to the movies, it is good to remind them that they are likely to encounter several attempts to change their attitudes.

Watch RESISTING PERSUASIVE EFFORTS

Revel Video

Resisting Peer Pressure

We've seen that many efforts to shape our attitudes consist of appeals to our emotions. Can we ward off this kind of opinion change technique just as we can ward off the effects of logical appeals? This is an important question, because many critical changes in attitudes and behaviors occur not in response to logic, but via more emotional appeals. Consider the way in which many adolescents begin to smoke, drink, or take drugs. Often they do so in response to pressure from their peers, at an age when they are particularly susceptible to such pressure. Indeed, one of the best predictors of whether an adolescent smokes cigarettes or marijuana is whether he or she has friends who also do so (Allen, Donohue, & Griffin, 2003; Haas & Schaefer, 2014).

Think about how this occurs. It is not as if peers present a set of logical arguments ("Hey, Jake, did you know that recent studies show that moderate drinking may have health benefits?"). Instead, peer pressure is linked to people's values and emotions, playing on their fear of rejection and their desire for freedom and autonomy. In adolescence, peers become an important source of social approval—perhaps the most important—and can dispense powerful rewards for holding certain attitudes or behaving in certain ways, some of which may be positive, but others of which are problematic, such as using drugs or engaging in unprotected sex. What is needed is a technique that will make young people more resistant to attitude change attempts via peer pressure so that they will be less likely to engage in dangerous behaviors.

One possibility is to extend the logic of McGuire's inoculation approach to more affectively based persuasion techniques such as peer pressure. In addition to inoculating people with doses of logical arguments that they might hear, we could also inoculate them with samples of the kinds of emotional appeals they might encounter. Consider Jake, a 13-year-old who is hanging out with some classmates, many of whom are smoking cigarettes. The classmates begin to tease Jake about not smoking, calling him names. One of them even lights a cigarette and holds it in front of Jake, daring him to take a puff. Many 13-year-olds, facing such pressure, would cave in and smoke that cigarette. But suppose that we have immunized Jake from such social pressures by exposing him to mild versions of them ahead of time, and showing him ways to combat these pressures. We might have him role-play a situation where a friend calls him a loser for not smoking a cigarette and teach him to respond by saying, "I'd be more of a loser if I did it just to impress you." Would this help him resist the more powerful pressures exerted by his classmates?

Several programs designed to prevent smoking in adolescents suggest that it would. In one, psychologists used a role-playing technique with seventh graders, very much like the one we just described (McAlister et al., 1980). The researchers found that these students were significantly less likely to smoke 3 years after the study, compared to a control group that had not participated in the program. This result is encouraging and has been replicated in similar programs designed to reduce smoking and drug abuse (Botvin & Griffin, 2004; Chou et al., 1998).

A number of interventions designed to prevent smoking in adolescents have had some success. Many celebrities have lent their names and pictures to the effort, such as actor Jackie Chan, who was the spokesperson for an anti-smoking campaign in Taiwan.

When Persuasion Attempts Backfire: Reactance Theory

Suppose you want to make sure that your child never smokes. "Might as well err on the side of giving too strong a message," you might think, absolutely forbidding your child to even look at a pack of cigarettes. "What's the harm?" you figure. "At least this way my child will get the point about how serious this is."

Actually, there is harm to administering strong prohibitions: The stronger they are, the more likely they will backfire, actually causing an *increase* in interest in the prohibited activity. According to **reactance theory** (Brehm, 1966), people do not like feeling that their freedom to do or think whatever they want is being threatened. When they feel that their freedom is threatened, an unpleasant state of reactance is aroused, and people can reduce this reactance by performing the threatened behavior (e.g., smoking, dating the person your parents told you to stay away from). Have you ever been at a restaurant and had your server warn you, "careful, that plate is hot," but you decided to touch it anyway? Or done something simply because your teachers or other authority figures explicitly told you that you couldn't? Well, that's reactance.

In one study, for example, researchers placed one of two signs in the bathrooms on a college campus, in an attempt to get people to stop writing graffiti on the restroom walls (Pennebaker & Sanders, 1976). One sign read, "Do not write on these walls under any circumstances." The other gave a milder prohibition: "Please don't write on these walls." The researchers returned 2 weeks later and observed how much graffiti was written after they posted the signs. As predicted, significantly more people wrote graffiti in the bathrooms with the "Do not write ..." sign than with the "Please don't write ..." sign. Similarly, people who receive strong admonitions against smoking, taking drugs, or getting their nose pierced become more likely to perform these

Reactance Theory

The idea that when people feel their freedom to perform a certain behavior is threatened, an unpleasant state of resistance is aroused, which they can reduce by performing the prohibited behavior

Watch SURVIVAL TIPS! HOW TO WARD OFF EFFORTS TO CHANGE YOUR MIND

Revel Video

behaviors to restore their sense of personal freedom and choice (Erceg, Hurn, & Steed, 2011; Miller et al., 2007). And recent research demonstrates that when service employees specifically ask customers to give them positive evaluations on a postpurchase satisfaction survey, they actually end up getting lower ratings as a result (Jones, Taylor, & Reynolds, 2014). Reactance strikes again!

All of which is to say that despite the long list of attitude change strategies cataloged in this chapter, efforts at persuasion are not always effective. We aren't hopelessly at the mercy of those who would seek to change how we think and act. So the next time you are watching television and an ad comes on for a particular brand of pain relief medicine (or you see a product placement in a movie), you can actively consider what steps you might take to resist the impact of advertising. That is, assuming that you do not want to be at the mercy of the advertising industry—you might not think it is worth the effort to muster your defenses against ads for pain relievers. But what about attempts to get you to vote for a particular political candidate or to develop positive attitudes toward cigarettes? So remember, despite the extensive research literature demonstrating the wide range of factors that can change our attitudes, we are not automatons that must march blindly to the tune of anyone who tries to influence how we think. Sometimes it is worth the cognitive effort to ask ourselves how much we want to be influenced by persuasive communications and then take specific steps to avoid that influence.

Review Questions

1. The concept of attitude inoculation indicates that we are better able to resist a later attempt to change our attitudes when we are first exposed to arguments that
   a. support our existing attitude.
   b. are weakened versions of arguments we might hear later.
   c. prevent us from considering alternative viewpoints ahead of time.
   d. lead us to pay more attention to peripheral cues.

2. Which of the following is the best explanation for why product placement can be effective at changing attitudes?
   a. It tends to operate via the central route to persuasion.
   b. The audience is often unaware that an effort at attitude change is occurring.
   c. It usually leads to a reactance response.
   d. Cognitively based efforts at persuasion tend to have longer-lasting effects.

3. Peer pressure effects tend to be linked most often to what type of attitude?
   a. Cognitively based attitudes
   b. Affectively based attitudes

   c. Inoculated attitudes
   d. Negative attitudes

4. Which of the following concepts relates to the ironic research finding that the stronger the warning against a certain attitude or behavior, the more people sometimes wish to exhibit it?
   a. Attitude inoculation
   b. Peer pressure
   c. Implicit attitude
   d. Reactance theory

5. Cameron and Mitchell want to convince their daughter to stop leaving her toys scattered all around the floor, so they leave her a sign by her toy box. According to reactance theory, which of the following signs would be most effective?
   a. "Please try to remember to clean up your toys when you are done with them."
   b. "All toys MUST be put away after they are used."
   c. "Do not leave toys lying around!."
   d. "Your job is to clean up after yourself."

Summary

LO 7.1 Describe the types of attitudes and what they are based on.

- **The Nature and Origin of Attitudes** An *attitude* is a person's enduring evaluation of people, objects, and ideas.

  - **Where Do Attitudes Come From?** Although some attitudes may have a genetic component, they are based mostly on our experiences. *Cognitively based attitudes* are based mostly on people's beliefs about the properties of the attitude object. *Affectively based attitudes* are based more on people's emotions and values; they can be created through *classical conditioning* or *operant conditioning*. *Behaviorally based attitudes* are based on people's actions toward the attitude object.

  - **Explicit Versus Implicit Attitudes** Once an attitude develops, it can exist at two levels. *Explicit attitudes* are ones we consciously endorse and can easily report. *Implicit attitudes* operate outside of conscious awareness.

LO 7.2 Analyze the conditions under which attitudes can predict behavior.

- **When Do Attitudes Predict Behavior?** Under what conditions will people's attitudes dictate how they actually behave?

  - **Predicting Spontaneous Behaviors** Attitudes predict spontaneous behaviors only when they are relatively accessible. *Attitude accessibility* refers to the strength of the association between an object and an evaluation of it.

  - **Predicting Deliberative Behaviors** According to the *theory of planned behavior*, deliberative (nonspontaneous) behaviors are a function of people's attitudes toward the specific act in question, subjective norms (people's beliefs about how others view the behavior in question), and how much people believe they can control the behavior.

LO 7.3 Explain how internal and external factors lead to attitude change.

- **How Do Attitudes Change?** Both internal and external factors influence our attitudes.

  - **Changing Attitudes by Changing Behavior: Cognitive Dissonance Theory Revisited** One way that attitudes change is when people engage in counterattitudinal advocacy for low external justification. When this occurs, we tend to find internal justification for our behavior, bringing our attitudes in line with our behavior.

- **Persuasive Communications and Attitude Change** Attitudes can also change in response to a *persuasive communication*. According to the *Yale Attitude Change approach*, the effectiveness of a persuasive communication depends on aspects of the communicator, or source of the message; aspects of the message itself (e.g., its content); and aspects of the audience. The *elaboration likelihood model* specifies when people are persuaded more by the strength of the arguments in the communication and when they are persuaded more by surface characteristics. When people have both the motivation and ability to pay attention to a message, they take the *central route to persuasion*, where they pay close attention to the strength of the arguments. When they have low motivation or ability, they take the *peripheral route to persuasion*, where they are swayed by surface characteristics, such as the attractiveness of the speaker.

- **Emotion and Attitude Change** Emotions influence attitude change in a number of ways. *Fear-arousing communications* can cause lasting attitude change if a moderate amount of fear is aroused and people believe they will be reassured by the content of the message. Emotions can also be used as heuristics to gauge one's attitude; if people feel good in the presence of an object, they often infer that they like it, even if those good feelings were caused by something else. Finally, the effectiveness of persuasive communications also depends on the type of attitude people have. Appeals to emotion and social identity work best if the attitude is based on emotion and social identity.

- **Attitude Change and the Body** People's confidence in their thoughts about an attitude object affects how much they will be influenced by a persuasive communication. People's confidence can be affected by such things as whether they are nodding or shaking their head while listening to a persuasive message.

LO 7.4 Describe how advertising changes people's attitudes.

- **The Power of Advertising** Advertising has been found to be effective at changing people's attitudes, as indicated by successful public health campaigns.

  - **How Advertising Works** Advertising works by targeting affectively based attitudes with emotions, by targeting cognitively based attitudes with facts, and by making a product seem personally relevant.

- **Subliminal Advertising: A Form of Mind Control?** There is no evidence that subliminal messages in advertisements have any influence on people's behavior. Subliminal influences have been found, however, under controlled laboratory conditions.

- **Advertising and Culture** Analyses of *culture and advertising* reveal interesting differences that converge with other cross-cultural findings in social and self-perception.

LO 7.5 **Identify strategies for resisting efforts at persuasion.**

- **Resisting Persuasive Messages** Researchers have studied a number of ways by which people can avoid being influenced by persuasive messages.

- **Attitude Inoculation** One way is to expose people to small doses of arguments against their position, which makes it easier for them to defend themselves against a persuasive message they hear later.

- **Being Alert to Product Placement** Increasingly, advertisers are paying to have their products shown prominently in TV shows and movies. Forewarning people about attempts to change their attitudes, such as product placement, makes them less susceptible to attitude change.

- **Resisting Peer Pressure** Teaching kids how to resist peer pressure ahead of time can make them less vulnerable to it later on.

- **When Persuasion Attempts Backfire: Reactance Theory** According to *reactance theory*, people experience an unpleasant state called reactance when their freedom of choice is threatened. Attempts to manage people's attitudes can backfire if they make people feel that their choices are limited.

Revel Interactive

Shared Writing **What Do You Think?**

What is one specific lesson you can take from this chapter in trying to be more effective in persuasive communications (or more effective about resisting the persuasive efforts of others)?

Test Yourself

1. All of the following are true about attitudes *except* one. Which one is false?

    a. Attitudes are related to our temperament and personality.

    b. Attitudes rarely change over time.

    c. Attitudes can be changed with persuasive communications.

    d. Under the right conditions attitudes predict people's behavior.

2. Paige wants to buy a puppy. She does some research and decides to buy an English Springer Spaniel rather than a Great Dane because they are smaller, more active, and good with children. Which type of attitude influenced her decision?

    a. Affectively based attitude

    b. Behaviorally based attitude

    c. Explicitly based attitude

    d. Cognitively based attitude

3. On a survey, Marquel reports that he agrees with wearing a seat belt. According to the theory of planned behavior, which of the following would be the best predictor of whether Marquel will wear a seat belt on a given day?

   a. He generally agrees that safe driving is important.

   b. His best friend, Trevor, who is always talking about how important it is to wear a seat belt, is in the car with him.

   c. His attitude toward seat belts is not very accessible.

   d. Marquel believes that it is hard to remember to wear his seat belt.

4. People will be most likely to change their attitudes about smoking if an antismoking advertisement

   a. uses extremely graphic pictures of how smoke can harm the body and warns of the risks of smoking.

   b. gives people subliminal messages about the risks of smoking as well as recommendations of how to quit.

   c. uses graphic pictures of the damages of smoking on the body and then provides specific recommendations on how to quit smoking.

   d. uses success stories of how people quit smoking.

5. Emilia would be most likely to pay attention to facts about the danger of AIDS during a school assembly *and* remember the facts for a long time if

   a. the speaker emphasized statistical information about AIDS throughout the world.

   b. the speaker emphasized how the disease has spread in her community and there isn't anything distracting Emilia from listening.

   c. the speaker emphasized how the disease has spread in her community and at the same time Emilia's best friend is whispering to her about a big party that weekend.

   d. the speaker is a nationally known expert on AIDS.

6. You are trying to sell a new electronic toothbrush at the airport to busy, distracted travelers. Which of the following strategies is *least* likely to be successful at getting people to buy a toothbrush?

   a. Make up a flier that gives convincing reasons why the toothbrush is so good.

   b. Make a large sign that says, "9 out of 10 dentists recommend this toothbrush!"

   c. Put up a large banner featuring a picture of your friend who looks like Brad Pitt posing with the toothbrush.

   d. Stop people and say, "Do you know that this is the toothbrush that is used the most by Hollywood stars?"

7. Under which of the following conditions would people be most likely to vote for a political candidate? They

   a. like the candidate's policies but have negative feelings toward him or her.

   b. know little about the candidate's policies but have positive feelings toward him or her.

   c. see subliminal ads supporting the candidate on national television.

   d. see television ads supporting the candidate while they are distracted by their children.

8. Suppose that while you are watching a film at a movie theater the words "Drink Coke" are flashed on the screen at speeds too quick for you to see consciously. According to research on subliminal perception, which of the following is true?

   a. You will get up and buy a Coke, but only if other people start to do so first.

   b. You will get up and buy a Coke, but only if you prefer Coke to Pepsi.

   c. You will be *less* likely to get up and buy a Coke.

   d. You will be no more likely to buy a Coke than if the subliminal messages were not flashed.

9. All of the following are examples of ways to resist persuasion *except*

   a. making people immune to change of opinions by initially exposing them to small doses of arguments against their position.

   b. warning people about advertising techniques such as product placement.

   c. forbidding people to buy a product.

   d. role-playing using milder versions of real-life social pressures.

10. According to reactance theory, what of the following public service messages would be *least* likely to get people to wear seat belts?

   a. "Please wear your seat belt every time you drive."

   b. "Wear your seat belt to save lives."

   c. "It's the law—you must wear your seat belt."

   d. "Buckle up your children—you might save their lives."

Chapter 8
Conformity and Obedience
Influencing Behavior

Chapter Outline and Learning Objectives

WHAT DO YOU THINK?

Survey	**What Do You Think?**	
SURVEY		RESULTS

Have you ever participated in the social media phenomenon known as the ALS ice bucket challenge?

○ Yes

○ No

Pete Frates grew up in Beverly, Massachusetts, where he was a high school honor roll student and three-sport varsity athlete. He went on to Boston College, where he double-majored in communications and history and played on the baseball team. By his senior year, the 6'2", 225-pound left-handed outfielder was named captain. In the summers he played baseball in Connecticut, Maryland, and Hawaii. After graduation he spent time in Germany, playing professionally and coaching German youth on the sport.

If the name Pete Frates is familiar to you, though, it likely isn't for his exploits in college baseball. In 2012, just 5 years after he graduated, Frates suddenly started having trouble hitting in the rec league in which he was playing, his batting average tumbling from .400 to .250. One game he was hit by a pitch on his wrist, and the hand never seemed to get better. This led to a series of medical appointments, culminating in a neurologist diagnosing the 27-year-old Frates with amyotrophic lateral sclerosis (ALS), also known as Lou Gehrig's disease. Two summers later, Frates' Tweets and online posts helped inspire the "ice bucket challenge," which went viral on social media.

You remember the ice bucket challenge, right? Though variations on the phenomena occurred before and since, the summer of 2014 was its heyday, as Facebook exploded with videos of people dumping ice water on themselves and challenging specific friends to do the same. In one version of the challenge, those who were called out by name were supposed to donate $10 to the ALS Association if they agreed to a public soaking within 24 hours, $100 if they didn't. By August 2014, the ice bucket challenge was everywhere, with celebrity participants including LeBron James, Bill Gates, Kerry Washington, Lady Gaga, and George W. Bush joining in. Then-President Barack Obama was challenged but didn't soak himself, opting instead to donate $100. Justin Bieber took the challenge, though he had to do it twice after his first effort was widely criticized for leaving out one critical detail … ice.

Pete Frates, inspiration for the ALS ice bucket challenge.

According to the ALS Association website, that summer more than 17 million people uploaded ice bucket videos, which were watched by 440 million people a total of 10 billion times. Some critics derided the phenomenon as a narcissistic exercise in "slacktivism," suggesting that people were more interested in having fun online than saving lives. But it's hard to argue with the numbers: the ALSA reports that donations during the height of the craze totaled more than $115 million, up from less than $3 million during the same time period the year before (ALSA, 2014).

What would compel millions and millions of individuals—including, according to our opening survey question, many of you reading this—to dump ice-cold water on themselves or watch videos of other people doing so? Sure, it was for a good cause, but there are a lot of good causes out there. Something about the ice bucket challenge seemed to be contagious. Something about seeing other people douse themselves in frigid water made people want to do this too, to conform

In August 2014, the "ice bucket challenge" exploded on social media, capitalizing on processes related to conformity to raise unprecedented amounts of money in the battle against ALS. Here, one of millions of participants takes her turn with the challenge, with a little help from an overeager friend and photographer.

to the behavior in front of them. Later in this chapter we will revisit the ice bucket challenge and consider what specific aspects of it made it particularly likely to "go viral" and elicit conformity.

More generally, every day, we make decisions about whether to conform to the behavior of others or strike out on a more independent path. On a regular basis, people try to get us to do what they want—to conform to their influence—sometimes through direct requests and sometimes through more subtle processes. A subtle version of this social influence occurs when others indirectly indicate to us what is appropriate, and we come to sense that it is in our best interest to conform, or go along with them, such as decisions about what clothes, hairstyles, or slang terms are fashionable. An even more powerful and direct type of social influence comes in the form of obedience, and occurs when an authority figure gives an order that we feel pressure to follow. In this chapter, we will focus on the potentially positive and negative effects of these social influence processes, beginning with more subtle examples of conformity and moving on to obedience to authority.

Conformity: When and Why

LO 8.1   **Define conformity, and explain why it occurs.**

American culture often stresses the importance of not conforming (Cohen & Varnum, 2016; Kim & Markus, 1999; Kitayama et al., 2009, 2010). Americans picture themselves as a nation of rugged individualists, people who think for themselves, stand up for the underdog, and go against the tide to fight for what they think is right. This cultural self-image has been shaped by the manner in which the nation was founded, by a system of government, and by this society's historical experience with western expansion—the "taming" of the Wild West (Kitayama et al., 2006; Turner, 1932).

American mythology has celebrated the rugged individualist in many ways. For example, one of the longest-running and most successful advertising campaigns in American history featured the "Marlboro Man." As far back as 1955, the photograph of a lone cowboy on the range was an archetypal image. It also sold a lot of cigarettes. Clearly, it told Americans something about themselves that they want and like to hear: that they make up their own minds and that they're not spineless, weak conformists (Cialdini, 2009; Pronin, Berger, & Molouki, 2007). More recently, consider the example of Apple Computer, one of the most valuable publicly traded companies in the world (Gaffen, 2016). For several years, Apple's advertising slogan captured a similar sentiment of nonconformity: "Think different."

But are we, in fact, nonconforming creatures? Are the decisions we make always based on what we think, or do we use other people's behavior to help us decide what to do? Despite Apple's advertising telling customers to "think different," take a careful look around the lecture hall next time you're in class and count how many glowing Apple logos stare back at you from the laptops of your fellow students. The computer of the nonconformist is now everywhere.

On a far more sobering note, as we saw in Chapter 6, the mass suicide of the Heaven's Gate cult members suggests that people sometimes conform in extreme and astonishing ways—even when making as crucial a decision as whether to take their own lives. But, you might argue, surely this is an extremely unusual case. Perhaps the followers of Marshall Applewhite were disturbed people who were somehow predisposed to do what a charismatic leader told them to do. There is, however, another, more chilling possibility: Maybe many of us would have acted the same way had we been exposed to the same long-standing, powerful conformity pressures as were the members of Heaven's Gate.

If this statement is true, we should be able to find other situations in which seemingly ordinary people, placed under strong social pressures, conformed to a surprising degree. And, in fact, we can. For example, in 1961, activists in the American civil rights movement incorporated Mohandas Gandhi's principles of nonviolent protest into their demonstrations to end segregation. They trained their "Freedom Riders" (so named because they boarded buses and disobeyed "back of the bus" seating rules) in the passive acceptance of violent treatment. Thousands of southern African Americans, joined by a smaller number of northern Whites, many from college campuses, demonstrated against the segregationist laws of the South. In confrontation after confrontation, the civil rights activists adhered to the principles of nonviolence that others had taught them; they remained stoic as they were beaten, clubbed, hosed, whipped, and even killed by southern sheriffs and police (Nelson, 2010; Powledge, 1991). New recruits conformed to the nonviolent

During the American civil rights movement, informational social influence was used to train people in the art of nonviolent demonstration. Experienced protestors modeled for new protestors how to remain calm in the face of harassment including cigarette smoke, threats, racist language, and actual violence.

responses the existing members modeled, and this contagious commitment to non-violent protest helped usher in a new era in America's fight for racial equality.

But just a few years later, social pressure resulted in a tragic rather than heroic course of events. On the morning of March 16, 1968, American soldiers in Vietnam boarded helicopters that would take them to the village of My Lai. One pilot radioed that he saw enemy soldiers below, and so the Americans jumped off the helicopters, rifles blazing. They soon realized that there were no enemy soldiers—only women, children, and elderly men cooking breakfast over small fires. Inexplicably, the leader of the platoon ordered one of the soldiers to kill the villagers. Other soldiers began firing too, and the carnage spread, ending with the deaths of approximately 500 Vietnamese civilians (Hersh, 1970). Similar processes of social influence have been implicated in more recent military atrocities, including the humiliating abuse of Iraqi captives at the Abu Ghraib prison starting in 2003 (Hersh, 2004) and American soldiers urinating on the corpses of Taliban fighters in Afghanistan in 2011 (Martinez, 2012). Social pressures like these have also been implicated in concerns about teenage "suicide clusters," when a school or community experiences multiple deaths in a short period of time (Rosin, 2015).

In all these examples, people found themselves caught in a web of social influence. In response, they altered their behavior to conform to the expectations of others (O'Gorman, Wilson, & Miller, 2008). For social psychologists, this is the essence of **conformity**: changing one's behavior due to the real or imagined influence of other (Aarts & Dijksterhuis, 2003; Kiesler & Kiesler, 1969; Sorrentino & Hancock, 2014). As these examples show, the consequences of conformity span a wide range, from bravery to tragedy. But why did these people conform? Some conformed because they did not know what to do in a confusing or unusual situation. The behavior of the people around them served as a cue as to how to respond, and they decided to act in a similar manner. Other people conformed because they did not wish to be ridiculed or punished for being different from everybody else. They chose to act the way the group expected so that they wouldn't be rejected or thought less of by group members. Let's see how each of these reasons for conforming operates.

Conformity

A change in one's behavior due to real or imagined influence of other people

Under strong social pressure, individuals will conform to the group even when this means doing something immoral. In 2004, American soldiers' degrading abuse of Iraqis held at the Abu Ghraib prison sparked an international scandal and a great deal of soul-searching back home. Why did the soldiers humiliate their captives? As you read this chapter, you will see how the social influence pressures of conformity can contribute to decent people committing indecent acts.

Review Questions

1. Which of the following is the most direct and powerful example of social influence?
   a. Complying with a polite request made by a friend
   b. Conforming to a group norm
   c. Obedience to an order from an authority figure
   d. Emotion-based attitudes

2. Which of the following statements best captures the relationship between cultural beliefs and conformity?
   a. There is little variability in how people from different cultures think about conformity.
   b. Compared to many cultures, Americans tend to have relatively negative attitudes toward conformity.
   c. Compared to many cultures, Americans tend to have relatively positive attitudes toward conformity.
   d. Americans' beliefs about conformity have become more and more negative over the years.

3. Conformity always includes
   a. positive and moral behavior.
   b. negative and immoral behavior.
   c. the real or imagined influence of other people.
   d. an authority figure.

Informational Social Influence: The Need to Know What's "Right"

LO 8.2   Explain how informational social influence motivates people to conform.

Life is full of ambiguous and confusing situations. How should you address your psychology professor—as Dr. Aronson, Professor Aronson, Mr. Aronson, or Elliot? Do you cut a piece of sushi or eat it whole? Did the scream you just heard in the hallway come from a person joking with friends or from the victim of a mugging? In these and many other scenarios, we feel uncertain about what to think or how to act. We simply don't know enough to make a good or accurate choice. Luckily, we have a powerful and useful source of knowledge available to us—the behavior of other people.

Sometimes we simply ask directly about the appropriate way to act. Many times, though, we watch others, observing their behavior to help us achieve a better definition of the situation (Kelley, 1955; Thomas, 1928). When we subsequently act like everyone else, we are conforming, but this doesn't mean we are spineless individuals lacking in self-reliance. Instead, the influence of others leads us to conform because we see those people as a valuable source of information to guide our behavior. We conform because we believe that others' interpretation of an ambiguous set of circumstances is accurate and will help us choose an appropriate course of action. This is called **informational social influence** (Cialdini & Goldstein, 2004; Deutsch & Gerard, 1955; Smith & Mackie, 2016).

As an illustration of how other people can be a source of information, imagine that you are a participant in the following experiment by Muzafer Sherif (1936). In the first phase of the study, you are seated alone in a dark room and asked to focus your attention on a dot of light 15 feet away. The experimenter asks you to estimate in inches how far the light moves. You stare earnestly at the light, and, yes, it seems to move a little. You say, "about 2 inches," though it is not easy to tell exactly. The light disappears and then comes back; you are asked to judge again. The light seems to move a little more this time, and you say, "4 inches." After several of these trials, the light seems to move about the same amount each time—somewhere in the neighborhood of 2 to 4 inches.

The interesting thing about this task is that the light is not actually moving at all. It looks as if it was because of a visual illusion called the autokinetic effect: If you stare at a bright light in a uniformly dark environment (e.g., a star on a dark night), the light will appear to waver a bit back and forth. This occurs because you have no stable visual reference point with which to anchor the position of the light. In Sherif's

Informational Social Influence
Relying on other people as a source of information to guide our behavior, which leads to conformity because we believe that others' interpretation of an ambiguous situation is correct

Eight thousand pumpkins meet the Eiffel Tower. While the holiday is based on ancient British and Irish traditions surrounding All Hallows' Eve, Halloween as we know it is a completely American phenomenon—until October 1997, that is, when "Ah-lo-ween" was introduced to the French public by retailers in an effort to boost consumer spending to spark a sagging French economy (R. Cohen, 1997). Informational social influence is how the French literally learned what this holiday is about. As of Halloween 1997, they had no idea of what "treek au treeting" was. However, just a few years later, French shops were decorated in Black and orange, carved pumpkins were displayed, and nightclubs held costume competitions.

(Associated Press, 2002)

Private Acceptance

Conforming to other people's behavior out of a genuine belief that what they are doing or saying is right

experiment, the participants arrived at their own stable estimate during the first phase of the study, but these estimates differed across people. Some thought the light was moving only an inch or so; others thought it was moving as much as 10 inches.

Sherif chose the autokinetic effect because he wanted a situation that would be ambiguous—where the correct definition of the situation would be unclear to his participants. In the second phase of the experiment, a few days later, the participants were paired with two other people, each of whom had had the same prior experience alone with the light. Now the situation became a truly social one, as all three made their judgments out loud. Now the autokinetic effect is experienced differently by different people: Some see a lot of movement, and some see not much at all. After hearing their partners give judgments that were different from their own, what did people in Sherif's study do?

Over the course of several trials as a group, people converged on a common estimate, and each member of the group tended to conform to that estimate. These results indicate that people were using each other as a source of information, coming to believe that the group estimate was the correct one (see Figure 8.1). An important feature of informational social influence is that it can lead to **private acceptance**, when people conform to the behavior of others because they genuinely believe that these other people are right.

It might seem equally plausible that people publicly conformed to the group but privately maintained the belief that the light was moving only a small amount. For example, maybe someone privately believed that the light was moving 10 inches but announced that it had moved 3 inches, the group consensus, in an effort to avoid

Figure 8.1 One Group's Judgments in Sherif's (1936) Autokinetic Studies

People estimated how far a point of light appeared to move in a dark room. When they saw the light by themselves, their estimates varied widely. When they were brought together in groups and heard other people announce their estimates, people conformed to the group's estimate of how much the light moved, adjusting their private beliefs based on the information other group members provided.

(Data from Sherif, 1936)

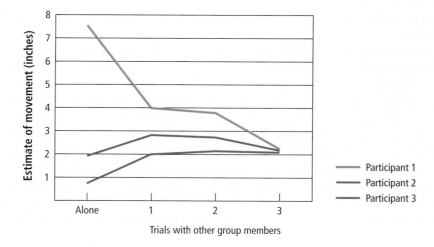

standing out from the crowd or looking foolish. This would be a case of **public compliance**, conforming publicly without necessarily believing in what the group is doing. Sherif cast doubt on this interpretation of his study, however, by asking people to judge the lights one more time, this time back on their own. Even though they no longer had to worry about how they looked in front of other participants, they continued to give the answer the group had given earlier. One study even found that people still conformed to the group estimate when they participated individually a full year later (Rohrer, Baron, Hoffman, & Swander, 1954). These results suggest that people were relying on each other to define reality and came to privately accept the wisdom of the group estimate.

The power of conformity to produce private acceptance has been demonstrated in several areas of life, including energy conservation. In one study, Jessica Nolan and her colleagues (2008) gave a sample of California residents information urging them to conserve electricity. The household members received one of four messages. Three of these presented basic reasons to conserve: to protect the environment, to benefit society, or to save money. The fourth message contained information designed to promote conformity: The participants were told that the majority of their neighbors conserved electrical energy. The researchers then measured actual energy usage from the homes' electrical meters. They found that the fourth message, the one containing information about the behavior of one's neighbors, caused people to conserve more energy than did the other three messages (Nolan et al., 2008). Similarly, Goldstein, Cialdini, and Griskevicius (2008) managed to increase hotel guests' compliance with a "reuse your bath towels" request, a widely used hotel management technique that hasn't always proved popular with guests. The researchers found that an informational sign in the bathroom stating that the majority of guests in this very room had reused their towels, was more effective than the general "Help the Environment" appeal usually used by hotels.

The Importance of Being Accurate

Later research extended Sherif's classic study on informational conformity in interesting ways (Baron, Vandello, & Brunsman, 1996; Levine, Higgins, & Choi, 2000; Muchnik, Aral, & Taylor, 2013). This research employed judgment tasks that are more like real life than the autokinetic effect. It also revealed another variable that affects informational social influence: how important it is to be accurate at the task.

For example, in one study, research participants were given an involving but ambiguous task: eyewitness identification (Baron et al., 1996). Just like eyewitnesses of a real crime, the participants were asked to pick a "perpetrator" out of a lineup, though in this instance they were asked to do it several times. For each of the 13 lineups, the participants were first shown a slide of a man—the perpetrator. Next, they saw a slide of a lineup composed of four men, one of whom was the perpetrator (he was sometimes dressed differently than he had been in the prior slide). The participant's job was to pick him out. The task was made difficult (and ambiguous) by presenting the slides extremely quickly: Participants saw each slide for only half a second. The study took place in a group consisting of the participant and three confederates. Each of the four said their answers out loud after viewing each pair of slides. On the critical seven trials, where informational social influence would be measured, the three confederates answered before the participant—and all the confederates gave the same wrong answer.

The researchers also manipulated how important it was to the research participants to be accurate at the task. In the high-importance condition, they were told that the upcoming task was a real test of eyewitness identification ability and that police departments and courts would soon be using it to differentiate good eyewitnesses from poor ones. Participants' scores would therefore establish standards against which future eyewitness performance would be judged. In addition, those who were most accurate at the

Public Compliance

Conforming to other people's behavior publicly without necessarily believing in what the other people are doing or saying

Even for judgments of the utmost importance—such as when an eyewitness to a crime later tries to identify the culprit—informational social influence influences our perceptions.

task would receive a $20 bonus from the experimenters. In contrast, in the low-importance condition, the research participants were told that the study was a first attempt to study eyewitness identification and that the slide task was still being developed. Thus, as the participants began the task, they were in two very different states of mind. Half thought their performance was very important and would have ramifications for real-life legal proceedings. They were motivated to do well. The other half saw this as just a basic research study like any other. Their performance didn't seem like it was all that important.

The high-importance condition mirrors the concerns of many situations in everyday life—your judgments and decisions have consequences, and you're motivated to "get things right." Does that make you more or less susceptible to informational social influence? The researchers found that it makes you *more* susceptible. In the low-importance condition, participants conformed to the confederates' judgments and gave the same wrong answers on just 35% of the critical trials. In the high-importance condition, participants conformed to the confederates' judgments on 51% of the critical trials.

But relying on other people as a source of information is a strategy that also comes with risks. In a different eyewitness study, pairs of eyewitnesses each watched separate videos of what they believed to be the exact same event (Gabbert, Memon, & Allan, 2003). Unbeknownst to participants, each member of the pair viewed a slightly different video. Among pairs that were allowed to discuss the video before each eyewitness took an individual memory test, 71% of witnesses went on to mistakenly recall personally having seen items that only their partner had actually seen. This experiment illustrates the major risk of using other people around you for information: What if those other people are wrong? Indeed, this is why most police procedures require that when there are multiple eyewitnesses in a case, each one is to be interviewed individually by investigators and view a lineup individually as well. Informational social influence among eyewitnesses is not welcome in the courtroom (Levett, 2013).

When Informational Conformity Backfires

A dramatic form of informational social influence occurs during crises, when an individual is confronted with a frightening, potentially dangerous situation to which he or she is ill equipped to respond (Killian, 1964). The person may have no idea of what is really happening or what he or she should do. When one's personal safety is involved, the need for information is acute—and the behavior of others is very informative.

Consider what happened on Halloween night in 1938. Orson Welles, the gifted actor and film director, and the Mercury Theater broadcast a radio play based loosely on H. G. Wells's science fiction fantasy *War of the Worlds*. Remember, this was the era before television; radio was a primary source of entertainment, and it was the only source for fast-breaking news. That night, the drama that Welles and his fellow actors broadcast—portraying

Watch INFORMATIONAL CONFORMITY

Revel Video

INFORMATIONAL SOCIAL INFLUENCE GONE AWRY

Orson Welles, renowned actor and director, whose War of the Worlds radio broadcast in 1938 sparked a public scare that spread, in large part, due to informational social influence. When listeners tried to figure out whether an attack was really happening, the anxious responses of those around them added to their own sense of panic.

Quito, Ecuador. In 1949, radio producers put on their own version of Welles's War of the Worlds broadcast, and once again, many listeners became convinced that an alien attack was imminent. When they discovered that the program was fiction, angry crowds stormed the radio station, set fires, and at least six people were killed in the rioting.

In contemporary society, misinformation spreads easily from person to person via social media and email. Internet hoaxes, erroneous updates about ongoing news stories, and email urban legends are all examples of informational social influence that fails to get us any closer to the "right" answer about the issues in question.

"That's fake news" has become a common argument that politicians use to try to discredit unflattering media coverage, even when the investigation in question seems based on solid and well-sourced reporting. But there is no doubt that during the 2016 U.S. presidential election, numerous factually inaccurate stories—some deliberate efforts at misinformation—were posted and spread widely. The degree to which these problematic stories influenced voter attitudes and behavior is difficult to quantify.

the invasion of Earth by hostile Martians—was so realistic that untold numbers of listeners became frightened and alerted the police; many were so panic stricken that they tried to flee the "invasion" in their cars (Cantril, 1940).

Why were Americans convinced that what they heard was a real news report of an actual invasion by aliens? Hadley Cantril (1940), who studied this real-life "crisis," suggested two reasons. One was that the play parodied existing radio news shows very well, and many listeners missed the beginning of the broadcast (when it was clearly identified as a play) because they had been listening to a popular show on another station. The other culprit, however, was informational social influence. Many people were listening with friends and family. As the *War of the Worlds* scenario became increasingly frightening, they naturally turned to each other, out of uncertainty, to see whether they should believe what they heard. Seeing looks of concern and worry on their loved ones' faces added to the panic people were beginning to feel. "We all kissed one another and felt we would all die," reported one listener (Cantril, 1940, p. 95).

Of course, this was decades ago, when people were much less savvy about differentiating reality from fiction—today, informational social influence rarely backfires in such a widespread fashion. Right? Well, maybe not…. Most of us have seen friends or family members post, tweet, or e-mail stories that send up red flags regarding their accuracy. Urban legends and unfounded conspiracy theories run rampant on social media. And the 2016 U.S. presidential election witnessed a record-breaking number of "fake news" stories that spread like wildfire, from baseless claims about Hillary Clinton and violent criminal behavior to allegations that Democrats sought to impose Islamic Law in Florida to claims that the Pope had endorsed Donald Trump (Holan, 2016). None of these stories were remotely true, but that didn't stop people from posting and sharing them, providing very recent examples of informational social influence gone awry. Orson Welles would have been proud (or perhaps a bit horrified).

When Will People Conform to Informational Social Influence?

Let's review the situations that are the most likely to produce conformity because of informational social influence.

WHEN THE SITUATION IS AMBIGUOUS Ambiguity is the most crucial variable for determining how much people use each other as a source of information. When you are unsure of the correct response, the appropriate behavior, or the right idea, you will be most open to influence from others. The more uncertain you are, the more you will rely on others (Huber, Klucharev, & Rieskamp, 2014; Tesser, Campbell, & Mickler, 1983; Walther et al., 2002). Situations such as the military atrocities discussed earlier were ambiguous for the people involved—ideal circumstances for informational social influence to take hold. Most of the soldiers were young and inexperienced. When they saw other soldiers shooting at the villagers or humiliating prisoners, many of them thought this was what they were supposed to do, and they joined in.

WHEN THE SITUATION IS A CRISIS Crisis often occurs simultaneously with ambiguity. In a crisis situation, we usually do not have time to stop and think about exactly which course of action we should take. We need to act—immediately. If we panic and are uncertain what to do, it is only natural for us to see how other people are responding and to do likewise. Unfortunately, the people we imitate may also panic and not be behaving rationally.

Soldiers, for example, are undoubtedly on edge during their tours of duty. Further, in many wars, it is not easy to tell who the enemy is. In the Vietnam War, civilians who were sympathizers of the Vietcong were known to have laid mines in the path of U.S. soldiers, fired guns from hidden locations, and thrown or planted grenades. Similarly, in Iraq and Afghanistan, it was (and remains) difficult to tell if people were civilians or combatants, allies or enemies. It is perhaps not surprising, then, that these soldiers often turned to others around them to gauge the proper course of action. Had these individuals not been in the midst of a chronic crisis situation and instead had more time to think about their actions, perhaps tragedy and scandal would have been avoided.

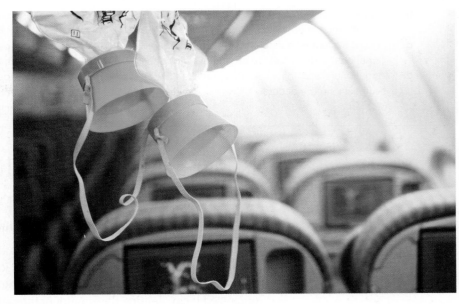

Consider a passenger who sees smoke coming out of an airplane engine or the sudden appearance of oxygen masks and wishes to determine if she is in the midst of a true emergency. Informational social influence suggests that she will probably look first to the reactions of the flight attendants, those with more expertise, rather than the reactions of her fellow seatmates.

WHEN OTHER PEOPLE ARE EXPERTS Typically, the more expertise or knowledge a person has, the more valuable he or she will be as a guide in an ambiguous situation (Cialdini & Trost, 1998; Williamson, Weber, & Robertson, 2013). For example, if you're visiting a foreign city and come across an unfamiliar street sign, you will probably check out the reactions of the locals rather than those of your fellow tourists. However, experts are not always reliable sources of information. Imagine the fear felt by the young man listening to the *War of the Worlds* broadcast who called his local police department for an explanation, only to learn that the police too thought the events described on the radio were actually happening (Cantril, 1940)!

Review Questions

1. Informational social influence occurs
  a. when we believe that other people's reactions can help us arrive at an accurate reading of a situation.
  b. through public but not private conformity.
  c. only in a crisis.
  d. autokinetically.

2. Which of the following statements regarding Sherif's (1936) study of perceptions of the autokinetic effect is true?
  a. Participants conformed publicly but not privately.
  b. Participants did conform, but the effects of this conformity were short lived as they reverted to their previous, individually given responses once they were no longer part of a group.
  c. Participants conformed because they were in a group with their friends, and they simply wanted to fit in with the group.
  d. Participants conformed because they believed the other people's responses were accurate.

3. The more important it is to people to make an accurate decision,
  a. the less likely they are to conform to informational social influence.
  b. the more likely they are to conform to informational social influence.
  c. the more they seek to make that decision on their own, uninfluenced by what the people around them have to say.
  d. the more they will prefer public to private conformity.

4. Which of the following statements best captures the relationship between informational social influence and eyewitness performance in legal proceedings?
  a. Because the stakes are so high in a criminal trial, eyewitnesses do not conform to informational social influence.

b. Eyewitnesses are encouraged to use informational social influence in providing their testimony at trial.

c. The legal system takes steps to prevent conformity to informational social influence among eyewitnesses.

d. Informational social influence always makes eyewitnesses more accurate.

5. Informational social influence is most likely to occur when

a. a situation is unambiguous and not a crisis.

b. the other people around are not experts and the situation is not a crisis.

c. the other people around are experts and the situation is ambiguous.

d. a situation is a crisis but also unambiguous.

Normative Social Influence: The Need to Be Accepted

LO 8.3 **Explain how normative social influence motivates people to conform.**

They're called polar plunges, and they started out as charity fund-raisers: sanctioned events in which people take a quick swim in ice-cold water to attract donations and attention to a worthwhile cause. Groups like the Special Olympics carefully planned and organized them, limiting the amount of time people spent in the cold temperatures and making sure that medical personnel were on hand in case of complications. But a few years ago, school districts across New England (and other cold-climate locales) began e-mailing parents to warn them about polar plunge dares that were spreading among adolescents via social media (Wilson, 2014). Teenagers were challenging each other to jump into freezing water without life vests, with no adult supervision, and often at night—when temperatures were even lower and visibility was poor. Many accepted the dares, filming their dangerous feats and then posting them online. But some weren't so lucky, with multiple injuries and at least one death reported in New Hampshire, where melting snow increased water levels and the speed of river currents (Phillip, 2014).

Why do people engage in such risky behavior? Why does anyone follow the group's lead when the resulting behavior is far from sensible and may even be fatal? We doubt that the do-it-yourself polar plungers risked their lives due to informational conformity. It is difficult to argue that a high school student staring at a rushing winter river filled with ice and other debris would say, "Gee, I don't know what to do. I guess jumping in there makes sense." This example suggests that there must be something else besides the need for information that can explain conformity. And there is: We also conform so that we will be liked and accepted by other people (Maxwell, 2002). We conform to the group's **social norms**—implicit (and sometimes explicit) rules for acceptable behaviors, values, and beliefs (Deutsch & Gerard, 1955; Kelley, 1955; Miller & Prentice, 1996; Sanfey, Stallen, & Chang, 2014). Groups have certain expectations about how their members should behave, and members in good standing conform to these rules. Members who do not are perceived as different, difficult, and eventually deviant. In the social media era, these norms are transmitted faster than ever.

Of course, conformity to social norms isn't always dangerous. It isn't even always a bad thing—after all, as discussed earlier, the ice bucket challenge raised enough to money to improve and even save lives. What was it about this particular challenge that led conformity to spread so far and wide, and so quickly? Research indicates that a critical predictor of what "goes viral" is that we are most likely to share content that leads to emotional arousal (Berger, 2011). Watching people dump icy water on themselves produces a variety of emotions including surprise and amusement, rendering it precisely the type of video we are most likely to share. Also, the challenge provided people with an opportunity to post visible evidence of themselves as they were "doing good." And one of the most critical aspects of the challenge is that it required people to identify specific friends by name, calling them out individually and placing pressure (albeit a fun kind of pressure) on them to respond. It is, of course, easier to resist a generic call for help than it is to sit quietly when someone asks you by name—publicly—to take action.

Social Norms

The implicit or explicit rules a group has for the acceptable behaviors, values, and beliefs of its members

CONFORMITY GONE VIRAL

"Going viral." The phrase itself has become a ubiquitous way to describe the dramatic and sudden popularity of certain videos, memes, stories, or ideas. Indeed, every day seems to bring with it a new example of something that people just can't resist forwarding, posting, sharing, or tweeting. What factors predict which ideas reach "viral" status? Any effort to answer this question certainly draws upon issues related to social influence, contagion, and the general focus of this chapter, conformity.

One factor underlying many examples of "going viral" is emotional response. For example, Rosanna Guadagno (2013) and colleagues found that students reported a greater likelihood of sharing videos that led them to feel happiness or surprise–perhaps some of the very emotions you experienced the first time you saw a clip of people freezing in place in response to the once-popular "mannequin challenge."

Not all of the emotions associated with the viral spread of ideas are positive ones. Sometimes we share a story or adopt a cause because of arousal inducing anger or outrage (Berger, 2011). Consider the quick spread of knitted pink hats among anti-Trump protesters in the wake of Election Day 2016, in response to vulgar comments he had made about women years earlier.

In short, while multiple psychological factors can help us understand ideas that "go viral," many times the popularity of a video or meme catches most of us off guard. What do you think, can you come up with any hypotheses to help account for the sudden popularity of bottle flipping videos among youth in the past few years?

More generally, why is normative conformity like that demonstrated by polar plungers and ice bucket challengers so powerful? Primarily because acceptance by others is incredibly important to us. Rejection hurts. Keep in mind that we human beings are by nature a social species. Few of us could live happily as hermits, never seeing or talking to another person. Other people are extraordinarily important to our sense of well-being. Research on individuals who have been isolated for long periods of time indicates that being deprived of human contact is stressful, traumatic, and psychologically painful (Baumeister & Leary, 1995; Schachter, 1959; Williams & Nida, 2011). We seek to avoid isolation or anything else that might cause a group to reject us.

Indeed, deviant group members—those who go against the flow—are often punished, ridiculed or even rejected by other group members (Abrams et al.,

2014; James & Olson, 2000; Miller & Anderson, 1979). For example, in Japan, a whole school will sometimes turn against one student perceived as different, alternately harassing and shunning the individual—treatment that can have tragic results. Another phenomenon in Japan is the *hikikomori*, teenagers (mostly male) who have withdrawn from all social interaction. They spend all their time alone, in their bedrooms in their parents' homes, some for over a decade. Japanese psychologists believe that many *hikikomori* were the victims of severe bullying before their withdrawal (M. Jones, 2006). Recently, researchers in various countries have begun to study cyberbullying in middle and secondary schools. This form of bullying, using cell phones and the Internet, is increasingly frequent, affecting anywhere from 10% to 35% of school children surveyed in nations including the United States, United Kingdom, Canada, and Australia (Kowalski et al., 2014; Wilton & Campbell, 2011).

Given this fundamental human need for social companionship, it is not surprising that we often conform to gain acceptance from others. Conformity for normative reasons occurs in situations where we do what other people are doing, not because we are using them as a source of information but so that we won't be made fun of, get into trouble, or be ostracized. Thus, **normative social influence** occurs when the influence of other people leads us to conform in order to be liked and accepted. This type of conformity results in public compliance with the group's beliefs and behaviors but not necessarily in private acceptance (Cialdini, Kallgren, & Reno, 1991; Deutsch & Gerard, 1955; Huang, Kendrick, & Yu, 2014).

You probably don't find it too surprising that people sometimes conform to be liked and accepted by others. You might be thinking, where's the harm? If the group is important to us and wearing the right clothes or using the right slang will gain us acceptance, why not go along? But when it comes to more important kinds of behaviors, such as hurting another person, surely we will resist such conformity pressures. And, of course, we won't conform when we are certain of the correct way of behaving and the pressures are coming from a group that we don't care all that much about. Or will we?

Normative Social Influence

Going along with what other people do to be liked and accepted by them, which leads to public conformity with the group's beliefs and behaviors but not always private acceptance of them

Conformity and Social Approval: The Asch Line-Judgment Studies

Solomon Asch (1951, 1956) conducted a series of now-classic studies exploring the power of normative social influence. Asch devised the studies assuming that there are limits to how much people will conform. Naturally, people conformed in the Sherif studies, he reasoned, because the situation was highly ambiguous—trying to guess how many inches a light was moving. But when a situation was wholly unambiguous, Asch expected that people would act like rational, objective problem solvers. When the group said or did something that contradicted an obvious truth, surely people would resist social pressures and decide for themselves what was going on, he figured.

To test his hypothesis, Asch conducted the following study. Had you been a participant, you would have been told that this was an experiment on perceptual judgment and that you'd be taking part with seven other students. Here's the scenario: The experimenter shows everyone two cards, one with a single line on it and the other with three lines labeled 1, 2, and 3. He asks each of you to judge and then announce out loud which of the three lines on the second card is closest in length to the line on the first card (see Figure 8.2).

It is crystal clear that the correct answer is the second line. Not surprisingly, each participant says, "Line 2." Your turn comes next to last, and, of course, you say, "Line 2" as well. The last participant concurs. The experimenter then presents a new set of cards and asks the participants again to make their judgments and announce them out loud.

Figure 8.2 Asch's Line-Judgment Task

In a series of studies of normative social influence, participants judged which of the three comparison lines on the right card was closest in length to the standard line on the card on the left. The correct answer was always obvious (as it is here). However, members of the group (actually confederates) sometimes gave the wrong answer out loud. Now the participant faced a dilemma: Give the right answer and go against the whole group, or conform to their behavior and give an obviously wrong answer?

(Adapted from Asch, 1956)

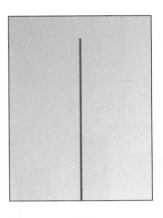

Standard line

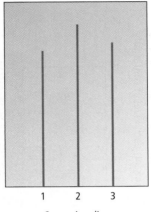

1   2   3

Comparison lines

Again, the answer is obvious, and everyone gives the correct answer. At this point, you are probably thinking, "What a waste of time. I've got a paper due tomorrow. I need to get out of here."

As your mind starts to wander, though, something surprising happens. The experimenter presents a third set of lines, and again the answer is obvious; line 3 is clearly the closest in length to the target line. But the first participant announces that the correct answer is line 1! "This guy must be so bored that he fell asleep," you think. Then the second person announces that line 1 is the correct answer. The third, fourth, fifth, and sixth participants all agree; it's now your turn. Startled at this point, you are probably looking at the lines very closely to see if you missed something. But no, line 3 is clearly the right answer. What will you do? Will you stand up for what you believe to be the truth, blurting out, "Line 3," or will you go along with the group and give the obviously wrong answer, "Line 1"?

As you can see, Asch set up a situation to discover if people would conform even when the right answer was absolutely obvious. In each group, all the individuals except for the actual participant were confederates of the research team who had been instructed to give the wrong answer on 12 of the 18 trials. What happened? Contrary to what Asch expected, a considerable amount of conformity occurred: 76% of the participants conformed and gave an obviously incorrect response on at least one trial. On average, people conformed on about one-third of the trials on which the accomplices gave an incorrect answer (see Figure 8.3).

Why did people conform so often? Participants couldn't have needed information from others to help them make a decision, as they did in the Sherif study, because the situation was not ambiguous. The right

Participants in an Asch line study. The real participant is seated in the middle. He is surrounded by the experimenter's accomplices, who have just given the wrong answer on the line task.

Figure 8.3 Results of the Asch Line-Judgment Study

Participants in the Asch line study showed a surprising level of conformity, given how obvious it was that the group was wrong in its judgments. Seventy-six percent of the participants conformed on at least one trial; only 24% of participants never conformed at all (see bar labeled zero). Most participants conformed on one to three of the 12 trials in which the group gave the wrong answer. However, a sizable number of participants conformed to the group's incorrect response nearly every single time (see the two bars on the right).

(Adapted from Asch, 1957)

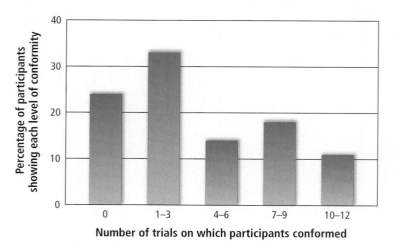

answers were so obvious that when people in a control group made the judgments by themselves, they were accurate more than 98% of the time. Instead, normative pressures came into play. Even though the other participants were strangers, the fear of being the lone dissenter was so strong that most people conformed, at least occasionally. One participant explained, "Here was a group; they had a definite idea; my idea disagreed; this might arouse anger … I was standing out [like] a sore thumb … I didn't want particularly to make a fool of myself … I felt I was definitely right … [but] they might think I was peculiar" (Asch, 1956).

These are classic normative reasons for conforming: People go along so as not to feel peculiar or look foolish. Notably, in contrast to informational social influence, normative pressures usually result in *public compliance without private acceptance*; people go along with the group even if they think it is wrong or do not believe in what they are doing.

What was especially surprising about Asch's results is that people were concerned about looking foolish even in front of complete strangers. It is not as if the participants were in danger of being ostracized by a group that was important to them. Yet decades of research since the original Asch study have indicated that conformity for normative reasons can occur simply because we do not want to risk social disapproval, even from complete strangers we will never see again (Bond & Smith, 1996; Chen, Wu, et al., 2012; Cialdini & Goldstein, 2004).

In a variation of his study, Asch (1957) demonstrated just how powerful social disapproval can be in shaping behavior. As before, the confederates gave the wrong answer 12 out of 18 times, but in this version the actual participants were the only ones allowed to write down their answers instead of saying them out loud. Now people did not have to worry about what the group thought of them because the

Watch ASCH'S LINE STUDY

group would never find out what their answers were. Conformity dropped dramatically, occurring on an average of only 1.5 of the 12 trials (Insko et al., 1985; Nail, 1986). As psychologist Serge Moscovici (1985) observed, the Asch studies are "one of the most dramatic illustrations of conformity, of blindly going along with the group, even when the individual realizes that by doing so he turns his back on reality and truth" (p. 349).

Research by Gregory Berns and colleagues has provided neural evidence for just how unpleasant and uncomfortable it is to resist normative social influence (Berns et al., 2005). Berns and his research team used functional magnetic resonance imaging (fMRI) to examine the changes in brain activity of research participants as they either normatively conformed to a group's judgment or maintained their independence and disagreed with the group.

Instead of judgments of line length, the task in this study involved mental rotation. While in the fMRI scanner, participants were shown a three-dimensional figure and then asked if a second figure (rotated in a different direction) was the same as the first figure or different. They indicated their answers by pushing a button. The task was slightly more difficult than Asch's line-judgment task; the baseline error rate, when participants made judgments alone, was 13.8%, compared to Asch's (1951, 1956) baseline error rate of 2%.

Before being placed in the fMRI scanner, participants met and interacted with four other participants who were, as you've probably guessed, actually confederates. These four would be doing the same mental rotation task, but only the participant would have his or her brain activity monitored. During the task, the participant completed one-third of the trials with no knowledge of the answers of the other four people. On the remaining two-thirds of the trials, the participant saw the other four group members' answers on a visual display. Half of the time, the group had all chosen the wrong answer, and the other half of the time, they had all chosen the right answer.

Now, what did the participants do, and, most important, what areas of their brains were more active when they did it? First, as with the original Asch study, participants conformed to the group's wrong answers a fair amount of the time (41% of the trials, to be exact). On the baseline trials, when the participants answered alone, the fMRI results indicated increased activity in the posterior brain areas dedicated to vision and perception. When the participants conformed to the group's wrong answers, activation occurred in the same areas; however, when participants chose to give the right answer and thus disagree with the group's unanimous wrong answer, the visual/perceptual areas of the brain were not activated. Instead, different areas of the brain became more active, in particular the amygdala, an area associated with, among other functions, negative emotional states and modulating social behavior (Berns et al., 2005). Thus, more recent research has continued to explore the same issues Asch first examined six decades ago and has provided support for the idea that normative social influence occurs because people feel arousing emotions, such as discomfort and tension, when they go against the group (Gaither et al., 2017; Hatcher et al., 2016; Shestakova et al., 2013).

The Importance of Being Accurate, Revisited

Now, you may be thinking, "Okay, so we conform to normative social influence, but hey, only when it's something minor. Who cares whether you give the right answer on a line-judgment task? It doesn't matter, nothing is at stake—I'd never conform to the group's wrong answer if something important were involved!" And this would be a very good criticism. Recall our discussion of importance in connection with informational social influence; we found that in ambiguous situations, the more important the decision is, the more someone will conform for informational reasons. What about in nonambiguous situations? Maybe the more important the decision is, the less the person would conform? When it's important to you to be right, are you strong enough to withstand group pressure and disagree with the group?

Recall the first study of eyewitness identification that we discussed earlier, in which participants viewed pairs of slides, one of the perpetrator alone and one of the perpetrator in a lineup (Baron et al., 1996). When studying informational conformity, the researchers made the task fiendishly difficult and ambiguous—the slides were projected for only half a second. To study normative social influence, however, the researchers made the same task easy: The participants viewed each slide for a full 5 seconds, and they were shown each pair of slides twice. Now the task became analogous to Asch's line-judging task; basically, if you were awake, you'd get the right answer. Indeed, when individuals in a control group viewed the slides alone, they answered correctly on 97% of the trials.

Baron and colleagues again manipulated the importance of the participants being accurate, in the same ways we discussed earlier. Half were led to believe that it was very important that they give the right answers, and half were told it really didn't matter how they did. How did participants respond when the confederates give the obviously wrong answer? Did they conform to the group on at least some of the trials, as the participants in the Asch study did? Or did the participants who believe accuracy is very important give the correct answers every time, standing up to the group and ignoring the normative pressure to agree with them?

The researchers found that participants in the low-importance condition conformed to the group on 33% of the critical trials—very close to the rate in Asch's line-judgment task. What happened to the participants in the high-importance condition? Rather than standing up to the group across the board, they caved on at least some trials. They did conform less to the obviously wrong answers of the group; on only 16% of the critical trials did they echo the group's blatantly wrong answer. But they still conformed sometimes! These findings underscore the power of normative social influence: Even when the group is wrong, the right answer is obvious, and there are strong incentives to be accurate, some people still find it difficult to risk social disapproval, even from strangers (Baron et al., 1996; Hornsey et al., 2003).

Normative social influence most closely reflects the negative stereotype of conformity we referred to earlier: the belief that those who conform are spineless and weak. Ironically, while this type of social pressure can be difficult to resist, people are often quick to deny that they've been influenced by normative considerations. Recall the energy conservation study by Nolan and colleagues (2008) described previously. In this study, researchers assessed the effectiveness of different arguments for reducing electricity use among Californians. The most effective persuasive message was telling consumers that their neighbors were conserving energy. But participants *believed* that this message had little effect on them, especially compared to participants who received information regarding protecting the environment or saving money. As Nolan and her coauthors conclude, we often underestimate the power of normative social influence.

But your denial that normative pressures affect you doesn't stop others from trying to exert influence through such processes. How else to explain why some television producers hire professional laughers to sit in the studio audience to make their comedies seem funnier (Warner, 2011)? Or why some sports teams pay abnormally enthusiastic fans to rile up fellow spectators at their home games (Sommers, 2011)? Clearly, the desire to fit in and be accepted is part of human nature, whether or not we're willing to admit it. Just think of the role normative social influence plays in daily decisions

Fads are a frivolous example of normative social influence. By 2007, the Crocs fad was in full force as kids (and parents) everywhere could be found out and about in these plastic clogs with Swiss-cheese holes. Just a few years later, reviews were already decidedly more mixed: quite quickly, anti-Croc pages with more than a million followers sprouted up on Facebook and Twitter.

about what to wear. Normative social influence is at work whenever we notice a particular look shared by people in a certain group, and helps explain why, no matter what it is, it will look outdated just a few years later until the fashion industry revives it in a new trend.

The Consequences of Resisting Normative Social Influence

One way to observe the power of normative social pressure is to examine the consequences when people manage to resist it. Indeed, entire television empires have been built around this very premise, that violating norms has consequences, and those consequences can be entertaining—at least when it's someone else suffering them and not you. *Curb Your Enthusiasm, Broad City, Louie, Inside Amy Schumer*, and other shows that inspire a potent mixture of laughter and cringing among viewers have become cult (and sometimes mainstream) classics by mining the comedic landscape that is resisting normative social influence.

In your own life, if a person refuses to do as the group asks and thereby violates its norms, what happens? Think about the norms that operate in your group of friends. Some friends have an egalitarian norm for making group decisions. For example, when choosing a movie, everyone gets to state a preference; the choice is then discussed until agreement is reached. What would happen if, in a group with this kind of norm, you stated at the outset that you wanted to see only *Rebel Without a Cause* and would not agree to watch anything else? Your friends would be surprised by your behavior; they would also be annoyed with you or even angry. If you continued to disregard the friendship norms of the group by failing to conform, two things would most likely happen. First, the group would try to bring you "back into the fold," chiefly through increased communication. Teasing comments and long discussions would ensue as your friends tried to figure out why you were acting so strangely and tried to get you to conform to their expectations, and if these tactics didn't work, your friends would most likely say negative things to you and about you and start to withdraw from you (Festinger & Thibaut, 1951; Packer, 2008b). Now, in effect, you've been rejected (Abrams et al., 2000; Jetten & Hornsey, 2014).

Stanley Schachter (1951) demonstrated how the group responds to an individual who ignores normative influence. He asked groups of college students to read and discuss a case history of "Johnny Rocco," a juvenile delinquent. Most of the students took a middle-of-the-road position about the case, believing that Rocco should receive a judicious mixture of love and discipline. Unbeknownst to the participants, however, Schachter had planted an accomplice in the group who was instructed to disagree with the group's recommendations. The accomplice consistently argued that Rocco should receive the harshest amount of punishment, regardless of what the other group members argued.

How was the deviant treated? He became the target of the most comments and questions from the real participants throughout most of the discussion, and then, near the end, communication with him dropped sharply. The other group members had tried to convince the deviant to agree with them; when it appeared that it wouldn't work, they started to ignore him altogether. In addition, they punished him. After the discussion, they were asked to fill out questionnaires that supposedly pertained to future discussion meetings of their group. The participants were asked to nominate one group member who should be eliminated from further discussions if the group size had to be reduced. They nominated the deviant. They were also asked to assign group members to various tasks in future discussions. They assigned the unimportant or boring jobs, such as taking notes, to the deviant. Social groups are well versed in how to bring a nonconformist into line. No wonder we respond as often as we do to normative pressures! You can find out what it's like to resist normative social influence in the following Try It!

Whether through stand-up routines in which she explores taboo topics and embarrassing revelations that most of us would never address in public or via her provocative show *Inside Amy Schumer*, Amy Schumer is one contemporary comedian who produces many of her laughs by exploring the consequences of norm violation.

Try It!

Unmasking Normative Social Influence by Breaking the Rules

Every day, you likely talk to a wide range of people—friends, professors, coworkers, strangers. When you have a conversation, whether long or short, you follow certain interaction "rules" that operate in your culture. These rules for conversation include nonverbal forms of behavior that others consider "normal" as well as "polite." You can find out how powerful these norms are by breaking them and noting how people respond to you; their responses demonstrate the power of normative social influence.

For example, in conversation, we stand a certain distance from each other—not too far and not too close. About 2 to 3 feet is typical in mainstream U.S. culture. In addition, we maintain a good amount of eye contact when we are listening to the other person; in comparison, when we're talking, we look away from the person more often.

What happens if you break these normative rules? Try having a conversation with a friend and stand either too close or too far away (e.g., 1 foot or 7 feet). Have a typical, normal conversation with your friend—only the spacing you use with this person should be different. Note how your friend responds. If you're too close, your friend will probably back away; if you continue to keep the distance small, he or she may act uncomfortable and even end your conversation sooner than usual. If you're too far away, your friend will probably come closer; if you back up, he or she may think you are in a strange mood. In either case, your friend's response will probably include looking at you a lot, having a puzzled look on his or her face, acting uncomfortable, and talking less than normal.

You have acted in a nonnormative way, and your conversational partner is, first, trying to figure out what is going on and, second, responding in a way to get you to stop acting oddly. From this one brief exercise, you will get the idea of what would happen if you behaved oddly all the time—people would try to get you to change, and then they would probably start avoiding or ignoring you.

When you're finished, "debrief" your friend, explaining the exercise, so that your behavior is understood. Note the tremendous relief you feel on revealing why you were acting so peculiarly. This is yet one more demonstration of the strength of normative pressure and the challenge inherent to resisting it!

When Will People Conform to Normative Social Influence?

Social Impact Theory
The idea that conforming to social influence depends on the group's importance, immediacy, and the number of people in the group

Although conformity is common, people don't always cave in to peer pressure. After all, we certainly do not all agree on many major issues, such as abortion, affirmative action, or same-sex marriage. And if 75% of participants in Asch's line-judging studies conformed during the course of the study, that means that 25% never did—indeed, 95% of participants disagreed with the rest of the group at least one time. Exactly when are people most likely to conform to normative pressures? Some answers to this question are provided by Bibb Latané's (1981) **social impact theory**. According to his theory, the likelihood that you will respond to social influence depends on three variables regarding the group in question:

1. *Strength:* How important to you is the group? The more important a group is to us, the more likely we will be to conform to its normative pressures, according to social impact theory.

2. *Immediacy:* How close is the group to you in space and time during the attempt to influence you? Conformity is also predicted to increase the closer group members are to us physically.

3. *Number:* How many people are in the group? As the size of the group increases, so does the normative pressure it exerts, but each additional person has less of an influencing effect. That is, going from three people to four makes much more of a difference than going from 53 people to 54. In short, it does not take an extremely large group to create normative social influence, but the larger the group, the stronger the social pressure (see Figure 8.4 for a depiction of this conclusion in Asch's conformity research).

Latané constructed a mathematical model that captures these hypothesized effects of strength, immediacy, and number and has applied this formula to the results of many

Figure 8.4 Effects of Group Size on Conformity

Asch varied the size of the unanimous majority in his study and found that once the majority numbered four, adding more people had little influence on conformity.

(Based on Asch, 1955)

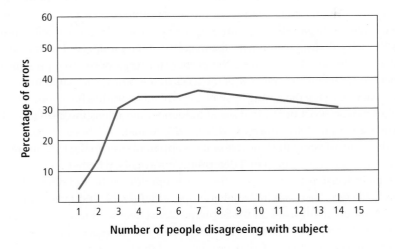

conformity studies (Bourgeois & Bowen, 2001; Latané & Bourgeois, 2001; Wolf, 2014). For example, gay men who live in communities highly involved in AIDS awareness activities (where strength, immediacy, and number would all be high) report feeling more social pressure to avoid risky sexual behavior and stronger intentions to do so than gay men who live in less involved communities (Fishbein et al., 1993). Similarly, a recent study of hetero-sexual dating couples (a relationship typically high in strength and immediacy) reveals that an individual's own tendency to engage in heavy drinking is significantly predicted by the norm set by his or her partner's drinking tendencies (Mushquash et al., 2011).

Let's see in more detail what social impact theory says about the conditions under which people will conform to normative social pressures.

WHEN THE GROUP IS IMPORTANT   The strength of the group—defined as how im-portant the group is to us—makes a difference. Normative pressures are much stronger when they come from people whose friendship, love, and respect we cherish because there is a large cost to losing this love and respect (Abrams et al., 1990; Guimond, 1999; Nowak, Szamrej, & Latané, 1990). One consequence of this conclusion is that it can be dangerous to have policy decisions made by highly cohesive groups because they care more about pleasing each other and avoiding conflict than arriving at the best, most logical decision. We will see several examples of this phenomenon in Chapter 9.

We should note, however, that the very act of conforming normatively to important groups *most* of the time can earn you the right to deviate occasionally without serious consequences. This interesting observation was made by Edwin Hollander (1960, 1985), who stated that conforming to a group over time earns you **idiosyncrasy credits**, much like putting money in the bank to save for future use. It's as if your past conformity allows you, at some point in the future, to deviate from the group (to "make withdrawals") with-out getting into too much trouble. Let's say, for example, that your friends are all in agree-ment that they want to go out for Chinese food. You, however, feel like Mexican food tonight, and rather than simply going along with group consensus, you decide to stick to your guns and lobby for burritos. If you have typically followed their friendship norms in other areas in the past, your friends will be less likely to become upset with you for your current nonconformity, for you've earned the right to deviate from their normative rules in this area on this occasion (Hornsey et al., 2007; Jetten & Hornsey, 2014).

WHEN ONE HAS NO ALLIES IN THE GROUP   Normative social influence is most powerfully felt when everyone in the group says or believes the same thing—for example,

Idiosyncrasy Credits

The tolerance a person earns, over time, by conforming to group norms; if enough credits are earned, the person can, on occasion, deviate from the group without retribution

when your group of friends all believe that *The Lord of the Rings* was the greatest movie trilogy ever made. Resisting such unanimous social influence is difficult unless you have an ally. If another person disagrees with the group—say, by nominating the original *Star Wars* movies as the best trilogy ever—this behavior will help you buck the tide as well.

To test the importance of having an ally, Asch (1955) conducted another version of his conformity experiment. He had six of the seven confederates give the wrong answer, while one confederate gave the right answer on every trial. The participant was no longer alone. Although still disagreeing with the majority of the group, having one ally dramatically changed the situation, helping the participant resist normative pressures. People conformed on an average of only 6% of the trials in this study, compared to 32% when all of the confederates gave the wrong answer. Several other studies have found that observing another person resist normative social influence emboldens the individual to do the same (Allen & Levine, 1969; Morris & Miller, 1975; Nemeth & Chiles, 1988).

The difficulty of being the lone dissenter is apparent even in the U.S. Supreme Court. After hearing a case, the justices first determine, informally, whether they are unanimous or split in their decision. Some justices then write opinion drafts and others decide which draft they will sign. There are informal attempts at influence, and eventually all make a decision. A content analysis of all the Supreme Court decisions from 1953 to 2001 (4,178 decisions, involving 29 different justices) indicated that the most common decision was 9–0, the unanimous one (35% of all decisions). And the least common decision? The one that required one justice to disagree with all of his or her colleagues, the 8–1 split, which accounted for only 10% of decisions over 48 years (Granberg & Bartels, 2005).

WHEN THE GROUP'S CULTURE IS COLLECTIVISTIC "In America, the squeaky wheel gets the grease. In Japan, the nail that stands out gets pounded down" (Markus & Kitayama, 1991, p. 224). Indeed, the society in which one is raised seems to predict the frequency of normative social influence (Milgram, 1961). In a cross-cultural study of normative social influence, people in Brazil, Hong Kong, and Lebanon conformed to a similar extent (both to each other and to the American sample), whereas participants from the Bantu tribe of Zimbabwe conformed to a much greater degree (Whittaker & Meade, 1967). As the researchers pointed out, conformity has a very high social value in Bantu culture.

Although Japanese culture tends to be more conforming than American culture in many areas, two Asch-type studies found that when the group unanimously gave the incorrect answer, Japanese students were less conformist in general than North Americans (Frager, 1970; Williams & Sogon, 1984). In Japan, cooperation and loyalty are directed to the groups to which one belongs and with which one identifies; there is little expectation that one should conform to the behavior of strangers, especially in such an artificial setting as a psychology experiment. Similarly, conformity was much higher in a British sample when the participants thought the other group members were psychology majors like themselves rather than art history majors (Abrams et al., 1990). Similarly, German research participants have shown less conformity in the Asch experiment than North Americans (Timaeus, 1968); in Germany, conformity to strangers is less valued than conformity to a few well-defined groups (Moghaddam, Taylor, & Wright, 1993).

A more systematic review of the role of culture in conformity is provided by a meta-analysis of 133 Asch line-judgment studies conducted in 17 countries (Bond & Smith, 1996). Participants from more collectivistic cultures showed higher rates of conformity on the line task than participants from more individualistic cultures. In collectivistic cultures, conformity is seen as a valued trait, not as a somewhat negative one. Agreeing with others is viewed not as an act of submission or cowardice in collectivist cultures but as an act of tact and sensitivity (Hodges & Geyer, 2006; Smith & Bond, 1999). Because the emphasis is on the group and not the individual, people in collectivistic cultures value normative social influence because it promotes harmony and supportive relationships in the group (Kim et al., 1994; Markus et al., 1996; Zhang et al., 2007).

The extent to which conformity is valued varies across cultures. In the Opening Ceremony of the 2008 Beijing Olympics, a worldwide television audience was mesmerized by the sight of 2,008 drummers performing in perfect synchronization.

#trending

Social Norms and Bigotry

According to FBI data, hate crimes in the United States increased by almost 7% from 2014 to 2015. Though most hate crimes continue to be motivated by race (over half are targeted toward Black or African Americans), much of the recent increase is from attacks against Muslims. In the days and weeks following the 2016 U.S. presidential election, reports of hate crimes and other forms of racial and religious harassment also spiked. It may be years before we have precise data on hate crimes for 2016 and 2017, and the causes of such an uptick in overt acts of bigotry are likely multiple and complex. But some social psychologists have argued that one relevant factor is normative social influence.

Keith Payne, a social psychologist at the University of North Carolina, has suggested that when people—especially those in positions of influence and authority—fail to condemn episodes of bias, a social norm is reinforced by which these biases become seen as more acceptable. In one study, for example, research participants—none of whom were Black—were given a measure of unconscious or implicit racial biases (a topic covered in more detail in Chapter 13; Payne, Burkley, & Stokes, 2008). Some of these participants were told by the experimenter in charge of the study that everyone is vulnerable to subtle prejudice, but that one way we can overcome it is to be vigilant against bias. Other participants were told that they should express their attitudes in the study as honestly as possible, even if they aren't "politically correct."

Payne and colleagues found that in a follow-up task, those participants who had been told that they shouldn't worry about political correctness expressed more negative feelings toward African American faces than did other participants. In other words, when the experimenter indicated that their biases were acceptable, the participants felt liberated to act on them. Creating a norm that tolerates or even encourages bigotry seems to allow bigotry to spread, much as research on social influence would predict.

This brings us back to the most recent presidential election. The 2016 campaign and its aftermath were marked by many instances of bias. Donald Trump campaigned on the premise that Mexican immigrants are a primary source of social and economic problems in America. He also promised to ban Muslims from entering the country and within weeks of taking office signed a controversial executive order that placed a travel ban on citizens from several predominantly Muslim nations. In August 2017, many criticized President Trump for failing to more explicitly blame Neo-Nazis and White supremacists for violence at a rally and counter-protest in Charlottesville, Virginia. As the research reviewed above indicates, when people in prominent and powerful positions sanction (or fail to criticize) biased ideas about certain groups, it can embolden others to voice and act on such bias as well. The trickle-down effect ultimately serves to normalize—there's that word "norm" again—hate and divisiveness, as can be seen by the Ku Klux Klan feeling emboldened enough to put out a full-page endorsement of Trump days before the election and by the maskless, tiki torch-bearing marchers in Charlottesville 10 months later.

Indeed, as Payne himself has written, "Maintaining social norms against prejudice means consciously rejecting our own implicit biases. Then it means speaking up, regardless of who you voted for, to say loudly and clearly in personal conversations and on social media that bias is not our way, and bigotry is unacceptable. Rejecting prejudice is not, and cannot be, a partisan issue." Like they do for so many other aspects of daily life, when it comes to bigotry and bias, social norms matter.

Minority Influence: When the Few Influence the Many

We shouldn't leave our discussion of normative social influence with the impression that groups affect individuals but the individual never has an effect on the group. As Serge Moscovici (1985, 1994; Moscovici, Mucchi-Faina, & Maass, 1994) says, if groups always succeeded in silencing nonconformists, rejecting deviants, and persuading everyone to go along with the majority point of view, how could change ever be introduced into the system? We would all be little robots, marching along with everyone else in monotonous synchrony, never able to adapt to changing reality. Clearly, this is not the case (Imhoff & Erb, 2009).

Minority Influence

The case where a minority of group members influences the behavior or beliefs of the majority

Instead, an individual or minority of group members can indeed influence the behavior or beliefs of the majority (Horcajo, Briñol, & Petty, 2014; Mucchi-Faina & Pagliaro, 2008; Sinaceur et al., 2010). This is called **minority influence**. The key is consistency: People with minority views must express the same view over time, and different members of the minority must agree with one another. If a person in the minority wavers between two different viewpoints or if two individuals express different minority views, the majority will dismiss them as people who have peculiar and groundless opinions. If, however, the minority expresses a consistent, unwavering view, the majority is more likely to take notice and even adopt the minority view (Moscovici & Nemeth, 1974). For example, in the 1970s, a minority of scientists began to call attention to evidence of human-caused climate change. Today, despite some vocal exceptions, the majority is paying attention, and political leaders from most industrialized nations have met to discuss possible worldwide solutions.

In a meta-analysis of nearly 100 studies, Wendy Wood and her colleagues describe how minority influence operates (Wood et al., 1994). People in the majority can cause other group members to conform through normative influence. As in the Asch experiments, the conformity that occurs may be a case of public compliance without private acceptance. People in the minority, however, can rarely influence others through normative means. Majority group members may be hesitant to agree publicly with the minority; they don't want anyone to think that they side with those unusual, strange views. Minorities therefore exert their influence on the group via the other principal method: informational social influence. The minority can introduce new and unexpected information to the group and cause the group to examine the issues more carefully. Such careful examination may cause the majority to realize that the minority view has merit, leading the group to adopt all or part of the minority's view. In short, majorities often obtain public compliance because of normative social influence, whereas when minorities are persuasive, it is more likely to be through private acceptance because of informational social influence (De Dreu & De Vries, 2001; Levine, Moreland, & Choi, 2001; Wood et al., 1996).

Review Questions

1. Societal rules regarding acceptable behavior are known as
   a. conformity.
   b. social norms.
   c. minority influence.
   d. convergence.

2. Asch's line-judgment research indicated that
   a. participants demonstrated public conformity without private acceptance.
   b. every single participant conformed at least one time.

   c. conformity was greater when participants wrote down their responses rather than said them aloud.
   d. conformity occurs only on a task that is of personal importance to the individual.

3. Compared to informational social influence, normative social influence
   a. leads to more internalized, private attitude change.
   b. is more consistent across different cultures.

c. has less to do with being accurate and more to do with fitting in.

d. is a tendency about which most Americans hold positive attitudes.

4. A 12-person jury is deliberating on a murder trial. Eleven members of the jury want to vote guilty and convict the defendant; only one juror wants to vote not guilty. The holdout juror, Henry, digs in and will not change his mind. According to research, what is the best prediction for how the rest of the group will react to Henry's deviance?

a. They will eventually come to ignore him and try to punish him by being generally unpleasant toward him.

b. They will come to appreciate his principled stand the longer he holds out in defiance of their position.

c. They will seek to change his opinion by using idiosyncrasy credits.

d. They will try to use minority influence to change his mind.

5. Which of the following conclusions is consistent with the predictions of social impact theory?

a. Conformity is more likely among groups of strangers than within established groups that are important to us.

b. Social influence increases in a linear fashion as a group grows in size; in other words, each new member added to a group adds the same amount of social influence as the previous member added.

c. The more immediate a group is, the more social influence it tends to exert.

d. Conformity is less prevalent in collectivist cultures than it is in individualistic cultures.

6. The key to minority influence is

a. normative social pressure.

b. immediacy.

c. creativity.

d. consistency.

Conformity Tactics

LO 8.4 **Describe how people can use their knowledge of social influence to influence others.**

We have seen how informational and normative conformity occurs. Even in a highly individualistic culture such as the United States, conformity of both types is common. Are there ways that we can put this tendency to productive use? Can we capitalize on conformity to change behavior for the common good? The answer is a resounding yes.

Consider a "61-million-person" experiment conducted via Facebook during the 2010 U.S. congressional elections (Bond et al., 2012). On Election Day, researchers arranged for millions of Facebook users to receive either an informational or a social message about voting (a control group received no message at all). The informational message appeared at the top of their "News Feed" and provided a link for finding their local polling place as well as an "I Voted" button they could click to update friends with the news that they had voted. The social message included this same information but with one addition: It told users how many of their own Facebook friends had also voted, showing them a randomly selected set of six photos of these voting friends. Compared to the control condition, the informational message had little impact on users' own likelihood of voting. But Facebook users who received the social message were significantly more likely to vote, as measured by their likelihood of clicking the site's "I Voted" button as well as actual voting records (Bond et al., 2012). These findings highlight just how powerful it can be to learn what others are up to—in fact, Bond et al. (2012) found that even seeing the social message posted to a friend's News Feed (not by one of *your* friends but by someone else your friend knows) was enough to have an indirect influence on a Facebook user's own voting behavior.

We can capitalize on the tendency to conform to change behavior for the common good, as in the effort to use social media messages to increase voter turnout.

The Role of Injunctive and Descriptive Norms

Robert Cialdini, Raymond Reno, and Carl Kallgren have suggested that social norms are particularly useful for subtly inducing people to conform to positive, socially approved behavior (Cialdini, Kallgren, & Reno, 1991; Jacobson, Mortensen, & Cialdini, 2011; Kallgren, Reno, & Cialdini, 2000). For example, we all know that littering is wrong. But when we've finished enjoying a snack at the beach or in a park, what determines whether we toss the wrapper on the ground or carry it with us until we come to a trash can? Let's say we wanted to decrease littering (or increase recycling or blood donations or contributions to other worthwhile causes). How would we go about doing it?

Cialdini and colleagues (1991) suggest that first we need to focus on what kind of norm is operating in the situation. A culture's social norms are of two types. **Injunctive norms** have to do with what we *think* other people approve or disapprove of. Injunctive norms motivate behavior by promising rewards (or punishments) for normative (or nonnormative) behavior. For example, an injunctive norm in our culture is that littering is wrong and that donating blood is a good thing to do. In other words, injunctive norms have to do with what people believe they *should* do in a given situation.

Descriptive norms concern our perceptions of the way people actually behave in a given situation, regardless of whether the behavior is approved or disapproved of by others. Descriptive norms motivate behavior by informing people about what is effective or adaptive behavior. For example, while we all know that littering is wrong (an injunctive norm), we also all know that there are situations when people are likely to do it (a descriptive norm)—for example, dropping peanut shells on the ground at a baseball game or leaving trash at your seat in a movie theater. Descriptive norms also tell us that relatively few people donate blood and that only a small percentage of registered voters actually vote. In other words, descriptive norms have to do with what people actually do in a given situation (Crane & Platow, 2010; Kallgren et al., 2000; White et al, 2009).

In a series of studies, Cialdini and colleagues explored how injunctive and descriptive norms affect people's likelihood of littering. For example, in one field experiment, people were returning to their cars in the parking lot when a confederate approached them (Reno, Cialdini, & Kallgren, 1993). In the control group, the confederate just walked by. In the *descriptive norm condition*, the confederate dropped an empty bag from a fast-food restaurant on the ground before passing the participant. By littering, the confederate was subtly communicating that "this is what people do in this situation." In the *injunctive norm condition*, the confederate was not carrying anything but instead picked up a littered fast-food bag from the ground before passing the participant. By picking up someone else's litter, the confederate was subtly communicating that "littering is wrong." These three conditions occurred in one of two environments: Either the parking lot was heavily littered (ahead of time by the experimenters), or the area was clean and unlittered (previously cleaned up by the experimenters).

At this point, research participants have been exposed to one of two types of norms about littering. And all this has happened in a littered or a clean environment. How were participants' own littering tendencies affected? When they got back to their cars, they found a large flyer that the experimenters had left on their windshield. The participant had two

Injunctive Norms

People's perceptions of what behaviors are approved or disapproved of by others

Descriptive Norms

People's perceptions of how people actually behave in given situations, regardless of whether the behavior is approved or disapproved of by others

Infomercials, those long, late-night advertisements for zany inventions and wild, new products, used to end as follows: "Operators are waiting; please call now." These days, they're more likely to instruct viewers: "If operators are busy, please call again." This new call to action has led to increases in calls from new customers. Can you use the concept of descriptive norms to explain why this new wording seems to be so effective?

Figure 8.5 The Effect of Injunctive and Descriptive Norms on Littering

The data for the control group (left) indicate that 37% to 38% of people litter a flyer found on their car windshield whether the environment (a parking lot) is littered or clean. When a descriptive norm is made salient, littering decreases significantly only in the clean environment (middle). When an injunctive norm is made salient, littering decreases significantly in both types of environment, indicating that injunctive norms are more consistently effective at changing behavior.

(Adapted from Reno, Cialdini, & Kallgren, 1993)

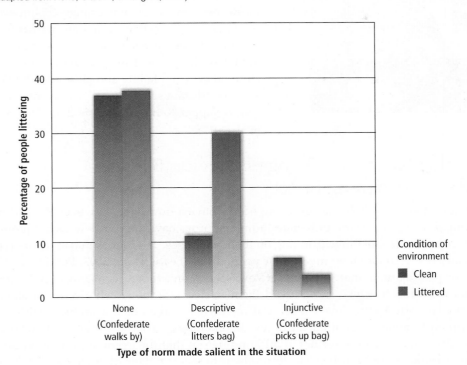

choices: throw the flyer on the ground, littering, or bring the flyer inside their car to dispose of it later.

The control group indicates that slightly more than one-third of people threw the flyer on the ground, regardless of whether the area was already littered or clean (see Figure 8.5). In the descriptive norm condition, the confederate's littering communicated two different messages, depending on the condition of the parking lot. In the littered lot, the confederate's behavior reminded participants that people often litter here—the confederate served as just one salient example of the type of behavior that had led to such a mess in the first place. In the clean parking lot, however, the confederate's behavior communicated a different message. Now, the behavior stood out as unusual—it reminded participants that most people don't litter in this area. Hence, we would expect the confederate's littering behavior to remind participants of a descriptive norm against littering, and this is what the researchers found. Finally, what about the injunctive norm condition? This kind of norm was less context dependent: Seeing the confederate picking up someone else's litter invokes the injunctive norm that littering is wrong in both the clean and the littered environments, thereby leading to the lowest amount of littering in the study (Reno et al., 1993).

In light of studies such as this one, researchers have concluded that injunctive norms are more powerful than descriptive norms in producing desirable behavior (Kallgren et al., 2000). This should not surprise you because injunctive norms tap into normative conformity; we conform (e.g., refraining from littering) because someone's behavior reminds us that our society disapproves of littering. We will look like selfish slobs if we litter, and we will feel embarrassed if other people see us litter. Although

Watch SURVIVAL TIPS! KEEPING PARTIES CLEAN

Revel Video

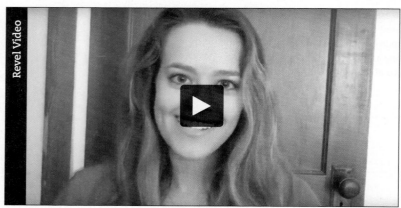

norms are always present to some extent—we *know* that littering is bad—they are not always *salient* to us (Jonas et al., 2008; Kallgren et al., 2000). To promote socially beneficial behavior, something in the situation needs to draw our attention to the relevant norm. Thus, anything that highlights injunctive norms can be used to create positive behavioral change (Bodimeade et al., 2014). Injunctive norms are particularly good predictors of behavior when the sense of approval/disapproval in question comes from close others (e.g., family and close friends) versus more distant sources (e.g., "the average person") (Napper, Kenney, & LaBrie, 2015; Pederson et al., 2017).

Using Norms to Change Behavior: Beware the "Boomerang Effect"

Efforts to change behavior by using norms have a downside, however. As one example, in recent years, university administrators have tried a new technique for decreasing alcohol binge drinking on their campuses. The idea is that students typically overestimate how much their peers drink (Lewis et al., 2007; Perkins, 2007). Thus, telling them that "students at your school, on average, consume only X number of drinks a week" should lead them to decrease their own alcohol intake as they conform to this lower level. But researchers have noted a problem with this approach: Sometimes, it backfires, or "boomerangs." That is, for students who already drink very little (or not at all), finding out that the average student on campus drinks more than they do leads them to *increase* their own alcohol intake to be more like everyone else! In short, the public service message meant to decrease alcohol consumption can actually have the effect of increasing it (Perkins, Haines, & Rice, 2005). Accordingly, your efforts to change others' behavior through processes of conformity must consider that there are different types of people receiving your message: those performing the undesirable behavior at an *above-average* level (whom you want to convince to decrease the behavior) and those already performing the undesirable behavior at a *below-average* level (who you want to continue doing what they're doing rather than to boomerang by increasing the undesirable behavior).

P. Wesley Shultz and colleagues tested this idea by focusing on a desirable behavior we've already discussed in this chapter: conserving electricity (Shultz et al., 2007). Residents of a California neighborhood agreed to take part in the study. Their baseline energy usage was measured, and they were divided into two groups: those whose energy consumption was above the neighborhood average and those whose energy consumption was below the average. The households were then randomly assigned to receive one of two kinds of feedback over several weeks. In the *descriptive norm condition*, they were told how much energy they had used that week, told how much energy the average household in their neighborhood had used, and given suggestions for energy conservation. In the *descriptive norm plus injunctive norm condition*, they received all of the above information plus one subtle but important addition: If they had consumed less energy than the average household, the researcher drew a smiley face next to the information. If they had consumed more energy than the average household, the researcher drew a sad face instead. The happy or sad face communicated the *injunctive* part of the message—the recipients were receiving either approval or disapproval for the amount of energy they had used.

❄ **Last Winter Comparison** | You used **5% LESS** natural gas than your efficient neighbors.

Your usage last winter:

*Therms: Standard unit of measuring heat energy

Smiley faces aren't just for texting. In this case, they're part of an effort from a utility company to use injunctive norms to convince consumers to cut down on their energy use.

Weeks later, researchers measured energy usage again. Did the messages help convince people to conserve energy? Did those who already used low amounts stray from the path of conservation righteousness and boomerang, deciding that it would not be so bad for them to be a little less efficient just like their wasteful neighbors? First, the results indicated that the descriptive norm message had a positive effect on those who consumed more energy than average; they cut back and conserved. However, the descriptive norm message had a boomerang effect on those who consumed less energy than average. Once they learned what their neighbors were doing (using electricity like crazy), they felt liberated to increase their own usage!

On the other hand, the "descriptive norm plus injunctive norm" message was uniformly successful. Those whose consumption was more than average decreased their usage when they received this message. Most important, those whose consumption was below average to begin with did not boomerang; they maintained their same, low level of energy use as before the study started. The smiley face reminded them that they were doing the right thing, and they kept on doing it (Schultz et al., 2007). This study has had a major impact on energy conservation strategies in the United States. The use of smiley and sad faces to give injunctive norm feedback, combined with descriptive norm energy-usage information, is now being used by utility companies in various major metropolitan areas in the United States, United Kingdom, and elsewhere (National Energy Study, 2014).

Other Tactics of Social Influence

The savvy practitioner of social influence has more than one trick up his or her sleeve. Using norms is not the only way to change other people's behavior. Indeed, anyone who has ever tried to buy a car, join a gym, or negotiate with any of a variety of salespeople, door-to-door petitioners, or telemarketers knows that there is a wide range of techniques that people use to try to get you to go along with what they'd like you to do.

Indeed, many of the most effective techniques for changing other people's behaviors psychologists have catalogued have been identified after observing masters of social influence at work—the successful salesperson, marketer, and negotiator. One important lesson that researchers have learned is that the sequence in which a series of requests is made contributes to its effectiveness. Consider the following scenario: You are approached by someone identifying himself as a member of a group called Citizens for Safe Driving. His hope is that you'll be willing to support his group's campaign by placing a sign in your front yard for a week. He then shows you a photo of the sign in question. It's huge! It blocks much of the house in the picture, completely concealing the front door. To be honest, it's not a particularly attractive sign either; the "Drive Carefully" lettering even looks a bit crooked. Oh, and did we mention that it will probably require making holes in your lawn?

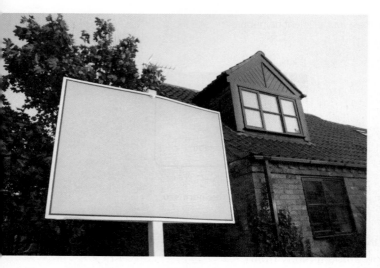

Would you agree to put a big sign in your yard, blocking the front of your house? Research on the foot-in-the-door technique suggests that your answer might depend on whether or not you have already agreed to a smaller request first.

Foot-in-the-Door Technique

Social influence strategy in which getting people to agree first to a small request makes them more likely to agree later to a second, larger request

Door-in-the-Face Technique

Social influence strategy in which first asking people for a large request that they will probably refuse makes them more likely to agree later to a second, smaller request

Our guess is that you aren't too excited at the prospects of adding this sign to your property, even on a temporary basis. Indeed, when Jonathan Freedman and Scott Fraser (1966) made this very request of homeowners in Palo Alto, California, they found just 17% willing to put the sign in their yard. But the researchers also figured out a way to make the same request seem much more agreeable: by first getting people to comply with a smaller request. Specifically, in another condition, the researchers first asked participants if they would place in their window a small, 3-inch sign that read, "Be a safe driver." Then, 2 weeks later, these participants were asked about putting up the larger (and uglier) yard sign, and a whopping 76% now agreed (Freedman & Fraser, 1966). This increase in compliance based on an earlier, smaller request is the **foot-in-the-door technique** in action—so named for the traveling salesman whose underlying strategy is to get at least one foot inside your house so you can't slam the door shut on him.

Why does this work? Think about what happens when you get people to agree to any request, even a small one. They start to see themselves as agreeable people. They feel committed to a helpful course of action. To say no to a follow-up request—even if it comes from a different person—could trigger uncomfortable feelings of inconsistency or dissonance (Cantatero, Gamian-Wilk, & Doliński, 2017; Cialdini, 2009; Pascual et al., 2013).

Interestingly, the opposite tactic also works. That is, another way to get people to agree to a request is first to ask them for a much larger commitment, one to which you know they'll say no. This is the **door-in-the-face technique**. In one study, Cialdini and colleagues (1975) approached college students and asked if they would be willing to spend 2 hours chaperoning a group of troubled children on a field trip to the local zoo. Only 17% of students agreed to this request. But consider the experience of other participants who were first asked about their willingness to volunteer every week for a minimum of 2 years at a local juvenile detention center. Every single one of the students refused this large request. But when they were then asked about chaperoning the 2-hour zoo trip, 50% agreed.

In short, people are also more likely to agree to the request you really care about when you first hit them up for a bigger favor that forces them to say no. One reason is that the first, bigger request makes the second "ask" seem less daunting by comparison. Another reason has to do with feelings of reciprocity (Chan & Au, 2011). After all, it seems like you—the requestor—have made some concessions here, coming down from your initially huge favor to a more much manageable later request. To the target of your requests, it feels as if the least they can do is negotiate a bit as well, meeting you halfway and agreeing to something smaller. Of course, little do they know that it was this second, smaller request that you really cared about all along.

Are these strategies for social influence ones you can envision using in your own life? Or maybe you bristle at the thought of such conscious efforts to manipulate others? At the very least, newly aware of their existence, perhaps now you'll be on the lookout for those times when other people attempt to use them on you. The ethics of such tactics make for an interesting discussion. Less debatable, though,

Watch TACTICS OF SOCIAL INFLUENCE

Revel Video

is the conclusion that social influence *can* be used to pursue illegal, immoral, and unconscionable aims. Consider the extraordinary example of **propaganda**, especially as perfected by the Nazi regime in the 1930s. Propaganda has been defined as "the deliberate, systematic attempt to shape perceptions, manipulate cognitions, and direct behavior to achieve a response that furthers the desired intent of the propagandist" (Jowett & O'Donnell, 1999, p. 6).

Adolf Hitler was well aware of the power of propaganda as a tool of the state. In 1933, he appointed Joseph Goebbels head of the newly created Nazi Ministry of Popular Enlightenment and Propaganda. It was a highly efficient agency that permeated every aspect of Germans' lives, controlling all forms of media, including newspapers, films, and radio. The Nazis also disseminated their ideology through the extensive use of posters and "spectacles"—lavish public rallies that aroused powerful emotions of loyalty and patriotism among massive crowds (Jowett & O'Donnell, 1999). Nazi propaganda was taught in schools and further promoted in Hitler Youth groups. It always presented a consistent, dogmatic message: The German people must act to protect their racial purity and to increase their *Lebensraum* (living space) through conquest (Staub, 1989).

The concerns with *Lebensraum* led to World War II; the concerns with racial purity led to the Holocaust. How could the German people have acquiesced to the destruction of European Jewry? A major factor was prejudice (which we will discuss further in Chapter 13). Anti-Semitism was not a new idea; it had existed in Germany and the rest of Europe for hundreds of years. Propaganda is most successful when it taps into an audience's preexisting beliefs. Thus, the German people's anti-Semitism was strengthened and expanded by Goebbels's ministry. Jews were described in the Nazi propaganda as destroyers of Aryan racial purity and thus a threat to German survival. They were "pests, parasites, bloodsuckers" (Staub, 1989, p. 103) and were compared to "a plague of rats that needed to be exterminated" (Jowett & O'Donnell, 1999, p. 242). Still, anti-Semitism alone is not a sufficient explanation for the Holocaust. Germany was initially no more prejudiced against Jews than were its neighbors (or even the United States) in the 1930s, but none of these other countries came up with the genocidal concept of a "final solution" as Germany did (Tindale et al., 2002).

One answer to the question of what made the Holocaust possible is propaganda, which operated in the form of persuasive messages leading to attitude change. But the propaganda also initiated social influence processes, persuading many Germans through informational conformity. They learned new "facts" (which were really lies) about the Jews and new solutions to what the Nazis had defined as the "Jewish question." The propaganda did an excellent job of convincing Germans that the Jews were a threat. As we saw previously, people experiencing a crisis—in this case, runaway inflation and economic collapse in Germany—are more likely to conform to information provided by others.

But surely, you are thinking, there must have been Germans who did not agree with the Nazi propaganda. Yes, there were, but it certainly wasn't easy to be one of them. The Nazi ideology so permeated daily life that children and teenagers in Hitler Youth groups were encouraged to spy on their own parents and report them to the Gestapo if they were not "good" Nazis (Staub, 1989). Neighbors, coworkers, store clerks, or passersby on the street—they could all turn you in if you said or did something that indicated disloyalty. This situation is ripe for normative conformity, through

Nazi propaganda permeated all facets of German life in the 1930s and 1940s. Here, huge crowds attend the 1934 Nuremberg rally. Such large public gatherings were a technique frequently used by Goebbels and Hitler to promote loyalty and conformity to the Nazi party.

Propaganda

A deliberate, systematic attempt to advance a cause by manipulating mass attitudes and behaviors, often through misleading or emotionally charged information

which public compliance can occur even without private acceptance. Rejection, ostracism, and even torture or death were strong motivators for normative conformity, and many ordinary Germans conformed to Nazi propaganda. Whether they did so for informational or normative reasons, their conformity permitted the Holocaust to occur.

Review Questions

1. A ____ norm involves perceptions of which behaviors society approves of; a ____ norm involves perceptions of how people actually behave.
   a. public; private
   b. private; public
   c. descriptive; injunctive
   d. injunctive; descriptive

2. ____ norms are most powerful for changing people's behaviors.
   a. Informational
   b. Normative
   c. Injunctive
   d. Descriptive

3. Which of the following provides an illustration of how the use of norms to change behavior can backfire and produce a "boomerang effect"?
   a. Jerry finds out that everyone in his building is conserving water by installing a low-flow shower head, so he decides that he doesn't need to worry about conserving, and he begins taking even longer showers than usual.
   b. Elaine notices that the new, attractive guy at the office brings a reusable cup instead of bottled water, so she goes out of her way to show off her reusable cup whenever he is in the vicinity in order to win his affection.
   c. Kramer finds out that he is using more electricity than most people in the neighborhood, so he cuts down on his usage by shutting off his computer, lights, and hot tub every time he leaves his apartment.
   d. George finds out that all of his neighbors are stealing cable television, so he decides that he will get an illegal cable hookup as well.

4. The foot-in-the-door technique
   a. works only when the second request comes from the same person as the first request.
   b. capitalizes on people's desire for self-consistency.
   c. is an example of propaganda.
   d. works only when the requests come from someone in a position of authority.

5. The door-in-the-face technique
   a. is an example of informational social influence.
   b. illustrates the importance of people's desire to be accurate.
   c. relies at least in part on norms of reciprocity.
   d. is more likely to work during a time of crisis.

Obedience to Authority

LO 8.5 **Summarize studies that have demonstrated people's willingness to obey authority figures.**

On April 9, 2004, a man called a McDonald's restaurant in Mount Washington, Kentucky, and identified himself as a police detective. He told the assistant manager she had a problem: One of her employees had stolen from the restaurant. He said he had talked to corporate headquarters and to the store manager, whom he named correctly. The policeman gave the assistant manager a rough description of the perpetrator, a teenage female, and she identified one of her employees (whom we will refer to as Susan, to protect her identity). The police detective told the assistant manager that she needed to search Susan immediately for the stolen money, or else Susan would be arrested, taken to jail, and searched there (Wolfson, 2005).

You might be thinking that this all sounds a bit odd. The assistant manager said later that she was initially confused, but the caller was very authoritative and presented his information in a convincing manner. And, after all, he was a policeman—we're supposed to obey the police. During the phone call, she thought she heard police radios in the background.

So she called Susan into a small room and locked the door. The man on the phone told the assistant manager what to do and what to say. Following his instructions, she ordered Susan to take off her clothing, one item at a time, until she was standing naked. She put all the clothes in a bag and put the bag outside the room, as instructed by the caller. Susan was now crying, fearful of the allegations and humiliated by the strip search.

Susan was not the first fast-food employee to be victimized in this manner. Phone calls to restaurant managers, ordering them to abuse their employees, had been occurring around the country for years. It just took law enforcement time to put the picture together. In all, managers of 70 restaurants, representing a dozen different chains in 32 states, received these phone calls and obeyed the caller's instructions (Barrouquere, 2006; Gray, 2004; Wolfson, 2005). The caller, as you have probably guessed, was not actually a policeman but was perpetrating a horrible hoax.

After Susan had been standing naked in the small, locked room for an hour, the "policeman" told the assistant manager to find someone else to guard Susan. She called her fiancé, who agreed to come to the restaurant and locked himself in the room with the naked and increasingly terrified teenager. At this point, the events become even more disturbing. This man also believed the caller was who he said he was, and in a series of escalating demands over 3 hours, the "detective" told him to force Susan to acquiesce to various sexual demands. The caller also talked directly to Susan, threatening her with what would happen if she didn't obey. "I was scared because they were a higher authority to me. I was scared for my safety because I thought I was in trouble with the law," she said (Wolfson, 2005, p. 3).

After an investigation that involved several states, a 38-year-old Florida man was ultimately arrested and charged as the telephone hoaxer. The assistant manager and her (no longer) fiancé pleaded guilty to various charges. Susan, who now suffers from panic attacks, anxiety, and depression, sued the McDonald's corporation for failing to warn employees nationally after the first hoaxes occurred at their restaurants. She was awarded $6.1 million in damages by a Kentucky jury (Barrouquere, 2006; Wolfson, 2005).

What could lead seemingly ordinary people to behave in this manner, following the orders of a complete stranger to humiliate and abuse an innocent teenager? We have explored different types of social influence in this chapter, from internalized pressures of group norms to direct requests. But to understand the fast-food restaurant hoax, we must consider one of the strongest forms of social influence: **obedience** to authority. Indeed, from a young age, we are socialized to obey authority figures whom we perceive as legitimate (Blass, 2000; Staub, 1989). We internalize this norm of obedience such that we usually adhere to rules and laws even when the authority figure isn't present—you stop at red lights even if the cops aren't parked around the corner—and this isn't necessarily a bad thing. However, as you've discovered in this chapter, obedience can have tragic consequences too.

Obedience

A change in one's behavior due to the direct influence of an authority figure

The Milgram Study

As with many eras, the past century was marked by repeated atrocities and genocides—in Germany, yes, but also the rest of Europe, Armenia, Ukraine, Rwanda, Cambodia, Bosnia, Sudan, and elsewhere. One of the most important questions facing the world's inhabitants, therefore, becomes, where does the role played by social influence end and personal responsibility begin? The philosopher Hannah Arendt (1965) was particularly interested in understanding the causes of the Holocaust. How could Hitler's Nazi regime in Germany carry out the murder of millions based on religion, ethnicity, sexual orientation, physical disability, and political beliefs? Arendt argued that most participants in the Holocaust were not sadists or psychopaths who enjoyed mass murder but rather ordinary citizens subjected to complex and powerful social pressures. As a journalist, she covered the trial of Adolf Eichmann, the Nazi official responsible for the transportation of Jews to the death camps, and concluded that he was not the

Multiple geopolitical, economic, cultural, and psychological factors contributed to the Nazi genocide of World War II, some of the horrific results of which are depicted above in a scene from the Bergen-Belsen concentration camp, 1945. But the Holocaust would not have been possible without obedience to authority, as Nazi soldiers as well as ordinary citizens went along with and facilitated a regime led by individuals who promoted mass deportation, internment, and extermination of millions of people.

bloodthirsty monster that many people made him out to be but rather a common bureaucrat who did what he was told without questioning his orders (A. G. Miller, 1995).

Our point is not that Eichmann—or the soldiers at My Lai or the Khmer Rouge in Cambodia or the Serbs in Bosnia—should be excused for the crimes they committed. The point is that it is too easy to explain their behavior as the acts of madmen. It is more fruitful—and more frightening—to view much of their behavior as the acts of ordinary people exposed to extraordinary social influence. How can we be sure that these atrocities were not caused solely by evil, psychopathic people but also by powerful social forces operating on people of all types? The way to find out is to study social pressure with an empirical research eye under controlled conditions. We could take a sample of ordinary citizens, subject them to various kinds of social influence, and see to what extent they will obey. Can an experimenter influence ordinary people to commit immoral acts, such as inflicting severe pain on an innocent bystander? Stanley Milgram (1963, 1974, 1976) decided to find out in what has become the most famous series of studies in social psychology.

Imagine that you were a participant in one of Milgram's studies. You answer an ad in the newspaper, asking for participants in a study on memory and learning. When you arrive at the laboratory, you meet another participant, a 47-year-old, somewhat overweight, pleasant-looking fellow. The experimenter, wearing a White lab coat, explains that one of you will play the role of a teacher and the other the role of a learner. You draw a slip of paper out of a hat and discover that you will be the teacher. It turns out that your job is to read to the other participant a list of word pairs (e.g., *blue–box, nice–day*) and then test him on his memory for the list. The experimenter instructs you to deliver an electric shock to the learner whenever he makes a mistake because the purpose of the study is to examine the effects of punishment on learning.

You watch as the other participant—the learner—is strapped into a chair in an adjacent room and electrodes are attached to his arm. You are seated in front of a shock generator whose 30 switches deliver varying levels of shock in 15-volt increments, starting at 15 volts and going all the way up to 450 volts. There are labels accompanying these switches, from "Slight Shock" to "Danger: Severe Shock" to an ominous "XXX" next to the highest levels (see the photos below). The experimenter tells you that the first time the learner makes a mistake, you should give him a shock of 15 volts, and then you will increase that amount by 15 volts for each subsequent mistake he makes. So that you will know what the shocks are like, the experimenter gives you a sample shock of 45 volts, which proves surprisingly painful.

You read the list of word pairs to the learner and then begin the testing phase. After announcing the first word of each pair, you give four possible answers; the

Left: The shock generator used in Milgram's research. *Right:* The learner (an accomplice of the experimenter) is strapped into the chair, and electrodes are attached to his arm.

(Adapted from Milgram, 1974)

Figure 8.6 Milgram Transcript and Prompts

Transcript of the learner's protests in Milgram's obedience study and of the prods used by the experimenter to compel people to continue giving shocks.

(Based on Milgram, 1963, 1974)

Learner's Protests

75 volts: Ugh!

90 volts: Ugh!

105 volts: Ugh! (louder)

120 volts: Ugh! Hey this really hurts.

135 volts: Ugh!!

150 volts: Ugh!!! Experimenter! That's all. Get me out of here. I told you I had heart trouble. My heart's starting to bother me now. Get me out of here, please. My heart's starting to bother me. I refuse to go on. Let me out.

165 volts: Ugh! Let me out! (shouting)

180 volts: Ugh! I can't stand the pain. Let me out of here! (shouting)

195 volts: Ugh! Let me out of here. Let me out of here. My heart's bothering me. Let me out of here! You have no right to keep me here! Let me out! Let me out of here! Let me out! Let me out of here! My heart's bothering me. Let me out! Let me out!

210 volts: Ugh! Experimenter! Get me out of here. I've had enough. I won't be in the experiment anymore.

225 volts: Ugh!

240 volts: Ugh!

255 volts: Ugh! Get me out of here.

270 volts: Ugh! (agonized scream) Let me out of here. Let me out of here. Let me out of here. Let me out. Do you hear? Let me out of here.

285 volts: Ugh! (agonized scream)

300 volts: Ugh! (agonized scream) I absolutely refuse to answer anymore. Get me out of here. You can't hold me here. Get me out. Get me out of here.

315 volts: Ugh! (intensely agonized scream) I told you I refuse to answer. I'm no longer part of this experiment.

330 volts: Ugh! (intense and prolonged agonized scream) Let me out of here. Let me out of here. My heart's bothering me. Let me out, I tell you. (hysterically) Let me out of here. Let me out of here. You have no right to hold me here. Let me out! Let me out! Let me out of here! Let me out!

Instructions Used by the Experimenter to Achieve Obedience

Prod 1: Please continue *or* Please go on.

Prod 2: The experiment requires that you continue.

Prod 3: It is absolutely essential that you continue.

Prod 4: You have no other choice; you must go on.

The prods were always made in sequence: Only if prod 1 had been unsuccessful could prod 2 be used. If the subject refused to obey the experimenter after prod 4, the experiment was terminated. The experimenter's tone of voice was at all times firm but not impolite. The sequence was begun anew on each occasion that the subject balked or showed reluctance to follow orders.

Special prods. If the subject asked whether the learner was likely to suffer permanent physical injury, the experimenter said:

Although the shocks may be painful, there is no permanent tissue damage, so please go on. [Followed by prods 2, 3, and 4 if necessary.]

If the subject said that the learner did not want to go on, the experimenter replied: Whether the learner likes it or not, you must go on until he has learned all the word pairs correctly. So please go on. [Followed by prods 2, 3, and 4 if necessary.]

learner responds by pressing one of four switches, illuminating a light on the answer box in front of you. Everything begins smoothly as the learner gets the first few right. Then he gets some wrong, and, as instructed, you deliver a shock each time. At this point, you are probably getting concerned about the number and severity of the shocks you will have to give. When you get to the 75-volt level, the learner, whom you can hear over an intercom, emits a painful "Ugh!" Perhaps you pause and ask the experimenter what you should do. "Please continue," he responds without hesitation. As the learner continues to make mistakes, you deliver more shocks. The learner protests, shouting, "Ugh! Experimenter! That's all! Get me out of here!" You look at the experimenter with concern. He tells you calmly, "It is absolutely essential that you continue" (see Figure 8.6).

What would you do? How many people do you think would continue to obey the experimenter, increasing the levels of shock all the way up the shock panel until they had delivered the maximum amount of 450 volts?

Revel Video

When this question was posed to psychology majors at Yale University, they estimated that less than 1% of the population would go to this extreme. A sample of middle-class adults and a panel of psychiatrists made similar predictions. Based on our discussion of conformity thus far, however, perhaps you are not as optimistic. Indeed, most of Milgram's participants succumbed to the pressure of the authority figure. The average maximum shock delivered was 360 volts, and 62.5% of the participants went all the way to the end of the panel, delivering the 450-volt shock. A full 80% of the participants continued giving the shocks even after the learner, who earlier had mentioned that he had a heart condition, screamed, "Let me out of here! Let me out of here! My heart's bothering me. Let me out of here! … Get me out of here! I've had enough. I won't be in the experiment any more" (Milgram, 1974, p. 56).

It is important to note that the learner was actually an accomplice of the experimenter who was acting rather than suffering; he did not receive any actual shocks. It is equally important to note that the study was very convincingly done so that people believed they really were shocking the learner. Here is Milgram's description of one participant's response to the teacher role:

> I observed a mature and initially poised businessman enter the laboratory smiling and confident. Within 20 minutes he was reduced to a twitching, stuttering wreck, who was rapidly approaching a point of nervous collapse. He constantly pulled on his earlobe, and twisted his hands. At one point he pushed his fist into his forehead and muttered, "Oh God, let's stop it." And yet he continued to respond to every word of the experimenter, and obeyed to the end. (Milgram, 1963, p. 377)

These research participants ranged in age from the twenties to the fifties and included people with a variety of occupations. Although participants in the original 1963 study were all men, in a follow-up Milgram found nearly identical obedience rates among women. Why did so many of these individuals obey the experimenter, to the point where they genuinely believed they were inflicting great pain on another human being? Why were the college students, middle-class adults, and psychiatrists so wrong in their predictions about what people would do? In a dangerous way, a variety of factors contributed to cause Milgram's participants to obey—just as many Germans did during the Holocaust and soldiers have done during more recent atrocities in Iraq and Afghanistan. Let's take a closer look at Milgram's research.

The Role of Normative Social Influence

First, it is clear that normative pressures made it difficult for people in Milgram's studies to refuse to continue. As we have seen, if someone really wants us to do something, it can be difficult to say no. This is particularly true when the person is in a position of authority. Milgram's participants probably believed that if they refused to continue, the experimenter would be disappointed or maybe even angry—all of which put pressure on them to continue. It is important to note that this study, unlike the Asch study, was set up so that the experimenter actively attempted to get people to conform, giving commands such as "It is absolutely essential that you continue." When an authority figure is so insistent that we obey, it is difficult to say no (Blass, 2000, 2003; Doliński & Grzyb, 2016; Meeus & Raaijmakers, 1995).

The fact that normative pressures were present in the Milgram study is clear from a variation that he conducted. This time, there were three teachers, two of whom were

Figure 8.7 Results of Different Versions of the Milgram Study

In the standard version of Milgram's study, obedience was 62.5%. This rate dropped when the study took place in a nondescript office location rather than the Yale Psychology Department. It dropped further when the teacher had to physically place the learner's hand on a shock plate, when the experimenter issuing commands was located remotely, and when two other "teachers" (actually confederates) refused to continue with the study. Finally, when participants were left on their own to determine the level of shock, almost none of them went to the end of the shock panel. The variation in these bars demonstrates just how context-dependent obedience to authority can be.

(Data from Milgram, 1974)

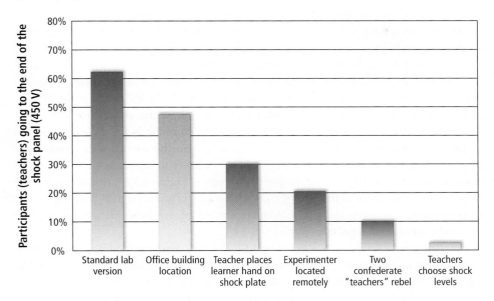

confederates. One confederate was instructed to read the list of word pairs and the other to tell the learner whether his response was correct. The (real) participant's job was to deliver the shocks, increasing their severity with each error, as in the original study. At 150 volts, when the learner gave his first vehement protest, the first confederate refused to continue despite the experimenter's command that he do so. At 210 volts, the second confederate refused to continue. The result? Seeing their peers disobey made it much easier for the actual participants to disobey too. Only 10% of the participants gave the maximum level of shock in this version of the study (see Figure 8.7). This result is similar to Asch's finding that people did not conform nearly as much when one accomplice bucked the majority.

The Role of Informational Social Influence

Despite the power of the normative pressures in Milgram's original study, they are not the sole reason people complied. The experimenter was authoritative and insistent, but he was hardly pointing a gun at participants and telling them to "conform or else"; the participants were free to get up and leave anytime they wanted to. Why didn't they, especially when the experimenter was a stranger they had never met before and probably would never see again?

As we saw previously, when people are in confusing circumstances and unsure what they should do, they use other people to help define the situation. Informational social influence is especially powerful when the situation is ambiguous, when it is a crisis, and when the other people in the situation have some expertise. All three of these characteristics describe the situation Milgram's participants faced. The scenario—a study of the effects of punishment on learning—seemed straightforward enough when the experimenter explained it, but it quickly turned into something else altogether. The learner cried out in pain, but the experimenter told the participant that the shocks did not cause permanent damage. The participant didn't want to hurt anyone, but he or she had agreed to be in the study and to follow the directions. When in such a state of conflict, it was only natural for the participants to use an expert—the experimenter in the scientific-looking white lab coat—to help them decide what was the right thing to do (Krakow & Blass, 1995; A. G. Miller, 1986; Miller, Collins, & Brief, 1995).

Another version of Milgram's study supports the idea that informational influence was operative. This version was identical to the original except for three critical changes: First, the experimenter never said which shock levels were to be given, leaving this decision up to the participant. Second, before the study began, the experimenter received a telephone call and had to leave the room, telling the participant to continue without him. Third, there was a confederate playing the role of an additional teacher, whose job was to record how long it took the learner to respond to each word pair. When the experimenter left, this other "teacher" said that he had just thought of a good system: How about if they increased the level of shock each time the learner made a mistake? He insisted that the real participant follow this procedure.

Note that in this situation, the person giving the commands has no expertise: He was just a regular person, no more knowledgeable than the participants themselves. Because he lacked expertise, people were much less likely to use him as a source of information about how they should respond. As seen in Figure 8.7, in this version, only 20% of participants went to the end of the shock panel. (The fact that 20% still gave the maximum shock suggests that some people were so uncertain about what to do that they used even a nonexpert as a guide.)

An additional variation conducted by Milgram underscores the importance of authority figures as experts in eliciting such obedience. In this variation, two experimenters gave the real participants their orders. At 150 volts, when the learner first cried out that he wanted to stop, the two experimenters began to disagree about whether they should continue the study. At this point, every single one of the participant-teachers stopped responding. Note that nothing the victim ever did caused all the participants to stop obeying; however, when the authorities' definition of the situation became unclear, the participants broke out of their obedient role.

Other Reasons Why We Obey

Both normative and informational social influences were very strong in Milgram's research; however, these reasons for complying still fall short of fully explaining why people acted in a manner that seems so inhumane. They account for why people initially obeyed the experimenter's instructions, but after it became increasingly obvious what was happening to the learner, why didn't participants realize that what they were doing was terribly wrong and stop? Just as the fast-food restaurant managers continued to abuse their employees long after the demands of the "policeman" on the phone shifted from merely bizarre to obviously illegal, many of Milgram's participants pressed the shock levers time after time after time despite the cries of anguish from a fellow human being.

ADHERING TO THE WRONG NORM   To understand this continued obedience, we need to consider additional aspects of the situation. We don't mean to imply that Milgram's participants were completely mindless or unaware of what they were doing. As video of the sessions clearly shows, they were terribly concerned about the plight of the victim. The problem was that they were caught in a web of conflicting norms, and it was difficult to determine which ones to follow. At the beginning of the study, it was perfectly reasonable to heed the norm that says, "Obey expert, legitimate authority figures." Moreover as Alexander Haslam and colleagues have argued, Milgram's participants were not merely following an authority figure's orders—they were also engaged in what they believed to be a just and worthwhile scientific endeavor (Haslam, Reicher, & Birney, 2016). After all, the teacher had been deputized as a de facto member of the research team, suggesting that participants believed that they were doing something good in the name of science and on behalf of a fellow researcher. In short, the experimenter was confident and knowledgeable, and the study seemed like a reasonable test of an interesting hypothesis. So why not cooperate and do as you are told?

But, gradually, the rules of the game changed, and these norms of "obey authority" and "all in the name of science" became less and less appropriate. The experimenter, who seemed so reasonable before, was now asking people to inflict great pain on their fellow participant. But once people follow a norm, it can be difficult to switch midstream, to realize that this norm is no longer appropriate, or to recognize that another norm—in this instance, "Do not inflict needless harm on a fellow human being"—should be followed. For example, suppose the experimenter had explained, at the outset, that he would like people to deliver possibly fatal shocks to the other participant. How many people would have agreed? Very few, we suspect, because it would have been clear that this violated an important social and personal norm about harming others. Instead, the experimenter pulled a kind of "bait and switch" routine, whereby he first made it look like an "obey authority" norm was appropriate and then only later gradually revealed just how he planned to use his authority in this situation (Collins & Brief, 1995).

It was particularly difficult for people to abandon the initial norms in the Milgram study because the study was fast paced, preventing the participants from stopping to reflect on what they were doing. They were busy recording the learner's responses, keeping track of the word pairs, and determining whether the learner's responses were right or wrong. Given that they had to attend carefully to these details and move along at a fast pace, it was difficult for them to realize that the initial norms guiding their behavior were, after a while, no longer appropriate (Conway & Schaller, 2005; Modigliani & Rochat, 1995). We suspect that if, halfway through the study, Milgram's participants had been told to take a break or had been left in the room by themselves for a period of time, many more would have successfully redefined the situation and refused to continue.

SELF-JUSTIFICATION   Another important aspect of the situation in the Milgram study is that, as alluded to above, the experimenter asked people to increase the shocks in small increments. The participants did not go from giving a small shock to giving a potentially lethal one. Instead, at any given point, they only faced a smaller decision about whether to increase by a meager 15 volts the amount of shock they had just given. As we saw in Chapter 6, every time a person makes an important or difficult decision, dissonance is produced, along with resulting pressures to reduce it. An effective way of reducing dissonance produced by a difficult decision is to decide that the decision was fully justified. But because reducing dissonance provides a justification for the preceding action, it can make a person vulnerable to further escalating a now-justified activity.

Thus, in the Milgram study, the participants' initial agreement to administer the first shock created internal pressure on them to continue to obey. As the participants administered each successive level of shock, they had to justify it in their own minds. After they had justified a particular shock level, it became very difficult for them to decide on a place where they should draw the line and stop. How could they say, in effect, "Okay, I gave him 200 volts, but not 215—never 215!" Justifying one level of shock then laid the groundwork for the next level of shock, and quitting would have produced dissonance: 215 volts is not *that* different from 200, and 230 is not *that* different from 215. Those who did break off the series did so against enormous internal pressure to continue (Darley, 1992; Gilbert, 1981; Miller et al., 1995). The incremental nature of the shock task was essential to the level of obedience Milgram observed, much in the

Self-justification can also help explain why people sometimes go along with an increasingly humiliating and even dangerous sequence of hazing activities when trying to join an organization. New members might tell themselves that since they just went along with one embarrassing or degrading act, how can they now say no to the next request? And in this manner, their loyalty to the group is reinforced.

same way that incrementally increasing a series of requests allows the foot-in-the-door technique to operate, as described earlier.

THE LOSS OF PERSONAL RESPONSIBILITY
Sometimes when you are the research participant (or the employee) and the other person is a legitimate authority figure (the experimenter, the boss, the military commander, the police officer), you become the "puppet," with them pulling the strings. They can define what it is you are supposed to do, and they are responsible for the end results—after all, it was their idea, and you were "just following orders." Milgram (1974) stressed that the loss of a sense of personal responsibility for one's actions was a critical component explaining the results of the obedience studies.

When faced with the prospect of acting in unpleasant or unseemly ways, it becomes easier to do so when you can offload personal responsibility for those actions to someone else. An example of a particularly disturbing job is that of prison guards who must carry out a capital punishment sentence. How do these guards respond to a job in which they are told to kill another person? Clearly, they need to reduce their cognitive dissonance. Taking a life is a supremely problematic and disturbing act, so they often need to engage in self-justification in order to do it. Michael Osofsky, Albert Bandura, and Philip Zimbardo (2005) studied guards on the execution teams of three southern state prisons and compared them to their fellow guards who did not conduct executions. All the guards responded anonymously to a questionnaire that asked them to rate their level of agreement with statements such as "Because of the nature of their crime, murderers have lost the right to live" and "Those who carry out state executions should not be criticized for following society's wishes."

The researchers found a significant difference in the attitudes of the two types of guards. The execution-team guards demonstrated much more "moral disengagement" from their work than did the other guards. The execution-team guards denied all personal responsibility for the executions. They felt they were just implementing orders—in this case, those of a judge and jury. They also engaged in justification in other areas. Compared to the regular prison guards, they dehumanized the prisoners more, seeing them as lacking important human qualities. They perceived the prisoners as more of a threat to society, such that it was necessary that they be killed. All these attitudes helped the execution guards reduce their qualms about the morality of what they did at work. As one guard put it, "I had a job to do, that's what we did. Our job was to execute this man and we were going to do it in a professional manner" (Osofsky, Bandura, & Zimbardo, 2005, p. 386).

The Obedience Studies, Then and Now

Stanley Milgram's study of obedience is widely considered to be one of the most important contributions to the field of psychology (Benjamin & Simpson, 2009). His work, conducted in the early 1960s, was replicated in the following years by researchers in 11 countries, involving approximately 3,000 research participants (Blass, 2000). However, Milgram's research paradigm also ignited a storm of protest (and soul-searching) in the research community over the ethical treatment of research participants.

Milgram's research has been criticized as unethical on several different levels. First, the study involved *deception*. Participants were told it was a study on memory and learning, when of course it was not; participants were told the electric shocks were real, when of course they were not. Second, there was not fully *informed consent* on the part of participants. When they agreed to be in the study, they were not informed as to its true nature, and thus they never really consented to take part in the scenario they eventually experienced. Third, their role as teacher caused them *psychological distress* during the course of the study. Fourth, it was not made clear to participants that they had the *right to withdraw* from the study at any time; in fact, the experimenter stated the exact opposite—for example, that they "had to continue." Fifth, the participants experienced *inflicted insight*. When the study ended, some of them had learned unpleasant things about themselves that they had not agreed to beforehand (Baumrind, 1964, 1985; A. G. Miller, 2009). More recent critiques have focused on disturbing allegations that Milgram misrepresented his debriefing methods in his published papers and that many research participants actually left the study unaware that the learner had been a confederate and the shocks had been fake (Nicholson, 2011; Perry, 2013).

Although the ethical issues surrounding Milgram's study were not, as is often suggested, the reason that formal ethical guidelines for research participants were created in the United States in 1966 (they were created primarily to protect participants in medical research), these new guidelines made conducting obedience research such as Milgram's increasingly challenging (Benjamin & Simpson, 2009). Indeed, decades would pass without researchers conducting follow-up studies of obedience using Milgram's procedure (Blass, 2009), and many students learned in their psychology courses that such studies could never be run again. But that all changed when Jerry M. Burger (2009) conducted the first Milgram-style obedience study in the United States in decades.

In order to conduct this study under modern ethical guidelines, Burger (2009) made a number of changes to the procedure. First, he reduced the psychological distress experienced by participants by stopping the study after 150 volts, when the learner is first heard yelling that he wants out and refuses to go on. Analysis of data from eight of Milgram's study versions indicated that when disobedience occurred, it was most likely to happen at this point in the study; most previous participants who passed the 150-volt mark tended to go all the way to end of the shock panel anyway (Packer, 2008a). Second, participants were prescreened by a clinical psychologist, and those who were identified as even slightly likely to have a negative reaction to the experience were excluded from the study. Finally, Burger explicitly and repeatedly told his participants that they could leave the study at any time, as could the learner.

In most respects, though, Burger's (2009) study was like the original. His experimenter used the same basic verbal "prods" that Milgram's used (e.g., "It is absolutely essential that you continue") when participants began to waver. Burger's participants, like Milgram's, were adult men and women recruited through newspaper advertisements and flyers. Their age range of 20 to 81 years was broader than Milgram's, though their average age of about 43 years was similar. They were more ethnically diverse than Milgram's participants, and they were also more highly educated. Finally, because the Milgram obedience studies are quite well known, Burger excluded participants who had taken more than two college-level psychology courses.

What did Burger find? Are people more disobedient today than they were in Milgram's time? The answer is no. Burger found no significant difference in obedience rates between his participants and Milgram's. After the critical 150-volt shock had been delivered, 70% of Burger's participants obeyed and were ready to continue. A few years later, Dariusz Doliński and colleagues (2017) used Burger's modified procedure in a study in Poland and found that 90% of their participants were obedient through the 150-volt level. These recent rates of obedience observed among American and Polish samples are not statistically different than the 82.5% rate Milgram himself reported at the 150-volt mark.

Note that Burger's ethically necessary changes in methodology also complicate a direct comparison to Milgram's results (A. G. Miller, 2009; Twenge, 2009). Stopping the study after 150 volts may have made the procedure more ethical, but it also means we have no idea how many participants, today, would go all the way to the 450-volt level. Much of the extraordinary power of the Milgram obedience studies came from participants' choices after 150 volts, as they continued step by small step to the last switch on the shock generator. It is during this part of the study that participants felt the most conflicted and anxious. It is here that they revealed their response to a pressing moral conflict (Miller, 2009). This information is lost in the recent replications. And, as such, it reminds us that scientific inquiry has two sometimes competing aims: to discover new knowledge and to do no harm.

Review Questions

1. Which of the following was a goal of Milgram's obedience research?
   a. To identify the abnormal personality characteristics associated with sadistic behavior
   b. To justify and exonerate the behaviors linked to genocide and other inhuman acts
   c. To better understand the social forces that contribute to destructive and immoral behavior
   d. To identify cultural differences in aggression

2. Which of the following illustrates the role played by normative social influence in the obedience of Milgram's participants?
   a. When other "teachers" (actually confederates) refused to continue with the study, participants' obedience rates declined significantly.
   b. Men and women exhibited similar levels of obedience in the research.
   c. The "learner" (actually a confederate) announced before the study began that he had a preexisting heart condition.
   d. Many participants showed signs of nervous laughter during the course of the study.

3. Which of the following was *not* one of the instruction prods used by the experimenter in the Milgram studies?
   a. "The experiment requires that you continue."
   b. "Please continue."
   c. "It is absolutely essential that you continue."
   d. "If you do not continue, you will not be paid for your participation."

4. Which of the following is a common ethical concern raised about the Milgram study?
   a. Participants' compensation was low.
   b. Participants were forced to learn unpleasant things about themselves without agreeing to that ahead of time.
   c. Participants were never given the chance to serve in the role of learner.
   d. Participants had to receive a sample shock of 75 volts before the study began.

5. Which of the following is a change that Burger (2009) made from the original Milgram study when he replicated the research several decades later?
   a. He examined only female participants.
   b. The study was stopped once participants went past 150 volts.
   c. He told participants that the study was part of research on the effects of punishment on learning.
   d. He paid participants for their involvement.

Summary

LO 8.1 Define conformity, and explain why it occurs.

- **Conformity: When and Why** Conformity occurs when people change their behavior due to the real (or imagined) influence of others. There are two main reasons people conform: informational and normative social influences.

LO 8.2 Explain how informational social influence motivates people to conform.

- **Informational Social Influence: The Need to Know What's "Right"** *Informational social influence* occurs when people do not know the correct (or best) action to take. They look to the behavior of others as an important source of information, using it to choose appropriate courses of action for themselves. Informational social influence usually results in *private acceptance*, in which people genuinely believe in what other people are doing or saying.

- **The Importance of Being Accurate** In situations where it is important to be accurate, the tendency to conform to other people through informational social influence increases.

- **When Informational Conformity Backfires** Using other people as a source of information can backfire when they are wrong about what's going on.

- **When Will People Conform to Informational Social Influence?** People are more likely to conform to informational social influence when the situation is ambiguous, when they are in a crisis, or if experts are present.

LO 8.3 Explain how normative social influence motivates people to conform.

- **Normative Social Influence: The Need to Be Accepted** *Normative social influence* occurs when we change our behavior to match that of others because we want to remain a member of the group in good standing and continue to gain the advantages of group membership. We conform to the group's *social norms*, implicit or explicit rules for acceptable behaviors, values, and attitudes. Normative social influence usually results in *public compliance* but not private acceptance of other people's ideas and behaviors.

  - **Conformity and Social Approval: The Asch Line-Judgment Studies** In a series of classic studies, Solomon Asch found that people would conform, at least some of the time, to the obviously wrong answer of the group.

  - **The Importance of Being Accurate, Revisited** When it is important to be accurate, people are more likely to resist normative social influence and go against the group, giving the right answer. But public conformity still occurs.

  - **The Consequences of Resisting Normative Social Influence** Resisting normative social influence can lead to ridicule, ostracism, and rejection by the group.

  - **When Will People Conform to Normative Social Influence?** *Social impact theory* specifies when normative social influence is most likely to occur by referring to the strength, immediacy, and size of the group. We are more likely to conform when the group is one we care about, when the group members are unanimous in their thoughts or behaviors, when the group has three or more members, and when we are members of collectivist cultures. Past

conformity gives people *idiosyncrasy credits*, allowing them to deviate from the group without serious consequences.

- **Minority Influence: When the Few Influence the Many** Under certain conditions, an individual (or small number of people) can influence the majority. The key is consistency in the presentation of the minority viewpoint.

LO 8.4 Describe how people can use their knowledge of social influence to influence others.

- **Conformity Tactics** Knowing about the tendency to conform can inform our strategic efforts to change the behavior of others

  - **The Role of Injunctive and Descriptive Norms** Communicating *injunctive norms*, expectations regarding the behaviors that society approves of, is a more powerful way to create change than communicating *descriptive norms*, expectations regarding how people actually behave.

  - **Using Norms to Change Behavior: Beware the "Boomerang Effect"** One must be careful that descriptive norms do not create a boomerang effect, making an undesirable behavior more likely than it previously was.

  - **Other Tactics of Social Influence** Other efforts to change people's behavior via direct request, include the *foot-in-the-door technique*, in which the requestor first secures agreement with a small favor before following up with a larger request, and the *door-in-the-face technique*, in which the requester first asks for a large favor that will certainly be rejected before following up with a smaller, second request. *Propaganda*, as used in Nazi Germany, is yet another, often nefarious strategy.

LO 8.5 Summarize studies that have demonstrated people's willingness to obey authority figures.

- **Obedience to Authority** In the most famous series of studies in social psychology, Stanley Milgram examined *obedience*, when people change their behavior in response to an authority figure. He found chilling levels of obedience, to the point where a majority of participants administered what they thought were potentially lethal shocks to a fellow human being.

- **The Milgram Study?**

  - **The Role of Normative Social Influence** Normative pressures make it difficult for people to stop obeying authority figures. They want to please the authority figure by doing a good job.

  - **The Role of Informational Social Influence** The obedience studies created a confusing situation for participants, with competing, ambiguous demands. Unclear about how to define what was going on, they followed the orders of the expert.

- **Other Reasons Why We Obey** Participants conformed to the wrong norm: They continued to follow the norms of "obey authority" and "all in the name of science" even when it was no longer appropriate to do so. It was difficult for them to abandon these initial norms because of the fast-paced nature of the study, the fact that the shock levels increased in small increments, and their loss of a feeling of personal responsibility.

- **The Obedience Studies, Then and Now** Milgram's research design was criticized on ethical grounds, involving deception, informed consent, psychological distress, the right to withdraw, and inflicted insight. A recent U.S. replication found that the level of obedience in the early 21st century was not significantly different from that found in the classic study in the 1960s.

Revel Interactive

Shared Writing   What Do You Think?

In what ways do you think conformity was a key motivator for the millions of people who have participated in the ALS ice bucket challenge? What other factors that you've read about in this chapter might have influenced the movement?

Test Yourself

1. All of the following are examples of informational social influence *except*

   a. you are running a race, but because you are unsure of the route, you wait to check which of two roads the other runners follow.

   b. you've just started work at a new job, and a fire alarm goes off; you watch your coworkers to see what to do.

   c. when you get to college, you change the way you dress so that you "fit in" better—that is, so that people will like you more.

   d. you ask your adviser which classes you should take next semester.

2. Which of the following is true, according to social impact theory?

   a. People conform more to others who are physically close than to others who are physically distant.

   b. People conform more if the others are important to them.

   c. People conform more to three or more people than to one or two people.

   d. All of the answers are true.

3. In Asch's line studies, participants who were alone when asked to report the length of the lines gave the correct answer 98% of the time. However, when they were with the confederates who sometimes gave an obviously wrong answer, 76% of participants gave the wrong answer at least once. This suggests that Asch's studies are an illustration of

   a. public compliance with private acceptance.

   b. public compliance without private acceptance.

   c. informational influence.

   d. private compliance.

4. Which of the following is most true about informational social influence?

   a. When deciding whether to conform, people should ask themselves whether the other people know more about what is going on than they do.

   b. People should always try to resist it.

   c. People are most likely to conform when others have the same level of expertise as they do.

   d. Often, people publicly conform but do not privately accept this kind of influence.

5. Brandon knows that society considers underage drinking to be wrong; he also knows, however, that on a Saturday night at his university, many of his friends will engage in this behavior. His belief that most of the public would disapprove of underage drinking is ____, while his perception that many teenagers drink under certain circumstances is ____.

   a. an injunctive norm; a descriptive norm

   b. a descriptive norm; an injunctive norm

   c. a descriptive norm; conformity

   d. an injunctive norm; conformity

6. Tom is a new student at his university. During the first week of classes, he notices a fellow student from one of his classes getting on a bus. Tom decides to follow the student and discovers that this bus takes him right to the building where his class meets. This best illustrates what kind of conformity?

   a. Obedience to authority

   b. Informational social influence

   c. Public compliance

   d. Normative social influence

7. Which of the following best describes an example of normative social influence?

   a. Carrie is studying with a group of friends. When comparing answers on the practice test, she discovers that they all answered the question differently than she had. Instead of speaking up and telling them she thinks the answer is something else, she agrees with their answer because she figures they must be right.

   b. Samantha is supposed to bring a bottle of wine to a dinner party she is attending. She doesn't drink wine herself but figures she can just ask the store clerk for advice on what kind to buy.

   c. Miranda is out to lunch with her boss and coworkers. Her boss tells a joke that makes fun of a certain ethnic group, and everyone else laughs. Miranda doesn't think the joke is funny but laughs anyway.

   d. Charlotte is flying on an airplane for the first time. She is worried when she hears the engine make a strange noise but feels better after she looks at the flight attendants and sees that they are not alarmed.

8. American mythology and culture often emphasize the importance of

   a. not conforming.

   b. following authority.

   c. setting descriptive norms.

   d. normative social influence.

9. Which of the following strategies of social influence creates a situation similar to that experienced by Milgram's study in that it relies on requests that increase in severity in incremental fashion?

   a. Contagion

   b. Foot-in-the-door technique

   c. Door-in-the-face technique

   d. Descriptive norms

10. Which of the following had the *least* influence on participants' willingness to keep giving shocks in the Milgram studies?

   a. Loss of personal responsibility

   b. Self-justification

   c. Informational social influence

   d. Participants' aggression

Chapter 9
Group Processes
Influence in Social Groups

 ## Chapter Outline and Learning Objectives

WHAT DO YOU THINK?

Revel Interactive	Survey	**What Do You Think?**	
	SURVEY		RESULTS
	Have you ever written or posted something anonymously online that you know you never would have had the nerve to say or do in person?		
	○ Yes		
	○ No		

As the evening of November 8 turned to the early morning of November 9, it became clear that the 2016 Election Day outcome very, very few had predicted was coming to fruition: Donald Trump would become the 45th president of the United States, defeating Hillary Clinton. Almost immediately, pundits and prognosticators began to generate potential explanations for the surprise result. Some pointed fingers at James Comey, the FBI Director who had announced the revival of an inquiry into Clinton's private e-mail server less than 2 weeks previously. Others suggested that perhaps some Trump voters had been unwilling to admit their support for the controversial candidate during pre-election polls, skewing reported results in an unrealistically pro-Clinton direction.

There were likely many reasons for Clinton's loss, including some that were outside her control: the Comey letter, reluctance to elect a female president, and even, potentially, Russian efforts to influence the election. There is little doubt, however, that Clinton and her seasoned team of campaign experts also blundered in some critical strategic decisions. Consider, for example, the following episode, which took place slightly more than a week before Election Day. Union organizers—a strong Clinton base of support—were growing concerned about an unexpectedly close race in Michigan. They decided to send more campaign volunteers to Detroit, hoping to bolster a state that the Democrats needed to win. Union leadership called top Clinton campaign aides to share their plan.

Turn those buses around! came the response from central command at Team Clinton in New York. There was no need, they asserted, to send resources to Michigan, a state that their statistical models projected as a 5-point win for their candidate (Dovere, 2016).

Similar stories were playing out in other supposed Democratic strongholds. Local campaign operatives in Wisconsin had to scramble to raise their own money for a get-out-the-vote effort after Clinton headquarters didn't earmark funds for the effort. (Stein, 2016). And while Clinton held a celebrity-filled rally in Philadelphia on election eve, some critics noted that her November travel schedule also included ultimately fruitless stops in Arizona and Utah, two traditionally "red states."

Had Hillary Clinton won Michigan, Wisconsin, and Pennsylvania, she would have been elected president. She ended up losing all three by a relatively paltry combined total of less than 70,000 votes. It appears to have been a catastrophic blunder for her team of advisors to assume that these states were safely in their column. Could a few more volunteers here, a few rallies there, and a different allocation of campaign dollars have been enough to change the outcome? Maybe. We will never know.

Social psychologists who study groups would pose a different, yet related set of questions: How could one of the most experienced, knowledgeable, and previously successful campaign teams ever assembled seemingly have gotten this wrong? Aren't groups of experts supposed to make better decisions than are individuals? Presidential campaigns have at their disposal a huge number of talented people, and it might seem that drawing on this combined expertise should inevitably lead to the best decisions. But groups don't always make good decisions. In this chapter, we will focus on questions about the nature of groups and how they influence people's behavior, which are some of the oldest topics in social psychology (Forsyth & Burnette, 2010; Kerr & Tindale, 2004; Wittenbaum & Moreland, 2008; Yuki & Brewer, 2014).

What Is a Group?

LO 9.1   Explain what groups are and why people join them.

Group

Two or more people who interact and are interdependent in the sense that their needs and goals cause them to influence each other

Six students studying independently at tables in the library are not a group. But if they meet to study for their psychology final together, they are. A **group** consists of two or more people who interact and are interdependent in the sense that their needs and goals cause them to influence each other (Cartwright & Zander, 1968; Lewin, 1948; J. C. Turner, 1982). However, groups are usually larger than two, with two people sometimes referred to as a dyad instead (Moreland, 2010). Like a president's advisers working together to reach a foreign policy decision or people who have gathered to blow off steam at a party, groups consist of people who have assembled for a common purpose.

Think for a moment of the number of groups to which you belong. Don't forget to include your family, campus groups (such as clubs or political organizations), community groups, sports teams, and more temporary groups (such as your classmates in a small seminar). All of these count as groups because you interact with the other members and you are interdependent: You influence them, and they influence you.

Why Do People Join Groups?

Joining forces with others allows us to accomplish objectives that would be more difficult to meet individually. Ever try to move to a new dorm room or apartment on your own? Much quicker and less painful if you can get others to help you. Forming relationships with other people also fulfills a number of basic human needs—so basic, in fact, that there may be an innate need to belong to groups. Some researchers argue that in our evolutionary past, there was a substantial survival advantage to establishing bonds with other people (Baumeister & Leary, 1995; DeWall & Richman, 2011; Reitz, Motti-Stefanidi, & Asendorpf, 2016). People who bonded together were better able to hunt for and grow food, find mates, and care for children. Consequently, researchers argue, the need to belong has become entrenched in all societies. Consistent with this view, people in all cultures are motivated to form relationships with other people, monitor their status in groups, and remain vigilant for any sign that they might be rejected (Blackhart et al., 2009; Gardner, Pickett, & Brewer, 2000; Kerr & Levine, 2008).

Not only do people have a strong need to belong to social groups, but they also have a need to feel distinctive from those who do *not* belong to the same groups. If you go to a large university, you might have a sense of belonging, but being a member of such a large collective is unlikely to make you feel distinctive from others. Groups that are relatively small can fulfill both functions by giving us a sense of belonging with our fellow group members and also making us feel special and distinctive. This helps explain why people are attracted to smaller groups within their college environments, whether fraternities and sororities, clubs and organizations, or dramatic or other performance ensembles (Brewer, 2007).

Groups have a number of benefits. They are an important part of our identity, helping us define who we are, and are a source of social norms, the explicit or implicit rules defining what is acceptable behavior. Groups also help us accomplish goals that we could not complete on our own.

Another important function of groups is that they help us define who we are. As we saw in Chapter 8, other people can be an important source of information, helping us resolve ambiguity about the nature of the social world (Darley, 2004). Groups provide a lens through which we can understand the world and our place in it (Baumeister, Ainsworth, & Vohs, 2016; Hogg, Hohman, & Rivera, 2008). So groups become an important part of our identity—witness the number of times people wear shirts emblazoned with the name of one of their groups (e.g., a sports team, a university or college, any campus organization). Groups also help establish social norms, the explicit or implicit rules defining what is acceptable behavior.

The Composition and Functions of Groups

The groups to which you belong probably vary in size from a few members to several dozen members. Most groups, however, have three to six members (Desportes & Lemaine, 1988; Levine & Moreland, 1998). If groups become too large, you cannot interact with all the members; for example, the college or university that you attend is not, on its own, a group because you are unlikely to meet and have interdependent goals with every other student. In the sections to follow, we will consider factors that influence how individuals behave within groups and how groups themselves function.

SOCIAL NORMS   All societies have norms about which behaviors are acceptable, some of which all members are expected to obey (e.g., we should be quiet in libraries) and some of which vary from group to group (e.g., what is appropriate to wear to weddings and funerals). If you live in a dorm, you can probably think of social norms that govern behavior in your group, such as whether alcoholic beverages are consumed at parties there and how you are supposed to feel about rival dorms. It is unlikely that your singing group, drama ensemble, or other groups to which you belong share these same exact norms. The power of norms to shape behavior becomes clear when we violate them too often: We are shunned by other group members and, in extreme cases, pressured to leave the group (Jetten & Hornsey, 2014; Marques, Abrams, & Serodio, 2001; Schachter, 1951).

SOCIAL ROLES   Most groups have a number of well-defined **social roles**, which are shared expectations in a group about how particular people are supposed to behave (Ellemers & Jetten, 2013; Hare, 2003). Whereas norms specify how all group members should act, roles specify how people who occupy certain positions in the group should behave. In a business, a boss and an employee occupy different roles and are expected to act in different ways in that setting. Like social norms, roles can be very helpful because people know what to expect from each other. When members of a group follow a set of clearly defined roles, they tend to be satisfied and perform well (Barley & Bechky, 1994; Bettencourt & Sheldon, 2001).

However, people can get so far into a role that their personal identities and personalities get lost. To test this idea, Philip Zimbardo and colleagues conducted a highly unusual (and controversial) study. They built a mock prison in the basement of the psychology department at Stanford University and paid students to play the role of guard or prisoner (Haney, Banks, & Zimbardo, 1973; Zimbardo, 2007). Which role a participant played—guard or prisoner—was determined by the simple flip of a coin. Guards were outfitted with a uniform of khaki shirts and pants, a whistle, a police nightstick, and reflective sunglasses. Prisoners were given a loose-fitting smock with an identification number stamped on it, rubber sandals, a nylon stocking cap, and a chain attached to one ankle.

Social Roles

Shared expectations in a group about how particular people are supposed to behave

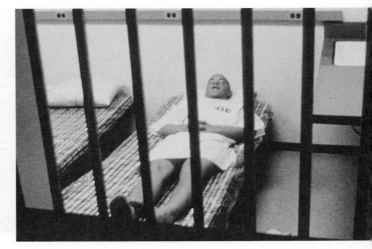

Zimbardo and his colleagues randomly assigned students to play the role of prisoner or guard in a mock prison. The students assumed these roles all too well.

One of the guards from Zimbardo's prison experiment at Stanford.

The researchers planned to observe the students for 2 weeks to see whether they began to act like real prison guards and prisoners. As it turned out, the students quickly assumed these roles—so much so that the researchers ended the experiment after only 6 days. Many of the guards became abusive, coming up with increasingly creative ways of verbally harassing and humiliating the prisoners. The prisoners became passive, helpless, and withdrawn. Some prisoners, in fact, became so anxious and depressed that they had to be released from the study early. Remember, everyone knew that they were in a psychology experiment and that the prison was only make-believe. But the roles of guard and prisoner were so compelling and powerful that this simple truth was often overlooked. People got so far into their roles that their personal identities and sense of decency somehow got lost. In fact, one major methodological criticism of Zimbardo's study—beyond the obvious ethical questions regarding the treatment of research participants—is that the students quickly figured out what the study was about and role-played in the manner that they thought was expected of them (Banuazizi & Movahedi, 1975; Kulig, Pratt, & Cullen, 2017).

But what is clear is that it didn't take coercion, bribery, or weeks of training to prompt these "guards" and "prisoners" to slip easily into their roles and that, in particular, some of the student guards clearly and quickly took things much too far. Does this sound familiar? As mentioned in Chapter 8, in 2004 it came to light that American military guards had been abusing prisoners in Abu Ghraib, a prison in Iraq (Hersh, 2004). The American public was shocked by pictures of U.S. soldiers smiling as they stood in front of naked Iraqi prisoners, as if they were posing in front of local landmarks for the folks back home. Did a few bad apples happen to end up in the unit guarding the prisoners? Not according to Zimbardo (2007). "What's bad is the barrel," Zimbardo argued. "The barrel is the barrel I created by my prison—and we put good boys in, just as in this Iraqi prison. And the barrel corrupts. It's the barrel of the evil of prisons—with secrecy, with no accountability—which gives people permission to do things they ordinarily would not" (quoted in O'Brien, 2004).

This is not to say that the soldiers should be excused for their actions. The abuse came to light when 24-year-old Joe Darby, an army reservist at Abu Ghraib, reported what was happening. As in Zimbardo's study, not everyone was caught in the web of their social roles, unable to resist. But as much as we would like to think that we would be one of these heroes, the lesson from the Zimbardo prison study—and Milgram's studies of obedience—is that many if not most of us would not fully resist the social influences in these powerful situations and would perhaps perform acts we thought we were incapable of.

GROUP COHESIVENESS Another important aspect of how a group functions is how cohesive it is. **Group cohesiveness** refers to the qualities of a group that bind members together and promote mutual liking (Dion, 2000; Holtz, 2004; Rosh, Offermann, & Van Diest, 2012). If a group has formed primarily for social reasons, such as a group of friends who go to the movies together on weekends, then the more cohesive the group is, the better. This is pretty obvious;

Group Cohesiveness

Qualities of a group that bind members together and promote liking between them

Watch ZIMBARDO'S PRISON STUDY

Revel Video

would you rather spend your free time with a bunch of people who don't care much for each other or a tight-knit and committed bunch? As you would expect, the more cohesive a group is, the more its members are likely to stay in the group, take part in group activities, and try to recruit new like-minded members (Levine & Moreland, 1998; Pickett, Silver, & Brewer, 2002; Spink et al., 2014).

If the function of the group is to work together and solve problems, however—as it is for a military unit or sales team at a company—then the story is not quite so simple. Doing well on a task causes a group to become more cohesive (Mullen & Cooper, 1994; Picazo et al., 2014), but is the reverse true? Does cohesiveness cause a group to perform well? It does if the task requires close cooperation between the group members, such as the case of a football team executing a difficult play or a military unit carrying out a complicated maneuver (Casey-Campbell & Martens, 2009; Gully, Devine, & Whitney, 1995). Sometimes, however, cohesiveness can get in the way of optimal performance if maintaining good relations among group members becomes more important than finding good solutions to a problem. Is it possible, for example, that the cohesiveness and sense of confidence shared by Hillary Clinton and her campaign advisers got in the way of clear thinking about how best to plot their electoral strategy? We will return to this question later in the chapter when we discuss group decision making.

GROUP DIVERSITY   Related to cohesiveness is the matter of how diverse a group's composition is. More often than not, members of a group tend to be alike in age, sex, beliefs, and opinions (Apfelbaum, Phillips, & Richeson, 2014; Levine & Moreland, 1998). There are at least two reasons for the relative homogeneity of groups. First, many groups tend to attract people who are already similar before they join (Alter & Darley, 2009; Feld, 1982). As we'll see in Chapter 10, people are attracted to others who share their attitudes and thus are likely to recruit fellow group members who are similar to them. Second, groups tend to operate in ways that encourage similarity in the members, as discussed in Chapter 8.

In short, people tend to gravitate toward groups with similar others, and such similarity predicts group cohesiveness. Consider a study conducted by McLeod, Lobel, and Cox (1996) in which college students were assigned to brainstorming groups ranging in size from three to five. Half of these groups were comprised entirely of White students. That is, these groups were not diverse at all with regard to race; they were racially homogeneous. The other half of the groups were racially diverse, including White students as well as Asian American, African American, or Latino students. All groups, regardless of their diversity, were assigned the same task: to spend 15 minutes brainstorming ideas for how best to attract more tourists to the United States. At the end of each session, participants were asked how much they liked the other members of their group. As you might predict based on the conclusion that homogeneous groups are often cohesive, members of all-White groups reported liking their fellow group members more than did members of diverse groups.

But remember that just because a group is cohesive does not mean it is performing at its optimal level. Indeed, when McLeod and colleagues (1996) analyzed the ideas each group developed for boosting tourism, they found that the diverse groups had come up with more feasible and effective possibilities. Participants may have enjoyed being in a group with similar others, but their performance was strongest when in a diverse group. These findings are consistent with more general conclusions that although diversity—of all types, not just related to race—can sometimes come at the expense of a group's cohesiveness and morale, a diversity of backgrounds or perspectives often predicts improved performance in terms of group creativity, information sharing, and flexible problem solving (Phillips et al., 2004; Savitsky et al., 2016; Sommers, 2006).

There is no simple answer to the question of how diversity affects groups (Apfelbaum et al., 2014; Mannix & Neale, 2005; van Knippenberg, van Ginkel, & Homan, 2013). For that matter, as we just alluded to, there are many ways to define a group's diversity—in

Figure 9.1 Racial and Gender Diversity and Business Performance

To examine the relationship between a business's performance and its racial and gender diversity, Herring (2009) conducted a correlational study of more than 1,000 U.S. workplaces and found a positive association between both types of diversity with (a) sales revenue and (b) number of customers. These results indicate a positive relationship between diversity and a business's bottom line. But as you know, because these data are only correlational, we cannot draw conclusions here regarding one variable causing another.

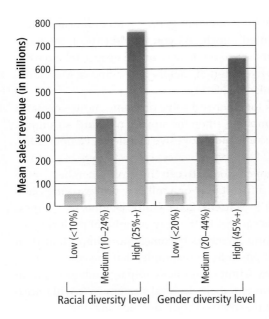

terms of race and other social demographics, sure, but also diversity in terms of experience, education, attitude, and other dimensions. Increasingly, though, a variety of organizations seem to be betting on the positive potential of diversity. There is a reason why institutions such as universities, the military, and *Fortune 500* companies currently spend effort and resources to achieve diversity in their ranks: They believe that it will lead to improved performance, whether in terms of the learning environment or the corporate bottom line (Herring, 2009; Page, 2008). Figure 9.1 suggests that—in correlational terms at least—they are often right. Similarly, in a recent experimental study using a stock market simulation, researchers found that traders randomly assigned to an ethnically diverse marketplace made better, more accurate decisions about how to price stocks than did equally experienced traders assigned to a homogeneous market, supporting the conclusion that the friction caused by diversity can upend conformity and improve decision making (Levine et al., 2015).

#trending

Diversity Research and the Affirmative Action Controversy

With some regularity, the U.S. Supreme Court has heard cases involving the use of affirmative action in college admissions. Most recently, in 2016, the Court issued its ruling in *Fisher v. University of Texas*, in which a White student, Abigail Fisher, had argued that the university's policy of taking into consideration an applicant's race—as one among many demographic, academic, and extracurricular factors—was unconstiutional. The Court ruled in favor of the University of Texas's policy, and against Fisher, but by no means will this be the final word in the legal machinations surrounding affirmative action in college admissions.

There are, of course, many arguments that colleges and universities make in favor of factoring race and ethnicity into admissions decisions. The justifications offered for affirmative action typically include righting historical wrongs and overcoming current obstacles to equal access for all demographic groups. Opponents of affirmative action sometimes argue that such policies are unfair and that admissions should be based solely on "objective criteria" such as test scores and GPA. But at the heart of the affirmative action debate resides a critical, social psychological question: what are the effects of a diverse student body on social and academic outcomes?

In one investigation, Gaither and Sommers (2013) followed roommate pairs over the course of their first year of college. These roommates had been assigned at random by their university housing office, resulting in both same-race pairs and interracial pairs. After one semester, White students who lived with an other-race roommate reported having a more diverse set of friends than did Whites who had a White roommate. In a follow-up study, Whites assigned to a non-White roommate were found to be less anxious and warmer during a laboratory conversation with a non-White stranger, suggesting that diverse living arrangements also affected students' more general social tendencies in new situations.

What about the effects of campus diversity on students of color? In another roommate study, Shook and Clay (2012) found that minority students randomly assigned to an interracial roommate pairing reported an increased sense of belonging on campus after one semester. And in terms of academic outcomes, minority students completed their first year with a higher GPA when they had been part of an interracial roommate pair, in large part because of the aforementioned increased sense of belonging at the university.

There is no question that affirmative action is a complex issue. And as you read previously in this chapter, the effects of a group's diversity on its performance are also complicated. Studies of college roommates have indicated, though, that there is some empirical evidence to support the claim of college and university admissions offices that the potential exists for a diverse student body to predict a variety of positive social and academic outcomes on campus.

Review Questions

1. Which of the following is *not* an example of a group?
   a. Six students studying together for an exam
   b. The 12-person cast of a musical theater production
   c. A four-person work team collaborating on a project via Web conferencing
   d. Seven commuters waiting together silently at a bus stop

2. One reason people join groups is to
   a. avoid having to deal with normative social influence.
   b. accomplish objectives that are more difficult or impossible to accomplish alone.
   c. decrease their cohesiveness.
   d. avoid well-defined social roles.

3. Group cohesiveness is particularly important for a group when
   a. the group has formed for primarily social reasons.
   b. the group's primary objective is problem solving.
   c. the group is diverse in terms of gender but not when it is diverse in terms of race.
   d. financial decision making is involved.

4. From an evolutionary perspective, groups
   a. are more productive when they have two or three members as opposed to when they are larger.

   b. help fulfill a basic human need to affiliate and belong with others.
   c. often lead to immoral behavior, such as that observed among abusive prison guards.
   d. are better able than individuals to avoid the influence of social norms.

5. With the redistricting of the school system, Coach Taylor's football team for the upcoming season is more diverse than usual, with kids from a wide range of backgrounds, including socioeconomic status, race and ethnicity, family status, sexual orientation, and even football experience. Research suggests which of the following conclusions regarding a diverse group such as this?
   a. His team will definitely win more games than will less diverse teams.
   b. His team will likely experience deficits in performance, creativity, and problem solving when compared to less diverse teams.
   c. His team is likely to experience threats to morale and group cohesion, but these challenges will probably lessen as the season goes on.
   d. His team will avoid relying on clear social roles.

Individual Behavior in a Group Setting

LO 9.2   Describe how individuals perform differently when others are around.

Thus far, we have focused on why people join groups and how groups function. But another question we might ask is, what are the effects of being in a group on the performance of individual people? Do you act differently when others are around? When do we "choke" under the pressure of having people watching us? When does having other people around lead us to raise our game and perform better than usual? Simply being in the presence of other people can have a variety of interesting effects on our behavior. We will begin by looking at how a group affects your performance on something with which you are no doubt very familiar—taking a test in a class.

Social Facilitation: When the Presence of Others Energizes Us

It is time for the final exam in your psychology class. You have spent hours studying the material, and you feel ready. When you arrive, you see that the exam is scheduled in a tiny room already packed with students. You squeeze into an empty desk, elbow to elbow with your classmates. The professor arrives and says that if any students are bothered by the close quarters, they can take the test by themselves in one of several smaller rooms down the hall. What should you do?

The question is whether being with others will affect your performance (Guerin, 1993; Monfardini et al., 2016; Zajonc, 1965). The presence of other people can mean one of two things: (a) performing a task with coworkers who are doing the same thing you are or (b) performing a task in front of an audience that is not doing anything but

Figure 9.2 Cockroaches and Social Facilitation

In the maze on the left, cockroaches had a simple task: to go from the starting point down the runway to the darkened box. They performed this feat faster when other roaches were watching than when they were alone. In the maze on the right, the cockroaches had a more difficult task. It took them longer to solve this maze when other roaches were watching than when they were alone.

(Based on data in Zajonc, Heingartner, & Herman, 1969)

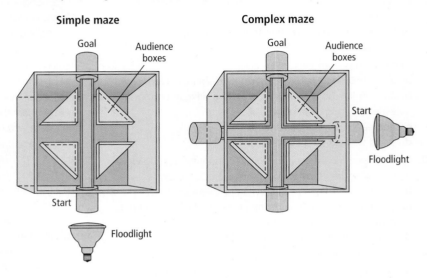

observing you. Note that the question is a basic one about the effects of the mere presence of others, even if they are not part of a group that is interacting. Does the simple fact that other people are around you make a difference, even if you never speak or interact with them in any way?

To answer this question, we need to talk about insects—cockroaches, in fact. Believe it or not, a classic study using cockroaches as research subjects helps us answer the question of how you should opt to take your psychology test. Robert Zajonc and his colleagues (Zajonc, Heingartner, & Herman, 1969) built a contraption to see how a cockroach's behavior was influenced by the presence of its peers. The researchers placed a bright light (which cockroaches dislike) at the end of a runway and timed how long it took a roach to escape the light by running to the other end, where it could scurry into a darkened box (see the left side of Figure 9.2). The question was, did roaches perform this simple feat faster when they were by themselves or when they were in the presence of other cockroaches?

Research on social facilitation finds that people do better on a well-learned task when in the presence of others than when they are alone. If students have studied hard and know the material well, they might be better off taking an exam in a room with lots of other people.

You might be wondering how the researchers managed to persuade other cockroaches to be spectators. They simply placed other roaches in clear plastic boxes next to the runway. These roaches were in the bleachers, so to speak, observing the solitary cockroach do its thing (see Figure 9.2). As predicted, the individual cockroaches performed the task faster when other roaches were there watching than when they were by themselves.

We would not give advice on how you should take your psychology test based only on one study of cockroaches. But the story does not end here. Dozens of studies have been done on the effects of the mere presence of others, involving human beings as well as other species, such as ants and birds (Demolliens et al., 2017; Krasheninnikova & Schneider, 2014; Sharma et al., 2010). The findings of these studies are consistent: As long as the task is a relatively simple, well-learned one—as escaping a light is for cockroaches—the mere presence of others improves performance.

SIMPLE VERSUS DIFFICULT TASKS Before concluding that you should stay in the crowded classroom to take your exam, we need to consider a different set of findings. Remember that we said that the presence of others enhances performance on *simple, well-learned* tasks, like cockroaches escaping a light. What happens when we give people a more difficult task to do and place them in the presence of others? To find out, Zajonc and his colleagues (1969) included another condition in the cockroach experiment. This time, the cockroaches had to solve a maze that had several runways, only one of which led to the darkened box (see the right side of Figure 9.2). When working on this more difficult task, the opposite pattern of results occurred: The roaches took *longer* to solve it when other roaches were present than when they were alone. Many other studies have also found that people and animals do worse in the presence of others when the task is difficult (Aiello & Douthitt, 2001; Augustinova & Ferrand, 2012; Geen, 1989).

AROUSAL AND THE DOMINANT RESPONSE In an influential article, Zajonc (1965) offered an elegant theoretical explanation for why the presence of others facilitates a well-learned response but inhibits a less practiced or new response. He argued that the presence of others increases physiological arousal (i.e., our bodies become more energized). When such arousal exists, it is easier to perform a dominant response (e.g., something we're good at) but harder to do something complex or learn something new. Consider, for example, a behavior that is second nature to you, such as riding a bicycle or writing your name. Arousal caused by the presence of other people watching you should make it even easier to perform these well-learned tasks. But let's say you have to do something more complex, such as learning a new sport or working on a difficult math problem. Now arousal will lead you to feel flustered and do less well than if you were alone (Schmitt et al., 1986). This phenomenon became known as **social facilitation**, which is the tendency for people to do better on simple tasks and worse on complex tasks when they are in the presence of others and their individual performance can be evaluated.

WHY THE PRESENCE OF OTHERS CAUSES AROUSAL Why does the presence of others lead to arousal? Researchers have developed three theories to explain the role of arousal in social facilitation: Other people cause us to become particularly alert and vigilant, they make us apprehensive about how we're being evaluated, and they distract us from the task at hand.

The first explanation suggests that the presence of other people makes us more alert. When we are by ourselves reading a book, we don't have to pay attention to anything but the book; we don't have to worry that the lamp will ask us a question. When someone else is in the room, however, we have to be alert to the possibility that he or she will do something that requires us to respond. Because other people are less predictable than lamps, we are in a state of greater alertness in their presence. This alertness, or vigilance, causes mild arousal. The beauty of this explanation is that it explains both the animal and the human studies. A solitary cockroach need not worry about what the cockroach in the next room is doing; however, it needs to be alert when in the presence of another member of its species—and the same goes for human beings.

The second explanation focuses on the fact that unlike cockroaches, people are often concerned about how others are evaluating them. When other people can see how you are doing, the stakes are raised: You feel as if the other people are evaluating you; you will be embarrassed if you do poorly and pleased if you do well. This concern about being judged, called *evaluation apprehension*, can cause arousal. According to this view, then, it is not the mere presence of others but rather the presence of others who are evaluating us that causes arousal and subsequent social facilitation (Blascovich et al., 1999; Muller & Butera, 2007).

Social Facilitation

When people are in the presence of others and their individual performance can be evaluated, the tendency to perform better on simple tasks and worse on complex tasks

Figure 9.3 Social Facilitation and Social Loafing

The presence of others can lead to social facilitation or social loafing. The important variables that distinguish the two are evaluation, arousal, and the complexity of the tasks.

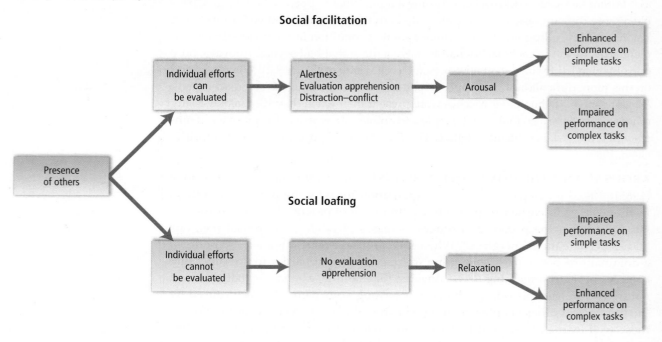

The third explanation centers on how distracting other people can be (Feinberg & Aiello, 2006; Muller, Atzeni, & Fabrizio, 2004). It is similar to Zajonc's (1980) notion that we need to be alert when in the presence of others, except that it focuses on the idea that any source of distraction—be it the presence of other people or noise from the party going on in the apartment upstairs—will put us in a state of conflict because it is difficult to pay attention to two things at the same time. This divided attention produces arousal, as any student knows who has ever tried to get work done in the presence of a roommate who is listening to loud music, talking on the phone, or otherwise making it hard to focus. Consistent with this interpretation, nonsocial sources of distraction, such as a flashing light, can cause the same kinds of social facilitation effects as the presence of other people (Baron, 1986).

We have summarized research on social facilitation in the top half of Figure 9.3 (we will discuss the bottom half in a moment). This figure illustrates that there is more than one reason why the presence of other people is arousing. The consequences of this arousal, however, are the same: When you are around other people, you do better on tasks that are simple and well learned, but you do worse on tasks that are complex and require you to learn something new. Where, then, should you take your psychology exam? We recommend that you stay in the regular classroom, assuming you know the material well, so that it is relatively simple for you to recall it. But when you study for an exam—that is, when you learn new material—you should do so by yourself, away from other people.

Social Loafing: When the Presence of Others Relaxes Us

When you take your psychology exam, your individual efforts will be evaluated (i.e., you will be graded on the test). This is typical of the research on social facilitation: People are working on something either alone or in the presence of others, and their individual efforts are easily evaluated. Often when you are in the presence of others, however, your individual efforts cannot be distinguished from those of the people around you. Such is the case when you clap after a concert (no one can tell how loudly you as an individual are clapping) or when you play an instrument in a marching band (your instrument blends in with all the others).

These situations are the opposite of the social facilitation settings we have just considered. In social facilitation, the presence of others puts the spotlight on you, making you aroused. But if being with other people means we can merge into a group, becoming less noticeable than when we are alone, we should become relaxed. Because no one can tell how well we are doing, we should feel less evaluation apprehension. What happens then? Will this relaxation produced by becoming lost in the crowd lead to better or worse performance? Again, the answer depends on whether we are working on a simple, unimportant task or a complex task.

Sometimes being surrounded by others allows us to slack off (or "loaf"), demonstrating that there's not a single, simple answer to the question of how the presence of other people affects individual performance.

The question of how working with others would influence performance on a basic task was first studied in the 1880s by a French agricultural engineer, Max Ringelmann (1913). He found that when a group pulled on a rope, each individual exerted less effort than when doing so alone. In other words, eight individuals pulling on the rope did not exert eight times the force as one person pulling alone. A century later, social psychologists Bibb Latané, Kipling Williams, and Stephen Harkins (2006) called this **social loafing**, which is the tendency for people to relax when they are in the presence of others and their individual performance cannot be evaluated, such that they do worse on simple tasks that they don't care about but better on complex tasks that are important to them. Social loafing in groups has since been found on a variety of simple tasks, such as clapping your hands, cheering loudly, and thinking of as many uses for an object as you can (Karau & Williams, 2001; Lount & Wilk, 2014; Shepperd & Taylor, 1999).

Social Loafing

When people are in the presence of others and their individual performance cannot be evaluated, the tendency to perform worse on simple or unimportant tasks but better on complex or important tasks

What about complex tasks? Recall that when performance in a group cannot be identified, people become more relaxed. Recall also our earlier discussion of the effects of arousal on performance: Arousal enhances performance on simple tasks but impairs performance on complex tasks. By the same reasoning, becoming relaxed impairs performance on simple tasks—as we have just seen—but can improve performance on complex tasks (Jackson & Williams, 1985). This process is illustrated in the bottom part of Figure 9.3.

Gender and Cultural Differences in Social Loafing: Who Slacks Off the Most?

Kate and William are working with several classmates on a class project, and no one will be able to assess their individual contributions. Who is more likely to slack off and let the other do most of the work: Kate or William? If you said William, you are probably right. In a review of more than 150 studies of social loafing, the tendency to loaf was found

Watch SOCIAL LOAFING

Revel Video

to be stronger in men than in women (Karau & Williams, 1993). Women tend to be higher than men in *relational interdependence*, which is the tendency to focus on and care about personal relationships with other individuals. Perhaps it is this focus that makes women less likely to engage in social loafing when in groups (Gabriel & Gardner, 1999).

Research has also found that the tendency to loaf is stronger in Western cultures than Asian cultures, which may be due to the different self-definitions prevalent in these cultures (Karau & Williams, 1993). Asians are more likely to have an *interdependent view of the self*, which is a way of defining oneself in terms of relationships to other people. This self-definition may reduce the tendency toward social loafing when in groups. We should not, however, exaggerate these gender and cultural differences. Women and members of Asian cultures do engage in social loafing when in groups; they are just less relatively likely to do so than men or members of Western cultures (Chang & Chen, 1995; Hong, Wyer, & Fong, 2008). Moreover, the composition of the entire group is an important consideration: Research indicates that people are more likely to loaf when they expect to work together with team members from a different culture (Meyer, Schermuly, & Kauffeld, 2016). This seems to occur because we more easily develop bonds and a sense of accountability to similar others, and also come to expect less cooperation from dissimilar others.

To summarize, you need to know two things to predict whether the presence of others will help or hinder your performance: whether your individual efforts can be evaluated and whether the task is simple or complex. If your performance can be evaluated, the presence of others will make you alert and aroused. This will lead to social facilitation effects, where people do better on simple tasks but worse on complex tasks (see the top of Figure 9.3). If your efforts cannot be evaluated (i.e., you are one cog in a machine), you are likely to become more relaxed. This leads to social loafing effects, where people do worse on simple tasks that they don't care about but better on complex ones (see the bottom of Figure 9.3).

These findings have numerous implications for the way in which groups should be organized. On the one hand, if you are a manager who wants your employees to work on a relatively simple problem, a little evaluation apprehension is not such a bad thing—it may very well improve performance. You shouldn't place your employees in groups where their individual performance cannot be observed because lowered performance on simple tasks is likely to result due to social loafing. On the other hand, if you want your employees to work on a difficult, complex task, then lowering their evaluation apprehension—by placing them in groups in which their individual performance cannot be observed—is likely to result in better performance.

Deindividuation

The loosening of normal constraints on behavior when people can't be identified (such as when they are in a crowd)

Watch SURVIVAL TIPS! KEEPING THE BAND MOTIVATED

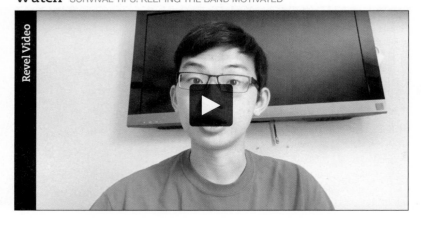

Revel Video

Deindividuation: Getting Lost in the Crowd

The consequences of feeling anonymous can be much more serious than loafing on a group task, however. Being in a group can also cause **deindividuation**, which is the loosening of normal constraints on behavior when people can't be identified (Lea, Spears, & de Groot, 2001). In other words, getting lost in a crowd can lead to an unleashing of behaviors that we would never dream of exhibiting by ourselves. Throughout history, there have been many examples of groups of people committing horrendous acts that few individuals would do on their own, such as military atrocities; acts of looting, arson, and violence; hysterical fans at rock concerts trampling each other to death; and other examples sometimes referred to more colloquially as resulting from a "mob mentality."

One particularly troubling example in the United States is the shameful history of Whites—often cloaked in the anonymity of hooded robes—lynching African Americans. Brian Mullen (1986) content-analyzed newspaper accounts of 60 lynchings committed between 1899 and 1946 and discovered that the more people there were in the mob in question, the greater the savagery and viciousness with which they killed their victims. Similar results were observed by Robert Watson (1973), who studied 24 cultures and found that warriors who hid their identities before going into battle—for example, by using face and body paint—were significantly more likely to kill, torture, or mutilate captive prisoners than were warriors who did not hide their identities.

DEINDIVIDUATION MAKES PEOPLE FEEL LESS ACCOUNTABLE Why does deindividuation lead to and exacerbate impulsive (often violent) acts? One reason is that people feel less accountable for their actions when they recognize there is a reduced likelihood that they can be singled out and blamed for their behavior (Diener, 1980; Postmes & Spears, 1998; Zimbardo, 1970). In Harper Lee's novel *To Kill a Mockingbird*, for example, a mob of White southerners assembled to lynch Tom Robinson, a Black man accused (falsely) of rape. Here is a classic case of deindividuation: It was night, the men were dressed alike, and it was difficult to tell one from another. But then Scout, the 8-year-old daughter of Robinson's attorney, Atticus, recognized one of the farmers and greeted him by name. She unwittingly performed a brilliant social psychological intervention by making the mob feel more like individuals who were accountable for their actions. And, indeed, the mob disbanded and went home.

DEINDIVIDUATION INCREASES OBEDIENCE TO GROUP NORMS In a meta-analysis of more than 60 studies, researchers found that becoming deindividuated also increases the extent to which people obey the group's norms (Postmes & Spears, 1998). Sometimes the norms of a specific group to which we belong conflict with the norms of other groups or of society at large. When these group members are together and deindividuated, they become more likely to act according to the group norms than societal norms. Thus, it is not just that deindividuation reduces the likelihood that one person will stand out and be blamed, but also that it increases adherence to the local group's norms (Reicher et al., 2016).

Consequently, deindividuation does not always lead to aggressive or antisocial behavior; it depends on what the group's norm is. Imagine that you are at a rowdy party at which everyone is dancing wildly to loud music. To the extent that you feel deindividuated—it is dark, and you are dressed similarly to other people—you are more likely to join the group and let loose on the dance floor, rather than if the room was bright and no one was dancing. Thus, it is the specific norm of the group that determines whether deindividuation will lead to positive or negative behaviors (Hirsh, Galinsky, & Zhong, 2011; Johnson & Downing, 1979). If the group is angry and the norm is to act violently, deindividuation will make people in the group act aggressively. If we are at a party and the norm is to eat a lot, being deindividuated will simply increase the likelihood that we eat the entire bowl of guacamole.

The robes and hoods of the Ku Klux Klan cloak its members in anonymity; their violent behavior is consistent with research on deindividuation.

DEINDIVIDUATION ONLINE Deindividuation doesn't require face-to-face contact. In fact, it thrives with less physical forms of interaction. Anyone who has ever read the comments

Beginning in 2014, several women video game developers and journalists—including media critic Anita Sarkeesian, pictured above—were targeted by vicious online attacks and false accusations in what quickly became known as "Gamergate." The sexist and often violent harassment was usually perpetrated by anonymous individuals, demonstrating once again that the phenomenon of the internet "troll" is a modern example of deindividuation.

section at the bottom of online article, blog, or YouTube clip has witnessed deindividuation at work, whereby people feel less inhibited about what they write because of their anonymity. In many respects, the internet is ideal terrain for the emergence of deindividuation (Coles & West, 2016; Lee, 2004). Given how quickly many online forums deteriorate into strings of insulting "trolling" or obscene comments, numerous sites have moved away from allowing anonymous participation, now requiring users to sign in with a social media account or other identifying information before they are allowed to post.

In the pre-internet era, angry readers and others seeking to stir up debate would have written letters to a newspaper editor or vented their feelings to coworkers at the watercooler. In both cases, their discourse would have likely been more civil, free of the profanities used in many online forums, in large part because people are not anonymous in such settings. Online anonymous communication does have certain advantages in terms of free and open discussion of difficult topics. But there is also a cost, namely, an apparent reduction in common civility. And one of the chief culprits responsible is deindividuation.

The good news? Perhaps understanding deindividuation can also help combat online trolling and make the internet a more civilized—at least slightly—place. In a recent study, Kathleen Van Royen and her colleagues (2017) tried out a series of potential interventions with adolescents active on social media. Specifically, the participants in this study were presented with a scenario in which a hypothetical user had posted about another girl who had "stolen" her boyfriend. The researchers were particularly interested in those participants who reported that they would be likely, in such a scenario, to respond by calling the other girl offensive names like "slut" and "whore."

One intervention message they tried with one group of youth who said they were likely to use this type of language was a reminder that such comments could be read by their parents. Another intervention told participants that many other people would disapprove of such comments. And yet another reminded participants that this sort of comment could be hurtful for the girl it targeted. Any of these three warning messages decreased a teenager's reported likelihood of going through with the sexist post, but particularly effective was the reminder that one's parents might read the offensive language. Why? Because it emphasized other influential norms, those related to family. And, presumably, because it also reminded participants of their own, unique personal identity.

Review Questions

1. The concept of *social facilitation* is so named because of the idea that when the presence of others is arousing,
   a. this arousal facilitates better task performance.
   b. this arousal facilitates a well-learned, dominant response.
   c. hard tasks are facilitated, but easy tasks are impeded.
   d. deindividuation is facilitated.

2. Which of the following is *not* an explanation for why the presence of other people can be arousing?
   a. The presence of other people is distracting and causes conflict, as individuals have to decide what they should pay attention to.
   b. When other people are around, an individual has to be on alert in anticipation of what might happen next.

     c. When other people are around, individuals become more concerned about how they are being evaluated.

     d. Having other people around makes an individual feel less accountable for his or her own actions.

3. Your social psychology professor calls you up to the front of the classroom and asks you to answer a series of course-related questions out loud. Even though you feel the eyes of your classmates on you, you find the questions to be easy. According to the model of _____, you should perform _____ on these questions than you would have if you had been asked them in private, without an audience.

     a. social facilitation; worse

     b. social facilitation; better

     c. social loafing; worse

     d. social loafing; better

4. Which of the following individuals would you expect to be most likely to engage in social loafing?

     a. Serena, an American woman

     b. Li, a Chinese woman

     c. Andy, a British man

     d. Kei, a Japanese man

5. Individuals experiencing deindividuation

     a. feel increasingly accountable for their actions.

     b. exhibit greater conformity to specific group norms.

     c. are less likely to engage in destructive or immoral behavior.

     d. are unlikely to experience this feeling online, as deindividuation is much less common in virtual environments.

Group Decisions: Are Two (or More) Heads Better Than One?

LO 9.3   **Compare the decision-making outcomes of individuals versus groups, and explain the impact of leadership in group outcomes.**

We have just seen that the presence of other people influences individual behavior in a number of interesting ways. We turn now to one of the major functions of groups: making decisions. Many important decisions are made by groups because it is assumed that groups are better decision makers than individuals. In the American judicial system, for example, most verdicts are determined by groups (juries), not individuals. The U.S. Supreme Court is made up of nine justices, not just one. Similarly, governmental and corporate decisions are often made by groups of people who meet to discuss the issues; U.S. presidents have a cabinet and the National Security Council to advise them.

    Is it true that two (or more) heads are better than one? Most of us assume the answer is yes. A lone individual may be subject to all sorts of whims and biases, whereas several people together can exchange ideas, catch each other's errors, and reach better decisions. We have all taken part in group decisions in which we listened to someone else and thought to ourselves, "Hmm, that's a really good point; I never would have thought of that." In general, groups can perform better than individuals when group members freely contribute independent opinions from a variety of viewpoints, if people are motivated to search for the answer that is best for the entire group and not just for themselves, or when they rely on group members' unique areas of expertise (De Dreu, Nijstad, & van Knippenberg, 2008; Surowiecki, 2004). Sometimes, though, two or more heads are not better than one—or at least no better than two heads working alone (Kerr & Tindale, 2004). Several factors can cause groups to make worse decisions than individuals would.

Process Loss: When Group Interactions Inhibit Good Problem Solving

One potential problem is that a group can perform well only if the most expert or talented members can convince the others that they are

Watch THE WISDOM OF CROWDS

Revel Video

Process Loss

Any aspect of group interaction that inhibits good problem solving

right. This is not always easy, given that many of us bear a strong resemblance to mules when it comes to admitting we are wrong. You undoubtedly know what it's like to try to convince a group to follow your idea, be faced with opposition and disbelief, and then have to sit there and watch the group make the wrong decision. This is an example of **process loss**, which is any aspect of group interaction that inhibits good problem solving (Steiner, 1972; Tidikis & Ash, 2013). Process loss can occur for a number of reasons. Groups might not try hard enough to find out who the most competent members are and instead rely on someone who really doesn't know what he or she is talking about. Perhaps the most competent members find it difficult to disagree with everyone else in the group. Other causes of process loss involve communication problems, such as failure to listen or one person being allowed to dominate the discussion while others tune out (Sorkin, Hays, & West, 2001; Watson et al., 1998).

FAILURE TO SHARE UNIQUE INFORMATION Suppose you are meeting with three other people to decide whether to support a particular candidate for Student Senate president. You all know some of the same things about the candidate (you have "shared" information), such as the fact that she was president of her sophomore class and is an economics major. But each of you also has information that only you know (i.e., "unique" information). Maybe you are the only one who knows that she was punished for underage drinking in her first-year dorm, whereas one of the other group members is the only one who knows that she volunteers every week at a local homeless shelter. Obviously, the four of you will make the best decision if you share with each other everything you know about the candidate.

But there is a funny thing about groups: They tend to focus on the information they already collectively share, talking less about facts known to only some members of the group (McLeod, 2013; Toma & Butera, 2009; Lu, Yuan, & McLeod, 2012). One study, for example, used a situation similar to the one we have just described, in which students decided who among several candidates was most qualified to be student body president (Stasser & Titus, 1985). In the shared information condition, groups of four participants were given the same packet of information to read, all of which indicated that Candidate A was the best choice for office. Not surprisingly, when the groups met to discuss the candidates, almost all of the members chose Candidate A. In the unique information condition, each participant in the group received a different packet of information. All participants learned that Candidate A had the same four negative qualities, but each learned that Candidate A also had two unique positive qualities—that is, positive qualities that were different from those listed in other participants' packets. Thus, if the four participants shared with each other the information in their packets, they would learn that Candidate A had a total of eight positive qualities and four negative qualities. Instead, most of the groups in the unique information condition never realized that Candidate A had more good than bad qualities because they focused on the information they already shared collectively rather than on the information they did not. As a result, few of these groups chose Candidate A.

Subsequent research has focused on ways to get groups to focus more on unique information (Scholten et al., 2007; Toma & Butera, 2015). Unique information is more likely to be brought up later in the discussion, suggesting that group discussions should last long enough to get beyond what everyone already knows (Fraidin, 2004; Larson et al., 1998). It also helps to tell group members not to share what their initial preferences are at the outset of the discussion; if they do, they will focus less on unique, unshared information (Mojzisch & Schulz-Hardt, 2010). Another approach is to assign different group members to specific areas of expertise so that they know that they alone are responsible for certain types of information (Stasser, Vaughn, & Stewart, 2000; Stewart & Stasser, 1995).

This last lesson has been learned by many couples, who know to rely on each other's memories for different kinds of information. One party might be responsible for remembering the times of social engagements, whereas the other might be responsible for remembering when to pay the bills. When the combined memory of a group is more efficient than the memory of its individual members, we call it **transactive memory** (Peltokorpi, 2008; Rajaram & Pereira-Pasarin, 2010; Wegner, 1995). By learning to specialize their memories and knowing what their partner is responsible for, couples often do quite well in remembering important information. The same can be true of groups if they develop a system whereby different people are responsible for remembering different parts of a task (Ellis, Porter, & Wolverton, 2008; Lewis et al., 2007; Mell, van Knippenberg, & van Ginkel, 2014). In sum, the tendency for groups to fail to consider important unique information can be overcome if people learn who is responsible for what kinds of information and take the time to discuss these unshared data (Stasser, 2000).

GROUPTHINK: MANY HEADS, ONE MIND   Earlier we mentioned that group cohesiveness can get in the way of clear thinking and good decision making. Using real-world events, Irving Janis (1972, 1982) developed an influential theory of group decision making that he called **groupthink**, a kind of thinking in which maintaining group cohesiveness and solidarity is more important than considering the facts in a realistic manner. According to Janis's theory, groupthink is most likely to occur when certain preconditions are met, such as when the group is highly cohesive, isolated from contrary opinions, and ruled by a directive leader.

Many a presidential decision gone awry has been chalked up to groupthink. Janis (1982) himself famously cited as an example the ill-fated decision of President John F. Kennedy and his advisers to try to overthrow Cuban leader Fidel Castro via the Bay of Pigs invasion in 1961. Some have suggested that President George W. Bush's decision to invade Iraq in 2003 was an example of groupthink. More recently, as discussed in the opening of this chapter, one might argue that the surprise failure of Hillary Clinton's 2016 presidential campaign also exhibited telltale signs of groupthink, as she and her team of advisers seemed to assume from the start that they had the election in the bag, sometimes turning away voices (and data) that went against that narrative.

None of these decisions can be reduced to just one explanation. But they all seem to meet many of the circumstances likely to elicit groupthink: tight-knit, homogeneous groups following the lead of a confident individual who made clear what he or she thought was the best course of action. Consider, for example, this assessment from Bush's former press secretary, Scott McClellan, who wrote that once the president made his view known, "it was rarely questioned" because "that is what Bush expected and made known to his top advisers" (McClellan, 2008, p. 128). The antecedents, or preconditions, of groupthink can be found on the left of Figure 9.4. Originally, it was believed that all of these preconditions had to be met for groupthink to occur; today, however, researchers propose that groupthink can occur even when only a few are present (Baron, 2005; Henningsen et al., 2006; Mok & Morris, 2010).

When preconditions of groupthink are met, several symptoms appear (see center box of Figure 9.4). The group begins to feel that it is invulnerable and can do no wrong. People exercise self-censorship, failing to voice contrary views because they are afraid of dampening the group's morale or because they fear being criticized by others. If anyone does voice a contrary viewpoint, the rest of the group is quick to criticize, pressuring the

Transactive Memory

The combined memory of a group that is more efficient than the memory of the individual members

Groupthink

A kind of decision process in which maintaining group cohesiveness and solidarity is more important than considering the facts in a realistic manner

Henry Martin/The New Yorker Collection/The Cartoon Bank

"All those in favor say 'Aye.'"
"Aye."
"Aye."
"Aye."
"Aye."
"Aye."

Figure 9.4 Groupthink: Antecedents, Symptoms, and Consequences

Under some conditions, maintaining group cohesiveness and solidarity becomes more important to a group than considering the facts in a realistic manner (see "Antecedents"). When this happens, certain symptoms of groupthink occur, such as the illusion of invulnerability (see "Symptoms"). These symptoms lead to defective decision making.

(Based on data in Janis & Mann, 1977)

Antecedents of groupthink	Symptoms of groupthink	Consequences of groupthink
The group is highly cohesive: The group is valued and attractive, and people very much want to be members.	**Illusion of invulnerability:** The group feels it is invincible and can do no wrong.	**Incomplete survey of alternatives:** The group fails to consider all other possible viewpoints and outcomes.
Group isolation: The group is isolated, protected from hearing alternative viewpoints.	**Belief in the moral correctness of the group:** "God is on our side."	**Failure to examine the risks of the favored alternative:** Discussion focuses on the good things expected to happen, at expense of considering bad things that might.
A directive leader: The leader controls the discussion and makes his or her wishes known.	**Stereotyped views of out-group:** Opposing sides are viewed in a simplistic, stereotyped manner.	**Poor information search:** The group selectively relies upon information that supports its viewpoint.
High stress: The members perceive threats to the group.	**Self-censorship:** People decide not to voice contrary opinions so as not to "rock the boat."	**Failure to develop contingency plans:** Overly confident in its decision, the group does not consider a Plan B (or C or D).
Poor decision-making procedures: No standard methods to consider alternative viewpoints.	**Direct pressure on dissenters to conform:** If people do voice contrary opinions, they are pressured by others to conform to the majority.	
	Illusion of unanimity: An illusion is created that everyone agrees—for example, by not calling on people known to disagree.	
	Mindguards: Group members protect the leader from contrary viewpoints.	

person to conform to the majority view. This kind of behavior creates an illusion of unanimity where it looks as if everyone agrees, even if, under the surface, they privately do not.

The perilous state of groupthink leads to an inferior decision-making process (Packer, 2009; Tetlock et al., 1992; Turner et al., 2006). As seen on the right of Figure 9.4, the group does not consider the full range of alternatives, develop contingency plans, or adequately consider the risks of its preferred choice. Can you think of other real-life examples—presidential or more personal—of decisions that may have been plagued by groupthink?

Research has demonstrated that groups and their leaders can take several steps to make groupthink less likely (McCauley, 1989; Pratkanis & Turner, 2013; Zimbardo & Andersen, 1993):

The concept of groupthink has become widely known in the general culture, and writers and pundits alike have blamed it for many bad decisions. A *New York Times* article, for example, claimed that experts on the Federal Reserve Board should have predicted the mortgage-based financial crisis of 2007 but didn't because they exhibited symptoms of groupthink (Shiller, 2008).

- **Remain impartial.** A leader should not take a directive role but should remain impartial.
- **Seek outside opinions.** The group should invite outside opinions from people who are not members and who are thus less concerned with maintaining group cohesiveness.
- **Create subgroups.** A leader can divide the group into subgroups that first meet separately and then meet together to discuss their different recommendations.
- **Seek anonymous opinions.** A group might also take a secret ballot or ask members to write down their opinions anonymously; doing so ensures that people give their true opinions, uncensored by a fear of recrimination from the group.

Group Polarization: Going to Extremes

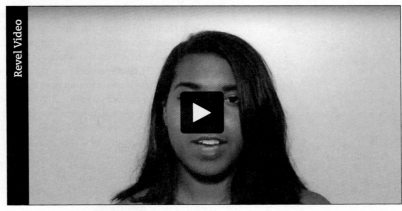

Revel Video

Okay, so groups sometimes make poor decisions. Surely, though, groups will usually make less risky decisions than a lone individual will. One individual might be willing to go all in on a risky proposition, but if others help make the decision, they will interject reason and moderation. Or will they? In examining the question of whether groups or individuals make riskier decisions, many initial studies found, surprisingly, that groups make riskier decisions than individuals do.

For example, in one study, people were asked to consider the following scenario: A low-ranked participant in a national chess tournament, playing an early match against a highly favored opponent, has the choice of whether to attempt a risky maneuver that might lead to quick victory if it is successful but almost certain defeat if it fails. When deciding alone, people said that the chess player should make the risky gambit only if there were at least a 30% chance of success. But after discussing the problem in a group, people said that the chess player should go for it even if there were only a 10% chance of success (Wallach, Kogan, & Bem, 1962). Findings such as these became known as the *risky shift*. But further research made clear that such shifts are not the full story. It turns out that groups tend to make decisions that are more extreme in the same direction as the initial predispositions of their members. So if the individual members of a group are already leaning toward a risky decision, group discussion will usually exaggerate that risky tendency. But when people are initially inclined to be conservative, groups tend to make even more conservative decisions than individuals do.

Consider this problem: Soo-Min, a young woman with two children, has a secure but low-paying job and no savings. Someone gives her a tip about a stock that will triple in value if the company's new product is successful but will plummet if the new product fails. Should Soo-Min sell her life insurance policy and invest in the company? Most people recommend a safe course of action here: Soo-Min should buy the stock only if the new product is very certain to succeed. When they talk it over in a group, they become even more conservative, deciding that the new product would have to have a nearly 100% chance of success before they would recommend that Soo-Min buy the stock. This tendency for groups to make decisions that are more extreme than the initial inclination of its members—toward greater risk if people's initial tendency is to be risky and toward greater caution if people's initial tendency is to be cautious—is known as **group polarization** (Brown, 1965; Keating, van Boven, & Judd, 2016; Palmer & Loveland, 2008).

Group polarization occurs for two main reasons. According to the *persuasive arguments* interpretation, all individuals bring to the group a set of arguments supporting their initial recommendation. One aspect of being in a group is that you might be exposed to persuasive arguments you hadn't thought of before. For example, in considering Soo-Min's investment strategy, one member of the group might stress that cashing in the life insurance policy is an unfair risk to Soo-Min's children should she die prematurely. Another group member might not have considered this possibility; thus, he or she becomes more conservative as well. A series of studies supports this interpretation of group polarization, whereby each member presents arguments that other members have not considered (Burnstein & Vinokur, 1977; El-Shinnawy & Vinze, 1998).

According to the *social comparison* interpretation, when people discuss an issue in a group, they first check out how everyone else feels. What does the group value: being risky or being cautious? In an effort to fit in and be liked, many people then take a position

Group Polarization

The tendency for groups to make decisions that are more extreme than the initial inclinations of their members

Figure 9.5 Increasing Partisanship in America

Joining a group is likely to lead an individual's attitudes to become more extreme through group polarization. Though this process isn't inevitable, it appears we are becoming more politically polarized as a country. One contributing factor could be social media. Social media feeds tend to vary widely based on a user's stated preferences. Someone who has clicked "like" on the *New York Times,* NPR, and Planned Parenthood is likely to be exposed to a much more progressive/liberal feed of posts than someone who has "liked" Fox News, Ann Coulter, and the NRA. As such, these two individuals, who had very different attitudes to begin with, are likely to find themselves even further apart ideologically through processes of polarization, as demonstrated below by the change over two decades in how people rate their own political values on a 10-item scale.

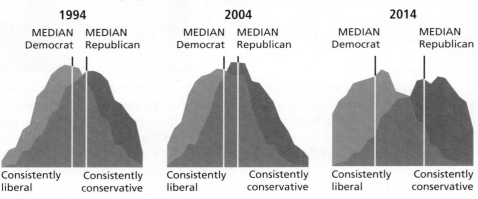

(Adapted from Pew, 2014)

that is similar to everyone else's but even just a little bit more extreme. In this way, individuals support the group's values and also present themselves in a positive light—as "good" group members. For example, consider the alcohol-related attitudes of new college students. Those who arrive on campus positively inclined toward drinking may soon find themselves surrounded by similar others, their own attitudes shifting even further in a positive direction in order to fit in. Those wary of alcohol may also seek out and find like-minded friends, growing even more wary of drinking as the group's values become clear.

Both the persuasive arguments and the social comparison interpretations of group polarization have received research support (Boos et al., 2013; Brauer, Judd, & Gilner, 1995), though notably, individuals tend to underestimate just how polarizing being in a group can be (Keating et al., 2016). That is, we as individuals are often unaware of the polarizing effects that group membership has on our own attitudes, perceiving instead that our beliefs have remained unbiased and stable over time. For example, Figure 9.5 depicts the political polarization that has taken place in the U.S. over the past two decades.

Leadership in Groups

Another critical issue related to group decision making is the role of a leader. The question of what makes a great leader has intrigued psychologists, historians, and political scientists for some time (Fiedler, 1967; Haslam, Reicher, & Platow, 2013; Lord et al., 2017). One of the best-known answers to this question is the **great person theory**, which maintains that certain key personality traits make a person a good leader, regardless of the nature of the situation the leader faces.

If the great person theory is true, we ought to be able to isolate the key aspects of personality that make someone an effective leader. Is it a combination of intelligence, charisma, and courage? Is it better to be introverted or extroverted? Should we add a dollop of ruthlessness to the mix as well, as Niccolò Machiavelli suggested in 1513 in his famous treatise on leadership, *The Prince*? Or do highly moral people make the best leaders?

LEADERSHIP AND PERSONALITY People of all different personality types can become successful leaders. Compared to nonleaders, for example, leaders tend to be only slightly more intelligent, extraverted, charismatic, open to new experiences, confident,

Great Person Theory

The idea that certain key personality traits make a person a good leader, regardless of the situation

and assertive (Ames & Flynn, 2007; Judge et al., 2002; Van Vugt, 2006). Surprisingly few personality characteristics correlate strongly with leadership effectiveness, and the relationships that have been found tend to be modest (Avolio, Walumbwa, & Weber, 2009; von Wittich & Antonakis, 2011). For example, Dean Simonton (1987, 2001) gathered information about 100 personal attributes of all U.S. presidents, such as their family backgrounds, educational experiences, occupations, and personalities. Tall presidents, those from small families, and those who had published books before taking office were most likely to become effective leaders, as rated by historians. The other 97 characteristics, including personality traits, were not related to leadership effectiveness at all.

LEADERSHIP STYLES Although great leaders may not have specific kinds of personalities, they do appear to adopt specific kinds of leadership styles. **Transactional leaders** set clear, short-term goals and reward people who meet them. **Transformational leaders**, on the other hand, inspire followers to focus on common, long-term goals (Bass, 1998; Haslam et al., 2013). So although transactional leaders do a good job of making things run smoothly, it is transformational leaders who think outside the box and inspire their followers to exert themselves to meet big-picture goals.

Interestingly, these leadership styles are not closely linked with personality traits; it is not as if people are "born to be" one type of leader or the other (Judge, Colbert, & Ilies, 2004; Nielsen & Cleal, 2011). Further, these styles are not mutually exclusive; in fact, the most effective leader is one who adopts both styles (Judge & Piccolo, 2004). If no one was minding the day-to-day operation of an organization or people were not being rewarded for meeting short-term objectives, the organization would suffer. At the same time, it is important to have a charismatic leader who inspires people to think about long-term objectives.

THE RIGHT PERSON IN THE RIGHT SITUATION As you know by now, one of the most important tenets of social psychology is that, to understand behavior, it is not enough to consider personality alone—we must take the situation into account as well. For example, a business leader can be highly successful in some situations but not in others. Consider the late Steve Jobs, who, at age 21, founded Apple Computer with Stephen Wozniak. Jobs was anything but a traditional suit-and-tie corporate leader; he turned to computers only after experimenting with LSD, traveling to India, and living on a communal fruit farm. In the days when there were no personal computers, Jobs's offbeat style was well suited to starting a new industry. Indeed, within 5 years, he had become the leader of a billion-dollar company.

But Jobs's unorthodox style was ill suited to managing a large corporation in a competitive market. Apple's earnings began to suffer, and in 1985 Jobs was forced out. Undeterred, Jobs cofounded Pixar in 1986, the first major company to make computer-generated animation, and then sold it to the Disney Company in 2006 for $7.4 billion. And in the 1990s, Apple faced some of the same technological challenges it had at its inception, needing to revamp the operating system for its Macintosh computers and regain market share. Whom did Apple hire to lead this new challenge? Jobs, of course, whose ability to think creatively and inspire his workforce to take risks made him the right person to lead these companies in times when a new direction was called for.

A comprehensive theory of leadership thus needs to focus on the characteristics of the leader, the followers, and the situation. The best-known theory of this type is the **contingency theory of leadership**, which argues that leadership effectiveness depends both on how task oriented or relationship oriented the leader is and on the amount of control and influence the leader has over the group (Fiedler, 1967; Yukl,

Transactional Leaders

Leaders who set clear, short-term goals and reward people who meet them

Transformational Leaders

Leaders who inspire followers to focus on common, long-term goals

Contingency Theory of Leadership

The idea that the effectiveness of a leader depends both on how task- or relationship-oriented the leader is and on the amount of control the leader has over the group

What determines whether someone, such as Martin Luther King, Jr., is a great leader? Is it a certain constellation of personality traits, or is it necessary to have the right person in the right situation at the right time?

Figure 9.6 Fiedler's Contingency Theory of Leadership

According to Fiedler, task-oriented leaders perform best when situational control is high or low, whereas relationship-oriented leaders perform best when situational control is moderate.

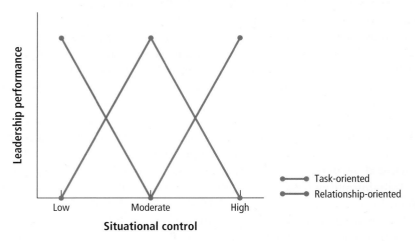

Task-Oriented Leaders

Leaders who are concerned more with getting the job done than with workers' feelings and relationships

Relationship-Oriented Leaders

Leaders who are concerned more with workers' feelings and relationships

2011). There are basically two kinds of leaders, the theory argues: **task-oriented leaders**, who are concerned more with getting the job done than with workers' feelings and relationships, and **relationship-oriented leaders**, who are concerned more with workers' feelings and relationships.

Task-oriented leaders do well in *high-control work situations*, when the leader's position in the company is clearly perceived as powerful and the work needing to be done by the group is structured and well defined (e.g., a corporate manager with control over each worker's performance review and merit raise). They also do well in *low-control work situations*, when the leader is not perceived as powerful and the work needing to be done is not clearly defined (e.g., the supervisor of a newly formed group of volunteers). What about relationship-oriented leaders? They are most effective in *moderate-control work situations*. Under these conditions, the wheels are turning fairly smoothly, but important work still needs to be done; the leader who can promote strong relations between individual employees will be the most successful (see Figure 9.6). The contingency theory of leadership has been supported in studies of numerous types of leaders, including business managers, college administrators, and military commanders (Ayman, 2002; Chemers, 2000; Lord et al., 2017).

GENDER AND LEADERSHIP The U.S. workforce today is approximately half female. But are women as likely as men to become leaders in business, politics, and other organizations? Not yet, but this is changing. The barriers between women and high-level advancement are breaking down, with one vivid example being Hillary Clinton's historic run in 2016. Still, there is work to be done. In 2016, only 21 of the chief executive officers of *Fortune 500* companies were women, and the boards of directors of U.S. companies included only 15% women (Catalyst, 2017). Things are not much different elsewhere. That 15% figure is actually among the highest in the world; among the few countries with higher rates include Norway (47%), Sweden (34%), France (34%), and Australia (23%). Taiwan (5%), South Korea (4%), and Japan (4%) came in at the low end of this survey. One reason why it is difficult for women to achieve leadership positions is that many people believe that good leaders have *agentic* traits (e.g., assertive, controlling, dominant, independent), which are traditionally associated with men. In contrast, women are stereotypically expected to be more

If women seeking leadership roles conform to society's expectations about how they ought to behave, by being warm and communal, they are often perceived as having low leadership potential. If they become leaders and act in ways that leaders are expected to act—namely, in agentic, forceful ways—they are often perceived negatively.

communal (e.g., concerned with the welfare of others, warm, helpful, affectionate). Thus, if women behave in the way they are "supposed" to behave, they are often viewed as having less leadership potential. But if women succeed in attaining a leadership position and act in ways that leaders are expected to act—namely, in agentic, forceful fashion—they are criticized for not "acting like a woman should" (Brescoll, Dawson, & Uhlmann, 2010; Eagly & Karau, 2002; Koenig et al., 2011).

Here's another danger that women leaders face: Because they are perceived as being more communal, they are often thought to be better at managing crises, particularly ones involving interpersonal conflicts. That might seem like a good thing—trusting women leaders to solve problems—but it has a downside in which women are more likely to be put in precarious, high-risk positions where it is difficult to succeed. Michelle Ryan and her colleagues have called this a "glass cliff" (Ryan et al., 2008, 2011). Even when women have broken through the "glass ceiling" into top leadership positions, they are more likely than men to be put in charge of units that are in crisis and in which the risk of failure is high. Ryan and her colleagues found this to be true in studies of hiring in real-world companies as well as in controlled laboratory studies in which people read descriptions of companies and recommended people for leadership positions. Participants were more likely to recommend a woman when an organizational unit was in crisis and a man when the unit was running smoothly—tendencies that make it more likely that women will fail in their leadership positions.

The better news is that prejudice against women leaders appears to be lessening over time. In a Gallup poll conducted in 1953, 66% of people said that they preferred a man as a boss, and only 5% preferred a woman (25% had no preference). In a similar poll conducted in 2011, 32% preferred a man as a boss, 22% preferred a woman, and 46% had no preference. Further, there is some evidence that people are becoming more accepting of women who act in stereotypically "male" ways (Twenge, 1997) and that there is a growing recognition that effective leaders must be able to act in communal as well as agentic ways (Eagly & Karau, 2002; Koenig et al., 2011).

In 2012, Yahoo hired Marissa Mayer (*left*) as its new CEO, hoping she could turn around its sagging fortunes as an internet portal that was quickly being left behind in an era of social media, mobile apps, and, of course, Google. Two years later, in 2014, Mary Barra (*right*) became the first female CEO of a major global automaker, in this case General Motors. Within months, she had to announce a recall of more than 11 million cars due to defective design components that the company had known about for a decade. Both Meyer and Barra seemed prime candidates to be women who broke through a "glass ceiling" only to find themselves on a "glass cliff." Meyer recently stepped down, with Yahoo still struggling, though its stock value soared during her time with the company. Barra, however, continues to enjoy what has been, by most metrics, a highly successful tenure at the helm of GM.

CULTURE AND LEADERSHIP   Most research on leadership has been conducted in Western countries; thus, the question arises as to how much the results apply to leadership in other cultures. For this reason, researchers have recently turned their attention to the kinds of traits people value in leaders and actual leadership styles in different cultures (Aktas, Gelfand, & Hanges, 2016; Aycan et al., 2013; Eagly & Chin, 2010). One ambitious study examined leadership practices and attitudes toward leaders in 62 different countries. The researchers gave questionnaires to 17,000 managers in 951 organizations in those countries, conducted extensive interviews, convened group discussions, and analyzed media content in each country. Not surprisingly, different cultures valued different traits in leaders. For example, autonomous leadership, defined as being independent of one's superiors and spending a lot of time working alone, was valued more in Europe than in Latin America. But there was universal agreement about the value of two leadership qualities: charisma and being team oriented (House et al., 2004). Questions about cultural differences in leadership are receiving increasing attention because in a global economy, work groups are becoming more diverse and managers from different cultures have increasingly frequent contact.

Review Questions

1. Which of the following is *not* an example of process loss?
   a. Transactive memory
   b. Group polarization
   c. Failure to share uniquely held information
   d. Groupthink

2. One step that can be taken to reduce the likelihood of groupthink is
   a. putting in place a strong, directive group leader.
   b. taking group votes aloud rather than relying on secret ballot or other anonymous methods.
   c. creating subgroups that meet on their own first before reconvening and sharing the content of their discussions with the group at large.
   d. emphasizing the importance of being unanimous.

3. Walt, Jesse, Mike, and Gus are business partners trying to decide whether they should invest in a risky new direction for their company. Jesse gets the feeling that his partners are leaning toward the risky option. To convince his partners that he is a valued member of the company and a "good" group member, Jesse speaks up in strong, public terms in favor of the risky decision, and he leaves the meeting even more convinced than he was before that they should take the risk. Jesse's personal shift in the risky direction illustrates the _____ explanation for group polarization.
   a. social comparison
   b. counterattitudinal
   c. persuasive arguments
   d. social facilitation

4. Research on personality type and leadership indicates that
   a. the great person theory is the best explanation for leadership success.
   b. people of all different personality types can become successful leaders.
   c. the most successful U.S. presidents (as rated by historians) tended to share major personality traits, such as extraversion, openness to new experience, and empathy.
   d. most successful leaders embrace agentic traits but avoid communal traits.

5. A _____ leader is one who sets clear, short-term goals and rewards people for meeting them.
   a. contingent
   b. transformational
   c. communal
   d. transactional

Conflict and Cooperation

LO 9.4   **Summarize the factors that determine whether individual and group conflict will escalate or be resolved.**

We have already examined how people work together to make decisions; in these situations, group members have a common goal. Often, however, people have incompatible goals, placing them in conflict with each other. This can be true of two individuals, such as domestic partners who disagree about who should clean the kitchen, or two groups, such as a labor union and company management who disagree over wages and working conditions. It can also be true of nations. Indeed, the opportunity for interpersonal conflict exists whenever two or more people interact. Sigmund Freud (1930) went so far as to argue that conflict is an inevitable by-product of civilization because the goals and needs of individuals often clash with the goals and needs of their fellow human beings. The nature of conflict and how it can be resolved has been the topic of a great deal of social psychological research (Cohen & Insko, 2008; De Dreu, 2014; Thibaut & Kelley, 1959).

Many conflicts are resolved peacefully, with little rancor. Couples often find a way to resolve their differences in a mutually acceptable manner, and labor disputes are sometimes settled with a handshake. All too often, however, conflict erupts into open hostilities. The divorce rate in the United States remains high. People sometimes resort to violence to resolve their differences. Warfare between nations remains an all-too-common solution to international disputes. Obviously, it is of great importance to find ways of resolving conflicts peacefully.

Sometimes people are able to resolve conflicts peacefully, such as a couple that works out its differences or even has an amicable divorce. At other times conflicts escalate into rancor and violence. Social psychologists have performed experiments to test ways in which conflict resolution is most likely to occur.

Social Dilemmas

One of the reasons why we have conflicts in the first place is because very often, what is best for an individual is not always best for the group as a whole. Consider a recent venture from the Panera restaurant chain. A few years ago, they began opening Panera Cares restaurants, which look and operate like other Paneras except for one thing: People aren't required to pay anything. There are suggested prices for all menu items, but customers are allowed to pay whatever they want. The chief executive officer and founder of the restaurant chain, Ronald Shaich, had a vision in which people in need could come get a good meal and pay what they could afford; the costs would be offset, he anticipated, by customers who could afford to pay more than the suggested prices.

Panera has devised a classic **social dilemma**, a conflict in which the most beneficial action for an individual will, if chosen by most people, be harmful to everyone (Van Lange et al., 2013; Wang et al., 2017; Weber, Kopelman, & Messick, 2004). It is to any individual's financial advantage to eat at Panera Cares free of charge and let other people worry about paying. However, if too many people take this approach, everyone will lose because the restaurant will not remain solvent and will eventually have to close.

In the first years of the Panera Cares experiment, about three in five people paid the suggested prices, one in five paid less, and one in five paid more. Some customers did take advantage of the system, such as three college students who paid $3 for a $40 meal simply because they felt like it. Of course, Panera's hope was that enough people would pay more than the suggested price to offset those who pay less. The verdict on Panera Cares has been a mixed one: three of the first five stores closed their doors, with those in Boston and St. Louis continuing to operate. What is it that determines whether people respond selfishly or selflessly in social dilemmas such as this one? Social psychologists have attempted to find out by studying such conflicts experimentally, testing both their causes and resolutions in the laboratory.

One of the most common ways of studying social dilemmas uses of a set-up referred to as the "prisoner's dilemma." This curious name derives from a scenario in which two (literal) partners in crime have been captured by police and are being held separately. Both criminals—let's call them Piper and Alex—are offered the

Social Dilemma

A conflict in which the most beneficial action for an individual will, if chosen by most people, have harmful effects on everyone

same deal: betray your partner and confess to the crime, and you'll receive a lighter sentence. The dilemma is that the precise sentence that both criminals receive depends on what their partner chooses to do. If they both decide to keep quiet, remaining loyal to each other, the police only have enough evidence to send them to prison for a short time. If they both betray each other, their sentence will be a bit longer. Easy choice, right? It seems like they should both keep quiet. But not so fast … if Piper keeps quiet but Alex confesses? Alex goes free while Piper serves the maximum sentence. And if Piper confesses but Alex keeps quiet? Then Piper goes free and Alex serves a long prison stint.

Luckily for research participants, psychologists have figured out laboratory variations on the prisoner's dilemma that do not involve the risk of jail time. In these studies, two players have to choose one of two options without knowing what the other player will choose. The number of points they win depends on the options chosen by both people. Suppose that you were playing the game with a friend. As shown in the following Try It! exercise, you have to choose Option X or Option Y. Just like it was for Piper and Alex, your payoff—in this case, the amount of money you win or lose—also depends on the choices made by your friend. For example, if both of you choose Option X, you both win $3. If, however, you choose Option Y and your friend chooses Option X, you win $6 and your friend loses $6. Which option would you choose, knowing that you won't find out what your partner chooses until afterward?

Option Y frequently seems like the safest choice in scenarios such as this one (Rapoport & Chammah, 1965). The dilemma is that both players may come to think this way, ensuring that both sides lose out on a potential payday. People's actions in these games seem to mirror many conflicts in everyday life. To find a solution desirable to both parties, people must trust each other. Often they do not, and this lack of trust leads to an escalating series of competitive moves so that in the end no one wins (Insko & Schopler, 1998; Kelley & Thibaut, 1978; Lount et al., 2008). Two countries locked in a weapons race, for example, may feel that they cannot afford to disarm out of fear that the other side will take advantage of their weakened position. The result is that both sides add furiously to their stockpile of weapons, neither gaining superiority and both spending money they could use to solve domestic problems instead

Try It!

The Prisoner's Dilemma

Your Friend's Options	Your Options	
	Option X	**Option Y**
Option X	You win $3 Your friend wins $3	You win $6 Your friend loses $6
Option Y	You lose $6 Your friend wins $6	You lose $1 Your friend loses $1

Play this version of the prisoner's dilemma game with a friend. First, show the table to the friend and explain how the game works: On each trial, you and your friend can choose Option X or Option Y, without knowing what the other will choose. You should each write your choice on folded pieces of paper that are opened at the same time. The numbers in the table represent imaginary money that you and your friend win or lose on each trial. For example, if you choose Option X on the first trial and your friend chooses Option Y, you lose an imaginary $6 and your friend wins an imaginary $6. If both of you choose Option Y, you both lose an imaginary $1. Play the game for 10 trials and keep track of how much each of you wins or loses. Did you and your friend choose the cooperative option (Option X) or the competitive option (Option Y) more often? Why? Did a pattern of trust or mistrust develop over the course of the game?

(Deutsch, 1973). Such an escalation of conflict is also seen all too often among couples who are divorcing. Sometimes the goal seems more to hurt the other person than to further one's own needs (or the children's). In the end, everyone suffers because, metaphorically speaking, both sides choose Option Y too often.

INCREASING COOPERATION IN THE PRISONER'S DILEMMA Such escalating conflict, though common, is not inevitable. Many studies have found that when people play the prisoner's dilemma game, they will, under certain conditions, adopt the more cooperative response (Option X), ensuring that both sides end up with a positive outcome. Not surprisingly, if people are playing the game with a friend or a partner with whom they expect to interact in the future, they are more likely to adopt a cooperative strategy that maximizes everyone's profits (Cohen & Insko, 2008; Grueneisen & Tomasello, 2017).

Subtly changing the norms about what kind of behavior is expected can also have large effects on how cooperative people are. One study found that simply changing the name of a game from the "Wall Street Game" to the "Community Game" increased the percentage of people who played cooperatively from 33% to 71% (Liberman et al., 2004). Another study, conducted with Chinese college students in Hong Kong, found that showing people symbols of Chinese culture before the game (e.g., a Chinese dragon) made people more cooperative, whereas showing people symbols of American culture (e.g., an American flag) made them more competitive (Wong & Hong, 2005).

Another option is the **tit-for-tat strategy**, a way of encouraging cooperation by at first acting cooperatively but then always responding the way your opponent did (cooperatively or competitively) in the previous trial. This strategy communicates a willingness to cooperate and an unwillingness to sit back and be exploited if the partner is selfish. The tit-for-tat strategy is often successful in getting the other person to respond with a trusting response (Klapwijk & Van Lange, 2009; Leite, 2011; Wubben, De Cremer, & van Dijk, 2009). Using this tactic in the arms race would mean matching not only any military buildup made by an unfriendly nation but also any conciliatory gestures, such as a ban on nuclear testing.

And one more proven strategy is to allow individuals rather than opposing groups to resolve a conflict. Two individuals who play the prisoner's dilemma are more likely to cooperate with each other than two groups who play the same game (Schopler & Insko, 1999). As discussed in Chapter 8, being in a group can be deindividuating; you also know now that groups produce more extreme and polarized attitudes. As a result of these phenomena, when two rival groups distrust each other, sometimes single representatives from each side are better able to bridge that gap and foster communication and negotiation. In short, social dilemmas have been the subject of a great deal of psychological research, though it is worth noting that not all of it has focused on the prisoner's dilemma. See the photo gallery on the next page for examples of social dilemmas based on management of shared resources.

Tit-for-Tat Strategy

A means of encouraging cooperation by at first acting cooperatively but then always responding the way your opponent did (cooperatively or competitively) on the previous trial

Using Threats to Resolve Conflict

When involved in a conflict, many of us are tempted to use threats to get the other party to cave to our wishes, believing that we should, in the words of Teddy Roosevelt, "speak softly and carry a big stick." Parents commonly use threats to get their children to behave, and teachers often threaten their students with detention or a visit to the principal. Threats are commonly used on an international scale as well to further the interests of one nation over another (Turner & Horvitz, 2001).

A classic series of studies by Morton Deutsch and Robert Krauss (1960, 1962) indicates that threats are not an effective means of reducing conflict. These researchers developed a game in which two participants imagined that they were in charge of trucking companies named Acme and Bolt. The goal of each company was to transport merchandise as quickly as possible to a destination. The participants were paid 60 cents for each "trip" but had 1 cent subtracted for every second it took them. The most direct route for each company was over a one-lane road that only one truck could travel

RESOURCE DILEMMAS

The prisoner's dilemma is not the only type of challenging social dilemma. Resource dilemmas involve shared use of a limited, finite resource. As with the prisoner's dilemma, an individual who opts for the selfish course of action stands to benefit, but if too few people cooperate, everyone will suffer the consequences.

Consider, for example, the tale of the tragedy of the commons, in which villagers sharing a common piece of grassy land are each allowed to place a certain number of cattle to graze there. Of course, by sneaking an extra animal or two onto the commons to eat, a villager could receive personal benefit—more (and fatter) cows! But if everyone does this, the grass will be gone and there won't be enough food for any cows (or, eventually, for the villagers).

One form of resource dilemma is when individuals use too much of a resource too quickly. Yet another is when not enough people contribute to a replenishable resource. If not enough individuals donate blood, there will not be enough supply when an emergency hits; if not enough individuals contribute taxes, infrastructure crumbles and people everywhere will suffer.

Many of the strategies reviewed in this chapter can help promote cooperation in resource dilemmas. Yet another possibility is to create a regulatory entity with the authority to sanction those who run afoul of pro-social, cooperative behavior. For example, the U.S. Environmental Protection Agency can levy large fines against corporations that violate national environmental standards.

at a time, which placed the two companies in direct conflict, as seen in Figure 9.7. If Acme and Bolt both tried to take the one-lane road, neither truck could pass, and both would lose money. Each company could take an alternate route, but this was much longer, guaranteeing that they would lose at least 10 cents per trial. After a while, most

Figure 9.7 The Deutsch and Krauss Trucking Game

Deutsch and Krauss (1962) studied cooperation (and the lack thereof) by asking participants to play a trucking game. In the game, players earned money by driving from one point to another as quickly as possible. As in the image below, the shortest route required crossing a one-lane road, but both companies could not use this road at the same time. When players were given gates they could use to restrict the other player's use of the one-lane road, both companies made even less money.

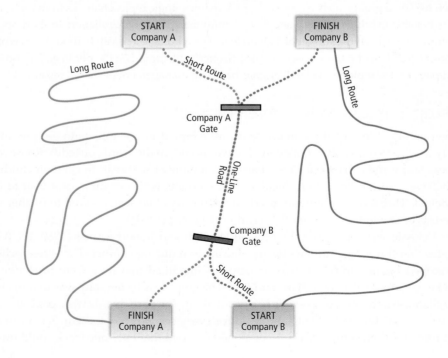

participants worked out a solution that allowed both trucks to make a modest amount of money, taking turns waiting for the other party to cross the one-lane road.

In another variation, the researchers gave Acme a gate that could be lowered over the one-lane road, thereby blocking Bolt from using that route. You might think that using force—the gate—would increase Acme's profits because all Acme had to do was to threaten Bolt to "stay off the one-lane road or else." In fact, the opposite happened. When one side had a gate, both participants lost more money than when neither side had a gate. Bolt did not like being threatened and often retaliated by parking its truck on the one-lane road, blocking the Acme truck's progress. Meanwhile, seconds ticked away, and both sides lost money. What happened when the situation was more equitable, with both sides having gates? Surely they would learn to cooperate then, recognizing the stalemate that would ensue if both of them used their gates—right? To the contrary, both sides lost even *more* money in the bilateral threat condition. Here, the owners of both trucking companies threatened to use their gates and did so with great frequency.

EFFECTS OF COMMUNICATION   There is an important way, however, in which the trucking game does not approximate real life: The two sides were not allowed to communicate with each other. Would the adversaries have worked out their differences if they could have talked them over? To find out, Deutsch and Krauss ran a version of their study in which the participants were required to communicate through an intercom on every trial. Alas, requiring people to communicate did not raise profits dramatically. Why not?

The problem with the communication in the trucking studies is that it did not foster trust. In fact, people used the opportunity to threaten each other. Krauss and Deutsch examined this tendency in yet another version of their study in which they specifically instructed people on how to communicate, telling them to work out a solution that was fair to both parties (i.e., one that they would be willing to accept if they were in the other person's shoes). Under these conditions, verbal communication did increase the amount of money both sides won because it fostered trust instead of adding fuel to the competitive fires (Deutsch, 1973; Deutsch, Coleman, & Marcus, 2011; Krauss & Deutsch, 1966).

Negotiation and Bargaining

In the laboratory games we have discussed so far, people's options are limited. They have to choose Option X or Y in the prisoner's dilemma, and they have only a couple of ways of getting their truck to its destination. In everyday life, we often have a wide array of options. Consider two people haggling over the price of a car. Both the buyer and the seller can give in to all of the other's demands, to some of them, or to none of them. Either party can walk away from the deal at any time. Given that there is considerable latitude in how people can resolve the conflict, communication between the parties becomes all the more important. By talking, bargaining, and negotiating, people can arrive at a satisfactory settlement. **Negotiation** is a form of communication between opposing sides in a conflict in which offers and counteroffers are made and a solution occurs only when both parties agree (Menon, Sheldon, & Galinsky, 2014; Thompson, Wang, & Gunia, 2010). How successful are people at negotiating mutually beneficial solutions?

One limit to successful negotiation is that people often assume that they are locked in a conflict in which only one party can come out ahead. They don't realize that a solution favorable to both parties is available. A couple getting a divorce, for example, might find it impossible to reach a financial settlement until they realize that they have different priorities. Perhaps it is most important to one person to keep the furniture and the baseball season tickets, whereas the other wants the fancy china and the vintage collection of vinyl records. This type of compromise, called an **integrative solution**, is an outcome to a conflict whereby the parties make trade-offs on issues according to their different interests; each side concedes the most on issues that are unimportant to it but are important to the other side.

It might seem that such integrative solutions would be easy to achieve. After all, the two parties simply have to sit down and figure out which issues are the most important to

Negotiation

A form of communication between opposing sides in a conflict in which offers and counteroffers are made and a solution occurs only when both parties agree

Integrative Solution

A solution to a conflict whereby the parties make trade-offs on issues, with each side conceding the most on issues that are unimportant to it but important to the other side

Neutral mediators often help solve labor disputes, legal battles, and divorce proceedings. Mediators can be in a better position to recognize that there are mutually agreeable solutions to a conflict.

each. However, people often find it difficult to identify integrative solutions (Moran & Ritov, 2007; Thompson, 1997). For example, the more people have at stake in a negotiation, the more biased their perceptions of their opponent. They will tend to distrust proposals made by the other side and to overlook interests they have in common (Kong, Dirks, & Ferrin, 2014; O'Connor & Carnevale, 1997). This is one reason why people often use neutral mediators to solve labor disputes, legal battles, and divorce proceedings: Mediators are often in a better position to recognize that there are mutually agreeable solutions to a conflict (Kressel & Pruitt, 1989; Ross & LaCroix, 1996; Wall & Dunne, 2012).

The *style* of communication is also critical to developing trust during negotiation (Rosette et al., 2012). It appears that trust is more easily established in old-fashioned face-to-face negotiations than in electronic communications such as e-mail, texting, and videoconferencing. The modern techniques have many advantages, of course, but one disadvantage is that it is harder to get to know people and learn to trust them. A meta-analysis of several studies found that negotiations conducted over electronic media were more hostile and resulted in lower profits than face-to-face negotiations (Stuhlmacher & Citera, 2005).

The bottom line? When you are negotiating with someone, it is important to keep in mind that integrative solutions are often available. Try to gain the other side's trust, communicate your own interests in an open manner and try taking the other person's perspective (Trötschel et al, 2011). Remember that the way you construe the situation is not necessarily the same as the way the other party construes it. You may well discover that the other side communicates its interests more freely as a result, increasing the likelihood that you will find a solution beneficial to both parties.

Review Questions

1. When it comes to social dilemmas,
   a. an individual who adopts a cooperative strategy will always be more profitable than one who is selfish.
   b. the most beneficial course of action for an individual will, if chosen by most people, be harmful to all in the long run.
   c. one always has to win, and one side always has to lose.
   d. laboratory studies cannot be useful in understanding the escalation and persistence of group conflicts.

2. Consider the prisoner's dilemma. You will receive the worst possible outcome for yourself as an individual if
   a. you are cooperative and so is your partner.
   b. you are cooperative but your partner is selfish.
   c. you are selfish and so is your partner.
   d. you are selfish but your partner is cooperative.

3. Two fishing companies, Hufflepuff and Ravenclaw, use the same body of water to catch fish. Both companies are considering building dams that would allow them to cut off the water supply and prevent the other company from fishing. Research on the power of threats indicates that if both companies build a dam and gain the ability to prevent the other from fishing,
   a. conflict will decrease because each side has equal threat capacity.
   b. conflict will increase because each side has equal threat capacity.
   c. conflict will increase slightly, but not as much as it would if only one side built a dam and had threat capacity.
   d. conflict will increase, but only if communication between the two companies is prevented.

4. A(n) _____ solution is an outcome to a negotiation in which each side concedes on issues that are unimportant to it but are important to the other side.
   a. tit-for-tat   b. transactive
   c. integrative   d. communal

5. According to Sigmund Freud, _____ is an inevitable by-product of civilization.
   a. negotiation   b. cooperation
   c. conflict   d. psychology

Summary

LO 9.1 **Explain what groups are and why people join them.**

- **What Is a Group?** A *group* consists of two or more (usually more) people who interact with each other and are interdependent.

  - **Why Do People Join Groups?** The *need to belong* to groups may be innate. Groups also allow us to accomplish difficult objectives, serve as a source of information about the social world, and are an important part of our social identities. People are sensitive to rejection from groups and do what they can to avoid it. Groups also make people feel distinctive from members of other groups.

  - **The Composition and Functions of Groups** Groups tend to consist of homogeneous members, in part because groups have *social norms* that people are expected to obey. Groups also have well-defined social roles, shared expectations about how people are supposed to behave. People can get so far into a social role that their personal identities and personalities get lost. Group cohesiveness, qualities of a group that bind members together and promote liking between members, is another important property of groups that influences the group's performance. So does a group's composition, with diversity sometimes negatively associated with group morale but positively associated with a range of performance outcomes.

LO 9.2 **Describe how individuals perform differently when others are around.**

- **Individual Behavior in a Group Setting** Research has compared the performance of people who are by themselves versus in groups.

  - **Social Facilitation: When the Presence of Others Energizes Us** When people's individual efforts on a task can be evaluated, the mere presence of others leads to social facilitation: Their performance is enhanced on simple tasks but impaired on complex tasks.

  - **Social Loafing: When the Presence of Others Relaxes Us** When people's individual efforts *cannot* be evaluated, the mere presence of others leads to relaxation and social loafing: Performance is impaired on simple or unimportant tasks but enhanced on complex tasks.

  - **Gender and Cultural Differences in Social Loafing: Who Slacks Off the Most?** Social loafing is more prevalent among men than women and more prevalent in Western than Asian cultures.

- **Deindividuation: Getting Lost in the Crowd** The mere presence of others can also lead to more serious consequences such as deindividuation, the loosening of normal constraints on behavior when people are in crowds.

LO 9.3 **Compare the decision-making outcomes of individuals versus groups, and explain the impact of leadership in group outcomes.**

- **Group Decisions: Are Two (or More) Heads Better Than One?** Research has compared how people make decisions when they are by themselves versus in groups.

  - **Process Loss: When Group Interactions Inhibit Good Problem Solving** Groups make better decisions than individuals if they are good at pooling independent ideas and listening to the expert members of the group. Often, however, process loss occurs, which is any aspect of group interaction that inhibits good decision making. For example, groups often focus on the information they have in common and fail to share unique information. Tightly knit, cohesive groups are also prone to groupthink, which occurs when maintaining group cohesiveness and solidarity becomes more important than considering the facts in a realistic manner.

  - **Group Polarization: Going to Extremes** Group polarization causes individuals to become more extreme in their attitudes than they were before group discussions; in this manner, group decisions can be more risky or more cautious than individual decisions, depending on which direction the individual members were initially leaning.

  - **Leadership in Groups** There is little support for the great person theory, which argues that good leadership is a matter of having the right personality traits. Leaders adopt specific kinds of leadership styles, such as transactional or transformational. Leadership effectiveness is a function of both the kind of person a leader is and the nature of the work situation. Although strides have been made, women are still underrepresented in leadership positions. Women who become leaders often face a "glass cliff" whereby they are put in charge of work units that are in crisis and in which the risk of failure is high. Further, there is a double bind for women leaders: If they conform to societal expectations about how they ought to behave, by being warm and communal, they are often perceived as having low leadership potential. If they succeed in attaining a leadership position and act in ways that leaders are expected to act—namely, in agentic, forceful ways—they are often perceived negatively for not "acting like a woman should."

LO 9.4 Summarize the factors that determine whether individual and group conflict will escalate or be resolved.

• **Conflict and Cooperation** Research has examined how people resolve conflicts when they have incompatible goals.

  • **Social Dilemmas** These occur when the most beneficial action for an individual will, if chosen by most people, have harmful effects for everyone. A commonly studied social dilemma is the prisoner's dilemma, in which two people must decide whether to look out for only their own interests or for their partner's interests as well. Creating trust is crucial in solving this kind of conflict, and a variety of situational factors can render individual cooperation more likely.

  • **Using Threats to Resolve Conflict** Research has found that using threats tends to escalate rather than resolve conflicts, even more so when both sides have equal threat capacity.

  • **Negotiation and Bargaining** When two sides are negotiating and bargaining, it is important to look for an integrative solution whereby each side concedes the most on issues that are unimportant to it but are important to its adversary.

Revel Interactive

Shared Writing   What Do You Think?

Why might deindividuation be particularly likely to occur in an online situation? How can websites prevent it from occurring?

Test Yourself

1. Why are groups often homogeneous (comprised of members who are alike in age, sex, beliefs, and opinions)?

  a. People who are already similar to each tend to be drawn to joining the same groups.

  b. Evolutionary pressures caused people with similar genes to join groups and people with dissimilar genes to avoid each other.

  c. Groups are more productive when they are homogeneous.

  d. Social loafing prevents us from seeking out new people and experiences.

2. Group cohesiveness is best defined as

  a. shared expectations in a group about how people are supposed to behave.

  b. qualities that bind members together and promote liking between members.

  c. expectations about the roles and behaviors of men and women.

  d. the tendency for people to do better on simple tasks and worse on complex tasks in the presence of others.

3. You are trying to decide whether to take a test in a lecture hall where you will be surrounded by lots of other people or in a room by yourself. Assuming that you have studied well for the test and find the material to be easy, you will perform best on the test in the _____ because it will result in _____.

  a. room by yourself; social loafing

  b. room by yourself; social facilitation

  c. lecture hall; social loafing

  d. lecture hall; social facilitation

4. The tendency to engage in social loafing is stronger in _____; it is also stronger in _____.

  a. men than women; Asian cultures than Western cultures

  b. women than men; Asian cultures than Western cultures

  c. men than women; Western cultures than Asian cultures

  d. women than men; Western cultures than Asian cultures

5. On his way back from class, Sanjeev encounters an angry mob ready to storm the dining hall to demand better food. Sanjeev likes the food as it is and wants to stop the mob. What would be the most effective solution?

   a. Increasing group cohesiveness by inviting the entire mob to his house for tea

   b. Passing out blue shirts for everyone to wear

   c. Reducing process loss in the group by making sure that its most expert members have the most influence

   d. Finding a friend in the group, calling out her name, and talking to her loudly in front of everyone

6. Four psychology students working on a group project together are trying to figure out how they should avoid groupthink when making decisions about their project. Which of these ideas would be the *least* helpful?

   a. Bonding by going to see a movie together before starting the project

   b. Assigning each group member to be responsible for a different chapter in their textbook so that they cover all the details

   c. Having a student who is not in their group review the project

   d. Designating a leader to oversee the project, one who is nondirective and encourages people to give honest feedback

7. Jim and Pam, a married couple, are buying a house and have narrowed their choice down to two options. Jim remembers that one house had a beautiful kitchen; Pam, however, remembers that there were roaches in the broom closet. By sharing this information with each other, Pam and Jim are using _____ to avoid _____.

   a. mindguards; groupthink

   b. social roles; deindividuation

   c. transactive memory; process loss

   d. subgroups; group polarization

8. Which of the following is most likely to lead to process loss in a committee?

   a. All members of the committee listen carefully to each other's opinions.

   b. The committee members are good friends and have known each other for years.

   c. Individual committee members share information that others lack.

   d. The most competent member on any given topic feels free to speak up.

9. Which of the following is true about research on leadership?

   a. Female leaders are more likely than male leaders to be put in precarious, high-risk positions where it is difficult to succeed.

   b. The best leaders are just born that way.

   c. People in all cultures value the same traits in leaders.

   d. If a woman succeeds in becoming a leader of an organization and acts in an agentic way, she is evaluated in the same way that male leaders are.

10. When is communication most effective for resolving conflict?

   a. When people communicate through electronic means (e.g., over e-mail)

   b. When it is required

   c. When the stakes are high and both sides of a conflict have the ability to issue threats

   d. When a mediator is used

Chapter 10
Attraction and Relationships
From Initial Impressions to Long-Term Intimacy

 ## Chapter Outline and Learning Objectives

WHAT DO YOU THINK?

Survey	What Do You Think?
SURVEY	**RESULTS**

Have you ever dated, hooked-up with, or had a relationship with someone you first met online or using a mobile app?

○ Yes

○ No

Janie Egan and Chris George are both huge basketball fans. So it comes as no surprise to friends who know the young couple that their first date was going to see second-round NCAA tournament games in nearby Salt Lake City. Janie had gotten tickets from a friend and, in an emoji-filled texting session, she convinced Chris to change his existing plans and go watch basketball with her instead. In truth, it didn't take that much convincing. Two days later they returned to the same arena to see third-round games. Within 7 months they were engaged.

There was one bump in the road of this whirlwind romance, however. The first time Chris met Janie's dad, he lied to the man who would eventually become his father-in-law. In fact, Janie asked him to. Because there was one aspect about the past that Janie wanted Chris to hide at all costs from her own parents. One skeleton in Chris's closet that she thought would be too much for her father to bear. What was it that Janie asked Chris to keep secret from her family? That the couple had met on Tinder.

Tinder is a mobile app that "hooks people up." A Tinder user is shown a series of photos of other users. You simply "swipe" your screen to the right for someone you might be interested in; you "swipe" left if you're not interested. Meanwhile, other users in your area are seeing your photo as well, and if someone whom you've right-swiped does the same to you, the app notifies you both of the match. Whether, where, and how far you take things from there is then up to the two of you.

Chris and Janie aren't the only couple out there to have met on Tinder. According to the app's website, by early 2017, 26 million matches were offered to users per day—the result of 1.6 billion daily swipes—with more than 20 billion matches across more than 190 countries since its inception. Still, Janie didn't want her parents to know any of this. It wasn't that they wouldn't understand what Tinder was. Quite the contrary: they were all too familiar with the app. They had been on her case for how much time she spent on it, and they didn't care for some of the other men she had met while using it. Indeed, when Chris showed up to the house that night for their first date, Janie's dad greeted him with, "You aren't one of those Tinder boys, are you?" And so, heeding the warnings of the woman who would one day become his wife, the very first words Chris uttered to his future father-in-law were a lie: "No, sir." Janie and Chris have since come clean with Mr. Egan. With the whole world, in fact, via their blog titled "Right Swiped: The Ultimate Tinder Success Story."

As the couple's backstory illustrates, attraction takes many forms and emerges from many places. A college dormitory or party. Happy hour at the local bar. A library, the gym, a work meeting, the grocery store … and, increasingly these days, online, whether in the form of dating websites—like OkCupid, Match.com, or eHarmony—or mobile apps like Tinder, Grindr, Hinge, PlentyOfFish, and others. Clearly, interpersonal attraction is something that's often on our minds (and tablets and phones). And like much of human nature, it can also be studied scientifically.

This is a good thing, because many of our assumptions about attraction and falling in love turn out to be false. One example is the belief that opposites attract: Research offers the clear conclusion that similarity is a stronger predictor of who we're drawn to (Heine, Foster, & Spina, 2009; West et al., 2014). How about the idea that women are pickier than men in selecting mates? This is often true, but not for the reasons you might assume (Finkel & Eastwick, 2009). In this chapter, we will explore what makes us feel attracted to other people, whether as friends or lovers, and how relationships develop and progress, both face-to-face and online.

What Predicts Attraction?

LO 10.1   Describe how people decide whom they like and want to get to know better.

When social psychologist Ellen Berscheid asked people of various ages what made them happy, at or near the top of their lists were making friends and having positive, warm relationships (Berscheid, 1985; Berscheid & Reis, 1998). The absence of meaningful relationships with others makes people feel lonely, worthless, hopeless, helpless, and powerless (Baumeister & Leary, 1995; Cacioppo & Patrick, 2008; Hartup & Stevens, 1997). In fact, social psychologist Arthur Aron has suggested that a central human motivation is "self-expansion." This is the desire to overlap or blend with another person, so that you have access to that person's knowledge, insights, and experience and thus broaden and deepen your own experience of life (Aron, Aron, & Norman, 2004; Fivecoat et al., 2014). We will begin this chapter by discussing the antecedents of attraction, from the initial liking of people meeting for the first time to the love that develops in close relationships.

The Person Next Door: The Propinquity Effect

One of the simplest determinants of interpersonal attraction is *propinquity* (also known as proximity). The people who, by chance, are the ones you see and interact with the most often are the most likely to become your friends and lovers (Berscheid & Reis, 1998).

Now, this might seem obvious. But the striking thing about the positive relationship that exists between proximity and attraction, or the **propinquity effect**, is that it works in a very narrow sense. For example, consider a classic study conducted in a housing complex for married students at MIT. Leon Festinger, Stanley Schachter, and Kurt Back (1950) tracked friendship formation among the couples in the various apartment buildings. One section of the complex, Westgate West, was composed of 17 two-story buildings, each having 10 apartments. Residents had been assigned to apartments at random, and nearly all were strangers when they moved in. The researchers asked residents to name their three closest friends in the complex. Just as the propinquity effect would predict, 65% of the friends mentioned lived in their same building, even though the other buildings were not far away.

Even more striking was the pattern of friendships *within* a building. Each Westgate West building was designed with front doors only 19 feet apart, and the greatest distance between apartment doors was only 89 feet. The researchers found that 41% of the next-door neighbors indicated that they were close friends, 22% of those who lived two doors apart said so, and only 10% of those who lived on opposite ends of the hall indicated that they were close friends.

Festinger and his colleagues (1950) demonstrated that attraction and propinquity rely not only on actual physical distance but also on "functional distance," which refers to aspects of architectural design that determine which people you cross paths with most often. For example, living at the foot of the stairs or near the

Propinquity Effect

The finding that the more we see and interact with people, the more likely they are to become our friends

Close friendships are often made in college, in part because of prolonged propinquity.

MERE EXPOSURE AND LIKING

One of the earliest and most famous demonstrations of the mere exposure effect was conducted by Robert Zajonc (1968) who asked American participants to guess the meaning of a series of Chinese characters. The more frequently a character was shown to them, the more positive a meaning people guessed for it, demonstrating that mere exposure tends to predict positive attitudes.

Advertising also capitalizes on the mere exposure effect. From the effectiveness of product placement to the catchiness of a commercial jingle, the idea is that the more times consumers see or hear about a product, they more they will like it and be willing to spend money on it.

One demonstration of the power of mere exposure to shape our feelings about people is provided by Moreland and Beach (1992). In their study, female students who were not registered for a class sat in a classroom 5, 10, or 15 times during the semester, never actually interacting with anyone else. When students were later asked to rate how attractive a series of faces were, their ratings of these women were higher the more times the individual had visited their classroom.

Mere exposure is about more than physical attractiveness and romantic attraction. It can also facilitate prejudice reduction. In one recent study, participants expressed less prejudice after reading a vignette about transgender people and seeing images of associated faces (Flores et al., 2017). Mere exposure would seem to have the potential to draw people to one another as well as bridge gaps that otherwise might exist between them.

mailboxes meant that one would see upstairs residents quite often. Sure enough, throughout the complex, residents in such apartments had more upstairs friends than did those who lived in the other first-floor apartments.

Propinquity works because of familiarity, or the **mere exposure effect**: The more exposure we have to a stimulus, the more apt we are to like it (Kawakami & Yoshida, 2014; Moreland & Topolinski, 2010; Zajonc, 1968). In reality, familiarity doesn't usually breed contempt; it breeds liking. We typically associate positive feelings with things that are familiar, like comfort food, songs we remember from childhood, and even certain corporate logos. The same is true for the people we encounter. The more often we see certain people, and the more familiar they become, the more friendship blooms. However, there is a caveat: If the person in question is obnoxious, then, not surprisingly, the more exposure you have, the greater your dislike becomes (Norton, Frost, & Ariely, 2007). But in the absence of negative qualities, familiarity tends to breed attraction and liking (Bornstein, 1989; Montoya et al., 2017; Reis et al., 2011).

Mere Exposure Effect

The finding that the more exposure we have to a stimulus, the more apt we are to like it

Similarity

As we saw, propinquity increases familiarity, which leads to liking. But more than that is needed to fuel a growing friendship or a romantic relationship. (Otherwise, every pair of roommates would be best friends!) That "fuel" is often *similarity*—a match between interests, attitudes, values, background, or personality. Folk wisdom captures this idea in the expression "Birds of a feather flock together" (the concept of *similarity*). But folk wisdom also has another saying, "Opposites attract" (the concept of *complementarity*). Luckily, we don't have to remain forever confused by contradictory advice from old sayings; research evidence demonstrates that it is overwhelmingly similarity and not complementarity that draws people together (Heine et al., 2009; McPherson, Smith-Lovin, & Cook, 2001; Montoya & Horton, 2013).

OPINIONS AND PERSONALITY   A large body of research indicates that the more similar someone's opinions are to yours, the more you will like the person (Byrne & Nelson, 1965; Lutz-Zois et al., 2006; Tidwell, Eastwick, & Finkel, 2013). For example, in a classic study, Theodore Newcomb (1961) randomly assigned male students at the University of Michigan to be roommates in a particular dormitory at the start of the school year. Would similarity predict friendship formation? The answer was yes: Men became friends with those who were demographically similar (e.g., shared a rural background), as well as with those who were similar in attitudes and values (e.g., were also engineering majors or also held comparable political views). It's not just attitudes or demographics that are important. Similar personality characteristics also promote liking and attraction. For example, in a study of gay men's relationships, those who scored high on a test of stereotypically male traits desired most of all a partner who was logical—another stereotypically masculine trait. Gay men who scored high on a test of stereotypically female traits desired most of all a partner who was expressive—another stereotypically feminine trait (Boyden, Carroll, & Maier, 1984). Similar personality characteristics are important for heterosexual couples and for friends as well (Gonzaga, Campos, & Bradbury, 2007; Smith et al., 2014; Weaver & Bosson, 2011).

INTERESTS AND EXPERIENCES   The situations you choose to be in are usually populated by people who have chosen them for similar reasons. You're sitting in a social psychology class, surrounded by people who also chose to take social psychology this semester. You sign up for salsa dance lessons; the others in your class also want to learn Latin dancing. Thus, we choose to enter into certain social situations where we then find similar others. For example, in a study of academic "tracking" (when schools group students by academic ability), researchers found that students were significantly more likely to choose friends from inside their track than from outside it (Kubitschek & Hallinan, 1998; Whyte & Torgler, 2017). Clearly, propinquity and initial similarity play a role in the formation of these friendships. However, the researchers add that similarity plays yet another role: Over time, students in the same academic track share many of the same experiences, which are different from the experiences of those in other tracks. Thus, new similarities are created and discovered, fueling the friendships. In short, shared experiences promote attraction (Pinel et al., 2006; Pinel & Long, 2012).

APPEARANCE   Similarity also operates when it comes to more superficial considerations. Sean Mackinnon, Christian Jordan, and Anne Wilson (2011) conducted a series of studies examining physical similarity and seating choice. In one study, they simply analyzed the seating arrangement of college students in a library computer lab, making observations multiple times over the course of several different days. Results indicated that, for instance, students who

"I don't care if she is a tape dispenser. I love her."

Sam Gross/The New Yorker
Collection/The Cartoon Bank

wore glasses sat next to other students with glasses far more often than random chance alone would predict. A second study found the same pattern by hair color.

In a third study, participants arrived at a psychology lab and were introduced to a partner who was already sitting. Handed a chair, they were told to have a seat, at which point the research team secretly measured how close to the partner's chair they put down their own chair. A separate set of researchers later evaluated photos of both the participant and the partner. Pairs judged as more physically similar had sat, on average, closer to each other. Without even realizing it, we are often drawn to those who look like us, to the point where people are even more likely to ask out on dates others who are similar to them in terms of attractiveness level (Taylor et al., 2011; Walster et al., 1966).

Watch ATTRACTION AND THE MATCHING HYPOTHESIS

Revel Video

GENETICS   People also tend to be drawn to others who are genetically similar to them. That is, friends tend to have more similar DNA than do strangers. This is the surprising conclusion of research conducted by Nicholas Christakis and James Fowler (2014). Their study included close to 2,000 participants, some of whom were friends and some of whom were strangers, and analyzed close to 1.5 million markers of gene variation. Christakis and Fowler (2014) found that participants shared more DNA with their friends than with strangers, to a degree that participants were as genetically similar to their average friend as they would be to someone who shared a great-great-great grandparent. Of course, these data do not prove that our genes *cause* friendships or that our DNA drives people toward certain others. As noted previously, people tend to make friends with others who live near them, and individuals of similar genetic ancestry may be more likely to share such geographical propinquity. And perhaps certain genetic predispositions—say, an athletic build and good lung capacity—make people more likely to select certain activities and frequent certain locales—say, joining a running club—which means that genetically similar individuals often end up doing the same thing at the same time in the same place. These and other possibilities provide intriguing explanations for Christakis and Fowler's provocative findings, which suggest interesting interactions between our genetic and social tendencies.

SOME FINAL COMMENTS ABOUT SIMILARITY   Here are two additional points about similarity. First, although similarity is very important in close relationships, it is important to make a distinction between *actual* similarity and *perceived* similarity (Morry, 2007; Tidwell et al., 2013). In a meta-analysis, R. Matthew Montoya and his colleagues found that in long-term relationships, individuals' *beliefs* about how similar they were to another person predicted liking and attraction better than their *actual* similarity did. Thus, feeling similar to another is what's really important—so much so that we will sometimes create beliefs about the similarity between ourselves and intimate others even when they don't exist (Montoya, Horton, & Kirchner, 2008).

Second, similarity appears to be far more important when we want a serious, committed relationship, and less so when we just want a "fling" (Amodio & Showers, 2005). Indeed, in low-commitment relationships (i.e., "one-night stands" or "hook-ups"), we sometimes go out of our way to choose someone who is

We often prioritize different characteristics in a romantic partner when looking for a long-term relationship versus a fling. Can you think of specific examples?

#trending

"Hook-Up Culture" and Today's Youth

In America today, teenagers and young adults are having unprecedent levels of casual, quick, and commitment-free sexual encounters with a regularly rotating number of new partners.

Does this sound familiar? Have you heard claims like this about a newly emerging "hook-up culture" among young people on college campuses and elsewhere? The suggestion is often that the contemporary social landscape for sexual behavior stands in stark contrast to more traditional ideas of courtship, dating, and committed relationships that were more common in the past.

It's a compelling narrative, but is it accurate? Recent research suggests that "hook-up culture" may be more myth than reality. First, what does the term "hook-up" really even mean? Many seem to believe that the phrase implies sexual intercourse, but a recent survey of college women indicates that only about one-half of the encounters they describe in this manner involved any sort of genital contact, with closer to just one-fourth involving actual sexual intercourse (Fielder & Carey, 2010). Furthermore, these women reported that almost half of their "hook-ups" were with a familiar, repeat partner. So even if it were the case that increasing numbers of college students talk about "hooking up," only a small percentage of these encounters appear to consist of one-time sex with first-time partners.

But what about the claim that casual sexual encounters are more prevalent now than ever? Analysis of nationwide data from the U.S. General Social Survey indicates that between the years 1988 and 1996, 49% of young adults reported having two or fewer sex partners since the age of 18. From 2004 to 2012, in a more modern era of online dating, Tinder, and supposedly relaxed sexual norms, this rate has remained basically unchanged at 51% (Monto & Carey, 2014). The more recent sample did not report having more sex than young people did two to three decades ago, nor did they report a greater number of total sexual partners.

Findings such as these have led researchers to draw skeptical conclusions regarding any sort of explosion of casual sex, or "hooking-up," among today's young people. Indeed, the sex life of today's youth seems to be, in many respects, not that different from that of past generations, at least in terms of quantity of partners and encounters. Of course, young adults today have at their disposal a wider range of means for easily meeting new partners, from social media to mobile apps to dating websites—but so do middle-aged and older adults! The idea of "hook-up" culture seems to be an illustrative example of how expectations and common sense assumptions about human sexuality do not always align with scientific data and real behavior.

The finding that we like people who like us suggests that the strategy of "playing hard-to-get" can sometimes backfire. Research suggests that the strategy tends to decrease how much another person *likes* you, all the while potentially increasing how much that person *wants* to be with you (Dai, Dong, & Jia, 2014). Consider yourselves warned!

strikingly different from us. A relationship with this sort of person represents more of an adventure, but, as we'll see as we progress through this chapter, relationships based on differences, rather than similarities, can be difficult to maintain.

Reciprocal Liking

We like to be liked. In fact, just knowing that a person likes us fuels our attraction to that individual. Liking is so powerful that it can even make up for the absence of similarity. For example, in one experiment, when a young woman expressed interest in male research participants simply by maintaining eye contact, leaning toward them, and listening attentively, the men expressed great liking for her despite the fact that they knew she disagreed with them on important issues (Gold, Ryckman, & Mosley, 1984). Whether the clues are nonverbal or verbal, perhaps the most crucial determinant of whether we like person A is the extent to which we believe person A likes us (Berscheid & Walster, 1978; Luo & Zhang, 2009; Montoya & Insko, 2008).

Just how powerful is reciprocal liking? Powerful enough to neutralize our basic tendency to pay more attention to attractive faces. Nicolas Koranyi and Klaus Rothermund (2012) used a computer program to present a series of opposite-sex faces to German research participants. Immediately after each photo appeared, a geometrical shape was shown that required participants to respond quickly using a keyboard. This procedure also allowed the researchers to measure which faces elicited the most visual attention from the respondents, and the results indicated, as you might predict, that we have a tendency to linger and look longer at good-looking faces.

But not all respondents showed this bias to stare a bit longer at attractive faces. Who was able to break the spell of the pretty face? Participants who had previously been asked to imagine that they had just learned that someone whom they had a crush on also had feelings for them. As the researchers suggest, it makes sense that this type of interest from someone else would disrupt our otherwise default focus on the attractive alternatives out there. Think about it: If our attention were repeatedly hijacked by *every* pretty face that passed by, we'd never get the chance to turn initial interactions into more meaningful, sustained romantic relationships. Basking in the glow of reciprocated liking is enough to stop a wandering eye and convince you, at least for a while, that the grass may not be greener on the other side.

Physical Attractiveness

Speaking of pretty faces, propinquity, similarity, and reciprocal liking are not the only predictors of whom we come to like. How important is physical appearance to our first impressions? In field experiments investigating actual behavior (rather than simply what people *say* they will do), people overwhelmingly go for physical attractiveness. In one classic study, Elaine Walster Hatfield and her colleagues (Walster, et al., 1966) randomly matched 752 incoming students at the University of Minnesota for a blind date at a dance during freshman orientation week. Although the students had previously taken a battery of personality and aptitude tests, the researchers paired them up totally at random. On the night of the dance, the couples spent a few hours together dancing and chatting. They then evaluated their date and indicated the strength of their desire to see that person again. Of the many possible characteristics that could have determined whether they liked each other—such as their partner's intelligence, independence, sensitivity, or sincerity—the overriding determinant was physical attractiveness.

What's more, there was no great difference between men and women on this count. Indeed, several studies have found that men and women pay equal attention to the physical attractiveness of others (Eastwick et al., 2011; Lynn & Shurgot, 1984), but other studies have reported that men value attractiveness more than women do (Buss, 1989; Meltzer et al., 2014). A meta-analysis of many studies found that although both sexes value attractiveness, men value it a bit more (Feingold, 1990); however, this gender difference was greater when men's and women's attitudes were being measured than when their actual behavior was being measured. Thus, it may be that men are more likely than women to *say* that physical attractiveness is important to them, but when it comes to actual behavior, men and women are fairly similar in how they respond to physical attractiveness. Across multiple studies, both genders rated physical attractiveness as the single-most important characteristic that triggers sexual desire (Graziano et al., 1993; Regan & Berscheid, 1997), a finding that has been observed among straight as well as gay men and women (Ha et al., 2012; Sergios & Cody, 1985).

WHAT IS ATTRACTIVE?   Okay, big surprise—attractiveness is important. But what makes someone attractive? Is physical attractiveness "in the eye of the beholder," or do we all share the same notions of what is beautiful? For now, let's focus on American culture; we'll get to potential cross-cultural differences in a moment. From early childhood, the media tell us what is attractive, and they tell us that beauty is associated with goodness. For example, illustrators of most traditional children's books, as well as Disney movies, have taught us that heroines—and the princes who woo and win them—have a specific look. The female protagonists have small, pert noses; big eyes; shapely lips; blemish-free complexions; and slim, athletic bodies—often rather like Barbie dolls.

One indicator of just how important physical appearance is in attraction is our nearly chronic tendency to shift visual attention to attractive others in our immediate vicinity.

Models represent standards of beauty for men and women.

Bombarded as we are with media depictions of attractiveness, it is not surprising to learn that we often share criteria for defining beauty (Fink & Penton-Voak, 2002; Yan & Bissell, 2014). Michael Cunningham (1986) designed a creative study to determine these standards of beauty. He asked college men to rate the attractiveness of 50 photographs of women, taken from a college yearbook and from an international beauty-pageant program. Cunningham then carefully measured the relative size of the facial features in each photograph. He found that high attractiveness ratings for female faces were associated with large eyes, a small nose, a small chin, prominent cheekbones, high eyebrows, large pupils, and a big smile. Researchers then examined women's ratings of male beauty in the same way (Cunningham, Barbee, & Pike, 1990). They found that male faces with large eyes, prominent cheekbones, a large chin, and a big smile received higher attractiveness ratings.

CULTURAL STANDARDS OF BEAUTY Are people's perceptions of beauty similar across cultures? The answer is a surprising yes (Coetzee et al., 2014; Rhodes et al., 2001; Zebrowitz et al., 2012). Even though racial and ethnic groups do vary in their specific facial features, people from a wide range of cultures agree on what is physically attractive in the human face. For example, one review of the literature that has compared how people from various countries, ethnicities, and racial groups rate attractiveness found that the correlations between participants' ratings were strong, ranging from 0.66 to 0.93 (Langlois & Roggman, 1990). A meta-analysis of several studies by Judith Langlois and her colleagues (2000) also found evidence for cross-cultural agreement in what constitutes an attractive face. In short, perceivers across cultural backgrounds think some faces are just better looking than others.

How can we explain these results? Researchers have suggested that humans came to find certain dimensions of faces attractive during the course of our evolution (Langlois & Roggman, 1990; Langlois, Roggman, & Musselman, 1994). For example, we know that even infants prefer the same photographs as adults do (Langlois et al., 1991). So what specific facial characteristics do people, including babies, tend to find attractive? One dimension that is preferred—in both men and women—is symmetry, where the size, shape, and location of the features on one side of the face match those on the other (Langlois et al., 2000; Little et al., 2008; Rhodes, 2006). Evolutionary psychologists suggest that we're attracted to symmetrical features because they serve as markers of good health and reproductive fitness—that is, facial symmetry is an indicator of "good genes" (Jones et al., 2001; Nedelec & Beaver, 2014).

A series of studies explored this preference by creating composite photographs of faces. Faces were morphed (i.e., combined digitally) to create the mathematical average of the features of multiple faces; ultimately, 32 faces were combined into a single composite. When shown to research participants, composite photographs were judged

Langlois and Roggman (1990) created composites of faces using a computer. Pictured here is the first step in the process: The first two women's photos are merged to create the "composite person" at the far right. This composite person has facial features that are the mathematical average of the facial features of the two original women. Research has shown that people typically find composite faces to be more attractive than the individual faces that comprise them.

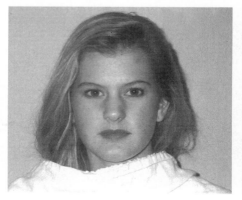
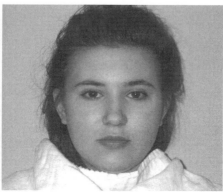

as more attractive than were all the separate faces that had created them, and this held true for both male and female photographs (Langlois & Roggman, 1990; Langlois et al., 1994). The "averaged" composite face was more attractive because it had lost some of the atypical or asymmetrical variation that was present in the individual faces.

Does this mean that we find "average" faces the most attractive? Clearly not, for we respond to the physical appearance of movie stars and models and consider their looks to be "above average" compared to most humans. So by "average" here we don't mean "average looking," but features that appear to be of average size and dimension. David Perret and his colleagues made this point clear in the following study (Perret, May, & Yoshikawa, 1994). They created composite faces of two types: One composite was based on 60 photographs that had each been rated as average in attractiveness. The other composite was based on 60 photographs that had each been rated as highly attractive. Composites of these two types were made using photographs of Caucasian women, Caucasian men, Japanese women, and Japanese men. Research participants in Great Britain and Japan then rated all the composite faces for attractiveness. The composites of highly attractive faces were rated as significantly more attractive than the composites of average attractiveness faces. Japanese and British participants showed the same pattern when judging the faces, reinforcing the idea that similar perceptions of facial attractiveness exist cross-culturally (Perrett et al., 1994). Of course, it's also worth noting that this study only included two cultures, leaving unanswered the question of whether people from, say, Borneo or Egypt or El Salvador would respond the same way.

THE POWER OF FAMILIARITY   In the end, the crucial variable on which much of interpersonal attraction hinges may be familiarity. We've seen that "averaging" faces together produces one face that looks typical, familiar, and physically attractive (see also Halberstadt & Rhodes, 2000). Research has also uncovered an even more startling familiarity effect: When participants rated the attractiveness of faces, they preferred those faces that most resembled their own! The researchers morphed a picture of each participant's face (without the participant's knowledge) with one of a person of the opposite sex. When presented with this photo of their opposite-sex "clone," participants gave it high ratings of attractiveness (Little & Perrett, 2002). Familiarity also underlies many of the other concepts we've discussed thus far: propinquity (people we see frequently become familiar through mere exposure), similarity (people who are similar to us will also seem familiar to us), and reciprocal liking (people who like each other get to know and become familiar with each other). All of these factors predicting attraction may be thought of as different examples of our basic preference for the comfortable, familiar, and safe over the unknown and unfamiliar.

ASSUMPTIONS ABOUT ATTRACTIVE PEOPLE   It's important to realize that beauty matters—even when it shouldn't. We're attracted to that which is beautiful, and this can lead to inequity in everyday life. A particularly chilling example of the unfair benefit of beauty was discovered by Lina Badr and Bahia Abdallah (2001), who rated the facial attractiveness and health status of premature infants born in hospitals in Beirut, Lebanon. They found that physical attractiveness significantly predicted the health outcomes of these infants above and beyond factors such as their medical condition. The more attractive the infant, the more quickly he or she gained weight and the shorter his or her stay in the hospital. The neonatal nurses appeared to respond more to the "prettier" infants and gave them better care.

Physical attractiveness is associated with a variety of benefits. People of above-average looks tend to earn 10% to 15% more than those of below-average appearance (Judge, Hurst, & Simon, 2009; Mobius & Rosenblat, 2006). College professors perceived as attractive tend to receive higher student evaluation ratings (Rinolo et al., 2006). Attractiveness even helps win elections. Niclas Berggren and his colleagues (2010) presented photographs of Finnish political candidates to research participants in other countries (who would have no prior knowledge of these candidates) and asked them to rate

It's no coincidence that in children's movies, the hero is traditionally attractive and the villain ugly. In addition to finding it pleasing to look at attractive others, we also tend to assume that "what is beautiful is good."

Halo Effect

A cognitive bias by which we tend to assume that an individual with one positive characteristic also possesses other (even unrelated) positive characteristics

the politicians on a variety of attributes, including attractiveness. They found that the ratings of attractiveness were the best predictors of the actual number of votes each candidate had gotten in the real elections. A higher beauty rating predicted an increase of between 2.5 and 2.8 percentage points in the vote total for female candidates and between 1.5 and 2.1 percentage points for male candidates, amounts that could tip the balance of a close election (Berggren, Jordahl, & Poutvaara, 2010).

Many studies have found that physical attractiveness affects the attributions people make about others (and vice versa). This tendency provides a specific example of what psychologists refer to as the **halo effect** (Forgas, 2011; Thorndike, 1920). The halo effect is a cognitive bias in which the perception that an individual possesses one positive characteristic makes us more likely to believe that he or she also possesses other (even unrelated) positive characteristics. Specifically, when it comes to attractiveness, we tend to attribute to beautiful people other good qualities, including some that have nothing to do with their looks, buying into a "what is beautiful is good" stereotype (Dion et al., 1972; Lemay, Clark, & Greenberg, 2010; Zebrowitz & Franklin, 2014). Meta-analyses have revealed that physical attractiveness has its largest effect on attributions related to social competence: The beautiful are thought to be more sociable, extroverted, assertive, sexual, and popular than the less attractive (Eagly et al., 1991; Feingold, 1992b; Wertheim & Sommers, 2016). The "halo" provided by being good-looking extends to the online realm as well: One study of dating websites found that those users who posted more attractive photos were also rated as having written more attractive profile descriptions (Brand et al., 2012).

Do these stereotypes about the beautiful operate across cultures? The answer appears to be yes (Anderson, Adams, & Plaut, 2008; Chen, Shaffer, & Wu, 1997). For example, college students in South Korea were asked to rate a number of yearbook photographs (Wheeler & Kim, 1997). Both male and female participants thought the more physically attractive people would also be more socially skilled, friendly, and well adjusted—the same traits that North American participants thought went with physical attractiveness (see Table 10.1). But Korean and North American students differed in some of the other

Table 10.1 Culture and the "What Is Beautiful Is Good" Stereotype

The "what is beautiful is good" stereotype has been explored in both individualistic cultures (e.g., North America) and collectivistic cultures (e.g., Asia). Male and female participants in the United States, Canada, and South Korea rated photographs of people with varying degrees of physical attractiveness. Responses indicated that some of the traits that make up the stereotype are the same across cultures, while other traits associated with the stereotype are different in the two cultures. In both cultures, the physically attractive are seen as having more of the characteristics that are valued in that culture than do the less physically attractive.

Traits Shared in the Korean, American, and Canadian Stereotype		
sociable	extraverted	likable
happy	popular	well-adjusted
friendly	mature	poised
sexually warm/responsive		
Additional Traits Present in the American and Canadian Stereotype		
strong	assertive	dominant
Additional Traits Present in the Korean Stereotype		
sensitive	empathic	generous
honest	trustworthy	

(Based on Eagly et al., 1991; Feingold, 1992b; Wheeler & Kim, 1997)

traits they assigned to the beautiful, highlighting that there are some differences in what is considered important in each culture (Markus et al., 1996; Triandis, 1995). For the American and Canadian students—who live in more individualistic cultures that value independence, individuality, and self-reliance—the "beautiful" stereotype included traits of personal strength. These traits were not part of the Korean "beautiful" stereotype. Instead, for these students, who live in a more collectivistic culture that values harmonious group relations, the "beautiful" stereotype included integrity and concern for others (see Table 10.1).

Interestingly, the stereotype that the beautiful are particularly gifted in the area of social competence has some empirical support. That is, highly attractive people *do* actually develop good social interaction skills and report having more satisfying interactions with others than do less-attractive people (Feingold, 1992b; Langlois et al., 2000; Meier et al., 2010). Why does this "kernel of truth" emerge in the stereotype? A leading explanation is that because the beautiful, from a young age, receive a great deal of attention that in turn helps them develop good social skills. You probably recognize the self-fulfilling prophecy at work here: Our expectations of people can affect how they actually come to behave. If others always treat you as if they expect you to be socially proficient (whether because of your physical appearance or otherwise), this then provides you with ample opportunities to actually develop superior social skills.

Can a "regular" person be made to act like a "beautiful" one through the self-fulfilling prophecy? To find out, researchers gave college men a photo and a packet of information about a woman with whom they were about to have a phone conversation (Snyder, Tanke, & Berscheid, 1977). But the photograph was rigged; at random, the men were either given a photo that a previous group of raters had judged to be attractive or one that a previous group had rated as unattractive. In both cases, this photo was *not* of the actual woman they were about to speak with. The experimental purpose of the photograph was to invoke the men's stereotype that "what is beautiful is good"—to test the possibility that a woman would be more likable, poised, and fun to talk to if her male conversation partner believed she was attractive. Again, the prediction here was not just that the men would *perceive* the woman as more fun to talk to when they thought she was attractive, but that the men's beliefs about her appearance would actually change the reality of how the woman behaved.

Did the researchers find evidence of an attractiveness-based self-fulfilling prophecy? In short, yes! The men who thought they were talking to an attractive woman responded to her in a warmer, more sociable manner than the men who thought they were talking to an unattractive woman. And the men's behavior actually influenced how the women behaved: When independent observers listened to a tape recording of only the woman's half of the conversation (without knowing anything about the photo the men had seen), they rated the women whose male partners thought they were attractive as more confident, animated, and warmer. In other words, because the male partner thought he was talking to an attractive woman, he spoke to her in a way that brought out her most sparkling qualities. Subsequent studies have found similar results with the gender roles reversed (Andersen & Bem, 1981), reminding us that it is a myth that physical attractiveness only affects how men perceive women: both men and women are treated differently based on their physical appearance. (Eagly et al., 1991; Langlois et al., 2000; Zhang et al., 2014).

Evolution and Mate Selection

The poet Robert Browning asked, "How do I love thee? Let me count the ways." For psychologists, the question is "*Why* do I love thee?" Some researchers believe that the answer lies in an evolutionary approach to mate selection. The basic tenet of evolutionary biology is that an animal's "fitness" is measured by its reproductive success (i.e., its capability to pass on genes to the next generation). Reproductive success is not just part of the game; it *is* the game. This biological concept has been applied to social behavior by some psychologists, who define evolutionary psychology as the attempt to explain social behavior in terms of genetic factors that have evolved over time according to the principles of natural selection. For example, as detailed earlier, one explanation for people's tendency to find symmetrical faces more attractive is that symmetry indicates positive health and "good genes."

EVOLUTION AND SEX DIFFERENCES   Evolutionary psychology also makes some interesting (and controversial) predictions regarding sex differences in mate preference. Specifically, evolutionary psychologists argue that men and women have very different agendas when it comes to mate selection, due to their differing roles in producing (and raising) offspring. For females, reproduction is costly in terms of time, energy, and effort: They must endure the discomforts of pregnancy, the risks of childbirth, and, traditionally, the primary responsibility for caring for the infant until maturity. Reproducing, then, is serious business, so females, the theory goes, must consider carefully when and with whom to reproduce. In comparison, reproduction is a low-cost, short-term investment for males. The evolutionary approach to mate selection concludes that reproductive success for the two sexes translates into two very different behavior patterns: Throughout the animal world, males' reproductive success is measured by the *quantity* of their offspring. They pursue frequent pairings with many females in order to maximize their number of surviving progeny. In contrast, females' reproductive success lies in successfully raising each of their offspring to maturity. They pair less frequently and only with carefully chosen males, because the cost to them of raising and ensuring the survival of each offspring is so high (Griffith, Pryke, & Buettemer, 2011; Symons, 1979).

Now, what does all of this have to do with how people fall in love? David Buss and his colleagues argue that the evolutionary approach explains the different strategies and tendencies of men and women in romantic relationships (Buss, 1985, 1988a; Buss & Schmitt, 1993). Buss (1988b) argues that finding (and keeping) a mate requires one to display resources—the aspects of oneself that will appear attractive to potential mates. He proposes that, across millennia, human beings have been selected through evolution to respond to certain external cues in the opposite sex. Women, facing high reproductive costs, will look for a man who can supply the resources and support she needs to raise a child. Men will look for a woman who appears capable of reproducing successfully. More precisely, the argument goes, men will respond to the physical appearance of women because age and health denote reproductive fitness, and women will respond to the economic and career achievements of men because these variables represent resources they and their offspring need (Buss, 1988b).

Many studies have provided support for these predictions. For example, Buss and colleagues (Buss, 1989; Buss et al., 1990) asked thousands of adults in 37 countries how desirable various characteristics were in a marriage partner. In general, women valued ambition, industriousness, and earning capacity in a potential mate more than the men did. The men valued physical attractiveness in a mate more than the women did. It should be noted, however, that the top characteristics on both men's and women's lists were the same: honesty, trustworthiness, and a pleasant personality (Hatfield & Sprecher, 1995; Regan & Berscheid, 1997; Sprecher, Sullivan, & Hatfield, 1994). Further evidence for the importance of reproductive considerations in human attraction comes from more recent research that has examined the relationship between a woman's menstrual cycle, her perceptions of potential mates, and how potential mates view her. Kelly Gildersleeve and colleagues (2014) conducted a meta-analysis that examined 50 studies and found reliable support for the hypothesis that as they near ovulation and peak fertility, women tend to exhibit greater preference for men who exhibit outward signs of reproductive fitness:

Research has linked perceptions of attractiveness to reproductive concerns. For example, as ovulation nears, women tend to rate as more attractive men with highly masculine faces and body types (Gildersleeve et al., 2014).

a symmetrical face, a masculine face (e.g., sharp, pronounced jawline), and a muscular physique (Gildersleeve, Haselton, & Fales, 2014).

ALTERNATE PERSPECTIVES ON SEX DIFFERENCES   The evolutionary approach to attraction and love has inspired its share of debate. For example, one could argue that evolutionary advantages to having multiple sexual partners should not be limited to men, but should also apply to women. With multiple partners, females would increase the odds of getting resources for their offspring, as well as benefit from genetic diversity. Females could choose an attractive male with "good genes" with whom to procreate and another male with whom to raise the offspring (Campbell, 2002; Gangestad & Simpson, 2000). It may also be the case that men value physical attractiveness in a partner not because of evolved tendencies, but simply because they have been taught by society to value it—that they have been conditioned by decades of advertising, media images, and other cultural messages to prioritize beauty in women and to have a more recreational approach to sex than women do (Hatfield & Rapson, 1993; Lefkowitz et al., 2014). Similarly, research has found that in some situations, women value physical attractiveness just as much as men— specifically, when they are considering a potential sexual partner as opposed to a potential marriage partner (Regan & Berscheid, 1997; Simpson & Gangestad, 1992).

Other researchers argue that the preference for different qualities in a mate can be explained without relying on evolutionary principles: Around the world, women typically have less power, status, wealth, and other resources than men do. Therefore, in many societies women need to rely on men to achieve economic security. To test this hypothesis, Steven Gangestad (1993) correlated the extent to which women in several countries had access to financial resources and the extent to which women reported male physical attractiveness as an important variable in a mate. He found that the more economic power women had in a given culture, the more highly women prioritized a man's physical attractiveness.

As you can see, when discussing human mate preference, it is often difficult to disentangle "nature" (inborn preferences) from "nurture" (cultural norms and gender roles). When we hear about sex differences related to mate selection and attraction, our first instinct is often to turn to biological or evolutionary explanations (Conley et al., 2011). But a closer look often reveals that many of these differences are also attributable to situational factors. Take, for instance, the proposition that women are pickier than men when it comes to selecting a mate. Indeed, whether you look at online dating, speed-dating events, or old-fashioned face-to-face date requests, research indicates that women are significantly more discriminating about who they'll go out with than men are (Clark & Hatfield, 1989; Hitsch, Hortaçsu, & Ariely, 2010; Schützwohl et al., 2009). This makes sense from the evolutionary perspective that women *have* to be picky because they can't afford to make mistakes; unlike men, their fertility window is relatively narrow across the life span, and each decision to reproduce requires more time and resources.

But consider the provocative results of a speed-dating study conducted by Eli Finkel and Paul Eastwick (2009). College students in this research had brief conversations with a dozen different opposite-sex individuals. In these speed-dating sessions, the women remained seated while the men rotated in a circle, spending 4 minutes with each prospective dating partner before moving on to the next person. After each of the 12 women had been visited by each of the 12 men, all participants completed a questionnaire assessing these potential mates. Women were, indeed, more selective than men, reporting lower levels of romantic desire and identifying fewer prospective mates that they'd like to get to know better.

Watch   SPEED-DATING AND THE SCIENCE OF RELATIONSHIPS

Revel Video.

But an interesting thing happened when the researchers made a minor tweak to the speed-dating situation. In a second set of dating events, they had men and women swap roles. Now the men remained seated and the women rotated around. Instead of women sitting still while men paraded in a circle, now the men remained stationary as women approached them. The "dates" themselves were still the same: 4-minute conversations after which both parties were asked for their impressions. But from a situational standpoint, this was traditional dating in reverse (Conley et al., 2011). And in this dating world where women did the approaching, women were no longer pickier than men. If anything, the female participants now reported more chemistry with their partners and identified more prospective mates that they wanted to see again. Finkel and Eastwick's (2009) results suggest that gender differences in mate selectivity do not simply reflect evolution or biology, but are also attributable to the established dating paradigm in most societies, in which men are the approachers and women the approachees. Being approached gives you control, regardless of sex or gender; being approached also means feeling in demand and having options. And so it is that, as with many aspects of human nature, we need both "nature" and "nurture" explanations to fully understand the psychology of attraction and mate selection.

Review Questions

1. Which of the following examples best illustrates how functional distance plays a role in the propinquity effect?
   a. Bart doesn't like his next-door neighbor, primarily because of his habit of playing loud music that makes it difficult to get to sleep at night.
   b. Marge, whose cubicle is right next to both the kitchen and the elevator, is one of the most popular people in the entire office.
   c. Homer prefers to take the stairs rather than the elevator because it decreases his likelihood of running into people he finds annoying.
   d. Lisa made more friends in her sophomore-year dorm than in her freshman-year dorm.

2. The _____ suggests that the more times we encounter someone or something, the more we tend to like it.
   a. evolutionary perspective
   b. halo effect
   c. mere exposure effect
   d. reciprocal liking effect

3. Similarity in terms of which of the following dimensions has been found to predict increased attraction?
   a. attitudes
   b. attractiveness level
   c. genetics
   d. All of the above

4. Which of the following statements about perceptions of physical attractiveness is true?
   a. Asymmetrical faces are typically viewed as more attractive because they are so distinctive.
   b. Large cross-cultural differences emerge in terms of what is seen as physically attractive in the human face.
   c. The more someone looks like us, the less attractive we typically find him or her to be.

   d. Perceivers tend to believe that someone who is attractive also possesses a range of other (unrelated) positive characteristics.

5. Which of the following is *not* identified as a major predictor of attraction in long-term romantic relationships?
   a. similarity
   b. reciprocity
   c. complementarity
   d. propinquity

6. Research indicates that a face's symmetry is a reliable predictor of how attractive it is seen to be. An evolutionary psychology explanation for this finding would be that
   a. symmetrical faces remind us of ourselves and therefore elicit positive feelings.
   b. symmetry is a sign of health and that a potential mate has good genes.
   c. "Western" cultures place a greater emphasis on physical attractiveness than do "Eastern" cultures.
   d. All of the above

7. You and your friends decide to hold a heterosexual "speed-dating" event on campus. At this event, male students sit at tables arranged in a circle and have 3-minute conversations with a series of women. After each 3-minute period has ended, the women rotate in a clockwise direction and sit down with a new male student. When asked about their "dating" experiences after the event, research suggests that
   a. the men should be somewhat pickier in terms of rating which women they would like to see again.
   b. the women should be somewhat pickier in terms of rating which men they would like to see again.
   c. the men should focus less on facial symmetry in assessing their dates' attractiveness.
   d. the women should focus less on facial symmetry in assessing their dates' attractiveness.

Making Connections in the Digital World

LO 10.2 **Explain how new technologies shape attraction and social connections.**

A time-traveler from just 20 years ago would barely recognize much of what passes for social interaction today. It isn't unusual to see a group out to a meal, faces (and thumbs) buried in devices, perhaps all the while carrying on a conversation of sorts with others at the table, and taking pictures of their food to post on social media. The opportunities presented by these amazing handheld technologies are plentiful, but are there also social costs to being tethered to technology? Research suggests that there might be. Consider a field experiment in which researchers visited cafes in the Washington D.C. area, observed 100 real-life interactions between pairs of people, and then asked the individuals involved questions about the conversation they just had. Among pairs who had at least one mobile device (e.g., phone, laptop, tablet) present during the conversation, ratings of connectedness to and empathy for the other person were significantly lower than they were among pairs who interacted in the absence of such a device (Misra et al., 2016).

As amazing as the technologies are, mobile devices like smartphones can also impair our feelings of social connectedness to others during the course of face-to-face interaction.

This finding is a correlational one, though. Perhaps you're saying to yourself, *I'm not like that; even when I have my phone, I'm engaged with the people around me.* Perhaps. But experiments have also demonstrated a causal link between the presence of a mobile device and decreased social connection. In one such experiment, Andrew Przybylski and Netta Weinstein (2013) brought pairs of strangers into their lab for a 10-minute conversation. Half of these conversations took place with a phone or tablet sitting on the small table between them; in another condition, there was no phone present. The researchers found that the mere presence of the device decreased participants' feelings of trust, closeness, and empathy with their conversation partner. These effects were particularly pronounced when the pairs were instructed to discuss a personally meaningful topic, a scenario that, in the absence of a phone, would be expected to foster a sense of closeness among strangers meeting for the first time (Przybylski & Weinstein, 2013).

These findings give pause for thought. If the mere presence of a phone that isn't even yours can impair aspects of social interaction, just imagine how distracting our own devices can be, even when they aren't ringing, chiming, or vibrating (Brown, Manago, & Tribble, 2016)! Technologies like these are here to stay, but social psychological research does provide additional support for the emerging movement to unplug once in a while and force ourselves to take periodic vacations from technology (Huffington, 2014).

Attraction 2.0: Mate Preference in an Online Era

One way to explore how our rapidly developing technological world affects processes of attraction and relationship formation is to revisit some of the classic findings regarding propinquity, similarity, and familiarity, examining how these factors operate in the internet age. For example, consider how propinquity operates in an era when physical distance no longer creates the same obstacles to interaction that it once did (Chan & Cheng, 2004; Dodds, Muhamad, & Watts, 2003; Leskovec & Horvitz, 2007). Research demonstrates empirically what many of us now take for granted: in the modern world, there aren't nearly as many degrees of separation between strangers as

Watch SMARTPHONES AND CONNECTEDNESS

Revel Video

there once were, putting a whole new spin on the relationship between propinquity and attraction that we discussed earlier.

Similarity continues to have value in technologically driven relationships. We have already discussed the tendency to be attracted to people of similar appearance, right down to people being attracted to others who are the same *level* of physical attractiveness as they are. Recent research indicates that this tendency to be drawn to comparable others who are "in our own league" is also evident when relationships go online. Lindsay Taylor and colleagues (2011) assessed the popularity of more than 3,000 heterosexual users of a dating website, testing the hypothesis that profiles would be most popular among other users who shared the same attractiveness level. They defined popularity as the number of opposite-sex individuals who sent unsolicited messages to a particular profile. To increase the validity of this measure, the researchers did not count messages sent in response to contact initiated by the user himself or herself (or subsequent messages sent during an ongoing exchange), meaning that there was no way for the users in the study to increase their own popularity count once they posted a profile.

Taylor and colleagues (2011) found that users who qualified as popular contacted other popular users at a rate greater than would be expected by chance—a finding that probably does not surprise you. After all, who wouldn't want to reach out to the popular potential mates? The less popular users of the site, that's who. The researchers also found that users lower in popularity contacted other low-popularity users more often. A follow-up study with over 1 million users produced a comparable result: People tend to select (and be selected by) others with similar levels of popularity, and this tendency to try to "match up" with mates of comparable popularity was no different for men than for women. As the researchers concluded, "one reason that established couples tend to be similar is that matching is at play from the earliest stages of dating" (Taylor et al., 2011, p. 952).

One question surrounding attraction is how tendencies regarding mate preference that have evolved over generations play out in the modern era of internet dating and apps, speed-dating events, and social media.

And what about familiarity? As you will recall, research has demonstrated that familiarity typically promotes attraction, to the point where even mere exposure to an object or person increases liking. But you may also recall that mere exposure works in the opposite direction when the additional encounters reveal negative characteristics of the object or person in question. Of course, this is a risk with any type of dating, but particularly with online dating when people sometimes come to learn that aspects of their initial impression (based on an ambiguous or less than honest website profile) turn out to be inaccurate. Actually meeting someone in person typically reveals additional information, some of which may highlight incompatibilities and dissimilarities that make a successful relationship less likely (Norton et al., 2007; see Finkel et al., 2015).

The Promise and Pitfalls of Meeting People Online

Participation on dating websites and apps is at an all-time high and attitudes toward internet dating have never been more positive than they are today. These developments are understandable, particularly given that dating websites advertise three primary services: (1) aggregating a large number of profiles for browsing, (2) providing opportunity for communication with potential mates, and (3) matching users based on analyses of compatibility (Finkel et al., 2012). Clearly, online dating services have a lot to offer those who are looking for love (Blackhart, Fitzpatrick, & Williamson, 2014), and social psychologists are increasingly directing their attention to the study of dating websites and apps (Sevi, Aral, & Eskenazi 2017; Timmermans & De Caluwé, 2017).

Some of this research, though, is quick to point out that meeting people online is not always all that it's cracked up to be. As one example, Eli Finkel and colleagues (2012) reviewed data regarding online dating and concluded that although the practice has never been more popular, many of the promises made by websites and apps go unfulfilled. Specifically, the idea of mathematical algorithms that can point users toward ideally compatible mates finds little in the way of empirical support. Sure, more Americans than ever are pairing up online, but the success rate for dates facilitated in this manner is no higher than for dates engineered through more old-fashioned routes, like meeting at a party or getting fixed up by friends (Finkel et al., 2012).

The compatibility analyses of online dating services don't live up to their promises for a variety of reasons, according to Finkel and colleagues. First, as you read about in Chapter 5, sometimes we don't have a good sense of why we do what we do or what will make us happy. By the same token, we aren't always accurate when it comes to predicting the mate characteristics that will lead to a satisfying relationship. Second, most online dating algorithms focus on matching people by personality traits or other stable characteristics. But many of the best predictors of relationship satisfaction—like communication style and sexual compatibility—can't be assessed until people actually get to know each other (Finkel et al., 2012).

Another potential pitfall, as we alluded to earlier, is that online profiles aren't always accurate (Ellison, Hancock, & Toma, 2012)! For example, Catalina Toma and Jeffrey Hancock examined potential differences in how men and women describe themselves online. In one study, they interviewed 84 online daters, presenting them with a printout of their own dating profile and asking them how accurate they believed they were in describing their height, weight, and age (Toma, Hancock, & Ellison, 2008). The researchers were able to compare these self-assessments of accuracy to objective measures of participants' actual height, weight, and age. Results indicated that a full 81% of participants provided inaccurate information in their profile for at least one characteristic, with the most lies coming about weight, followed by age, then height. Interestingly, no gender differences emerged: Men and women were equally likely to try to stretch the truth. Participants' self-reported estimates of their profile accuracy were reasonably good predictors of actual accuracy, indicating that the discrepancies observed did not result from unconscious tendencies to view the self through rose-colored glasses, but rather intentional efforts to fudge facts.

A slightly different pattern emerges from analysis of photos used in dating profiles. Here, Hancock and Toma (2009) found that distortions are often less conscious, especially among women. Following a similar procedure to their previous study, the researchers interviewed online daters about how accurate they believed their profile photo to be. They then had a separate group of college students look at a series of two images side by side: (1) each participant's dating profile photo and (2) a photo taken of the participant during the recent interview. The college students were asked to evaluate how accurate a depiction the profile photograph was of the participant's current physical appearance. In total, 32% of profile photographs were judged to be deceptive or misleading, and females' photos were found to be less accurate than males'. Common inaccuracies included daters looking

"On the Internet, nobody knows you're a dog."

Peter Steiner/The New Yorker Collection/The Cartoon Bank

thinner in the profile photo than they currently do, having more hair in the profile photo than they do now, or using profile photos that were retouched or airbrushed. Unlike with written profiles, users' self-assessed accuracy ratings were not reliable predictors of the actual accuracy of their photo (as rated by the students), particularly among female daters.

In light of these inaccuracies—both intentional and unintentional—what's an internet dater to do? Luckily, the same research techniques that uncovered these inaccurate portrayals can also be used to identify which potential online mates are the most (and least) honest (Toma, 2017). Specifically, Toma and Hancock (2012) suggest three giveaways that the profile you're checking out online may not pass a reality check. First, deceptive profiles tend to have fewer first-person pronouns like *I* and *me*. The researchers explain that this is one way for those who lie or exaggerate to distance themselves psychologically from their half-truths. Second, deceptive profiles make more use of negations, or negative turns of phrase (e.g., "not judgmental" instead of "open-minded"; "not averse to taking risks" instead of "adventurous"). Third, deceptive profiles simply include fewer total words than accurate profiles. Stretching the truth is hard work and cognitively demanding; the fewer inaccurate statements you put in your profile, the fewer fabrications you have to remember later on when you meet someone in person. In short, online dating offers users a much larger pool of potential mates than do more traditional methods that are constrained by geography and other practical limitations. At the same time, in some important respects, dating sites and apps sometimes fall short of the promises they make to users.

Review Questions

1. Research on the influence of phones on social interaction indicates that
   a. contrary to what some critics believe, the availability of mobile phones has no negative effect on social engagement.
   b. men are more easily distracted by the presence of a phone during a conversation than are women.
   c. even if a phone isn't being used during a conversation, it can still pose a distraction that comes at the expense of social engagement.
   d. while laptops and tablets can be distracting during face-to-face interaction, phones are not.

2. Research on the effectiveness of dating websites and apps indicates that
   a. websites and apps using mathematical algorithms to match couples by compatibility are far more successful than more traditional ways of meeting a partner such as getting fixed up by friends.

   b. people tend to send messages to fellow website users whose attractiveness and popularity levels are similar to their own.
   c. these sites and apps are very popular among gay and lesbian users, but not among heterosexuals.
   d. the more you find out about someone you met online the more you tend to like that person.

3. Which of the following statements is true regarding how people tend to represent themselves in online dating profiles?
   a. Misrepresentation in online profiles tends to be of both the intentional and unintentional varieties.
   b. Deceptive web profiles tend to be longer and more detailed than accurate profiles.
   c. There are no gender differences in how men and women represent themselves online.
   d. The vast majority of people post inaccurate or misleading photos of themselves in online profiles.

Love and Close Relationships

LO 10.3 Examine the cultural, personality, and biological factors that are associated with different types of love.

By this point in the chapter, you have learned enough about attraction to make a favorable first impression the next time you meet someone. Suppose you want Sophia to like you. You should hang around her so that you become familiar, emphasize your similarity to her, and let her know you enjoy her company. But what if you want to do more than make a good impression? What if you want to have a close friendship or a romantic relationship?

Until recently, social psychologists had little to say in answer to this question—research on attraction focused almost exclusively on first impressions. Why? Primarily because long-term relationships are much more difficult to study scientifically than first impressions are. As you know by now, random assignment to different conditions is the hallmark of the experimental method. When studying first impressions, a researcher can randomly assign you to a get-acquainted session with someone who is similar or dissimilar to you. But a researcher can't randomly assign you to the similar or dissimilar "lover" condition and make you have a relationship! In addition, the feelings and intimacy associated with close relationships can be difficult to measure. Psychologists face a daunting task when trying to analyze such complex feelings as love and passion.

Defining Love: Companionship and Passion

Despite the difficulties inherent to studying close relationships, social psychologists have made interesting discoveries about the nature of love, how it develops, and how it flourishes. Let's begin with perhaps the most difficult question: What, exactly, is love? Early attempts to define love distinguished between liking and loving, showing that, as you might expect, love is something different from "lots of liking"—and not just in terms of sexual desire (Aumer, 2016; Sternberg, 1987).

For Shakespeare's Romeo and Juliet, love was passionate, turbulent, and full of longing. Perhaps your grandparents, if they've remained married for a long time, exemplify a calmer, more tranquil kind of love. We use the word *love* to describe all of these relationships, though each one seems to be of a different kind (Berscheid & Meyers, 1997; Fehr, 2013; Vohs & Baumeister, 2004).

Social psychologists have recognized that a good definition of love must include the passionate, giddy feelings of romantic love as well as the deep, long-term devotion of married couples, lifelong friends, or siblings. In defining love, then, we generally distinguish between *companionate love* and *passionate love* (Hatfield & Rapson, 1993; Hatfield & Walster, 1978). **Companionate love** consists of feelings of intimacy and affection we have for someone that are not accompanied by passion or physiological arousal. People can experience companionate love in nonsexual close friendships, or in romantic relationships in which they experience great feelings of intimacy but not as much of the heat and passion as they once felt.

Passionate love involves an intense longing for another person, characterized by the experience of physiological arousal—the feeling of shortness of breath and a thumping heart in someone's presence (Fisher, 2004; Ratelle et al., 2013; Regan & Berscheid, 1999). When things are going well (the other person loves us too), we feel great fulfillment and ecstasy. When things are not going well (our love is unrequited), we feel great sadness and despair. Elaine Hatfield and Susan Sprecher (1986) developed a questionnaire to measure passionate love, assessing strong, uncontrollable thoughts; intense feelings; and overt acts toward the target of one's affection. Find out if you are experiencing (or have experienced) passionate love by filling out the questionnaire in the following Try It! exercise.

Companionate Love

The feelings of intimacy and affection we have for someone that are not accompanied by passion or physiological arousal

Passionate Love

An intense longing we feel for a person, accompanied by physiological arousal

The relationship between Tris and Four in *Divergent* exemplifies the early stages of passionate love.

Try It!

Passionate Love Scale

These items ask you to describe how you feel when you are passionately in love. Think of the person whom you love most passionately right now. If you are not in love right now, think of the last person you loved passionately. If you have never been in love, think of the person you came closest to caring for in that way. Choose your answers as you remember how you felt when your feelings were the most intense.

For each of the 15 items, choose the number between 1 and 9 that most accurately describes your feelings. The answer scale ranges from 1 (not at all true) to 9 (definitely true). Write the number you choose next to each item.

```
1    2    3    4    5    6    7    8    9
↑                   ↑                   ↑
Not at all true   Moderately true   Definitely true
```

1. I would feel deep despair if _____ left me.
2. Sometimes I feel I can't control my thoughts; they are obsessively on _____.
3. I feel happy when I am doing something to make _____ happy.
4. I would rather be with _____ than anyone else.
5. I'd get jealous if I thought _____ were falling in love with someone else.

6. I yearn to know all about _____.
7. I want _____—physically, emotionally, mentally.
8. I have an endless appetite for affection from _____.
9. For me, _____ is the perfect romantic partner.
10. I sense my body responding when _____ touches me.
11. _____ always seems to be on my mind.
12. I want _____ to know me—my thoughts, my fears, and my hopes.
13. I eagerly look for signs indicating _____'s desire for me.
14. I possess a powerful attraction for _____.
15. I get extremely depressed when things don't go right in my relationship with _____.

Scoring: Add up your scores for the 15 items. The total score can range from a minimum of 15 to a maximum of 135. The higher your score, the more your feelings for the person reflect passionate love; the items to which you gave a particularly high score reflect those components of passionate love that you experience most strongly.

(Adapted from Hatfield & Rapson, 1990, p. 146.)

Figure 10.1 Sternberg's Triangular Theory of Love

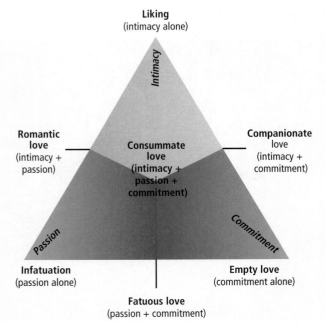

Perhaps you bristle a bit at the effort to scientifically define and classify an experience as mystical as love. Can we really capture different "types of love" in a theoretical model? Or perhaps you're having the opposite reaction: don't some relationships have characteristics of both companionate and passionate love? Are two types of love enough to capture such a complex set of feelings and interactions? If you find yourself asking this second set of questions, then, boy, do we have the theory for you! Robert Sternberg's (1986) *triangular theory* proposes that there are three major components to love. First, there is intimacy, which he defines as feelings of closeness and connectedness. Second, there's passion, involving physical attraction and drives that lead to sexual relations. And third, commitment over time.

Sternberg proposed that these three components could be present (or absent) in any combination, with each combination translating into a different type of love (see Figure 10.1). Intimacy plus passion? That would be romantic love, according to Sternberg. Commitment by itself, without either intimacy or passion? Empty love, according to the theory. When you take a look at the figure on the left, what do you think? Are any types of love still missing from Stenberg's model?

Culture and Love

The process of finding a romantic partner varies across the world. For example, in villages in Nepal, dating is forbidden, and even casual meetings between young men and women are considered inappropriate. Traditionally, a future spouse is chosen by one's parents, who focus on the potential mate's social standing: family, caste, and economic resources. In these arranged marriages, the bride and groom often speak to each other for the first time on their wedding day (Goode, 1999). Many of these unions turn out to be successful, especially considering the high divorce rate of unarranged marriages in the United States. That said, others might point out that the freedom to even consider seeking a divorce in an unhappy marriage is also something that varies by culture.

Beyond differences in custom and ceremony, cultures also differ with regard to how people think about, define, and experience love. As we have discussed throughout this book, Western and Eastern cultures vary with respect to how they conceptualize the needs of individuals, groups, and societies (Kim & Markus, 1999; Markus, Kitayama, & Heiman, 1996; Triandis, 1995). Social psychologists have noted that, although romantic love is deemed an important, even crucial, basis for marriage in individualistic societies, it is less emphasized in collectivistic ones. In individualistic societies, one immerses oneself in a new partner, virtually ignoring friends and family for a while. The decision regarding whom to become involved with or marry is for the most part a personal one. In comparison, in collectivistic societies, the individual in love must consider the wishes of family and other group members, which sometimes includes agreeing to an arranged marriage (Dion & Dion, 1993; Kamble et al., 2014; Levine et al., 1995). Interestingly, though, in recent decades Western ways of finding a partner have begun to permeate collectivistic cultures (Hatfield & Rapson, 2002). In Nepal, for example, prospective brides and grooms now write each other letters, getting to know each other a bit before the wedding (Goode, 1999).

Although people all over the world experience love, how love is defined can vary across cultures.

Cross-cultural research indicates that American couples tend to value passionate love more than Chinese couples do, and Chinese couples tend to value companionate love more than American couples do (Gao, 1993; Jankowiak, 1995; Ting-Toomey & Chung, 1996). In comparison, the Taita of Kenya, in East Africa, value both equally; they conceptualize romantic love as a combination of companionate and passionate love. The Taita consider this the best kind of love, and achieving it is a primary goal in their society (Bell, 1995). Reviewing the anthropological research on 166 societies, William Jankowiak and Edward Fischer (1992) found evidence for passionate love in 147 of them, as you can see in Table 10.2.

The results of studies such as these indicate that we all love, but we do not necessarily all love in the same way (Dion & Dion, 1996; Hatfield & Rapson, 2002; Li et al., 2010)—or at least we don't describe it in the same way (Landis & O'Shea, 2000). For example, the Japanese use the word *amae* as an extremely positive emotional state in which one is a totally passive love object, indulged and taken care of by one's romantic partner, much like a mother-infant relationship. Amae has no equivalent word in English or in any other Western language; the closest is the word *dependency*, an emotional state that Western cultures consider unhealthy in adult relationships (Dion & Dion, 1993; Doi, 1988; Farrer, Tsuchiya, & Bagrowicz, 2008).

Table 10.2 Cross-Cultural Evidence for Passionate Love Based on Anthropological Research in 166 Societies

Cultural Area	Passionate Love Present	Passionate Love Absent
Mediterranean	22 (95.7%)	1 (4.3%)
Sub-Saharan Africa	20 (76.9%)	6 (23.1%)
Eurasia	32 (97.0%)	1 (3.0%)
Insular Pacific	27 (93.1%)	2 (6.9%)
North America	24 (82.8%)	5 (17.2%)
South and Central America	22 (84.6%)	4 (15.4%)

(Based on data from Jankowiak & Fischer, 1992)

Similarly, the Chinese concept of *gan qing* differs from the Western view of romantic love. Gan qing is achieved by helping and working for another person; for example, a "romantic" act would be fixing someone's bicycle or helping someone learn new material (Gao, 1996). In Korea, a special kind of relationship is expressed by the concept of *jung*. Much more than "love," jung is what ties two people together. Couples in new relationships may feel strong love for each other, but they have not yet developed jung—that takes time and mutual experiences. Interestingly, jung can develop in negative relationships too—for example, between business rivals who dislike each other. Jung may unknowingly grow over time, with the result that they will feel that a strange connection exists between them (Kline, Horton, & Zhang, 2008; Lim & Choi, 1996).

Thus, it appears that romantic love is nearly universal in the human species, but cultural rules alter how that emotional state is experienced, expressed, and remembered (Higgins et al., 2002; Jackson et al., 2006). As one final example, Shuangyue Zhang and Susan Kline (2009) found two major differences in American and Chinese dating couples' decisions to marry. When describing how they would decide whether or not to marry their partners, Chinese students placed a heavier emphasis on two concepts central to their collectivistic culture: xiao (the obedience and devotion shown by children to their parents) and guanxi (relationships as a network of connections). In contrast, American students placed importance on receiving support, care, and "living a better life." As Robert Moore (1998) noted in summarizing his research in the People's Republic of China, "Young Chinese do fall deeply in love and experience the same joys and sorrows of romance as young Westerners do. But they do so according to standards that require ... the individual [to] sacrifice personal interests for the sake of the family ... This means avoiding fleeting infatuations, casual sexual encounters, and a dating context [where] family concerns are forgotten" (p. 280).

Attachment Styles in Intimate Relationships

Much as the culture in which we grow up shapes how we think about and experience love, so do our interactions in the early years of life with parents or caregivers. Specifically, one approach to examining intimate relationships among adults focuses on **attachment styles** and draws on the groundbreaking work of John Bowlby (1969, 1973, 1980) and Mary Ainsworth (Ainsworth et al., 1978) concerning how infants form bonds with their primary caregivers (usually their mothers or fathers).

Ainsworth and her colleagues (1978) identified three types of relationships between infants and their caregivers. They did so by creating a situation in which a caregiver briefly left his or her infant in an unfamiliar room with a stranger before returning. The infant's reactions upon separation and reunion with the parent were observed. Infants with a **secure attachment style** cry and show signs of distress when their parent leaves the room and are quite happy when he or she returns. These infants tend to trust their caregivers, show positive emotions when interacting with them, and are not particularly worried about abandonment. Infants with an **avoidant attachment style** do not react

Attachment Styles
The expectations people develop about relationships with others based on the relationship they had with their primary caregiver when they were infants

Secure Attachment Style
An attachment style characterized by trust, a lack of concern with being abandoned, and the view that one is worthy and well liked

Avoidant Attachment Style
An attachment style characterized by difficulty developing intimate relationships because previous attempts to be intimate have been rebuffed

much at their parent's departure or return. They desire to be close to their caregiver but learn to suppress this need, as if they know that such attempts will be rejected, sometimes by a caregiver who is aloof, distant, or busy. Infants with an **anxious/ambivalent attachment style** seem distressed even before the parent leaves the room and can be difficult to soothe even upon the parent's return, their response often a mixture of anger and indifference. These infants are unusually anxious, sometimes owing to an inability to predict when and how their caregivers will respond to their needs.

The key assumption of attachment theory is that the particular attachment style we learn in infancy becomes our working model or schema for what all relationships are like throughout adult life (Fraley & Shaver, 2000; Konrath et al., 2014; Mikulincer et al., 2009). Thus, people who as children had a secure relationship with their parents or caregivers are better able to develop mature, lasting relationships as adults; people who had avoidant relationships with their parents are less able to trust others and find it difficult to develop close, intimate relationships; and people who had anxious/ambivalent relationships with their parents want to become close to their adult partners but often worry that their partners will not return their affections (Collins & Feeney, 2000; Rholes, Simpson & Friedman, 2006; Simpson et al., 2007). This has been borne out in numerous studies using questionnaires to measure adults' attachment styles and analyzing correlations between attachment style and the quality of adult romantic relationships. For example, in one study researchers asked adults to choose one of the three statements shown in Table 10.3, according to how they typically feel in romantic relationships (Hazan & Shaver, 1987). Each statement was designed to capture one of the three kinds of attachment styles we described.

When researchers correlate adults' responses to questions about attachment style with their answers to questions about their current relationships, they find results consistent with an attachment theory perspective (Feeney, Cassidy, & Ramos-Marcuse, 2008; Feeney, Noller, & Roberts, 2000; Hazan & Shaver, 1994). For example, securely attached individuals tend to have the most enduring romantic relationships of the three attachment types. They experience the highest level of commitment to relationships as well as the highest level of satisfaction with their relationships. The anxious/ambivalently attached individuals have the most short-lived romantic relationships. They enter into relationships the most quickly, often before they know their partner well. One study conducted at a marriage license bureau found that anxious men acquired marriage licenses after a shorter courtship than did either secure or avoidant men (Senchak & Leonard, 1992). They are also the most upset and angriest of the three types when their love is not reciprocated. The third group, avoidant individuals, is the least likely to enter into a relationship and the most likely to report never having been in love. They maintain their emotional distance and have the lowest level of commitment to their relationships of the three types (Campbell et al., 2005; Collins et al., 2006; Keelan, Dion, & Dion, 1994).

It is important to note, however, that attachment theory does not suggest that people who had unhappy relationships with their parents are doomed to repeat this same kind of unhappy relationship with everyone they ever meet, or that secure attachment as an infant guarantees a healthy adult love life (Simms, 2002). Some researchers have recontacted their research participants months or years after their original studies and asked them to take the attachment-style scale again. They have found

Anxious/Ambivalent Attachment Style

An attachment style characterized by a concern that others will not reciprocate one's desire for intimacy, resulting in higher-than-average levels of anxiety

Attachment theory predicts that the attachment style we learn as infants and young children stays with us throughout life and generalizes to all of our relationships with other people.

Table 10.3 Measuring Adult Attachment Styles

As part of a survey of attitudes toward love published in a newspaper, people were asked to choose the statement that best described their romantic relationships. The attachment style each statement was designed to measure and the percentage of people who chose each alternative are indicated.

Secure style	56%	"I find it relatively easy to get close to others and am comfortable depending on them and having them depend on me. I don't often worry about being abandoned or about someone getting too close."
Avoidant style	25%	"I am somewhat uncomfortable being close to others; I find it difficult to trust them completely, difficult to allow myself to depend on them. I am nervous when anyone gets close, and often love partners want me to be more intimate than I feel comfortable being."
Anxious style	19%	"I find that others are reluctant to get as close as I would like. I often worry that my partner doesn't really love me or won't stay with me. I want to merge completely with another person, and this desire sometimes scares people away."

(Adapted from Hazan & Shaver, 1987)

that 25% to 30% of participants change from one attachment style to another (Feeney & Noller, 1996; Kirkpatrick & Hazan, 1994). People can and do change; their experiences in relationships can help them learn new ways of relating to others than what they experienced as children. Moreover, other research suggests that, at any given time, the attachment style that people display is the one that is called into play by their partner's behavior and the type of relationship that they've created as a couple. Thus, people can respond to situational variables in their relationships, displaying a more secure attachment style in one relationship and a more anxious one in another, or evolving in their attachment style within one relationship as time goes by (Fraley, 2002; Hadden et al., 2014; Simpson et al., 2003).

Your Body and Brain in Love

Falling in love is an extraordinary feeling, experienced by people in many different cultures with many different early childhood experiences. You feel giddy and euphoric. In the presence of your beloved, your heart races, your breathing quickens, and your body feels alert and full of energy. Indeed, most of us think of these bodily changes as symptoms of love. They can be. But it is also the case that bodily changes like these can make us more likely to fall for other people. That is, sometimes physiological arousal is a cause, rather than effect, of our attraction to others (Laird & Lacasse, 2014).

For example, in Chapter 5 we discussed Dutton and Aron's (1974) bridge studies, in which men whose hearts were still racing after they walked across an arousal-inducing suspension bridge showed greater signs of attraction to a female researcher who approached them. More recent research has also demonstrated this tendency to transfer feelings of physiological arousal to romantic feelings. Cindy Meston and Penny Frohlich (2003) approached men and women at an amusement park, surveying them either right before or after they rode a roller coaster. Participants who had just gone on the ride rated the stranger they were sitting next to as more attractive than did those about to go on the ride. These findings again demonstrate the bidirectional relationship between arousal and love. They also suggest that you may be more primed to meet that next special someone at the gym or on a hike rather than at the library or grocery store.

Psychologists have also studied what happens in our brains when we fall in love. One team of researchers recruited college students in the greater New York area who described themselves as currently being "intensely in love" (Aron et al., 2005). They asked these research participants to bring two photographs to the experimental session: one of their beloved and one of an acquaintance of the same age and sex as their beloved. After filling out some questionnaires (including the Try It! Passionate Love Scale you completed earlier), the participants were ready for the main event. They slid into a functional MRI (fMRI) scanner, which records increases and decreases in blood flow in the brain, thus indicating which regions of the brain have changes in neural activity at any given time. While the participant was in the scanner, the experimenters alternated projecting on a screen one photograph and then the other, interspersed with a mathematical distraction task.

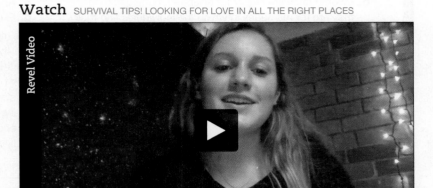

Watch SURVIVAL TIPS! LOOKING FOR LOVE IN ALL THE RIGHT PLACES

Revel Video

The researchers found that two specific areas, deep within the brain, showed evidence of increased activation when participants looked at the photograph of their romantic partner, but not when they looked at the photograph of their acquaintance (or when they engaged in the math task). Furthermore, those participants who self-reported higher levels of romantic love showed greater activation in these areas when looking at their beloved than those who reported lower levels (Aron et al., 2005). These two brain areas were the ventral tegmental area (VTA) and the caudate nucleus, which communicate with each other as part of a circuit.

Prior research has found that the VTA becomes active when we engage in rewarding behaviors, such as when people ingest cocaine—a drug that induces feelings of pleasure, euphoria, restlessness, sleeplessness, and loss of appetite (reactions that, wouldn't you know it, are also reminiscent of falling in love). The VTA, rich in the neurotransmitter dopamine, also fires when people eat chocolate. In short, the VTA and the caudate nucleus constitute a major reward and motivation center of the brain. For example, fMRI studies of gamblers' brains show greatly increased activity in these dopamine-rich areas when they win—a rewarding and motivating event (Aron et al., 2005). Thus, when people say that falling in love is "addictive," "like a drug," or "like winning the lottery," they're right. All these experiences predict greater activation in the same areas of the brain: dopamine-rich centers of pleasure, reward, and motivation (Bartels & Zeki, 2004; Fisher, 2004; Scheele et al., 2013).

Review Questions

1. Whereas _____ love is characterized by feelings of intimacy and affection, _____ love tends to include intense longing and physiological arousal.
   a. platonic; romantic
   b. tranquil; sexual
   c. companionate; passionate
   d. empty; erotic

2. Which of the following is not one of the three major components of love, according to Sternberg's triangular theory of love?
   a. Intimacy
   b. Passion
   c. Reciprocity
   d. Commitment

3. Which of the following is *not* one of the cross-cultural research findings about love and relationships reported in this chapter?
   a. Unlike in the United States where it is conventional for married couples to live together, in many areas of West Africa, married couples live apart, prioritizing the connection with extended family over that with a spouse.
   b. As indicated by the concept of *yuan*, Chinese are more likely to believe that relationship outcomes are determined by fate than are Americans.
   c. Romantic love seems universal among humans, even as culture shapes how that emotional state is experienced and expressed.

d. Divorce rates are higher for arranged marriages than they are for marriages in which the individuals find their own spouse.

4. Which attachment style below is best captured by the following sentiment: "I am uncomfortable being close to others and find it difficult to trust people completely. I am nervous when anyone gets close, and often my partners want me to be more intimate than I feel comfortable being."
   a. Secure attachment style
   b. Avoidant attachment style
   c. Anxious/ambivalent attachment style
   d. Exchange attachment style

5. The regions of the brain that exhibit signs of increased activity when someone thinks about feelings of romantic love are the same regions that exhibit signs of increased activity when a person
   a. sleeps.
   b. ingests cocaine.
   c. cries.
   d. is anxious about being the focus of attention.

Assessing Relationships: Satisfaction and Breaking Up

LO 10.4 **Analyze different theories of measuring relationship satisfaction and research regarding romantic breakups.**

So far, we've examined attraction and the ways in which people define and experience love. But how exactly do individuals assess how their relationships are going? What factors shape how happy they are with their current mate or with their "love life" more generally? What determines whether people remain committed to a current relationship or start considering alternatives? And if they do decide to end a relationship, what are the psychological consequences of breaking up? We turn now to theories of relationship satisfaction and dissolution in the attempt to provide empirically based answers to these most intimate of questions.

Theories of Relationship Satisfaction

Relationships are not like the stock market or presidential approval ratings. Few of us keep daily charts or graphs in which we record precisely how happy we are with our current partner (which is likely a good thing!). That said, many of us periodically take stock of how our relationships are going more generally, perhaps on a significant anniversary or because someone asks directly. Or maybe because a fight or other aggravation with a partner makes us stop to ponder just how satisfied we really are. Below we review two influential theories regarding relationship satisfaction: social exchange theory and equity theory.

SOCIAL EXCHANGE THEORY   Many of the variables we have discussed as antecedents of attraction can be thought of as examples of social rewards. It is pleasing to have our attitudes validated; thus, the more similar a person's attitudes are to ours, the more rewarded we are by spending time together. Likewise, it is rewarding to be around someone who likes us, particularly when that person is physically attractive. In other words, the more social rewards (and the fewer costs) a person provides us with, the more we like the person. The flip side of this equation is that if a relationship costs (e.g., in terms of emotional turmoil) far more than it gives (e.g., in terms of validation or praise), chances are that it will not last.

This simple notion that relationships operate on an economic model of costs and benefits, much like other marketplaces, has been expanded by researchers into complex theories of social exchange (Cook et al., 2013; Kelley & Thibaut, 1978; Thibaut & Kelley, 1959). **Social exchange theory** holds that how people feel about a relationship will depend on their perceptions of the rewards they receive from it, their perceptions of the costs they incur, their beliefs regarding what kind of relationship they deserve,

Social Exchange Theory

The idea that people's feelings about a relationship depend on their perceptions of its rewards and costs, the kind of relationship they deserve, and their chances for having a better relationship with someone else and the probability that they could find a better relationship with someone else. In essence, we "buy" the best relationship we can get—one that gives us the most value for our emotional dollar based on the options on the table. The basic concepts of social exchange theory are reward, cost, outcome, and comparison level.

Rewards are the gratifying aspects of a relationship that make it worthwhile and reinforcing. They include the kinds of personal characteristics and behaviors of our relationship partner, and our ability to acquire external resources by virtue of knowing this person (e.g., gaining access to money, status, activities, or other interesting people; Lott & Lott, 1974). For example, in Brazil, friendship is openly used as an exchange value. Brazilians will readily admit that they need a *pistolão* (literally, a big, powerful handgun), meaning that they need a person who will use personal connections to help them get what they want (Rector & Neiva, 1996). Costs are, obviously, the other side of the coin, and all friendships and romantic relationships have some costs attached, such as putting up with those annoying habits and characteristics of the other person. The outcome of the relationship is a direct comparison of its rewards and costs; you can think of it as a mathematical formula where outcome equals rewards minus costs. If you come up with a negative number, your relationship is not in good shape.

In addition to rewards and costs, how satisfied you are with your relationship depends on another variable: your **comparison level**, or what you *expect* the outcome of your relationship to be in terms of costs and rewards (Kelley & Thibaut, 1978; Thibaut & Kelley, 1959). Over time, you have amassed a long history of relationships with others, and this history has led you to have certain expectations as to what your current and future relationships should be like. Some people have a high comparison level, expecting lots of rewards and few costs in their relationships. If a given relationship doesn't match this lofty expected comparison level, they quickly will grow unhappy and unsatisfied. In contrast, people who have a low comparison level would be happy in the same relationship because they expect their relationships to be difficult and costly.

Finally, your satisfaction with a relationship also depends on your perception of the likelihood that you could replace it with a better one—or your **comparison level for alternatives**. As the saying goes, there are plenty of fish in the sea. Could a relationship with a different person give you a better outcome than your current one? People who have a high comparison level for alternatives—either because they believe the world is full of fabulous people dying to meet them or because they know of one particular fabulous person dying to meet them—are more likely to take the plunge, change things up, and hit the market for a new friend or lover. People with a low comparison level for alternatives will be more likely to stay in a costly relationship, because, in their mind, what they have may not be great, but it's better than what they expect they could find elsewhere (Etcheverry, Le, & Hoffman, 2013; Lehmiller & Agnew, 2006; Simpson, 1987).

Social exchange theory has received a great deal of empirical support. Friends and romantic couples often do pay attention to the costs and rewards in their relationships, and these perceptions predict how positively people feel about the status of the relationship (Bui, Peplau, & Hill, 1996; Cook et al., 2013; Rusbult, 1983). Such findings have been observed for intimate relationships in cultures as different as Taiwan and the Netherlands (Le & Agnew, 2003; Lin & Rusbult, 1995; Van Lange et al., 1997). Generally speaking, when relationships are seen as offering a lot of rewards, people report feeling happy and satisfied.

However, many people do not leave their partners even when they are dissatisfied and their other alternatives look bright. Research indicates that we need to consider

According to social exchange theory, this couple's relationship satisfaction will depend on the two individuals' perceptions of benefits and costs, but also their more general expectations for how rewarding relationships should be.

Comparison Level

People's expectations about the level of rewards and costs they are likely to receive in a particular relationship

Comparison Level for Alternatives

People's expectations about the level of rewards and costs they would receive in an alternative relationship

Investment Model

The theory that people's commitment to a relationship depends not only on their satisfaction with the relationship, but also on how much they have invested in the relationship that would be lost by ending it

at least one additional factor to understand close relationships: a person's level of investment in the relationship (Carter et al., 2013; Goodfriend & Agnew, 2008; Rusbult et al., 2001). In her **investment model** of close relationships, Caryl Rusbult (1983) defines *investment* as anything people have put into a relationship that will be lost if they leave it. Examples include tangible things, such as financial resources, possessions, and property, as well as intangible things, such as the emotional welfare of one's children, the time and emotional energy spent building the relationship, and the sense of personal integrity that will be lost if one gets divorced. As seen in Figure 10.2, the greater the investment individuals have in a relationship, the less likely they are to leave, even when satisfaction is low and other alternatives look promising. In short, to predict whether people will stay in an intimate relationship, we need to know (1) how satisfied they are with the relationship, (2) what they think of their alternatives, and (3) how great their investment in the relationship is.

To test this model, Rusbult (1983) asked college students involved in heterosexual dating relationships to fill out questionnaires over the course of 7 months. Every 3 weeks, people answered questions about each of the components of the model shown in Figure 10.2. Rusbult also kept track of whether the students stayed in the relationships or broke up. As you can see in Figure 10.3, satisfaction, alternatives, and investments all predicted how committed people were to the relationship and whether it lasted. (The higher the number on the scale, the more each factor predicted the commitment to and length of the relationship.) Subsequent studies have found results similar to those shown in Figure 10.3 for married couples of different ages, lesbian and gay couples, nonsexual friendships, and residents of both the United States and Taiwan (Kurdek, 1992; Lin & Rusbult, 1995; Rusbult & Buunk, 1993).

Does the same model hold for destructive relationships? To find out, Rusbult and a colleague interviewed women who had sought refuge at a shelter for victims of domestic abuse (Rusbult & Martz, 1995). Why had these women stayed in these relationships, even to the point where some of them returned to an abusive partner? As

Figure 10.2 The Investment Model of Commitment

People's commitment to a relationship depends on several variables. First, their *satisfaction* with the relationship is based on their comparing their *rewards* to their costs and determining if the outcome exceeds their general expectation of what they should get in a relationship (or *comparison level*). Next, their *commitment* to the relationship depends on three variables: how *satisfied* they are, how much they feel they have *invested* in the relationship, and whether they have good *alternatives* to this relationship. These commitment variables in turn predict how stable the relationship will be. For example, a woman who feels her relationship has more costs and fewer rewards than she considers acceptable would have low satisfaction. If she also felt she had little invested in the relationship and an attractive person had just asked her for a date, she would have a low level of commitment. The end result is low stability; most likely, she will break up with her current partner.

(Adapted from Rusbult, 1983)

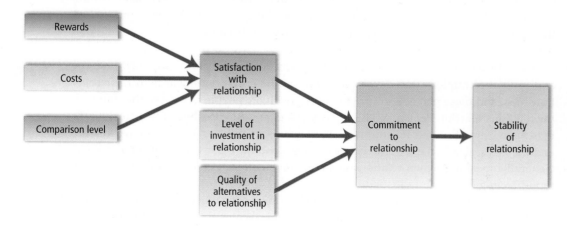

Figure 10.3 A Test of the Investment Model

This study examined the extent to which college students' satisfaction with a relationship, their comparison level for alternatives, and their investment in the relationship predicted their commitment to the relationship and their decision about whether to break up with their partner. The higher the number, the more each variable predicted commitment and breakup, independent of the two other variables. All three variables were good predictors of how committed people were and whether or not they broke up.

(Adapted from Rusbult, 1983)

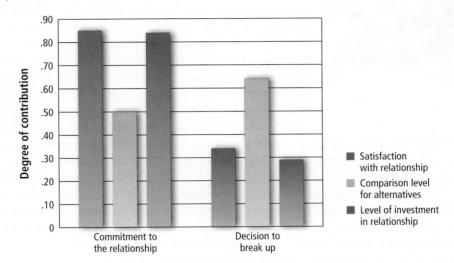

the theory predicts, feelings of commitment to the abusive relationship were greater among women who had poorer economic alternatives to the relationship or were more heavily invested in the relationship. In long-term relationships, then, commitment is based on more than just the amount of rewards and costs a partner elicits; it also depends on people's perceptions of their investments in, satisfaction with, and alternatives to the relationship.

EQUITY THEORY   Some researchers have criticized social exchange theory for ignoring an essential variable in relationships—the notion of fairness, or equity. Proponents of **equity theory** argue that people don't engage in relationships the way they do board games, doing anything they can to end up with the most reward in the bank. We aren't just out to get the most rewards for the least cost, the argument goes: We are also concerned about equity or the idea that the rewards and costs we experience should be roughly equal to those of the other person involved (Bowles, 2016; Kalmijn & Monden, 2012; Walster, Walster, & Berscheid, 1978). Indeed, these theorists describe equitable relationships as the happiest and most stable, whereas, inequitable relationships result in one person feeling overbenefited (getting a lot of rewards, incurring few costs, having to devote little time or energy to the relationship) and the other feeling underbenefited (getting few rewards, incurring a lot of costs, having to devote a lot of time and energy to the relationship).

According to equity theory, both underbenefited and overbenefited partners should feel uneasy about this state of affairs, and both should be motivated to restore equity to the relationship. This makes sense for the underbenefited person—after all, who wants to feel miserable and unappreciated? But why should the overbenefited individual want to give up what social exchange theory indicates is a cushy deal, lots of rewards for little cost and little work? Theorists argue that equity is a powerful social norm and that people will eventually feel uncomfortable and guilty if they keep getting more than they deserve in a relationship. Still, being overbenefited isn't as bad as being underbenefited, and research has indicated that inequity is perceived as *more* of a problem by the underbenefited individual (Buunk & Schaufeli, 1999; Guerrero, La Valley, & Farinelli, 2008; Sprecher, 2016).

Equity Theory

The idea that people are happiest with relationships in which the rewards and costs experienced by both parties are roughly equal

Close relationships can have either exchange or communal properties. Family relationships are typically communal.

Exchange Relationships

Relationships governed by the need for equity (i.e., for an equal ratio of rewards and costs)

Communal Relationships

Relationships in which people's primary concern is being responsive to the other person's needs

Of course, this whole notion of equity implies that partners in a relationship are keeping track of who is benefiting, who is getting shortchanged, and by how much. Some might suggest that many people in happy relationships don't spend so much time and energy keeping tabs in this manner. Indeed, the more we get to know someone, the more reluctant we are to believe that we are simply exchanging favors or expecting compensation for every kind gesture. Sure, in casual relationships, we trade "in kind"—you lend someone your class notes, she buys you lunch. But in intimate relationships, we're trading different types of resources, so even if we wanted to, determining whether or not equity has been achieved becomes difficult. Does taking out your significant other to a nice dinner one night balance out the fact that you had to work late the previous two nights? In other words, long-term, intimate relationships may be governed by a looser give-and-take notion of equity rather than a rigid tit-for-tat strategy (Kollack, Blumstein, & Schwartz, 1994; Laursen & Hartup, 2002; Vaananen et al., 2005).

According to Margaret Clark and Judson Mills (1993), interactions between new acquaintances are governed by equity concerns and are called **exchange relationships**. As you can see in Figure 10.4, in exchange relationships, people keep track of who is contributing what and feel taken advantage of when they feel they are putting more into the relationship than they are getting out of it. In comparison, longer-term interactions between close friends, family members, and romantic partners are governed less by an equity norm and more by a desire to help each other as needed. In these **communal relationships**, people give in response to the other's needs, regardless of whether

Figure 10.4 Exchange Versus Communal Relationships

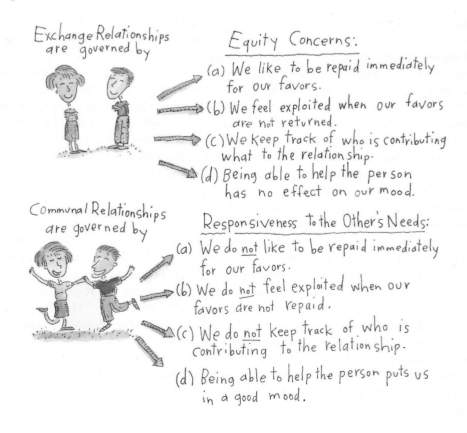

Exchange Relationships are governed by

Equity Concerns:
(a) We like to be repaid immediately for our favors.
(b) We feel exploited when our favors are not returned.
(c) We keep track of who is contributing what to the relationship.
(d) Being able to help the person has no effect on our mood.

Communal Relationships are governed by

Responsiveness to the Other's Needs:
(a) We do _not_ like to be repaid immediately for our favors.
(b) We do _not_ feel exploited when our favors are not repaid.
(c) We do _not_ keep track of who is contributing to the relationship.
(d) Being able to help the person puts us in a good mood.

they get paid back (Abele & Brack, 2013; Mills & Clark, 2011; Vaananen et al., 2005). In this manner, communal interactions are the hallmark of long-term, intimate relationships. Research comparing heterosexual couples to same-sex couples has found that they are equally committed and communal in their relationships: if anything, gay men and lesbians report greater compatibility and less conflict than heterosexual couples do (Balsam et al., 2008; Roisman et al., 2008).

Are people in communal relationships completely unconcerned with equity? Not necessarily. As we saw previously, people do feel distressed if they believe their intimate relationships are inequitable (Canary & Stafford, 2001; Walster et al., 1978); however, equity takes on a somewhat different form in communal relationships than it does in less intimate ones. In communal relationships, the partners are more relaxed about what constitutes equity at any given time, believing that things will eventually balance out and a rough kind of equity will be achieved over the long run (Lemay & Clark, 2008; Lemay, Clark, & Feeney, 2007). If this doesn't happen—if they continue to feel that there is an imbalance—the relationship may ultimately end.

The Process and Experience of Breaking Up

The American divorce rate is nearly 50% and has been for the past few decades (Kennedy & Ruggles, 2014; National Center for Health Statistics, 2005). An examination of data from 58 societies, taken from the *Demographic Yearbook of the United Nations*, indicates that the majority of separations and divorces occur after just three or four years of marriage (Fisher, 2004). And, of course, countless romantic relationships between unmarried individuals end every day. Ending a romantic relationship is one of life's more painful experiences, and below we consider research about what prompts couples to break up and the disengagement strategies they use when doing so (Frazier & Cook, 1993; Rusbult & Zembrodt, 1983; Sprecher, Zimmerman, & Fehr, 2014).

For example, Steve Duck (1982) reminds us that relationship dissolution is not a single event but a process with many steps (see Figure 10.5). Duck theorizes that there are four stages to dissolving a relationship, ranging from the intrapersonal

---

Figure 10.5 Steps in Dissolving Close Relationships

(Based on Duck, 1982)

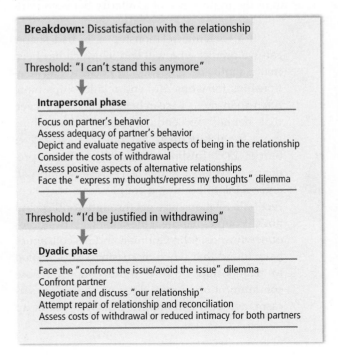

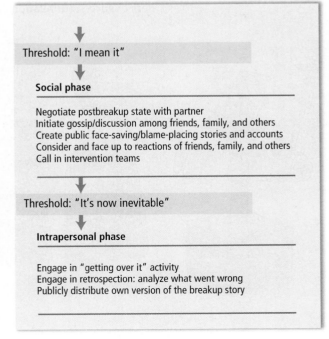

Breakdown: Dissatisfaction with the relationship

Threshold: "I can't stand this anymore"

Intrapersonal phase

Focus on partner's behavior
Assess adequacy of partner's behavior
Depict and evaluate negative aspects of being in the relationship
Consider the costs of withdrawal
Assess positive aspects of alternative relationships
Face the "express my thoughts/repress my thoughts" dilemma

Threshold: "I'd be justified in withdrawing"

Dyadic phase

Face the "confront the issue/avoid the issue" dilemma
Confront partner
Negotiate and discuss "our relationship"
Attempt repair of relationship and reconciliation
Assess costs of withdrawal or reduced intimacy for both partners

Threshold: "I mean it"

Social phase

Negotiate postbreakup state with partner
Initiate gossip/discussion among friends, family, and others
Create public face-saving/blame-placing stories and accounts
Consider and face up to reactions of friends, family, and others
Call in intervention teams

Threshold: "It's now inevitable"

Intrapersonal phase

Engage in "getting over it" activity
Engage in retrospection: analyze what went wrong
Publicly distribute own version of the breakup story

(the individual thinks a lot about his or her dissatisfaction with the relationship) to the dyadic (the individual discusses the breakup with the partner) to the social (the breakup is announced to other people) and back to the intrapersonal (the individual recovers from the breakup and forms an internal account of how and why it happened). In terms of the last stage in the process, John Harvey and colleagues (Harvey, 1995; Harvey, Flanary, & Morgan, 1986) have found that the honest version of "why the relationship ended" that we present to close friends can be very different from the official version that we present to coworkers or neighbors.

Why relationships end has been studied from several angles (Bui et al., 1996; Drigotas & Rusbult, 1992). For example, Caryl Rusbult has identified four types of behavior that occur in troubled relationships (Rusbult, 1987; Rusbult & Zembrodt, 1983). The first two are destructive behaviors: actively harming the relationship (e.g., abusing the partner, threatening to break up, actually leaving) and passively allowing the relationship to deteriorate (e.g., refusing to deal with problems, ignoring the partner or spending less time together, putting no energy into the relationship). The other two responses are positive, constructive behaviors: actively trying to improve the relationship (e.g., discussing problems, trying to change, going to a therapist) and passively remaining loyal to the relationship (e.g., waiting and hoping that the situation will improve, being supportive rather than fighting, remaining optimistic). Rusbult and her colleagues have found that destructive behaviors harm a relationship a lot more than constructive behaviors help it. When one partner acts destructively and the other partner responds constructively to save the relationship, a common pattern, the relationship is likely to continue, but when both partners act destructively, the relationship typically ends (Rusbult, Johnson, & Morrow, 1986; Rusbult, Yovetich, & Verette, 1996).

Another approach to studying why relationships end considers what attracted the people to each other in the first place. For example, in one study, college men and women were asked to focus on a former romantic relationship to list the qualities that first attracted them to the person and the characteristics they ended up disliking the most about the person (Femlee, 1995, 1998). In 30% of these breakups, the very qualities that were initially so attractive became the very reasons why the relationship ended. For example, "He's so unusual and different" became "He and I have nothing in common." "She's so exciting and unpredictable" became "I can never count on her." This type of breakup reminds us again of the importance of similarity between partners to successful relationships.

If a romantic relationship is in bad shape, can we predict who will end it? Much has been made about the tendency in heterosexual relationships for women to end relationships more often than men. Research has found, however, that neither sex ends romantic relationships more frequently than the other (Hagestad & Smyer, 1982; Rusbult et al., 1986). A better predictor of whether and when a relationship will end seems to be how a couple deals with conflict. All relationships go through conflict, but not all couples handle it the same way. In studies of newlyweds, John Gottman and his colleagues have found that when discussing issues related to relationship conflict, those couples whose communication shows signs of contempt, sarcasm, and criticism are more likely to break up (and break up sooner) than other couples (Gottman, 2014; Gottman & Levenson, 2002). Couples better able to weather the storms of conflict are those who wait to calm down before hashing out a disagreement and those who exhibit an ability to listen without automatically getting defensive.

Other research has examined the experience of breaking up, seeking to predict the different ways people will act and feel when their relationship ends (Connolly & McIsaac, 2009; Helgeson, 1994; Lloyd & Cate, 1985). Some research has indicated that investment plays a role in postbreakup interactions, as couples with higher rates of satisfaction and investment during the course of their relationship are also more likely to remain friends afterward (Tan et al., 2014). And while remaining friends with an ex-partner may be a positive outcome for many formerly intimate relationships, other research indicates that efforts to stay in contact or even monitor the new exploits of a former lover—perhaps simply by continuing to keep track of that person's activity via social media—can also be distressing and render it more challenging to adjust to the breakup (Belu, Lee, & O'Sullivan, 2016).

Indeed, from an emotional standpoint, it will come as little surprise to learn that research indicates that breaking up can be quite difficult. For example, Kimberly Balsam, Sharon Rostosky, and Ellen Riggle (2017) conducted interviews with women who had been in same-sex relationships that had recently ended. These interviews revealed three main themes in terms of these women's emotional reactions to their break-up: shame/guilt; feelings of failure; a sense of isolation and loneliness. Other research indicates that men and women tend to exhibit similar levels of distress after a breakup, and that, as one would expect, while even initiating a breakup can be stressful, being broken up with tends to lead to an even stronger negative emotional response (Sprecher, 1994).

In short, the social psychological research literature on close relationships spans the entire range of our most intimate of connections with others—from initial attraction and mate selection, to sexual behavior, to relationship satisfaction, to the heartbreak of breaking up … and then, in many instances, starting at least part of that trajectory all over again.

Review Questions

1. Although her girlfriend treats her well, always puts her needs first, and doesn't demand much in the way of relationship effort from her, Courtney feels unsatisfied with the relationship because a little voice in her head keeps telling her there must be an even better mate out there for her somewhere. Courtney seems to have
   a. a high comparison level.
   b. a low comparison level.
   c. a low comparison level for alternatives.
   d. a high sense of investment.

2. Equity theory suggests that if a relationship is not equitable
   a. the overbenefited individual will still be satisfied with it.
   b. both the underbenefited and the overbenefited individuals will still be satisfied with it.
   c. both the underbenefited and the overbenefited individuals will be unsatisfied with it.
   d. it will transition from a communal relationship to an exchange relationship.

3. Which of the following is an example of an intrapersonal stage to relationship dissolution?
   a. The breakup is announced to other people.
   b. One member of the couple thinks a lot about his or her relationship dissatisfaction.
   c. One member of the couple discusses the potential breakup with the other person.
   d. The couple decides to get back together.

4. Which of the following findings regarding breakups is true?
   a. Initiating a breakup is even more distressing than being broken up with.
   b. The dissolution of same-sex relationships is not marked by the same type and amount of negative emotional response as is the dissolution of cross-sex relationships.
   c. Staying in contact and up-to-date on the new exploits of an ex-partner can have both positive and negative effects on an individual after a breakup.
   d. On average, men are not nearly as upset by breakups as are women.

Summary

LO 10.1 Describe how people decide whom they like and want to get to know better.

- **What Predicts Attraction?**

  - **The Person Next Door: The Propinquity Effect** In the first part of this chapter, we discussed the variables that cause initial attraction between two people. One such variable is physical proximity, or the *propinquity effect*: People who you come into contact with the most are the most likely to become your friends and lovers. This occurs because of the *mere exposure effect*: Exposure to a stimulus increases liking for it.

  - **Similarity** Similarity between people, whether in attitudes, values, demographic characteristics, physical appearance, and even genetics is also a powerful predictor of attraction and liking. Similarity is more associated with attraction than complementarity, the idea that opposites attract, especially for long-term relationship formation.

  - **Reciprocal Liking** In general, we like others who behave as if they like us.

  - **Physical Attractiveness** Physical attractiveness also plays an important role in liking. People from different cultures perceive facial attractiveness quite similarly. The "what is beautiful is good" stereotype is an example of a *halo effect*, the tendency to believe that an individual who possesses one positive characteristic also possesses other, unrelated positive traits. Specifically, people assume that physical attractiveness is associated with a variety of other desirable traits, sometimes leading to self-fulfilling prophecies.

  - **Evolution and Mate Selection** Evolutionary psychology explains love in terms of genetic factors that have evolved over time according to the principles of natural selection. According to this perspective, which is not without its critics, men and women are attracted to different characteristics because this maximizes their reproductive success.

LO 10.2 Explain how new technologies shape attraction and social connections.

- **Making Connections in the Digital World**

  - New technologies provide social psychologists with new questions to ask about attraction and relationships, including whether phones and other mobile devices can undermine social connectedness.

  - **Attraction 2.0: Mate Preference in an Online Era** Basic predictors of attraction such as propinquity, similarity, and familiarity manifest themselves differently in the modern era of text messages, the internet, and social media.

  - **The Promise and Pitfalls of Meeting People Online** Online and mobile app-based dating expands your pool of potential mates, but carries its own risks, including unproven compatibility algorithms and deceptive profile descriptions and photos.

LO 10.3 Examine the cultural, personality, and biological factors that are associated with different types of love.

- **Love and Close Relationships**

  - **Defining Love: Companionship and Passion** One definition of love makes a distinction between *companionate love*, feelings of intimacy that are not accompanied by intense longing and arousal, and *passionate love*, feelings of intimacy that are accompanied by intense longing and arousal.

  - **Culture and Love** Although love is a universal emotion, there are cultural variations in the practice and definition of love. Love has a somewhat different emphasis in collectivistic and individualistic cultures.

  - **Attachment Styles in Intimate Relationships** People's past relationships with their caregivers are significant predictors of the quality of their close relationships as adults. There are three types of attachment relationships: *secure, avoidant*, and *anxious/ambivalent*.

  - **Your Body and Brain in Love** The experience of falling in love can also be examined at the level of the brain. Functional magnetic resonance imaging studies indicate that thinking about someone with whom you are in love leads to greater activation in regions of the brain also activated by other pleasurable rewards.

LO 10.4 Analyze different theories of measuring relationship satisfaction and research regarding romantic breakups.

- **Assessing Relationships: Satisfaction and Breaking Up**

  - **Theories of Relationship Satisfaction** Social Exchange Theory states that how people feel about their relationship depends on their perception of the rewards they receive and the costs they incur. In order to determine whether people will stay in a relationship, we need to know their *comparison level* (expectations about the outcomes of their relationship), their *comparison level for alternatives* (expectations about how happy they would be in other relationships), as well as their *investment* in the relationship. Equity theory states that the most important determinant of satisfaction is that both parties feel comparably rewarded by the relationship. People are less likely to track costs and rewards in communal relationships than in exchange relationships.

- **The Process and Experience of Breaking Up** Strategies for responding to problems in a romantic relationship include both constructive and destructive behaviors. The breaking-up process is often composed of stages. Various factors predict how people will act and feel after a break-up, though continued contact with an ex-partner can have both positive and negative effects.

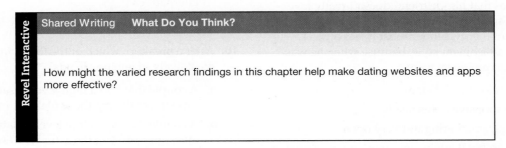

Revel Interactive

Shared Writing   **What Do You Think?**

How might the varied research findings in this chapter help make dating websites and apps more effective?

Test Yourself

1. Sam has his eye on Julie and wants her to like him. According to research in social psychology, which of the following is *least* likely to work?

  a. Emphasizing how similar their attitudes are

  b. Arranging to work with her on a class project so that he can spend time with her

  c. Emphasizing that they have complementary personalities and that opposites attract

  d. Making himself look as physically attractive as he can

2. Which of the following is a benefit of online dating?

  a. The ability to achieve propinquity with a wider range of people

  b. Mathematical formulas that are highly effective at creating compatibility matches

  c. People tend to be more honest about themselves online

  d. With online dating, there's no such thing as potential mates feeling "out of your league"

3. Which of the following is *false*?

  a. People in communal relationships tend to keep track of who is contributing what to the relationship.

  b. People find "average" faces to be more attractive than unusual faces.

  c. People like others who like them.

  d. The more we see and interact with people, the more we will like them.

4. Katie and Madeline are dating. According to the *investment model of close relationships*, which of the following will influence their commitment to the relationship?

  a. Their satisfaction with the relationship

  b. Their level of investment in the relationship

  c. The availability and quality of alternative partners

  d. All of these answers are correct.

5. _____ involves intense longing for another person, accompanied by physiological arousal.

  a. Passionate love

  b. Companionate love

  c. Exchange love

  d. Communal love

6. Which of the following statements regarding attachment style is true?

  a. Few if any individuals change their attachment style once they reach adulthood.

  b. A majority of adults have been found to exhibit an avoidant attachment style.

  c. The attachment style that adults display is shaped by their partner's behavior and the type of relationship they've created as a couple.

  d. Your attachment style as an infant typically has little to do with the attachment style you have in your adult relationships.

7. Marquel and Eric have been friends since the beginning of the school year. According to equity theory, their friendship will suffer if

   a. Eric is much more likely to help Marquel out when he needs it than Marquel is to help Eric.

   b. Eric has a "makeover" and suddenly becomes far more attractive than Marquel.

   c. Eric and Marquel stop having similar interests.

   d. Eric and Marquel are romantically interested in the same person.

8. Elliot worries that his girlfriend doesn't really love him and he smothers her with attention. According to attachment theory, Elliot probably has a(n) _____ attachment style, because when he was an infant, his caregivers were _____.

   a. avoidant; aloof and distant

   b. secure; responsive to his needs

   c. communal; smothering but very open

   d. anxious/ambivalent; inconsistent and overbearing

9. You are considering breaking up with your significant other after 1 month of being a couple. While the relationship gives you lots of rewards and has few costs, you have recently met someone new whom you anticipate will give you even more rewards for even fewer costs. Your dilemma stems from the fact that you have a _____ and a _____.

   a. low comparison level; high comparison level for alternatives

   b. high comparison level; high comparison level for alternatives

   c. low comparison level; low comparison level for alternatives

   d. high comparison level; low equity level

10. After a breakup, which of the following couples is most likely to remain friends?

   a. A couple that had a high level of satisfaction and investment during the actual relationship.

   b. A couple that had a low level of satisfaction and investment during the actual relationship

   c. A couple that initially met online

   d. A couple in which one individual was overbenefited and the other was underbenefited

Chapter 11
Prosocial Behavior
Why Do People Help?

Chapter Outline and Learning Objectives

Basic Motives Underlying Prosocial Behavior: Why Do People Help?

LO 11.1 Describe the basic motives that determine whether people help others.

Evolutionary Psychology: Instincts and Genes
Social Exchange: The Costs and Rewards of Helping
Empathy and Altruism: The Pure Motive for Helping

Personal Qualities and Prosocial Behavior: Why Do Some People Help More than Others?

LO 11.2 Describe the personal qualities that influence whether a given individual will help.

Individual Differences: The Altruistic Personality
Gender Differences in Prosocial Behavior
Cultural Differences in Prosocial Behavior
Religion and Prosocial Behavior
The Effects of Mood on Prosocial Behavior

Situational Determinants of Prosocial Behavior: When Will People Help?

LO 11.3 Describe the situations in which people are more likely, or less likely, to help others.

Environment: Rural Versus Urban
Residential Mobility
The Number of Bystanders: The Bystander Effect
Diffusion of Responsibility in Cyberspace
Effects of the Media: Video Games and Music Lyrics

How Can Helping Be Increased?

LO 11.4 Explain what can be done to promote prosocial behavior.

Increasing the Likelihood That Bystanders Will Intervene
Increasing Volunteerism

WHAT DO YOU THINK?

Survey	What Do You Think?	
SURVEY		RESULTS

Have you ever helped someone in an emergency, either directly (e.g., saving someone in danger) or by calling 911?

○ Yes

○ No

Revel Interactive

September 11, 2001, was truly a day of infamy in American history, with terrible loss of life at the World Trade Center, the Pentagon, and the field in Pennsylvania where United Airlines flight 93 crashed. It was also a day of incredible courage and sacrifice by people who did not hesitate to help their fellow human beings. Many people lost their lives while helping others, including 403 New York firefighters and police officers who died trying to rescue people from the World Trade Center.

Many of the heroes of September 11 were ordinary citizens who found themselves in extraordinary circumstances. Imagine that you were working in the World Trade Center towers when they were hit by the planes and how strong the desire would be to flee and seek personal safety. This is exactly what William Wik's wife urged him to do when he called her from the 92nd floor of the South Tower shortly after the attacks. "No, I can't do that; there are still people here," he replied (R. W. Lee, 2001, p. 28). Wik's body was found in the rubble of the South Tower after it collapsed; he was wearing work gloves and holding a flashlight.

Abe Zelmanowitz worked on the 27th floor of the North Tower and could easily have walked down the stairs to safety when the plane struck the floors above. Instead, he stayed behind with his friend Ed Beyea, a quadriplegic, waiting for help to carry him down the stairs. Both died when the tower collapsed.

Rick Rescorla was head of security for the Morgan Stanley brokerage firm. After the first plane hit the North Tower, Rescorla and the other employees in the South Tower were instructed to remain at their desks. Rescorla, who had spent years studying the security of the towers, had drilled his employees repeatedly on what to do in an emergency like this—find a partner, avoid the elevators, and evacuate the building. He invoked this plan immediately, and when the plane hit the South Tower, he was on the 44th floor supervising the evacuation, yelling instructions through a bullhorn. After most of the Morgan Stanley employees made it out of the building, Rescorla decided to do a final sweep of the offices to make sure no one was left behind, and he perished when the South Tower collapsed. Rescorla is credited with saving the lives of the 3,700 employees he guided to safety (Stewart, 2002).

And then there were the passengers on United flight 93. Based on phone calls made from the plane in the fateful minutes after it was hijacked, it appears that several passengers, including Todd Beamer, Jeremy Glick, and Thomas Burnett—all fathers of young children—stormed the cockpit and struggled with the terrorists. They could not prevent the plane from crashing, killing everyone on board, but they did prevent the plane from carrying out its likely mission: crashing into the White House or the U.S. Capitol.

Basic Motives Underlying Prosocial Behavior: Why Do People Help?

LO 11.1 Describe the basic motives that determine whether people help others.

Prosocial Behavior

Any act performed with the goal of benefiting another person

How can we explain acts of great self-sacrifice and heroism like these? Especially when people are also capable of acting in uncaring, heartless ways? In this chapter, we will consider the major causes of **prosocial behavior**—any act performed with the goal of benefiting another person (Batson, 2012; Penner et al., 2005). We are particularly concerned with prosocial behavior that is motivated by **altruism**, which is the desire to help another person even if it involves a cost to the helper. Someone might act in a prosocial way out of self-interest, hoping to get something in return. Altruism is helping purely out of the desire to benefit someone else, with no benefit (and often a cost) to oneself; the heroes of September 11, who gave their lives while helping strangers, are a clear example of altruism.

We begin by considering the basic origins of prosocial behavior and altruism: Is the willingness to help a basic impulse with genetic roots? Must it be taught and nurtured in childhood? Is there a pure motive for helping? Or do people typically help only when there is something in it for them? Let's see how psychologists have addressed these centuries-old questions (Crocker, Canevello, & Brown, 2017; Keltner et al., 2014; Piliavin, 2009; Tomasello & Vaish, 2013).

Altruism

The desire to help another person even if it involves a cost to the helper

Evolutionary Psychology: Instincts and Genes

According to Charles Darwin's (1859) theory of evolution, natural selection favors genes that promote the survival of the individual. Any gene that furthers our survival and increases the probability that we will produce offspring is likely to be passed on from generation to generation. Genes that lower our chances of survival, such as those causing life-threatening diseases, reduce the chances that we will produce offspring and thus are less likely to be passed on. Evolutionary psychologists attempt to explain social behavior in terms of genetic factors that have evolved over time according to the principles of natural selection (Buss, 2014; Neuberg, Kenrick, & Schaller, 2010; Tooby & Cosmides, 2005). In Chapter 10, we discussed how evolutionary psychology attempts to explain love and attraction; here we discuss its explanation of prosocial behavior (Arnocky et al., 2017; Hare, 2017; Simpson & Beckes, 2010).

Darwin realized early on that there was a problem with evolutionary theory: How can it explain altruism? If people's overriding goal is to ensure their own survival, why would they ever help others at a cost to themselves? It would seem that over the course of human evolution altruistic behavior would disappear, because people who acted that way would, by putting themselves at risk, produce fewer offspring than would people who acted selfishly. Genes promoting selfish behavior should be more likely to be passed on—or should they?

KIN SELECTION One way that evolutionary psychologists attempt to resolve this dilemma is with the notion of **kin selection**, the idea that behaviors that help a genetic relative are favored by natural selection (Carazo et al., 2014; Hamilton, 1964; Vasey & VanderLaan, 2010). People can increase the chances that their genes will be passed along not only by having their own children, but also by ensuring that their genetic relatives have children. Because a person's blood relatives share some of his or her genes, the more that person ensures their survival, the greater the chances that his or her genes will flourish in future generations. Thus, natural selection should favor altruistic acts directed toward genetic relatives.

In one study, for example, people reported that they would be more likely to help genetic relatives than nonrelatives in life-and-death situations, such as a house fire. People did not report that they would be more likely to help genetic relatives when the situation was nonlife-threatening, which supports the idea that people are most likely to help in ways that ensure the survival of their own genes. Interestingly, both males and females, and both American and Japanese participants, followed this rule of kin selection in life-threatening situations, suggesting that kin selection is not limited to one gender or a particular culture (Burnstein, Crandall, & Kitayama, 1994).

Kin Selection

The idea that behaviors that help a genetic relative are favored by natural selection

According to evolutionary psychology, prosocial behavior occurs in part because of kin selection.

Watch SUCCESSFUL AGING, EXTENDED FAMILY

Of course, in this study people reported what they thought they would do; this doesn't prove that in a real fire they would indeed be more likely to save their sibling than their cousin. Anecdotal evidence from real emergencies, however, is consistent with these results. Survivors of a fire at a vacation complex reported that when they became aware that there was a fire, they were much more likely to search for family members before exiting the building than they were to search for friends (Sime, 1983).

Evolutionary psychologists are not suggesting that people consciously weigh the biological importance of their behavior before deciding whether to help. According to evolutionary theory, however, kin selection may have become ingrained in human behavior, and as a result the genes of people who help their relatives are more likely to survive than the genes of people who do not (Archer, 2013; Vasey & VanderLaan, 2010).

Norm of Reciprocity

The expectation that helping others will increase the likelihood that they will help us in the future

THE RECIPROCITY NORM To explain altruism, evolutionary psychologists also point to the **norm of reciprocity**, which is the expectation that helping others will increase the likelihood that they will help us in the future. The idea is that as human beings were evolving, a group of completely selfish individuals, each living in his or her own cave, would have found it more difficult to survive than a group that had learned to cooperate. Of course, if people cooperated too readily, they might have been exploited by an adversary who never helped in return. Those who were most likely to survive, the argument goes, were people who developed an understanding with their neighbors about reciprocity: "I will help you now, with the agreement that when I need help, you will return the favor." Because of its survival value, such a norm of reciprocity may have become genetically based (Gray, Ward, & Norton, 2014; Krockow, Colman, & Pulford, 2016; Trivers, 1971). Some researchers suggest that the emotion of *gratitude*—the positive feelings that are caused by the perception that one has been helped by others—evolved in order to regulate reciprocity (Algoe, 2012; Algoe, Fredrickson, & Gable, 2013; Eibach, Wilmot, & Libby, 2015). That is, if someone helps us, we feel gratitude, which motivates us to return the favor in the future. The following Try It! describes how the reciprocity norm has been studied using economic games.

Try It!

The Dictator Game

Imagine that you take part in the following study: An experimenter gives you 10 one-dollar bills and says that you can keep all of the money or donate some of it to the next participant, whom you will never meet. The experimenter leaves you by yourself, with the instructions to put whatever amount you want to give to the next participant (if any) in a sealed envelope, after which you can leave. How much, if anything, would you donate?

This procedure, called the Dictator Game, has been used in dozens of studies to study human generosity. Although it would be in people's self-interest to keep all the money, most people donate some of it to the anonymous stranger they will never meet—on average, about $2.80 (Engel, 2010). In other words,

people act altruistically in this situation, by helping another person at some cost to themselves. Now imagine a slight twist in the game: When you arrive, the experimenter gives you an envelope containing money that a participant in another room sent to you as part of the Dictator Game. That is, the other person was given $10 and told that he or she could keep it all or give some of it to you, and the amount he or she donated—let's say it was $4.00—is in your hands.

Now the experimenter gives you an additional $10 and asks you to keep it or give some of it to that same participant in the next room. By the way, you will never meet this person, and the experimenter will never know how much you gave—after you make your decision you will leave without seeing the other participant. How much of the $10, if anything, will you give to the other participant?

If your answer was $4.00—the same amount that the other participant gave you—you answered like most people in a study that followed this exact procedure. In that study, almost all participants gave the person in the next room the same amount that that person had given them, or close to it (Ben-Ner, Putterman, Kong, & Magan, 2004). Thus, if the person had given you $4, you likely gave them $4 back, whereas if he or she had given you $1, you likely give them that much back. This study illustrates how sensitive people are to the *reciprocity norm*; we help others to the same degree that they help us.

GROUP SELECTION Classic evolutionary theory argues that natural selection operates on individuals: People who have traits that make them more likely to survive are more likely to reproduce and pass those traits on to future generations. Some argue that natural selection also operates at the group level. Imagine two neighboring villages, for example, that are often at war with each other. Village A is made up entirely of selfish individuals who refuse to put themselves at risk to help the village. Village B, on the other hand, has selfless sentries who put their lives at risk by alerting their comrades of an invasion. Which *group* is more likely to win the war and pass on its genes to later generations? The one with the selfless (altruistic) sentries, of course. Even though the *individual* sentries in Village B are at risk and likely to be captured and killed, their selfless behavior increases the likelihood that their *group* will survive—namely, the group that values altruism. Though the idea of group selection is controversial and not supported by all biologists, it has prominent proponents (Rand & Nowak, 2013; Wilson, Van Vugt, & O'Gorman, 2008; Wilson & Wilson, 2007).

In sum, evolutionary psychologists believe that people help others because of factors that have become ingrained in our genes. As we saw in Chapter 10, evolutionary psychology is a challenging and creative approach to understanding prosocial behavior, though it has its critics (Batson, 2011; LaFrance & Eagly, 2017; Panksepp & Panksepp, 2000; Wood & Eagly, 2002). How, for example, can evolutionary theory explain why complete strangers sometimes help each other, even when there is no reason for them to assume that they share some of the same genes or that their favor will ever be returned? It seems absurd to say that the heroes of September 11, who lost their lives while saving others, somehow calculated how genetically similar they were to the others before deciding to help. Further, just because people are more likely to save family members than strangers from a fire does not necessarily mean that they are genetically programmed to help genetic relatives. It may simply be that they cannot bear the thought of losing a loved one and therefore go to greater lengths to save the ones they love over people they have never met. We turn now to other possible motives behind prosocial behavior that do not necessarily originate in people's genes.

Social Exchange: The Costs and Rewards of Helping

Although some social psychologists disagree with evolutionary approaches to prosocial behavior, they share the view that altruistic behavior can be based on self-interest. In fact, *social exchange theory* (see Chapter 10) argues that much of what we do stems from the desire to maximize our rewards and minimize our costs (Cook & Rice, 2003; Homans, 1961; Thibaut & Kelley, 1959). The difference from evolutionary approaches is that social exchange theory doesn't trace this desire back to our evolutionary roots, nor does it assume that the desire is genetically based. Social exchange theorists assume that just as people in an economic marketplace try to maximize the ratio of their monetary profits to their monetary losses, people in their relationships with others try to maximize the ratio of social rewards to social costs.

Helping can be rewarding in a number of ways. As we saw with the norm of reciprocity, it can increase the likelihood that someone will help us in return. Helping

Study: Cavemen helped disabled

United Press International
NEW YORK—The skeleton of a dwarf who died about 12,000 years ago indicates that cave people cared for physically disabled members of their communities , a researcher said yesterday.

The skeleton of the 3-foot-high youth was initially discovered in 1963 in a cave in southern Italy but was lost to anthropologists until American researcher David W. Frayer reexamined the remains and reported his findings in the British journal Nature.

Frayer, a professor of anthropology at the University of Kansas at Lawrence, said in a telephone interview that the youth "couldn't have taken part in normal hunting of food or gathering activities so

he was obviously cared for by others."

Archaeologists have found the remains of other handicapped individuals who lived during the same time period, but their disabilities occurred when they were adults, Frayer said.

"This is the first time we've found someone who was disabled since birth . . . .", Frayer said. He said there was no indication that the dwarf, who was about 17 at the time of his death, had suffered from malnutrition or neglect.

He was one of six individuals buried in the floor of a cave and was found in a dual grave in the arms of a woman, about 40 years old.

This touching story of early hominid prosocial behavior is intriguing to think about in terms of different theories of prosocial behavior. Evolutionary psychologists might argue that the caregivers helped the dwarf because he was a relative and that people are programmed to help those who share their genes (kin selection). Social exchange theory would maintain that the dwarf's caregivers received sufficient rewards from their actions to outweigh the costs of caring for him. The empathy-altruism hypothesis would hold that the caregivers helped out of strong feelings of empathy and compassion for him—an interpretation supported by the article's final paragraph.

someone is an investment in the future, the social exchange being that someday someone will help us when we need it. Helping can also relieve the personal distress of a bystander. Considerable evidence indicates that people are aroused and disturbed when they see another person suffer and that they help at least in part to relieve their own distress (Dovidio, 1984; Dovidio et al., 1991; Eisenberg & Fabes, 1991). By helping others, we can also gain such rewards as social approval from others and increased feelings of self-worth.

The other side of the coin, of course, is that helping can be costly. Helping decreases when the costs are high, such as when it would put us in physical danger, result in pain or embarrassment, or simply take too much time (Dovidio et al., 1991; Piliavin et al., 1981; Piliavin, Piliavin, & Rodin, 1975). Perhaps Abe Zelmanowitz, who stayed behind with his friend Ed Beyea in the World Trade Center, found the prospect of walking away and letting his friend die too distressing. Basically, social exchange theory argues that true altruism, in which people help even when doing so is costly to them, does not exist. People help when the benefits outweigh the costs.

If you are like many of our students, you may think this is an overly cynical view of human nature. Is true altruism, motivated only by the desire to help someone else, really such a mythical act? Must we trace all prosocial behavior, such as large charitable gifts made by wealthy individuals, to the self-interest of the helper? Well, a social exchange theorist might reply, there are many ways in which people can obtain gratification, and we should be thankful that one way is by helping others. After all, wealthy people could decide to get their pleasure solely from lavish vacations, expensive cars, and meals at fancy restaurants. We should applaud their decision to give money to the disadvantaged, even if, ultimately, it is just a way for them to feel good about themselves. Prosocial acts are doubly rewarding in that they help both the giver and the recipient of the aid. Thus, it is to everyone's advantage to promote and praise such acts.

Still, many people are dissatisfied with the argument that all helping stems from self-interest. How can it explain why people give up their lives for others, as many of the heroes of September 11 did? According to some social psychologists, people do have hearts of gold and sometimes help only for the sake of helping.

Empathy and Altruism: The Pure Motive for Helping

C. Daniel Batson (1991) is the strongest proponent of the idea that people often help purely out of the goodness of their hearts. Batson acknowledges that people sometimes help others for selfish reasons, such as to relieve their own distress at seeing another person suffer. But he also argues that people's motives are sometimes purely altruistic, in that their only goal is to help the other person, even if doing so involves some cost to them. Pure altruism is likely to come into play, he maintains, when we feel **empathy** for the person in need of help, putting ourselves in the shoes of another person and experiencing events and emotions the way that person experiences them (Batson, 2011; Batson, Ahmad, & Stocks, 2011).

Empathy

The ability to put oneself in the shoes of another person and to experience events and emotions (e.g., joy and sadness) the way that person experiences them

Helping behavior is common in virtually all species of animals, and sometimes it even crosses species lines. In August 1996, a 3-year-old boy fell into a pit containing seven gorillas, at the Brookfield, Illinois, zoo. Binti, a 7-year-old gorilla, immediately picked up the boy. After cradling him in her arms, she placed the boy near a door where zookeepers could get to him. Why did she help? Evolutionary psychologists would argue that prosocial behavior is selected for and thus becomes part of the genetic makeup of the members of many species. Social exchange theorists would argue that Binti had been rewarded for helping in the past. In fact, because she had been rejected by her mother, she had received training in parenting skills from zookeepers, in which she was rewarded for caring for a doll (20 Years Ago Today, 2016).

Suppose that while you are food shopping, you see a man holding a baby and a bag full of diapers, toys, and rattles. As he reaches for a box of cereal, the man drops the bag, and everything spills onto the floor. Will you help him pick up his things? According to Batson, it depends first on whether you feel empathy for him. If you do, you will help, regardless of what you have to gain. Your goal will be to relieve the other person's distress, not to gain something for yourself. This is the crux of Batson's **empathy-altruism hypothesis**: When we feel empathy for another person, we will attempt to help that person for purely altruistic reasons, regardless of what we have to gain.

If you do not feel empathy, Batson says, social exchange concerns come into play. What's in it for you? If there is something to be gained, such as obtaining approval from the man or from onlookers, you will help the man pick up his things. If you will not profit from helping, you will go on your way without stopping. Batson's empathy-altruism hypothesis is summarized in Figure 11.1.

Batson and his colleagues would be the first to acknowledge that it can be difficult to isolate the exact motives behind complex social behaviors. If you saw someone help the man pick up his possessions, how could you tell whether the person was acting out of empathic concern or to gain some sort of reward, such as relieving his own distress? Consider a famous story about Abraham Lincoln. One day, while riding in a coach, Lincoln and a fellow passenger were debating the very question we are considering: Is helping ever truly altruistic? Lincoln argued that helping always stems from self-interest, whereas his fellow passenger took the view that true altruism exists. Suddenly, the men were interrupted by the screeching of a pig that was trying to save her piglets from drowning in a creek. Lincoln ordered the coach to stop, jumped out, ran down to the creek, and lifted the piglets to the safety of the bank. When he returned, his companion said, "Now, Abe, where does selfishness come in on this little episode?" "Why, bless your soul, Ed," Lincoln replied. "That was the very essence of selfishness. I should have had no peace of mind all day had I gone on and left that suffering old sow worrying over those pigs. I did it to get peace of mind, don't you see?" (Sharp, 1928, p. 75).

As this example illustrates, an act that seems truly altruistic is sometimes motivated by self-interest. How, then, can we tell which is which? Batson and his colleagues have devised a series of clever experiments to unravel people's motives (Batson, Ahmad, &

Empathy-Altruism Hypothesis
The idea that when we feel empathy for a person, we will attempt to help that person for purely altruistic reasons, regardless of what we have to gain

Figure 11.1 Empathy-Altruism Theory

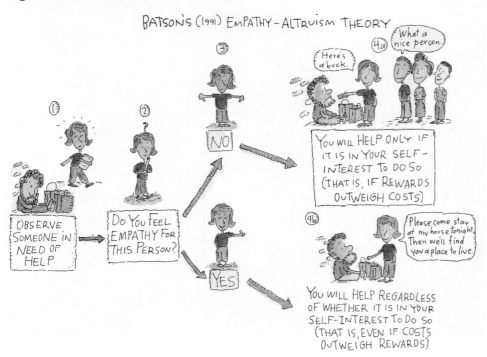

Stocks, 2004; Batson & Powell, 2003). Imagine that you were an introductory psychology student in one of these studies (Toi & Batson, 1982). You are asked to evaluate some recordings of new programs for the university radio station, one of which is called *News from the Personal Side*. There are lots of different submissions for this program, and you are told that only one person will be listening to each submission. The one you hear is an interview with a student named Carol Marcy. She says she was in a bad automobile accident in which both of her legs were broken and talks about how hard it has been to keep up with her class work as a result of the accident, especially because she is still in a wheelchair. Carol says she is especially concerned about how far she has fallen behind in her Introductory Psychology class and mentions that she will have to drop the class unless she can find another student to tell her what she has missed.

When you're done listening to the story, the experimenter hands you an envelope marked "To the student listening to the Carol Marcy submission." The experimenter says she doesn't know what's in the envelope but was asked by the professor supervising the research to hand it out. You open the envelope and find a note from the professor, saying that he was wondering if the student who listened to Carol's story would be willing to help her out with her psychology class. Carol was reluctant to ask for help, he says, but because she is so far behind in the class, she agreed to write a note to the person listening to her submission. The note asks if you could meet with her and share your Introductory Psychology lecture notes.

As you have probably guessed, the point of the study was to look at whether people agreed to help Carol and to pit two motives against each other: empathy versus self-interest. The researchers varied how much empathy people felt toward Carol by telling different participants to adopt different perspectives when listening to her story. In the high-empathy condition, people were told to try to imagine how Carol felt about what had happened to her and how it had changed her life. In the low-empathy condition, people were told to try to be objective and not be concerned with how Carol felt. As expected, people in the high-empathy condition reported feeling more empathy for Carol than people in the low-empathy condition did.

The researchers looked at self-interest by varying how costly it would be *not* to help Carol. In one condition, participants learned that she would start coming back to class the following week and happened to be in the same psychology section as they were; thus, they would see her every time they went to class and would be reminded that she needed help. This was the high-cost condition because it would be unpleasant to refuse to help Carol and then run into her every week in class. In the low-cost condition, people learned that Carol would be studying at home and would not be coming to class; therefore, they would never have to face her in her wheelchair and feel guilty about not helping her.

According to the empathy-altruism hypothesis, people should have been motivated purely by altruistic concerns and helped regardless of the costs—if empathy was high (see Figure 11.1). As you can see from the right side of Figure 11.2, this prediction was confirmed: In the high-empathy condition, about as many people agreed to help when they thought they would see Carol in class as when they thought they would not see her in class. This suggests that people had Carol's interests in mind and not their own. But in the low-empathy condition many more people agreed to help when they thought they would see Carol in class than when they thought they would not see her in class (see the left side of Figure 11.2). This suggests that when empathy was low, social exchange concerns came into play, in that people based their decision to help on the costs and benefits to themselves. They helped when it was in their interests to do so (i.e., when they would see Carol in her wheelchair and feel guilty for not helping), but not otherwise (i.e., when they thought they would never see her again).

Does this resolve the debate over whether helping can be purely altruistic? Well, as the "Carol" experiment illustrates, people will sometimes help out of a concern for others when there is no tangible benefit to themselves. But it is hard to prove that there was *nothing* in it for the people in the "high empathy" condition of that experiment. Indeed, some theorists have argued that what ultimately motivates people to help others, even when there are costs to doing so, is the good feeling that results. Consistent with this view, recent research shows that when people help others, the same parts of their brain are activated as when they receive such tangible rewards as food, water, and sex (Buchanan & Preston, 2016; Zaki & Mitchell, 2016).

In the end, this debate centers on how we define "self-interest." If by that we mean immediate, tangible, benefits to the self, such as praise from others or a promotion at work, then it is clear that such rewards are not the only reasons people help others. As Batson's work illustrates, when people feel empathy toward others, they will help even if it is not in their immediate self-interest to do so. But if we define "self-interest" more broadly, to include the glow people experience when they help others, and the relief they feel when they can alleviate another person's suffering, then yes, this kind of altruism is "selfish" as well (Crocker et al., 2017; Marsh, 2016). But isn't it a wonderful thing

---

Figure 11.2 Altruism Versus Self-Interest

Under what conditions did people agree to help Carol with the work she missed in her introductory psychology class? When empathy was high, people helped regardless of the costs and rewards (i.e., regardless of whether they would encounter her in their psychology class). When empathy was low, people were more concerned with the rewards and costs for themselves; they were more likely to help if they would encounter Carol in their psychology class and thus feel guilty about not helping.

(Adapted from Toi & Batson, 1982)

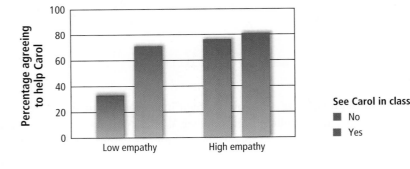

that human beings are so willing to help others even when there are costs to doing so? Sometimes people pay the ultimate cost, as seen by those who lost their lives helping others at the World Trade Centers or by those who die in military service to their country, and it is hard to argue that there was anything selfish about such heroic acts.

To sum up, we've identified three basic motives underlying prosocial behavior, each of which has its supporters and critics:

1. Helping is an instinctive reaction to promote the welfare of those genetically similar to us (evolutionary psychology).

2. The rewards of helping often outweigh the costs, so helping is in our self-interest (social exchange theory).

3. Under some conditions, powerful feelings of empathy and compassion for the victim prompt selfless giving (the empathy-altruism hypothesis).

Review Questions

1. Which of the following is the best example of altruistic behavior?
   a. Julia puts a dollar in the church collection basket because everyone else donates.
   b. Robert volunteers at his son's school to help out his class.
   c. Jawal anonymously donates $100 to a homeless shelter.
   d. Mary helps her husband with the dishes with the hope that he will cook dinner more often.

2. Evolutionary psychology would have the most trouble explaining which of the following incidents?
   a. When Usha was in a building that caught on fire, she let everyone else exit before her, even though she didn't know them.
   b. Clint risks his life to save his nephew who was drowning.
   c. Natasha runs in front of a moving car to keep her daughter from being hit.

   d. When Julio was put in the unfortunate situation of saving his cousin or his son in a boating accident, he chose to save his son.

3. According to social exchange theory, which of the following people is most likely to give money to a homeless person?
   a. Jade, who feels empathy for the homeless person
   b. Bill, who wants to impress his date by helping the homeless person
   c. Jack, who is related to the homeless person
   d. Emma, who has a genetic predisposition for helping people

4. According to Batson's empathy-altruism theory, which of the following people is *most* likely to give money to a homeless person?
   a. Jade, who feels empathy for the homeless person
   b. Bill, who wants to impress his date by helping the homeless person
   c. Jack, who is related to the homeless person
   d. Both Jade and Bill are likely to give money.

Personal Qualities and Prosocial Behavior: Why Do Some People Help More Than Others?

LO 11.2 Describe the personal qualities that influence whether a given individual will help.

If basic human motives fully explained prosocial behavior, why are some people so much more helpful than others? Clearly, we need to consider the personal qualities that distinguish the helpful person from the selfish one.

Individual Differences: The Altruistic Personality

As just noted, individuals have stood out for their incredibly altruistic acts throughout history, such as those who sheltered Jews during World War II, saving them from the death camps, often at great risk to themselves (Oliner & Oliner, 1988). The heroes of

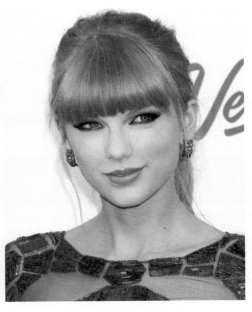

Some people have more of an altruistic personality than others. Taylor Swift and Beyoncé, for example, have topped lists of "Most Generous Celebrities" for helping to raise money for charities. Personality, however, is not the whole story; the nature of the social situation also determines whether people help.

Altruistic Personality
The qualities that cause an individual to help others in a wide variety of situations

September 11 are other examples—selfless, caring people who gave their lives to save others. It is natural to assume that such people have an **altruistic personality**, the qualities that cause an individual to help others in a wide variety of situations (Eisenberg, Spinrad, & Sadovsky, 2006; Habashi, Graziano, & Hoover, 2016; Hubbard et al., 2016; Zhao, Ferguson, & Smillie, 2016).

Clearly some people have more of an altruistic personality than others, and psychologists have developed instruments to measure this quality. Go ahead and fill out the empathic concern questionnaire in the Try It! exercise below, to see where you fall on this dimension.

Even if you have a high score on this measure, though, research shows that when it comes to predicting how helpful people actually are, personality is not the full story (Eisenberg et al., 2014; Graziano & Habashi, 2015; Hertz & Krettenauer, 2016). We need to consider several other critical factors as well, such as the situational pressures that are affecting people, their gender, the culture in which they grew up, how religious they are, and even their current mood (Graziano et al., 2007).

Whereas men are more likely to perform chivalrous and heroic acts, women are more likely to be helpful in long-term relationships that involve greater commitment.

Gender Differences in Prosocial Behavior

Consider two scenarios. In one, someone performs a dramatic, heroic act, like storming the cockpit of United flight 93 to fight terrorists. In the other, someone is involved in a long-term helping relationship, such as assisting a disabled neighbor with chores around the house. Are men or women more likely to help in each situation?

The answer is males in the first situation and females in the second (Eagly, 2009; Eagly & Koenig, 2006; Einolf, 2011). In virtually all cultures, norms prescribe different traits and behaviors for males and females, learned as boys and girls are growing up. In Western cultures, the male sex role includes being chivalrous and heroic; females are expected to be nurturing and caring and to value close, long-term relationships (Rand et al., 2016). Indeed, of the 7,000 people who received medals from the Carnegie Hero

Try It!

Empathic Concern

Instructions: The following statements inquire about your thoughts and feelings in a variety of situations. For each item, indicate how well it describes you by circling the appropriate number next to the statement. Please read each item carefully before responding. Answer as honestly as you can.

	Does Not Describe Me Very Well				Describes Me Very Well
1. I often have tender, concerned feelings for people less fortunate than me.	1	2	3	4	5
2. Sometimes I don't feel very sorry for other people when they are having problems.	1	2	3	4	5
3. When I see someone being taken advantage of, I feel kind of protective toward them.	1	2	3	4	5
4. Other people's misfortunes do not usually disturb me a great deal.	1	2	3	4	5
5. When I see someone being treated unfairly, I sometimes don't feel very much pity for them.	1	2	3	4	5
6. I am often quite touched by things that I see happen.	1	2	3	4	5
7. I would describe myself as a pretty soft-hearted person.	1	2	3	4	5

Scoring: On some of the questions a high score reflects low sympathy, so we first need to "reverse score" your answers to those questions. First, reverse your answers to Questions 2, 4, and 5. That is, if you answered 1 change it to 5, if you answered 2 change it to a 4, if you answered 3 keep it the same, if you answered 4 change it to a 2, and if you answered 5 change it to a 1. Now sum your answers to all the items and divide by 7 to get your average score.

Interpretation: These questions, from a scale by Davis (1983), are a measure of empathic concern (your feelings of sympathy for other people in need). The higher your score, the more empathic concern you expressed.

Empathy and Your Age: Research shows that your score might be a function of how old you are. Recall that in Chapter 5, we saw that narcissism has increased in college students over the past few decades. Unfortunately, people's empathic concern has decreased during that same time period (Konrath, O'Brien, & Hsing, 2011). Why has empathy decreased? No one knows for sure, though the authors speculate that it might have to do with the increase in the amount of time people spend on personal technology and media, to the extent that that decreases the amount of time people spend in meaningful, face-to-face interactions with others. The increase in reality television shows might also play a role, to the extent that they portray narcissistic people concerned mostly with themselves.

Watch 92-YEAR-OLD VOLUNTEER

Revel Video

Fund Commission for risking their lives to save a stranger, 91% have been men. In contrast, women are more likely than men to provide social support to their friends and to engage in volunteer work that involves helping others (Eagly & Koenig, 2006; Monin, Clark, & Lemay, 2008; Volunteering in the United States, 2013). Cross-cultural evidence suggests the same pattern. In a survey of adolescents in seven countries, more girls than boys reported doing volunteer work in their communities (Flanagan et al., 1998).

Cultural Differences in Prosocial Behavior

Suppose you find out that a student at your university needs help because she lost all of her possessions in a fire at her apartment building. She has no insurance and very little money, so a call goes out to donate to a fund to help her buy clothes and other necessities. Would you donate money? Well, let's take this example a little further: Suppose that in one case the student was similar to you; she is of the same race and has a similar background. Alternatively, suppose that she is a member of a different cultural group. Perhaps you grew up in the United States and she is an international student, or vice versa. Would this make a difference in your willingness to help her?

On the one hand, there is ample evidence that people often favor their **in-groups**, or the groups with which they identify as a member, and discriminate against members of **out-groups**, defined as groups with which they do not identify (P. B. Smith, 2015). Indeed, there is a long history of discrimination and prejudice against out-group members, including those of other races, cultures, and genders, as well as people with different sexual orientations. But on the other hand, people often go out of their way to help out-group members. People donate to charities that help disadvantaged strangers and rise to the occasion when an individual is in need, even if he or she belongs to a different group.

Recent research resolves this conundrum. It turns out that people often help both in-group and out-group members, but for different reasons. We are more likely to feel empathy toward members of our in-groups who are in need. Thus, if the student who lost her possessions in the apartment fire is a member of your in-group, you will probably feel empathy for her, and the more empathy you feel, the more likely you are to help. We tend to help out-group members for a different reason—we do so, to put it bluntly, when there is something in it for us, such as making us feel good about ourselves or making a good impression on others. Sound familiar? Recall that Batson's empathy-altruism theory posits two routes to helping others: When we feel empathy, we help regardless of whether there is something in it for us, but when we don't feel empathy, we help only if there is something in it for us (see Figure 11.1). Research on intergroup helping suggests that we are more likely to take the first route when the person in need is an in-group member, but more likely to take the second route when the person in need is an out-group member (van Leeuwen & Täuber, 2010; Stürmer & Snyder, 2010).

More generally, are there differences in cultural values that make people in one culture more likely to help than people in another culture? One such value is *simpatía*. Prominent in Spanish-speaking countries, simpatía refers to a range of social and emotional traits, including being friendly, polite, good-natured, pleasant, and helpful toward others (interestingly, it has no direct English translation). One study tested the hypothesis that helping would be higher in cultures that value simpatía than in cultures that do not (Levine, 2003; Levine, Norenzayan, & Philbrick, 2001; Ramírez-Esparza et al., 2012). The researchers staged helping incidents in large cities in 23 countries and observed what people did. In one scenario, for example, a researcher posing as a blind person stopped at a busy intersection and observed whether pedestrians offered help in crossing or informed the researcher when the light turned green.

If you look at Table 11.1, you'll see that the percentage of people who helped (averaged across the different incidents) in countries that value simpatía was higher than in countries that did not, 83% to 66%. The researchers noted that these results are only suggestive, because the five Latin American and Spanish countries differed from the others in ways other than the value they placed on simpatía. And some countries not known for their simpatía had high rates of helping. Nevertheless, if a culture strongly values friendliness and prosocial behavior, people may be more likely to help strangers on city streets (Janoff-Bulman & Leggatt, 2002).

In-Group

The group with which an individual identifies as a member

Out-Group

Any group with which an individual does not identify

Table 11.1 Helping in 23 Cities

In 23 cities around the world, researchers observed how many people helped in three situations: helping a person with a leg brace who dropped a pile of magazines, helping someone who did not notice that he or she had dropped a pen, and helping a blind person across a busy intersection. The percentages in the table are averaged across the three situations. The cities in boldface are in countries that have the cultural value of *simpatía*, which prizes friendliness, politeness, and helping others.

City	Percent Helping
Rio de Janeiro, Brazil	**93**
San José, Costa Rica	**91**
Lilongwe, Malawi	86
Calcutta, India	83
Vienna, Austria	81
Madrid, Spain	**79**
Copenhagen, Denmark	78
Shanghai, China	77
Mexico City, Mexico	**76**
San Salvador, El Salvador	**75**
Prague, Czech Republic	75
Stockholm, Sweden	72
Budapest, Hungary	71
Bucharest, Romania	69
Tel Aviv, Israel	68
Rome, Italy	63
Bangkok, Thailand	61
Taipei, Taiwan	59
Sofia, Bulgaria	57
Amsterdam, Netherlands	54
Singapore	48
New York, United States	45
Kuala Lumpur, Malaysia	40

(Based on Levine, Norenzayan, & Philbrick, 2001)

Religion and Prosocial Behavior

Most religions teach some version of the Golden Rule, urging us to do unto others as we would have others do unto us. Are religious people more likely to follow this advice than nonreligious people? That is, do religious people engage in more prosocial behavior?

The answer, it turns out, is a qualified yes. A very important feature of religion is that it binds people together and creates strong social bonds. As a result, religious people are more likely to help than other people are, with an important qualification: if the person in need of help shares their religious beliefs (Galen, 2012; Graham & Haidt, 2010). Indeed, some have argued that religion was partly responsible for the dramatic increase in human population that occurred roughly 12,000 years ago. Prior to that time, human beings lived in small-scale societies in which most people knew each other. From that time forward, large scale societies began to flourish, in which strangers lived together in large towns and cities. How did strangers learn to live together peacefully in such large numbers? One reason, according to Ara Norenzayan and colleagues (2016), is that members of those societies shared religious beliefs that stressed cooperation with like-minded individuals, even if they were strangers.

One study, for example, examined 200 utopian communities that arose in the United States in the 19th century. Which ones lasted longer, those that were based on shared religious beliefs or those that were nonreligious? As seen in

#trending

Helping Across the Political Divide

As just seen, people are more likely to help in-group members than out-groups members. And, in Chapter 13, we will see how prone human beings are to divide people in to in-groups and out-groups, resulting in stereotyping and prejudice toward those who are "not like me." But in this chapter we also saw that people *will* help a stranger, across group lines, if they feel empathy toward that person. This is what seems to have happened on Monday, January 23, 2017, in a Washington D.C. restaurant.

Jason White, a White dentist from West Texas, was in town for Donald Trump's inauguration. A Trump supporter from the beginning, he and two friends had spent the weekend celebrating President Trump's election. At breakfast that Monday morning, their server was Rosalynd Harris, a 25-year-old African American dancer who was working there to make ends meet. In contrast to her three patrons, Ms. Harris was not a Trump supporter and was in fact feeling quite energized by the Women's March on Washington that had occurred the day after the presidential inauguration.

Think about how this encounter could have gone wrong: Given the partisan divide in America, one can imagine any number of ways that two people of different races at opposite ends of the political spectrum might have acted suspiciously, or even with hostility, toward each other. Instead they had a warm and friendly conversation. They joked, they chatted cheerfully, they learned a little bit about each other. "You automatically assume if someone supports Trump that they have ideas about you," she [Ms. Harris] said, "but [the customer was] more embracing than even some of my more liberal friends, and there was a real authenticity in our exchange" (Itkowitz, 2017).

After White had finished his meal and left, Harris noticed that he had written something on the receipt: "We may come from different cultures and may disagree on certain issues," she read, "but if everyone would share their smile and kindness like your beautiful smile, our country will come together as one people. Not race. Not gender. Just American" (Itkowitz, 2017). And, accompanying the note was a $450 tip.

Based on what you've read in this chapter, why do you think White acted so generously toward a complete stranger who differed from him in so many ways? According to Batson's empathy-altruism hypothesis, it is because he felt empathy toward her and realized she could probably use the money. This doesn't mean there was nothing in it for him, as we discussed earlier, he may well have experienced the satisfaction and glow that results from helping another person. But this example shows that under the right circumstances, people will reach out and help others who are not members of their in-group.

Figure 11.3, religious ones lasted longer, possibly because their religious values increased the likelihood that the members of the commune cooperated with each other (Solis, 2000).

Note that this evidence concerns how likely religious people are to help in-group members, namely those who share their religious values. Are religious people more likely to help out-group members, namely those who don't necessarily share their values? The evidence suggest that the answer is no. When it comes to helping strangers, for example, such as donating blood, or tipping a waiter or waitress, religious people are no more helpful than nonreligious people (Batson, Schoenrade, & Ventis, 1993; Galen, 2012; Preston, Ritter, & Hernandez, 2010). And, there is some evidence that religious beliefs *increase* hostilities toward outgroup members who do not share those beliefs (Hobson & Inzlicht, 2016). Religion is likely another example of in-group favoritism, which, as we saw in the previous section on cultural differences in helping, occurs because people feel more empathy toward in-group than out-group members.

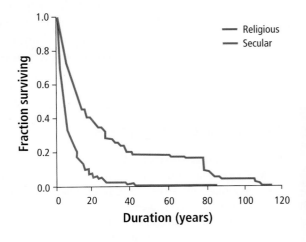

Figure 11.3 The Duration of Religious and Non-Religious Communes in the 19th Century

Nineteenth-century communes whose members shared religious beliefs lasted longer than nonreligious communes. From Solis, 2000.

The Effects of Mood on Prosocial Behavior

It turns out that it also matters what mood people are in. Whether people are in good, bad, or neutral moods can have surprising effects on how helpful they will be.

EFFECTS OF POSITIVE MOODS: FEEL GOOD, DO GOOD In a classic study, researchers wanted to see whether people's mood influenced the likelihood that they would help a stranger in a real world setting (Isen & Levin, 1972). To find out, they staged a helping opportunity at a shopping mall, whereby a man "accidentally" dropped a manila folder full of papers in front of stranger who was by himself or herself. The researchers then observed whether the stranger stopped and helped the man pick up the papers. But how did they experimentally manipulate the stranger's mood? They did so in a clever way, namely by leaving a dime in the coin-return slot of a public telephone at the mall and then waiting for someone to find it. (Note that when this study was done there were no cell phones, so people relied on pay phones, and also that 10 cents then would be like finding 50 cents today.) Half of the time the research assistant dropped the folder in front of a stranger who had just found the planted dime, and thus had just gotten a temporary mood boost, and half of the time he dropped the folder in front of a stranger who had just used the phone without a planted dime. Now, it might not seem like finding a dime would influence people's moods very much, or affect their likelihood of helping a stranger, but the results were dramatic: Only 4% of the people who did not find a dime helped the man pick up his papers, whereas a whopping 84% of the people who found a dime stopped to help.

This "feel good, do good" effect has been replicated many times with different ways of boosting people's moods (including giving positive feedback on a test, giving gifts, and playing cheerful music; North, Tarrant, & Hargreaves, 2004) and with many different ways of measuring helping (e.g., whether people help someone find a lost contact lens, tutor another student, donate blood, or help coworkers on the job; Carlson, Charlin, & Miller, 1988; Isen, 1999; Kayser et al., 2010).

FEEL BAD, DO GOOD Should you avoid asking people to help when they are in a bad mood? Given that feeling happy leads to greater helping, it might seem that feeling sad would lower it. Surprisingly, however, sadness can also lead to an increase in helping, because when people are sad, they are motivated to engage in activities that make them feel better. And, because helping others is rewarding, it can lift people out of the doldrums. Thus, you might have luck asking people to help with your community service project if they are in sad moods (as opposed to neutral moods; Cialdini & Fultz, 1990; Wegener & Petty, 1994; Yue, Wang, & Groth, 2016).

Another kind of bad mood also increases helping: feeling guilty (Ahn, Kim, & Aggarwal, 2014; Xu, Bègue, & Bushman, 2012). People often act on the idea that good deeds cancel out bad deeds. When they have done something that has made them feel guilty, helping another person balances things out, reducing their guilty feelings. For example, one study found that Catholic churchgoers were more likely to donate money to charities before attending confession than afterward, presumably because confessing to a priest reduced their guilt (Harris, Benson, & Hall, 1975).

Review Questions

1. Which of the following is true?
 a. People with high scores on tests of altruism are *not* that much more likely to help another person than people with low scores.
 b. People with high scores on tests of altruism *are* much more likely to help another person than people with low scores.
 c. If a person has an altruistic personality, then they are quite likely to overcome situational pressures preventing them from helping someone.

 d. The genes for an altruistic personality have been identified by evolutionary psychologists.

2. _____ is most likely to dive into a pond to save a drowning child, whereas _____ is most likely to do errands for an elderly neighbor every week.
 a. A woman; a man
 b. A man; a woman
 c. An East Asian citizen; a Western citizen
 d. A Western citizen; an East Asian citizen

3. In which city are people most likely to help a blind person cross a street?
   a. New York, USA
   b. Amsterdam, Netherlands
   c. Budapest, Hungary
   d. Rio de Janeiro, Brazil
4. Which person is *least* likely help a blind person cross the street?

a. Marco, who is having a normal day and is in a neutral mood
b. Silvi, who just got an A on a paper and is thus in a good mood
c. Olivia, who just got a D on a paper and is thus feeling sad
d. Brandon, who just cheated on his girlfriend and is thus feeling guilty

Situational Determinants of Prosocial Behavior: When Will People Help?

LO 11.3   Describe the situations in which people are more likely, or less likely, to help others.

Personality, gender, culture, religion, and mood all contribute a piece to the puzzle of why people help others, but they do not complete the picture. To understand more fully why people help, we also need to consider the social situation in which people find themselves.

Environment: Rural Versus Urban

Here's another helping scenario for you. Suppose you are walking down the street one day when you see a man suddenly fall down and cry out with pain. He rolls up his pants leg, revealing a bandaged shin that is bleeding heavily. What would you do? When this event was staged in small towns, about half the people who walked by stopped and offered to help the man. But in large cities, only 15% of passersby stopped to help (Amato, 1983). Other studies have found that people in small towns are more likely to help when asked to find a lost child, give directions, and return a lost letter. Increased helping in small towns has been found in several countries (Hedge & Yousif, 1992; Oishi, 2014; Steblay, 1987).

Why are people more likely to help in small towns? One possibility is that people who grow up in a small town are more likely to internalize altruistic values.

People are less helpful in big cities than in small towns, not because of a difference in values, but because the stress of urban life causes them to keep to themselves.

Urban Overload Hypothesis

The theory that people living in cities are constantly bombarded with stimulation and that they keep to themselves to avoid being overwhelmed by it

If this were the case, people who grew up in small towns would be more likely to help, even if they were visiting a big city. Alternatively, the immediate surroundings might be the key and not people's internalized values. Stanley Milgram (1970), for example, suggested that people living in cities are constantly bombarded with stimulation and that they keep to themselves to avoid being overwhelmed by it. According to this **urban overload hypothesis**, if you put urban dwellers in a calmer, less stimulating environment, they would be as likely as anyone else to reach out to others. Research has supported the urban overload hypothesis more than the idea that living in cities makes people less altruistic by nature. Thus, to predict whether people will help, it is more important to know whether they are currently in a rural or urban area than it is to know where they happened to grow up (Levine et al., 1994; Steblay, 1987).

Residential Mobility

In many areas of the world, it is common for people to move far away from where they were raised (Hochstadt, 1999). In the year 2000, for example, nearly one in five Americans (18%) were living in a different state than they were in 1995 (Migration and Geographic Mobility, 2003), and in many urban areas, fewer than half of the residents were living in the same house as they were in 1995 (Oishi et al., 2007).

As it turns out, people who have lived for a long time in one place are more likely to engage in prosocial behaviors that help their community. Residing in one place leads to a greater attachment to the community, more interdependence with one's neighbors, and a greater concern with one's reputation in the community (O'Brien, Gallup, & Wilson, 2012; Oishi, 2014; Oishi et al., 2015). For all these reasons, long-time residents are more likely to engage in prosocial behaviors. Shigehiro Oishi and colleagues (2007), for example, found that people who had lived for a long time in the Minneapolis-St. Paul area were more likely to purchase "critical habitat" license plates, compared to people who had recently moved to the area. (These license plates cost an extra $30 a year and provide funds for the state to purchase and manage natural habitats.)

Perhaps it is not surprising that people who have lived in one place for years feel more of a stake in their community. Oishi and his colleagues (2007) also found, though, that this increase in helping can arise quite quickly, even in a one-time laboratory setting. Imagine that you are in a study in which you are playing a trivia contest against four other students, where the winner will win a $10 gift certificate. The experimenter says that people in the group can help each other if they want, but that doing so might lower the helper's chances of winning the prize. As the game progresses, one of your fellow group members keeps sighing and commenting that he doesn't know the answers to the questions. Would you offer him some help or let him continue to struggle on his own?

The answer, it turns out, depends on how long you have been in the group with the struggling student. The study by Oishi and colleagues involved a total of four tasks; the trivia contest was the last one. Half of the participants remained together and worked on all the tasks throughout the study, whereas the other half switched to a new group after each task. Thus, in the former condition people had more of an opportunity to get to know each other and form a sense of community, whereas the latter group was more analogous to moving from one community to another. As the researchers predicted, people in the "stable community" condition were more likely to help their struggling companion than were people in the "transient" group condition. Another reason that people might be less helpful in big cities, then, is that residential mobility is higher in cities than in rural areas. People are more likely to have just moved to a city and thus feel less of a stake in the community.

The Number of Bystanders: The Bystander Effect

On March 11, 2011, in Bethesda, Maryland, Jayna Murray was brutally murdered by a coworker inside the clothing store where they worked. Two employees in an Apple store next door heard the murder through the walls, including cries for help from Murray, but did nothing to help (Johnson, 2011). In October of 2011 in Southern China, a 2-year-old girl was run over by two vans, minutes apart, and lay in the street dying. Neither car stopped, and a dozen people walked or rode past the girl without offering help (Branigan, 2011). In September of 2013 in Philadelphia, a transit police officer was beaten by a man he was trying to arrest, in front of more than a dozen onlookers, none of whom intervened or called 911 (Ubinas, 2013).

Why did the bystanders fail to come to the aid of a fellow human being who was in dire need of help? We have just discussed one possibility, namely that the passersby kept to themselves because they were overloaded with urban stimulation (all of the events took place in large cities). Although this may be part of the reason, these kinds of failures to help are not limited to big cities. In Fredericksburg, Virginia, for example, a town of 28,000 residents, a convenience store clerk was beaten in front of customers, who did nothing to help, even after the assailant had fled and the clerk lay bleeding on the floor (Hsu, 1995).

Maybe the answer is that people are just too afraid or cowardly to do anything. That was the premise of the movie *Kick-Ass*, in which the main character, a nerdy high school student who gets picked on by bullies, decides to become a superhero to help those in need. Unlike superheroes in comic books he doesn't have any super powers, but donning a costume and assuming an alternative identity gives him the courage to confront bullies and bad guys. But as entertaining as the movie is, it misses a key social psychological point: Often, the fact that many people fail to help in emergencies is not because of who they are, but because of the nature of the social situation.

Bibb Latané and John Darley (1970) were the first to propose this idea and put it to the test. The key situational variable, they thought, might be the number of bystanders who witness an emergency. Paradoxically, they reasoned, the greater the number of bystanders who observe an emergency, the less likely any one of them is to help. In each of the three brutal incidents we described earlier, more than one bystander witnessed the emergency, and this may have been the key to why no one intervened.

In a series of now-classic experiments, Latané and Darley (1970) found support for this hypothesis. Think back to the seizure experiment we discussed in Chapter 2. In that study, people sat in individual cubicles, participating in a group discussion of college life (over an intercom system) with students in other cubicles. One of the other students suddenly had a seizure, crying out for help, choking, and finally falling silent. There was actually only one real participant in the study. The other "participants," including the one who had the seizure, were prerecorded voices. The point of the study was to see whether the real participant would attempt to help the seizure victim by trying to find him or by summoning the experimenter, or whether the participant would simply sit there and do nothing.

As Latané and Darley anticipated, the answer depended on how many people the participant thought witnessed the emergency. When people believed they were the only ones listening to the student having the seizure, most of them (85%) helped within 60 seconds. By 2 1/2 minutes, 100% of the people who thought they were the only bystander had offered assistance (see Figure 11.4). In comparison, when the research

Figure 11.4 Bystander Intervention: The Presence of Bystanders Reduces Helping

When people believed they were the only one witnessing a student having a seizure, when they were the lone bystander, most of them helped him immediately, and all did so within a few minutes. When they believed that someone else was listening as well, that there were two bystanders, they were less likely to help and did so more slowly. And when they believed that four others were listening, that there were five bystanders, they were even less likely to help.

(Based on Darley & Latané, 1968)

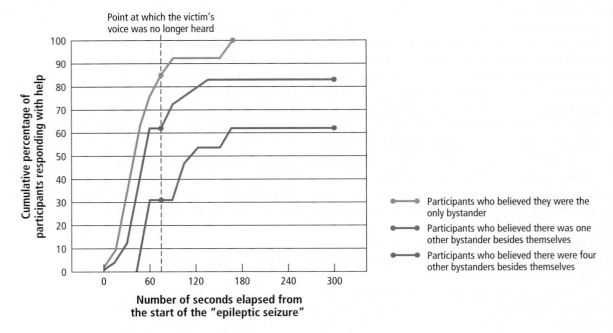

participants believed there was one other student listening, fewer helped—only 62% within 60 seconds; helping occurred more slowly when there were two bystanders and never reached 100%, even after 6 minutes, when the experiment was ended. Finally, when the participants believed there were four other students listening in addition to themselves, the percentage of people who helped dropped even more dramatically. Only 31% helped in the first 60 seconds, and after 6 minutes only 62% had offered help. Dozens of other studies, conducted in the laboratory and in the field, have found the same thing: The greater the number of bystanders who witness an emergency, the less likely any one of them is to help the victim—a phenomenon called the **bystander effect** (Fischer et al., 2011).

Why is it that people are less likely to help when others are present? Latané and Darley (1970) developed a five-step tree that describes how people decide whether to intervene in an emergency (see Figure 11.5). Part of this description is an explanation of how the number of bystanders can make a difference. But let's begin with the first step—whether people notice that someone needs help.

NOTICING AN EVENT   If you are hurrying down a crowded street, you might not notice that someone has collapsed in a doorway. Obviously, if people don't notice that an emergency situation exists, they will not intervene and offer to help. What determines whether people notice an emergency?

John Darley and Daniel Batson (1973) demonstrated that something as seemingly trivial as how much of a hurry people are in can make more of a difference than what kind of people they are. These researchers conducted a study that mirrored the parable of the Good Samaritan, wherein many passersby failed to stop to help a man lying unconscious at the side of the road. The research participants were people we might think would be extremely altruistic—seminary students preparing to devote their lives to the ministry. The students were asked to walk to another building,

Bystander Effect

The finding that the greater the number of bystanders who witness an emergency, the less likely any one of them is to help

Figure 11.5 Bystander Intervention Decision Tree: Five Steps to Helping in an Emergency

Latané and Darley (1970) showed that people go through five decision-making steps before they help someone in an emergency. If bystanders fail to take any one of the five steps, they will not help. Each step is outlined here, along with the possible reasons why people decide not to intervene.

(Based on Darley & Latané, 1968)

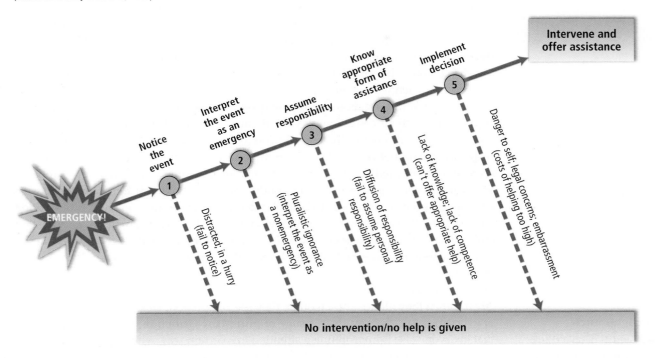

where the researchers would record them making a brief speech. Some were told that they were late and should hurry to keep their appointment. Others were told that there was no rush because the assistant in the other building was running a few minutes behind schedule. As they walked to the other building, each of the students passed a man who was slumped in a doorway. The man (an accomplice of the experimenters) coughed and groaned as each student walked by. Did the seminary students stop and offer to help him? If they were not in a hurry, most of them (63%) did. If they were hurrying to keep their appointment, however, only 10% stopped to help. Many of the students who were in a hurry did not even notice the man.

Surely if people were deeply religious, they would be less influenced by such a small matter as how hurried they were. Surprisingly, though, Darley and Batson (1973) found that the seminary students who were the most religious were no more likely to help than those who were the least religious. What about if they were thinking about helping people in need? The researchers also varied the topic of the speech they asked the students to give. Some were asked to discuss the kinds of jobs seminary students preferred; others were asked to discuss the parable of the Good Samaritan. You might think that seminary students who were thinking about the parable of the Good Samaritan would be especially likely to stop and help a man slumped in a doorway, given the similarity of this incident to the parable, but the topic of the speech made little difference in whether they helped. Students in a hurry were unlikely to notice the man and help, even if they were very religious and about to give a speech about the Good Samaritan.

INTERPRETING THE EVENT AS AN EMERGENCY Even if people do notice someone slumped in a doorway, they might not stop and help. The next determinant of helping is whether the bystander interprets the event as an emergency—as a situation where help is needed (see Figure 11.5). Sometimes, of course, there is little doubt that an emergency has occurred, such as when we witness a car accident and see that people have been seriously injured. Under these circumstances, the number of by-standers is less likely to matter, because people know that help is needed (Fischer et al., 2011). Often, however, the situation is more ambiguous.

Is the person in the doorway drunk or seriously ill? Did the scream we just heard come from someone having a good time at a party or is someone being attacked? If people assume that what they witnessed is not an emergency, then obviously they will not help.

In ambiguous situations such as these, the number of bystanders makes a difference in a curious way: The greater the number of people who witness an emergency, the less likely they are to *know* that it is an emergency. To understand why, think back to our discussion of informational social influence in Chapter 8. This type of social influence occurs when we use other people to help us define reality. Suppose, for example, that you are sitting in class one day and notice that some white vapor or smoke is coming out of an air conditioning vent. Because you aren't sure what to make of this, you do what comes naturally to us all; you look around and see how other people are responding. You notice that the person to your left is looking at the vent and doesn't seem at all concerned, so you conclude that there is nothing to worry about. "Probably just some water vapor from the air conditioning system," you think. As we saw in Chapter 8, using other people to help us interpret an ambiguous event is often a good strategy. The danger is that no one may know exactly what is going on, and mistakenly assume that everyone else does. For example, the guy sitting to your left in the class may look unconcerned because he saw that *you* weren't panicking. Emergencies are often confusing and sudden events, and bystanders tend to freeze, watching with blank expressions as they try to figure out what is happening (Van den Bos & Lind, 2013). When they glance at each other, they see an apparent lack of concern on the part of everyone else. This results in a state of **pluralistic ignorance**, wherein people think that everyone else is interpreting a situation in a certain way, when in fact they are not.

This white-smoke scenario is taken from another classic experiment by Latané and Darley (1970) and illustrates the dangers of pluralistic ignorance. Again, imagine you were a participant and arrive at the appointed time for a study of people's attitudes toward the problems of urban life. A sign tells you to fill out a questionnaire while you're waiting for the study to begin, so you take a seat and get started. Then you notice something odd: White smoke is trickling into the room through a small vent in the wall. Before long, the room is so filled with smoke that you can barely see the questionnaire. What will you do?

In fact, there was no real danger—the experimenters were pumping smoke into the room to see how people would respond to this potential emergency. Not surprisingly, when people were alone, most of them took action. Within 2 minutes, 50% of the participants left the room and found the experimenter down the hall, reporting that there may have been a fire in the building; by 6 minutes, 75% of the participants had left the room to alert the experimenter.

But what would happen if people were not alone? Given that 75% of the participants who were by themselves reported the smoke, it would seem that the larger the group, the greater the likelihood that someone would report the smoke. In fact, this can be figured mathematically: If there is a 75% chance that any one person will report the smoke, then there is a 98% chance that at least one person in a three-person group will do so.

To find out if there really is safety in numbers, Latané and Darley (1970) included a condition

Pluralistic Ignorance

The case in which people think that everyone else is interpreting a situation in a certain way, when in fact they are not

Watch PLURALISTIC IGNORANCE AND EMERGENCIES

Revel Video

in which three participants took part at the same time. Everything was identical except that three people sat in the room as the smoke began to seep in. Surprisingly, in only 12% of the three-person groups did someone report the smoke within 2 minutes, and in only 38% of the groups did someone report the smoke within 6 minutes. In the remaining groups, the participants sat there filling out questionnaires even when they had to wave away the smoke with their hands to see what they were writing. What went wrong?

Unsure whether the smoke signaled an emergency, participants used each other as a source of information. If the people next to you glance at the smoke and then continue filling out their questionnaires, you will feel reassured that nothing is wrong; otherwise, why would they be acting so unconcerned? The problem is that they are probably looking at you as well, and if you seem untroubled, they too are reassured that everything is OK. In short, each group member is reassured because they assume that everyone else knows more about what's going on than they do. And when the event is ambiguous—as when smoke is coming from a vent—people in groups will convince each other that nothing is wrong, resulting in potentially tragic cases of pluralistic ignorance (Clark & Word, 1972; Solomon, Solomon, & Stone, 1978).

Emergency situations can be confusing. Does this man need help? Have the bystanders failed to notice him or has the behavior of the others led each of them to interpret the situation as a nonemergency—an example of pluralistic ignorance?

ASSUMING RESPONSIBILITY   Sometimes it is obvious that an emergency is occurring, such as when the bystanders in Philadelphia witnessed the transit officer being attacked by a man he was trying to arrest. That they did nothing indicates that even if we interpret an event as an emergency, we have to decide that it is *our* responsibility, not someone else's, to do something about it. Here again the number of bystanders is a crucial variable.

Think back to the Latané and Darley (1968) seizure experiment in which participants believed they were the only one listening to the student while he had a seizure. The responsibility was totally on their shoulders. If they didn't help, no one would, and the student might die. As a result, in this condition most people helped almost immediately, and all helped within a few minutes.

But what happens when there are many witnesses? A **diffusion of responsibility** occurs: Each bystander's sense of responsibility to help decreases as the number of witnesses increases. Because other people are present, no single bystander feels a strong personal responsibility to act. Recall from our previous discussion that helping often entails costs: We might be putting ourselves in danger or end up looking foolish by overreacting or doing the wrong thing. Why should we risk these costs when many other people who can help are present? One study found that a diffusion of responsibility even among 5-year-olds. When an experimenter "accidentally" knocked over a glass of water, 95% of children helped clean it up, if they were the only person to witness the accident. But when two other children were present and didn't help (they were accomplices

Diffusion of Responsibility

The phenomenon wherein each bystander's sense of responsibility to help decreases as the number of witnesses increases

Watch SURVIVAL TIPS! DIFFUSION OF RESPONSIBILITY IN FIELD HOCKEY

Revel Video

of the experimenter and were instructed to do nothing), then only 55% of the children helped (Plötner et al., 2015).

A diffusion of responsibility is particularly likely to occur when people cannot tell whether someone else has already intervened. When participants in the seizure experiment believed that other students were witnesses as well, they couldn't tell whether another student had already helped, because the intercom system allowed only the voice of the student having the seizure to be transmitted. Each student probably assumed that he or she did not have to help, thinking that surely someone else had already done so. The same is true in many real-life emergencies; when we drive by a car accident on the highway, for example, we assume that someone else has already called 911.

KNOWING HOW TO HELP   Even if people have made it this far in the helping sequence, another condition must still be met (Step 4 in Figure 11.5): They must decide what kind of help is appropriate. Suppose that on a hot summer day you see a woman collapse in the street. No one else seems to be helping, so you decide it is up to you. But what should you do? Has the woman had a heart attack? Is she suffering from heatstroke? Should you call an ambulance, administer CPR, or try to get her out of the sun? If people don't know what form of assistance to give, obviously they will be unable to help.

DECIDING TO IMPLEMENT THE HELP   Finally, even if you know exactly what kind of help is appropriate, there are still reasons why you might decide not to intervene. For one thing, you might not be qualified to deliver the right kind of help. Even if the woman is complaining of chest pains, indicating a heart attack, you may not know how to give her CPR. Or you might be afraid of making a fool of yourself, of doing the wrong thing and making matters worse, or even of placing yourself in danger by trying to help. Consider the fate of three television network technicians who in 1982 saw a man beating a woman in a New York parking lot, tried to intervene, and were shot and killed by the assailant. Even when we know what kind of intervention is needed, we have to weigh the costs of trying to help.

Diffusion of Responsibility in Cyberspace

People increasingly interact on social media sites and chat rooms and sometimes encounter requests for help. Are people less likely to help each other as the number of people in the chat room increases, as Latané and Darley's model predicts? Researchers in one study entered chat groups on Yahoo! Chat where 2 to 19 people were discussing a wide variety of topics (Markey, 2000). The researchers posed as either a male or female participant and typed this request for help: "Can anyone tell me how to look at someone's profile?" (p. 185). The message was addressed either to the group as a whole or to one randomly selected person in the chat room. Then the researchers timed how long it took someone in the group to respond to the request for help.

When the request was addressed to the group as a whole, Latané and Darley's results were replicated closely: The more people there were in the chat room, the longer it took for anyone to respond to the request for help. But when the request was directed to a specific person, that person responded quickly, regardless of the size of the group. These results suggest that the diffusion of responsibility was operating. When a general request for help is made, a large group makes people feel that they do not have much responsibility to respond. When addressed by name, though, people are more likely to feel a responsibility to help, even when many others are present (van Bommel et al., 2012).

Effects of the Media: Video Games and Music Lyrics

When we think about the effects of the media on behavior, we usually think about negative influences, such as whether violence on television or playing violent video games makes people more aggressive. There are indeed such negative effects, which we discuss in Chapter 12. But can the opposite also occur, such that seeing people act in prosocial ways or playing prosocial video games makes people more cooperative? Recent research suggests that it can.

Tobias Greitemeyer and his colleagues have conducted a number of studies that follow the same procedure: First, participants come into the lab and play a video game for about 10 minutes. Half are randomly assigned to play a game that involves prosocial acts, such as *Lemmings*, in which the goal is to care for a group of small beings and save them by helping them find the exit out of different worlds. The other half play a neutral video game such as *Tetris*, where the goal is to rotate falling geometric figures so that they cover the bottom of the screen. Participants then take part in what they think is an unrelated study, in which they are given the opportunity to help someone. The helping opportunities include relatively easy actions such as helping an experimenter pick up a cup of pencils that he or she accidentally knocked over, more time-consuming commitments such as volunteering to participate in future studies without compensation; and potentially dangerous actions such as helping a female experimenter when an ex-boyfriend enters the room and starts harassing her. As seen in Figure 11.6, people who had just played a prosocial video game were more likely to help in all of these ways than were people who had just played a neutral video game (Greitemeyer & Osswald, 2010; Prot et al., 2014).

It isn't just prosocial video games that can make people more helpful—listening to songs with prosocial lyrics works too. Studies have found that people who listen to songs such as Michael Jackson's *Heal the World* or the Beatles' *Help* are more likely to help someone than people who listened to songs with neutral lyrics such as the Beatles' *Octopus's Garden* (Greitemeyer, 2009, 2011; North et al., 2004).

Why does playing a prosocial video game or listening to prosocial song lyrics make people more helpful? It works in at least two ways: by increasing people's empathy toward someone in need of help and increasing the accessibility of thoughts about helping others (Greitemeyer, Osswald, & Brauer, 2010). So, if you ever find yourself in need of help and see someone approaching with headphones on, hope that he or she is listening to music with prosocial lyrics!

Figure 11.6 Effects of Playing Prosocial Video Games on the Likelihood of Helping

(Based on Greitemeyer & Osswald, 2010)

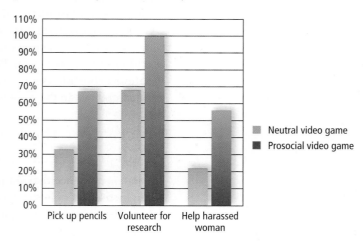

Review Questions

1. Which of the following people is most likely to agree to help clean up a park in a large city?
   a. Brian, who just moved to that city
   b. Rachel, who grew up in a small town
   c. Jiaying, who has lived in that city her entire life
   d. David, who just played a violent video game

2. Which one of the following is *not* part of the Bystander Intervention Decision Tree?
   a. Having an altruistic personality
   b. Interpreting an event as an emergency
   c. Assuming responsibility
   d. Knowing the appropriate form of assistance

3. Suppose that Jinyi sends a tweet asking for someone to help her move a couch into her apartment. Under which of these conditions is one of her followers mostly likely to agree to help?
   a. Jinyi has a very large number of followers.
   b. Jinyi just began tweeting and has only a few followers.
   c. Jinyi lives in a very large city.
   d. Jinyi grew up in the United States.

4. Which of the following people is *least* likely to help someone who dropped a folder of papers on her way to class?
   a. Julia, who just listened to Michael Jackson's song *Heal the World*
   b. Owen, who just played the videogame *Lemmings*
   c. Chanel, who just listened to the Beatles song *Help*
   d. Ben, who just played the videogame *Tetris*

How Can Helping Be Increased?

LO 11.4 **Explain what can be done to promote prosocial behavior.**

What can we do to get people to help those in need? Before addressing this question, we should point out that people do not always want to be helped. Imagine that you are sitting in a coffee shop and are trying to figure out how to upload a video from your phone to a new social media site. You're having trouble getting it to work when a guy you know saunters over, looks over your shoulder for a few minutes and then says, "You have a lot to learn. Let me show you how to do it." How would you react? You might feel gratitude, but you will probably also feel some resentment. His offer of help comes with a message: "You are too stupid to figure this out for yourself." Because receiving help can make people feel inadequate and dependent, they do not always react positively when someone offers them aid. People do not want to appear incompetent, so they often decide to suffer in silence, even if doing so lowers their chances of successfully completing a task (Alvarez & Van Leeuwen, 2011; Halabi, Nadler, & Dovidio, 2013).

Nevertheless, the world would be a better place if more people helped those in need. How can we increase everyday acts of kindness, such as looking out for an elderly neighbor or volunteering to read to kids at the local school? The answer to this question lies in our discussion of the causes of prosocial behavior. For example, we saw that several personal characteristics of potential helpers are important, and promoting those factors can increase the likelihood that these people will help (Clary et al., 1994; Snyder, 1993). But even kind, altruistic people will fail to help if certain situational constraints are present, such as being in an urban environment or witnessing an emergency in the presence of numerous bystanders.

Increasing the Likelihood That Bystanders Will Intervene

There is evidence that simply being aware of the barriers to helping in an emergency can increase people's chances of overcoming those barriers. A few years ago at Cornell University, several students intervened to prevent another student from committing suicide. As is often the case with emergencies, the situation was very confusing, and at first the bystanders were not sure what was happening or what they should do. The student who led the intervention said that she was reminded of a lecture she had heard on bystander intervention in her introductory psychology class a few days before and realized that if she didn't act, no one would (Savitsky, 1998). Or consider an incident at Vassar College not long ago where students saw someone being attacked by a mugger. As so often happens with incidents like this, most of the bystanders did nothing, probably because they assumed that somebody else had already called the police. One of the students, however, immediately called the campus police because she was struck by how similar the situation was to the studies on bystander intervention she had read about in her social psychology course—even though she had taken the class more than a year earlier (Coats, 1998).

These are not controlled experiments, of course, and we cannot be certain that these helpful people were spurred on by what they had learned in their psychology classes. Fortunately, this question has been addressed experimentally (Beaman et al., 1978). The researchers randomly assigned students to listen to a lecture about Latané and Darley's (1970) bystander intervention research or a lecture on an unrelated topic. Two weeks later, all the students participated in what they thought was a completely unrelated sociology study, during which they came across a student lying on the floor. Was he in need of help? Had he fallen and injured himself, or was he simply a student who had fallen asleep after pulling an all-nighter? As we have seen, when in an ambiguous situation such as this one, people look to see how other people are reacting. Because an accomplice of the experimenter (posing as another participant) intentionally acted unconcerned, the natural thing to do was to assume that nothing was wrong. This is exactly what most participants did if they had not heard the lecture about bystander intervention research; in this condition, only 25% of them stopped to help the student. However, if the participants had heard the lecture about bystander intervention, 43% stopped to help the student. Thus, knowing how we can be unwittingly influenced by others can by itself help overcome this type of social influence and make us more likely to intervene in a possible emergency.

Would it help to train people more broadly to "not be a bystander" and help when needed? Consider, for example, the all-too-common problem of violence in our society, including sexual violence, bullying, and stalking. Many of us have probably had the experience of seeing someone who might be at risk for such violence but we failed to intervene, because we weren't sure what to do or because there were lots of other people available to help. Suppose, for example, that you are at a college party and see a man gripping a woman by the arm and leading her out of the room. She doesn't seem to be leaving voluntarily, or is she? It's probably OK, you think. After all, no one else is doing anything about it. The man is probably a friend of the woman's and is helping her home because she has had too much to drink.

But by now you know that the other bystanders might be in the same position as you, failing to help because they don't see anyone else reacting with alarm (including you!). And now that you know about the bystander effect and diffusion of responsibility, we hope you are more likely to jump in and ask the woman if she is OK.

Indeed, this is the premise behind bystander intervention training programs such as Green Dot—that people can be trained to be better bystanders by understanding the difficulties of helping in situations such as the one we just described. Many colleges have adopted programs such as this, and although they are new, there is some initial evidence that they work. In one study, for example, researchers tracked the incidence of sexual violence in 26 high schools, after randomly assigning half of them to get Green Dot bystander intervention training and half to a control group that did not get the training. Over a 5-year period, there were significantly fewer reports of sexual violence in the schools that got the training (Coker et al., 2017).

Another approach is simply to remind ourselves that it can be important to overcome our inhibitions and do the right thing. When people find themselves in situations that are surprising and difficult to understand—which is certainly the case when emergencies arise—they naturally "freeze" and try to make sense of what is happening around them (van den Bos & Lind, 2013). This is particularly likely to happen when people are in public and worry about "doing the wrong thing" in front of others.

Maybe people who are concerned about doing the wrong thing in public would be more likely to help if they thought about times in the past when they overcame their inhibitions. To test

Why did this person help, even when several other bystanders witnessed the same emergency and didn't help? Perhaps this person learned about the barriers to bystander intervention in a social psychology class.

that hypothesis, Kees van den Bos and colleagues (2009) asked people to fill out one of two versions of a questionnaire. In the disinhibition condition, people wrote about times when they had acted in an uninhibited way despite what other people thought. In the control condition, people wrote about how they behaved on normal days. Next the researchers staged a helping situation to see which group of people was most likely to come to the aid of someone in need. As they predicted, it was the people in the disinhibition condition. In one study, for example, 53% of individuals who had filled out the disinhibition questionnaire helped a man pick up pens that he dropped as he was rushing to catch a train, compared to only 7% of individuals in the control condition. As natural as it is to hang back and do nothing in situations such as this one, reminding ourselves of times in the past when we overcame our inhibitions can make us more likely to help (Van den Bos & Lind, 2013).

Increasing Volunteerism

There are many important kinds of prosocial behavior besides intervening in emergencies, including volunteerism and community service. Social psychologists have studied this kind of helping as well, wherein people commit to helping strangers on a more long-term basis (Johnson & Post, 2017; Mannino, Snyder, & Omoto, 2011; Piliavin, 2010).

Surveys of Western European and North American countries have found that many people engage in volunteer work, with the highest rate in the United States (47%; Ting & Piliavin, 2000). This level of volunteerism is a tremendous source of support for many members of our society, including children, the homeless, immigrants, and many others. It is also a great source of support for those doing the volunteering (Layous et al., 2017). Older adults who engage in volunteer work, have better health, less depression, and even a longer life (Anderson et al., 2014). These benefits are so substantial that some medical professionals have argued that doctors should prescribe two hours a week of volunteer behavior to all their patients (Johnson & Post, 2017). Similar to our previous discussion of empathy and helping, volunteerism is a case where there are benefits both to the helper and those being helped.

Because of this, some institutions have responded by requiring their members to perform community service. Some high schools, colleges, and businesses, for example, require their students or employees to engage in volunteer work. These programs have the benefit of increasing the pool of volunteers available to help community organizations such as homeless shelters, medical clinics, and day-care centers.

But the question arises as to the effect of such "mandatory volunteerism" on the motivation of the people who do the helping. As we discussed in Chapter 5, giving people strong external reasons for performing an activity can actually undermine their intrinsic interest in that activity. This is called the *overjustification effect*: People see their behavior as caused by compelling extrinsic reasons (e.g., being required to do volunteer work), making them underestimate the extent to which their behavior was caused by intrinsic reasons (e.g., that they like to do volunteer work). Consistent with this research, the more that people feel they are volunteering because of external requirements, the *less* likely they are to volunteer freely in the future (Bringle, 2005; Kunda & Schwartz, 1983; Stukas, Snyder, & Clary, 1999). The moral? It is best to encourage people to volunteer while at the same time preserving the sense that they freely choose to do so. Under these conditions volunteering will increase people's well-being and their intentions to volunteer again in the future (Piliavin, 2008; Stukas et al., 1999).

An increasing number of schools and businesses are requiring people to perform community service. These programs can actually lower interest in volunteering if people feel they are helping because of an external requirement. Encouraging people to volunteer while preserving the sense that they freely choose to do so is likely to increase people's intentions to volunteer again in the future.

Review Questions

1. Which of the following is true?
   a. People are always grateful for offers to help them.
   b. As a result of learning about the social psychology of prosocial behavior, you may be more likely to help someone in need in the future.
   c. If someone doesn't want to help others there isn't much we can do to change that.
   d. Hearing a lecture about prosocial behavior and bystander intervention isn't likely to change how people behave in a real emergency.

2. A company is considering offering its employees the opportunity to do community service. Which of the following would you recommend they do, based on research in social psychology?
   a. Make the community service mandatory
   b. Offer incentives for doing the community service such as extra vacation days
   c. Make sure that people feel that doing the community service is voluntary
   d. Assign people to different community agencies

3. Which of the following people would be most admired by his or her peers?
   a. Victoria volunteers at a hospital because she thinks it will look good on her college applications.
   b. Kevin works at a soup kitchen each week as part of a mandatory community service requirement at his job.
   c. Jun failed to help in an emergency because he thought someone else had already called 911.
   d. Shamika volunteers at a shelter for homeless families because she really likes working with the kids.

Summary

LO 11.1 Describe the basic motives that determine whether people help others.

- **Basic Motives Underlying Prosocial Behavior: Why Do People Help?** This chapter examined the causes of *prosocial behavior*, acts performed with the goal of benefiting another person. What are the basic origins of prosocial behavior?

  - **Evolutionary Psychology: Instincts and Genes** Evolutionary theory explains prosocial behavior in three ways. *Kin selection*, the idea that behaviors that help a genetic relative are favored by natural selection. The *norm of reciprocity*, which is the expectation that helping others will increase the likelihood that they will help us in the future. The third is *group selection*, the idea that social groups with altruistic members are more likely to survive in competition with other groups.

  - **Social Exchange: The Costs and Rewards of Helping** Social exchange theory argues that prosocial behavior is not necessarily rooted in our genes. Instead, people help others in order to maximize social rewards and minimize social costs.

  - **Empathy and Altruism: The Pure Motive for Helping** People can be motivated by *altruism*, the desire to help another person even if it involves a cost to the helper. According to the *empathy-altruism hypothesis*, when people feel *empathy* toward another person (they experience events and emotions the other person experiences), they attempt to help that person purely for altruistic reasons.

LO 11.2 Describe the personal qualities that influence whether a given individual will help.

- **Personal Qualities and Prosocial Behavior: Why Do Some People Help More Than Others?** Basic motives are not all there is to understanding prosocial behavior—personal qualities matter as well.

  - **Individual Differences: The Altruistic Personality** Although some people have altruistic personalities that make them more likely to help others, we need to consider several other critical factors when predicting who will help and who will not.

  - **Gender Differences in Prosocial Behavior** In many cultures, the male sex role includes helping in chivalrous and heroic ways, whereas the female sex role includes helping in close, long-term relationships.

  - **Cultural Differences in Prosocial Behavior** People are willing to help both *in-group* and *out-group* members, but for different reasons. People are more likely to feel empathy toward members of their in-groups who are in need, and the more empathy they feel, the more likely they are to help. People help out-group members for a different reason: They do so when they have something to gain, such as feeling good about themselves or making a good impression on others.

- **Religion and Prosocial Behavior** There is a pervasive stereotype that religious people are more moral and engage in more prosocial behavior than nonreligious people. When it comes to actual behavior, it is true that religious people are more likely to help than other people are *if* the person in need of help shares their beliefs, but religious people are not more likely to help strangers. This is an example of in-group favoritism, in that people show preference to in-group members over out-group members. Thus, it may not be religiosity per se that causes people to be more helpful, but rather that people are more helpful toward people who belong to the same groups they do.

- **The Effects of Mood on Prosocial Behavior** People are more likely to help if they are in especially good moods, but also if they are in especially bad moods.

LO 11.3 Describe the situations in which people are more likely, or less likely, to help others.

- **Situational Determinants of Prosocial Behavior: When Will People Help?** To understand why people help others, we also need to consider the nature of the social situation.

  - **Environment: Rural Versus Urban** People are less likely to help in dense, urban settings because of the *urban overload hypothesis*—the idea that people living in cities are constantly bombarded with stimulation and that they keep to themselves to avoid being overwhelmed by it.

  - **Residential Mobility** People who have lived for a long time in one place are more likely to engage in prosocial behaviors than are people who have recently moved to an area.

  - **The Number of Bystanders: The Bystander Effect** To help in an emergency, people must meet five conditions: They must notice the event, interpret it as an emergency, assume responsibility, know how to help, and implement their decision to help. As the number of bystanders who witness an emergency increases, the more difficult it is to meet two of these conditions—interpreting the event as an emergency and assuming responsibility. This produces the *bystander effect*: The larger the number of bystanders, the less likely any one of them is to help.

  - **Diffusion of Responsibility in Cyberspace** The bystander effect has also been observed in online chat rooms. The more people there were in a chat room, the longer it took for anyone to respond a user's request for help.

  - **Effects of the Media: Video Games and Music Lyrics** Playing a prosocial video game or listening to a song with prosocial lyrics makes people more likely to help others in a variety of ways.

LO 11.4 Explain what can be done to promote prosocial behavior.

- **How Can Helping Be Increased?** Prosocial behavior can be increased in a number of ways.

  - **Increasing the Likelihood That Bystanders Will Intervene** Research shows that teaching people about the barriers to bystander intervention increases the likelihood that they will help in emergencies. Reminding people of times they acted in uninhibited ways can work as well.

  - **Increasing Volunteerism** Organizations that encourage their employees to engage in volunteer work should be careful about how they do so. If people feel that they are volunteering only because they have to, they may actually become less likely to volunteer in the future. Encouraging people to volunteer while preserving the sense that they freely choose to do so has been shown to increase people's sense of well-being and their intentions to volunteer again in the future.

Revel Interactive

Shared Writing   **What Do You Think?**

Think about a time in the past when you were in a position to help someone, either in an emergency or not in an emergency. Why did you help or not help the person?

Test Yourself

1. Which of the following is *not* a way in which evolutionary theory explains prosocial behavior?

   a. Social exchange
   b. Kin selection
   c. Reciprocity norm
   d. Group selection

2. Amy is walking across campus and sees someone on her hands and knees looking for a ring that slipped off her finger. Under which of the following conditions is Amy *least* likely to help the person look for the ring, according to the empathy-altruism hypothesis?

   a. Amy feels empathy toward the person, and thinks she will be admired by passersby if she stops to help.
   b. Amy feels empathy toward the person, but she doesn't think she has much to gain by helping.
   c. Amy doesn't feel empathy toward the person but recognizes her as a TA in her English class. Amy really wants to get a good grade in that class.
   d. Amy doesn't feel empathy toward the person and doesn't think she has much to gain by helping.

3. Research on prosocial behavior finds that religious people:

   a. help others more than nonreligious people do in virtually all ways.
   b. show more compassion toward needy strangers than do nonreligious people.
   c. are more likely to help than other people are if the person in need of shares their beliefs, but are not more likely to help strangers.
   d. actually help others less than do nonreligious people.

4. Frank has recently graduated from college and moved from New York City back to the small town in Ohio where he grew up. He now finds that he is much more inclined to engage in prosocial behavior. What is the most likely reason for this change?

   a. Growing up in a small town caused him to internalize altruistic values.
   b. The change in his immediate surroundings changed his likelihood of helping.
   c. College students are less likely to help because they are more susceptible to the bystander effect.
   d. Frank is more likely to engage in negative-state relief when he is in the small town.

5. Luke listened to a lecture in his history class that he found very confusing, but at the end of the class when the professor asked whether there was anything students didn't understand, Luke didn't raise his hand. Because no other hands were raised, Luke assumed that other students had understood the material and that he just didn't pay enough attention. In fact, many students hadn't understood the material and were in the same situation as Luke. This is an example of:

   a. empathy-altruism hypothesis.
   b. reciprocity norm.
   c. social exchange.
   d. pluralistic ignorance.

6. Which of the following is *not* a reason why being in a good mood tends to increase prosocial behavior?

   a. Good moods make us view situations more positively, and thus we are more likely to give people the benefit of the doubt.
   b. Helping prolongs good moods.
   c. Good moods make us pay more attention to the possible rewards for helping.
   d. Good moods increase how much attention we pay to ourselves, which makes us more likely to act according to our values.

7. Which of the following is true?

   a. Listening to song lyrics with prosocial lyrics makes people more helpful.
   b. If we want someone to say yes when we ask for a date, it doesn't really work to have him or her listen to a song with romantic lyrics.
   c. Playing prosocial video games has no effect on how helpful people will be.
   d. Playing violent video games makes people more helpful.

8. Meghan lives in a single room in a college dormitory. Late one night, she hears a scream coming from just outside her dorm. She is pretty sure that the person needs help because the person yelled, "Help me! I think I broke my leg!" Meghan goes back to sleep, only to find out the next day that the person was on the ground for 45 minutes before someone helped. Which of the following best explains why Meghan didn't help?

   a. Informational influence
   b. A diffusion of responsibility
   c. She didn't interpret it as an emergency
   d. Pluralistic ignorance

9. Which of the following is true about prosocial behavior?

    a. How often people have moved from one place to another influences how helpful they are.

    b. There is no effect of personality on prosocial behavior.

    c. Being in a bad mood decreases prosocial behavior.

    d. Being in a good mood decreases prosocial behavior.

10. It's a busy day at the motor vehicles office and many people are waiting for their turn. As one man gets up to leave, he accidentally drops a folder he was carrying and papers go everywhere. Which person is *least* likely to help him pick up the papers?

    a. Meghan, who was just thinking about times in her past when she acted in uninhibited ways

    b. Joe, who is taking social psychology and heard a lecture about Latané and Darley's decision tree earlier in the week

    c. Michael, who is feeling guilty because he should be home helping his roommates clean their apartment

    d. Maggie, who is very religious but doesn't know the man who dropped the papers

Chapter 12

Aggression
Why Do We Hurt Other People?
Can We Prevent It?

Chapter Outline and Learning Objectives

Is Aggression Innate, Learned, or Optional?

LO 12.1 **Distinguish evolutionary, cultural, and learning explanations of aggression.**

The Evolutionary View

Culture and Aggression

Gender and Aggression

Learning to Behave Aggressively

Some Physiological Influences

Social Situations and Aggression

LO 12.2 **Describe situational and social causes of aggression.**

Frustration and Aggression

Provocation and Reciprocation

Weapons as Aggressive Cues

Putting the Elements Together: The Case of Sexual Assault

Violence and the Media

LO 12.3 **Explain how observing violence increases violence.**

Studying the Effects of Media Violence

The Problem of Determining Cause and Effect

How to Decrease Aggression

LO 12.4 **Identify ways aggression can be diminished.**

Does Punishing Aggression Reduce Aggression?

Can We Release Anger by Indulging It?

What Are We Supposed to Do with Our Anger?

Disrupting the Rejection-Rage Cycle

WHAT DO YOU THINK?

Survey	What Do You Think?	
SURVEY		RESULTS

Do you regularly play first-person shooter video games or watch TV shows or movies that depict acts of violence?

○ Yes
○ No

The mass murder at Columbine High School in Littleton, Colorado, casts a long shadow in American culture. There, in 1999, Eric Harris and Dylan Klebold went on a rampage with assault weapons, killing a teacher and 12 of their fellow students. They then turned their guns on themselves. As horrendous as it was, the death toll could have been much higher. The two shooters had made a videotape prior to the massacre in which they announced that they had prepared and planted 95 explosive devices (fortunately, due to a technical error, these failed to go off). The videotape shows the perpetrators gleefully predicting that, before the day was over, they would have killed 250 people.

Since then, dozens of troubled teenagers have apparently used Columbine as a template for revenge against the classmates they believe have taunted, bullied, or rejected them; some researchers even call this the "Columbine effect." For example, in 2012, Adam Lanza carried out a similar rampage at the Sandy Hook Elementary School in Newton, Connecticut. The police investigation discovered that Lanza was particularly obsessed with the Columbine massacre.

In the aftermath of every mass shooting, the country invariably seeks someone to blame. Were the parents at fault? Does our country make weapons too easily accessible? Does the media show too much violence, influencing our society's behavior? Were all of the shooters crazy? Obviously, anyone who commits mass murder is not emotionally stable, but mental illness itself cannot explain most of these tragic outbursts; most mentally ill people, after all, are not mass murderers.

The violence that human beings inflict on one another comes in all too many varieties: war, mass shootings, fistfights and brawls, murder, sexual coercion and rape, and domestic abuse. In this chapter, we will try to understand some of the diverse causes of aggression. Are human beings innately aggressive? You rarely hear about a woman going on a shooting rampage; does that mean men are innately more aggressive than women? Can healthy people be inspired to commit violence by watching violent characters in films or playing violent video games? Can a society, a school, or a parent do anything to reduce aggression? If so, what specifically?

Needless to say, social psychologists don't have all the answers, but we do have some of them. By the time you get to the end of this chapter, we hope you will have gained some insight into why humans would hurt other humans.

Is Aggression Innate, Learned, or Optional?

LO 12.1 Distinguish evolutionary, cultural, and learning explanations of aggression.

For social psychologists, **aggression** is defined as intentional behavior aimed at causing either physical or psychological pain. The intention to do harm is a necessary component of the psychological definition of aggression, and what makes aggression different from assertiveness. When people fight for their rights, compete in a sports

Aggression

Intentional behavior aimed at causing physical harm or psychological pain to another person

match, or act ambitiously in the business world, they are being assertive without being aggressive, because true aggression involves the intent to harm another. Aggressive action might be physical or verbal; it might succeed in its goal or not. If someone throws a beer bottle at your head and you duck so that the bottle misses you, it was still an aggressive act. By the same token, if a drunk driver unintentionally hits you while you're attempting to cross the street, that is not an act of aggression, even though the damage would be far greater than that caused by the beer bottle that missed. The important thing is the intention. "Violence" is an extreme form of aggression, as in acts of war, murder, and assault.

It is also useful to distinguish between types of aggression (Berkowitz, 1993). **Hostile aggression** is an act of aggression stemming from feelings of anger and is aimed at inflicting pain or injury. **Instrumental aggression** is an act of aggression that is an intermediary step toward a nonaggressive goal. Imagine you are going down the stairs toward a subway platform and you see the train paused with its doors open. You need to get on this train because you will miss your doctor's appointment if you don't. The problem is, all the passengers who deboarded the train are going up the stairs without giving equal room to the people who are trying to go down. You suddenly decide that you cannot wait and must rush forward to make your train. So, you use your shoulders and arms to push people out of your way, even though you know you could bruise someone or even knock people down. If you behaved aggressively purely out of the desire to make your train, then this is instrumental aggression. If, however, you felt angry that the people going up the stairs weren't sharing the space fairly and felt a desire to dole out a few bruises, then the same act (i.e., pushing people out of your way while going downstairs) would be hostile aggression.

Today, social psychologists and other scientists have made great strides in understanding the biological, social, cultural, and situational causes of aggressive behavior. Research has found that aggression has many complex causes and comes in many forms—from direct assault to indirect cruelty—but it's important to note that such behavior is not inevitable and that we possess the power to limit its frequency and consequences.

The Evolutionary View

It seems obvious that men are more aggressive than women. More than 90% of all mass murders (defined as killing at least four people in one location) are committed by men (Hillshafer, 2013). Men are more likely than women to get into spontaneous, unprovoked acts of "picking a fight" with a stranger, join in a flash mob bent on destruction and looting, and commit crimes of violence (murder, aggravated assault, rape). But as we will see, this fact doesn't necessarily mean that women are the shy, retiring, peaceful sex.

Evolutionary psychologists argue that physical aggression is genetically programmed into men because it enables them to defend their group and perpetuate their genes. In cultures all over the world—as diverse as the United States, Switzerland, and Ethiopia—male aggressiveness starts in childhood: Little boys are far more likely than little girls to engage in "nonplayful" pushing, shoving, and hitting (Deaux & La France, 1998; Maccoby & Jacklin, 1974). Males are theorized to aggress for two reasons: first, to establish dominance over other males and secure the highest possible status and, second, males aggress out of sexual jealousy to ensure that their mate is not having sex with other men, thereby ensuring their own paternity (Buss, 2004, 2005; Kaighobadi, Shackelford, & Goetz, 2009). When females behave aggressively, in the evolutionary view, it is generally to protect their offspring. Do not get in the way of a mother bear—or, for that matter, a mother bird.

It is commonly believed that the hormone that fuels male aggression is testosterone, which both sexes have, although in higher proportion in males. Laboratory

Hostile Aggression

Aggression stemming from feelings of anger with the goal of inflicting pain or injury

Instrumental Aggression

Aggression that is done as a means to achieve some goal other than causing pain

Boys are more likely than girls, the world over, to roughhouse and pummel each other. Is this evidence of hostile or instrumental aggression—or just of physical play?

Challenge Hypothesis

Testosterone relates to aggression only when there are opportunities for reproduction

Dual-Hormone Hypothesis

Testosterone relates to dominance-seeking behavior only when the stress hormone, cortisol, is not elevated

animals whose testosterone is removed become less aggressive, and those injected with testosterone become more aggressive (Moyer, 1983; Sapolsky, 1998). Testosterone levels are significantly higher among prisoners convicted of violent crimes than among those convicted of nonviolent crimes (Dabbs, 2000; Dabbs et al., 1995). Testosterone may lead to aggression by reducing our ability to control impulses. Testosterone is related to reduced activity in the orbitofrontal cortex, which is a key brain area for self-regulation and impulse control, and activity in the orbitofrontal cortex in turn predicts responding aggressively to unfair offers in a resource-allocation game (Mehta & Beer, 2010).

However, the link between testosterone and aggression heavily depends on the social situation. The **Challenge Hypothesis** states that testosterone and aggression are only related when opportunities for reproduction are high (Buss, 2002). Similarly, the **Dual-Hormone Hypothesis** states that testosterone only relates to dominance behaviors when the stress hormone, cortisol, is low (Mehta & Josephs, 2010). Research on the Dual-Hormone Hypothesis shows that, in stressful or dangerous times (i.e., when cortisol is elevated), testosterone is related to systematically *less* aggressive and dominance-seeking behaviors. In other words, testosterone only predicts aggression when there is a chance to gain something from that aggression, suggesting a specific relationship between testosterone and instrumental aggression. Both the Challenge Hypothesis and the Dual-Hormone Hypothesis support the evolutionary explanation for aggression serving as a means for establishing dominance and securing mates.

It's also easy (and wrong) to get carried away with claims that men suffer from "testosterone poisoning." Most of the studies have been correlational, which suggests that causality can (and does) flow in both directions: That is, testosterone itself can slightly increase aggression, but being in an aggressive, competitive, or sexual situation increases the production of testosterone (Mazur, Booth, & Dabbs, 1992; Trumble et al., 2012). Moreover, testosterone shares a chemical precursor with the other primary sex hormone, estradiol, that is higher in women than men. Estradiol relates to similar psychological variables as testosterone, such as aggression and sexuality. In fact, the neurons that regulate the synthesis of estradiol also regulate aggression in both men and women (Unger et al., 2015), but we know that estradiol is higher in women than men. Understanding the nuanced differences between the way that testosterone and estradiol relate to aggression is an active research area that seeks to understand the biological contributions to sex differences in aggression.

AGGRESSION IN OTHER ANIMALS To determine the extent to which aggressiveness is innate or learned, some scientists have turned to experiments with nonhuman species. Consider the common belief that cats will instinctively stalk and kill rats. More than a half-century ago, biologist Zing Yang Kuo (1961) performed a simple experiment: He raised a kitten in the same cage with a rat. Not only did the cat refrain from attacking the rat, but the two became close companions. When given the opportunity, the cat refused either to chase or to kill other rats; thus, the benign behavior was not confined to his one buddy but generalized to rats the cat had never met.

Although this experiment is charming, it fails to prove that aggressive behavior is not instinctive in cats; it merely demonstrates that early experience can override it. What if an organism grows up without any contact with other organisms? Will it or won't it show aggressive tendencies? It turns out that rats raised in isolation, without any experience in fighting other rats, will attack a fellow rat when one is introduced into the cage; the isolated rats use the same pattern of threat and attack that experienced rats use (Eibl-Eibesfeldt, 1963). So even though aggressive behavior can be modified by experience, as shown by Kuo's experiment, some kinds of aggressive behavior apparently do not need to be learned.

We can gain still greater insight into our own biological heritage by observing the behavior of those animals with whom we have the most genetic similarity. Our closest relatives in the animal kingdom are two primates: the chimpanzees and the bonobos. Both species have 98% of their DNA in common with human beings, and chimps, bonobos, and humans all directly evolved from the same ancestor (Prüfer et al., 2012). Nonetheless, aggression differs a lot between us. The chimpanzee is known for its aggressive behavior; the females too can be pretty mean (Miller et al., 2014). It is the only nonhuman species in which groups of male members hunt and kill other members of their own kind—indeed, at about the same rate that humans in hunter-gatherer societies kill each other (Wrangham, Wilson, & Muller, 2006). Based on the research on chimps, we might conclude that humans, especially males, are genetically programmed for aggressive behavior.

However, living across the river from the chimpanzees and out of their reach are the bonobos, our equally close genetic relative. Unlike the chimp, the bonobo is known for its nonaggressive behavior. In fact, bonobos are often referred to as the "make love, not war" ape. Prior to engaging in activities that could otherwise lead to conflict, bonobos have sex, an activity that functions to diffuse potential conflict (De Waal, 1995). Thus, when the group arrives at a feeding ground, they first enjoy some sexual play and then proceed to eat peacefully. In contrast, when chimps arrive at a feeding ground, they compete aggressively for the food. Also, unlike the chimps, bonobos form female-dominated societies, keeping males in line and often behaving with remarkable sensitivity to others in their group (Parish & de Waal, 2000).

Unfortunately, the bonobo way of life is rare in the animal kingdom. The near universality of aggression strongly suggests that aggressiveness has evolved and has been maintained because it has survival value (Buss, 2004; Lore & Schultz, 1993). At the same time, nearly all organisms also seem to have evolved strong inhibitory mechanisms that enable them to suppress aggression when it is in their best interests to do so. Aggression is determined by the animal's previous experiences as well as by the specific social context in which the animal finds itself.

When people say that aggression is "natural," they often point to our primate relatives. Chimpanzees (top) are indeed pretty belligerent and aggressive, but bonobos (bottom) would rather make love than war.

Culture and Aggression

Most social psychologists, therefore, believe that aggression is an optional strategy: We humans are born with the *capacity* for aggressive behavior, but how, whether, when, and where we express it is learned and depends on our circumstances and culture (Berkowitz, 1993). All males and females have testosterone and estradiol, after all, but their rates of aggression and violence around the world vary dramatically. Likewise, we seem to have an inborn tendency to respond to certain provocative stimuli by striking out against the perpetrator, but whether we actually do so depends on a complex interplay between these innate tendencies, a variety of learned inhibitory responses, and the precise nature of the social situation. You may be angry if a police officer stops you for speeding when all the cars around you were speeding, but it is likely that you will control your temper—and your behavior.

Thus, although many animals, from insects to apes, will usually attack another animal that invades their territory, we cannot conclude that human beings are similarly programmed to protect their territory and behave aggressively in response to specific stimuli. Three major lines of evidence support this more complex view of aggression: studies of cultures across time, studies across cultures, and laboratory experiments.

CHANGES IN AGGRESSION ACROSS TIME AND CULTURES Within a given culture, changing social conditions frequently lead to significant changes in aggressive behavior. Consider the Iroquois of North America. For hundreds of years, the Iroquois lived peacefully as a hunting nation, without fighting other tribes. But in the seventeenth century, barter with the newly arrived Europeans brought the Iroquois into direct competition with the neighboring Hurons over furs, which dramatically increased in value because they could now be traded for manufactured goods. A series of skirmishes with the Hurons ensued, and within a short time, the Iroquois developed into ferocious warriors. It would be hard to argue that they became ferocious warriors because of some innate aggressive impulse; rather, their aggressive shift almost certainly came about because a social change produced increases in competition (Hunt, 1940).

It works in the other direction, too. Psychologist Steven Pinker (2011) amassed evidence that aggressive acts like war, crime, torture, and murder—though unquestionably still prevalent—have actually been steadily declining over the centuries (see Figure 12.1). Genocidal eruptions such as the Holocaust and contemporary wars are interruptions on a trajectory showing that violence has declined in the family, in neighborhoods, and between nations. We now live in an era, Pinker argues, that is less violent, less cruel, and more peaceful than any previous period of human history. So, if you feel like times are pretty violent now, then imagine what life was like 3000 years ago! We are the same species as the people who lived then, so any innate human aggression has remained constant between us. What changed was the civilizing processes of settled communities and nation-states, and the rising belief in human rights. Many societies that were once warlike—such as the Scandinavians or Portuguese—have become the most peaceful on the planet. "Violence as entertainment" now takes place on movie screens and not in gladiator arenas where actual people were once torn apart to the cheers of audiences.

Moreover, not all societies have been equally warlike. Cultures embedded with cooperative, collectivist values have had lower levels of aggressive behavior than European societies (Bergeron & Schneider, 2005). Certain tribes, such as the Lepchas of Sikkim, the Pygmies of Central Africa, and the Arapesh of New Guinea, live in apparent peace and harmony, with acts of aggression being extremely rare (Baron & Richardson, 1994). In close-knit cultures that depend on cooperation for the group's survival, anger and aggression are considered dangerous and disruptive, and an offender will be ostracized or punished. When men live in cultures that lack internal and external threats to their survival—and, admittedly, not many cultures are so blessed—they are not raised to be aggressive, sex differences are minimized, and cooperation is encouraged (Gilmore, 1990; Kimmel, 2012).

For example, the Teduray, a hunter-gatherer culture in the Philippine rain forest, have established institutions and norms specifically designed to prevent aggression among themselves. In their societies, people are expected to pay special attention to the effect of their actions on the feelings of others. When a situation arises, such as adultery, in which there is significant risk that anger will lead to violence, specific members of a Teduray village work to placate the injured individuals. The Teduray believe that human beings are aggressive by nature but do all they can to reduce its expression within their group. They will, however, behave aggressively to protect themselves from aggression from outsiders (Schlegel, 1998). Altogether, if human aggression was a reliable response to provocative stimuli, then humans in all cultures would be equally aggressive.

Figure 12.1 Homicide rates have been steadily decreasing in America over the last 300 years

Claude Fischer

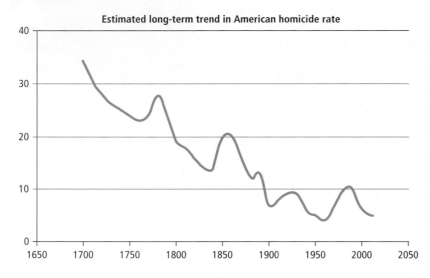

Estimated long-term trend in American homicide rate

CULTURES OF HONOR   Perhaps the strongest evidence against the notion that "men are naturally aggressive because of their testosterone" comes from experiments showing how cultural norms and expectations literally "get inside" people, causing them to behave differently under similar provocation.

For example, in the United States, there are some major regional differences in aggressive behavior and in the kinds of events that trigger violence. Homicide rates for White males from the South and Southwest are substantially higher than those for White northern males, especially in rural areas. Richard Nisbett (1993) hypothesized that the higher rates of violence derive from economic causes: Higher rates of violence occur in cultures that were originally based on herding, in contrast to cultures based on agriculture. Why would this be so? People who depend economically on agriculture tend to develop cooperative strategies for survival. But people who depend on their herds are extremely vulnerable; their livelihoods can be lost in an instant by the theft of their animals. To reduce the likelihood of theft, Nisbett theorized, herders learn to be hyperalert to any threatening act (real or perceived) and respond to it immediately with force. This would explain why cattle rustling and horse thievery were capital crimes in the Old West and why Mediterranean and Middle Eastern herding cultures even today place a high value on male aggressiveness. And indeed, when Nisbett looked at agricultural practices *within* the South, he found that homicide rates were more than twice as high in the hills and dry plains areas (where herding occurs) as in farming regions.

The emphasis on aggressiveness and vigilance in herding communities fosters, in turn, a *culture of honor* in which even small disputes put a man's reputation for toughness on the line, requiring him to respond aggressively to restore his status (Cohen, 1998). Although the herding economy has become much less important in the South and West, the legacy of its culture of honor remains. These regions have rates of honor-related homicides (such as murder to avenge a perceived insult to one's family) that are five times higher than in other regions of the country. High school students in culture-of-honor states are far more likely than students from other states to bring a weapon to school and to use that weapon. These states have more than twice as many school shootings per capita than do other states (Brown, Osterman, & Barnes, 2009). Whereas Pinker (2011) found that violence declines in democracies that allow the government to manage justice and determine the proper punishment for offenders—thereby removing the burden of revenge from individual citizens—men in cultures of honor tend to distrust governments and believe they are the ones who have the obligation to retaliate, personally and sometimes violently.

Gender and Aggression

If women aren't very likely to get into fistfights, start riots, or shoot someone to defend their family's reputation, does that mean that they are inherently less aggressive than men? Gender differences in aggression are obvious in the larger social world; in the private world of families and relationships, these differences aren't always so clear.

The Teduray culture in the Philippines have developed norms and practices that mitigate aggression.

The early economies of the American South and West created a "culture of honor" in which a man was literally quick on the trigger if he thought another man was about to smear his reputation—or steal his cattle.

PHYSICAL AGGRESSION   Most cases of *extreme* violence in the family are perpetrated by men: For example, 8 in 10 murderers who kill a family member are male. And when men beat up their victims, they inflict more serious injury than women abusers do. According to the Centers for Disease Control's national survey of violence between partners, women have a significantly higher lifetime prevalence of severe physical violence by an intimate partner (24.3%) compared to men (13.8%; Breiding, Chen, & Black, 2014; see Figure 12.2), but the rates for men are not as low as societal views assume. When it comes to hitting, slapping, throwing objects, and battering, women, dare we say, don't pull their punches. In a study of nearly 500 first-year American college women who reported violence with their boyfriends, most reported reciprocal abuse (Testa, Hoffman, & Leonard, 2011). A few years ago, a review of more than 200 studies of community samples found no significant gender differences in the percentage of men and women who are physically aggressive with their partners (Straus, 2011). The causes are the same for both parties—including sexual jealousy, anger, to get partner's attention, revenge for perceived emotional abuse, and self-defense (Langhinrichsen-Rohling et al., 2012).

There is often great overlap between males' and females' aggressive behavior. Indeed, in some studies that compared young boys and girls in levels of physical aggression, most of the boys and girls were similarly nonaggressive (Archer, 2004). Among adults, the sex difference in the willingness to inflict physical harm often vanishes when both sexes feel provoked and entitled to retaliate (Matlin, 2012). Adult women do not differ from men, on average, in their willingness to yell, be verbally abusive, humiliate or punish their children, and express aggression in similar ways (Archer, 2004). In a cultural community that admires physical aggression, both sexes may rely on violent tactics: In one international study, women from Australia and New Zealand showed greater evidence of aggressiveness than men from Sweden and Korea (Archer & McDaniel, 1995). A study of all known female suicide bombers throughout the world since 1981 found that "the main motives and circumstances that drive female suicide bombers are quite similar to those that drive men"—loyalty to their country or religion, anger at being occupied by a foreign military, and revenge for loved ones killed by the enemy (O'Rourke, 2008).

RELATIONAL AGGRESSION   When we move out of the realm of physical aggression, sex differences actually flip: Girls and women are more likely than males to commit *relational aggression*—harming another person through the manipulation of relationships, usually in

Figure 12.2 Lifetime Prevalence of Physical Violence by an Intimate Partner

(U.S. Women and Men, NISVS 2010)

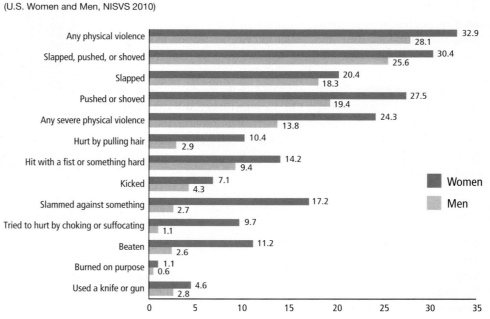

such covert acts as talking behind someone's back, spreading false rumors about the target person, shunning or excluding that person (Archer, 2004; McFadyen-Ketchum et al., 1996; Richardson, 2014). While relational aggression may seem more benign than physical aggression, its consequences can be equally severe. Phoebe Prince, a 15-year-old Irish girl living in Massachusetts, was targeted by a group known as the Mean Girls after she had a brief relationship with a popular boy at her school. Seven girls and two boys began a relentless campaign against her of verbal assault (including calling her "Irish slut" and "whore" on Facebook and other social media) and threats of bodily harm. After 4 months of being slandered and harassed, Prince committed suicide.

The average gender difference in relational aggression starts early: In one study of 3- to 5-year-old children playing in groups of three, the kids were instructed to use a crayon to color in a picture on a white sheet of paper. Three crayons were provided, but only one was a color (orange), and the other two were white. Naturally, the children all wanted the orange crayon. The boys used physical aggression to get it, hitting or pushing the child who had the orange crayon. The girls used relational aggression, spreading rumors about the child with the orange crayon or ignoring her to make her cry (Ostrov et al., 2004).

One especially harmful form of relational aggression is online bullying. Physical bullying, in which a stronger person intentionally humiliates or physically abuses a weaker one, has long been a fact of school life, and cyberbullying simply translates that impulse into a newer technology (Rivers, Chesney, & Coyne, 2011). Cyberbullying ranges from the less severe (prank calls and mild insults on instant messaging) to extremely severe acts (posting unpleasant or sexual photos on websites; distributing insults, nasty text messages, ugly rumors, etc.). According to a review prepared for the government on Child Safety and Online Technologies, the greatest source of danger that teenagers face on the Internet does not come from pornography, predatory adults, or sexting, but rather bullying and harassment, most often by peers (Palfrey, Boyd, & Sacco, 2010).

What is your own experience with gender differences in physical and relational aggression? See the Try It!

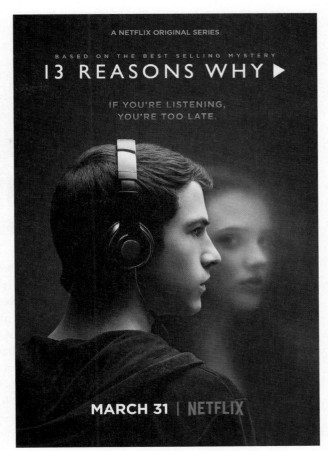

As depicted in the show *13 Reasons Why*, relational aggression can sometimes have devastating and tragic consequences.

Learning to Behave Aggressively

Most of us take our cues from other people. If we want to know whether aggressive behavior is okay, we will look to see what others are doing or what others are saying about it—and whether they get away with it or are punished. We learn, almost

---

Revel Interactive

Survey	**Is All Aggression Equal**	
	SURVEY	RESULTS

Which type of aggression is more hurtful?

○ Physical aggression

○ Relational aggression

Watch BOBO DOLL EXPERIMENT

Revel Video

Social-Cognitive Learning Theory

The theory that people learn social behavior (e.g., aggression or altruism) in large part through observation and imitation of others and by cognitive processes such as plans, expectations, and beliefs

unconsciously, what our culture's rules are and what the norms are for men and women. Either way, those situations can shape, direct, encourage, or suppress people's individual wishes to behave aggressively or peacefully.

Social-cognitive learning theory holds that we learn social behavior, from aggression to altruism, in large part by observing others and imitating them—a process called *observational learning*. But observational learning in human beings cannot be fully understood without taking into account the thought processes and perceptions of the learner; that's the "cognitive" part of social-cognitive learning theory (Mischel & Shoda, 1995). It's the reason that you and a friend can see the same vampire movie and one of you thinks it's stupid and the other thinks it's funny.

Children are especially susceptible to observational learning. In a classic series of experiments, Albert Bandura and his associates demonstrated the power of social learning on children's aggressive behavior (Bandura, Ross, & Ross, 1961, 1963). Their basic procedure was to have an adult knock around a plastic, air-filled Bobo doll, the kind that bounces back after it's been knocked down. The adult would smack the doll around with the palm of a hand, strike it with a mallet, kick it, and yell aggressive things at it. The kids were then allowed to play with the doll. In these experiments, the children imitated the aggressive adults and treated the doll in almost exactly the same ways, as you can see in Figure 12.3. Some of them went beyond mere imitation, coming up with inventive new forms of beating up the doll. Children who did not see the

Figure 12.3 The Bobo Doll Experiment

Children learn aggressive behavior through imitation. In this classic study, the experimenter (top row) modeled some rather violent treatment of the doll—and the children imitated her perfectly (middle and bottom rows).

aggressive adult in action almost never unleashed any aggression against the hapless doll. This research offers strong support for the social learning of aggressive behavior—the power of watching and imitating the behavior of others.

In general, the more respected a person or institution is, the greater their influence as a role model. Brad Bushman and his colleagues (2007) explored the impact of religiously sanctioned stories of violence. They found that when a violent story was attributed to the Bible and when, in that story, God sanctioned the violence, the reader was more likely to behave aggressively afterward. The effect held for nonreligious as well as religious participants. Sports are another hallowed institution, in which the more aggressive players usually achieve the greatest fame and the highest salaries, and the more aggressive teams win more games. It usually doesn't pay to be a gentle soul.

Similarly, when children watch their parents or other adults they admire yelling, kicking, and acting in other aggressive ways, that is the behavior they will copy. One of the main predictors of whether women will commit physical aggression against their male partners, for example, is their having grown up in a household where they saw their mothers hitting their fathers (Testa et al., 2011).

What happens if we reverse things and expose children to nonaggressive models—to people who, when provoked, express themselves in a restrained, rational, pleasant manner? This question has been tested in several experiments (Baron, 1972; Donnerstein & Donnerstein, 1976; Vidyasagar & Mishra, 1993). Children first watched youngsters behaving peacefully even when provoked. Later, when the children were put in a situation in which they themselves were provoked, they were much less likely to respond aggressively than were children who had not seen the nonaggressive models.

Some Physiological Influences

It is hardly news that when people are drunk, hot, or in considerable pain, they are more likely to lash out at others, getting into fights and quarrels, than if they feel completely fine, sipping lemonade on a cool spring day. But why does the chance of aggression increase under these physical influences? Does it always?

THE EFFECTS OF ALCOHOL   As most college students know, alcohol is a social lubricant that lowers our inhibitions against acting in ways frowned on by society, including acts of aggression (Desmond, 1987; Taylor & Leonard, 1983). Remember that the relationship between testosterone and aggression is partly explained by a relationship between testosterone and reduced activity in the orbitofrontal cortex that regulates impulse control (Mehta & Beer, 2010). Just like testosterone, alcohol lower inhibitions. The link between alcohol and aggressive behavior has been well documented, and it appears even among people who have not been provoked and who do not usually behave aggressively when sober (Bailey & Taylor, 1991; Bushman & Cooper, 1990; Graham et al., 2006). This might explain why fistfights frequently break out in bars and nightclubs and why family violence is often associated with alcohol abuse. In fact, consuming alcohol in the last 4 hours makes you 3.6 times more likely to become a perpetrator of physical aggression and 1.36 times more likely to perpetrate relational aggression (Testa & Derrick, 2014).

How can alcohol increase aggressive behavior? Alcohol reduces anxiety and lowers social inhibitions, making us less cautious than we usually are (MacDonald, Zanna, & Fong, 1996). But it is more than that. By impairing the part of the brain involved in planning and controlling behavior, alcohol also disrupts the way we usually process information (Bushman, 1997; Bushman & Cooper, 1990; Hanson et al., 2011). This is why intoxicated people often respond to the most obvious aspects of a social situation and tend to miss the subtleties. If you are sober and someone steps on your toe, you would notice that the person didn't do it on purpose. But if you were drunk, you might miss the subtlety of the situation and respond as if that person had purposely stomped on your foot. If you and the offender are males, you might slug him. This response is typical of the kinds of ambiguous situations that men tend to interpret as provocative, especially under the influence of alcohol (Pedersen et al., 2014).

There is another way in which alcohol facilitates aggression, however, and this is through what has been called the "think-drink" effect: When people *expect* alcohol to have certain effects on them, it often does (Marlatt & Rohsenow, 1980). Indeed, when people expect that alcohol will "release" their aggressive impulses, they often do become more aggressive—even when they are drinking something nonalcoholic. In a study of 116 men ages 18 to 45, experimenters gave one-third of the men a nonalcoholic drink, one-third a drink targeting a modest blood alcohol level, and one-third a stronger drink targeting a high blood alcohol level. Within each of these three groups, the researchers manipulated the drinkers' expectancies of how much alcohol they were getting. They then measured the men's behavior toward a research confederate who had behaved aggressively toward them. Remarkably, the actual quantity of alcohol that the men drank was less related to their aggressive behavior than their *expectations* were. The more alcohol the men believed they were drinking, the more aggressively they behaved toward the confederate (Bègue et al., 2009).

Of course, alcohol does have potent physiological effects on cognition and behavior. But those effects interact with what people have learned about alcohol, such as whether it provides an excuse to behave aggressively (or, as we will see, sexually) and how they expect to feel after consuming (Davis & Loftus, 2004).

THE EFFECTS OF PAIN AND HEAT   If an animal is in pain and cannot flee the scene, it will almost invariably attack; this is true of rats, mice, hamsters, foxes, monkeys, crayfish, snakes, raccoons, alligators, and a host of other creatures (Azrin, 1967; Hutchinson, 1983). In those circumstances, animals will attack members of their own species, members of different species, or anything else in sight, including stuffed dolls and tennis balls. Do you think this is true of human beings as well? You probably will say yes. Most of us feel a flash of irritation when we hit our thumb with a hammer and know the feeling of wanting to lash out at the nearest available target. Indeed, in a series of experiments, students who underwent the pain of having their hand immersed in very cold water were far more likely to act aggressively against other students than were those who had not suffered the pain (Berkowitz, 1983).

Other forms of bodily discomfort—such as heat, humidity, air pollution, crowds, and offensive odors—also lower the threshold for aggressive behavior (Stoff & Cairns, 1997). In major American cities from Houston, Texas, to Des Moines, Iowa, the hotter it is on a given day or a given average year, the greater the likelihood that violent crimes will occur (Anderson, 2012; Anderson et al., 2000; Rotton & Cohn, 2004). Figure 12.4 plots violent crimes on days that were below the average temperature through days that were higher than average. Smaller "crimes" increase, too: In the desert city of Phoenix, Arizona, drivers in non–air-conditioned cars are more likely to honk their horns in traffic jams than drivers in air-conditioned cars (Kenrick & MacFarlane, 1986). Even on the baseball field, heat and hostility go together. In major league baseball games when the temperature rises above 90 degrees, significantly more batters are hit by pitched balls (Larrick et al., 2011). In the National Football League, more penalties for aggressive infractions are given when games are played in hotter weather (Craig et al., 2016).

As you know by now, one must be cautious about interpreting events that take place outside the laboratory. The scientist in you might be tempted to ask whether increases in aggression are due to the temperature itself or merely to the fact that more people are apt to be outside (getting in one another's way) on hot days than on cold or rainy days. So how might we determine that it's the heat causing the aggression and not merely the greater

Figure 12.4 The Long, Hot Summer

Warm temperatures predict an increased likelihood of violent crime and other aggressive acts.

(Adapted from Hsiang et al., 2013)

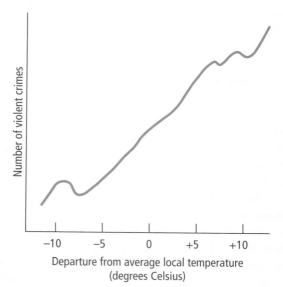

opportunity for contact? We can bring the phenomenon into the laboratory. In one such experiment, students took the same test under different conditions: Some worked in a room at normal room temperature, while others worked in a room where the temperature reached 90 degrees (Griffitt & Veitch, 1971). The students in the hot room not only reported feeling more aggressive but also expressed more hostility toward a stranger whom they were asked to describe and evaluate. Similar results have been reported by a number of investigators (Anderson, 2012; Anderson et al., 2000; Rule, Taylor, & Dobbs, 1987).

Review Questions

1. From a social-psychological perspective, a problem with evolutionary theories of aggression is that they fail to account for
   a. different levels of testosterone among men.
   b. different rates of aggression across cultures.
   c. genetic influences on behavior.
   d. differences between bonobos and chimpanzees.

2. Which of the following men is most likely to act aggressively toward someone who insults him?
   a. Ray, who grew up in Minnesota
   b. Randy, who grew up in Massachusetts
   c. Richard, who grew up in Louisiana
   d. Ricky, who grew up in Maine

3. Which of the following statements about gender differences in aggression is true?
   a. In families, almost all acts of physical aggression are committed by men.
   b. Girls are more likely than boys to express aggressive feelings indirectly, as by shunning or slandering a target.

   c. Gender differences in physical aggression increase when men and women are insulted.
   d. Because violence is so rare in women, female suicide bombers are much crazier than males who carry out these attacks.

4. After watching his teenage brother beat up a classmate in a fistfight and walk away with the admiration of their friends, a little boy takes a swipe at another boy in the playground. He has acquired this behavior through a process of
   a. cognitive learning.
   b. parental support.
   c. playing violent video games.
   d. observational learning.

5. What does the "think-drink" effect refer to?
   a. If you think you'd like a drink, you'll get one.
   b. If you think alcohol releases your anger, it will.
   c. If you think alcohol is harmful, you won't drink.
   d. If you think alcohol is healthy, you'll drink too much.

Social Situations and Aggression

LO 12.2   **Describe situational and social causes of aggression.**

Imagine that your friend Kevin is driving you to the airport so that you can fly home for the Christmas holidays. Kevin has picked you up a bit later than you feel comfortable with; he accuses you of being overly anxious and assures you that he knows the route well and that you will arrive there with plenty of time to spare. Halfway to the airport, you are standing still in bumper-to-bumper traffic. Kevin assures you that there is plenty of time, but this time he sounds less confident. After 10 more minutes, your palms are sweating. You open the car door and survey the road ahead: Not a car is moving as far ahead as you can see. You get back in the car, slam the door, and glare at Kevin. He smiles lamely and says, "How was I supposed to know there would be so much traffic?" Should he be prepared to duck?

Is road rage an inevitable outcome of frustration with fellow drivers? If so, how come not every driver gets as angry as this woman?

Frustration and Aggression

As this all-too-familiar story suggests, frustration is a major cause of aggression. Frustration occurs when a person is thwarted on the way to an expected goal or gratification. All of us have felt frustrated from time to time—at least three

Many experiences in daily life are frustrating—and can lead to aggression.

Frustration-Aggression Theory

The theory that frustration—the perception that you are being prevented from attaining a goal—increases the probability of an aggressive response

or four times a week, if not three or four times a day! According to **frustration-aggression theory**, people's perception that they are being prevented from attaining a goal will increase the probability of an aggressive response (Dollard et al., 1939). This is especially true when the frustration is unpleasant, unwelcome, and uncontrollable.

Several things can increase frustration and, accordingly, will increase the probability that some form of aggression will occur. One such factor involves your closeness to the goal or the object of your desire. The closer the goal, the greater the expectation of pleasure that is thwarted; the greater the expectation, the more likely the aggression. In one field experiment, a confederate cut in line in front of people who were waiting in a variety of places—for movie tickets, outside crowded restaurants, and at the checkout counter of a supermarket. On some occasions, the confederate cut in front of the second person in line; at other times, in front of the twelfth person. The results were clear: The people standing right behind the intruder were much more aggressive when the confederate cut into the second place in line (Harris, 1974).

However, frustration does not always produce aggression. Rather, it seems to produce anger or annoyance and a *readiness* to aggress if other things about the situation are conducive to aggressive behavior (Berkowitz, 1989, 1993; Gustafson, 1989). What are those other things? Well, an obvious one would be the size and strength of the person responsible for your frustration as well as that person's ability to retaliate. It is undoubtedly easier to become impatient and rude with an incompetent customer-service person who is miles away and has no idea who you are than to take out your anger against your frustrator if he turned out to be the middle linebacker of the Green Bay Packers and was staring you right in the face. Similarly, if the frustration is understandable, legitimate, and unintentional, the tendency to aggress will be reduced.

We want to emphasize that frustration is not the same as deprivation: Children who don't have toys do not aggress more than children who do. In the crayon experiment discussed earlier, frustration and aggression occurred because the children with white crayons were set up to expect that they would be coloring. This expectation was thwarted when they discovered their crayons did not leave marks on the white paper, prompting the aggression toward the child with the orange crayon. Frustration is about goal attainment, whereas deprivation is about resources.

Watch SURVIVAL TIPS! AWARENESS OF THE FRUSTRATION-AGGRESSION HYPOTHESIS

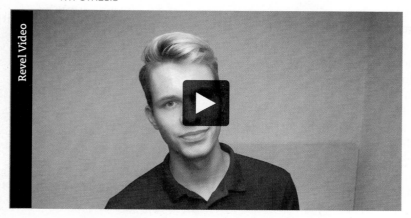

On a national scale, thwarted expectations combined with frustration can produce riots and revolutions. Social scientists have found that it is often not *absolute* deprivation that creates anger and aggression but *relative* deprivation, which occurs when people see a discrepancy between what they have and what they expect to have (Moore, 1978). Relative deprivation theory can explain why riots seem to coincide with generally positive social movements; the movements inspire people to expect equal treatment, so they become frustrated when their expectations shift faster than their living conditions improve. For example, in 1967 and 1968, nationwide race riots occurred in the middle of rising expectations and increased social spending to fight poverty. The most serious riots did not erupt in the geographic areas of greatest poverty; instead, they exploded in Los Angeles and Detroit, where things were not nearly as bad for African Americans as they were in most other large urban centers. But conditions were bad relative to the rioters' perception of how White people were doing and relative to the positive changes many African Americans had a right to expect.

Similarly, the discrepancy between political hopes and realities can drive people to war. Syrians lived under autocratic rule for decades, but they expected this to change when President Bashar al-Assad took over the government. When Al-Assad did not deliver the anticipated reforms, unrest grew (Brownlee, Masoud, & Reynolds, 2013). Research on contemporary suicide bombers in the Middle East—including Mohamed Atta, who led the 9/11 attack on the World Trade Center, and the Tsarnaev brothers, who bombed the Boston marathon in 2013—shows that they usually have no psychopathology and are often quite educated and affluent (Krueger, 2007; Sageman, 2008; Silke, 2003). But they were motivated by anger over the perceived discrepancy between what they had and what they felt their nation and religion were entitled to. Thus, an important cause of aggression is relative deprivation: the perception that you (or your group) have less than you deserve, less than what you have been led to expect, or less than what people similar to you have.

Provocation and Reciprocation

Suppose you are working at your part-time job behind the counter, flipping hamburgers in a crowded fast-food restaurant. Today, you are working harder than usual because the other short-order cook went home sick, and the customers are lining up at the counter, clamoring for their burgers. In your eagerness to speed up the process, you spin around too fast and knock over a large jar of pickles that smashes on the floor just as the boss enters the workplace. "I'm gonna dock your pay $10 for that one!" he shouts. "Grab a broom and clean it up, moron!" You glare at him. You'd love to tell him what he can do with this lousy job.

Aggression frequently stems from the need to reciprocate after being provoked by aggressive behavior from another person. Although the Christian plea to "turn the other cheek" is wonderful advice, most people don't take it, as has been demonstrated in countless experiments in and out of the laboratory. In one experiment, participants prepared an advertisement for a new product; their ad was then evaluated and criticized by an accomplice of the experimenter. In one condition, the criticism, though strong, was done in a gentle and considerate manner ("I think there's a lot of room for improvement"); in the other condition, the criticism was given in an insulting manner ("I don't think you could be original if you tried"). When provided with an opportunity to retaliate, those people who were criticized harshly were far more likely to do so than those in the "gentle criticism" condition (Baron, 1988).

Provocation and aggression are so strongly linked that they appear to overpower gender differences in aggression. While men are more aggressive than women under neutral conditions, provocation leads to aggression for both sexes (Bettencourt & Miller, 1996). Why would this be the case? Both men and women get angry when they are provoked, and anger reduces impulse control (Denson et al., 2011). So, similar to testosterone and alcohol, provocation leads to aggression through impeded self-control.

But to curtail an aggressive response, we must be aware of those mitigating circumstances at the time of the provocation. In one study, students were insulted by the experimenter's assistant. Half of them were first told that the assistant was upset after receiving an unfair low grade on a chemistry exam; the other students received this information only after the insult was delivered. All subjects later had an opportunity to retaliate by choosing the level of unpleasant noise with which to zap the assistant. Those students who knew about the mitigating circumstances before being insulted delivered weaker bursts of noise (Johnson & Rule, 1986). Why the difference? At the time of the insult, the informed students simply did not take it personally and therefore felt no need to retaliate. This interpretation is bolstered by evidence of their physiological arousal: At the time of the insult, the heart rates of the insulted students did not increase as rapidly if they knew about the assistant's unhappy state of mind beforehand.

To help you identify your own triggers and responses to provocation, take this Try It!

Try It!

Insults and Aggression

Think about the last time you felt insulted by another person. Note down your answers to these questions:
- Who insulted you?
- What were the circumstances?
- Did you take it personally or not?

- How did you respond—with anger, patience, amusement, or something else?
- How do your answers relate to the material you have just finished reading?

Weapons as Aggressive Cues

Certain stimuli seem to impel us to action. Is it conceivable that the mere presence of an aggressive stimulus—an object that is associated with aggressive responses—might increase the probability of aggression?

In a classic experiment, Leonard Berkowitz and Anthony Le Page (1967) purposely angered college students by insulting them. Some of the students were in a room in which a gun was left lying around (ostensibly from a previous experiment) and others in a room in which a neutral object (a badminton racket) was substituted for the gun. Participants were then given the opportunity to administer what they believed were electric shocks to a fellow college student. Those individuals who had been angered in the presence of the gun administered stronger electric shocks than those angered in the presence of the racket (see Figure 12.5). The presence of a gun seems to trigger—so to speak—an aggressive response when a person is already primed to respond that way because of frustration or anger (Anderson, Benjamin, & Bartholow, 1998).

This provocative finding, which has been replicated many times in the United States and Europe, is now referred to as the **weapons effect**—an increase in aggression that can occur because of the mere presence of a gun or other weapon (Benjamin & Bushman, 2017). The effect is physiological as well as psychological: Male

Figure 12.5 The Trigger Can Pull the Finger

Aggressive cues, such as weapons, tend to increase levels of aggression.

(Based on Berkowitz & Le Page, 1967)

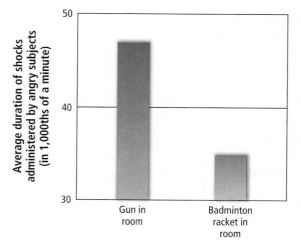

college students asked to interact with a gun for 15 minutes show higher testosterone levels than do students playing a children's game for the same amount of time (Klinesmith, Kasser, & McAndrew, 2006). Such findings point to a conclusion opposite to the familiar slogan often used by opponents of gun control, that "guns don't kill; people do." As Leonard Berkowitz (1981) put it, "The finger pulls the trigger, but the trigger may also be pulling the finger."

Putting the Elements Together: The Case of Sexual Assault

One of the most troubling kinds of aggression is sexual assault, which can take many forms. Although "rape" is an upsetting word to many people, it is important to define it so that everyone agrees on what it means—and so that the law can reflect that meaning. For example, the law used to exempt married men, who were legally allowed to have forcible sex with their wives. In 2013, the Department of Justice revised the definition of *rape* to include the penetration of any bodily orifice with any part of the body or with any object, without the consent of the victim. Sexual assault is the broader term, including various other acts, but lack of consent remains the key criterion. In this section, we will consider how social psychologists draw on various kinds of evidence to help understand this phenomenon.

MOTIVATIONS FOR RAPE Some men commit rape out of a desire to dominate, humiliate, or punish their victims. This motive is apparent among soldiers who rape captive women during war and then often kill them (Olujic, 1998) and among men who rape other men, usually by anal penetration (King & Woollett, 1997). The latter form of rape often occurs in youth gangs, where the intention is to humiliate rival gang members, and in prison, where the motive, in addition to the obvious sexual one, is to conquer and degrade the victim. Men can be sexually assaulted and raped by women also, although many men are ashamed to admit it (Stemple & Meyer, 2014).

When most people think of a "rapist," they imagine a violent stranger or a serial predator. Some rapists are exactly that. They are often unable to empathize with women, may feel hostility and contempt toward women, and feel entitled to have sexual relations with whatever woman they choose. This may be why sexual violence is often committed by high-status men, including high school and college athletic stars, powerful politicians, and celebrities, who could easily find consenting sexual partners. They equate feelings of power with sexuality, angrily accuse women of provoking them, and endorse rape myths (Nunes, Hermann, & Ratcliffe, 2013; Thompson et al., 2011).

But the fact is that about 85% of all rapes or attempted rapes occur between people who know each other; the victim may even be having a relationship with the assailant (Koss, 2011; McMullin & White, 2006). Rape may occur as a result of *physical force* (having sex under actual or threatened violence), or through *incapacitation*: having sex with a victim who has been induced into a blackout with Rohypnol ("roofies"), who is drunk or otherwise drugged, or who has passed out (Breiding, Chen, & Black, 2014).

SEXUAL SCRIPTS AND THE PROBLEM OF CONSENT Everyone understands that a sexual predator who rapes a woman by overt force, threats of violence, or drugs used to render her unconscious has committed a serious crime. But what is going on with the large, additional numbers of women assaulted through "incapacitation" caused by their voluntary enjoyment of alcohol and other drugs? One answer may stem from the different **sexual scripts** that males and females learn as part of their gender roles in American society (Laumann & Gagnon, 1995). Sexual scripts are schemas for how sexual encounters play out between potential

Weapons Effect

The increase in aggression that can occur because of the mere presence of a gun or other weapon

Sexual Scripts

Sets of implicit rules that specify proper sexual behavior for a person in a given situation, varying with the person's gender, age, religion, social status, and peer group

A lot of campus rapes start here.

Whenever there's drinking or drugs, things can get out of hand.
So it's no surprise that many campus rapes involve alcohol.
But you should know that under any circumstances, sex without
the other person's consent is considered rape. A felony, punishable
by prison. And drinking is no excuse.
That's why, when you party, it's good to know what your limits are.
You see, a little sobering thought now can save you from a big
problem later.

©1990 Rape Treatment Center, Santa Monica Hospital

partners. Sexual scripts vary according to one's culture, sexual orientation, ethnicity, and geographic region, and they change over time. One dominant script in America for young straight women and men is that the female's role is to resist the male's sexual advances and that the male's role is to be persistent. In films, TV, and magazines, male characters frequently act out this traditional male script; many female characters still play the part of "sex object" and are judged by their sexual conduct (Hust et al., 2014; Kim et al., 2007). Sexual scripts for gay men and lesbians tend to be more flexible than heterosexual scripts because partners are not following traditional gender roles (Kurdek, 2005).

The existence of scripts that dictate notions about appropriate sexual behavior may explain why many people are confused or angry over the meaning of the word *no* in a sexual context. The repeated message of antirape groups—"What part of 'no' don't you understand?"—seems obvious. But American sexual scripts hold mixed messages regarding the meaning of this word; even if a woman wants sex, she is not supposed to seem too eager, which makes a *"no"* seem less absolute. In one survey of high school students, although almost 100% of the males and females agreed that the man should stop his sexual advances as soon as the woman says no, nearly half of those same students also believed that when a woman says no, she doesn't always mean it (Monson, Langhinrichsen-Rohling, & Binderup, 2000). The resulting confusion may also explain why some college women feel they need to drink heavily as a prelude to sex (Cole, 2006; Howard, Griffin, & Boekeloo, 2008; Villalobos, Davis, & Leo, 2015). After all, if they are inebriated, they haven't said "yes," and if they haven't explicitly said "yes," no one can accuse them of being promiscuous.

Further complicating matters is that most couples communicate sexual interest and intentions—including a wish *not* to have sex—indirectly through hints, body language, eye contact, and other nonverbal behaviors. Studies find that sometimes young women try to convey "no" without saying no, such as by stepping a few inches back or pretending not to notice the man's advances. For their part, many men are motivated to overinterpret women's nonverbal actions as signs of sexual interest rather than just friendliness (La France et al., 2009). Given that nonverbal behaviors are ambiguous by nature, the most common cues people use are also the most likely to be misunderstood.

As a result of all of these reasons for miscommunication, the sexes often disagree on whether a rape has even occurred (Hamby & Koss, 2003; Villalobos et al., 2015; Yoffe, 2014). In a nationally representative survey of more than 3,000 Americans ages 18 to 59, nearly one-fourth of the women said that a man, usually a husband or boyfriend, had forced them to do something sexually that they did not want to do, yet only about 3% of the men said that they had ever forced a woman into a sexual act (Laumann et al., 1994).

Review Questions

1. According to frustration-aggression theory,
   a. when people are frustrated, they almost always become aggressive.
   b. when people behave aggressively, they feel frustrated.
   c. frustration increases the likelihood of aggression.
   d. frustration caused by deprivation causes aggression.

2. Noah was counting on his roommate George to help him on moving day, but George never showed up, and Noah is plenty annoyed. What might he say to himself to reduce his wish to retaliate or tell George off?
   a. "That's just his personality; he's always thoughtless."
   b. "I'm a better person than he is."
   c. "I don't need his help anyway."
   d. "I bet George is under a lot of stress about exams this week."

3. What is relative deprivation?
   a. When people feel deprived of having close relatives they can count on
   b. When people live in poverty and feel they have no hope of improvement
   c. When people feel there is an unfair discrepancy between what they have and what they expect to get
   d. When some people earn relatively less than others for doing the same work

4. The "weapons effect" refers to the fact that
   a. many people have an emotional response to seeing a weapon.
   b. the mere presence of a gun can provoke an aggressive response.
   c. the mere presence of a gun makes people feel safer.
   d. some weapons provoke more aggression than others.

5. Which of the following statements about rape is true?
   a. Men who commit rape tend to be mentally ill.
   b. Most rapes are committed by men who attack unknown women.
   c. Most rapes are committed in the context of an acquaintance or ongoing relationship.
   d. Men cannot be raped.

6. Having sexual intercourse with a woman who is drunk or otherwise incapacitated
   a. is against the law.
   b. may be morally wrong but is not illegal.
   c. is acceptable if she seemed to consent.
   d. is acceptable if she did consent.

7. "Sexual scripts" refer to
   a. a stage director's instructions for actors in a love scene.
   b. a set of rules governing notions of "appropriate" sexual behavior that people acquire in learning gender roles.
   c. a set of unchanging rules that govern men's and women's sexual behavior.
   d. rules that govern the sexual behavior of straight people but not of gay men or lesbians.

Violence and the Media

LO 12.3   Explain how observing violence increases violence.

Most American children are immersed in images of violence in all types of media: from television and movies to video games and the Internet. In fact, they are not only immersed, they are marinated in it! They see an unending parade of beatings, explosions, and bad guys committing brutal acts as well as good guys doing brutal things to catch them. Violence in films has more than doubled since 1950, and gun violence in PG-13-rated films has more than tripled since 1985. In fact, PG-13-rated films now contain as much violence as R-rated films (Bushman et al., 2013).

Many people—psychologists as well as the general public—are worried about all the mayhem that children and teenagers observe; they figure there *must* be significant consequences, starting with making guns seem cool and exciting (Bushman & Pollard-Sacks, 2014). For them, it is as obvious as the Bobo doll study that children imitate the violence they see on TV and in the movies and are otherwise affected emotionally by it. If *prosocial* videos can increase helpful behavior in children who watch them (see Chapter 11), surely the far more common antisocial, violent videos can increase anti-social, violent behavior.

For just as many others, though, this is a nonissue. How powerful can media violence be, they ask, if during the same years that gun violence in PG-13 movies tripled, real-world gun violence and overall violent crime by young people decreased to record lows? Besides, they add, media violence consists of cartoon-like stories and images that "everyone knows" are not real. Indeed, that was the reasoning behind the Supreme Court's 2011 decision that video games can be sold to minors no matter how violent the games are, including the popular *Mortal Kombat* and *Grand Theft Auto* series.

And so the debate rages on. In this section we want to sort through the evidence on both sides and come to what we think is the most sensible resolution.

Studying the Effects of Media Violence

How would you study the possible effects of media violence? Countless stories in the news would seem to provide a compelling answer. For example, several years ago, a man drove his truck through the window of a crowded cafeteria in Killeen, Texas; emerged from the cab; and began shooting people at random, killing 22. In his pocket, police found a ticket stub to *The Fisher King*, a film depicting a deranged man firing

a shotgun into a crowded bar, killing several people. Dylan Klebold and Eric Harris, the Columbine killers, enjoyed the video game *Doom*, and the Columbine murders themselves spurred many copycat acts across the United States (Aronson, 2000). Two teenagers in Tennessee took their guns and went out sniping at passing cars on a freeway, killing one driver, because they wanted to act out their favorite video game, *Grand Theft Auto*. And then there is the case of a man who, having seen a movie showing women dancing on screen, became convinced that all women were immoral and deserved to die. He then committed four brutal rape-murders before he was caught. The film that set him off was *The Ten Commandments*.

But social scientists know that anecdotes, no matter how interesting they may be, are not sufficient to answer the question of the effects of media violence. It's too easy to cherry-pick

Does watching violent movies make children and adults numb to what violence really does?

your examples to make a case either way; you could select examples of kids who play *Grand Theft Auto* and then go off to do their homework and take piano lessons. Accordingly, researchers have conducted experimental and field studies to try to untangle this complicated question.

EXPERIMENTAL STUDIES The beauty of the laboratory experiment is that it allows us to determine whether images in the media have any impact at all on the behavior of a random sample of people (see Chapter 2). In such an experiment, the situation is completely controlled; every factor can be held constant except for exposure to violence. The dependent variable, the participant's behavior, can likewise be carefully measured.

Most of the experimental evidence demonstrates that watching violence does increase the frequency of aggressive behavior, angry emotions, and hostile thoughts (Bushman, Gollwitzer, & Cruz, 2015; Greitemeyer & McLatchie, 2011; Huesmann, Dubow, & Yang, 2013). In one early experiment, a group of children watched an extremely violent episode of a police drama. In a control condition, a similar group watched an exciting but nonviolent televised sporting event for the same length of time. Each child was then allowed to play in another room with a group of other children. Those who had watched the violent police drama later behaved far more aggressively with their playmates than did those who had watched the sporting event—the Bobo doll effect (Liebert & Baron, 1972). The research is not consistent, however, and some reviews of the experimental literature have found minimal or no effects (Ferguson, 2009, 2013; Sherry, 2001).

However, actively playing violent video games seems to have a stronger influence: Games that directly reward violence—for example, by awarding points or moving the player to the next level after a "kill"—are especially likely to increase feelings of hostility, aggressive thoughts, and aggressive acts, and this is true not only for American kids but also for those in other nations (Anderson et al., 2010; Carnagey & Anderson, 2005). A meta-analysis of 98 studies, with nearly 37,000 participants, found that both violent video games and prosocial video games have direct effects on their players (Greitemeyer & Mügge, 2014).

Another detrimental consequence of a diet of violence might be numbing people to difficult, violent, or unpleasant events (Thomas, 1982). In general, our bodies respond over time to repeated stimuli with either progressively less arousal—termed "habituation"—or more arousal—termed "sensitization." If exposure to one violent event affects responses to the next violent event, then we can observe processes of either habituation or sensitization through people's physiology. In one of the earliest experiments on this issue, researchers measured the physiological responses of young men while they were watching a brutal and bloody boxing match (Cline, Croft, & Courrier, 1973). The results supported the hypothesis that we habituate to violence. Those who had watched a lot of television in their daily lives seemed relatively indifferent to the mayhem in the ring; they showed little physiological evidence of excitement, anxiety, or other arousal. They were unmoved by the violence. But those who watched relatively little TV showed major physiological arousal; the violence really agitated them. Today, that "brutal and bloody boxing match" from a 40-year-old experiment seems tame compared to *Game of Thrones* or *The Walking Dead*. The very fact that violence has had to increase in gruesomeness and intensity to get the same reaction from audiences that mild violence once did may be the perfect illustration of the numbing effects of a diet of violence.

Although psychic numbing may protect us from feeling upset, it may also have the unintended effect of increasing our indifference to real victims of violence and others who need help. In one field study, people who had just seen a violent movie took longer to come to the aid of a woman struggling to pick up her crutches than did people who had seen a nonviolent movie or people still waiting to see one of the two movies (Bushman & Anderson, 2009).

Does playing first-person shooter video games make people more violent or are people who have violent tendencies to begin with drawn to such games? Or could it be both?

And if the person needing help is not "one of us," watch out. When you are playing a violent video game, you are likely to see yourself as the hero who is blasting those evil creatures out of existence. That's fun, as far as it goes, but some research suggests it can go further: Once players get in the habit of dehumanizing the "enemy," that habit can be carried over into how players come to regard real people, not just robots and life-like cartoons. In two experiments in England, researchers found that participants (male and female) who played a violent video game (*Lamers*) were later more likely to dehumanize

immigrants to Britain, seeing them as somehow less human and deserving than native Britons, in contrast to the students who played a prosocial version of the game (*Lemmings*) or a neutral game (*Tetris*) (Greitemeyer & McLatchie, 2011; see also Greitemeyer, 2014).

Exposure to media violence, especially playing video games, may have these effects for three reasons: They increase physiological arousal and excitement, they trigger an automatic tendency to imitate the hostile or violent characters, and they activate existing aggressive ideas and expectations, making people more likely to act on them (Anderson et al., 2003). Movies and games also model social *scripts*, approved ways of behaving when we are frustrated, angry, or hurt. Violent media shows the public how to commit violence while simultaneously making it cool (i.e., normative).

LONGITUDINAL STUDIES Taken together, these experiments show that under controlled conditions, media violence has an impact on children and teenagers. The lab allows us to demonstrate that something of significance is happening, but it has a major limitation: Experiments cannot begin to capture the effects on a person who plays video games 20 or 30 hours a week and lives on a steady diet of action and horror films over weeks, months, and years.

To investigate that effect, we need to use longitudinal studies in which children are followed for a year or longer. The researcher has less control over the factors being studied, but it is a better way of determining the effects of what a child is *really* being exposed to. In addition, unlike most laboratory experiments that must use artificial measures of aggression (such as administering fake electric shocks or loud noises to the victim), longitudinal studies can examine seriously aggressive behavior. The disadvantage of this method is that people's lives are full of many other factors that can enhance or mitigate the effects of media violence.

Longitudinal research finds that the more violence children watch, the more aggressively they behave later as teenagers and young adults (Anderson et al., 2003; Eron, 1987, 2001). For example, one study followed more than 700 families over a period of 17 years. The amount of time spent watching television during adolescence and early adulthood was strongly related to the likelihood of later committing violent acts against others, including assault. This association was significant regardless of parental education, family income, and extent of neighborhood violence (Johnson et al., 2002). A more recent study followed 430 elementary-age children in the third to fifth grades over the course of a school year. The investigators measured three types of aggression—verbal, relational, and physical—and exposure to violence in television, movies, and video games. They measured both aggressive and prosocial behaviors in the children twice during the year, interviewing the children's peers and teachers as well as observing the children directly. They found that the children's consumption of media violence early in the school year predicted higher rates of all three kinds of aggression (verbal, relational, and physical) and less prosocial behavior later in the year (Gentile, Coyne, & Walsh, 2011).

The Problem of Determining Cause and Effect

Longitudinal studies find another consequence of watching a heavy dose of media violence: the magnification of danger. If I am watching all this murder and mayhem on the home screen, wouldn't it be logical for me to conclude that it isn't safe to leave the house, especially after dark? That is exactly what many heavy viewers do conclude. Adolescents and adults who watch TV for more than 4 hours per day are more likely than people who watch less than 2 hours per day to have an exaggerated view of the degree of violence taking place outside their own homes, and they have a much greater fear of being personally assaulted (Gerbner et al., 2002).

Now, it is possible that watching violence made them fearful. But it is just as likely that they spend a lot of time indoors because they think there is danger in the streets. Then, being at home with nothing to do, they watch a lot of television. As this example illustrates, the greatest challenge involved in trying to interpret the data in most nonexperimental longitudinal studies and survey research is teasing apart cause and effect. The usual assumption has been that watching violence makes people more aggressive, but aggressive people are also drawn to watching violence. Moreover, another entirely independent factor may be causing both. Some children are born with a mental or emotional predisposition toward violence; or learn it as toddlers from the way they are treated by abusive parents or siblings; or in other ways develop aggressiveness as a personality trait. In turn, this trait or predisposition manifests itself in both their aggressive behavior *and* their liking for watching violence or playing aggressive games (Bushman, 1995; Ferguson, 2013).

Violent media does not potentiate violence in all children. Children who are predisposed to violence also prefer violent media, which amplifies the likelihood of aggressive behavior.

In an experiment investigating the interaction between temperament and exposure to violence, children watched either a film depicting a great deal of police violence or an exciting but nonviolent film about bike racing. They then played a game of floor hockey. Watching the violent film did increase the number of aggressive acts the children committed during the hockey game—but primarily by those who had previously been rated as highly aggressive by their teachers. These kids hit others with their sticks, threw elbows, and yelled aggressive things at their opponents to a much greater extent than did either the kids rated as nonaggressive who had also watched the violent film or the kids rated as aggressive who had watched the nonviolent film (Josephson, 1987).

Likewise, a few longitudinal studies have shown that exposure to violence in media or video games has the strongest relationship in children who are already predisposed to violence (Anderson & Dill, 2000). Thus, it may be that watching media violence merely serves to give them permission to express their aggressive inclinations (Ferguson & Kilburn, 2009). The same conclusions apply to the research on violent pornography (in contrast to nonviolent erotica). Meta-analyses repeatedly conclude that although there is, for men, a positive correlation between watching violent pornography and hostile, aggressive attitudes toward women, that association is largely due to men who already have high levels of hostility toward women and are predisposed to sexual aggression (Malamuth, Hald, & Koss, 2012).

Taking all this research together, we conclude that frequent exposure to violent media, especially in the form of violent video games, does have an impact on average children and adolescents, but the impact is greatest on those who are already prone to violent behavior. Obviously, most people do not become motivated to behave aggressively or commit an act of violence as a result of what they observe. As social-cognitive learning theory predicts, people's interpretation of what they are watching, their personality dispositions, and the social context can all affect how they respond (Feshbach & Tangney, 2008). Children and teens watch many different programs and movies and have many models to observe besides those they see in the media, including parents and peers. But the fact that some people *are* influenced by violent entertainments, with tragic results, cannot be denied.

One of the leading researchers who study media violence argues that it is "time to move forward with a more sophisticated perspective on media effects that focuses less on moral objections to certain content and more on media consumers and their motivations" (Ferguson, 2014). Given the research just discussed, we think there are at least five distinct reactions that explain why exposure to violence might increase aggression in those vulnerable "media consumers":

1. **Norms**: *If they can do it, so can I.* When people see characters behaving violently, it may weaken their previously learned inhibitions against violent behavior.

2. **Observational Learning**: *Oh, so that's how you do it!* When people see characters behaving violently, it might trigger imitation, providing them with ideas as to how they might go about it.

3. **Misattribution**: *Those feelings I am having must be real anger rather than merely my reaction to a stressful day.* Watching violence may put people more in touch with their feelings of anger and make an aggressive response more likely through priming. Having recently viewed violence, someone might interpret his or her own feelings of mild irritation as intense anger and then be more likely to lash out.

4. **Habituation**: *Ho-hum, another brutal beating. What's on the other channel?* Watching a lot of mayhem seems to reduce both our sense of horror about violence and our sympathy for the victims, making it easier for us to live with violence and perhaps easier for us to act aggressively.

5. **Self-fulfilling Prophecy**: *I had better get him before he gets me!* If watching a lot of television makes people think the world is a dangerous place, they might be more apt to be hostile to a stranger who approaches them on the street.

Finally, however, let's put this issue in larger perspective. The effects of the media pale in comparison to the biological, social, economic, and psychological factors that are far more powerful predictors of aggressive behavior: a child's genetic predispositions to violence, low feelings of self-control, being socially rejected by peers (which we will discuss further at the end of this chapter), criminal opportunity, being the victim of childhood physical abuse, being in a peer group that endorses and encourages violence, and living in a community where aggression is a way of life (Crescioni & Baumeister, 2009; Ferguson & Kilburn, 2009).

Review Questions

1. Which of the following statements is true?
   a. Watching violent shows makes most young children likely to imitate them.
   b. Watching violent shows makes some children more likely to imitate them.
   c. Playing violent video games has less of an impact on children than watching violence on TV or in the movies does.
   d. Viewing television violence has no effect on people's response to others in trouble.

2. According to social-cognitive learning theory, which of these factors intervenes between a person's observation of media violence and his or her likelihood of imitating it?

   a. Violence portrayed as part of a religious story
   b. Violence endorsed by the government
   c. How the observer interprets the violent story
   d. Whether the observer is in a good mood

3. Watching violence in the media and behaving aggressively are positively correlated. What does this mean?
   a. Watching violent shows makes children more aggressive.
   b. Aggressive children are more likely to watch violent shows.
   c. Growing up in a violent environment makes children aggressive and more likely to watch violent shows.
   d. Answers a and c are correct.
   e. All of the answers are correct.

4. What do experimental studies of media violence tend to find?
   a. Watching violent films has little effect on aggressive behavior.
   b. Playing violent video games has a stronger effect than watching violent shows.
   c. Playing violent video games makes children feel better and less angry.
   d. Children get used to media violence quickly, so it doesn't affect them.

5. What is the main problem in interpreting longitudinal studies of the effects of media violence?
   a. Teasing apart whether media violence causes aggression or whether aggressive people are drawn to media violence
   b. Separating studies of TV violence from those of violent video games
   c. Identifying which children are more vulnerable to TV violence
   d. Finding out if children who play video games will also prefer violent pornography

How to Decrease Aggression

LO 12.4   Identify ways aggression can be diminished.

"Stop hitting your brother!" "Turn off the TV and go to your room *right now*!" Most parents, trying to curb the aggressive behavior of their children, use some form of punishment. Some deny privileges; others shout, threaten, or use force, believing in the old saying, "Spare the rod and spoil the child." How well does punishment work? On the one hand, you might think that punishing any behavior would reduce its frequency. On the other hand, if the punishment takes the form of an aggressive act, parents who are administering the penalty are actually modeling aggressive behavior—thereby inducing their child to imitate them.

Does Punishing Aggression Reduce Aggression?

Let's consider the complexities of punishment. As we discussed in Chapter 6, several experiments with preschoolers demonstrated that the threat of relatively severe punishment for committing a transgression does not make the transgression less appealing to the child. But the threat of *mild* punishment, of a degree just powerful enough to get the child to stop the undesired activity temporarily, leads the child to try to justify his or her restraint and, as a result, can make the behavior less appealing (Aronson & Carlsmith, 1963; Freedman, 1965).

However, the use of *harsh* punishments to reduce aggression usually backfires; it may put a halt to a child's aggressive behavior in the short term, but children who are physically punished tend to become more aggressive and antisocial over time (Durrant & Ensom, 2012). Harsh punishments backfire for several other reasons, too. People may shout things they don't mean or, out of frustration, use severe methods to try to control the behavior of their children. The target of all this noise and abuse is then likely to respond with anxiety or anger rather than with a reaction of "Thanks, I'd better correct that aggressive habit you don't like." In some cases, angry attention may be just what the offender is hoping to get. If a mother yells at her daughter who is throwing a tantrum, the very act of yelling may give her what she

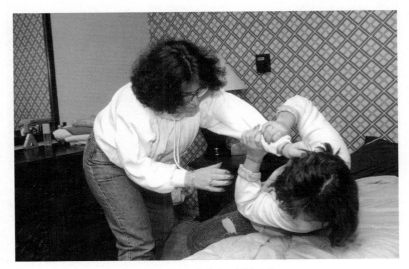

Many tired, exasperated parents punish their children's misbehavior by shouting at them or hitting or grabbing them. But this usually backfires, making the child angry and resentful without stopping the misbehavior. On the contrary, it teaches children what to do when they are tired and exasperated—hit someone.

wants, namely a reaction from Mom. More seriously, extreme punishment like spanking and physical abuse is a risk factor in children for the development of depression, low self-esteem, violent behavior, and many other problems (Gershoff, 2002; Gershoff & Grogan-Kaylor, 2016). And, finally, punishment often fails because it tells the target what not to do, but it does not communicate what the person should do. Spanking a little boy for hitting his sister will not teach him to play cooperatively with her.

Because of these drawbacks, most psychologists believe that harsh punishment is a poor way to eliminate aggressive or other unwanted behavior. In certain cases, for example, when a bully is hitting a classmate, temporary physical restraint is usually called for. But is that the best strategy to keep a bully from behaving aggressively when the adult leaves the room?

USING PUNISHMENT ON VIOLENT ADULTS   The criminal justice system of most cultures administers harsh punishments both as retribution and as a means of deterring violent crimes like murder, manslaughter, and rape. Does the threat of harsh punishments make such crimes less likely? Do people who are about to commit violent crimes say to themselves, "I'd better not do this because if I get caught, I'm going to jail for a long time; I might even be executed"?

Laboratory experiments indicate that punishment can indeed act as a deterrent but only if two conditions are met: Punishment must be (a) prompt and (b) certain (Bower & Hilgard, 1981). It must follow quickly after the aggression occurred, and it must be unavoidable. In the real world, these conditions are almost never met. In most American cities, the probability that a person who commits a violent crime will be apprehended, charged, tried, and convicted is not high. Given the volume of cases in our courts, punishment is delayed by months or even years. Because many things influence crime rates—the proportion of young versus older people in the population, poverty levels, drug policies, discriminatory arrest patterns—the relationship between incarceration rates and crime rates in the United States varies considerably from state to state (Harrington & Gelfand, 2014). Consequently, in the complex world of criminal justice, severe punishment is unlikely to have the kind of deterrent effect that it does in the controlled conditions of the laboratory.

Given these realities, severe punishment is not likely to deter violent crime. Countries that invoke the death penalty for murder do not have fewer murders per capita than those without it (Fajnzylber et al., 2002). American states that have abolished the death penalty have not had an increase in capital crimes, as some experts predicted; the death penalty seems generally unrelated to homicide rates (National Research Council, 2012). Imagine someone in the throes of a murderous rage: It's not the moment when most people would stop and reason through their decision.

Watch PHYSICAL PUNISHMENT AND AGGRESSION

Revel Video

Catharsis

The notion that "blowing off steam"—by behaving aggressively or watching others do so—relieves built-up anger and aggressive energy and hence reduces the likelihood of further aggressive behavior

Can We Release Anger by Indulging It?

Conventional wisdom suggests that one way to reduce feelings of aggression is to do something aggressive. "Get it out of your system" has been common advice for decades: If you are feeling angry, yell, scream, curse, throw a dish at the wall; express the anger, and it won't build up into something uncontrollable. This belief stems from

Sigmund Freud's psychoanalytic notion of **catharsis** (Dollard et al., 1939; Freud, 1933). Freud held a "hydraulic" idea of aggressive impulses: Unless people were allowed to express ("sublimate") their aggression in harmless or constructive ways, he believed, their aggressive energy would be dammed up, pressure would build, and the energy would seek an outlet, either exploding into acts of extreme violence or manifesting itself as symptoms of mental illness.

Unfortunately, Freud's theory of catharsis has been greatly oversimplified into the notion that people should vent their anger or they will suffer physically and emotionally; by venting that anger, they will become less likely to commit aggressive acts in the future. When we are feeling frustrated or angry, many of us do temporarily feel less tense after blowing off steam by yelling, cursing, or perhaps kicking the sofa. But do any of those actions reduce the chance that we will commit further aggression? Does the notion of catharsis square with the data?

THE EFFECTS OF AGGRESSIVE ACTS ON SUBSEQUENT AGGRESSION

Following Freud, many psychoanalysts believed that playing competitive games served as a harmless outlet for aggressive energies. But they were wrong. In fact, the reverse is true: Competitive games often make participants and observers *more* aggressive.

In one demonstration of this fact, the hostility levels of high school football players were measured 1 week before the football season began and 1 week after it ended. If the intense competitiveness and aggressive behavior that are part of playing football serve to reduce the tension caused by pent-up aggression, the players would be expected to show a decline in hostility over the course of the season. Instead, the results showed that feelings of hostility *increased* significantly (Patterson, 1974).

What about watching aggressive games? Will that reduce aggressive behavior? Unfortunately, no. Research on sports fans has focused more on their aggression than any other aspect of fandom (Wann et al., 2015). While you might think that sports fans would riot when their team loses, it seems like fans of a winning team are the most volatile. "Avid" baseball fans watched videos of baseball plays while in an fMRI, which measures brain activity. The more the reward-processing areas of the brain were activated by watching their team win, the more fans of the winning team said they wanted to do things like throw food or drinks at fans of the other team (Cikara, Botvinick, Fiske, 2011).

Outside the lab, in the real world, we see the same phenomenon: Verbal acts of aggression are followed by more of the same. Many people feel worse, both physically and mentally, after an angry confrontation. When people ruminate about their anger, talk to others incessantly about how angry they are, or vent their feelings in hostile acts, their blood pressure shoots up, they often feel angrier, and they behave even *more* aggressively later than if they had just let their feelings of anger subside (Bushman et al., 2005).

Contrary to the catharsis hypothesis, many fans who watch aggressive sports do not become less aggressive; they may become more aggressive than if they hadn't watched at all.

BLAMING THE VICTIM OF OUR AGGRESSION Repeated aggression is a downward spiral. When you hurt another person, you experience cognitive dissonance: The cognition "I hurt Darion" is dissonant with the cognition "I am a decent, kind person." A good way for you to reduce dissonance is to convince yourself that hurting Darion was not a bad thing to do. You can accomplish this by ignoring Darion's virtues and emphasizing his faults, convincing yourself that Darion is a bad person who deserved to be hurt. And you would be especially likely to reduce dissonance this way if Darion were an innocent victim of your aggression. In the experiments described in Chapter 6,

participants inflicted either psychological or physical harm on an innocent person who had not hurt them (Davis & Jones, 1960; Glass, 1964). Participants then persuaded themselves that their victims were not nice people and therefore deserved what they got. This certainly reduces dissonance, but it also sets the stage for further aggression because once a person has succeeded in finding reasons to dislike someone, it is easier to harm that victim again.

What happens, though, if the victim isn't totally innocent? What if the victim has done something that did hurt or disturb you and therefore, in your opinion, deserves your retaliation? Here the situation becomes more complex and more interesting. Acting aggressively toward someone who harmed you *increases* your hostility towards that person, thus feeding the anger; that originally made you aggress (Kahn, 1966).

What Are We Supposed to Do with Our Anger?

If aggression leads to self-justification, which in turn breeds more aggression, what should we do with our angry feelings toward someone? Stifling anger, sulking around the house, and hoping the other person will read our mind doesn't seem to be a good solution, and neither are brooding and ruminating by ourselves, which just prolong and intensify the anger (Bushman et al., 2005; Rusting & Nolen-Hoeksema, 1998). But if keeping our feelings bottled up and expressing them are both harmful, what is the alternative?

First, it is possible to control anger by actively enabling it to dissipate. *Actively enabling* means using such simple devices as counting to 10 (or 100!) before shooting your mouth off. Taking deep breaths or getting involved in a pleasant, distracting activity (playing a game, taking a bike ride, or even doing a good deed) are active ways of enabling the anger to fade away. If this advice sounds suspiciously like something your grandmother could have told you, well, that's because it is! Your grandmother often knows what she is talking about. But there is more to anger than merely controlling it, as you will see.

VENTING VERSUS SELF-AWARENESS   Dissipating anger is not always best for you or for a relationship. If your close friend or partner does something that makes you angry, you may want to express that anger in a way that helps you gain insight into yourself and the dynamics of the relationship. You may also wish to express yourself in a way that solves the problem without escalating it by arousing anger in the other person. But for that to happen, you must express your feelings in a way that is neither hostile nor demeaning.

You can do this (after counting to 10) by calmly stating that you are feeling angry and describing, nonjudgmentally, what you believe the other person did to bring about those feelings. Such a statement in itself will probably make you feel better to have "cleared the air," and because you haven't harmed the target of your anger with verbal or physical abuse, your response will not set in motion the

It's possible to actively dissipate feelings of anger.

cognitive processes that would lead you to justify your behavior by ridiculing your friend or escalating the argument. It is important that you speak in a way that does not cause your listener to become defensive or counterattack. Instead, you want to speak in a way that invites problem solving ("Look, we seem to have different notions about housework. Can we figure out how to resolve this?"). When such feelings are expressed between friends or partners in a straightforward, nonconfrontational manner, greater mutual understanding and a strengthening of the friendship can result (Christensen, Doss, & Jacobson, 2014).

Although it is probably best to reveal your anger to the friend who provoked it—at least if you are hoping to resolve the problem between you—sometimes the target of your anger is unavailable. Perhaps the person did something to you many years ago, or he or she has died or moved away. When you want to feel less angry about a bygone offense, one trick is to recall it from a third-person perspective. Students who recalled an angry experience from a first-person perspective reported feeling intense emotions and had an increase in blood pressure, whereas students who recalled an angry experience from a distanced, third-person perspective had less intense emotions and no increase in blood pressure (Ayduk & Kross, 2008). To see whether this technique can help you let go of anger over an unexpressed experience, take the Try It!

Research also finds it can be helpful to write down your feelings in a journal. In experiments with people undergoing traumatic events or who had been carrying a burdensome secret they had never shared with anyone, those who were instructed simply to write their "deepest thoughts and feelings" about the event or the secret felt healthier and even had fewer physical illnesses 6 months to a year later than did people who suffered in silence, who wrote about trivial topics, or who wrote about the details of the traumatic events without revealing their own underlying feelings. The benefits of "opening up" are due not to the venting of feeling but primarily to the insights and self-awareness that usually accompany such self-disclosure (Pennebaker, 1990, 2002). For example, one young woman realized that she had been carrying a lot of anger since her childhood over something another child had done to her. When she saw what she had written about the incident, she realized, "My god, we were both just kids."

TRAINING IN COMMUNICATION AND PROBLEM-SOLVING SKILLS   Feeling angry is part of being human, but we have to learn the right skills to express anger or annoyance constructively and nonviolently. In most societies, it is precisely the people who lack those social skills who are most prone to violent solutions to problems in relationships (Langhinrichsen-Rohling et al., 2012). One way to reduce aggression, then, is to teach people such techniques as how to communicate anger or criticism in constructive ways, how to negotiate and compromise when conflicts arise, and how to apologize when they need to (Christensen et al., 2014).

Try It!

Controlling Your Anger

Are you feeling angry about a personal matter in your life? Try to describe the event from a third-person perspective. Think about the space in which the event took place, where you and others were positioned, and the clothing of all people involved. Think about what you looked like from the outside, including your facial expressions during the event. Does viewing the situation differently in your mind's eye lessen your anger?

Many elementary and secondary schools now train students to use nonaggressive strategies for resolving conflict, along with problem-solving skills, emotional control, and conflict resolution (Barnes, Smith, & Miller, 2014; Wilson & Lipsey, 2007). For example, in one major longitudinal study, kindergarten boys who were already showing high levels of aggression were randomly assigned to either a 10-year intervention or a control group. The intervention included teaching them to feel more *competent* in managing their emotions, getting along with peers, and succeeding in school. At age 26, more than 10 years after the intervention was over, the young men were brought into a laboratory, where they played a game with a (fictitious) partner who provoked them to anger by stealing points from them. Those who had been in the intervention not only behaved less aggressively when given the chance to retaliate but even showed reduced testosterone reactivity to the provocation (Carré et al., 2014).

GETTING APOLOGIES RIGHT   What if you are not the person who is feeling angry, but the one who caused it in someone else? How should you apologize in a way that won't make the other person even angrier? Typically, any apology sincerely given and in which the perpetrator takes full responsibility is effective. Notice the "sincerely" part and the "full responsibility" part. The bland, token apologies offered by many public figures or corporate leaders when they've been caught doing something illegal or immoral don't count (Smith, 2014). Corporate Twitter accounts spend more time apologizing to user complaints posted on Twitter than tweeting new content (Page, 2014). To maximize the likelihood that someone will accept your apology, you must genuinely say you are sorry and reassure the person that you will not do the same thing again. Do not try to explain your behavior at the moment of the apology.

The person will be most likely to forgive you without aggressive retaliation if you follow that formula (Eaton & Struthers, 2006).

Of course, the offender must believe that an apology is even necessary, and here we see a gender difference. In a study in which young women and men kept daily diaries noting whether they committed an offense or experienced one, the researchers found that men simply have a higher threshold for what constitutes an offensive action warranting an apology. When everyone was asked to evaluate actual offenses they had experienced in the past or come up with imaginary ones, again the men rated them all as being less severe than women did. You can imagine the unfortunate consequences of this discrepancy in cross-sex close relationships: A woman might feel angry or slighted that her partner doesn't even notice an offense that she thinks is serious enough to warrant an apology, and the man might feel angry that she is being oversensitive and thin-skinned (Schumann & Ross, 2010).

COUNTERING DEHUMANIZATION BY BUILDING EMPATHY   As we saw, most people find it difficult to inflict pain on a stranger unless they can find a way to justify it, and the most common way of justifying it is to dehumanize the victim (Caselman, 2007). By building empathy among people, aggressive acts should be

#trending

"Re-accommodation": The United Airlines Debacle

On the evening of Sunday, April 9, 2017, the passengers of United Flight 3411 had just finished settling in their seats aboard a flight from Chicago, Illinois to Louisville, Kentucky. Unbenownst to them, four United Airlines employees arrived at the gate just after boarding and told the flight crew that they needed to get to Louisville immediately to service a flight leaving from that airport the next day. Flight 3411's crew offered the passengers $400 and then $800 to give up their seats, but no one was willing to do it for that price. So, the flight attendants announced they would pick passengers at random to be removed from the flight.

One of their random choices was a 69-year-old medical doctor from Elizabethtown, Kentucky, David Dao, but Dr. Dao said he would not deboard the plane because he had to see patients the next morning. Airport security was called, and disturbing cellphone videos taken by other passengers show the security guards forcibly removing Dr. Dao from the plane, banging his face on an armrest and dragging him, bloodied and disoriented, off the plane while other passengers gasp and cry, "My God, what are you doing?" and "No, this is wrong!" Dr. Dao suffered a concussion, had a broken nose, and lost two of his front teeth.

Perhaps needless to say, the Internet was outraged. But it was not until United's CEO, Oscar Munoz, provided the compassionless apology "for having to re-accommodate [the passenger]" and said that United had "followed established procedures" that the backlash on social media surged. Twitter erupted with hashtags that mocked United Airlines, such as #NewUnitedAirlinesMottos and #BoycottUnited. At the heart of the public outcry was the question: How could such disproportionate violence occur in the course of a commonplace business transaction? Instead of expressing remorse and promising that this would never happen to any future United Airlines passenger, Munoz tried to justify the beating, thus botching the opportunity to make things right.

Instances of especially bad customer service are coupled with rising rates of anger and aggression among airline passengers—a phenomenon known as "air rage." The foundation for this phenomenon is relative deprivation; airlines sell the idea that flying is a luxury service through their advertisements, but most travelers' experiences can hardly be described as "luxe." The mismatch between flyers expectations and airline service delivery coincides with increases in air rage (Hunter, 2006). In turn, dealing with angry customers takes its toll on service employees, leading to burn-out and increasing the chance that the employee may act more aggressively if a conflict breaks out with new customer (Grandey, Dickter, & Sin, 2004). In this case, Dr. Dao's minor provocation, folding his arms tightly when the officer told him to get off the plane, was perceived as an insult and violence ensued.

The frustration-aggression hypothesis also explains actions on both sides. Dr. Dao was *so* close to his goal of flying home—he was already in his seat!—before he was told to leave, thus increasing his frustration and making him less likely to comply with the request. For the flight attendants and airport security, there were two goals that were being thwarted: finding seats for the United employees and ensuring the plane took off reasonably close to the scheduled departure time. When Dr. Dao became an obstacle to the achievement of these goals, aggressive impulses took over.

more difficult to commit. The research data lend strong support to this contention. In one study, students who had been trained to empathize—that is, to take the perspective of the other person—behaved far less aggressively toward that person than did students who had not received the training (Richardson et al., 1994). In a similar study, Japanese students were told to shock another student as part of an alleged learning experiment (Ohbuchi, Ohno, & Mukai, 1993). In one condition, the "victims" first revealed something personal about themselves; in the other condition, they were not given this opportunity. Participants gave weaker shocks to the victim who had revealed personal information. It's harder to harm a stranger if you have made a personal connection with that person, and this is true whether the stranger is your neighbor, a homeless person, a sales clerk, or a civilian enemy.

Norma Feshbach (1989, 1997), who has pioneered the teaching of empathy in elementary schools, designed a 30-hour empathy-training program for children.

Children who are taught to put themselves in others' shoes often have higher self-esteem, are more generous, and are less aggressive than children who lack skills of empathy.

The kids had to think hard about questions such as "What would the world look like to you if you were as small as a cat?" and "What birthday present would make each member of your family happiest?" Thinking about the answers expands children's ability to put themselves in another's situation. The children also listened to stories and then retold them from the point of view of each of the different characters in each story. The children played the role of each of the characters, and their performances were videotaped. The children then viewed the tapes and talked about how people look and sound when they express different feelings. At the end of the program, the children not only had learned to be more empathic but also had higher self-esteem, were more generous, and were less aggressive than were students who had not participated in the program. As perspective-taking requires cognitive flexibility, it should not surprise us to learn that students who develop greater empathic ability also tend to have higher academic achievement (Feshbach & Feshbach, 2009).

Disrupting the Rejection-Rage Cycle

At the beginning of this chapter, we described the massacre at Columbine High School and discussed some of the speculations about what might have caused that horrifying event and the many other school shootings like it. Could these tragedies have been prevented?

To be sure, many of the shooters were severely mentally ill. Seung-Hui Cho, who murdered 32 of his fellow students at Virginia Tech University in 2007, had a lifelong history of mental problems, delusions, and aberrant behavior that had been increasing in the previous year; as a boy, he had written that he wanted to "repeat Columbine" (Hillshafer, 2013). The Sandy Hook Elementary School shooter, Adam Lanza, and Elliot Rodger, who killed six people in Santa Barbara, California, in 2014, had a history, since childhood, of mental problems that had recently been worsening. Some investigators have concluded that Harris might have been a psychopath who was easily able to fool adults, including his own psychiatrist; Klebold suffered from major depression (Cullen, 2010). But it would be a mistake to dismiss the Columbine massacre and most other school shootings as being a result of individual pathology and let it go at that. Such an explanation leads nowhere, because Harris and Klebold had been functioning effectively. They were getting good grades, attended class regularly, and did not present serious behavior problems to their parents or to the school authorities. Klebold had even gone to his prom three days earlier. True, they were loners, but so were many other students at Columbine High School.

Thus, to dismiss their horrifying deed as solely the result of mental illness would lead us to miss something of vital importance, something that might help us prevent similar tragedies: the power of the social situation. Elliot Aronson (2000) argued that Harris and Klebold were reacting in an extreme manner to a school atmosphere that creates an environment of exclusion and mockery, making life difficult for a sizable number of students. Most high schools are cliquish places where students are shunned if they belong to the "wrong" ethnic group, come from the poor part of town, wear the "wrong" clothes, or are too short, too fat, too tall, or too smart. After the shootings, Columbine students recalled that Harris and Klebold had been taunted and bullied. Indeed, one student justified this behavior by saying, "Most kids didn't want them there. They were into witchcraft. They were into voodoo. Sure we teased them. But what do you expect with kids who come to school with weird hairdos and horns on their hats? If you want to get rid of someone, usually you tease 'em. So the whole school would call them homos" (Gibbs & Roche, 1999).

In the video they left behind, Harris and Klebold spoke angrily about the insults and bullying they endured at Columbine. "Perhaps now we will get the respect we deserve," said Klebold, brandishing a sawed-off shotgun. Indeed, the motivation behind the vast majority of rampage killings is an attempt to transform feelings of shame, humiliation, and rejection into feelings of pride. Social rejection is the most significant risk factor for teenage suicide, despair, and violence (Crescioni & Baumeister, 2009; Leary, Twenge, & Quinlivan, 2006; Stillman et al., 2009). When a team of researchers investigated 15 school shootings that occurred between 1995 and 2001, they found that in 13 of them, the killers had been angered by bullying and social rejection (Leary et al., 2003). In the immediate aftermath of the Columbine massacre, countless young people posted messages online, describing their anguish over being rejected and taunted by their popular classmates. None of these teenagers condoned the shootings, yet their Internet postings revealed a high degree of empathy for the suffering that they assumed Harris and Klebold must have endured. A 16-year-old girl wrote, "I know how they feel. Parents need to realize that a kid is not overreacting all the time [when] they say that no one accepts them?"

In the past decade, many schools have adopted bullying prevention programs to change norms regarding a form of aggression that can otherwise become dangerously prevalent among adolescents.

How do we stop the cycle of bullying and aggressive retaliation? Over the school year of 2013 to 2014, a massive bullying intervention involving more than 24,000 middle school students was conducted in New Jersey by Elizabeth Levy-Paluck and her colleagues (Paluck, Shepherd, & Aronow, 2016). The intervention was designed on the idea that social norms are best conveyed by people who are well-known and liked in their communities, like popular kids who were cool with lots of different social circles. The researchers first mapped out the social networks of 56 middle schools and then randomly assigned students in some of the schools to create an "anticonflict intervention group." Students in the anticonflict intervention groups designed anti-bullying campaigns with high-quality print media and easily sharable digital images that were implemented in their schools. One year later, schools with anticonflict intervention groups showed a 30% reduction in disciplinary reports for peer conflict. Notably, this effect was stronger for schools where more popular, well-liked kids were involved in designing the anti-bullying campaigns.

Research from social psychology shows that it should be possible to make our schools safer, as well as more pleasant and humane, by bringing about a change in the negative, exclusionary social atmosphere and by building empathy among schoolchildren. And, by the way, Columbine High School now has an antibullying program in place.

Review Questions

1. Suppose you want to reduce the chances that your children will act aggressively toward other people. Which of the following strategies is most likely to work?
   a. Be a good role model; do not be verbally or physically abusive.
   b. Let your children play all the violent video games they want.
   c. Order them to behave nicely with other children and punish them if they don't.
   d. Encourage them to play sports where they can vent their frustrations on the playing field.

2. Tiffany is angry at Whitney for forgetting her birthday. To defuse her anger, Tiffany should
   a. think about other times Whit annoyed her and then confront Whit with all the evidence of what a bad friend she is.
   b. write about her feelings privately for 20 minutes a day for a few days to get some perspective.
   c. post her feelings about Whit on her Facebook page.
   d. get back at Whit by complaining about her to all their mutual friends.

3. Tiffany finally decides she is ready to confront Whitney directly. How should she express her anger (assuming she wants to keep the friendship)?

   a. She should "let it all out" so that she will feel better, and Whit will know exactly how she feels.
   b. She should invite Whitney to play a game of tennis and then really try to clobber her.
   c. She should explain why she feels upset and hurt, as calmly as she can, without blame and accusation.
   d. She should explain why she feels upset and hurt, but let Whit know that she blames her for her thoughtless behavior.

4. Which form of apology is most likely to be accepted and believed?
   a. "If I hurt your feelings, I'm really sorry."
   b. "I'm sorry I hurt your feelings, but look, we were both to blame here."
   c. "I'm really sorry, and I understand what I did wrong; it won't happen again."
   d. "I'm sorry."

5. What is the most significant risk factor for teenage suicide and violence?
   a. Doing poorly in school
   b. Having strict parents
   c. Having a genetic predisposition
   d. Being socially rejected

Summary

LO 12.1 Distinguish evolutionary, cultural, and learning explanations of aggression.

- **Is Aggression Innate, Learned, or Optional?** **Aggression** is intentional behavior aimed at doing harm or causing physical or psychological pain to another person. **Hostile aggression** is defined as having as one's goal the harming of another; **instrumental aggression** inflicts harm as a means to some other end.

- **The Evolutionary View** Evolutionary psychologists argue that aggression is genetically programmed into men because it enables them to defend their group and perpetuate their genes; males also aggress out of sexual jealousy to protect their paternity. A hormone involved in male aggression is testosterone (which both sexes have in varying levels), but the aggression-testosterone link is modest, and each affects the other. Two evolutionary theories believe this link depends on the social situation: the **Dual-Hormone Hypothesis** shows that testosterone only leads to aggression when there is a potential to dominate such that, under times of stress, testosterone even predicts *less* aggressive behavior whereas the

Challenge Hypothesis states that testosterone only leads to aggression when there is the potential to mate. There is substantial variation in the degree of aggressiveness among human males and also among our two closest animal relatives, chimpanzees and bonobos. Even if aggressive behavior has survival value, nearly all animals have also evolved strong inhibitory mechanisms that enable them to suppress aggression when they need to.

- **Culture and Aggression** Most social psychologists believe that human beings are born with the capacity for aggression, but whether or not it is expressed is influenced by situational and cultural factors and is therefore modifiable. There is a great variation in the levels of aggression across cultures; under some conditions, groups have had to become more aggressive, and under other conditions, they have become more peaceful. Cooperative, collectivist cultures have low levels of aggression, and in the past few centuries, war, murder, and torture have been steadily declining around the world. In *cultures of honor*, however, such as those in the American

South and Southwest and in the Middle East, men are raised to respond aggressively to perceptions of threat and disrespect, a response that originated in economic conditions. In such cultures, the rate of physical abuse of women is often higher than elsewhere because such abuse is regarded as a male prerogative. Multiple factors shape whether or not a culture tends to nurture aggressive behavior, including the extent to which male aggression fulfills a central part of the male role and identity.

- **Gender and Aggression** Men and boys are much more likely than women to commit *physical aggression* in provocative situations, to pick fights with strangers, and to commit crimes of violence. However, gender differences in physical aggression are reduced when women are as provoked as men or when cultural norms foster female aggression. Husbands are far more likely to murder their wives than vice versa, but community studies find no significant gender differences in rates of less extreme partner abuse, such as hitting. Girls and women are more likely to commit *relational aggression*, acts that harm another person through manipulation of the relationship (e.g., spreading rumors, shunning).

- **Learning to Behave Aggressively** Social-cognitive learning theory holds that people often learn social behavior, including aggression, through *observational learning*—observing and imitating others, especially people or institutions they respect. But their actual behavior also depends on their beliefs, perceptions, and interpretations of what they observe.

- **Some Physiological Influences** Alcohol can increase aggressive behavior because it serves as a disinhibitor, reducing a person's inhibitions. Alcohol also disrupts the way people usually process information so that they may respond to the most obvious aspects of a social situation and fail to pick up its subtle elements. But thanks to the "think-drink" effect, when people expect alcohol to have certain effects, it often does. When people are in pain or in a very hot environment, they are more likely to act aggressively.

LO 12.2 Describe situational and social causes of aggression.

- **Social Situations and Aggression**

  - **Frustration and Aggression** The frustration-aggression theory states that frustration can increase the probability of an aggressive response. Frustration is more likely to produce aggression if one is thwarted on the way to a goal in a manner that is either illegitimate or unexpected. Also, *relative deprivation*—the feeling that you have less than what you deserve or less than people similar to you have—is more likely to cause frustration

and aggressive behavior than absolute deprivation, as illustrated by protests and revolutions from the civil rights movement to Eastern Europe to the Middle East.

- **Provocation and Reciprocation** Individuals frequently aggress to reciprocate the aggressive behavior of others. This response is reduced if there are mitigating circumstances or the recipient believes the other person's behavior was unintentional.

- **Weapons as Aggressive Cues** The mere presence of a gun, an aggressive stimulus, in an otherwise neutral situation increases the degree of aggressive behavior, especially if a person is already feeling angry or frustrated. In a classic study, participants angered in the presence of a gun administered stronger electric shocks to their "victim" than those angered in the same setting in which a tennis racket was substituted for the gun.

- **Putting the Elements Together: The Case of Sexual Assault** Most crimes of rape are committed by assailants known to the victim (acquaintance or date rape). Rape may occur as a result of *physical force* or through *incapacitation*, when the victim has been drugged or is drunk or unconscious. Sexually aggressive males who commit these acts are often unable to empathize with women, may feel hostility and contempt toward women, and feel entitled to have sexual relations with whatever woman they choose. Date rape may also occur because of misunderstandings and ambiguities in the **sexual scripts** that men and women follow regarding sexual norms. Because most couples communicate sexual interest and intentions—including a wish *not* to have sex—indirectly through hints, body language, eye contact, and other nonverbal behaviors, the possibility of misunderstanding one another is greatly increased. The topics in this chapter lend themselves to understanding the factors involved in sexual assault: the importance of social and cultural norms; the power of perceptions and beliefs; the role of observational learning from role models, peers, and the media; why "testosterone made me do it" is an excuse, not an explanation; and the disinhibiting effects of alcohol and the "think-drink" effect.

LO 12.3 Explain how observing violence increases violence.

- **Violence and the Media**

  - **Studying the Effects of Media Violence** To try to determine what effect all the violence in media and video games might have on children and adults, researchers have conducted laboratory experiments and longitudinal studies. Watching violence is associated with an increase in aggressive behavior, especially in children, but not all studies find a relationship. Exposure to violent pornography, in contrast to nonviolent erotica, increases acceptance of sexual violence toward women; the effects are strongest on men who already have hostile attitudes toward women and are predisposed to behave aggressively with them. In the laboratory, playing violent video games does increase hostile feelings and aggressive behavior and also has a "numbing" effect, increasing people's indifference to the needs of others, especially if the others are not "one of us." Longitudinal studies show that the more television violence observed by children, the greater the amount of violence they exhibit as teenagers and young adults. Viewing violence also exaggerates people's perceptions of danger in the outside world.

- **The Problem of Determining Cause and Effect** The relationship between media violence and actual aggression, however, is a two-way street: Children who are already predisposed to aggression are more likely to seek out aggressive shows and games to watch and play. The effects of violence in the media have the greatest effect on children already predisposed to violence because of a genetic predisposition, living in a violent family, or a personality trait. And many other factors have a far more powerful influence on aggression, including growing up with violent or otherwise abusive parents, living in a violent community, and being rejected socially.

LO 12.4 Identify ways aggression can be diminished.

- **How to Decrease Aggression**
  - **Does Punishing Aggression Reduce Aggression?** If punishment is itself aggressive, it actually models such behavior to children and may engender greater aggressiveness. Punishment may also enhance the attractiveness of the transgression to the child, get the attention that the child is hoping for, or backfire by making the child anxious and angry. Punishment often fails to reduce aggression because it does not communicate what the target should do, only what he or she should not do. For punishment to serve as a deterrent to misbehavior or criminal acts, it must

be both prompt and certain. For that reason, in the complex world of criminal justice, severe punishment is unlikely to deter violent crime.

- **Can We Release Anger by Indulging It?** The theory of **catharsis** predicts that venting one's anger or watching others behave aggressively would serve to "get it out of your system" and make people less likely to behave aggressively themselves. Research shows the contrary: Acting aggressively or observing aggressive events or sports increases the likelihood of aggressive behavior in players and fans. Ventilating anger directly toward someone who has insulted or otherwise angered you also increases blood pressure, feelings of anger, and acts of aggression. In turn, because of self-justification and the need to reduce dissonance, each act of "righteous aggression" a person commits increases the likelihood that it will be repeated.

- **What Are We Supposed to Do with Our Anger?** Venting anger usually causes more harm than good, but stifling serious feelings is often not useful either. It is more effective to become aware of the anger and then to deal with it in ways that are more constructive than yelling or hitting: cooling off; remembering the angering event from a distanced perspective; becoming more self-aware (perhaps through writing down your feelings privately); learning to communicate your feelings in a clear but nonjudgmental or noninsulting way; taking responsibility for acts that anger others, through understanding and apology; learning how to solve the problem that has made you and the other person angry; and strengthening empathic skills.

- **Disrupting the Rejection-Rage Cycle** Social rejection is the most significant risk factor for teenage suicide, despair, and violence. Most of the teenagers who have committed horrifying murders in their schools felt angry and vengeful at having been bullied and rejected by their peers. Changing the structure and atmosphere of schools through awareness, empathy training, and bullying-reduction programs that take advantage of existing social dynamics can reduce bullying and improve the lives of children and teenagers.

Revel Interactive

Shared Writing   What Do You Think?

What are three different explanations for why exposure to violent media can create violent tendencies among certain individuals?

Test Yourself

1. _____ aggression stems from feelings of anger and is aimed at inflicting pain, whereas _____ aggression serves as a means to some goal other than pain.

   a. Hostile; instrumental

   b. Direct; passive

   c. Instrumental; hostile

   d. Passive; direct

2. What does the research on cultures of honor suggest about the relationship between testosterone and aggression?

   a. It explains why men are more aggressive than women across cultures.

   b. It shows that testosterone and aggression are unrelated.

   c. It shows that culture affects when and why men can be provoked to become aggressive.

   d. It shows that culture has little effect on the basic biology of testosterone in men.

3. *Relational aggression* refers to

   a. behaving violently against one's relations.

   b. the negative effects of aggression on one's relationships.

   c. expressing aggression indirectly by manipulating a relationship.

   d. having sexual relations with the target of one's aggression.

4. In terms of *physical aggression*, men are more likely than women to

   a. engage in public displays of violence.

   b. behave aggressively to defend their honor or status.

   c. hit or slap a spouse or partner.

   d. All of the answers are correct.

   e. Answers a and b are correct.

5. Social-cognitive learning theory explains why, when people are provoked,

   a. they respond aggressively if they think aggression is justified.

   b. they respond aggressively if they are tired or hungry.

   c. they automatically respond aggressively.

   d. they seek their friends' opinions of what to do.

6. John has consumed enough alcohol to make him legally drunk. Under which of the following conditions is he most likely to become aggressive?

   a. He is partying with his friends.

   b. A stranger says hello to him.

   c. He is walking to work on a cold winter day.

   d. A stranger bumps into him in a crowded restaurant.

7. What does research suggest is the most reasonable conclusion about the effects of media violence?

   a. They have an effect, but primarily on children already predisposed to aggression.

   b. They have a strong effect, making most young children more aggressive.

   c. They have virtually no effect.

   d. Their effects depend on whether children are watching cartoons, television, or movies.

8. In the United States rape occurs most often because of

   a. force by a stranger.

   b. force by an acquaintance.

   c. incapacitation of the perpetrator.

   d. incapacitation of the victim.

9. What does research find about the validity of the catharsis theory?

   a. Supported: It is usually beneficial to ventilate anger and get it out of your system.

   b. Supported: Playing or watching violent sports reduces aggression.

   c. Disconfirmed: Expressing anger often makes people angrier.

   d. Disconfirmed: Acting out anger is healthy for physical but not psychological reasons.

   e. Both answers a and b are correct.

10. Jim has been convicted of assault and offers many reasons for his behavior. How many of the following of Jim's arguments have social psychologists studied scientifically?

    a. "There was a gun in the room when it happened."

    b. "I used to watch my older brother beat up neighborhood kids."

    c. "I had just been fired from a job I really wanted."

    d. "I grew up on a cattle ranch in the Southwest."

    e. "I was justified—the other guy started it."

    f. Answers a, b, and e are correct.

    g. Answers a, c, and d are correct.

    h. All of the answers are correct.

Chapter 13
Prejudice
Causes, Consequences, and Cures

NO DOGS NEGROES MEXICANS

20 FEB. 1942

LONESTAR RESTAURANTS ASSN.
Dallas, Texas

 ## Chapter Outline and Learning Objectives

Defining Prejudice

LO 13.1   Summarize the three components of prejudice.

The Cognitive Component: Stereotypes
The Affective Component: Emotions
The Behavioral Component: Discrimination

Detecting Hidden Prejudices

LO 13.2   Explain how we measure prejudices that people don't want to reveal—or that they don't know they hold.

Ways of Identifying Suppressed Prejudices
Ways of Identifying Implicit Prejudices

The Effects of Prejudice on the Victim

LO 13.3   Describe some ways that prejudice affects its targets.

The Self-Fulfilling Prophecy
Social Identity Threat

Causes of Prejudice

LO 13.4   Describe three aspects of social life that can cause prejudice.

Pressures to Conform: Normative Rules
Social Identity Theory: Us versus Them
Realistic Conflict Theory

Reducing Prejudice

LO 13.5   Summarize the conditions that can reduce prejudice.

The Contact Hypothesis
Cooperation and Interdependence: The Jigsaw Classroom

WHAT DO YOU THINK QUESTION

Revel Interactive	Survey **What Do You Think?**	
	SURVEY	RESULTS
	What is prejudice? How does it come about? How can it be reduced?	
	○ Yes	
	○ No	

Of all the social behaviors we discuss in this book, prejudice is among the most common and the most dangerous. Consider these examples:

- One Wednesday evening of February 24, 2017, two Indian immigrants, Srinivas Kuchibhotla and Alok Madasani, were enjoying drinks at the bar they frequented in Olathe, Kansas. A man they did not know, Adam Purinton, began to call them racial slurs against "Arabs." The bar staff kicked Purinton out, but he returned shortly and yelled "Get out of my country!" before opening fire on the two friends. For racism against a group that wasn't even their own, Kuchibhotla lost his life and Madasani was seriously wounded.

- When trying to rent or buy a house, Asian Americans and African Americans are 17% less likely to be told about available homes by real estate agents than White clients. Discrimination even shows up in temporary housing like AirBnB, where requesters with Black-sounding names are 16% less likely to be accepted than requesters with White-sounding names.

- More than 300 people were dancing away their Saturday night at Pulse, a gay nightclub in Orlando, Florida, when Omar Mateen opened fire with a semi-automatic rifle. Forty-nine people did not make it out alive. Although Mateen identified himself as a terrorist in social media posts, both his family and coworkers said he was virulently homophobic, and they assumed that was why he carried out the attack at Pulse. Indeed, the FBI announced that they considered the attack to be both a hate crime and an act of terrorism.

None of us emerges completely unscathed by prejudice; it is a problem common to all humankind. When prejudice escalates into extreme hatred, it can lead to brutality, murder, war, and even genocide. During the past half-century, social psychologists have contributed greatly to our understanding of the psychological processes underlying prejudice and have begun to identify some possible solutions. What is prejudice? How does it come about? How can it be reduced?

Defining Prejudice

LO 13.1   Summarize the three components of prejudice.

Prejudice is an attitude—an emotionally powerful one. Attitudes are made up of three components: a cognitive component, involving the beliefs or thoughts (cognitions) that make up the attitude; an affective or emotional component, representing both the type of emotion linked with the attitude (e.g., anger, warmth) and the intensity of the emotion (e.g., mild uneasiness, outright hostility); and a behavioral component, relating to one's actions. (See Chapter 7.) People don't only hold attitudes; they usually act on them as well.

In this context, a **prejudice** is a hostile or negative attitude toward people in a distinguishable group, based *solely* on their membership in that group. Thus, when we say that someone is prejudiced against a certain group, we mean that he or she is

Prejudice

A hostile or negative attitude toward people in a distinguishable group based solely on their membership in that group; it contains cognitive, emotional, and behavioral components

primed to behave coolly or with hostility toward the members of that group and that he or she feels that all members of the group are pretty much the same. The characteristics this individual assigns to the members of that group are negative and applied to the group as a whole. The individual traits or behaviors of the individual target of prejudice will either go unnoticed or be dismissed. Prejudices have a cognitive element (a stereotype) and can influence behavior (in the form of discrimination).

We are all victims or potential victims of prejudice for no other reason than our membership in an identifiable group, whether on the basis of ethnicity, skin color, religion, gender, age, national origin, sexual orientation, body size, or disability, to name just a few. And it is not only minority groups that are the targets of prejudice at the hands of the dominant majority. Prejudice is a two-way street; it often flows from the minority group to the majority group as well as in the other direction.

To be sure, enormous progress has been made. The numbers of people who admit to believing that Blacks are inferior to Whites, women inferior to men, and gays inferior to straights have been steadily dropping (Weaver, 2008). Fifty years ago, the overwhelming majority of Americans were opposed to racial integration and could not imagine ever voting for any Black candidate, let alone for president of the United States. Many other changes have swept the country. Fifty years ago, few could imagine that it would one day become routine to see female lawyers, doctors, bartenders, Supreme Court justices, astronauts, or marine biologists. Gay men and lesbians lived in fear of anyone discovering their sexual orientation, and few could imagine that same-sex marriage would ever be a possibility, let alone become legal. Inspired by the civil rights movement, the National Association to Advance Fat Acceptance was formed in 1969, "dedicated to ending size discrimination in all of its forms," and Disability Rights Advocates likewise have organized to fight discrimination against anyone with a disability.

And yet it's clear that prejudice continues. Hate groups in the United States have more than doubled since the turn of the century. Between 2015 and 2017, there was a 197% increase in the total number of anti-Muslim hate groups in the United States (Potok, 2017). The rise in extremist attitudes has been attributed to reactions to demographic shifts throughout the country. Some people—definitely not all people—think that more freedom for another group must come at the cost of less freedom for their own group. If you view the world in this way, then the relationship between local demographics and prejudice make sense. For example, some White Americans feel that reductions in anti-Black bias must necessarily be accompanied by a rise in anti-White bias (Norton & Sommers, 2011; Wilkins & Kaiser, 2014); when confronted with information that the country is becoming more ethnically diverse and that the proportion of Whites is declining, these same people respond not with tolerance but with fear and increased prejudice toward Latinos, African Americans, and Asian Americans (Craig & Richeson, 2014). Online, hundreds of thousands of self-identified White nationalists proudly express their contempt for gays, Blacks, Mexicans, and, primarily, Jews (Stephens-Davidowitz, 2014). Sometimes prejudice erupts overtly, as in the stories we described above, along with hate crimes, vandalism, bigoted jokes. Most of its expressions are more subtle and low-level, however, being reflected in our bodies and the way we process information.

The Cognitive Component: Stereotypes

The human mind cannot avoid creating categories, putting some people into one group based on certain characteristics and others into another group based on their different characteristics (Brewer, 2007; Dovidio & Gaertner, 2010). Researchers in the field of *social neuroscience* find that creating categories is an adaptive mechanism, one built into the human brain; humans begin creating categories almost as soon as they are born (Cikara & Van Bavel, 2014). Newborns have no preferences for faces of one race or another, but if they live in a "monoracial" world, they will show a preference for faces of their own race by only

3 months of age (Anzures et al., 2013). If they repeatedly see faces of two or more races, however, they show no preference. This research illustrates a major theme of social-psychological approaches to prejudice: We are born with the ability to notice different categories, but experience shapes that ability, right from the get-go.

Just as we make sense out of the physical world by grouping animals and plants into taxonomies, we make sense out of our social world by grouping people according to characteristics that are important, most notably gender, age, and race. We rely on our perceptions of what people with similar characteristics have been like in the past to help us determine how to react to someone else with the same ones (Andersen & Klatzky, 1987; Macrae & Bodenhausen, 2000). As a result, when you think about a social group, concepts that you associate with that group become more accessible (Greenwald & Banaji, 1995). As a result, stereotype-consistent information is given more attention and remembered more easily than the "exceptions" to the stereotype (Macrae & Bodenhausen, 2000). When asked to evaluate a drug addict's honesty or dishonesty, more people remembered being told that he found some money on the street and pocketed it than being told that he returned it to its rightful owner (Wigboldus, Dijksterhuis, & van Knippenberg, 2003). The resulting categories are both useful and necessary, but they have profound consequences. They do not inevitably generate prejudices, but they are the first step.

We tend to categorize according to what we regard as normative. And within a given culture, what people regard as normative is similar, in part because these images are perpetuated and broadcast widely by the media. Stereotyping, however, goes a step beyond simple categorization. A **stereotype** is a generalization about a group of people in which identical characteristics are assigned to virtually all members of the group, regardless of actual variation among the members. Walter Lippmann (1922), a distinguished journalist who was the first to introduce the term *stereotype*, described the distinction between the world "out there" and "the little pictures we carry around inside our heads." Within a given culture, these pictures tend to be remarkably similar.

We know that there are male cheerleaders and nurses, female computer programmers, and Black classical musicians. So, why do we use stereotypes? The world is too complicated for us to have highly differentiated attitudes about everything, we maximize our cognitive time and energy by constructing nuanced, accurate attitudes about some topics while relying on simple, error-prone beliefs about others. Gordon Allport (1954) described stereotyping as "the law of least effort." Given our limited capacity for processing information, it allows human beings to behave like "cognitive misers"—to adopt certain rules of thumb in our attempt to understand other people (Ito & Urland, 2003). We develop stereotypes based on our own experience and what we learn through the media and local culture. Even when a given stereotype is accurate, it blinds us to a person's individuality, which can be extremely maladaptive for all parties. (See the Try It!) Stereotypes certainly harm their targets. Across the world, when occupations are segregated by gender, many people form gender stereotypes about the requirements of such careers: Female jobs

At birth, newborns have no preference for faces of one race or another, and if they repeatedly see faces of two or more races, they continue to show no preference.

Stereotype

A generalization about a group of people in which certain traits are assigned to virtually all members of the group, regardless of actual variation among the members

Watch RACE AND THE BIKE THIEF

Revel Video

What is this woman's occupation? Most Western non-Muslims hold the stereotype that Muslim women who wear the full-length Black *niqab* must be repressed sexually as well as politically. But Wedad Lootah, a Muslim living in Dubai, United Arab Emirates, is a marriage counselor and sexual activist, and the author of a best-selling Arabic sex manual.

require kindness and nurturance; male jobs require strength and smarts. These stereotypes, in turn, stifle many people's aspirations to enter a nontraditional career and also create prejudices in employers that motivate them to discriminate (Agars, 2004; Cejka & Eagly, 1999; Eccles, 2011).

Do stereotypes have a "kernel of truth" to them, as some pundits like to argue? Some do, some don't. To the extent that a stereotype is based on experience and accurately identifies certain attributes of a group overall, it can be an adaptive, shorthand way of dealing with complex situations (Jussim et al., 2009; Lee, McCauley, & Jussim, 2013). But, some stereotypes do not reflect experience at all. Consider the pop-psych stereotype that women are "more talkative" than men. To test this assumption, psychologists wired up a sample of men and women with voice recorders that tracked their conversations while they went about their daily lives. There was no significant difference in the number of words spoken: Both sexes used about 16,000 words per day on average, with large individual differences among the participants (Mehl et al., 2007). To know if a stereotype is true or not, you have to be open to evidence that disconfirms it.

ARE POSITIVE STEREOTYPES GOOD? Not all stereotypes are negative. Sometimes we may assume someone is honest because of their group membership: We would be surprised if a Catholic priest stole money from a cash register. While it may seem like a good thing to hold positive beliefs about a group of people, positive stereotypes also disadvantage both parties. For the person holding the stereotype, it is more maladaptive to mistakenly view someone positively than to mistakenly view them negatively. For example, in a zombie apocalypse, if you mistake a zombie for a human, then you will be killed or turned into a zombie, but if you mistake a human for a zombie then it's at most a missed opportunity. For the target of the stereotype, positive stereotypes still mean that you are still being interpreted as a category instead of an individual and possibly mistreated as a result.

For example, Asian Americans have often been labeled a "model minority," a culture of people who are hardworking, ambitious, and intelligent. But many Asian Americans themselves object to this blanket characterization because it sets up expectations for those who are not interested in academic achievement, who don't like science and math and don't do well in those subjects, and who in general don't appreciate being treated as a category rather than as individuals (Thompson & Kiang, 2010). Moreover,

Try It!

Stereotypes and Aggression

Close your eyes. Imagine an aggressive construction worker. How is this person dressed, where is this person located, and what, specifically, is this person doing to express aggression? Write your answers, being specific about the person's actions.

Now imagine an aggressive lawyer. How is this person dressed, where is this person located, and what, specifically, is this person doing to express aggression? Write your answers, being specific about the person's actions.

If you are like the experimental participants in one research study, your stereotypes of the construction worker and the lawyer will have influenced the way you have construed the term *aggression*: Most of the study subjects imagined the construction worker using physical aggression and the lawyer using verbal aggression (Kunda, Sinclair, & Griffin, 1997). And, by the way, in your visualization, are the construction worker and lawyer both men? Young? What is their race or ethnicity? Unless you are Asian American, we are pretty sure that neither one of the people you are imagining is Asian American. How come?

the stereotype lumps together *all* Asian Americans, ignoring differences across Asian cultures (rather like referring to Swedes, Germans, the Irish, the French, and Greeks as all one bunch of "European Americans"). A study of Cambodian, Chinese, Korean, Lao, and Vietnamese students in America found many average differences in values, motivations, and goals across these groups (S. J. Lee, 2009).

Or consider the stereotype that "White men can't jump" and its implied corollary of positive stereotypes that (all) Black men *can* jump. This is a negative stereotype about White men and a positive stereotype about Black men, but neither group wins. Currently, more than 80% of National Basketball Association (NBA) players are Black, yet African Americans constitute only 13% of the U.S. population. Certainly, some of this discrepancy is driven by the impact of negative stereotypes on White boys' baller aspirations. So, what in this stereotype is insulting to the minority? The problem is that this assumption obscures the overlap in the distributions—that is, it blurs the fact that many Black kids are not adept at basketball and that many White kids are. To say that 80% of NBA players are Black does not mean that 80% of all Black men are capable of becoming NBA players. Thus, if someone meets a young Black man and is astonished at his ineptitude on the basketball court, then, in a real sense, the Black man is being denied his individuality. He is being relegated to a category of "good athlete" rather than, say, "smart professional." This creates hurtful experiences like the one described by a Black law professor: At an elegant restaurant with her two young sons, the maître d' came by and casually asked her if they would become rappers or ball players. She replied that doctor or lawyer was more likely. "Aiming kind of high, aren't we?" he said (Cashin, 2014).

Nonetheless, the use and depiction of positive stereotypes has been increasing steadily in America. As it has become less acceptable to overtly express prejudice, people have begun to systematically replace negative stereotypes with more positive stereotypes during conversations and communications with others (Bergsieker et al., 2012). However, people who endorse a lot of positive stereotypes also tend to endorse more negative stereotypes. For example, research involving 15,000 men and women in 19 nations shows that positive gender stereotypes fuel a form of sexism called *benevolent sexism*, where women are idealized as being better than men for stereotypically female qualities like being caring and good cooks (Glick & Fiske, 2001). In comparison, *hostile sexism* describes what we typically think of as sexism: The belief that women are inferior to men and the endorsement of negative stereotypes of

Do you have a stereotype of Asian women, blond women, tattooed women, or muscular women? This woman is all four. Are any or all of those four stereotypes positive or negative for you?

women. Because benevolent sexism lacks a tone of hostility to women, it doesn't seem like a prejudice to many people, but benevolent sexism and hostile sexism are strongly correlated, meaning that benevolent sexists are likely also hostile sexists (Glick & Fiske, 1996). We're not just talking about men here: many women also endorse benevolent sexism (e.g., wanting men to hold doors for them), and those who do are less motivated to support action for women's equal rights (Becker & Wright, 2001). Thus, both positive and negative stereotypes legitimize discrimination and can be used to justify relegating people to stereotyped roles (Christopher & Wojda, 2008; Glick 2006).

Watch SURVIVAL TIPS! DEALING WITH POSITIVE STEREOTYPES

Revel Video

Revel Video

Prejudice
an attitude towards people from another group

The Affective Component: Emotions

If you've ever argued with people who hold deep-seated prejudices, you know how hard it is to get them to change their minds. Even people who are usually reasonable about most topics become immune to rational, logical arguments when it comes to the topic of their prejudice. Why is this so? It is primarily the emotional aspect of attitudes that makes a prejudiced person so hard to argue with; logical arguments are not always effective in countering emotions.

The difficulty of using reason to change prejudice was beautifully illustrated by Gordon Allport (1954) in his landmark book *The Nature of Prejudice*. He reports a dialogue between Mr. X and Mr. Y:

> *Mr. X:* The trouble with the Jews is that they only take care of their own group.
>
> *Mr. Y:* But the record of the Community Chest campaign shows that they gave more generously, in proportion to their numbers, to the general charities of the community than did non-Jews.
>
> *Mr. X:* That shows they are always trying to buy favor and intrude into Christian affairs. They think of nothing but money; that is why there are so many Jewish bankers.
>
> *Mr. Y:* But a recent study shows that the percentage of Jews in the banking business is negligible, far smaller than the percentage of non-Jews.
>
> *Mr. X:* That's just it; they don't go in for respectable business; they are only in the movie business or run nightclubs.

This dialogue shows how we can be motivated to protect certain beliefs. Because Mr. X is emotionally caught up in his beliefs about Jews, his responses are not logical. Rather than challenging the data presented by Mr. Y, he distorts the facts so that they support his hatred of Jews, or he simply ignores them and initiates a new line of attack. The prejudiced attitude remains intact, despite the fact that the specific arguments Mr. X began with are each refuted. That is the signal that emotional reasoning is at work: It is impervious to logic or evidence. The result, as Allport observed long ago, is that "defeated intellectually, prejudice lingers emotionally" (p. 328). He meant that the emotional component of prejudice, its deep-seated negative feelings, may persist even when a person knows consciously that the prejudice is wrong.

An early pair of studies on prejudice, began by asking college students to rank and rate 20 ethnic and national groups (e.g., Argentines, Canadians, Turks). Later, the students came to the lab and were connected to a skin conductance machine to measure physiological arousal while they listened to *good* statements about their most disliked group, such as "The world will undoubtedly come to recognize them as honest, wise and completely unselfish," and *bad* statements about their most liked group, such as "They certainly can be said to have caused more trouble for humanity than they are worth." They also heard good and bad statements about two neutral groups they had ranked in the middle. Students skin conductance spiked when they heard their most disliked group complimented or their most liked group derogated compared to the equivalent statements about neutral groups. Even more interesting, in the second study, Cooper (1959) was able to predict individual student's group rankings based on how aroused they became to statements about each of the 20 groups. Thus, prejudice is such a strong attitude that it literally gets under your skin to hear someone say something nice about a group you do not like.

Stereotypes also shape our emotional reactions to different groups. Susan Fiske, Amy Cuddy, and Peter Glick (2007) argue that all group stereotypes can be classified along two universal dimensions of person perception: warmth and competence. For example, we tend to view rich people as competent but not warm and the elderly as warm but not competent, and we feel different emotions toward them as a result (see Figure 13.1). Groups that are perceived as competent but not warm are envied, whereas groups that are warm but not competent are pitied. How warm and competent groups are viewed predict people's emotional reactions to them. We admire groups that we consider to be both warm and competent (e.g., the Middle Class), and feel contempt toward groups that we view as neither warm nor competent (e.g., the homeless).

Throughout this book, we have seen that none of us is 100% reliable when it comes to processing social information that is important to us. The human mind does not tally events objectively; our emotions, needs, and self-concepts get in the way (Fine, 2008; Gilovich, 1991; Westen et al., 2006). That is why a prejudice—a blend of a stereotype and emotional "heat" toward a particular group—is so hard to change. We see only the information that confirms how right we are about "those people" and, like Mr. X, dismiss information that might require us to change our minds. What negative feelings do you hold toward some group—perhaps even in spite of your wishes not to have those feelings? (See the Try It!)

Figure 13.1 Emotional responses as a function of groups' perceived warmth and competence

Groups are generally perceived along the dimensions of warmth and competence. Based on how the stereotypes of a group fall along these dimensions, different groups elicit different emotional reactions in people.

(Adapted from Fiske, Cuddy, & Glick, 2007)

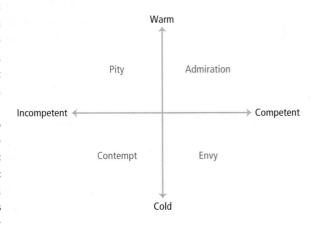

The Behavioral Component: Discrimination

Prejudice often leads to **discrimination**, which is unjust treatment of someone based solely on their membership in group. The discrimination may be obvious or subtle. In a culture that relentlessly endorses "thin is beautiful," for example, overweight people are often targets of jokes, harassment, and humiliation; they are less likely than slender people to be hired and promoted; and they are less likely to receive appropriate medical treatment from their physicians (Finkelstein, DeMuth, & Sweeney, 2007; Miller et al., 2013). This kind of discrimination has mortal consequences. Take the case of Rebecca Hiles, who first began seeking medical treatment for a cough that wouldn't go away—and sometimes came up with blood—when she was just 17. Over the next 5 years, she went to multiple doctors who all assumed the same thing: her problems were due to her weight. A doctor finally took her problems seriously and Rebecca was diagnosed with cancer. At that point, the only choice was to remove an entire lung. The surgeon later told her that she would still have her lung if she had been diagnosed 5 years earlier.

Discrimination

Unjustified negative or harmful action toward a member of a group solely because of his or her membership in that group

Try It!

Identifying Your Prejudices

Is there some group of people you "can't stand"? Who evokes the strongest prejudice in you? Is it a category defined by their looks, fashion choices, weight, age, occupation, ethnicity, religion, sexual orientation, gender, race, or even the type of music they listen to? Think about the factors that cause prejudice: Which one or ones might be contributing to your negative feelings? Think about the changes in experience and attitudes that might reduce your prejudice: What would have to happen before you could let go of it?

INSTITUTIONALIZED DISCRIMINATION We opened this chapter with many examples where discrimination was clear, but most obvious forms of discrimination in hospitals, schools, and the workplace are now illegal in America. Nonetheless, stereotypes and prejudices affect behavior in subtle ways that are difficult to document. For example, both male and female science professors at leading universities were contacted and asked to evaluate the applications of a student for a laboratory manager position in their labs. Although the applications were identical except for a randomly assigned male or female name, professors thought the male applicant was significantly more competent than the female applicant. They were more willing to hire him, and they offered him a higher starting salary and more career mentoring than they offered the female (Moss-Racusin et al., 2012).

As a result of hiring discrimination, people resort to strategies that minimize their social identities. The process of "whitening" a résumé is when a non-White person removes references to their ethnicity in their résumé, like removing any awards given by a cultural organization. Sadly, this stripping of one's social identity may be effective: In a massive study, Whitened and non-Whitened résumés of fictitious Black and Asian college graduates were sent to 1600 job ads posted to major career sites over the summer of 2015. The applications with Whitened résumés were twice as likely to receive a callback as applications with non-Whitened résumés (Kang, DeCelles, Tilcsik, & Jun, 2016). Despite the widespread perception that affirmative action has given an advantage to Black job candidates, especially those who are college graduates, studies show that they remain at a disadvantage in tough economic times.

Discrimination appears institutionalized in our criminal justice system, too. Consider the fact that our national "war against drugs," which began in the 1980s, has perhaps done tremendous social and economic harm to the Black community. Legal scholar Michelle Alexander in her book *The New Jim Crow* (2012) has called the mass incarceration of Black men based in large part on the war on drugs as the newest form of legal segregation. Across the country, relative to their numbers in the general population and among drug offenders, African Americans are disproportionately arrested, convicted, and incarcerated on drug charges (Blow, 2011). A typical illustration comes from a study in Seattle, which is 70% White. The great majority of those who use or sell serious drugs are White, yet almost two-thirds of those who are arrested are Black. Whites constitute the majority of those who use or sell methamphetamine, ecstasy, powder cocaine, and heroin; Blacks are the majority of those who use or sell crack. But the police virtually ignore the White market and concentrate on crack arrests. The researchers said they could not find a "racially neutral" explanation for this difference. The focus on crack offenders did not appear to be related to the frequency of crack transactions compared to other drugs, public safety or health concerns, crime rates, or citizen complaints. The researchers concluded that the police department's drug enforcement efforts reflect the unconscious impact of race on official perceptions of who is the cause of the city's drug problem (Beckett, Nyrop, & Pfingst, 2006).

One unobtrusive measure of social distance and "microaggressions" is to notice how people respond, nonverbally, to people with disabilities.

EVERYDAY DISCRIMINATION However, discrimination is not limited to major life events. Discrimination can subtly occur through *microaggressions*, defined as the "slights, indignities, and put-downs" that many minorities routinely encounter (Dovidio, Pagotto, & Hebl, 2011; Nadal et al., 2011; Sue, 2010). Derald Sue (2010) offers these examples: A White professor compliments an Asian American graduate student on his "excellent English," although the student has lived in the United States his whole life. Employers spend less time interviewing people they are uncomfortable with, making less eye contact and being less verbally positive (Hebl et al., 2002).

FROM PREJUDICE TO DISCRIMINATION One evening shortly after Independence Day 2016 in Minneapolis, a Black couple, Philando Castile and Diamond Reynolds, and her 4-year-old daughter were stopped in their car by Officer Jeronimo Yanez. Castile declared to Yanez he had a permitted gun in the car and 6 seconds later the officer shot seven times into the car, killing Castile. An audio recording captured Castile repeatedly telling Yanez he was not reaching for his gun, while Yanez is yelling at Castile not to touch it. Yanez told everyone later that he felt afraid when he thought Castile was reaching for the gun. He began yelling at Reynolds to not touch the gun, at which point, she began using Facebook Live to stream what was happening. Millions of people watched the horrifying and utterly sad aftermath of the shooting. Yanez was charged with second-degree manslaughter and endangering Reynolds and her daughter by firing into the car, but he was acquitted on all charges less than 1 year after the shooting. Yanez' defense hinged on the fear he felt in the moment.

This image shows the forensic team investigating the car where Philando Castile was killed. Castile is part of a tragic ongoing pattern of Black males being killed because their shooters claimed to have perceived them as dangerous. Research on implicit bias and discrimination is relevant to the effort to understand and prevent such tragedies.

At the end of the day, justice for Castile boiled down to what Yanez *felt* instead of the officer's objective level of danger. This is where prejudice turns into the deadliest form of discrimination. Research has shown that White Americans attribute some "super human" qualities to African Americans, such as exceptional strength (Waytz, Hoffman, & Trawalter, 2014). When making snap judgements of the danger of a moment, this set of beliefs weighs in. Moreover, police officers are often forced to make quick decisions under conditions of extreme stress and have little time to stop and analyze whether someone poses a threat, requiring them to rely on the faster, association-based thinking of stereotypes. Is that person reaching for an ID or a gun? Is the decision to open fire influenced by the victim's race? Would the officer have acted any differently if Castile had been White? In 2015, police shot five times as many unarmed Black people as unarmed White people.

This question led researchers to try to recreate the situation in the laboratory. In one study, White participants saw videos of young men in realistic settings, such as in a park, at a train station, and on a city sidewalk (Correll et al., 2002). Half of the men were African American, and half were White. And half of the men in each group were holding a handgun, and half were holding nonthreatening objects, such as a cell phone, wallet, or camera. Participants were instructed to press a button labeled "shoot" if the man in the video had a gun and a button labeled "don't shoot" if he did not. Like a police officer, they had less than a second to make up their minds. Participants won or lost points on each round: They won 5 points for not shooting someone who did not have a gun and 10 points for shooting someone who did have a gun; they lost 20 points if they shot someone who was not holding a gun and lost 40 points if they failed to shoot someone who was holding a gun (which would be the most life-threatening situation for a police officer).

The results? The White participants were especially likely to pull the trigger when the men in the videos were Black, whether or not they were holding a gun. This "shooter bias" meant that people made relatively few errors when a Black person was actually holding a gun; it also meant, however, that they

Figure 13.2 Errors Made in "Shooting" People in a Video Game

Participants played a video game in which they were supposed to "shoot" a man if he was holding a gun and withhold fire if he was holding a harmless object, such as a cell phone. As the graph shows, players' most common error was to "shoot" an unarmed Black man.

(Adapted from Correll et al., 2002)

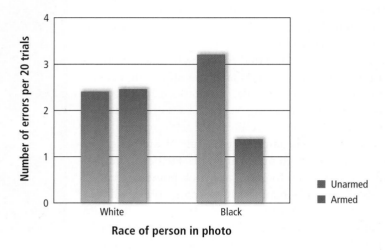

made the most errors (shooting an unarmed person) when a Black person was not holding a gun (see Figure 13.2). When the men in the picture were White, participants made about the same number of errors whether the men were armed or unarmed. When this experiment was done with police officers, the officers showed the same association between Black men and guns, taking less time to shoot an armed Black man than an armed White man, even when the background situation looked safe and unthreatening. Many variations of these experiments have replicated the basic findings (Correll et al., 2011; Ma & Correll, 2011; Plant & Peruche, 2005).

Discrimination can also be activated when a person is angered or insulted (Rogers & Prentice-Dunn, 1981). White students were told they would be inflicting electric shock on another student, the "learner," whom they were told was either White or African American, as part of an apparent study of biofeedback. The students initially gave a *lower* intensity of shock to Black learners than to White ones—reflecting a desire, perhaps, to show that they were not prejudiced. The students then overheard the learner making derogatory comments about them, which, naturally, made them angry. Now, given another opportunity to inflict electric shock, the students who were working with a Black learner administered *higher* levels of shock than did students who worked with a White learner (see Figure 13.3). The same pattern appears in studies of how English-speaking Canadians behave toward French-speaking Canadians, straights toward gays, non-Jewish students toward Jews, and men toward women (Fein & Spencer, 1997; Maass et al., 2003; Meindl & Lerner, 1985).

#BlackLivesMatter is a movement that formed after George Zimmerman was acquitted for killing 17-year-old Trayvon Martin to fight the dehumanization of Black Americans.

Figure 13.3 The Unleashing of Prejudice Against African Americans

Prejudices can be activated when people feel angry or insulted. In this experiment, White participants gave less shock to a Black "learner" than to a White learner when they were feeling fine. But once insulted, the White students gave higher levels to the Black learner.

(Adapted from Rogers & Prentice-Dunn, 1981)

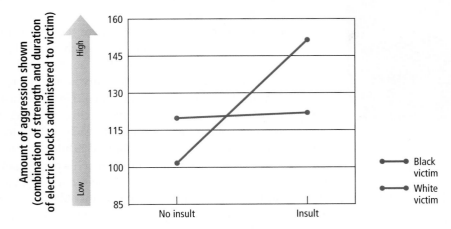

These findings suggest that prejudices often lurk just beneath the surface. It doesn't take much to activate them, and once activated, they can have tragic consequences for how we perceive and treat a particular member of an out-group.

Review Questions

1. Findings from social neuroscience suggest that
   a. it has been evolutionarily beneficial for the brain to be able to rapidly form categories.
   b. the tendency to form categories and stereotypes is determined largely by experience.
   c. people in some cultures are more likely to form stereotypes than other people.
   d. experience plays almost no role in the ability to notice different categories.

2. Suppose you're a bartender and you have a stereotype about people with full-arm tattoos: You think they are more likely to get into fights at your bar than people without tattoos. Your perception illustrates which aspect(s) of stereotypes?
   a. You are noticing people who confirm your stereotype and overlooking those who don't.
   b. You are paying attention to nonaggressive people with tattoos.
   c. You are paying attention to aggressive people without tattoos.
   d. Your stereotype is accurate.

3. *Benevolent sexism* refers to people who think that women are naturally superior to men in kindness and nurturance. What does international research show is a consequence of this belief?
   a. Women have higher self-esteem than men.
   b. Men envy women for having more positive traits than they have.

   c. It can legitimize discrimination against women and justify relegating them to traditional roles.
   d. It can cause people to overlook sexism directed against men.

4. What leads us to envy a social group?
   a. The group is stereotyped as being incompetent and not warm.
   b. The group is stereotyped as being competent but not warm.
   c. The group is stereotyped as being incompetent but warm.
   d. The group is stereotyped as being competent and warm.

5. Because the law has made most forms of discrimination in the United States illegal, the expression of prejudice
   a. has declined markedly.
   b. is more likely to be revealed in microaggressions.
   c. has not changed.
   d. can be activated when a person is under stress, angry, or frustrated.
   e. has less of an impact on minority group members.
   f. both b and d.
   g. b, d, and e.

The election of America's first Black president was an exhilarating milestone for many Americans, but it awakened prejudices in others.

Detecting Hidden Prejudices

LO 13.2 Explain how we measure prejudices that people don't want to reveal—or that they don't know they hold.

When Barack Obama was first elected president, many people hoped the nation was entering a "postracial" era, but before long it became apparent that we're not there yet. Highly prejudiced people realized that it would have been uncool to oppose him on transparently racial grounds, so their prejudice took the form of questioning his nationality and religion: He wasn't born in the United States (he was). He is a Muslim (he is Christian). He wasn't a legitimate citizen (he is). He wasn't, in short, "one of us." A study of nearly 300 students, Black and White, found that for prejudiced Whites, President Obama's perceived "non-Americanism" affected their evaluation of his performance, but not of Vice President Joe Biden's performance (Hehman, Gaertner, & Dovidio, 2011). In effect, these students could say, "I'm not prejudiced against Black people—it's just that Obama isn't really an American *and* is a lousy president." In contrast, Black students and unprejudiced White students could be either supportive or critical of Obama, but belief in his American status was irrelevant to their personal evaluation of him. Perhaps ironically, the subsequent president, Donald Trump, was a leader in the "birther" movement that insisted Obama was not a U.S. citizen.

Now, it is unclear whether it is socially acceptable to express prejudice. On the one hand, we saw Trump win the presidency while overtly expressing negative beliefs about Muslims and Mexican immigrants—among other groups. But simultaneously, we see high-profile people like Frank Artiles, the Florida state senator who resigned in April 2017 after a drunken tirade where he called his fellow state senators by racist and sexist slurs. Because of these mixed messages, some prejudiced people suppress their true feelings to avoid being labeled as racist, sexist, or homophobic by others, whereas other prejudiced people suppress their true feelings out of a genuine desire to change and be non-prejudiced (Devine et al., 2002; Plant & Devine, 2009). In either case, these people will keep their prejudices private. And some people, as we saw in Chapter 7, hold *implicit* prejudices that they might not even be aware of consciously—slight biases and rarely activated stereotypes as well as our fuzzy attitudes of a group having more "goodness" or "badness." Social psychologists have developed a variety of *implicit measures* to try to identify the prejudices that people don't want to admit—to others or to themselves (De Houwer et al., 2009).

Ways of Identifying Suppressed Prejudices

One method to identify suppressed prejudices is to send identical résumés to potential employers, varying only a name that indicates gender (e.g., John or Jennifer), implies race (a name or membership in an African American organization), mentions religious affiliation, or describes an applicant as obese (Acquisti & Fong, 2014; Agerström & Rooth, 2011; Rooth, 2010). Does the employer show bias in responding?

We saw that the answer is often yes, but this method can reveal other prejudices, too, especially when combined with social media. Today, more than a third of U.S. employers check an applicant's Facebook page or other online sources for information they would be prohibited from asking the candidate directly because of state or federal laws. One research team sent out more than 4,000 fabricated résumés to private firms across the country that had posted job openings. They then created fake Facebook pages containing information that the candidate was Muslim or Christian, or gay or straight. The researchers found incredible progress in the acceptance of gay men and lesbians: Employers did not discriminate on the basis of sexual orientation anywhere in the country. But employers in the most conservative states revealed an anti-Muslim bias: Christian applicants were much more likely to get a callback than Muslim applicants were—17% to 2.3% (Acquisti & Fong, 2014).

Because people tend to believe they can't fool a machine, another way of identifying people's explicit but suppressed prejudices calls on technology. An early version of this method was named the *bogus pipeline*. Participants were hooked up to an impressive-looking machine and told it was a kind of lie detector; actually, it was just a pile of electronic hardware that did nothing. Participants were randomly assigned to one of two conditions in which they indicated their attitudes either on a questionnaire (where it was easy to give socially correct responses) or by using the bogus pipeline (where they believed the machine would reveal their true attitudes if they lied). People expressed more racial prejudice when the bogus pipeline was used (Jones & Sigall, 1971; Roese & Jamieson, 1993; Sigall & Page, 1971). Similarly, college men and women expressed almost identically positive attitudes about women's rights and women's roles in society on a questionnaire. When the bogus pipeline was used, however, most of the men revealed their true feelings, which were far less sympathetic to women's issues (Tourangeau, Smith, & Rasinski, 1997). The bogus pipeline has also been used to reveal people's hostility toward Jews and Israel, feelings that would otherwise be masked as socially inappropriate (Cook et al., 2012).

Ways of Identifying Implicit Prejudices

The methods such as the bogus pipeline are employed based on the assumption that people know what they really feel but prefer to hide those feelings from others. But some people may harbor implicit prejudices that are hidden from themselves. Psychologists have developed several ways of measuring implicit prejudice.

One method that has garnered national and international attention is the **Implicit Association Test (IAT)**, which measures the speed of people's positive and negative associations to a target group (Banaji & Greenwald, 2013; Greenwald, McGhee, & Schwartz, 1998). Here's how it works. You sit at a computer and are shown a series of faces you must sort as quickly as you can—pressing a left key for a Black face, say, and a right key for a White face. Now you have to do the same for a series of positive or negative words—press the left key for positive words (such as *triumph, joy, honest*) and the right key for negative words (such as *devil, maggot, failure*). Once you've mastered these sorting tasks, the faces and words are combined: Now, as quickly as possible, you must press the left key when you see a Black face or a positive word and the right key when you see a White face or a negative word. You are given a rapid set of combinations: *Black + triumph, Black + poison, White + peace, White + hatred*. The key pairing then switches so that the left key is for Black faces and negative words and the right key is for White faces and positive words.

Repeatedly, people respond more quickly when White faces are paired with positive words and when Black faces are paired with negative words. That speed difference is said to be a measure of their implicit attitudes toward African Americans because it's harder for their unconscious minds to link African Americans with positive words. Versions of the IAT have been administered using many target groups, including people who are young or old, male or female, Asian or White, disabled or not, gay or straight, overweight or thin. More than 15 million people of all ages and walks of life, all over the world, have taken the test online, in school, or in their workplaces, and most learn that they hold implicit prejudices (Nosek, Greenwald, & Banaji, 2007; Miller et al., 2013).

Implicit Association Test (IAT)

A test that measures the speed with which people can pair a target face (e.g., Black or White, old or young, Asian or White) with positive or negative stimuli (e.g., the words *honest* or *evil*) reflecting unconscious (implicit) prejudices

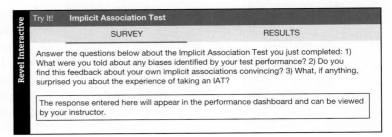

Watch MAHZARIN BANAJI ON THE IAT

The developers of the IAT, Mahzarin Banaji and Anthony Greenwald (2013), report that people are often surprised and alarmed to be told they have prejudices they are unaware of. Banaji herself, a woman of color who was born and raised in India, says that she "failed" the racial IAT, revealing anti-Black associations that she consciously repudiates. One gay activist they describe was stunned to learn that "her own mind contained stronger gay = bad associations than gay = good associations." Young people have faster reaction times to *old + bad* than to *old + good*, but the great majority of old people do also. And writer Malcolm Gladwell, who is biracial, likewise was shocked by his responses on the IAT. The researchers quote from his interview with Oprah Winfrey: "The person in my life [his mother] who I love more than almost anyone else is Black, and here I was taking a test, which said, frankly, I wasn't too crazy about Black people, you know?" (quoted in Banaji & Greenwald, 2013, p. 57).

Well, not so fast, Malcolm! The IAT could mean you are prejudiced, but it might not. Psychological scientists have debated the ambiguities surrounding interpretations of the test. If Gladwell's response to *Black + good* is a few milliseconds slower than to *Black + bad*, that could mean that he holds an unconscious (implicit) bias. But it could also mean that the IAT is not always measuring what it says it's measuring (De Houwer et al., 2009; Kinoshita & Peek-O'Leary, 2005; Rothermund & Wentura, 2004). Some psychological scientists think it simply captures a cultural association or stereotype, in the same way that people would be quicker to pair *bread + butter* than *bread + avocado*. Thus, old people may really be as biased against other old people as young people are, but it could also be that old and young share the same cultural stereotypes and associations about the elderly (Arkes & Tetlock, 2004; Olson & Fazio, 2004). Even if we adopt this interpretation, individual differences in the IAT suggest that some people hold these stereotypes more strongly than others.

One way to judge the IAT's validity is to see if a high score predicts actual behavior toward people who are elderly, overweight, transgender, or any other group. Some studies do show that the higher a person's IAT score, the more likely he or she is to discriminate against the target in some way (Green et al., 2007; Greenwald et al., 2009). For example, one study found that Whites who reveal racial bias on the IAT tend to find Blacks less trustworthy (Stanley et al., 2011), and another found that Whites with high scores don't communicate as warmly with Blacks in professional settings as they would with Whites (Cooper et al., 2012). Cancer doctors with higher IAT scores spent less time in the treatment room with Black patients and they thought Black patients had milder cancer symptoms than White patients. This differentiated behavior is not seen among oncologists with low IAT scores (Penner et al., 2016).

Typical stimuli used in the IAT to measure implicit racism.

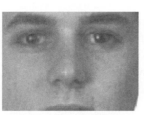

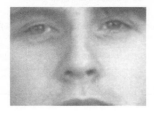

However, some people claim that the IAT measures biases that are hidden from even yourself, such that you would be surprised to hear how implicitly prejudiced you were toward different groups. To the contrary, it seems that people are "surprisingly accurate" when predicting their implicit prejudice toward five different groups on the IAT (Hahn et al., 2014). This suggests that, if the implicit bias exists, you probably know it. Thus, although it is clear that people can and do hold unconscious prejudices that govern their behavior in ways they do not always recognize (see Chapter 7), the debate over how best to identify them continues.

Review Questions

1. What is a *suppressed* prejudice?
 a. A person holds a prejudice without being aware of it.
 b. A person has a tendency to become prejudiced under the right circumstances.
 c. A person knows he or she is prejudiced but chooses not to express it in public.
 d. A person reveals a prejudice subtly, by *implying* a bias rather than saying so outright.

2. What is an *implicit* prejudice?
 a. A person holds a prejudice without being aware of it.
 b. A person has a tendency to become prejudiced under the right circumstances.
 c. A person knows he or she is prejudiced but chooses not to express it in public.
 d. A person reveals a prejudice subtly, by *implying* a bias rather than saying so outright.

3. When people are attached to a "bogus pipeline" or other technological "lie detectors," how does this affect their willingness to admit their prejudices?
 a. They are more likely admit prejudices that they would otherwise suppress.
 b. They are more likely to admit unconscious prejudices.
 c. They are less likely to admit any kind of prejudice.

 d. They are less likely to reveal sexism but more likely to reveal anti-Semitism.

4. What is one of the main problems with the Implicit Association Test?
 a. People can't respond to the pairs of associations rapidly enough.
 b. It is pretty good at identifying racism but not other kinds of prejudice.
 c. It may reflect cultural norms more than individual prejudices.
 d. It is a better test of explicit prejudice than implicit prejudice.

5. The Implicit Association Test might be measuring implicit prejudice, but what other explanations might account for the findings it produces?
 a. It is capturing cultural stereotypes rather than people's real feelings.
 b. It reflects actual associations between two traits but not necessarily prejudices.
 c. It doesn't measure speed of associations quickly enough.
 d. All of the answers are correct.
 e. Answers a and b are correct.

The Effects of Prejudice on the Victim

LO 13.3   **Describe some ways that prejudice affects its targets.**

Thus far, we have been looking at prejudice from the perspective of the perpetrator, but let's shift the focus now to the victim. A common result of being the target of prejudice is to internalize society's views of one's group as being inferior, unattractive, or incompetent. But, another common response is to reappropriate these negative stereotypes and turn them into a source of empowerment, motivation, and pride. What predicts one response or the other? Here we will discuss two kinds of self-defeating problems that can occur as a result of those internalized feelings as well as strategies that people with stigmatized identities use to be resilient in the face of stigma.

The Self-Fulfilling Prophecy

All other things being equal, if you believe that Amy is not very bright and treat her accordingly, chances are that she will not say a lot of clever things in your presence. This is the well-known **self-fulfilling prophecy**. (See Chapter 3.) How does it work? Given your belief in her low intelligence, you probably will not ask her interesting questions, and you will not listen intently while she is talking; you might even look out the window or yawn. You behave this way because of a simple expectation: Why waste energy paying attention to Amy if she is unlikely to say anything smart or interesting? Your behavior, in turn, is bound to influence Amy's behavior, for if the people she is talking to aren't paying much attention, she will feel uneasy. She will probably clam up and not come out with all the poetry and wisdom within her. Her silence then serves to confirm the belief you had about her in the first place. The circle is closed; the self-fulfilling prophecy is

Self-Fulfilling Prophecy

An expectation of one's own or another person's behavior that comes true because of the tendency of the person holding it to act in ways that bring it about.

complete. And it is complete for Amy as well: As people continue to ignore her observations, she develops a self-concept that she is stupid and boring.

Researchers demonstrated the relevance of this phenomenon to stereotyping and discrimination in an elegant experiment (Word, Zanna, & Cooper, 1974). White college undergraduates were asked to interview several job applicants, some White, some African American. The White students displayed discomfort and lack of interest when interviewing African American applicants. They sat farther away, tended to stammer, and ended the interview far sooner than when they were interviewing White applicants. Then, in a second experiment, the researchers systematically varied the behavior of the interviewers (actually their confederates) so that it coincided with the way the original interviewers had treated the African American or White interviewees in the first experiment. But in the second experiment, all of the people being interviewed were White. The researchers videotaped the proceedings and had the applicants rated by independent judges. Applicants who were interviewed the way African Americans had been interviewed in the first experiment were judged to be far more nervous and far less effective than those who were interviewed the way White applicants had originally been interviewed. Their behavior, in short, reflected the *interviewer's* expectations (see Figure 13.4).

On a societal level, the insidiousness of the self-fulfilling prophecy goes even further. Suppose that there is a general belief that a particular group is irredeemably uneducable and fit only for low-paying jobs. Why waste educational resources on them? Hence, they are given inadequate schooling and fail to acquire the skills they need for well-paying careers. Hence, they face a limited number of jobs that are available and that they can do. Thirty years later, what do you

Figure 13.4 An Experiment Demonstrating Self-Fulfilling Prophecies

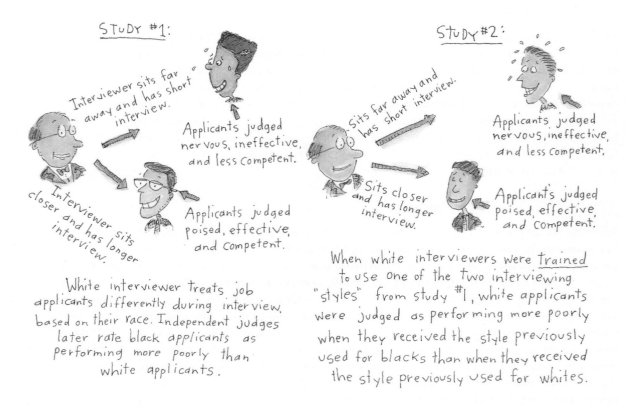

White interviewer treats job applicants differently during interview, based on their race. Independent judges later rate black applicants as performing more poorly than white applicants.

When white interviewers were trained to use one of the two interviewing "styles" from study #1, white applicants were judged as performing more poorly when they received the style previously used for blacks than when they received the style previously used for whites.

find? For the most part, members of the targeted group will be severely limited in the jobs available to them and otherwise disadvantaged compared to the rest of the population. "See? I was right all the while," says the bigot. "How fortunate that we didn't waste our precious educational resources on such people!" The self-fulfilling prophecy strikes again.

Social Identity Threat

Have you ever been talking with other people and, either because someone directly mentioned it or the conversation topic was relevant, you suddenly become hyper-aware of your group identity? You suddenly realize that the other people may view you more as a representative of your group instead of an individual. Could be to do with your race, religion, or sexual orientation, but it could also do with less "weighty" categorizations, such as your political affiliations, being part of a certain organization or sports team, or even the color of your hair. When this happens, there is a lot more weight on your shoulders to disprove negative stereotypes about your group and prove that you are a smart, well-rounded, and good-natured person. This burden uses up your cognitive resources to focus on the task at hand, which hinders your ability to show off your skills and true self.

Researchers call the feelings and behaviors elicited by knowing that you are being evaluated as a member of your group **social identity threat** (Inzlicht & Kang, 2010). This experience of being evaluated through the lens of negative stereotypes about your group used to be termed *stereotype threat* (Steele & Aronson, 1995a, b), but the experience seems to extend to any situation where you feel at risk to be devalued on the basis of your identity. Research shows that social identity threat reduces our working memory capacity (Schmader & Johns, 2003), so you do not have as many cognitive resources left to enable you to perform at your best. The extra burden of representing your whole social group creates an apprehension that interferes with your ability to perform well.

In one of their experiments, Claude Steele and Joshua Aronson administered a difficult test (the GRE) individually to African American and White students at Stanford University. Half of the students of each race were led to believe that the investigator was interested in measuring their intellectual ability. The other half were led to believe that the investigator was examining the process of test taking but didn't care about the students' abilities. The results confirmed the researchers' predictions. White students performed equally well (or poorly) regardless of whether or not they believed the test was being used as a diagnostic tool. The African American students who believed their abilities were not being measured performed as well as the White students. But the African American students who thought the test *was* measuring their abilities did not perform as well as the African Americans in the other group. The African Americans who thought the researchers were investigating test-taking performed equally well as the White students. Steele and Aronson subsequently found that one of the triggers of social identity threat is the salience of social identity: If test takers are asked to indicate their race prior to taking the test, Black students perform significantly worse than they would otherwise. This detail has no effect on the performance of White test takers.

Social identity threat is truly about whichever of your social identities is currently salient in a given situation. In some cases, you may have social identities with conflicting stereotypes. For example, would society stereotype Asian American women as being good or bad at math? On the one hand, American culture has a stereotype that men are better at math than women are, despite the fact that the sexes' math skills overlap far more than they diverge (Else-Quest, Hyde, & Linn, 2010). However, American culture also has a stereotype that Asians are better at math than non-Asians. So, how do Asian American women perform on math?

Social Identity Threat

The threat elicited when people perceive that others are evaluating them as a member of their group instead of as an individual

Whether or not you feel "social identity threat" depends on what category you are identifying with at the time. Asian women do worse on math tests when they see themselves as "women" (stereotype = poor at math) rather than as "Asians" (stereotype = good at math).

The answer depends on whether they are thinking about their ethnic identity or gender identity: Asian American women do worse on math tests when they are reminded of their gender than when they are reminded of their cultural identity (Shih, Pittinsky, & Ambady, 1999). The phenomenon applies to White males too: They performed less well on a math exam when they thought they would be compared with Asian males (Aronson, Lustina, et al., 1999).

The impact of social identity threat extends beyond the situation that triggered it. University students whose social identities were triggered subsequently exhibited less self-control in other areas—in one study they ate more unhealthy food and in another study they behaved more aggressively (Inzlicht & Kang, 2010)—because their motivation for self-control had been sapped by the experience of social identity threat. Social identity threat affects people's everyday lives, too. One study followed the daily experiences of male and female engineers for 2 weeks (10 work days). Overall, female engineers felt like their gender affected the way their colleagues interacted with them in the workplace more than male engineers. Moreover, on days when female engineers experienced more social identity threat, they also felt more burnt out and disengaged from their jobs (Hall, Schmader, & Croft, 2015).

How can the effects of social threat be reversed? Joshua Aronson and his colleagues reasoned in the following way: If thinking about a negatively stereotyped identity can harm performance, then drawing on an identity that has a counter-stereotype ought to help performance. In one experimental condition, they reminded women and men who were about to take a difficult test of spatial ability that they were students at a "selective northeastern liberal arts college." This reminder was enough to completely eliminate the male–female gap that occurred in the control condition, in which the test takers were merely reminded of the fact that they were "residents of the Northeast" (McGlone & Aronson, 2006). Similar results have been found for advanced calculus students at the university level and with middle school students on actual standardized tests (for a review, see Aronson & McGlone, 2009).

We have discussed *self-affirmation*, the practice of reminding yourself—realistically—of your good qualities or experiences that made you feel successful or proud. Self-affirmation is a counter-stereotype approach, as well. Experimental and field studies have found that thinking about important social identities other than the negatively stereotyped one can help to counteract the effects of feeling stigmatized, disrespected, or incompetent (Cohen, Purdie-Vaughns, & Garcia, 2012; Hall, Zhao, & Shafir, 2014). This practice puts poor performance in that one area into broader perspective; their worth does not depend on performance in one domain alone (Sherman et al., 2013). Even learning about social identity threat—like you are right now—is sufficient for improving test performance, because people know to attribute feelings of anxiety to the social situation instead of their abilities (Johns, Schmader, & Martens, 2005).

Now that we have described the universality and consequences of prejudice, it is time to look at some of its causes.

Watch SOCIAL IDENTITY THREAT

Revel Video

Review Questions

1. Noah's teachers don't think that Noah is very smart, so they stop paying attention to him or asking him questions. After a few years, Noah decides there is no point trying to do well in school because he's dumb. He has become a victim of
   a. the justification of effort.
   b. a self-fulfilling prophecy.
   c. implicit prejudice.
   d. stereotype threat.

2. Jenny, who is Asian American, is taking a math test. Under which of these conditions is she likely to do best?
   a. When she's made aware that women don't do as well as men at math
   b. When she's made aware that she is not at a top-notch university
   c. When she's made aware of her Asian identity
   d. Since Jenny is very good at math, none of these conditions will affect her performance.

3. What is an aspect of social identity threat?
   a. Feeling threatened by prejudices we wish we didn't have
   b. Feeling threatened by stereotypes we hold about other people

   c. Feeling threatened by people who confirm our stereotypes
   d. Feeling threatened by stereotypes that others hold of our group

4. How can test takers reduce the effects of social identity threat on their performance?
   a. By reminding themselves of their skills and good qualities
   b. By denying that stereotypes affect them
   c. By studying harder
   d. By blaming cultural prejudices in society

5. Which of these ways of thinking can reduce the power of social identity threat?
   a. Understanding that people's abilities are pretty fixed, so it's not worth being upset if you don't do well on a test
   b. Being aware that anxiety about taking tests is normal, especially for members of stigmatized groups
   c. Accepting the cultural stereotype as one that is likely to be based on actual group differences
   d. Spend 5 minutes before the test reflecting on your stigmatized group identity and how it defines you

Causes of Prejudice

LO 13.4 **Describe three aspects of social life that can cause prejudice.**

Prejudice is created and maintained by many forces in the social world. Some operate on the level of the group or institution, which demands conformity to normative standards or rules in the society. Some operate within the individual, such as in the ways we process information and assign meaning to observed events. And some forces operate on whole groups of people, such as the effects of competition, conflict, and frustration.

Pressures to Conform: Normative Rules

Most people, simply by living in a society where stereotypical information abounds and where discriminatory behavior is the norm, will develop prejudiced attitudes and behave in discriminatory ways to some extent. Under conditions of **institutional discrimination**, when companies and other institutions are legally permitted—or socially encouraged—to discriminate on the basis of race, gender, or other categories, prejudice will seem normal. If you grow up in a society where few minority group members and women have professional careers and where most people in these groups hold menial jobs, the likelihood of your developing negative attitudes about the inherent abilities of minorities and women will be increased. This will happen without anyone actively teaching you that minorities and women are inferior and without any law or decree banning minorities and women from college faculties, boardrooms, or medical schools. Instead, social barriers create a lack of opportunity for these groups that makes their success unlikely.

As social norms change, often as a result of changing laws and customs, so does prejudice. For decades, prejudice against the LGBTQ community was institutionalized in law and custom, just as segregation was. "Sodomy" (anal sex and certain

Institutional Discrimination

Practices that discriminate, legally or illegally, against a minority group by virtue of its ethnicity, gender, culture, age, sexual orientation, or other target of societal or company prejudice

Children often learn prejudice from parents and grandparents.

Normative Conformity

The tendency to go along with the group in order to fulfill the group's expectations and gain acceptance

When the mayor of Latta, South Carolina, fired 20-year force veteran Crystal Moore (below) from her position as police chief in 2014, he made little secret of the fact that it was because of her sexual orientation. But the citizens of Latta were outraged, rallying behind Chief Moore and forcing a vote on a referendum that allowed the town council to reinstate her. By reacting vocally to examples of prejudice in our immediate environment, we have the potential to create norms that combat bias.

other forms of sexual behavior, practiced by people of all sexual orientations) was against the law until the Supreme Court struck down state laws against sodomy in 2003. The 1996 Defense of Marriage Act, which had defined marriage as the union of one man and one woman, was ruled unconstitutional in 2013, and by 2017, 64% of all Americans thought same-sex marriage should be allowed (Gallup, 2017), up from only 27% in 1996. But gay marriage is a nonissue for most young people, whereas it remains highly contentious among many of their elders. Seventy-one percent of Americans younger than 35 support same-sex marriage, compared to only 38% of Americans older than age 72 (Pew Research Center, 2016).

The tendency to go along with the group to fulfill the group's expectations and gain acceptance is known as **normative conformity**. (See Chapter 8.) An understanding of normative conformity helps explain why people who hold deep prejudices might not act on them, and why people who are not prejudiced might behave in a discriminatory way: They are conforming to the norms of their social groups or institutions. A vivid example of the influence of social norms occurred in a small mining town in West Virginia many decades ago, when racial segregation was rigidly enforced: African American miners and White miners worked together with total integration while they were underground but observed the norms of total segregation while they were above ground (Minard, 1952).

Being a nonconformist is not easy; your friends might reject you, or your employer might fire you. Many people would rather go along with the prevailing view of their friends and culture rather than rock the boat. It's as if people say, "Everybody else thinks Xs are inferior; if I behave warmly toward Xs, people won't like me. They'll say bad things about me. I could lose my job. I don't need the hassle. I'll just go along with everybody else." What happens to people who think it is important to confront friends or colleagues who make racist or sexist remarks, but, when it actually happens, decide not to, preferring to go along rather than speak up? In a series of experiments, college women were put in a group allegedly to discuss group decision making; one male member (a confederate of the experimenter) repeatedly made sexist remarks. The women who valued confronting—but did not say anything when given the opportunity—later evaluated the confederate *more highly* than women who didn't care about speaking out. Moreover, the self-silencers later decided that confronting guys who make sexist remarks is less important than they originally thought: "I guess what he said wasn't that bad" (Rasinski, Geers, & Czopp, 2013). This is too bad, because people who witness someone confront prejudice later exhibit less prejudice and stereotyping (Czopp, Monteith, & Mark, 2006). In other words, confronting prejudice works. The crucial message of this research is that silence has a price: It not only affects the target of the racist or sexist remark, who mistakenly assumes everyone else in the room agrees with it, but it also affects the people who remain silent. They reduce dissonance by justifying their inaction—and thereby increasing the chance that they won't speak up in the future.

#trending

Everyday Discrimination in Professional Sports

On the evening of May 1, 2017, major league baseball fans were setting up to enjoy the opening game of a series between the Baltimore Orioles and the Boston Red Sox in Boston's historic Fenway Park. Fans were enjoying classic ballpark treats like peanuts and hot dogs, but at least one fan felt more hate than hunger. Orioles' All-Star center fielder, Adam Jones, suddenly found himself being repeatedly called racial slurs (the "n-word") and even had a bag of peanuts chucked at him. That fan was ejected from the stadium, but no assault charges were filed.

The next day, Jones spoke out about his experience, sending sports fans into a social media tailspin. In solidarity with Jones, other Black baseball players spoke out about their own experiences with racism from fans, including the Red Sox's David Price who reported being the target of racial slurs in Fenway during his first year on the team. Other baseball players were less sympathetic. Former Red Sox' pitcher, Curt Shilling, came out publicly in media interviews to say that Jones was "lying," saying "I think this is bulls***. I think this is somebody creating a situation." This is a common response to people who confront prejudice. The confronter is derogated, especially if they are a member of the targeted group. When prejudiced people witness someone confront prejudice, they tend to be irritated and antagonistic (Czopp & Monteith, 2003). It was important to Shilling to deny and dismiss Jones's experience of discrimination, and he did so by publicly attacking his credibility.

The Orioles and the Red Sox were playing again at Fenway the following night. Prior to the game, Red Sox player Mookie Betts tweeted that he wished fans would "Literally stand up for [Jones] tonight and say no to racism." That evening, as Jones stepped up to bat, the crowded stadium of fans spontaneously lept up and gave him a standing ovation. The Red Sox pitcher, Chris Sale, stepped off the pitcher's mound to allow the ovation to continue. Betts took off his hat in respect and joined in the applause. Jones said he thought the response by the Red Sox and the MLB was "tremendous" and expeditious. All the same, the pain of discrimination lingers. Despite the positive outcomes that arose from this incident, he later wrote that the incident still "breaks my heart."

Thus, people can conform to the prejudices of others and to the pressures of institutional discrimination without being prejudiced themselves, just as they can suppress their own prejudices when the norms and situation demand. But how do prejudices get "inside" us in the first place and become so difficult to eradicate?

Social Identity Theory: Us versus Them

Each of us develops a personal identity that is based on our particular personality and unique life history. But we also develop a **social identity** based on the groups we belong to, including our national, religious, political, and occupational groups (Brewer & Brown, 1998; Tajfel & Turner, 1986). Social identities give us a sense of place and position in the world. It feels good to be part of an "us." But does that mean that we must automatically feel superior to "them"? As we already saw with social identity threat, these social identities also form the basis on which others judge us.

ETHNOCENTRISM   The belief that your own culture, nation, or religion is superior to all others is called **ethnocentrism**. It is universal, probably because it aids survival by increasing people's attachment to their own group and their willingness to work on its behalf. It rests on a fundamental category: us. As soon as people have created an "us," however, they perceive everybody else as "not us." The impulse to feel suspicious of "outsiders" seems to be part of a biological survival mechanism inducing us to favor our own family, tribe, or race and to protect our tribe from external threat. But that statement doesn't go far enough, because human beings are also biologically prepared to be friendly, open, and cooperative (Cikara & Van Bavel, 2014; Kappeler & van Schaik, 2006).

Social neuroscientists investigate which parts of the brain might be involved in forming stereotypes, holding prejudiced beliefs, and feeling disgust, anger, or anxiety about an ethnic or stigmatized group (Harris & Fiske, 2006; Stanley, Phelps, & Banaji, 2008). In one study, when African Americans and Whites saw pictures of each other, activity in

Social Identity

The part of a person's self-concept that is based on his or her identification with a nation, religious or political group, occupation, or other social affiliation

Ethnocentrism

The belief that one's own ethnic group, nation, or religion is superior to all others

Dressing alike is a way of demonstrating membership in an in-group.

In-Group Bias

The tendency to favor members of one's own group and give them special preference over people who belong to other groups; the group can be temporary and trivial as well as significant

the amygdala (the brain structure associated with fear and other negative emotions) was elevated; it was not elevated when people saw pictures of members of their own group. Yet when participants were registering the faces as individuals or as part of a simple visual test rather than as members of the category "Blacks," there was no increased activation in the amygdala. The brain is designed to register differences, it appears, but any negative associations with those differences depend on context and learning (Wheeler & Fiske, 2005). That is why social psychologists strive to identify the *conditions* under which prejudice and hostility toward out-groups are fostered or reduced.

IN-GROUP BIAS Even when people have almost nothing else in common, a bond can form immediately between people who share social identities. There is a presumption that in-group members will treat you fairly. For example, investors put 10.9% more money into mutual funds managed by someone with an American-sounding last name (Kumar, Niessen-Ruenzi, & Spalt, 2015). This **in-group bias** refers to the positive feelings and special treatment we give to people we have defined as being part of our in-group; unfortunately, it often leads to unfair treatment of others merely because we have defined them as being in the out-group. Indeed, social psychologists Anthony Greenwald and Thomas Pettigrew (2014) argue that in-group bias is an even more powerful reason for discrimination than outright prejudice and hostility are. People prefer being with others who are familiar, who are similar to them in norms and customs, and whom they perceive as being "like them" in other important ways. But this bias can lead to unintended negative outcomes, such as preference for the in-group in hiring and promotion.

To get at the pure, unvarnished mechanisms behind this phenomenon, British social psychologist Henri Tajfel and his colleagues created entities called *minimal groups* (Tajfel, 1982; Tajfel & Turner, 1986). In their experiments, complete strangers are formed into groups using the most trivial criteria imaginable. For example, in one, British schoolboys were shown a set of slides with varying numbers of dots on them. The boys were asked to guess how many dots there were. The boys were arbitrarily told that they were "overestimators" or "underestimators" and were then asked to work on another task. In this phase, they had a chance to give points to other boys identified as overestimators or underestimators. Although each boy worked alone in his cubicle, almost every single one assigned far more points to boys he thought were like him, an overestimator or an underestimator. As the boys emerged from their rooms, they were asked, "Which were you?" The answers received either cheers or boos from the others.

In short, even when the reasons for differentiation are minimal, being in the in-group makes you want to win against members of the out-group and leads you to treat the latter unfairly, because such tactics build your self-esteem and feeling of "belongingness." When your group does win, it strengthens your feelings of pride and identification with that group. How do you feel about being a student of your

Watch MINIMAL GROUPS

Revel Video

university following a winning or losing football season? Robert Cialdini and his colleagues (Cialdini et al., 1976; see also Cialdini, 2009) counted the number of college insignia T-shirts and sweatshirts worn to classes on the Monday following a football game at seven different universities. The results? You guessed it: Students were more likely to wear their university's insignia after victory than after defeat. "We" won. But if our team loses, we say "they" lost.

OUT-GROUP HOMOGENEITY   Besides the in-group bias, another consequence of social categorization is the perception of **out-group homogeneity**, the belief that "they" are all alike (Linville, Fischer, & Salovey, 1989; Quattrone, 1986). In-group members tend to perceive those in the out-group as more similar to each other (homogeneous) than they really are. Does your college have a traditional rival, whether in athletics or academics? If so, as an in-group member, you probably value your institution more highly than you value the rival (thereby raising and protecting your self-esteem), and you probably perceive students at this rival school to be more alike than you perceive students at your own college to be.

Consider a study of students in two rival universities: Princeton and Rutgers. The rivalry between these institutions has long been based on athletics, academics, and even social-class consciousness (Princeton is private, and Rutgers is public). Male students at the two schools watched videotaped scenes in which three different young men were asked to make a decision, such as whether he wanted to listen to rock music or classical music while participating in an experiment on auditory perception (Quattrone & Jones, 1980). The participants were told that the man was either a Princeton or a Rutgers student, so for some of them, the student in the videotape was an in-group member and for others an out-group member. Participants had to predict what the man in the videotape would choose. After they saw the man make his choice (e.g., rock or classical music), they were asked to predict what percentage of male students at that institution would make the same choice. Did the predictions vary due to the in-group or the out-group status of the target men?

As you can see in Figure 13.5, the results support the out-group homogeneity hypothesis: When the target person was an out-group member, the participants believed his choice was more predictive of what his peers would choose than when he was an in-group member (a student at their own school). In other words, if you know something about one out-group member, you are more likely to feel you know something about all of them. Similar results have been found in a wide variety of experiments (Park & Rothbart, 1982).

BLAMING THE VICTIM   Try as they might, people who have rarely been discriminated against have a hard time fully understanding what it's like to be a target of prejudice. Well-intentioned members of the majority will sympathize with groups that are targets of discrimination, but true empathy is difficult for those who have routinely been judged on the basis of their own merit and not their racial, ethnic, religious, or other group membership. And when empathy is absent, it is hard to avoid falling into the attributional trap of **blaming the victim** for his or her plight.

Ironically, this tendency to blame victims for their victimization—attributing their predicaments to inherent deficits in their abilities and character—is typically motivated by an understandable desire to see the world as a fair and just place, one where

Out-Group Homogeneity

The perception that individuals in the out-group are more similar to each other (homogeneous) than they really are, as well as more similar than members of the in-group are

Blaming the Victim

The tendency to blame individuals (make dispositional attributions) for their victimization, typically motivated by a desire to see the world as a fair place

Figure 13.5 Judgments About In-Group and Out-Group Members

After watching a target person choose between two alternatives, Rutgers students and Princeton students had to estimate what percentage of students at their school (their in-group) versus their rival school (the out-group) would make the same choice. Students thought that out-group members were more alike, whereas they noticed variation within their own group. This "homogeneity bias" was especially pronounced among Rutgers students (blue line).

(Adapted from Quattrone & Jones, 1980)

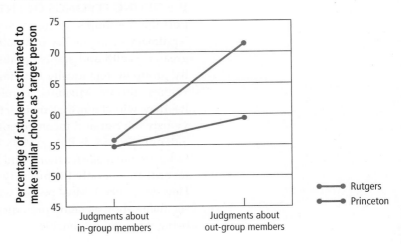

people get what they deserve and deserve what they get. (See Chapter 4.) The stronger a person's belief in a just world, the more likely he or she is to blame the poor and homeless for their own plight, or to blame overweight people for being lazy, rather than consider economic conditions, genetic predispositions, mental illness, lack of opportunities, and so forth (Crandall et al., 2001; Furnham & Gunter, 1984). Similarly, most people, when confronted with evidence of an unfair outcome that is otherwise hard to explain, find a way to blame the victim (Aguiar et al., 2008; Lerner, 1980, 1991; Lerner & Grant, 1990). In one experiment, two people worked equally hard on the same task, and by the flip of a coin, one received a sizable reward, and the other received nothing. After the fact, observers tended to reconstruct what happened and convince themselves that the unlucky person must not have worked as hard.

Most of us are good at reconstructing situations after the fact to support our belief in a just world. It simply requires making a dispositional attribution (it's the victim's fault) rather than a situational one (scary, random events can happen to anyone at any time). In a fascinating experiment, college students who were provided with a description of a young woman's friendly behavior toward a man judged that behavior as completely appropriate (Janoff-Bulman, Timko, & Carli, 1985). Another group of students was given the same description, plus the information that the encounter ended with the young woman being raped by the man. This group rated the young woman's behavior as inappropriate; she was judged as having brought the rape on herself.

How can we account for such harsh attributions? When something bad happens to another person, we will feel sorry for the person but at the same time relieved that this horrible thing didn't happen to us. We will also feel scared that such a thing might happen to us in the future. We can protect ourselves from that fear by convincing ourselves that the person must have done something to cause the tragedy. We feel safer, then, because we believe that *we* would have behaved more cautiously (Jones & Aronson, 1973).

How does the belief in a just world lead to the perpetuation of prejudice? Most of us find it frightening to think that we live in a world where people, through no fault of their own, can be discriminated against, deprived of equal pay for equal work, or denied the basic necessities of life. It is much more reassuring to believe that they brought their fates on themselves. One variation of blaming the victim is the "well-deserved reputation" excuse. It goes something like this: "If the Jews have been victimized throughout their history, they must have been doing something to deserve it." Such reasoning constitutes a demand that members of the out-group conform to more stringent standards of behavior than those the majority have set for themselves.

JUSTIFYING FEELINGS OF ENTITLEMENT AND SUPERIORITY Prejudices support the in-group's feeling of superiority, its religious or political identity, and the legitimacy of inequality in wealth, status, and power ("our group is entitled to its greater wealth and status because 'those people' are inferior"). Wherever a majority group systematically discriminates against a minority to preserve its power—Whites, Blacks, Muslims, Hindus, Japanese, Hutu, Christians, Jews, you name it—they will claim that their actions are legitimate because the minority is so obviously inferior and incompetent (Jost, Nosek, & Gosling, 2008; Morton et al., 2009; Sidanius, Pratto, & Bobo, 1996). In a series of experiments in Bangladesh, Muslims (who are the majority there) and Hindus (a minority) both revealed strong in-group favoritism, but only the majority Muslims denigrated the minority Hindus (Islam & Hewstone, 1993). Most people who are in dominant positions in their society do not see themselves as being prejudiced; they regard *their* beliefs about the out-group as being perfectly reasonable.

Christian Crandall and Amy Eshleman (2003) argue that most people struggle between their urge to express a prejudice they hold and their need to maintain a positive self-concept as someone who is not a bigot, both in their own eyes and in the eyes of others. But suppressing prejudiced impulses requires constant energy, so people are always on the lookout for information that will enable them to convince themselves that they are justified in disliking a particular out-group. Once they find that justification, they can discriminate all they want and still feel that they are not bigots (thus avoiding cognitive dissonance). Remember the experiments in which supposedly unprejudiced people administered more punishment to the out-group when they had been insulted or angered? They had a justification for their increased aggression: "I'm not a bad or prejudiced person, but he insulted me! She hurt me!" In this way, as Crandall and Eshleman (2003, p. 425) put it, "Justification undoes suppression, it provides cover, and it protects a sense of egalitarianism and a non-prejudiced self-image."

Many people justify their beliefs, including their prejudiced beliefs, by calling on religious doctrine. For example, it's not uncommon for people to defend their antigay feelings by citing the Bible, either claiming that the Bible prohibits homosexuality or that they are fighting for "family values" rather than against gays and lesbians. The problem with using the Bible in this way is that equally religious people use the Bible to support their belief in acceptance of and equality for gay men and lesbians, and many religious denominations now endorse gay marriage and approve of gay clergy. In their book *What God Has Joined Together: The Christian Case for Gay Marriage*, David Myers and Letha Scanzoni (2006) argued that there are far more verses in the Bible celebrating compassion, love, and justice than the very few that refer vaguely to homosexuality. As Gordon Allport (1954, p. 444) wrote, "The role of religion is paradoxical. It makes prejudice and it unmakes prejudice."

The Bible has been used to promote tolerance and compassion—as well as to justify and inflame many prejudices.

Realistic Conflict Theory

Finally, one of the most obvious sources of conflict and prejudice is competition—for scarce resources, for political power, and for social status. **Realistic conflict theory** holds that limited resources lead to conflict between groups and result in prejudice and discrimination (J. W. Jackson, 1993; Sherif, 1966; White, 1977). In a classic experiment, Muzafer Sherif and his colleagues (1961) tested realistic conflict theory using the natural environment of a Boy Scout camp called Robber's Cave. The participants in the camp were healthy 12-year-old boys who were randomly assigned to one of two groups, the Eagles or the Rattlers. Each group stayed in its own cabin; the cabins were located quite a distance apart to reduce contact between the two groups. The boys were placed in situations designed to increase the cohesiveness of their own group, such as going hiking and swimming, working together on building projects, and preparing group meals.

After feelings of cohesiveness developed within each group, the researchers set up a series of competitive activities in which the two groups were pitted against each other—in football, baseball, and tug-of-war, where prizes were awarded to the winning team. These competitive games aroused feelings of conflict and tension between the two groups. The investigators created other situations to further intensify the conflict: A camp party was arranged, but each group was told that it started at a different time, thereby ensuring that the Eagles would arrive well before the Rattlers. Also, the refreshments at the party consisted of two different kinds of food. Half the food was fresh, appealing, and appetizing, while the

Realistic Conflict Theory
The idea that limited resources lead to conflict between groups and result in increased prejudice and discrimination

Economic competition drives a good deal of prejudice. When unemployment rises, so does resentment against minorities.

other half was squashed, ugly, and unappetizing. As you'd expect, the early-arriving Eagles ate well, and the late-coming Rattlers were not happy with what they found. They began to curse the Eagles for being greedy. Because the Eagles believed they deserved what they got (first come, first served), they resented the name-calling and responded in kind. Name-calling escalated into food throwing, and within a short time punches were thrown and a full-scale riot ensued.

In today's economic climate, intergenerational tensions have grown due to how each generation feels resources are being allocated. Some young people are feeling resentful, believing that the old are getting more of society's benefits and opportunities than they deserve. Some older people, on the other hand, feel that all the focus is on the young. Both old and young now complain that they are victims of age discrimination (North & Fiske, 2012). Many young people complain that they are unfairly labeled as lazy and entitled by the older generations. But they too may be ageist, regarding old people as incompetent, irrelevant, stubborn, or stingy.

In his classic study of prejudice in a small industrial town, John Dollard (1938) was among the first to document the relationship between discrimination and economic competition. At first, there was no discernible hostility toward the new German immigrants who had arrived in the town; prejudice flourished, however, as jobs grew scarce. Local Whites became hostile and aggressive toward the newcomers. They began to express scornful, derogatory opinions about the Germans, to whom the native White people felt superior. "The chief element in the permission to be aggressive against the Germans," wrote Dollard, "was rivalry for jobs and status in the local woodenware plants" (pp. 25–26).

In politics, weak leaders and governments often select a minority group to use as a scapegoat—"those people are the reason for all our problems." This is an effort to unify their citizens ("us") against "them" and thereby distract everyone's attention from "our" failures to run the country (Staub, 1999). Rodrigo Duterte was elected president of the Philippines in the summer of 2016 during a surge of unemployment due to dips in oil prices. Almost immediately, he launched his #WarOnDrugs where he urged Filipino citizens to kill drug addicts. He pitted the money the state spent on caring for drug users against the money it could be spending to create jobs for the unemployed, the message being that the economy would get back on track if we simply didn't have the drug addicts. Less than a year later, it is estimated more than 7000 Filipino drug users have been murdered by police and random citizens in Duterte's #WarOnDrugs (Bueza, 2017).

Today, Mexicans are viewed in the same way the Chinese were, particularly the Mexican migrant workers whose labor is needed in many American states but who are perceived as costing American workers their jobs. As competition—real and imagined—has increased, violence against Latinos has risen as well, and Mexicans and other Latinos have become the main focus of White anger about working-class job loss. These changes in the target of a majority group's anger suggest that when times are tough and resources are scarce, in-group members will feel more threatened by the out-group. Accordingly, incidents of prejudice, discrimination, and violence toward out-group members will increase.

Review Questions

1. According to realistic conflict theory, prejudice and discrimination are likely to increase when
   a. a country has a history of racism.
   b. people who hold stereotypes about a target group are frustrated.
   c. people know that their close friends are prejudiced.
   d. people are competing for jobs and security.
   e. prejudice is explicit rather than implicit.

2. Rebecca is covering her college's football game against its arch rival for the school newspaper. At the game, she interviews six students from her college but decides she needs to interview only one student from the rival school to represent their view of the game. Rebecca is demonstrating
   a. in-group bias.
   b. out-group homogeneity.
   c. entitlement.
   d. blaming the victim.

3. Following are some explanations of prejudice that social psychologists investigate. Which one doesn't fit?
   a. Pressures to conform
   b. Ethnocentrism

   c. Realistic economic conflicts
   d. The need for catharsis
   e. Institutional discrimination

4. John knows and likes most of his Latino classmates but privately believes that his Anglo culture is superior to all others. His belief is evidence of his
   a. anti-Latino prejudice.
   b. stereotyping a minority.
   c. ethnocentrism.
   d. out-group homogeneity.

5. The Robber's Cave study created hostility between two groups of boys by
   a. putting them in competitive situations with prizes for the winners.
   b. allowing them to freely express their feelings of anger.
   c. randomly giving one group more privileges.
   d. letting the boys set their own rules and games.

Reducing Prejudice

LO 13.5   Summarize the conditions that can reduce prejudice.

Sometimes prejudice feels so ubiquitous, it is easy to find yourself questioning whether it is also inevitable. As we saw in discussing stereotypes earlier, when people are presented with an example or two that seems to refute their existing stereotype, most of them do not change their general belief. In one experiment, some people presented with this kind of disconfirming evidence actually *strengthened* their stereotypical belief because the disconfirming evidence challenged them to come up with additional reasons for holding on to their prejudice (Kunda & Oleson, 1997). Does this mean that prejudice is an essential aspect of human social interaction and will therefore always be with us? We social psychologists do not take such a pessimistic view. We tend to agree with Henry David Thoreau that "it is never too late to give up our prejudices." People can change. But how? What can we do to reduce this noxious aspect of human social behavior?

Because stereotypes and prejudice are typically based on false information, for many years social activists believed that education was the answer: All we needed to do was expose people to the truth, and their prejudices would disappear. But, as we saw earlier, this expectation proved to be naive. Because of the underlying emotional aspects of prejudice, as well as some of the cognitive ruts we get into, stereotypes based on misinformation are difficult to modify merely by providing people with the facts. But there is hope. Repeated contact with members of an out-group can modify stereotypes and prejudice (Pettigrew & Tropp, 2006). But mere contact is not enough; it must be a special kind of contact. What exactly does this mean?

After the attacks on the World Trade Center and the Pentagon on September 11, 2001, scapegoating of Muslims increased.

The Contact Hypothesis

In 1954, when the U.S. Supreme Court outlawed segregated schools, social psychologists were excited and optimistic. They believed that desegregating the schools—increasing the contact between White children and Black children—would increase the self-esteem of minority children and herald the beginning of the end of prejudice. The view that social interactions between social groups would reduce prejudice came to be called the *contact hypothesis*.

There was good reason for this optimism because empirical evidence also supported the power of contact among races (Van Laar, Levin, & Sidanius, 2008). As early as 1951, Morton Deutsch and Mary Ellen Collins examined the attitudes of White Americans toward African Americans in two public housing projects that differed in their degree of racial integration. In one, Black and White families had been randomly assigned to separate buildings in the same project. In the other project, Black and White families lived in the same building. After several months, White residents in the integrated project reported a greater positive change in their attitudes toward Black neighbors than residents of the segregated project did, even though the former had not chosen to live in an integrated building initially (Deutsch & Collins, 1951). Similarly, when White southerners joined the U.S. Army—after army units became integrated in the early 1950s—their racism gradually decreased (Pettigrew, 1958; Watson, 1950).

Today's multiethnic college campuses are a living laboratory of the contact hypothesis. White students who have roommates, friends, and relationships across racial and ethnic lines tend to become less prejudiced and find commonalities across group borders (Van Laar et al., 2008). A longitudinal study of Black and Latino students at a predominantly White university found that friendships with White students increased their feelings of belonging and reduced their feelings of dissatisfaction with the school. The effect of friendship was strongest for students who tended to expect other people to reject them for their race (Mendoza-Denton & Page-Gould, 2008) (see Figure 13.6).

The contact hypothesis has been supported by many studies in the laboratory and in the real world. Contact with other groups eases prejudice for a variety of groups, such as young people's attitudes toward the elderly, healthy people's attitudes toward the mentally ill, nondisabled children's attitudes toward the disabled, and heterosexual people's prejudices toward the LGBTQ community (Herek & Capitanio, 1996; Wilner, Walkley, & Cook, 1955). Although the effectiveness of contact varies across different groups—contact between heterosexuals and gays and lesbians has the strongest effect in decreasing prejudice whereas contact with the elderly has the weakest—more intergroup contact is nonetheless associated with decreasing prejudice in 94% of the more than 700 samples where it has been investigated (Pettigrew & Tropp, 2006). But, while the promise of the contact hypothesis for improving intergroup relations is great—some call it "our best hope" (Wright, Brody, & Aron, 2005)—there remain a number of barriers that limit its potential impact.

One problem with the classic contact hypothesis is that it requires each person to directly experience intergroup contact in order to reduce prejudice. But what if you do not have the opportunity for contact? Some people live in homogenous areas and have

Figure 13.6 The Impact of Cross-Ethnic Friendships on Minority Students' Well-Being

In a longitudinal study of minority Black students at a predominantly White university, many Black students at first felt dissatisfied and excluded from school life. But the more White friends they made, the higher their sense of belonging (orange bar) and satisfaction with the university (red bar). This finding was particularly significant for minority students who had been the most sensitive to rejection and who had felt the most anxious and insecure about being in a largely White school. The study was later replicated by creating cross-group friendships among White and Latino students at a predominantly White university.

(Based on Mendoza-Denton & Page-Gould, 2008)

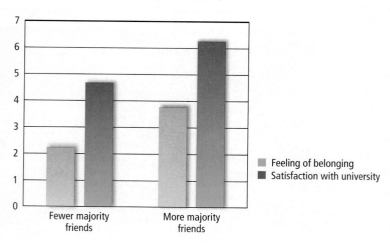

■ Feeling of belonging
■ Satisfaction with university

little exposure to people who are different from them. It turns out there are many indirect forms of contact that also predict less prejudice. The *extended contact effect* shows that simply knowing an in-group member has out-group friends is sufficient to reduce prejudice (Wright et al., 1997). Thus, if you gain a new cross-group friend, then you are helping to reduce the prejudice of all your friends. Intergroup contact can also be spread *en mass* through the media. *Media contact* occurs through the media in two ways: (a) getting emotionally connected to and invested in certain characters or celebrities from other social groups, which is called *parasocial contact*; (b) vicariously witnessing intergroup contact occur through vignettes in the news and entertainment media, which is called *vicarious contact* (Joyce & Harwood, 2012; Schiappa, Gregg & Hewes, 2005). Indirect forms of contact hold particular promise for improving prejudice at the population level.

Another problem with the contact hypothesis is that social interactions between members of different groups, termed *intergroup interaction*, tend to be characterized by mistrust and anxiety (Stephan & Stephan, 1985; Trawalter, Richeson, & Shelton, 2009). These feelings of anxiety during intergroup interactions are a core reason people avoid interacting with people of other groups (Plant & Butz, 2006). The discomfort of intergroup interaction can run deep, such that people show physiological patterns of threat when interacting with people who have stigmatized identities (Blascovich et al., 2001). But, these negative experiences may be relegated to when you are a relative intergroup novice (MacInnis & Page-Gould, 2015). People's expectations for intergroup interactions tend to be worse than intergroup interactions actually are (Mallett, Wilson, & Gilbert, 2008) and most intergroup interactions in everyday life are relatively benign (Page-Gould, 2012). With more contact, the psychological differences between intergroup interactions and in-group interactions disappear. Indeed, people with lots of intergroup contact do not show physiological threat during interracial interactions (Blascovich et al., 2001).

The biggest problem with the contact hypothesis is that, sometimes, contact can make intergroup relations more hostile and even increase prejudice (Saguy et al., 2011). Take, for example, the time of "The Troubles" in Ireland, when regular violence between Catholics and Protestants in Northern Ireland led to more than 65% of people reporting the serious injury of themselves or a loved one (Paolini et al., 2004). Especially in situations marked by extreme intergroup violence, mere contact does not seem to reduce prejudice and can even make it worse (Islam & Hewstone, 1993). However, even in these violent intergroup contexts, *high-quality contact* like cross-group friendship still predicts less prejudice and greater desire for reconciliation (Paolini et al., 2004).

What increases the quality of intergroup contact to the extent that it will improve prejudice? Allport (1954) stated that contact can reduce prejudice only when four conditions are met: both groups are of equal status; both share a common goal that generates awareness of their shared interests and common humanity; the contact involves intergroup cooperation; and their contact is supported by law or local custom (social norms). Thomas Pettigrew and Linda Tropp (2006) looked at 134 studies that included Allport's optimal conditions compared to studies that did not. True to Allport's intuition, studies that included all optimal conditions found a stronger link between contact and prejudice reduction than studies involving nonoptimal contact, but nonoptimal contact still predicted less prejudice. So, while the optimal conditions are helpful, they are not as necessary for the contact hypothesis as was once thought.

That being said, contact reliably reduces prejudice when different groups must work together to achieve a common goal. In the Robber's Cave experiment, Sherif created conditions of **interdependence**, placing the two groups of boys in situations where they needed one another to get something that was important to both sides (see Figure 13.7). One time, the investigators set up an emergency situation by damaging

Intergroup contact can occur through the media when people get personally invested in the lives of celebrities like Armenian reality TV star, Kim Kardashian West. One hundred years ago, Armenians were barred from being able to loan money or buy houses in certain neighborhoods in the United States. With tens of millions of followers on Instagram and Twitter, the *parasocial relationships* that people have with Kardashian West represent a high-quality form of intergroup contact.

Interdependence

The situation that exists when two or more groups need to depend on one another to accomplish a goal that is important to each of them

Figure 13.7 How Cooperation Fosters Intergroup Relations

When the Eagles and the Rattlers were in competition, few of the boys in each group had friends from the other side. Intergroup tensions were eased only after the boys had to cooperate to get shared privileges and the boys began to make friends across "enemy lines."

(Based on data in Sherif, Harvey, White, Hood, & Sherif, 1961)

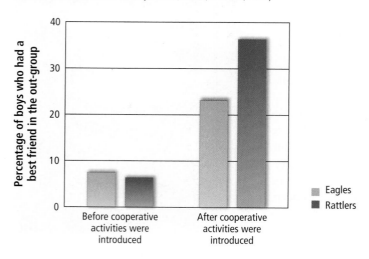

This image from the Robber's Cave experiment shows the Eagles and the Rattlers working together to pull the camp truck, using their former tug-of-war rope as an ironic touch.

the water supply system; the only way the system could be repaired was if all the Rattlers and Eagles cooperated immediately. On another occasion, the camp truck broke down while the boys were on a camping trip. To get the truck going again, it was necessary for all of them to work in harmony to pull it up a steep hill.

WHERE CONTACT CAN GO WRONG Although contact between ethnic groups is generally a good thing, the desegregation of schools did not work as smoothly as most knowledgeable people had expected. Far from producing the hoped-for harmony, school desegregation frequently led to tension and turmoil in the classroom. In his analysis of the research examining the impact of desegregation, Walter Stephan (1978) found that in 53% of studies on school desegregation, prejudice actually increased; in 34% of the studies, no change in prejudice occurred. And if you had taken an aerial photograph of the school yards of most desegregated schools, you would have found almost no integration: White kids tended to cluster with White kids, Black kids tended to cluster with Black kids, Hispanic kids tended to cluster with Hispanic kids, and so on (Aronson & Gonzalez, 1988; Aronson & Thibodeau, 1992; Schofield, 1986). Clearly, in this instance, mere contact did not work as anticipated. What went wrong? Why did desegregated housing work better than desegregated schools?

Knowing now what conditions help contact work, we can better understand the problems that occurred when schools were first desegregated. Imagine this scenario: Carlos, a Mexican American sixth grader, has been attending schools in an underprivileged neighborhood his entire life. Because the schools in his neighborhood were not well equipped or well staffed, his first 5 years of education were somewhat deficient. Suddenly, without much warning or preparation, he is bused to a school in a predominantly White, middle-class neighborhood.

As most students know from experience, the traditional classroom is a highly competitive environment. The typical scene involves the teacher asking a question; immediately, several hands go into the air as the children strive to show the teacher that they know the answer. When a teacher calls on one child, several others groan because they've missed an opportunity to show the teacher how smart they are. If the child who is called on hesitates or comes up with the wrong answer, there is a renewed and intensified flurry of hands in the air, perhaps even accompanied by whispered, derisive comments directed at the student who failed. Carlos finds he must compete against White, middle-class students who have been doing it this way all along. They are used to raising one's hand enthusiastically whenever the teacher asks a question, but Carlos has been thrust into this highly competitive situation for the first time. After a few failures, Carlos, feeling defeated, humiliated, and dispirited, stops raising his hand and can hardly wait for the bell to ring to signal the end of the school day.

How could we change the atmosphere of the classroom so that it comes closer to Allport's prescription for the effectiveness of contact? How could we get White students and minority students to be of equal status, interdependent, and in pursuit of common goals?

Cooperation and Interdependence: The Jigsaw Classroom

In 1971, Austin, Texas, desegregated its schools. Within just a few weeks, African American, White, and Mexican American children were in open conflict; fistfights broke out in the corridors and school yards. Austin's school superintendent called on Elliot Aronson, then a professor at the University of Texas, to find a way to create a more harmonious environment. After spending a few days observing the dynamics of several classrooms, Aronson and his graduate students were reminded of the situation that existed in the Robber's Cave experiment of Sherif and colleagues (1961). With the findings of that study in mind, they developed a technique that created an interdependent classroom atmosphere designed to place the students of various racial and ethnic groups in pursuit of common goals. They called it the **jigsaw classroom** because it resembled the assembling of a jigsaw puzzle (Aronson, 1978; Aronson & Bridgeman, 1979; Aronson & Gonzalez, 1988; Aronson & Patnoe, 1997; Walker & Crogan, 1998; Wolfe & Spencer, 1996).

Here is how the jigsaw classroom works: Students are placed in diverse six-person learning groups. The day's lesson is divided into six segments, and each student is assigned one segment of the written material. Thus, if the students are to learn the life of Eleanor Roosevelt, her biography is broken into six parts and distributed to the six students, each of whom has possession of a unique and vital part of the information, which, like the pieces of a jigsaw puzzle, must be put together before anyone can view the whole picture. Each student must learn his or her own section and teach it to the other members of the group, who do not have any other access to that material. Therefore, if Alicia wants to do well on the exam about the life of Eleanor Roosevelt, she must pay close attention to Carlos (who is explaining Roosevelt's girlhood years), to Shamika (who is explaining Roosevelt's years in the White House), and so on.

Unlike the traditional classroom, where students are competing against each other, the jigsaw classroom has students depending on each other. In the traditional classroom, if Carlos, because of anxiety and discomfort, is having trouble reciting, the other students can easily ignore him or put him down in their zeal to show the teacher how smart they are. But in the jigsaw classroom, if Carlos is having trouble reciting, it is now in the best interests of the other students to be patient, make encouraging comments, and even ask friendly, probing questions to make it easier for Carlos to bring forth the knowledge that only he has.

Through the jigsaw process, the children begin to pay more attention to each other and to show respect for each other. A child such as Carlos would respond to this treatment by simultaneously becoming more relaxed and more engaged; this would inevitably produce an improvement in his ability to communicate. After a couple of weeks, the other students were struck by their realization that Carlos was a lot smarter than they had thought he was. They began to like him. Carlos began to enjoy school more and began to see the White students in his group not as tormentors, but as helpful and responsible teammates. In turn, as he began to feel increasingly comfortable in class and started to gain more confidence in himself, Carlos's academic performance began to improve. As his academic performance improved, so did his self-esteem. The vicious circle had been broken; the elements that had been causing a downward spiral were changed, and the spiral moved upward.

The formal data gathered from the jigsaw experiments confirmed the observations of the experimenters and the teachers: Compared to students in traditional classrooms,

Jigsaw Classroom

A classroom setting designed to reduce prejudice and raise the self-esteem of children by placing them in small, multiethnic groups and making each child dependent on the other children in the group to learn the course material

Watch THE JIGSAW CLASSROOM

students in jigsaw groups became less prejudiced and liked their groupmates more, both within and across ethnic boundaries. Children in the jigsaw classrooms did better on exams, had higher self-esteem, and began to like school better than did the children in traditional classrooms. Finally, the jigsaw children became more truly integrated: In the school yard, there was far more intermingling among ethnic groups than on the grounds of schools using more traditional classroom techniques.

WHY DOES JIGSAW WORK? One reason for the success of this technique is that the process of participating in a cooperative group breaks down in-group versus out-group perceptions and allows the individual to develop the cognitive category of "oneness" (Gaertner et al., 1990). In addition, the cooperative strategy places people in a "favor-doing" situation. In Chapter 6, we discussed an experiment demonstrating that people who act in a way that benefits others subsequently come to feel more favorable toward the people they helped (Leippe & Eisenstadt, 1998).

Jigsaw learning produces positive outcomes for another reason: It encourages the development of empathy. In the competitive classroom, the goal is to show the teacher how smart you are. You don't have to pay much attention to the other students in your classroom. But to participate effectively in the jigsaw classroom, you have to pay close attention to whichever member of the group is reciting. In doing so, the participants learn how to approach each classmate in a way that is tailored to fit his or her special needs. Alicia may learn that Carlos is a bit shy and needs to be prodded gently, while Trang is so talkative that she might need to be reined in occasionally. Darnell can be joked with, but Peter responds only to serious suggestions.

If our analysis is sound, it should follow that working in jigsaw groups would lead to the sharpening of a child's general empathic ability, a change that will reduce the tendency to rely on stereotypes. To test this notion, Diane Bridgeman conducted a clever experiment with 10-year-old children. Just prior to her experiment, half of the children had spent 2 months participating in jigsaw classes and the other half in traditional classrooms. Bridgeman (1981) showed the children a series of cartoons aimed at testing their ability to put themselves in the shoes of the cartoon characters. In one cartoon, the first panel shows a little boy looking sad as he waves good-bye to his father at the airport. In the next panel, a letter carrier delivers a package to the boy. In the third panel, the boy opens the package, finds a toy airplane inside, and bursts into tears. Bridgeman asked the children why they thought the little boy burst into tears at the sight of the airplane. Nearly all of the children could answer correctly: because the toy airplane reminded him of how much he missed his father. Then Bridgeman asked the crucial question: "What did the letter carrier think when he saw the boy open the package and start to cry?"

The children in the control group thought that the letter carrier would know the boy was sad because the gift reminded him of his father leaving. But those who had participated in the jigsaw classroom responded differently. They had developed the ability to take the perspective of the letter carrier—to put themselves in his shoes—and they realized

When the classroom is structured so that students of various ethnic groups work together cooperatively, prejudice decreases and self-esteem increases.

Try It!

Jigsaw-Type Group Study

The next time a quiz is coming up in one of your courses, try to organize a handful of your classmates into a jigsaw-type group for purposes of studying for the quiz.

Assign each person a segment of the reading. That person is responsible for becoming the world's greatest expert on that material. That person will organize the material into a report that will be given to the rest of the group. The rest of the group will feel free to ask questions to make sure they fully understand the material. At the end of the session, ask the group members the following questions:

1. Compared to studying alone, was this more or less enjoyable?
2. Compared to studying alone, was this more or less efficient?
3. How are you feeling about each of the people in the group, compared to how you felt about them prior to the session?
4. Would you like to do this again?

You should realize that this situation is probably less influential than the jigsaw groups described in this book. Why?

---

that he would be confused at seeing the boy cry over receiving a nice present because he hadn't witnessed the farewell scene at the airport. Offhand, this might not seem important. Who cares whether kids have the ability to figure out what is in the mind of a cartoon character? We should all care. The extent to which children can develop the ability to see the world from the perspective of another human being has profound implications for empathy, generosity, and learning to get along with others (Todd et al., 2011). (To find out if the jigsaw method will benefit you, see the Try It!)

When we develop the ability to understand what another person is going through, it increases the probability that our heart will open to that person. Once our heart opens to another person, it becomes almost impossible to feel prejudice against that person, to bully that person, to humiliate that person.

THE GRADUAL SPREAD OF COOPERATIVE AND INTERDEPENDENT LEARNING The jigsaw approach was first tested in 1971; since then, educational researchers have developed a variety of similar cooperative techniques (J. Aronson, 2010; Cook, 1985; Johnson & Johnson, 1987; Slavin & Cooper, 1999). The striking results that Aronson and his colleagues obtained years ago in Austin have now been replicated in hundreds of classrooms, for children of all ages and in many regions of the country and abroad (Hänze & Berger, 2007; Jürgen-Lohmann, Borsch, & Giesen, 2001; Sharan, 1980; Walker & Crogan, 1998). This method is now generally accepted as one of the most effective ways of improving relations between ethnic groups, increasing acceptance of stigmatized individuals such as people with mental illness, building empathy, and improving instruction (Desforges et al., 1991; Deutsch, 1997; McConahay, 1981; Slavin, 1996). What began as a simple experiment in one school system is slowly becoming an important force in public education. Unfortunately, the operative word in the preceding sentence is *slowly*. The educational system, like all other bureaucracies, tends to resist change.

But it is a goal worth pursuing. It is impossible to overstate the power that a simple change in the classroom structure can have on the life of a child. Some three decades ago, Elliot Aronson, the inventor of the jigsaw classroom, received a letter from a college student. He has saved it all these years, as an eloquent reminder that under all the scientific research and statistical analyses, there are living, breathing human beings who are affected every day by prejudice and by how the social situation treats them—individuals who can rise and flourish when the classroom structure makes it possible for them to do so. Here is the letter in its entirety:

Dear Professor Aronson:

I am a senior at—University. Today I got a letter admitting me to the Harvard Law School. This may not seem odd to you, but let me tell you something. I am the 6th of 7 children my parents had—and I am the only one who ever went to college, let alone graduate, or go to law school.

By now, you are probably wondering why this stranger is writing to you and bragging to you about his achievements. Actually, I'm not a stranger although we never met. You see, last year I was taking a course in social psychology and we were using a book you wrote, *The Social Animal*, and when I read about prejudice and jigsaw it all sounded very familiar—and then, I realized that I was in that very first class you ever did jigsaw in—when I was in the 5th grade. And as I read on, it dawned on me that I was the boy that you called Carlos. And then I remembered you when you first came to our classroom and how I was scared and how I hated school and how I was so stupid and didn't know anything. And you came in—it all came back to me when I read your book—you were very tall—about 6 1/2 feet—and you had a big Black beard and you were funny and made us all laugh.

And, most important, when we started to do work in jigsaw groups, I began to realize that I wasn't really that stupid. And the kids I thought were cruel became my friends and the teacher acted friendly and nice to me and I actually began to love school, and I began to love to learn things and now I'm about to go to Harvard Law School.

You must get a lot of letters like this but I decided to write anyway because let me tell you something. My mother tells me that when I was born I almost died. I was born at home and the cord was wrapped around my neck and the midwife gave me mouth to mouth and saved my life. If she was still alive, I would write to her too, to tell her that I grew up smart and good and I'm going to law school. But she died a few years ago. I'm writing to you because, no less than her, you saved my life too.

Sincerely,
"Carlos"

Review Questions

1. Increasing contact between groups will reduce prejudice if the following conditions are met except one. Which one?
   a. Common goals
   b. Higher status of the minority group
   c. Cooperation between groups
   d. Approval of authorities

2. What strategy does the Robber's Cave study suggest for reducing hostility between groups?
   a. Sharing social norms
   b. Being together in the same environment
   c. Working together in pursuit of common goals
   d. Playing fun competitive games like tug-of-war

3. Why did early attempts at desegregation fail to reduce prejudice between ethnic groups?
   a. The students were given equal status.
   b. The classroom environments were highly competitive.
   c. The minority students didn't try hard enough to make friends.

   d. The majority students shared the same goals as the minority students.

4. What is the key feature of the jigsaw classroom?
   a. Kids of different ethnicities need each other to solve problems.
   b. Kids of different ethnicities have a chance to show their individual talents.
   c. Minority kids get to work in their own language and preferred pace.
   d. Teachers stop calling on individual students.

5. What is one of the main reasons that the jigsaw method is effective?
   a. It requires kids to behave in polite and empathic ways.
   b. It sets clear rules for good behavior.
   c. It allows kids to express their real feelings toward one another.
   d. It breaks down in-group versus out-group perceptions and stereotypes.

Summary

LO 13.1 Summarize the three components of prejudice.

- **Defining Prejudice** Prejudice is a widespread phenomenon, present in all societies of the world. What varies across societies are the particular social groups that are the victims of prejudice and the degree to which societies enable or discourage discrimination. Social psychologists define **prejudice** as a hostile or negative attitude toward a distinguishable group of people based solely on their group membership. It contains cognitive, emotional, and behavioral components.

  - **The Cognitive Component: Stereotypes** A **stereotype** is a generalization about a group of people in which identical characteristics are assigned to virtually all members of the group, regardless of actual variation among the members. A stereotype may be positive or negative, and it can be a useful, adaptive mental tool to organize the social world. However, by obliterating individual differences within a group of people, it can be come maladaptive and unfair both to the person holding the stereotype and to the target. Even positive stereotypes of a group can be limiting and demeaning to members of the stereotyped group. Modern stereotypes of gender—which can take the form of *hostile sexism* or *benevolent sexism*—justify discrimination against women and their relegation to traditional roles.

  - **The Affective Component: Emotions** The deep emotional aspect of prejudice is what makes a prejudiced person so hard to argue with; logical arguments are not effective in countering emotions. This is the reason that prejudices can linger unconsciously long after a person wishes to be rid of them. People tend to react to groups with the emotions of admiration, pity, contempt, or envy, based on the warmth and competence conveyed in stereotypes about those groups.

  - **The Behavioral Component: Discrimination** An unjustified negative or harmful action directed toward members of a group solely because of their membership in that group is a sign of **discrimination**. Examples include police focus on Black drug users rather than on the much larger number of White drug users; *institutionalized discrimination* in hiring and the justice system; and *microaggressions*, the small insults and put-downs that many members of minority groups experience. When people are stressed, angry, have suffered a blow to their self-esteem, or otherwise are not in full control of their conscious intentions, they often behave with greater aggression or hostility toward a stereotyped target than toward members of their own group.

LO 13.2 Explain how we measure prejudices that people don't want to reveal—or that they don't know they hold.

- **Detecting Hidden Prejudices** Because of a shift in normative rules about prejudice, many people have learned to hide their prejudices in situations where they might be labeled as racist, sexist, anti-Semitic, homophobic, and so on. Accordingly, researchers have developed ways to detect hidden prejudices.

  - **Ways of Identifying Suppressed Prejudices** Researchers have developed unobtrusive measures to identify suppressed prejudices, such as sending out identical résumés that vary only the applicant's name or another identifying feature to see whether employers are biased against a particular group; or using the "bogus pipeline," in which participants believe a machine is registering their real attitudes.

  - **Ways of Identifying Implicit Prejudices** A popular method of identifying unconscious (implicit) prejudices is the **Implicit Association Test (IAT)**, a measure of the speed of people's associations between a target group and negative attributes. However, controversy exists about what the IAT actually measures.

LO 13.3 Describe some ways that prejudice affects its targets.

- **The Effects of Prejudice on the Victim**

  - **The Self-Fulfilling Prophecy** The prevalence of stereotypes and prejudices can create a **self-fulfilling prophecy** both for members of the majority and for victims of prejudice.

  - **Social Identity Threat** One cause of the average difference in academic performance is **social identity threat**, the anxiety that some groups feel when a stereotype about their group is activated or they could be devalued on the basis of their social identity.

LO 13.4 Describe three aspects of social life that can cause prejudice.

- **Causes of Prejudice** Three aspects of social life that increase the likelihood of prejudice are conformity to social rules, the importance of social identities and "us-them" thinking, and realistic conflict over resources or power.

- **Pressures to Conform: Normative Rules** Institutional discrimination reflects society's norms. Normative conformity, or the desire to be accepted and fit in, leads many people to go along with stereotyped beliefs and their society's dominant prejudices and not challenge them. As norms change, so, often, does prejudice.

- **Social Identity Theory: Us versus Them** Prejudice is enabled by the human tendency to organize people into in-groups and out-groups. It begins with **ethnocentrism**, the universal human inclination to see our own groups as superior to all others, and the need for a **social identity**, the part of the self-concept based on our membership in groups that are important to us. Ethnocentrism may originally have served as a survival mechanism inducing people to favor their own families and tribes, but human beings are also biologically designed to be friendly and cooperative. Social psychologists therefore strive to identify the conditions under which intergroup prejudice is fostered or reduced. Ethnocentrism and "us-them" categorization leads to **in-group bias** (the tendency to treat members of our own group more positively than members of the out-group) and **out-group homogeneity** (the mistaken perception that "they" are all alike). One common out-group attribution is **blaming the victim** for one's own prejudices and discriminatory behavior. Blaming the victim also promotes the in-group's feelings of superiority, its religious or political identity, and the legitimacy of its power.

- **Realistic Conflict Theory** According to **realistic conflict theory**, prejudice is the inevitable by-product of real conflict between groups for limited resources, whether involving economics, power, or status. Competition for resources leads to denigration of and discrimination against the competing out-group, as happened with Chinese immigrants in

the nineteenth century and as happens with Mexican and other Latino immigrants today. Scapegoating is a process whereby frustrated and angry people tend to displace their aggression from its real source to a convenient target—an out-group that is disliked, visible, and relatively powerless.

LO 13.5 Summarize the conditions that can reduce prejudice.

- **Reducing Prejudice** Prejudice may be universal, but social psychologists have investigated many of the conditions under which intergroup hostility can be reduced and better relationships fostered. It is not enough simply to provide prejudiced people with information that they are stereotyping the out-group; they will often cling even more tightly to their beliefs.

- **The Contact Hypothesis** According to the *contact hypothesis*, the most important way to reduce prejudice between racial and ethnic groups is through contact, bringing in-group and out-group members together. Such contact has been shown to be effective in many situations, from integrating housing projects and the military to fostering friendships across ethnic lines at universities. However, mere contact is not enough and can even exacerbate existing negative attitudes. Contact is optimal when it involves intergroup cooperation, a common goal, equal status, and the contact is approved by authorities. Contact is especially effective when groups are interdependent and need each other to achieve a superordinate goal.

- **Cooperation and Interdependence:** The **Jigsaw Classroom** The **jigsaw classroom** is a form of cooperative learning in which children from different ethnic groups must cooperate in order to learn a lesson. It has been shown to improve minority students' self-esteem and performance, increase empathy, and promote intergroup friendships.

Revel Interactive

Shared Writing   **What Do You Think?**

How might college campuses combat the negative effects of social identity threat on the academic performance of some students?

Test Yourself

1. A *prejudice* is

   a. a hostile attitude toward members of a group, based solely on their membership in that group.

   b. a feeling held by members of a majority group toward members of a minority group.

   c. generally unaffected by societal events.

   d. usually acquired in childhood and lasts a lifetime.

2. A *stereotype* is

   a. the cognitive form of a prejudice.

   b. a negative impression of a group of people.

   c. always inaccurate.

   d. a cognitive summary that can be positive or negative.

3. "Hostile sexists" think women are inferior to men; "benevolent sexists" think women are superior to men. What do they have in common? Both

   a. reveal a dislike of women.

   b. legitimize discrimination against women.

   c. share an underlying admiration for women.

   d. share an underlying dislike of men.

4. When Gordon Allport said that "defeated intellectually, prejudice lingers emotionally," what did he mean?

   a. You can't argue intellectually with a prejudiced person.

   b. A prejudiced person cannot intellectually defend his or her attitude.

   c. A person's implicit prejudices may decline while explicit prejudices remain.

   d. A person's explicit prejudices may decline while implicit prejudices remain.

5. Which of the following measures of unconscious prejudice describes the IAT?

   a. A person's keeping greater distance from a member of a group he or she dislikes

   b. A person's slower associations between a target image and positive words than with negative words

   c. A person's making subtle slights and put-downs about a target person

   d. A group's ignoring the comments and contributions of its lone minority member

6. According to realistic conflict theory, what might be the major reason for the changing levels of prejudice and discrimination by White Americans toward the Chinese, Japanese, Irish, and Mexicans in American history?

   a. Competition for work and political status

   b. Degree of White familiarity with the minorities

   c. Percentage of minorities enrolled in colleges

   d. Differences in job training and skills

7. What is social identity threat?

   a. It is the fear that a concealable identity will be revealed in a social group.

   b. It is the anxiety felt by members of a stereotyped group when they are made aware of a stereotype about them.

   c. It is threats to the values and customs that comprise a person's social identity.

   d. It is when members of a minority group threaten to retaliate against the stereotypes they find unfair.

8. Which of the following describes a consequence of in-group bias?

   a. A self-fulfilling prophecy

   b. Feelings of inadequacy about our own in-group

   c. A tendency to discriminate against members of an out-group

   d. A greater vulnerability to stereotype threat

9. What is implied by the extended contact hypothesis?

   a. Intergroup contact can be broadcast to the masses through the news and entertainment media.

   b. Contact effects extend to the regional level.

   c. You will reduce prejudice among all your friends if they know you have cross-group friends.

   d. Contact must be experienced directly to be effective.

10. What is the main social psychological mechanism that makes the jigsaw classroom effective?

    a. It requires cooperation in pursuit of shared goals.

    b. It relies on ethnocentrism.

    c. It emphasizes individual achievement to demonstrate minority competence.

    d. It measures and overcomes implicit prejudices.

Social Psychology in Action 1
Using Social Psychology to Achieve a Sustainable and Happy Future

Chapter Outline and Learning Objectives

Applied Research in Social Psychology

SPA 1.1 Describe how social psychological principles can be used to improve people's lives.

Capitalizing on the Experimental Method
Social Psychology to the Rescue

Using Social Psychology to Achieve a Sustainable Future

SPA 1.2 Describe how social psychology can help people to live in a sustainable manner.

Conveying and Changing Social Norms

Keeping Track of Consumption
Introducing a Little Competitiveness
Inducing Hypocrisy
Removing Small Barriers to Achieve Big Changes

Happiness and a Sustainable Lifestyle

SPA 1.3 Describe how to apply social psychology to make people happier.

What Makes People Happy?
Do People Know What Makes Them Happy?

WHAT DO YOU THINK?

Survey	**What Do You Think?**	
SURVEY		RESULTS

Do you think that living in a way that is environmentally sustainable means giving up things that make you happy?

○ Yes

○ No

When Jankel Aleman drives to work at an electronics store in Miami, Florida, he is sure to bring along some plastic bags and rubber bands, which he uses to cover his shoes as he walks from his car to the store. Otherwise, his feet would be soaked by the sea water that often comes through drains and floods the street in front of the store. As sea levels rise flooding is increasingly common on the streets of Miami—even on sunny days—efforts are underway to prevent the city from becoming an underwater metropolis. The first phase of the project will involve raising the height of roads and installing new sewer mains and pumps, at a cost of $100 million. And that is just the beginning of fixes that are likely to cost billions of dollars (Davenport, 2014; Flechas, 2017). "We are past the point of debating the existence of climate change and are now focusing on adapting to current and future threats," said Miami's mayor, Philip Levine (Davenport, 2014).

Miami is in worse shape than other coastal cities in the United States, because it rests on porous limestone that allows sea water to bubble up through drains and into the streets. But rising sea levels threatens other cities as well. In Norfolk, Virginia, the congregation of the Unitarian Church of Norfolk became fed up with walking through water to get to church and relocated to higher ground. "I don't know many churches that have to put the tide chart on their Web site," said Reverend Jennifer Slade, which she did so that members of the congregation knew whether there would be sea water lapping at the entrance to the sanctuary (Montgomery, 2014, p. A1). The U.S. Naval Station in Norfolk is also vulnerable to rising seas and could be underwater for days if a big storm hits. The navy is already in the process of raising several of its piers at a cost of $60 million each ("On the Front Line of Rising Seas," 2016).

To review some basic facts, Planet Earth has always had a supply of "greenhouse" gases that capture heat from the sun and keep the earth warm. But ever since the Industrial Revolution in the eighteenth century, humans have been adding to these gases—chiefly carbon dioxide (CO_2), which is released when we burn fossil fuels (e.g., in power plants, factories, and automobiles). The amount of CO_2 we are now releasing far exceeds the amount that the earth can absorb naturally. As a result, global temperatures are on the rise. For example, 16 of the last 17 years have been the hottest ever recorded (Mooney, 2017). Shelf ice in Antarctica and Greenland has been melting at an alarming rate. Experts estimate that sea levels will rise several feet by the end of the century (Sheridan, 2017). Further, many scientists believe that the frequency and severity of hurricanes is getting worse because of a rise in ocean

Rising sea levels due to global warming are already impacting American cities, including Miami, Florida, and Norfolk, Virginia.

Watch THE GREAT PACIFIC GARBAGE PATCH

Watch THE GREAT PACIFIC GARBAGE PATCH

Revel Video

temperatures. By some estimates, deaths attributable to global warming have already reached 400,000 people a year—far more than have died in terrorist attacks (Leber, 2015).

Unfortunately, global warming is not the only environmental problem that human beings are causing. We are using up the world's oil, coal, fresh water, and other nonrenewable natural resources at a precipitous rate. Where to put all of our trash is another problem. As far back as 1987, a barge called the *Mobro 4000* set out from New York City in search of a place to dump its cargo of trash, because landfills in that area were overflowing. It made ports of call in North Carolina, Florida, Alabama, Mississippi, Louisiana, Mexico, Belize, and the Bahamas, but no one was willing to dump New York's trash in their landfills. Finally, after a 6,000-mile voyage, the *Mobro 4000* returned home, and local authorities convinced a landfill outside of New York City to incinerate and bury the trash. Where else is our trash going? In the 1990s, researchers discovered that a huge patch of the Pacific Ocean (an area larger than the United States, by some estimates) has become an enormous garbage dump; similar "trash vortex" areas have since been identified in other areas of the world's oceans (Lovett, 2010). The problem is that a great deal of plastic material is produced, and it is then discarded into rivers and oceans near coastlines. Because the plastic is not biodegradable, it floats along currents into the ocean, which has become the final resting place for used toothbrushes, disposable cigarette lighters, plastic bags, and umbrella handles ("Plastic oceans," 2008).

The root cause of all of these environmental problems is that there are so many of us; the worldwide human population is 7.5 billion and counting. As seen in Figure SPA-1.1, the human population was relatively constant until the Industrial

Figure SPA-1.1 The Growth of World Population

The size of the human race increased only very gradually until the Industrial Revolution in the eighteenth century. It has been growing exponentially ever since.

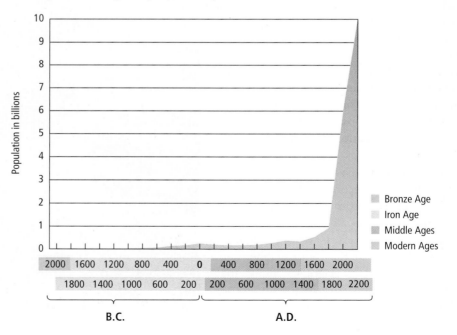

Revolution, at which point people began to reproduce like crazy. Around that time, English clergyman Thomas Malthus warned that the human population was expanding so rapidly that soon there would not be enough food to feed everyone. Malthus was wrong about when such a calamity would occur, chiefly because of technological advances in agriculture that have vastly improved grain yields. But he was right that, as the food supply has dwindled, the number of malnourished people in the world has increased. By some estimates, one out of every nine people in the world today is hungry (World Hunger, 2016). Malthus's timing may have been a little off, but many scientists fear that his predictions are becoming truer every day.

What can we do? Basically, there are three solutions: First, we can try to curb population growth. The good news is that the rate of growth has slowed in the past few decades, although the population is still rapidly expanding ("Population Growth Rate," n.d.). Second, we can hope that improved technology bails us out—such as the development of more-efficient grains and renewable energy sources including wind and solar power. Although advances are being made in these areas, they are unlikely to solve environmental problems on their own. Third, people can adopt a more sustainable lifestyle by using fewer of the world's resources. This is easier said than done, of course; no one likes to be told that they have to consume less, and entrenched habits are hard to change. But if change we must, how can we encourage people to act in more environmentally responsible ways?

By now you know that this is a classic social psychological question. In earlier chapters, we talked about how people form and change attitudes, how people are influenced by other people's behavior, the power of social norms, and so on. We turn now to a general discussion of how social psychology can be used to address social and psychological problems, followed by a specific discussion of research on how to get people to adopt more-sustainable lifestyles. Then, in the following chapters, we discuss two other major areas of applied social psychological research—namely, health and the law.

In 1987, a barge called the *Mobro 4000* left New York City in search of a place to dump its load of trash. After traveling 6,000 miles and finding no takers, it returned to New York and dumped it in an overflowing landfill outside of the city.

Mick Stevens/The New Yorker Collection/ The Cartoon Bank

Applied Research in Social Psychology

SPA 1.1 Describe how social psychological principles can be used to improve people's lives.

Since its inception, the field of social psychology has been interested in applying what it knows to solve practical problems. Kurt Lewin (1946), generally recognized as the founder of empirical social psychology, made three key points:

- Social psychological questions are best tested with the experimental method.

"Gentlemen, it's time we gave some serious thought to the effects of global warming."

- These studies can be used to understand basic psychological processes and to develop theories about social influence.
- Social psychological theories and methods can be used to address pressing social problems.

To many of us in the field, the beauty of social psychology is that by its very nature it addresses both basic and applied questions about human behavior. Research on stereotyping and prejudice, for example, investigates basic theoretical questions about the ways in which people form impressions of each other, as well as applied questions about how stereotyping and prejudice can be reduced.

As we discussed in Chapter 2, though, a distinction can still be made between *basic research* that is concerned primarily with theoretical issues and *applied research* that is concerned primarily with addressing specific real-world problems. Although much of the research we have discussed so far has touched on practical problems, it falls squarely in the category of basic research. As Kurt Lewin (1951) said, "There is nothing so practical as a good theory," by which he meant that to solve difficult social problems, we must first understand the underlying psychological dynamics of human nature and social influence. Increasingly, though, social psychologists are conducting studies designed specifically to address practical problems. In fact, social psychologists are better equipped to study applied problems than researchers in many other disciplines, for reasons we now discuss.

Capitalizing on the Experimental Method

One of the most important lessons of social psychology is the value of conducting experiments to answer questions about social influence. Nowhere is this more important than in finding ways to solve applied questions, such as getting people to reduce energy consumption. Only by conducting experiments (as opposed to observational or correlational studies; see Chapter 2) can we hope to discover which solutions will work the best.

Most people seem to understand this lesson in other domains, such as research on medical treatments. Suppose that a chemist found a new compound that seems to be an effective pain killer; the initial studies with animals look very promising, but studies with people have not yet been conducted. Should we allow a drug company to go ahead and market the drug to people? Not so fast, most of us would think. Who knows how safe the drug is for humans; it might turn out to have dangerous side effects, as seems to have been the case with the pain killer Vioxx and the psoriasis drug Raptiva. There should be extensive clinical trials in humans, in which people are randomly assigned to receive the new drug or a placebo, to see whether it really does reduce pain and whether it has any serious side effects. Indeed, federal law requires extensive testing and approval by the U.S. Food and Drug Administration (FDA) before drugs become available to the public.

We have laxer standards when it comes to testing psychological and social "treatments." If someone wants to try a new energy conservation technique, a new educational initiative, or a program to reduce prejudice, they can usually do so without a lot of rigorous testing of the intervention. A company might try a new program to reduce energy usage or institute a mandatory diversity training program, for example, before such techniques have been tested experimentally.

Well, you might think, what's the harm? Trying a new energy conservation program hardly puts people at risk, and we certainly don't want to inhibit innovation by subjecting people to cumbersome testing guidelines. And can't we find out whether these interventions work simply by interviewing people afterward or seeing whether their behavior changes (e.g., if they use less energy after the conservation program)? Unfortunately, it's not so simple. It is difficult to test the effectiveness of an intervention without a randomly assigned control group, and failing to conduct such tests can have serious consequences.

ASSESSING THE EFFECTIVENESS OF INTERVENTIONS As an example, consider a psychological intervention that has been widely implemented across the world to help people who have experienced traumatic events, such as rescue workers who witness multiple deaths in a natural disaster or plane crash. The basic idea of the program, called Critical Incident Stress Debriefing (CISD), is to bring people together as soon as possible after the trauma for a 3- to 4-hour session in which participants describe their experiences in detail and discuss their emotional reactions to the events. This cathartic experience is supposed to prevent later psychiatric symptoms, including posttraumatic stress disorder (PTSD). Numerous fire and police departments have made CISD the treatment of choice for officers who witness terrible human tragedies. It is also widely used with civilians who experience traumatic events. Following the September 11, 2001, terrorist attacks, more than 9,000 counselors rushed to New York City to help survivors deal with the trauma and stress and prevent PTSD, many using psychological debriefing techniques.

Psychological debriefing makes sense, doesn't it? An ounce of prevention is worth a pound of cure, and getting people to openly discuss their reactions to traumas rather than bottling them up seems like a good thing. "Seems like" and "really is" are not the same thing, however, and an interesting thing about CISD is that it was widely implemented before social scientists conducted rigorous tests of its effectiveness. Once they did, by randomly assigning some people to undergo CISD and others to an untreated control condition, and then giving everyone a battery of psychological measures; the results were not encouraging. In a comprehensive review of the literature, Harvard psychologist Richard McNally and his colleagues concluded that there is "no convincing evidence" that psychological debriefing techniques prevent PTSDs (McNally, Bryant, & Ehlers, 2003, p. 72).

Following the September 11, 2001, terrorists attacks, more than 9,000 counselors rushed to New York City to help survivors deal with the trauma and stress and prevent posttraumatic stress disorder. Many used a technique called Critical Incident Stress Debriefing. Was this technique adequately tested before it was widely used? Does it work or actually do harm? (See the text for the answer.)

POTENTIAL RISKS OF SOCIAL INTERVENTIONS Even if CISD doesn't work as well as people said it did, what's the big deal? Surely getting people together to talk about their experiences can't do any harm. But here's another problem with social and psychological interventions: People use common sense to assess their effectiveness, and common sense is sometimes wrong. Not only has CISD been found to be ineffective at preventing PTSD, it may in fact do harm. In one study, participants who had been severely burned and admitted to the hospital were randomly assigned to receive CISD or to be a part of a control group that did not. All participants completed various psychological measures over the next several months and were interviewed at home by a researcher who was unaware of whether they had undergone CISD. The results were sobering: Thirteen months after the intervention, the CISD group had a significantly *higher* incidence of PTSD, scored *higher* on psychological measures of anxiety and depression, and reported significantly *less* contentedness with their lives (Carlier, Voerman, & Gersons, 2000). Similar results have been found in studies testing the effectiveness of CISD with emergency workers. In their review of the literature, McNally and colleagues (2003) noted that "some evidence suggests that it [CISD] may impede natural recovery" and recommended that "for scientific and ethical reasons, professionals should cease compulsory debriefing of trauma-exposed people" (p. 72).

It turns out that right after a traumatic event, when people are experiencing considerable negative emotions, may not be the best time to focus on the event and discuss it with others. Instead, as we will see in Chapter SPA-2, people are often quite resilient when left alone (Bonanno, 2004). Forcing people to talk about and relive traumatic experiences may make them more likely to remember those experiences later (Paterson, Whittle, & Kemp, 2014). If people don't succeed in recovering on their own, they might do better to let some time pass before reliving the trauma, at a point when they have distance from it and can think about the event more objectively (Pennebaker, 2001).

Think of the consequences of implementing CISD so widely before it was adequately tested. Not only has it been a colossal waste of time, effort, and money, but also thousands of police, fire, and rescue workers have been forced to undergo a debriefing procedure that may have harmed more of them than it helped. If this were a medical intervention, there would be a huge public outcry (followed by the inevitable lawsuits).

Social Psychology to the Rescue

Social psychologists are in a unique position to find solutions to applied problems and to avoid fiascos such as the widespread use of CISD. First, the field of social psychology is a rich source of theories about human behavior that people can draw upon to devise solutions to problems. Second, and of equal importance, social psychologists know how to perform rigorous experimental tests of these solutions to see if they work (Walton, 2014; Wilson, 2011). We will see many examples of such applied research in the next two chapters. We return now to the issue with which we began this chapter: how to get people to act in ways that will help ensure a sustainable future.

Review Questions

1. Which of the following is *not* one of Kurt Lewin's three points about how social psychologists should be applying what they know to solve practical problems?
   a. Social psychological questions are best tested with the experimental method.
   b. Experimental studies can be used to understand basic psychological processes and to develop theories about social influence.
   c. Some social problems are so pressing that we should try to solve them before we have time to conduct experiments.
   d. Social psychological theories and methods can be used to address pressing social problems.

2. A team of social psychologists has designed a new intervention to get people to use less energy in their homes. Which of the following should they do?
   a. Conduct a study in which a large sample of homeowners gets the intervention to see if energy use declines over time in these homes.
   b. Conduct an experiment in which some homeowners are randomly assigned to get the intervention and other

homeowners are randomly assigned to a control group that doesn't get the intervention, and then measure the energy consumption of both groups.
   c. Given the importance of conserving energy, they should deliver the intervention to all homeowners in a particular city as soon as possible.
   d. Conduct a survey in which homeowners are asked whether they think the intervention would be effective.

3. Which of the following is true about Critical Incident Stress Debriefing (CISD)?
   a. It is a good way to help college students who have experienced a traumatic event.
   b. It is most effective when people undergo CISD as soon as possible after they have experienced a traumatic event.
   c. It is a good way to help emergency workers and first responders who have witnessed traumatic events.
   d. Not only has CISD been found to be ineffective at preventing PTSD, it may do more harm than good.

Using Social Psychology to Achieve a Sustainable Future

SPA 1.2   Describe how social psychology can help people to live in a sustainable manner.

Social psychologists have adopted a variety of approaches to get people to act in more environmentally responsible ways. The approaches were inspired by social psychological theories and used the experimental method to see if they were successful (Clayton et al., 2016; Schultz & Kaiser, 2012; Stern, 2011).

Conveying and Changing Social Norms

One approach to getting people to behave more environmentally responsibly is to remind them of social norms, the rules a group has for the acceptable behaviors, values, and beliefs of its members. As we discussed in Chapter 8, people follow two kinds of norms: *injunctive norms*, which are people's perceptions of what behaviors are approved or disapproved of by others, and *descriptive norms*, those that are people's perceptions of how people actually behave. If people believe that a certain kind of behavior is strongly frowned upon by their social group and they observe that others are obeying the norm, they are likely to follow the norm as well (Cialdini, 2012; Jacobson, Mortensen, & Cialdini, 2011).

Robert Cialdini and his colleagues have illustrated the power of social norms in encouraging people to act in environmentally friendly ways. Take littering, for example. Throwing trash on the ground may not seem to be all that serious a matter. Although billboards implore us to "keep America beautiful," many people seem to think it isn't a big deal to leave their paper cup at the side of the road instead of in a trash barrel. Unfortunately, those paper cups add up. Americans discard 51 billion pieces of trash on roadsides each year, and it costs more than $11 billion per year to clean up that litter ("Litter Prevention," n.d.).

In Chapter 8, we discussed a field experiment by Reno and his colleagues (1993) in which an experimental accomplice conveyed an injunctive norm against littering, by picking up a fast-food bag that had been discarded on the ground. The researchers hypothesized that seeing the accomplice pick up the bag would be a vivid reminder of the injunctive norm—that littering is bad and other people disapprove of it—and hence would lower people's inclination to litter. They were right; almost no one who saw the accomplice pick up the fast-food bag took a handbill that had been placed on the windshield of their car and tossed it on the ground. In a control condition, in which there was no bag on the ground and the accomplice simply walked by, 37% threw the handbill on the ground.

What is the best way to communicate *descriptive* norms against littering? The most straightforward way, it would seem, would be to clean up all the litter in an environment, to illustrate that "no one litters here." In general, this is true: The less litter there is in an environment, the less likely people are to litter (Huffman et al., 1995; Krauss, Freedman, & Whitcup, 1978; Reiter & Samuel, 1980).

There is, however, an interesting exception to this finding. Cialdini, Reno, and Kallgren (1990) figured that seeing one conspicuous piece of litter on the ground spoiling an otherwise clean environment would be a better reminder of descriptive norms than seeing a completely clean environment. The single piece of trash sticks out like a sore thumb,

"Help!"

Mick Stevens/The New Yorker Collection/ The Cartoon Bank

Figure SPA-1.2 Descriptive Norms and Littering

Who littered the least—people who saw that no one else had littered, people who saw one piece of litter on the floor, or people who saw several pieces of litter? As shown in the figure, it was people who saw one piece of litter. Seeing the single piece of litter was most likely to draw people's attention to the fact that most people had not littered, making people less likely themselves to litter.

(Based on Cialdini, Reno, & Kallgren, 1990)

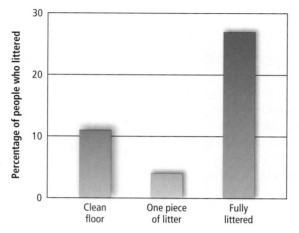

reminding people that no one has littered here except one thoughtless person. In contrast, if there is no litter on the ground, people might be less likely to think about what the descriptive norm is. Ironically, then, littering may be more likely to occur in a totally clean environment than in one containing a single piece of litter.

To test this hypothesis, the researchers stuffed students' mailboxes with handbills and then observed from a hidden vantage point how many of the students dropped the handbills on the floor (Cialdini et al., 1990). In one condition, the researchers cleaned up the mailroom so that there were no other pieces of litter to be seen. In another condition, they placed one very noticeable piece of litter on the floor—a hollowed-out piece of watermelon. In a third condition, they not only put the watermelon rind on the floor, but also spread out dozens of discarded handbills. As predicted, the lowest rate of littering occurred in the condition where there was a single piece of trash on the floor (see Figure SPA-1.2). The single violation of a descriptive norm highlighted the fact that no one had littered but the one doofus who had dropped the watermelon rind on the floor. Now that people's attention was focused on the descriptive norm against littering, virtually none of the students littered. The highest percentage of littering occurred when the floor was littered with lots of handbills; here it was clear that there was a descriptive norm in favor of littering, and many of the students followed suit.

Another way of conveying descriptive norms is simply to tell people what most others do—particularly in situations in which you can't directly observe others' behavior. If you have ever stayed in a hotel, for example, you might have seen a sign asking you to reuse your towels, because washing towels every day wastes environmental resources (e.g., water and electricity). Do these appeals work? Not as much as conveying a descriptive norm about what people *actually* do. Researchers found that the standard appeal to help the environment worked less well than one that said, "Join your fellow guests in helping to save the environment" and went on to communicate that 75% of guests reuse their towels (Baca-Motes et al., 2013; Goldstein et al., 2008; Terrier & Marfaing, 2015). The simple message that "other people do it" can be enough to get people to do the right thing (Nolan et al., 2008). See the Try It! below for an example of how you might apply this study to getting people to recycle more.

Try It!

Reducing Littering with Descriptive Norms

Can you think of ways of getting people to act in more environmentally friendly ways, based on the findings of the Goldstein et al. (2008) hotel study? For example, suppose that you decided to make a sign to put in a dormitory, urging people to recycle their bottles and cans. Based on what you have read so far, which of these signs do you think would work the best?

(a) "Help to save the environment—recycle your bottles and cans."

(b) "Join your fellow students in helping to save the environment—75% of residents of this dorm recycle their bottles and cans."

(c) "Many people in this dorm don't recycle their bottles and cans. You can do better!"

The correct answer is (b) because it conveys a descriptive norm that most people are recycling, which can motivate others to conform to that norm. Option (c) could have a negative effect, because it conveys the descriptive norm that most people *don't* recycle, and others might conform to that norm.

Clearly, drawing people's attention to both injunctive and descriptive norms can nudge them into acting in more environmentally responsible ways. But what happens when there are no norms for acting in the proper way, or even norms for behaving in the opposite manner? Suppose, for example, that you are a member of a fraternity or sorority in which many people drive gas-guzzling SUVs. Perhaps that is the vehicle of choice for you and your peers; maybe it's even a sign of status and prestige. No one likes to "break the rules," and though you might have been thinking about trading in your Jeep Grand Cherokee for a smaller car with a hybrid engine, you worry about what your friends will say.

But would it really be so bad? Sometimes people overestimate the consequences of violating an injunctive norm—in other words, how much your friends would really care if you traded in your SUV. Research shows that college students overestimate other injunctive norms, such as what their friends think about

Besides being unsightly, litter can cost millions of dollars to clean up. Social psychologists have found that emphasizing different kinds of social norms against littering is an effective way to prevent it.

drinking alcohol. Many college students believe that their peers are more in favor of drinking than they actually are (Neighbors et al., 2008; Prince & Carey, 2010). The same might be true about cars; people might not care as much as you think about what kind of car you drive.

Even if your friends would look disparagingly at your purchase of a hybrid car, someone has to be the first to change an injunctive norm. As we saw in Chapter 8, it is easier to buck the tide if we can get just one other person to go along with us, so you might first try to convince a friend who is looking to buy a car to consider a hybrid. If this doesn't work, just go for it. You might be surprised by how much you alone can change a norm, especially if you keep reminding people how much you are saving on gas and that SUVs are not nearly as safe as people think they are (Gladwell, 2005).

Keeping Track of Consumption

A problem with some types of consumption is that it is not easy for people to keep track of how much of a resource they are using—such as gas, electricity, or water. During a drought, for example, people may be asked to conserve water, but it is not easy for them to monitor how many gallons a month they are using. One pair of researchers reasoned that making it easy for people to keep track of their water consumption would make it easier for them to act on their concern for the greater good (Van Vugt & Samuelson, 1999). They compared two communities in the Hampshire region of England during a severe drought in the summer of 1995. The houses in one community had been equipped with water meters that allowed residents to monitor how much water they were consuming. The houses in the other community did not have meters. As expected, when people felt that the water shortage was severe, those in the metered houses consumed less water than those in the unmetered houses.

What if we got people to keep track of the energy they were saving, rather than the energy they were consuming? For example, what if we asked drivers to keep track of the miles they *avoided* driving, by walking, riding a bike, taking public transportation, or getting a ride with a friend? Making people more mindful of opportunities to avoid driving might make them more willing to leave their car at home. To find out, Graham, Koo, and Wilson (2011) asked college students to keep track of the number of miles they avoided driving and to record that figure on a website every other day for 2 weeks. As predicted, students who kept track of the miles they saved drove their cars less than did students in a control group who did not keep track of the miles they saved. This finding is consistent with research showing that simply keeping track of one's behavior is the first step to changing it.

Graham and colleagues (2011) also examined whether there would be an added benefit to giving the students different kinds of feedback about the miles they saved. After students entered how many miles they had avoided driving, some received feedback about how much money they had saved on gas and maintenance costs. Others received feedback about savings in air pollution (e.g., how many carbon dioxide and hydrocarbon emissions weren't emitted). Some got both kinds of feedback. It turned out that this latter group—the one that learned both how much money they had saved and how much pollution wasn't emitted—was especially likely to avoid driving their cars. Keeping track of one's behavior that avoids environmental damage and receiving concrete feedback about the savings, then, turned out to be an effective way to get college students to drive their cars less. (If you would like to try this on your own, you can download a spreadsheet with instructions how to use it at people.virginia.edu/~tdw/Driving.file.htm.)

Introducing a Little Competitiveness

Other researchers have demonstrated that a little competitiveness helps people conserve energy in the workplace (Siero et al., 1996). At one unit of a factory in the Netherlands, the employees were urged to engage in energy-saving behaviors. For example, announcements were placed in the company magazine asking people to close windows during cold weather and to turn off lights when leaving a room. In addition, the employees got weekly feedback on their behavior; graphs were posted that showed how much they had improved their energy-saving behaviors, such as how often they had turned off the lights. This intervention resulted in modest improvement. By the end of the program, for example, the number of times people left the lights on decreased by 27%.

Another unit of the factory took part in an identical program, with one difference: In addition to receiving weekly feedback on their own energy-saving actions, they got to see how the other unit was doing. The researchers hypothesized that this social comparison information would motivate people to do better than their colleagues in the other unit. As seen in Figure SPA-1.3, they were right. By the end of the program, the number of times people left lights on had decreased by 61%. Engaging people's competitive spirit can have a large impact on their behavior (Staats, Harland, & Wilke, 2004).

Inducing Hypocrisy

In many areas of the world, fresh water is becoming an increasingly scarce resource. Part of the reason is population growth in areas that have limited water supplies, such as the southwestern United States. Another cause is droughts, which are becoming increasingly frequent as the temperature of the earth rises. In 1975, 10% to 15% of the earth was drought stricken; by 2005, that figure was closer to 30% ("Drought's Growing Reach," 2005).

Figure SPA-1.3 Effects of Comparative Feedback on Energy-Saving Behaviors

Two units of a factory were urged to conserve energy and received feedback about how their unit was doing. Only one of the units, however, received comparative feedback about how it was doing relative to the other unit. As seen in the graph, this second unit improved its behavior the most, especially by turning off lights more.

(Based on Siero, Bakker, Dekker, & Van Den Burg, 1996)

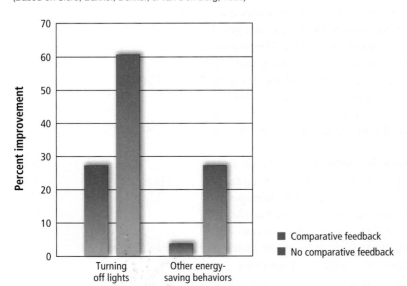

One study estimates that by the middle of this century, a third of the counties in the continental United States will be at high risk for water shortages ("Climate Change, Water, and Risk," 2010). It is thus important to find ways to encourage people to conserve water, especially when drought conditions exist.

Several years ago, when California was experiencing severe water shortages, administrators at one campus of the University of California realized that an enormous amount of water was being wasted by students using the university athletic facilities. The administrators posted signs in the shower rooms of the gymnasiums, exhorting students to conserve water by taking briefer, more efficient showers. The signs appealed to the students' conscience by urging them to take brief showers and to turn off the water while soaping up. The administrators were confident that the signs would be effective, because the vast majority of students at this campus were ecology minded and believed in preserving natural resources. However, systematic observation revealed that fewer than 15% of the students complied with the conservation message on the posted signs.

Many parts of the United States are experiencing extreme drought conditions, and many more will as global warming increases. What are some ways that social psychology can be used to increase water conservation?

The administrators were puzzled; perhaps the majority of the students hadn't paid attention to the signs. After all, a sign on the wall is easy to ignore. So they made each sign more obtrusive, putting it on a tripod at the entrance to the showers so that the students needed to walk around the sign in order to get into the shower room. Although this increased compliance slightly (19% turned off the shower while soaping up), it apparently made a great many students angry; the sign was continually being knocked over and kicked around, and a large percentage of students took inordinately long showers, apparently as a reaction against being told what to do. The sign was doing more harm than good, puzzling the administrators even more. Time to call in the social psychologists.

Elliot Aronson and his students (Dickerson et al., 1992) decided to apply a technique called "the hypocrisy procedure," which they had successfully used before to get people to increase their use of condoms (see a description of this study in Chapter 6). The procedure involved intercepting female students who were on their way from the swimming pool to the women's shower room, introducing the experimental manipulations, and then having a female research assistant casually follow them into the shower room to time their showers. Experimental manipulations in one condition asked research participants to respond to a brief questionnaire about their water use, a task designed to make them mindful of how they sometimes wasted water while showering. In another condition, research participants were asked to make a public commitment, exhorting others to take steps to conserve water. Specifically, these participants were asked to sign their names to a public poster that read, "Take shorter showers. Turn shower off while soaping up. If I can do it, so can *you*!" In this crucial condition—the "hypocrisy" condition—the participants were not only made mindful of their own wasteful behavior, but they also had to indicate publicly (on the poster) that they were practicing water conservation, even though up to this point they weren't. In short, they were made aware that they were preaching behavior they themselves were not practicing.

Just as in the condom study described in Chapter 6, those participants who were made to feel like hypocrites changed their behavior so that they could feel good about themselves. In this case, they took briefer showers than participants in the other conditions. The hypocrisy procedure has been found to increase other environmentally sound practices as well, such as recycling (Fried & Aronson, 1995).

Removing Small Barriers to Achieve Big Changes

Sometimes the best way to change people's behavior is simply to make it easy for them to do so. Consider recycling. Many cities encourage their residents to recycle, and we all know recycling reduces waste. But as you know, it can be inconvenient to do so; in some areas, you have to load your car with boxes of cans and bottles and drop them off at a recycling center, which might be several miles from your house. Other cities have curbside recycling, whereby a truck picks up recycling materials that you set out at the curb on a designated day, but you often have to separate your cans, bottles, and paper products from the rest of the trash. We thus have a classic *social dilemma*, which as we saw in Chapter 9, is a conflict in which the easiest action for an individual (in this case, not bothering to recycle) will, if chosen by most people, have harmful effects on everyone. As you might imagine, several social psychologists have turned their attention to ways of getting people to recycle more.

There have been two general approaches to this problem. First, some psychologists have focused on changing people's attitudes (namely in a pro-environment direction), because doing so often leads to changes in behavior (e.g., recycling more; see Chapter 7). Several studies have found that people's attitudes toward recycling are in fact good predictors of their recycling behaviors, suggesting that a mass media campaign that targets people's attitudes is a good way to go (Knussen, Yule, & MacKenzie, 2004; Oskamp et al., 1998; Schwab, Harton, & Cullum, 2014).

Sometimes, however, we fail to act consistently with our attitudes, despite our best intentions. Perhaps the recycling center is too far away or we just can't find the time to sort our trash, even though we know we should. Kurt Lewin (1947), one of the founders of social psychology, made the observation that big social changes can sometimes occur by removing small barriers from people's environments (Ross & Nisbett, 1991). When it comes to recycling, it might be better simply to make it hassle free, such as instituting curbside recycling, than to try to change people's attitudes toward the environment. A number of studies have found this to be true. Increasing the number of recycling bins in a community, instituting curbside recycling, and allowing residents to mix materials instead of having to sort them have all been found to increase people's recycling behaviors (Domina & Koch, 2002; Ludwig, Gray, & Rowell, 1998; Schultz, Oskamp, & Mainieri, 1995).

Consider a natural experiment that was conducted in Fairfax County, Virginia (Guagnano, Stern, & Dietz, 1995). Curbside recycling had recently begun in the county, but only about a quarter of the residents had received plastic bins for collecting their recyclable materials. Others had to find their own containers in which to put their bottles and cans. Now, it might seem as if this would not be much of an impediment to recycling; if people really cared about the environment, they should be able to find their own box. As Lewin argued, however, sometimes little barriers have big effects, and, indeed, the people who had the bins were much more likely to recycle.

The researchers also measured people's attitudes toward recycling, to see if those with positive attitudes were more likely to recycle than those who were not. Interestingly, people's attitudes predicted behavior only when they did *not* possess a recycling bin. When there was a barrier preventing easy compliance (e.g., people had to search through the garage to find a suitable box), only those with positive attitudes made the effort to circumvent the barrier. When there was no barrier (e.g., people had a convenient container provided by the county), attitudes did not matter as much. In this latter case, people were likely to conform even if they did not have strong pro-environmental attitudes. One study, for example, found that providing office workers with a recycling box that they could keep next to their desks dramatically increased the amount of paper they recycled (Holland, Aarts, & Langendam, 2006). The simple convenience of putting paper in a box next to their desk—as opposed to taking it to a central location—was enough to alter people's behavior. There may be, however, a downside to convenience: one study found that when a recycling bin for paper towels was placed in a public restroom, people used more paper towels. Thus, when recycling is easy people will do it, but they may also consume more of the product they are recycling (Catlin & Wang, 2013). The moral? Keep a recycling bin handy, but resist the temptation to increase consumption of recyclable products.

Of course, we can't make every behavior easy to perform. How else can we nudge people into doing the right thing? The same study found that it works to get people to form *implementation intentions*, which are people's specific plans about where, when, and how they will fulfill a goal (Gollwitzer & Oettingen, 2011). The researchers also measured the extent to which people recycled plastic cups, which had to be taken to a central location (that is, the workers did not have boxes in their offices in which they could deposit used cups). Workers in the implementation intention condition were first asked to visualize and write down exactly when, where, and how they would recycle their cups, whereas workers in a control condition were not. People in the former condition recycled nearly four times as many cups as those in the latter, suggesting that the best-laid plans of mice and men often go awry (to paraphrase the poet Robert Burns), *unless* we first visualize how we are going to make those plans come true.

Now that you have read about several approaches for changing people's behavior in ways that help the environment, you are in a position to try them out yourself.

Review Questions

1. Suppose that where you work, people often fail to recycle. In the copy room, for example, there is both a recycling box and a trash bin, and many people put used paper in the trash instead of the recycling box. Which of the following is *most* likely to get people to recycle more?
   a. Put up a sign that says, "Many of you are putting paper in the trash; please recycle it instead."
   b. Put up a sign that says, "Please recycle. We're already doing better than other units in the company, but there is room to improve."
   c. Set an example by cleaning up the copy room and putting all the paper that was in the trash bin into the recycling box.
   d. Put all the paper that was in the trash bin into the recycling box, except for one big, noticeable paper product (e.g., a poster) into the trash bin.

2. Suppose there is a drought in your area and you want to get college students living in a dorm to use less water. Which of the following is *least* likely to work?
   a. Put up signs in public areas of the dorm urging students to conserve water.
   b. Install devices that show students exactly how much water they used when they took showers.

   c. Start a competition with a neighboring dormitory to see who can conserve the most water in the next month.
   d. Ask students to complete a questionnaire that makes them mindful of times they wasted water, then ask them to sign a public poster endorsing the idea of taking shorter showers.

3. Suppose that there is a college dormitory in which it is difficult for the residents to recycle, because students have to carry their recyclable materials to a bin that is far away from the dorm. Which of the following residents of the dorm is *least* likely to recycle?
   a. Alex, who is strongly in favor of recycling.
   b. Heather, who doesn't care that much about recycling, but whose roommate agrees to take her recycling goods to the bin, if Heather will put them in a box in their room.
   c. Savannah, who is only moderately in favor of recycling and believes that most of the other students in the dorm don't care much about it either.
   d. Eugene, who is only moderately in favor of recycling, but decides to write down exactly when, where, and how he would take his recyclable materials to the bin outside the dorm.

Happiness and a Sustainable Lifestyle

SPA 1.3 **Describe how to apply social psychology to make people happier**

The research we have been discussing thus far might seem sobering or even depressing. There are lots of environmental problems, and drastic steps are necessary to prevent them. We need to cut back on our use of energy, buy less, recycle more, and in general tighten our belts. This doesn't sound like a recipe for a happy life, does it? Actually, it might be. We end this chapter on an optimistic note by discussing research showing that consumption isn't nearly as important to happiness as people often assume. It is entirely possible to adopt a sustainable lifestyle and be a very happy person (Kjell, 2011).

What Makes People Happy?

A good place to start is with the question of what makes people happy. Philosophers and psychologists have debated this question for centuries, and there is no simple answer that applies to everyone. For one thing, part of the recipe for happiness is outside of our control. Most psychologists agree, for example, that happiness is partly genetic; some of us are born with a happier temperament than are others (Lykken & Tellegen, 1996). Further, we can't control all the outside circumstances that impact our happiness, such as political upheavals or crushing environmental disasters (Inglehart & Klingemann, 2000). Nonetheless, research shows that there are things that people *can* control that influence their happiness (Diener et al., 2017). Four of the most important factors are having satisfying relationships with other people, becoming engaged in something you love, pursuing experiences more than things, and helping others.

SATISFYING RELATIONSHIPS Perhaps the best predictor of whether someone is happy is the quality of his or her social relationships. In one study, for example, extremely happy college students were compared to their less-happy peers, and the main thing that set them apart was that happy people spent more time with other people and were more satisfied with their relationships (Diener & Biswas-Diener, 2008; Diener & Seligman, 2004). Now, being a good social psychologist, you know that this is a correlational finding and that there are three possible explanations for it: Good social relationships make people happy, happy people are more likely to have good relationships, or a third variable, such as being extraverted, makes people happier and more likely to have good relationships. These possibilities are not mutually exclusive; in fact, we suspect that all three are true. But researchers generally agree that having high-quality relationships is a major source of happiness (Diener & Oishi, 2005; Kawamichi et al., 2016; Siedlecki et al., 2014).

In fact, even a brief positive interaction with a stranger can improve people's mood, as shown in a study that randomly assigned customers entering a coffee shop to one of two conditions. Half were asked to have a brief, friendly conversation with the cashier, whereas the other half were asked to minimize conversation with the cashier and make their interaction as efficient as possible (Sandstrom & Dunn, 2014). Then, as they were leaving the store, all participants completed a questionnaire on which they rated their mood and how connected they felt to other people at that moment. Those who had been asked

Very happy people are more likely to spend time with other people and are more satisfied with their relationships than are less-happy people.

to have a brief chat with the cashier were in a significantly better mood and felt more connected to other people than those who were asked to have an efficient interaction. So, the next time you are in a store or restaurant, exchange a few pleasant words with the salesperson or waitperson—you will likely feel better as a result.

FLOW: BECOMING ENGAGED IN SOMETHING YOU ENJOY Think back to a time when you worked very hard to achieve a highly valued goal and your efforts paid off. Perhaps you were on a sports team that won a championship or in an orchestra that performed a concert to rave reviews. Now think back to when you were the happiest: Was it after you achieved the goal or while you were working toward the goal? In a sport, for example, did you feel happiest when the game ended and you were the champion, or when you were playing well and your team was ahead but you didn't know for sure whether you would win? Although it can be gratifying to have our dreams come true, there is evidence that people are happier when they are working at something they enjoy and making progress (Haidt, 2006).

There are a couple of reasons for this. First, when people are working toward a goal, they are often in a highly desired state called *flow*, which occurs when people are "lost" in a task that is challenging but attainable (Csikszentmihalyi, 1997; Csikszentmihalyi & Nakamura, 2010; Harmat et al., 2016). Flow is what people feel when they are highly absorbed in a task and have the sense that they are making progress, such as when they are playing sports, engaged in creative activities such as writing, composing, or performing, or simply working on an enjoyable puzzle. Flow is such a pleasurable and absorbing state that people often lose track of how much time has passed and exactly where they are. When people achieve their goal—the game is over or they complete a work of art—the flow stops. People may be very gratified with what they have accomplished, but they are no longer "lost" in the pursuit of their goal (Keller & Bless, 2008).

Second, when people are working toward a goal but are not certain that they will obtain it, it is hard to think about anything else. The uncertainty about the outcome focuses their attention on the task, and other matters fade from view. After a goal is obtained, however, people's thoughts invariably turn to other matters—such as how much homework they have and the fact that they need to do their laundry. People usually adapt quickly to their successes, in the sense that sooner or later their accomplishment comes to seem normal, perhaps even expected, and not something that they think about all that much (Wilson & Gilbert, 2008). In short, pursuing something in an enjoyable way often makes us happier than getting it.

ACCUMULATE EXPERIENCES, NOT THINGS You may have noticed an important omission from our recipe for happiness—wealth. Surely it is the case that people who make a lot of money are happier than those who don't? Well, the story here is not as straightforward as you might think (Diener, Tay, & Oishi, 2013; Dunn, Gilbert, & Wilson, 2011; Hershfield, Mogilner, & Barnea, 2016). It is true that people who are very poor and have trouble getting food and shelter are less happy than others. After people have the basic necessities of life, however, having more money doesn't increase happiness much at all (Oishi & Gilbert, 2016; Kahneman & Deaton, 2010).

Helping others increases happiness more than does spending money on material things for ourselves.

One reason for this is that it is not material things that make people happy. In fact, people who are materialistic—those who place a high value on money and possessions—are *less* happy than people who are not as concerned with money and possessions (Banerjee & Dittmar, 2008; Tatzel, 2014). In contrast, research shows that over time, experiences make people happier than things. By "experiences" we mean activities that people engage in such as concerts, vacations, and family gatherings, as opposed to material possessions such as clothing, jewelry, cars, and electronic gadgets. People are happier when they think about past experiences they have had than when they think about material things they have purchased (Howell & Guevarra, 2013; Van Boven & Gilovich, 2003).

There are at least three reasons why experiences bring more happiness than things. First, experiences tend to bind us to other people more than do possessions; we go to concerts with other people, for example, whereas we are more likely to play with the newest electronic gadget by ourselves. And, as we saw, interactions with other people make us happy (Yamaguchi et al., 2016). Second, we are more likely to view experiences as expressions of who we truly are. That is, going to concerts and plays and movies are better ways of expressing our preferences and identities than are buying things, which makes the former more satisfying (Carter & Gilovich, 2012). Third, people derive more pleasure from anticipating an upcoming experience (e.g., looking forward to going to a concert) than they do anticipating a material purchase (Kumar, Killingsworth, & Gilovich, 2014). The moral is that there is no need to be materialistic to be happy; having nice experiences will work better.

HELPING OTHERS   Instead of having experiences or buying things, we could use our time and money to help other people—which research shows is another important ingredient of happiness. Imagine, for example, that you are walking across campus one morning when a researcher approaches you and gives you an envelope with $20 in it. She asks you to spend it on yourself by 5:00 P.M. that day, such as by buying yourself a gift or paying off a bill. Pretty nice windfall, right? What would you spend it on? Now imagine that you were randomly assigned to another condition. Here you also get $20, but the researcher asks you to spend it on someone else by 5:00 P.M., such as by taking a friend out for lunch or donating it to a charity. How would that make you feel? It turns out that when the researchers contacted people that evening and asked how happy they were, those assigned to the "spend it on others" condition were happier than those asked to spend the money on themselves (Dunn, Aknin, & Norton, 2008). Why does helping others increase happiness? One reason is that helping increases positive interactions with other people. Spending $20 on a gift for ourselves is nice but doesn't do much for our social life, whereas taking a friend out for lunch connects us more to another person. Another reason is that helping others makes us feel like good people—that is, it improves our self-image (Dunn, Aknin, & Norton, 2014). Now that you know about some ways to increase happiness, see if you can apply them to your own life in the Try It! Exercise below.

Try It!

Applying the Research to Your Own Life

This chapter describes four ways in which people can become happier. Can you apply these to your own life?

Satisfying Relationships: In what ways could you spend high-quality time with your friends and loved ones?

Flow: How could you increase the amount of time you spend on "flow" activities?

Experiences instead of Things: How could you spend more time on satisfying experiences and less on accumulating material possessions?

Helping Others: What are some concrete ways in which you could help other people?

Do People Know What Makes Them Happy?

Although each of us knows what makes us happy to some extent, research on **affective forecasting**—the extent to which people can predict the intensity and duration of their emotional reactions to future events—has found that we haven't figured it out completely (Gilbert, 2005; Gilbert & Wilson, 2007; Wilson & Gilbert, 2003). When it comes to understanding the recipe for happiness, sometimes we even get it backward.

When we talk with our undergraduate advisees about their career plans, for example, many of them mention that their goal is to make a lot of money. There is nothing wrong with wanting to achieve a comfortable lifestyle, of course. But as we have discussed, money itself does not make people happy, especially if it breeds materialism.

We also saw that one of the best predictors of happiness is having satisfying social relationships. And yet Americans are becoming increasingly isolated from each other (Putnam, 2000). In 1985, about 75% of the people surveyed said they had a close friend with whom they could talk about their problems, but by 2004, only half the people said they had such a friend (Vedantam, 2006).

In short, people often strive for things that are unlikely to make them happier (e.g., earning lots of money) and overlook things that will make them happier (e.g., spending time with close friends and loved ones). And, ironically, striving for money and more consumption is a source of many environmental problems, whereas the things that really make people happy (e.g., social relationships) are not. When it comes to achieving a sustainable lifestyle, the kinds of changes we may need to make can be done without sacrificing the things that truly make people happy.

Suppose, for example, you could choose between two lives. In Life A, you live in a huge house in the suburbs and earn $500,000 a year, which you spend on lots of nice things: beautiful furniture, expensive cars, designer clothes. The downside is that you have a long commute to a job you don't really enjoy very much. In Life B, you live in an apartment and earn $50,000 a year. You don't own a car; most days you ride your bicycle or walk the short distance to your job as a teacher. You can't wait to get to work each morning because you love what you do. You have lots of friends at work, as well as a tightly knit group of friends from college with whom you get together nearly every weekend. You have many interests and hobbies that keep you busy; you recently started taking salsa dance lessons, for example, and you volunteer with a literacy group that helps adults improve their reading skills.

These are extreme examples, of course, and you might argue that we have stacked the deck in favor of Life B (there is no reason, for example, the person in Life A couldn't take salsa lessons as well). But we hope the point is clear: Life B includes the recipe for happiness—namely, lots of satisfying social relationships, plenty of flow experiences (at work and during leisure time), and ample opportunities to help others. Life A satisfies none of these things. Further, Life A is much less sustainable than Life B in terms of the amount of resources a person living it would consume—the energy required to heat and cool the huge house, the gasoline needed to commute to work, the resources needed to produce all the consumer items the person buys. The environmental problems we face are severe, but the good news is that we can meet the challenges without sacrificing the things that make us truly happy.

Affective Forecasting

The extent to which people can predict the intensity and duration of their emotional reactions to future events

---

Review Questions

1. Chantal wins $5,000 in the lottery. Which of the following ways of spending the money will make her the happiest, according to social psychological research?
   a. Buying a new wardrobe of clothes
   b. Taking her three closest friends on a vacation in the Caribbean
   c. Buying new furniture for her apartment
   d. Buying a new TV and sound system for her apartment

2. Which of the following is true, based on social psychological research?
   a. The things that make people happy tend to be bad for the environment.

b. The more money people earn, the happier they tend to be.

c. It is possible to adopt a lifestyle that is good for the environment without sacrificing the things that make us happy.

d. The cars that people enjoy owning the most tend to get the worst gas mileage.

3. According to social psychological research, which of the following people is likely to be *least* happy?

a. Nicole, who works 60 hours a week on a tedious job and makes $300,000 a year.

b. Rasia, who mentors underprivileged teens.

c. Navin, who is passionate about his hobby and spends hours working on it.

d. Rebecca, who is very close to her family and has a tight-knit group of friends who she spends a lot of time with.

Summary

SPA 1.1 Describe how social psychological principles can be used to improve people's lives.

- **Applied Research in Social Psychology** By its very nature, social psychology addresses both basic and applied questions about human behavior. Social psychologists have conducted a good deal of applied research on important social and psychological issues, such as how people can adopt a more sustainable lifestyle.

  - **Capitalizing on the Experimental Method** One of the most important lessons of social psychology is the value of conducting experiments to answer questions about social influence. This is important when testing the effectiveness of interventions designed to solve an applied problem. Some interventions have backfired and had negative effects because they were not adequately tested.

  - **Social Psychology to the Rescue** Social psychologists are in a unique position to find solutions to applied problems. First, the field of social psychology is a rich source of theories about human behavior that people can draw upon to devise solutions to problems. Second, social psychologists know how to perform rigorous experimental tests of these solutions to see if they work.

SPA 1.2 Describe how social psychology can help people to live in a sustainable manner.

- **Using Social Psychology to Achieve a Sustainable Future** The human population is expanding at an exponential rate, with severe environmental consequences. Famine and malnutrition are spreading, natural resources are being depleted, and global warming is an alarming, immediate problem. Social psychologists have devised several approaches to encourage people to adopt a more sustainable lifestyle.

  - **Conveying and Changing Social Norms** One approach is to remind people of both *injunctive* and *descriptive* norms against environmentally damaging acts, such as littering. For example,

communicating descriptive norms—that other people act in environmentally friendly ways—has been shown to reduce the extent to which passersby litter and increase the extent to which hotel-room guests reuse their towels.

- **Keeping Track of Consumption** One simple technique is to make it easier for people to know how much energy they are using, for example, by providing them with water meters that are easy to read. College students who kept track of the number of miles they avoided driving their cars (e.g., by walking or taking the bus) drove their cars less.

- **Introducing a Little Competitiveness** Units in a company that were competing with each other to conserve energy were more successful than units that were encouraged to save but did not compete.

- **Inducing Hypocrisy** It works to arouse dissonance in people by making them feel that they are not practicing what they are preaching; for example, that even though they believe in water conservation, they are taking long showers.

- **Removing Small Barriers to Achieve Big Changes** Removing barriers that make pro-environmental behaviors difficult, such as instituting curbside recycling and providing people with recycling bins, has been shown to be effective. It also helps to get people to form implementation intentions, which are people's specific plans about where, when, and how they will fulfill a goal, such as the goal to recycle.

SPA 1.3 Describe how to apply social psychology to make people happier.

- **Happiness and a Sustainable Lifestyle** It is possible to adopt a sustainable lifestyle and be a happy person.

  - **What Makes People Happy?** Happiness is partly a matter of the temperament with which we are born and partly a matter of environmental conditions outside of our control, such as the political stability of the government. Four things we can control also influence our happiness: the quality of our social relationships, opportunities for "flow" experiences, pursuing experiences instead of things, and helping others. Further, people who are materialistic—those who place a high value on money and possessions—tend to be less happy than people who place less value on money and possessions.

- **Do People Know What Makes Them Happy?** When it comes to understanding the recipe for happiness, some people get it backward: They focus too much on wealth and materialism, and too little on social relationships, flow, and helping others. The moral is that people can achieve a sustainable lifestyle without sacrificing the things that make people truly happy.

Revel Interactive

Shared Writing   **What Do You Think?**

What kind of changes could you make in your life that would be good for the environment but have little or no impact on your happiness?

Test Yourself

1. According to what you read in this chapter, which of the following is likely to be *least* effective at solving environmental problems?

    a. Finding more-efficient ways of getting rid of the trash human beings generate.

    b. Slowing the population growth of human beings.

    c. Developing new technologies such as more-efficient grains and renewable energy sources such as wind and solar power.

    d. Getting people to adopt a more sustainable lifestyle by using fewer of the world's resources.

2. Which of the following statements is *least* true about the social psychological approach to solving applied problems?

    a. Applied questions are best tested with the experimental method.

    b. There is nothing as practical as a good theory.

    c. Social psychological theories and methods can be used to address pressing social problems.

    d. Given how pressing many problems are, it is a good idea to implement solutions before we are able to test them experimentally.

3. Meghan is a first-year college student and is trying to figure out what the norms are about dating at her school. Which of the following is the best example of an *injunctive norm*?

    a. Meghan believes that most students disapprove of people who have casual "hookups" with other people.

    b. Meghan believes that many students do hook up with other students.

    c. Meghan believes that most students do not hook up with other students.

    d. Meghan has no idea how many students hook up with other students.

4. Suppose you want people in your apartment building to stop throwing their junk mail on the floor of the mailroom. Which of the following would be *least* likely to work?

    a. Set an example by picking up the litter yourself when people are watching.

    b. Post a sign informing people that there is a recycling center on the other side of town that accepts junk mail.

    c. Clean up all the litter in the mailroom, but leave one very noticeable piece of trash on the floor.

    d. Post a sign in the mailroom that says, "Join your fellow residents in helping to keep things clean; 90% of residents recycle their junk mail."

5. Suppose you live in a dorm and want to get people who live there to act in more environmentally responsible ways, such as recycling more. Which of the following would be *least* likely to work, according to social psychological research?

    a. Measure how much the dorm recycles each month, and post graphs of these figures where everyone can see them.

    b. Set up a competition with another dorm, in which the one that recycles more each month wins free pizzas.

   c. Make a point of taking soda cans out of the trash and putting them in a recycling bin in a public area where lots of people can see you do this.

   d. Post a sign asking people to recycle more.

6. Suppose you wanted to get people to use less electricity where you work by getting them to turn off lights when they leave. Which of the following is *most* likely to succeed, based on research in social psychology?

   a. Get people to sign a public pledge that they will turn off lights when they leave.

   b. Ask people to write about times when they forgot to turn off lights when they left.

   c. Ask people to do both—sign the public pledge and write about times they didn't turn off the lights.

   d. Ask people to sign the public pledge and write about times they did turn off the lights when they left.

7. Which of the following is *least* likely to make people happy?

   a. Helping other people

   b. Having satisfying relationships with other people

   c. Earning enough money to be able to afford a lot of luxury possessions

   d. Having "flow" activities in which people become highly engaged

8. Which of the following is true about research on happiness?

   a. People have a very good idea of what will make them happy in the future.

   b. One of the best predictors of happiness is having satisfying social relationships, but Americans are becoming increasingly isolated from each other.

   c. When choosing a career, the most important thing to consider is how much money you will earn.

   d. Acting in ways that will help the environment will probably make people less happy.

Social Psychology in Action 2
Social Psychology and Health

 ## Chapter Outline and Learning Objectives

Stress and Human Health

SPA 2.1 Define stress, and describe what effect it has on our health.

Resilience

Effects of Negative Life Events

Perceived Stress and Health

Feeling in Charge: The Importance of Perceived Control

Coping with Stress

SPA 2.2 Explain how people can cope and recover after a stressful experience.

Gender Differences in Coping with Stress

Social Support: Getting Help from Others

Reframing: Finding Meaning in Traumatic Events

Prevention: Promoting Healthier Behavior

SPA 2.3 Describe how we can apply social psychology to help people live healthier lives.

Joanne Hill suffered an unimaginable amount of loss over a 4-year period. It started when her husband, Ken, died of heart failure at the age of 55. Shortly after that, Hill lost her brother, stepfather, mother, aunt, two uncles, two cousins, her cousin's partner, her stepmother, and, finally, her son, who died suddenly of a heart attack at the age of 38. Joanne helped care for several of these loved ones before they died, including her mother, who suffered from Alzheimer's and breast cancer; her brother, who died of lung cancer; and her aunt, who died of liver cancer. "Everyone I loved seemed to need help," she said (Hill, 2002, p. 21).

How could anyone endure so much loss? Surely any one of these tragedies would stop us in our tracks, and suffering so many in such a short time would surely push most of us to the breaking point, taking a toll on our physical and emotional well-being. But rather than crawl under a rock, Joanne made it through what she calls her "locust years" with strength, grace, and resilience. She was the executor of several of her relatives' estates and dealt successfully with complicated legal issues. She provided help and support to numerous friends and family members. She also went back to college, traveled to Europe, and wrote a book about her experiences. Life is "filled with both bright sunny places and dark stormy times," she says. "Within each I looked for the golden nuggets of wisdom and truth that helped me grow stronger, happier and healthier" (Hill, n.d.).

Maybe Joanne is one of those rare people born with a huge reservoir of inner strength, allowing her to weather any storm. But she didn't always find it easy to deal with life's slings and arrows. She had struggled with depression in childhood and beyond, was addicted to prescription medication early in her marriage, and suffered from debilitating physical ailments—so many that she had difficulty buying life insurance. "Today," she reports in her book, "in spite of one trauma after another for several years, I am healthy in body and whole in mind. Not because of Lady Luck, but because I decided to make different choices" (p. 133). Hill attributes her survival to a series of "rainbow remedies" that she learned, through hard experience, to apply to her life.

This chapter is concerned with the application of psychology to physical and mental health, which is a flourishing area of research. We will focus primarily on topics that connect social psychology and health: how people cope with stress in their lives, the relationship between their coping styles and their physical and mental health, and how we can get people to behave in healthier ways. Along the way we will return to Joanne Hill's story, discuss her "rainbow remedies," and see that at least some of them are backed up by research in social psychology and health.

Stress and Human Health

SPA 2.1 Define stress, and describe what effect it has on our health.

There is more to our physical health than germs and disease; we also need to consider the amount of stress in our lives and how we deal with that stress (Park, 2010; Segerstrom & O'Connor, 2012; Taylor, 2015). Early research in this area documented some extreme cases in which people's health was influenced by stress. Consider these examples, reported by psychologist W. B. Cannon (1942):

- A New Zealand woman eats a piece of fruit and then learns that it came from a forbidden supply reserved for the chief. Horrified, her health deteriorates, and the next day she dies—even though it was a perfectly fine piece of fruit.

- A man in Africa has breakfast with a friend, eats heartily, and goes on his way. A year later, he learns that his friend had made the breakfast from a wild hen, a food strictly forbidden in his culture. The man immediately begins to tremble and is dead within 24 hours.

- An Australian man's health deteriorates after a witch doctor casts a spell on him. He recovers only when the witch doctor removes the spell.

These examples probably sound bizarre, but let's shift to the present in the United States, where many similar cases of sudden death occur following a psychological trauma. When people undergo a major upheaval in their lives, such as losing a spouse, declaring bankruptcy, or being forced to resettle in a new culture, their chance of dying increases (Morse, Martin, & Moshonov, 1991). Soon after a major earthquake in the Los Angeles area on January 17, 1994, there was an increase in the number of people who died suddenly of heart attacks (Leor, Poole, & Kloner, 1996). And many people experienced psychological and physical problems after the terrorist attacks on September 11, 2001 (Neria, DiGrande, & Adams, 2011; Silver et al., 2002). One study measured the heart rates of a sample of adults in New Haven, Connecticut, the week after the attacks. Compared to a control group of people studied before the attacks, the post–September 11 sample showed lower heart rate variability, which is a risk factor for sudden death (Gerin et al., 2005; Lampert et al., 2002). On the other hand, as we will see in a moment, studies of the long-term effects of the 9/11 attacks have found relatively little evidence of prolonged negative reactions. What exactly are the effects of stress on our psychological and physical health, and how can we learn to cope most effectively?

Resilience

The first thing to note is that humans are remarkably resilient. To be sure, we all must contend with the blows that life deals us, including day-to-day hassles and major, life-altering events. And although it is true that such events can have negative effects on psychological and physical health, many people, such as Joanne Hill, cope with them extremely well. Researchers have examined people's reactions over time to major life events, including the death of loved ones and the 9/11 terrorist attacks. The most common response to such traumas is **resilience**, which can be defined as mild, transient reactions to stressful events, followed by a quick return to normal, healthy functioning (Bonanno, 2005; Kalisch, Müller, & Tüscher, 2015; Sullivan et al., 2016).

Resilience

Mild, transient reactions to stressful events, followed by a quick return to normal, healthy functioning

Take life's most difficult challenge—dealing with the loss of a loved one. For years, mental health professionals assumed that the "right" way to grieve was to go through an intense period of sadness and distress, in which people confronted and worked through their feelings, eventually leading to acceptance of the loss. People who did not show symptoms of extreme distress were said to be in a state of denial that would lead to greater problems down the road. When researchers looked systematically at how people respond to the death of loved ones, however, an interesting fact emerged: Many

Watch OPTIMISM AND RESILIENCE

Revel Video

People are surprisingly resilient in the face of stressful events. Studies of reactions to the 9/11 terrorist attacks, for example, have found that relatively few people showed long-term signs of depression or other mental health problems.

people never experienced significant distress and recovered quickly (Bookwala, 2014; Wortman & Silver, 1989). Studies of bereaved spouses, for example, typically find that fewer than half show signs of significant, long-term distress (Bonanno, Boerner, & Wortman, 2008; Bonanno et al., 2005). The remainder, like Joanne Hill, show no signs of depression and are able to experience positive emotions.

Although one might think that such people are in a state of denial, or that they were never very attached to their spouses, there is little evidence to support these possibilities. Rather, there is increasing evidence that although life's traumas can be quite painful, many people have the resources to recover from them quickly. The same pattern has been found in people's responses to other highly stressful events, such as emergency workers' reactions to the bombing of the federal building in Oklahoma City in 1995 and New Yorkers' reactions to the 9/11 terrorist attacks. Surprisingly few people show prolonged, negative reactions to these tragedies (Dekel et al., 2013; Seery et al., 2008; Updegraff, Silver, & Holman, 2008). Nonetheless, some people do have severe negative reactions to stressful events. What determines whether people bounce back quickly or buckle under stress?

Effects of Negative Life Events

Among the pioneers in research on stress is Hans Selye (1956, 1976), who defined *stress* as the body's physiological response to threatening events. Selye focused on how the human body adapts to threats from the environment, regardless of the source—be it a psychological or physiological trauma. Later researchers have examined what it is about a life event that makes it threatening. Holmes and Rahe (1967), for example, suggested that stress is the degree to which people have to change and readjust their lives in response to an external event. The more change that is required, the greater the stress we experience. For example, if a spouse or partner dies, just about every aspect of a person's life is disrupted, leading to a great deal of stress. Holmes and Rahe's definition of stress applies to happy events as well if the event causes big changes in one's daily routine. Getting married is a happy occasion, but it can also be stressful because of the planning involved and the potential for family friction.

What makes life stressful for college students? To find out, researchers made a long list of potential stressors and had college students rate how often they had experienced them and how stressful they were (Renner & Mackin, 1998). You can take an abridged version of this stress inventory in the Try It! exercise below. Studies have shown that the higher people score on stress inventories such as this one, the worse their mental and physical health (Armata & Baldwin, 2008; Dohrenwend, 2006; Seta, Seta, & Wang, 1990).

LIMITS OF STRESS INVENTORIES It may seem obvious that the more stress people are experiencing, the more likely they are to feel anxious and get sick. But the findings aren't all that straightforward. One problem, as you may have recognized, is that most studies in this area use correlational, not experimental designs. As you now know, just because life changes are correlated with health problems does not mean that the life changes caused the health problems. Some researchers have argued persuasively for the role of "third variables," whereby certain kinds of people are more likely to be experiencing difficult life changes and to report that they are ill (Schroeder & Costa, 1984; Watson & Pennebaker, 1989). According to these researchers, it is not life changes that cause health problems. Instead, people with certain personality traits, such as the tendency to experience negative moods, are more likely to experience life difficulties and to have health problems.

Another problem with measures such as the College Life Stress Inventory is that they focus on stressors experienced by the middle class and underrepresent stressors experienced by the poor and members of minority groups. Variables such as poverty and racism are potent causes of stress (Gibbons, Gerrard, & Cleveland, 2004;

Try It!

The College Life Stress Inventory

Instructions: Copy the "stress rating" number into the right column for any event that has happened to you in the past year; then add these scores. Keep in mind that some of the events you will be asked to read about below may be upsetting to think about.

Event	Stress Rating	Your Score
Being raped	100	_____
Finding out that you are HIV-positive	100	_____
Death of a close friend	97	_____
Death of a close family member	96	_____
Contracting a sexually transmitted disease (other than AIDS)	94	_____
Concerns about being pregnant	91	_____
Finals week	90	_____
Concerns about your partner being pregnant	90	_____
Oversleeping for an exam	89	_____
Flunking a class	89	_____
Having a boyfriend or girlfriend cheat on you	85	_____
Ending a steady dating relationship	85	_____
Serious illness in a close friend or family member	85	_____
Financial difficulties	84	_____
Writing a major term paper	83	_____
Being caught cheating on a test	83	_____
Drunk driving	82	_____
Cheating on your boyfriend or girlfriend	77	_____
Negative consequences of drinking or drug use	75	_____
Depression or crisis in your best friend	73	_____
Difficulties with parents	73	_____
Competing or performing in public	69	_____
Difficulties with a roommate	66	_____
Job changes (applying, new job, work hassles)	65	_____
Declaring a major	65	_____
Taking a class you hate	62	_____
Drinking or use of drugs	61	_____
Starting a new semester	58	_____
Going on a first date	57	_____
Maintaining a steady dating relationship	55	_____
Commuting to campus or work, or both	54	_____
Peer pressures	53	_____
Being away from home for the first time	53	_____
Concerns about your appearance	52	_____
Getting straight A's	51	_____
Making new friends; getting along with friends	47	_____
Falling asleep in class	40	_____
Sum of Your Score		_____

These may be happy events, but they can also cause stress. Can you think of positive developments or good news in your life that has somehow also been stressful?

Lick, Durso, & Johnson, 2013; Myers, 2009). Moreover, the way in which these variables are related to health is not always obvious. It might not surprise you to learn that the more racism minority groups experience, the worse their health (Mouzon et al., 2017; Prather et al., 2016). It might come as more of a surprise to learn that majority groups who express the most racist attitudes also experience diminished health (Jackson & Inglehart, 1995). Racism is often associated with hostility and aggression, and there is evidence that hostility is related to health problems such as coronary heart disease. Clearly, to understand the relationship between stress and health, we need to understand better such community and cultural variables as poverty and racism.

Perceived Stress and Health

There is another problem with measures such as the College Life Stress Inventory: They violate a basic principle of social psychology—namely, that subjective situations have more of an impact on people than objective situations (Dohrenwend, 2006; Griffin & Ross, 1991). Of course, some situational variables are hazardous to our health regardless of how we interpret them (Jackson & Inglehart, 1995; Taylor, Repetti, & Seeman, 1997). Children growing up in smog-infested areas such as Los Angeles and Mexico City, for example, have been found to have physiological and psychological deficits, compared to children who grow up in less-polluted areas (Calderón-Garcidueñas & Torres-Jardón, 2012; Ferguson et al., 2013; Peters et al., 1999).

Nonetheless, some environmental events are open to interpretation and seem to have negative effects only on people who construe these events in certain ways. To some students, writing a term paper is a major hassle; for others, it's a minor inconvenience (or even an enjoyable challenge). For some people, a major life change such as getting divorced is a liberating escape from an unhappy relationship; for others, it is a devastating personal failure (Crum, Salovey, & Achor, 2013; Yeager et al., 2014). As recognized by Richard Lazarus (1966, 2000) in his pioneering work on stress, it is subjective, not objective, stress that causes problems. An event is stressful for people only if they interpret it as stressful; thus, we can define **stress** as the negative feelings and beliefs that occur whenever people feel unable to cope with demands from their environment (Lazarus & Folkman, 1984).

Stress

The negative feelings and beliefs that arise whenever people feel unable to cope with demands from their environment

Consider the number of losses Joanne Hill experienced in a 4-year period. According to research on life events, she should have been experiencing a great deal of stress—enough to put her at risk for severe physical problems. The fact that she made it through with grace and strength suggests that there are limits to trying to predict people's reactions from a count of the number of stressful events in their lives. We need to take into account how different people *interpret* disruptions and challenges in their lives.

Studies using the subjective definition of stress confirm the idea that negative life experiences are bad for our health. In fact, stress caused by negative interpretations of events can directly affect our immune systems, making us more susceptible to disease. Consider the common cold. When people are exposed to the virus that causes a cold, only 20% to 60% of them become sick. Is it possible that stress is one determinant of who will be in this category? To find out, researchers asked volunteers to spend a week at a research institute in southern England (Cohen, Tyrrell, & Smith, 1991, 1993). As a measure of stress, the participants listed recent events that they perceived to have had a negative impact on their lives.

The researchers then gave participants nasal drops that contained either the virus that causes the common cold or saline (salt water). The participants were subsequently quarantined for several days so that they had no contact with other people. The results? The more stress people were experiencing, the more likely they were to catch a cold from the virus (see Figure SPA-2.1).

Among people who reported the least amount of stress, about 27% came down with a cold. This rate increased steadily the more stress people reported, topping out at a rate of nearly 50% in the group that was experiencing the most stress. This effect of stress was found even when several other factors that influence catching a cold were taken into account, such as the time of year people participated and the participants' age, weight, and gender. This study, along with others like it, shows that the more stress people experience, the lower their immunity to disease (Cohen et al., 2008; Marsland, Bachen, & Cohen, 2012).

You may have noticed, though, that this study used a correlational design, which means we must be cautious about its interpretation. It is possible that stress itself did not lower people's immunity but rather that some third variable did. For example, maybe having a pessimistic outlook on life lowers people's immunity and increases the likelihood that they will experience stress. It would have been ethically impermissible, of course, to conduct an experimental study in which people were randomly assigned to a condition in which they experienced a great deal of prolonged stress. There are studies, however, in which people's immune responses are measured before and after undergoing mildly stressful tasks in the laboratory, such as solving mental arithmetic problems continuously for 6 minutes or giving speeches on short notice. Even relatively mild stressors such as these can lead to a suppression of the immune system (Cacioppo, 1998; Cacioppo et al., 1998).

The finding that stress negatively predicts health raises an important question: What exactly is it that makes people perceive a situation as stressful? One important determinant is the amount of control they believe they have over the event.

Figure SPA-2.1 Stress and the Likelihood of Catching a Cold

People were first exposed to the virus that causes the common cold and then isolated. The greater the amount of stress they were experiencing, the greater the likelihood that they caught a cold from the virus.

(Based on Cohen, Tyrrell, & Smith, 1991)

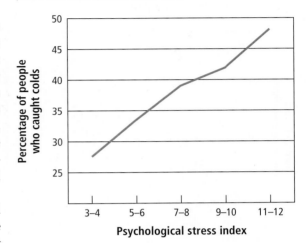

Feeling in Charge: The Importance of Perceived Control

"There are times in life when we feel so out of control that helplessness and hopelessness become constant companions," writes Joanne Hill. "But choice, like breath, is something that is part of us. *We always have a choice*" (Hill, 2002, p. 128). Research

Figure SPA-2.2 Beliefs in Internal-External Locus of Control in College Students over Time

As seen in the graph, in the past 50 years there is a trend whereby college students in the United States endorse more external beliefs about locus of control. This means that they increasingly believe that good and bad things in life are outside of their control.

(Data from Twenge, Zhang, & Im, 2004)

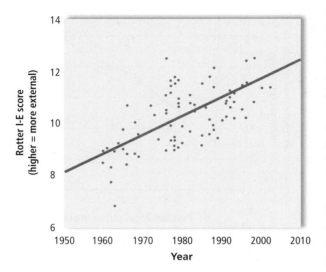

Internal-External Locus of Control

The tendency to believe that things happen because we control them versus believing that good and bad outcomes are out of our control

Perceived Control

The belief that we can influence our environment in ways that determine whether we experience positive or negative outcomes

shows, however, that some people feel this way more than others. For example, suppose you read a series of pairs of statements such as "people's misfortunes result from mistakes they make" versus "many of the unhappy things in people's lives are partly due to bad luck." Which of these two do you think is more true? These statements are part of a test of **internal-external locus of control** (Johnson, Rosen, & Lin, 2016; Levenson, 1981; Rotter, 1966), which is the tendency to believe that things happen because we control them versus believing that good and bad outcomes are out of our control. The first statement above reflects an internal locus of control, which is the belief that people can control their fates. The second statement reflects an external locus of control, which is the belief that our fates are more a matter of happenstance.

Research by Jean Twenge and her colleagues (Twenge, Gentile, & Campbell, 2015; Twenge, Zhang, & Im, 2004) has found that between the years 1960 and 2002, college students in the United States have scored more and more on the external end of the locus-of-control scale. That is, as seen in Figure SPA-2.2, college students are becoming more convinced that good and bad things in life are outside of their control. The reasons for this trend are not entirely clear; it may be part of an increased sense of alienation and distrust among younger generations in the United States (Fukuyama, 1999; Putnam, 2000).

Feelings of control are not something that we either have or do not have. These feelings vary from day to day; on some days, people feel like they are on top of the world, whereas other days, they feel like they are butting their heads against the wall to no avail. These beliefs are important, because on the days that people feel like they are in control, they engage in healthier behaviors such as exercising and eating well (Ryon & Gleason, 2014). More generally, having a sense of **perceived control**—defined as the belief that we can influence our environment in ways that determine whether we experience positive or negative outcomes—is associated with good physical and mental health (Frazier et al., 2011; Infurna, Ram, & Gerstorf, 2013; Roepke & Grant, 2011).

If people become seriously ill, feeling in control is especially important. Shelley Taylor and her colleagues (Taylor, Lichtman, & Wood, 1984; Taylor, 2015) interviewed women with breast cancer and found that many of them believed they could control whether their cancer returned. Here is how one man described his wife: "She got books, she got pamphlets, she studied, she talked to cancer patients. She found out everything that was happening to her and she fought it. She went to war with it. She calls it 'taking in her covered wagons and surrounding it'" (quoted in Taylor, 1989, p. 178). The researchers found that women who believed their cancer was controllable were better adjusted psychologically (Folkman & Moskowitz, 2000). Similar results have been found with people who have other medical issues, such as those who underwent a coronary angioplasty because of diseased arteries. Those who had a high sense of control over their futures were less likely to experience subsequent heart problems than people with a low sense of control (Helgeson, 2003; Helgeson & Fritz, 1999). Joanne Hill recognized this lesson; one of her rainbow remedies is that the "Power of Choice is an empowering remedy that truly makes the difference whether we survive and thrive, or wither and die" (Hill, n.d.).

INCREASING PERCEIVED CONTROL IN NURSING HOMES Some of the most dramatic effects of perceived control have been found in studies of older people in nursing homes. Many people who end up in nursing homes and hospitals feel they have lost control of their lives (Raps et al., 1982; Sherwin & Winsby, 2011). People are often placed in long-term care facilities against their wishes and, when there, have little say in what they do, whom they see, or what they eat. Two psychologists believed that boosting their feelings of control would help such people (Langer & Rodin, 1976). They asked the director of a nursing home in Connecticut to convey to the residents that, contrary to what they might think, they had a lot of responsibility for their own lives. Here is an excerpt of his speech:

> Take a minute to think of the decisions you can and should be making. For example, you have the responsibility of caring for yourselves, of deciding whether or not you want to make this a home you can be proud of and happy in. You should be deciding how you want your rooms to be arranged—whether you want it to be as it is or whether you want the staff to help you rearrange the furniture. You should be deciding how you want to spend your time.... If you are unsatisfied with anything here, you have the influence to change it.... These are just a few of the things you could and should be deciding and thinking about now and from time to time every day. (Langer & Rodin, 1976, pp. 194–195)

The director went on to say that a movie would be shown on two nights the next week and that the residents should decide which night they wanted to attend. Finally, he offered each resident a gift of a house plant, emphasizing that it was up to the resident to decide whether to take one (they all did) and to take care of it. The director also gave a speech to residents assigned to a comparison group. This speech was different in one crucial way: All references to making decisions and being responsible for oneself were deleted. He emphasized that he wanted the residents to be happy, but he did not say anything about the control they had over their lives. He said that a movie would be shown on two nights the next week but that the residents would be assigned to see it on one night or the other. He gave plants to these residents as well but said that the nurses would take care of the plants.

Nursing home residents who have a sense of control over their lives have been found to do better, both physically and psychologically.

The director's speech might not seem like a major change in the lives of the residents. The people in the induced-control group heard one speech about the responsibility they had for their lives and were given one plant to water. That might not seem like very strong stuff. But to an institutionalized person who feels helpless and constrained, even a small boost in control can have a dramatic effect. Indeed, the residents in the induced-control group became happier and more active than residents in the comparison group (Langer & Rodin, 1976). Most dramatically of all, the intervention improved the residents' health and reduced the likelihood that they would die in the next year and a half (Rodin & Langer, 1977). Eighteen months after the director's speech, 15% of the residents in the induced-control group had died, compared to 30% in the comparison condition (see the left side of Figure SPA-2.3).

Another researcher increased feelings of control in residents of nursing homes in a different way (Schulz, 1976). Undergraduates visited the residents of a North Carolina nursing home once a week for 2 months. In the induced-control condition, the residents decided when their visits would occur and how long they would last. In a randomly assigned comparison condition, it was the students, not the residents, who decided when the visits would occur and how long they would last. Thus, the residents received visits in both conditions, but in only one could they control the visits' frequency and duration. This may seem like a minor difference, but again, giving the residents some semblance of control over their lives had dramatic effects. After 2 months, those in the induced-control condition were happier, healthier, more active, and taking fewer medications than those in the comparison group.

Figure SPA-2.3 Perceived Control and Mortality

In two studies, elderly residents in nursing homes were made to feel more in control of their lives. In one (Rodin & Langer, 1977), the intervention endured over time, so that people continued to feel in control. As seen on the left side of the figure, this intervention had positive effects on mortality rates. Those who received it were more likely to be alive 18 months later than those who did not. In the other study (Schulz & Hanusa, 1978), the intervention was temporary. Being given control and then having it taken away had negative effects on mortality rates, as seen on the right side of the figure.

(Based on Rodin & Langer, 1977; Schulz & Hanusa, 1978)

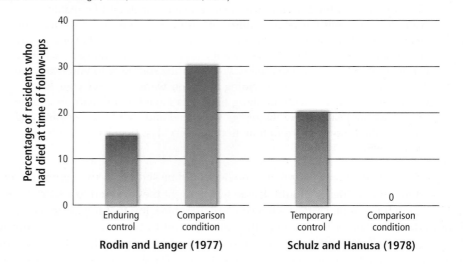

The researchers returned to the nursing home several months later to assess the long-term effects of their intervention, including its effect on mortality rates. Based on the results of the Langer and Rodin (1976) study, we might expect that the residents who could control the students' visits would be healthier than the residents who could not. But there is a crucial difference between the two studies: The residents in the Langer and Rodin study were given an enduring sense of control, whereas the residents in the Schulz study experienced control and then lost it. That is, Langer and Rodin's participants could continue to choose which days to participate in different activities, continue to take care of their plant, and continue to feel that they could make a difference in what happened to them, even after the study ended. By contrast, when Schulz's study was over, the student visits ended. The residents who could control the visits suddenly had that control removed.

Unfortunately, Schulz's intervention had an unintended effect: After the program ended, the people in the induced-control group did worse (Schulz & Hanusa, 1978). Compared to people in the comparison group, they were more likely to have experienced deteriorating health and zest for life, and they were more likely to have died (see the right side of Figure SPA-2.3). This study has sobering implications for the many college-based volunteer programs in which students visit residents of nursing homes, prisons, and mental hospitals. These programs might be beneficial in the short run but cause more harm than good after they end. But the most important conclusions to emerge from these studies several decades later are that there are clear benefits of perceived control for older adults when it comes to physical, mental, and psychological well-being (Mallers, Claver, & Lares, 2014), but that benefits are more likely to be realized and maintained in some interventions than in others (Walton, 2014).

DISEASE, CONTROL, AND WELL-BEING We end this discussion with some words of caution. First, the relationship between perceived control and distress is more important to Western cultures than to Asian cultures. Research shows that

Asians report that perceived control is less important to them than to Westerners and that there is less of a relationship between perceived control and psychological distress among Asians than Westerners (Cheng et al., 2013; Sastry & Ross, 1998). In Western cultures, where individualism and personal achievement are prized, people are more likely to be distressed if they feel that they cannot personally control their destinies. A lowered sense of control is less of an issue in Asian cultures, because Asians place greater value on collectivism and putting the social group ahead of individual goals.

Second, even in Western societies, there is a danger in exaggerating the relationship between perceived control and health. Certainly it can be problematic if people come to blame illness on some kind of human frailty, such as a lack of faith, a moral weakness, or a broken heart, even to the point where they do not seek effective treatment. Although it helps people to feel that they are in control of their illnesses, the downside of this strategy is that if they do not get better, they may blame themselves for failing to recover. Tragically, diseases such as cancer can be fatal no matter how much control a person feels. It only adds to the tragedy if people with serious diseases feel a sense of moral failure, blaming themselves for a disease that is unpredictable and incurable.

For people living with serious illnesses, keeping some form of control has benefits, even when their health is failing. Researchers have found that when people who are seriously ill with cancer or AIDS felt no control over the disease, many of them still believed they could control the consequences of the disease, such as their emotional reactions and some of the physical symptoms, such as how tired they felt. And the more people felt they could control the consequences of their disease, the better adjusted they were, even if they knew they could not control the eventual course of their illness. In short, it is important to feel in control of something, even if it is not the disease itself. Maintaining such a sense of control is likely to improve one's psychological well-being, even if one's health fails (Heckhausen & Schulz, 1995; Morling & Evered, 2006; S. C. Thompson, 2002).

Review Questions

1. Michael's roommate has come down with a cold. In which of the following circumstances is Michael most likely to catch his roommate's cold?
   a. Michael's girlfriend just broke up with him, but he knew it was coming and doesn't view it as all that bad a thing.
   b. Michael's goldfish just died, which he views as a very negative event.
   c. Michael hasn't been exercising very much lately.
   d. It doesn't matter what is going on in Michael's life; all that matters is whether he is exposed to the virus that causes the cold.

2. Which of the following is true?
   a. Someone who is exposed to the cold virus is almost certainly going to come down with a cold.
   b. For people with serious diseases such as cancer, it doesn't matter how much control they feel they have over the disease or its consequences.

   c. If a college student experiences one or more of the stressful life events at the top of the College Life Stress Inventory, he or she will almost certainly get sick.
   d. Many people who experience the death of a loved one do not experience severe distress and recover quickly.

3. Which of the following is true? In the last 60 years or so, college students have:
   a. scored more on the external end of the locus-of-control scale.
   b. scored more on the internal end of the locus-of-control scale.
   c. scored higher on a measure of resiliency.
   d. scored lower on a measure of resiliency.

4. Which of the following is most associated with good health?
   a. Low perceived control
   b. Low perceived stress
   c. A small number of negative life events
   d. Low resiliency

Coping with Stress

SPA 2.2 Explain how people can cope and recover after a stressful experience.

No one always feels in control, of course, and sometimes it is difficult to avoid being pessimistic after something bad happens. The death of a loved one, an acrimonious divorce, and the loss of a job are extremely stressful events. Considerable research indicates that people exhibit various reactions, or **coping styles**, in the face of such events (Aspinwall & Taylor, 1997; Lazarus & Folkman, 1984; Taylor, 2015). We examine a few coping styles here, beginning with research on gender differences in the ways people respond to stress.

Coping Styles

The ways in which people react to threatening events

Fight-or-Flight Response

Responding to stress by either attacking the source of the stress or fleeing from it

Tend-and-Befriend Response

Responding to stress with nurturing activities designed to protect oneself and one's offspring (tending) and creating social networks that provide protection from threats (befriending)

Gender Differences in Coping with Stress

If you have ever been to a dog park, you know that dogs respond in one of two ways when they are attacked: Sometimes they respond in kind, and a dogfight occurs, with owners scrambling to remove their dogs from the melee. Other times, the dog who is attacked will take off as fast as it can, tail between its legs. Walter Cannon (1932) termed this the **fight-or-flight response**, defined as responding to stress by either attacking the source of the stress or fleeing from it. For years, the fight-or-flight response has been viewed as the way in which all mammals respond to stress. When under threat, mammals are energized by the release of hormones such as norepinephrine and epinephrine, and, like the dogs in the park, they either go on the attack or retreat as quickly as they can.

That, at least, has been the accepted story for many years. Shelley Taylor and her colleagues (Taylor, 2012; Taylor et al., 2000; Taylor & Master, 2011) pointed out that there is another way to deal with stress, namely the **tend-and-befriend response**. Instead of fighting or fleeing, people can respond to stress with nurturing activities designed to protect oneself and one's offspring (tending) and creating social networks that provide protection from threats (befriending). Although both men and women exhibit the tend-and-befriend response (von Dawans et al., 2012), it is especially prevalent among women. Why? Taylor and her colleagues argue that the fight-or-flight response does not work well for females because they typically play a greater role in caring for children. Fighting is not always a good option for a pregnant female or one tending offspring. Similarly, fleeing is difficult when an adult is responsible for the care of young children or in the later months of pregnancy. Indeed, research shows that when under stress the hormone oxytocin is released, which is sometimes called the "bonding hormone," because it is associated with the desire to be close to other people. And, whereas both men and women have oxytocin, its effects are enhanced by the presence of estrogen, a female hormone (Taylor, 2012).

Females are somewhat more likely than males to develop intimate friendships, cooperate with others, and focus their attention on social relationships, particularly when under stress. This is called a *tend-and-befriend* coping strategy.

We should be careful not to oversimplify gender differences such as these. Although gender differences in coping do exist, the magnitude of these differences is not very large (Tamres et al., 2002). Further, seeking social support can benefit both women and men—as seen in the next section.

Social Support: Getting Help from Others

Joanne Hill could not have gotten through her "locust years" without the support of a good many family members and friends. When she got the devastating news that her son had died, she was at a gathering of the National Speakers Association (NSA). Joanne turned immediately to her friend Mitchell, a man who had survived both a motorcycle accident and a plane crash. Although badly scarred and wheelchair bound, Mitchell had overcome his adversity and become a successful public speaker. On that terrible day, he held Joanne's hand, shared her grief, and rode with her to the airport. Others helped too: The president of the NSA and her husband took charge of the travel arrangements, and Barbara, a woman Joanne had met just a couple of days earlier at the convention, insisted on accompanying her home.

Watch DO WOMEN AND MEN COPE WITH STRESS DIFFERENTLY?

Revel Video

Social support, perceiving that others are responsive and receptive to one's needs, is very helpful for dealing with stress (Hostinar, Sullivan, & Gunnar, 2014; Lakey & Orehek, 2011; Lam & Dickerson, 2013). But researchers have wondered: Does social support help people physically as well as emotionally? There is some evidence that it does. Studies have shown that interventions designed to increase social support and decrease stress in cancer patients improve the functioning of their immune systems (Andersen et al., 2004; Antoni & Lutgendorf, 2007; Weihs, Enright, & Simmens, 2008). And, social support seems to prolong the lives of healthy people as well. In a study of a large sample of American men and women in the years 1967 to 1969, those with a low level of social support were significantly more likely to die over the next dozen years than people with a high level of social support (House, Robbins, & Metzner, 1982), a finding that has been replicated in other studies (Holt-Lunstad, Smith, & Layton, 2010). To get an idea of the amount of social support you feel is available in your life, complete the Try It! exercise on the next page.

Though it may seem obvious that social support is beneficial, it turns out that there are some interesting qualifications in when and how it helps. First, when things are tough, the kind of social support we get matters. To illustrate, imagine that you are struggling in one of your classes and attend a study session for the final exam. Sarah, a friend of yours in the group, greets you by saying, "I know you aren't doing very well in this class, so how about if we all focus on the material you don't understand and give you an extra hand?" On the one hand, you appreciate the support and extra help. But who likes being singled out as the person who "isn't doing very well"? People don't like receiving help when it comes with the message "you are too incompetent to do it yourself." Now suppose that Sarah was a little more subtle in her support. She knows that you are having trouble with the material in the last chapter of the textbook, but rather than singling you out, she says, "A lot of us are struggling with the material in this chapter—I know I am. How about if we focus on that?" She steers help your way without singling you out or communicating that you are incompetent.

Research has demonstrated that the latter kind of help, which is called *invisible support*, is much more effective. This kind of support provides people with assistance without sending the message that they are incapable of doing it themselves. The former type of help, which is called *visible support*, is a two-edged sword, because it singles out beneficiaries as needy and as people who can't help themselves. The moral?

Social Support

The perception that others are responsive and receptive to one's needs

Try It!

Social Support

This list contains statements that may or may not be true about you. For each statement that is probably true about you, circle T; for each that is probably not true about you, circle F.

You may find that many of the statements are neither clearly true nor clearly false. In these cases, try to decide quickly whether probably true (T) or probably false (F) is more descriptive of you. Although some questions will be difficult to answer, it is important that you pick one alternative or the other. Circle only one of the alternatives for each statement.

Read each item quickly but carefully before responding. This is not a test, and there are no right or wrong answers.

1.	There is at least one person I know whose advice I really trust.	T	F
2.	There is really no one I can trust to give me good financial advice.	T	F
3.	There is really no one who can give me objective feedback about how I'm handling my problems.	T	F
4.	When I need suggestions for how to deal with a personal problem, I know there is someone I can turn to.	T	F
5.	There is someone I feel comfortable going to for advice about sexual problems.	T	F
6.	There is someone I can turn to for advice about handling hassles over household responsibilities.	T	F
7.	I feel that there is no one with whom I can share my most private worries and fears.	T	F
8.	If a family crisis arose, few of my friends would be able to give me good advice about how to handle it.	T	F
9.	There are very few people I trust to help solve my problems.	T	F
10.	There is someone I could turn to for advice about changing my job or finding a new one.	T	F

1. You get 1 point each time you answered true (T) to questions 1, 4, 5, 6, and 10 and 1 point for each time you answered false (F) to questions 2, 3, 7, 8, and 9.

2. This scale was developed to measure what the researchers call appraisal social support, or "the perceived availability of someone to talk to about one's problems" (Cohen et al., 1985, pp. 75–76). One of the findings was that when people were not under stress, those low in social support had no more physical symptoms than people high in social support did. When people were under stress, however, those low in social support had more physical symptoms than did people high in social support. Another finding was that women scored reliably higher on the social support scale than men did. If you scored lower than you would like, you might want to consider reaching out to others more when you are under stress.

(Adapted from Cohen, Mermelstein, Kamarack, & Hoberman, 1985)

If you have a friend who is under a great deal of stress, find a way to help him or her unobtrusively without making a big deal of it (Bolger & Amarel, 2007; Girme, Overall, & Simpson, 2013; Maisel & Gable, 2009).

Second, social support operates differently in different cultures. Who do you think is more likely to seek support from other people when things get tough: members of Western cultures that stress individualism and independence, or members of East Asian cultures that stress collectivism and interdependence? It might seem as though cultures that stress collectivism would be more likely to seek help from each other, but research has found just the opposite: When under stress, members of East Asian cultures are *less* likely to seek social support than are members of Western cultures (Chen et al., 2012; Kim, Sherman, & Taylor, 2008; Mojaverian & Kim, 2013). The reason? Members of collectivistic cultures are concerned that seeking support from others will disrupt the harmony of the group and open them up to criticism from others.

Does this mean that members of collectivistic cultures receive less support from others and benefit less from it when they do receive it? Not at all. The main difference is in *how* people in different cultures seek and obtain social support. Because members of collectivistic cultures are concerned with upsetting group harmony and criticism from others, they are less likely to ask directly for help in a way that shows they are having problems. For example, they are less likely to say to a friend, "Hey, I'm having a hard time here. Can you give me a hand?" They do benefit from interacting with supportive others, as long as they do not have to disclose that they are having problems (Kim et al., 2008).

Reframing: Finding Meaning in Traumatic Events

When something traumatic happens to you, is it best to try to bury it as deep as you can and never talk about it, or to spend time thinking about the event and discuss it with others? Although folk wisdom has long held that it is best to open up, only recently has this assumption been put to the test. James Pennebaker and his colleagues (Pennebaker, 1997; Sloan et al., 2008; Smyth, Pennebaker, & Arigo, 2012) have conducted a number of interesting experiments on the value of writing about traumatic events. Pennebaker and Beale (1986), for example, asked college students to write—for 15 minutes on each of 4 consecutive nights—about a traumatic event that had happened to them. Students in a control condition wrote for the same amount of time about a trivial event. The traumas that people chose to write about included tragedies such as rape and the death of a sibling.

Not surprisingly writing about these events was upsetting, at least in the short run: Students who wrote about traumas reported more negative moods and showed greater increases in blood pressure. But there were dramatic long-term benefits: The same students were less likely to visit the student health center during the next 6 months, and they reported having fewer illnesses. Similarly, a wide range of participant samples including first-year college students who wrote about the problems of entering college, survivors of the Holocaust who wrote about their experiences, and patients who had had a heart attack and wrote about it exhibited improved health over several months after putting their experiences in writing (Pennebaker, Barger, & Tiebout, 1989; Pennebaker, Colder, & Sharp, 1990; Willmott et al., 2011).

What is it about opening up that leads to better health? People who write about negative events construct a more meaningful narrative or story that reframes the event. Pennebaker (1997) has analyzed the hundreds of pages of writing his participants provided and found that the people who improved the most were those who began with rather incoherent, disorganized descriptions of their problem and ended with coherent, organized stories that explained the event and gave it meaning. Subsequent research has shown that reframing is especially likely to occur when people take a step back and write about a negative life event like an observer would, rather than immersing themselves in the event and trying to relive it (Kross & Ayduk, 2011; Kross

Research by James Pennebaker shows that there are long-term health benefits to writing or talking about one's personal traumas, particularly if enough time has passed to allow people to gain a new perspective on the traumatic events.

et al., 2014). The result? Once people have reframed a traumatic event in this way, they think about it less and are less likely to try to suppress thoughts about it when it does come to mind. Trying to suppress negative thoughts can lead to a preoccupation with those very thoughts, because the act of trying not to think about them can actually make us think about them more, leading to intrusive memories (Wegner, 1994).

You may recall that in Chapter SPA-1 we discussed an intervention called Critical Incident Stress Debriefing (CISD), in which people who have witnessed a horrific event are asked to relive the event as soon as possible in a 3- to 4-hour session, describing their experiences in detail and discussing their emotional reactions to the event. As we saw, CISD has been shown, in well-controlled studies, *not* to be beneficial. But why does

writing about an event help people recover when reliving it in a CISD session does not? One reason appears to be the timing. The writing exercise works best if enough time has passed to allow people to gain a new perspective on the incident. In contrast, right after the event occurs is not a good time to try to relive it, reframe it, or understand it in a different way. In fact, one problem with CISD is that it can solidify memories of the bad things that occurred, rather than helping people to reframe them.

In sum, research shows that humans are often remarkably resilient in the face of adversity, particularly if they can maintain a sense of control. Seeking social support can help. If people continue to be troubled by the memories of stressful events, it may help to use Pennebaker's writing technique to help make sense of what happened and what it means.

Review Questions

1. Which of the following is true?
   a. Only women exhibit the tend-and-befriend response because they have higher levels of oxytocin.
   b. Most mammals exhibit a fight-or-flight response to stress, though human beings are much more likely to "fight" than "flight."
   c. Both men and women exhibit the tend-and-befriend response, but it is especially prevalent in women.
   d. Women benefit more from social support than men do.

2. Which of the following is true?
   a. Receiving social support helps people emotionally but has no effect on their physical health.
   b. Women who receive social support tend to live longer but receiving social support is unrelated to how long men live.
   c. When under stress, members of East Asian cultures are more likely to seek social support than are members of Western cultures.

   d. Interventions designed to increase social support and decrease stress in patients with cancer improved the functioning of their immune systems.

3. Under which of the following conditions will people be most likely to recover from a traumatic event that happened to them?
   a. If they write about the event right after it occurs
   b. If they let some time pass and then take a step back and write about the traumatic event like an observer would, rather than immersing themselves in the event and trying to relive it
   c. If they immerse themselves in the traumatic event and try to relive it
   d. If they do their best to suppress any thoughts about the traumatic event

Prevention: Promoting Healthier Behavior

SPA 2.3 Describe how we can apply social psychology to help people live healthier lives.

According to the World Health Organization, more than half of the deaths worldwide are due to preventable chronic diseases (Reardon, 2011). The same is true in the United States, where tobacco use remains the leading cause of preventable deaths. What is number two? It might surprise you to learn that it is obesity, an area in which Americans are not doing such a good job (see Table SPA-2.1). More than one in three Americans are obese, which is associated with such health problems as high blood pressure, diabetes, heart disease, and cancer of the breast, prostate, and colon (NCHS Data Brief, 2015; "Adult obesity," 2011).

Another problem is alcohol consumption. Binge drinking, defined as five or more drinks in a short period of time for men and four or more for women (Wechsler & Austin, 1998), is a problem on many college campuses. Binge drinkers are at heightened risk for a number of health problems, including high blood pressure, heart disease, liver disease, meningitis, and sexually transmitted infections. They are

Table SPA-2.1 Behavioral Causes of Health Problems in the United States

Behavior	Health Risks	How Are Americans Doing?
Tobacco Use	Cigarette smoking accounts for more than 480,000 deaths each year in the US*	18% of adults in the US smoke cigarettes*
Overeating (Obesity)	Obese people are at a higher risk for heart disease, diabetes, some forms of cancer, gynecological problems, and erectile dysfunction**	More than a third of American adults are obese; 17% of American children are obese*
Excessive Alcohol Use	Excessive drinking causes 88,000 deaths each year*	17% of Americans binge drink at least four times a month*
Lack of Exercise	Regular exercise can help prevent heart disease, diabetes, and some cancers*	52% of adults in the US do not meet recommendations for exercise*
Poor Diet	Poor diets have been linked to a number of diseases, such as heart disease, some forms of cancer, and diabetes*	38% of adults in the US eat fruit less than once a day, and 23% eat vegetables less than once a day*
Unsafe Sex	About 15,000 Americans with HIV die each year*	More than one million people in the US are HIV-positive*
Exposure to Sun, Indoor Tanning Rays	More than 60,000 adults in the US are diagnosed with melanomas of the skin each year*	Only 58% of adults reported that they regularly protect themselves from the sun by using sunscreen, wearing protective clothing, or avoiding the sun*

*Center for Disease Control and Prevention (2014)
**Mayo Clinic (n.d.)

also more likely to be in car accidents, die by drowning, have unwanted pregnancies, experience domestic violence, and have sexual dysfunction (Naimi et al., 2003; "Quick stats," 2008).

More than 36 million people worldwide are currently infected with the HIV virus, and in 2015, more than one million people died of AIDS ("Global Health Observatory," n.d.). Most cases are in sub-Saharan Africa, although no continent is free of the disease. Most of these cases could have been avoided if people had used condoms during sexual intercourse. Fortunately, the use of condoms is increasing in the United States; one survey found that among teenagers, 80% of males used a condom the first time they had sex. But that means that 20% did not (Martinez, Copen, & Abma, 2011). And although condom use is increasing in some African countries, in others it is decreasing ("Global report," 2013).

Many serious health problems are preventable, including those resulting from unsafe sex, smoking, and overeating. Social psychologists have designed many successful interventions to improve health habits, such as programs that encourage people to use condoms.

We realize that we have just maligned what many people consider to be the chief pleasures of life: sex, eating, drinking (and even smoking). Health problems resulting from these behaviors are prevalent precisely because they are so pleasurable—and in some cases, addictive. It is thus a challenge to find ways to change people's attitudes and behaviors in ways that lead to better health habits. How might we do so?

By now you know that this is a classic social psychological question. It should be possible to put theories into action theories of attitude change and social influence to help people to act in healthier ways. Indeed, there is a great deal of research on this very issue, and social psychologists have had considerable success in designing programs to get people to use condoms, quit smoking, drink less, and engage in a variety of

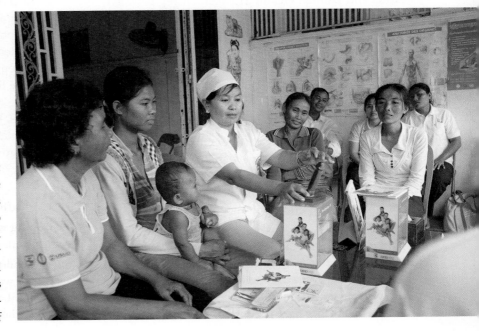

preventive behaviors, such as using sunscreen (Klein, Rothman, & Cameron, 2013; Noar, Benac, & Harris, 2007; Taylor, 2015). Many of these programs use principles covered elsewhere in this text—for example, the attitude-change techniques discussed in Chapter 7 and social norms techniques described in Chapters 8 and SPA1. For example, one study found that women living in Phoenix, Arizona, had incorrect perceptions of injunctive norms about sun exposure: They overestimated how much other women thought that tanned skin was attractive, and underestimated how much other women approved of protecting skin from the sun. Researchers found that correcting these misperceptions caused women to protect themselves more from the sun by using sunscreen and wearing protective clothing (Reid & Aiken, 2013). Perhaps you can think of ways to adopt some of these approaches in your own life. Behavior change isn't easy, but armed with the social psychological techniques you have learned in this book, we are convinced that you can do it.

Review Questions

1. Which of the following is *false*?
   a. The number one cause of preventable deaths in the United States is tobacco use.
   b. Binge drinkers are at a heightened risk for high blood pressure, heart disease, liver disease, meningitis, and sexually transmitted diseases.
   c. The use of condoms is increasing in the United States.
   d. There is little people can do to prolong their lives because most diseases are genetically caused.

2. Which of the following is *false*?
   a. AIDS is no longer a major health crisis because there are drugs to treat it.
   b. Social psychologists have had considerable success in designing programs to get people to act in healthier ways.
   c. One study used social norms techniques to convince women to protect themselves from the sun more.
   d. Binge drinkers are more likely to be in car accidents, die by drowning, have unwanted pregnancies, experience domestic violence, and have difficulty performing sexually.

Summary

SPA 2.1 Define stress, and describe what effect it has on our health.

- **Stress and Human Health** The relationship between stress and human health has received a great deal of attention from social psychologists.

  - **Resilience** People have been found to be surprisingly resilient when they experience negative events, often showing only mild, transient reactions, followed by a quick return to normal, healthy functioning.

  - **Effects of Negative Life Events** Nonetheless, stressful events can have debilitating effects on people's psychological and physical health. Some studies calculate the number of stressful events people are experiencing and use that to predict their health.

  - **Perceived Stress and Health** Stress is best defined as the negative feelings and beliefs that arise when people feel unable to cope with demands from their environment. The more stress people experience, the more likely they are to get sick (e.g., catch a cold).

- **Feeling in Charge: The Importance of Perceived Control** People perceive negative events as stressful if they feel they cannot control them. In the past several decades, college students have increasingly adopted an external locus of control, which is the tendency to believe that good and bad outcomes are out of their control. The less control people believe they have, the more likely it is that the event will cause them physical and psychological problems. For example, the loss of control experienced by many older people in nursing homes can have negative effects on their health.

SPA 2.2 Explain how people can cope and recover after a stressful experience.

- **Coping with Stress** Coping styles refer to the ways in which people react to stressful events.

  - **Gender Differences in Coping with Stress** There are two ways of responding to stress. One is the **fight-or-flight reaction**, which involves attacking the source of the stress or fleeing from it. Another is the

tend-and-befriend reaction, which involves nurturing activities designed to protect oneself and one's offspring (tending) and creating social networks that provide protection from threats (befriending). Although both men and women exhibit the tend-and-befriend response, it is especially prevalent in women.

- **Social Support: Getting Help from Others** Social support—the perception that other people are responsive to one's needs—is beneficial for men and women. The form of social support, however, is important. People react better to invisible than visible support. People from individualistic cultures react well when they directly ask for support, whereas people from collectivistic cultures react well when they get support without disclosing that they are having problems.

- **Reframing: Finding Meaning in Traumatic Events** Other researchers focus on ways of coping with stress that everyone can adopt. Several studies show that reframing traumatic events, by writing or talking about one's problems, has long-term health benefits.

SPA 2.3 **Describe how we can apply social psychology to help people live healthier lives.**

- **Prevention: Promoting Healthier Behavior** It is also important to find ways to help people change their health habits more directly. Numerous studies have used social psychological techniques to do so, such as correcting people's beliefs about injunctive norms.

Revel Interactive

Shared Writing   **What Do You Think?**

According to the research discussed in this chapter, what are some good ways to seek and provide social support?

Test Yourself

1. After her husband died, Rachel did not experience significant distress. Within a few weeks she had returned to her usual activities and regained a cheerful outlook on life. Which is most true, according to research discussed in this chapter?

   a. Rachel's lack of distress indicates the likelihood of poor psychological adjustment.

   b. Because Rachel did not experience extreme grief, she was probably in a troubled marriage and did not love her husband very much.

   c. Although life's traumas can be quite painful, many people have the resources to recover from them quickly.

   d. Rachel is showing "delayed grief syndrome" and will probably experience grief later.

2. Bob's grandmother died recently, and he just found out that his girlfriend cheated on him. He is also in the middle of final exams. According to research on stress and health, which is true?

   a. Because Bob is experiencing so many negative life events, he will almost certainly get sick.

   b. These life events will be stressful for Bob only if he interprets them as stressful; in other words, if he feels unable to cope with the events.

   c. When under stress, a person's immune system is stimulated. Therefore, Bob is less likely to get sick now than he normally would.

   d. If Bob feels more in control of these events than he really is, he is especially likely to get sick.

3. Lindsay does an internship at a nursing home. According to research discussed in this chapter, which of the following would be most likely to benefit the residents?

   a. Lindsay encourages the residents to talk to her about any stressful issues in their lives.

   b. Lindsay allows the residents to choose what time she will come to visit them, and when her internship ends, she decides to keep visiting the residents when they ask her to.

   c. Lindsay allows the residents to choose what time she will come to visit them, but when her internship ends, she doesn't visit the nursing home anymore.

   d. Lindsay gives the residents a plant and makes sure to water it for them.

4. Which of the following is true about research on social support?

   a. Social support of all kinds has been found to be beneficial to people in all cultures.

   b. If you are thinking of helping someone, it is better to give them invisible rather than visible social support.

   c. If you are thinking of helping someone, it is better to given them visible rather than invisible social support.

   d. Members of East Asian cultures are more likely to seek help from others than are members of Western cultures.

5. Which of the following is true of research on coping styles?

   a. Women are most likely to show the fight-or-flight response.

   b. Men are most likely to show the tend-and-befriend response.

   c. Women are mostly likely to show the tend-and-befriend response.

   d. Men and women tend to cope with stress in the same ways.

6. Navneet has had a hard time getting over her parents' divorce. According to social psychological research, which of the following would probably help Navneet the most?

   a. She should spend 15 minutes a night on four consecutive nights writing about her feelings about the divorce.

   b. She should try to attribute the divorce to internal, global, stable things about herself.

   c. She should avoid talking about the divorce with her closest friends because it would probably just depress them.

   d. She should focus on the fact that she has low self-efficacy to improve her relationship with her parents.

7. Which of the following is true?

   a. Although obesity is increasing in the United States, it is not a major health problem.

   b. Many serious health problems are preventable, and social psychological interventions have been developed to get people to act in healthier ways.

   c. There is not much that social psychologists can do to get people to act in healthier ways.

   d. Smoking tobacco is no longer a major cause of preventable deaths.

8. According to social psychological research, which of the following would be most likely to succeed in reducing binge drinking on college campuses?

   a. Point out that college can be a stressful time in people's lives.

   b. Point out that many students can't control how much they drink.

   c. Point out that many college students are resilient.

   d. Point out that many college students overestimate how much their peers approve of binge drinking.

Social Psychology in Action 3
Social Psychology and the Law

 ## Chapter Outline and Learning Objectives

Eyewitness Testimony

SPA 3.1 Explain what psychology indicates about the accuracy of eyewitness testimony.

Why Are Eyewitnesses Often Wrong?
Judging Whether Eyewitnesses Are Mistaken
The Recovered Memory Debate

Juries: Group Processes in Action

SPA 3.2 Describe how social psychology helps explain how juries make decisions.

How Jurors Process Information during the Trial
Confessions: Are They Always What They Seem?
Deliberations in the Jury Room

WHAT DO YOU THINK?

Survey	What Do You Think?	
SURVEY		RESULTS

Can you remember a time when you were absolutely confident that a certain event in your life happened in a certain way only to find out later that you were actually mistaken?

○ Yes

○ No

You be the jury.

How would you vote after hearing the following testimony from an actual case in Texas? On a cold, dark November night, police officer Robert Wood and his partner pulled over a car with its headlights off. Wood signaled up to the driver's side, but before he could even speak, the driver aimed a handgun and shot him, killing the trooper instantly. Wood's partner emptied her revolver at the car as it sped away, but the killer escaped.

A month later, the police picked up a suspect, 16-year-old David Harris. Harris admitted that he had stolen a neighbor's car and gun the day before the murder, that this same car was the one Officer Wood had pulled over that night, and that he was in the car when the shooting occurred. Harris denied, however, that he was shooter. He said he had picked up a hitchhiker by the name of Randall Adams and it was Adams, he claimed, who reached under the seat, grabbed the weapon, and shot the officer. When the police questioned Randall Adams, he admitted that he had gotten a ride from David Harris but said that Harris had dropped him off at his motel 3 hours before the murder.

Who was telling the truth? It was Harris's word against Adams's—until the police found three eyewitnesses who corroborated Harris's story. Emily and Robert Miller testified that they drove by just before Officer Wood was shot. Though it was dark, they said they got a good look at the driver, and both identified him as Randall Adams. "When he rolled down the window, that's what made his face stand out," said Robert Miller. "He had a beard, mustache, kind of dishwater blond hair" (Morris, 1988). Indeed, Randall Adams fit the Millers' description; David Harris, on the other hand, was clean-shaven (see the photos on the left). Michael Randell, a salesman, also happened to be driving by right before the murder and claimed to have seen two people in the car. He, too, said the driver had long hair and a mustache, matching the appearance of Randall Adams.

Who do you think committed this real-life murder? The jury in the case believed the eyewitnesses and convicted Adams, sentencing him to death. However, as Adams languished in jail, waiting for the courts to hear his appeals, several experts began to doubt that he was guilty. New evidence came to light (largely because of a documentary film made about the case, *The Thin Blue Line*), and it is now almost certain that David Harris was the actual murderer. Harris was later convicted of another murder and, while on death row, strongly implied that he, not Randall Adams, had shot Officer Wood. Finally, an appeals court overturned Adams's conviction. He was a free man—but only after spending 12 years in prison for a crime he did not commit.

If Adams was innocent, why had eyewitnesses said that the driver of the car had long hair and a mustache? And why did the jury believe them? How common are such miscarriages of justice? In this chapter, we will discuss the answers to these questions, focusing on the role social psychological processes play in the legal system.

Before we begin, a brief review of the American justice system: When someone commits a crime and the police arrest a suspect, a judge or a grand jury decides

Randall Adams (top) and David Harris (bottom). The fact that eyewitnesses said the murderer had long hair and a mustache was the main reason Adams was convicted of murdering Officer Wood.

whether there is enough evidence to press formal charges. If there is, lawyers for the defense and the prosecution gather evidence and negotiate with each other. As a result of these negotiations, the defendant often pleads guilty to a lesser charge. Fewer than 10% of criminal cases actually go to a trial in which a jury decides the defendant's fate (Edkins, 2011; Redlich et al., 2017).

Social psychologists have studied the legal system a great deal in recent years, both because it offers an excellent applied setting in which to study basic psychological processes and because of its importance in daily life (Brewer & Williams, 2017; Greene & Heilbrun, 2013). If you, through no fault of your own, become the accused in a criminal case, what do you need to know to convince the system of your innocence? If you ever find yourself seated on a jury, how might your expertise in social psychology help you to make a better, more informed decision in the case? We will begin our discussion with eyewitness testimony, the most troubling aspect of the Randall Adams story.

Eyewitness Testimony

SPA 3.1 Explain what psychology indicates about the accuracy of eyewitness testimony.

Randall Adams was convicted largely because of the eyewitnesses who identified him, even though in other ways the case against him was weak. Unfortunately, wrongful convictions based on faulty eyewitness identification are not uncommon. The website of the Innocence Project (www.innocenceproject.com) lists more than 350 cases in which someone has been exonerated with DNA evidence after being convicted of a crime—often, like Randall Adams, after already having spent many years in prison. In approximately 75% of these cases, the conviction was based, at least in part, on faulty eyewitness testimony. Sometimes, as in Randall Adams's case, *multiple* eyewitnesses got it wrong. In short, one of the most common causes of an innocent person being convicted of a crime is an erroneous eyewitness (Brewer & Wells, 2011; Pezdek, 2012; Wells, 2014).

Why Are Eyewitnesses Often Wrong?

The problem is that our minds are not like video cameras, which can record an event, store it over time, and play it back later with perfect accuracy. To be an accurate eyewitness, a person must successfully complete three stages of memory processing: encoding, storage, and retrieval of the events witnessed. **Encoding** refers to the process whereby people notice and pay attention to information in their environment, transforming sensory data into some sort of mental representation. Because people cannot perceive everything that is happening around them, they encode only a subset of the information. **Storage** is the process by which people maintain in memory this new information they have encoded. **Retrieval** refers to the process by which people recall information stored in their memories (see Figure SPA-3.1). Eyewitnesses can be inaccurate because of difficulties that arise at any of these three stages.

ENCODING   The amount of information about a crime that people take in at the encoding stage is limited by several factors, such as how much time they have to watch an event and the nature of the viewing conditions. As obvious as this may sound, people sometimes overlook how these factors can limit eyewitness reports of crimes. Crimes usually occur under the very conditions that make encoding difficult: quickly, unexpectedly, under poor viewing conditions (e.g., at night), and under stress. These conditions certainly describe the scene of the murder of Officer Wood. Eyewitnesses were driving down a dimly lit road, past a pulled-over car, when the unexpected happened—shots were fired and a police officer fell to the ground.

Encoding

The process by which people attend to information in their environment and transform this sensory data into a mental representation

Storage

The process by which people maintain in memory information they have encoded from the environment

Retrieval

The process by which people recall information stored in their memories

Figure SPA-3.1 Encoding, Storage, and Retrieval

To be an accurate eyewitness, people must complete three stages of memory processing. Errors may creep in at each of the three stages.

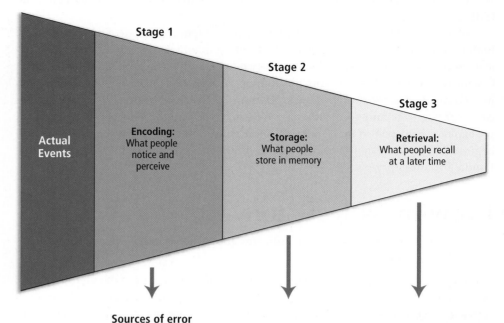

Sources of error

- Poor viewing conditions
- People see what they expect to see
- Focus on weapons
- Own-race bias
- Change blindness

- Misleading questions
- Source monitoring errors

- "Best guess" problem in lineup identification
- Negative effects of verbalization

When eyewitnesses are the victims of a crime, they are usually terribly afraid, and this alone can make it difficult to take in everything that is happening. The more stress people are under, the worse their memory the details of a crime or the people involved (Deffenbacher, Bornstein, & Penrod, 2004; Morgan et al., 2013). Another reason why victims of crimes have a poor memory for faces is that they focus their attention mostly on any weapon they see and less on a culprit's features (Fawcett et al., 2013; Pickel, 2007; Saunders, 2009). If someone points a gun at you and demands your money, your attention is likely to be more on the gun than on what color the robber's eyes are.

The information witnesses notice and pay attention to is also influenced by what they expect to see. Consider our friend Alan, a social psychologist who is an expert on social perception. One Sunday, Alan was worried because his neighbor, a frail woman in her 80s, did not appear for church. After knocking on her door repeatedly and receiving no response, Alan jimmied open a window and searched her house. Soon his worst fears were realized: The woman was lying dead on the floor of her bedroom.

Shaken, Alan went back to his house and telephoned the police. A detective spent a great deal of time in the woman's house, after which he asked Alan some pointed questions, such as whether he had noticed any suspicious activity in the past day or two. Alan was confused by this line of questioning and finally burst out, "Why are you asking me these questions? Isn't it obvious that my neighbor died of old age? Shouldn't we be notifying her family?" Now it was the detective's turn to look puzzled. "Aren't you the one who discovered the body?" he asked. Alan said he was. "Well," said the detective, "didn't you notice that her bedroom had been ransacked, that there was broken glass everywhere, and that there was a belt tied around her neck?"

It turned out that Alan's neighbor had been strangled by a man who had come to spray her house for insects. There had been a fierce struggle, and the fact that the woman was murdered could not have been more obvious. But Alan saw none of the signs. He was worried that his elderly neighbor had passed away. When he discovered that she had in fact died, he was quite upset, and the furthest thing from his mind was that she had been murdered. As a result, he saw what he expected and failed to see what he did not expect. When the police later showed him photographs of the crime scene, he felt as though he had never been there. He recognized almost nothing.

Watch ATTENTIONAL BLINDNESS

Research has confirmed that people are poor at noticing the unexpected. In one study, participants watched a videotape of two teams passing a basketball back and forth and counted the number of times one team passed the ball to the other. Thirty-five seconds into the film, something weird happened: A woman wearing a gorilla costume walked into the middle of the basketball game, turned toward the camera, thumped her chest, and then walked away. Meanwhile, the basketball players continued with their passing game. Although it seems as if everyone would notice such a bizarre interruption, only half did. The other half simply didn't see the gorilla at all (Chabris & Simons, 2010; Simons & Chabris, 1999). Given that crimes are almost always highly unexpected events, it is no surprise that people often fail to notice key details in the crime scene (Rensink, 2002; Simons & Ambinder, 2005; Wilford & Wells, 2010).

Even if we notice a person or event, we might not remember it very well if we are unfamiliar with it. For example, people are better at recognizing faces that are of the same race as they are, a phenomenon known as **own-race bias** (or sometimes referred to as the cross-race effect). Whites are better at recognizing White faces than Black or Asian faces, Blacks are better at recognizing Black than White faces, and Asians are better at recognizing Asian than White faces (Brigham et al., 2007; McGuire & Pezdek, 2014; Wan et al., 2017). Studies have found similar effects with gender and age (Man & Hills, 2017; Wright & Stroud, 2002).

One reason for the own-race bias is that people have more contact with members of their own race, allowing them to learn better how to distinguish one individual from another (Meissner & Brigham, 2001). Another is that when people examine same-race faces, they often pay close attention to individuating features that distinguish that face from others, such as the height of the cheekbones or the contour of the forehead. When people examine different-race faces, however, they are drawn more to features that distinguish that face from their own race, rather than individuating features (Hugenberg et al., 2010; Levin, 2000). Daniel Levin, a researcher who has investigated this hypothesis, puts it like this: "When a White person looks at another White person's nose, they're likely to think to themselves, 'That's John's nose.' When they look at a Black person's nose, they're likely to think, 'That's a Black nose'" (quoted in Carpenter, 2000, p. 44). Because people usually have less experience with features that characterize individuals of other races, they are often not as good at telling members of that race apart.

Own-Race Bias

The tendency for people to be better at recognizing faces of their own race than those of other races

STORAGE   In the preceding discussion of encoding, we have seen that several variables limit what people perceive and thus what they are able to store in their memories. After a piece of information is in memory, it might seem as if it stays there, unaltered like a photograph in an album, until we recall it at a later time.

In reality, few of us have photographic memories. Memories, like printed photographs, fade with age. Further, it is tempting to believe that a picture, once stored, cannot be altered or retouched, and that details cannot be added to or subtracted from the image. If the shooter we saw was clean-shaven, surely we will not pencil in a mustache at some later time, right? Hence, the fact that the witnesses who testified at the Randall Adams trial remembered that the driver of the car had long hair and a mustache seems like pretty incriminating evidence against Randall Adams.

Unfortunately, however, memories are far from indelible. People can get mixed up about where they heard or saw something; memories from one time or situation can get confused with memories in another. As a result, people can have quite inaccurate recall about what they saw. This is the conclusion reached after years of research on **reconstructive memory**: the distortion of memories of an event by information encountered after the event occurred (Blank & Launay, 2014; Loftus, 1979, 2005). According to this research, information we obtain after witnessing an event can change our memories of the event.

In one classic study, Elizabeth Loftus and colleagues (1978) showed students 30 slides depicting different stages of an automobile accident. The content of one slide varied; some students saw a car stopped at a stop sign, and others saw the same car stopped at a yield sign. After the slide show, the students were asked several questions about the car accident they had "witnessed." The key question varied how the traffic sign was described. In one version, the question asked whether another car passed the red car "while it was stopped at the stop sign." In the other version, the question was whether the red car had been passed "while it was stopped at the yield sign." Thus, for half the participants, the question described the traffic sign as they had in fact seen it. But for the other half, the wording of the question subtly introduced new information—that they had seen a stop sign, when in fact they had seen a yield sign. Would this small change (akin to what might occur when witnesses are being questioned by police investigators or attorneys) influence people's memories of the actual event?

All the students were shown the two pictures and asked which one they had originally seen. Most people (75%) who were asked about the sign they had actually seen chose the correct picture; that is, if they had seen a stop sign and were asked about a stop sign, most of them correctly identified the stop sign photograph (note that 25% still got it wrong, making a crucial mistake on what would seem to be an easy question). However, of those who had received the misleading question, only 41% chose the correct photograph (Loftus, Miller, & Burns, 1978). This study allowed Loftus and colleagues to demonstrate the power of leading questions asked after an incident to influence people's actual memory for the event itself.

Reconstructive Memory

The process whereby memories of an event become distorted by information encountered after the event occurred

---

Watch LEADING QUESTIONS AND MEMORY

Revel Video

In subsequent experiments, Loftus and her colleagues found that misleading questions could change people's minds about how fast a car was going, whether broken glass was at the scene of an accident, whether a traffic light was green or red, and—of relevance to the Randall Adams trial—whether or not a suspect had a mustache (Loftus, 1979). Her studies show that the way in which the police and lawyers question witnesses can change the witnesses' reports about what they saw. (Indeed, there is some suspicion that in the Randall Adams case the police may have led the witnesses by asking questions that implicated Adams and not Harris. At the time of the murder, Harris was a juvenile and could not receive the death penalty for killing a police officer; Adams was in his thirties and was eligible for the death penalty, allowing them to pursue the most severe of penalties for someone who they believed had killed one of their colleagues.)

Misleading questions can cause a problem with **source monitoring**, the process people use to try to identify the basis for their memories (Hyman et al., 2014; Johnson, Verfaellie, & Dunlosky, 2008; Qin, Ogle, & Goodman, 2008). In the Loftus studies, for example, people who saw a stop sign but received a misleading question about a yield sign then had two different pieces of information in memory—the stop sign and the yield sign. This is all well and good as long as they could remember where these memories came from: the stop sign from the accident they saw earlier and the yield sign from the question they were asked later. The problem is that people often get mixed up about where they heard or saw something, mistakenly believing, for instance, that the yield sign looks familiar because they saw it during the slide show. It's easy to get confused; when information gets stored in memory, it is not always well "tagged" as to where it came from.

The implications for legal testimony are sobering. Eyewitnesses who are asked misleading questions often report seeing things that were not really there. In addition, eyewitnesses might be confused as to why a suspect looks familiar. It is likely, for example, that the eyewitnesses in the Randall Adams trial saw pictures of Adams in the newspaper before they testified about what they saw the night of the murder. When asked to remember what they saw that night, they might have become confused because of a source monitoring error, recalling Adams's photo from the newspaper—depicting a man with long hair and a mustache—rather than thinking about what they actually saw on the night of the shooting.

RETRIEVAL   Suppose you are an eyewitness to a crime. The police have arrested a suspect and want to see if you identify him or her as the person you saw commit the crime. Typically, the police arrange a lineup or photo array at the police station, where you will be asked whether one of several people is the perpetrator. You might be asked to look through a one-way mirror at a live lineup of the suspect and some foils (people known not to have committed the crime); more likely, you would view a series of photographs of the suspect and the foils. In either case, if you identify the suspect as the perpetrator, that suspect is likely to be charged and convicted of the crime. After all, if an eyewitness saw the suspect commit the crime and subsequently picked him out of a lineup, that's pretty good evidence that the suspect is the guilty party, isn't it? Well, maybe not.

Just as there are problems with acquisition and storage of information, so too can there be problems with how people retrieve information from their memories (Brewer & Wells, 2011; Malpass, Tredoux, & McQuiston-Surrett, 2007; Wells & Quinlivan, 2009). Unfortunately, a number of things other than the image of a person that is stored in memory can influence whether eyewitnesses will pick someone out of a lineup. For example, witnesses often choose the person in a lineup who most resembles the criminal, a major problem if the actual perpetrator isn't actually in the lineup!

In short, eyewitnesses who view a photo array or live lineup often complete the task much the same way as a student takes a multiple-choice test: they use a process of elimination. This means that, just like in a multiple-choice test, a variety of seemingly trivial factors have the potential to greatly influence performance, including who is administering the test, the instructions given to the test-taker, and the other response options available for each question. To avoid this process-of-elimination guessing, as well as other problems with lineup identifications, psychologists have made several recommendations about how the police should conduct lineups. These are summarized in Table SPA-3.1.

Source Monitoring

The process whereby people try to identify the source of their memories

Table SPA-3.1 Research-Based Recommendations for How to Conduct Lineups

Recommendation	Why It Is Important
Make sure everyone in the lineup resembles the witness's description of the suspect.	Doing so minimizes the possibility that the witness will simply choose the person who looks most like the culprit relative to the other photos available (Fitzgerald, Oriet, & Price, 2014; Wells et al., 1998).
Tell the witnesses that the person suspected of the crime may or may not be in the lineup.	If witnesses assume that the culprit is present, they are much more likely to choose the person who looks most like what they remember, rather than saying that they aren't sure if the person is there. As a result, false identifications are less likely to occur when people are instructed that the culprit may or may not be in the lineup (Clark, 2005; Steblay, 1997; Wells et al., 2000).
Make sure that the police officer administering the lineup does not know which person in the lineup is the suspect.	This avoids the possibility that the person will (intentionally or unintentionally) communicate to the witness who the suspect is (Greene & Evelo, 2014; Wells et al., 1998).
If using photographs of people, present the pictures sequentially, one at a time, instead of simultaneously, or all at once.	Doing so makes it more difficult for witnesses to compare all the pictures and choose the one that most resembles the criminal even when the criminal is not actually in the lineup (Lindsay & Wells, 1985; Meissner, Tredoux, & Parker, 2005; Steblay et al., 2001), though recent research suggests that such a procedure may also make eyewitnesses less likely to identify *anyone* in the lineup, even the actual perpetrator (Dobolyi, & Dodson, 2013; Gronlund, Wixted, & Mickes, 2014).
Don't count on witnesses knowing whether their selections were biased.	To determine whether a witness's selection was biased, attorneys or judges sometimes ask them, for example, "Do you think your choice of suspect was influenced by how the pictures were presented or what the police told you?" Unfortunately, people don't have sufficient access to their thought processes to detect whether they were biased (Charman & Wells, 2008; Nisbett & Wilson, 1977).

Judging Whether Eyewitnesses Are Mistaken

Suppose you are a member of a jury who is listening to a witness describe a suspect. How can you tell whether her memory is accurate or whether she is making one of the mistakes in memory we have just documented? It might seem that the answer to this question is straightforward: Pay careful attention to how confident the witness is. Consider the case of Jennifer Thompson, who was raped when she was a 22-year-old college student. During the rape, Thompson reports, she "studied every single detail on the rapist's face" to help her identify him. She was determined that if she survived, she was going to make sure he was caught and went to prison. After the ordeal, she went to the police station and looked through hundreds of police photos. When she saw Ronald Cotton's picture, she knew right away that he was the rapist. "I knew this was the man. I was completely confident. I was sure."

The police brought Cotton in and put him in a lineup, and Thompson picked him out without hesitation. Certain that Cotton was the man who had raped her, she testified against him in court. "I was sure. I knew it. I had picked the right guy." On the basis of her convincing testimony, Cotton was sentenced to life in prison.

A few years later, the police asked Thompson to go to court and look at another man, Bobby Poole, who had been bragging in prison that he had committed the rape. Some people thought that Poole looked a lot like Cotton, others that they bore only a passing resemblance to one another. When asked if she recognized Poole, Thompson replied, "I have never seen him in my life. I have no idea who he is."

As the years passed, and Cotton remained in jail for the rape, DNA testing became more widely available. The police decided to see if evidence from the case matched Cotton's or Poole's DNA. In 1995, 11 years after the crime, the police informed Thompson of the results: "I was standing in my kitchen when the detective and the district attorney visited. They were good and decent people who were trying to do their jobs—as I had done mine, as anyone would try to do the right thing. They told me: 'Ronald Cotton didn't rape you. It was Bobby Poole.'" (Thompson, 2000, p. 15). Cotton was released from prison after serving 11 years for a crime he did not commit.

This example illustrates that eyewitness confidence is not always a good indicator of eyewitness accuracy. In fact, numerous studies have shown that witnesses' confidence is inconsistently related to their accuracy (Charman, Wells, & Joy, 2011; Douglass & Pavletic, 2012; Eisenstadt & Leippe, 2010). When law enforcement officials and jurors assume that a witness who is very confident is also correct, they can make serious mistakes.

Why isn't confidence always a sign of accuracy? One reason is that the things that influence people's confidence are not necessarily the same things that influence their accuracy. After identifying a suspect, for example, a person's confidence increases if he or she finds out that other witnesses identified the same suspect and decreases if he or she finds out that other witnesses identified a different suspect (Busey et al., 2000). Of course, this change in confidence doesn't influence the accuracy of the actual identification made earlier. Therefore, just because a witness is confident does not mean that he or she is accurate, as the cases of Randall Adams and Ronald Cotton illustrate so tragically. However, confidence in combination with another way of responding might indeed suggest that people are accurate—namely, if people identify a face quickly.

RESPONDING QUICKLY   In a study by David Dunning and Lisa Beth Stern (1994), participants watched a film in which a man stole some money from a woman's wallet; they then tried to identify the thief in a photo lineup. Some participants were able to make their choices quickly, saying that the perpetrator's face just "popped out" at them. Others needed to take their time, deliberately comparing one face to another. Who was more likely to correctly identify the thief? It turned out to be the fast responders, for whom the man's face "popped out." We should thus be more willing to believe a witness who says, "I knew it was the defendant as soon as I saw him in the lineup" than one who says, "I compared everyone in the lineup to each other, thought about it, and decided it was the defendant"—particularly if the first witness made the judgment in 10 seconds or less (Dunning & Perretta, 2002). Of course, being quick does

Time and again, research studies demonstrate that being an accurate eyewitness and correctly identifying a perpetrator from a lineup is much more challenging than we assume it to be.

Understandably, jurors place a great deal of weight on how confident an eyewitness appears to be when they assess the accuracy of his memory. But various factors, including post-identification feedback, can inflate the confidence of even erroneous eyewitnesses.

not guarantee being accurate: we saw with the example of Jennifer Thompson that even when eyewitnesses make judgments quickly, and are very confident in their judgments, they can still be incorrect. But, witnesses who respond quickly are more likely to be correct than those who think about it for awhile.

POST-IDENTIFICATION FEEDBACK   Another factor that can influence an eyewitness's confidence is feedback after an identification is made. Note that in Table SPA-3.1, one recommendation for improving lineup procedure is making sure that the person administering the lineup does not know who the suspect is. Keeping the lineup administrator "blind" in this fashion guarantees that nothing he or she says or does will affect who the eyewitness chooses or how confident the eyewitness becomes in that identification. Consider the dangers of the alternative: Laura Smalarz and Gary Wells (2014) conducted a two-part study in which college students were asked to be eyewitnesses and watch video of a theft at an airport. In the first phase of the study, eyewitnesses were asked to identify the culprit from a six-photo array (because they had made the video, the researchers also knew whether the eyewitnesses were accurate or inaccurate in making an identification). In the second phase, the eyewitnesses recorded video testimony in which they described what they had seen and the identification that they had made; these videos were then shown to a separate group of participants, who you could think of as the equivalent of jurors, whose job it was to determine whether each eyewitness had made a correct identification. In a baseline condition, these Phase II observers were, indeed, significantly more likely to believe the testimony of accurate versus inaccurate eyewitnesses. That's good! We would hope that observers, such as jurors, would be able to differentiate between accurate and inaccurate eyewitnesses.

But in another condition of the study, the Phase II observers became unable to tell which eyewitnesses had gotten the identification right. This was the condition in which the eyewitnesses had received positive feedback immediately after making their identification. Specifically, eyewitnesses in this condition made a selection from the photo array, at which point the administrator in charge had remarked, "Good job, you got the suspect." Smalarz and Wells (2014) found that this simple comment (which was made regardless of whether or not the eyewitness was actually correct) inflated eyewitness's confidence in the reliability of their memory. It also made it next to impossible for outside observers to figure out which eyewitnesses were accurate and which ones weren't, a finding with sobering implications for jurors who have to make such determinations in real trials.

To sum up, several factors can contribute to making eyewitness testimony inaccurate, leading to all too many false identifications. Research suggests that perhaps the United States legal system should rely less on eyewitness testimony than it now does. For example, in the legal systems of some countries, a suspect cannot be convicted on the basis of a sole eyewitness; at least two independent witnesses are needed. Of course, adopting this more stringent standard in the effort to curtail false convictions would also raise the risk that some guilty people go free. The following Try It! exercise provides an opportunity to see how accurate you and your friends are at eyewitness testimony and to illustrate some of the pitfalls of human memory.

Try It!

The Accuracy of Eyewitness Testimony

Try this demonstration with a group of friends who you know will be gathered in one place, such as a dorm room or an apartment. The idea is to stage an incident in which someone comes into the room suddenly, acts in a strange manner, and then leaves. Your friends will then be asked to recall as much as they can about this person, to see if they are good eyewitnesses. Here are some specific instructions about how you might do this.

1. Take one friend, whom we will call the actor, into your confidence before you do this exercise. Ideally, the actor should be a stranger to the people who will be the eyewitnesses. The actor should suddenly rush into the room where you and your other friends are gathered and act in a strange (but nonthreatening) manner. For example, the actor could hand someone a flower and say, "The flower man cometh!" Or he or she could go up to each person and say something unexpected, like "Meet me in Moscow at the mosque." Ask the actor to hold something in his or her hand during this episode, such as a pencil, shoelace, or banana.

2. *Important note:* The actor should not act in a violent or threatening way or make the eyewitnesses uncomfortable. The goal is to act in unexpected and surprising ways, not to frighten people.

3. After a few moments, the actor should leave the room. Inform your friends that you staged this event as a demonstration of eyewitness testimony and that, if they are willing, they should try to remember in as much detail as possible what occurred. Ask them to write down answers to these questions:
   a. What did the actor look like? Write down a detailed description.
   b. What did the actor say? Write down his or her words as best as you can remember.
   c. How much time did the actor spend in the room?
   d. Did the actor touch anyone? If yes, whom?
   e. What was the actor holding in his or her hand?

4. After all participants have answered these questions, ask them to read their answers aloud. How much did they agree? How accurate were people's answers? Discuss with your friends why they were correct or incorrect in their descriptions.

Note: This demonstration will work best if you have access to a video camera and can record the actor's actions. That way, you can play back the video to assess the accuracy of the eyewitnesses' descriptions. If you cannot video record it, keep track of how much time elapsed, so that you can judge the accuracy of people's time estimates.

The Recovered Memory Debate

Sometimes an eyewitness is also a victim. One form of memory that has received a great deal of attention is the case in which a person recalls having been the victim of a crime, typically sexual abuse, after many years of not consciously remembering it. Not surprisingly, the accuracy of such **recovered memories** has been hotly debated (McNally, 2017; Schooler & Eich, 2000).

In the 1980s and 1990s, some psychotherapists came to believe that traumatic events are routinely "repressed" and can be retrieved in therapy through hypnosis, "dream analysis," and other suggestive techniques. This coincided with a nationwide epidemic of claims: people going into therapy and coming out making charges that their fathers, daycare workers, teachers, or other adults had routinely abused them for years, only for the abuse to then be forgotten. With so many cases being brought, psychological scientists began to examine the assumptions of recovered-memory therapy by doing empirical research, and they found that many assumptions about recovered memories were simply wrong. Traumas are not usually repressed; on the contrary, most sufferers have difficulty forgetting them. They found that memories are not stored perfectly in the brain, but are subject to confabulation, distortion, and social influence (e.g., Loftus, Garry, & Hayne, 2008; McNally & Geraerts, 2009; Ofshe & Watters, 1994).

This research led to the notion of **false memory syndrome**: People recalling past traumatic experiences that are objectively false but that they believe to be

Recovered Memories
Recollections of a past event, such as sexual abuse, that have been forgotten or repressed

False Memory Syndrome
Remembering a past traumatic experience that is objectively false but is nevertheless accepted by the person as true

One infamous case of alleged recovered memory of abuse occurred in 1988 in Olympia, Washington, when Paul Ingram's daughters accused him of sexual abuse, Satanic rituals, and murder—events they claimed to have suddenly recalled years after they occurred. The police could find no evidence for the crimes, and Ingram (center, above) initially denied that they had ever taken place. Eventually, though, after a series of interviews that included hypnosis, he became convinced that he too had repressed his past behavior and must have committed the crimes, even though he could not remember having done so. According to experts who have studied this case, Ingram's daughters made their allegations after returning from a group religious retreat intended to encourage women to reveal past incidents of Satanic abuse. They genuinely believed that the ritualistic abuse had occurred, as did Ingram himself, but they were wrong. What they thought they remembered were actually false memories (Wright, 1994).

true (Kihlstrom, 1996). Extensive evidence now exists that people can acquire vivid memories of events that never occurred, especially if another person—such as a psychotherapist—suggests that the events occurred (Loftus et al., 2008; Meyersburg et al., 2009; Schooler & Eich, 2000). In addition to numerous laboratory demonstrations of false memories, evidence from everyday life also indicates that memories of abuse can be false. Often, these memories are contradicted by objective evidence (e.g., no evidence of abuse); sometimes people who suddenly acquire such memories decide later that the events never occurred; and sometimes the memories are so bizarre (e.g., alien abduction) as to strain credibility. Accordingly, psychotherapists have to consider that the risk of suggesting past abuse is implanting false memories rather than helping clients remember real events.

In one examination of such memories, Elke Geraerts and her colleagues (2007) placed advertisements in the newspaper to recruit people who reported having memories of childhood sexual abuse. The researchers divided the sample into two groups: those who had continuous memories (that is, they had never forgotten their abuse) and those who believed they had recovered a memory of abuse. This second group was further divided into those who recovered their memory of abuse outside of psychotherapy and those who did so in psychotherapy. All participants were asked to report any knowledge they had of corroborating evidence for the abuse, such as whether other individuals had reported being abused by the same perpetrator or if the perpetrator had confessed to the abuse. Although not perfect, the reported existence of corroborating information gives some indication related to the likelihood that the memories were accurate.

As seen in Figure SPA-3.2, people whose memories of sexual abuse had been recovered in therapy were *least* likely to be able to provide corroborating evidence of the abuse. In fact, no one in this group could do so. Does this prove that everyone who recovered a memory of abuse with the help of a psychotherapist was incorrect and that no such abuse occurred? Certainly not; in cases like these, we can't be 100% sure how accurate memories are. But these results do suggest that claims of abuse cannot be simply taken on faith, especially if they are the result of suggestions from others. Of course, sexual abuse and other childhood traumas *are* a terrible problem and *are* more common than we would like to think. But the scientific evidence now shows quite clearly that abuse is not usually repressed, and suggests that it can be dangerous for therapists to repeatedly encourage clients with no memory of abuse to consider the possibility that they were victimized.

Figure SPA-3.2 Corroborating Evidence for Remembered Childhood Sexual Abuse

People who reported that they had been sexually abused in childhood were divided into three groups: those who had never forgotten the abuse, those who had recovered a memory of the abuse outside of psychotherapy, and those who had recovered a memory of the abuse in psychotherapy. All participants reported whether there was any corroborating evidence of the abuse, such as the perpetrator confessing. As seen here, people who recovered memories of abuse in psychotherapy were less likely to report corroborating evidence.

(Based on Geraerts et al., 2007)

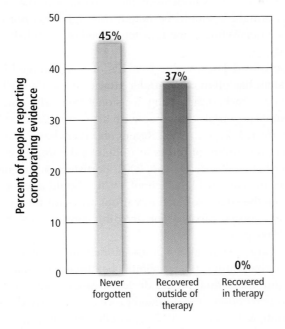

Review Questions

1. Which of the following is *not* one of the stages of memory processing?
   a. Storage
   b. Retrieval
   c. Schema
   d. Encoding

2. Andy, a White American, committed a crime in front of several eyewitnesses in downtown New York City. Research suggests that which of the following witnesses will be most likely to make an accurate identification of Andy in a lineup?
   a. Mariano, who was born and raised in Panama, but has worked in the United States for several years
   b. Matt, a White male who lived in St. Louis for several years but recently moved to New York City
   c. C.C., who is African American
   d. Masahiro, who is Japanese and just came to the United States this year

3. The recommendation that the police investigator who administers a lineup should not know which person is the suspect is
   a. not supported by psychological research findings.
   b. intended to prevent post-identification feedback.
   c. likely to make the own-race bias worse.
   d. the best solution to the problems caused by witness verbalization.

4. Which of the following statements about eyewitness memory is true?
   a. Jurors often have a difficult time determining whether or not an eyewitness is accurate.
   b. The best indicator of an eyewitness' accuracy is his or her confidence.
   c. Eyewitnesses who take their time and look at all the photographs presented to them before making an identification tend to be more accurate then those who make a judgment quickly.
   d. When presenting photographs to an eyewitness, the recommendation is that police show all of the photos at once instead of presenting them one at a time.

5. Researchers who have studied recovered memories of abuse have found that
   a. all supposedly recovered memories are false.
   b. false memory syndrome does not exist.
   c. memories recovered outside of psychotherapy are more likely to have corroborating evidence than memories recovered in a psychotherapy setting.
   d. hypnosis is an effective way to prevent people from coming to believe in what turn out to be false memories.

Juries: Group Processes in Action

SPA 3.2 Describe how social psychology helps explain how juries make decisions.

The right to be tried by a jury of one's peers has a long tradition in English and American law. Trial by jury was an established institution in England at the beginning of the seventeenth century, and the people who founded the first permanent English settlement in North America—at Jamestown, Virginia—carried this tradition with them (although, it should be noted, this right was not granted to Native Americans or other non-Whites, nor to a few rebellious English settlers who were summarily hanged).

Despite the perceived fairness and benefits of being judged by a jury of one's peers, the jury system has often come under attack. In the Randall Adams trial, it is now clear that the jury reached the wrong decision. One study found that judges who presided over criminal jury trials disagreed with the verdict rendered by the jury a full 25% of the time (Kalven & Zeisel, 1966). Recent observers have also criticized the jury system, questioning the ability of jurors to understand complex evidence and reach a dispassionate verdict (Arkes & Mellers, 2002; Bornstein & Greene, 2011). As noted by a former dean of the Harvard Law School, "Why should anyone think that 12 persons brought in from the street, selected in various ways for their lack of general ability, should have any special capacity for deciding controversies between persons?" (Kalven & Zeisel, 1966, p. 5).

Of course, the jury system also has its staunch supporters, and few people on either side of the debate argue that it should be abolished. Sometimes juries seem to "get it wrong," but individual judges deciding cases would also be susceptible to many of the biased perceptions and decision processes we have discussed in previous chapters (Robbennolt, & Eisenberg, 2017). And allowing citizens to participate in important decisions such as these also can boost public perceptions of how fair our legal system is. The point is that the jury system is not perfect and many researchers continue to devote their efforts to better understanding the ways in which it sometimes goes awry and how the process can be improved (Devine, 2012; Semmler, Brewer, & Douglass, 2012; Sommers & Marotta, 2014).

How Jurors Process Information during the Trial

How do individual jurors think about the evidence they hear during a trial? As we saw in Chapter 3, people often construct theories and schemas to interpret the world around them, and the same is true of jurors (V. L. Smith, 1991; Weinstock, 2011). Some psychologists have proposed a **story model** for jury decision making, namely that as jurors hear evidence in a case, they decide on one story that best explains everything they hear. They then try to fit this story to the possible verdicts they are allowed to render, and if one of those verdicts fits well with their preferred story, they are likely to vote to convict on that charge (Hastie, 2008; Hastie & Pennington, 2000). The story model has important implications for how lawyers present their cases. Lawyers typically present the evidence in one of two ways. One is *story order*, in which they present the evidence in the sequence in which the events occurred, corresponding as closely as possible to the story they want the jurors to believe. Another is called *witness order*, in which attorneys present witnesses in the sequence they think will have the greatest impact, even if this means that events are described out of order. For example, a lawyer might save his or her best witness for last so that the trial ends on a dramatic note, even if this witness describes events that occurred early on in the alleged criminal incident.

Story Model

The theory that jurors try to fit the evidence they hear at trial into a coherent story, and ultimately reach a verdict that best fits the story they have created

If you were a lawyer, in which order would you present the evidence? Given that jurors are ultimately swayed by the story or schema they think best explains the sequence of events, the best strategy should be to present the evidence in story order, not witness order. To test this hypothesis, researchers asked mock jurors to listen to a simulated murder trial and varied the order in which the prosecuting and defense attorneys presented their cases (Pennington & Hastie, 1988). In one condition, both used story order, whereas in another condition, both used witness order. In other conditions, one attorney used story order and the other used witness order.

The results provided clear support for the story-order strategy. As seen in Table SPA-3.2, when the prosecutor used story order and the defense used witness order, the jurors were most likely to believe the prosecutor—78% voted to convict the defendant. When the prosecutor used witness order and the defense used story order, the tables were turned—only 31% voted to convict. One reason the conviction rate in felony trials in the United States is so high—approximately 80%—may be that in real trials prosecutors are more likely to present evidence in story order. If you are a budding lawyer, remember this when you are preparing for trial!

"Your Honor, we're going to go with the prosecution's spin."

Mike Twohy/The New Yorker Collection/The Cartoon Bank

Confessions: Are They Always What They Seem?

Imagine that you are a member of a jury at a murder trial. The prosecution presents what seems to be ironclad evidence—namely, a videotape of the defendant confessing to the crime. "OK, yes," you hear the defendant say, "I was the one who pulled the trigger." More than likely, you would vote to convict. Why would the defendant admit to the crime if he was innocent? And many cases never go to trial, because the defendant pleads guilty after confessing to the crime.

Confessions, however, are not always what they seem. Consider the high-profile case of the Central Park jogger, a woman who was raped and brutally beaten while jogging in New York City in 1989. The victim, who suffered a fractured skull and traumatic brain injuries, was in a coma for several days, and when she awoke, she had no memory of the attack. Despite her inability to point to a perpetrator, the police arrested five teenagers, all either African American or Hispanic, who had been in the park that night. The boys confessed to the crime and ultimately provided lurid details of what had happened. Four of the confessions were videotaped and played at the trial, and largely on this basis, all of the teenagers were convicted and given long prison sentences.

Table SPA-3.2 How Should Lawyers Present a Case?

A lawyer can present a case in a variety of ways. This study found that story order, in which a lawyer presents the evidence in the order that corresponds most closely to the story he or she wants the jurors to believe, works best.

	Percentage of People Voting to Convict the Defendant	
	Defense Evidence	
Prosecution Evidence	Story Order	Witness Order
Story order	59%	78%
Witness order	31%	63%

(Adapted from Pennington & Hastie, 1988)

The problem with some confessions is that they are not autobiographical at all, but false.

"For me, a confession is much too autobiographical."

Frank Cotham/The New Yorker Collection/The Cartoon Bank

The only problem is that, 13 years later, as detailed in Ken Burns's documentary *The Central Park Five*, it became clear that the boys were innocent. Another man, in prison for three rapes and a murder, confessed to the crime, admitting he had acted alone. His DNA matched samples recovered from the victim (none of the teenagers' DNA matched), and he gave details of the crime scene that were known only to the police. In 2002, a judge vacated the convictions of all five boys.

If the boys were innocent, then why did they confess to the crime? Unfortunately, the police interrogation process can go wrong in ways that elicit false confessions, even to the point where innocent suspects come to believe that they actually committed the crime (Gudjonsson et al., 2014; Hasel & Kassin, 2012; Kassin et al., 2010). One problem is that police investigators are often convinced that the suspect is guilty, and this belief biases how they conduct the interrogation. They ask leading questions, isolate suspects and put them under considerable stress, and sometimes make false promises. The suspects in the Central Park jogger case, for example, were questioned for up to 30 hours, and the police detectives implied that they could go home if they would sign a confession. After many hours of prolonged interrogation, innocent people can become so psychologically fatigued that they don't know what to think and may even come to believe that they are guilty. This may seem relatively unproblematic to you if the suspect really is guilty, and if the techniques succeed in making him or her confess. However, people—even trained investigators—are not very good at telling whether someone is lying, which means that innocent people are sometimes subjected to these techniques as well. In fact, in a large number of cases in which DNA evidence has exonerated defendants who have been falsely convicted of a crime, the defendant has confessed (Kassin, Bogart, & Kerner, 2012).

One solution to the problem of false confessions is requiring that interrogations be videotaped, as several states now do. This rule ensures that the jury can view the recording and judge for itself whether the defendant was coerced into admitting things he or she didn't do. Although recording interrogations is a step forward, it also raises another potential problem. Almost all videos of interrogations focus on the suspect, rather than on the interrogator asking the questions. Well, you might wonder, what's wrong with that?

People sometimes confess to crimes they did not commit when they are subjected to long, stressful interrogations.

The problem is that viewers tend to think that whoever the camera is focused on is more in charge of the situation than they actually are. Some studies have showed people a video of the same confession from different camera angles—similar to what we discussed in Chapter 4 regarding how the angle at which you see a speaker affects your impressions of who has control over the conversation—and then asked them to judge how voluntary or coerced the confession appeared to be. People thought that the confession was most voluntary (i.e., the least coerced) when the camera focused on the suspect; here, people had the sense that the suspect was in charge of what was happening. When the camera showed both the suspect and the interrogator, people thought the confession was less voluntary. And when the camera focused only on the interrogator, people thought the confession was the most coerced (Lassiter, 2010). Remember, everyone heard the same confession; all that differed was their visual perspective. In part because of this research, some states are now beginning to require that both the suspect and the questioner be shown in videotaped interviews.

Deliberations in the Jury Room

As any trial lawyer can tell you, the crucial part of the jury process occurs out of sight, when jurors deliberate in the attempt to reach a unanimous verdict. Even if most jurors are inclined to vote in one direction, there might be a persuasive minority able to change the other jurors' minds. That said, in most jury deliberations, the initial majority ultimately determines the verdict (Bornstein & Greene, 2011; Kalven & Zeisel, 1966; MacCoun, 1989). In the Randall Adams trial, for example, a majority of the 12-person jury (7 men and 5 women) initially voted to convict Adams. After 8 hours of deliberations, this majority prevailed: The holdouts changed their minds, and the jury voted unanimously to convict. In a study of more than 200 juries in actual criminal trials, researchers found that in 97% of the cases the jury's final decision was the same as the one favored by a majority of the jurors on the initial vote (Kalven & Zeisel, 1966). Thus, just as we saw when exploring the topic of conformity, majority opinion usually carries the day in a group.

If jury deliberation is stacked toward the initial majority opinion, why not just abandon the deliberation process, letting the jury's initial vote determine a defendant's guilt or innocence? For at least two reasons, this would not be a good idea. First, forcing jurors to reach a unanimous verdict makes them consider the evidence more carefully rather than simply assuming that their initial impressions of the case were correct (Hastie, Penrod, & Pennington, 1983; Sommers, 2006). Second, even if the jury minority seldom succeeds in persuading the majority to change its mind about guilt or innocence, a jury minority sometimes does change people's minds about the degree to which a person is guilty. In criminal trials, juries may have some discretion about the type of guilty verdict they can reach. In a murder trial, for example, they can often decide whether to convict the defendant of first-degree murder, second-degree murder, or manslaughter. One study found that people on a jury who have a minority point of view often convince fellow jurors to change their minds about the specific charge on which to convict (Pennington & Hastie, 1990). Thus, while a minority of jurors is less likely to convince a majority of jurors to change a verdict from first-degree murder to not guilty, these jurors might well convince the others to switch from first-degree to second-degree murder.

Review Questions

1. Research indicates that _____ tends to be the most persuasive way of presenting evidence to a jury.
   a. witness order
   b. schema order
   c. blind order
   d. story order
2. Videotaping interrogations of suspects
   a. is illegal in the United States.
   b. can help identify and prevent false confessions, but it makes a big difference who the camera is focused on.
   c. can help identify and prevent false confessions, but it makes a big difference whether or not the police officers know they are being recorded.
   d. is what helped authorities in the Central Park jogger case figure out that the wrong people had been convicted of the crime.
3. When it comes to jury decision making, minority influence
   a. never occurs.
   b. is more effective in 12-person juries than in 6-person juries.
   c. can be more effective in changing which charge the jury convicts on as opposed to actually changing the jury's verdict from, say, guilty to not guilty.
   d. works best when done in witness order.

Summary

SPA 3.1   Explain what psychology indicates about the accuracy of eyewitness testimony.

- **Eyewitness Testimony** Eyewitness testimony is often of questionable accuracy because of the way people naturally observe and remember unexpected events.

  - **Why Are Eyewitnesses Often Wrong?** A number of factors bias the **encoding, storage**, and **retrieval** of what people observe, sometimes leading to the false identification of criminals. For example, research on **own-race bias** shows that people find it more difficult to recognize members of other races than members of their own race. Research on **reconstructive memory** indicates that errors in **source monitoring** can occur when people become confused about where they saw or heard something. Recognizing the problems people have retrieving information from memory, social psychology research has contributed to new guidelines for how police lineups should be conducted.

  - **Judging Whether Eyewitnesses Are Mistaken** There is no surefire way of telling whether a witness is making an accurate or inaccurate identification, although there is some evidence that people who identify a suspect from an array of pictures within 10 seconds *and* express very high confidence in their choice are especially likely to be correct. Post-identification feedback from a lineup administrator can inflate an eyewitness's confidence, making it even harder for jurors to determine whether or not the witness's memory is accurate.

  - **The Recovered Memory Debate** Although **recovered memories** may be accurate in some instances, they can also be the result of **false memory syndrome**, whereby people come to believe that a memory is true when it actually is not. False memories are especially likely to occur when another person, such as a psychotherapist, plants the suggestion that an event likely occurred.

SPA 3.2   Describe how social psychology helps explain how juries make decisions.

- **Juries: Group Processes in Action** Juries are of particular interest to social psychologists, because the way they reach verdicts is directly relevant to social psychological research on group processes and social interaction. Jurors are susceptible to the same kinds of biases and social pressures we have documented in earlier chapters (though it's only fair to note that so, too, are individual judges).

  - **How Jurors Process Information during the Trial** According to the **story model** of jury decision making, during a trial, jurors attempt to make sense out of the testimony and often decide on one story that explains all of the evidence. Juries are thus most swayed by lawyers who present the evidence in a way that tells a consistent story.

  - **Confessions: Are They Always What They Seem?** The interrogation techniques used by the police can sometimes produce false confessions. The video recording of interrogations is a safeguard against this, although focusing the camera solely on the suspect increases the likelihood that viewers will think he or she voluntarily confessed.

  - **Deliberations in the Jury Room** During deliberations, jurors with minority views are often pressured into conforming to the view of the majority; thus, verdicts usually correspond to the initial feelings of the majority of jurors.

<table>
<tr><td rowspan="3">**Revel Interactive**</td><td>Shared Writing</td><td>**What Do You Think?**</td></tr>
<tr><td colspan="2"></td></tr>
<tr><td colspan="2">What are two (or more) lineup strategies that the legal system can adopt to make mistaken eyewitness identification less likely?</td></tr>
</table>

Test Yourself

1. Which of the following is *least* true about eyewitness testimony?

   a. Jurors and law enforcement professionals rely heavily on eyewitness testimony when they are deciding whether someone is guilty.

   b. Jurors tend to overestimate the accuracy of eyewitnesses.

   c. People are better at recognizing faces of people of their own race than faces of people of different races.

   d. Writing down a description of someone you saw will make it easier for you to recognize that person later.

2. Gloria was working the night shift at a convenience store. A man came in, pulled out a gun, and demanded that Gloria give him all the money in the cash register. When the police interview Gloria about the crime, which of the following will she most likely be able to tell them?

   a. The size of the gun the man had

   b. The type of clothes the man wore

   c. The height of the man

   d. The color of the man's eyes

3. You are an assistant district attorney trying to decide which suspect to try for a burglary case. Each of five eyewitnesses picked a different suspect from a photo lineup. Based on social psychological research, which eyewitness would you find most credible?

   a. Phil, who carefully compared each of the faces against the others

   b. Luke, who wrote down a description of the suspect right after the robbery

   c. Hayley, who reported that the suspect's face just "popped out" at her

   d. Alex, who said that she was "extremely confident" that she was correct

4. Which of the following is *not* a recommendation that social psychologists have made about how the police should conduct lineups?

   a. Make sure everyone in the lineup resembles the witness's description of the suspect.

   b. Tell the witness that the person suspected of the crime may or may not be in the lineup.

   c. Before seeing the lineup, have the witness reconstruct the face of the suspect, using face-composite computer programs.

   d. Don't assume that witnesses know whether their selections were biased.

5. Research has supported which of the following statements about recovered memories?

   a. False memory syndrome does not exist.

   b. People who recover memories of sexual abuse in psychotherapy are almost always correct that the abuse really occurred.

   c. There may be instances in which people do suddenly remember traumatic events that really did occur.

   d. Judges are more likely to believe them than are juries.

6. Which of the following recommendations have social psychologists made to the legal profession?

   a. The police should try as hard as they can to get suspects to confess to a crime, because if the suspects confess, they are surely guilty.

   b. Lawyers should present witnesses in the sequence they think will have the greatest impact, even if this means that events of the case are described out of order.

   c. The police should videotape all interrogations and make sure that the camera angle shows both the interrogator and the suspect.

   d. Hypnosis is a useful way for producing accurate eyewitness memories.

7. Which of the following statistics about juries is accurate?

   a. Ninety-seven percent of mistaken convictions of the innocent result from eyewitness errors.

   b. Judges and juries agree on the appropriate verdict in a case 75% of the time.

   c. In 55% of cases, the jury's final decision was the same as the one favored by a majority of the jurors on the initial vote during deliberations.

   d. Twenty-five percent of juries get the verdict wrong in criminal cases.

8. Which of the following is *most true* about research on social psychology and the law?

   a. In police interrogations, people sometimes confess to a crime they did not commit and even come to believe that they did commit the crime.

   b. When jury deliberations begin, if a couple of jurors disagree with everyone else, they are easily able to persuade the majority to change from a guilty to a not-guilty verdict.

   c. People have pretty good memories for events they witness, and it is hard to convince them that they saw something they did not.

d. If a witness picks a suspect out of a lineup and is extremely confident that he or she has identified the right person, then he or she is almost certainly correct.

9. One explanation for why eyewitnesses might be confident in an inaccurate identification is

a. the story model.

b. post-identification feedback.

c. own-race bias.

d. recovered memory.

10. Raj is having trouble remembering whether he actually saw a white van speeding away from the scene of the bank robbery or whether he just heard other people talking about a white van. Raj is having difficulty with

a. composite memory.

b. verbalization effects.

c. storage.

d. source monitoring.

Glossary

Accessibility The extent to which schemas and concepts are at the forefront of people's minds and are therefore likely to be used when making judgments about the social world

Affect Blends Facial expressions in which one part of the face registers one emotion while another part of the face registers a different emotion

Affective Forecasting The extent to which people can predict the intensity and duration of their emotional reactions to future events

Affectively Based Attitude An attitude based more on people's feelings and values than on their beliefs about the nature of an attitude object

Aggression Intentional behavior aimed at causing physical harm or psychological pain to another person

Altruism The desire to help another person even if it involves a cost to the helper

Altruistic Personality The qualities that cause an individual to help others in a wide variety of situations

Analytic Thinking Style A type of thinking in which people focus on the properties of objects without considering their surrounding context; this type of thinking is common in Western cultures

Anxious/Ambivalent Attachment Style An attachment style characterized by a concern that others will not reciprocate one's desire for intimacy, resulting in higher-than-average levels of anxiety

Applied Research Studies designed to solve a particular social problem

Archival Analysis A form of the observational method in which the researcher examines the accumulated documents, or archives, of a culture (e.g., diaries, novels, magazines, and newspapers)

Attachment Styles The expectations people develop about relationships with others based on the relationship they had with their primary caregiver when they were infants

Attitude Accessibility The strength of the association between an attitude object and a person's evaluation of that object, measured by the speed with which people can report how they feel about the object

Attitude Inoculation Making people immune to attempts to change their attitudes by initially exposing them to small doses of the arguments against their position

Attitudes Evaluations of people, objects, and ideas

Attribution Theory A description of the way in which people explain the causes of their own and other people's behavior

Automatic Thinking Thinking that is nonconscious, unintentional, involuntary, and effortless

Availability Heuristic A mental rule of thumb whereby people base a judgment on the ease with which they can bring something to mind

Avoidant Attachment Style An attachment style characterized by difficulty developing intimate relationships because previous attempts to be intimate have been rebuffed

Base Rate Information Information about the frequency of members of different categories in the population

Basic Dilemma of the Social Psychologist The trade-off between internal and external validity in conducting research; it is very difficult to do one experiment that is both high in internal validity and generalizable to other situations and people

Basic Research Studies that are designed to find the best answer to the question of why people behave as they do and that are conducted purely for reasons of intellectual curiosity

Behaviorally Based Attitude An attitude based on observations of how one behaves toward an object

Behaviorism A school of psychology maintaining that to understand human behavior, one need only consider the reinforcing properties of the environment

Belief in a Just World A form of defensive attribution wherein people assume that bad things happen to bad people and that good things happen to good people

Belief Perseverance The tendency to stick with an initial judgment even in the face of new information that should prompt us to reconsider

Bias Blind Spot The tendency to think that other people are more susceptible to attributional biases in their thinking than we are

Blaming the Victim The tendency to blame individuals (make dispositional attributions) for their victimization, typically motivated by a desire to see the world as a fair place

Bystander Effect The finding that the greater the number of bystanders who witness an emergency, the less likely any one of them is to help

Catharsis The notion that "blowing off steam"—by behaving aggressively or watching others do so—relieves built-up anger and aggressive energy and hence reduces the likelihood of further aggressive behavior

Causal Theories Theories about the causes of one's own feelings and behaviors; often we learn such theories from our culture (e.g., "absence makes the heart grow fonder")

Central Route to Persuasion The case in which people have both the ability and the motivation to elaborate on a persuasive communication, listening carefully to and thinking about the arguments presented

Challenge Hypothesis Testosterone relates to aggression only when there are opportunities for reproduction

Classical Conditioning The phenomenon whereby a stimulus that elicits an emotional response is repeatedly paired with a neutral stimulus that does not, until the neutral stimulus takes on the emotional properties of the first stimulus

Cognitive Dissonance The discomfort that people feel when two cognitions (beliefs, attitudes) conflict, or when they behave in ways that are inconsistent with their conception of themselves

Cognitively Based Attitude An attitude based primarily on people's beliefs about the properties of an attitude object

Communal Relationships Relationships in which people's primary concern is being responsive to the other person's needs

Companionate Love The feelings of intimacy and affection we have for someone that are not accompanied by passion or physiological arousal

Comparison Level People's expectations about the level of rewards and costs they are likely to receive in a particular relationship

Comparison Level for Alternatives People's expectations about the level of rewards and costs they would receive in an alternative relationship

Conformity A change in one's behavior due to the real or imagined influence of other people

Consensus Information   Information about the extent to which other people behave the same way toward the same stimulus as the actor does

Consistency Information   Information about the extent to which the behavior between one actor and one stimulus is the same across time and circumstances

Construal   The way in which people perceive, comprehend, and interpret the social world

Contingency Theory of Leadership   The idea that the effectiveness of a leader depends both on how task- or relationship-oriented the leader is and on the amount of control the leader has over the group

Controlled Thinking   Thinking that is conscious, intentional, voluntary, and effortful

Coping Styles   The ways in which people react to threatening events

Correlation Coefficient   A statistical technique that assesses how well you can predict one variable from another—for example, how well you can predict people's weight from their height

Correlational Method   The technique whereby two or more variables are systematically measured and the relationship between them (i.e., how much one can be predicted from the other) is assessed

Counterattitudinal Behavior   Acting in a way that runs counter to one's private belief or attitude

Counterfactual Thinking   Mentally changing some aspect of the past as a way of imagining what might have been

Covariation Model   A theory that states that to form an attribution about what caused a person's behavior, we systematically note the pattern between the presence or absence of possible causal factors and whether the behavior occurs

Cover Story   A description of the purpose of a study, given to participants, that is different from its true purpose and is used to maintain psychological realism

Cross-Cultural Research   Research conducted with members of different cultures, to see whether the psychological processes of interest are present in both cultures or whether they are specific to the culture in which people were raised

Debriefing   Explaining to participants, at the end of an experiment, the true purpose of the study and exactly what transpired

Deception   Misleading participants about the true purpose of a study or the events that will actually transpire

Decode   To interpret the meaning of the nonverbal behavior other people express, such as deciding that a pat on the back was an expression of condescension and not kindness

Deindividuation   The loosening of normal constraints on behavior when people can't be identified (such as when they are in a crowd)

Dependent Variable   The variable a researcher measures to see if it is influenced by the independent variable; the researcher hypothesizes that the dependent variable will depend on the level of the independent variable

Descriptive Norms   People's perceptions of how people actually behave in given situations, regardless of whether the behavior is approved or disapproved of by others

Diffusion of Responsibility   The phenomenon wherein each bystander's sense of responsibility to help decreases as the number of witnesses increases

Discrimination   Unjustified negative or harmful action toward a member of a group solely because of his or her membership in that group

Display Rules   Culturally determined rules about which nonverbal behaviors are appropriate to display

Distinctiveness Information   Information about the extent to which one particular actor behaves in the same way to different stimuli

Door-in-the-Face Technique   Social influence strategy in which first asking people for a large request that they will probably refuse makes them more likely to agree later to a second, smaller request

Downward Social Comparison   Comparing ourselves to people who are worse than we are with regard to a particular trait or ability

Dual-Hormone Hypothesis   Testosterone relates to dominance-seeking behavior only when the stress hormone, cortisol, is not elevated

Elaboration Likelihood Model   A model explaining two ways in which persuasive communications can cause attitude change: *centrally*, when people are motivated and have the ability to pay attention to the arguments in the communication, and *peripherally*, when people do not pay attention to the arguments but are instead swayed by surface characteristics

Emblems   Nonverbal gestures that have well-understood definitions within a given culture; they usually have direct verbal translations, such as the OK sign

Empathy   The ability to put oneself in the shoes of another person and to experience events and emotions (e.g., joy and sadness) the way that person experiences them

Empathy-Altruism Hypothesis   The idea that when we feel empathy for a person, we will attempt to help that person for purely altruistic reasons, regardless of what we have to gain

Encode   To express or emit nonverbal behavior, such as smiling or patting someone on the back

Encoding   The process by which people attend to information in their environment and transform this sensory data into a mental representation

Equity Theory   The idea that people are happiest with relationships in which the rewards and costs experienced by both parties are roughly equal

Ethnocentrism   The belief that one's own ethnic group, nation, or religion is superior to all others

Ethnography   The method by which researchers attempt to understand a group or culture by observing it from the inside, without imposing any preconceived notions they might have

Evolutionary Psychology   The attempt to explain social behavior in terms of genetic factors that have evolved over time according to the principles of natural selection

Exchange Relationships   Relationships governed by the need for equity (i.e., for an equal ratio of rewards and costs)

Experimental Method   The method in which the researcher randomly assigns participants to different conditions and ensures that these conditions are identical except for the independent variable (the one thought to have a causal effect on people's responses)

Explicit Attitudes   Attitudes that we consciously endorse and can easily report

External Attribution   The inference that a person is behaving a certain way because of something about the situation he or she is in; the assumption is that most people would respond the same way in that situation

External Justification   A reason or an explanation for dissonant personal behavior that resides outside the individual (e.g., to receive a large reward or avoid a severe punishment)

External Validity   The extent to which the results of a study can be generalized to other situations and to other people

Extrinsic Motivation   The desire to engage in an activity because of external rewards or pressures, not because we enjoy the task or find it interesting

False Memory Syndrome   Remembering a past traumatic experience that is objectively false but is nevertheless accepted by the person as true

Fear-Arousing Communication   Persuasive message that attempts to change people's attitudes by arousing their fears

Field Experiments Experiments conducted in natural settings rather than in the laboratory

Fight-or-Flight Response Responding to stress by either attacking the source of the stress or fleeing from it

Fixed Mindset The idea that we have a set amount of an ability that cannot change

Foot-in-the-Door Technique Social influence strategy in which getting people to agree first to a small request makes them more likely to agree later to a second, larger request

Frustration-Aggression Theory The theory that frustration—the perception that you are being prevented from attaining a goal—increases the probability of an aggressive response

Fundamental Attribution Error The tendency to overestimate the extent to which other people's behavior is as a result of internal, dispositional factors and to underestimate the role of situational factors

Gestalt Psychology A school of psychology stressing the importance of studying the subjective way in which an object appears in people's minds rather than the objective, physical attributes of the object

Great Person Theory The idea that certain key personality traits make a person a good leader, regardless of the situation

Group Two or more people who interact and are interdependent in the sense that their needs and goals cause them to influence each other

Group Cohesiveness Qualities of a group that bind members together and promote liking between them

Group Polarization The tendency for groups to make decisions that are more extreme than the initial inclinations of their members

Groupthink A kind of decision process in which maintaining group cohesiveness and solidarity is more important than considering the facts in a realistic manner

Growth Mindset The idea that our abilities are malleable qualities that we can cultivate and grow

Halo Effect A cognitive bias by which we tend to assume that an individual with one positive characteristic also possesses other (even unrelated) positive characteristics

Heuristic–Systematic Model of Persuasion An explanation of the two ways in which persuasive communications can cause attitude change: either systematically processing the merits of the arguments or using mental shortcuts or heuristics

Hindsight Bias The tendency for people to exaggerate, after knowing that something occurred, how much they could have predicted it before it occurred

Holistic Thinking Style A type of thinking in which people focus on the overall context, particularly the ways in which objects relate to each other; this type of thinking is common in East Asian cultures (e.g., China, Japan, and Korea)

Hostile Aggression Aggression stemming from feelings of anger and aimed at inflicting pain or injury

Hypocrisy Induction The arousal of dissonance by having individuals make statements that run counter to their behaviors and then reminding them of the inconsistency between what they advocated and their behavior; the purpose is to lead individuals to more responsible behavior

Idiosyncrasy Credits The tolerance a person earns, over time, by conforming to group norms; if enough credits are earned, the person can, on occasion, deviate from the group without retribution

Implementation Intentions People's specific plans about where, when, and how they will fulfill a goal

Implicit Association Test (IAT) A test thought to measure unconscious (implicit) prejudices according to the speed with which people can pair a target face (e.g., black or white, old or young, Asian or white) with a positive or negative association (e.g., the words *honest* or *evil*)

Implicit Attitudes Attitudes that exist outside of conscious awareness

Impression Management The attempt by people to get others to see them as they want to be seen

In-Group The group with which an individual identifies as a member

In-Group Bias The tendency to favor members of one's own group and give them special preference over people who belong to other groups; the group can be temporary and trivial as well as significant

Independent Variable The variable a researcher changes or varies to see if it has an effect on some other variable

Independent View of the Self A way of defining oneself in terms of one's own internal thoughts, feelings, and actions and not in terms of the thoughts, feelings, and actions of other people

Informational Social Influence Relying on other people as a source of information to guide our behavior; we conform because we believe that others' interpretation of an ambiguous situation is correct and can help us choose an appropriate course of action

Informed Consent Agreement to participate in an experiment, granted in full awareness of the nature of the experiment, which has been explained in advance

Ingratiation The process whereby people flatter, praise, and generally try to make themselves likable to another person, often of higher status

Injunctive Norms People's perceptions of what behaviors are approved or disapproved of by others

Institutional Discrimination Practices that discriminate, legally or illegally, against a minority group by virtue of its ethnicity, gender, culture, age, sexual orientation, or other target of societal or company prejudice

Institutional Review Board (IRB) A group made up of at least one scientist, one nonscientist, and one member not affiliated with the institution that reviews all psychological research at that institution and decides whether it meets ethical guidelines; all research must be approved by the IRB before it is conducted

Instrumental Aggression Aggression as a means to some goal other than causing pain

Insufficient Punishment The dissonance aroused when individuals lack sufficient external justification for having resisted a desired activity or object, usually resulting in individuals devaluing the forbidden activity or object

Integrative Solution A solution to a conflict whereby the parties make trade-offs on issues, with each side conceding the most on issues that are unimportant to it but important to the other side

Interdependence The situation that exists when two or more groups need to depend on one another to accomplish a goal that is important to each of them

Interdependent View of the Self A way of defining oneself in terms of one's relationships to other people, recognizing that one's behavior is often determined by the thoughts, feelings, and actions of others

Internal-External Locus of Control The tendency to believe that things happen because we control them versus believing that good and bad outcomes are out of our control

Internal Attribution The inference that a person is behaving in a certain way because of something about the person, such as attitude, character, or personality

Internal Justification The reduction of dissonance by changing something about oneself (e.g., one's attitude or behavior)

Internal Validity Making sure that nothing besides the independent variable can affect the dependent variable; this is accomplished by controlling all extraneous variables and by randomly assigning people to different experimental conditions

Intrinsic Motivation The desire to engage in an activity because we enjoy it or find it interesting, not because of external rewards or pressures

Introspection The process whereby people look inward and examine their own thoughts, feelings, and motives

Investment Model The theory that people's commitment to a relationship depends not only on their satisfaction with the relationship, but also on how much they have invested in the relationship that would be lost by ending it

Jigsaw Classroom A classroom setting designed to reduce prejudice and raise the self-esteem of children by placing them in small, multiethnic groups and making each child dependent on the other children in the group to learn the course material and do well in the class

Judgmental Heuristics Mental shortcuts people use to make judgments quickly and efficiently

Justification of Effort The tendency for individuals to increase their liking for something they have worked hard to attain

Kin Selection The idea that behaviors that help a genetic relative are favored by natural selection

Lowballing An unscrupulous strategy whereby a salesperson induces a customer to agree to purchase a product at a low cost, subsequently claims it was an error, and then raises the price; frequently, the customer will agree to make the purchase at the inflated price

Mere Exposure Effect The finding that the more exposure we have to a stimulus, the more apt we are to like it

Meta-Analysis A statistical technique that averages the results of two or more studies to see if the effect of an independent variable is reliable

Minority Influence The case where a minority of group members influences the behavior or beliefs of the majority

Misattribution of Arousal The process whereby people make mistaken inferences about what is causing them to feel the way they do

Naïve Realism The conviction that we perceive things "as they really are," underestimating how much we are interpreting or "spinning" what we see

Narcissism The combination of excessive self-love and a lack of empathy toward others

Negotiation A form of communication between opposing sides in a conflict in which offers and counteroffers are made and a solution occurs only when both parties agree

Nonverbal Communication The way in which people communicate, intentionally or unintentionally, without words; nonverbal cues include facial expressions, tone of voice, gestures, body position and movement, the use of touch, and gaze

Normative Conformity The tendency to go along with the group in order to fulfill the group's expectations and gain acceptance

Normative Social Influence Going along with what other people do to be liked and accepted by them; we publicly conform with the group's beliefs and behaviors but do not always privately accept them

Norm of Reciprocity The expectation that helping others will increase the likelihood that they will help us in the future

Obedience A change in one's behavior due to the direct influence of an authority figure

Observational Method The technique whereby a researcher observes people and systematically records measurements or impressions of their behavior

Operant Conditioning The phenomenon whereby behaviors we freely choose to perform become more or less frequent, depending on whether they are followed by a reward or punishment

Out-Group Any group with which an individual does not identify

Out-Group Homogeneity The perception that individuals in the out-group are more similar to each other (homogeneous) than they really are, as well as more similar than members of the in-group are

Overjustification Effect The tendency for people to view their behavior as caused by compelling extrinsic reasons, making them underestimate the extent to which it was caused by intrinsic reasons

Own-Race Bias The tendency for people to be better at recognizing faces of their own race than those of other races

Passionate Love An intense longing we feel for a person, accompanied by physiological arousal

Perceived Control The belief that we can influence our environment in ways that determine whether we experience positive or negative outcomes

Perceptual Salience The seeming importance of information that is the focus of people's attention

Performance-Contingent Rewards Rewards that are based on how well we perform a task

Peripheral Route to Persuasion The case in which people do not elaborate on the arguments in a persuasive communication but are instead swayed by more superficial cues

Persuasive Communication A message advocating a particular side of an issue

Planning Fallacy The tendency for people to be overly optimistic about how soon they will complete a project, even when they have failed to get similar projects done on time in the past

Pluralistic Ignorance The case in which people think that everyone else is interpreting a situation in a certain way, when in fact they are not

Postdecision Dissonance Dissonance aroused after making a decision, typically reduced by enhancing the attractiveness of the chosen alternative and devaluating the rejected alternatives

Prejudice A hostile or negative attitude toward people in a distinguishable group based solely on their membership in that group; it contains cognitive, emotional, and behavioral components

Primacy Effect When it comes to forming impressions, the first traits we perceive in others influence how we view information that we learn about them later

Priming The process by which recent experiences increase the accessibility of a schema, trait, or concept

Private Acceptance Conforming to other people's behavior out of a genuine belief that what they are doing or saying is right

Probability Level (*p*-value) A number calculated with statistical techniques that tells researchers how likely it is that the results of their experiment occurred by chance and not because of the independent variable or variables; the convention in science, including social psychology, is to consider results *significant* (trustworthy) if the probability level is less than 5 in 100 that the results might be due to chance factors and not the independent variables studied

Process Loss Any aspect of group interaction that inhibits good problem solving

Propaganda A deliberate, systematic attempt to advance a cause by manipulating mass attitudes and behaviors, often through misleading or emotionally charged information

Propinquity Effect The finding that the more we see and interact with people, the more likely they are to become our friends

Prosocial Behavior Any act performed with the goal of benefiting another person

Psychological Realism The extent to which the psychological processes triggered in an experiment are similar to psychological processes that occur in everyday life

Public Compliance Conforming to other people's behavior publicly without necessarily believing in what the other people are doing or saying

Random Assignment to Condition A process ensuring that all participants have an equal chance of taking part in any condition of an experiment; through random assignment, researchers can be relatively certain that differences in the participants' personalities or backgrounds are distributed evenly across conditions

Random Selection A way of ensuring that a sample of people is representative of a population by giving everyone in the population an equal chance of being selected for the sample

Reactance Theory The idea that when people feel their freedom to perform a certain behavior is threatened, an unpleasant state of resistance is aroused, which they can reduce by performing the prohibited behavior

Realistic Conflict Theory The idea that limited resources lead to conflict between groups and result in increased prejudice and discrimination

Reconstructive Memory The process whereby memories of an event become distorted by information encountered after the event occurred

Recovered Memories Recollections of a past event, such as sexual abuse, that have been forgotten or repressed

Relationship-Oriented Leaders Leaders who are concerned more with workers' feelings and relationships

Replications Repeating a study, often with different subject populations or in different settings

Representativeness Heuristic A mental shortcut whereby people classify something according to how similar it is to a typical case

Resilience Mild, transient reactions to stressful events, followed by a quick return to normal, healthy functioning

Retrieval The process by which people recall information stored in their memories

Schemas Mental structures people use to organize their knowledge about the social world around themes or subjects and that influence the information people notice, think about, and remember

Sexual Scripts Sets of implicit rules that specify proper sexual behavior for a person in a given situation, varying with the person's gender, age, religion, social status, and peer group

Secure Attachment Style An attachment style characterized by trust, a lack of concern with being abandoned, and the view that one is worthy and well liked

Self-Affirmation Theory The idea that people can reduce threats to their self-esteem by affirming themselves in areas unrelated to the source of the threat

Self-Awareness Theory The idea that when people focus their attention on themselves, they evaluate and compare their behavior to their internal standards and values

Self-Concept The overall set of beliefs that people have about their personal attributes

Self-Control The ability to subdue immediate desires to achieve long-term goals.

Self-Esteem People's evaluations of their own self-worth—that is, the extent to which they view themselves as good, competent, and decent

Self-Evaluation Maintenance Theory The idea that people experience dissonance when someone close to us outperforms us in an area that is central to our self-esteem. This dissonance can be reduced by becoming less close to the person, changing our behavior so that we now outperform them, or deciding that the area is not that important to us after all.

Self-Fulfilling Prophecy An expectation of one's own or another person's behavior that comes true because of the tendency of the person holding it to act in ways that bring it about

Self-Handicapping The strategy whereby people create obstacles and excuses for themselves so that if they do poorly on a task, they can avoid blaming themselves

Self-Perception Theory The theory that when our attitudes and feelings are uncertain or ambiguous, we infer these states by observing our behavior and the situation in which it occurs

Self-Serving Attributions Explanations for one's successes that credit internal, dispositional factors and explanations for one's failures that blame external, situational factors

Social-Cognitive Learning Theory The theory that people learn social behavior (e.g., aggression or altruism) in large part through observation and imitation of others and by cognitive processes such as plans, expectations, and beliefs

Social Cognition How people think about themselves and the social world; more specifically, how people select, interpret, remember, and use social information to make judgments and decisions

Social-Cognitive Learning Theory The theory that people learn social behavior (e.g., aggression or altruism) in large part through observation and imitation of others and by cognitive processes such as plans, expectations, and beliefs

Social Comparison Theory The idea that we learn about our own abilities and attitudes by comparing ourselves to other people

Social Dilemma A conflict in which the most beneficial action for an individual will, if chosen by most people, have harmful effects on everyone

Social Exchange Theory The idea that people's feelings about a relationship depend on their perceptions of its rewards and costs, the kind of relationship they deserve, and their chances for having a better relationship with someone else

Social Facilitation When people are in the presence of others and their individual performance can be evaluated, the tendency to perform better on simple tasks and worse on complex tasks

Social Identity The part of a person's self-concept that is based on his or her identification with a nation, religious or political group, occupation, or other social affiliation

Social Identity Threat The threat elicited when people perceive that others are evaluating them as a member of their group instead of as an individual

Social Impact Theory The idea that conforming to social influence depends on the group's importance, immediacy, and the number of people in the group

Social Influence The effect that the words, actions, or mere presence of other people have on our thoughts, feelings, attitudes, or behavior

Social Loafing When people are in the presence of others and their individual performance cannot be evaluated, the tendency to perform worse on simple or unimportant tasks but better on complex or important tasks

Social Norms The implicit or explicit rules a group has for the acceptable behaviors, values, and beliefs of its members

Social Perception The study of how we form impressions of and make inferences about other people

Social Psychology The scientific study of the way in which people's thoughts, feelings, and behaviors are influenced by the real or imagined presence of other people

Social Roles Shared expectations in a group about how particular people are supposed to behave

Social Support The perception that others are responsive and receptive to one's needs

Social Tuning   The process whereby people adopt another person's attitudes

Source Monitoring   The process whereby people try to identify the source of their memories

Stereotype   A generalization about a group of people in which certain traits are assigned to virtually all members of the group, regardless of actual variation among the members

Storage   The process by which people maintain in memory information they have acquired from the environment

Story Model   The theory that jurors try to fit the evidence they hear at trial into a coherent story, and ultimately reach a verdict that best fits the story they have created

Stress   The negative feelings and beliefs that arise whenever people feel unable to cope with demands from their environment

Subliminal Messages   Words or pictures that are not consciously perceived but may nevertheless influence judgments, attitudes, and behaviors

Surveys   Research in which a representative sample of people are asked (often anonymously) questions about their attitudes or behavior

Task-Contingent Rewards   Rewards that are given for performing a task, regardless of how well the task is done

Task-Oriented Leaders   Leaders who are concerned more with getting the job done than with workers' feelings and relationships

Tend-and-Befriend Response   Responding to stress with nurturing activities designed to protect oneself and one's offspring (tending) and creating social networks that provide protection from threats (befriending)

Terror Management Theory   The theory that holds that self-esteem serves as a buffer, protecting people from terrifying thoughts about their own mortality

Theory of Planned Behavior   The idea that people's intentions are the best predictors of their deliberate behaviors, which are determined by their attitudes toward specific behaviors, subjective norms, and perceived behavioral control

Thin-Slicing   Drawing meaningful conclusions about another person's personality or skills based on an extremely brief sample of behavior

Tit-for-Tat Strategy   A means of encouraging cooperation by at first acting cooperatively but then always responding the way your opponent did (cooperatively or competitively) on the previous trial

Transactional Leaders   Leaders who set clear, short-term goals and reward people who meet them

Transactive Memory   The combined memory of a group that is more efficient than the memory of the individual members

Transformational Leaders   Leaders who inspire followers to focus on common, long-term goals

Two-Factor Theory of Emotion   The idea that emotional experience is the result of a two-step self-perception process in which people first experience physiological arousal and then seek an appropriate explanation for it

Two-Step Attribution Process   Analyzing another person's behavior first by making an automatic internal attribution and only then thinking about possible situational reasons for the behavior, after which one may adjust the original internal attribution

Upward Social Comparison   Comparing ourselves to people who are better than we are with regard to a particular trait or ability

Urban Overload Hypothesis   The theory that people living in cities are constantly bombarded with stimulation and that they keep to themselves to avoid being overwhelmed by it

Weapons Effect   The increase in aggression that can occur because of the mere presence of a gun or other weapon

Yale Attitude Change Approach   The study of the conditions under which people are most likely to change their attitudes in response to persuasive messages, focusing on the source of the communication, the nature of the communication, and the nature of the audience

References

Aaker, J. L. (2000). Accessibility or diagnosticity? Disentangling the influence of culture on persuasion processes and attitudes. *Journal of Consumer Research, 26,* 340–357.

Aarts, H., & Dijksterhuis, A. (2003). The silence of the library: Environment, situational norm, and social behavior. *Journal of Personality and Social Psychology, 84,* 18–28.

Aarts, H., & Elliot, A. J. (Eds.). (2012). *Goal-directed behavior.* New York: Taylor & Francis.

Abele, A. E., & Brack, S. (2013). Preference for other persons' traits is dependent on the kind of social relationship. *Social Psychology, 44,* 84–94.

Abelson, R. P., Kinder, D. R., Peters, M. D., & Fiske, S. T. (1982). Affective and semantic components in political person perception. *Journal of Personality and Social Psychology, 42,* 619–630.

Abrams, D., Marques, J. M., Bown, N., & Henson, M. (2000). Pro-norm and anti-norm deviance within and between groups. *Journal of Personality and Social Psychology, 78,* 906–912.

Abrams, D., Palmer, S. B., Rutland, A., Cameron, L., & Van de Vyer, J. (2014). Evaluations of and reasoning about normative and deviant ingroup and outgroup members: Development of the black sheep effect. *Developmental Psychology, 50,* 258–270.

Abrams, D., Viki, G. T., Masser, B., & Bohner, G. (2003). Perceptions of stranger and acquaintance rape: The role of benevolent and hostile sexism in victim blame and rape proclivity. *Journal of Personality and Social Psychology, 84,* 111–125.

Abrams, D., Wetherell, M., Cochrane, S., Hogg, M. A., & Turner, J. C. (1990). Knowing what to think by knowing who you are: Self-categorization and the nature of norm formation, conformity and group polarization. *British Journal of Social Psychology, 29,* 97–119.

Acquisti, A., & Fong, C. M. (2014, October 26). An experiment in hiring discrimination via online social networks. Available at SSRN: http://ssrn.com/abstract=2031979 or http://dx.doi.org/10.2139/ssrn.2031979

Adams, R. B., Jr., & Kleck, R. E. (2003). Perceived gaze direction and the processing of facial displays of emotion. *Psychological Science, 14,* 644–647.

Adams, R. B., Jr., Franklin, R. G., Jr., Rule, N. O., Freeman, J. B., Kveraga, K., Hadjikhani, N., et al. (2010). Culture, gaze, and the neural processing of fear expressions. *Social Cognitive and Affective Neuroscience, 5,* 340–348.

Adolfsson, K., & Strömwall, L. A. (2017). Situational variables or beliefs? A multifaceted approach to understanding blame attributions. *Psychology, Crime & Law,* 1–26.

Adult obesity. (2011). Centers for Disease Control and Prevention. Retrieved November 1, 2011, from www.cdc.gov/obesity/data/adult.html

Agars, M. D. (2004). Reconsidering the impact of gender stereotypes on the advancement of women in organizations. *Psychology of Women Quarterly, 28,* 103–111.

Agerström, J., & Rooth, D-O. (2011). The role of automatic obesity stereotypes in real hiring discrimination. *Journal of Applied Psychology, 96,* 790–805.

Aguiar, P., Vala, J., Correia, I., & Pereira, C. (2008). Justice in our world and in that of others: Belief in a just world and reactions to victims. *Social Justice Research, 21,* 50–68.

Ahler, D. J., Citrin, J., Dougal, M. C., & Lenz, G. S. (2016). Face value? Experimental evidence that candidate appearance influences electoral choice. *Political Behavior, 39,* 1–26.

Ahn, H.-K., Kim, H. J., & Aggarwal, P. (2014). Helping fellow beings: Anthropomorphized social causes and the role of anticipatory guilt. *Psychological Science, 25*(1), 224–229.

Aiello, J. R., & Douthitt, E. A. (2001). Social facilitation from Triplett to electronic performance monitoring. *Group Dynamics: Theory, Research, and Practice, 5,* 163–180.

Ainsworth, M. D. S., Blehar, M. C., Waters, E., & Wall, S. (1978). *Patterns of attachment: A psychological study of the strange situation.* Hillsdale, NJ: Erlbaum.

Ajzen, I. (1985). From intentions to actions: A theory of planned behavior. In J. Kuhl & J. Beckmann (Eds.), *Action control: From cognition to behavior* (pp. 11–39). Heidelberg, Germany: Springer-Verlag.

Ajzen, I., & Fishbein, M. (1980). *Understanding attitudes and predicting social behavior.* Englewood Cliffs, NJ: Prentice Hall.

Ajzen, I., & Sheikh, S. (2013). Action versus inaction: Anticipated affect in the theory of planned behavior. *Journal of Applied Social Psychology, 43,* 155–162.

Aktas, M., Gelfand, M. J., & Hanges, P. J. (2016). Cultural tightness–looseness and perceptions of effective leadership. *Journal of Cross-Cultural Psychology, 47,* 294–309.

Albarracín, D., Johnson, B. T., Fishbein, M., & Muellerleile, P. A. (2001). Theories of reasoned action and planned behavior as models of condom use: A meta-analysis. *Psychological Bulletin, 127,* 142–161.

Albarracín, D., Kumkale, G. T., & Poyner-Del Vento, P. (2017). How people can become persuaded by weak messages presented by credible communicators: Not all sleeper effects are created equal. *Journal of Experimental Social Psychology, 68,* 171–180.

Alexander, M. (2012). *The New Jim Crow: Mass Incarceration in the Age of Colorblindness.* New York: The New Press.

Algoe, S. B. (2012). Find, remind, and bind: The functions of gratitude in everyday relationships. *Social and Personality Psychology Compass, 6*(6), 455–469. doi:10.1111/j.1751-004.2012.00439.x

Algoe, S. B., Fredrickson, B. L., & Gable, S. L. (2013). The social functions of the emotion of gratitude via expression. *Emotion, 13,* 605–609. doi:10.1037/a0032701

Allen, M., Donohue, W. A., & Griffin, A. (2003). Comparing the influence of parents and peers on the choice to use drugs. *Criminal Justice and Behavior, 30,* 163–186.

Allen, V. L., & Levine, J. M. (1969). Consensus and conformity. *Journal of Personality and Social Psychology, 5,* 389–399.

Allport, G. W. (1954). *The nature of prejudice.* Reading, MA: Addison-Wesley.

Allport, G. W. (1985). The historical background of social psychology. In G. Lindzey & E. Aronson (Eds.), *The handbook of social psychology* (3rd ed., Vol. 1, pp. 1–46). New York: McGraw-Hill.

ALSA. (2014). The ALS Association expresses sincere gratitude to over three million donors. Retrieved August 29, 2014, from www.alsa.org/news/media/press-releases/ice-bucket-challenge-082914.html

Alter, A. L., & Darley, J. M. (2009). When the association between appearance and outcome contaminates social judgment: A bidirectional model linking group homogeneity and collective treatment. *Journal of Personality and Social Psychology, 9,* 776–795. doi:10.1037/a0016957

Alvarez, K., & Van Leeuwen, E. (2011). To teach or to tell? Consequences of receiving help from experts and peers. *European Journal of Social Psychology, 41*(3), 397–402. doi:10.1002/ejsp.789

Amato, P. R. (1983). Helping behavior in urban and rural environments: Field studies based on a taxonomic organization of helping episodes. *Journal of Personality and Social Psychology, 45,* 571–586.

Ambady, N., & Rosenthal, R. (1992). Thin slices of expressive behavior as predictors of interpersonal consequences: A meta-analysis. *Psychological Bulletin, 111,* 256–274.

Ambady, N., & Rosenthal, R. (1993). Half a minute: Predicting teacher evaluations from thin slices of nonverbal behavior and physical attractiveness. *Journal of Personality and Social Psychology, 64,* 431–441.

Ambady, N., LaPlante, D., Nguen, T., Rosenthal, R., & Levinson, W. (2002). Surgeon's tone of voice: A clue to malpractice history. *Surgery, 132,* 5–9.

American Psychological Association. (2010). Ethical principles of psychologists and code of conduct. Retrieved March 22, 2010, from www.apa.org/ethics/code/index.aspx

Ames, D. R., & Flynn, F. J. (2007). What breaks a leader: The curvilinear relation between assertiveness and leadership. *Journal of Personality and Social Psychology, 92,* 307–324.

Ames, D. R., & Johar, G. V. (2009). I'll know what you're like when I see how you feel: How and when affective displays influence behavior-based impressions. *Psychological Science, 20,* 586–593.

Ames, D. R., Rose, P., & Anderson, C. P. (2006). The NPI-16 as a short measure of narcissism. *Journal of Research in Personality, 40,* 440–450.

Amodio, D. M., & Showers, C. J. (2005). 'Similarity breeds liking' revisited: The moderating role of commitment. *Journal of Social and Personal Relationships, 22,* 817–836.

Andersen, B., Farrar, W. B., Golden-Kreutz, D. M., Glaser, R., Emery, C. F., & Crespin, T. R. (2004). Psychological, behavioral, and immune changes after a psychological intervention: A clinical trial. *Journal of Clinical Oncology, 22,* 3570–3580.

Andersen, S. M. (1984). Self-knowledge and social inference: II. The diagnosticity of cognitive/affective and behavioral data. *Journal of Personality and Social Psychology, 46,* 294–307.

Andersen, S. M., & Bem, S. L. (1981). Sex typing and androgyny in dyadic interaction: Individual differences in responsiveness to physical attractiveness. *Journal of Personality and Social Psychology, 41,* 74–86.

Andersen, S. M., & Klatzky, R. L. (1987). Traits and social stereotypes: Levels of categorization in person perception. *Journal of Personality and Social Psychology, 53,* 235–246.

Andersen, S. M., & Ross, L. D. (1984). Self-knowledge and social inference: I. The impact of cognitive/affective and behavioral data. *Journal of Personality and Social Psychology, 46,* 280–293.

Anderson, C. A. (1995). Implicit personality theories and empirical data: Biased assimilation, belief perseverance and change, and covariation detection sensitivity. *Social Cognition, 13,* 25–48.

Anderson, C. A. (1999). Attributional style, depression, and loneliness: A cross-cultural comparison of American and Chinese students. *Personality and Social Psychology Bulletin, 25,* 482–499.

Anderson, C. A. (2012). Climate change and violence. In D. J. Christie (Ed.), *The encyclopedia of peace psychology.* New York: Wiley-Blackwell.

Anderson, C. A., & Bushman, B. J. (1997). External validity of "trivial" experiments: The case of laboratory aggression. *Review of General Psychology, 1,* 19–41.

Anderson, C. A., & Dill, K. E. (2000). Video games and aggressive thoughts, feelings, and behavior in the laboratory and in life. *Journal of Personality and Social Psychology, 78,* 772–790.

Anderson, C. A., Anderson, K. B., Dorr, N., DeNeve, K. M., & Flanagan, M. (2000). Temperature and aggression. In M. P. Zanna (Ed.), *Advances in experimental social psychology* (Vol. 32, pp. 63–133). San Diego, CA: Academic Press.

Anderson, C. A., Benjamin, A. J., Jr., & Bartholow, B. D. (1998). Does the gun pull the trigger? Automatic priming effects of weapon pictures and weapon names. *Psychological Science, 9,* 308–314.

Anderson, C. A., Berkowitz, L., Donnerstein, E., Huesmann, L. R., Johnson, J. D., et al. (2003). The influence of media violence on youth. *Psychological Science in the Public Interest, 4,* 81–110.

Anderson, C. S., Shibuya, A., Ihori, N., Swing, E. L., Bushman, B. J., Sakamoto, A., Rothstein, H. R., & Saleem, M. (2010). Violent video game effects on aggression, empathy, and prosocial behavior in Eastern and Western countries: A meta-analytic review. *Psychological Bulletin, 136,* 151–173.

Anderson, E., Siegel, E., White, D., & Barrett, L. F. (2012). Out of sight but not out of mind: Unseen affective faces influence evaluations and social impressions. *Emotion, 12*(6), 1210–1221. doi:10.1037/a0027514

Anderson, J. R., & Gallup, G. G., Jr. (2015). Mirror self-recognition: A review and critique of attempts to promote and engineer self-recognition in primates. *Primates, 56,* 317–326.

Anderson, N. D., Damianakis, T., Kröger, E., Wagner, L. M., Dawson, D. R., Binns, M.A., Bernstein, S., Caspi, E., Cook, S. L., & The BRA-VO Team (2014). The benefits associated with volunteering among seniors: A critical review and recommendations for future research. *Psychological Bulletin, 140,* 1505–1533.

Anderson, S. L., Adams, G., & Plaut, V. C. (2008). The cultural grounding of personal relationship: The importance of attractiveness in everyday life. *Journal of Personality and Social Psychology, 95,* 352–368.

Andrade, E. B., & Van Boven, L. (2010). Feelings not forgone: Underestimating affective reactions to what does not happen. *Psychological Science, 21*(5), 706–711.

Antoni, M. H., & Lutgendorf, S. (2007). Psychosocial factors and disease progression in cancer. *Current Directions in Psychological Science, 16,* 42–46.

Anzures, G., Quinn, P. C., Pascalis, O., Slater, A. M., Tanaka, J. W., & Lee, K. (2013). Developmental origins of the other-race effect. *Current Directions in Psychological Science, 22,* 173–178.

Apfelbaum, E. P., Phillips, K. W., & Richeson, J. A. (2014). Rethinking the baseline in diversity research: Should we be explaining the effects of homogeneity? *Perspectives on Psychological Science, 9,* 235–244.

Applebome, P. (1991, November 10). Duke: The ex-Nazi who would be governor. *The New York Times.* Retrieved February 17, 2015, from http://www.nytimes.com/1991/11/10/us/duke-the-ex-nazi-who-would-be-governor.html

AP-GfK Poll. (2016). Retrieved April 16, 2017, from http://ap-gfkpoll.com/main/wp-content/uploads/2016/04/March-2016-AP-GfK-Poll-FINAL_Obama.pdf

Aquino, A., Haddock, G., Maio, G. R., Wolf, L. J., & Alparone, F. R. (2016). The role of affective and cognitive individual differences in social perception. *Personality and Social Psychology Bulletin, 42,* 798–810.

Archer, D. (1997). Unspoken diversity: Cultural differences in gestures. *Qualitative Sociology, 20,* 79–105.

Archer, D., & Akert, R. M. (1984). Problems of context and criterion in nonverbal communication: A new look at the accuracy issue. In M. Cook (Ed.), *Issues in person perception* (pp. 114–144). New York: Methuen.

Archer, D., & McDaniel, P. (1995). Violence and gender: Differences and similarities across societies. In R. B. Ruback & N. A. Weiner (Eds.), *Interpersonal violent behaviors: Social and cultural aspects* (pp. 63–88). New York: Springer-Verlag.

Archer, J. (2004). Sex differences in aggression in real-world settings: A meta-analytic review. *Review of General Psychology, 8,* 291–322.

Archer, J. (2013). Can evolutionary principles explain patterns of family violence? *Psychological Bulletin, 139*(2), 403–440. doi:10.1037/a0029114

Arend, R. J., Cao, X., Grego-Nagel, A., Im, J., Yang, X., & Canavati, S. (2016). Looking upstream and downstream in entrepreneurial cognition: Replicating and extending the Busenitz and Barney (1997) study. *Journal of Small Business Management, 54,* 1147–1170.

Arendt, H. (1965). *Eichmann in Jerusalem: A report on the banality of evil.* New York: Viking.

Arigo, D., Suls, J. M., & Smyth, J. M. (2014). Social comparisons and chronic illness: Research synthesis and clinical implications. *Health Psychology Review, 8,* 154–214.

Arkes, H. R., & Mellers, B. A. (2002). Do juries meet our expectations? *Law and Human Behavior, 26,* 625–639.

Arkes, H., & Tetlock, P. (2004). Attributions of implicit prejudice, or "Would Jesse Jackson 'fail' the Implicit Association Test?" *Psychological Inquiry, 15,* 257–278.

Armata, P. M., & Baldwin, D. R. (2008). Stress, optimism, resiliency, and cortisol with relation to digestive symptoms or diagnosis. *Individual Differences Research, 6,* 123–138.

Arnocky, S., Piché, T., Albert, G., Ouellette, D. & Barclay, P. (2017). Altruism predicts mating success in humans. *British Journal of Psychology, 108,* 416–435.

Aron, A., Aron, E. N., & Norman, C. (2004). Self-expansion model of motivation and cognition in close relationships and beyond. In M. B. Brewer & M. Hewstone (Eds.), *Self and social identity* (pp. 99–123). Malden, MA: Blackwell Publishing.

Aron, A., Fisher, H., Mashek, D. J., Strong, G., Li, H., & Brown, L. L. (2005). Reward, motivation, and emotion systems associated with early-stage intense romantic love. *Journal of Neurophysiology, 94,* 327–337.

Aronson, E. (1969). The theory of cognitive dissonance: A current perspective. In L. Berkowitz (Ed.), *Advances in experimental social psychology* (Vol. 4, pp. 1–34). New York: Academic Press.

Aronson, E. (1978). *The jigsaw classroom.* Beverly Hills, CA: Sage.

Aronson, E. (1997). The theory of cognitive dissonance: The evolution and vicissitudes of an idea. In C. McGarty & S. A. Haslam (Eds.), *The message of social psychology: Perspectives on mind in society* (pp. 20–35). Malden, MA: Blackwell.

Aronson, E. (1998). Dissonance, hypocrisy, and the self-concept. In E. Harmon-Jones & J. S. Mills (Eds.), *Cognitive dissonance theory: Revival with revisions and controversies* (pp. 21–36). Washington, DC: American Psychological Association.

Aronson, E. (1999). *The social animal* (8th ed.). New York: Worth/Freeman.

Aronson, E. (2000). *Nobody left to hate: Teaching compassion after Columbine.* New York: Worth/Freeman.

Aronson, E. (2007). The evolution of cognitive dissonance theory: A personal appraisal. In A. Pratkanis (Ed.), *The science of social influence.* New York: Psychology Press.

Aronson, E. (2008). *The social animal* (11th ed.). New York: W. H. Freeman.

Aronson, E., & Bridgeman, D. (1979). Jigsaw groups and the desegregated classroom: In pursuit of common goals. *Personality and Social Psychology Bulletin, 5,* 438–446.

Aronson, E., & Carlsmith, J. M. (1962). Performance expectancy as a determinant of actual performance. *Journal of Abnormal and Social Psychology, 65,* 178–182.

Aronson, E., & Carlsmith, J. M. (1963). Effect of severity of threat in the devaluation of forbidden behavior. *Journal of Abnormal and Social Psychology, 66,* 584–588.

Aronson, E., & Carlsmith, J. M. (1968). Experimentation in social psychology. In G. Lindzey & E. Aronson (Eds.), *The handbook of social psychology* (Vol. 2, pp. 1–79). Reading, MA: Addison-Wesley.

Aronson, E., & Gonzalez, A. (1988). Desegregation, jigsaw, and the Mexican-American experience. In P. A. Katz & D. Taylor (Eds.), *Towards the elimination of racism: Profiles in controversy* (pp. 310–330). New York: Plenum.

Aronson, E., & Mills, J. S. (1959). The effect of severity of initiation on liking for a group. *Journal of Abnormal and Social Psychology, 59,* 177–181.

Aronson, E., & Patnoe, S. (1997). *Cooperation in the classroom: The jigsaw method.* New York: Longman.

Aronson, E., & Patnoe, S. (2011). *Cooperation in the classroom: The jigsaw method.* London, England: Pinter & Martin. Available in the U.S. through Amazon Digital Services as a Kindle edition.

Aronson, E., & Thibodeau, R. (1992). The jigsaw classroom: A cooperative strategy for reducing prejudice. In J. Lynch, C. Modgil, & S. Modgil (Eds.), *Cultural diversity in the schools* (pp. 110–118). London: Falmer Press.

Aronson, E., Ellsworth, P. C., Carlsmith, J. M., & Gonzalez, M. H. (1990). *Methods of research in social psychology* (2nd ed.). New York: McGraw-Hill.

Aronson, E., Fried, C., & Stone, J. (1991). Overcoming denial and increasing the intention to use condoms through the induction of hypocrisy. *American Journal of Public Health, 81,* 1636–1638.

Aronson, E., Wilson, T. D., & Brewer, M. B. (1998). Experimental methods. In D. T. Gilbert, S. T. Fiske, & G. Lindzey (Eds.), *The handbook of social psychology* (4th ed., Vol. 1, pp. 99–142). New York: McGraw-Hill.

Aronson, J. (2010). Jigsaw, social psychology, and the nurture of human intelligence. In *The scientist and the humanist: A festschrift in honor of Elliot Aronson.* New York: Taylor & Francis.

Aronson, J., Cohen, G., & Nail, P. R. (1999). Self-affirmation theory: An update and appraisal. In E. Harmon-Jones & J. S. Mills (Eds.), *Cognitive dissonance: Progress on a pivotal theory in social psychology* (pp. 127–147). Washington, DC: American Psychological Association.

Aronson, J., Lustina, M. J., Good, C., Keough, K., Steele, C. M., & Brown, J. (1999). When white men can't do math: Necessary and sufficient factors in stereotype threat. *Journal of Experimental Social Psychology, 35,* 29–46.

Aronson, J., & McGlone, M. (2009). Stereotype threat. In T. Nelson (Ed.), *The handbook of prejudice, stereotyping, and discrimination* (pp. 153–179). New York: Psychology Press.

Arsena, A., Silvera, D. H., & Pandelaere, M. (2014). Brand trait transference: When celebrity endorsers acquire brand personality traits. *Journal of Business Research.* Advance online publication. doi: http://dx.doi.org/10.1016/j.jbusres.2014.01.011

Asch, S. E. (1946). Forming impressions of personality. *Journal of Abnormal and Social Psychology, 41,* 258–290.

Asch, S. E. (1951). Effects of group pressure upon the modification and distortion of judgment. In H. Guetzkow (Ed.), *Groups, leadership, and men* (pp. 76–92). Pittsburgh, PA: Carnegie Press.

Asch, S. E. (1955). Opinions and social pressure. *Scientific American, 193,* 31–35.

Asch, S. E. (1956). Studies of independence and conformity: A minority of one against a unanimous majority. *Psychological Monographs, 7* (9, Whole No. 416).

Asch, S. E. (1957). An experimental investigation of group influence. In Walter Reed Army Institute of Research, *Symposium on preventive and social psychiatry* (pp. 15–17). Washington, DC: U.S. Government Printing Office.

Aspinwall, L. G., & Taylor, S. E. (1993). Effects of social comparison direction, threat, and self-esteem on affect, evaluation, and expected success. *Journal of Personality and Social Psychology, 64,* 708–722.

Aspinwall, L. G., & Taylor, S. E. (1997). A stitch in time: Self-regulation and proactive coping. *Psychological Bulletin, 121,* 417–436.

Associated Press. (2002, November 1). Halloween is debated by French. *The Boston Globe,* p. A20.

Aucouturier, J., Johansson, P., Hall, L., Segnini, R., Mercadié, L., & Watanabe, K. (2016). Covert digital manipulation of vocal emotion alter speakers' emotional states in a congruent direction. *Proceedings of the National Academy of Sciences of the United States of America, 113,* 948–953.

Augustinova, M., & Ferrand, L. (2012). The influence of mere social presence of Stroop interference: New evidence from the semantically-based Stroop task. *Journal of Experimental Social Psychology, 48,* 1213–1216.

Aumer, K. (2016). *The psychology of love and hate in intimate relationships.* Springer: Switzerland.

Aune, K. S., & Aune, R. K. (1996). Cultural differences in the self-reported experience and expression of emotions in relationships. *Journal of Cross-Cultural Psychology, 27,* 67–81.

Avolio, B. J., Walumbwa, F. O., & Weber, T. J. (2009). Leadership: Current theories, research, and future directions. *Annual Review of Psychology, 60,* 421–449.

Aycan, Z., Schyns, B., Sun, J., Felfe, J., & Saher, N. (2013). Convergence and divergence of paternalistic leadership: A cross-cultural investigation of prototypes. *Journal of International Business Studies, 44,* 962–969.

Ayduk, Ö., & Kross, E. (2008). Enhancing the pace of recovery: Self-distanced analysis of negative experiences reduces blood pressure reactivity. *Psychological Science, 19,* 229–231.

Ayman, R. (2002). Contingency model of leadership effectiveness. In L. L. Neider & C. A. Schriesheim (Eds.), *Leadership* (pp. 197–228). Greenwich, CT: Information Age.

Azrin, N. H. (1967, May). Pain and aggression. *Psychology Today,* pp. 27–33.

Baca-Motes, K., Brown, A. Gneezy, A., Keenan, E. A., & Nelson, L. D. (2013). Commitment and behavior change: Evidence from the field. *Journal of Consumer Research, 39,* 1070–1084.

Badr, L. K., & Abdallah, B. (2001). Physical attractiveness of premature infants affects outcome at discharge from the NICU. *Infant Behavior and Development, 24,* 129–133.

Bailey, D. S., & Taylor, S. P. (1991). Effects of alcohol and aggressive disposition on human physical aggression. *Journal of Research in Personality, 25*(3), 334–342.

Baird, B., Smallwood, J., Fishman, D. J. F., Mrazek, M. D., & Schooler, J. W. (2013). Unnoticed intrusions: Dissociations of meta-consciousness in thought suppression. *Consciousness and Cognition: An International Journal, 22*(3), 1003–1012.

Balsam, K. F., Beauchaine, T. P., Rothblum, E. D., & Solomon, S. E. (2008). Three-year follow-up of same-sex couples who had civil unions in Vermont, same-sex couples not in civil unions, and heterosexual married couples. *Developmental Psychology, 44,* 102–116.

Balsam, K. F., Rostosky, S. S., & Riggle, E. D. (2017). Breaking up is hard to do: Women's experience of dissolving their same-sex relationship. *Journal of Lesbian Studies, 21,* 30–46.

Banaji, M. R., & Greenwald, A. G. (2013). *Blindspot: Hidden biases of good people.* New York: Delacorte.

Banaji, M. R., & Heiphetz, L. (2010). Attitudes. In S. T. Fiske, D. T. Gilbert, & G. Lindzey (Eds.), *Handbook of social psychology* (5th ed., Vol. 1, pp. 353–393). Hoboken, NJ: Wiley.

Banas, J. A., & Miller, G. (2013). Inducing resistance to conspiracy theory propaganda: Testing inoculation and metainoculation strategies. *Human Communication Research, 39,* 184–207.

Bandura, A., Ross, D., & Ross, S. (1961). Transmission of aggression through imitation of aggressive models. *Journal of Abnormal and Social Psychology, 63,* 575–582.

Bandura, A., Ross, D., & Ross, S. (1963). Imitation of film-mediated aggressive models. *Journal of Abnormal and Social Psychology, 66,* 3–11.

Banerjee, R., & Dittmar, H. (2008). Individual differences in children's materialism: The role of peer relations. *Personality and Social Psychology Bulletin, 34,* 17–31.

Banuazizi, A., & Movahedi, S. (1975). Interpersonal dynamics in a simulated prison: A methodological analysis. *American Psychologist, 30,* 152–160.

Bar, M., Neta, M., & Linz, H. (2006). Very first impressions. *Emotion, 6,* 269–278.

Bar-Anan, Y., Wilson, T. D., & Hassin, R. R. (2010). Inaccurate self-knowledge formation as a result of automatic behavior. *Journal of Experimental Social Psychology, 46*(6), 884–894. doi:10.1016/j.jesp.2010.07.007

Bargh, J. A. (1996). Automaticity in social psychology. In E. T. Higgins & A. W. Kruglanski (Eds.), *Social psychology: Handbook of basic principles* (pp. 169–183). New York: Guilford Press.

Bargh, J. A., & Pietromonaco, P. (1982). Automatic information processing and social perception: The influence of trait information presented outside of conscious awareness on impression formation. *Journal of Personality and Social Psychology, 43,* 437–449.

Bargh, J. A., Schwader, K. L., Hailey, S. E., Dyer, R. L., & Boothby, E. J. (2012). Automaticity in social-cognitive processes. *Trends in Cognitive Sciences, 16*(12), 593–605. doi:10.1016/j.tics.2012.10.002

Bargh, J. (2017). *The hidden mind: The simple reasons we do what we do.* New York: Random House.

Barkan, R., Ayal, S., Gino, F., & Ariely, D. (2012). The pot calling the kettle black: Distancing response to ethical dissonance. *Journal of Experimental Psychology: General, 141,* 757–773.

Barley, S. R., & Bechky, B. A. (1994). In the backrooms of science: The work of technicians in science labs. *Work and Occupations, 21,* 85–126.

Barnes, T. N., Smith, S. W., & Miller, M. D. (2014). School-based cognitive-behavioral interventions in the treatment of aggression in the United States: A meta-analysis. *Aggression and Violent Behavior, 19,* 311–321.

Baron, R. A. (1972). Reducing the influence of an aggressive model: The restraining effects of peer censure. *Journal of Experimental Social Psychology, 8,* 266–275.

Baron, R. A. (1988). Negative effects of destructive criticism: Impact on conflict, self-efficacy, and task performance. *Journal of Applied Psychology, 73,* 199–207.

Baron, R. A., & Richardson, D. R. (1994). *Human aggression* (2nd ed.). New York: Plenum.

Baron, R. M., & Misovich, S. J. (1993). Dispositional knowing from an ecological perspective. *Personality and Social Psychology Bulletin, 19,* 541–552.

Baron, R. S. (1986). Distraction/conflict theory: Progress and problems. In L. Berkowitz (Ed.), *Advances in experimental social psychology* (Vol. 19, pp. 1–40). Orlando, FL: Academic Press.

Baron, R. S. (2005). So right it's wrong: Groupthink and the ubiquitous nature of polarized group decision making. In M. P. Zanna (Ed.), *Advances in experimental social psychology* (Vol. 37, pp. 219–253). San Diego, CA: Academic Press.

Baron, R. S., Vandello, J. A., & Brunsman, B. (1996). The forgotten variable in conformity research: Impact of task importance on social influence. *Journal of Personality and Social Psychology, 71,* 915–927.

Barrouquere, B. (2006, June 15). A call, a hoax, a nationwide search for the man on the phone. *Associated Press.*

Barsalou, L. W. (2008). Grounded cognition. *Annual Review of Psychology, 59,* 617–645.

Bartels, A., & Zeki, S. (2004). The neural correlates of maternal and romantic love. *Neuroimage, 21,* 1155–1166.

Bartlett, F. C. (1932). *Remembering.* Cambridge, UK: Cambridge University Press.

Bashar al-Assad's Opera House Speech. (2013, January). Retrieved May 21, 2017, from http://carnegie-mec.org/diwan/50513?lang=en

Bass, B. M. (1998). *Transformational leadership: Industry, military, and educational impact.* Mahwah, NJ: Erlbaum.

Batson, C. D. (1991). *The altruism question: Toward a social-psychological answer.* Hillsdale, NJ: Erlbaum.

Batson, C. D. (2011). *Altruism in humans.* New York: Oxford University Press.

Batson, C. D. (2012). A history of prosocial behavior research. In A. W. Kruglanski & W. Stroebe (Eds.), *Handbook of the history of social psychology* (pp. 243–264). New York: Psychology Press.

Batson, C. D., & Powell, A. A. (2003). Altruism and prosocial behavior. In T. Millon & M. J. Lerner (Eds.), *Handbook of psychology: Personality and social psychology* (Vol. 5, pp. 463–484). New York: Wiley.

Batson, C. D., Ahmad, N., & Stocks, E. L. (2004). Benefits and liabilities of empathy-induced altruism. In A. G. Miller (Ed.), *The social psychology of good and evil* (pp. 359–385). New York: Guilford.

Batson, C. D., Ahmad, N., & Stocks, E. L. (2011). Four forms of prosocial motivation: Egoism, altruism, collectivism, and principlism. In D. Dunning (Ed.), *Frontiers of social psychology. Social motivation* (pp. 103–126). New York: Psychology Press.

Batson, C. D., Schoenrade, P., & Ventis, W. L. (1993). *Religion and the individual.* New York: Oxford University Press.

Battle for your brain. (1991, August). *Consumer Reports,* pp. 520–521.

Baumeister, R. (Ed.). (1993). *Self-esteem: The puzzle of low self-regard.* New York: Plenum.

Baumeister, R. F. (1991). *Escaping the self: Alcoholism, spirituality, masochism, and other flights from the burden of selfhood.* New York: Basic Books.

Baumeister, R. F., & Leary, M. R. (1995). The need to belong: Desire for interpersonal attachment as a fundamental human motivation. *Psychological Bulletin, 117,* 497–529.

Baumeister, R. F., & Masicampo, E. J. (2010). Conscious thought is for facilitating social and cultural interactions: How mental simulations serve the animal–culture interface. *Psychological Review, 117*(3), 945–971. doi:10.1037/a0019393

Baumeister, R. F., & Vohs, K. D. (2016). Misguided effort with elusive implications. *Perspectives on Psychological Science, 11,* 574–575.

Baumeister, R. F., Campbell, J. D., Krueger, J. I., & Vohs, K. D. (2003). Does high self-esteem cause better performance, interpersonal success, happiness, or healthier lifestyles? *Psychological Science in the Public Interest, 4,* 1–44. doi:10.1111/1529-1006.01431

Baumeister, R. F., Ainsworth, S. E., & Vohs, K. D. (2016). Are groups more or less than the sum of their members? The moderating role of individual identification. *Behavioral and Brain Sciences, 39.* doi:10.1017/S0140525X15000618

Baumeister, R. F., Masicampo, E. J., & Dewall, C. N. (2009). Prosocial benefits of feeling free: Disbelief in free will increases aggression and reduces helpfulness. *Personality and Social Psychology Bulletin, 35,* 260–268.

Baumeister, R. F., Masicampo, E. J., & Vohs, K. D. (2015). Conscious thoughts and the causation of behavior. In M. Mikulincer & P. R. Shaver (Eds.), *APA Handbook of Personality and Social Psychology: Vol. 1. Attitudes and Social Cognition* (pp. 231–250). Washington, D.C.: American Psychological Association.

Baumeister, R., Vohs, K., & Tice, D. (2007). The strength model of self-control. *Current Directions in Psychological Science, 16,* 351–355.

Baumrind, D. (1964). Some thoughts on ethics of research: After reading Milgram's "Behavioral study of obedience." *American Psychologist, 19,* 421–423.

Baumrind, D. (1985). Research using intentional deception: Ethical issues revisited. *American Psychologist, 40,* 165–174.

Beach, S. R. H., Tesser, A., Mendolia, M., & Anderson, P. (1996). Self-evaluation maintenance in marriage: Toward a performance ecology of the marital relationship. *Journal of Family Psychology, 10,* 379–396.

Beaman, A. L., Barnes, P. J., Klentz, B., & McQuirk, B. (1978). Increasing helping rates through informational dissemination: Teaching pays. *Personality and Social Psychology Bulletin, 4,* 406–411.

Beaman, A. L., Klentz, B., Diener, E., & Svanum, S. (1979). Objective self-awareness and transgression in children: A field study. *Journal of Personality and Social Psychology, 37,* 1835–1846.

Beauvois, J., & Joule, R. (1996). *A radical dissonance theory.* London: Taylor & Francis.

Becker, D. V., Kenrick, D. T., Neuberg, S. L., Blackwell, K. C., & Smith, D. M. (2007). The confounded nature of angry men and happy women. *Journal of Personality and Social Psychology, 92*, 179–190.

Becker, J. C., & Wright, S. C. (2011). Yet another dark side of chivalry: Benevolent sexism undermines and hostile sexism motivates collective action for social change. *Journal of Personality and Social Psychology, 101*, 62–77.

Beckett, K., Nyrop, K., & Pfingst, L. (2006). Race, drugs, and policing: Understanding disparities in drug delivery arrests. *Criminology, 44*, 105–137.

Beer, J. S., Chester, D. S., & Hughes, B. L. (2013). Social threat and cognitive load magnify self-enhancement and attenuate self-deprecation. *Journal of Experimental Social Psychology, 49*(4), 706–711. doi:10.1016/j.jesp.2013.02.017

Bègue, L., Subra, B., Arvers, P., Muller, D., Bricout, V., & Zorman, M. (2009). A message in a bottle: Extrapharmacological effects of alcohol on aggression. *Journal of Experimental Social Psychology, 45*, 137–142.

Bell, J. (1995). Notions of love and romance among the Taita of Kenya. In W. Jankowiak (Ed.), *Romantic passion: A universal experience?* (pp. 152–165). New York: Columbia University Press.

Bell, S. T., Kuriloff, P. J., & Lottes, I. (1994). Understanding attributions of blame in stranger-rape and date-rape situations: An examination of gender, race, identification, and students' social perceptions of rape victims. *Journal of Applied Social Psychology, 24*, 1719–1734.

Belu, C. F., Lee, B. H., & O'Sullivan, L. F. (2016). It hurts to let you go: Characteristics of romantic relationships, breakups and the aftermath among emerging adults. *Journal of Relationships Research, 7.* doi:10.1017/jrr.2016.11

Bem, D. J. (1972). Self-perception theory. In L. Berkowitz (Ed.), *Advances in experimental social psychology* (Vol. 6, pp. 1–62). New York: Academic Press.

Benedetti, P. (2007). Ontario removes video slot machines flashing winning images. *CBC News.* http://www.cbc.ca/news/canada/ontario-removes-video-slot-machines-flashing-winning-images-1.631835

Benjamin, A. J., & Bushman, B. J. (2017). The Weapons Effect. *Current Opinion in Psychology, 19*, 93–97.

Benjamin, L. T., Jr, & Simpson, J. A. (2009). The power of the situation: The impact of Milgram's obedience studies on personality and social psychology. *American Psychologist, 64*, 12–19.

Ben-Ner, A., Putterman, L., Kong, F., & Magan, D. (2004). Reciprocity in a two-part dictator game. *Journal of Economic Behavior and Organization, 53*, 333–352.

Berger, J. (2011). Arousal increases social transmission of information. *Psychological Science, 22*, 891–893.

Bergeron, N., & Schneider, B. H. (2005). Explaining cross-national differences in peer-directed aggression: A quantitative synthesis. *Aggressive Behavior, 31*, 116–137.

Berggren, N., Jordahl, H., & Poutvaara, P. (2010). The looks of a winner: Beauty and electoral success. *Journal of Public Economics, 94*, 8–15.

Bergsieker, H. B., Leslie, L. M., Constantine, V. S., & Fiske, S. T. (2012). Stereotyping by omission: eliminate the negative, accentuate the positive. *Journal of Personality and Social Psychology, 102*, 1214–1238.

Berke, R. L. (2000, September 12). Democrats see, and smell, "rats" in GOP ad. *The New York Times on the Web,* www.nytimes.com

Berkowitz, L. (1981). *When the "trigger" pulls the finger.* Washington, D.C., US: American Psychological Association.

Berkowitz, L. (1983). Aversively simulated aggression. *American Psychologist, 38*, 1135–1144.

Berkowitz, L. (1989). Frustration-aggression hypothesis: Examination and reformulation. *Psychological Bulletin, 106*, 59–73.

Berkowitz, L. (1993). *Aggression: Its causes, consequences, and control.* New York: McGraw-Hill.

Berkowitz, L., & Le Page, A. (1967). Weapons as aggression-eliciting stimuli. *Journal of Personality and Social Psychology, 7*, 202–207.

Bermeitinger, C., Goelz, R., Johr, N., Neumann, M., Ecker, U. K. H., & Doerr, R. (2009). The hidden persuaders break into the tired brain. *Journal of Experimental Social Psychology, 45*(2), 320–326. doi:10.1016/j.jesp.2008.10.001

Berns, G. S., Chappelow, J., Zink, C. F., Pagnoni, G., Martin-Skurski, M. E., & Richards, J. (2005). Neurobiological correlates of social conformity and independence during mental rotation. *Biological Psychiatry, 58*, 245–253.

Bernstein, D. M., Aßfalg, A., Kumar, R., & Ackerman, R. (2016). Looking backward and forward on hindsight bias. In J. Dunlosky & S. K. Tauber (Eds.), *Oxford library of psychology. The Oxford handbook of metamemory* (pp. 289–304). New York: Oxford University Press.

Berscheid, E. (1985). Interpersonal attraction. In G. Lindzey & E. Aronson (Eds.), *The handbook of social psychology* (3rd ed., Vol. 3, pp. 413–484). New York: McGraw-Hill.

Berscheid, E., & Meyers, S. A. (1997). The language of love: The difference a preposition makes. *Personality and Social Psychology Bulletin, 23*, 347–362.

Berscheid, E., & Reis, H. T. (1998). Attraction and close relationships. In D. T. Gilbert, S. T. Fiske, & L. Gardner (Eds.), *The handbook of social psychology* (4th ed., pp. 193–281). New York: McGraw-Hill.

Berscheid, E., & Walster, E. (1978). *Interpersonal attraction.* Reading, MA: Addison-Wesley.

Berscheid, E., Boye, D., & Walster, E. (1968). Retaliation as a means of restoring equity. *Journal of Personality and Social Psychology, 10*, 370–376.

Bertrand, M., & Mullainathan, S. (2004). Are Emily and Greg more employable than Lakisha and Jamal? A field experiment on labor market discrimination. *The American Economic Review, 94*, 991–1013.

Bettencourt, B. A., & Miller, N. (1996). Gender differences in aggression as a function of provocation: A meta-analysis. *Psychological Bulletin, 119*, 422–447.

Bettencourt, B. A., & Sheldon, K. (2001). Social roles as mechanism for psychological need satisfaction within social groups. *Journal of Personality and Social Psychology, 81*, 1131–1143.

Blackhart, G. C., Fitzpatrick, J., & Williamson, J. (2014). Dispositional factors predicting use of online dating sites and behaviors related to online dating. *Computers in Human Behavior, 33*, 113–118.

Blackhart, G. C., Nelson, B. C., Knowles, M. L., & Baumeister, R. F. (2009). Rejection elicits emotional reactions but neither causes immediate distress nor lowers self-esteem: A meta-analytic review of 192 studies on social exclusion. *Personality and Social Psychology Review, 13*(4), 269–309. doi:10.1177/1088868309346065

Blank, H., & Launay, C. (2014). How to protect eyewitness memory against the misinformation effect: A meta-analysis of post-warning studies. *Journal of Applied Research in Memory and Cognition, 3*, 77–88.

Blascovich, J., Mendes, W. B., Hunter, S. B., & Salomon, K. (1999). Social "facilitation" as challenge and threat. *Journal of Personality and Social Psychology, 77*, 68–77.

Blascovich, J., Mendes, W. B., Hunter, S. B., Lickel, B., & Kowai-Bell, N. (2001). Perceiver threat in social interactions with stigmatized others. *Journal of Personality and Social Psychology, 80*, 253–267.

Blass, T. (2000). *Obedience to authority: Current perspectives on the Milgram paradigm.* Mahwah, NJ: Erlbaum.

Blass, T. (2003). The Milgram paradigm after 35 years: Some things we now know about obedience to authority. *Journal of Applied Social Psychology, 29*, 955–978.

Blass, T. (2009). From New Haven to Santa Clara: A historical perspective on the Milgram obedience experiments. *American Psychologist, 64*, 37–45.

Blow, C. (2011, June 11). Drug bust. *The New York Times.* Op-ed page.

Bochner, S. (1994). Cross-cultural differences in the self-concept: A test of Hofstede's individualism/collectivism distinction. *Journal of Cross-Cultural Psychology, 25*, 273–283.

Boden, M. T., Berenbaum, H., & Gross, J. J. (2016). Why do people believe what they do? A functionalist perspective. *Review of General Psychology, 20*, 399–411.

Bodimeade, H., Anderson, E., La Macchia, S., Smith, J. R., Terry, D. J., & Louis, W. R. (2014). Testing the direct, indirect, and interactive roles of referent group injunctive and descriptive norms for sun protection in relation to the theory of planned behavior. *Journal of Applied Social Psychology, 44*, 739–750.

Boduroglu, A., Shah, P., & Nisbett, R. E. (2009). Cultural differences in allocation of attention in visual information processing. *Journal of Cross-Cultural Psychology, 40*(3), 349–360. doi:10.1177/0022022108331005

Bohner, G., & Dickel, N. (2011). Attitudes and attitude change. *Annual Review of Psychology, 62*, 391–417. doi:10.1146/annurev.psych.121208.131609

Bolger, N., & Amarel, D. (2007). Effects of social support visibility on adjustment to stress: Experimental evidence. *Journal of Personality and Social Psychology, 92*, 458–475.

Bolino, M., Long, D., & Turnley, W. (2016). Impression management in organizations: Critical questions, answers, and areas for future research. *Annual Review of Organizational Psychology and Organizational Behavior, 3*, 377–406.

Bonanno, G. A. (2004). Loss, trauma, and human resilience: Have we underestimated the human capacity to thrive after extremely aversive events? *American Psychologist, 59*, 20–28.

Bonanno, G. A. (2005). Resilience in the face of potential trauma. *Current Directions in Psychological Science, 14*, 135–138.

Bonanno, G. A., Moskowitz, J. T., Papa, A., & Folkman, S. (2005). Resilience to loss in bereaved spouses, bereaved parents, and bereaved gay men. *Journal of Personality and Social Psychology, 88*, 827–843.

Bonanno, G. A., Boerner, K., & Wortman, C. (2008). Trajectories of grieving. In M. S. Stroebe, R. O. Hansson, H. Schut, W. Stroebe, & E. Van den Blink (Eds.), *Handbook of bereavement research and practice: Advances in theory and intervention* (pp. 287–307). Washington, DC: American Psychological Association.

Bond, M. H. (1996). Chinese values. In M. H. Bond (Ed.), *The handbook of Chinese psychology* (pp. 208–226). Hong Kong: Oxford University Press.

Bond, M. H. (Ed.). (1988). *The cross-cultural challenge to social psychology.* Newbury Park, CA: Sage.

Bond, R. M., Fariss, C. J., Jones, J. J., Kramer, A. D. I., Marlow, C., Settle, J. E., et al. (2012). A 61-million-person experiment in social influence and political mobilization. *Nature, 489*, 295–298.

Bond, R., & Smith, P. B. (1996). Culture and conformity: a meta-analysis of studies using Asch's (1952b, 1956) line judgment task. *Psychological Bulletin, 119*, 111–137.

Bookwala, J. (2014). Spouse health status, depressed affect, and resilience in mid and late life: A longitudinal study. *Developmental Psychology, 50*, 1241–1249.

Boos, M., Schauenberg, B., Strack, M., & Belz, M. (2013). Social validation of shared and non-validation of unshared information in group discussions. *Small Group Research, 44*, 257–271.

Bornstein, B. H., & Greene, E. (2011). Jury decision making: Implications for and from psychology. *Current Directions in Psychological Science, 20*(1), 63–67. doi:10.1177/0963721410397282

Bornstein, R. F. (1989). Exposure and affect: Overview and meta-analysis of research, 1968–1987. *Psychological Bulletin, 106*, 265–289.

Botvin, G. J., & Griffin, K. W. (2004). Life skills training: Empirical findings and future directions. *Journal of Primary Prevention, 25*, 211–232.

Bourgeois, M. J., & Bowen, A. (2001). Self-organization of alcohol-related attitudes and beliefs in a campus housing complex: An initial investigation. *Health Psychology, 20*, 434–437.

Bower, G. H., & Hilgard, E. R. (1981). *Theories of learning* (15th ed.). Englewood Cliffs, NJ: Prentice Hall.

Bowlby, J. (1969). *Attachment and loss: Vol. 1. Attachment.* New York: Basic Books.

Bowlby, J. (1973). *Attachment and loss: Vol. 2. Separation: Anxiety and anger.* New York: Basic Books.

Bowlby, J. (1980). *Attachment and loss: Vol. 3. Loss.* New York: Basic Books.

Bowles, T. V. (2016). Who's the fairest of them all and does it really matter? Positive and negative affective responses to levels of relational equity in adolescent relationships. *Journal of Relationships Research, 7.* https://doi.org/10.1017/jrr.2016.14

Boyden, T., Carroll, J. S., & Maier, R. A. (1984). Similarity and attraction in homosexual males: The effects of age and masculinity-femininity. *Sex Roles, 10,* 939–948.

Brand, R. J., Bonatsos, A., D'Orazio, R., & DeShong, H. (2012). What is beautiful is good, even online: Correlations between photo attractiveness and text attractiveness in men's online dating profiles. *Computers in Human Behavior, 28,* 166–170.

Branigan, T. (2011, October 21). Chinese toddler dies after hit-and-run ordeal. *The Guardian.* Retrieved November 21, 2011, from www.guardian.co.uk/world/2011/oct/21/chinese-toddler-dies-hit-and-run

Brannon, L. A., & Brock, T. C. (1994). The subliminal persuasion controversy. In S. Shavitt & T. C. Brock (Eds.), *Persuasion: Psychological insights and perspectives* (pp. 279–293). Needham Heights, MA: Allyn & Bacon.

Brauer, M., Judd, C. M., & Gliner, M. D. (1995). The effects of repeated expressions on attitude polarization during group discussions. *Journal of Personality and Social Psychology, 68,* 1014–1029.

Breckler, S. J., & Wiggins, E. C. (1989). On defining attitude and attitude theory: Once more with feeling. In A. R. Pratkanis, S. J. Breckler, & A. G. Greenwald (Eds.), *Attitude structure and function* (pp. 407–427). Hillsdale, NJ: Erlbaum.

Brehm, J. W. (1956). Postdecision changes in the desirability of alternatives. *Journal of Abnormal and Social Psychology, 52,* 384–389.

Brehm, J. W. (1966). *A theory of psychological reactance.* New York: Academic Press.

Breiding, M. J., Chen J., & Black, M. C. (2014). *Intimate partner violence in the United States—2010.* Atlanta: National Center for Injury Prevention and Control, Centers for Disease Control and Prevention.

Brescoll, V. L., Dawson, E., & Uhlmann, E. L. (2010). Hard won and easily lost: The fragile status of leaders in gender-stereotype-incongruent occupations. *Psychological Science, 21*(11), 1640–1642. doi:10.1177/0956797610384744

Brewer, M. B. (1979). In-group bias in the minimal intergroup situation: A cognitive-motivational analysis. *Psychological Bulletin, 86,* 307–324.

Brewer, M. B. (2007). The importance of being we: Human nature and intergroup relations. *American Psychologist, 62*(8), 728–738. doi:10.1037/0003-066X.62.8.728

Brewer, M. B., & Brown, R. J. (1998). *Intergroup Relations.* McGraw-Hill.

Brewer, N., & Wells, G. L. (2011). Eyewitness identification. *Current Directions in Psychological Science, 20,* 24–27.

Brewer, N., & Williams, K. D. (Eds.). (2017). *Psychology and law: An empirical perspective.* New York: Guilford Publications.

Bridgeman, D. L. (1981). Enhanced role taking through cooperative interdependence: A field study. *Child Development, 52,* 1231–1238.

Brigham, J., Bennett, L., Meissner, C., & Mitchell, T. (2007). The influence of race on eyewitness memory. In R. C. L. Lindsay, D. F. Ross, D. J. Read, & M. P. Toglia (Eds.). *The handbook of eyewitness psychology, Vol. II: Memory for people* (pp. 257–281). Mahwah, NJ: Erlbaum.

Bringle, R. G. (2005). Designing interventions to promote civic engagement. In A. M. Omoto (Ed.), *Processes of community change and social action* (pp. 167–187). Mahwah, NJ: Erlbaum.

Briñol, P., & Petty, R. E. (2003). Over head movements and persuasion: A self-validation analysis. *Journal of Personality and Social Psychology, 4,* 1123–1139.

Briñol, P., & Petty, R. E. (2009). Persuasion: Insights from the self-validation hypothesis. In M. P. Zanna (Ed.), *Advances in experimental social psychology* (Vol. 41, pp. 69–118). New York: Elsevier.

Briñol, P., & Petty, R. E. (2012). Knowing our attitudes and how to change them. In S. Vazire & T. D. Wilson (Eds.), *Handbook of self-knowledge.* New York: Guilford.

Brophy, J. E. (1983). Research on the self-fulfilling prophecy and teacher expectations. *Journal of Educational Psychology, 75,* 631–661.

Brosch, T., Schiller, D., Mojdehbakhsh, R., Uleman, J. S., & Phelps, E. A. (2013). Neural mechanisms underlying the integration of situational information into attribution outcomes. *Social Cognitive and Affective Neuroscience, 8,* 640–646.

Brown, G., Manago, A. M., & Trimble, J. E. (2016). Tempted to text: College students' mobile phone use during a face-to-face interaction with a close friend. *Emerging Adulthood, 4,* 440–443.

Brown, G. R., & Cross, C. P. (2017). Evolutionary approaches to human psychology. In J. Call, G. M. Burghardt, I. M. Pepperberg, C. T. Snowdon, T., & Zentall (Eds.). *APA handbook of comparative psychology: Basic concepts, methods, neural substrate, and behaviour* (Vol. 1, pp. 299–313). Washington, D.C.: APA.

Brown, R. (1965). *Social psychology.* New York: Free Press.

Brown, R. P., Osterman, L. L., & Barnes, C. D. (2009). School violence and the culture of honor. *Psychological Science, 20,* 1400–1405.

Brownlee, J., Masoud, T., & Reynolds, A. (2013). Why the modest harvest? *Journal of Democracy, 24,* 29–44.

Buchanan, T. W., & Preston, S. D. (2016). When feelings and doing diverge: Neural and physiological correlates of the empathy-altruism divide. In J. D. Greene, I. Morrison, & M. E. P. Seligman, *Positive neuroscience* (pp. 69–104). New York: Oxford University Press.

Buehler, R., Griffin, D., & Peetz, J. (2010). The planning fallacy: Cognitive, motivational, and social origins. In M. P. Zanna (Ed.), *Advances in experimental social psychology* (Vol. 43, pp. 1–62). San Diego, CA: Academic Press.

Buehler, R., Griffin, D., & Ross, M. (1994). Exploring the "planning fallacy": Why people underestimate their task completion times. *Journal of Personality and Social Psychology, 67,* 366–381.

Bueza, M. (2017). "In numbers: The Philippines' 'war on drugs'." Rappler IQ. Retrieved from http://www.rappler.com/nation/169921-death-rate-down-police-operations-dilg-pnp

Buffone, A., Gabriel, S., & Poulin, M. (2016). There but for the grace of god: Counterfactuals influence religious belief and images of the divine. *Social Psychological and Personality Science, 7*(3), 256–263.

Bui, K.-V. T., Peplau, L. A., & Hill, C. T. (1996). Testing the Rusbult model of relationship commitment and stability in a 15-year study of heterosexual couples. *Personality and Social Psychology Bulletin, 22,* 1244–1257.

Bülbül, C., & Menon, G. (2010). The power of emotional appeals in advertising: The influence of concrete versus abstract affect on time-dependent decision. *Journal of Advertising Research, 50,* 169–180.

Bullens, L., van Harreveld, F., Förster, J., & van der Pligt, J. (2013). Reversible decisions: The grass isn't merely greener on the other side; it's also very brown over here. *Journal of Experimental Social Psychology, 49,* 1093–1099.

Burger, J. M. (1981). Motivational biases in the attribution of responsibility for an accident: A meta-analysis of the defensive-attribution hypothesis. *Psychological Bulletin, 90,* 496–512.

Burger, J. M. (2009). Replicating Milgram: Would people still obey today? *American Psychologist, 64,* 1–11.

Burgoon, J. K., Guerrero, L. K., & Floyd, K. (2016). *Nonverbal communication.* Abington, UK: Routledge.

Burkley, E. (2008). The role of self-control in resistance to persuasion. *Personality and Social Psychology Bulletin, 34,* 419–431.

Burnstein, E., & Vinokur, A. (1977). Persuasive argumentation and social comparison as determinants of attitude polarization. *Journal of Experimental Social Psychology, 13,* 315–332.

Burnstein, E., Crandall, C. S., & Kitayama, S. (1994). Some neo-Darwinian decision rules for altruism: Weighing cues for inclusive fitness as a function of the biological importance of the decision. *Journal of Personality and Social Psychology, 67,* 773–789.

Busey, T. A., Tunnicliff, J., Loftus, G. R., & Loftus, E. F. (2000). Accounts of the confidence-accuracy relation in recognition memory. *Psychonomic Bulletin and Review, 7,* 26–48.

Bushman, B. J. (1995). Moderating role of trait aggressiveness in the effects of violent media on aggression. *Journal of Personality and Social Psychology, 69,* 950–960.

Bushman, B. J. (1997). Effects of alcohol on human aggression: Validity of proposed explanations. In M. Galanter (Ed.), *Recent developments in alcoholism: Vol. 13. Alcohol and violence: Epidemiology, neurobiology, psychology, family issues* (pp. 227–243). New York: Plenum.

Bushman, B. J., & Anderson, C. A. (2009). Comfortably numb: Desensitizing effects of violent media on helping others. *Psychological Science, 20,* 273–277.

Bushman, B. J., & Baumeister, R. F. (2002). Does self-love or self-hate lead to violence? *Journal of Research in Personality, 36,* 543–545.

Bushman, B. J., & Cooper, H. M. (1990). Alcohol and human aggression: An integrative research review. *Psychological Bulletin, 107,* 341–354.

Bushman, B. J., & Pollard-Sacks, D. (2014). Supreme Court decision on violent video games was based on the First Amendment, not scientific evidence. *American Psychologist, 69,* 306–307.

Bushman, B. J., Bonacci, A. M., Pedersen, W. C., Vasquez, E. A., & Miller, N. (2005). Chewing on it can chew you up: Effects of rumination on triggered displaced aggression. *Journal of Personality and Social Psychology, 88,* 969–983.

Bushman, B. J., Gollwitzer, M., & Cruz, C. (2015). There is broad consensus: Media researchers agree that violent media increase aggression in children, and pediatricians and parents concur. *Psychology of Popular Media Culture, 4,* 200–214.

Bushman, B. J., Jamieson, P. E., Weitz, I., & Romer, D. (2013). Gun violence trends in movies. *Pediatrics, 132,* 1014–1018.

Bushman, B. J., Ridge, R. D., Das, E., Key, C. W., & Busath, G. L. (2007). When God sanctions killing: The effect of scriptural violence on aggression. *Psychological Science, 18*(3), 204–207.

Buss, D. (2005). *The handbook of evolutionary psychology.* New Jersey: John Wiley & Sons.

Buss, D. M. (1985). Human mate selection. *American Scientist, 73,* 47–51.

Buss, D. M. (1988a). The evolution of human intrasexual competition. *Journal of Personality and Social Psychology, 54,* 616–628.

Buss, D. M. (1988b). Love acts: The evolutionary biology of love. In R. J. Sternberg & M. L. Barnes (Eds.), *The psychology of love* (pp. 110–118). New Haven, CT: Yale University Press.

Buss, D. M. (1989). Sex differences in human mate preferences: Evolutionary hypotheses tested in 37 cultures. *Behavioral and Brain Sciences, 12,* 1–49.

Buss, D. M. (2002). Human mate guarding. *Neuroendocrinology Letters, 23,* 23–29.

Buss, D. M. (2004). *Evolutionary psychology: The new science of the mind* (2nd ed.). Boston: Allyn & Bacon.

Buss, D. M. (Ed.). (2005). *The handbook of evolutionary psychology.* Hoboken, NJ: Wiley.

Buss, D. M. (2014). *Evolutionary psychology: The new science of the mind* (5th ed.). New York: Psychology Press.

Buss, D. M., & Schmitt, D. P. (1993). Sexual strategies theory: An evolutionary perspective on human mating. *Psychological Bulletin, 100,* 204–232.

Buss, D. M., Abbott, M., Angleitner, A., Biaggio, A., Blanco-Villasenor, A., Bruchon-Schweitzer, M., et al. (1990). International preferences in selecting mates: A study of 37 cultures. *Journal of Cross-Cultural Psychology, 21*, 5–47.

Buunk, B. P., & Gibbons, F. X. (2013). *Health, coping, and well-being: Perspectives from social comparison theory*. New York: Psychology Press.

Buunk, B. P., & Schaufeli, W. B. (1999). Reciprocity in interpersonal relationships: An evolutionary perspective on its importance for health and well-being. In W. Stroebe & M. Hewstone (Eds.), *European review of social psychology* (Vol. 10, pp. 259–291). New York: Wiley.

Byrne, D., & Nelson, D. (1965). Attraction as a linear function of positive reinforcement. *Journal of Personality and Social Psychology, 1*, 659–663.

Cacioppo, J. T. (1998). Somatic responses to psychological stress: The reactivity hypothesis. In M. Sabourin & F. Craik (Eds.), *Advances in psychological science: Biological and cognitive aspects* (Vol. 2, pp. 87–112). Hove, England: Psychology Press.

Cacioppo, J. T., & Cacioppo, S. (2013). Social neuroscience. *Perspectives on Psychological Science, 8*, 667–669. doi:10.1177/1745691613507456

Cacioppo, J. T., & Patrick, W. (2008). *Loneliness: Human nature and the need for social connection*. New York: Norton & Company.

Cacioppo, J. T., Berntson, G. G., Malarkey, W. B., Kiecolt-Glaser, J. K., Sheridan, J. F., Poehlmann, K. M., Burleson, M. H., Ernst, J. M., Hawkley, L. C., & Glaser, R. (1998). Autonomic, neuroendocrine, and immune responses to psychological stress: The reactivity hypothesis. In S. M. McCann & J. M. Lipton (Eds.), *Annals of the New York academy of sciences* (Vol. 840, pp. 664–673). New York: New York Academy of Sciences.

Cacioppo, J. T., Marshall-Goodell, B. S., Tassinary, K., & Petty, R. E. (1992). Rudimentary determinants of attitudes: Classical conditioning is more effective when prior knowledge about the attitude stimulus is low than high. *Journal of Experimental Social Psychology, 28*, 207–233.

Cai, H., Luo, Y. L., Shi, Y., Liu, Y., & Yang, Z. (2016). Male = science, female = humanities: Both implicit and explicit gender-science stereotypes are heritable. *Social Psychological and Personality Science, 7*, 412–419.

Calder, B. J., & Staw, B. M. (1975). Self-perception of intrinsic and extrinsic motivation. *Journal of Personality and Social Psychology, 31*, 599–605.

Calderón-Garcidueñas, L., & Torres-Jardón, R. (2012). Air pollution, socioeconomic status, and children's cognition in megacities: The Mexico City scenario. *Frontiers in Psychology, 3*, Article 217.

Campbell, A. (2002). *A mind of her own*. New York: Oxford University Press.

Campbell, D. T., & Stanley, J. C. (1967). *Experimental and quasi-experimental designs for research*. Chicago: Rand McNally.

Campbell, L., Simpson, J. A., Boldry, J., & Kashy, D. A. (2005). Perceptions of conflict and support in romantic relationships: The role of attachment anxiety. *Journal of Personality and Social Psychology, 88*, 510–531.

Campbell, W. K., Miller, J. D., & Buffardi, L. E. (2010). The United States and the "Culture of narcissism": An examination of perceptions of national character. *Social Psychological and Personality Science, 1*, 222–229.

Canary, D. J., & Stafford, L. (2001). Equity in the preservation of personal relationships. In J. Harvey & A. Wenzel (Eds.), *Close romantic relationships: Maintenance and enhancement* (pp. 133–151). Mahwah, NJ: Erlbaum.

Cannon, W. B. (1932). *The wisdom of the body*. New York: Norton.

Cannon, W. B. (1942). "Voodoo" death. *American Anthropologist, 44*, 169–181.

Cantatero, K., Gamian-Wilk, M., & Doliński, D. (2017). Being inconsistent and compliant: The moderating role of preference for consistency in the door-in-the-face technique. *Personality and Individual Differences*. http://dx.doi.org/10.1016/j.paid.2016.07.005

Cantril, H. (1940). *The invasion from Mars: A study in the psychology of panic*. New York: Harper & Row.

Capella, M. L., Webster, C., & Kinard, B. R. (2011). A review of the effect of cigarette advertising. *International Journal of Research in Marketing, 28*(3), 269–279. doi:10.1016/j. ijresmar.2011.05.002

Carazo, P., Tan, C.c K. W., Allen, F., Wigby, S., & Pizzari, T. (2014). Within-group male relatedness reduces harm to females in Drosophila. *Nature, 505*, 672–675.

Carlier, I. V. E., Voerman, A. E., & Gersons, B. P. R. (2000). The influence of occupational debriefing on post-traumatic stress symptomatology in traumatized police officers. *British Journal of Medical Psychology, 73*, 87–98.

Carlson, M., Charlin, V., & Miller, N. (1988). Positive mood and helping behavior: A test of six hypotheses. *Journal of Personality and Social Psychology, 55*, 211–229.

Carnagey, N. L., & Anderson, C. A. (2005). The effects of reward and punishment in violent video games on aggressive affect, cognition, and behavior. *Psychological Science, 16*, 882–889.

Carpenter, S. (2000, December). Why do "they all look alike"? *Monitor on Psychology*, pp. 44–45.

Carré, J. M., Iselin, A. R., Welker, K. M., Hariri, A. R., & Dodge, K. A. (2014). Testosterone reactivity to provocation mediates the effect of early intervention on aggressive behavior. *Psychological Science, 25*, 1140–1146.

Carter, A. M., Fabrigar, L. R., MacDonald, T. K., & Monner, L. J. (2013). Investigating the interface of the investment model and adult attachment theory. *European Journal of Social Psychology, 43*, 661–672.

Carter, E. C., Kofler, L. M., Forster, D. E., & McCulloch, M. E. (2015). A series of meta-analytic tests of the depletion effect: Self-control does not seem to rely on a limited resource. *Journal of Experimental Psychology: General, 144*, 796–815.

Carter, T. J., & Gilovich, T. (2012). I am what I do, not what I have: The differential centrality of experiential and material purchases to the self. *Journal of Personality and Social Psychology, 102*, 1304.

Cartwright, D., & Zander, A. (1968). *Group dynamics: Research and theory*. New York: Harper & Row.

Caruso, E. M. (2008). Use of experienced retrieval ease in self and social judgments. *Journal of Experimental Social Psychology, 44*(1), 148–155.

Carver, C. S. (2003). Self-awareness. In M. R. Leary & J. P. Tangney (Eds.), *Handbook of self and identity* (pp. 179–196). New York: Guilford Press.

Carver, C. S., & Scheier, M. F. (1981). *Attention and self-regulation: A control-theory approach to human behavior*. New York: Springer-Verlag.

Carver, C. S., & Scheier, M. F. (1998). *On the self-regulation of behavior*. New York: Cambridge University Press.

Caselman, T., (2007). *Teaching children empathy*. New York: YouthLight.

Casey-Campbell, M., & Martens, M. L. (2009). Sticking it all together: A critical assessment of the group cohesion-performance literature. *International Journal of Management Reviews, 11*, 223–246.

Cashin, S. (2014). *Place, not race: A new vision of opportunity in America*. Boston: Beacon Press.

Catalyst (2017). Women on corporate boards globally. Retrieved April 24, 2017, from http://www.catalyst.org/knowledge/women-corporate-boards-globally

Catlin, J. R., & Wang, Y. (2013). Recycling gone bad: When the option to recycle increases resource consumption. *Journal of Consumer Psychology, 23*, 122–127.

Cejka, M., & Eagly, A. H. (1999). Gender-stereotypic images of occupations correspond to the sex segregation of employment. *Personality and Social Psychology Bulletin, 25*, 413–423.

Centers for Disease Control and Prevention. (2014). Chronic disease prevention and health promotion. Retrieved August 19, 2014, from http://www.cdc.gov/chronicdisease/index.htm

Centers for Disease Control and Prevention. (2014, January). Current cigarette smoking among adults—United States, 2005–2012. *Morbidity and Mortality Weekly Report*. Retrieved April 26, 2014, from http://www.cdc.gov/mmwr/preview/mmwrhtml/mm6302a2.htm

Centers for Disease Control and Prevention. (n.d.). Retrieved June 6, 2011, from profiles.nlm.nih.gov/ps/access/NNBCPH.pdf

Centers for Disease Control and Prevention (2017). Current Cigarette Smoking Among Adults in the United States. Retrieved June 13, 2017, from https://www.cdc.gov/tobacco/data_statistics/fact_sheets/adult_data/cig_smoking/

Chabris, C., & Simons, D. (2010). *The invisible gorilla: And other ways our intuitions deceive us*. New York: Harmony.

Chaiken, S. (1980). Heuristic versus systematic information processing and the use of source versus message cues in persuasion. *Journal of Personality and Social Psychology, 39*, 752–766.

Chaiken, S., & Baldwin, M. W. (1981). Affective-cognitive consistency and the effect of salient behavioral information on the self-perception of attitudes. *Journal of Personality and Social Psychology, 41*, 1–12.

Chaiken, S., & Stangor, C. (1987). Attitudes and attitude change. *Annual Review of Psychology, 38*, 575–630.

Chan, A., & Au, T. K. (2011). Getting children to do more academic work: Foot-in-the-door versus door-in-the-face. *Teaching and Teacher Education, 27*, 982–985.

Chan, D. K.-S., & Cheng, G. H.-L. (2004). A comparison of offline and online friendship qualities at different stages of relationship development. *Journal of Personal and Social Relationships, 21*, 305–320.

Chang, C., & Chen, J. (1995). Effects of different motivation strategies on reducing social loafing. *Chinese Journal of Psychology, 37*, 71–81.

Chaplin, W. F., Phillips, J. B., Brown, J. D., & Clanton, N. R. (2000). Handshaking, gender, personality, and first impressions. *Journal of Personality and Social Psychology, 79*, 110–117.

Charman, S. D., Wells, G. L., & Joy, S. W. (2011). The dud effect: Adding highly dissimilar fillers increases confidence in lineup identifications. *Law and Human Behavior, 35*(6), 479–500. doi:10.1007/s10979-010-9261-1

Charman, S., & Wells, G. (2007). Applied lineup theory. *The handbook of eyewitness psychology*, Vol II: *Memory for people* (pp. 219–254). Mahwah, NJ: Erlbaum.

Charman, S., & Wells, G. (2008). Can eyewitnesses correct for external influences on their lineup identifications? The actual/counterfactual assessment paradigm. *Journal of Experimental Psychology: Applied, 14*, 5–20.

Chemers, M. M. (2000). Leadership research and theory: A functional integration. *Group Dynamics: Theory, Research, and Practice, 4*, 27–43.

Chen, J. M., Kim, H. S., Mojaverian, T., & Morling, B. (2012). Culture and social support provision: Who gives what and why. *Personality and Social Psychology Bulletin, 38*, 3–13.

Chen, J., Wu, Y., Tong, G., Guan, X., & Zhou, X. (2012). ERP correlates of social conformity in a line judgment task. *BMC Neuroscience, 13*. doi:10.1186/1471-2202-13-43

Chen, M., & Bargh, J. A. (1997). Nonconscious behavioral confirmation processes: The self-fulfilling consequences of automatic stereotype activation. *Journal of Experimental Social Psychology, 33*, 541–560.

Chen, N. Y., Shaffer, D. R., & Wu, C. H. (1997). On physical attractiveness stereotyping in Taiwan: A revised sociocultural perspective. *Journal of Social Psychology, 137*, 117–124.

Chen, S., & Andersen, S. M. (1999). Relationships from the past in the present: Significant-other representations and transference in interpersonal life. In M. P. Zanna (Ed.), *Advances in experimental social psychology* (Vol. 31, pp. 123–190). San Diego, CA: Academic Press.

Chen, S. X., Lam, B. C. P., Wu, W. C. H., Ng, J. C. K., Buchtel, E. E., Guan, Y., & Deng, H. (2016). Do people's world views matter? The why and how. *Journal of Personality and Social Psychology, 110*(5), 743–765.

Cheng, C., Cheung, S.-F., Chio, J. H.-M., & Chan, M.-P. S. (2013). Cultural meaning of perceived control: A meta-analysis of locus of control and psychological symptoms across 18 cultural regions. *Psychological Bulletin, 139*, 152–188.

Chernyak, N., & Kushnir, T. (2013). Giving preschoolers choice increases sharing behavior. *Psychological Science, 24*, 1971–1979.

Cheung, B. Y., Chudek, M., & Heine, S. J. (2011). Evidence for a sensitive period for acculturation: Younger immigrants report acculturating at a faster rate. *Psychological Science, 22*(2), 147–152. doi:10.1177/0956797610394661

Choi, I., Dalal, R., Kim-Prieto, C., & Park, H. (2003). Culture and judgment of causal relevance. *Journal of Personality and Social Psychology, 84*, 46–59.

Choi, S. M., Lee, W. N., & Kim, H. J. (2005). Lessons from the rich and famous: A cross-cultural comparison of celebrity endorsement in advertising. *Journal of Advertising, 34*, 85–98.

Choi, Y., He, M., & Harachi, T. (2008). Intergenerational cultural dissonance, parent-child conflict and bonding, and youth problem behaviors among Vietnamese and Cambodian immigrant families. *Journal of Youth and Adolescence, 37*, 85–96.

Chou, C., Montgomery, S., Pentz, M., Rohrbach, L., Johnson, C., Flay, B., & MacKinnon, D. P. (1998). Effects of a community-based prevention program in decreasing drug use in high-risk adolescents. *American Journal of Public Health, 88*, 944–948.

Christakis, N. A., & Fowler, J. H. (2014). Friendship and natural selection. *Proceedings of the National Academy of Sciences.* doi:10.1073/pnas.1400825111

Christensen, A., Doss, B., & Jacobson, N. S. (2014). *Reconcilable differences* (2nd ed.). New York: Guilford Press.

Christensen, L. (1988). Deception in psychological research: When is its use justified? *Personality and Social Psychology Bulletin, 14*, 664–675.

Christopher, A. N., & Wojda, M. R. (2008). Social dominance orientation, right-wing authoritarianism, sexism, and prejudice toward women in the workforce. *Psychology of Women Quarterly, 32*, 65–73.

Cialdini, R. B. (2009). *Influence: Science and practice* (5th ed.). Upper Saddle River, NJ: Prentice Hall.

Cialdini, R. B. (2012). The focus theory of normative conduct. In P. A. M. Van Lange, A. W. Kruglanski, & E. T. Higgins (Eds.), *Handbook of theories of social psychology* (Vol. 2, pp. 295–312). Thousand Oaks, CA: Sage Publications.

Cialdini, R. B., & Fultz, J. (1990). Interpreting the negative mood-helping literature via "mega"-analysis: A contrary view. *Psychological Bulletin, 107*, 210–214.

Cialdini, R. B., & Goldstein, N. J. (2004). Social influence: Compliance and conformity. *Annual Review of Psychology, 55*, 591–621.

Cialdini, R. B., & Trost, M. R. (1998). Social influence: Social norms, conformity, and compliance. In D. T. Gilbert, S. T. Fiske, & G. Lindzey (Eds.), *The handbook of social psychology* (4th ed., Vol. 2, pp. 151–192). New York: McGraw-Hill.

Cialdini, R. B., Borden, R. J., Thorne, A., Walker, M. R., Freeman, S., & Sloan, L. R. (1976). Basking in reflected glory: Three (football) field studies. *Journal of Personality and Social Psychology, 34*, 366–375.

Cialdini, R. B., Cacioppo, J. T., Basset, R., & Miller, J. (1978). Low-ball procedure for producing compliance: Commitment, then cost. *Journal of Personality and Social Psychology, 36*, 463–476.

Cialdini, R. B., Kallgren, C. A., & Reno, R. R. (1991). A focus theory of normative conduct: A theoretical refinement and reevaluation of the role of norms in human behavior. In M. P. Zanna (Ed.), *Advances in experimental social psychology* (Vol. 24, pp. 201–234). San Diego, CA: Academic Press.

Cialdini, R. B., Reno, R. R., & Kallgren, C. A. (1990). A focus theory of normative conduct: Recycling the concept of norms to reduce littering in public places. *Journal of Personality and Social Psychology, 58*, 1015–1026.

Cialdini, R. B., Vincent, J. E., Lewis, S. K., Catalan, J., Wheeler, D., & Darby, B. L. (1975). Reciprocal concessions procedure for inducing compliance: The door-in the face technique. *Journal of Personality and Social Psychology, 31*, 206–215.

Cikara, M., & Van Bavel, J. J. (2014). The neuroscience of intergroup relations: An integrative review. *Perspectives on Psychological Science, 9*, 245–274.

Cikara, M., Botvinick, M. M., & Fiske, S. T. (2011). Us versus them: Social identity shapes neural responses to intergroup competition and harm. *Psychological science, 22*, 306–313.

Clark, M. S., & Mills, J. (1993). The difference between communal and exchange relationships: What it is and is not. *Personality and Social Psychology Bulletin, 19*, 684–691.

Clark, R. D., III, & Hatfield, E. (1989). Gender differences in receptivity to sexual offers. *Journal of Psychology and Human Sexuality, 2*, 39–55.

Clark, R. D., III, & Word, L. E. (1972). Why don't bystanders help? Because of ambiguity? *Journal of Personality and Social Psychology, 24*, 392–400.

Clark, S. E. (2005). A re-examination of the effects of biased lineup instructions in eyewitness identification. *Law and Human Behavior, 29*, 575–604.

Clarkson, J. J., Otto, A. S., Hirt, E. R., & Egan, P. M. (2016). The malleable efficacy of willpower theories. *Personality and Social Psychology Bulletin, 42*, 1490–1504.

Claro, S., Paunesku, D., & Dweck, C. S. (2016). Growth mindset tempers the effects of poverty on academic achievement. *Proceedings of the National Academy of Sciences, 113*, 8664–8668.

Clary, E. G., Snyder, M., Ridge, R. D., Miene, P. K., & Haugen, J. A. (1994). Matching messages to motives in persuasion: A functional approach to promoting volunteerism. *Journal of Applied Social Psychology, 24*, 1129–1149.

Claypool, H. M., Hall, C. E., Mackie, D. M., & Garcia-Marques, T. (2008). Positive mood, attribution, and the illusion of familiarity. *Journal of Experimental Social Psychology, 44*, 721–728.

Clayton, S., Devine-Wright, P., Swim, J., Bonnes, M., Steg, L., Whitmarsh, L., & Carrico, A. (2016). Expanding the role for psychology in addressing environmental challenges. *American Psychologist, 71*, 199–215.

Climate change, water, and risk: Current water demands are not sustainable. (2010). National Resources Defense Council. Retrieved July 23, 2014, from http://www.nrdc.org/globalwarming/watersustainability/files/WaterRisk.pdf

Cline, V. B., Croft, R. G., & Courrier, S. (1973). Desensitization of children to television violence. *Journal of Personality and Social Psychology, 27*, 360–365.

Clobert, M., van Cappellen, P., Bourdon, M., & Cohen, A. B. (2016). Good day for Leos: Horoscope's influence on perception, cognitive performances, and creativity. *Personality and Individual Differences, 101*, 348–355.

Coan, J. A., & Maresh, E. L. (2014). Social baseline theory and the social regulation of emotion. In J. J. Gross (Ed), *Handbook of emotion regulation* (2nd ed., pp. 221–236). New York: Guilford Press.

Coane, J. H., & Balota, D. A. (2009). Priming the holiday spirit: Persistent activation due to extraexperimental experiences. *Psychonomic Bulletin & Review, 16*(6), 1124–1128. doi:10.3758/PBR.16.6.1124

Coats, E. (1998, March 20). Bystander intervention [E-mail response to G. Mumford, Tobacco update]. Retrieved from www.stolaf.edu/cgibin/mailarchivesearch.pl?directory=/home/www/people/huff/SPSP&listname=archive98

Coetzee V., Greeff, J. M., Stephen, I. D., & Perrett, D. I. (2014). Cross-cultural agreement in facial attractiveness preferences: The role of ethnicity and gender. *PLoS ONE, 9*, e99629.

Cogsdill, E. J., Todorov, A. T., Spelke, E. S., & Banaji, M. R. (2014). Inferring character from faces: A developmental study. *Psychological Science.* Retrieved March 25, 2014. doi:10.1177/0956797614523297

Cohen, A. B., & Varnum, M. E. W. (2016). Beyond East vs. West: Social class, region, and religion as forms of culture. *Current Opinion in Psychology, 8*, 5–9.

Cohen, D. (1998). Culture, social organization, and patterns of violence. *Journal of Personality and Social Psychology, 75*(2), 408–419.

Cohen, F., Jussim, L., Harber, K. D., & Bhasin, G. (2009). Modern anti-Semitism and anti-Israeli attitudes. *Journal of Personality and Social Psychology, 97*, 290–306.

Cohen, G. L., & Sherman, D. K. (2014). The psychology of change: Self-affirmation and social psychological intervention. *Annual Review of Psychology, 65*, 333–371.

Cohen, R. (1997, October 31). AH-lo-ween: An American holiday in Paris? *The New York Times*, pp. A1, A4.

Cohen, S., Alper, C., Doyle, W., Adler, N., Treanor, J., & Turner, R. (2008). Objective and subjective socioeconomic status and susceptibility to the common cold. *Health Psychology, 27*, 268–274.

Cohen, S., Mermelstein, R., Kamarack, T., & Hoberman, H. (1985). Measuring the functional components of social support. In I. G. Sarason & B. R. Sarason (Eds.) *Social support: Theory, research, and applications* (pp. 73–94). The Hague, Netherlands: Martines Nijhoff.

Cohen, S., Tyrrell, D. A. J., & Smith, A. P. (1991). Psychological stress in humans and susceptibility to the common cold. *New England Journal of Medicine, 325*, 606–612.

Cohen, S., Tyrrell, D. A. J., & Smith, A. P. (1993). Negative life events, perceived stress, negative affect, and susceptibility to the common cold. *Journal of Personality and Social Psychology, 64*, 131–140.

Cohen, T. R., & Insko, C. A. (2008). War and peace: Possible approaches to reducing intergroup conflict. *Perspectives on Psychological Science, 3*, 87–93.

Coker, A. L., Bush, H. M., Cook-Craig, P. G., DeGue, S. A., Clear, E. R., Brancato, C. J., Fisher, B. S., & Recktenwald, E. A. (2017). RCT testing bystander effectiveness to reduce violence. *American Journal of Preventive Medicine, 52*, 566–578.

Cole, T. B. (2006). Rape at U.S. colleges often fueled by alcohol. *Journal of the American Medical Association, 296*, 504–505.

Coleman, M. D. (2010). Sunk cost and commitment to medical treatment. *Current Psychology: A Journal for Diverse Perspectives on Diverse Psychological Issues, 29*, 121–134.

Coles, B. A., & West, M. (2016). Trolling the trolls: Online forum users constructions of the nature and properties of trolling. *Computers in Human Behavior, 60*, 233–244.

Collins, B. E., & Brief, D. E. (1995). Using person-perception vignette methodologies to uncover the symbolic meanings of teacher behaviors in the Milgram paradigm. *Journal of Social Issues, 51*, 89–106.

Collins, N. L., & Feeney, B. C. (2000). A safe haven: An attachment theory perspective on support seeking and caregiving in intimate relationships. *Journal of Personality and Social Psychology, 78*, 1053–1073.

Collins, N. L., Ford, M. B., Guichard, A. C., & Allard, L. M. (2006). Working models of attachment and attribution processes in intimate relationships. *Personality and Social Psychology Bulletin, 32*, 201–219.

Compton, J., Jackson, B., & Dimmock, J. A. (2016). Persuading others to avoid persuasion: Inoculation theory and resistant health attitudes. *Frontiers in Psychology, 7.* doi:10.3389/fpsyg.2016.00122

Conley, T. D., Moors, A. C., Matsick, J. L., Ziegler, A., & Valentine, B. A. (2011). Women, men, and the bedroom: Methodological and conceptual insights that narrow, reframe, and eliminate gender differences in sexuality. *Current Directions in Psychological Science, 20*, 296–300.

Connelly, J. J. & Morris, J. P. (2016). Epigenetics and social behavior. In J. Y. Chiao, S. Li, R. Seligman, & R. Turner (Eds.) *The Oxford handbook of cultural neuroscience* (pp. 299–313). New York: Oxford University Press.

Conner, M., Rhodes, R. E., Morris, B., McEachan, R., & Lawton, R. (2011). Changing exercise through targeting affective or cognitive attitudes. *Psychology & Health, 26*(2), 133–149. doi:10.1080/08870446.2011.531570

Connolly, J., & McIsaac, C. (2009). Adolescents' explanations for romantic dissolutions: A developmental perspective. *Journal of Adolescence, 32*, 1209–1223.

Conway, L. G., III, & Schaller, M. (2005). When authorities' commands backfire: Attributions about consensus and effects on deviant decision making. *Journal of Personality and Social Psychology, 89*, 311–326.

Cook, J. E., Purdie-Vaughns, V., Garcia, J., & Cohen, G. L. (2012). Chronic threat and contingent belonging: protective benefits of values affirmation on identity development. *Journal of Personality and Social Psychology, 102*, 479–496.

Cook, K. (2014). *Kitty Genovese: The murder, the bystanders, the crime that changed America*. New York: W. W. Norton.

Cook, K. S., Cheshire, C., Rice, E. R. W., & Nakagawa, S. (2013). Social exchange theory. In J. DeLamater & A. Ward (Eds.), *Handbook of social psychology*. Netherlands: Springer.

Cook, K., & Rice, E. (2003). Social exchange theory. In J. Delamater (Ed.), *Handbook of social psychology* (pp. 53–76). New York: Kluwer Academic/Plenum.

Cook, S. W. (1985). Experimenting on social issues: The case of school desegregation. *American Psychologist, 40*, 452–460.

Cooley, C. H. (1902). *Human nature and social order*. New York: Scribners.

Cooper, J. (1980). Reducing fears and increasing assertiveness: The role of dissonance reduction. *Journal of Experimental Social Psychology, 16*, 199–213.

Cooper, J. (2010). Riding the D train with Elliot. In M. H. Gonzales, C. Tavris, & J. Aronson (Eds.), *The scientist and the humanist: A festschrift in honor of Elliot Aronson* (pp. 159–174). New York: Psychology Press.

Cooper, J. (2012). Cognitive dissonance theory. In P. Van Lange, A. W. Kruglanski, & E. T. Higgins (Eds.), *Handbook of theories of social psychology* (Vol. 1, pp. 377–397). Thousand Oaks, CA: Sage.

Cooper, J., Bennett, E. A., & Sukel, H. L. (1996). Complex scientific testimony: How do jurors make decisions? *Law and Human Behavior, 20*, 379–394.

Cooper, J. B. (1959). Emotion in prejudice. *Science, 130*, 314–318.

Cooper, L. A., Roter, D. L., Carson, K. A., Beach, M. C., Sabin, J. A., et al. (2012). The associations of clinicians' implicit attitudes about race with medical visit communication and patient ratings of interpersonal care. *American Journal of Public Health, 102*, 979–987.

Correll, J., Park, B., Judd, C. M., & Wittenbrink, B. (2002). The police officer's dilemma: Using ethnicity to disambiguate potentially threatening individuals. *Journal of Personality and Social Psychology, 83*, 1314–1329.

Correll, J., Wittenbrink, B., Park, B., Judd, C. M., & Goyle, A. (2011). Dangerous enough: Moderating racial bias with contextual threat cues. *Journal of Experimental Social Psychology, 47*, 184–189.

Courbet, D., Fourquet-Courbet, M., Kazan, R., & Intartaglia, J. (2014). The long-term effects of e-advertising: The influence of internet pop-ups viewed at a low level of attention in implicit memory. *Journal of Computer-Mediated Communication, 19*, 274–293.

Craig, C., Overbeek, R. W., Condon, M. V., & Rinaldo, S. B. (2016). A relationship between temperature and aggression in NFL football penalties. *Journal of Sport and Health Science, 5*, 205–210.

Craig, M. A., & Richeson, J. A. (2014). More diverse yet less tolerant? How the increasingly diverse racial landscape affects white Americans' racial attitudes. *Personality and Social Psychology Bulletin, 40*, 750–761.

Crandall, C. S., & Eshleman, A. (2003). A justification-suppression model of the expression and experience of prejudice. *Psychological Bulletin, 129*(3), 414–446.

Crandall, C. S., & Greenfield, B. S. (1986). Understanding the conjunction fallacy: A conjunction of effects? *Social Cognition, 4*, 408–419.

Crandall, C. S., D'anello, S., Sakalli, N., Lazarus, E., Wieczorkowska, G., & Feather, N. T. (2001). An attribution-value model of prejudice: Anti-fat attitudes in six nations. *Personality and Social Psychology Bulletin, 27*, 30–37.

Crandall, C. S., Silvia, P. J., N'Gbala, A. N., Tsang, J.-A., & Dawson, K. (2007). Balance theory, unit relations, and attribution: The underlying integrity of Heiderian theory. *Review of General Psychology, 11*, 12–30.

Crane, M. F., & Platow, M. J. (2010). Deviance as adherence to injunctive group norms: The overlooked role of social identification in deviance. *British Journal of Social Psychology, 49*, 827–847.

Crawford, M. T. (2007). The renegotiation of social identities in response to a threat to self-evaluation maintenance. *Journal of Experimental Social Psychology, 43*, 39–47.

Crescioni, A. W., & Baumeister, R. F. (2009). Alone and aggressive: Social exclusion impairs self-control and empathy and increases hostile cognition and aggression. In M. J. Harris (Ed.), *Bullying, rejection, and peer victimization: A social-cognitive neuroscience perspective* (pp. 251–277). New York: Springer.

Crocker, J., Canevello, A., & Brown, A. A. (2017). Social motivation: Costs and benefits of selfishness and otherishness. *Annual Review of Psychology, 68*, 299–325.

Croyle, R. T., & Jemmott, J. B., III. (1990). Psychological reactions to risk factor testing. In J. A. Skelton & R. T. Croyle (Eds.), *The mental representation of health and illness* (pp. 121–157). New York: Springer-Verlag.

Crum, A. J., Salovey, P., & Achor, S. (2013). Rethinking stress: The role of mindsets in determining the stress response. *Journal of Personality and Social Psychology, 104*, 716–733. doi:10.1037/a0031201

Csikszentmihalyi, M. (1997). *Finding flow*. New York: Basic Books.

Csikszentmihalyi, M., & Nakamura, J. (2010). Effortless attention in everyday life: A systematic phenomenology. In B. Bruya (Ed.), *Effortless attention: A new perspective in the cognitive science of attention and action* (pp. 179–189). Cambridge, MA: MIT Press.

Cuddy, A. J., Wilmuth, C. A., Yap, A. J., & Carney, D. R. (2015). Preparatory power posing affects nonverbal presence and job interview performance. *Journal of Applied Psychology, 100*, 1286–1295.

Cullen, D. (2010). *Columbine*. New York: Twelve.

Cunningham, M. R. (1986). Measuring the physical in physical attractiveness: Quasi-experiments on the sociobiology of female facial beauty. *Journal of Personality and Social Psychology, 50*, 925–935.

Cunningham, M. R., & Baumeister, R. F. (2016). How to make nothing out of something: Analyses of the impact of study sampling and statistical interpretation in misleading meta-analytic conclusions. *Frontiers in Psychology, 7*, Article 1639. doi:0.3389/fpsyg.2016.01639

Cunningham, M. R., Barbee, A. P., & Pike, C. L. (1990). What do women want? Facial metric assessment of multiple motives in the perception of male facial physical attractiveness. *Journal of Personality and Social Psychology, 59*, 61–72.

Czopp, A. M., & Monteith, M. J. (2003). Confronting prejudice (literally): Reactions to confrontations of racial and gender bias. *Personality and Social Psychology Bulletin, 29*, 532–544.

Czopp, A. M., Monteith, M. J., & Mark, A. M. (2006). Standing up for a change: Reducing bias through interpersonal confrontation. *Journal of Personality and Social Psychology, 90*, 784–803.

Dabbs, J. M., Jr. (2000). *Heroes, rogues, and lovers*. New York: McGraw-Hill.

Dabbs, J. M., Jr., Carr, T. S., Frady, R. L., & Riad, J. K. (1995). Testosterone, crime, and misbehavior among 692 male prison inmates. *Personality and Individual Differences, 18*, 627–633.

Dai, X., Dong, P., & Jia, J. S. (2014). When does playing hard to get increase romantic attraction? *Journal of Experimental Psychology: General, 132*, 521–526.

Dalbert, C., & Yamauchi, L. A. (1994). Belief in a just world and attitudes toward immigrants and foreign workers: A cultural comparison between Hawaii and Germany. *Journal of Applied Social Psychology, 24*, 1612–1626.

Dang, J. (2016). Commentary: A multilab preregistered replication of the ego-depletion effect. *Frontiers in Psychology, 7*, Article 1155. doi:10.3389/fpsyg.2016.01155

Dann, C. (2014, May 12). In polling Obamacare, a label makes a big difference. *NBC News*. Retrieved April 1, 2017, from http://www.nbcnews.com/politics/first-read/polling-obamacare-label-makes-big-difference-n102861

Darley, J. M. (1992). Social organization for the production of evil. *Psychological Inquiry, 3*, 199–218.

Darley, J. M. (2004). Social comparison motives in ongoing groups. In M. B. Brewer & M. Hewstone (Eds.), *Emotion and motivation* (pp. 281–297). Malden, MA: Blackwell.

Darley, J. M., & Batson, C. D. (1973). From Jerusalem to Jericho: A study of situational and dispositional variables in helping behavior. *Journal of Personality and Social Psychology, 27*, 100–108.

Darley, J. M., & Latané, B. (1968). Bystandar intervention in emergencies: Diffusion of responsibility. *Journal of Personality and Social Psychology, 8*, 377–383.

Dar-Nimrod, I., & Heine, S. J. (2011). Genetic essentialism: On the deceptive determinism of DNA. *Psychological Bulletin, 137*, 800–818.

Darwin, C. R. (1859). *The origin of species*. London: Murray.

Darwin, C. R. (1872). *The expression of the emotions in man and animals*. London: Murray.

Davenport, C. (2014, May 7). Miami finds itself ankle-deep in Climate Change debate. *The New York Times*. Retrieved July 15, 2014, from http://www.nytimes.com/2014/05/08/us/florida-finds-itself-in-the-eye-of-the-storm-on-climate-change.html?emc=eta1

Davidov, E., Meuleman, B., Cieciuch, J., Schmidt, P., & Billiet, J. (2014). Measurement equivalence in cross-national research. *Annual Review of Sociology, 40*, 55–75.

Davidson, A. R., & Jaccard, J. J. (1979). Variables that moderate the attitude-behavior relation: Results of a longitudinal survey. *Journal of Personality and Social Psychology, 37*, 1364–1376.

Davis, A. L., & Fischhoff, B. (2014). Communicating uncertain experimental evidence. *Journal of Experimental Psychology: Learning, Memory, and Cognition, 40*, 261–274.

Davis, D., & Loftus, E. F. (2003). What's good for the goose cooks the gander: Inconsistencies between the law and psychology of voluntary intoxication and sexual assault. In W. T. O'Donohue & E. Levensky (Eds.), *Handbook of Forensic Psychology: Resources for Mental Health and Legal Professionals* (pp. 997–1032). New York: Elsevier Academic Press.

Davis, K. E., & Jones, E. E. (1960). Changes in interpersonal perception as a means of reducing cognitive dissonance. *Journal of Abnormal and Social Psychology, 61*, 402–410.

Davis, M. H. (1983). Measuring individual differences in empathy: Evidence for a multidimensional approach. *Journal of Personality and Social Psychology, 44*, 113–126.

DeBono, K. G., & Snyder, M. (1995). Acting on one's attitudes: The role of a history of choosing situations. *Personality and Social Psychology Bulletin, 21*, 629–636.

De Dreu, C. K. W. (2014). *Social conflict within and between groups*. East Sussex: Psychology Press.

De Dreu, C. K. W., & De Vries, N. K. (Eds.). (2001). *Group consensus and minority influence: Implications for innovation*. Oxford, England: Blackwell Publishers.

De Dreu, C., Nijstad, B., & van Knippenberg, D. (2008). Motivated information processing in group judgment and decision making. *Personality and Social Psychology Review, 12*, 22–49.

De Houwer, J. (2011). Evaluative conditioning: A review of procedure knowledge and mental process theories. In T. Schachtman & S. Reilly (Eds.), *Applications of learning and conditioning*. Oxford, UK: Oxford University Press.

De Houwer, J., Gawronski, B., & Barnes-Holmes, D. (2013). A functional-cognitive framework for attitude research. *European Review of Social Psychology, 24*, 252–287.

De Houwer, J., Teige-Mocigemba, S., Spruyt, A., & Moors, A. (2009). Implicit measures: A normative analysis and review. *Psychological Bulletin, 135*, 347–368.

de Mooij, M. (2014). International and cross-cultural consumer behavior. In H. Cheng (Ed.), *The handbook of international advertising research* (Vol. 1, pp. 128–148).

De Waal, F. B. M. (1995, March). Bonobo sex and society: The behavior of a close relative challenges assumptions about male supremacy in human evolution. *Scientific American*, 82–88.

Deaux, K., & La France, M. (1998). Gender. In D. T. Gilbert, S. T. Fiske, & G. Lindzey (Eds.), *The handbook of social psychology*. Boston: McGraw Hill.

Deci, E. L. (2016). Intrinsic motivation: The inherent tendency to be active. In R. J. Sternberg, S. T. Fiske, & D. J. Foss (Eds.). *Scientists making a difference: One hundred eminent behavioral and brain scientists talk about their most important contributions* (pp. 288–292). New York: Cambridge University Press.

Deci, E. L., & Ryan, R. M. (1985). *Intrinsic motivation and self-determination in human behavior*. New York: Plenum.

Deci, E. L., Koestner, R., & Ryan, R. M. (1999a). A meta-analytic review of experiments examining the effects of extrinsic rewards. *Psychological Bulletin, 125*, 627–668.

Deci, E. L., Koestner, R., & Ryan, R. M. (1999b). The undermining effect is a reality after all—extrinsic rewards, task interest, and self-determination: Reply to Eisenberger, Pierce, and Cameron (1999) and Lepper, Henderlong, and Gingras (1999). *Psychological Bulletin, 125*, 692–700.

Deffenbacher, K. A., Bornstein, B. H., & Penrod, S. D. (2004). A meta-analytic review of the effects of high stress on eyewitness memory. *Law and Human Behavior, 28*, 687–706.

Dekel, S., Ein-Dor, T., Gordon, K. M., Rosen, J. B., & Bonanno, G. A. (2013). Cortisol and PTSD symptoms among male and female high-exposure 9/11 survivors. *Journal of Traumatic Stress, 26*, 621–625.

DeMarree, K. G., Loersch, C., Briñol, P., Petty, R. E., Payne, B. K., & Rucker, D. D. (2012). From primed construct to motivated behavior: Validation processes in goal pursuit. *Personality and Social Psychology Bulletin, 38*, 1659–1670.

DeMarree, K. G., Clark, C. J., Wheeler, S. C., Briñol, P., & Petty, R. E. (2017). On the pursuit of desired attitudes: Wanting a different attitude affects information processing and behavior. *Journal of Experimental Social Psychology, 70*, 129–142.

Demolliens, M., Isbaine, F., Takerkart, S., Huguet, P., & Boussaoud, D. (2017). Social and asocial prefrontal cortex neurons: A new look at social facilitation and the social brain. *Social Cognitive and Affective Neuroscience*. doi:10.1093/scan/nsx053

Dennett, D. C. (1991). *Consciousness explained*. Boston: Little, Brown.

Denson, T. F., Pedersen, W. C., Friese, M., Hahm, A., & Roberts, L. (2011). Understanding impulsive aggression: Angry rumination and reduced self-control capacity are mechanisms underlying the provocation–aggression relationship. *Personality and Social Psychology Bulletin, 37*, 850–862.

Department of Health and Human Services. (2010). *National Intimate Partner and Sexual Violence Survey*. Atlanta, GA: Centers for Disease Control and Prevention.

DePaulo, B. M. (1992). Nonverbal behavior and self-presentation. *Psychological Bulletin, 111*, 203–243.

Deppe, R. K., & Harackiewicz, J. M. (1996). Self-handicapping and intrinsic motivation: Buffering intrinsic motivation from the threat of failure. *Journal of Personality and Social Psychology, 70*, 868–876.

Derzon, J. H., & Lipsey, M. W. (2002). A meta-analysis of the effectiveness of mass communication for changing substance-use knowledge, attitudes, and behavior. In W. D. Crano & M. Burgoon (Eds.), *Mass media and drug prevention: Classic and contemporary theories and research* (pp. 231–258). Mahwah, NJ: Erlbaum.

Descheemaeker, M., Spruyt, A., Fazio, R. H., & Hermans, D. (2016). On the generalization of attitude accessibility after repeated attitude expression. *European Journal of Social Psychology*. doi:10.1002/ejsp.2206

Desforges, D. M., Lord, C. G., Ramsey, S. L., Mason, J. A., Van Leeuwen, M. D., et al. (1991). Effects of structured cooperative contact on changing negative attitudes toward stigmatized social groups. *Journal of Personality and Social Psychology, 60*, 531–544.

Desmond, E. W. (1987, November 30). Out in the open. *Time*, pp. 80–90.

Desportes, J. P., & Lemaine, J. M. (1998). The sizes of human groups: An analysis of their distributions. In D. Canter, J. C. Jesuino, L. Soczka, & G. M. Stephenson (Eds.), *Environmental social psychology* (pp. 57–65). Dordrecht, Netherlands: Kluwer.

Deutsch, M. (1973). *The resolution of conflict: Constructive and destructive processes*. New Haven, CT: Yale University Press.

Deutsch, M. (1997, April). *Comments on cooperation and prejudice reduction*. Paper presented at the symposium Reflections on 100 Years of Social Psychology, Yosemite National Park, CA.

Deutsch, M., & Collins, M. E. (1951). *Interracial housing: A psychological evaluation of a social experiment*. Minneapolis: University of Minnesota Press.

Deutsch, M., & Gerard, H. G. (1955). A study of normative and informational social influence upon individual judgment. *Journal of Abnormal and Social Psychology, 51*, 629–636.

Deutsch, M., & Krauss, R. M. (1960). The effect of threat upon interpersonal bargaining. *Journal of Abnormal and Social Psychology, 61*, 181–189.

Deutsch, M., & Krauss, R. M. (1962). Studies of interpersonal bargaining. *Journal of Conflict Resolution, 6*, 52–76.

Deutsch, M., Coleman, P. T., & Marcus, E. C. (2011). *The handbook of conflict resolution: Theory and practice*. Hoboken, NJ: Wiley.

Devine, D. J. (2012). *Jury decision making: The state of the science*. New York: NYU Press.

Devine, P. G. (1989). Stereotypes and prejudice: Their automatic and controlled components. *Journal of Personality and Social Psychology, 56*, 5–18.

Devine, P. G., Plant, E. A., Amodio, D. M., Harmon-Jones, E., & Vance, S. L. (2002). The regulation of explicit and implicit race bias: The role of motivations to respond without prejudice. *Journal of Personality and Social Psychology, 82*(5), 835–848.

DeWall, C. N., & Richman, S. B. (2011). Social exclusion and the desire to reconnect. *Social and Personality Psychology Compass, 5*, 919–932. doi:10.1111/j.1751-9004.2011.00383.x

DeWall, C. N., Pond, R. S., Jr., Campbell, W. K., & Twenge, J. M. (2011, March 21). Tuning in to psychological change: Linguistic markers of psychological traits and emotions over time in popular U.S. song lyrics. *Psychology of Aesthetics, Creativity, and the Arts*. Advance online publication. doi:10.1037/a0023195

Dickerson, C., Thibodeau, R., Aronson, E., & Miller, D. (1992). Using cognitive dissonance to encourage water conservation. *Journal of Applied Social Psychology, 22*, 841–854.

Diener, E. (1980). Deindividuation: The absence of self-awareness and self-regulation in group members. In P. B. Paulus (Ed.), *Psychology of group influence* (pp. 209–242). Hillsdale, NJ: Erlbaum.

Diener, E., & Biswas-Diener, R. (2008). *Happiness: Unlocking the mysteries of psychological wealth*. Boston: Wiley-Blackwell.

Diener, E., & Oishi, S. (2005). The nonobvious social psychology of happiness. *Psychological Inquiry, 16*, 162–167.

Diener, E., & Seligman, M. E. P. (2004). Beyond money: Toward an economy of well-being. *Psychological Science in the Public Interest, 5*, 1–31.

Diener, E., & Wallbom, M. (1976). Effects of self-awareness on antinormative behavior. *Journal of Research in Personality, 10*, 107–111.

Diener, E., Heintzelman, S. J., Kushlev, K., Tay, L., Wirtz, D., Lutes, L. D., & Oishi, S. (2017). Findings all psychologists should know from the new science on subjective well-being. *Canadian Psychology/Psychologie canadienne, 58*, 87–104.

Diener, E., Tay, L., & Oishi, S. (2013). Rising income and the subjective well-being of nations. *Journal of Personality and Social Psychology, 104*, 267–276.

Dijksterhuis, A., & Strick, M. (2016). A case for thinking without consciousness. Perspectives on *Psychological Science, 11*(1), 117–132.

Dijksterhuis, A., Aarts, H., & Smith, P. K. (2005). The power of the subliminal: On subliminal persuasion and other potential applications. In R. R. Hassin, J. S. Uleman, & J. A. Bargh (Eds.), *The new unconscious* (pp. 77–106). New York: Oxford University Press.

Dion, K. K., & Dion, K. L. (1993). Individualistic and collectivistic perspectives on gender and the cultural context of love and intimacy. *Journal of Social Issues, 49*, 53–69.

Dion, K. K., & Dion, K. L. (1996). Cultural perspectives on romantic love. *Personal Relationships, 3*, 5–17.

Dion, K. L. (2000). Group cohesion: From "fields of forces" to multidimensional construct. *Group Dynamics, 4*, 7–26.

Dion, K. L., & Dion, K. K. (1993). Gender and ethnocultural comparisons in styles of love. *Psychology of Women Quarterly, 17*, 463–473.

Dion, K., Berscheid, E., & Walster, E. (1972). What is beautiful is good. *Journal of Personality and Social Psychology, 24*, 285–290.

Dobolyi, D. G., & Dodson, C. S. (2013). Eyewitness confidence in simultaneous and sequential lineups: A criterion shift account for sequential mistaken identification overconfidence. *Journal of Experimental Psychology: Applied, 19*, 345–357.

Dodds, P. S., Muhamad, R., & Watts, D. J. (2003). An experimental study of search in global social networks. *Science, 301*, 827–829.

Dohrenwend, B. (2006). Inventorying stressful life events as risk factors for psychopathology: Toward resolution of the problem of intracategory variability. *Psychological Bulletin, 132*, 477–495.

Doi, T. (1988). *The anatomy of dependence*. New York: Kodansha International.

Doliński, D., & Grzyb, T. (2016). One serious shock versus gradated series of shocks: Does 'multiple feet-in-the-door' explain obedience in Milgram studies? *Basic and Applied Social Psychology, 38*, 276–283.

Doliński, D., Grzyb, T., Folwarczny, M., Grzybała, P., Krzyszycha, K., Martynowska, K., & Trojanowski, J. (2017). Would you deliver an electric shock in 2015? Obedience in the experimental paradigm developed by Stanley Milgram in the 50 years following the original studies. *Social Psychological and Personality Science*. doi: 10.1177/1948550617693060

Dollard, J. (1938). Hostility and fear in social life. *Social Forces, 17*, 15–26.

Dollard, J., Doob, L., Miller, N., Mowrer, O. H., & Sears, R. R. (1939). *Frustration and aggression*. New Haven, CT: Yale University Press.

Domina, T., & Koch, K. (2002). Convenience and frequency of recycling: Implications for including textiles in curbside recycling programs. *Environment and Behavior, 34*, 216–238.

Donnelly, G. E., Ksendzova, M., Howell, R. T. Vohs, K. D., & Baumeister, R. F. (2016). Buying to blunt negative feelings: Materialistic escape from the self. *Review of General Psychology, 20*, 272–316.

Donnerstein, E., & Berkowitz, L. (1981). Victim reactions in aggressive erotic films as a factor in violence against women. *Journal of Personality and Social Psychology, 41*, 710–724.

Donnerstein, E., & Donnerstein, M. (1976). Research in the control of interracial aggression. In R. G. Green & E. C. O'Neal (Eds.), *Perspectives on aggression* (pp. 133–168). New York: Academic Press.

Douglass, A. B., & Pavletic, A. (2012). Eyewitness confidence malleability. In B. L. Cutler (Ed.), *Conviction of the innocent: Lessons from psychological research* (pp. 149–165). Washington, DC: American Psychological Association.

Douthwaite, Julia V. (2002). *The wild girl, natural man, and the monster: Dangerous experiments in the age of enlightenment*. Chicago: University of Chicago Press.

Dovere, E-I (2016). How Clinton lost Michigan—and blew the election. Retrieved April 17, 2017, from http://www.politico.com/story/2016/12/michigan-hillary-clinton-trump-232547

Dovidio, J. F. (1984). Helping behavior and altruism: An empirical and conceptual overview. In L. Berkowitz (Ed.), *Advances in experimental social psychology* (Vol. 17, pp. 361–427). New York: Academic Press.

Dovidio, J. F., & Gaertner, S. L. (1996). Affirmative action, unintentional racial biases, and intergroup relations. *Journal of Social Issues, 52*, 51–75.

Dovidio, J. F., Kawakami, K., & Gaertner, S. L. (2002). Implicit and explicit prejudice and interracial interaction. *Journal of Personality and Social Psychology, 82*, 62–68.

Dovidio, J. F., Pagotto, L., & Hebl, M. R. (2011). Implicit attitudes and discrimination against people with physical disabilities. In R. L. Wiener & S. L. Willborn (Eds.), *Disability and aging discrimination: Perspectives in law and psychology* (pp. 157–183). New York: Springer Science 1 Business Media.

Dovidio, J. F., Piliavin, J. A., Gaertner, S. L., Schroeder, D. A., & Clark, R. D., III. (1991). The arousal cost-reward model and the process of intervention. In M. S. Clark (Ed.), *Review of personality and social psychology* (Vol. 12, pp. 86–118). Newbury Park, CA: Sage.

Draper, R. (2008). *Dead certain*. New York: Free Press.

Drigotas, S. M., & Rusbult, C. E. (1992). Should I stay or should I go? A dependence model of breakups. *Journal of Personality and Social Psychology, 62*, 62–87.

Dropp, K., & Nyhan, B. (2017). One-third don't know Obamacare and Affordable Care Act are the same. Retrieved April 21, 2017, from https://www.nytimes.com/2017/02/07/upshot/one-third-dont-know-obamacare-and-affordable-care-act-are-the-same.html?_r=0

Drought's growing reach: NCAR study points to global warming as key feature. (2005, Jan. 10). University Corportation for Atmospheric Research. Retrieved July 25, 2017, from http://www.ucar.edu/news/releases/2005/drought_research.shtml

Du, S., Tao, Y., & Martinez, A. M. (2014). Compound facial expressions of emotion. *Proceedings of the National Academy of Sciences*. doi:10.1073/pnas.1322355111

Duck, S. W. (1982). A typography of relationship disengagement and dissolution. In S. W. Duck (Ed.), *Personal relationships 4: Dissolving personal relationships* (pp. 1–32). London: Academic Press.

Duckworth, A. L., Gendler, T. S., & Gross, J. J. (2016). Situational strategies for self-control. *Perspectives on Psychological Science, 11*, 35–55.

Dunn, A. (1997, May 14). If Deep Blue wrote Hamlet would it change the endgame? *The New York Times*. Retrieved June 11, 2017, from https://partners.nytimes.com/library/cyber/surf/051497mind.html

Dunn, E. W., Aknin, L. B., & Norton, M. (2008). Spending money on others promotes happiness. *Science, 319*, 1687–1688.

Dunn, E. W., Aknin, L. B., & Norton, M. I. (2014). Prosocial spending and happiness: Using money to benefit others pays off. *Current Directions in Psychological Science, 23*, 41–47.

Dunn, E. W., Gilbert, D. T., & Wilson, T. D. (2011). If money doesn't make you happy, then you probably aren't spending it right. *Journal of Consumer Psychology, 21*, 115–125.

Dunning, D., & Perretta, S. (2002). Automaticity and eyewitness accuracy: A 10- to 12-second rule for distinguishing accurate from inaccurate positive identifications. *Journal of Applied Psychology, 87*, 951–962.

Dunning, D., & Stern, L. B. (1994). Distinguishing accurate from inaccurate eyewitness identifications via inquiries about decision processes. *Journal of Personality and Social Psychology, 67*, 818–835.

Durrant, J., & Ensom, R. (2012). Physical punishment of children: Lessons from 20 years of research. *Canadian Medical Association Journal, 184*, 1373–1377.

Dutton, D. G., & Aron, A. P. (1974). Some evidence for heightened sexual attraction under conditions of high anxiety. *Journal of Personality and Social Psychology, 30*, 510–517.

Duval, T. S., & Silvia, P. J. (2001). *Self-awareness and causal attributions: A dual-systems theory*. Boston: Kluwer Academic.

Duval, T. S., & Silvia, P. J. (2002). Self-awareness, probability of improvement, and the self-serving bias. *Journal of Personality and Social Psychology, 82*, 49–61.

Duval, T. S., & Wicklund, R. A. (1972). *A theory of objective self-awareness*. New York: Academic Press.

Dweck, C. S. (2006). *Mindset: The new psychology of success*. New York: Random House.

Eagly, A. H. (2009). The his and hers of prosocial behavior: An examination of the social psychology of gender. *American Psychologist, 64*(8), 644–658. doi:10.1037/0003-066X.64.8.644

Eagly, A. H., & Chaiken, S. (1975). An attribution analysis of communicator characteristics on opinion change: The case of communicator attractiveness. *Journal of Personality and Social Psychology, 32*, 136–244.

Eagly, A. H., & Chaiken, S. (1993). *The psychology of attitudes*. Fort Worth, TX: Harcourt Brace.

Eagly, A. H., & Chaiken, S. (2007). The advantages of an inclusive definition of attitude. *Social Cognition, 25*, 582–602.

Eagly, A. H., & Chin, J. L. (2010). Diversity and leadership in a changing world. *American Psychologist, 65*, 216–224.

Eagly, A. H., & Karau, S. J. (2002). Role congruity theory of prejudice toward female leaders. *Psychological Review, 109*, 573–598.

Eagly, A. H., & Koenig, A. M. (2006). Social role theory of sex differences and similarities: Implication for prosocial behavior. In K. Dindia & D. J. Canary (Eds.), *Sex differences and similarities in communication* (2nd ed., pp. 161–177). Mahwah, NJ: Erlbaum.

Eagly, A. H., Ashmore, R. D., Makhijani, M. G., & Longo, L. C. (1991). What is beautiful is good, but …: A meta-analytic review of research on the physical attractiveness stereotype. *Psychological Bulletin, 110*, 109–128.

Eastwick, P. W., Eagly, A. H., Finkel, E. J., & Johnson, S. E. (2011). Implicit and explicit preferences for physical attractiveness in a romantic partner: A double dissociation in predictive validity. *Journal of Personality and Social Psychology, 101*, 993–1011.

Eaton, J., & Struthers, C. W. (2006). The reduction of psychological aggression across varied interpersonal contexts through repentance and forgiveness. *Aggressive Behavior, 32*, 195–206.

Ebert, J. P., & Wegner, D. M. (2011). Mistaking randomness for free will. *Consciousness and Cognition: An International Journal, 20*, 965–971. doi:10.1016/j.concog.2010.12.012

Eccles, J. S. (2011). Understanding women's achievement choices: Looking back and looking forward. *Psychology of Women Quarterly, 35*, 520–516.

Edelman, B. (2009). Red light states: Who buys online adult entertainment? *Journal of Economic Perspectives, 23*, 209–230.

Edkins, V. A. (2011). Defense attorney plea recommendations and client race: Does zealous representation apply equally to all? *Law and Human Behavior, 35*, 413–425.

Egan, P. M., Hirt, E. R., & Karpen, S. C. (2012). Taking a fresh perspective: Vicarious restoration as a means of recovering self-control. *Journal of Experimental Social Psychology, 48*(2), 457–465. doi:10.1016/j.jesp.2011.10.019

Ehrlinger, J., Gilovich, T., & Ross, L. (2005). Peering into the bias blind spot: People's assessments of bias in themselves and others. *Personality and Social Psychology Bulletin, 31*, 680–692.

Eibach, R. P., Wilmot, M. O., & Libby, L. (2015). The system-justifying function of gratitude norms. *Social and Personality Psychology Compass, 9*, 348–358.

Eibl-Eibesfeldt, I. (1963). Aggressive behavior and ritualized fighting in animals. In J. H. Masserman (Ed.), *Science and psychoanalysis: Vol. 6. Violence and war* (pp. 8–17). New York: Grune & Stratton.

Einolf, C. J. (2011). Gender differences in the correlates of volunteering and charitable giving. *Nonprofit and Voluntary Sector Quarterly, 40*, 1092–1112.

Eisenberg, N., & Fabes, R. A. (1991). Prosocial behavior and empathy: A multimethod developmental perspective. In M. S. Clark (Ed.), *Review of personality and social psychology* (Vol. 12, pp. 34–61). Newbury Park, CA: Sage.

Eisenberg, N., Hofer, C., Sulik, M. J., & Liew, J. (2014). The development of prosocial moral reasoning and a prosocial orientation in young adulthood: Concurrent and longitudinal correlates. *Developmental Psychology, 50*, 58–70.

Eisenberg, N., Spinrad, T. L., & Sadovsky, A. (2006). Empathy-related responding in children. In M. Killen & J. G. Smetana (Eds.), *Handbook of moral development* (pp. 517–549). Mahwah, NJ: Erlbaum.

Eisenstadt, D., & Leippe, M. R. (2010). Social influences on eyewitness confidence: The social psychology of memory self-certainty. In R. M. Arkin, K. C. Oleson, & P. J. Carroll (Eds.), *Handbook of the uncertain self* (pp. 36–61). New York: Psychology Press.

Eitam, B., & Higgins, E. T. (2010). Motivation in mental accessibility: Relevance of a Representation (ROAR) as a new framework. *Social and Personality Psychology Compass, 4*(10), 951–967. doi:10.1111/j.1751-9004.2010.00309.x

Ekman, P. (1993). Facial expression and emotion. *American Psychologist, 48*, 384–392.

Ekman, P., & Davidson, R. J. (Eds.). (1994). *The nature of emotion: Fundamental questions*. New York: Oxford University Press.

Ekman, P., & Friesen, W. V. (1971). Constants across cultures in the face and emotion. *Journal of Personality and Social Psychology, 17*, 124–129.

Ekman, P., & Friesen, W. V. (1975). *Unmasking the face*. Englewood Cliffs, NJ: Prentice Hall.

Ekman, P., Friesen, W. V., O'Sullivan, M., Chan, A., Diacoyanni-Tarlatzis, I., Heider, K., et al. (1987). Universals and cultural differences in the judgments of facial expressions of emotions. *Journal of Personality and Social Psychology, 53*, 712–717.

Ekman, P., O'Sullivan, M., & Matsumoto, D. (1991). Confusions about content in the judgment of facial expression: A reply to "Contempt and the relativity thesis." *Motivation and Emotion, 15*, 169–176.

Elfenbein, H. A., & Ambady, N. (2002). On the universality and cultural specificity of emotion recognition: A meta-analysis. *Psychological Bulletin, 128*, 203–235.

Ellemers, N., & Jetten, J. (2013). The many ways to be marginal in a group. *Personality and Social Psychology Review, 17*, 3–21.

Ellis, A. P. J., Porter, C. O. L. H., & Wolverton, S. A. (2008). Learning to work together: An examination of transactive memory system development in teams. In V. I. Sessa & M. London (Eds.), *Work group learning: Understanding, improving and assessing how groups learn in organizations* (pp. 91–115). New York: Erlbaum.

Else-Quest, N. M., Hyde, J. S., & Linn, M. C. (2010). Cross-national patterns of gender differences in mathematics: A meta-analysis. *Psychological Bulletin, 136*, 103–127.

Ellison, N. B., Hancock, J. T., & Toma, C. L. (2012). Profile as promise: A framework for conceptualizing veracity in online dating self-presentations. *New Media and Society, 14*, 45–62.

El-Shinnawy, M., & Vinze, A. S. (1998). Polarization and persuasive argumentation: A study of decision making in group settings. *Management Information Systems Quarterly, 22*, 165–198.

Emery, S. L., Szczypka, G., Abril, E. P., Kim, Y., & Vera, L. (2014). Are you scared yet? Evaluating fear appeal messages in tweets about the Tips campaign. *Journal of Communication, 64*, 278–295.

Engel, C. (2010). Dictator games: A meta study. Retrieved June 13, 2014, from http://www.coll.mpg.de/pdf_dat/2010_07online.pdf

Epley, E., & Huff, C. (1998). Suspicion, affective response, and education benefit as a result of deception in psychology research. *Personality and Social Psychology Bulletin, 24*, 759–768.

Erceg-Hurn, D. M., & Steed, L. G. (2011). Does exposure to cigarette health warnings elicit psychological reactance in smokers? *Journal of Applied Social Psychology, 41*(1), 219–237. doi:10.1111/j.1559-1816.2010.00710.x

Eron, L. D. (1987). The development of aggressive behavior from the perspective of a developing behaviorism. *American Psychologist, 42*, 435–442.

Eron, L. D. (2001). Seeing is believing: How viewing violence alters attitudes and aggressive behavior. In A. C. Bohart & D. J. Stipek (Eds.), *Constructive and destructive behavior: Implications for family, school, and society* (pp. 49–60). Washington, DC: American Psychological Association.

Etcheverry, P. E., Le, B., & Hoffman, N. G. (2013). Predictors of friend approval for romantic relationships. *Personal Relationships, 20*, 69–83.

Ethical Principles of Psychologists and Code of Conduct. (2017). Downloaded September 1, 2017, from http://www.apa.org/ethics/code/.

Eyink, J., Hirt, E. R., Hendrix, K. S., & Galante, E. (2017). Circadian variations in claimed self-handicapping: Exploring the strategic use of stress as an excuse. *Journal of Experimental Social Psychology, 69*, 102–110.

Fabrigar, L. R., & Petty, R. E. (1999). The role of affective and cognitive bases of attitudes in susceptibility to affectively and cognitively based persuasion. *Personality and Social Psychology Bulletin, 25*, 363–381.

Fajnzylber, P., Lederman, D., & Loayza, N. (2002). What causes violent crime? *European Economic Review, 46*, 1323–1357.

Farrer, J., Tsuchiya, H., & Bagrowicz, B. (2008). Emotional expression in tsukiau dating relationships in Japan. *Journal of Social and Personal Relationships, 25*, 169–188.

Fawcett, J. M., Russell, E. J., Peace, K. A., & Christie, J. (2013). Of guns and geese: A meta-analytic review of the 'weapon focus' literature. *Psychology, Crime, and Law, 19*, 35–66.

Fazio, R. H. (1990). Multiple processes by which attitudes guide behavior: The MODE model as an integrative framework. In M. P. Zanna (Ed.), *Advances in experimental social psychology* (Vol. 23, pp. 75–109). San Diego, CA: Academic Press.

Fazio, R. H. (2007). Attitudes as object–evaluation associations of varying strength. *Social Cognition, 25*, 603–637.

Fazio, R. H., & Olson, M. A. (2003). Implicit measures in social cognition research: Their meaning and uses. *Annual Review of Psychology, 54*, 297–327.

Fazio, R. H., Ledbetter, J. E., & Towles-Schwen, T. (2000). On the costs of accessible attitudes: detecting that the attitude object has changed. *Journal of Personality and Social Psychology, 78*, 197–210.

Feeney, B. C., Cassidy, J., & Ramos-Marcuse, F. (2008). The generalization of attachment representations to new social situations: Predicting behavior during initial interactions with strangers. *Journal of Personality and Social Psychology, 95*, 1481–1498.

Feeney, J. A., & Noller, P. (1996). *Adult attachment.* Thousand Oaks, CA: Sage.

Feeney, J. A., Noller, P., & Roberts, N. (2000). Attachment and close relationships. In C. Hendrick & S. S. Hendrick (Eds.), *Close relationships: A sourcebook* (pp. 185–201). Thousand Oaks, CA: Sage.

Feeney, M. (2005, October 25). Rosa Parks, civil rights icon, dead at 92. *Boston Globe*, pp. A1, B8.

Fehr, B. (2013). The social psychology of love. In J. A. Simpson & L. Campbell (Eds.), *Oxford handbook of close relationships* (pp. 201–233). New York, NY: Oxford University Press.

Fein, S., & Spencer, S. J. (1997). Prejudice as self-image maintenance: Affirming the self through derogating others. *Journal of Personality and Social Psychology, 73*, 31–44.

Feinberg, J. M., & Aiello, J. R. (2006). Social facilitation: A test of competing theories. *Journal of Applied Social Psychology, 36*, 1087–1109.

Feinberg, M., & Willer, R. (2011). Apocalypse soon? Dire messages reduce belief in global warming by contradicting just-world beliefs. *Psychological Science, 22*, 34–38.

Feingold, A. (1990). Gender differences in effects of physical attractiveness on romantic attraction: A comparison across five research paradigms. *Journal of Personality and Social Psychology, 59*, 981–993.

Feingold, A. (1992). Good-looking people are not what we think. *Psychological Bulletin, 111*, 304–341.

Felberbaum, M. (2013, March 19). US to revise cigarette warning labels. Retrieved May 22, 2014, from http://bigstory.ap.org/article/apnews-break-us-revise-cigarette-warning-labels

Feld, S. L. (1982). Social structural determinants of similarity among associates. *American Sociological Review, 47*, 797–801.

Feldman, G. (2017). Making sense of agency: Belief in free will as a unique and important construct. *Social and Personality Psychology Compass, 11*(1). http://dx.doi.org/10.1111/spc3.12293

Femlee, D. H. (1995). Fatal attractions: Affection and disaffection in intimate relationships. *Journal of Social and Personal Relationships, 12*, 295–311.

Femlee, D. H. (1998). "Be careful what you wish for …": A quantitative and qualitative investigation of "fatal attractions." *Personal Relationships, 5*, 235–253.

Fenigstein, A., Scheier, M. F., & Buss, A. H. (1975). Public and private self-consciousness: Assessment and theory. *Journal of Consulting and Clinical Psychology, 43*, 522–527.

Ferguson, C. J. (2009). Media violence effects: Confirmed truth or just another X-File? *Journal of Forensic Psychology Practice, 9*, 103–126.

Ferguson, C. J. (2013). Violent video games and the Supreme Court: Lessons for the scientific community in the wake of *Brown v. Entertainment Merchants Association. American Psychologist, 68*, 57–74.

Ferguson, C. J. (2014). A way forward for video game violence research. *American Psychologist, 69*, 307–309.

Ferguson, C. J., & Kilburn, J. (2009). The public health risks of media violence: A meta-analytic review. *Journal of Pediatrics, 154*, 759–763.

Ferguson, K. T., Cassells, R. C., MacAllister, J. W., & Evans, G. W. (2013). The physical environment and child development: An international review. *International Journal of Psychology, 48*, 437–468.

Fernández-Dols, J. M., & Crivelli C. (2013). Emotion and expression: Naturalistic studies. *Emotion Review, 5*, 24–29.

Ferris, T. (1997, April 14). The wrong stuff. *New Yorker*, p. 32.

Feshbach, N. D. (1989). Empathy training and prosocial behavior. In J. Groebel & R. A. Hinde (Eds.), *Aggression and war: Their biological and social bases* (pp. 101–111). New York: Cambridge University Press.

Feshbach, N. D. (1997). Empathy—the formative years: Implications for clinical practice. In A. C. Bohart & L. S. Greenberg (Eds.), *Empathy reconsidered: New directions in psychotherapy* (pp. 33–59). Washington, DC: American Psychological Association.

Feshbach, N. D., & Feshbach, S. (2009). Empathy and education: Social neuroscience. In J. Decety & W. Ickes (Eds.), *The social neuroscience of empathy* (pp. 85–97). Cambridge, MA: MIT Press.

Feshbach, S., & Tangney, J. (2008). Television viewing and aggression: Some alternative perspectives. *Perspectives on Psychological Science, 3*, 387–389.

Festinger, L. (1954). A theory of social comparison processes. *Human Relations, 7*, 117–140.

Festinger, L. (1957). *A theory of cognitive dissonance.* Stanford, CA: Stanford University Press.

Festinger, L. (1980). Looking backward. In L. Festinger (Ed.), *Retrospections in social psychology* (pp. 236–254). New York: Oxford University Press.

Festinger, L., & Carlsmith, J. M. (1959). Cognitive consequences of forced compliance. *Journal of Abnormal and Social Psychology, 58*, 203–211.

Festinger, L., & Thibaut, J. (1951). Interpersonal communication in small groups. *Journal of Abnormal and Social Psychology, 46*, 92–99.

Festinger, L., Riecken, H. W., & Schachter, S. (1956). *When prophecy fails.* Minneapolis: University of Minnesota Press.

Festinger, L., Schachter, S., & Back, K. (1950). *Social pressures in informal groups: A study of human factors in housing.* New York: Harper.

Fiedler, F. (1967). *A theory of leadership effectiveness.* New York: McGraw-Hill.

Fiedler, K., Walther, E., & Nickel, S. (1999). Covariation-based attribution: On the ability to assess multiple covariations of an effect. *Personality and Social Psychology Bulletin, 25*, 607–622.

Fielder, R. L., & Carey, M. P. (2010). Predictors and consequences of sexual "hookups" among college students: A short-term prospective study. *Archives of Sexual Behavior, 39*, 1105–1119.

Fincham, F. D., Bradbury, T. N., Arias, I., Byrne, C. A., & Karney, B. R. (1997). Marital violence, marital distress, and attributions. *Journal of Family Psychology, 11*, 367–372.

Fine, C. (2008). *A mind of its own: How your brain distorts and deceives.* New York: W.W. Norton.

Fine, G. A., & Elsbach, K. D. (2000). Ethnography and experiment in social psychological theory building: Tactics for integrating qualitative field data with quantitative lab data. *Journal of Experimental Social Psychology, 36*, 51–76.

Fink, B., & Penton-Voak, I. (2002). Evolutionary psychology of facial attractiveness. *Current Directions in Psychological Science, 11*, 154–158.

Finkel, E. J., & Eastwick, P. W. (2009). Arbitrary social norms influence sex differences in romantic selectivity. *Psychological Science, 20*, 1291–1295.

Finkel, E. J., Eastwick, P. W., Karney, B. R., Reis, H. T., & Sprecher, S. (2012). Online dating: A critical analysis from the perspective of psychological science. *Psychological Science in the Public Interest.* doi:10.1177/1529100612436522

Finkel, E. J., Norton, M. I., Reis, H. T., Ariely, D., Caprariello, P. A., Eastwick, P. W., Frost, J. H., & Maniaci, M. R. (2015). When does familiarity promote versus undermine interpersonal attraction? A proposed integrative model from erstwhile adversaries. *Perspectives on Psychological Science, 10*, 3–19.

Finkelstein, L. M., DeMuth, R. L. F., & Sweeney, D. L. (2007). Bias against overweight job applicants: Further explorations of when and why. *Human Resource Management, 46*, 203–222.

Finney, P. D. (1987). When consent information refers to risk and deception: Implications for social research. *Journal of Social Behavior and Personality, 2*, 37–48.

Fischer, P., Krueger, J. I., Greitemeyer, T., Vogrincic, C., Kastenmüller, A., Frey, D., Heene, M., Wicher, M., & Kainbacher, M. (2011). The bystander-effect: A meta-analytic review on bystander intervention in dangerous and non-dangerous emergencies. *Psychological Bulletin, 137*(4), 517–537. doi:10.1037/a0023304

Fishbein, M., & Ajzen, I. (2010). *Predicting and changing behavior: The reasoned action approach.* New York: Psychology Press.

Fishbein, M., Chan, D., O'Reilly, K., Schnell, D., Wood, R., Beeker, C., & Cohn, C. (1993). Factors influencing gay men's attitudes, subjective norms, and intentions with respect to performing sexual behaviors. *Journal of Applied Social Psychology, 23*, 417–438.

Fisher, H. (2004). *Why we love: The nature and chemistry of romantic love*. New York: Macmillan.

Fiske, S. T., & Taylor, S. E. (2013). *Social cognition: From brains to culture* (2nd ed.). Thousand Oaks, CA: Sage.

Fiske, S. T., & Taylor, S. E. (2017). *Social cognition: From brains to culture* (3rd ed.). Thousand Oaks, CA: Sage.

Fiske, S. T., Cuddy, A. J., & Glick, P. (2007). Universal dimensions of social cognition: Warmth and competence. *Trends in Cognitive Sciences, 11*, 77–83.

Fiske, S. T., Cuddy, A. J., Glick, P., & Xu, J. (2002). A model of (often mixed) stereotype content: competence and warmth respectively follow from perceived status and competition. *Journal of Personality and Social Psychology, 82*, 878–902.

Fiske, S. T., Cuddy, A. J. C., & Glick, P. (2006). Universal dimensions of social cognition: Warmth and competence. *Trends in Cognitive Sciences, 11*, 77–83.

Fitzgerald, R. J., Oriet, C., & Price, H. L. (2014). Suspect filler similarity in eyewitness lineups: A literature review and a novel methodology. *Law and Human Behavior*. doi:10.1037/lhb0000095

Fivecoat, H. C., Tomlinson, J. M., Aron, A., & Caprariello, P. A. (2014). Partner support for individual self-expansion opportunities: Effects on relationship satisfaction in long-term couples. *Journal of Social and Personal Relationships*. doi:10.1177/0265407514533767

Flanagan, C. A., Bowes, J. M., Jonsson, B., Csapo, B., & Sheblanova, E. (1998). Ties that bind: Correlates of adolescents' civic commitments in seven countries. *Journal of Social Issues, 54*, 457–475.

Flechas, J. (2017). Miami Beach to begin new $100 million flood prevention project in face of sea level rise. *Miami Herald*. Retrieved May 29, 2017, from http://www.miamiherald.com/news/local/community/miami-dade/miami-beach/article129284119.html

Flick, U. (2014). *An introduction to qualitative research methods*. Thousand Oaks, CA: Sage.

Flores, A. R., Haider-Markel, D. P., Lewis, D. C., Miller, P. R., Tadlock, B. L., & Taylor, J. K. (2017). Challenged expectations: Mere exposure effects on attitudes about transgender people and rights. *Political Psychology*. doi:10.1111/pops.12402

Folkman, S., & Moskowitz, J. T. (2000). The context matters. *Personality and Social Psychology Bulletin, 26*, 150–151.

Forer, B. R. (1949). The fallacy of personal validation: A classroom demonstration of gullibility. *Journal of Abnormal and Social Psychology, 44*, 118–123.

Forgas, J. P. (2011). She just doesn't look like a philosopher…? Affective influences on the halo effect in impression formation. *European Journal of Social Psychology, 41*, 812–817.

Forgas, J. P. (2013). Don't worry, be sad! On the cognitive, motivational, and interpersonal benefits of negative mood. *Current Directions in Psychological Science, 22*, 225–232.

Forsyth, D. R., & Burnette, J. (2010). Group processes. In R. F. Baumeister & E. J. Finkel (Eds.), *Advanced social psychology: The state of the science* (pp. 495–534). New York: Oxford.

Foster, J. D., Campbell, W. K., & Twenge, J. M. (2003). Individual differences in narcissism: Inflated self views across the lifespan and around the world. *Journal of Research in Personality, 37*, 469–486.

Fotuhi, O., Fong, G. T., Zanna, M. P., Borland, R., Yong, H., & Cummings, K. M. (2013). Patterns of cognitive dissonance-reducing beliefs among smokers: A longitudinal analysis from the International Tobacco Control (ITC) Four Country Survey. *Tobacco Control: An International Journal, 22*, 52–58.

Fox, C. (2006). The availability heuristic in the classroom: How soliciting more criticism can boost your course ratings. *Judgment and Decision Making, 1*, 86–90.

Frager, R. (1970). Conformity and anticonformity in Japan. *Journal of Personality and Social Psychology, 15*, 203–210.

Fraidin, S. N. (2004). When is one head better than two? Interdependent information in group decision making. *Organizational Behavior and Human Decision Processes, 93*, 102–113.

Fraley, R. C. (2002). Attachment stability from infancy to adulthood: Meta-analysis and dynamic modeling of developmental mechanisms. *Personality and Social Psychology Review, 6*, 123–151.

Fraley, R. C., & Shaver, P. R. (2000). Adult romantic attachment: Theoretical developments, emerging controversies, and unanswered questions. *Review of General Psychology, 4*, 132–154.

Franklin, B. (1868/1900). *The autobiography of Benjamin Franklin* (J. Bigelow, Ed.). Philadelphia: Lippincott.

Frazier, P. A., & Cook, S. W. (1993). Correlates of distress following heterosexual relationship dissolution. *Journal of Social and Personal Relationships, 10*, 55–67.

Frazier, P., Keenan, N., Anders, S., Perera, S., Shallcross, S., & Hintz, S. (2011). Perceived past, present, and future control and adjustment to stressful life events. *Journal of Personality and Social Psychology, 100*, 749–765. doi:10.1037/a0022405

Freedman, J. L. (1965). Long-term behavioral effects of cognitive dissonance. *Journal of Experimental and Social Psychology, 1*, 145–155.

Freedman, J. L., & Fraser, S. C. (1966). Compliance without pressure: The foot-in-the-door technique. *Journal of Personality and Social Psychology, 4*, 195–202.

Freijy, T., & Kothe, E. J. (2013). Dissonance-based interventions for health behaviour change: A systematic review. *British Journal of Health Psychology, 18*, 310–337.

Freud, S. (1930). *Civilization and its discontents* (J. Riviere, Trans.). London: Hogarth Press.

Freud, S. (1933). *New introductory lectures on psychoanalysis*. New York: Norton.

Fried, C., & Aronson, E. (1995). Hypocrisy, misattribution, and dissonance reduction: A demonstration of dissonance in the absence of aversive consequences. *Personality and Social Psychology Bulletin, 21*, 925–933.

Friese, M., Smith, C. T., Koever, M., & Bluemke, M. (2016). Implicit measures of attitudes and political voting behavior. *Social and Personality Psychology Compass, 10*, 188–201.

Fukuyama, F. (1999). *The great disruption: Human nature and the reconstitution of social order*. New York: Free Press.

Furman, C. R., Luo, S., & Pond, R. S. (2017). A perfect blame: Conflict-promoting attributions mediate the association between perfectionism and forgiveness in romantic relationships. *Personality and Individual Differences, 111*, 178–186.

Furnham, A. (1993). Just world beliefs in twelve societies. *Journal of Social Psychology, 133*, 317–329.

Furnham, A. (2003). Belief in a just world: Research progress over the past decade. *Personality and individual differences, 34*, 795–817.

Furnham, A., & Gunter, B. (1984). Just world beliefs and attitudes toward the poor. *British Journal of Social Psychology, 23*, 265–269.

Furnham, A., & Procter, E. (1989). Beliefs in a just world: Review and critique of the individual difference literature. *British Journal of Social Psychology, 28*, 365–384.

Furnham, A., Richards, S. C., & Paulhus, D. L. (2013). The dark triad of personality: A 10 year review. *Social and Personality Psychology Compass, 7*, 199–216.

Gabbert, F., Memon, A., & Allan, K. (2003). Memory conformity: Can eyewitnesses influence each other's memories for an event? *Applied Cognitive Psychology, 17*, 533–543.

Gabriel, S., & Gardner, W. L. (1999). Are there "his" and "hers" types of interdependence? The implications of gender differences in collective versus relational interdependence for affect, behavior, and cognition. *Journal of Personality and Social Psychology, 77*, 642–655.

Gaertner, S. L., Mann, J. A., Dovidio, J. F., & Murrell, A. J. (1990). How does cooperation reduce intergroup bias? *Journal of Personality and Social Psychology, 59*, 692–704.

Gaffen, D. (2016, February 1). Alphabet passes Apple to become most valuable traded U.S. Company. http://www.reuters.com/article/us-apple-alphabet-value-idUSKCN0VA3JA

Galdi, S., Arcuri, L., & Gawronski, B. (2008). Automatic mental associations predict future choices of undecided decision makers. *Science, 321*, 1100–1102.

Galen, L. W. (2012). Does religious belief promote prosociality? A critical examination. *Psychological Bulletin, 138*, 876–906.

Gallup (2017). "US Support for Gay Marriage Edges to New High." Gallup Poll Social Series. Retrieved from http://www.gallup.com/poll/210566/support-gay-marriage-edges-new-high.aspx

Gallup, G. (1997). On the rise and fall of self-conception in primates. In J. G. Snodgrass & R. L. Thompson (Eds.), *The self across psychology: Self-recognition, self-awareness, and the self concept* (pp. 73–82). New York: New York Academy of Sciences.

Gallup, G. G., Jr., Anderson, J. R., & Shillito, D. J. (2002). The mirror test. In M. Bekoff & C. Allen (Eds.), *Cognitive animal: Empirical and theoretical perspectives on animal cognition* (pp. 325–333). Cambridge, MA: MIT Press.

Gangestad, S. W. (1993). Sexual selection and physical attractiveness: Implications for mating dynamics. *Human Nature, 4*, 205–235.

Gangestad, S. W., & Simpson, J. A. (2000). The evolution of human mating: Trade-offs and strategic pluralism. *Behavioral and Brain Sciences, 23*, 573–587.

Gangitano, A. (May 10, 2016). Poll: Two-thirds of Trump backers think Obama is Muslim. Retreived September 12, 2017, from https://www.rollcall.com/politics/poll-two-thirds-trump-supporters-think-obama-muslim.

Gao, G. (1993, May). *An investigation of love and intimacy in romantic relationships in China and the United States*. Paper presented at the annual conference of the International Communication Association, Washington, DC.

Gao, G. (1996). Self and other: A Chinese perspective on interpersonal relationships. In W. B. Gudykunst, S. Ting-Toomey, & T. Nishida (Eds.), *Communication in personal relationships across cultures* (pp. 81–101). Thousand Oaks, CA: Sage.

Gardner, W. L., Pickett, C. L., & Brewer, M. B. (2000). Social exclusion and selective memory: How the need to belong influences memory for social events. *Personality and Social Psychology Bulletin, 26*, 486–496.

Garrison, K. E., Tang, D., & Schmeichel, B. J. (2016). Embodying power: A preregistered replication and extension of the power pose effect. *Social Psychological and Personality Science, 7*, 623–630.

Gaither, S. E., & Sommers, S. R. (2013). Living with an other-race roommate shapes Whites' behavior in subsequent diverse settings. *Journal of Experimental Social Psychology, 49*, 272–276.

Gaither, S. E., Apfelbaum, E. P., Birnbaum, H. J., Babbitt, L. G., & Sommers, S. R. (2017). Mere membership in racially diverse groups reduces conformity. *Social Psychological and Personality Science*.

Gawronski, B. (2003). Implicational schemata and the correspondence bias: On the diagnostic value of situationally constrained behavior. *Journal of Personality and Social Psychology, 84*, 1154–1171.

Gawronski, B., & Bodenhausen, G. V. (2012). Self-insight from a dual-process perspective. In S. Vazire, & T. D. Wilson (Eds.), *Handbook of self-knowledge*. New York: Guilford Press.

Geen, R. G. (1989). Alternative conceptions of social facilitation. In P. B. Paulus (Ed.), *Psychology of group influence* (2nd ed., pp. 15–51). Hillsdale, NJ: Erlbaum.

Gelfand, M. J., Chiu, C., & Hong, Y. (Eds.). (2014). *Advances in culture and psychology* (Vol. 4). New York: Oxford University Press.

Gendron, M., Roberson, D., van der Vyver, J. M., & Barrett, L. F. (2014). Perceptions of emotion from facial expressions are not culturally universal: Evidence from a remote culture. *Emotion, 14,* 251–262.

Gentile, D. A., Coyne, S., & Walsh, D. A. (2011). Media violence, physical aggression, and relational aggression in school age children: A short-term longitudinal study. *Aggressive Behavior, 37,* 193–206.

Geraerts, E., Schooler, J., Merckelbach, H., Jelicic, M., Hauer, B., & Ambadar, Z. (2007). The reality of recovered memories: Corroborating continuous and discontinuous memories of childhood sexual abuse. *Psychological Science, 18,* 564–568.

Gerard, H. B., & Mathewson, G. C. (1966). The effects of severity of initiation on liking for a group: A replication. *Journal of Experimental Social Psychology, 2,* 278–287.

Gerbner, G., Gross, L., Morgan, M., Signorielli, N., & Shanahan, J. (2002). Growing up with television: Cultivation processes. In J. Bryant & D. Zillmann (Eds.), *Media effects: Advances in theory and research* (pp. 43–67). Mahwah, NJ: Erlbaum.

Gerdes, E. P. (1979). College students' reactions to social psychological experiments involving deception. *Journal of Social Psychology, 107,* 99–110.

Gerin, W., Chaplin, W., Schwartz, J. E., Holland, J., Alter, R., Wheeler, R., Duong, D., & Pickering, T. G. (2005). Sustained blood pressure increase after an acute stressor: The effects of the 11 September 2001 attack on the New York City World Trade Center. *Journal of Hypertension, 23,* 279–284.

Gershoff, E. T. (2002). Parental corporal punishment and associated child behaviors and experiences: A meta-analytic and theoretical review. *Psychological Bulletin, 128,* 539–579.

Gershoff, E. T., & Grogan-Kaylor, A. (2016). Spanking and child outcomes: Old controversies and new meta-analyses. *Journal of Family Psychology, 30,* 453–469.

Ghrear, S. E., Birch, S. A. J., & Bernstein, D. M. (2016). Outcome knowledge and false belief. *Frontiers in Psychology, 7,* Article ID 118.

Gibbons, F. X. (1978). Sexual standards and reactions to pornography: Enhancing behavioral consistency through self-focused attention. *Journal of Personality and Social Psychology, 36,* 976–987.

Gibbons, F. X., Eggleston, T. J., & Benthin, A. C. (1997). Cognitive reactions to smoking relapse: The reciprocal relation between dissonance and self-esteem. *Journal of Personality and Social Psychology, 72,* 184–195.

Gibbons, F. X., Gerrard, M., & Cleveland, M. J. (2004). Perceived discrimination and substance use in African American parents and their children: A panel study. *Journal of Personality and Social Psychology, 86,* 517–529.

Gibbs, N., & Roche, T. (1999, December 20). The Columbine tapes. *Time,* p. 154.

Gigerenzer, G. (2016). Taking heuristics seriously: Introduction. In A. Samson (Ed.), *The behavioral economics guide 2016.* Retrieved from http://www.behavioraleconomics.com/the-behavioral-economics-guide-2016/ (pp. V–XI). London: Behavioral Science Solutions.

Gilbert, D. T. (1989). Thinking lightly about others: Automatic components of the social inference process. In J. S. Uleman & J. A. Bargh (Eds.), *Unintended thought* (pp. 189–211). New York: Guilford Press.

Gilbert, D. T. (1991). How mental systems believe. *American Psychologist, 46,* 107–119.

Gilbert, D. T. (1993). The assent of man: Mental representation and the control of belief. In D. M. Wegner & J. W. Pennebaker (Eds.), *The handbook of mental control* (pp. 57–87). Englewood Cliffs, NJ: Prentice Hall.

Gilbert, D. T. (2006). *Stumbling on happiness.* New York: Knopf.

Gilbert, D. T., & Ebert, E. J. (2002). Decisions and revisions: The affective forecasting of changeable outcomes. *Journal of Personality and Social Psychology, 82*(4), 503–514.

Gilbert, D. T., & Hixon, J. G. (1991). The trouble of thinking: Activation and applications of stereotypical beliefs. *Journal of Personality and Social Psychology, 60,* 509–517.

Gilbert, D. T., & Jones, E. E. (1986). Perceiver-induced constraint: Interpretations of self-generated reality. *Journal of Personality and Social Psychology, 50,* 269–280.

Gilbert, D. T., & Malone, P. S. (1995). The correspondence bias. *Psychological Bulletin, 117,* 21–38.

Gilbert, D. T., & Osborne, R. E. (1989). Thinking backward: Some curable and incurable consequences of cognitive busyness. *Journal of Personality and Social Psychology, 57,* 940–949.

Gilbert, D. T., & Wilson, T. D. (2007). Prospection: Experiencing the future. *Science, 317,* 1351–1354.

Gilbert, D. T., King, G., Pettigrew, S., & Wilson, T. D. (2016. March 4). Comment on "Estimating the reproducibility of psychological science." *Science, 351,* 1037. http://science.sciencemag.org/content/351/6277/1037.2

Gilbert, D. T., Pelham, B. W., & Krull, D. S. (1988). On cognitive busyness: When person perceivers meet persons perceived. *Journal of Personality and Social Psychology, 54,* 733–740.

Gilbert, S. J. (1981). Another look at the Milgram obedience studies: The role of the gradated series of shocks. *Personality and Social Psychology Bulletin, 4,* 690–695.

Gildersleeve, K., Haselton, M. G., & Fales, M. R. (2014). Do women's mate preferences change across the ovulatory cycle? A meta-analytic review. *Psychological Bulletin.*doi:10.1037/a0035438

Gilmore, D. D. (1990). *Manhood in the making: Cultural concepts of masculinity.* New Haven, CT: Yale University Press.

Gilovich, T. (1991). *How we know what isn't so: The fallibility of human reason in everyday life.* New York: Free Press.

Gilovich, T., & Griffin, D. W. (2002). Introduction: Heuristics and biases, now and then. In T. Gilovich, D. W. Griffin, & D. Kahneman (Eds.), *Heuristics and biases: The psychology of intuitive judgment* (pp. 1–18). New York: Cambridge University Press.

Girl born to Japan's princess. (2001, December 1). *The New York Times,* p. 8.

Girme, Y. U., Overall, N. C., & Simpson, J. A. (2013). When visibility matters: Short-term versus long-term costs and benefits of visible and invisible support. *Personality and Social Psychology Bulletin, 39,* 1441–1454.

Gladwell, M. (2005). *Blink: The power of thinking without thinking.* New York: Little, Brown.

Gladwell, M. (2005, January 12). Big and bad: How the S.U.V. ran over automotive safety. *New Yorker.*

Glasman, L. R., & Albarracín, D. (2006). Forming attitudes that predict future behavior: A meta-analysis of the attitude-behavior relation. *Psychological Bulletin, 132,* 778–822.

Glass, D. C. (1964). Changes in liking as a means of reducing cognitive discrepancies between self-esteem and aggression. *Journal of Personality, 32,* 531–549.

Glick, P. (2006). Ambivalent sexism, power distance, and gender inequality across cultures. In S. Guimond (Ed.), *Social comparison and social psychology: Understanding cognition, intergroup relations, and culture.* New York: Cambridge University Press.

Glick, P., & Fiske, S. T. (1996). The ambivalent sexism inventory: Differentiating hostile and benevolent sexism. *Journal of Personality and Social Psychology, 70,* 491–512.

Glick, P., & Fiske, S. (2001). An ambivalent alliance: Hostile and benevolent sexism as complementary justifications for gender inequality. *American Psychologist, 56,* 109–118.

"Global Health Observatory." n.d. World Health Organization. Retrieved June 5, 2017, from http://gamapserver.who.int/mapLibrary/app/searchResults.aspx

Global Report: UNAIDS Report on the Global Aids Epidemic 2013. (2013). Retrieved August 19, 2014, from http://www.unaids.org/en/media/unaids/contentassets/documents/epidemiology/2013/gr2013/UNAIDS_Global_Report_2013_en.pdf

Goethals, G. R., & Darley, J. M. (1977). Social comparison theory: An attributional approach. In J. M. Suls & R. L. Miller (Eds.), *Social comparison processes: Theoretical and empirical perspectives* (pp. 259–278). Washington, DC: Hemisphere/Halsted.

Goffman, E. (1959). *Presentation of self in everyday life.* Garden City, NY: Anchor/Doubleday.

Gold, J. A., Ryckman, R. M., & Mosley, N. R. (1984). Romantic mood induction and attraction to a dissimilar other: Is love blind? *Personality and Social Psychology Bulletin, 10,* 358–368.

Golder, S. A., & Macy, M. W. (2011). Diurnal and season mood vary with work, sleep, and daylength across diverse cultures. *Science, 333,* 1878–1881. doi:10.1126/science.1202775

Goldinger, S. D., Kleider, H. M., Azuma, T., & Beike, D. R. (2003). "Blaming the victim" under memory load. *Psychological Science, 14,* 81–85.

Goldstein, N. J., Cialdini, R. B., & Griskevicius, V. (2008). A room with a viewpoint: Using social norms to motivate environmental conservation in hotels. *Journal of Consumer Research, 35,* 472–482.

Gollwitzer, P. M. (2014). Weakness of the will: Is a quick fix possible? *Motivation and Emotion, 38,* 305–322.

Gollwitzer, P. M., & Oettingen, G. (2011). Planning promotes goal striving. In K. D. Vohs & R. F. Baumeister (Eds.), *Handbook of self-regulation: Research, theory, and applications* (2nd ed., pp. 162–185). New York: Guilford.

Gonzaga, G. C., Campos, B., & Bradbury, T. (2007). Similarity, convergence, and relationship satisfaction in dating and married couples. *Journal of Personality and Social Psychology, 93,* 34–48.

Goode, E. (1999, February 9). Arranged marriage gives way to courtship by mail. *The New York Times,* p. D3.

Goodfriend, W., & Agnew, C. R. (2008). Sunken costs and desired plans: Examining different types of investments in close relationships. *Personality and Social Psychology Bulletin, 34,* 1639–1652.

Goodwin, G. P., Piazza, J., & Rozin, P. (2014). Moral character predominates in person perception and evaluation. *Journal of Personality and Social Psychology, 106,* 148–168.

Gosling, S. (2008). *Snoop: What your stuff says about you.* London: Profile Books Ltd.

Gosling, S. D., Augustine, A. A., Vazire, S., Holtzman, N., & Gaddis, S. (2011). Manifestations of personality in online social networks: Self-reported Facebook-related behaviors and observable profile information. *Cyberpsychology, Behavior, and Social Networking, 14,* 483–488.

Goto, S. G., Ando, Y., Huang, C., Yee, A., & Lewis, R. S. (2010). Cultural differences in the visual processing of meaning: Detecting incongruities between background and foreground objects using the N400. *Social Cognitive and Affective Neuroscience, 5,* 242–253.

Goto, S. G., Yee, A., Lowenberg, K., & Lewis, R. R. (2013). Cultural differences in sensitivity to social context: Detecting affective incongruity using the N400. *Social Neuroscience, 8,* 63–74.

Gottman, J. M. (2014). *What predicts divorce?: The relationship between marital processes and marital outcomes.* New York, NY: Psychology Press.

Gottman, J. M., & Levenson, R. W. (2002). A two-factor model for predicting when a couple will divorce: Exploratory analyses using 14-year longitudinal data. *Family Process, 41,* 83–96.

Goyer, J. P., Garcia, J., Purdie-Williams, V., Binning, K. R., Cook, J. E., Reeves, S. L., Apfel, N., Taborsky-Barba, S., Sherman, D. K., & Cohen, G. L. (2017). Into swifter currents: Self-affirmation nudges minority middle schoolers onto a college trajectory. *Proceedings of the National Academy of Sciences.*

Graham, J., & Haidt, J. (2010). Beyond beliefs: Religion binds individuals into moral communities. *Personality and Social Psychology Review, 14,* 140–150.

Graham, J., Koo, M., & Wilson, T. D. (2011). Conserving energy by inducing people to drive less. *Journal of Applied Social Psychology, 41,* 106–118.

Graham, K., Osgood, D. W., Wells, S., & Stockwell, T. (2006). To what extent is intoxication associated with aggression in bars? A multilevel analysis. *Journal of Studies on Alcohol, 67*, 382–390.

Granberg, D., & Bartels, B. (2005). On being a lone dissenter. *Journal of Applied Social Psychology, 35*, 1849–1858.

Grandey, A. A., Dickter, D. N., & Sin, H. P. (2004). The customer is not always right: Customer aggression and emotion regulation of service employees. *Journal of Organizational Behavior, 25*, 397–418.

Gray, K., Ward, A. F., & Norton, M. I. (2014). Paying it forward: Generalized reciprocity and the limits of generosity. *Journal of Experimental Psychology: General, 143*(1), 247–254. doi:10.1037/a0031047

Gray, S. (2004, March 30). Bizarre hoaxes on restaurants trigger lawsuits. *Wall Street Journal,* Retrieved June 5, 2006, from online.wsj.com/article_print/SB108061045899868615.html

Graziano, W. G., & Habashi, M. M. (2015). Searching for the prosocial personality. In D. A. Schroeder & W. G. Graziano (Eds.), *The Oxford handbook of prosocial behavior* (pp. 231–255). New York: Oxford University Press.

Graziano, W. G., Habashi, M. M., Sheese, B. E., & Tobin, R. M. (2007). Agreeableness, empathy, and helping: A person × situation perspective. *Journal of Personality and Social Psychology, 93*, 583–599.

Graziano, W. G., Jensen-Campbell, L. A., Shebilske, L. J., & Lundgren, S. R. (1993). Social influence, sex differences, and judgments of beauty: Putting the interpersonal back in interpersonal attraction. *Journal of Personality and Social Psychology, 65*, 522–531.

Green, A. R., Carney, D. R., Pallin, D. J., Ngo, L. H., Raymond, K. L., et al. (2007). Implicit bias among physicians and its prediction of thrombolysis decisions for black and white patients. *Journal of General Internal Medicine, 22*, 1231–1238.

Green, M. A., Willis, M., Fernandez-Kong, K., Reyes, S., Linkhart, R., Johnson, M., Thorne, T., Kroska, E., Woodward, H., & Lindberg, J. (2017). Dissonance-based eating disorder program reduces cardiac risk: A preliminary trial. *Health Psychology, 36*, 346–355.

Greenberg, J., & Musham, C. (1981). Avoiding and seeking self-focused attention. *Journal of Research in Personality, 15*, 191–200.

Greenberg, J., Pyszczynski, T., & Solomon, S. (1982). The self-serving attributional bias: Beyond self-presentation. *Journal of Experimental Social Psychology, 18*, 56–67.

Greenberg, J., Solomon, S., & Pyszczynski, T. (1997). Terror management theory of self-esteem and social behavior: Empirical assessments and conceptual refinements. In M. P. Zanna (Ed.), *Advances in experimental social psychology* (Vol. 29, pp. 61–139). New York: Academic Press.

Greene, D., Sternberg, B., & Lepper, M. R. (1976). Overjustification in a token economy. *Journal of Personality and Social Psychology, 34*, 1219–1234.

Greene, E., & Evelo, A. (2014). Cops and robbers (and eyewitnesses): A comparison of lineup administration by robbery detectives in the U.S. and Canada. *Psychology, Crime, and Law.* doi:10.1080/1068316X.2014.952236

Greene, E., & Helbrun, K. (2013). *Wrightsman's Psychology and the Legal System.* New York: Cengage.

Greenwald, A. G., & Banaji, M. R. (1995). Implicit social cognition: Attitudes, self-esteem, and stereotypes. *Psychological Review, 102*, 4–27.

Greenwald, A. G., McGhee, D. E., & Schwartz, J. L. K. (1998). Measuring individual differences in implicit cognition: The Implicit Association Test. *Journal of Personality and Social Psychology, 74*, 1464–1480.

Greenwald, A. G., Poehlman, T. A., Uhlmann, E. L., & Banaji, M. R. (2009). Understanding and using the Implicit Association Test: III. Meta-analysis of predictive validity. *Journal of Personality and Social Psychology, 97*(1), 17–41. doi:10.1037/a0015575

Greenwald, A. G., Spangenberg, E. R., Pratkanis, A. R., & Eskenazi, J. (1991). Double-blind tests of subliminal self-help audiotapes. *Psychological Science, 2*, 119–122.

Greenwald, A., & Pettigrew, T. (2014). With malice toward none and charity for some: Ingroup favoritism enables discrimination. *American Psychologist.* doi:10.1037/a0036056

Greitemeyer, T. (2009). Effects of songs with prosocial lyrics on prosocial behavior: Further evidence and a mediating mechanism. *Personality and Social Psychology Bulletin, 35*(11), 1500–1511. doi:10.1177/0146167209341648

Greitemeyer, T. (2011). Exposure to music with prosocial lyrics reduces aggression: First evidence and test of the underlying mechanism. *Journal of Experimental Social Psychology, 47*(1), 28–36. doi:10.1016/j.jesp.2010.08.005

Greitemeyer, T. (2014). Playing violent video games increases intergroup bias. *Personality and Social Psychology Bulletin, 40*, 70–78.

Greitemeyer, T., & McLatchie, N. (2011). Denying humanness to others: A newly discovered mechanism by which violent video games increase aggressive behavior. *Psychological Science, 22*, 659–665.

Greitemeyer, T., & Mügge, D. O. (2014). Video games do affect social outcomes: A meta-analytic review of the effects of violent and prosocial video game play. *Personality and Social Psychology Bulletin, 40*, 578–589.

Greitemeyer, T., & Osswald, S. (2010). Effects of prosocial video games on prosocial behavior. *Journal of Personality and Social Psychology, 98*(2), 211–221. doi:10.1037/a0016997

Greitemeyer, T., Osswald, S., & Brauer, M. (2010). Playing prosocial video games increases empathy and decreases schadenfreude. *Emotion, 10*(6), 796–802. doi:10.1037/a0020194

Grice, E. (2006, July 17). Cry of an enfant sauvage. *The Telegraph.* Retrieved March 28, 2017, from http://www.telegraph.co.uk/culture/tvandradio/3653890/Cry-of-an-enfant-sauvage.html

Griffin, D. W., & Ross, L. (1991). Subjective construal, social inference, and human misunderstanding. In L. Berkowitz (Ed.), *Advances in experimental social psychology* (Vol. 24, pp. 319–359). San Diego, CA: Academic Press.

Griffin, D., & Kahneman, D. (2003). Judgmental heuristics: Human strengths or human weaknesses? In L. G. Aspinwall & U. M. Staudinger (Eds.), *A psychology of human strengths: Fundamental questions and future directions for a positive psychology* (pp. 165–178). Washington, DC: American Psychological Association.

Griffith, S. C., Pryke, S. R., & Buettemer, W. A. (2011). Constrained mate choice in social monogamy and the stress of having an unattractive partner. *Proceedings of the Royal Society of London, Series B, 278*, 2798–2805.

Griffitt, W., & Veitch, R. (1971). Hot and crowded: influences of population density and temperature on interpersonal affective behavior. *Journal of Personality and Social Psychology, 17*(1), 92–98.

Gronlund, S. D., Wixted, J. T., & Mickes, L. (2014). Evaluating eyewitness identification procedures using receiver operating characteristic analysis. *Current Directions in Psychological Science, 23*, 3–10.

Grubbs, J. B., & Exline, J. J. (2016). Trait entitlement: A cognitive-personality source of vulnerability to psychological distress. *Psychological Bulletin, 142*, 1204–1226.

Guadagno, R. E., Rempala, D. M., Murphy, S., & Okdie, B. M. (2013). What makes a video go viral? An analysis of emotional contagion and Internet memes. *Computers in Human Behavior, 29*, 2312–2319.

Grueneisen, S., & Tomasello, M. (2017). Children coordinate in a recurrent social dilemma by taking turns and along dominance asymmetries. *Developmental psychology, 53*, 265–273.

Guagnano, G. A., Stern, P. C., & Dietz, T. (1995). Influences on attitude-behavior relationships: A natural experiment with curbside recycling. *Environment and Behavior, 27*, 699–718.

Gudjonsson, G. H., Sigurdsson, J. F., Sigurdardottir, A. S., Steinthorsson, H., & Sigurdardottir, V. M. (2014). The role of memory distrust in cases of internalised false confession. *Applied Cognitive Psychology, 28*, 336–348.

Gudykunst, W. B. (1988). Culture and intergroup processes. In M. H. Bond (Ed.), *The cross-cultural challenge to social psychology* (pp. 165–181). Newbury Park, CA: Sage.

Gudykunst, W. B., Ting-Toomey, S., & Nishida, T. (1996). *Communication in personal relationships across cultures.* Thousand Oaks, CA: Sage.

Guerin, B. (1993). *Social facilitation.* Cambridge: Cambridge University Press.

Guerrero, L. K., La Valley, A. G., & Farinelli, L. (2008). The experience and expression of anger, guilt, and sadness in marriage: An equity theory explanation. *Journal of Social and Personal Relationships, 25*, 699–724.

Guimond, S. (1999). Attitude change during college: Normative or informational social influence? *Social Psychology of Education, 2*, 237–261.

Gully, S. M., Devine, D. J., & Whitney, D. J. (1995). A meta-analysis of cohesion and performance: Effects of level of analysis and task interdependence. *Small Groups Research, 26*, 497–520.

Gustafson, R. (1989). Frustration and successful vs. unsuccessful aggression: A test of Berkowitz's completion hypothesis. *Aggressive Behavior, 15*, 5–12.

Ha, T., van den Berg, J. E. M., Engels, R. C. M. E., & Lichtwarck-Aschoff, A. (2012). Effects of attractiveness and status in dating desire in homosexual and heterosexual men and women. *Archives of Sexual Behavior, 41*, 673–682.

Haas, S. A., & Schaefer, D. R. (2014). With a little help from my friends? Asymmetrical social influence on adolescent smoking initiation and cessation. *Journal of Health and Social Behavior, 55*, 126–143.

Habashi, M. M., Graziano, W.G., & Hoover, A. E. (2016). Searching for the prosocial personality: A big five approach to linking personality and prosocial behavior. *Personality and Social Psychology Bulletin, 42*, 1177–1192.

Hadden, B. W., Smith, C. V., & Webster, G. D. (2014). Relationship duration moderates associations between attachment and relationship quality: Meta-analytic support for the temporal adult romantic attachment model. *Personality and Social Psychology Review, 18*, 42–58.

Haddock, G., Maio, G. R., Arnold, K., & Huskinson, T. (2008). Should persuasion be affective or cognitive? The moderating effects of need for affect and need for cognition. *Personality and Social Psychology Bulletin, 34*, 769–778.

Hafer, C. L., & Begue, L. (2005). Experimental research on just-world theory: Problems, developments, and future challenges. *Psychological Bulletin, 131*(1), 128–167.

Hagestad, G. O., & Smyer, M. A. (1982). Dissolving long-term relationships: Patterns of divorcing in middle age. In S. W. Duck (Ed.), *Personal relationships: Vol. 4. Dissolving personal relationships* (pp. 155–188). London: Academic Press.

Hagger, M. S., Chatzisarantis, N. L. D., Alberts, H., Anggono, C. O., Batailler, C., Birt, A. R., … Zwienenberg, M. (2016). A multilab preregistered replication of the ego-depletion effect. *Perspectives on Psychological Science, 11*, 546–573.

Hahn, A., Judd, C. M., Hirsh, H. K., & Blair, I. V. (2014). Awareness of implicit attitudes. *Journal of Experimental Psychology: General, 143*, 1369–1392.

Haidt, J. (2006). *The happiness hypothesis: Finding modern truth in ancient wisdom.* New York: Basic Books.

Halabi, S., Nadler, A., & Dovidio, J. F. (2013). Positive responses to intergroup assistance: The roles of apology and trust. *Group Processes & Intergroup Relations, 16*(4), 395–411. doi:10.1177/1368430212453863

Halberstadt, J. B., & Rhodes, G. (2000). The attractiveness of nonface averages: Implications for an evolutionary explanation of the attractiveness of average faces. *Psychological Science, 11*, 285–289.

Hall, C. C., Zhao, J., & Shafir, E. (2014). Self-affirmation among the poor: Cognitive and behavioral implications. *Psychological Science, 25,* 619–625.

Hall, E. T. (1969). *The hidden dimension.* Garden City, NY: Doubleday.

Hall, J. A., Gunnery, S. D., & Andrzejewski, S. A., (2011). Nonverbal emotion displays, communication modality, and the judgment of personality. *Journal of Research in Personality, 45*(1), 77–83.

Hall, J. A., Mast, M. S., & West, T. V. (2016). *The social psychology of perceiving others accurately.* Cambridge, UK: Cambridge University Press.

Hall, J. A., Murphy, N. A., & Schmid Mast, M. (2007). Nonverbal self-accuracy in interpersonal interaction. *Personality and Social Psychology Bulletin, 33,* 1675–1685.

Hall, W. M., Schmader, T., & Croft, E. (2015). Engineering Exchanges Daily Social Identity Threat Predicts Burnout Among Female Engineers. *Social Psychological and Personality Science, 6,* 528–534.

Halliwell, E., & Diedrichs, P. C. (2014). Testing a dissonance body image intervention among young girls. *Health Psychology, 33,* 201–204.

Hamby, S. L., & Koss, M. P. (2003). Shades of gray: A qualitative study of terms used in the measurement of sexual victimization. *Psychology of Women Quarterly, 27,* 243–255.

Hamilton, W. D. (1964). The genetical evolution of social behavior. *Journal of Theoretical Biology, 7,* 1–52.

Han, S., & Shavitt, S. (1994). Persuasion and culture: Advertising appeals in individualistic and collectivistic societies. *Journal of Experimental Social Psychology, 30,* 326–350.

Hancock, J. T., & Toma, C. L. (2009). Putting your best face forward: The accuracy of online dating photographs. *Journal of Communication, 59,* 367–286.

Haney, C., Banks, C., & Zimbardo, P. (1973). Interpersonal dynamics in a simulated prison. *International Journal of Criminology and Penology, 1,* 69–97.

Hansen, K., Gerbasi, M., Todorov, A., Kruse, E., & Pronin, E. (2014). People claim objectivity after knowingly using biased strategies. *Personality and Social Psychology Bulletin.* doi:10.1177/0146167214523476

Hanson, K. L., Medina, K. L., Padula, C. B., Tapert, S. F., & Brown, S. A. (2011). Impact of adolescent alcohol and drug use on neuropsychological functioning in young adulthood: 10-year outcomes. *Journal of Child & Adolescent Substance Abuse, 20,* 135–154.

Hänze, M., & Berger, R. (2007). Cooperative learning, motivational effects, and student characteristics: An experimental study comparing cooperative learning and direct instruction in 12th grade physics classes. *Learning and Instruction, 17,* 29–41.

Harackiewicz, J. M. (1979). The effects of reward contingency and performance feedback on intrinsic motivation. *Journal of Personality and Social Psychology, 37,* 1352–1363.

Harackiewicz, J. M. (1989). Performance evaluation and intrinsic motivation processes: The effects of achievement orientation and rewards. In D. M. Buss & N. Cantor (Eds.), *Personality psychology: Recent trends and emerging directions* (pp. 128–137). New York: Springer-Verlag.

Harackiewicz, J. M., & Elliot, A. J. (1993). Achievement goals and intrinsic motivation. *Journal of Personality and Social Psychology, 65,* 904–915.

Harackiewicz, J. M., & Elliot, A. J. (1998). The joint effects of target and purpose goals on intrinsic motivation: A mediational analysis. *Personality and Social Psychology Bulletin, 24,* 675–689.

Harackiewicz, J. M., & Hulleman, C. S. (2010). The importance of interest: The role of achievement goals and task values in promoting the development of interest. *Social and Personality Psychology Compass, 4,* 42–52. doi:10.1111/j.1751-9004.2009.00207.x

Harackiewicz, J. M., Manderlink, G., & Sansone, C. (1984). Rewarding pinball wizardry: The effects of evaluation and cue value on intrinsic interest.

Harackiewicz, J. M., Canning, E. A., Tibbetts, Y., Giffen, C. J., & Hyde, J. S. (2014). Closing the social class achievement gap for first-generation students in undergraduate biology. *Journal of Educational Psychology, 106,* 375–389.

Hardin, C. D., & Higgins, E. T. (Eds.). (1996). *Shared reality: How social verification makes the subjective objective.* New York: Guilford Press.

Hare, A. P. (2003). Roles, relationships, and groups in organizations: Some conclusions and recommendations. *Small Group Research, 34,* 123–154.

Hare, B. (2017). Survival of the friendliest: *Homo sapiens* evolved via selection for prosociality. *Annual Review of Psychology, 68,* 155–186.

Harmat, L., Ørsted Andersen, F., Ullén, F., Wright, J., Sadlo, G. (Eds.). (2016). *Flow experience: Empirical research and applications.* Cham, Switzerland: Springer International Publishing.

Harmon-Jones, C., Schmeichel, B. J., Mennitt, E., & Harmon-Jones, E. (2011). The expression of determination: Similarities between anger and approach-related positive affect. *Journal of Personality and Social Psychology, 100,* 172–181.

Harrington, J. R., & Gelfand, M. J. (2014). Tightness–looseness across the 50 United States. *Proceedings of the National Academy of Sciences, 111,* 7990–7995.

Harris, L. T., & Fiske, S. T. (2006). Dehumanizing the lowest of the low: Neuro-imaging responses to extreme outgroups. *Psychological Science, 17,* 847–853.

Harris, M. B. (1974). Mediators between frustration and aggression in a field experiment. *Journal of Experimental and Social Psychology, 10,* 561–571.

Harris, M. B., Benson, S. M., & Hall, C. (1975). The effects of confession on altruism. *Journal of Social Psychology, 96,* 187–192.

Harrison, J. A., & Wells, R. B. (1991). Bystander effects on male helping behavior: Social comparison and diffusion of responsibility. *Representative Research in Social Psychology, 19,* 53–63.

Hart, D., & Damon, W. (1986). Developmental trends in self-understanding. *Social Cognition, 4,* 388–407.

Hart, D., & Matsuba, M. K. (2012). The development of self-knowledge. In S. Vazire & T. D. Wilson (Eds.), *The handbook of self-knowledge* (pp. 7–21). New York: Guilford Press.

Hart, W., Albarracín, D., Eagly, A. H., Brechan, I., Lindberg, M. J., & Merrill, L. (2009). Feeling validated versus being correct: A meta-analysis of selective exposure to information. *Psychological Bulletin, 135,* 555–588.

Harter, S. (2003). The development of self-representations during childhood and adolescence. In M. R. Leary & J. P. Tangney (Eds.), *Handbook of self and identity* (pp. 610–642). New York: Guilford Press.

Hatfield, E., & Rapson, R. L. (1990). Passionate love in intimate relationships. In B. S. Moore & A. M. Isen (Eds.), *Affect and social behavior* (pp. 126–151). Cambridge: Cambridge University Press.

Hartup, W. W., & Stevens, N. (1997). Friendships and adaptation in the life course. *Psychological Bulletin, 121,* 355–370.

Harvey, J. H. (1995). *Odyssey of the heart: The search for closeness, intimacy, and love.* New York: Freeman.

Harvey, J. H., Flanary, R., & Morgan, M. (1986). Vivid memories of vivid loves gone by. *Journal of Personal and Social Relationships, 3,* 359–373.

Harwood, J., & Joyce, N. (2012). Intergroup contact and communication. In H. Giles (Ed.), *Handbook of Intergroup Communication* (pp. 167–180). London, UK: Routledge.

Hasel, L. E., & Kassin, S. M. (2012). False confessions. In B. L. Cutler (Ed.), *Conviction of the innocent: Lessons from psychological research* (pp. 53–77). Washington, DC: American Psychological Association.

Haslam, S. A., Reicher, S. D., & Platow, M. J. (2013). *The new psychology of leadership: Identity, influence, and power.* East Sussex: Psychology Press.

Haslam, S. A., Reicher, S. D., & Birney, M. E. (2016). Questioning authority: New perspectives on Milgram's 'obedience' research and its implications for intergroup relations. *Current Opinion in Psychology, 11,* 6–9.

Hassin, R. R. (2013). Yes it can: On the functional abilities of the human unconscious. *Perspectives in Psychological Science, 8*(2), 195–207.

Hassin R. R., Aviezer H., & Bentin S. (2013). Inherently ambiguous: Facial expressions of emotions, in context. *Emotion Review, 5,* 60–65.

Hastie, R. (2008). What's the story? Explanations and narratives in civil jury decisions. In B. H. Bornstein, R. L. Wiener, R. Schopp, & S. L. Willborn (Eds.), *Civil juries and civil justice: Psychological and legal perspectives* (pp. 23–34). New York: Springer.

Hastie, R., & Pennington, N. (2000). Explanation-based decision making. In T. Connolly & H. R. Arkes (Eds.), *Judgment and decision making: An interdisciplinary reader* (2nd ed., pp. 212–228). New York: Cambridge University Press.

Hastie, R., Penrod, S. D., & Pennington, N. (1983). *Inside the jury.* Cambridge, MA: Harvard University Press.

Hatcher, J. W., Cares, S., Detrie, R., Dillenbeck, T., Goral, E., Troisi, K., & Whirry-Achten, A. M. (2016). Conformity, arousal, and the effect of arbitrary information. *Group Processes and Intergroup Relations.* doi:10.1177/1368430216670525

Hatfield, E., & Rapson, R. L. (1993). *Love, sex, and intimacy: Their psychology, biology, and history.* New York: HarperCollins.

Hatfield, E., & Rapson, R. L. (2002). Passionate love and sexual desire: Cultural and historical perspectives. In A. L. Vangelisti, H. T. Reis, & M. A. Fitzpatrick (Eds.), *Stability and change in relationships* (pp. 306–324). New York: Cambridge University Press.

Hatfield, E., & Sprecher, S. (1986). Measuring passionate love in intimate relationships. *Journal of Adolescence, 9,* 383–410.

Hatfield, E., & Sprecher, S. (1995). Men's and women's preferences in marital partners in the United States, Russia, and Japan. *Journal of Cross-Cultural Psychology, 26,* 728–750.

Hatfield, E., & Walster, G. W. (1978). *A new look at love.* Reading, MA: Addison-Wesley.

Hazan, C., & Shaver, P. (1987). Romantic love conceptualized as an attachment process. *Journal of Personality and Social Psychology, 52,* 511–524.

Hazan, C., & Shaver, P. (1994). Deeper into attachment theory. *Psychological Inquiry, 5,* 68–79.

Heatherton, T. F., & Sargent, J. D. (2009). Does watching smoking in movies promote teenage smoking? *Current Directions in Psychological Science, 18,* 63–67.

Hebl, M., Foster, J., Bigazzi, J., Mannix, L., & Dovidio, J. (2002). Formal and interpersonal discrimination: A field study of bias toward homosexual applicants. *Personality and Social Psychology Bulletin, 28,* 815–825.

Heckhausen, J., & Schulz, R. (1995). A life-span theory of control. *Psychological Review, 102,* 284–304.

Hedden, T., Ketey, S., Aron, A., Markus, H. R., & Gabrieli, J. D. E. (2008). Cultural influence on neural substrates of attentional control. *Psychological Science, 19,* 12–17.

Hedge, A., & Yousif, Y. H. (1992). Effects of urban size, urgency, and cost on helpfulness. *Journal of Cross-Cultural Psychology, 23,* 107–115.

Hehman, E., Gaertner, S. L., & Dovidio, J. F. (2011). Evaluations of presidential performance: Race, prejudice, and perceptions of Americanism. *Journal of Experimental Social Psychology, 47,* 430–435.

Heider, F. (1944). Social perception and phenomenal causality. *Psychological Review, 51,* 358–374.

Heider, F. (1958). *The psychology of interpersonal relations.* New York: Wiley.

Heine, S. J. (2010). Cultural psychology. In S. T. Fiske, D. T. Gilbert, & G. Lindzey (Eds.), *Handbook of social psychology* (5th ed., Vol. 2, pp. 1423–1464). Hoboken, NJ: John Wiley.

Heine, S. J., Foster, J. B., & Spina, R. (2009). Do birds of a feather universally flock together? Cultural variation in the similarity-attraction effect. *Asian Journal of Psychology, 12*, 247–258.

Heine, S. J., Lehman, D. R., Peng, K., & Greenholtz, J. (2002). What's wrong with cross-cultural comparisons of subjective Likert scales?: The reference-group effect. *Journal of Personality and Social Psychology, 82*, 903–918.

Heine, S., Proulx, T., & Vohs, K. (2006). The meaning maintenance model: On the coherence of social motivations. *Personality and Social Psychology Review, 10*, 88–110.

Heinzen, T. E., Lilienfeld, S. O., & Nolan, S. A. (2015). *The horse that won't go away: Clever Hans, facilitated communication, and the need for clear thinking.* New York: Worth.

Heitland, K., & Bohner, G. (2010). Reducing prejudice via cognitive dissonance: Individual differences in preference for consistency moderate the effects of counter-attitudinal advocacy. *Social Influence, 5*, 164–181.

Helgeson, V. S. (1994). Long-distance romantic relationships: Sex differences in adjustment and breakup. *Personality and Social Psychology Bulletin, 20*, 254–265.

Helgeson, V. S. (2003). Cognitive adaptation, psychological adjustment, and disease progression among angioplasty patients: 4 years later. *Health Psychology, 22*, 30–38.

Helgeson, V. S., & Fritz, H. L. (1999). Cognitive adaptation as a predictor of new coronary events after percutaneous transluminal coronary angioplasty. *Psychosomatic Medicine, 61*, 488–495.

Hendrix, K. S., & Hirt, E. R. (2009). Stressed out over possible failure: The role of regulatory fit on claimed self-handicapping. *Journal of Experimental Social Psychology, 45*, 51–59. doi:10.1016/j.jesp.2008.08.016

Henningsen, D., Henningsen, M., Eden, J., & Cruz, M. (2006). Examining the symptoms of groupthink and retrospective sensemaking. *Small Group Research, 37*, 36–64.

Henrich, J., Heine, S. J., & Norenzayan, A. (2010). The weirdest people in the world? *Behavioral and Brain Sciences, 33*(2–3), 61–83. doi:10.1017/S0140525X0999152X

Herek, G. M., & Capitanio, J. P. (1996). "Some of My Best Friends:" Intergroup contact, concealable stigma, and heterosexuals' attitudes toward Gay men and Lesbians. *Personality and Social Psychology Bulletin, 22*, 412–424.

Herring, C. (2009). Does diversity pay? Race, gender, and the business case for diversity. *American Sociological Review, 74*, 208–224.

Hersh, S. M. (1970). *My Lai 4: A report on the massacre and its aftermath.* New York: Vintage Books.

Hersh, S. M. (2004, May 10). Torture at Abu Ghraib. *New Yorker.*

Hershfield, H. E., Mogilner, C., & Barnea, U. (2016). People who choose time over money are happier. *Social Psychological and Personality Science, 7*, 697–706.

Hertz, S. G., & Krettenauer, T. (2016). Does moral identity effectively predict moral behavior?: A meta-analysis. *Review of General Psychology, 20*, 129–140

Heschl, A., & Burkart, J. (2006). A new mark test for mirror self-recognition in non-human primates. *Primates, 47*, 187–198.

Hibbard, L. (2011, November 8). Virginia Beach high schools pay students for good grades. *Huffington Post.* Retrieved January 10, 2012, from www.huffingtonpost.com/2011/11/08/high-school-pays-students_n_1082488.html

Higgins, E. T. (1996). Knowledge application: Accessibility, applicability, and salience. In E. T. Higgins & A. R. Kruglanski (Eds.), *Social psychology: Handbook of basic principles* (pp. 133–168). New York: Guilford Press.

Higgins, E. T., & Bargh, J. A. (1987). Social cognition and social perception. *Annual Review of Psychology, 38*, 369–425.

Higgins, E. T., Rholes, W. S., & Jones, C. R. (1977). Category accessibility and impression formation. *Journal of Experimental Social Psychology, 13*, 141–154.

Higgins, L. T., Zheng, M., Liu, Y., & Sun, C. H. (2002). Attitudes to marriage and sexual behaviors: A survey of gender and culture differences in China and United Kingdom. *Sex Roles, 46*, 75–89.

Hill, J. K. (2002). *Rainbow remedies for life's stormy times.* South Bend, IN: Moorhill Communications.

Hill, J. K. (n.d.). How I survived the deaths of twelve family members. Retrieved December 21, 2008, from www.resiliencycenter.com/stories/2002stories/0201hill.shtml

Hillshafer, D. (2013). The mass murder problem. *Skeptic, 18*, 24–32.

Hilton, D. J., Smith, R. H., & Kim, S. H. (1995). Process of causal explanation and dispositional attribution. *Journal of Personality and Social Psychology, 68*, 377–387.

Hilton, J. L., Fein, S., & Miller, D. T. (1993). Suspicion and dispositional inference. *Journal of Personality and Social Psychology, 19*, 501–512.

Hirsh, J. B., Galinsky, A. D., & Zhong, C. (2011). Drunk, powerful, and in the dark: How general processes of disinhibition produce both prosocial and antisocial behavior. *Perspectives on Psychological Science, 6*, 415–427.

Hirt, E. R., & McCrea, S. M. (2009). Man smart, woman smarter? Getting to the root of gender differences in self-handicapping. *Social and Personality Psychology Compass, 3*, 260–274. doi:10.1111/j.1751-9004.2009.00176.x

Hirt, E. R., McCrea, S. M., & Boris, H. I. (2003). "I know you self-handicapped last exam": Gender differences in reactions to self-handicapping. *Journal of Personality and Social Psychology, 84*, 177–193.

Hirt, E. R., Melton, J. R., McDonald, H. E., & Harackiewicz, J. M. (1996). Processing goals, task interest, and the mood-performance relationship: A mediational analysis. *Journal of Personality and Social Psychology, 71*, 245–261.

Hitsch, G., Hortaçsu, A., & Ariely, D. (2010). What makes you click? Mate preferences in online dating. *Quantitative Marketing and Economics, 8*, 393–427.

Hobson, N. M., & Inzlicht, M. (2016). Recognizing religion's dark side: Religious ritual increases antisociality and hinders self-control. *Behavioral and Brain Sciences, 39*, Article e14.

Hochstadt, S. (1999). *Mobility and modernity: Migration in Germany, 1820–1989.* Ann Arbor: University of Michigan Press.

Hodges, B. H., & Geyer, A. L. (2006). A nonconformist account of the Asch experiments: Values, pragmatics, and moral dilemmas. *Personality and Social Psychology Review, 10*, 2–19.

Hofmann, W., De Houwer, J., Perugini, M., Baeyens, F., & Crombez, G. (2010). Evaluative conditioning in humans: A meta-analysis. *Psychological Bulletin, 136*, 390–421.

Hogg, M. A., Hohman, Z. P., & Rivera, J. E. (2008). Why do people join groups? Three motivational accounts from social psychology. *Social and Personality Psychology Compass, 2*, 1269–1280.

Hogh-Olessen, H. (2008). Human spatial behavior: The spacing of people, objects and animals in six cross-cultural samples. *Journal of Cognition and Culture, 8*, 245–280.

Holan, A. D. (2016, December 13). 2016 Lie of the Year: Fake news. http://www.politifact.com/truth-o-meter/article/2016/dec/13/2016-lie-year-fake-news/

Holland, R. W., Aarts, H., & Langendam, D. (2006). Breaking and creating habits on the working floor: A field-experiment on the power of implementation intentions. *Journal of Experimental Social Psychology, 42*, 776–783.

Hollander, E. P. (1960). Competence and conformity in the acceptance of influence. *Journal of Abnormal and Social Psychology, 61*, 361–365.

Hollander, E. P. (1985). Leadership and power. In G. Lindzey, and E. Aronson (Eds.) *The Handbook of Social Psychology:* Vol. 11, (pp. 485–537). New York: Random House.

Hollenbaugh, E. E., & Ferris, A. L. (2015). Predictors of honesty, intent, and valence of Facebook self-disclosure. *Computers in Human Behavior, 50*, 456–464.

Holmes, T. H., & Rahe, R. H. (1967). The social readjustment rating scale. *Journal of Psychosomatic Research, 11*, 213–218.

Holt-Lunstad, J., Smith, T. B., & Layton, J. B. (2010). Social relationships and mortality risk: A meta-analytic review. *PLoS Medicine, 7*(7), e1000316.

Holtz, R. (2004). Group cohesion, attitude projection, and opinion certainty: Beyond interaction. *Group Dynamics: Theory, Research, and Practice, 8*, 112–125.

Homans, G. (1961). *Social Behavior: Its Elementary Forms.* New York: Harcourt Brace Jovanovich.

Hong, Y., Benet-Martínez, V., Chiu, C., & Morris, M. W. (2003). Boundaries of cultural influence: Construct activation as a mechanism for cultural differences in social perception. *Journal of Cross-Cultural Psychology, 34*, 453–464.

Hong, Y., Wyer, R. S., Jr., & Fong, C. P. S. (2008). Chinese working in groups: Effort dispensability versus normative influence. *Asian Journal of Social Psychology, 11*, 187–195. doi:10.1111/j.1467-839X.2008.00257.x

Hong, Y.-Y., Chiu, C.-Y., & Kung, T. M. (1997). Bringing culture out in front: Effects of cultural meaning system activation on social cognition. In K. Leung, Y. Kashima, U. Kim, & S. Yamaguchi (Eds.), *Progress in Asian social psychology* (Vol. 1, pp. 135–146). Singapore: Wiley.

Hong, Y.-Y., Morris, M. W., Chiu, C.-Y., & Benet-Martinez, V. (2000). Multicultural minds: A dynamic constructivist approach to culture and cognition. *American Psychologist, 55*, 709–720.

Hood, K. B., & Shook, N. J. (2014). Who cares what others think?: The indirect effect of other's attitudes on condom use intentions. *International Journal of Sexual Health, 26*, 282–294.

Hoog, N., Stroebe, W., & de Wit, J. B. F. (2005). The impact of fear appeals on processing and acceptance of action recommendations. *Personality and Social Psychology Bulletin, 31*, 24–33.

Hoorens, V., & Van Damme, C. (2012). What do people infer from social comparisons? Bridges between social comparison and person perception. *Social and Personality Psychology Compass, 6*(8), 607–618. doi:10.1111/j.1751-9004.2012.00451.x

Horcajo, J., Briñol, P., & Petty, R. E. (2014). Multiple roles for majority versus minority source status on persuasion when source status follows the message. *Social Influence, 9*, 37–51.

Horgan, R. (2013). Bat area firm claims last laugh with Jason Headsets.com gambit. *Adweek.* http://www.adweek.com/digital/jason-headsets-auction-cnnmoney-techcrunch-huffingtonpost/

Hormes, J. M., Rozin, P., Green, M. C., & Fincher, K. (2013). Reading a book can change your mind, but only some changes last for a year: Food attitude changes in readers of *The Omnivore's Dilemma. Frontiers in Psychology, 4.* doi:10.3389/fpsyg.2013.00778

Hornsey, M. J., Grice, T., Jetten, J., Paulsen, N., & Callan, V. (2007). Group-directed criticisms and recommendations for change: Why newcomers arouse more resistance than old-timers. *Personality and Social Psychology Bulletin, 32*, 1620–1632.

Hornsey, M. J., Majkut, L., Terry, D. J., & McKimmie, B. M. (2003). On being loud and proud: Non-conformity and counter-conformity to group norms. *British Journal of Social Psychology, 42*, 319–335.

Hostinar, C. E., Sullivan, R. M., & Gunnar, M. R. (2014). Psychobiological mechanisms underlying the social buffering of the hypothalamic–pituitary–adrenocortical axis: A review of animal models and human studies across development. *Psychological Bulletin, 140*, 256–282.

House, J. S., Robbins, C., & Metzner, H. L. (1982). The association of social relationships and activities with mortality: Prospective evidence from the Tecumseh Community Health Study. *American Journal of Epidemiology, 116*, 123–140.

House, R. J., Hanges, P. J., Javidan, M., Dorfman, P. W., & Gupta, V. (2004). *Culture, leadership, and organizations: The GLOBE study of 62 societies.* Thousand Oaks, CA: Sage.

Hovland, C. I., Janis, I. L., & Kelley, H. H. (1953). *Communication and persuasion: Psychological studies of opinion change*. New Haven, CT: Yale University Press.

Howard, D. E., Griffin, M. A., & Boekeloo, B. O. (2008). Prevalence and psychosocial correlates of alcohol-related sexual assault among university students. *Adolescence, 43*, 733–750.

Howell, R. T., & Guevarra, D. A. (2013). Buying happiness: Differential consumption experiences for material and experiential purchases. *Advances in Psychology Research, 98*, 57–69.

Howerton, D. M., Meltzer, A. L., & Olson, M. A. (2012). Honeymoon vacation: Sexual-orientation prejudice and inconsistent behavioral responses. *Basic and Applied Social Psychology, 34*, 146–151.

Hsiang, S. M., Burke, M., & Miguel, E. (2013, September). Quantifying the influence of climate on human conflict. *Science, 341*. doi:10.1126/science.1235367

Hsu, S. S. (1995, April 8). Fredericksburg searches its soul after clerk is beaten as 6 watch. *Washington Post*, pp. A1, A13.

Hu, T., Zhang, D., & Ran, G. (2016). Self-serving attributional bias among Chinese adolescents. *Personality and Individual Differences, 91*, 80–83.

Huang, Y, Kendrick, K. M., & Yu, R. (2014). Conformity to the opinions of other people lasts for no more than 3 days. *Psychological Science, 25*, 1388–1393.

Hubbard, J., Harbaugh, W. T., Srivastava, S., Degras, D., & Mayr, U. (2016). A general benevolence dimension that links neural, psychological, economic, and life-span data on altruistic tendencies. *Journal of Experimental Psychology: General, 145*, 1351–1358.

Huber, R. E., Klucharev, V., & Rieskamp, J. (2014). Neural correlates of informational cascades: Brain mechanisms of social influence on belief updating. *Social Cognitive and Affective Neuroscience, 10*, 589–597.

Huesman, L. R., Dubow, E. F., & Yang, G. (2013). Why it is hard to believe that media violence causes aggression. In K. E. Dill (Ed.), *The Oxford handbook of media psychology* (pp. 159–171). Oxford: Oxford University Press.

Huffington, A. (2014). *Thrive: The third metric to redefining success and creating a life of well-being, wisdom, and wonder*. New York, NY: Harmony.

Huffman, K. T., Grossnickle, W. F., Cope, J. G., & Huffman, K. P. (1995). Litter reduction: A review and integration of the literature. *Environment and Behavior, 27*, 153–183.

Hugenberg, K., Young, S. G., Bernstein, M. J., & Sacco, D. F. (2010). The categorization-individuation model: An integrative account of the other-race recognition deficit. *Psychological Review, 117*(4), 1168–1187. doi:10.1037/a0020463

Hughes, S. M., & Miller, N. E. (2016). What sounds beautiful looks beautiful stereotype The matching of attractiveness of voices and faces. *Journal of Social and Personal Relationships, 33*, 984–996.

Hulleman, C. S., Schrager, S. M., Bodmann, S. M., & Harackiewicz, J. M. (2010). A meta-analytic review of achievement goal measures: Different labels for the same constructs or different constructs with similar labels? *Psychological Bulletin, 136*, 422–449. doi:10.1037/a0018947

Hunt, G. T. (1940). *The wars of the Iroquois*. Madison: University of Wisconsin Press.

Hunter, J. (2006). Correlational study of how airline customer service and consumer perception of airline customer service affect the air rage phenomenon. *Journal of Air Transportation, 11*, 78–109.

Huntsinger, J., & Sinclair, S. (2010). When it feels right, go with it: Affective regulation of affiliative social tuning. *Social Cognition, 28*, 290–305.

Hurley, D., & Allen, B. P. (1974). The effect of the number of people present in a nonemergency situation. *Journal of Social Psychology, 92*, 27–29.

Hust, S. J. T., Marett, E. G., Ren, C., Adams, P. M., Willoughby, J. F., Lei, M., et al. (2014). Establishing and adhering to sexual consent: The association between reading magazines and college students' sexual consent negotiation. *Journal of Sex Research, 51*, 280–290.

Hutchinson, R. R. (1983). The pain-aggression relationship and its expression in naturalistic settings. *Aggressive Behavior, 9*, 229–242.

Huwaë, S., & Schaafsma, J. (2016). Cross-cultural differences in emotion suppression in everyday interactions. *International Journal of Psychology*. doi:10.1002/ijop.12283

Hyman, I. E., Jr., Roundhill, R. F., Wener, K. M., & Rabiroff, C. A. (2014). Collaboration inflation: Egocentric source monitoring errors following collaborative remembering. *Journal of Applied Research in Memory and Cognition*.doi:10.1016/j.jarmac.2014.04.004

Ibrahim, J. K., & Glantz, S. A. (2007). The rise and fall of tobacco control media campaigns, 1967–2006. *American Journal of Public Health, 97*, 1383–1396.

Imada, T., & Kitayama, S. (2010). Social eyes and choice justification: Culture and dissonance revisited. *Social Cognition, 28*, 589–608.

Imhoff, R., & Erb, H. (2009). What motivates non-comformity? Uniqueness seeking blocks majority influence. *Personality and Social Psychology Bulletin, 35*, 309–320.

Infurna, F. J., Ram, N., & Gerstorf, D. (2013). Level and change in perceived control predict 19-year mortality: Findings from the Americans' changing lives study. *Developmental Psychology, 49*, 1833–1847.

Inglehart, R., & Klingemann, H. (2000). Genes, culture, democracy, and happiness. In E. Diener & D. M. Suh (Eds.), *Culture and subjective well-being* (pp. 165–183). Cambridge, MA: MIT Press.

Insko, C. A., & Schopler, J. (1998). Differential trust of groups and individuals. In C. Sedikides & J. Schopler (Eds.), *Intergroup cognition and intergroup behavior* (pp. 75–107). Mahwah, NJ: Erlbaum.

Insko, C. A., Smith, R. H., Alicke, M. D., Wade, J., & Taylor, S. (1985). Conformity and group size: The concern with being right and the concern with being liked. *Personality and Social Psychology Bulletin, 11*, 41–50.

Inzlicht, M., & Kang, S. K. (2010). Stereotype threat spillover: how coping with threats to social identity affects aggression, eating, decision making, and attention. *Journal of Personality and Social Psychology, 99*, 467–481.

Isen, A. M. (1999). Positive affect. In T. Dalgleish & M. J. Power (Eds.), *Handbook of cognition and emotion* (pp. 521–539). Chichester, UK: Wiley.

Isen, A. M., & Levin, P. A. (1972). Effect of feeling good on helping: Cookies and kindness. *Journal of Personality and Social Psychology, 21*, 384–388.

Islam, M. R., & Hewstone, M. (1993). Intergroup attributions and affective consequences in majority and minority groups. *Journal of Personality and Social Psychology, 64*, 936–950.

Ito, K., Masuda, T., & Li, M. W. (2013). Agency and facial emotion judgment in context. *Personality and Social Psychology Bulletin, 39*, 763–776.

Ito, T. A., & Urland, G. R. (2003). Race and gender on the brain: Electrocortical measures of attention to the race and gender of multiply categorizable individuals. *Journal of Personality and Social Psychology, 85*, 616–626.

Itkowitz, C. (2017, January 25). A white Trump voter explains why he left a Black waitress a $450 tip with an uplifting note. *Washington Post*. https://www.washingtonpost.com/news/inspired-life/wp/2017/01/24/not-race-not-gender-just-american-these-white-men-left-their-black-waitress-an-uplifting-note-and-a-450-tip/?utm_term=.1b81c820b118

Jack, R. E., Garrod, O. G., Yu, H., Caldara, R., & Schyns, P. G. (2012). Facial expressions of emotion are not culturally universal. *Proceedings of the National Academy of Sciences, 109*, 7241–7244.

Jackson, J. M., & Williams, K. D. (1985). Social loafing on difficult tasks: Working collectively can improve performance. *Journal of Personality and Social Psychology, 49*, 937–942.

Jackson, J. S., & Inglehart, M. R. (1995). Reverberation theory: Stress and racism in hierarchically structured communities. In S. E. Hobfoll & M. W. De Vries (Eds.), *Extreme stress and communities: Impact and intervention* (pp. 353–373). Dordrecht, Netherlands: Kluwer.

Jackson, J. S., Brown, T. N., Williams, D. R., Torres, M., Sellers, S. L., & Brown, K. (1996). Racism and the physical and mental health status of African Americans: A thirteen-year national panel study. *Ethnicity and Disease, 6*, 132–147.

Jackson, J. W. (1993). Realistic group conflict theory: A review and evaluation of the theoretical and empirical literature. *Psychological Record, 43*, 395–413.

Jackson, T., Chen, H., Guo, C., & Gao, X. (2006). Stories we love by conceptions of love among couples from the People's Republic of China and the United States. *Journal of Cross-Cultural Psychology, 37*, 446–464.

Jacobs, P., & Landau, S. (1971). *To serve the devil* (Vol. 2). New York: Vintage Books.

Jacobson, R. P., Mortensen, C. R., & Cialdini, R. B. (2011). Bodies obliged and unbound: Differentiated response tendencies for injunctive and descriptive social norms. *Journal of Personality and Social Psychology, 100*(3), 433–448. doi:10.1037/a0021470

James, L. M., & Olson, J. M. (2000). Jeer pressure: The behavioral effects of observing ridicule of others. *Personality and Social Psychology Bulletin, 26*, 474–485.

Janis, I. L. (1972). *Victims of groupthink*. Boston: Houghton Mifflin.

Janis, I. L. (1982). *Groupthink: Psychological studies of policy decisions and fiascoes* (2nd ed.). Boston: Houghton Mifflin.

Janis, I. L., & Feshbach, S. (1953). Effects of fear-arousing communications. *Journal of Abnormal and Social Psychology, 49*, 78–92.

Janis, I. L., & Mann, L. (1977). *Decision Making*. New York: The Free Press.

Jankowiak, W. R. (1995). Introduction. In W. R. Jankowiak (Ed.), *Romantic passion: A universal experience?* (pp. 1–19). New York: Columbia University Press.

Jankowiak, W. R., & Fischer, E. F. (1992). A cross-cultural perspective on romantic love. *Ethnology, 31*, 149–155.

Janoff-Bulman, R., & Leggatt, H. K. (2002). Culture and social obligation: When "shoulds" are perceived as "wants." *Journal of Research in Personality, 36*, 260–270.

Janoff-Bulman, R., Timko, C., & Carli, L. L. (1985). Cognitive biases in blaming the victim. *Journal of Experimental Social Psychology, 21*, 161–177.

Jecker, J., & Landy, D. (1969). Liking a person as a function of doing him a favor. *Human Relations, 22*, 371–378.

Jennings, K. (2011, February 16). My puny human brain. *Slate.com*. Retrieved April 18, 2011, from www.slate.com/id/2284721/

Jetten, J., & Hornsey, M. J. (2014). Deviance and dissent in groups. *Annual Review of Psychology, 65*, 461–485.

Job, V., Bernecker, K., Miketta, S., & Friese, M. (2015). Implicit theories about willpower predict the activation of a rest goal following self-control exertion. *Journal of Personality and Social Psychology, 109*, 694–706.

Job, V., Dweck, C. S., & Walton, G. M. (2010). Ego depletion—Is it all in your head? Implicit theories about willpower affect self-regulation. *Psychological Science, 21*, 1686–1693.

Johansson, P., Hall, L., Skiström, S., & Olsson, A. (2005). Failure to detect mismatches between intention and outcome in a simple decision task. *Science, 310*, 116–119.

Johns, M., Schmader, T., & Martens, A. (2005). Knowing is half the battle: Teaching stereotype threat as a means of improving women's math performance. *Psychological Science, 16*, 175–179.

Johnson, C. (2012). Behavioral responses to threatening social comparisons: From dastardly deeds to rising above. *Social and Personality Psychology Compass, 6*(7), 515–524. doi:10.1111/j.1751-9004.2012.00445.x

Johnson, D. W., & Johnson, R. T. (1987). *Learning together and alone: Cooperative, competitive, and individualistic learning* (2nd ed.). Englewood Cliffs, NJ: Prentice Hall.

Johnson, J. G., Cohen, P., Smailes, E. M., Kasen, S., & Brook, J. (2002). Television viewing and aggressive behavior during adolescence and adulthood. *Science, 295*, 2468–2471.

Johnson, J. (2011, Nov. 4). The bystander effect: Why those who heard the Lululemon murder didn't help. *Washington Post*. Retrieved June 23, 2017, from https://www.washingtonpost.com/opinions/the-bystander-effect-why-those-who-heard-the-lululemon-murder-didnt-help/2011/11/03/gIQAHIWYmM_story.html?utm_term=.d83667f381e5

Johnson, L. B. (1971). *The vantage point: Perspectives of the presidency, 1963–69*. New York: Holt, Rinehart and Winston.

Johnson, M., Verfaellie, M., & Dunlosky, J. (2008). Introduction to the special section on integrative approaches to source memory. *Journal of Experimental Psychology: Learning, Memory, and Cognition, 34*, 727–729.

Johnson, R. D., & Downing, R. L. (1979). Deindividuation and valence of cues: Effects of prosocial and antisocial behavior. *Journal of Personality and Social Psychology, 37*, 1532–1538.

Johnson, R. E., Rosen, C. C., & Lin, S. H. J. (2016). Assessing the status of locus of control as an indicator of core self-evaluations. *Personality and Individual Differences, 90*, 155–162.

Johnson, S. S., & Post, S. G. (2017). Rx It's good to be good (G2BG) 2017 commentary: Prescribing volunteerism for health, happiness, resilience, and longevity. *American Journal of Health Promotion, 31*, 163–172.

Johnson, T. E., & Rule, B. G. (1986). Mitigating circumstance information, censure, and aggression. *Journal of Personality and Social Psychology, 50*, 537–542.

Jonas, E., Martens, A., Kayser, D. N., Fritsche, I., Sullivan, D., & Greenberg, J. (2008). Focus theory of normative conduct and terror-management theory: The interactive impact of mortality salience and norm salience on social judgment. *Journal of Personality and Social Psychology Bulletin, 95*, 1239–1251.

Jonas, K. J. (2013). Automatic behavior—Its social embedding and individual consequences. *Social and Personality Psychology Compass, 7*, 689–700. doi:10.1111/spc3.12060

Jones, B. C., Little, A. C., Penton-Voak, I. S., Tiddeman, B. P., Burt, D. M., & Perrett, D. I. (2001). Facial symmetry and judgements of apparent health: Support for a "good genes" explanation of the attractiveness-symmetry relationship. *Evolution and Human Behavior, 22*, 417–429.

Jones, C., & Aronson, E. (1973). Attribution of fault to a rape victim as a function of the respectability of the victim. *Journal of Personality and Social Psychology, 26*, 415–419.

Jones, E. E. (1964). *Ingratiation: A social psychological analysis*. New York: Appleton-Century-Crofts.

Jones, E. E. (1979). The rocky road from acts to dispositions. *American Scientist, 34*, 107–117.

Jones, E. E., & Harris, V. A. (1967). The attribution of attitudes. *Journal of Experimental Social Psychology, 3*, 1–24.

Jones, E. E., & Nisbett, R. E. (1972). The actor and the observer: Divergent perceptions of the causes of behavior. In E. E. Jones, D. E. Kanouse, H. H. Kelley, R. E. Nisbett, S. Valins, & B. Weiner (Eds.), *Attribution: Perceiving the causes of behavior* (pp. 79–94). Morristown, NJ: General Learning Press.

Jones, E. E., & Pittman, T. S. (1982). Toward a general theory of strategic self-presentation. In J. Suls (Ed.), *Psychological perspectives on the self* (pp. 231–262). Hillsdale, NJ: Erlbaum.

Jones, E. E., & Sigall, H. (1971). The bogus pipeline: A new paradigm for measuring affect and attitude. *Psychological Bulletin, 76*, 349–364.

Jones, E. E., & Wortman, C. B. (1973). *Ingratiation: An attributional approach*. Morristown, NJ: General Learning Press.

Jones, M. (2006, January 15). Shutting themselves in. *The New York Times*, Sec. 6, pp. 46–51.

Jones, M. A., Taylor, V. A., & Reynolds, K. E. (2014). The effect of requests for positive evaluations on customer satisfaction ratings. *Psychology and Marketing, 31*, 161–170.

Jordan, M., & Sullivan, K. (1995, September 8). A matter of saving face: Japanese can rent mourners, relatives, friends, even enemies to buff an image. *Washington Post*, pp. A1, A28.

Jordan, C. H., Spencer, S. J., Zanna, M. P., Hoshino-Browne, E., & Correll, J. (2003). Secure and defensive high self-esteem. *Journal of Personality and Social Psychology, 85*, 969–978.

Josephson, W. D. (1987). Television violence and children's aggression: Testing the priming, social script, and disinhibition prediction. *Journal of Personality and Social Psychology, 53*, 882–890.

Jost, J. T., Nosek, B. A., & Gosling, S. D. (2008). Ideology: Its resurgence in social, personality, and political psychology. *Perspectives on Psychological Science, 3*, 126–136.

Jostmann, N. B., Lakens, D., & Schubert, T. W. (2009). Weight as an embodiment of importance. *Psychological Science, 20*, 1169–1174. doi:10.1111/j.1467-9280.2009.02426.x

Jowett, G. S., & O'Donnell, V. (1999). *Propaganda and persuasion*. Thousand Oaks, CA: Sage.

Judge, T. A., & Piccolo, R. F. (2004). Transformational and transactional leadership: A meta-analytic test of their relative validity. *Journal of Applied Psychology, 89*, 755–768.

Judge, T. A., Bono, J. E., Ilies, R., & Gerhardt, M. W. (2002). Personality and leadership: A qualitative and quantitative review. *Journal of Applied Psychology, 87*, 765–780.

Judge, T. A., Colbert, A. E., & Ilies, R. (2004). Intelligence and leadership: A quantitative review and test of theoretical propositions. *Journal of Applied Psychology, 89*, 542–552.

Judge, T. A., Hurst, C., & Simon, L. S. (2009). Does it pay to be smart, attractive, or confident (or all three)? Relationships among general mental ability, physical attractiveness, core self-evaluations, and income. *Journal of Applied Psychology, 94*, 742–755.

Juhl, J., & Routledge, C. (2016). Putting the terror in terror management theory: Evidence that the awareness of death does cause anxiety and undermine psychological well-being. *Current Directions in Psychological Science, 25*, 99–103.

Jürgen-Lohmann, J., Borsch, F., & Giesen, H. (2001). Kooperatives Lernen an der Hochschule: Evaluation des Gruppenpuzzles in Seminaren der Pädagogischen Psychologie. *Zeitschrift für Pädagogische Psychologie, 15*, 74–84.

Jussim, L. (2012). *Social perception and social reality: Why accuracy dominates bias and self-fulfilling prophecy*. New York: Oxford University Press.

Jussim, L., Cain, T. R., Crawford, J. T., Harber, K., & Cohen, F. (2009). The unbearable accuracy of stereotypes. In T. Nelson (Ed.), *The handbook of prejudice, stereotyping, and discrimination* (pp. 199–227). New York: Psychology Press.

Kahn, M. (1966). The physiology of catharsis. *Journal of Personality and Social Psychology, 3*, 278–298.

Kahneman, D. (2011). *Thinking, fast and slow*. New York: Farrar, Straus, & Giroux.

Kahneman, D., & Deaton, A. (2010). High income improves evaluation of life but not emotional well-being. *Proceedings of the National Academy of Sciences, 10*, 16489–16493.

Kahneman, D., & Frederick, S. (2002). Representativeness revisited: Attribute substitution in intuitive judgment. In T. Gilovich, D. W. Griffin, & D. Kahneman (Eds.), *Heuristics and biases: The psychology of intuitive judgment* (pp. 49–81). New York: Cambridge University Press.

Kahneman, D., & Tversky, A. (1973). On the psychology of prediction. *Psychological Review, 80*, 237–251.

Kahneman, D., & Tversky, A. (1979). Intuitive prediction: Biases and corrective procedures. *TIMS Studies in Management Science, 12*, 313–327.

Kaighobadi, F., Shackelford, T. K., & Goetz, A. T. (2009). From mate retention to murder: Evolutionary psychological perspectives on men's partner-directed violence. *Review of General Psychology, 13*, 327–334.

Kalanthroff, E., Aslan, C., & Dar, R. (2017). Washing away your sins will set your mind free: Physical cleansing modulates the effect of threatened morality on executive control. *Cognition and Emotion, 31*(1), 185–192. http://dx.doi.org/10.1080/02699931.2015.1086313

Kalisch, R., Müller, M. B., & Tüscher, O. (2015). A conceptual framework for the neurobiological study of resilience. *Behavioral and Brain Sciences, 38*. doi:10.1017/S0140525X1400082X, e92

Kalisch, R., Müller, M. B., & Tüscher, O. (2014). A conceptual framework for the neurobiological study of resilience. *Behavioral and Brain Sciences*, 1–49.

Kallgren, C. A., Reno, R. R., & Cialdini, R. B. (2000). A focus theory of normative conduct: When norms do and do not affect behavior. *Personality and Social Psychology Bulletin, 26*, 1002–1012.

Kalmijn, M., & Monden, C. W. S. (2012). The division of labor and depressive symptoms at the couple level: Effects of equity of specialization? *Journal of Social and Personal Relationships*. doi:10.1177/0265407511431182

Kalven, H., Jr., & Zeisel, H. (1966). *The American jury*. Boston: Little, Brown.

Kamble, S., Shackelford, T. K., Pham, M. N., & Buss, D. M. (2014). Indian mate preferences: Continuity, sex differences, and cultural change across a quarter of a century. *Personality and Individual Differences, 70*, 150–155.

Kamide, H., & Daibo, I. (2009). Application of a self-evaluation maintenance model to psychological health in interpersonal contexts. *The Journal of Positive Psychology, 4*, 557–565.

Kang, C. (2008). Product placement on TV targeted. *Washington Post*. http://www.washingtonpost.com/wp-dyn/content/article/2008/06/26/AR2008062603632.html

Kang, S. K., DeCelles, K. A., Tilcsik, A., & Jun, S. (2016). Whitened resumes: Race and self-presentation in the labor market. *Administrative Science Quarterly, 61*, 469–502.

Kappas, A. (1997). The fascination with faces: Are they windows to our soul? *Journal of Nonverbal Behavior, 21*, 157–162.

Kappes, A., & Crockett, M. J. (2017). The benefits and costs of a rose-colored hindsight. *Trends in Cognitive Sciences, 20*, 644–646.

Kappeler, P., & van Schaik, C. P. (Eds.). (2006). *Cooperation in primates and humans: Mechanisms and evolution*. Berlin: Springer.

Karau, S. J., & Williams, K. D. (1993). Social loafing: A meta-analytic review and theoretical integration. *Journal of Personality and Social Psychology, 65*, 681–706.

Karau, S. J., & Williams, K. D. (2001). Understanding individual motivation in groups: The collective effort model. In M. E. Turner (Ed.), *Groups at work—theory and research: Applied social research* (pp. 113–141). Mahwah, NJ: Erlbaum.

Karremans, J. C., Stroebe, W., & Claus, J. (2006). Beyond Vicary's fantasies: The impact of subliminal priming and brand choice. *Journal of Experimental Social Psychology, 42*, 792–798.

Kassin, S. M., Bogart, D., & Kerner, J. (2012). Confessions that corrupt: Evidence from the DNA exoneration case files. *Psychological Science, 23*, 41–45.

Kassin, S. M., Drizin, S. A., Grisso, T., Gudjonsson, G. H., Leo, R. A., & Redlich, A. D. (2010). Police-induced confessions, risk factors, and recommendations: Looking ahead. *Law and Human Behavior, 34*(1), 49–52. doi:10.1007/s10979-010-9217-5

Katz, D. (1960). The functional approach to the study of attitudes. *Public Opinion Quarterly, 24*, 163–204.

Kauffman, D. R., & Steiner, I. D. (1968). Conformity as an ingratiation technique. *Journal of Experimental Social Psychology, 4*, 404–414.

Kawakami, N., & Yoshida, F. (2014). How do implicit effects of subliminal mere exposure become explicit? Mediating effects of social interaction. *Social Influence*. doi:10.1080/15534510.2014.901245

Kawamichi, H., Sugawara, S. K., Hamano, Y. H., Makita, K., Matsunaga, M., Tanabe, H. C., Ogino, Y., Saito, S., & Sadato, N. (2016). Being in a romantic relationship is associated with reduced gray matter density in striatum and increased subjective happiness. *Frontiers in Psychology, 7*, Article 1763.

Kayser, D. N., Greitemeyer, T., Fischer, P., & Frey, D. (2010). Why mood affects help giving, but not moral courage: Comparing two types of prosocial behaviour. *European Journal of Social Psychology, 40*(7), 1136–1157. doi:10.1002/ejsp.717

Keating, J., Van Boven, L., & Judd, C. M. (2016). Partisan underestimation of the polarizing influence of group discussion. *Journal of Experimental Social Psychology, 65,* 52–58.

Keelan, J. P. R., Dion, K. L., & Dion, K. K. (1994). Attachment style and heterosexual relationships among young adults: A short-term panel study. *Journal of Social and Personal Relationships, 11,* 201–214.

Keller, J., & Bless, H. (2008). Flow and regulatory compatibility: An experimental approach to the flow model of intrinsic motivation. *Personality and Social Psychology Bulletin, 34,* 196–209.

Kelley, H. H. (1950). The warm-cold variable in first impressions of persons. *Journal of Personality, 18,* 431–439.

Kelley, H. H. (1955). The two functions of reference groups. In G. E. Swanson, T. M. Newcomb, & E. L. Hartley (Eds.), *Readings in social psychology* (2nd ed., pp. 410–414). New York: Henry Holt.

Kelley, H. H. (1967). Attribution theory in social psychology. In D. Levine (Ed.), *Nebraska Symposium on Motivation* (Vol. 15, pp. 192–238). Lincoln: University of Nebraska Press.

Kelley, H. H. (1973). The process of causal attribution. *American Psychologist, 28,* 107–128.

Kelley, H. H., & Thibaut, J. W. (1978). *Interpersonal relations: A theory of interdependence.* New York, NY: Wiley.

Keltner, D., & Shiota, M. N. (2003). New displays and new emotions: A commentary on Rozin and Cohen. *Emotion, 3,* 86–91.

Keltner, D., Kogan, A., Piff, P. K., & Saturn, S. R. (2014). The sociocultural appraisals, values, and emotions (SAVE) framework of prosociality: Core processes from gene to meme. *Annual Review of Psychology, 65,* 425–460.

Kennedy, S., & Ruggles, S. (2014). Breaking up is hard to count: The rise of divorce in the United States, 1980–2010. *Demography, 51,* 587–598.

Kenrick, D. T., & MacFarlane, S. W. (1986). Ambient temperature and horn honking: A field study of the heat/aggression relationship. *Environment and Behavior, 18,* 179–191.

Kerr, N. L., & Tindale, R. S. (2004). Groups performance and decision making. *Annual Review of Psychology, 55,* 623–655.

Kerr, N., & Levine, J. (2008). The detection of social exclusion: Evolution and beyond. *Group Dynamics: Theory, Research, and Practice, 12,* 39–52.

Kertzer, J. D., Powers, K. E., Rathbun, B. C., & Iyer, R. (2014). Moral support: How moral values shape foreign policy attitudes. *The Journal of Politics, 76,* 825–840.

Kessels, L. T., Ruiter, R. A. C., Wouters, L., & Jansma, B. M. (2014). Neuroscientific evidence for defensive avoidance of fear appeals. *International Journal of Psychology, 49,* 80–88.

Kestemont, J., Ma, N., Baetens, K., Clément, N., Van Overwalle, F., & Vandekerckhove, M. (2014). Neural correlates of attributing causes to the self, another person, and the situation. *Social Cognitive and Affective Neuroscience.* doi:10.1093/scan/nsu030

Key, Wilson B. (1973). *Subliminal seduction.* Englewood Cliffs, NJ: Signet Books.

Key, Wilson B. (1989). *Age of manipulation: The con in confidence and the sin in sincere.* New York: Henry Holt.

Kiesler, C. A., & Kiesler, S. B. (1969). *Conformity.* Reading, MA: Addison-Wesley.

Kihlstrom, J. F. (1996). The trauma-memory argument and recovered memory therapy. In J. Pezdek & W. P. Banks (Eds.), *The recovered memory/false memory debate* (pp. 297–311). San Diego, CA: Academic Press.

Kilduff, G. J., & Galinsky, A. D. (2017). The spark that ignites: Mere exposure to rivals increases Machiavellianism and unethical behavior. *Journal of Experimental Social Psychology, 69,* 156–162.

Killian, L. M. (1964). Social movements. In R. E. Farris (Ed.), *Handbook of modern sociology* (pp. 426–455). Chicago: Rand McNally.

Kim, H. S., Sherman, D. K., & Taylor, S. E. (2008). Culture and social support. *American Psychologist, 63,* 518–526.

Kim, H., & Markus, H. R. (1999). Deviance or uniqueness, harmony or conformity? A cultural analysis. *Journal of Personality and Social Psychology, 77,* 785–800.

Kim, H., Park, K., & Schwarz, N. (2010). Will this trip really be exciting? The role of incidental emotions in product evaluation. *Journal of Consumer Research, 36*(6), 983–991. doi:10.1086/644763

Kim, J. L., Sorsoli, C. L., Collins, K., Zylbergold, B. A., Schooler, D., & Tolman, D. L. (2007). From sex to sexuality: Exposing the heterosexual script on primetime network television. *Journal of Sex Research, 44,* 145–157.

Kim, U., Triandis, H. C., Kagitcibasi, C., Choi, S. C., & Yoon, G. (Eds.). (1994). *Individualism and collectivism: Theory, method, and applications.* Thousand Oaks, CA: Sage.

Kimmel, M. (2012). *The gendered society* (5th ed.). New York: Oxford University Press.

King, M., & Woollett, E. (1997). Sexually assaulted males: 115 men consulting a counseling service. *Archives of Sexual Behavior, 26,* 579–588.

Kinoshita, S., & Peek-O'Leary, M. (2005). Does the compatibility effect in the race Implicit Association Test reflect familiarity or affect? *Psychonomic Bulletin Review, 12,* 442–452.

Kirkpatrick, L. A., & Hazan, C. (1994). Attachment styles and close relationships: A four-year prospective study. *Personal Relationships, 1,* 123–142.

Kitayama, S., & Cohen, D. (Eds.). (2007). *Handbook of cultural psychology.* New York: Guilford.

Kitayama, S., & Markus, H. R. (1994). Culture and the self: How cultures influence the way we view ourselves. In D. Matsumoto (Ed.), *People: Psychology from a cultural perspective* (pp. 17–37). Pacific Grove, CA: Brooks/Cole.

Kitayama, S., & Uchida, Y. (2003). Explicit self-criticism and implicit self-regard: Evaluating self and friend in two cultures. *Journal of Experimental Social Psychology, 39,* 476–482.

Kitayama, S., & Uchida, Y. (2005). Interdependent agency: An alternative system for action. In R. L. Sorrentino & D. Cohen (Eds.), *Cultural and social behavior: The Ontario Symposium* (Vol. 10, pp. 137–164). Mahwah, NJ: Erlbaum.

Kitayama, S., Conway, L. G., Pietromonaco, P. R., Park, H., & Plaut, V. C. (2010). Ethos of independence across regions in the United States: The production-adoption model of cultural change. *American Psychologist, 65,* 559–574.

Kitayama, S., Ishii, K., Imada, T., Takemura, K., & Ramaswamy, J. (2006). Voluntary settlement and the spirit of independence: Evidence from Japan's 'northern frontier.' *Journal of Personality and Social Psychology, 91,* 369–384.

Kitayama, S., Park, H., Sevincer, A. T., Karasawa, M., & Uskul, A. K. (2009). A cultural task analysis of implicit independence: Comparing North America, Western Europe, and East Asia. *Journal of Personality and Social Psychology, 97,* 236–255.

Kitayama, S., Tompson, S., & Chua, H. F. (2014). Cultural neuroscience of choice justification. In J. P. Forgas & E. Harmon-Jones (Eds.), *Motivation and its regulation: The control within* (pp. 313–330). New York: Psychology Press.

Kjell, O. N. E. (2011). Sustainable well-being: A potential synergy between sustainability and well-being research. *Review of General Psychology, 15*(3), 255–266. doi:10.1037/a0024603

Klapwijk, A., & Van Lange, P. A. M. (2009). Promoting cooperation and trust in "noisy" situations: The power of generosity. *Journal of Personality and Social Psychology, 96,* 83–103.

Klein, W. M. P., Rothman, A. J., & Cameron, L. D. (2013). Theoretical innovations in social and personality psychology and implications for health: Introduction to special issue. *Health Psychology, 32,* 457–459.

Kleinjan, M., van den Eijnden, R. J., & Engels, R. C. (2009). Adolescents' rationalizations to continue smoking: The role of disengagement beliefs and nicotine dependence in smoking cessation. *Addictive Behaviors, 34,* 440–445.

Kline, S. L., Horton, B., & Zhang, S. (2008). Communicating love: Comparisons between American and East Asian university students. *International Journal of Intercultural Relations, 32,* 200–214.

Klinesmith, J., Kasser, T., & McAndrew, F. T. (2006). Guns, testosterone, and aggression an experimental test of a mediational hypothesis. *Psychological Science, 17,* 568–571.

Klug, W., O'Dwyer, A., Barry, D., Dillard, L., Polo-Neil, H., & Warriner, M. (2011). The burden of combat: Cognitive dissonance in Iraq war veterans. In D. Kelly, S. Howe-Barksdale, & D. Gitelson (Eds.), *Treating young veterans: Promoting resilience through practice and advocacy* (pp. 33–79). New York: Springer.

Kluger, R. (1996). *Ashes to ashes: America's hundred-year cigarette war, the public health, and the unabashed triumph of Philip Morris.* New York: Knopf.

Knapp, M. L., Hall, J. A., & Horgan, T. G. (2014). *Nonverbal communication in human interaction.* Belmont, CA: Wadsworth.

Knobe, J., Buckwalter, W., Nichols, S., Robbins, P., Sarkissian, H., & Sommers, T. (2012). Experimental philosophy. *Annual Review of Psychology, 63,* 81–99.

Knowles, E. D., Morris, M. W., Chiu, C., & Hong, Y. (2001). Culture and the process of person perception: Evidence for automaticity among East Asians in correcting for situational influences on behavior. *Personality and Social Psychology Bulletin, 27,* 1344–1356.

Knoll, M. A. Z., & Arkes, H. R. (2016). The effects of expertise on the hindsight bias. *Journal of Behavioral Decision Making.* Advance online publication. http://dx.doi.org/10.1002/bdm.1950

Knox, R., & Inkster, J. (1968). Postdecision dissonance at post time. *Journal of Personality and Social Psychology, 8,* 319–323.

Knussen, C., Yule, F., & MacKenzie, J. (2004). An analysis of intentions to recycle household waste: The roles of past behaviour, perceived habit, and perceived lack of facilities. *Journal of Environmental Psychology, 24,* 237–246.

Koehler, J. J. (1993). The base rate fallacy myth. *Psycoloquy, 4,* 49.

Koehler, J. J. (1996). The base rate fallacy reconsidered: Descriptive, normative, and methodological challenges. *Behavioral and Brain Sciences, 19,* 1–53.

Koenig, A. M., Eagly, A. H., Mitchell, A. A., & Ristikari, T. (2011). Are leader stereotypes masculine? A meta-analysis of three research paradigms. *Psychological Bulletin, 137*(4), 616–642. doi:10.1037/a0023557

Kokkoris, M. D., & Kühnen, U. (2013). Choice and dissonance in a European cultural context: The case of Western and Eastern Europeans. *International Journal of Psychology, 48,* 1260–1266.

Kollack, P., Blumstein, P., & Schwartz, P. (1994). The judgment of equity in intimate relationships. *Social Psychology Quarterly, 57,* 340–351.

Kong, D. T., Dirks, K. T., & Ferrin, D. L. (2014). Interpersonal trust within negotiations: Meta-analytic evidence, critical contingencies, and directions for future research. *Academy of Management Journal, 57,* 1235–1255.

Konrath, S. H., Chopik, W. J., Hsing, C. K., & O'Brien, E. (2014). Changes in adult attachment styles in American college students over time. *Personality and Social Psychology Review.* doi:10.1177/1088868314530516

Konrath, S. H., O'Brien, E. H., & Hsing, C. (2011). Changes in dispositional empathy in American college students over time: A meta-analysis. *Personality and Social Psychology Review, 15,* 180–198.

Koppel, J., & Bensten, D. (2014). The cultural life script as cognitive schema: How the life script shapes memory for fictional life stories, *Memory, 22,* 949–971.

Koranyi, N., & Rothermund, K. (2012). When the grass on the other side of the fence doesn't matter: Reciprocal romantic interest neutralizes attentional bias towards attractive alternatives. *Journal of Experimental Social Psychology, 48,* 186–191.

Koss, M. P. (2011). Hidden, unacknowledged, acquaintance, and date rape: Looking back, looking forward. *Psychology of Woman Quarterly, 35,* 348–354.

Kotabe, H. P., & Hoffmann, W. (2015). On integrating the components of self-control. *Perspectives on Psychological Science, 10*, 618–638.

Kowalski, R. M., Giumetti, G. W., Schroeder, A. N., & Lattanner, M. R. (2014). Bullying in the digital age: A critical review and meta-analysis of cyberbullying research among youth. *Psychological Bulletin, 140*, 1073–1137.

Krakow, A., & Blass, T. (1995). When nurses obey or defy inappropriate physician orders: Attributional differences. *Journal of Social Behavior and Personality, 10*, 585–594.

Krasheninnikova, A., & Schneider, J. M. (2014). Testing problem-solving capacities: Differences between individual testing and social group setting. *Animal Behavior.* doi:10.1007/s10071-014-0744-1

Krauss, R. M., & Deutsch, M. (1966). Communication in interpersonal bargaining. *Journal of Personality and Social Psychology, 4*, 572–577.

Krauss, R. M., Freedman, J. L., & Whitcup, M. (1978). Field and laboratory studies of littering. *Journal of Experimental Social Psychology, 14*, 109–122.

Kressel, K., & Pruitt, D. G. (1989). A research perspective on the mediation of social conflict. In K. Kressel & D. G. Pruitt (Eds.), *Mediation research: The process and effectiveness of third party intervention* (pp. 394–435). San Francisco: Jossey-Bass.

Krishna, A., & Schwarz, N. (2014). Sensory marketing, embodiment, and grounded cognition: A review and introduction. *Journal of Consumer Psychology, 24*(2), 159–168. http://dx.doi.org/10.1016/j.jcps.2013.12.006

Krockow, E. M., Colman, A. M., & Pulford, B. D. (2016). Cooperation in repeated interactions: A systematic review of Centipede game experiments, 1992–2016. *European Review of Social Psychology, 27*, 231–282.

Krosnick, J. A., & Alwin, D. F. (1989). Aging and susceptibility to attitude change. *Journal of Personality and Social Psychology, 57*, 416–425.

Kross, E., & Ayduk, O. (2011). Making meaning out of negative experiences by self-distancing. *Current Directions in Psychological Science, 20*(3), 187–191. doi:10.1177/0963721411408883

Kross, E., Bruehlman-Senecal, E., Park, J., Burson, A., Dougherty, A., Shablack, H., et al. (2014). Self-talk as a regulatory mechanism: How you do it matters. *Journal of Personality and Social Psychology, 106*, 304–324.

Krueger, A. B. (2007). *What makes a terrorist: Economics and the roots of terrorism.* Princeton, NJ: Princeton University Press.

Krull, D. S. (1993). Does the grist change the mill? The effect of the perceiver's inferential goal on the process of social inference. *Personality and Social Psychology Bulletin, 19*, 340–348.

Krull, D. S., Loy, M. H., Lin, J., Wang, C., Chen, S., & Zhao, X. (1999). The fundamental correspondence bias in individualist and collectivist cultures. *Personality and Social Psychology Bulletin, 25*, 1208–1219.

Kubitschek, W. N., & Hallinan, M. T. (1998). Tracking and students' friendships. *Social Psychology Quarterly, 61*, 1–15.

Kulig, T. C., Pratt, T. C., & Cullen, F. T. (2017). Revisiting the Stanford prison experiment: A case study in organized skepticism. *Journal of Criminal Justice Education, 28*, 74–111.

Kumar, A., Killingsworth, M. A., & Gilovich, T. (2014). Waiting for Merlot: Anticipatory consumption of experiential and material purchases. *Psychological Science, 25*, 1924–1931.

Kumar, A., Niessen-Ruenzi, A., & Spalt, O. G. (2015). What's in a name? Mutual fund flows when managers have foreign-sounding names. *Review of Financial Studies, 28*, 2281–2321.

Kunda, Z., & Oleson, K. C. (1997). When exceptions prove the rule: How extremity of deviance determines the impact of deviant examples on stereotypes. *Journal of Personality and Social Psychology, 72*, 965–979.

Kunda, Z., & Schwartz, S. H. (1983). Undermining intrinsic moral motivation: External reward and self-presentation. *Journal of Personality and Social Psychology, 45*, 763–771.

Kunda, Z., Sinclair, L., & Griffin, D. W. (1997). Equal ratings but separate meanings: Stereotypes and the construal of traits. *Journal of Personality and Social Psychology, 72*, 720–734.

Kuo, Z. Y. (1961). *Instinct.* Princeton, NJ: Van Nostrand.

Kurdek, L. A. (1992). Relationship stability and relationship satisfaction in cohabiting gay and lesbian couples: A prospective longitudinal test of the contextual and interdependence models. *Journal of Social and Personal Relationships, 9*, 125–142.

Kurdek, L. A. (2005). What do we know about gay and lesbian couples? *Current Directions in Psychological Science, 14*, 251–254.

Kurdi, B., & Banaji, M. R. (2017). Repeated evaluative pairings and evaluative statements: How effectively do they shift implicit attitudes? *Journal of Experimental Psychology: General, 146*, 194–213.

Kwan, L. Y., & Chiu, C. (2014). Holistic versus analytic thinking explains collective culpability attribution. *Basic and Applied Social Psychology, 36*, 3–8.

La France, B. H., Henningsen, D. D., Oates, A., & Shaw, C. M. (2009). Social-sexual interactions? Meta-analyses of sex differences in perceptions of flirtatiousness, seductiveness, and promiscuousness. *Communication Monographs, 76*, 263–285.

LaFrance, M., & Eagly, A. H. (2017). Omitted evidence undermines sexual motives explanation for attractiveness bias. *Behavioral and Brain Sciences, 40*, Article e31.

LaPiere, R. T. (1934). Attitudes vs. actions. *Social Forces, 13*, 230–237.

Laird, J. D., & Lacasse, K. (2014). Bodily influences on emotional feelings: Accumulating evidence and extensions of William James's theory of emotion. *Emotion Review, 6*, 27–34.

Lakey, B., & Orehek, E. (2011). Relational regulation theory: A new approach to explain the link between perceived social support and mental health. *Psychological Review, 118*(3), 482–495. doi:10.1037/a0023477

Lakoff, G., & Johnson, M. (1999). *Philosophy in the flesh: The embodied mind and its challenge to Western thought.* New York: Basic Books.

Lalwani, A. K., & Shavitt, S. (2009). The "me" I claim to be: Cultural self-construal elicits self-presentational goal pursuit. *Journal of Personality and Social Psychology, 97*, 88–102. doi:10.1037/a0014100

Lam, S., & Dickerson, S. S. (2013). Social relationships, social threat, and health. In M. L. Newman & N. A. Roberts (Eds.), *Health and social relationships: The good, the bad, and the complicated* (pp. 19–38). Washington, DC: American Psychological Association.

Lamb, C. S., & Crano, W. D. (2014). Parents' beliefs and children's marijuana use: Evidence for a self-fulfilling prophecy effect. *Addictive Behaviors, 39*, 127–132.

Lampert, R., Baron, S. J., McPherson, C. A., & Lee, F. A. (2002). Heart rate variability during the week of September 11, 2001. *Journal of the American Medical Association, 288*, 575.

Landau, M. J., Meier, B. P., & Keefer, L. A. (2010). A metaphor-enriched social cognition. *Psychological Bulletin, 136*(6), 1045–1067. doi:10.1037/a0020970

Landis, D., & O'Shea, W. A. (2000). Cross-cultural aspects of passionate love: An individual differences analysis. *Journal of Cross-Cultural Psychology, 31*, 752–777.

Lane, K. A., Banaji, M. R., & Nosek, B. A. (2007). Understanding and using the implicit association test: IV: What we know (so far) about the method. In B. Wittenbrink & N. Schwarz (Eds.), *Implicit measures of attitudes* (pp. 59–102). New York: Guilford.

Langer, E. J., & Rodin, J. (1976). The effects of choice and enhanced personal responsibility for the aged: A field experiment. *Journal of Personality and Social Psychology, 34*, 191–198.

Langhinrichsen-Rohling, J., Misra, T. A., Selwyn, C., & Rohling, M. L. (2012). Rates of bi-directional versus unidirectional intimate partner violence across samples, sexual orientations, and race/ethnicities: A comprehensive review. *Partner Abuse, 3*, 199–230.

Langlois, J. H., & Roggman, L. A. (1990). Attractive faces are only average. *Psychological Science, 1*, 115–121.

Langlois, J. H., Kalakanis, L., Rubenstein, A. J., Larson, A., Hallam, M., & Smoot, M. (2000). Maxims or myths of beauty? A meta-analytic and theoretical review. *Psychological Bulletin, 126*, 390–423.

Langlois, J. H., Ritter, J. M., Roggman, L. A., & Vaughn, L. S. (1991). Facial diversity and infant preferences for attractive faces. *Developmental Psychology, 27*, 79–84.

Langlois, J. H., Roggman, L. A., & Musselman, L. (1994). What is average and what is not average about attractive faces? *Psychological Science, 5*, 214–220.

Larrick, R. P., Timmerman, T. A., Carton, A. M., & Abrevaya, J. (2011). Temper, temperature, and temptation: Heat-related retaliation in baseball. *Psychological Science, 22*, 423–428.

Larson, J. R., Jr., Christensen, C., Franz, T. M., & Abbott, A. S. (1998). Diagnosing groups: The pooling, management, and impact of shared and unshared case information in team-based medical decision making. *Journal of Personality and Social Psychology, 75*, 93–108.

Lassiter, G. D. (2010). Psychological science and sound public policy: Video recording of custodial interrogations. *American Psychologist, 65*(8), 768–779. doi:10.1037/0003-066X.65.8.768

Lassiter, G. D., Diamond, S. S., Schmidt, H. C., & Elek, J. K. (2007). Evaluating videotaped confessions: Expertise provides no defense against the camera perspective effect. *Psychological Science, 18*, 224–226.

Lassiter, G. D., Geers, A. L., Munhall, P. J., Ploutz-Snyder, R. J., & Breitenbecher, D. L. (2002). Illusory causation: Why it occurs. *Psychological Science, 13*, 299–305.

Lassiter, G. D., Ratcliff, J. J., Ware, L. J., & Irvin, C. R. (2006). Videotaped confessions: Panacea or Pandora's Box? *Law and Policy, 28*, 192–210.

Latané, B. (1981). The psychology of social impact. *American Psychologist, 36*, 343–356.

Latané, B., & Bourgeois, M. J. (2001). Successfully simulating dynamic social impact: Three levels of prediction. In J. P. Forgas & K. D. Williams (Eds.), *Social influence: Direct and indirect processes* (pp. 61–76). Philadelphia: Psychology Press.

Latané, B., & Dabbs, J. M. (1975). Sex, group size, and helping in three cities. *Sociometry, 38*, 108–194.

Latané, B., & Darley, J. M. (1968). Group inhibition of bystander intervention. *Journal of Personality and Social Psychology, 10*, 215–221.

Latané, B., & Darley, J. M. (1970). *The unresponsive bystander: Why doesn't he help?* Englewood Cliffs, NJ: Prentice Hall.

Latané, B., & Nida, S. (1981). Ten years of research on group size and helping. *Psychological Bulletin, 89*, 308–324.

Latané, B., Williams, K., & Harkins, S. (2006). Many hands make light the work: The causes and consequences of social loafing. In J. M. Levine & R. L. Moreland (Eds.), *Small groups* (pp. 297– 308). New York: Psychology Press.

Lau, R. R., & Russell, D. (1980). Attributions in the sports pages: A field test of some current hypotheses about attribution research. *Journal of Personality and Social Psychology, 39*, 29–38.

Laumann, E. O., & Gagnon, J. H. (1995). A sociological perspective on sexual action. In R. G. Parker & J. H. Gagnon (Eds.), *Conceiving sexuality: Approaches to sex research in a postmodern world.* New York: Routledge.

Laumann, E. O., Gagnon, J. H., Michael, R. T., & Michaels, S. (1994). *The social organization of sexuality.* Chicago: University of Chicago Press.

Laursen, B., & Hartup, W. W. (2002). The origins of reciprocity and social exchange in friendships. In L. Brett & W. G. Graziano (Eds.), *Social exchange in development: New directions for child and adolescent development* (pp. 27–40). San Francisco: Jossey-Bass/Pfeiffer.

Layous, K., Nelson, S. K., Kurtz, J. L., & Lyubomirsky, S. (2017). What triggers prosocial effort? A positive feedback loop between positive activities, kindness, and well-being. *The Journal of Positive Psychology, 12*, 385–398.

Lazarus, R. S. (1966). *Psychological stress and the coping process*. New York: McGraw-Hill.

Lazarus, R. S. (2000). Toward better research on stress and coping. *American Psychologist, 55*, 665–673.

Lazarus, R. S., & Folkman, S. (1984). *Stress, appraisal, and coping*. New York: Springer-Verlag.

Le, B., & Agnew, C. R. (2003). Commitment and its theorized determinants: A meta-analysis of the investment model. *Personal Relationships, 10*, 37–57.

Lea, M., Spears, R., & de Groot, D. (2001). Knowing me, knowing you: Anonymity effects on social identity processes within groups. *Personality and Social Psychology Bulletin, 27*, 526–537.

Leary, M. R. (2004). *The curse of the self: Self-awareness, egotism, and the quality of human life*. New York: Oxford University Press.

Leary, M. R., & Kowalski, R. M. (1990). Impression management: A literature review and two-component model. *Psychological Bulletin, 107*, 34–47.

Leary, M. R., & Tate, E. B. (2010). The role of self-awareness and self-evaluation in dysfunctional patterns of thought, emotion, and behavior. In J. E. Maddux & J. P. Tangney (Eds.), *Social psychological foundations of clinical psychology* (pp. 19–35). New York: Guilford Press.

Leary, M. R., Kowalski, R. M., Smith, L., & Phillips, S. (2003). Teasing, rejection, and violence: Case studies of the school shootings. *Aggressive Behavior, 29*, 202–214.

Leary, M. R., Twenge, J. M., & Quinlivan, E. (2006). Interpersonal rejection as a determinant of anger and aggression. *Personality and Social Psychology Review, 10*, 111–132.

Leber, R. (2015, Feb. 11). Obama is right: Climate change kills more people than terrorism. *New Republic*. Retrieved May 29, 2017, from https://newrepublic.com/article/121032/map-climate-change-kills-more-people-worldwide-terrorism

Lee, E. (2004). Effects of visual representation on social influence in computer-mediated communication: Experimental tests of the social identity model of deindividuation effects. *Human Communication Research, 30*, 234–259.

Lee, R. W. (2001). Citizen heroes. *New American, 17*, 19–32.

Lee, S. J. (2009). *Unraveling the "Model Minority" stereotype: Listening to Asian American youth* (2nd ed.). New York: Teachers College, Columbia University.

Lee, Y., & Seligman, M. E. P. (1997). Are Americans more optimistic than the Chinese? *Personality and Social Psychology Bulletin, 23*, 32–40.

Lee, Y-T., McCauley, C., & Jussim, L. (2013). Stereotypes as valid categories of knowledge and human perceptions of group differences. *Social and Personality Psychology Compass, 7*, 470–486.

Lefkowitz, E. S., Shearer, C. L., Gillen, M. M., & Espinosa-Hernandez, G. (2014). How gendered attitudes relate to women's and men's sexual behaviors and beliefs. *Sexuality and Culture*. doi:10.1007/s12119-014-9225-6

Lehmiller, J. J., & Agnew, C. R. (2006). Marginalized relationships: The impact of social disapproval on romantic relationship commitment. *Personality and Social Psychology Bulletin, 32*, 40–51.

Lien, J. W., & Yuan, J. (2015). The cross-sectional "Gambler's Fallacy": Set representativeness in lottery number choices. *Journal of Economic Behavior & Organization, 109*, 163–172.

Leippe, M. R., & Eisenstadt, D. (1994). Generalization of dissonance reduction: Decreasing prejudice through induced compliance. *Journal of Personality and Social Psychology, 67*, 395–413.

Leippe, M. R., & Eisenstadt, D. (1998). A self-accountability model of dissonance reduction: Multiple modes on a continuum of elaboration. In E. Harmon-Jones & J. S. Mills (Eds.), *Cognitive dissonance theory: Revival with revisions and controversies*. Washington, DC: American Psychological Association.

Leite, F. P. (2011). Larger reward values alone are not enough to entice more cooperation. *Thinking & Reasoning, 17*(1), 82–103. doi:10.1080/13546783.2010.537521

Lemay, E. P., Jr., & Clark, M. S. (2008). How the head liberates the heart: Projection of communal responsiveness guides relationship promotion. *Journal of Personality and Social Psychology, 94*, 647–671.

Lemay, E. P., Jr., Clark, M. S., & Feeney, B. C. (2007). Projection of responsiveness to needs and the construction of satisfying communal relationships. *Journal of Personality and Social Psychology, 92*, 834–853.

Lemay, E. P., Jr., Clark, M. S., & Greenberg, A. (2010). What is beautiful is good because what is beautiful is desired: Physical attractiveness stereotyping as projection of interpersonal goals. *Personality and Social Psychology Bulletin, 36*, 339–353.

Leor, J., Poole, W. K., & Kloner, R. A. (1996). Sudden cardiac death triggered by an earthquake. *New England Journal of Medicine, 334*, 413–419.

Lepper, M. R. (1995). Theory by numbers? Some concerns about meta-analysis as a theoretical tool. *Applied Cognitive Psychology, 9*, 411–422.

Lerner, M. J. (1980). *The belief in a just world: A fundamental decision*. New York: Plenum.

Lerner, M. J. (1991). The belief in a just world and the "heroic motive": Searching for "constants" in the psychology of religious ideology. *International Journal for the Psychology of Religion, 1*, 27–32.

Lerner, M. J. (1998). The two forms of belief in a just world. In L. Montada & M. J. Lerner (Eds.), *Responses to victimization and belief in a just world* (pp. 247–269). New York: Plenum Press.

Lerner, M. J., & Grant, P. R. (1990). The influences of commitment to justice and ethnocentrism on children's allocations of pay. *Social Psychology Quarterly, 53*, 229–238.

Lerner, M. J., & Miller, D. T. (1978). Just world research and the attribution process: Looking back and ahead. *Psychological Bulletin, 85*, 1030–1051.

Leskovec, J., & Horvitz, E. (2007). *Worldwide buzz: Planetary-scale views on an instant-messaging network* (Vol. 60). Technical report, Microsoft Research.

Leung, K. (1996). Beliefs in Chinese culture. In M. H. Bond (Ed.), *The handbook of Chinese psychology* (pp. 247–262). Hong Kong: Oxford University Press.

Levenson, H. (1981). Differentiating between internality, powerful others, and chance. In H. M. Lefcourt (Ed.), *Research with the locus of control construct* (Vol. 1, pp. 15–63). New York, NY: Academic Press.

Leventhal, H., Watts, J. C., & Pagano, F. (1967). Effects of fear and instructions on how to cope with danger. *Journal of Personality and Social Psychology, 6*, 313–321.

Levett, L. M. (2013). Co-witness information influences whether a witness is likely to choose from a lineup. *Legal and Criminological Psychology, 18*, 168–180.

Levin, D. T. (2000). Race as a visual feature: Using visual search and perceptual discrimination tasks to understand face categories and the cross-race recognition deficit. *Journal of Experimental Psychology: General, 129*, 559–574.

Levine, J. M., & Moreland, R. L. (1998). Small groups. In D. T. Gilbert, S. T. Fiske, & G. Lindzey (Eds.), *The handbook of social psychology* (4th ed., Vol. 2, pp. 415–469). New York: McGraw-Hill.

Levine, J. M., Higgins, E. T., & Choi, H.-S. (2000). Development of strategic norms in groups. *Organizational Behavior and Human Decision Processes, 82*, 88–101.

Levine, J. M., Moreland, R. L., & Choi, S. (2001). Group socialization and newcomer innovation. In M. Hogg & S. Tindale (Eds.), *Blackwell handbook of social psychology: Group processes* (pp. 86–106). Oxford, England: Blackwell Publishers.

Levine, R. V. (2003). The kindness of strangers: People's willingness to help someone during a chance encounter on a city street varies considerably around the world. *American Scientist, 91*, 226–233.

Levine, R. V., Martinez, T. S., Brase, G., & Sorenson, K. (1994). Helping in 36 U.S. cities. *Journal of Personality and Social Psychology, 67*, 69–82.

Levine, R. V., Norenzayan, A., & Philbrick, K. (2001). Cross-cultural differences in helping strangers. *Journal of Cross-Cultural Psychology, 32*, 543–560.

Levine, R., Sato, S., Hashimoto, T., & Verma, J. (1995). Love and marriage in eleven cultures. *Journal of Cross-Cultural Psychology, 26*, 554–571.

Levine, S. S., Apfelbaum, E. P., Bernard, M., Bartelt, V. L., Zajac, E. J., & Stark, D. (2015). Ethnic diversity deflates price bubbles. *Proceedings of the National Academy of Sciences*. doi:10.1073/pnas.1407301111

Levitan, L. C., & Visser, P. S. (2008). The impact of the social context on resistance to persuasion: Effortful versus effortless responses to counter-attitudinal information. *Journal of Experimental Social Psychology, 44*, 640–649.

Lewin, K. (1943). Defining the "field at a given time." *Psychological Review, 50*, 292–310.

Lewin, K. (1946). Action research and minority problems. *Journal of Social Issues, 2*, 34–46.

Lewin, K. (1947). Frontiers in group dynamics. *Human Relations, 1*, 5–41.

Lewin, K. (1948). *Resolving social conflicts: Selected papers in group dynamics*. New York: Harper.

Lewin, K. (1951). Problems of research in social psychology. In D. Cartwright (Ed.), *Field theory in social science* (pp. 155–169). New York: Harper.

Lewis, G. J., Kandler, C., & Riemann, R. (2014). Distinct heritable influences underpin in-group love and out-group derogation. *Social Psychology and Personality Science, 5*, 407–413.

Lewis, K., Belliveau, M., Herndon, B., & Keller, J. (2007). Group cognition, membership change, and performance: Investigating the benefits and detriments of collective knowledge. *Organizational Behavior and Human Decision Processes, 103*, 159–178.

Lewis, M., & Ramsay, D. (2004). Development of self-recognition, personal pronoun use, and pretend play during the 2nd year. *Child Development, 75*, 1821–1831.

Lewis, R. S., Goto, S. G., & Kong, L. (2008). Culture and context: East Asian American and European American differences in P3 event-related potential. *Personality and Social Psychology Bulletin, 34*, 623–634.

Li, Y. J., Johnson, K. A., Cohen, A. B., Williams, M. J., & Knowles, E. D. (2012). Fundamental(ist) attribution error: Protestants are dispositionally focused. *Journal of Personality and Social Psychology, 102*, 281–290.

Li, Z., Connolly, J., Jiang, D., Pepier, D., & Craig, W. (2010). Adolescent romantic relationships in China and Canada: A cross-national comparison. *International Journal of Behavioral Development, 34*, 113–120.

Liberman, V., Samuels, S. M., & Ross, L. D. (2004). The name of the game: Predictive power of reputations versus situational labels in determining Prisoner's Dilemma Game moves. *Personality and Social Psychology Bulletin, 30*, 1175–1185.

Lick, D. J., Durso, L. E., & Johnson, K. L. (2013). Minority stress and physical health among sexual minorities. *Perspectives on Psychological Science, 8*, 521–548.

Lieberman, M. D. (2013). *Social: Why our brains are wired to connect*. New York: Crown.

Liebert, R. M., & Baron, R. A. (1972). Some immediate effects of televised violence on children's behavior. *Developmental Psychology, 6*, 469–475.

Lilienfeld, S. O., & Byron, R. B. (2013). Your brain on trial. *Scientific American Mind, 23*, 44–53.

Liljenquist, K. A., Zhong, C., & Galinsky, A. D. (2010). The smell of virtue: Clean scents promote reciprocity and charity. *Psychological Science, 21*, 381–383.

Lim, T.-S., & Choi, H.-S. (1996). Interpersonal relationships in Korea. In W. B. Gudykunst, S. Ting-Toomey, & T. Nishida (Eds.), *Communication in personal relationships across cultures* (pp. 122–136). Thousand Oaks, CA: Sage.

Lin, Y. H. W., & Rusbult, C. E. (1995). Commitment to dating relationships and cross-sex friendships in America and China. *Journal of Social and Personal Relationships, 12*, 7–26.

Lindsay, R. C. L., & Wells, G. L. (1985). Improving eyewitness identifications from lineups: Simultaneous versus sequential lineup presentation. *Journal of Applied Psychology, 70*, 556–564.

Linville, P. W., Fischer, G. W., & Salovey, P. (1989). Perceived distributions of characteristics of in-group and out-group members: Empirical evidence and a computer simulation. *Journal of Personality and Social Psychology, 57,* 165–188.

Lippmann, W. (1922). *Public opinion.* New York: Free Press.

Litter prevention (n.d.). Keep America Beautiful. Retrieved September 5, 2011, from www.kab.org/site/PageServer?pagename=focus_litter_prevention#COSTS

Little, A. C., & Perrett, D. I. (2002). Putting beauty back in the eye of the beholder. *Psychologist, 15,* 28–32.

Little, A. C., Jones, B. C., Waitt, C., Tiddeman, B. P., Feinberg, D. R., Perrett, D. I., Apicella, C. L., & Marlowe, F. W. (2008). Symmetry is related to sexual dimorphism in faces: Data across culture and species. *PLoS One, 3,* e2106.

Livesley, W. J., & Bromley, D. B. (1973). *Person perception in childhood and adolescence.* New York: Wiley.

Livingston, R. W., & Pearce, N. A. (2009). The teddy-bear effect: Does having a baby face benefit Black chief executive officers? *Psychological Science, 20,* 1229–1236.

Lloyd, S. A., & Cate, R. M. (1985). The developmental course of conflict in dissolution of premarital relationships. *Journal of Social and Personal Relationships, 2,* 179–194.

Loersch, C., & Payne, B. K. (2011). The situated inference model: An integrative account of the effects of primes on perception, behavior, and motivation. *Perspectives on Psychological Science, 6*(3), 234–252. doi:10.1177/1745691611406921

Loftus, E. F. (1979). *Eyewitness testimony.* Cambridge, MA: Harvard University Press.

Loftus, E. F. (2005). Planting misinformation in the human mind: A 30-year investigation of the malleability of memory. *Learning and Memory, 12,* 361–366.

Loftus, E. F., Garry, M., & Hayne, H. (2008). Repressed and recovered memory. In E. Borgida & S. T. Fiske (Eds.), *Beyond common sense: Psychological science in the courtroom* (pp. 177–194). Malden, MA: Blackwell.

Loftus, E. F., Miller, D. G., & Burns, H. J. (1978). Semantic integration of verbal information into a visual memory. *Journal of Experimental Psychology: Human Learning and Memory, 4,* 19–31.

Lonner, W., & Berry, J. (Eds.). (1986). *Field methods in cross-cultural research.* Beverly Hills, CA: Sage.

Lord, C. G., Lepper, M. R., & Preston, E. (1984). Considering the opposite: A corrective strategy for social judgment. *Journal of Personality and Social Psychology, 47,* 1231–1243.

Lord, R. G., Day, D. V., Zaccaro, S. J., Avolio, B. J., & Eagly, A. H. (2017). Leadership in applied psychology: Three waves of theory and research. *Journal of Applied Psychology, 102,* 434–451.

Lore, R. K., & Schultz, L. A. (1993). Control of human aggression. *American Psychologist, 48,* 16–25.

Lott, A. J., & Lott, B. E. (1974). The role of reward in the formation of positive interpersonal attitudes. In T. L. Huston (Ed.), *Foundations of interpersonal attraction* (pp. 171–189). New York: Academic Press.

Lount, R. B., Jr., & Wilk, S. L. (2014). Working harder or hardly working? Posting performance eliminates social loafing and promotes social laboring in workgroups. *Management Science, 60,* 1098–1106.

Lount, R. B., Jr., Zhong, C.-B., Sivanathan, N., & Murnighan, J. K. (2008). Getting off on the wrong foot: The timing of a breach and the restoration of trust. *Personality and Social Psychology Bulletin, 34*(12), 1601–1612. doi:10.1177/0146167208324512

Lovett, R. A. (2010, March 2). Huge garbage patch found in Atlantic too. *National Geographic News.* National Geographic Society. Retrieved March 8, 2012, from news.nationalgeographic.com/news/2010/03/100302-new-ocean-trash-garbage-patch/

Lu, L., Yuan, Y. C., & McLeod, P. L. (2012). Twenty-five years of hidden profiles in group decision making: A meta-analysis. *Personality and Social Psychology Review, 16,* 54–75.

Lu, M., Fung, H. H., & Doosje, B. (2017). Intergroup conflicts: When interdependent individuals feel less dialectical than independent individuals. *Personality and Individual Differences, 105,* 150–157.

Ludwig, T. D., Gray, T. W., & Rowell, A. (1998). Increasing recycling in academic buildings: A systematic replication. *Journal of Applied Behavior Analysis, 31,* 683–686.

Luo, S., & Zhang, G. (2009). What leads to romantic attraction: Similarity, reciprocity, security, or beauty? Evidence from a speed dating study. *Journal of Personality, 77,* 933–964.

Lupien, S. P., Seery, M. D., & Almonte, J. L. (2010). Discrepant and congruent high self-esteem: Behavioral self-handicapping as a preemptive defensive strategy. *Journal of Experimental Social Psychology, 46,* 1105–1108. doi:10.1016/j.jesp.2010.05.022

Lutz-Zois, C. J., Bradley, A. C., Mihalik, J. L., & Moorman-Eavers, E. R. (2006). Perceived similarity and relationship success among dating couples: An idiographic approach. *Journal of Social and Personal Relationships, 23,* 865–880.

Lykken, D., & Tellegen, A. (1996). Happiness is a stochastic phenomenon. *Psychological Science, 7,* 186–189.

Lynn, M., & Shurgot, B. A. (1984). Responses to lonely hearts advertisements: Effects of reported physical attractiveness, physique, and coloration. *Personality and Social Psychology Bulletin, 10,* 349–357.

Lyubomirsky, S., Layous, K., Chancellor, J., & Nelson, S. K. (2015). Thinking about rumination: The scholarly contributions and intellectual legacy of Susan NolenHoeksema. *Annual Review of Clinical Psychology, 11,* 1–22.

Ma, D. S., & Correll, J. (2011). Target prototypicality moderates racial bias in the decision to shoot. *Journal of Experimental Social Psychology, 47,* 391–396.

Maass, A., Cadinu, M., Guarnieri, G., & Grasselli, A. (2003). Sexual harassment under social identity threat: The computer harassment paradigm. *Journal of Personality and Social Psychology, 85,* 853–870.

Maccoby, E. E., & Jacklin, C. N. (1974). *The psychology of sex differences.* Stanford, CA: Stanford University Press.

MacCoun, R. J. (1989). Experimental research on jury decision-making. *Science, 244,* 1046–1050.

MacDonald, T. K., Zanna, M. P., & Fong, G. T. (1996). Why common sense goes out the window: Effects of alcohol on intentions to use condoms. *Personality and Social Psychology Bulletin, 22,* 763–775.

MacInnis, C. C., & Page-Gould, E. (2015). How can intergroup interaction be bad if intergroup contact is good? Exploring and reconciling an apparent paradox in the science of intergroup relations. *Perspectives on Psychological Science, 10,* 307–327.

Mackie, D. M. (1987). Systematic and nonsystematic processing of majority and minority persuasive communications. *Journal of Personality and Social Psychology, 53,* 41–52.

MacKinnon, C. (1993, July–August). Turning rape into pornography: Postmodern genocide. *Ms.,* pp. 24–30.

Mackinnon, S. P., Jordan, C. H., & Wilson, A. E. (2011). Birds of a feather sit together: Physical similarity predicts seating choice. *Personality and Social Psychology Bulletin, 37,* 879–892.

Maclean, N. (1983). *A river runs through it.* Chicago: University of Chicago Press.

Macrae, C. N., & Bodenhausen, G. V. (2000). Social cognition: Thinking categorically about others. *Annual Review of Psychology, 51,* 93–120.

Madon, S., Guyll, M., Buller, A. A., Scherr, K. C., Willard, J., & Spoth, R. (2008). The mediation of mothers' self-fulfilling effects on their children's alcohol use: Self-verification, informational conformity, and modeling processes. *Journal of Personality and Social Psychology, 95*(2), 369–384. doi:10.1037/0022-3514.95.2.369

Madon, S., Guyll, M., Spoth, R. L., Cross, S. E., & Hilbert, S. J. (2003). The self-fulfilling influence of mother expectations on children's under-age drinking. *Journal of Personality and Social Psychology, 84*(6), 1188–1205. doi:10.1037/0022-3514.84.6.1188

Madon, S., Jussim, L., & Eccles, J. (1997). In search of the powerful self-fulfilling prophecy. *Journal of Personality and Social Psychology, 72,* 791–809. doi:10.1037/0022-3514.72.4.791

Madon, S., Willard, J., Guyll, M., & Scherr, K. C. (2011). Self-fulfilling prophecies: Mechanisms, power, and links to social problems. *Social and Personality Psychology Compass, 5*(8), 578–590. doi:10.1111/j.1751-9004.2011.00375.x

Maio, G. R., Olson, J. M., Allen, L., & Bernard, M. M. (2001). Addressing discrepancies between values and behavior: The motivating effect of reasons. *Journal of Experimental Social Psychology, 37,* 104–117.

Maisel, N. C., & Gable, S. L. (2009). The paradox of received social support: The importance of responsiveness. *Psychological Science, 20*(8), 928–932. doi:10.1111/j.1467-9280.2009.02388.x

Malamuth, N. M., Addison, T., & Koss, M. (2000). Pornography and sexual aggression: Are there reliable effects and can we understand them? *Annual Review of Sex Research 11,* 26–91.

Malamuth, N. M., Hald, G., & Koss, M. (2012). Pornography, individual differences in risk and men's acceptance of violence against women in a representative sample. *Sex Roles, 66,* 427–439.

Mallers, M. H., Claver, M., & Lares, L. A. (2014). Perceived control in the lives of older adults: The influence of Langer and Rodin's work on gerontological theory, policy, and practice. *The Gerontologist, 54,* 67–74.

Mallett, R. K., Wilson, T. D., & Gilbert, D. T. (2008). Expect the unexpected: failure to anticipate similarities leads to an intergroup forecasting error. *Journal of Personality and Social Psychology, 94,* 265–277.

Malloy, T. E. (2001). Difference to inference: Teaching logical and statistical reasoning through online interactivity. *Behavior Research Methods, Instruments, and Computers, 33,* 270–273.

Malpass, R. S., Tredoux, C. G., & McQuiston-Surrett, D. (2007). Lineup construction and lineup fairness. *The handbook of eyewitness psychology,* Vol II: *Memory for people* (pp. 155–178). Mahwah, NJ: Lawrence Erlbaum.

Man, T. W., & Hills, P. J. (2017). Eye-tracking the own-gender bias in face recognition: Other-gender faces are viewed differently to own-gender faces. *Visual Cognition,* 1–12.

Mannes, A. E., Soll, J. B., & Larrick, R. P. (2014). The wisdom of select crowds. *Journal of Personality and Social Psychology, 107,* 276–299. http://dx.doi.org/10.1037/a0036677

Manning, M. (2009). The effects of subjective norms on behaviour in the theory of planned behaviour: A meta-analysis. *British Journal of Social Psychology, 48*(4), 649–705. doi:10.1348/014466608X393136

Mannino, C. A., Snyder, M., & Omoto, A. M. (2011). Why do people get involved? Motivations for volunteerism and other forms of social action. In D. Dunning (Ed.), *Frontiers of social psychology. Social motivation* (pp. 127–146). New York: Psychology Press.

Mannix, E., & Neale, M. A. (2005). What differences make a difference? The promise and reality of diverse teams in organizations. *Psychological Science in the Public Interest, 6,* 31–55.

Marien, H., Aarts, H., & Custers, R. (2016). How goals control behavior: The role of action-outcome and reward information. In T. S. Braver (Ed.), *Motivation and cognitive control* (pp. 145–163). New York: Routledge/Taylor & Francis Group.

Marion, R. (1995, August). The girl who mewed. *Discover,* pp. 38–40.

Markey, P. M. (2000). Bystander intervention in computer-mediated communication. *Computers in Human Behavior, 16,* 183–188.

Markman, K. D., Karadogan, F., Lindberg, M. J., & Zell, E. (2009). Counterfactual thinking: Function and dysfunction. In K. D. Markman, W. M. P. Klein, & J. A. Suhr (Eds.), *Handbook of imagination and mental simulation* (pp. 175–193). New York: Psychology Press.

Markoff, J. (2011, February 16). Computer wins on "Jeopardy!": Trivial, it's not. *The New York Times.* Retrieved April 18, 2011, from www.nytimes.com/2011/02/17/science/17jeopardy-watson.html?pagewanted=2

Markus, H. R. (1977). Self-schemata and processing information about the self. *Journal of Personality and Social Psychology, 35,* 63–78.

Markus, H. R., & Kitayama, S. (1991). Culture and the self: Implications for cognition, emotion, and motivation. *Psychological Review, 98,* 224–253.

Markus, H. R., & Kitayama, S. (2010). Cultures and selves: A cycle of mutual constitution. *Perspectives on Psychological Science, 5*(4), 420–430. doi:10.1177/1745691610375557

Markus, H. R., & Zajonc, R. B. (1985). The cognitive perspective in social psychology. In G. Lindzey & E. Aronson (Eds.), *Handbook of social psychology* (3rd ed., Vol. 1, pp. 137–230). New York: McGraw-Hill.

Markus, H. R., Kitayama, S., & Heiman, R. J. (1996). Culture and "basic" psychological principles. In E. T. Higgins & A. W. Kruglanski (Eds.), *Social psychology: Handbook of basic principles* (pp. 857–913). New York: Guilford Press.

Markus, H. R., Uchida, Y., Omoregie, H., Townsend, S. S., & Kitayama, S. (2006). Going for the gold models of agency in Japanese and American contexts. *Psychological Science, 17,* 103–112.

Marlatt, G. A., & Rohsenow, D. J. (1980). Cognitive processes in alcohol use: Expectancy and the balanced placebo design. In N. K. Mello (Ed.), *Advances in substance abuse* (Vol. 1). Greenwich, CT: JAI Press.

Marques, J., Abrams, D., & Serodio, R. (2001). Being better by being right: Subjective group dynamics and derogation of in-group deviants when generic norms are undermined. *Journal of Personality and Social Psychology, 81,* 436–447.

Marsland, A., Bachen, E. A., & Cohen, S. (2012). Stress, immunity, and susceptibility to upper respiratory infectious disease. In A. Baum, T. A. Revenson, & J. Singer (Eds.), *Handbook of health psychology* (2nd ed., pp. 717–738). New York, NY: Psychology Press.

Marsh, A. A. (2016). Extraordinary altruism. In J. D. Greene, I. Morrison, & M. E. P. Seligman, *Positive neuroscience* (pp. 143–158). New York: Oxford University Press.

Martin, P. Y., & Martin, R. (2013). Morningness–eveningness orientation and attitude change: Evidence for greater systematic processing and attitude change at optimal time-of-day. *Personality and Individual Differences, 54,* 551–556.

Martinez, G., Copen, C. E., & Abma J. C. (2011). Teenagers in the United States: Sexual activity, contraceptive use, and childbearing, 2006–2010 National Survey of Family Growth. National Center for Health Statistics. *Vital Health Statistics, 23*(31). Retrieved November 1, 2011, from www.cdc.gov/nchs/data/series/sr_23/sr23_031.pdf

Martinez, L. (2012, January 11). U.S. Marines allegedly urinate on Taliban corpses. *ABC News.* Available online at: http://abcnews.go.com/Blotter/marines-allegedly-urinate-taliban-corpes/story?id=15341700#.T1GNRcxLWpc

Masicampo, E. J., & Ambady, N. (2014). Predicting fluctuations in widespread interest: Memory decay and goal-related memory accessibility in Internet search trends. *Journal of Experimental Psychology: General, 143,* 205–214.

Mason, M. F., & Morris, M. W. (2010). Culture, attribution and automaticity: A social cognitive neuroscience view. *Social Cognitive and Affective Neuroscience, 5,* 292–306.

Masuda, T., & Nisbett, R. E. (2006). Culture and change blindness. *Cognitive Science: A Multidisciplinary Journal, 30,* 381–399.

Masuda, T., Ellsworth, P. C., & Mesquita, B. (2008). Placing the face in context: Cultural differences in the perception of facial emotion. *Journal of Personality and Social Psychology, 94*(3), 365–381.

Masuda, T., Ishii, K., & Kimura, J. (2016). When does the culturally dominant mode of attention appear or disappear? Comparing patterns of eye movement during the visual flicker task between European Canadians and Japanese. *Journal of Cross-Cultural Psychology, 47*(7), 997–1014.

Matlin, M. W. (2012). *Psychology of women* (7th ed.). Belmont, CA: Wadsworth.

Matsumoto, D., & Hwang, H. S. (2010). Judging faces in context. *Social and Personality Psychology Compass, 4,* 393–402.

Matsumoto, D., & Willingham, B. (2006). The thrill of victory and the agony of defeat: Spontaneous expressions of medal winners of the 2004 Athens Olympic games. *Journal of Personality and Social Psychology, 91,* 568–581.

Maxwell, K. A. (2002). Friends: The role of peer influence across adolescent risk behaviors. *Journal of Youth and Adolescence, 31,* 267–277.

Mayo Clinic. (n.d.). Diseases and conditions. Retrieved August 19, 2014, from http://www.mayoclinic.org/diseases-conditions

Mazur, A., Booth, A., & Dabbs, J. M. (1992). Testosterone and chess competition. *Social Psychology Quarterly, 55,* 70–77.

McAlister, A., Perry, C., Killen, J. D., Slinkard, L. A., & Maccoby, N. (1980). Pilot study of smoking, alcohol, and drug abuse prevention. *American Journal of Public Health, 70,* 719–721.

McArthur, L. Z. (1972). The how and what of why: Some determinants and consequences of causal attribution. *Journal of Personality and Social Psychology, 22,* 171–193.

McCauley, C. (1989). The nature of social influence in groupthink: Compliance and internalization. *Journal of Personality and Social Psychology, 57,* 250–260.

McClellan, S. (2008). *What happened: Inside the Bush White House and Washington's culture of deception.* New York: Public Affairs.

McConahay, J. B. (1981). Reducing racial prejudice in desegregated schools. In W. D. Hawley (Ed.), *Effective school desegregation.* Beverly Hills, CA: Sage.

McCrea, S., Hirt, E., & Milner, B. (2008). She works hard for the money: Valuing effort underlies gender differences in behavioral self-handicapping. *Journal of Experimental Social Psychology, 44,* 292–311.

McFadyen-Ketchum, S. A., Bates, J. E., Dodge, K. A., & Pettit, G. S. (1996). Patterns of change in early childhood aggressive-disruptive behavior: Gender differences in predictions from early coercive and affectionate mother-child interactions. *Child Development, 67,* 2417–2433.

McGlone, M., & Aronson, J. (2006). Social identity salience and stereotype threat. *Journal of Applied Developmental Psychology, 27,* 486–493.

McGuire, M., & Pezdek, K. (2014). Birds of a feather get misidentified together: High entativity decreases recognition accuracy for groups of other-race faces. *Legal and Criminological Psychology.* doi:10.1111/lcrp.12066

McGuire, W. J. (1964). Inducing resistance to persuasion. In L. Berkowitz (Ed.), *Advances in experimental social psychology* (Vol. 1, pp. 192–229). New York: Academic Press.

McKown, C., & Weinstein, R. (2008). Teacher expectations, classroom context, and the achievement gap. *Journal of School Psychology, 46*(3), 235–261. doi:10.1016/j.jsp.2007.05.001

McLeod, P. L. (2013). Distributed people and distributed information: Vigilant decision-making in virtual teams. *Small Group Research, 44,* 627–657.

McLeod, P. L., Lobel, S. A., & Cox, T. H., Jr. (1996). Ethnic diversity and creativity in small groups. *Small Group Research, 27,* 248–264.

McMillan, W., Stice, E., & Rohde, P. (2011). High-and low-level dissonance-based eating disorder prevention programs with young women with body image concerns: An experimental trial. *Journal of Consulting and Clinical Psychology, 79,* 129–134.

McMullin, D., & White, J. W. (2006). Long-term effects of labeling a rape experience. *Psychology of Women Quarterly, 30,* 96–105.

McNally, R. J. (2017). False memories in the laboratory and in life: Commentary on Brewin and Andrews (2016). *Applied Cognitive Psychology, 31,* 40–41.

McNally, R. J., & Geraerts, E. (2009). A new solution to the recovered memory debate. *Perspectives on Psychological Science, 4*(2), 126–134. doi:10.1111/j.1745-6924.2009.01112.x

McNally, R. J., Bryant, R. A., & Ehlers, A. (2003). Does early psychological intervention promote recovery from posttraumatic stress? *Psychological Science in the Public Interest, 4,* 45–79.

McNulty, J. K., O'Mara, E. M., & Karney, B. R. (2008). Benevolent cognitions as a strategy of relationship maintenance: "Don't sweat the small stuff" … But it is not all small stuff. *Journal of Personality and Social Psychology, 94,* 631–646.

McPherson, M., Smith-Lovin, L., & Cook, J. M. (2001). Birds of a feather: Homophily in social networks. *Annual Review of Sociology, 27,* 415–444.

Medvec, V. H., Madey, S. F., & Gilovich, T. (1995). When less is more: Counterfactual thinking and satisfaction among Olympic medalists. *Journal of Personality and Social Psychology, 69,* 603–610.

Meeus, W. H. J., & Raaijmakers, Q. A. W. (1995). Obedience in modern society: The Utrecht studies. *Journal of Social Issues, 51,* 155–175.

Mehl, M. R., Vazire, S., Ramírez-Esparza, N., & Pennebacker, J. W. (2007). Are women really more talkative than men? *Science, 317,* 82.

Mehta, P. H., & Beer, J. (2010). Neural mechanisms of the testosterone–aggression relation: the role of orbitofrontal cortex. *Journal of Cognitive Neuroscience, 22,* 2357–2368.

Mehta, P. H., & Josephs, R. A. (2010). Testosterone and cortisol jointly regulate dominance: Evidence for a dual-hormone hypothesis. *Hormones and Behavior, 58,* 898–906.

Meier, B. P., Robinson, M. D., Carter, M. S., & Hinsz, V. B. (2010). Are sociable people more beautiful? A zero-acquaintance analysis of agreeableness, extraversion, and attractiveness. *Journal of Research in Personality, 44,* 293–296.

Meier, B. P., Schnall, S., Schwarz, N., & Bargh, J. A. (2012). Embodiment in social psychology. *Topics in Cognitive Science, 4,* 705–716.

Meindl, J. R., & Lerner, M. J. (1985). Exacerbation of extreme responses to an out-group. *Journal of Personality and Social Psychology, 47,* 71–84.

Meissner, C. A., & Brigham, J. C. (2001). Thirty years of investigating the own-race bias in memory for faces: A meta-analytic review. *Psychology, Public Policy, and Law, 7,* 3–35.

Meissner, C. A., Tredoux, C. G., & Parker, J. F. (2005). Eyewitness decisions in simultaneous and sequential lineups: A dual-process signal detection theory analysis. *Memory and Cognition, 33,* 783–792.

Mell, J. N., van Knippenberg, D., & van Ginkel, W. P. (2014). The catalyst effect: The impact of transactive memory system structure on team performance. *Academy of Management Journal, 57,* 1154–1173.

Meltzer, A. L., McNulty, J. K., Jackson, G. L., & Karney, B. R. (2014). Sex differences in the implications of partner physical attractiveness for the trajectory of marital satisfaction. *Journal of Personality and Social Psychology, 106,* 418–428.

Mendoza-Denton, R., & Page-Gould, E. (2008). Can cross-group friendships influence minority students' well-being at historically white universities? *Psychological Science, 19,* 933–939.

Menon, T., Morris, M. W., Chiu, C., & Hong, Y. (1999). Culture and the construal of agency: Attribution to individual versus group dispositions. *Journal of Personality and Social Psychology, 76,* 701–717.

Menon, T., Sheldon, O. J., & Galinsky, A. D. (2014). Barriers to transforming hostile relations: Why friendly gestures can backfire. *Negotiation and Conflict Management Research, 7,* 17–37.

Meston, C. M., & Frohlich, P. F. (2003). Love at first fright: Partner salience moderates roller-coaster-induced excitation transfer. *Archives of Sexual Behavior, 32*(6), 537–544.

Meyer, B., Schermuly, C. C., & Kauffeld, S. (2016). That's not my place: The interacting effects of faultlines, subgroup size, and social competence on social loafing behaviour in work groups. *European Journal of Work and Organizational Psychology, 25,* 31–49.

Meyersburg, C. A., Bogdan, R., Gallo, D. A., & McNally, R. J. (2009). False memory propensity in people reporting recovered memories of past lives. *Journal of Abnormal Psychology, 118*(2), 399–404. doi:10.1037/a0015371

Mezulis, A. H., Abramson, L. Y., Hyde, J. S., & Hankin, B. L. (2004). Is there a universal positivity bias in attributions? A meta-analytic review of individual, developmental, and cultural differences in the self-serving attributional bias. *Psychological Bulletin, 130*(5), 711–747.

Migration and geographic mobility in metropolitan and nonmetropolitan America, 1995–2000 (2003). United States Census Bureau. Accessed on April 16, 2006, at www.census.gov/prod/2003pubs/censr-9.pdf

Mikulincer, M., Shaver, P. R., Sapir-Lavid, Y., & Avihou-Kanza, N. (2009). What's inside the minds of securely and insecurely attached people? The secure-base script and its associations with attachment-style dimensions. *Journal of Personality and Social Psychology, 97*, 615–633.

Milgram, S. (1961). Nationality and conformity. *Scientific American, 205*, 45–51.

Milgram, S. (1963). Behavioral study of obedience. *Journal of Abnormal and Social Psychology, 67*, 371–378.

Milgram, S. (1970). The experience of living in cities. *Science, 167*, 1461-1468.

Milgram, S. (1974). *Obedience to authority: An experimental view.* New York: Harper & Row.

Milgram, S. (1976). Obedience to criminal orders: The compulsion to do evil. In T. Blass (Ed.), *Contemporary social psychology: Representative readings* (pp. 175–184). Itasca, IL: Peacock.

Mill, J. S. (1843). *A system of logic ratiocinative and inductive.* London.

Miller, A. G. (1986). *The obedience experiments: A case study of controversy in social science.* New York: Praeger.

Miller, A. G. (1995). Constructions of the obedience experiments: A focus upon domains of relevance. *Journal of Social Issues, 51*, 33–53.

Miller, A. G. (2009). Reflections on 'Replicating Milgram' (Burger, 2009). *American Psychologist, 64*, 20–27.

Miller, A. G., Ashton, W., & Mishal, M. (1990). Beliefs concerning the features of constrained behavior: A basis for the fundamental attribution error. *Journal of Personality and Social Psychology, 59*, 635–650.

Miller, A. G., Collins, B. E., & Brief, D. E. (1995). Perspectives on obedience to authority: The legacy of the Milgram experiments. *Journal of Social Issues, 51*, 1–19.

Miller, C. E., & Anderson, P. D. (1979). Group decision rules and the rejection of deviates. *Social Psychology Quarterly, 42*, 354–363.

Miller, C. H., Lane, L. T., Deatrick, L. M., Young, A. M., & Potts, K. A. (2007). Psychological reactance and promotional health messages: The effects of controlling language, lexical concreteness, and the restoration of freedom. *Human Communication Research, 33*, 219–240.

Miller, C. T. (1982). The role of performance-related similarity in social comparison of abilities: A test of the related attributes hypothesis. *Journal of Experimental Social Psychology, 18*, 513–523.

Miller, D. P., Jr., Spangler, J. G., Vitolins, M. Z., Davis, S. W., Ip, E. H., et al. (2013). Are medical students aware of their anti-obesity bias? *Academic Medicine, 88*, 978–982.

Miller, D. T., & Prentice, D. A. (1996). The construction of social norms and standards. In E. T. Higgins & A. W. Kruglanski (Eds.), *Social psychology: Handbook of basic principles* (pp. 799–829). New York: Guilford Press.

Miller, D. T., & Ross, M. (1975). Self-serving biases in the attribution of causality: Fact or fiction? *Psychological Bulletin, 82*, 213–225.

Miller, D., & Taylor, B. (2002). Counterfactual thought, regret, and superstition: How to avoid kicking yourself. In T. Gilovich, D. Griffiin, & D. Kahneman (Eds.), *Heuristics and biases: The psychology of intuitive judgement* (pp. 367–378). New York: Cambridge University Press.

Miller, J. A., Pusey, A. E., Gilby, I. C., Schroepfer-Walker, K., Markham, A. C., & Murray, C. M. (2014). Competing for space: female chimpanzees are more aggressive inside than outside their core areas. *Animal Behaviour, 87*, 147–152.

Miller, J. G. (1984). Culture and the development of everyday social explanation. *Journal of Personality and Social Psychology, 46*, 961–978.

Minard, R. D. (1952). Race relations in the Pocahontas coal field. *Journal of Social Issues, 8*, 29–44.

Mischel, W., & Shoda, Y. (1995). A cognitive affective system theory of personality: Reconceptualizing situations, dispositions, dynamics, and invariance in personality structures. *Psychological Review, 102*, 246–268.

Mischel, W., Zeiss, A. R., & Ebbesen, E. B. (1972). Cognitive and attentional mechanisms in delay of gratification. *Journal of Personality and Social Psychology, 21*, 204–218.

Misra, S., Cheng, L., Genevie, J., & Yuan, M. (2016). The iPhone effect: The quality of in-person social interactions in the presence of mobile devices. *Environment and Behavior, 48*, 275–298.

Miyake, A., Kost-Smith, L. E., Finkelstein, N. D., Pollock, S. J., Cohen, G. L., & Ito, T. A. (2010). Reducing the gender achievement gap in college science: A classroom study of values affirmation. *Science, 330*, 1234–1237.

Miyamoto, Y. (2013). Culture and analytic versus holistic cognition: Toward multilevel analyses of cultural influences. *Advances in Experimental Social Psychology, 47*, 131–188.

Miyamoto, Y., & Kitayama, S. (2002). Cultural variation in correspondence bias: The critical role of attitude diagnosticity of socially constrained behavior. *Journal of Personality and Social Psychology, 83*, 1239–1248.

Mobius, M. M., & Rosenblat, T. S. (2006). Why beauty matters. *The American Economic Review, 96*, 222–235.

Modigliani, A., & Rochat, F. (1995). The role of interaction sequences and the timing of resistance in shaping obedience and defiance to authority. *Journal of Social Issues, 51*, 107–123.

Moghaddam, F. M., Taylor, D. M., & Wright, S. (1993). *Social psychology in cross-cultural perspective.* New York: Freeman.

Mojaverian, T., & Kim, H. S. (2013). Interpreting a helping hand: Cultural variation in the effectiveness of solicited and unsolicited social support. *Personality and Social Psychology Bulletin, 39*, 88–99.

Mojzisch, A., & Schulz-Hardt, S. (2010). Knowing others' preferences degrades the quality of group decisions. *Journal of Personality and Social Psychology, 98*(5), 794–808. doi:10.1037/a0017627

Mok, A., & Morris, M. W. (2010). An upside to bicultural identity conflict: Resisting groupthink in cultural ingroups. *Journal of Experimental Social Psychology, 46*(6), 1114–1117. doi:10.1016/j.jesp.2010.05.020

Monfardini, E., Redouté, J., Hadj-Bouziane, F., Hynaux, C., Fradin, J., Huguet, P., ... & Meunier, M. (2016). Others' sheer presence boosts brain activity in the attention (but not the motivation) network. *Cerebral Cortex, 26*, 2427–2439.

Monga, A. (S.) B., & Williams, J. D. (2016). Cross-cultural styles of thinking and their influence on consumer behavior. *Current Opinion in Psychology, 10*, 65–69.

Monin, J., Clark, M., & Lemay, E. (2008). Communal responsiveness in relationships with female versus male family members. *Sex Roles, 59*, 176–188.

Monson, C. M., Langhinrichsen-Rohling, J., & Binderup, T. (2000). Does "no" really mean "no" after you say "yes"? Attributions about date and marital rape. *Journal of Interpersonal Violence, 15*, 1156–1174.

Montemayor, R., & Eisen, M. (1977). The development of self-conceptions from childhood to adolescence. *Developmental Psychology, 13*, 314–319.

Montgomery, L. (2014, June 1). Evidence of climate change laps at Norfolk's feet. *Washington Post*, pp. A1, A9.

Monto, M. A., & Carey, A. G. (2014). A new standard of sexual behavior? Are claims associated with the hookup culture" supported by general social survey data? *Journal of Sex Research, 51*, 605–615.

Montoya, R. M., & Horton, R. S. (2013). A meta-analytic investigation of the processes underlying the similarity-attraction effect. *Journal of Social and Personal Relationships, 30*, 64–94.

Montoya, R. M., & Insko, C. A. (2008). Toward a more complete understanding of the reciprocity of liking effect. *European Journal of Social Psychology, 38*, 477–498.

Montoya, R. M., Horton, R. S., & Kirchner, J. (2008). Is actual similarity necessary for attraction? A meta-analysis of actual and perceived similarity. *Journal of Social and Personal Relationships, 25*, 889–922.

Montoya, R. M., Horton, R. S., Vevea, J. L., Citkowicz, M., & Lauber, E. A. (2017). A re-examination of the mere exposure effect: The influence of repeated exposure on recognition, familiarity, and liking. *Psychological Bulletin, 143*, 459–498.

Mooney, C. (2017, Jan. 18). U.S. scientists officially declare 2016 the hottest year on record. That makes three in a row. *Washington Post.* Retrieved May 29, 2017, from https://www.washingtonpost.com/news/energy-environment/wp/2017/01/18/u-s-scientists-officially-declare-2016-the-hottest-year-on-record-that-makes-three-in-a-row/?utm_term=.a919bf5f55cc

Moore, B., Jr. (1978). *Injustice: The social bases of obedience and revolt.* White Plains, NY: Sharpe.

Moore, R. L. (1998). Love and limerance with Chinese characteristics: Student romance in the PRC. In V. C. de Munck (Ed.), *Romantic love and sexual behavior* (pp. 251–283). Westport, CT: Praeger.

Moors, A., & De Houwer, J. (2006). Automaticity: A theoretical and conceptual analysis. *Psychological Bulletin, 132*, 297–326.

Mor, N., Doane, L. D., Adam, E. K., Mineka, S., Zinbarg, R. E., Griffith, J. W., ... Nazarian, M. (2010). Within-person variations in self-focused attention and negative affect in depression and anxiety: A diary study. *Cognition and Emotion, 24*, 48–62. doi:10.1080/02699930802499715

Moran, J. M., Jolly, E., & Mitchell, J. O. (2014). Spontaneous mentalizing predicts the fundamental attribution error. *Journal of Cognitive Neuroscience, 26*, 569–576.

Moran, S., & Ritov, I. (2007). Experience in integrative negotiations: What needs to be learned? *Journal of Experimental Social Psychology, 43*, 77–90.

Moreland, R. L. (2010). Are dyads really groups? *Small Group Research, 41*(2), 251–267. doi:10.1177/1046496409358618

Moreland, R. L., & Beach, S. R. (1992). Exposure effects in the classroom: The development of affinity among students. *Journal of Experimental Social Psychology, 28*, 255–276.

Moreland, R. L., & Topolinski, S. (2010). The mere exposure phenomenon: A lingering melody by Robert Zajonc. *Emotion Review, 2*, 329–339.

Morgan, C. A. III, Southwick, S., Steffian, G., Hazlett, G. A., & Loftus, E. F. (2013). Misinformation can influence memory for recently experienced, highly stressful events. *International Journal of Law and Psychiatry, 36*, 11–17.

Morin, A. (2011). Self-awareness Part 1: Definition, measures, effects, functions, and antecedents. *Social and Personality Compass, 5*, 807–823.

Morling, B. (2016). Cultural difference, inside and out. *Social and Personality Psychology Compass, 10*, 693–706.

Morling, B., & Evered, S. (2006). Secondary control reviewed and defined. *Psychological Bulletin, 132*, 269–296.

Morling, B., & Lamoreaux, M. (2008). Measuring culture outside the head: A meta-analysis of individualism-collectivism in cultural products. *Personality and Social Psychology Review, 12*, 199–221.

Morris, E. (Director). (1988). *The thin blue line* [Film]. New York: HBO Videos.

Morris, W. N., & Miller, R. S. (1975). The effects of consensus-breaking and consensus-preempting partners on reduction of conformity. *Journal of Experimental Social Psychology, 11*, 215–223.

Morry, M. M. (2007). The attraction-similarity hypothesis among cross-sex friends: Relationship satisfaction, perceived similarities, and self-serving perceptions. *Journal of Social and Personal Relationships, 24*, 117–138.

Morse, D. R., Martin, J., & Moshonov, J. (1991). Psychosomatically induced death relative to stress, hypnosis, mind control, and voodoo: Review and possible mechanisms. *Stress Medicine, 7,* 213–232.

Morton, T. A., Postmes, T., Haslam, S. A., & Hornsey, M. J. (2009). Theorizing gender in the face of social change: Is there anything essential about essentialism? *Journal of Personality and Social Psychology, 96,* 653–664.

Moscovici, S. (1985). Social influence and conformity. In G. Lindzey & E. Aronson (Eds.), *Handbook of social psychology* (3rd ed., Vol. 2, pp. 347–412). New York: McGraw-Hill.

Moscovici, S. (1994). Three concepts: Minority, conflict, and behavioral style. In S. Moscovici, A. Mucchi-Faina, & A. Maass (Eds.), *Minority influence* (pp. 233–251). Chicago: Nelson-Hall.

Moscovici, S., & Nemeth, C. (1974). Minority influence. In C. Nemeth (Ed.), *Social psychology: Classic and contemporary integrations* (pp. 217–249). Chicago: Rand McNally.

Moscovici, S., Mucchi-Faina, A., & Maass, A. (Eds.). (1994). *Minority influence.* Chicago: Nelson-Hall.

Moss-Racusin, C. A., Dovidio, J. F., Brescoll, V. L., Graham, M. J., & Handelsman, J. (2012). Science faculty's subtle gender biases favor male students. *PNAS, 109,* 16474–16479.

Mostert, M. P. (2010). Facilitated communication and its legitimacy—Twenty-first century developments. *Exceptionality, 18*(1), 31–41. doi:10.1080/09362830903462524

Mouzon, D. M., Taylor, R. J., Woodward, A. T., & Chatters, L. M. (2017). Everyday racial discrimination, everyday non-racial discrimination, and physical health among African-Americans. *Journal of Ethnic and Cultural Diversity in Social Work, 26,* 68–80.

Moyer, K. E. (1976). *The Psychobiology of Aggression.* New York: Harper & Row.

Moynihan, A. B., Igou, E. R., & van Tilburg, W. A. P. (2017). Free, connected, and meaningful: Free will beliefs promote meaningfulness through belongingness. *Personality and Individual Differences, 107,* 54–65.

Mucchi-Faina, A., & Pagliaro, S. (2008). Minority influence: The role of ambivalence toward the source. *European Journal of Social Psychology, 38,* 612–623.

Muchnik, L., Aral, S., & Taylor, S. J. (2013). Social influence bias: A randomized experiment. *Science, 341,* 647–651.

Mueller, P. A., & Oppenheimer, D. M. (2014). The pen is mightier than the keyboard: Advantages of longhand over laptop note taking. *Psychological Science, 25,* 1159–1168.

Mullen, B. (1986). Atrocity as a function of lynch mob composition: A self-attention perspective. *Personality and Social Psychology Bulletin, 12,* 187–197.

Mullen, B., & Cooper, C. (1994). The relation between group cohesiveness and performance: An integration. *Psychological Bulletin, 115,* 210–227.

Muller, D., & Butera, F. (2007). The focusing effect of self-evaluation threat in coaction and social comparison. *Journal of Personality and Social Psychology, 93,* 194–211.

Muller, D., Atzeni, T., & Fabrizio, B. (2004). Coaction and upward social comparison reduce the illusory conjunction effect: Support for distraction-conflict theory. *Journal of Experimental Social Psychology, 40,* 659–665.

Mun, C. Jung, Karoly, P., Okun, M. A., Kim, H., & Tennen, H. (2016). Affect, work-goal schemas, and work-goal striving among adults with chronic pain: A multilevel structural equation analysis. *Journal of Behavioral Medicine, 39,* 288–299.

Muraven, M., Tice, D. M., & Baumeister, R. F. (1998). Self-control as limited resource: Regulatory depletion patterns. *Journal of Personality and Social Psychology, 74,* 774–789.

Murr, A., & Smalley, S. (2003, March 17). White power, minus the power. *Newsweek,* pp. 42–45.

Mushquash, A. R., Stewart, S. H., Sherry, S. B., Mackinnon, S. P., Antony, M. M., & Sherry, D. L. (2011). Heavy episodic drinking among dating partners: A longitudinal actor-partner interdependence model. *Psychology of Addictive Behaviors.* Available online. doi:10.1037/a0026653

Mussweiler, T., & Förster, J. (2000). The sex-aggression link: A perception-behavior dissociation. *Journal of Personality and Social Psychology, 79,* 507–520.

Myers, A. L., McCrea, S. M., & Tyser, M. P. (2014). The role of thought-content and mood in the preparative benefits of upward counterfactual thinking. *Motivation and Emotion, 38*(1), 166–182.

Myers, D. G., & Scanzoni, L. D. (2006). *What God has joined together: The Christian case for gay marriage.* Harper Collins: San Francisco.

Myers, H. F. (2009). Ethnicity and socioeconomic status-related stresses in context: An integrative review and conceptual model. *Journal of Behavioral Medicine, 32*(1), 9–19. doi:10.1007/s10865-008-9181-4

Nadal, K., Griffin, K. E., Vargas, V. M., Issa, M., Lyons, O. B., & Tobio, M. (2011). Processes and struggles with racial microaggressions from the White American perspective: Recommendations for workplace settings. In M. A. Paludi, C. A. Paludi, Jr., & E. R. DeSouza (Eds.), *Praeger handbook on understanding and preventing workplace discrimination* (pp. 155–180). Santa Barbara, CA: Praeger/ABC-CLIO.

Nail, P. R. (1986). Toward an integration of some models and theories of social response. *Psychological Bulletin, 100,* 190–206.

Naimi, T., Brewer, B., Mokdad, A., Serdula, M., Denny, C., & Marks, J. (2003). Binge drinking among U.S. adults. *Journal of the American Medical Association, 289,* 70–75.

Napper, L. E., Kenney, S. R., & LaBrie, J. W. (2015). The longitudinal relationships among injunctive norms and hooking up attitudes and behaviors in college students. *Journal of Sex Research, 52,* 499–506.

Nasco, S. A., & Marsh, K. L. (1999). Gaining control through counter-factual thinking. *Personality and Social Psychology Bulletin, 25,* 556–568.

National Center for Health Statistics. (2005). Marriage and divorce. Retrieved September 19, 2006, from www.cdc.gov/nchs/fastats/divorce.html2

National Energy Study. (2014). A study of the effects of feedback on domestic energy use. Available: http://cdn2.hubspot.net/hub/63188/file-1082558786-pdf/docs/NES_report_final_-_public_version.pdf

National Research Council. (2012). *Deterrence and the death penalty.* National Academies Press.

Naughton, F., Eborall, H., & Sutton, S. (2012). Dissonance and disengagement in pregnant smokers. *Journal of Smoking Cessation, 8,* 24–32.

NCHS Data Brief (2015). Prevalence of obesity among adults and youth: United States, 2011–2014. Available: https://www.cdc.gov/nchs/data/databriefs/db219.pdf

Nedelec, J. L., & Beaver, K. M. (2014). Physical attractiveness as a phenotypic marker of health: An assessment using a nationally representative sample of American adults. *Evolution and Human Behavior.* doi:10.1016/j.evolhumbe-hav.2014.06.004

Neighbors, C., O'Connor, R. M., Lewis, M. A., Chawla, N., Lee, C. M., & Fossos, N. (2008). The relative impact of injunctive norms on college student drinking: The role of reference group. *Psychology of Addictive Behaviors, 22,* 576–581.

Nelson, M. R. (2008). The hidden persuaders: Then and now. *Journal of Advertising, 37,* 113–126. doi:10.2753/JOA0091-3367370109

Nelson, S. (Writer, Producer, Director). (2010). *Freedom riders* [motion picture]. United States: American Experience (Public Broadcasting Service: WGBH, Boston). Available from http://www.pbs.org/wgbh/americanexperience/freedomriders/

Nemeth, C. J., & Chiles, C. (1988). Modeling courage: The role of dissent in fostering independence. *European Journal of Social Psychology, 18,* 275–280.

Neria, Y., DiGrande, L., & Adams, B. G. (2011). Posttraumatic stress disorder following the September 11, 2001, terrorist attacks: A review of the literature among highly exposed populations. *American Psychologist, 66*(6), 429–446. doi:10.1037/a0024791

Neuberg, S. L. (1988). Behavioral implications of information presented outside of awareness: The effect of subliminal presentation of trait information on behavior in the prisoner's dilemma game. *Social Cognition, 6,* 207–230.

Neuberg, S. L., Kenrick, D. T., & Schaller, M. (2010). Evolutionary social psychology. In S. T. Fiske, D. T. Gilbert, & G. Lindzey (Eds.), *Handbook of social psychology* (5th ed., Vol. 2, pp. 761–796). Hoboken, NJ: John Wiley.

Newcomb, T. M. (1961). *The acquaintance process.* New York: Holt, Rinehart and Winston.

Newkirk, V. R. (2016, Nov. 9). What went wrong with the 2016 polls? *The Atlantic.* Retrieved January 30, 2017, from http://www.theatlantic.com/politics/archive/2016/11/what-went-wrong-polling-clinton-trump/507188/

Newman, L. S. (1996). Trait impressions as heuristics for predicting future behavior. *Personality and Social Psychology Bulletin, 22,* 395–411.

Newman, L. S., & Bakina, D. A. (2009). Do people resist social-psychological perspectives on wrongdoing? Reactions to dispositional, situational, and interactionist explanations. *Social Influence, 4,* 256–273.

Nicholson, I. (2011). "Torture at Yale": Experimental subjects, laboratory torment, and the "rehabilitation" of Milgram's "Obedience to Authority." *Theory and Psychology, 21,* 737–761.

Nielsen, K., & Cleal, B. (2011). Under which conditions do middle managers exhibit transformational leadership behaviors?—An experience sampling method study on the predictors of transformational leadership behaviors. *Leadership Quarterly, 22*(2), 344–352. doi:10.1016/j.leaqua.2011.02.009

Nisbett, R. E. (1993). Violence and U.S. regional culture. *American Psychologist, 48,* 441–449.

Nisbett, R. E. (2003). *The geography of thought: How Asians and Westerners think differently … and why.* New York: Free Press.

Nisbett, R. E. (2015). *Mindware: Tools for smart thinking.* New York: Farrar, Straus and Giroux.

Nisbett, R. E., & Masuda, T. (2003). Culture and point of view. *Proceedings of the National Academy of Sciences, 100,* 11163–11170.

Nisbett, R. E., & Ross, L. (1980). *Human inference: Strategies and shortcomings of human judgment.* Englewood Cliffs, NJ: Prentice Hall.

Nisbett, R. E., & Wilson, T. D. (1977). Telling more than we can know: Verbal reports on mental processes. *Psychological Review, 84,* 231–259.

Nisbett, R. E., Fong, G. T., Lehman, D. R., & Cheng, P. W. (1987). Teaching reasoning. *Science, 238,* 625–631.

Nixon, R. M. (1990). *In the arena: A memoir of victory, defeat, and renewal.* New York: Simon & Schuster.

Noar, S. M., Benac, C. N., & Harris, M. S. (2007). Does tailoring matter? Meta-analytic review of tailored print health behavior change interventions. *Psychological Bulletin, 133,* 673–693.

Nolan, J., Schultz, P., Cialdini, R., Goldstein, N., & Griskevicius, V. (2008). Normative social influence is underdetected. *Personality and Social Psychology Bulletin, 34,* 913–923.

Norenzayan, A., & Heine, S. J. (2005). Psychological universals: What are they and how can we know? *Psychological Bulletin, 131,* 763–784.

Norenzayan, A., & Nisbett, R. E. (2000). Culture and causal cognition. *Current Direction in Psychological Science, 9,* 132–135.

Norenzayan, A., Choi, I., & Peng, K. (2007). Perception and cognition. In S. Kitayama & D. Cohen (Eds.), *Handbook of cultural psychology* (pp. 569–594). New York: Guilford.

Norenzayan, A., Shariff, A. F., Gervais, W. M., Willard, A. K., McNamara, R. A., Slingerland, E., & Henrich, J. (2016). The cultural evolution of prosocial religions. *Behavioral and Brain Sciences, 39,* 1–65.

Normand, A., & Croizet, J.-C. (2013). Upward social comparison generates attentional focusing when the dimension of comparison is self-threatening. *Social Cognition, 31*(3), 336–348.

North, A. C., Tarrant, M., & Hargreaves, D. J. (2004). The effects of music on helping behavior: A field study. *Environment and Behavior, 36,* 266–275.

North, M. S., & Fiske, S. T. (2012). An inconvenienced youth? Ageism and its potential intergenerational roots. *Psychological Bulletin, 138,* 982–997.

Norton, M. I., & Sommers, S. R. (2011). Whites see racism as a zero-sum game that they are now losing. *Perspectives on Psychological Science, 6,* 215–218.

Norton, M. I., Frost, J. H., & Ariely, D. (2007). Less is more: The lure of ambiguity, or why familiarity breeds contempt. *Journal of Personality and Social Psychology, 92,* 97–105.

Nosek, B. A., Greenwald, A. G., & Banaji, M. R. (2007). The Implicit Association Test at 7: A methodological and conceptual review. In J. A. Bargh (Ed.), *Social psychology and the unconscious.* New York: Psychology Press.

Nowak, A., Szamrej, J., & Latané, B. (1990). From private attitude to public opinion: A dynamic theory of social impact. *Psychological Review, 97,* 362–376.

Nunes, K. L., Hermann, C. A., & Ratcliffe, K. (2013). Implicit and explicit attitudes toward rape are associated with sexual aggression. *Journal of Interpersonal Violence, 28,* 2657–2675.

O'Brien, D. T., Gallup, A. C., & Wilson, D. S. (2012). Residential mobility and prosocial development within a single city. *American Journal of Community Psychology, 50,* 26–36.

O'Brien, S. (2004, May 21). Researcher: It's not bad apples, it's the barrel. Retrieved January 20, 2005, from CNN.com, www.cnn.com/2004/US/05/21/zimbarbo.access/J

O'Connor, K. M., & Carnevale, P. J. (1997). A nasty but effective negotiation strategy: Misrepresentation of a common-value issue. *Personality and Social Psychology Bulletin, 23,* 504–515.

O'Gorman, R., Wilson, D. S., & Miller, R. R. (2008). An evolved cognitive bias for social norms. *Evolution and Human Behavior, 29,* 71–78.

O'Rourke, L. (2008, August 2). Behind the woman behind the bomb. *The New York Times,* Op-ed page.

Obrecht, N. A., & Chesney, D. L. (2016). Prompting deliberation increases baserate use. *Judgment and Decision Making, 11*(1), 1–6.

Ochsner, K. (2007). Social cognitive neuroscience: Historical development, core principles, and future promise. In A. W. Kruglanski & E. T. Higgins (Eds.), *Social psychology: Handbook of basic principles* (2nd ed., pp. 39–66). New York: Guilford.

Oettingen, G., & Reininger, K. M. (2016). The power of prospection: Mental contrasting and behavior change. *Social and Personality Psychology Compass, 10,* 591–604.

Ofshe, R., & Watters, E. (1994). *Making monsters: False memories, psychotherapy, and sexual hysteria.* New York: Scribner.

Ohbuchi, K., Ohno, T., & Mukai, H. (1993). Empathy and aggression: Effects of self-disclosure and fearful appeal. *Journal of Social Psychology, 133,* 243–253.

Oishi, S. (2014). Socioecological psychology. *Annual Review of Psychology, 65,* 581–609.

Oishi, S., & Gilbert, E. A. (2016). Current and future directions in culture and happiness research. *Current Opinion in Psychology, 8,* 54–58.

Oishi, S., Rothman, A. J., Snyder, M., Su, J., Zehm, K., Hertel, A. W., et al. (2007). The socioecological model of procommunity action: The benefits of residential stability. *Journal of Personality and Social Psychology, 93,* 831–844.

Oishi, S., Talhelm, T., Lee, M., Komiya, A., & Akutsu, S. (2015). Residential mobility and low-commitment groups. *Archives of Scientific Psychology, 3,* 54–61.

Oishi, S., Wyer, R. S., & Colcombe, S. J. (2000). Cultural variation in the use of current life satisfaction to predict the future. *Journal of Personality and Social Psychology, 78,* 434–445.

Oliner, S. P., & Oliner, P. M. (1988). *The altruistic personality: Rescuers of Jews in Nazi Europe.* New York: The Free Press.

Olmsted, L. (2012, April 10). James Bond ditches martinis for beer 007 fans cry sell out. *Forbes.* Retrieved May 1, 2014, from http://www.forbes.com/sites/larryolmsted/2012/04/10/james-bond-ditches-martinis-for-beer-007-fans-cry-sell-out/

Olson, J. M., Vernon, P. A., Harris, J. A., & Jang, K. L. (2001). The heritability of attitudes: A study of twins. *Journal of Personality and Social Psychology, 80*(6), 845–860.

Olson, J., & Stone, J. (2005). The influence of behavior on attitudes. In D. Albarracín, B. T. Johnson, & M. P. Zanna (Eds.), *The handbook of attitudes* (pp. 223–271). Mahwah, NJ: Erlbaum.

Olson, M. A., & Fazio, R. H. (2004). Reducing the influence of extrapersonal associations on the implicit association test: Personalizing the IAT. *Journal of Personality and Social Psychology, 86,* 653–667.

Olujic, M. (1998). Embodiment of terror: Gendered violence in peacetime and wartime in Croatia and Bosnia-Herzegovina. *Medical Anthropology Quarterly, 12,* 31–50.

On the Front Lines of Rising Seas: Naval Station Norfolk, Virginia (2016, July 27). Union of Concerned Scientists. Retrieved May 29, 2017, from http://www.ucsusa.org/global-warming/global-warming-impacts/sea-level-rise-flooding-naval-station-norfolk#.WStjvmgrI2w

Open Science Collaboration. (2015). Estimating the reproducibility of psychological science. *Science, 349*(6251). doi:10.1126/science.aac4716

Orbell, S., & Henderson, C. J. (2016). Automatic effects of illness schema activation on behavioral manifestations of illness. *Health Psychology, 35,* 1144–1153.

Orizio, R. (2003). *Talk of the devil: Encounters with seven dictators.* New York: Walker & Company.

Oskamp, S., Burkhardt, R. I., Schultz, P. W., Hurin, S., & Zelezny, L. (1998). Predicting three dimensions of residential curbside recycling: An observational study. *Journal of Environmental Education, 29,* 37–42.

Osofsky, M. J., Bandura, A., & Zimbardo, P. G. (2005). The role of moral disengagement in the execution process. *Law and Human Behavior, 29,* 371–393.

Ostrov, J. M., Woods, K. E., Jansen, E. A., Casas, J. F., & Crick, N. R. (2004). An observational study of delivered and received aggression, gender, and social-psychological adjustment in preschool. *Early Childhood Research Quarterly, 19,* 355–371.

Oyserman, D., & Lee, S. (2008). Does culture influence what and how we think? Effects of priming individualism and collectivism. *Psychological Bulletin, 134,* 311–342.

Pachur, T., Hertwig, R., & Steinmann, F. (2012). How do people judge risks: Availability heuristic, affect heuristic, or both? *Journal of Experimental Psychology: Applied, 18,* 314–330.

Packer, D. J. (2008a). Identifying systematic disobedience in Milgram's obedience experiments: A meta-analytic review. *Perspectives on Psychological Science, 3,* 301–304.

Packer, D. J. (2008b). On being both with us and against us: A normative conflict model of dissent in social groups. *Personality and Social Psychology Review, 12,* 50–72.

Packer, D. J. (2009). Avoiding groupthink: Whereas weakly identified members remain silent, strongly identified members dissent about collective problems. *Psychological Science, 20*(5), 546–548. doi:10.1111/j.1467-9280.2009.02333.x

Page, R. (2014). Saying 'sorry': Corporate apologies posted on Twitter. *Journal of Pragmatics, 62,* 30–45.

Page, S. (2008). *The difference: How the power of diversity creates better groups, firms, schools, and societies.* Princeton, NJ: Princeton University Press.

Page-Gould, E. (2012). To whom can I turn? Maintenance of positive intergroup relations in the face of intergroup conflict. *Social Psychological and Personality Science, 3,* 462–470.

Palfrey, J., Boyd, D., & Sacco, D. (2010). *Enhancing child safety and online technologies.* The Berkman Center for Internet & Society at Harvard University. Durham, NC: Carolina Academic Press. Available online http://www.cap-press.com/pdf/1997.pdf

Palmer, J., & Loveland, J. (2008). The influence of group discussion on performance judgments: Rating accuracy, contrast effects, and halo. *Journal of Psychology: Interdisciplinary and Applied, 142,* 117–130.

Paluck, E. L., Shepherd, H., & Aronow, P. M. (2016). Changing climates of conflict: A social network experiment in 56 schools. *Proceedings of the National Academy of Sciences, 113,* 566–571.

Panksepp, J., & Panksepp, J. (2000). The seven sins of evolutionary psychology. *Evolution and Cognition, 6,* 108–131.

Paolini, S., Hewstone, M., Cairns, E., & Voci, A. (2004). Effects of direct and indirect cross-group friendships on judgments of Catholics and Protestants in Northern Ireland: The mediating role of an anxiety-reduction mechanism. *Personality and Social Psychology Bulletin, 30,* 770–786.

Parish, A. R., & de Waal, F. B. M. (2000). The other closest living relative: How bonobos (*pan paniscus*) challenge traditional assumptions about females, dominance, inter- and intrasexual interactions and hominid evolution. *Proceedings of the New York Academy of Sciences, 907,* 97–113.

Park, B., & Rothbart, M. (1982). Perception of out-group homogeneity and levels of social categorization: Memory for the subordinate attributes of in-group and out-group members. *Journal of Personality and Social Psychology, 42,* 1051–1068.

Park, C. L. (2010). Making sense of the meaning literature: An integrative review of meaning making and its effects on adjustment to stressful life events. *Psychological Bulletin, 136,* 257–301.

Park, H. S., & Smith, S. W. (2007). Distinctiveness and influence of subjective norms, personal descriptive and injunctive norms, and societal descriptive and injunctive norms on behavioural intent: A case of two behaviours critical to organ donation. *Human Communication Research, 33,* 194–218.

Parkinson, B. (2013). Contextualizing facial activity. *Emotion Review, 5,* 97–103.

Pascual, A., Guéguen, N., Pujos, S., & Felonneau, M. (2013). Foot-in-the-door and problematic requests: A field experiment. *Social Influence, 8,* 46–53.

Paterson, H. M., Whittle, K., & Kemp, R. I. (2014). Detrimental effects of post-incident debriefing on memory and psychological responses. *Journal of Police and Criminal Psychology.* Advance online publication. doi:10.1007/s11896-014-9141-6

Patterson, A. (1974, September). *Hostility catharsis: A naturalistic quasi-experiment.* Paper presented at the annual meeting of the American Psychological Association, New Orleans.

Payne, B. K., & Gawronski, B. (2010). A history of implicit social cognition: Where is it coming from? Where is it now? Where is it going? In B. Gawronski & B. K. Payne (Eds.), *Handbook of implicit social cognition: Measurement, theory, and applications* (pp. 1–15). New York: Guilford.

Payne, B. K., Burkley, M. A., & Stokes, M. B. (2008). Why do implicit and explicit attitude tests diverge? The role of structural fit. *Journal of Personality and Social Psychology, 94,* 16–31.

Pechmann, C., & Knight, S. J. (2002). An experimental investigation of the joint effects of advertising and peers on adolescents' beliefs and intentions about cigarette consumption. *Journal of Consumer Research, 29,* 5–19.

Pedersen, E. R., Osilla, K. C., Miles, J. N. V., Tucker, J. S., Ewing, B. A., Shih, R. A., & D'Amico, E. (2017). The role of perceived injunctive alcohol norms in adolescent drinking behavior. *Addictive Behaviors, 67,* 1–7.

Pedersen, W. C., Vasquez, E. A., Bartholow, B. D., Grosvenor, M., & Truong, A. (2014). Are you insulting me? Exposure to alcohol primes increases aggression following ambiguous provocation. *Personality and Social Psychology Bulletin, 40,* 1037–1049.

Pelonero, C. (2014). *Kitty Genovese: A true account of a public murder and its private consequences.* New York: Skyhorse Publishing.

Peltokorpi, V. (2008). Transactive memory systems. *Review of General Psychology, 12*(4), 378–394. doi:10.1037/1089-2680.12.4.378

Pennebaker, J. W. (1990). *Opening up: The healing powers of confiding in others.* New York: Morrow.

Pennebaker, J. W. (1997). Writing about emotional experiences as a therapeutic process. *Psychological Science, 8,* 162–166.

Pennebaker, J. W. (2001). Dealing with a traumatic experience immediately after it occurs. *Advances in Mind-Body Medicine, 17,* 160–162.

Pennebaker, J. W. (2002). Writing, social processes, and psychotherapy: From past to future. In S. J. Lepore & J. M. Smyth (Eds.), *The writing cure: How expressive writing promotes health and emotional well-being.* Washington, DC: American Psychological Association.

Pennebaker, J. W., & Beale, S. K. (1986). Confronting a traumatic event: Toward an understanding of inhibition and disease. *Journal of Abnormal Psychology, 95,* 274–281.

Pennebaker, J. W., & Sanders, D. Y. (1976). American graffiti: Effects of authority and reactance arousal. *Personality and Social Psychology Bulletin, 2,* 264–267.

Pennebaker, J. W., Barger, S. D., & Tiebout, J. (1989). Disclosure of traumas and health among Holocaust survivors. *Psychosomatic Medicine, 51,* 577–589.

Pennebaker, J. W., Colder, M., & Sharp, L. K. (1990). Accelerating the coping process. *Journal of Personality and Social Psychology, 58,* 528–537.

Penner, L. A., Dovidio, J. F., Gonzalez, R., Albrecht, T. L., Chapman, R., Foster, T., ... & Gadgeel, S. (2016). The effects of oncologist implicit racial bias in racially discordant oncology interactions. *Journal of Clinical Oncology, 34,* 2874–2880.

Penner, L. A., Dovidio, J. F., Piliavin, J. A., & Schroeder, D. A. (2005). Prosocial behavior: Multilevel perspectives. *Annual Review of Psychology, 56,* 365–392.

Pennington, N., & Hastie, R. (1988). Explanation-based decision making: Effects of memory structure on judgment. *Journal of Experimental Psychology: Learning, Memory, and Cognition, 14,* 521–533.

Pennington, N., & Hastie, R. (1990). Practical implications of psychological research on juror and jury decision making. *Personality and Social Psychology Bulletin, 16,* 90–105.

Perkins, H. W. (2007). Misperceptions of peer drinking norms in Canada: Another look at the "reign of error" and its consequences among college students. *Addictive Behaviors, 32,* 2645–2656.

Perkins, H., Haines, M. P., & Rice, R. (2005). Misperceiving the college drinking norm and related problems: A nationwide study of exposure to prevention information, perceived norms and student alcohol misuse. *Journal of Studies on Alcohol and Drugs, 66,* 470–478.

Perlstein, L. (1999, November 14). The sweet rewards of learning: Teachers motivate students with tokens for fries and candy. *Washington Post,* pp. A1, A14.

Perrett, D. I., May, K. A., & Yoshikawa, S. (1994). Facial shape and judgments of female attractiveness. *Nature, 368,* 239–242.

Perry, G. (2013). *Behind the shock machine: The untold story of the notorious Milgram psychology experiments.* New York: New Press.

Peters, J. M., Avol, E., Gauderman, W. J., Linn, W. S., Navidi, W., London, S. J., Margolis, H., Rappaport, E., Vora, H., Gong, H. Jr., & Thomas, D. B. (1999). A study of twelve Southern California communities with differing levels and types of air pollution: II. Effects on pulmonary function. *American Journal of Respiratory and Critical Care Medicine, 159,* 768–775.

Peterson, A. A., Haynes, G. A., & Olson, J. M. (2008). Self-esteem differences in the effects of hypocrisy induction on behavioral intentions in the health domain. *Journal of Personality, 76,* 305–322.

Petrocelli, J. V., Kammrath, L. K., Brinton, J. E., Uy, M. R. Y., & Cowens, D. F. L. (2015). Holding on to what might have been may loosen (or tighten) the ties that bind us: A counterfactual potency analysis of previous dating alternatives. *Journal of Experimental Social Psychology, 56,* 50–59.

Pettigrew, T. F. (1958). Personality and sociocultural factors and intergroup attitudes: A cross-national comparison. *Journal of Conflict Resolution, 2,* 29–42.

Pettigrew, T. F., & Tropp, L. R. (2006). A meta-analytic test of intergroup contact theory. *Journal of Personality and Social Psychology, 90,* 751–783.

Petty, R. E. (1995). Attitude change. In A. Tesser (Ed.), *Advanced social psychology* (pp. 195–255). New York: McGraw-Hill.

Petty, R. E., & Briñol, P. (2012). The elaboration likelihood model. In P. A. M. Van Lange, A. Kruglanski, & E. T. Higgins (Eds.), *Handbook of theories of social psychology* (Vol. 1, pp. 224–245). London: Sage.

Petty, R. E., & Briñol, P. (2015). Emotion and persuasion: Cognitive and meta-cognitive processes impact attitudes. *Cognition and Emotion, 1.*

Petty, R. E., & Brock, T. C. (1981). Thought disruption and persuasion: Assessing the validity of attitude change experiments. In R. E. Petty, T. M. Ostrom, & T. C. Brock (Eds.), *Cognitive responses in persuasion* (pp. 55–79). Hillsdale, NJ: Erlbaum.

Petty, R. E., & Cacioppo, J. T. (1986). *Communication and persuasion: Central and peripheral routes to attitude change.* New York: Springer-Verlag.

Petty, R. E., & Krosnick, J. A. (2014). *Attitude strength: Antecedents and consequences.* New York: Psychology Press.

Petty, R. E., & Wegener, D. T. (1999). The elaboration likelihood model: Current status and controversies. In S. Chaiken & Y. Trope (Eds.), *Dual-process theories in social psychology* (pp. 41–72). New York: Guilford Press.

Petty, R. E., & Wegener, D. T. (2014). Thought systems, argument quality, and persuasion. In R. S. Wyer, Jr., & T. K. Srull (Eds.), *Advances in social cognition* (Vol. IV, pp. 147–161). New York: Psychology Press.

Petty, R. E., Barden, J., & Wheeler, S. C. (2009). The Elaboration Likelihood Model of persuasion: Developing health promotions for sustained behavioral change. In R. J. DiClemente, R. A. Crosby, & M. C. Kegler (Eds.), *Emerging theories in health promotion practice and research* (2nd ed., pp. 185–214). San Francisco: Jossey-Bass.

Petty, R. E., Cacioppo, J. T., & Goldman, R. (1981). Personal involvement as a determinant of argument-based persuasion. *Journal of Personality and Social Psychology, 41,* 847–855.

Pew Research Center. (2016). "Changing Attitudes on Gay Marriage." Religion & Public Life. Retrieved from https://login.proxy.bib. uottawa.ca/login?url=http://poll.orspub.com/document.php?id=quest12.out_4650&type=hitlist&num=1

Pezdek, K. (2012). Fallible eyewitness memory and identification. In B. L. Cutler (Ed.), *Conviction of the innocent: Lessons from psychological research* (pp. 105–124). Washington, DC: American Psychological Association.

Phillip, A. (2014, April 29). The latest social media "challenge" is dangerous, but probably won't be around for long. *Washington Post.* Retrieved May 26, 2014, from www.washingtonpost.com/news/post-nation/wp/2014/04/29/the-latest-social-media-challenge-is-dangerous-but-probably-wont-be-around-for-long

Phillips, A. G., & Silva, P. J. (2005). Self-awareness and the emotional consequences of self-discrepancies. *Personality & Social Psychology Bulletin, 31,* 703–713.

Phillips, K. W., Mannix, E. A., Neale, M. A., & Gruenfeld, D. H. (2004). Diverse groups and information sharing: The effects of congruent ties. *Journal of Experimental Social Psychology, 40,* 495–510.

Picazo, C., Gamero, N., Zornoza, A., & Peiró, J. M. (2014). Testing relations between group cohesion and satisfaction in project teams: A cross-level and cross-lagged approach. *European Journal of Work and Organizational Psychology.* doi:10.1080/1359432X.2014.894979

Pickel, K. (2007). Remembering and identifying menacing perpetrators: Exposure to violence and the weapon focus effect. In R. C. L. Lindsay, D. F. Ross, J. D. Read, & M. P. Toglia (Eds.), *The handbook of eyewitness psychology,* Vol. II: *Memory for people* (pp. 339–360). Mahwah, NJ: Erlbaum.

Pickett, C. L., Silver, M. D., & Brewer, M. B. (2002). The impact of assimilation and differentiation needs on perceived group importance and judgments of ingroup size. *Personality and Social Psychology Bulletin, 28,* 546–558.

Piliavin, I. M., Piliavin, J. A., & Rodin, J. (1975). Costs, diffusion, and the stigmatized victim. *Journal of Personality and Social Psychology, 32,* 429–438.

Piliavin, J. A. (2008). Long-term benefits of habitual helping: Doing well by doing good. In B. A. Sullivan, M. Snyder, & J. L. Sullivan (Eds.), *Cooperation: The political psychology of effective human interaction* (pp. 241–258). Malden, MA: Blackwell.

Piliavin, J. A. (2009). Altruism and helping: The evolution of a field: The 2008 Cooley-Mead Presentation. *Social Psychology Quarterly, 72*(3), 209–225. doi:10.1177/019027250907200305

Piliavin, J. A. (2010). Volunteering across the life span: Doing well by doing good. In S. Stürmer & M. Snyder (Eds.), *The psychology of prosocial behavior: Group processes, intergroup relations, and helping* (pp. 157–172). Oxford, UK: Wiley-Blackwell.

Piliavin, J. A., & Piliavin, I. M. (1972). The effect of blood on reactions to a victim. *Journal of Personality and Social Psychology, 23,* 253–261.

Piliavin, J. A., Dovidio, J. F., Gaertner, S. L., & Clark, R. D., III. (1981). *Emergency intervention.* New York: Academic Press.

Pinel, E. C., & Long, A. E. (2012). When I's meet: Sharing subjective experience with someone from the outgroup. *Personality and Social Psychology Bulletin, 38,* 296–307.

Pinel, E. C., Long, A. E., Landau, M. J., Alexander, K., & Pyszczynski, T. (2006). Seeing I to I: A pathway to interpersonal connectedness. *Journal of Personality and Social Psychology, 90,* 243–257.

Pinker, S. (2011). *The better angels of our nature.* New York: Penguin.

Pitt, R. N. (2010). "Killing the messenger": Religious Black gay men's neutralization of anti-gay religious messages. *Journal for the Scientific Study of Religion, 49,* 56–72.

Plant, E. A., & Butz, D. A. (2006). The causes and consequences of an avoidance-focus for interracial interactions. *Personality and Social Psychology Bulletin, 32,* 833–846.

Plant, E. A., & Devine, P. G. (2009). The active control of prejudice: Unpacking the intentions guiding control efforts. *Journal of Personality and Social Psychology, 96,* 640–652.

Plant, E. A., & Peruche, B. M. (2005). The consequences of race for police officers' responses to criminal suspects. *Psychological Science, 16,* 180–183.

Plastic oceans. (2008, November 13). Spencer Michels, reporter. *The Newshour with Jim Lehrer,* Public Broadcasting System.

Pleban, R., & Tesser, A. (1981). The effects of relevance and quality of another's performance on interpersonal closeness. *Social Psychology Quarterly, 44,* 278–285.

Plötner, M., Over, H., Carpenter, M., & Tomasello, M. (2015). Young children show the bystander effect in helping situations. *Psychological Science, 26,* 499–506.

Population Growth Rate. (n.d.). The World Bank Group. Retrieved July 15, 2014, from http://www.worldbank.org/depweb/english/modules/social/pgr/print.html

Posada, S., & Colell, M. (2007). Another gorilla (Gorilla gorilla gorilla) recognizes himself in a mirror. *American Journal of Primatology, 69*(5), 576–583.

Postmes, T., & Spears, R. (1998). Deindividuation and antinormative behavior: A meta-analysis. *Psychological Bulletin, 123,* 238–259.

Potok, M. (2017). The year in hate and extremism. *Intelligence Report* (Spring). Montgomery, AL: Southern Poverty Law Center.

Powledge, F. (1991). *Free at last? The civil rights movement and the people who made it.* Boston: Little, Brown.

Pratarelli, M. E. (2012). When human nature confronts the need for a global environmental ethics. *Journal of Social, Evolutionary, and Cultural Psychology, 6,* 384–403.

Prather, C., Fuller, T. R., Marshall, K. J., & Jeffries W.L., IV (2016). The impact of racism on the sexual and reproductive health of African American women. *Journal of Women's Health, 25,* 664–671.

Pratkanis, A. R., & Turner, M. E. (2013). Methods for counteracting groupthink risk: A critical appraisal. *International Journal of Risk and Contingency Management, 2,* 18–38.

Preston, J. L., Ritter, R. S., & Hernandez, J. I. (2010). Principles of religious prosociality: A review and reformulation. *Social and Personality Psychology Compass, 4*(8), 574–590. doi:10.1111/j.1751-9004.2010.00286.x

Prince, M. A., & Carey, K. B. (2010). The malleability of injunctive norms among college students. *Addictive Behaviors, 35,* 940–947.

Pronin, E., Berger, J., & Moluki, S. (2007). Alone in a crowd of sheep: Asymmetric perceptions of conformity and their roots in an introspection illusion. *Journal of Personality and Social Psychology, 92,* 585–595. doi:10.1037/0022-3514.92.4.585

Pronin, E., Gilovich, T., & Ross, L. (2004). Objectivity in the eye of the beholder: Divergent perceptions of bias in self versus others. *Psychological Review, 111,* 781–799.

Pronin, E., Lin, D. Y., & Ross, L. (2002). The bias blind spot: Perceptions of bias in self versus others. *Personality and Social Psychology Bulletin, 28,* 369–381.

Proost, K., Schreurs, B., De Witte, K., & Derous, D. (2010). Ingratiation and self-promotion in the selection interview: The effects of using single tactics or a combination of tactics on interviewer judgments. *Journal of Applied Social Psychology, 40*(9), 2155–2169. doi:10.1111/j.1559-1816.2010.00654.x

Prot, S., Gentile, D. A., Anderson, C. A., Suzuki, K., Swing, E., Lim, K. M., et al. (2014). Long-term relations among prosocial-media use, empathy, and prosocial behavior. *Psychological Science, 25*(2), 358–368.

Prüfer, K., Munch, K., Hellmann, I., Akagi, K., Miller, J. R., Walenz, B., ... & Knight, J. R. (2012). The bonobo genome compared with the chimpanzee and human genomes. *Nature, 486,* 527–531.

Przybylski, A. K., & Weinstein, N. (2013). Can you connect with me now? How the presence of mobile communication technologies influences face-to-face conversation quality. *Journal of Social and Personal Relationships, 30,* 237–246.

Pulfrey, C., Darnon, C., & Butera, F. (2013). Autonomy and task performance: Explaining the impact of grades on intrinsic motivation. *Journal of Educational Psychology, 105,* 39–57. doi:10.1037/a0029376

Putnam, R. D. (2000). *Bowling alone: The collapse and revival of American community.* New York: Simon & Schuster.

Pyszczynski, T., & Taylor, J. (2016). When the buffer breaks: Disrupted terror management in post-traumatic stress disorder. *Current Directions in Psychological Science, 25,* 286–290.

Qin, J., Ogle, C., & Goodman, G. (2008). Adults' memories of childhood: True and false reports. *Journal of Experimental Psychology: Applied, 14,* 373–391.

Quattrone, G. A. (1982). Behavioral consequences of attributional bias. *Social Cognition, 1,* 358–378.

Quattrone, G. A. (1986). On the perception of a group's variability. In S. Worchel & W. G. Austin (Eds.), *Psychology of intergroup relations* (2nd ed.). Chicago: Nelson-Hall.

Quattrone, G. A., & Jones, E. E. (1980). The perception of variability within ingroups and outgroups: Implications for the law of small numbers. *Journal of Personality and Social Psychology, 38,* 141–152.

Quick stats binge drinking. (2008). Department of Health and Human Services, Center for Disease Control and Prevention. Retrieved December 30, 2008, from www.cdc.gov/alcohol/quickstats/binge_drinking.htm

Rajaram, S., & Pereira-Pasarin, L. P. (2010). Collaborative memory: Cognitive research and theory. *Perspectives on Psychological Science, 5*(6), 649–663. doi:10.1177/1745691610388760

Ramirez, A. (2005, December 2). New Yorkers take a tribute standing up. *The New York Times,* p. B1.

Ramírez-Esparza, N., Chung, C. K., Sierra-Otero, G., & Pennebaker, J. W. (2012). Cross-cultural constructions of self-schemas: Americans and Mexicans. *Journal of Cross-Cultural Psychology, 43*(2), 233–250. doi:10.1177/0022022110385231

Rand, D. G., & Nowak, M. A. (2013). Human cooperation. *Trends in Cognitive Sciences, 17*(8), 413–425. doi:10.1016/j.tics.2013.06.003

Rand, D. G., Brescoll, V. L., Everett, J. A. C., Capraro, V., & Barcelo, H. (2016). Social heuristics and social roles: Intuition favors altruism for women but not for men. *Journal of Experimental Psychology: General, 145,* 389–396.

Randles, D., Inzlicht, M., Proulx, T., Tullett., A., & Heine, S. J. (2015). Is dissonance reduction a special case of fluid compensation? Evidence that dissonant cognitions cause compensatory affirmation and abstraction. *Journal of Personality and Social Psychology, 108,* 697–710.

Ranganath, K. A., & Nosek, B. A. (2008). Implicit attitude generalization occurs immediately, explicit attitude generalization takes time. *Psychological Science, 19,* 249–254.

Rao, L. (2016). Here's how artificial intelligence is going to replace middle class jobs. *Fortune.* Retrieved February 5, 2017, from http://fortune.com/2016/10/17/human-workforce-ai/

Rapoport, A., & Chammah, A. M. (1965). *Prisoner's dilemma: A study in conflict and cooperation.* Ann Arbor: University of Michigan Press.

Raps, C. S., Peterson, C., Jonas, M., & Seligman, M. E. P. (1982). Patient behavior in hospitals: Helplessness, reactance, or both? *Journal of Personality and Social Psychology, 42,* 1036–1041.

Rasinski, H. M., Geers, A. L., & Czopp, A. M. (2013). "I guess what he said wasn't that bad": Dissonance in nonconfronting targets of prejudice. *Personality and Social Psychology Bulletin, 39,* 856–869.

Raskin, R., & Terry, H. (1988). A principle-components analysis of the Narcissistic Personality Inventory and further evidence of its construct validity. *Journal of Personality and Social Psychology, 54,* 890–902.

Ratelle, C. F., Carbonneau, N., Vallerand, R. J., & Mageau, G. (2013). Passion in the romantic sphere: A look at relational outcomes. *Motivation and Emotion, 37,* 106–120.

Ratliff, K. A., & Oishi, S. (2013). Gender differences in implicit self-esteem following a romantic partner's success or failure. *Journal of Personality and Social Psychology, 105*(4), 688–702. doi:10.1037/a0033769

Ratliff, K. A., Howell, J., & Redford, L. (2017). Attitudes toward the prototypical environmentalist predict environmentally-friendly behavior. *Journal of Environmental Psychology.*

Ravizza, S. M., Uitvlugt, M. G., & Fenn, K. M. (2016). Logged in and zoned out: How laptop internet use relates to classroom learning. *Psychological Science, 28,* 171–180.

Reardon, S. (2011, April 27). Preventable chronic diseases are now the world's biggest killers. *ScienceInsider.* Retrieved August 19, 2014, from http://news.sciencemag.org/2011/04/preventable-chronic-diseases-are-now-worlds-biggest-killers

Rector, M., & Neiva, E. (1996). Communication and personal relations in Brazil. In W. B. Gudykunst, S. Ting-Toomey, & T. Nishida (Eds.), *Communication in personal relationships across cultures* (pp. 156–173). Thousand Oaks, CA: Sage.

Redlawsk, D. P. (2002). Hot cognition or cool consideration? Testing the effects of motivated reasoning on political decision making. *Journal of Politics, 64,* 1021–1044.

Redlich, A. D., Bibas, S., Edkins, V. A., & Madon, S. (2017). The psychology of defendant plea decision making. *American Psychologist, 72,* 339–352.

Regan, P. C., & Berscheid, E. (1997). Gender differences in characteristics desired in a potential sexual and marriage partner. *Journal of Psychology and Human Sexuality, 9,* 25–37.

Regan, P. C., & Berscheid, E. (1999). *Lust: What we know about human sexual desire.* Thousand Oaks, CA: Sage.

Regnerus, M., Gordon, D., & Price, J. (2016). Documenting pornography use in America: A comparative analysis of methodological approaches. *Journal of Sex Research, 53,* 873–881.

Reicher, S. D., Spears, R., Postmes, T., & Kende, A. (2016). Disputing deindividuation: Why negative group behaviours derive from group norms, not group immersion. *Behavioral and Brain Sciences, 39.* doi:10.1017/S0140525X15001491

Reid, A. E., & Aiken, L. S. (2013). Correcting injunctive norm misperceptions motivates behavior change: A randomized controlled sun protection intervention. *Health Psychology, 32,* 551–560.

Riemer, H., Shavitt, S., Koo, M., & Markus, H. R. (2014). Preferences don't have to be personal: Expanding attitude theorizing with a cross-cultural perspective. *Psychological Review, 121,* 619–648.

Reis, H. T., & Gosling, S. D. (2010). Social psychological methods outside the laboratory. In S. T. Fiske, D. T. Gilbert, & G. Lindzey (Eds.), *Handbook of social psychology* (5th ed., Vol. 1, pp. 82–114). Hoboken, NJ: John Wiley.

Reis, H. T., & Judd, C. M. (Eds.). (2000). *Handbook of research methods in social and personality psychology.* New York: Cambridge University Press.

Reis, H. T., Maniaci, M. R., Caprariello, P. A., Eastwick, P. W., & Finkel, E. J. (2011). Familiarity does indeed promote attraction in live interaction. *Journal of Personality and Social Psychology, 101,* 557–570.

Reiter, S. M., & Samuel, W. (1980). Littering as a function of prior litter and the presence or absence of prohibitive signs. *Journal of Applied Social Psychology, 10,* 45–55.

Reitz, A. K., Motti-Stefanidi, F., & Asendorpf, J. B. (2016). Me, us, and them: Testing sociometer theory in a socially diverse real-life context. *Journal of Personality and Social Psychology, 110,* 908.

Renner, M. J., & Mackin, R. S. (1998). A life stress instrument for classroom use. *Teaching of Psychology, 25,* 46–48.

Reno, R. R., Cialdini, R. B., & Kallgren, C. A. (1993). The transsituational influence of social norms. *Journal of Personality and Social Psychology, 64,* 104–112.

Rensink, R. A. (2002). Change detection. *Annual Review of Psychology, 53,* 245–277.

Rexrode, C. (2011, November 3). Twitter changes business of celebrity endorsements. *USA Today.* Retrieved December 22, 2011, from www.usatoday.com/tech/news/story/2011-11-03/celebrity-twitter-endorsements/51058228/1

Rhodes, G. (2006). The evolutionary psychology of facial beauty. *Annual Review of Psychology, 57,* 199–226.

Rhodes, G., Yoshikawa, S., Clark, A., Lee, K., McKay, R., & Akamatsu, S. (2001). Attractiveness of facial averageness and symmetry in non-Western cultures: In search of biologically based standards of beauty. *Perception, 30,* 611–625.

Rhodes, N., & Wood, W. (1992). Self-esteem and intelligence affect influenceability: The mediating role of message reception. *Psychological Bulletin, 111,* 156–171.

Rhodewalt, F., Sanbonmatsu, D. M., Tschanz, B., Feick, D. L., & Waller, A. (1995). Self-handicapping and interpersonal trade-offs: The effects of claimed self-handicaps on observers' performance evaluations and feedback. *Personality and Social Psychology Bulletin, 21,* 1042–1050.

Rholes, W. S., Simpson, J. A., & Friedman, M. (2006). Avoidant attachment and the experience of parenting. *Personality and Social Psychology Bulletin, 32*, 275–285.

Richard, F. D., Bond, C. F., Jr., & Stokes-Zoota, J. J. (2001). 'That's completely obvious … and important": Lay judgments of social psychological findings. *Personality and Social Psychology Bulletin, 27*, 497–505.

Richardson, D. S. (2014). Everyday aggression takes many forms. *Psychological Science, 23*, 220–224.

Richardson, D., Hammock, G., Smith, S., & Gardner, W. (1994). Empathy as a cognitive inhibitor of interpersonal aggression. *Aggressive Behavior, 20*, 275–289.

Richter, C. P. (1957). On the phenomenon of sudden death in animals and man. *Psychosomatic Medicine, 19*, 191–198.

Ringelmann, M. (1913). Recherches sur les moteurs animés: Travail de l'homme [Research on driving forces: Human work]. *Annales de l'Institut National Agronomique*, series 2, *12*, 1–40.

Rinolo, R. C., Johnson, K. C., Sherman, T. R., & Misso, J. A. (2006). Hot or not? Do professors perceived as physically attractive receive higher student evaluations? *Journal of General Psychology, 133*, 19–35.

Rise, J., Sheeran, P., & Hukkelberg, S. (2010). The role of self-identity in the theory of planned behavior: A meta-analysis. *Journal of Applied Social Psychology, 40*(5), 1085–1105. doi:10.1111/j.1559-1816.2010.00611.x

Risen, J. L., & Gilovich, T. (2007). Target and observer differences in the acceptance of questionable apologies. *Journal of Personality and Social Psychology, 92*, 418–433.

Rivers, I., Chesney, T., & Coyne, I. (2011). Cyberbullying. In C. P. Monks & I. Coyne (Eds.), *Bullying in different contexts* (pp. 211–230). New York: Cambridge University Press.

Robbennolt, J. K., & Eisenberg, T. (2017). Juries compared with what? The need for a baseline and attention to real-world complexity. In M. B. Kovera (Ed.), *The psychology of juries* (pp. 109–129). Washington, DC: American Psychological Association.

Robins, R. W., & Schriber, R. A. (2009). The self-conscious emotions: How are they experienced, expressed, and assessed? *Social and Personality Psychology Compass, 3*, 887–898.

Rodin, J., & Langer, E. J. (1977). Long-term effects of a control-relevant intervention with the institutional aged. *Journal of Personality and Social Psychology, 35*, 897–902.

Rodriguez, R., Marchand, E., Ng, J., & Stice, E. (2008). Effects of a cognitive dissonance-based eating disorder prevention program are similar for Asian American, Hispanic, and White participants. *International Journal of Eating Disorders, 41*, 618–625.

Roepke, S. K., & Grant, I. (2011). Toward a more complete understanding of the effects of personal mastery on cardiometabolic health. *Health Psychology, 30*, 615–632. doi:10.1037/a0023480

Roesch, S. C., & Amirkhan, J. H. (1997). Boundary conditions for self-serving attributions: Another look at the sports pages. *Journal of Applied Social Psychology, 27*, 245–261.

Roese, N. J. (1997). Counterfactual thinking. *Psychological Bulletin, 121*, 133–148.

Roese, N. J., & Jamieson, D. W. (1993). Twenty years of bogus pipeline research: A critical review and meta-analysis. *Psychological Bulletin, 114*, 363–375.

Roese, N. J., & Olson, J. M. (1997). Counterfactual thinking: The intersection of affect and function. In M. P. Zanna (Ed.), *Advances in experimental social psychology* (Vol. 29, pp. 1–59). San Diego, CA: Academic Press.

Rogers, R., & Prentice-Dunn, S. (1981). Deindividuation and anger-mediated interracial aggression: Unmasking regressive racism. *Journal of Personality and Social Psychology, 41*, 63–73.

Rohrer, J. H., Baron, S. H., Hoffman, E. L., & Swander, D. V. (1954). The stability of autokinetic judgments. *Journal of Abnormal and Social Psychology, 49*, 595–597.

Roisman, G. I., Clausell, E., Holland, A., Fortuna, K., & Elieff, C. (2008). Adult romantic relationships as contexts of human development: A multimethod comparison of same-sex couples with opposite-sex dating, engaged, and married dyads. *Developmental Psychology, 44*, 91–101.

Romero-Canyas, R., Downey, G., Reddy, K. S., Rodriguez, S., Cavanaugh, T. J., & Pelayo, R. (2010). Paying to belong: When does rejection trigger ingratiation? *Journal of Personality and Social Psychology, 99*(5), 802–823. doi:10.1037/a0020013

Rooth, D. O. (2010). Automatic associations and discrimination in hiring: Real world evidence. *Labour Economics, 17*, 523–534.

Rosenberg, J., & Egbert, N. (2011). Online impression management: Personality traits and concerns for secondary goals as predictors of self-presentation tactics on Facebook. *Journal of Computer-Mediated Communication, 17*, 1–18.

Rosenberg, M. J., Davidson, A. J., Chen, J., Judson, F. N., & Douglas, J. M. (1992). Barrier contraceptives and sexually transmitted diseases in women: A comparison of female-dependent methods and condoms. *American Journal of Public Health, 82*, 669–674.

Rosenthal, R. (1994). Interpersonal expectancy effects: A 30-year perspective. *Current Directions in Psychological Science, 3*, 176–179.

Rosenthal, R., & Jacobson, L. (1968/2003). *Pygmalion in the classroom: Teacher expectation and pupils' intellectual development* (revised ed.). Norwalk, CT: Crown.

Rosette, A. S., Brett, J. M., Barsness, Z., & Lytle, A. L. (2012). When cultures clash electronically: The impact of email and social norms on negotiation behavior and outcomes. *Journal of Cross-Cultural Psychology, 43*, 628–643.

Rosh, L., Offermann, L. R., & Van Diest, R. (2012). Too close for comfort? Distinguishing between team intimacy and team cohesion. *Human Resource Management Review, 22*, 116–127.

Rosin, J. (2015). The Silicon Valley suicides: Why are so many kids with bright prospects killing themselves in Palo Alto? *The Atlantic.* https://www.theatlantic.com/magazine/archive/2015/12/the-silicon-valley-suicides/413140/

Ross, L. (1977). The intuitive psychologist and his shortcomings: Distortions in the attribution process. In L. Berkowitz (Ed.), *Advances in experimental social psychology* (Vol. 10, pp. 173–220). Orlando, FL: Academic Press.

Ross, L. (2010). Dealing with conflict: Experiences and experiments. In M. H. Gonzales, C. Tavris, & J. Aronson (Eds.), *The scientist and the humanist: A festschrift in honor of Elliot Aronson* (pp. 39–66). New York: Psychology Press.

Ross, L., & Nisbett, R. E. (1991). *The person and the situation: Perspectives of social psychology.* New York: McGraw-Hill.

Ross, L., & Ward, A. (1996). Niave realism in everyday life: Implications for social conflict and misunderstanding. In E. S. Reed, E. Turiel, & T. Brown (Eds.), *Values and knowledge* (pp. 103–135). Hillsdale, NJ: Erlbaum.

Ross, L., Amabile, T. M., & Steinmetz, J. L. (1977). Social roles, social control, and biases in social perception. *Journal of Personality and Social Psychology, 35*, 485–494.

Ross, L., Lepper, M. R., & Hubbard, M. (1975). Perseverance in self-perception and social perception: Biased attributional processes in the debriefing paradigm. *Journal of Personality and Social Psychology, 32*, 880–892.

Ross, M., & Wilson, A. E. (2003). Autobiographical memory and conceptions of self: Getting better all the time. *Current Directions in Psychological Science, 12*, 66–69.

Ross, W., & La Croix, J. (1996). Multiple meanings of trust in negotiation theory and research: A literature review and integrative model. *International Journal of Conflict Management, 7*, 314–360.

Rothermund, K., & Wentura, D. (2004). Underlying processes in the Implicit Association Test: Dissociating salience from associations. *Journal of Experimental Psychology: General, 133*, 139–165.

Rotter, J. B. (1966). Generalized expectancies for internal versus external control of reinforcement. *Psychological Monographs, 80*, 1–28 (Whole No. 609).

Rottman, B. M., & Hastie, R. (2014). Reasoning about causal relationships: Inferences on causal networks. *Psychological Bulletin, 140*, 109–139.

Rotton, J., & Cohn, E. G. (2004). Outdoor temperature, climate control, and criminal assault: The spatial and temporal ecology of violence. *Environment & Behavior, 36*, 276–306.

Rudman, L., Phelan, J., & Heppen, J. (2007). Developmental sources of implicit attitudes. *Personality and Social Psychology Bulletin, 33*, 1700–1713.

Ruiter, R. A. C., Abraham, C., & Kok, G. (2001). Scary warnings and rational precautions: A review of the psychology of fear appeals. *Psychology and Health, 16*, 613–630.

Rule, B. G., Taylor, B. R., & Dobbs, A. R. (1987). Priming effects of heat on aggressive thoughts. *Social Cognition, 5*, 131–143.

Rule, N. O., & Ambady, N. (2010). First impressions of the face: Predicting success. *Social and Personality Psychology Compass, 4*, 506–516.

Rule, N. O., Ambady, N., & Hallett, K. C. (2009). Female sexual orientation is perceived accurately, rapidly, and automatically from the face and its features. *Journal of Experimental Social Psychology, 45*, 1245–1251.

Rule, N. O., Ambady, N., Adams, R. B., Jr., & Macrae, C. N. (2008). Accuracy and awareness in the perception and categorization of male sexual orientation. *Journal of Personality and Social Psychology, 95*, 1019–1028.

Rule, N. O., Krendl, A. C., Ivcevic, Z., & Ambady, N. (2013). Accuracy and consensus in judgments of trustworthiness from faces: Behavioral and neural correlates. *Journal of Personality and Social Psychology, 104*, 409–426.

Rusbult, C. E. (1983). A longitudinal test of the investment model: The development (and deterioration) of satisfaction and commitment in heterosexual involvements. *Journal of Personality and Social Psychology, 45*, 101–117.

Rusbult, C. E. (1987). Responses to dissatisfaction in close relationships: The exit-voice-loyalty-neglect model. In D. Perlman & S. W. Duck (Eds.), *Intimate relationships: Development, dynamics, and deterioration* (pp. 209–237). Newbury Park, CA: Sage.

Rusbult, C. E., & Buunk, B. P. (1993). Commitment processes in close relationships: An interdependence analysis. *Journal of Social and Personal Relationships, 10*, 175–204.

Rusbult, C. E., & Martz, J. M. (1995). Remaining in an abusive relationship: An investment model analysis of nonvoluntary dependence. *Personality and Social Psychology Bulletin, 21*, 558–571.

Rusbult, C. E., & Zembrodt, I. M. (1983). Responses to dissatisfaction in romantic involvements: A multidimensional scaling analysis. *Journal of Experimental Social Psychology, 19*, 274–293.

Rusbult, C. E., Johnson, D. J., & Morrow, G. D. (1986). Impact of couple patterns of problem solving on distress and nondistress in dating relationships. *Journal of Personal and Social Psychology, 50*, 744–753.

Rusbult, C. E., Olsen, N., Davis, N. L., & Hannon, P. (2001). Commitment and relationship maintenance mechanisms. In J. H. Harvey & A. Wenzel (Eds.), *Close romantic relationships: Maintenance and enhancement* (pp. 87–113). Mahwah, NJ: Erlbaum.

Rusbult, C. E., Yovetich, N. A., & Verette, J. (1996). An interdependence analysis of accommodation processes. In G. J. O. Fletcher & J. Fitness (Eds.), *Knowledge structures in close relationships: A social psychological approach* (pp. 63–90). Mahwah, NJ: Erlbaum.

Rusting, C. L., & Nolen-Hoeksema, S. (1998). Regulating responses of anger: Effects of rumination and distraction on angry mood. *Journal of Personality and Social Psychology, 74*, 790–803.

Ryan, M. K., Haslam, S. A., Hersby, M. D., & Bongiorno, R. (2011). Think crisis–think female: The glass cliff and contextual variation in the think manager–think male stereotype. *Journal of Applied Psychology, 96*(3), 470–484. doi:10.1037/a0022133

Ryan, M. K., Haslam, S. A., Hersby, M. D., Kulich, C., & Atkins, C. (2008). Opting out or pushed off the edge? The glass cliff and the precariousness of women's leadership positions. *Social and Personality Psychology Compass, 2*, www.blackwell-compass.com/subject/socialpsychology/

Ryan, R. M., & Deci, E. L. (2000). Intrinsic and extrinsic rewards: Classic definitions and new directions. *Current Educational Psychology, 25*, 54–67.

Rydell, R. J., & Durso, G. R. O. (2012). Can I borrow a feeling? Spillover of negative arousal from inconsistent information during attitude formation diminishes perceptions of well-being. *Journal of Experimental Social Psychology, 48*(2), 575–578. doi:10.1016/j.jesp.2011.10.018

Ryon, H. S., & Gleason, M. E. J. (2014). The role of locus of control in daily life. *Personality and Social Psychology Bulletin, 40*, 121–131.

Sacks, O. (1987). *The man who mistook his wife for a hat and other clinical tales.* New York: Harper & Row.

Saffer, H. (2002). Alcohol advertising and youth. *Journal of Studies on Alcohol, 14*, 173–181.

Sagarin, B. J., & Wood, S. E. (2007). Resistance to influence. In A. R. Pratkanis (Ed.), *Frontiers of social psychology. The science of social influence: Advances and future progress* (pp. 321–340). New York: Psychology Press.

Sageman, M. (2008). *Leaderless jihad: Terror networks in the twenty-first century.* Philadelphia: University of Pennsylvania Press.

Saguy, T., Tausch, N., Dovidio, J. F., Pratto, F., & Singh, P. (2011). Tension and harmony in intergroup relations. In P. R. Shaver & M. Mikulincer (Eds.), *Human aggression and violence: Causes, manifestations, and consequences* (Herzilya series on personality and social psychology, pp. 333–348). Washington, DC: American Psychological Association.

Sakai, H. (1999). A multiplicative power-function model of cognitive dissonance: Toward an integrated theory of cognition, emotion, and behavior after Leon Festinger. In E. Harmon-Jones & J. S. Mills (Eds.), *Cognitive dissonance: Progress on a pivotal theory in social psychology* (pp. 120–138). Washington, DC: American Psychological Association.

Sana, F., Weston, T., & Cepeda, N. J. (2013). Laptop multitasking hinders classroom learning for both users and nearby peers. *Computers & Education, 62*, 24–31.

Sandstorm, G. M., & Dunn, E. W. (2014). Is efficiency overrated? Minimal social interactions lead to belonging and positive affect. *Social Psychological and Personality Science, 5*, 437–442.

Sanfey, A. G., Stallen, M., & Chang, L. J. (2014). Norms and expectations in social decision-making. *Trends in Cognitive Sciences, 18*, 172–174.

Sapolsky, R. (1998). *The trouble with testosterone.* New York: Scribner.

Sastry, J., & Ross, C. E. (1998). Asian ethnicity and the sense of personal control. *Social Psychology Quarterly, 61*, 101–120.

Saunders, J. (2009). Memory impairment in the weapon focus effect. *Memory & Cognition, 37*(3), 326–335. doi:10.3758/MC.37.3.326

Savitsky, K. (1998). Embarrassment study [E-mails]. Society for Personal and Social Psychology e-mail list archive. Retrieved from www.stolaf.edu/cgi-bin/mailarchivesearch.pl?directory=/home/www/people/huff/SPSP&listname=archive98

Savitsky, K., Cone, J., Rubel, J., & Eibach, R. P. (2016). Haters are all the same: Perceptions of group homogeneity following positive vs. negative feedback. *Journal of Experimental Social Psychology, 64*, 50–56.

Schachter, S. (1951). Deviation, rejection, and communication. *Journal of Abnormal and Social Psychology, 46*, 190–207.

Schachter, S. (1959). *The psychology of affiliation.* Stanford, CA: Stanford University Press.

Schachter, S. (1964). The interaction of cognitive and physiological determinants of emotional state. In L. Berkowitz (Ed.), *Advances in experimental social psychology* (Vol. 1, pp. 49–80). New York: Academic Press.

Schachter, S., & Singer, J. E. (1962). Cognitive, social, and physiological determinants of emotional states. *Psychological Review, 69*, 379–399.

Schaller, M., Asp, C. H., Rosell, M. C., & Heim, S. J. (1996). Training in statistical reasoning inhibits formation of erroneous group stereotypes. *Personality and Social Psychology Bulletin, 22*, 829–844.

Scheele, D., Wille, A., Kendrick. K. M., Stoffel-Wagner, B., Becker, B., Güntürkün, O., et al. (2013). Oxytocin enhances brain reward system responses in men viewing the face of their female partner. *Proceedings of the National Academy of Sciences, 110*, 20308–20313.

Schiappa, E., Gregg, P. B., & Hewes, D. E. (2005). The parasocial contact hypothesis. *Communication Monographs, 72*, 92–115.

Schlegel, S. (1998). *Wisdom from a rainforest: The spiritual journey of an anthropologist.* Athens: University of Georgia Press.

Schlenker, B. R. (2003). Self-presentation. In M. R. Leary & J. P. Tangney (Eds.), *Handbook of self and identity* (pp. 492–518). New York: Guilford.

Schmader, T., & Johns, M. (2003). Converging evidence that stereotype threat reduces working memory capacity. *Journal of Personality and Social Psychology, 85*(3), 440–452.

Schmeichel, B. J., Gailliot, M. T., Filardo, E.-A., McGregor, I., Gitter, S., & Baumeister, R. F. (2009). Terror management theory and self-esteem revisited: The roles of implicit and explicit self-esteem in mortality salience effects. *Journal of Personality and Social Psychology, 96*(5), 1077–1087. doi:10.1037/a0015091

Schmidt, H. G., Mamede, S., van den Berge, K., van Gog, T., van Saase, J.,& Rikers, R. (2014). Exposure to media information about a disease can cause doctors to misdiagnose similar-looking clinical cases. *Academic Medicine, 89*, 285–291.

Schmitt, B. H., Gilovich, T., Goore, N., & Joseph, L. (1986). Mere presence and social facilitation: One more time. *Journal of Experimental Social Psychology, 22*, 228–241.

Schofield, J. W. (1986). Causes and consequences of the color-blind perspective. In J. F. Dovidio & S. L. Gaertner (Eds.), *Prejudice, discrimination, and racism* (pp. 231–253). Orlando, FL: Academic Press.

Scholten, L., van Knippenberg, D., Nijstad, B. A., & De Dreu, C. K. W. (2007). Motivated information processing and group decision-making: Effects of process accountability on information processing and decision quality. *Journal of Experimental Social Psychology, 43*, 539–552.

Schooler, J. W., & Eich, E. (2000). Memory for emotional events. In E. Tulving & F. I. M. Craik (Eds.), *The Oxford handbook of memory* (pp. 379–392). Oxford, UK: Oxford University Press.

Schopler, J., & Insko, C. A. (1999). The reduction of the interindividual-intergroup discontinuity effect: The role of future consequences. In M. Foddy & M. Smithson (Eds.), *Resolving social dilemmas: Dynamic, structural, and intergroup aspects* (pp. 281–293). Bristol, PA: Taylor & Francis.

Schriber, R. A., & Robbins, R. W. (2012). Self-knowledge: An individual differences perspective. In S. Vazire & T. D. Wilson (Eds.), *The handbook of self-knowledge* (pp. 105–127). New York: Guilford Press.

Schrift, R. Y., & Parker, J. R. (2014). Staying the course: The option of doing nothing and its impact on postchoice persistence. *Psychological Science, 25*, 772–780.

Schroeder, D. H., & Costa, P. T., Jr. (1984). Influence of life event stress on physical illness: Substantive effects or methodological flaws? *Journal of Personality and Social Psychology, 46*, 853–863.

Schultz, P. W., & Kaiser, F. G. (2012). Promoting pro-environmental behavior. In S. D. Clayton (Ed.), *Oxford library of psychology. The Oxford handbook of environmental and conservation psychology* (pp. 556–580). doi:10.1093/oxfordhb/9780199733026.013.0029.

Schultz, P. W., Oskamp, S., & Mainieri, T. (1995). Who recycles and when? A review of personal and situational factors. *Journal of Environmental Psychology, 15*, 105–121.

Schulz, R. (1976). Effects of control and predictability on the physical and psychological well-being of the institutionalized aged. *Journal of Personality and Social Psychology, 33*, 563–573.

Schulz, R., & Hanusa, B. H. (1978). Long-term effects of control and predictability-enhancing interventions: Findings and ethical issues. *Journal of Personality and Social Psychology, 36*, 1202–1212.

Schuman, H., & Kalton, G. (1985). Survey methods. In G. Lindzey & E. Aronson (Eds.), *Handbook of social psychology* (3rd ed., Vol. 1, pp. 635–697). New York: McGraw-Hill.

Schumann, K., & Ross, M. (2010). Why women apologize more than men: Gender differences in thresholds for perceiving offensive behavior. *Psychological Science, 21*, 1649–1655.

Schützwohl, A., Fuchs, A., McKibbin, W. F., & Schackelford, T. K. (2009). How willing are you to accept sexual requests from slightly unattractive to exceptionally attractive imagined requestors? *Human Nature, 20*, 282–293.

Schwab, N. (2014). Social influence constrained by the heritability of attitudes. *Personality and Individual Differences, 66*, 54–57.

Schwab, N., Harton, H. C., & Cullum, J. G. (2014). The effects of emergent norms and attitudes on recycling behavior. *Environment and Behavior, 46*, 403–422.

Schwarz, N., & Vaughn, L. A. (2002). The availability heuristic revisited: Ease of recall and content of recall as distinct sources of information. In T. Gilovich, D. W. Griffin, & D. Kahneman (Eds.), *Heuristics and biases: The psychology of intuitive judgment* (pp. 103–119). New York: Cambridge University Press.

Schwarz, N., Bless, H., & Bohner, G. (1991). Mood and persuasion: Affective states influence the processing of persuasive communications. *Advances in Experimental Social Psychology, 24*, 161–199.

Schwarz, N., Bless, H., Strack, F., Klumpp, G., Rittenauer-Schatka, H., & Simmons, A. (1991). Ease of retrieval as information: Another look at the availability heuristic. *Journal of Personality and Social Psychology, 61*, 195–202.

Schwarz, N., Groves, R. M., & Schuman, H. (1998). Survey methods. In D. T. Gilbert, S. T. Fiske, & G. Lindzey (Eds.), *The handbook of social psychology* (4th ed., Vol. 1, pp. 143–179). New York: McGraw-Hill.

Schwarz, N., Newman, E., & Leach, W. (2016). Making the truth stick & the myths fade: Lessons from cognitive psychology. *Behavioral Science & Policy, 2*, 85–95.

Schwinger, M., Wirthwein, L., Lemmer, G., & Steinmayr, R. (2014). Academic self-handicapping and achievement: A meta-analysis. *Journal of Educational Psychology.* Advance online publication. doi:10.1037/a0035832

Sedikides, C., & Anderson, C. A. (1994). Causal perceptions of intertrait relations: The glue that holds person types together. *Personality and Social Psychology Bulletin, 21*, 294–302.

Seery, M., Silver, R., Holman, E., Ence, W., & Chu, T. (2008). Expressing thoughts and feelings following a collective trauma: Immediate responses to 9/11 predict negative outcomes in a national sample. *Journal of Consulting and Clinical Psychology, 76*, 657–667.

Segerstrom, S. C., & O'Connor, D. B. (2012). Stress, health and illness: Four challenges for the future. *Psychology & Health, 27*, 128–140.

Selye, H. (1956). *The stress of life.* New York: McGraw-Hill.

Selye, H. (1976). *Stress in health and disease.* Woburn, MA: Butterworth.

Semmler, C., Brewer, N., & Douglass, A. B. (2012). Jurors believe eyewitnesses. In B. L. Cutler (Ed.), *Conviction of the innocent: Lessons from psychological research* (pp. 185–209). Washington, DC: American Psychological Association.

Senchak, M., & Leonard, K. E. (1992). Attachment styles and marital adjustment among newlywed couples. *Journal of Social and Personal Relationships, 9*, 51–64.

Sergios, P. A., & Cody, J. (1985). Physical attractiveness and social assertiveness skills in male homosexual dating behavior and partner selection. *Journal of Social Psychology, 125*, 505–514.

Seta, J. J., Seta, C. E., & Wang, M. A. (1990). Feelings of negativity and stress: An averaging-summation analysis of impressions of negative life experiences. *Personality and Social Psychology Bulletin, 17*, 376–384.

Sevi, B., Aral, T., & Eskenazi, T. (2017). Exploring the hook-up app: Low sexual disgust and high sociosexuality predict motivation to use Tinder for casual sex. *Personality and Individual Differences*, http://dx.doi.org/10.1016/j.paid.2017.04.053

Shah, A. K., & Oppenheimer, D M. (2008). Heuristics made easy: An effort-reduction framework. *Psychological Bulletin, 134*, 207–232.

Sharan, S. (1980). Cooperative learning in small groups. *Review of Educational Research, 50*, 241–271.

Shariff, A., & Norenzayan, A. (2007). God is watching you: Priming god concepts increases prosocial behavior in an anonymous economic game. *Psychological Science, 18*, 803–809.

Shariff, A. F., Willard, A. K., Andersen, T., & Norenzayan, A. (2015). Religious priming: A meta-analysis with a focus on prosociality. *Personality and Social Psychology Review, 20*(1), 27–48. http://dx.doi.org/10.1177/1088868314568811

Sharma, D., Booth, R., Brown, R., & Huguet, P. (2010). Exploring the temporal dynamics of social facilitation in the Stroop task. *Psychonomic Bulletin & Review, 17*(1), 52–58. doi:10.3758/PBR.17.1.52

Sharp, F. C. (1928). *Ethics*. New York: Century.

Sharpe, D., Adair, J. G., & Roese, N. J. (1992). Twenty years of deception research: A decline in subjects' trust? *Personality and Social Psychology Bulletin, 18*, 585–590.

Shavitt, S. (1990). The role of attitude objects in attitude function. *Journal of Experimental Social Psychology, 26*, 124–148.

Sheppard, J. A., & Taylor, K. M. (1999). Social loafing and expectancy-value theory. *Personality and Social Psychology Bulletin, 25*, 1147–1158.

Sheppard, J., Malone, W., & Sweeny, K. (2008). Exploring causes of the self-serving bias. *Social and Personality Psychology Compass, 2*, 895–908.

Sheridan, K. (2017, Jan. 24). US scientists raise bar for sea level by 2100. Phys.org. Retrieved May 29, 2017, from https://phys.org/news/2017-01-scientists-bar-sea.html

Sherif, M. (1936). *The psychology of social norms*. New York: Harper.

Sherif, M. (1966). *In common predicament: Social psychology of intergroup conflict and cooperation*. Boston: Houghton Mifflin.

Sherif, M., Harvey, O. J., White, J., Hood, W., & Sherif, C. W. (1961). *Intergroup conflict and cooperation: The robber's cave experiment*. Norman: Institute of Intergroup Relations, University of Oklahoma.

Sherman, D. K., Hartson, K. A., Binning, K. R., Purdie-Vaughns, V., Garcia, J., Taborsky-Barba, S., et al. (2013). Deflecting the trajectory and changing the narrative: How self-affirmation affects academic performance and motivation under identity threat. *Journal of Personality and Social Psychology, 104*, 591–618.

Sherry, J. L. (2001). The effects of violent video games on aggression: A meta-analysis. *Human Communication Research, 27*, 409–431.

Sherwin, S., & Winsby, M. (2011). A relational perspective on autonomy for older adults residing in nursing homes. *Health Expectations: An International Journal of Public Participation in Health Care & Health Policy, 14*, 182–190.

Shestakova, A., Rieskamp, J., Tugin, S., Ossadtchi, A., Krutitskaya, J., & Klucharev, V. (2013). Electrophysiological precursors of social conformity. *Social Cognitive and Affective Neuroscience, 8*, 756–763.

Shih, M., Pittinsky, T. L., & Ambady, N. (1999). Stereotype susceptibility: Identity salience and shifts in quantitative performance. *Psychological Science, 10*, 80–83.

Shiller, R. J. (2008, November 2). Challenging the crowd in whispers, not shouts. *The New York Times*, p. BU5. Retrieved July 9, 2011, from www.nytimes.com/2008/11/02/business/02view.html?pagewanted=1&_r=1&ref=business

Shipp, E. R. (2005, October 25). Rosa Parks, 92, Intrepid pioneer of civil rights movement, is dead. *The New York Times*, pp. A1, C18.

Shook, N. J., & Clay, R. (2012). Interracial roommate relationships: A mechanism for promoting sense of belonging at university and academic performance. *Journal of Experimental Social Psychology, 48*(5), 1168–1172.

Shotland, R. L., & Straw, M. K. (1976). Bystander response to an assault: When a man attacks a woman. *Journal of Personality and Social Psychology, 34*, 990–999.

Shteynberg, G. (2010). A silent emergence of culture: The social tuning effect. *Journal of Personality and Social Psychology, 99*, 683–689.

Sidanius, J., Pratto, F., & Bobo, L. (1996). Racism, conservatism, affirmative action, and intellectual sophistication: A matter of principled conservatism or group dominance? *Journal of Personality and Social Psychology, 70*, 476–490.

Siedlecki, K. L., Salthouse, T. A., Oishi, S., & Jeswani, S. (2014). The relationship between social support and subjective well-being across age. *Social Indicators Research, 117*, 561–576.

Siero, F. W., Bakker, A. B., Dekker, G. B., & Van Den Burg, M. T. C. (1996). Changing organizational energy consumption behavior through comparative feedback. *Journal of Environmental Psychology, 16*, 235–246.

Sigall, H., & Page, R. (1971). Current stereotypes: A little fading, a little faking. *Journal of Personality and Social Psychology, 18*, 247–255.

Silke, A. (Ed.). (2003). *Terrorists, victims, and society: Psychological perspectives on terrorism and its consequences*. New York: Wiley.

Silver, N. (2012, November 10). Which polls fared best (and worst) in the 2012 presidential race. *The New York Times*. Retrieved April 14, 2014, from http://fivethirtyeight.blogs.nytimes.com/2012/11/10/which-polls-fared-best-and-worst-in-the-2012-presidential-race/?_php=true&_type=blogs&_r=0

Silver, R., Holman, E. A., McIntosh, D. N., Poulin, M., & Gil-Rivas, V. (2002). Nationwide longitudinal study of psychological responses to September 11. *Journal of the American Medical Association, 2882*, 1235–1244.

Silverman, A., Logel, C., & Cohen, G. L. (2013). Self-affirmation as a deliberate coping strategy: The moderating role of choice. *Journal of Experimental Social Psychology, 49*, 93–98.

Silvia, P. J., & Abele, A. E. (2002). Can positive affect induce self-focused attention? Methodological and measurement issues. *Cognition and Emotion, 16*, 845–853.

Sime, J. D. (1983). Affiliative behavior during escape to building exits. *Journal of Environmental Psychology, 3*, 21–41.

Simmons, R. E., & Scheepers, L. (1996). Winning by a neck: Sexual selection in the evolution of giraffe. *The American Naturalist, 148*, 771–786.

Simms, L. J. (2002). The application of attachment theory to individual behavior and functioning in close relationships: Theory, research, and practical applications. In J. H. Harvey & A. Wenzel (Eds.), *A clinician's guide to maintaining and enhancing close relationships* (pp. 63–80). Mahwah, NJ: Erlbaum.

Simons, D. J., & Chabris, C. F. (1999). Gorillas in our midst: Sustained inattentional blindness for dynamic events. *Perception, 28*, 1059–1074.

Simons, D., & Ambinder. M. (2005). Change blindness: Theory and consequences. *Current Directions in Psychological Science, 14*, 44–48.

Simonton, D. K. (1987). *Why presidents succeed: A political psychology of leadership*. New Haven, CT: Yale University Press.

Simonton, D. K. (2001). Predicting presidential performance in the United States: Equation replication on recent survey results. *Journal of Social Psychology, 141*, 293–307.

Simpson, J. A. (1987). The dissolution of romantic relationships: Factors involved in relationship stability and emotional distress. *Journal of Personality and Social Psychology, 53*, 683–692.

Simpson, J. A. (2010). A tiller in the greening of relationship science. In M. H. Gonzales, C. Tavris, & J. Aronson (Eds.), *The scientist and the humanist: A festschrift in honor of Elliot Aronson* (pp. 203–210). New York: Psychology Press.

Simpson, J. A., & Beckes, L. (2010). Evolutionary perspectives on prosocial behavior. In M. Mikulincer & P. R. Shaver (Eds.), *Prosocial motives, emotions, and behavior: The better angels of our nature* (pp. 35–53). Washington, DC: American Psychological Association. doi:10.1037/12061-002

Simpson, J. A., & Gangestad, S. W. (1992). Sociosexuality and romantic partner choice. *Journal of Personality, 60*, 31–51.

Simpson, J. A., Collins, W. A., Tran, S., & Haydon, K. C. (2007). Attachment and the experience and expression of emotions in romantic relationships: A developmental perspective. *Journal of Personality and Social Psychology, 92*, 355–367.

Simpson, J. A., Rholes, W. S., Campbell, L., & Wilson, C. L. (2003). Changes in attachment orientations across the transition to parenthood. *Journal of Experimental Social Psychology, 39*, 317–331.

Sinaceur, M., Thomas-Hunt, M. C., Neale, M. A., O'Neill, O. A., & Haag, C. (2010). Accuracy and perceived expert status in group decisions: When minority members make majority members more accurate privately. *Personality and Social Psychology Bulletin, 3*, 423–437.

Sinclair, S., Lowery, B. S., Hardin, C. D., & Colangelo, A. (2005). Social tuning of automatic racial attitudes: The role of affiliative motivation. *Journal of Personality and Social Psychology, 89*(4), 583–592.

Singelis, T. M. (1994). The measurement of independent and interdependent self-construals. *Personality and Social Psychology Bulletin, 20*, 580–591.

Sirota, M., Kostovičová, L., & Vallée-Tourangeau, F. (2015). How to train your Bayesian: A problem-representation transfer rather than a format-representation shift explains training effects. *The Quarterly Journal of Experimental Psychology, 68*, 1–9.

Skinner, B. F. (1938). *The behavior of organisms: An experimental analysis*. New York: Appleton-Century-Crofts.

Skorinko, J. L., & Sinclair, S. A. (2013). Perspective taking can increase stereotyping: The role of apparent stereotype confirmation. *Journal of Experimental Social Psychology, 49*, 10–18.

Slavin, R. E. (1996). Cooperative learning in middle and secondary schools. (Special section: Young adolescents at risk.) *Clearing House, 69*, 200–205.

Slavin, R. E., & Cooper, R. (1999). Improving intergroup relations: Lessons learned from cooperative learning programs. *Journal of Social Issues, 55*, 647–663.

Slepian, M. L., Bogart, K. B., & Ambady, N. (2014). Thin-slice judgments in the clinical context. *Annual Review of Clinical Psychology, 10*, 16.1–16.23.

Sloan, D., Marx, B., Epstein, E., & Dobbs, J. (2008). Expressive writing buffers against maladaptive rumination. *Emotion, 8*, 302–306.

Smalarz, L., & Wells, G. L. (2014). Post-identification feedback to eyewitness impairs evaluators' abilities to discriminate between accurate and mistaken testimony. *Law and Human Behavior, 38*, 194–202.

Smith, A. (2017). Prince Harry opens up about mental health after Mom's death. *NBC News*. Retrieved April 19, 2017, from, http://www.nbc-news.com/news/world/prince-harry-opens-about-metal-health-after-mom-s-death-n747216

Smith, C. V., Hadden, B. W., Webster, G. D., Jonason, P. K., Gessekman, A. N., & Crysel, L. C. (2014). Mutually attracted or repulsed? Actor-partner interdependence models of Dark Triad traits and relationship outcomes. *Personality and Individual Differences, 67*, 35–41.

Smith, E. R., & Mackie, D. M. (2016). Representation and incorporation of close others' responses. *Personality and Social Psychology Review, 20*, 311–331.

Smith, M. B., Bruner, J., & White, R. W. (1956). *Opinions and personality*. New York: Wiley.

Smith, N. (2014). *Justice through apologies: Remorse, reform, and punishment*. New York: Cambridge University Press.

Smith, P. B. (2015). To lend helping hands: In-group favoritism, uncertainty avoidance, and the national frequency of pro-social behaviors. *Journal of Cross-Cultural Psychology, 46*, 759–771.

Smith, P. B., & Bond, M. H. (1999). *Social psychology across cultures*. Boston: Allyn & Bacon.

Smith, S. S., & Richardson, D. (1983). Amelioration of deception and harm in psychological research: The important role of debriefing. *Journal of Personality and Social Psychology, 44*, 1075–1082.

Smith, V. L. (1991). Prototypes in the courtroom: Lay representation of legal concepts. *Journal of Personality and Social Psychology, 61*, 857–872.

Smyth, J. M., Pennebaker, J. W., & Arigo, D. (2012). What are the health effects of disclosure? In A. Baum, T. A. Revenson, & J. Singer (Eds.), *Handbook of health psychology* (2nd ed., pp. 175–191). New York: Psychology Press.

Snodgrass, M., Shevrin, H., & Abelson, J. A. (2014). Extremely rigorous subliminal paradigms demonstrate unconscious influences on simple decisions. *Behavioral and Brain Sciences, 37*, 39–40.

Snyder, C. R., & Higgins, R. L. (1988). Excuses: Their effective role in the negotiation of reality. *Psychological Bulletin, 104*, 23–35.

Snyder, K. E., Malin, J. L., Dent, A. L., & Linnenbrink-Garcia, L. (2014). The message matters: The role of implicit beliefs about giftedness and failure experiences in academic self-handicapping. *Journal of Educational Psychology, 106*(1), 230–241.

Snyder, M. (1984). When belief creates reality. In L. Berkowitz (Ed.), *Advances in experimental social psychology* (Vol. 18, pp. 247–305). Orlando, FL: Academic Press.

Snyder, M. (1993). Basic research and practical problems: The promise of a "functional" personality and social psychology. *Personality and Social Psychology Bulletin, 19*, 251–264.

Snyder, M. (2016). When and why do expectations create reality? Reflections on behavioral confirmation in social interaction. In S. Trusz & P. Babel (Eds.), *Interpersonal and intrapersonal expectancies* (pp. 89–95). London: Routledge.

Snyder, M., & DeBono, K. G. (1989). Understanding the functions of attitudes: Lessons from personality and social behavior. In A. R. Pratkanis, S. J. Breckler, & A. G. Greenwald (Eds.), *Attitude structure and function* (pp. 361–381). Hillsdale, NJ: Lawrence Erlbaum.

Snyder, M., Tanke, E. D., & Berscheid, E. (1977). Social perception and interpersonal behavior: On the self-fulfilling nature of social stereotypes. *Journal of Personality and Social Psychology, 35*, 656–666.

Solis, R. (2000). Religion and intragroup cooperation: Preliminary results of a comparative analysis of utopian communities. *Cross-cultural Research, 34*, 70–87.

Solomon, L. Z., Solomon, H., & Stone, R. (1978). Helping as a function of number of bystanders and ambiguity of emergency. *Personality and Social Psychology Bulletin, 4*, 318–321.

Sommers, S. (2011). *Situations matter: Understanding how context transforms your world*. New York: Riverhead.

Sommers, S. R. (2006). On racial diversity and group decision-making: Identifying multiple effects of racial composition on jury deliberations. *Journal of Personality and Social Psychology, 90*, 597–612.

Sommers, S. R., & Marotta, S. A. (2014). Racial disparities in legal outcomes: On policing, charging decisions, and criminal trial proceedings. *Policy Insights from Behavioral and Brain Sciences, 1*, 103–111.

Son Hing, L. S., Li, W., & Zanna, M. P. (2002). Inducing hypocrisy to reduce prejudicial responses among aversive racists. *Journal of Experimental Social Psychology, 38*, 71–78.

Sorhagen, N. S. (2013). Early teacher expectations disproportionately affect poor children's high school performance. *Journal of Educational Psychology, 105*, 465–477.

Sorkin, R. D., Hays, C. J., & West, R. (2001). Signal-detection analysis of group decision making. *Psychological Review, 108*, 183–203.

Sorrentino, R. M., & Hancock, R. D. (2014). Information and affective value: A case for the study of individual difference and social influence. In M. P. Zanna, J. M. Olson, & C. P. Herman (Eds.), *Social influence: The Ontario Symposium* (Vol. 5, pp. 247–268). New York: Psychology Press.

Spink, K. S., Ulvick, J. D., Crozier, A. J., & Wilson, K. S. (2014). Group cohesion and adherence in unstructured exercise groups. *Psychology of Sport and Exercise, 15*, 293–298.

Sprecher, S. (1994). Two sides to the breakup of dating relationships. *Personal Relationships, 1*, 199–222.

Sprecher, S. (2016). Inequity leads to distress and a reduction in satisfaction: Evidence from a priming experiment. *Journal of Family Issues*. doi:10.1177/0192513X16637098

Sprecher, S., Sullivan, Q., & Hatfield, E. (1994). Mate selection preference: Gender differences examined in a national sample. *Journal of Personality and Social Psychology, 66*, 1074–1080.

Sprecher, S., Zimmerman, C., & Fehr, B. (2014). The influence of compassionate love on strategies used to end a relationship. *Journal of Social and Personal Relationships, 31*, 697–705.

Staats, H., Harland, P., & Wilke, H. A. M. (2004). Effecting durable change: A team approach to improve environmental behavior in the household. *Environment and Behavior, 36*, 341–367.

Stanley, D. A., Sokol-Hessner, P., Banaji, M. R., & Phelps, E. A. (2011). Implicit race attitudes predict trustworthiness judgments and economic trust decisions. *Proceedings of the National Academy of Sciences, 108*, 7710–7715.

Stanley, D., Phelps, E., & Banaji, M. (2008). The neural basis of implicit attitudes. *Current Directions in Psychological Science, 17*, 164–170.

Stanovich, K. E., West, R., & Toplak, M. E. (2013). Myside bias, rational thinking, and intelligence. *Psychological Science, 22*, 259–264.

Stapel, J. C., van Wijk, I. C., Bekkering, H. & Hunnius, S. (2016). Eighteen-month-old infants show distinct electrophysiological responses to their own faces. *Developmental Science*. doi: 10.1111/desc.12437

Stasser, G. (2000). Information distribution, participation, and group decision: Explorations with the DISCUSS and SPEAK models. In D. R. Ilgen & C. L. Hulin (Eds.), *Computational modeling of behavior in organizations: The third scientific discipline* (pp. 135–161). Washington, DC: American Psychological Association.

Stasser, G., & Titus, W. (1985). Pooling of unshared information in group decision making: Biased information sampling during discussion. *Journal of Personality and Social Psychology, 48*, 1467–1478.

Stasser, G., Vaughan, S. I., & Stewart, D. D. (2000). Pooling unshared information: The benefits of knowing how access to information is distributed among group members. *Organizational Behavior and Human Decision Processes, 82*, 102–116.

Staub, E. (1974). Helping a distressed person: Social, personality, and stimulus determinants. In L. Berkowitz (Ed.), *Advances in experimental social psychology* (Vol. 7, pp. 293–341). New York: Academic Press.

Staub, E. (1989). *The roots of evil: The origins of genocide and other group violence*. New York: Cambridge University Press.

Staub, E. (1999). The roots of evil: Social conditions, culture, personality, and basic human needs. *Personality and Social Psychology Review, 3*, 179–192.

Steblay, N. M. (1987). Helping behavior in rural and urban environments: A meta-analysis. *Psychological Bulletin, 102*, 346–356.

Steblay, N. M. (1997). Social influence in eyewitness recall: A meta-analytic review of lineup instruction effects. *Law and Human Behavior, 21*, 283–297.

Steblay, N. M., Dysart, J., Fulero, S. M., & Lindsay, R. C. L. (2001). Eyewitness accuracy rates in sequential and simultaneous lineup presentations: A meta-analytic comparison. *Law and Human Behavior, 25*, 459–473.

Steele, C. M. (1988). The psychology of self-affirmation: Sustaining the integrity of the self. In L. Berkowitz (Ed.), *Advances in experimental social psychology* (Vol. 21, pp. 261–302). New York: Academic Press.

Steele, C. M., (2010). *Whistling Vivaldi: And other clues to how stereotypes affect us*. New York: W.W. Norton & Co.

Steele, C. M., & Aronson, J. M. (1995a). Stereotype threat and the intellectual test performance of African-Americans. *Journal of Personality and Social Psychology, 69*, 797–811.

Steele, C. M., & Aronson, J. M. (1995b). Stereotype vulnerability and intellectual performance. In E. Aronson (Ed.), *Readings about the social animal* (7th ed.). New York: Freeman.

Steele, C. M., Hoppe, H., & Gonzales, J. (1986). *Dissonance and the lab coat: Self-affirmation and the free-choice paradigm*. Unpublished manuscript, University of Washington.

Steele, J. R., & Ambady, N. (2006). "Math is Hard!" The effect of gender priming on women's attitudes. *Journal of Experimental Social Psychology, 42*(4), 428–436. doi:10.1016/j.jesp.2005.06.003

Stein, S. (2016). The Clinton campaign was undone by its own neglect and a touch of arrogance, staffers say. Retrieved April 17, 2017, from http://www.huffingtonpost.com/entry/clinton-campaign-neglect_us_582cacb0e4b-058ce7aa8b861

Steiner, I. D. (1972). *Group process and productivity*. New York: Academic Press.

Stemple, L., & Meyer, I. H. (2014). The sexual victimization of men in America: New data challenge old assumptions. *American Journal of Public Health, 104*, e19–e26.

Stephan, W. G. (1978). School desegregation: An evaluation of predictions made in *Brown v. Board of Education*. *Psychological Bulletin, 85*, 217–238.

Stephan, W. G., & Stephan, C. W. (1985). Intergroup anxiety. *Journal of Social Issues, 41*, 157–175.

Stephens-Davidowitz, S. (2014, July 12). The data of hate. *The New York Times*, op-ed.

Stern, P. C. (2011). Contributions of psychology to limiting climate change. *American Psychologist, 66*(4), 303–314. doi:10.1037/a0023235

Sternberg, R. J. (1986). A triangular theory of love. *Psychological Review, 93*, 119–135.

Sternberg, R. J. (1987). Liking versus loving: A comparative evaluation of theories. *Psychological Bulletin, 102*, 331–345.

Stewart, D. D., & Stasser, G. (1995). Expert role assignment and information sampling during collective recall and decision making. *Journal of Personality and Social Psychology, 69*, 619–628.

Stewart, G. L., Dustin, S. L., Barrick, M. R., & Darnold, T. C. (2008). Exploring the handshake in employment interviews. *Journal of Applied Psychology, 93*, 1139–1146.

Stewart, J. B. (2002). *Heart of a soldier*. New York: Simon & Schuster.

Stice, E., Marti, C. N., Spoor, S., Presnell, K., & Shaw, H. (2008). Dissonance and healthy weight eating disorder prevention programs: Long-term effects from a randomized efficacy trial. *Journal of Consulting and Clinical Psychology, 76*, 329–340.

Stice, E., Shaw, H., Burton, E., & Wade, E. (2006). Dissonance and healthy weight eating disorders prevention programs: A randomized efficacy trial. *Journal of Consulting and Clinical Psychology, 74*, 263–275.

Stillman, T. F., Baumeister, R. F., Lambert, N. M., Crescioni, A. W., DeWall, C. N., & Fincham, F. D. (2009). Alone and without purpose: Life loses meaning following social exclusion. *Journal of Experimental Social Psychology, 45*, 686–694.

Stinson, D. A., Logel, C., Shepherd, S., & Zanna, M. P. (2011). Rewriting the self-fulfilling prophecy of social rejection: Self-affirmation improves relational security and social behavior up to 2 months later. *Psychological Science, 22*(9), 1145–1149. doi:10.1177/0956797611417725

Stoff, D. M., & Cairns, R. B. (Eds.). (1997). *Aggression and violence: Genetic, neurobiological, and biosocial perspectives*. Mahwah, NJ: Erlbaum.

Stone, J., Aronson, E., Crain, A. L., Winslow, M. P., & Fried, C. (1994). Inducing hypocrisy as a means of encouraging young adults to use condoms. *Personality and Social Psychology Bulletin, 20*, 116–128.

Storbeck, J., & Clore, G. L. (2008). Affective arousal as information: How affective arousal influences judgments, learning, and memory. *Social and Personality Psychology Compass, 2*(5), 1824–1843. doi:10.1111/j.1751-9004.2008.00138.x

Stormo, K. J., Lang, A. R., & Stritzke, W. G. K. (1997). Attributions about acquaintance rape: The role of alcohol and individual differences. *Journal of Applied Social Psychology, 27*, 279–305.

Story, L. (2007, January 15). Anywhere the eye can see, it's likely to see an ad. *The New York Times*. Retrieved July 12, 2011, from www.nytimes.com/2007/01/15/business/media/15everywhere.html?scp=1&sq=anywhere%20the%20eye%20can%20see&st=cse

Stouffer, S. A., Suchman, E. A., De Vinney, L. C., Star, S. A., & Williams, R. M., Jr. (1949). *The American soldier: Adjustment during army life* (Vol. 1). Princeton, NJ: Princeton University Press.

Strack, F., & Schwarz, N. (2016). Editorial overview: Social priming: Information accessibility and its consequences. *Current Opinion in Psychology, 12*, 4–7.

Straus, M. (2011). Gender symmetry and mutuality in perpetration of clinical-level partner violence: Empirical evidence and implications for prevention and treatment. *Aggression and Violent Behavior, 16*, 279–288.

Strohminger, N., & Nichols, S. (2014). The essential moral self. *Cognition, 131*, 159–171.

Stuhlmacher, A. F., & Citera, M. (2005). Hostile behavior and profit in virtual negotiation: A meta-analysis. *Journal of Business and Psychology, 20*, 69–93.

Stukas, A. A., Snyder, M., & Clary, E. G. (1999). The effects of "mandatory volunteerism" on intentions to volunteer. *Psychological Science, 10*, 59–64.

Sturman, E. D. (2012). Dehumanizing just makes you feel better: The role of cognitive dissonance in dehumanization. *Journal of Social, Evolutionary, and Cultural Psychology, 6*, 527–531.

Stürmer, S., & Snyder, M. (2010). Helping "us" versus "them": Towards a group-level theory of helping and altruism within and across group boundaries. In S. Stürmer & M. Snyder (Eds.), *The psychology of prosocial behavior: Group processes, intergroup relations, and helping* (pp. 33–58). Oxford, UK: Wiley-Blackwell.

Suddendorf, T., & Butler, D. L. (2013). The nature of visual self-recognition. *Trends in Cognitive Sciences, 17*(3), 121–127. doi:10.1016/j.tics.2013.01.004

Sue, D. W. (2010). *Microaggressions in everyday life: Race, gender, and sexual orientation*. Hoboken, NJ: John Wiley & Sons.

Sullivan, K. A., Kempe, C. B., Edmed, S. L., & Bonanno, G. A. (2016). Resilience and other possible outcomes after mild traumatic brain injury: A systematic review. *Neuropsychology Review, 26*, 173–185.

Suls, J. M., & Fletcher, B. (1983). Social comparison in the social and physical sciences: An archival study. *Journal of Personality and Social Psychology, 44*, 575–580.

Suls, J. M., & Miller, R. L. (Eds.). (1977). *Social comparison processes: Theoretical and empirical perspectives*. Washington, DC: Hemisphere/Halstead.

Suls, J. M., & Wheeler, L. (Eds.). (2000). *Handbook of social comparison: Theory and research*. New York: Kluwer/Plenum.

Suls, J., Martin, R., & Wheeler, L. (2000). Three kinds of opinion comparison: The Triadic Model. *Personality and Social Psychology Review, 4*, 219–237.

Surian, L., Caldi, S., & Sperber, D. (2007). Attribution of beliefs by 13-month-old infants. *Psychological Science, 18*, 580–586.

Surowiecki, J. (2004). *The wisdom of crowds: Why the many are smarter than the few and how collective wisdom shapes business, economies, societies and nations*. New York: Doubleday.

Susskind, J. M., Lee, D. H., Cusi, A., Feiman, R., Grabski, W., & Anderson, A. K. (2008). Expressing fear enhances sensory acquisition. *Nature Neuroscience, 11*, 843–850.

Sweldens, S., Corneille, O., & Yzerbyt, V. (2014). The role of awareness in attitude formation through evaluative conditioning. *Personality and Social Psychology Review, 18*, 187–209.

Swencionis, J. K.,& Fiske, S. T. (2014). How social neuroscience can inform theories of social comparison. *Neuropsychologia, 56*, 140–146.

Symons, D. (1979). *The evolution of human sexuality*. New York: Oxford University Press.

Sznycer, D., Al-Shawaf, L., Bereby-Meyer, Y., Curry, O. S., De Smet, D., Ermer, E., … Tooby, J. (2017). Cross-cultural regularities in the cognitive architecture of pride. *Proceedings of the National Academy of Sciences, 114*, 1874–1879.

Tajfel, H. (1982). Social psychology of intergroup relations. *Annual Review of Psychology, 33*, 1–39.

Tajfel, H., & Turner, J. C. (1986). The social identity theory of intergroup behavior. In S. Worchel & W. G. Austin (Eds.), *Psychology of intergroup relations*. Chicago: Nelson-Hall.

Takaku, S. (2006). Reducing road rage: An application of the dissonance-attribution model of interpersonal forgiveness. *Journal of Applied Social Psychology, 36*, 2362–2378.

Tamres, L. K., Janicki, D., & Helgeson, V. S. (2002). Sex differences in coping behavior: A meta-analytic review and an examination of relative coping. *Personality and Social Psychology Review, 6*, 2–30.

Tan, K., Agnew, C. R., VanderDrift, L. E., & Harvey, S. M. (2014). Committed to us: Predicting relationship closeness following nonmarital romantic relationship breakup. *Journal of Social and Personal Relationships*. doi:10.1177/0265407514536293

Tang, S., & Hall, V. (1995). The overjustification effect: A meta-analysis. *Applied Cognitive Psychology, 9*, 365–404.

Tang, Y., Newman, L. S., & Huang, L. (2014). How people react to social-psychological accounts of wrongdoing: The moderating effects of culture. *Journal of Cross-Cultural Psychology, 45*, 752–763.

The tangled web of porn in the office. (2008, December 8). *Newsweek*. Retrieved March 21, 2011, from www.newsweek.com/2008/11/28/the-tangled-web-of-porn-in-the-office.html

Taras, V., Sarala, R., Muchinsky, P., Kemmelmeier, M., Singelis, T. M., Avsec, A., et al. (2014). Opposite ends of the same stick? Multi-method test of the dimensionality of individualism and collectivism. *Journal of Cross-Cultural Psychology, 45*, 213–245.

Tatzel, M. (Ed.) (2014). *Consumption and well-being in the material world*. New York: Springer.

Tavris, C., & Aronson, E. (2007). *Mistakes were made (but not by me)*. New York: Harcourt.

Taylor, L. S., Fiore, A. T., Mendelsohn, G. A., & Cheshire, C. (2011). "Out of my league": A real-world test of the matching hypothesis. *Personality and Social Psychology Bulletin, 37*, 942–954.

Taylor, S. E. (1989). *Positive illusions: Creative self-deception and the healthy mind*. New York: Basic Books.

Taylor, S. E. (2012). Tend and befriend theory. In P. A. M. Van Lange, A. W. Kruglanski, & E. T. Higgins (Eds.), *Handbook of theories of social psychology* (Vol. 1, pp. 32–49). Thousand Oaks, CA: Sage Publications.

Taylor, S. E. (2015). Social cognition and health. In M. Mikulincer, P. R. Shaver, E. Borgida, & J. A. Bargh (Eds.), *APA handbooks in psychology. APA handbook of personality and social psychology, Vol. 1. Attitudes and social cognition* (pp. 339–361). Washington, DC: American Psychological Association.

Taylor, S. E., & Fiske, S. T. (1975). Point of view and perceptions of causality. *Journal of Personality and Social Psychology, 32*, 439–445.

Taylor, S. E., & Master, S. L. (2011). Social responses to stress: The tend-and-befriend model. In R. J. Contrada & A. Baum (Eds.), *The handbook of stress science: Biology, psychology, and health* (pp. 101–109). New York: Springer.

Taylor, S. E., Klein, L. C., Lewis, B. P., Gruenewald, T. L., Gurung, R. A. R., & Updegraff, J. A. (2000). Biobehavioral responses to stress in females: Tend-and-befriend, not fight-or-flight. *Psychological Review, 107*, 411–429.

Taylor, S. E., Lichtman, R. R., & Wood, J. V. (1984). Attributions, beliefs about control, and adjustment to breast cancer. *Journal of Personality and Social Psychology, 46*, 489–502.

Taylor, S. E., Repetti, R. L., & Seeman, T. (1997). Health psychology: What is an unhealthy environment and how does it get under the skin? *Annual Review of Psychology, 48*, 411–447.

Taylor, S. P., & Leonard, K. E. (1983). Alcohol and human physical aggression. In R. G. Geen & E. Donnerstein (Eds.), *Aggression: Theoretical and empirical reviews* (pp. 77–101). New York: Academic Press.

Terrier, L., & Marfaing, B. (2015).Using social norms and commitment to promote pro-environmental behavior among hotel guests. *Journal of Environmental Psychology, 44*, 10–15.

Tesser, A. (1980). Self-esteem maintenance in family dynamics. *Journal of Personality and Social Psychology, 39*, 77–91.

Tesser, A. (1988). Toward a self-evaluation maintenance model of social behavior. In L. Berkowitz (Ed.), *Advances in experimental social psychology*, Vol. 21. *Social psychological studies of the self: Perspectives and programs* (pp. 181–227). San Diego, CA: Academic Press.

Tesser, A., & Cornell, D. P. (1991). On the confluence of self processes. *Journal of Experimental Social Psychology, 27*, 501–526.

Tesser, A., & Paulus, D. (1983). The definition of self: Private and public self-evaluation management strategies. *Journal of Personality and Social Psychology, 44*, 672–682.

Tesser, A., Campbell, J. D., & Mickler, S. (1983). The role of social pressure, attention to the stimulus, and self-doubt in conformity. *European Journal of Social Psychology, 13*, 217–233.

Tesser, A., & Smith, J. (1980). Some effects of friendship and task relevance on helping: You don't always help the one you like. *Journal of Experimental Social Psychology, 16*, 583–590.

Testa, M., & Derrick, J. L. (2014). A daily process examination of the temporal association between alcohol use and verbal and physical aggression in community couples. *Psychology of Addictive Behaviors, 28*, 127–138.

Testa, M., Hoffman, J. H., & Leonard, K. E. (2011). Female intimate partner violence perpetration: Stability and predictors of mutual and nonmutual aggression across the first year of college. *Aggressive Behavior, 37*, 362–373.

Tetlock, P. E., Peterson, R. S., McGuire, C., Chang, S., & Field, P. (1992). Assessing political group dynamics: A test of the groupthink model. *Journal of Personality and Social Psychology, 63*, 403–425.

Teves, O. (2002, May 28). WHO warns Asia 25% of youth will die from smoking without curbed advertising. *Associated Press*.

Thibaut, J. W., & Kelley, H. H. (1959). *The social psychology of groups*. New York: Wiley.

Thomas, M. H. (1982). Physiological arousal, exposure to a relatively lengthy aggressive film, and aggressive behavior. *Journal of Research in Personality, 16*, 72–81.

Thomas, W. I. (1928). *The child in America*. New York: Knopf.

Thompson, J. (2000, June 18). I was certain, but I was wrong. *The New York Times*, p. D15.

Thompson, L. (1997). *The mind and heart of the negotiator*. Upper Saddle River, NJ: Prentice Hall.

Thompson, L. L., Wang, J., & Gunia, B. C. (2010). Negotiation. *Annual Review of Psychology, 61*, 491–515. doi:10.1146/annurev.psych.093008.100458

Thompson, M. P., Koss, M. P., Kingree, J. B., Goree, J., & Rice, J. (2011). Prospective mediational model of sexual aggression among college men. *Journal of Interpersonal Violence, 26*, 2716–2734.

Thompson, S. C. (2002). The role of personal control in adaptive functioning. In C. R. Snyder & S. J. Lopez (Eds.), *Handbook of positive psychology* (pp. 202–213). London: Oxford University Press.

Thompson, T. L., & Kiang, L. (2010). The model minority stereotype: Adolescent experiences and links with adjustment. *Asian American Journal of Psychology, 1,* 119–128.

Thorndike, E. L. (1920). A constant error in psychological ratings. *Journal of Applied Psychology, 4,* 25–29.

Thornton, D., & Arrowood, A. J. (1966). Self-evaluation, self-enhancement, and the locus of social comparison. *Journal of Experimental Social Psychology, 1*(Suppl.), 40–48.

Thorson, E. (2016). Belief echoes: The persistent effects of corrected misinformation. *Political Communication, 33,* 460–480.

Tidikis, V., & Ash, I. K. (2013). Working in dyads and alone: Examining process variables in solving insight problems. *Creativity Research Journal, 25,* 189–198.

Tidwell, N. D., Eastwick, P. W., & Finkel, E. J. (2013). Perceived, not actual, similarity predicts initial attraction in a live romantic context: Evidence from the speed dating paradigm. *Personal Relationships, 20,* 199–215.

Timaeus, E. (1968). Untersuchungen zum soge-nannten konformen Verhalten [Research into so-called conforming behavior]. *Zeitschrift für Experimentelle und Angewandte Psychologie, 15,* 176–194.

Timmermans, E., & De Caluwé, E. (2017). Development and validation of the Tinder Motives Scale (TMS). *Computers in Human Behavior, 70,* 341–350.

Tindale, R. S., Munier, C., Wasserman, M., & Smith, C. M. (2002). Group processes and the Holocaust. In L. S. Newman & R. Erber (Eds.), *Understanding genocide: The social psychology of the Holocaust* (pp. 143–161). New York: Oxford University Press.

Ting, J. C., & Piliavin, J. A. (2000). Altruism in comparative international perspective. In J. Phillips, B. Chapman, & D. Stevens (Eds.), *Between state and market: Essays on charities law and policy in Canada* (pp. 51–105). Kingston, Montreal: McGill-Queen's University Press.

Ting-Toomey, S., & Chung, L. (1996). Cross-cultural interpersonal communication: Theoretical trends and research directions. In W. B. Gudykunst, S. Ting-Toomey, & T. Nishida (Eds.), *Communication in personal relationships across cultures* (pp. 237–261). Thousand Oaks, CA: Sage.

Todd, A. R., Bodenhausen, G. V., Richeson, J. A., & Galinsky, A. D. (2011). Perspective taking combats automatic expressions of racial bias. *Journal of Personality and Social Psychology, 100,* 1027–1042.

Todorov, A., Said, C. P., Engell, A., & Oosterhof, N. N. (2008). Understanding evaluation of faces on social dimensions. *Trends in Cognitive Sciences, 12,* 455–460.

Toi, M., & Batson, C. D. (1982). More evidence that empathy is a source of altruistic motivation. *Journal of Personality and Social Psychology, 43,* 281–292.

Toma, C. (2017). Developing online deception literacy while looking for love. *Media, Culture, and Society, 39,* 423–428.

Toma, C., & Butera, F. (2009). Hidden profiles and concealed information: Strategic information sharing and use in group decision making. *Personality and Social Psychology Bulletin, 35*(6), 793–806. doi:10.1177/0146167209333176

Toma, C., & Butera, F. (2015). Cooperation versus competition effects on information sharing and use in group decision-making. *Social and Personality Psychology Compass, 9,* 455–467.

Toma, C. L., & Hancock, J. T. (2012). What lies beneath: The linguistic traces of deception in online dating profiles. *Journal of Communication, 62,* 78–97.

Toma, C. L., Hancock, J. T., & Ellison, N. B. (2008). Separating fact from fiction: An examination of deceptive self-presentation in online dating profiles. *Personality and Social Psychology Bulletin, 34,* 1023–1036.

Tomasello, M., & Vaish, A. (2013). Origins of human cooperation and morality. *Annual Review of Psychology, 64,* 231–255.

Tooby, J., & Cosmides, L. (2005). Conceptual foundations of evolutionary psychology. In D. M. Buss (Ed.), *The handbook of evolutionary psychology* (pp. 5–67). Hoboken, NJ: Wiley.

Tourangeau, R., Smith, T., & Rasinski, K. (1997). Motivation to report sensitive behaviors on surveys: Evidence from a bogus pipeline experiment. *Journal of Applied Social Psychology, 27,* 209–222.

Tracy, J. L., & Matsumoto, D. (2008). The spontaneous expression of pride and shame: Evidence for biologically innate nonverbal displays. *Proceedings of the National Academy of Sciences, 105,* 11655–11660.

Tracy, J. L., & Robins, R. W. (2004). Putting the self into self-conscious emotions: A theoretical model. *Psychological Inquiry, 15,* 103–125.

Tracy, J. L., & Robins, R. W. (2008). The nonverbal expression of pride: Evidence for cross-cultural recognition. *Journal of Personality and Social Psychology, 94,* 516–530.

Trappey, C. (1996). A meta-analysis of consumer choice and subliminal advertising. *Psychology and Marketing, 13,* 517–530.

Trawalter, S., Richeson, J. A., & Shelton, J. N. (2009). Predicting behavior during interracial interactions: A stress and coping approach. *Personality and Social Psychology Review.*

Triandis, H. C. (1989). The self and social behavior in differing cultural contexts. *Psychological Review, 96,* 506–520.

Triandis, H. C. (1995). *Individualism and collectivism.* Boulder, CO: Westview Press.

Trick, L., Watkins, E., Windeatt, S., & Dickens, C. (2016). The association of perseverative negative thinking with depression, anxiety and emotional distress in people with long term conditions: A systematic review. *Journal of Psychosomatic Research, 91,* 89–101.

Trivers, R. L. (1971). The evolution of reciprocal altruism. *Quarterly Review of Biology, 46,* 35–57.

Trötschel, R., Hüffmeier, J., Loschelder, D. D., Schwartz, K., & Gollwitzer, P. M. (2011). Perspective taking as a means to overcome motivational barriers in negotiations: When putting oneself into the opponent's shoes helps to walk toward agreements. *Journal of Personality and Social Psychology, 101,* 771–790. doi:10.1037/a0023801

Trumble, B. C., Cummings, D., von Rueden, C., O'Connor, A., Smith, E. A., Gurven, M., & Kaplan, H. (2012). Physical competition increases testosterone among Amazonian forager-horticulturalists: a test of the 'challenge hypothesis'. *Proceedings of the Royal Society B: Biological Sciences, 279,* 2907–2912.

Turner, F. J. (1932). *The significance of sections in American history.* New York: Henry Holt.

Turner, J. C. (1982). Towards a cognitive redefinition of the social group. In H. Tajfel (Ed.), *Social identity and intergroup relations* (pp. 15–40). Cambridge: Cambridge University Press.

Turner, M. E., & Horvitz, T. (2001). The dilemma of threat: Group effectiveness and ineffectiveness under adversity. In M. E. Turner (Ed.), *Groups at work: Theory and research* (pp. 445–470). Mahwah, NJ: Erlbaum.

Turner, M., Pratkanis, A., Probasco, P., & Leve, C. (2006). Threat, cohesion, and group effectiveness: Testing a social identity maintenance perspective on groupthink. *Small Groups* (pp. 241–264). New York: Psychology Press.

Tversky, A., & Kahneman, D. (1973). Availability: A heuristic for judging frequency and probability. *Cognitive Psychology, 5,* 207–232.

Tversky, A., & Kahneman, D. (1974). Judgment under uncertainty: Heuristics and biases. *Science, 185,* 1124–1131.

Twenge, J. M. (1997). Attitudes toward women, 1970–1995: A meta-analysis. *Psychology of Women Quarterly, 21,* 35–51.

Twenge, J. M. (2009). Change over time in obedience: The jury's still out, but it might be decreasing. *American Psychologist, 64,* 28–31.

Twenge, J. M., & Campbell, W. K. (2009). *The narcissism epidemic.* New York: Free Press.

Twenge, J. M., & Foster, J. D. (2010). Birth cohort increases in narcissistic personality traits among American college students, 1982–2009. *Social Psychological and Personality Science, 1,* 99–106.

Twenge, J. M., Campbell, W. K., & Gentile, B. (2013). Changes in pronoun use in American books and the rise of individualism, 1960–2008. *Journal of Cross-Cultural Psychology, 44,* 406–415.

Twenge, J. M., Konrath, S., Foster, J. D., Campbell, W. K., & Bushman, B. J. (2008). Egos inflating over time: A cross-temporal meta-analysis of the Narcissistic Personality Inventory. *Journal of Personality, 76,* 875–902. doi:10.1111/j.1467-6494.2008.00507.x

Twenge, J. M., Miller, J. D., & Campbell, W. K. (2014). The narcissism epidemic: Commentary on modernity and narcissistic personality disorder. *Personality Disorders: Theory, Research, and Treatment, 5,* 227–229.

Twenge, J. M., Zhang, L., & Im, C. (2004). It's beyond my control: A cross-temporal meta-analysis of increasing externality in locus of control, 1960–2002. *Personality and Social Psychology Review, 8,* 308–319.

Twenge, J. M., Gentile, B., & Campbell, W. K. (2015). Birth cohort differences in personality. In Mikilincer, M., Shaver, P. R., Cooper, M. L., & Larsen, R. J. (Eds.), *APA handbook of personality and social psychology, Volume 4: Personality processes and individual differences* (pp. 535–551). Washington, DC: American Psychological Association.

20 years ago today: Brookfield zoo gorilla helps boy who fell into habitat. (2016, Aug. 16). *Chicago Tribune.* Retrieved June 23, 2017, from http://www.chicagotribune.com/news/ct-gorilla-saves-boy-brookfield-zoo-anniversary-20160815-story.html

Ubinas, H. (2013, September 24). Smile, we've apparently lost our sense of civic duty. *Philly.com.* Retrieved April 22, 2014, from http://www.philly.com/philly/columnists/20130924_Smile_we_ve_apparently_lost_our_sense_of_civic_duty_.html

Ulloa, J. L., Puce, A., Hugueville, L., & George, N. (2014). Sustained neural activity to gaze and emotion perception in dynamic social scenes. *Social Cognitive and Affective Neuroscience, 9,* 350–357.

Unger, E. K., Burke, K. J., Yang, C. F., Bender, K. J., Fuller, P. M., & Shah, N. M. (2015). Medial amygdalar aromatase neurons regulate aggression in both sexes. *Cell Reports, 10,* 453–462.

Updegraff, J., Silver, R., & Holman, E. (2008). Searching for and finding meaning in collective trauma: Results from a national longitudinal study of the 9/11 terrorist attacks. *Journal of Personality and Social Psychology, 95,* 709–722.

Uzzell, D. (2000). Ethnographic and action research. In G. M. Breakwell, S. Hammond, & C. Fife-Schaw (Eds.), *Research methods in psychology* (2nd ed., pp. 326–337). Thousand Oaks, CA: Sage.

Vaananen, A., Buunk, B. P., Kivimaki, M., Pentti, J., & Vahteva, J. (2005). When is it better to give than to receive: Long-term health effects of perceived reciprocity in support exchange. *Journal of Personality and Social Psychology, 89,* 176–193.

van Bommel, M., van Prooijen, J.-W., Elffers, H., & Van Lange, P. A. M. (2012). Be aware to care: Public self-awareness leads to a reversal of the bystander effect. *Journal of Experimental Social Psychology, 48*(4), 926–930. doi:10.1016/j.jesp.2012.02.011

Van Boven, L., & Gilovich, T. (2003). To do or to have? That is the question. *Journal of Personality and Social Psychology, 85,* 1193–1202.

van de Ven, N., Zeelenberg, M., & Pieters, R. (2011). Appraisal patterns of envy and related emotions. *Motivation and Emotion, 36,* 195–204.

Van den Bos, K., & Lind, E. A. (2013). On sense-making reactions and public inhibition of benign social motives: An appraisal model of prosocial behavior. *Advances in Experimental Social Psychology, 48,* 1–58.

Van den Bos, K., Müller, P. A., & van Bussel, A. A. L. (2009). Helping to overcome intervention inertia in bystander's dilemmas: Behavioral disinhibition can improve the greater good. *Journal of Experimental Social Psychology, 45,* 873–878.

van Knippenberg, D., van Ginkel, W. P., & Homan, A. C. (2013). Diversity mindsets and the performance of diverse teams. *Organizational Behavior and Human Decision Processes, 121*, 183–193.

Van Laar, C., Levin, S., & Sidanius, J. (2008). Ingroup and outgroup contact: A longitudinal study of the effects of cross-ethnic friendships, dates, roommate relationships and participation in segregated organizations. In U. Wagner, L. R. Tropp, G. Finchilescu, & C. Tredoux (Eds.), *Improving intergroup relations: Building on the legacy of Thomas F. Pettigrew*. Malden, MA: Blackwell.

Van Lange, P. A. M., Joireman, J., Parks, C. D., & Van Dijk, E. (2013). The psychology of social dilemmas: A review. *Organizational Behavior and Human Decision Processes, 120*, 125–141.

Van Lange, P. A. M., Rusbult, C. E., Drigotas, S. M., Arriaga, X. B., Witcher, B. S., & Cox, C. L. (1997). Willingness to sacrifice in close relationships. *Journal of Personality and Social Psychology, 72*, 1373–1395.

van Leeuwen, E., & Täuber, S. (2010). The strategic side of out-group helping. In S. Stürmer & M. Snyder (Eds.), *The psychology of prosocial behavior: Group processes, intergroup relations, and helping* (pp. 81–99). Oxford, UK: Wiley-Blackwell.

Van Reijmersdal, E., Neijens, P., & Smit, E. G. (2009). A new branch of advertising: Reviewing factors that influence reactions to product placement. *Journal of Advertising Research, 49*(4), 429–449. doi:10.2501/S0021849909091065

Van Royen, K., Poels, K., Vandebosch, H., & Adam, P. (2017). "Thinking before posting?" Reducing cyber harassment on social networking sites through a reflective message. *Computers in Human Behavior, 66*, 345–352.

Van Vugt, M. (2006). Evolutionary origins of leadership and followership. *Personality and Social Psychology Review, 10*(4), 354–371.

Van Vugt, M., & Samuelson, C. (1999). The impact of personal metering in the management of a natural resource crisis: A social dilemma analysis. *Personality and Social Psychology Bulletin, 25*, 731–745.

Varnum, M. E. W. (2016). The emerging (social) neuroscience of SES. *Social and Personality Psychology Compass, 10*, 423–430.

Varnum, M. E. W., & Kitayama, S. (2011). What's in a name? Popular names are less common on frontiers. *Psychological Science, 22*, 176–183.

Varnum, M. E. W., Grossmann, I., Kitayama, S., & Nisbett, R. E. (2010). The origin of cultural differences in cognition: The social orientation hypothesis. *Current Directions in Psychological Science, 19*(1), 9–13. doi:10.1177/0963721409359301

Vasey, P. L., & VanderLaan, D. P. (2010). An adaptive cognitive dissociation between willingness to help kin and nonkin in Samoan Fa'afafine. *Psychological Science, 21*(2), 292–297. doi:10.1177/0956797609359623

Vedantam, S. (2006, June 23). Social isolation growing in U.S.

Verwijmeren, T., Karremans, J. C., Stroebe, W., & Wigboldus, D. (2011), The workings and limits of subliminal advertising: The role of habits. *Journal of Consumer Psychology, 21*, 206–213. doi:10.1016/j.jcps.2010.11.004

Verwijmeren, T., Karremans, J. C., Bernritter, S. F., Stroebe, W., & Wigboldus, D. H. (2013). Warning: You are being primed! The effect of a warning on the impact of subliminal ads. *Journal of Experimental Social Psychology, 49*, 1124–1129.

Vidyasagar, P., & Mishra, H. (1993). Effect of modelling on aggression. *Indian Journal of Clinical Psychology, 20*, 50–52.

Villalobos, J. G., Davis, D., & Leo, R. A. (2015). His story, her story: Sexual miscommunication, motivated remembering, and intoxication as pathways to honest false testimony regarding sexual consent. In R. Burnett (Ed.), *Vilified: Wrongful allegations of person abuse*. Oxford: Oxford University Press.

Vohs, K. D., & Baumeister, R. F. (2004). Sexual passion, intimacy and gender. In D. J. Mashek & A. Aron (Eds.), *Handbook of closeness and intimacy* (pp. 189–200). Mahwah, NJ: Erlbaum.

Vohs, K. D., & Baumeister, R. F. (Eds.). (2011). *Handbook of self-regulation*. New York: Guilford.

Vohs, K. D., Baumeister, R. F., & Schmeichel, B. J. (2012). Motivation, personal beliefs, and limited resources all contribute to self-control. *Journal of Experimental Social Psychology, 48*, 943–947.

Vohs, K. D., & Schooler, J. W. (2008). The value of believing in free will: Encouraging a belief in determinism increases cheating. *Psychological Science, 19*, 49–54.

Volunteering in the United States. (2013). Bureau of Labor Statistics, United States Department of Labor. Retrieved June 14, 2014, from http://www.bls.gov/news.release/volun.nr0.htm

von Dawans, B., Fischbacher, U., Kirschbaum, C., Fehr, E., & Heinrichs, M. (2012). The social dimension of stress reactivity: Acute stress increases prosocial behavior in humans. *Psychological Science, 23*, 651–660.

von Wittich, D., & Antonakis, J. (2011). The KAI cognitive style inventory: Was it personality all along? *Personality and Individual Differences, 50*(7), 1044–1049. doi:10.1016/j.paid.2011.01.022

Wakefield, M., Flay, B., & Nichter, M. (2003). Role of the media in influencing trajectories of youth smoking. *Addiction, 98*(Suppl. 1), Special issue: Contexts and adolescent tobacco use trajectories, 79–103.

Walker, I., & Crogan, M. (1998). Academic performance, prejudice, and the jigsaw classroom: New pieces to the puzzle. *Journal of Community and Applied Social Psychology, 8*, 381–393.

Wall, J. A., & Dunne, T. C. (2012). Mediation research: A current review. *Negotiation Journal, 28*, 217–244.

Wallach, M. A., Kogan, N., & Bem, D. J. (1962). Group influences on individual risk taking. *Journal of Abnormal and Social Psychology, 65*, 75–86.

Walster, E. (1966). Assignment of responsibility for an accident. *Journal of Personality and Social Psychology, 3*, 73–79.

Walster, E., Aronson, V., Abrahams, D., & Rottman, L. (1966). Importance of physical attractiveness in dating behavior. *Journal of Personality and Social Psychology, 5*, 508–516.

Walster, E., Walster, G. W., & Berscheid, E. (1978). *Equity: Theory and research*. Needham Heights, MA: Allyn & Bacon.

Walther, E., & Langer, T. (2010). For whom Pavlov's bell tolls: Processes underlying evaluative conditioning. In J. P. Forgas, J. Cooper, & W. D. Crano (Eds.), *The Sydney symposium of social psychology. The psychology of attitudes and attitude change* (pp. 59–74). New York: Psychology Press.

Walther, E., Bless, H., Strack, F., Rackstraw, P., Wagner, D., & Werth, L. (2002). Conformity effects in memory as a function of group size, dissenters and uncertainty. *Applied Cognitive Psychology, 16*, 793–810.

Walton, G. M. (2014). The new science of wise interventions. *Current Directions in Psychological Science, 23*, 73–82.

Wan, L., Crookes, K., Dawel, A., Pidcock, M., Hall, A., & McKone, E. (2017). Face-blind for other-race faces: Individual differences in other-race recognition impairments. *Journal of Experimental Psychology: General, 146*, 102–122.

Wang, O., & Ross, M. (2007). Culture and memory. In S. Kitayama & D. Cohen (Eds.), *Handbook of cultural psychology* (pp. 645–667). New York: Guilford.

Wang, Qi. (2016). Why should we all be cultural psychologists? Lessons from the study of social cognition. *Perspectives on Psychological Science, 11*, 583–596.

Wang, Z., Jusup, M., Wang, R. W., Shi, L., Iwasa, Y., Moreno, Y., & Kurths, J. (2017). Onymity promotes cooperation in social dilemma experiments. *Science Advances, 3*, e1601444.

Wann, D. L., Weaver, S., Belva, B., Ladd, S., & Armstrong, S. (2015). Investigating the impact of team identification on the willingness to commit verbal and physical aggression by youth baseball spectators. *Journal of Amateur Sport, 1*, 1-28.

Warneken, F., & Tomasello, M. (2014). Extrinsic rewards undermine altruistic tendencies in 20-month-olds. *Motivation Science, 1*(S), 43–48.

Warner, J. (2011, December 23). Laughter auditions: How I learned how to be a professional laugher. *LA Weekly Blogs*. Available at: blogs.laweekly.com/arts/2011/12/how_to_be_a_professional_laugh.php

Watkins, E. R., & Nolen-Hoeksema, S. (2014). A habit-goal framework of depressive rumination. *Journal of Abnormal Psychology, 123*, 24–34.

Watson, D., & Pennebaker, J. W. (1989). Health complaints, stress, and distress: Exploring the central role of negative affectivity. *Psychological Review, 96*, 234–254.

Watson, J. (1950). Some social and psychological situations related to change in attitude. *Human Relations, 3*, 15–56.

Watson, R. I. (1973). Investigation into deindividuation using a cross-cultural survey technique. *Journal of Personality and Social Psychology, 25*, 342–345.

Watson, W. E., Johnson, L., Kumar, K., & Critelli, J. (1998). Process gain and process loss: Comparing interpersonal processes and performance of culturally diverse and non-diverse teams across time. *International Journal of Intercultural Relations, 22*, 409–430.

Waytz, A., Hoffman, K. M., & Trawalter, S. (2015). A superhumanization bias in Whites' perceptions of Blacks. *Social Psychological and Personality Science, 6*, 352–359.

Weaver, C. N. (2008). Social distance as a measure of prejudice among ethnic groups in the United States. *Journal of Applied Social Psychology, 38*, 778–795.

Weaver, J., Filson Moses, J., & Snyder, M. (2016). Self-fulfilling prophecies in ability settings. *The Journal of Social Psychology, 156*, 179–189.

Weaver, J. R., & Bosson, J. K. (2011). I feel like I know you: Sharing negative attitudes of others promotes feelings of familiarity. *Personality and Social Psychology Bulletin, 37*, 481–491.

Webb, T. L., & Sheeran, P. (2006). Does changing behavioural intentions engender behavior change? A meta-analysis of the experimental evidence. *Psychological Bulletin, 132*, 249–268.

Weber, E. U., & Johnson, E. J. (2009). Mindful judgment and decision making. *Annual Review of Psychology, 60*, 53–85. doi:10.1146/annurev.psych.60.110707.163633

Weber, E. U., Bockenholt, U., Hilton, D. J., & Wallace, B. (1993). Determinants of diagnostic hypothesis generation: Effects of information, base rates, and experience. *Journal of Experimental Psychology: Learning, Memory, and Cognition, 19*, 1151–1164.

Weber, J. M., Kopelman, S., & Messick, D. M. (2004). A conceptual review of decision making in social dilemmas: Applying a logic of appropriateness. *Personality and Social Psychology Review, 8*, 281–307.

Webster, D. M. (1993). Motivated augmentation and reduction of the overattributional bias. *Journal of Personality and Social Psychology, 65*, 261–271.

Wechsler, H., & Austin, S. B. (1998). Binge drinking: The five/four measure. *Journal of Studies of Alcohol, 59*, 122–124.

Wegener, D. T., & Petty, R. E. (1994). Mood management across affective states: The hedonic contingency hypothesis. *Journal of Personality and Social Psychology, 66*, 1034–1048.

Wegner, D. M. (1986). Transactive memory: A contemporary analysis of the group mind. In B. Mullen & G. R. Goethals (Eds.), *Theories of group behavior* (pp. 185–208). New York: Springer-Verlag.

Wegner, D. M. (1992). You can't always think what you want: Problems in the suppression of unwanted thoughts. In M. P. Zanna (Ed.), *Advances in experimental social psychology* (Vol. 25, pp. 193–225). San Diego, CA: Academic Press.

Wegner, D. M. (1994). Ironic processes of mental control. *Psychological Review, 101*, 34–52.

Wegner, D. M. (1995). A computer network model of human transactive memory. *Social Cognition, 13*, 319–339.

Wegner, D. M. (2002). *The illusion of conscious will*. Cambridge, MA: MIT Press.

Wegner, D. M. (2004). Precis of the illusion of conscious will. *Behavioral & Brain Sciences, 27,* 649–659.

Wegner, D. M., Sparrow, B., & Winerman, L. (2004). Vicarious agency: Experiencing control over the movements of others. *Journal of Personality and Social Psychology, 86,* 838–848.

Wehrens, M. J. P. W., Kuyper, H., Dijkstra, P., Buunk, A. P., & Van Der Werf, M. P. C. (2010). The long-term effect of social comparison on academic performance. *European Journal of Social Psychology, 40*(7), 1158–1171. doi:10.1002/ejsp.706

Wehrle, T., Kaiser, S., Schmidt, S., & Scherer, K. R. (2000). Studying the dynamics of emotional expression using synthesized facial muscle movements. *Journal of Personality and Social Psychology, 78,* 105–119.

Weihs, K. L., Enright, T. M., & Simmens, S. J. (2008). Close relationships and emotional processing predict decreased mortality in women with breast cancer: Preliminary evidence. *Psychosomatic Medicine, 70*(1), 117–124. doi:10.1097/PSY.0b013e31815c25cf

Weiner, B. (1985). "Spontaneous" causal thinking. *Psychological Bulletin, 97,* 74–84.

Weiner, B. (2008). Reflections on the history of attribution theory and research. *Social Psychology, 39,* 151–156.

Weingarten, E., Chen, Q., McAdams, M., Yi, J., Hepler, J., & Albarracín, D. (2016). From primed concepts to action: A metaanalysis of the behavioral effects of incidentally presented words. *Psychological Bulletin, 142*(5), 472–497.

Weinstock, M. (2011). Knowledge-telling and knowledge-transforming arguments in mock jurors' verdict justifications. *Thinking & Reasoning, 17*(3), 282–314. doi:10.1080/13546783.2011.575191

Weir, W. (1984). Another look at subliminal "facts." *Advertising Age,* October 15, p. 46.

Wells, G. L. (2014). Eyewitness identification: Probative value, criterion shifts, and policy regarding the sequential lineup. *Current Directions in Psychological Science, 23,* 11–16.

Wells, G. L., & Quinlivan, D. S. (2009). Suggestive eyewitness identification procedures and the Supreme Court's reliability test in light of eyewitness science: 30 years later. *Law and Human Behavior, 33,* 1–24.

Wells, G. L., Malpass, R. S., Lindsay, R. C. L., Fisher, R. P., Turtle, J. W., & Fulero, S. M. (2000). From the lab to the police station. *American Psychologist, 55,* 581–598.

Wells, G. L., Small, M., Penrod, S., Malpass, R. S., Fulero, S. M., & Brimacombe, C. E. (1998). Eyewitness identification procedures: Recommendations for lineups and photospreads. *Law and Human Behavior, 22,* 603–647.

Wenzler, S., Levine, S., van Dick, R., Oertel-Knöchel, V., & Aviezer, H. (2016). Beyond pleasure and pain: Facial expression ambiguity in adults and children during intense situations. *Emotion, 16,* 807–814.

Werth, L., & Foerster, J. (2002). Implicit person theories influence memory judgments: The circumstances under which metacognitive knowledge is used. *European Journal of Social Psychology, 32,* 353–362.

Wertheim, L. J., & Sommers, S. (2016). *This is your brain on sports: The science of underdogs, the value of rivalry, and what we can learn from the t-shirt cannon.* New York: Crown.

West, T. V., Magee, J. C., Gordon, S. H., & Gullett, L. (2014). A little similarity goes a long way: The effects of peripheral but self-revealing similarities on improving and sustaining interracial relationships. *Journal of Personality and Social Psychology, 107,* 81–100.

Westen, D. (2007). *The political brain: The role of emotion in deciding the fate of the nation.* New York: Public Affairs Books.

Westen, D., Kilts, C., Blagov, P., et al. (2006). The neural basis of motivated reasoning: An fMRI study of emotional constraints on political judgment during the U.S. presidential election of 2004. *Journal of Cognitive Neuroscience, 18,* 1947–1958.

Weyant, J. M. (1996). Application of compliance techniques to direct-mail requests for charitable donations. *Psychology and Marketing, 13,* 157–170.

Wheeler, L., & Kim, Y. (1997). What is beautiful is culturally good: The physical attractiveness stereotype has different content in collectivistic cultures. *Personality and Social Psychology Bulletin, 23,* 795–800.

Wheeler, L., Koestner, R., & Driver, R. (1982). Related attributes in the choice of comparison others: It's there, but it isn't all there is. *Journal of Experimental Social Psychology, 18,* 489–500.

Wheeler, M. E., & Fiske, S. T. (2005). Controlling racial prejudice: Social-cognitive goals affect amygdala and stereotype activation. *Psychological Science, 16,* 56–63.

Wheeler, S. C., & DeMarree, K. G. (2009). Multiple mechanisms of prime-to-behavior effects. *Social and Personality Psychology Compass, 3*(4), 566–581. doi:10.1111/j.1751-9004.2009.00187.x

Wheeler, S. C., Briñol, P., & Hermann, A. D. (2007). Resistance to persuasion as self-regulation: Ego-depletion and its effects on attitude change processes. *Journal of Experimental Social Psychology, 43,* 150–156.

White, C., Baimel, A., & Norenzayan, A. (2017). What are the causes and consequences of belief in karma? *Religion, Brain & Behavior.* doi:10.1080/2153599X.2016.1249921

White, K. M., Smith, J. R., Terry, D. J., Greenslade, J. H., & McKimmie, B. M. (2009). Social influence in the theory of planned behaviour: The role of descriptive, injunctive, and in-group norms. *British Journal of Social Psychology, 48,* 135–158.

White, M. H. II, & Sheldon, K. M. (2014). The contract year syndrome in the NBA and MLB: A classic undermining pattern. *Motivation and Emotion, 38,* 196–205.

White, P. A. (2002). Causal attribution from covariation information: The evidential evaluation model. *European Journal of Social Psychology, 32,* 667–684.

White, R. K. (1977). Misperception in the Arab-Israeli conflict. *Journal of Social Issues, 33,* 190–221.

Whittaker, J. O., & Meade, R. D. (1967). Social pressure in the modification and distortion of judgment: A cross-cultural study. *International Journal of Psychology, 2,* 109–113.

Whyte, J., & Torgler, B. (2017). Things change with age: Educational assortment in online dating. *Personality and Individual Differences, 109,* 5–11.

Wicker, A. W. (1969). Attitudes versus actions: The relationship between verbal and overt behavioral responses to attitude objects. *Journal of Social Issues, 25,* 41–78.

Wigboldus, D. H., Dijksterhuis, A., & Van Knippenberg, A. (2003). When stereotypes get in the way: Stereotypes obstruct stereotype-inconsistent trait inferences. *Journal of Personality and Social Psychology, 84,* 470–484.

Wilford, M. M., & Wells, G. L. (2010). Does facial processing prioritize change detection? Change blindness illustrates costs and benefits of holistic processing. *Psychological Science, 21*(11), 1611–1615. doi:10.1177/0956797610385952

Wilkins, C. L., & Kaiser, C. R. (2014). Racial progress as a threat to the status hierarchy: Implications for perceptions of anti-white bias. *Psychological Science, 25,* 439–446.

Willard, J., & Madon, S. (2016). Understanding the connections between self-fulilling prophecies and social problems. In S. Trusz & P. Babel (Eds.), *Interpersonal and intrapersonal expectancies* (pp. 117–124). London: Routledge.

Willard, J., Madon, S., Guyll, M., Scherr, K. C., & Buller, A. A. (2012). The accumulating effects of shared expectations. *European Journal of Social Psychology, 42,* 497–508. doi:10.1002/ejsp.874

Williams, K. D., & Nida, S. A. (2011). Ostracism: Consequences and coping. *Current Directions in Psychological Science, 20,* 71–75.

Williams, L. E., & Bargh, J. A. (2008). Experiencing physical warmth promotes interpersonal warmth. *Science, 322*(5901), 606–607. doi:10.1126/science.1162548

Williams, T. P., & Sogon, S. (1984). Group composition and conforming behavior in Japanese students. *Japanese Psychological Research, 26,* 231–234.

Williamson, P., Weber, N., & Robertson, M-T (2013). The effect of expertise on memory conformity: A test of informational influence. *Behavioral Sciences and the Law, 31,* 607–623.

Willis, J., & Todorov, A. (2006). First impressions: Making up your mind after a 100-ms exposure to a face. *Psychological Science, 17,* 592–598.

Willmott, L., Harris, P., Gellaitry, G., Cooper, V., & Horne, R. (2011). The effects of expressive writing following first myocardial infarction: A randomized controlled trial. *Health Psychology, 30*(5), 642–650. doi:10.1037/a0023519

Wilner, D., Walkley, R., & Cook, S. (1955). *Human relations in interracial housing.* Minneapolis: University of Minnesota Press.

Wilson, A. E., & Ross, M. (2000). The frequency of temporal-self and social comparisons in people's personal appraisals. *Journal of Personality and Social Psychology, 78,* 928–942.

Wilson, C. (2011, February 15). Jeopardy, Schmeopardy: Why IBM's next target should be a machine that plays poker. *Slate.com.* Retrieved April 18, 2011, from www.slate.com/id/2285035/

Wilson, D. S., & Wilson E. O. (2007, November 3). Survival of the selfless. *New Scientist,* pp. 42–46.

Wilson, D. S., Van Vugt, M., & O'Gorman, R. (2008). Multilevel selection theory and major evolutionary transitions: Implications for psychological science. *Current Directions in Psychological Science, 17,* 6–9.

Wilson, I. (2014, April 10). Dangerous "polar plunge" trend causes concern for N.H. school districts. *Concord Monitor.* Retrieved May 26, 2014, from www.concordmonitor.com/news/11495396-95/dangerous-polar-plunge-trend-causes-concern-for-nh-school-districts

Wilson, R. E., Gosling, S. D., & Graham, L. T. (2012). A review of Facebook research in the social sciences. *Perspectives on Psychological Science, 7,* 203–220.

Wilson, S. J., & Lipsey, M. W. (2007). School-based interventions for aggressive and disruptive behavior: Update of a meta-analysis. *American Journal of Preventive Medicine, 33,* S130–S143.

Wilson, T. D. (2002). *Strangers to ourselves: Discovering the adaptive unconscious.* Cambridge, MA: Harvard University Press.

Wilson, T. D. (2011). *Redirect: The surprising new science of psychological change.* New York: Little, Brown.

Wilson, T. D. (2015). *Redirect: Changing the stories we live by.* New York: Little, Brown.

Wilson, T. D., & Bar-Anan, Y. (2008). The unseen mind. *Science, 321,* 1046–1047.

Wilson, T. D., & Brekke, N. (1994). Mental contamination and mental correction: Unwanted influences on judgments and evaluations. *Psychological Bulleting, 116,* 117–142.

Wilson, T. D., & Dunn, E. W. (2004). Self-knowledge: Its limits, value and potential for improvement. *Annual Review of Psychology, 55,* 493–518.

Wilson, T. D., & Gilbert, D. T. (2003). Affective forecasting. In M. P. Zanna (Ed.), *Advances in experimental social psychology* (Vol. 35, pp. 345–411). San Diego, CA: Academic Press.

Wilson, T. D., & Gilbert, D. T. (2008). Explaining away: A model of affective adaptation. *Perspectives on Psychological Science, 3,* 370–386.

Wilson, T. D., Aronson, E., & Carlsmith, K. (2010). The art of laboratory experimentation. In S. Fiske, D. Gilbert, & G. Lindzey (Eds.), *Handbook of social psychology* (5th ed., pp. 49–79). New York: Wiley.

Wilson, T. D., Houston, C. E., & Meyers, J. M. (1998). Choose your poison: Effects of lay beliefs about mental processes on attitude change. *Social Cognition, 16,* 114–132.

Wilson, T. D., Laser, P. S., & Stone, J. I. (1982). Judging the predictors of one's own mood: Accuracy and the use of shared theories. *Journal of Experimental Social Psychology, 18,* 537–556.

Wilson, T. D., Lindsey, S., & Schooler, T. Y. (2000). A model of dual attitudes. *Psychological Review, 107,* 101–126.

Wilson, T. D., Reinhard, D., Westgate, E. C., Gilbert, D. T., Ellerbeck, N., Hahn, C., Brown, C. L., & Shaked, A. (2014). Just think: The challenges of the disengaged mind. *Science, 345,* 75–77.

Wilton, C., & Campbell, M. A. (2011). An exploration of the reasons why adolescents engage in traditional and cyber bullying. *Journal of Educational Sciences and Psychology, 1,* 101–109.

Winkielman, P., Niedenthal, P., Wielgosz, J., Eelen, J., & Kavanagh, L. C. (2015). Embodiment of cognition and emotion. In M. Mikulincer, P. R. Shaver, E. Borgida, & J. A. Bargh (Eds.), *APA handbooks in psychology. APA handbook of personality and social psychology,* Vol. 1. *Attitudes and social cognition* (pp. 151–175). http://dx.doi.org/10.1037/14341-004

Wisman, A., Heflick, N., & Goldenberg, J. L. (2015). The great escape: The role of self-esteem and self-related cognition in terror management. *Journal of Experimental Social Psychology, 60,* 121-132.

Wittenbaum, G. M., & Moreland, R. L. (2008). Small-group research in social psychology: Topics and trends over time. *Social and Personality Psychology Compass, 2* 187–203.

Wojciszke, B. (2005). Affective concomitants of information on morality and competence. *European Psychologist, 10,* 60–70.

Wolf, S. (2014). Majority and minority influence: A social impact analysis. In M. P. Zanna, J. M. Olson, & C. P. Herman (Eds.), *Social influence: The Ontario Symposium* (Vol. 5, pp. 207–236). New York: Psychology Press.

Wolfe, C., & Spencer, S. (1996). Stereotypes and prejudice: Their overt and subtle influence in the classroom. *American Behavioral Scientist, 40,* 176–185.

Wolfson, A. (2005). A hoax most cruel. *The Courier-Journal,* October 9. Retrieved June 5, 2006, from www.courier-journal.com/apps/pbcs.d11/article?Date=20051009&category=NEWS01

Wong, E. M., Galinsky, A. D., & Kray, L. J. (2009). The counterfactual mind-set: A decade of research. In K. D. Markman, W. M. P. Klein, & J. A. Suhr (Eds.), *Handbook of imagination and mental simulation* (pp. 161–174). New York: Psychology Press.

Wong, R. Y., & Hong, Y. (2005). Dynamic influences of culture on cooperation in a Prisoner's Dilemma game. *Psychological Science, 16,* 429–434.

Wood, J. V., Taylor, S. E., & Lichtman, R. R. (1985). Social comparison in adjustment to breast cancer. *Journal of Personality and Social Psychology, 49,* 1169–1183.

Wood, W. (1982). Retrieval of attitude-relevant information from memory: Effects on susceptibility to persuasion and on intrinsic motivation. *Journal of Personality and Social Psychology, 42,* 798–810.

Wood, W., & Eagly, A. H. (2002). A cross-cultural analysis of the behavior of women and men: Implications for the origins of sex differences. *Psychological Bulletin, 128,* 699–727.

Wood, W., & Quinn, J. M. (2003). Forewarned and forearmed? Two meta-analytic syntheses of forewarnings of influence appeals. *Psychological Bulletin, 129,* 119–138.

Wood, W., Lundgren, S., Ouellette, J. A., Busceme, S., & Blackstone, T. (1994). Minority influence: A meta-analytic review of social influence processes. *Psychological Bulletin, 115,* 323–345.

Wood, W., Pool, G. J., Leck, K., & Purvis, D. (1996). Self-definition, defensive processing, and influence: The normative impact of majority and minority groups. *Journal of Personality and Social Psychology, 71,* 1181–1193.

Word, C. O., Zanna, M. P., & Cooper, J. (1974). The nonverbal mediation of self-fulfilling prophecies in interracial interaction. *Journal of Experimental Social Psychology, 10,* 109–120.

World Hunger and Poverty Facts and Statistics (2016, Dec. 28). *Hunger Notes.* Retrieved May 29, 2016, from http://www.worldhunger.org/2015-world-hunger-and-poverty-facts-and-statistics/

Wortman, C. B., & Silver, R. C. (1989). The myths of coping with loss. *Journal of Consulting and Clinical Psychology, 57,* 349–357.

Wrangham, R. W., Wilson, M. L., & Muller, M. N. (2006). Comparative rates of violence in chimpanzees and humans. *Primates, 47,* 14–26.

Wright, D. B., & Stroud, J. N. (2002). Age differences in lineup identification accuracy: People are better with their own age. *Law and Human Behavior, 26,* 641–654.

Wright, E. F., Lüüs, C. E., & Christie, S. D. (1990). Does group discussion facilitate the use of consensus information in making causal attributions? *Journal of Personality and Social Psychology, 59,* 261–269.

Wright, L. (1994). *Remembering Satan.* New York: Knopf.

Wright, P. J., Tokunaga, R. S., & Kraus, A. (2016). A meta-analysis of pornography consumption and actual acts of sexual aggression in general population studies. *Journal of Communication, 66,* 183–205.

Wright, S. C., Aron, A., McLaughlin-Volpe, T., & Ropp, S. A. (1997). The extended contact effect: Knowledge of cross-group friendships and prejudice. *Journal of Personality and Social Psychology, 73,* 73-90.

Wright, S. C., Brody, S. M., & Aron, A. (2005). Intergroup contact: Still our best hope for improving intergroup relations. In C.S. Crandall & M. Schaller (Eds.), *Social Psychology of Prejudice: Historical and Contemporary Issues* (pp. 115–142). Lawrence, KS: Lewinian Press.

Wubben, M. J. J., De Cremer, D., & van Dijk, E. (2009). How emotion communication guides reciprocity: Establishing cooperation through disappointment and anger. *Journal of Experimental Social Psychology, 45*(4), 987–990. doi:10.1016/j.jesp.2009.04.010

Wusik, M. F., & Axsom, D. (2016). Socially positive behaviors as self-handicapping. *Journal of Social and Clinical Psychology, 35,* 494–509.

Wyer, R. S., & Srull, T. K. (1989). *Memory and cognition in its social context.* Hillsdale, NJ: Erlbaum.

Xu, H., Bègue, L., & Bushman, B. J. (2012). Too fatigued to care: Ego depletion, guilt, and prosocial behavior. *Journal of Experimental Social Psychology, 48*(5), 1183–1186.

Xu, K., Nosek, B., & Greenwald, A. G. (2014). Psychology data from the Race Implicit Association Test on the Project Implicit Demo website. *Journal of Open Psychology Data, 2,* e3.

Xygalatas, D., Mitkidis, P., Fischer, R., Reddish, P., Skewes, J., Geertz, A. W., et al. (2013). Extreme rituals promote prosociality. *Psychological Science, 24,* 1602–1605.

Yahalom, N., & Schul, Y. (2016). Applying ease of retrieval in judgments: The role of contextual background. *Social Cognition, 34,* 217–237.

Yamaguchi, M., Masuchi, A., Nakanishi, D., Suga, S., Konishi, N., Yu, Y., & Ohtsubo, Y. (2016). Experiential purchases and prosocial spending promote happiness by enhancing social relationships. *The Journal of Positive Psychology, 11,* 480–488.

Yan, Y., & Bissell, K., (2014). The globalization of beauty: How is ideal beauty influenced by globally published fashion and beauty magazines? *Journal of Intercultural Communication Research.* doi:10.1080/17475759.2014.917432

Yan, X., Andrews, T. J., & Young, A. W. (2016). Cultural similarities and differences in perceiving and recognizing facial expressions of basic emotions. *Journal of Experimental Psychology: Human Perception and Performance, 42,* 423–440.

Yeager, D. S., Johnson, R., Spitzer, B. J., Trzesniewski, K. H., Powers, J., & Dweck, C. S. (2014). The far-reaching effects of believing people can change: Implicit theories of personality shape stress, health, and achievement during adolescence. *Journal of Personality and Social Psychology, 106,* 867–884.

Yeager, D. S., Romero, C., Paunesku, D., Hulleman, C. S., Schneider, B., Hinojosa, C., … Dweck, C. S. (2016). Using design thinking to improve psychological interventions: The case of the growth mindset during the transition to high school. *Journal of Educational Psychology, 108,* 374–391.

Yoffe, E. (2014, December 7). The college rape over-correction. *Slate.com.* http://www.slate.com/articles/double_x/doublex/2014/12/college_rape_campus_sexual_assault_is_a_serious_problem_but_the_efforts.html

Young, A. I., & Fazio, R. H. (2013). Attitude accessibility as a determinant of object construal and evaluation. *Journal of Experimental Social Psychology, 49,* 404–418.

Yue, Y., Wang, K. L., & Groth, M. (2016). Feeling bad and doing good: The effect of customer mistreatment on service employee's daily display of helping behaviors. *Personnel Psychology.* doi:10.1111/peps.12208

Yuki, M., & Brewer, M. (2014). *Culture and group processes.* New York: Oxford University Press.

Yukl, G. (2011). Contingency theories of effective leadership. In A. Bryman, D. L. Collinson, K. Grint, B. Jacksin, & M. Uhl-Bien (Eds.), *The Sage handbook of leadership* (pp. 286–298). Thousand Oaks, CA: Sage.

Zajonc, R. B. (1965). *Social facilitation.* Research Center for Group Dynamics, Institute for Social Research, University of Michigan.

Zajonc, R. B. (1968). Attitudinal effects of mere exposure. *Journal of Personality and Social Psychology, 9,* 1–27.

Zajonc, R. B. (1980). Feeling and thinking: Preferences need no inferences. *American Psychologist, 35,* 151–175.

Zajonc, R. B., Heingartner, A., & Herman, E. M. (1969). Social enhancement and impairment of performance in the cockroach. *Journal of Personality and Social Psychology, 13,* 83–92.

Zaki, J., & Mitchell, J. P. (2016). Prosociality as a form of reward seeking. In J. D. Greene, I. Morrison, & M. E. P. Seligman, *Positive neuroscience* (pp. 57–72). New York: Oxford University Press.

Zanna, M. P., & Rempel, J. K. (1988). Attitudes: A new look at an old concept. In D. Bar-Tal & A. W. Kruglanski (Eds.), *The social psychology of knowledge* (pp. 315–334). Cambridge, England: Cambridge University Press.

Zanot, E. J., Pincus, J. D., & Lamp, E. J. (1983). Public perceptions of subliminal advertising. *Journal of Advertising, 12,* 39–45.

Zebrowitz, L. A., & Franklin, R. G., Jr. (2014). The attractiveness halo effect and the babyface stereotype in older and younger adults: Similarities, own-age accentuation, and older adult positivity effects. *Experimental Aging Research, 40,* 375–393.

Zebrowitz, L. A., & Montepare, J. M. (2008). Social psychological face perception: Why appearance matters. *Social and Personality Psychology Compass, 2,* 1497–1517.

Zebrowitz, L. A., Wang, R., Bronstad, P. M., Eisenberg, D., Undurraga, E., Reyes-García, V., et al. (2012). First impressions from faces among US and culturally isolated Tsimane' people in the Bolivian rainforest. *Journal of Cross-Cultural Psychology, 43,* 119–134.

Zhang, D., Lowry, P. B., Zhou, L., & Fu, X. (2007). The impact of individualism-collectivism, social presence, and group diversity on group decision making under majority influence. *Journal of Management Information Systems, 23,* 53–80.

Zhang, H., You, J., Teng, F., & Chan, D. K. (2014). Differential roles of physical attractiveness and earning capability in explaining sense of power among dating individuals in China: A gender comparison. *Sex Roles, 70,* 343–355.

Zhang, Q., & Covey, J. (2014). Past and future implications of near-misses and their emotional consequences. *Experimental Psychology, 61,* 118–126.

Zhang, S., & Kline, S. L. (2009). Can I make my own decision? A cross-cultural study of perceived social network influence in mate selection. *Journal of Cross-Cultural Psychology, 40*, 3–23.

Zhao, K., Ferguson, E., & Smillie, L. D. (2016). Prosocial personality traits differentially predict egalitarianism, generosity, and reciprocity in economic games. *Frontiers in Psychology, 7*, Article 1137.

Zhong, C.-B., & Liljenquist, K. (2006). Washing away your sins: Threatened morality and physical cleansing. *Science, 313*, 1451–1452.

Zhu, Y., & Han, S. (2008). Cultural differences in the self: From philosophy to psychology and neuroscience. *Social and Personality Psychology Compass, 2*, 1799–1811.

Zillmann, D. (1978). Attributions and misattributions of excitatory reactions. In J. H. Harvey, W. Ickes, & R. F. Kidd, (Eds.), *New directions in attribution research* (Vol. 2). Hillsdale, NJ: Erlbaum.

Zimbardo, P. G. (1970). The human choice: Individuation, reason, and order versus deindividuation, impulse, and chaos. In W. J. Arnold & D. Levine (Eds.), *Nebraska Symposium on Motivation* (Vol. 17; pp. 237–307). Lincoln: University of Nebraska Press.

Zimbardo, P. G. (2007). *The Lucifer effect: Understanding how good people turn evil*. New York: Random House.

Zimbardo, P., & Andersen, S. (1993). Understanding mind control: Exotic and mundane mental manipulations. *Recover from cults: Help for victims of psychological and spiritual abuse*, pp. 104–125.

Credits

Photo Credits

Chapter 1   Page 1: pixelheadphoto digitalskillet/Shutterstock; Page 3: aberCPC/Alamy Stock Photo; Page 5: Xinhua/Alamy Stock Photo; Page 7: Glow Images; Page 8: Paul Chesley/National Geographic Creative; Page 12: Heritage Image Partnership Ltd/Alamy Stock Photo; Page 13: Interfoto/Alamy Stock Photo; Page 14: MediaPunch Inc/Alamy Stock Photo; Page 15: Estate of Francis Bello/Science Source; Page 16: THOMAS KIENZLE/EPA/Newscom; Page 17: Newscom; Page 18: Felix Choo/Alamy Stock Photo; Page 18: Pepsi Co.; Page 19: Byron Peter/Getty Images.

Chapter 2   Page 23: Chip Somodevilla/Getty Images; Page 26: kyodowc07440/Newscom; Page 29: Pixellover RM 8/Alamy Stock Photo; Page 31: Franklin D. Roosevelt Presidential Library & Museum; Page 32: Monkey Business/Fotolia; Page 38: Africa studio/Fotolia; Page 40: Justin Kase zninez/Alamy Stock Photo; Page 44: ton koene/Alamy Stock Photo; Page 44: Mark Harmel/Science Source; Page 45: ScienceCartoonsPlus.com.

Chapter 3   Page 51: AP Photo/Seth Wenig/AP Images; Page 52: Sean Nel/Shutterstock; Page 55: National Archives and Records Administration; Page 55: National Archives and Records Administration; Page 55: SeanShot/Getty Images; Page 60: Monkey Business/Fotolia; Page 62: Gina Sanders/Fotolia; Page 63: Feedough/Getty Images; Page 65: Darren Baker/Alamy; Page 70: Masuda and Nisbett (2006); Page 70: Masuda and Nisbett (2006); Page 73: RyanJLane/Getty Images; 75, Nikola Solic/Reuters.

Chapter 4   Page 83: David Dettmann/Channel 4/Netflix/courtesy Everett Collection; Page 86: Walt Disney Studios Motion Pictures/courtesy Everett Collection; Page 87: OJenny/Shutterstock; Page 87: pathdoc/Fotolia; Page 87: PhotosIndia.com RM 18/Alamy Stock Photo; Page 87: Jochem D Wijnands/Getty Images; Page 87: Ollyy/Shutterstock; Page 87: Maksym Bondarchuk/Shutterstock; Page 88: Marco Iorio/Alamy Stock Photo; Page 88: White House Photo/Alamy Stock Photo; Page 89: The Paul Ekman Group, LLC; Page 89: The Paul Ekman Group, LLC; Page 90: Fizkes/Shutterstock; Page 90: Carol Beckwith & Angela Fisher/HAGA/The Image Works; Page 90: Victor Tongdee/Shutterstock; Page 90: Andres Rodriguez/Fotolia; Page 90: Marco Destefanis/Alamy Stock Photo; Page 93: Kathy Hutchins/Shutterstock; Page 93: COURTESY OF WICHITA STATE UNIVERSITY; Page 94: mikeledray/Shutterstock; Page 95: FLUKY FLUKY/Shutterstock; Page 95: sjenner13/123RF; Page 95: Stasique/Shutterstock; Page 95: John Holcroft/Getty Images; Page 97: Tony Rivetti/Contributor/Getty Images; Page 98: Minerva Studio/Fotoilia; Page 101: Bebeto Matthews/AP Images; Page 108: Michael-John Wolfe/Shutterstock; Page 108: Mick Roessler/Getty Images; Page 108: deepblue/Getty Images; Page 108: Mario Mitsis/Alamy Stock Photo; Page 108: iqoncept/123RF; Page 111: Masuda, Takahiko; Page 111: Masuda, Takahiko; Page 112: trubach/Shutterstock; Page 112: Lissandra Melo/Shutterstock; Page 112: bigredlynx/Shutterstock; Page 112: Izmael/Shutterstock; Page 112: violetkaipa/Shutterstock; Page 114: PCN Photography/Alamy Stock Photo.

Chapter 5   Page 119: Alexander Image/Shutterstock; Page 121: serg_dibrova/Shutterstock; Page 122: The Asahi Shimbun via Getty Images; Page 132: Omika/Fotolia; Page 134: Pearson Education; Page 136: Greg Epperson/Shutterstock; Page 143: Library of Congress Prints and Photographs Division; Page 143: Lee Corkran/Contributor/Getty Images; Page 144: (c) Hit Entertainment. Courtesy: Everett Collection; Page 144: Don Arnold/WireImage/Getty Images.

Chapter 6   Page 149: Education Images/UIG via Getty Images; Page 152: Greatstock/Alamy Stock Photo; Page 154: RosaIreneBetancourt 10/Alamy Stock Photo; Page 155: Industrieblick/Fotolia; Page 156: moodboard/Fotolia; Page 157: Shariff Che'Lah/Fotolia; Page 158: Splash News/Newscom; Page 160: Library of Congress Prints and Photographs Division Washington[LC-USZC4-7214]; Page 161: Janine Wiedel Photolibrary/Alamy Stock Photo; Page 162: Glow Images;

Page 163: Shannon Fagan/The Image Bank/Getty Images; Page 165: Krasyuk/Fotolia; Page 173: The Durango Herald/AP Images; Page 173: AP Photo/KING-TV/AP Images; Page 173: AP Photo/Maeder family/AP Images; Page 173: AP Photo/Tribune Newspapers/AP Images; 174, Rodger Mallison/The Fort Worth Star-Telegram/AP Images; Page 176: SuperStock/Alamy Stock Photo.

Chapter 7   Page 181: Pictorial Press Ltd/Alamy Stock Photo; Page 183: Deseret Morning News, Keith Johnson/AP Images; Page 185: AP Photo/J Pat Cart er/AP Images; Page 187: © 2017 UCLA All Rights Reserved.; Page 190: Hero Images/Getty Images; Page 194: Joseph Sohm/Shutterstock; Page 194: Monkey Business Images; Page 194: SimpleB/Shutterstock; Page 194: Wavebreak Media Ltd/123RF GB; Page 195: Elizabeth Goodenough/Everett Collection/Alamy Stock Photo; Page 200: Martyn Evans/Alamy Stock Photo; Page 201: Henry Martin/The New Yorker (c) Conde Nast; Page 203: Craig Sjodin/ABC via Getty Images; Page 205: Bill Greenblat/News-makers/Getty Images; Page 206: Copyright ©2018 American Association of Advertising Agencies, Reprinted with Permission.; Page 208: Stacy Walsh Rosenstock/Alamy Stock Photo; Page 208: VCG/VCG via Getty Images; Page 209: turgaygundogdu/Shutterstock; Page 210: Moviestore collection Ltd/Alamy Stock Photo; Page 211: Kenny Wu/Reuters.

Chapter 8   Page 216: Rich Carey/Shutterstock; Page 218: Gregory Rec/Portland Press Herald via Getty Images; Page 219: Howard Sochurek/The LIFE Picture Collection/Getty Images; Page 220: Courtesy Wikepedia/ZUMA Press/Newscom; Page 222: Jeremy Bembaron/Sygma/Sygma via Getty Images; Page 224: RichLegg/GettyImages; Page 225: Library of Congress Prints and Photographs Division[LC-USZ62-119765; Page 225: Ecuadorpostales/Shutterstock; Page 225: Sergiy Tryapitsyn/Alamy Stock Photo; Page 225: Thomas Faull/GettyImages; Page 227: litabit/Shutterstock; Page 229: Simon Belcher/Alamy Stock Photo; Page 229: OnTheRoad/Alamy Stock Photo; Page 229: Jennifer Wright/Alamy Stock Photo; Page 231: "Reproduced with permission. Copyright © 1955 Scientific American, a division of Nature America, Inc. All rights reserved."; Page 234: Jeff Greenberg "0 people images/Alamy Stock Photo; Page 235: AF archive/Alamy Stock Photo; Page 239: Aflo Co., Ltd./Alamy Stock Photo; Page 241: Joe Belanger/Shutterstock; Page 242: SpeedKingz/Shutterstock; Courtesy of Elliot Aronson; Page 246: Enviromantic/Getty Images; Page 247: Pictorial Press Ltd/Alamy Stock Photo; Page 250: Prisma by Dukas Presseagentur GmbH/Alamy Stock Photo; Page 250: From the film Obedience © 1968 by Stanley Milgram. ©Renewed 1993 by Alexandra Milgram. Distributed by Alexander Press.; Page 250: From the film Obedience © 1968 by Stanley Milgram. ©Renewed 1993 by Alexandra Milgram. Distributed by Alexander Press.; Page 256: Tim Clayton/Corbis via Getty Images.

Chapter 9   Page 262: Justin Sullivan/Getty Images; Page 264: ESB Professional/Shutterstock; Page 265: Philip G. Zimbardo, Inc.; Page 266: Philip G. Zimbardo, Inc.; Page 270: Doyeol (David) Ahn/Alamy Stock Photo; Page 273: PhotoAlto/Alamy; Page 275: Library of Congress (Photoduplication); Page 276: Steve Mack/Getty Images; Page 279: Henry Martin/The New Yorker Collection/The Cartoon Bank; Page 280: Andy Dean Photography/Shutterstock; Page 283: File/AP Images; Page 284: Everett Collection Inc/Alamy; Page 285: The Collaborationist/Getty Images; Page 285: US Senate/Alamy Stock Photo; Page 287: WavebreakmediaMicro/Fotolia; Page 289: Bradley Kanaris/Getty Images; Page 289: gillmar/Shutterstock; Page 289: Top Photo Corporation/Alamy Stock Photo; Page 289: DedMityay/Shutterstock; Page 292: Rawpixel.com/Shutterstock.

Chapter 10   Page 296: Elena Elisseva/Shutterstock; Page 299: wklzzz/123RF; Page 299: Roberto Herrett/Alamy Stock Photo; Page 299: Monkey Business Images/Shutterstock; Page 299: oneinchpunch/Shutterstock; Page 300: Design Pics Inc/Alamy Stock Photo; Page 300: Sam Gross/The New Yorker (c) Conde Nast; Page 301: Dmitriy Shironosov/123RF; Page 302: Samuel R. Sommers; Page 303: Radius Images/Getty Images; Page 304: Trinette Reed/Blend/Glow Images; Page 304:

Text Credits

M. E. W., & Kitayama, S. (2011). What's in a name? Popular names are less common on frontiers. Psychological Science, 22, 176-183; Page **124**: Kitayama, S., & Markus, H. R. (1994). Culture and the self: How cultures influence the way we view ourselves. In D. Matsumoto (Ed.), People: Psychology from a cultural perspective (pp. **17–37**). Pacific Grove, CA: Brooks/Cole; Page **126**: Based on Carver, C. S., & Scheier, M. F. (1981). Attention and self-regulation: A control-theory approach to human behavior. New York: Springer-Verlag; Page **130**: Schachter, S., & Singer, J. E. (1962). Cognitive, social, and physiological determinants of emotional states. Psychological Review, 69, 379–399; Page **133**: Based on Dutton, D. G., & Aron, A. P. (1974). Some evidence for heightened sexual attraction under conditions of high anxiety. Journal of Personality and Social Psychology, 30, 510–517; Page **135**: Adapted from Greene, D., Sternberg, B., & Lepper, M. R. (1976). Overjustification in a token economy. Journal of Personality and Social Psychology, 34, 1219–1234; Page **139**: Sinclair et al., 2005, p. **588**; Page **140**: Adapted from Sinclair, S., Lowery, B. S., Hardin, C. D., & Colangelo, A. (2005). Social tuning of automatic racial attitudes: The role of affiliative motivation. Journal of Personality and Social Psychology, 89(4), 583–592.

Chapter 6   Page **150**: Ferris, T. (1997, April 14). The wrong stuff. New Yorker, p. **32**; Page **153**: Pitt, R. N. (2010). "Killing the messenger": Religious Black gay men's neutralization of anti-gay religious messages. Journal for the Scientific Study of Religion, 49, 56–72; Page **156**: Based on Aronson, E., & Mills, J. S. (1959). The effect of severity of initiation on liking for a group. Journal of Abnormal and Social Psychology, 59, 177–181; Page **159**: Franklin, B. (1900). The autobiography of Benjamin Franklin (J. Bigelow, Ed.). Philadelphia: Lippincott. (Originally published 1868); Page **160**: Based on data in Jecker, J., & Landy, D. (1969). Liking a person as a function of doing him a favor. Human Relations, 22, 371–378; Page **162**: Bashar al-Assad, Speech by Bashar al-Assad on Syrian crisis. Voltairenet.org, January 6, 2013. Retrieved from http://www.voltairenet.org/article177102.html; Page **164**: Based on data in Freedman, J. L. (1965). Long-term behavioral effects of cognitive dissonance. Journal of Experimental and Social Psychology, 1, 145–155; Page **166**: Takaku, S. (2006). Reducing road rage: An application of the dissonance-attribution model of interpersonal forgiveness. Journal of Applied Social Psychology, 36, 2362–2378; Page **171**: Norman Maclean, A river runs through it: University of Chicago Press, 1983; Page **172**: Nixon, R. M. (1990). In the arena: A memoir of victory, defeat, and renewal. New York: Simon & Schuster; Page **174**: Tavris, C. & Aronson, E. (2007). Mistakes were made (but not by me). New York: Harcourt; Page **177**: Based on Jean M. Twenge and Joshua D. Foster, Birth Cohort Increases in Narcissistic Personality Traits Among American College Students, 1982–2009," Social Psychological and Personality Science, vol. 12, no. 1, January 1, 2010.

Chapter 7   Page **190**: Data from Ajzen, I. (1985). From intentions to actions: A theory of planned behavior. In J. Kuhl & J. Beckmann (Eds.), Action control: From cognition to behavior (pp. **11–39**). Heidelberg, Germany: Springer-Verlag; Page **191**: Adapted from Davidson, A. R., & Jaccard, J. J. (1979). Variables that moderate the attitude-behavior relation: Results of a longitudinal survey. Journal of Personality and Social Psychology, 37, 1364–1376; Page **197**: Based on data in Petty, R. E., Cacioppo, J. T., & Goldman, R. (1981). Personal involvement as a determinant of argument-based persuasion. Journal of Personality and Social Psychology, 41, 847–855; Page **199**: Adapted from Leventhal, H., Watts, J. C., & Pagano, F. (1967). Effects of fear and instructions on how to cope with danger. Journal of Personality and Social Psychology, 6, 313–321; Page **202**: Figure adapted from Briñol, P. & Petty, R. E (2003). Overt head movements and persuasion: A self-validation analysis. Journal of Personality and Social Psychology, 84, 1123-1139; Page **203**: Don Draper, 1960. Inside the mind of Don Draper - understanding his marketing philosophy, Guardian News and Media; Page **204**: Battle for your brain. (1991, August). Consumer Reports, pp. **520–521**.

Chapter 8   Page **222**: Data from Sherif, M. (1936). The psychology of social norms. New York: Harper; Page **226**: Cantril, H. (1940). The invasion from Mars: A study in the psychology of panic. New York: Harper & Row; Page **231**: Adapted from Asch, S. E. (1956). Studies of independence and conformity: A minority of one against a unanimous majority. Psychological Monographs, 7 (9, Whole No. 416); Page **232**: Asch, S. E. (1956). Studies of independence and conformity: A minority of one against a unanimous majority. Psychological Monographs, 7 (9, Whole No. 416); Page **232**: ROBERT BOLT, A MAN FOR ALL SEASONS; Page **232**: Adapted from Asch, S. E. (1957). An experimental investigation of group influence. In Walter Reed Army Institute of Research, Symposium on preventive and social psychiatry (pp. **15–17**). Washington, DC:

U.S. Government Printing Office; Page **233**: Moscovici, S. (1985). Social influence and conformity. In G. Lindzey & E. Aronson (Eds.), Handbook of social psychology (3rd ed., Vol. 2, pp. **347–412**). New York: Random House. p. **349**; Page **237**: Based on Asch, 1955; Page **238**: Markus, H. R., & Kitayama, S. (1991). Culture and the self: Implications for cognition, emotion, and motivation. Psychological Review, 98, 224–253., Page **243**: Adapted from Reno, R. R., Cialdini, R. B., & Kallgren, C. A. (1993). The transsituational influence of social norms. Journal of Personality and Social Psychology, 64, 104–112; Page **247**: Jowett, G. S., & O'Donnell, V. (1999). Propaganda and persuasion. Thousand Oaks, CA: Sage.,p. **6**; Page **247**: Ervin Staub. The Roots of Evil: The Origins of Genocide and Other Group Violence. Cambridge University Press, 1989 p. **103**; Page **247**: Jowett & O'Donnell, 1999, p. **242**; Page **249**: Wolfson, A. (2005). "A hoax most cruel." The Courier-Journal, October 9. Retrieved June 5, 2006, from www.courier-journal.com/apps/pbcs.d11/article?Date=20051009&category=NEWS01 p. **3**; Page **251**: Based on Milgram, S. (1963). Behavioral study of obedience. Journal of Abnormal and Social Psychology, 67, 371–378; Page **251**: Milgram, S. (1974). Obedience to authority: An experimental view. New York: Harper & Row., Page **256**: Osofsky, Bandura, & Zimbardo, 2005, p. **386**).

Chapter 9   Page **266**: quoted in O'Brien, S. (2004, May 21). Researcher: It's not bad apples, it's the barrel. Retrieved on January 20, 2005, from CNN.com, www.cnn.com/2004/US/05/21/zimbarbo.access/J; Page **270**: Based on data in Zajonc, Heingartner, & Herman, 1969; Page **279**: McClellan, S. (2008). What happened: Inside the Bush White House and Washington's culture of deception. New York: Public Affairs., p. **128**; Page **280**: Based on data in Janis, I. L., Mann, L (1977). Decision Making. Copyright © 1977 by The Free Press, a Division of Macmillan Publishing Co., Inc.

Chapter 10   Page **306**: Based on Eagly, A. H., Ashmore, R. D., Makhijani, M. G., & Longo, L. C. (1991). What is beautiful is good, but ...: A meta-analytic review of research on the physical attractiveness stereotype. Psychological Bulletin, 110 109–128.; Feingold, A. (1992b). Good-looking people are not what we think. Psychological Bulletin, 111, 304–341. Wheeler, L., & Kim, Y. (1997). What is beautiful is culturally good: The physical attractiveness stereotype has different content in collectivistic cultures. Personality and Social Psychology Bulletin, 23, 795–800; Page **312**: Taylor, S. E., & Master, S. L. (2011). Social responses to stress: The tendand-befriend model. In R. J. Contrada & A. Baum (Eds.), The handbook of stress science: Biology, psychology, and health (pp. **101–109**). New York: Springer. p. **952**; Page **318**: Data from Jankowiak, W. R., & Fischer, E. F. (1992). A cross-cultural perspective on romantic love. Ethnology, 31, 149–155; Page **318**: Moore, R. L. (1998). Love and limerance with Chinese characteristics: Student romance in the PRC. In V. C. de Munck (Ed.), Romantic love and sexual behavior (pp. **251–283**). Westport, CT: Praeger; Page **319**: Adapted from Hazan, C., & Shaver, P. (1987). Romantic love conceptualized as an attachment process. Journal of Personality and Social Psychology, 52, 511–524; Page **324**: Adapted from Rusbult, C. E. (1983). A longitudinal test of the investment model: The development (and deterioration) of satisfaction and commitment in heterosexual involvements. Journal of Personality and Social Psychology, 45, 101–117; Page **325**: Adapted from Rusbult, C. E. (1983). A longitudinal test of the investment model: The development (and deterioration) of satisfaction and commitment in heterosexual involvements. Journal of Personality and Social Psychology, 45, 101–117; Page **327**: Data from Duck, S. W. (1982). A typography of relationship disengagement and dissolution. In S. W. Duck (Ed.), Personal relationships 4: Dissolving personal relationships (pp. **1–32**). London: Academic Press.

Chapter 11   Page **334**: Lee, A. Y. (2001). The mere exposure effect: An uncertainty reduction explanation revisited. Personality and Social Psychology Bulletin, 27, 1255–1266; Page **336**: Sa'di: The Bustan of Sadi (London: John Murray, 1911), trans. by A. Hart Edwards; Page **339**: Frank Chapman Sharp, Ethics, New York, London, Century [©1928]; Page **341**: Adapted from Toi, M., & Batson, C. D. (1982). More evidence that empathy is a source of altruistic motivation. Journal of Personality and Social Psychology, 43, 281–292. Page **346**: Based on Levine, R.V., Norenzayan, A., & Philbrick, K. (2001). Cultural differences in the helping of strangers. Journal of Cross Cultural Psychology, 32, 543-560; Page **347**: Itkowitz, 2017 Itkowitz, C. (2017, January 25). A white Trump voter explains why he left a Black waitress a $450 tip with an uplifting note. Washington Post. https://www.washingtonpost.com/news/inspired-life/wp/2017/01/24/not-race-not-gender-just-american-these-white-men-left-their-black-waitress-an-uplifting-note-and-a-450-tip/?utm_term=.1b81c820b118; Page **347**: Solis, R. (2000). Religion and intragroup cooperation: Preliminary results of a comparative analysis of utopian communities. Cross-cultural Research, 34, 70-87; Page 352: Based on Darley, J. M., & Latané, B. (1968). Bystandar intervention in emergencies: Diffusion of responsibility. Journal of Personality and Social Psychology, 8, 377–383; Page 353: Data from Latané, B., & Darley, J. M. (1970). The unresponsive bystander: Why doesn't he help? Englewood Cliffs, NJ: Prentice Hall.; Page 357: Based on Greitemeyer, T., & Osswald, S. (2010). Effects of prosocial video games on prosocial behavior. Journal of Personality and Social Psychology, 98(2), 211–221. doi:10.1037/a0016997;

Chapter 12 Page 372: Figure 2.1 from p. 15 here: http://www.futureswithoutviolence.org/userfiles/CDC_Intimate%20Partner%20Violence%20in%20the%20US%20%282010%29.pdf; Page 372: O'Rourke, L. (2008, August 2). Behind the woman behind the bomb. The New York Times, Op-ed page; Page 376: figure A from p. 6 here: http://www.sciencemag.org/content/341/6151/1235367.full.pdf; Page 380: Based on data in Berkowitz, L., & Le Page, A. (1967). Weapons as aggression-eliciting stimuli. Journal of Personality and Social Psychology, 7, 202–207; Page 381: Berkowitz L, Cochran ST, Embree MC, Physical pain and the goal of aversively stimulated aggression, J Pers Soc Psychol. 1981 Apr;40 (4):687-700; Page 388: Ferguson, C. J. (2014). A way forward for video game violence research. American Psychologist, 69, 307-309; Page 395: Mark Macias (2017),"It may be time for United to 're-accommodate' CEO Oscar Munoz", CNBC LLC,http://www.cnbc.com/2017/04/11/it-may-be-time-for-united-to-re-accommodate-ceo-oscar-munoz-commentary.html; Page 395: April 2017, United Airlines video: 'They'll kill me, I want to go home, 'says bleeding doctor David Dao who was dragged off flight so that staff could take his seat" Belfast Telegraph,http://www.belfasttelegraph.co.uk/news/world-news/united-airlines-video-theyll-kill-me-i-want-to-go-home-says-bleeding-doctor-david-dao-who-was-dragged-off-flight-so-that-staff-could-take-his-seat-35614293.html; Page 397: Gibbs, N., & Roche, T. (1999, December 20). The Columbine tapes. Time, p. 154; Page 397: March (1999), Basement Tapes", Columbine site, retrieved from http://www.acolumbinesite.com/quotes1.html; Page 397: Darrell Scott, Steve Rabey (2001), Chain Reaction: A Call to Compassionate Revolution", Harper Collins.

Chapter 13 Page 407: Cashin, S. (2014). Place, not race: A new vision of opportunity in America. Boston, MA: Beacon; Page 409: Adapted from Fiske, Cuddy, & Glick, 2007; Page 412: Adapted from Correll, J., Park, B., Judd, C. M., & Wittenbrink, B. (2002). The police officer's dilemma: Using ethnicity to disambiguate potentially threatening individuals. Journal of Personality and Social Psychology, 83, 1314–1329; Page 413: Adapted from Rogers, R., & Prentice-Dunn, S. (1981). Deindividuation and anger-mediated interracial aggression: Unmasking regressive racism. Journal of Personality and Social Psychology, 41, 63–73; Page 416: Banaji, M. R., & Greenwald, A. G. (2013). "Blindspot: Hidden biases of good people." Random House Publishing Group; Page 420: McGlone & Aronson (2006), Stereotype threat, identity salience, and spatial reasoning"2017 Elsevier B.V; Page 422: Heather M. Rasinski, Andrew L. Geers, Alexander M. Czopp, 2013 "I Guess What He Said Wasn't That Bad" Society for Personality and Social Psychology, Inc.; Page 423: Mookie Betts (@mookiebetts) May 2, 2017 Twitter post.; Page 424: Adapted from Quattrone, G. A., & Jones, E. E. (1980). The perception of variability within ingroups and outgroups: Implications for the law of small numbers. Journal of Personality and Social Psychology, 38, 141–152; Page 427: Crandall, C. S., & Eshleman, A. (2003). A justification-suppression model of the expression and experience of prejudice. Psychological Bulletin, 129(3), 414–446; Page 427: "Allport, G. W. (1954). The nature of prejudice. Reading, MA: Addison-Wesley; Page 428: Dollard, J. (1938). Hostility and fear in social life. Social Forces, 17, 15–26; Page 429: Carol Tavris, Elliot Aronson (2008),"Mistakes Were Made (But Not by Me): Why We Justify Foolish Beliefs, Bad Decisions, and Hurtful Acts", Houghton Mifflin Harcourt; Page 430: Mendoza-Denton, R., & Page-Gould, E. (2008). Can cross-group friendships influence minority students' well-being at historically white universities? Psychological Science, 19, 933–939; Page 432: Based on data in Sherif, M., Harvey, O. J., White, J., Hood, W., & Sherif, C. W. (1961). Intergroup conflict and cooperation: The robber's cave experiment. Norman: Institute of Intergroup Relations, University of Oklahoma.

SPA1 Page 441: Montgomery, L. (2014, June 1). Evidence of climate change laps at Norfolk's feet. Washington Post (p. A1, A9); Page 441: Davenport, C. (2014, May 7). Miami finds itself ankle-deep in Climate Change debate. New York Times. Retrieved July 15, 2014 from: http://www.nytimes.com/2014/05/08/us/florida-finds-itself-in-the-eye-of-the-storm-on-climate-change.html?emc=eta1; Page 444: Lewin, K. (1951). Problems of research in social psychology. In D. Cartwright (Ed.), Field theory in social science (pp. 155–169). New York: Harper; Page 445: McNally, R. J., Bryant, R. A., & Ehlers, A. (2003). Does early psychological intervention promote recovery from posttraumatic stress? Psycho- logical Science in the Public Interest, 4, 45–79; Page 448: Adapted from Cialdini, R. B., Reno, R. R., & Kallgren, C. A. (1990). A focus theory of normative conduct: Recycling the concept of norms to reduce littering in public places. Journal of Personality and Social Psychology, 58, 1015–1026; Page 448: "Goldstein, N. J., Cialdini, R. B., & Griskevicius, V. (2008). A room with a viewpoint: Using social norms to motivate environmental conservation in hotels. Journal of Consumer Research, 35, 472–482; Page 450: Adapted from Siero, F. W., Bakker, A. B., Dekker, G. B., & Van Den Burg, M. T. C. (1996). Changing organizational energy consumption behavior through comparative feedback. Journal of Environmental Psychology, 16, 235–246.

SPA2 Page 462: Hill, J. K. (2002). "Rainbow remedies for life's stormy times." South Bend, IN: Moorhill Communications.; Page 467: Adapted from Cohen, S., Tyrrell, D. A. J., & Smith, A. P. (1991). Psychological stress in humans and susceptibility to the common cold. New England Journal of Medicine, 325, 606–612; Page 467: Hill, J. K. (2002). "Rainbow remedies for life's stormy times." South Bend, IN: Moorhill Communications.; Page 468: Adopted from Twenge, J. M., Zhang, L., & Im, C. (2004). It's beyond my control: A cross-temporal meta-analysis of increasing externality in locus of control, 1960–2002. Personality and Social Psychology Review, 8, 308–319; Page 468: Taylor, 1989. Adjustment to threatening events: A theory of cognitive adaptation. American Psychologist, Vol 38(11), Nov 1983, 1161-1173. p.178; Page 468: Hill, J. K. (2002). "Rainbow remedies for life's stormy times." South Bend, IN: Moorhill Communications; Page 469: Langer, E. J., & Rodin, J. (1976). The effects of choice and enhanced personal responsibility for the aged: A Held experiment. Journal of Personality and Social Psychology, 34, 191–198.; Page 470: Adapted from Rodin, J., & Langer, E. J. (1977). Long-term effects of a control-relevant intervention with the institutional aged. Journal of Personality and Social Psychology, 35, 897–902.; Schulz, R., & Hanusa, B. H. (1978). Long-term effects of control and predictability-enhancing interventions: Findings and ethical issues. Journal of Personality and Social Psychology, 36, 1202–1212; Page 474: Adapted from Cohen, S., Mermelstein, R., Kamarack, T., & Hoberman, H. (1985). Measuring the functional components of social support. In I. G. Sarason & B. R. Sarason (Eds.). Social support: Theory, research, and applications (pp. 73–94). The Hague, Netherlands: Martines Nijhoff; Page 477: Center for Disease Control and Prevention (2014).

SPA3 Page 482: Morris, E. (Director). (1988). The thin blue line [Film]. New York: HBO Videos; Page 485: Carpenter, S. (2000, December). Why do "they all look alike?" Monitor on Psychology, pp. 44–45; Page 488: Thompson, J. (2000, June 18). "I was certain, but I was wrong." The New York Times, p. D15.; Page 489: Dunning, D., & Perretta, S. (2002). Automaticity and eyewitness accuracy: A 10- to 12-second rule for distinguishing accurate from inaccurate positive identifications. Journal of Applied Psychology, 87, 951–962; Page 490: Smalarz L; Wells GL (2014),"Post-identification feedback to eyewitnesses impairs evaluators' abilities to discriminate between accurate and mistaken testimony.", US National Library of Medicine National Institutes of Health; Page 493: Adapted from Geraerts, E., Schooler, J., Merckelbach, H., Jelicic, M., Hauer, B., & Ambadar, Z. (2007). The reality of recovered memories: Corroborating continuous and discontinuous memories of childhood sexual abuse. Psychological Science, 18, 564–568; Page 494: Kalven, H., Jr., & Zeisel, H. (1966). The American jury. Boston: Little, Brown; Page 495: Adapted from Pennington, N., & Hastie, R. (1988). "Explanation-based decision making: Effects of memory structure on judgment." Journal of Experimental Psychology: Learning, Memory, and Cognition, 14, 521–533.

Name Index

Page numbers followed by *f* and *t* indicate figures and tables.

Subject Index

Page numbers with *f* and *t* indicate figures and tables.